Dear Friend,

Welcome to your all-new *Better Homes and Gardens* NEW COOK BOOK! It's the very latest of the trusted "Red Plaids" that generations of good cooks have relied on to prepare many a great meal.

I think this new 12th Edition Red Plaid is the best ever. You'll find not only hundreds of all-new recipes, but also an entire chapter on crockery cooking. I suspect it will become your favorite kitchen resource.

Of course, there are over 300 <u>more</u> *Better Homes and Gardens* books that could become your favorites, too!

Dozens of <u>cookbooks</u> with kitchen-tested recipes, from breads and barbecue to heavenly desserts and holiday treats. Plus, hundreds of <u>how-to books</u> with ideas and guidance for decorating, gardening, crafts and health. Everything you need to support your love of home and family.

Every *Better Homes and Gardens* book comes with our over 70-year-old tradition of excellence and expertise. Your satisfaction is always 100% guaranteed. That's our promise to you.

You can find *Better Homes and Gardens* books wherever quality books are sold. Or, look for them on our Web site, **bhg.com.**

Speaking of our Web site, don't hesitate to join us at **bhg.com** when you need the answer now. You'll discover more than 10,000 delicious recipes, decorating and gardening how-to's, crafts ideas and so much more.

But right now, I'm guessing you're anxious to dive into your NEW COOK BOOK.

Thanks so much for joining our *Better Homes and Gardens* family. Happy cooking!

Sincerely,

Karol DeWulf Nickell

Editor in Chief
Better Homes and Gardens
Magazine

We understand your love of home and family

Beginning with our very first cookbook in 1930, *Better Homes and Gardens* Books has been committed to helping families like yours with the important basics that support your love of home – cooking, decorating, gardening, do-it-yourself, home improvement, crafts and health. Now, with more than 300 titles, *Better Homes and Gardens* Books is the leader in home and family books, a staple in millions of households across America.

Of course, the *Better Homes and Gardens* family of magazines is *also* committed to serving your home and family needs.

Whether you're yearning for a country garden or want to sew up an heirloom quilt, renovate your bathroom or simply change a window treatment, you'll find just the magazine you need to get it done to perfection. In addition to BH&G® Magazine itself, over 100 *Better Homes and Gardens* Special Interest Publications are focused on everything you need for success!

Be it a book or magazine, you can count on *Better Homes and Gardens* for accurate information, reliable answers, practical ideas and creative solutions. It's our promise to you.

When you need the answer NOW, go to bhg.com®. Help is just a click away!

Click on the **Recipe Center** for more than 10,000 recipes, instantly at your fingertips. Now you can customize menus and even create your own recipe files.

Click on the **Decorating Center** for real-life decorating advice, plus hundreds of stunning rooms to browse through to tap into your personal style.

You'll find ideas and inspiration for every aspect of your home at *bhg.com* – garden plans, garden projects, crafts, parenting, kids' activities, entertaining, discussion groups and so much more. You'll even find a comprehensive How-to Encyclopedia! All just a click away at *bhg.com*!

Better Homes and Gardens®

America's #1 Cookbook Since 1930

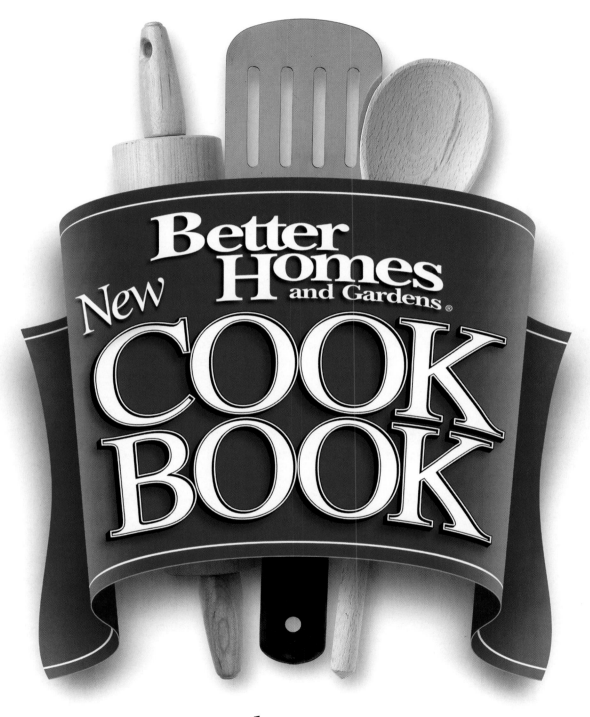

Better Homes and Gardens
New
COOK BOOK

12th Edition

Better Homes and Gardens® Books
Des Moines, Iowa

Better Homes and Gardens® Books
An imprint of Meredith® Books

Better Homes and Gardens® New Cook Book

Editor: Jennifer Dorland Darling
Contributing Editors: Joyce R. Trollope (Project Manager), Kristi Fuller, R.D., Linda J. Henry, Tami Leonard,
   Shelli McConnell, Jan Miller, R.D., Carrie Holcomb Mills, Winifred Moranville, Chuck Smothermon, Kay Springer
Senior Associate Art Director and Cover Designer: Ken Carlson
Copy Chief: Terri Fredrickson
Copy and Production Editor: Victoria Forlini
Editorial Operations Manager: Karen Schirm
Managers, Book Production: Pam Kvitne, Marjorie J. Schenkelberg
Contributing Copy Editor: Jennifer Speer Ramundt
Contributing Proofreaders: Maria Duryee, Gretchen Kauffman, Susan Kling, Sheila Mauk
Photographers: Mike Dieter, Pete Krumhardt, Scott Little
Food Stylists: Jill Lust, Dianna Nolin, Janet Pittman, Charles Worthington
Prop Stylist: Susan Strelecki
Indexer: Kathleen Poole
Electronic Production Coordinator: Paula Forest
Editorial and Design Assistants: Karen McFadden, Judy Bailey, Mary Lee Gavin
Test Kitchen Director: Lynn Blanchard
Test Kitchen Home Economists: Marilyn Cornelius (Product Supervisor), Judy Comstock, Juli Hale, Laura Harms,
   Jennifer Kalinowski, M.P.H., R.D., Maryellyn Krantz, Jill Moberly, Colleen Weeden, Lori Wilson
   Assistants: Barb Allen, Merry Bradley, Debra Cioccio, BJ Jones, Sherri Russell

Meredith® Books
Publisher and Editor in Chief: James D. Blume
Design Director: Matt Strelecki
Managing Editor: Gregory H. Kayko

Director, Operations: George A. Susral
Director, Production: Douglas M. Johnston

Vice President and General Manager: Douglas J. Guendel

Better Homes and Gardens® Magazine

Editor in Chief: Karol DeWulf Nickell
Deputy Editor, Food and Entertaining: Nancy Hopkins

Meredith Publishing Group
President, Publishing Group: Stephen M. Lacy
Vice President-Publishing Director: Bob Mate

Meredith Corporation
Chairman and Chief Executive Officer: William T. Kerr

Chairman of the Executive Committee: E. T. Meredith III

All of us at Better Homes and Gardens® Books are dedicated to providing you
with the information and ideas you need to create delicious foods. We welcome
your comments and suggestions. Write to us at: Better Homes and Gardens Books,
Cookbook Editorial Department, 1716 Locust St., Des Moines, IA 50309-3023.

If you would like to purchase any of our cooking, crafts, gardening, home
improvement, or home decorating and design books, check wherever quality
books are sold. Or visit us at bhgbooks.com

Our seal assures you that every
recipe in the *New Cook Book* has
been tested in the Better Homes
and Gardens® Test Kitchen. This
means that each recipe is
practical and reliable, and meets
our high standards of taste
appeal. We guarantee your
satisfaction with this book for as
long as you own it.

Contents

Creamy Caramel-Pecan Rolls
page 128

French Onion Soup
page 504

Sausage and Pepper Sandwiches
page 358

Baked Cavatelli
page 389

Peaches and Cream Tart
page 413

A Word from the Editor

Dear Friends,

From my first days as a young cook, I've relied on the *Better Homes and Gardens® New Cook Book* as my No. 1 reference guide in the kitchen. In fact, my very first cookbook was the *Better Homes and Gardens® Junior Cook Book.* It was a gift on my eighth birthday from a friend of my mother's who knew the Better Homes and Gardens® name meant, above all, trust. This cherished gift, and lots of coaching from my mom, fostered such an intense love of food and cooking that I chose it for a career. I've been a part of the Better Homes and Gardens® cookbook team for nearly 20 years now.

As we set out to revise the *Better Homes and Gardens® New Cook Book,* our goal was to keep the promise of earlier editions: to be the most relevant and trusted resource on the home cook's shelf. We want to provide you with everything you need to know to carry on the meaningful tradition of gathering family and friends over good food.

To do this, our talented cookbook staff and I have worked to completely revise, update, and expand this book for today's lifestyles. Many of you have told us that taste, convenience, and health are among your top priorities when preparing meals. So thanks to you, more than ever before, our recipe selections reflect these priorities.

We also know that when you take time out of your busy schedules to cook, you expect first-rate results. Be assured that every recipe in this book is guaranteed to work the first time—and every time—because all have been approved by the Better Homes and Gardens® Test Kitchen. At every step, our Test Kitchen staff looks for ways to make the recipes better tasting, faster, and easier to use, until every recipe meets our high standards. The result of our hard work is to provide you with recipes that taste delicious and work every time. These are recipes you'll be proud to share.

I hope our newest edition of this trusted kitchen companion brings joy and good eating to you, your family, and your friends for years to come.

Jennifer Dorland Darling

Jennifer Dorland Darling

Chapter 1
Cooking Basics

Measuring Ingredients

Getting consistently successful results from a recipe begins with measuring the ingredients correctly. To do this, stock up on the right utensils for the job and learn the correct method for measuring specific ingredients.

The Right Utensils

Graduated measuring cups: Also called dry measuring cups, these stackable cups come in increments of ¼, ⅓, ½, ⅔, ¾, and 1 cup and are used to measure dry ingredients and soft solids such as shortening. They're not used for liquids.

Liquid measuring cups: These clear glass or plastic cups hold 1, 2, or 4 cups liquid and have the incremental markings printed on the outside; a handle and a spout make for easy pouring.

Measuring spoons: Nested spoons commonly come in sets that measure ¼ teaspoon, ½ teaspoon, 1 teaspoon, and 1 tablespoon. These can be used for dry and liquid ingredients.

The Right Way to Measure

Dry ingredients: Spoon the ingredient into the appropriate dry measuring cup or measuring spoon and level off the excess with the straight edge of a knife or spatula.

Liquid ingredients: Place the liquid measuring cup on a level surface. Bend down so your eye is level with the markings on the cup. When measuring 1 tablespoon or less, fill the appropriate measuring spoon to the top without letting it spill over.

Ingredients That Require Extra Know-How

Brown sugar: Press firmly into a dry measure so it holds the shape of the cup when it is turned out.

Butter, margarine, or solid shortening: These ingredients are often packaged in stick form, with markings on the wrapper indicating tablespoon and cup measures. Use a sharp knife to cut off the amount needed. If the wrapper isn't marked, press the ingredient firmly into a dry measuring cup or spoon with a rubber scraper, then level the excess off with a straight edge.

Dried herbs: Lightly fill a measuring spoon to the top, keeping the herb as level with the top as pos-

Liquid measuring cups

Graduated measuring cups

Measuring spoons

sible; there's no need to level with a spatula. If a recipe specifies crushing the dried herb, empty the spoon's contents into your hand and crush the herb with the other hand. To crush rosemary, use a mortar and pestle (see page 27).

Flour: Stir flour in the bag or canister to lighten its volume. Sifting is not necessary, except for cake flour. Gently spoon flour into a dry measuring cup or a measuring spoon. Level off the top with the straight edge of a knife or spatula.

Weights and Measures

Tablespoon Math

3 teaspoons = 1 tablespoon
4 tablespoons = ¼ cup
5⅓ tablespoons = ⅓ cup
8 tablespoons = ½ cup
10⅔ tablespoons = ⅔ cup
12 tablespoons = ¾ cup
16 tablespoons = 1 cup

Measure	Equivalent Measure	Equivalent Ounces
1 tablespoon		½ fluid ounce
1 cup	½ pint	8 fluid ounces
2 cups	1 pint	16 fluid ounces
2 pints (4 cups)	1 quart	32 fluid ounces
4 quarts (16 cups)	1 gallon	128 fluid ounces

Note: For metric equivalents, see page 574.

Kitchen Appliances and Equipment

Select appliances, utensils, and gadgets to create a kitchen you'll love.

Cooking Knives

Choose your knives carefully and care for them on a regular basis.

Selecting the Right Knives

Choose knives that feel balanced and comfortable in your hand. A good choice is those made of high-carbon stainless steel with blades that run through the handles and are riveted in place. High-carbon stainless steel resists corrosion similarly to regular stainless steel, but it isn't as hard, so it sharpens more easily.

Useful Knives for the Home Cook

These knives should meet the needs of most home cooks:

Bread knife (8-inch blade): The serrated blade of this knife allows you to easily cut through breads, bagels, tomatoes, cakes, or other foods with tough exteriors and soft interiors.

Chef's or cook's knife (8-inch blade): Chop, dice, and mince foods with the wedge-shape blade.

Paring knife (3- or 4-inch blade): This knife is comfortable to handle when peeling and cutting fruits and vegetables or other small items.

Utility knife (6-inch blade): The thin blade of this knife makes it easy to smoothly slice sandwiches and other soft foods, such as fruit and cheese.

Nonessential Knives

Knives that are useful, but not essential, include:

Boning knife (5-inch blade): A narrow knife used to cut meat off bones.

Carving knife/slicer (10-inch blade): This long, thin knife makes it easy to slice cooked meats.

Fillet knife (7-inch blade): This knife's long, thin, flexible blade is useful for efficiently filleting fish.

Caring for Your Knives

Always cut on a cutting board. Wash knives in hot, soapy water immediately after using them; rinse and allow to air-dry. Do not let them soak in water, and do not wash them in the dishwasher. Store knives in a knife block or protective case.

In general, you should sharpen knives using a professional-style grind wheel or a whetstone, or take them to a professional service. Once sharp, occasionally realign the edge and remove nicks with a sharpening steel—a ridged rod made of diamond-coated steel or ceramic. Here's how:

■ Rest the sharpening steel vertically with the tip pressed against a stable cutting surface. Place the  knife edge near the knife's handle at a 20-degree angle to the steel near the sharpening steel's handle.

■ In one smooth, slow motion, draw the knife blade gently down the full length of the sharpening steel, pulling the knife toward you as it moves down the steel.

■ When you finish the stroke, the tip of the blade—still at an angle—should be near the tip of the steel. Repeat with the other side of the blade.

Bread knife

Chef's or cook's knife

Paring knife

Utility knife

Carving knife

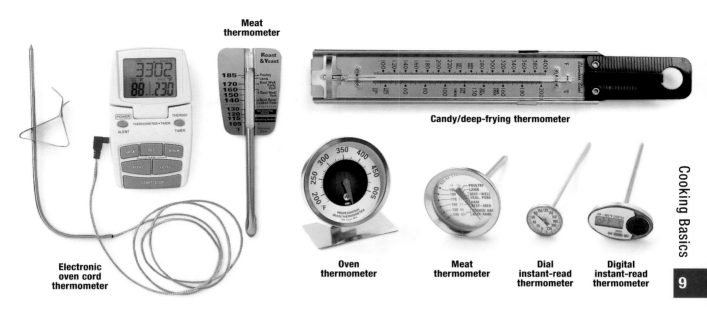

Meat
thermometer

Candy/deep-frying thermometer

Electronic
oven cord
thermometer

Oven
thermometer

Meat
thermometer

Dial
instant-read
thermometer

Digital
instant-read
thermometer

Kitchen Thermometers

Kitchen thermometers help ensure that foods are cooked and stored at proper temperatures as well as cooked to a safe internal temperature.

Appliance Thermometers

Oven thermometer: This allows you to check the temperature of your oven.

Refrigerator/freezer thermometer: This verifies whether the appliance is chilling correctly. For food safety, refrigerators should maintain a temperature of no higher than 40°F, and freezers should maintain a temperature of 0°F or less.

Food Thermometers

For information on the proper way to use meat thermometers, see page 331; for information on internal temperatures for cooked meats and poultry, see the charts at the end of the grilling, meat, and poultry chapters.

Candy/deep-frying thermometer: Use one when making candy, some frostings and syrups, and when frying foods in a large quantity of cooking oil or shortening. Used to measure extra-high temperatures, the thermometer is marked with candy-making stages, such as hard-crack; it's also marked for deep-fat frying. For more information on cooking and testing candy mixtures, see page 177.

Disposable temperature indicator (not pictured): Designed for specific temperature ranges, this single-use thermometer has a sensor that changes color when the appropriate temperature is reached. Follow manufacturer's directions and use it only for the foods for which it is designed.

Electronic oven cord thermometer: Best for roasts or large cuts of meats, this thermometer features a

probe designed to stay in the meat as it cooks. A stay-cool cord attaches to a magnet-backed unit that affixes to the oven door. An alarm sounds when the food reaches the desired temperature. Though they're designed for oven use, they can also be used to check foods cooking on the stove.

Fork thermometer (not pictured): Handy for grilling, fork thermometers can be used for most foods; however, they're not designed to be left in food while it is cooking. To ensure an accurate reading, be sure that the tine of the fork containing the sensor is fully inserted.

Instant-read thermometer: This can give an internal reading in seconds. The sensor in a digital instant-read thermometer is in the tip. Use this type of thermometer to verify internal temperatures of thin or thick foods. The sensor of a dial instant-read thermometer is in the stem, not the tip, so it must be inserted at least 2 inches into the food you are testing for an accurate reading (for thinner cuts, you may need to insert the thermometer sideways into the food). Also see page 331. Do not leave either type of thermometer in food while cooking.

Meat thermometer: Typically used to check the internal temperature of large cuts of meats, such as roasts and whole poultry, they are generally not appropriate for thin foods. Oven-safe meat thermometers may be left in a conventional oven, but not a microwave oven.

Pop-up thermometer (not pictured): Sometimes turkey or other meat comes with a thermometer that pops up when the food is done. Even when such a device is present, the food should be tested with a reliable food thermometer to ensure that it reaches the proper temperatures for safety and doneness.

Kitchen Gadgets

You can certainly get soup from pot to bowl without a ladle, but it's amazing how much easier (and neater) the task is with one in hand. That's the case with most kitchen gadgets. In general, having the right tools can make cooking more efficient and enjoyable.

Cooking Utensils and Gadgets Checklist

Here are some of the most helpful tools for cooking, including substitutions where possible.

Bottle/can opener.

Colander: Use this perforated bowl-shape utensil to rinse food or to drain liquids from solid food. When solids are very fine, use a sieve.

Corkscrew: Many models are available, so choose the type you're comfortable using. See page 112.

Cutting boards: Stock up on two that are easy to tell apart, and reserve one solely for raw meat, poultry, fish, and shellfish, and the other for ready-to-eat foods. See page 45.

Egg separator: Use to separate egg yolks from whites. See page 263. It is not safe to separate eggs by passing the yolk from shell to shell.

Food mill: If you don't have one, force food through a strainer set over a bowl or pan.

Fork, long-handled: Use when carving or moving large pieces of food, such as roasts.

Funnel: Helps avoid spills when pouring ingredients from one container to another.

Grater: This tool generally has a metal surface punched with sharp-edged holes or slits that are used to break foods into smaller pieces. Graters come in many shapes and sizes. Tools with larger holes are sometimes called shredders, while those with the largest holes are sometimes called slicers. The size of the holes or slits determines what task the grater is best suited for. Smaller holes or slits will break food into finer pieces. Box graters have different-sized holes or slits on each side.

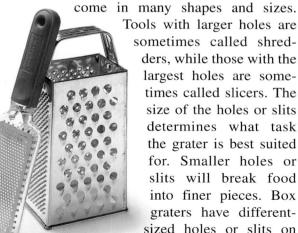

Colander

Sieves

Graters

Kitchen shears: Use for snipping everything from fresh herbs to kitchen string.

Knives: See page 8.

Ladle: In a pinch, substitute a heatproof cup.

Measuring cups and measuring spoons: See page 7.

Mixing bowls: For most cooks, a set of four mixing bowls in the following sizes will suffice: small (1 quart), medium (1½ quarts), large (2½ quarts), and very large (4 quarts).

Pastry blender: For cutting fat (such as shortening) into flour to make pastries, biscuits, etc. If you don't have one, cut in the fat using two knives in a crisscross motion.

Pastry blender

Pastry brush: Often used for brushing glazes over baked goods; also useful for greasing pans.

Pepper grinder: Because pepper is more flavorful when ground fresh, you should keep one of these on hand to grind whole peppercorns as needed.

Rolling pin: If you don't have one, try using a clean, heavy bottle with smooth sides.

Rotary beater: If you have an electric mixer or hand-held blender, you may not need one.

Rubber scrapers: Also known as rubber spatulas, these utensils are used for scraping batter from a bowl and for folding ingredients together.

Sharpening steel: See page 8.

Sieves: Stock up on one large and one small, and use these circular wire-mesh utensils to separate small particles from large ones. Also called strainers.

Sifter: If you don't have one, pour flour or powdered sugar into a sieve set over a bowl, then stir it to force the grains through the holes.

Skewers. These thin, pointed sticks are made of metal or wood and are used to hold pieces of meat, fruit, and vegetables in place. To use wooden skewers for grilling or broiling, be sure to first soak them in water for at least 30 minutes to prevent them from burning.

Slotted spoon, long-handled: Useful for removing solids from liquid mixtures.

Spatulas: These flat utensils can be made of metal, rubber, plastic, and wood. A turner-type spatula is used for flipping foods; a narrow, flexible, metal spatula works well for spreading. For rubber or plastic spatulas, see Rubber scrapers, above. When using a spatula for cooking on the range top, make sure the one you use is heatproof.

Other Useful Gadgets

These tools are not essential for everyday cooking, but the more you cook, the more you'll enjoy having them on hand:

Cheese slicer	Parchment paper
Citrus juicer/reamer	Pastry bag with tips
Citrus zester	Pizza cutter
Mandoline	Pizza stone
Meat mallet	Potato masher
Mortar and pestle	Salad spinner

Spoon, long-handled: Handy to stir large volumes.

Thermometers: See page 9.

Timer: Digital timers can help you time cooking steps to the second.

Tongs (metal): Great for lifting and turning foods.

Vegetable brush: Useful for scrubbing fruits and vegetables when skins will not be removed.

Vegetable peeler: Essential for peeling vegetables; in a pinch, peel skins with a paring knife.

Wire cooling rack: Allows air to circulate around baked goods to cool them quickly and keep them from getting soggy.

Wire whisks: These come in handy for beating ingredients such as eggs. They can also help you smooth out lumpy sauces; see page 477. In a pinch, substitute a rotary beater.

Wooden spoons (assorted sizes): Sturdy tools for stirring thick dough and batter. Also useful for stirring mixtures while they heat, as wooden handles stay cool longer than metal handles.

Pots and Pans

Pots and pans are made of a variety of materials. Aluminum pans and copper pans are the best heat conductors; however, all-copper pans are expensive and tarnish easily, while plain aluminum pans can react with certain foods. Therefore, good options for the home cook include heavy stainless-steel pans with copper bottoms, pans clad with aluminum sandwiched between stainless steel, and aluminum pans treated with a process known as hard anodization. Anodization creates a non-corrosive cookware that conducts heat well.

Heavy pans are often called for in our recipes because they heat foods evenly and gently. Copper-bottom, cast iron, enameled cast iron, anodized aluminum, and clad aluminum are all good choices for heavy-bottom pans.

Range Top Cookware Checklist

Cookware commonly used to prepare recipes in this cookbook includes:

Double boiler: Two pans that work together; one fits on top of the other. Water in the bottom pan simmers gently to cook the contents in the top pan. If you do not own a double boiler, substitute a metal or heat-resistant glass bowl and a saucepan. The bowl should be wide enough so it fits in the pan but doesn't touch the simmering water.

Dutch oven or kettle: These large, heavy pots with tight-fitting lids and handles on opposite sides of the rim are used for soups, stews, and braising meats. When canning, a kettle is often used.

Saucepan

Saucepan

Dutch oven

Straight-sided skillet
with lid

Flared-edge
skillet

Seasoning a Skillet

Cast-iron cookware needs to be seasoned to help it avoid rust and corrosion. Instructions for seasoning should come with the skillet. If no instructions are available, wash and dry the pan thoroughly. Brush shortening over the entire inside surface. Heat in a 350°F oven for 1 hour. Cool completely and wipe out the skillet. Season the skillet before the first use and periodically thereafter (especially after you've cleaned it well).

Saucepans (1-, 2-, and 3-quart, with lids): It's best to have a few different sizes of these versatile, long-handled pans.

Skillets: Sometimes referred to as a frying pan, a skillet is a long-handled, low-sided pan. Often the sides gently slope to allow steam to escape the pan. Large (10-inch) and extra-large (12-inch) skillets are most useful. A 10-inch nonstick skillet will also come in handy. Other sizes include small (6-inch) and medium (8-inch). If you need to use the skillet in the oven, make sure the handle can withstand high heat; if in doubt, wrap handle in a couple of layers of heavy-duty foil or select a skillet with a removable handle.

Vegetable steamer (collapsible or insert): A perforated basket that holds food over boiling water in a pan in order to steam it rather than boil it.

Specialty Pans

While not essential for most of our recipes, these specialty pans offer features that make preparing a specific food easier:

Griddles: This flat, often rimless pan makes flipping pancakes a cinch. Nonstick griddles also help you cook with a minimum amount of fat.

Grill pan: The grooves of this heavy, stove-top, griddle-type pan allow fat to drain away from food and add appetizing grill marks to the cooked items.

Omelet pans: Sloped sides and a nonstick surface make it easy to fold and slide omelets from the pan.

Woks: Available with rounded or flat bottoms, these pans offer deep, sloping sides that help keep food pieces in the pan when stir-frying.

About Nonstick Pans

It's not necessary to buy the most expensive nonstick pans you can afford because their coatings eventually will become damaged. However, don't buy the cheapest. Look for fairly heavy, moderately priced nonstick pans. With proper care, they will last three to five years before needing to be replaced.

Baking Pans and Dishes

For the recipes in this cookbook, a baking pan refers to a metal pan, and a baking dish refers to an oven-safe glass or ceramic container. (If substituting glass or ceramic cookware for recipes that call for baking pans, reduce baking temperature by about 25°F.)

Use Baking Pans (Metal)

■ For nicely browned baked goods. See pages 163 and 405 for information on choosing the right pans for cakes and pies.

■ For broiling. Do not use glass dishes or casseroles when broiling because the high temperatures may cause the glass to shatter. Therefore, when broiling, use only metal pans or bakeware suitable for broiling.

Use Baking Dishes (Glass or Ceramic)

■ For dishes made with eggs or with acidic ingredients such as tomatoes and lemon. Baking pans made of aluminum, iron, and tin can react with these foods and cause the foods to discolor.

Specialty Bakeware

Some desserts require specific bakeware:

Fluted tube pan: The fluted sides bring a decorative look to the finished product. It comes in various sizes; a 12-cup pan is the most common.

Springform pan (8- or 9-inch is most common; 10- and 11-inch are also available): This round pan, used for making cheesecakes and other desserts that are tricky to remove from their pans, has a bottom that is separate from the side. A clamp holds the pan together and opens to allow the side to easily be pulled away from the baked dessert.

Tart pan (10- to 11- inch) with removable bottom: The removable bottom makes it easy to neatly transfer a tart to a serving plate. (Shallow quiche or flan pans are one piece, without removable bottoms.)

Tube pan (10-inch): Also known as an angel food cake pan, this deep pan has a hollow tube in the center that promotes even baking. Most tube pans have removable bottoms.

Roasting pan with rack

Square baking dish

Covered casserole dish

Custard cups

Cookie sheet

15×10×1-inch baking pan

Ovenware Checklist

Outfit your kitchen with the following, and you'll be able to make just about any baking recipe in this book:

Baking dishes, rectangular: one 2-quart (12×7½×2-inch) and one 3-quart (13×9×2-inch) glass dish.

Baking dishes, square: one 2-quart (8×8×2-inch) glass dish.

Baking pans: one 9×9×2-inch, one 15×10×1-inch (jelly-roll), and one 13×9×2-inch metal pan.

Cake pans: two round (8×1½- or 9×1½-inch) metal pans. Cake pans that are 2 inches deep will also work for the recipes in this book.

Cookie sheets: at least two metal sheets with either no sides or low sides. In a pinch, substitute a 15×10×1-inch (jelly-roll) baking pan, though the rims may inhibit even browning.

Covered casseroles: Several various size round, deep glass dishes (1-, 2-, and 3-quart). If a recipe calls for a covered casserole, and you do not own one, use a baking dish covered with foil.

Custard cups (6-ounce): Six glass baking dishes for cooking custards and other individual desserts.

They can be used individually when measuring and preparing small amounts of ingredients, such as garlic, in advance so that the ingredients are ready when you need them in a recipe.

Loaf pans or dishes: Several metal or glass rectangular pans (7½×3½×2-inch, 8×4×2-inch, or 9×5×3-inch).

Muffin cups: One pan of twelve 2½-inch cups or several mini-muffin cups of twelve 1¾-inch cups. Muffin cups are also known as muffin pans.

Pie plates or pans: One 9-inch metal pie pan or glass pie plate; see page 405 regarding using shiny or dull metal pie pans.

Pizza pan: One round metal pan. In a pinch, substitute a baking sheet, but build up the pizza crust edges to hold toppings.

Roasting pan with rack: One large enough to accommodate a roast (be sure it fits in your oven). A rack helps promote even cooking and prevents the roast from stewing in the pan juices.

Soufflé dish: One round glass 1½-quart dish; in a pinch, substitute a straight-sided casserole with the same volume.

Specialty bakeware: See page 12.

Countertop Appliances

Here's a roundup of today's most common and most useful kitchen appliances.

Blender: With short blades that rotate quickly, this kitchen helper trims preparation time by instantly blending, chopping, and pureeing foods. For best results:

■ Blend large quantities of food in several small batches for better control.

■ Stop your blender often and check the size of the food pieces. Blenders work quickly and can easily overblend or overchop food.

■ Keep in mind that a blender cannot whip foods (such as whipped cream and potatoes).

■ In general, cut foods into 1/2- to 1-inch pieces before adding them to the blender.

■ When blending heated mixtures, cool hot foods slightly before blending and fill the blender container half full. Cover with lid and open vent. Cover blender container with a clean towel while operating. Begin blending warm mixtures on low speed, then increase to higher speed, as necessary.

Blenders, hand-held: Also called immersion blenders, these can blend, liquefy, or puree foods directly in pots or bowls. This saves on cleanup, because a blender container isn't needed.

Bread machine: This machine takes bread recipes through mixing, kneading, rising, punching down, and baking. See page 148.

Crockery cooker/continuous slow cooker: See the Crockery Cooking chapter, pages 227–240, for information on this appliance.

Electric mixer: This appliance is essential for efficiently mixing, whipping, and beating foods. Two types of mixers exist. A hand-held, portable mixer will do for most recipes. If you do a lot of cooking, you may want to invest in a heavy-duty stand mixer, which can handle large amounts of thick batter and allows you some freedom while it's operating. Also, many stand mixers can knead bread dough with special attachments.

Food processor: This appliance performs many of the same jobs as a blender or electric mixer. While it can't whip foods, it can slice and shred. When processing heated mixtures, cool mixture slightly; fill bowl only half full. Cover lid with a clean towel while operating.

Indoor grill: See page 328.

Toaster oven: Because these take little time to preheat, they're ideal for toasting several slices of bread at once and baking small amounts of food.

Cooking Appliances

These days, the home cook can choose from a variety of ranges. Innovations that go beyond the standard gas and electric options include:

Combination ovens: Combination microwave-convection ovens combine the speed of microwaving with the even cooking of convection baking.

Convection oven: A fan circulates hot air through this gas or electric oven, enabling food to cook faster and more evenly. Such even browning means superior results, especially when baking. Also, because the air circulates, more of the oven space can be used.

Converting Recipes for Convection Ovens

Most of the recipes in this book can be converted for use in a convection oven. Follow the specific instructions given by your oven manufacturer, keeping these general guidelines in mind:

■ When converting recipes from conventional to convection, use the temperature and time from the original recipe as a guideline, checking for doneness after three-quarters of the baking time has elapsed. Or, the original baking temperature may be reduced by 25°F in general. Open the oven door as little as possible during baking.

■ Because convection ovens offer superior results when browning and crisping foods, most recipes designed for convection ovens do not call for baking dishes to be covered. If you do use your convection oven to bake a standard recipe that calls for the dish to be covered, the temperature and time will likely be about the same. For covered long-baking recipes designed for a standard oven, you may reduce the temperature by 25°F to 50°F when using a convection oven.

■ Follow the user's manual for manufacturer's recommendations for preheating a convection oven. Be sure to position oven racks before you turn the oven on because they will heat up quickly.

■ To enable hot air to circulate around the food, place foods in the center of the oven; be sure to leave space between pans, and between pans and oven walls.

■ Always test food a few minutes before the minimum cooking time has elapsed, using the doneness test given in the recipe. Keep in mind that even when food appears golden brown, it may not be completely done.

Halogen/microwave combination oven: These combine light waves with microwaves to cook food four times faster than a conventional oven would—with the same oven-quality browning and crisping.

Microwave oven: These appliances use electromagnetic waves to cook and warm food in much less time than conventional ovens and stove tops—a great convenience for time-pressed cooks. While you should follow the manufacturer's directions for operating your microwave, here's some general know-how:

■ Our microwave timings are usually designed for a microwave with a cooking power of 850 to 1,000 watts. If you own a lower- or higher-wattage oven, adjust cooking times.

■ Use only microwave-safe utensils, materials, and containers in a microwave oven. Look for the words "microwave-safe" on product labels. Never use metal utensils or dishes or those that contain metal (such as dishes or plates with gold or silver trim) in the microwave.

■ Use the lid of the microwave-safe container or plastic wrap to cover containers when cooking foods such as casseroles, fish, poultry, and meat. Covering the food helps retain steam, prevent drying, and cook the food faster. Use waxed paper as a cover when heating foods that might spatter.

■ When using plastic wrap to cover, vent it by turning back one corner to allow steam to escape.

■ Microwave energy tends to penetrate the edges of food first, so stir food often. This way, the hotter portion on the outside will be mixed into the cooler center. If the food cannot be stirred (such as chicken pieces or fish fillets), rearrange it to ensure even cooking. Move the less-cooked food from the center to the edges of the baking dish. For foods in individual dishes, rearrange the dishes from the center of the oven to the edges. Some microwaves have a turntable to help food cook more evenly.

■ If the food can't be stirred or rearranged, and your microwave doesn't have a turntable, turn the dish or the food. When a recipe says to turn a food, rotate the dish halfway, unless it specifies otherwise. Turn over large pieces of food, checking for even cooking.

■ Always test food after the minimum cooking time in a recipe, using the doneness test given. Some microwaved foods may look as if they need more cooking, when they actually are done.

Microwave Timing Hints

Almonds (toasting): Place ½ to 1 cup slivered or sliced almonds in a 2-cup microwave-safe measure. Microwave, uncovered, on 100 percent power (high) for 1 minute; stir. Microwave 1½ to 3 minutes more, stirring every 30 seconds. At the first sign of toasting, spread nuts on paper towels. (They will continue to toast as they stand.) Let stand for at least 15 minutes before using.

Chocolate (melting): Place 1 cup (6 ounces) semisweet or milk chocolate pieces or 1 ounce unsweetened or semisweet chocolate, chopped, in a small microwave-safe bowl. Microwave, uncovered, on 70 percent power (medium-high) for 1 minute; stir. Microwave on 70 percent power (medium-high) for 1½ to 3 minutes more, stirring after every 15 seconds, until chocolate is melted and smooth.

Cream cheese (softening): In a microwave-safe bowl microwave cream cheese, uncovered, on 100 percent power (high). Allow 10 to 20 seconds for 3 ounces and 30 to 60 seconds for 8 ounces or until cream cheese begins to soften. Let stand for 5 minutes to completely soften.

Meat, ground: In a 1½-quart microwave-safe casserole crumble 1 pound ground beef, pork, lamb, or turkey. Microwave, covered, on 100 percent power (high) for 4 to 6 minutes or until meat is thoroughly cooked, stirring twice. Drain off fat.

Pancake syrup (heating): In a microwave-safe measure, microwave syrup, uncovered, on 100 percent power (high) for 20 to 30 seconds for ½ cup and 30 to 60 seconds for 1 cup or until syrup is warm.

Pie: To warm a slice of fruit pie, place it on a microwave-safe plate. Microwave, uncovered, on 100 percent power (high) for 20 to 30 seconds or until warm.

Potatoes (baking): Prick medium-size baking potatoes (6 to 8 ounces each) with a fork. Microwave, uncovered, on 100 percent power (high) until almost tender, rearranging once. Allow 4 to 6 minutes for 1 potato, 6 to 9 minutes for 2 potatoes, and 10 to 15 minutes for 4 potatoes. Let potatoes stand for 5 minutes.

Poultry: See page 450.

Tortillas (softening): Place flour tortillas between paper towels. Microwave on 100 percent power (high), allowing 20 to 30 seconds for four 6- to 9-inch tortillas and 30 to 40 seconds for six tortillas.

Vegetables: See pages 540-544.

Cooking at High Altitudes

When you cook at high altitudes, recipe adjustments need to be made to ensure the best results possible. Unfortunately, no simple formula exists for converting all recipes to high altitude recipes. If you live more than 1,000 feet above sea level, it will help you to understand ways in which altitude affects cooking and to become familiar with common cooking adjustments.

General High-Altitude Issues

At altitudes higher than 3,000 feet above sea level:
- Water boils at lower temperatures, causing moisture to evaporate more quickly. This can cause food to dry out during cooking and baking.
- Because of a lower boiling point, foods cooked in steam or boiling liquids take longer to cook.
- Lower air pressure may cause baked goods that use yeast, baking powder, baking soda, egg whites, or steam to rise excessively, then fall.

Suggestions for Baking

- For cakes leavened by air, such as angel food, beat the egg whites only to soft peaks; otherwise, the batter may expand too much.
- For cakes made with shortening, you may want to decrease the baking powder (start by decreasing it by $\frac{1}{8}$ teaspoon per teaspoon called for); decrease the sugar (start by decreasing by about 1 tablespoon for each cup called for); and increase the liquid (start by increasing it 1 to 2 tablespoons for each cup called for). These estimates are based on an altitude of 3,000 feet above sea level—at higher altitudes, you may need to alter these measures proportionately. You can also try increasing the baking temperature by 15°F to 25°F to help set the batter.
- When making a rich cake, reduce the shortening by 1 to 2 tablespoons per cup and add one egg (for a 2-layer cake) to prevent cake from falling.
- Cookies generally yield acceptable results, but if you're not satisfied, try slightly increasing the baking temperature; slightly decreasing the baking powder or soda, fat, and/or sugar; and/or slightly increasing the liquid ingredients and flour.
- Muffinlike quick breads and biscuits generally need little adjustment, but if you find that these goods develop a bitter or alkaline flavor, decrease the baking soda or powder slightly. Because cakelike quick breads are more delicate, you may need to follow adjustment guidelines for cakes.

- Yeast breads will rise more quickly at high altitudes. Allow unshaped dough to rise only until double in size, then punch the dough down. Repeat this rising step once more before shaping dough. Flour tends to be drier at high altitudes and sometimes absorbs more liquid. If your yeast dough seems dry, add more liquid and reduce the amount of flour the next time you make the recipe.
- Large cuts of meat may take longer to cook. Be sure to use a meat thermometer to determine proper doneness.

Suggestions for Range-Top Cooking

Candy-making: Rapid evaporation caused by cooking at high altitudes can cause candies to cook down more quickly. Therefore, decrease the final cooking temperature by the difference in boiling water temperature at your altitude and that of sea level (212°F). This is an approximate decrease of 2 degrees for every increase of 1,000 feet in elevation above sea level.

Canning and freezing foods: When canning at high altitudes, adjustments in processing time or pressure are needed to guard against contamination; when freezing, an adjustment in the blanching time is needed. See the Canning and Freezing chapter, especially the tip on page 190.

Deep-fat frying: At high altitudes, deep-fried foods can overbrown on the outside but remain underdone inside. While foods vary, a rough guideline is to lower the temperature of the fat about 3°F for every 1,000 feet in elevation above sea level.

Cooking Above 6,000 Feet

Cooking at altitudes higher than 6,000 feet above sea level poses further challenges because the dry air found at such elevations influences cooking. Call your local United States Department of Agriculture Extension Service Office for advice.

Further Information

For more information on cooking at high altitudes, contact your county extension office or write to Colorado State University, Department of Food Science and Human Nutrition Cooperative Extension, Fort Collins, CO 80523-1571. Please use this contact only for queries regarding high-altitude cooking.

Glossary of Cooking Ingredients, Terms, and Techniques

Definitions of terms and techniques used in this cookbook and others appear in this section. These pages also contain helpful information about ingredients, including both common staples and specialty ingredients enjoyed in a range of multi-cultural cooking styles. For topics not found here, look in relevant chapters (for example, look for pummelos in the fruit chapter) or in the index.

Adobo sauce: A dark-red Mexican sauce made from ground chiles, herbs, and vinegar. Chipotle peppers are packed in cans of adobo sauce.

Al dente: See page 393.

Almond paste: A creamy mixture made of ground, blanched almonds and sugar that's often used as a filling in pastries, cakes, and confections. For best baking results, use an almond paste without syrup or liquid glucose.

Anchovy paste: A mixture of ground anchovies, vinegar, and seasonings. Anchovy paste is available in tubes in the canned fish or gourmet section of the supermarket.

Artificial sweeteners: A category of sugar substitutes that have no nutritional value. Because they have unique attributes, they should not be substituted for other sweeteners unless a recipe calls for them specifically.

Bake: To cook food, covered or uncovered, using the direct, dry heat of an oven. The term is usually used to describe the cooking of cakes, other desserts, casseroles, and breads.

Baking ammonia: A compound also known as hartshorn powder that was once used as a leavening agent. It's most often used in Scandinavian baking and is available at pharmacies and through mail order. Cream of tartar is an acceptable substitute, although cookies made with it are less crisp than those made with baking ammonia. If you use baking ammonia for baking, use caution when opening the oven door because irritating ammonialike fumes may be produced.

Baking powder: A combination of dry acid, baking soda, and starch that has the ability to release carbon dioxide in two stages: when liquid ingredients are added and when the mixture is heated.

Baking Powder and Soda

Because recipes often call for such small amounts of baking powder and baking soda, you may think these ingredients are not essential for success. They are! These ingredients are leavening agents—without them, the baked products will not rise. And, because the chemical properties of the two ingredients are different, one cannot be substituted for another. It's best to keep both on hand.

When using baking soda, keep in mind that the soda and acid begin to react as soon as a liquid is added, so any product that uses only soda as the leaven should be baked immediately.

Baking soda: A chemical leavening agent that creates carbon dioxide and is used in conjunction with acidic ingredients, such as buttermilk, sour cream, brown sugar, or fruit juices, to create the bubbles that make the product rise.

Balsamic vinegar: Syrupy and slightly sweet, this dark-brown vinegar is made from the juice of the white Trebbiano grape. It gets its body, color, and sweetness from being aged in wooden barrels.

Basmati rice: An aromatic, long grain brown or white rice from India and California. Basmati rice is nutty and fluffy. Use as you would regular long grain rice.

Baste: To moisten foods during cooking or grilling with fats or seasoned liquids to add flavor and prevent drying. In general, recipes in this cookbook do not call for basting meat and poultry with pan juices or drippings. That's because basting tools, such as brushes and bulb basters, could be sources of bacteria if contaminated when dipped into uncooked or undercooked meat and poultry juices, then allowed to sit at room temperature and used later for basting.

Batter: An uncooked, wet mixture that can be spooned or poured, as with cakes, pancakes, and muffins. Batters usually contain flour, eggs, and milk as their base. Some thin batters are used to coat foods before deep frying.

Bean sauce, bean paste: Popular in Asian cooking, both products are made from fermented soybeans and have a salty bean flavor. Japanese bean paste is called miso.

Bean threads: Thin, almost transparent noodles made from mung bean flour. They also are called bean noodles or cellophane noodles.

Bean thread

Beat: To make a mixture smooth by briskly whipping or stirring it with a spoon, fork, wire whisk, rotary beater, or electric mixer. See "Beating Eggs," page 23.

Bias-slice: To slice a food crosswise at a 45-degree angle.

Bias-slice

Blackened: A popular Cajun cooking method in which seasoned fish or other foods are cooked over high heat in a superheated heavy skillet until charred, resulting in a crisp, spicy crust. At home, this is best done outdoors because of the large amount of smoke produced.

Blanch: To partially cook fruits, vegetables, or nuts in boiling water or steam to intensify and set color and flavor. This is an important step in preparing fruits and vegetables for freezing. Blanching also helps loosen skins from tomatoes, peaches, and almonds.

Blend: To combine two or more ingredients by hand, or with an electric mixer or blender, until smooth and uniform in texture, flavor, and color.

Boil: To cook food in liquid at a temperature that causes bubbles to form in the liquid and rise in a steady pattern, breaking at the surface. A rolling boil occurs when liquid is boiling so vigorously that the bubbles can't be stirred down. See also Simmer, page 32.

Bouillon: A bouillon cube is a compressed cube of dehydrated beef, chicken, fish, or vegetable stock. Bouillon granules are small particles of the same substance, but they dissolve faster. Both can be reconstituted in hot liquid to substitute for stock or broth.

Braise: To cook food slowly in a small amount of liquid in a tightly covered pan on the range top or in the oven. Braising is recommended for less-tender cuts of meat.

Breading: A coating of crumbs, sometimes seasoned, on meat, fish, poultry, and vegetables.

Breading is often made with soft or dry bread crumbs. See Crumbs, page 21.

Brine: Heavily salted water used to pickle or cure vegetables, meats, fish, and seafood.

Broil: To cook food a measured distance below direct, dry heat. When broiling, position the broiler pan and its rack so that the surface of the food (not the rack) is the specified distance from the heat source. Use a ruler to measure this distance.

Broil

Broth: The strained clear liquid in which meat, poultry, or fish has been simmered with vegetables and herbs. It is similar to stock and can be used interchangeably with it. Reconstituted bouillon can also be used when broth is specified.

Brown: To cook a food in a skillet, broiler, or oven to add flavor and aroma and develop a rich, desirable color on the outside and moistness on the inside.

Butter: For rich flavor, butter is usually the fat of choice. For baking, butter is recommended rather than margarine for consistent results (see Margarine, page 26). Salted and unsalted butter can be used interchangeably in recipes; however, if you use unsalted butter, you may want to increase the amount of salt in a recipe.

Butterfly: To split food, such as shrimp or pork chops, through the middle without completely separating the halves. Opened flat, the split halves resemble a butterfly.

Candied: A food, usually a fruit, nut, or citrus peel, that has been cooked or dipped in sugar syrup.

Capers: The buds of a spiny shrub that grows from Spain to China. Found next to the olives in the the supermarket, capers have an assertive flavor that can best be described as the marriage of citrus and olive, plus an added tang that comes from the salt and vinegar of their packaging brine. While the smaller buds bring more flavor than the larger buds, both can be used interchangeably in recipes.

Capers

Chiles

Chiles are spicy pods of the capsicum family of plants. Also known as chile peppers, they're available in many sizes and colors, with varying degrees of hotness (generally, the smaller the chile, the hotter it is). See tip, page 64, regarding safe handling of chiles. When shopping for fresh chiles, look for bright colors and avoid any that are shriveled, bruised, or broken. Store them, covered, in the refrigerator for up to 5 days. Dried chiles will keep for up to 1 year in airtight containers in a cool, dark place. A few varieties include:

Anaheim: Available in fresh and dried forms, these chiles are versatile and offer medium heat.

Ancho: The dried version of the poblano pepper, these are mild to medium-hot, with complex flavors.

Cascabel: These red chiles have a medium heat and are most often sold dried.

Chile de arbol: This long, slender, bright-to-deep-red chile is extremely hot. It comes in both dried and fresh forms.

Chipotle: Chipotle peppers are dried, smoked jalapeños, which are sometimes found canned in adobo, a spicy sauce.

Dried pequin: These tiny chiles are loaded with blistering heat. They should be used sparingly and with caution.

Habañero: Native to the Caribbean, these pack a searing heat and are available fresh and dried, with the fresh being the most popular.

Jalapeño: These are hot to extremely hot, with a short, oval shape and a green to reddish-green color.

Pasilla: These long, slender dried chiles have wrinkled skin and are medium to very hot, with a rich flavor. In some regions, they're also available fresh.

Poblano: This one is a mild to medium-hot chile with deep, complex flavors.

Serrano: The color of these hot, slender chiles is deep green, which sometimes ripens to bright red.

Thai: For spicing up Thai-inspired dishes, these colorful little chiles are the choice—they pack plenty of intense heat.

Anaheim (fresh)

Anaheim (dried)

Cascabel

Chile de arbol

Dried pequin

Chipotle peppers in adobo sauce

Habañero (fresh)

Jalapeño

Habañero (dried)

Pasilla

Poblano

Ancho

Serrano

Thai

Carve: To cut or slice cooked meat, poultry, fish, or game into serving-size pieces. To carve poultry, see page 440.

Cheese: See "Cheese," pages 276–278.

Cheesecloth: A thin 100-percent-cotton cloth with either a fine or coarse weave. Cheesecloth is used in cooking to bundle up herbs, strain liquids, and wrap rolled meats. Look for it among cooking supplies in supermarkets and specialty cookware shops.

Chiffonade

Chiffonade: In cooking, this French word, meaning "made of rags," refers to thin strips of fresh herbs or lettuce.

Chile: See page 19.

Chili oil: A fiery oil, flavored with chile peppers, that's used as a seasoning.

Chili paste: A condiment, available in mild or hot versions, that's made from chile peppers, vinegar, and seasonings.

Chill: To cool food to below room temperature in the refrigerator or over ice. When the recipes in this book call for chilling foods, it should be done in the refrigerator.

Chocolate: In general, six types of chocolate are available at the supermarket:

Milk chocolate is at least 10-percent pure chocolate with added cocoa butter, sugar, and milk solids.

Semisweet and bittersweet chocolate can be used interchangeably. They contain at least 35-percent pure chocolate with added cocoa butter and sugar.

Sweet chocolate is dark chocolate that contains at least 15-percent pure chocolate with extra cocoa butter and sugar.

Melting Chocolate

To melt chocolate on the range top, place it in a heavy saucepan or double boiler. Place the saucepan over low heat or the double boiler over hot, but not boiling, water. Stir the chocolate often to keep it from burning.

When melting chocolate, make sure the utensils you use are dry and avoid splashing water into the pan. Even a little water will cause the chocolate to seize up and get grainy and lumpy.

To melt chocolate in a microwave, see page 15.

Unsweetened chocolate is used for baking and cooking rather than snacking. This ingredient contains pure chocolate and cocoa butter with no sugar added.

Unsweetened cocoa powder is pure chocolate with most of the cocoa butter removed. Dutch-process or European-style cocoa powder has been treated to neutralize acids, making it mellower in flavor.

White chocolate, which has a mild flavor, contains cocoa butter, sugar, and milk solids. Products such as white baking bars, white baking pieces, white candy coating, and white confectionery bars are sometimes confused with white chocolate. While they are often used interchangeably in recipes, they are not truly white chocolate because they do not contain cocoa butter.

Chop: To cut foods with a knife, cleaver, or food processor into smaller pieces. See "Slicing, Dicing, and More," page 22.

Chorizo (chuh-REE-zoh): A spicy pork sausage used in Mexican and Spanish cuisine. Spanish chorizo is made with smoked pork, and Mexican chorizo is made with fresh pork.

Chutney: A condiment often used in Indian cuisine that's made of chopped fruit (mango is a classic), vegetables, and spices enlivened by hot peppers, fresh ginger, or vinegar.

Clarified butter: Sometimes called drawn butter, clarified butter is best known as a dipping sauce for seafood. It is butter that has had the milk solids removed. Because clarified butter can be heated to high temperatures without burning, it's also used for quickly browning meats. To clarify butter, melt the butter over low heat in a heavy saucepan without stirring. Skim off foam, if necessary. You will see a clear, oily layer on top of a milky layer. Slowly pour the clear liquid into a dish, leaving the milky layer in the pan. The clear liquid is the clarified butter; discard the milky liquid. Store clarified butter in the refrigerator up to 1 month.

Coat: To evenly cover food with crumbs, flour, or a batter. Often done to meat, fish, and poultry before cooking.

Coconut milk: A product made from water and coconut pulp that's often used in Southeast Asian and Indian cooking. Coconut milk is not the clear liquid in the center of the coconut, nor should it be confused with cream of coconut, a sweetened coconut concoction often used to make mixed drinks such as piña coladas.

Cooking oil: Liquids at room temperature made from vegetables, nuts, or seeds. Common types for general cooking include corn, soybean, canola, sunflower, safflower, peanut, and olive. For baking, cooking oils cannot be used interchangeably with solid fats because they do not hold air when beaten. See also Flavored oils, page 24.

Couscous (KOOS-koos): A granular pasta popular in North Africa that's made from semolina. Look for it in the rice and pasta section of supermarkets.

Cream (verb): To beat a fat, such as butter or shortening either alone or with sugar, to a light, fluffy consistency. May be done by hand with a wooden spoon or with an electric mixer. This process incorporates air into the fat so baked products have a lighter texture and a better volume.

Crème fraîche: A dairy product made from whipping cream and a bacterial culture, which causes the whipping cream to thicken and develop a sharp, tangy flavor. If you can't find crème fraîche in your supermarket, you can make a substitute by combining ½ cup whipping cream (do not use ultra-pasteurized cream) and ½ cup dairy sour cream. Cover the mixture and let it stand at room temperature for 2 to 5 hours or until it thickens. Cover and refrigerate for up to 1 week.

Crimp: To pinch or press pastry or dough together using your fingers, a fork, or another utensil. Usually done for a piecrust edge.

Crisp-tender: A term that describes the state of vegetables that have been cooked until just tender but still somewhat crunchy. At this stage, a fork can be inserted with a little pressure.

Crumbs: Fine particles of food that have been broken off a larger piece. Crumbs are often used as a coating, thickener, or binder, or as a crust in desserts. Recipes usually specify either soft or fine dry bread crumbs, which generally are not interchangeable. See above right.

Crush: To smash food into smaller pieces, generally using hands, a mortar and pestle, or a rolling pin. Crushing dried herbs releases their flavor and aroma.

Cube: See "Slicing, Dicing, and More," page 22.

Curdle: To cause semisolid pieces of coagulated protein to develop in a dairy product. This can occur

Making Crumbs

While some prepared crumbs, such as those made from graham crackers, chocolate wafers, and dry bread, are available at the supermarket, others are not. All are easy to make at home.

■ Dry bread, cookie, and cracker crumbs can be made by processing them to a fine consistency in a blender or food processor. Or place the ingredient in a heavy plastic bag and crush it to a fine consistency with a rolling pin. Leave one end of the bag open a bit so air can escape during rolling.

■ To make 1 cup of cracker or cookie crumbs, you'll need 28 saltine crackers, 14 graham cracker squares, 22 vanilla wafers, 19 chocolate wafers,15 gingersnaps, or 24 rich, round crackers.

■ To make fine dry bread crumbs or soft bread crumbs, see page 293.

when foods such as milk or sour cream are heated to too high a temperature or are combined with an acidic food, such as lemon juice or tomatoes.

Curry paste: A blend of herbs, spices, and fiery chiles that's often used in Indian and Thai cooking. Look for curry paste in Asian markets. Curry pastes are available in many varieties and are sometimes classified by color (green, red, or yellow), by heat (mild or hot), or by a particular style of curry (such as Panang or Masaman).

Cut in: To work a solid fat, such as shortening, butter, or margarine, into dry ingredients. This is usually done with a pastry blender, two knives in a crisscross fashion, your fingertips, or a food processor (see photo 1, page 417).

Dash: Refers to a small amount of seasoning that is added to food. It is generally between ¹⁄₁₆ and ⅛ teaspoon. The term is often used for liquid ingredients, such as bottled hot pepper sauce.

Deep-fat fry: See Fry, page 24.

Deglaze: Adding a liquid such as water, wine, or broth to a skillet that has been used to cook meat. After the meat has been removed, the liquid is poured into the pan to help loosen the browned bits and make a flavorful sauce.

Demi-glace (DEHM-ee-glahs): A thick, intense meat-flavor gel that's often used as a foundation for soups and sauces. Demi-glace is available in gourmet shops or through mail-order catalogs.

Dice: See "Slicing, Dicing, and More," below.

Dip: To immerse food for a short time in a liquid or dry mixture to coat, cool, or moisten it.

Direct grilling: Method of quickly cooking food by placing it on a grill rack directly over the heat source. A charcoal grill is often left uncovered, while a gas grill is generally covered.

Dissolve: To stir a solid food and a liquid food together to form a mixture in which none of the solid remains. In some cases, heat may be needed in order for the solid to dissolve.

Slicing, Dicing, and More

Not sure of the difference between chopping, mincing, slicing, or dicing? Here's a guide:

Chop means to cut foods with a knife or food processor into fine, medium, or coarse irregular pieces.

Cube means to cut food into uniform pieces, usually ½ inch on all sides.

Dice means to cut food into uniform pieces, usually ⅛ to ¼ inch on all sides.

Julienne means to cut food into thin matchlike sticks about 2 inches long. For easier cutting, first cut food into slices about 2 × ¼ inch; stack the slices and cut them lengthwise into strips ⅛ to ¼ inch wide.

Mince means to chop a food into tiny irregular pieces.

Slice means to cut food into flat, thin pieces.

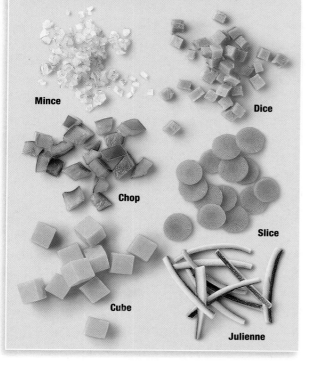

Mince

Dice

Chop

Slice

Cube

Julienne

Drawn: A term referring to a whole fish, with or without scales, that has had its internal organs removed. The term "drawn butter" refers to clarified butter. See Clarified butter, page 20.

Dredge: To coat a food, either before or after cooking, with a dry ingredient, such as flour, cornmeal, or sugar.

Drip pan: A metal or disposable foil pan placed under food to catch drippings when grilling. A drip pan can also be made from heavy-duty foil.

Drizzle: To randomly pour a liquid, such as powdered sugar icing, in a thin stream over food.

Dust: To lightly coat or sprinkle a food with a dry ingredient, such as flour or powdered sugar, either before or after cooking.

Egg roll skins: Pastry wrappers used to encase a savory filling and make egg rolls. Look for these products in the produce aisle of the supermarket or at Asian markets. Egg roll skins are similar to, but larger than, wonton skins.

Egg whites, dried: Pasteurized dried egg whites can be used where egg whites are needed; follow package directions for reconstituting them. Unlike raw egg whites, which must be thoroughly cooked before serving to kill harmful bacteria, pasteurized dried egg whites can be used in recipes that do not call for egg whites to be thoroughly cooked. Keep in mind that meringue powder may not be substituted, as it has added sugar and starch. Find dried egg whites in powdered form in the baking aisle of many supermarkets and through mail-order sources. Also see page 408.

Eggs: See page 263 regarding how to use eggs safely. Keep in mind that you should avoid eating foods that contain raw eggs. Eggs should be cooked until both the yolk and white are firm; scrambled eggs should not be runny. Cook casseroles and other dishes that contain eggs until they register 160°F on a food thermometer. If you have a recipe that calls for the eggs to be raw or undercooked (such as Caesar salads and homemade ice cream), use shell eggs that are clearly labeled as having been pasteurized to destroy salmonella; these are available at some retailers. Or use a widely available pasteurized egg product. If you have a recipe that calls for egg whites to be raw or undercooked, use pasteurized dried egg whites or pasteurized refrigerated liquid egg whites.

For cake recipes, allow eggs to stand at room temperature for 30 minutes before using. If the cake recipe calls for separated eggs, separate them immediately after removing them from the refrigerator and use them within 30 minutes. For all other recipes, use eggs straight from the refrigerator.

See tip, below, regarding equivalent egg sizes.

Emulsify: To combine two liquid or semiliquid ingredients, such as oil and vinegar, that don't naturally dissolve into each other. One way to do this is to gradually add one ingredient to the other while whisking rapidly with a fork or wire whisk.

Extracts, oils: Products based on the aromatic essential oils of plant materials that are distilled by various means. In extracts, the highly concentrated oils are usually suspended in alcohol to make them easier to combine with other foods in cooking and baking. Almond, anise, lemon, mint, orange, peppermint, and vanilla are some commonly available extracts.

Some undiluted oils are also available, usually at pharmacies. These include oil of anise, oil of cinnamon, oil of cloves, oil of peppermint, and oil of wintergreen. Do not try to substitute oils for ground spices in recipes. Oils are so concentrated that they're measured in drops, not teaspoons. Oil of cinnamon, for example, is 50 times stronger than ground cinnamon. You can, however, substitute 1 or 2 drops of an oil for ½ teaspoon extract in frosting or candy recipes.

Fats, oils: See specific ingredients, such as butter, margarine, shortening, lard, or cooking oil.

Fillet: A piece of meat or fish that has no bones. As a verb, fillet refers to the process of cutting meat or fish into fillets.

Fish sauce: A pungent brown sauce made by fermenting fish, usually anchovies, in brine. It's often used in Southeast Asian cooking.

Flake: To gently break food into small, flat pieces.

Egg Equivalents

Recipes in this book were developed and tested using large eggs. If you purchase eggs in other sizes, adjust the number you use to ensure success when preparing baked goods, soufflés, egg-thickened sauces, or recipes in which egg binds the ingredients together. For most other recipes, egg size isn't critical.

Large Eggs	Other Size Equivalents
1 large egg	1 jumbo, 1 extra-large, 1 medium, or 1 small egg
2 large eggs	2 jumbo, 2 extra-large, 2 medium, or 3 small eggs
3 large eggs	2 jumbo, 3 extra-large, 3 medium, or 4 small eggs
4 large eggs	3 jumbo, 4 extra-large, 5 medium, or 5 small eggs
5 large eggs	4 jumbo, 4 extra-large, 6 medium, or 7 small eggs
6 large eggs	5 jumbo, 5 extra-large, 7 medium, or 8 small eggs

Beating Eggs

Here's how to beat whole eggs, egg whites, or egg yolks to the right consistency called for in recipes:

Slightly beaten eggs: Use a fork to beat the whole egg until the yolk and white are combined and no streaks remain.

Beating egg whites until soft peaks form: Place the egg whites in a clean glass or metal bowl (do not use plastic). Beat the whites with an electric mixer on medium speed or with a rotary beater until they form peaks with tips that curl over when the beaters are lifted out. Any speck of fat, oil, or yolk in the bowl will prevent whites from developing the necessary whipped consistency.

Beating egg whites until stiff peaks form: Continue beating egg whites, now on high speed, until they form peaks with tips that stand straight when the beaters are lifted out.

Beating egg yolks: Beat the egg yolks with an electric mixer on high speed for about 5 minutes or until they are thick and lemon-color.

Slightly beaten eggs

Soft peaks

Stiff peaks

Beating egg yolks

Flavored oils: Commercially prepared oils flavored with herbs, spices, or other ingredients, including avocado, walnut, sesame, hazelnut, and almond. In addition to using them in recipes when called for, try brushing them over grilled vegetables or bread, or experiment with them in your favorite vinaigrette recipe.

Flavoring: An imitation extract made of chemical compounds. Unlike an extract or oil, a flavoring often does not contain any of the original food it resembles. Some common imitation flavorings available are banana, black walnut, brandy, cherry, chocolate, coconut, maple, pineapple, raspberry, rum, strawberry, and vanilla.

Flour: A milled food that can be made from many cereals, roots, and seeds, although wheat is the most popular. Store flour in an airtight container in a cool, dry place. All-purpose flour may be stored for up to 8 months. Bread flour, cake flour, gluten flour, whole wheat flour, and other whole grain flours may be stored up to 5 months. For longer storage, refrigerate or freeze the flour in a moisture- and vaporproof container. Bring chilled flour to room temperature before using in baking.

Here are the types of flour most commonly used in cooking:

All-purpose flour: This flour is made from a blend of soft and hard wheat flours and, as its name implies, can be used for many purposes, including baking, thickening, and coating. All-purpose flour usually is sold presifted and is available bleached or unbleached. Bleached flour has been made chemically whiter in appearance. Some cooks prefer the bleached flour to make their cakes and bread as white as possible, while other cooks prefer their flour to be processed as little as necessary. Both bleached and unbleached flour are suitable for home baking and can be used interchangeably.

Bread flour: This flour contains more gluten than all-purpose flour, making it ideal for baking breads, which rely on gluten for structure and height (see Gluten, page 25). If you use a bread machine, use bread flour instead of all-purpose flour for best results. Or use all-purpose flour and add 1 or 2 tablespoons of gluten flour (available in supermarkets or health food stores).

Cake flour: Made from a soft wheat, cake flour produces a tender, delicate crumb because the gluten is less elastic. It's too delicate for general baking, but to use it for cakes, sift it before measuring and use 1 cup plus 2 tablespoons of cake flour for every 1 cup all-purpose flour specified.

Gluten flour: Because whole-grain flours are low in gluten (see Gluten, page 25), some whole-grain bread recipes often call for a little gluten flour to help the finished loaf attain the proper texture. Sometimes called wheat gluten, gluten flour is made by removing most of the starch from high-protein, hard-wheat flour. If you can't find gluten flour at a supermarket, look for it at a health food store.

Pastry flour: A soft wheat blend with less starch than cake flour. It is used for making pastry.

Self-rising flour: An all-purpose flour with salt and a leavener, such as baking powder, added. It is generally not used for making yeast products.

Specialty flours: Specialty flours, such as whole wheat, graham, rye, oat, buckwheat, and soy, generally are combined with all-purpose flour in baking recipes because none has sufficient gluten to provide the right amount of elasticity on its own.

Flour (verb): To coat or dust a food or utensil with flour. Food may be floured before cooking to add texture and improve browning. Baking utensils sometimes are floured to prevent sticking.

Flute: To make a decorative impression in food, usually a piecrust (see photos, page 417).

Fold: A method of gently mixing ingredients without decreasing their volume. To fold, use a rubber spatula to cut down vertically through the mixture from the back of the bowl. Move the spatula across the bottom of the bowl, and bring it back up the other side, carrying some of the mixture from the bottom up over the surface. Repeat these steps, rotating the bowl one-fourth of a turn each time you complete the process.

Food coloring: Liquid, paste, or powdered edible dyes used to tint foods.

French: To cut meat away from the end of a rib or chop to expose the bone, as with a lamb rib roast.

Frost: To apply a cooked or uncooked topping, which is soft enough to spread but stiff enough to hold its shape, to cakes, cupcakes, or cookies.

Fruit: For tips on selecting and storing fresh fruits, see pages 531–533. For information on less-common fruits, see pages 536–539.

Fry: To cook food in a hot cooking oil or fat, usually until a crisp brown crust forms. To panfry is to cook food, which may have a very light breading or coating, in a skillet in a small amount of hot fat or oil. To deep-fat fry (or French fry) is to cook a food until it is crisp in enough hot fat or oil to cover the food. To shallow fry is to cook a food, usually breaded or coated with batter, in about an inch of hot fat or oil. To oven fry is to cook a food in a hot oven, using a small amount of fat to produce a healthier product.

Garlic: The strongly scented, pungent bulb of a plant related to an onion. A garlic clove is one of the several small segments that make up a garlic bulb. Elephant garlic is larger, milder, and more closely related to the leek.

Garlic bulb (head)

Store firm, fresh, plump garlic bulbs in a cool, dry, dark place; leave bulbs whole because individual cloves dry out quickly. Convenient substitutes are available; for each clove called for in a recipe use either ⅛ teaspoon garlic powder or ½ teaspoon bottled

Garlic cloves

minced garlic. For a recipe for Roasted Garlic Spread, see page 71.

Garnish: To add visual appeal to a finished dish.

Gelatin: A dry ingredient made from natural animal protein that can thicken or set a liquid. Gelatin is available in unflavored and flavored forms. When using, make sure the gelatin powder is completely dissolved.

To dissolve one envelope of unflavored gelatin: Place gelatin in a small saucepan and stir in at least ¼ cup water, broth, or fruit juice. Let it stand 5 minutes to soften, then stir it over low heat until the gelatin is dissolved.

Do not mix gelatin with figs, fresh pineapple (canned pineapple is not a problem), fresh ginger, guava, kiwifruit, and papaya, as these foods contain an enzyme that prevents gelatin from setting up.

Some recipes call for gelatin at various stages of gelling. "Partially set" means the mixture looks like unbeaten egg whites. At this point, solid ingredients may be added. "Almost firm" describes gelatin that is sticky to the touch. It can be layered at this stage. "Firm" gelatin holds a cut edge and is ready to be served.

Giblets: The edible internal organs of poultry, including the liver, heart, and gizzard. (Although sometimes packaged with the giblets, the neck is not part of the giblets.) Giblets are sometimes used to make gravy.

Ginger: The root of a semitropical plant that adds a spicy-sweet flavor to recipes (also called gingerroot). Ginger should be peeled before using. To peel, cut off one end of the root and use a vegetable peeler to remove the brown outer layer in strips. To grate ginger, use the fine holes of a grater. To mince ginger, slice peeled ginger with the grain (lengthwise) into thin sticks. Stack the sticks in a bundle and cut them finely. Ginger stays fresh two or three weeks in the refrigerator when wrapped loosely in a paper towel. For longer storage, place unpeeled ginger in a freezer bag and store in freezer. Ginger will keep indefinitely when frozen, and you can grate or slice the ginger while it's frozen. In a pinch, ground ginger can be used for grated fresh ginger. For 1 teaspoon grated fresh ginger, use ¼ teaspoon ground ginger.

Ginger, crystallized: A confection made from pieces of ginger (gingerroot) cooked in a sugar syrup, then coated with sugar. Also known as candied ginger. Store in a cool, dry, dark place.

Crystallized ginger

Glacé (gla-SAY): The French term for "glazed" or "frozen." In the United States, it describes a candied food. See Candied, page 18.

Glaze: A thin, glossy coating.

Gluten: An elastic protein present in flour, especially wheat flour, that provides most of the structure of baked products. Also see Knead, page 26.

Grate: To rub food, such as hard cheeses, vegetables, or whole nutmeg or ginger, across a grating surface to make very fine pieces. A food processor also may be used. See also Shred, page 32.

Grate

Grease: To coat a utensil, such as a baking pan or skillet, with a thin layer of fat or oil. A pastry brush works well to grease pans. Also refers to fat released from meat and poultry during cooking.

Grease

Grind: To mechanically cut a food into smaller pieces, usually with a food grinder or a food processor.

Herbs: See "Seasonings," pages 36–39.

Hoisin sauce: A sauce, popular in Asian cooking, that brings a multitude of sweet and spicy flavors to a dish: fermented soybeans, molasses, vinegar, mustard, sesame seeds, garlic, and chiles. Look for hoisin sauce alongside the soy sauce in most supermarkets or in Asian markets.

Honey: A sweet, sticky sweetener that's produced by bees from floral nectar. Honey is now available in more than 300 varieties in the United States. Its flavor depends on the flowers from which the honey is derived; most honey is made from clover, but other sources include lavender, thyme, orange blossom, apple, cherry, buckwheat, and tupelo. Generally, the lighter the color, the milder the flavor. Store honey at room temperature in a dark place. If it crystallizes (becomes solid), reliquefy it by warming the honey jar slightly in the microwave oven or in a pan of very hot tap water. If the honey smells or tastes strange, toss it out.

Note that honey should not be given to children who are younger than one year old because it can contain trace amounts of botulism spores. These spores could trigger a potentially fatal reaction in children with undeveloped immune systems.

Hors d'oeuvre (or-DERV): French term for small, hot or cold portions of savory food served as an appetizer.

Ice: To drizzle or spread baked goods with a thin frosting.

Indirect grilling: Method of slowly cooking food in a covered grill over a spot where there are no coals. Usually the food is placed on the rack over a drip pan, with coals arranged around the pan.

Jelly roll: Dessert made by spreading a filling on a sponge cake and rolling it up into a log shape (recipe, page 166). When other foods are shaped "jelly-roll-style," it refers to rolling them into a log shape with fillings inside.

Juice: The natural liquid extracted from fruits, vegetables, meats, and poultry. Also refers to the process of extracting juice from foods.

Julienne: See "Slicing, Dicing, and More," page 22.

Knead: To work dough with the heels of your hands in a pressing and folding motion until it becomes smooth and elastic. This is an essential step in developing the gluten in many yeast breads. (See photo 1, page 132, and page 133.)

Kosher salt: A coarse salt with no additives that many cooks prefer for its light, flaky texture and clean taste. It also has a lower sodium content than regular salt. Find it next to salt in the supermarket.

Lard: A product made from pork fat that is sometimes used for baking. It's especially noted for producing light, flaky piecrusts. Today, shortening is commonly used instead of lard.

Leavenings: Ingredients that are essential in helping batter and dough expand or rise during baking. If omitted, the baked products will be heavy and tough. See specific ingredients, such as yeast, baking powder, and baking soda, for more information.

Lemongrass

Lemongrass: A highly aromatic, lemon-flavored herb often used in Asian cooking. To use, trim the fibrous ends and slice what remains into 3- to 4-inch sections. Cut each section in half lengthwise, exposing the layers. Rinse pieces under cold water to remove any grit and slice the lemongrass thinly. In a pinch, substitute ½ teaspoon finely shredded lemon peel for 1 tablespoon lemongrass.

Marble: To gently swirl one food into another. Marbling is usually done with light and dark batters for cakes or cookies. Also see Vanilla Fudge Marble Cake, page 162.

Margarine: A product generally made from vegetable oil that was developed in the late 1800s as a substitute for butter. When baking, be sure to use a stick margarine that contains at least 80 percent fat. Check the nutritional information. It should have 100 calories per tablespoon. See page 222.

Marble

Marinade: A seasoned liquid in which meat, poultry, fish, shellfish, or vegetables are soaked to flavor and sometimes tenderize them. Most marinades contain an acid, such as wine or vinegar.

Marinate: To soak food in a marinade. When marinating foods, do not use a metal container, as it can react with acidic ingredients to give foods an off flavor. Always marinate foods in the refrigerator, never on the kitchen counter. To reduce cleanup, use a plastic bag set in a bowl or dish to hold the food you are marinating. Discard leftover marinade that has come in contact with raw meat. Or if it's to be used on cooked meat, bring leftover marinade to a rolling boil before using to destroy any bacteria that may be present.

Marsala: A fortified wine that can be either dry or sweet. Sweet Marsala is used both for drinking and cooking. Dry Marsala makes a nice predinner drink.

Mash: To press or beat a food to remove lumps and make a smooth mixture. This can be done with a fork, potato masher, food mill, food ricer, or electric mixer.

Measure: To determine the quantity or size of a food or utensil. (See "Measuring Ingredients," page 7.)

Melt: To heat a solid food, such as chocolate, margarine, or butter, over very low heat until it becomes liquid or semiliquid.

Meringue powder: See page 408.

Milk and milk products: Varieties include:

Buttermilk: Buttermilk is a low-fat or fat-free milk to which a bacterial culture has been added. It has a mildly acidic taste. Sour milk, made from milk and lemon juice or vinegar, can be substituted in baking recipes. See page 157.

Evaporated milk: Made from whole milk, canned evaporated milk has had about half of its water removed; it lends a creamy richness to many recipes, including pumpkin pie. Measure it straight from the can for recipes calling for evaporated milk; to use it in place of fresh milk, dilute it as directed on the can (usually with an equal amount of water) to make the quantity called for in the recipe. Evaporated milk is also available in low-fat and fat-free versions. Evaporated milk is not interchangeable with sweetened condensed milk.

Fat-free half-and-half: Made mostly from skim milk, with carrageenan for body, this product can bring a creamy flavor to recipes without added fat. Experiment using it in cornstarch or flour-thickened soup, sauce, and gravy recipes that call for regular half-and-half.

Light cream and half-and-half: Light cream contains 18 to 30 percent milk fat. Half-and-half is a mixture of milk and cream. They're interchangeable in most recipes; however, neither contains enough fat to be whipped.

Nonfat dry milk powder: When reconstituted, this milk product can be used in cooking.

Sour cream and yogurt: Sour cream is traditionally made from light cream with a bacterial culture added, while yogurt is made from milk with a bacterial culture added. Both are available in low-fat and fat-free varieties.

Sweetened condensed milk: This product is made with whole milk that has had water removed and sugar added. It is also available in low-fat and fat-free versions. Sweetened condensed milk is not interchangeable with evaporated milk or fresh milk.

Whipping cream: It contains at least 30 percent milk fat and can be beaten into whipped cream.

Whole, low-fat or light, reduced-fat, and fat-free milk: Because these milk types differ only in the amount of fat they contain and in the richness of flavor they lend to foods, they may be used interchangeably in cooking. Recipes in this cookbook were tested using reduced-fat (2 percent) milk.

Mince: See tip "Slicing, Dicing, and More," page 22.

Mix: To stir or beat two or more foods together until they are thoroughly combined. May be done with an electric mixer, a rotary beater, or by hand with a wooden spoon.

Moisten: To add enough liquid to a dry ingredient or mixture to make it damp but not runny.

Mortar and pestle: A set that includes a bowl-shape vessel (the mortar) to hold ingredients to be crushed by a club-shape utensil (the pestle).

Mortar and pestle

Mull: To slowly heat a beverage, such as cider, with spices and sugar.

Mushrooms, dried: Dried mushrooms swell into tender, flavorful morsels. Simply cover them in warm water and soak them for about 30 minutes. Rinse well and squeeze out the moisture. Remove and discard tough stems. Cook them in recipes as you would fresh mushrooms. Popular choices include oyster, wood ear, and shiitake.

Mushrooms, fresh: See photos, page 29. A plant in the fungus family, mushrooms come in many colors and shapes, with flavors ranging from mild and nutty to meaty, woodsy, and wild. Fresh varieties to look for include:

Beech: These small mushrooms, with their all-white or light-brown caps, offer a crunchy texture and a mild, sweet, nutty flavor that works well in stir-fries and in sauces for poultry and fish. When adding to recipes, add toward the end of cooking time to retain their texture.

Chanterelle (shant-uh-REL): Best in simple recipes, trumpet-shape chanterelle are bright yellow to orange in color and have a buttery flavor.

Crimini: Tan to rich brown in color, crimini mushrooms can be used in most any recipe that calls for white mushrooms. They're similar in taste but earthier in flavor.

Enoki (eh-NOH-kee): These white mushrooms with long, thin stems and tiny caps often come vacuum packed. Show off their delicate flavor and slight crunch in salads and as soup toppers.

Morel (more-EL): Great for refined sauces and other gourmet recipes, these tan, black, or yellow spongy-looking mushrooms have an intense rich and nutty flavor and aroma—and generally a high price tag. Morels are also available in dried form.

Oyster: Oyster mushrooms come in a variety of colors, from cream to gray, and sizes; all have a velvety texture and a mild taste that melds well with poultry, veal, and seafood dishes.

Porcini: Also known as cèpes, these pale-brown wild mushrooms are usually found dried. They are prized for their strong woodsy flavor. Try them in soups and pasta sauces.

Portobello: Often used to bring heartiness to vegetarian entrées, these velvety brown mushrooms boast a deep mushroom flavor; find them in large, medium, and small sizes.

Shiitake (shee-TAH-kee): This brown mushroom is prized for the meaty flavor and texture it brings to pasta dishes, soups, and other entrées. Remove stems before adding to recipes

White: This umbrella-shape creamy white to light brown mushroom, with a mild, woodsy flavor, is a good, all-purpose mushroom that can be served raw, sauteed, or grilled. The small ones are sometimes referred to as button mushrooms.

Wood ear: This variety is favored for its yielding, yet crunchy, texture.

For information on storing and selecting fresh mushrooms, see page 530.

Nonstick cooking spray: This convenient product reduces the mess associated with greasing pans; it can also help cut down on fat in cooking. Use the spray only on unheated baking pans or skillets because it can burn or smoke if sprayed onto a hot surface. For safety, hold pans over a sink or garbage can when spraying to avoid making the floor or counter slippery.

Nuts: Dried seeds or fruits with edible kernels surrounded by a hard shell or rind. Nuts are available in many forms, such as chopped, slivered, and halved. Use the form called for in the recipe. In most recipes, the nuts are selected for their particular flavor and appearance; however, in general, walnuts may be substituted for pecans, and almonds for hazelnuts, and vice versa.

When grinding nuts, take extra care not to overgrind them, or you may end up with a nut butter. If you're using a blender or processor to grind them, add 1 tablespoon of the sugar or flour from the recipe for each cup of nuts to help absorb some of the oil. Use a quick start-and-stop motion for better control over the fineness. For best results, grind the nuts in small batches and be sure to let the nuts cool after toasting and before grinding.

To toast nuts, see page 224.

Olive oil: See page 455.

Olives: See page 30.

Oven fry: See Fry, page 24.

Pan-broil: To cook a food, especially meat, in a skillet without added fat, removing any fat as it accumulates.

Pancetta: See page 31.

Parboil: To boil a food, such as vegetables, until it is partially cooked.

Parchment paper: A grease- and heat-resistant paper used to line baking pans, to wrap foods in packets for baking, or to make disposable pastry bags.

Pare: To cut off the skin or outer covering of a fruit or vegetable, using a small knife or a vegetable peeler.

Partially set: See Gelatin, page 25.

Pectin: A natural substance found in some fruits that makes fruit-and-sugar mixtures used in jelly- or jam-making set up. Commercial pectin is also available. See page 187.

Oyster

Shiitake

White

Beech

Crimini

Chanterelle

Morel

Wood ear

Porcini

Enoki

Portobello
(small)

Portobello
(large)

Peel: The skin or outer covering of a vegetable or fruit (also called the rind). Peel also refers to the process of removing this covering.

Pesto: Traditionally an uncooked sauce made from crushed garlic, basil, and nuts blended with Parmesan cheese and olive oil. Today's pestos may call on other herbs or greens and may be homemade or purchased. Tomato pesto is also available. Pesto adds a heady freshness to many recipes.

Phyllo dough (FEE-loh): Prominent in Greek, Turkish, and Near Eastern dishes, phyllo consists of tissue-thin sheets of dough that, when layered and baked, results in a delicate, flaky pastry. The word phyllo (sometimes spelled *filo*) is Greek for "leaf." Although phyllo can be made at home, a frozen commercial prod-

Pine nuts

uct is available and much handier to use. Allow frozen phyllo dough to thaw while it is still wrapped; once unwrapped, sheets of phyllo dough quickly dry out and become unusable. To preserve sheets of phyllo, keep the stack covered with plastic wrap while you prepare your recipe. Rewrap any remaining sheets and return them to the freezer.

Pinch: A small amount of a dry ingredient (the amount that can be pinched between a finger and the thumb).

Pine nut: A high-fat nut that comes from certain varieties of pine trees. Their flavor ranges from mild and sweet to pungent. They go rancid quickly; store in the refrigerator or freezer. In a pinch, substitute chopped almonds or, in cream sauces, walnuts.

Olives

The fruit of the olive tree is available in more than 75 varieties. Olives are sold pitted and unpitted. Although purchased pitted olives are more convenient to use in cooking than unpitted olives, pitting causes more of the olive to be exposed to the brine. This can cause the flesh to become softer and yield a different flavor. One way to remove a pit from an unpitted olive is to gently crush the long side of the olive with the heel of your hand, then pull out the pit. Here are some of the more flavorful olives available:

Alphonso: A huge, deep-purple olive from Chile with soft, meaty flesh and a slightly bitter, sour taste.

Arbequina: A green, brine-cured olive with a slightly bitter taste.

Cerignola: A huge, green or jet-black brine-cured olive with a lemon-apple flavor. This one is difficult to pit.

Gaeta: A small, reddish-brown olive with a slightly earthy flavor.

Kalamata: A greenish-black-purple, brine-cured olive with a pungent, lingering flavor.

La Catalan: A brine-cured Spanish olive that's marinated with curry, celery, and pepper. It has a crisp, dense flesh and an assertive curry flavor.

Niçoise: A small, brownish-purple, brine-cured olive that's fruity and juicy, but not oily.

Nyon: A black, dry-roasted, tender olive with a slightly bitter flavor.

Alphonso

Kalamata

La Catalan

Gaeta

Niçoise Arbequina

Nyon

Cerignola

Pipe: To force a semisoft food, such as whipped cream or frosting, through a pastry bag to decorate food.

Pit: To remove the seed from fruit.

Plump: To allow a food, such as raisins, to soak in a liquid, which generally increases its volume.

Poach: To cook a food by partially or completely submerging it in a simmering liquid.

Pound: To strike a food with a heavy utensil to crush it. Or, in the case of meat or poultry, to break up connective tissue in order to tenderize or flatten it.

Precook: To partially or completely cook a food before using it in a recipe.

Preheat: To heat an oven or a utensil to a specific temperature before using it.

Process: To preserve food at home by canning, or to prepare food in a food processor.

Proof: To allow a yeast dough to rise before baking. Also a term that indicates the amount of alcohol in a distilled liquor.

Prosciutto: See tip, right.

Puff pastry: A butter-rich, multilayered pastry. When baked, the butter produces steam between the layers, causing the dough to puff up into many flaky layers. Because warm, softened puff pastry dough becomes sticky and unmanageable, roll out one sheet of dough at a time, keeping what you're not using wrapped tightly in plastic wrap in the refrigerator.

Puree: To process or mash a food until it is as smooth as possible. This can be done using a blender, food processor, sieve, or food mill; also refers to the resulting mixture.

Reconstitute: To bring a concentrated or condensed food, such as frozen fruit juice, to its original strength by adding water.

Reduce: To decrease the volume of a liquid by boiling it rapidly to cause evaporation. As the liquid evaporates, it thickens and intensifies in flavor. The resulting richly flavored liquid, called a reduction, can be used as a sauce or as the base of a sauce. When reducing liquids, use the pan size specified in the recipe, as the surface area of the pan affects how quickly the liquid will evaporate.

Rice: See page 81 for many varieties of rice available. Rice also means to force food that has been cooked through a perforated utensil known as a ricer, giving the food a somewhat ricelike shape.

Rice noodles, rice sticks: Thin noodles, popular in Asian cooking, that are made from finely ground rice and water. When fried, they puff into light, crisp strands. They can also be soaked to use in stir-fries and soups. Thicker varieties are called rice sticks. Find in Asian markets; substitute vermicelli or capellini for thin rice noodles, linguine or fettuccine for thicker rice sticks.

Rice papers: These round, flat, edible papers, made from the pith of a rice-paper plant, are used for wrapping spring rolls.

Rice vinegar: A mild-flavored vinegar made from fermented rice. Rice vinegar is interchangeable with rice wine vinegar, which is made from fermented rice wine. Seasoned rice vinegar, with added sugar and salt, can be used in recipes calling for rice vinegar, though you may wish to adjust the seasonings. If you can't find rice vinegar, substitute white vinegar or white wine vinegar.

Pancetta and Prosciutto

These two time-honored Italian meats are becoming favorites for adding flavor to today's cooking. Look for both in well-stocked supermarkets, Italian grocery stores, or specialty food shops.

Prosciutto (proh-SHOO-toh): To Italians, prosciutto means "ham"; cooks in America use the term to refer to a type of ham that has been seasoned, salt-cured, and air-dried (rather than smoked). The process takes at least nine months and results in somewhat sweetly spiced, rose-color meats with a sheen. Parma ham from Italy (prosciutto di Parma) is considered to be the best. Sliced prosciutto dries out quickly and should be used within a day or frozen for longer storage.

Pancetta (pan-CHEH-tuh): Italian-style bacon that's made from the belly (or pancia) of a hog; unlike bacon, pancetta is not smoked, but instead seasoned with pepper and other spices and cured with salt. Pancetta is generally available packaged in a sausagelike roll. In a pinch, substitute regular bacon.

Rind: The skin or outer coating, usually rather thick, of a food.

Roast, roasting: A large piece of meat or poultry that's usually cooked by roasting. Roasting refers to a dry-heat cooking method used to cook foods, uncovered, in an oven. Tender pieces of meat work best for roasting.

Roll, roll out: To form a food into a shape. Dough, for instance, can be rolled into ropes or balls. The phrase "roll out" refers to mechanically flattening a food, usually a dough or pastry, with a rolling pin.

Roux (roo): A French term that refers to a mixture of flour and a fat cooked to a golden- or rich-brown color and used for a thickening in sauces, soups, and gumbos.

Salad oil: See page 455.

Salsa: A sauce usually made from finely chopped tomatoes, onions, chiles, and cilantro. It is often used in Mexican and Southwestern cuisine.

Saute: From the French word *sauter*, meaning "to jump." Sauteed food is cooked and stirred in a small amount of fat over fairly high heat in an open, shallow pan. Food cut into uniform size sautes the best.

Scald: To heat a liquid, often milk, to a temperature just below the boiling point, when tiny bubbles just begin to appear around the edge of the liquid.

Score: To cut narrow slits, often in a diamond pattern, through the outer surface of a food to decorate it, tenderize it, help it absorb flavor, or allow fat to drain as it cooks.

Scrape: To use a sharp or blunt instrument to rub the outer coating from a food, such as carrots.

Sea salt: This variety of salt is derived from the evaporation of sea water. Some cooks prefer it over table salt for its clean, salty flavor.

Sear: To brown a food, usually meat, quickly on all sides using high heat. This helps seal in the juices and may be done in the oven, under a broiler, or on top of the range.

Section: To separate and remove the membrane of segments of citrus fruits.

Section

To section oranges, use a paring knife to remove the peel and white rind. Working over a bowl to catch the juice, cut between one orange section and the membrane, slicing to the center of the fruit. Turn the knife and slide it up the other side of the section along the membrane, cutting outward. Repeat with remaining sections.

Sesame oil: See page 455.

Sherry: A fortified wine that ranges from dry to sweet, and light to dark. Sherry can be enjoyed as a predinner or after-dinner drink, and it is also used in cooking.

Shortening: A vegetable oil that has been processed into solid form. Shortening commonly is used for baking or frying. Plain and butter-flavor types can be used interchangeably. Store in a cool, dry place. Once opened, use within 6 months. Discard if it has an odor or appears discolored.

Shred, finely shred: To push food across a shredding surface to make long, narrow strips. Finely shred means to make long thin strips. A food processor also may be used. Lettuce and cabbage may be shredded by thinly slicing them. (See also Grate, page 25.)

Shred

Shrimp paste: A pungent seasoning made from dried, salted shrimp that's been pounded into a paste. Shrimp paste gives Southeast Asian dishes an authentic, rich flavor. The

Finely shred

salty shrimp taste mellows during cooking. In a pinch, substitute anchovy paste, though it's not as boldly flavored.

Shuck: To remove the shells from seafood, such as oysters and clams, or the husks from corn.

Sieve: To separate liquids from solids, usually using a sieve.

Sift: To put one or more dry ingredients, especially flour or powdered sugar, through a sifter or sieve to remove lumps and incorporate air.

Sieve

Simmer: To cook food in a liquid that is kept just below the boiling point; a liquid is simmering when a few bubbles form slowly and burst just before reaching the surface. See also Boil, page 18.

Skewer: A long, narrow metal or wooden stick that can be inserted through pieces of meat or vegetables for grilling. If using bamboo or wooden skewers, soak them in cold water for 30 minutes before you thread them to prevent burning.

Skim: To remove a substance, such as fat or foam, from the surface of a liquid. To skim fat from poultry or meat drippings, see photo, page 444. To skim fat from broth, see page 491.

Slice: A flat, usually thin, piece of food cut from a larger piece. Also the process of cutting flat, thin pieces. (See "Slicing, Dicing, and More," page 22.)

Snip: To cut food, often fresh herbs or dried fruit, with kitchen shears or scissors into very small, uniform pieces using short, quick strokes.

Snip

Soba noodles: Made from wheat and buckwheat flours, soba noodles are a favorite Japanese fast food. In a pinch, substitute a narrow whole wheat ribbon pasta, such as linguine.

Somen noodles: Made from wheat flour, these dried Japanese noodles are very fine and most often white. In a pinch, substitute angel hair pasta.

Soymilk: Made of the liquid pressed from ground soybeans, soymilk can be a good substitute for cow's milk for people who do not consume dairy products. Plain, unfortified soymilk offers high-quality proteins and B vitamins. Substituting soymilk for regular milk is possible in some cases, though the flavor may be affected. Experiment to see what is acceptable to you.

Spices: See Seasonings, pages 36–39.

Steam: To cook a food in the vapor given off by boiling water.

Steep: To allow a food, such as tea, to stand in water that is just below the boiling point in order to extract flavor or color.

Stew: To cook food in liquid for a long time until tender, usually in a covered pot. The term also refers to a mixture prepared this way.

Stir: To mix ingredients with a spoon or other utensil to combine them, to prevent ingredients

Soba noodles

from sticking during cooking, or to cool them after cooking.

Stir-fry: A method of quickly cooking small pieces of food in a little hot oil in a wok or skillet over medium-high heat while stirring constantly. See page 347.

Stock: The strained clear liquid in which meat, poultry, or fish has been simmered with vegetables or herbs. It is similar to broth but is richer and more concentrated. Stock and broth can be used interchangeably; reconstituted bouillon can also be substituted for stock.

Sugar: A sweetener that's primarily made from sugar beets or sugarcane. Sugar comes in a variety of forms:

Brown sugar: A mix of granulated sugar and molasses. Dark brown sugar has more molasses, and hence, more molasses flavor, than light brown sugar (also known as golden brown sugar). Unless otherwise specified, recipes in this cookbook were tested using light brown sugar. In general either can be used in recipes that call for brown sugar, unless one or the other is specified. Tip: To help keep brown sugar soft, store it in a heavy plastic bag or a rustproof, airtight container and seal well. If it becomes hard, you can resoften it by emptying the hardened sugar into a rustproof container and placing a piece of soft bread in the container; the sugar will absorb the moisture and soften in a day or two. After the sugar has softened, remove the bread and keep the container tightly closed.

Coarse sugar: Often used for decorating baked goods, coarse sugar (sometimes called pearl sugar) has much larger grains than regular granulated sugar; look for it where cake-decorating supplies are sold.

Granulated sugar: This white, granular, crystalline sugar is what to use when a recipe calls for sugar without specifying a particular type. White sugar is most commonly available in a fine granulation, though superfine (also called ultrafine or castor sugar), a finer grind, is also available. Because superfine sugar dissolves readily, it's ideal for frostings, meringues, and drinks.

Powdered sugar: Also known as confectioner's sugar, this is granulated sugar that has been milled to a fine powder, then mixed with cornstarch to prevent lumping. Sift powdered sugar before using.

Raw sugar: In the United States, true raw sugar is not sold to consumers. Products labeled and sold as raw sugar, such as Demerara sugar and turbinado sugar, have been refined in some way. Cleaned through a steaming process, turbinado sugar is a coarse sugar with a subtle molasses flavor. It is available in many health food stores.

Vanilla sugar: Infused with flavor from a dried vanilla bean, vanilla sugar tastes great stirred into coffee drinks and sprinkled over baked goods. To make vanilla sugar, fill a 1-quart jar with 4 cups sugar. Cut a vanilla bean in half lengthwise and insert both halves into sugar. Secure lid and store in a cool, dry place for several weeks before using. It will keep indefinitely.

Sweeteners: See Artificial Sweeteners, page 17; Honey, page 26; and Sugar, page 33.

Tahini: A flavoring agent, often used in Middle Eastern cooking, that's made from ground sesame seeds. Look for tahini in specialty food shops or Asian markets.

Tamari: A dark, thin sauce made from soybeans. Tamari is a slightly thicker, mellower cousin of soy sauce and is used to flavor Asian dishes. In a pinch, substitute soy sauce.

Tamarind paste: A thick, tart, brown Asian flavoring that comes from the fruit of a tamarind tree.

Thickeners: Food substances used to give a thicker consistency to sauces, gravies, puddings, and soups. Common thickeners include:

Flour and cornstarch: All-purpose flour and cornstarch are starches commonly used to thicken saucy mixtures. Cornstarch produces a more translucent mixture than flour and has twice the thickening power. Before adding one to a hot mixture, stir cold water into a small amount. You can also combine either flour or cornstarch with cold water in a screw-top

Thickening Math

Here are some guidelines when using flour and cornstarch for thickening sauces:

Generally, for each cup of medium-thick sauce, use 2 tablespoons flour mixed with ¼ cup cold water. Or use 1 tablespoon cornstarch mixed with 1 tablespoon cold water. Be sure to thoroughly mix the water with the starch (the flour or cornstarch) to prevent lumps. After stirring the combined starch and water into the liquid to be thickened, cook and stir over medium heat until thickened and bubbly. Cook and stir 1 minute more for flour and 2 minutes more for cornstarch to completely cook the starch.

jar and shake until thoroughly blended. It is critical that the starch-water mixture be free of lumps to prevent lumps in your sauce or gravy.

Quick-cooking tapioca: This is a good choice for foods that are going to be frozen because, unlike flour- and cornstarch-thickened mixtures, frozen tapioca mixtures retain their thickness when reheated. Tip: When using tapioca as a thickener for crockery cooking and freezer-bound foods, you can avoid its characteristic lumpy texture by grinding the tapioca with a mortar and pestle before adding to the recipe.

Toast: The process of browning, crisping, or drying a food by exposing it to heat. Toasting coconut, nuts, and seeds helps develop their flavor (see page 224). Also the process of exposing bread to heat so it becomes browner, crisper, and drier. See tip, below left.

Toasted sesame oil: See page 455.

Tofu: See page 90.

Tomatoes, dried: Sometimes referred to as sun-dried tomatoes, these shriveled-looking tomato pieces boast an intense flavor and chewy texture. They're available packed in olive oil or dry. Follow recipe directions for rehydrating dry tomatoes. If no directions are given, cover with boiling water, let stand about 10 minutes or until pliable, then drain well and pat dry. Snip pieces with scissors if necessary. Generally, dry and oil-packed tomatoes can be used interchangeably, though the dry tomatoes will need to be rehydrated, and the oil-packed will need to be drained and rinsed.

Tomatoes, dried

Toasting Tips

Toasting rolls and buns adds a little crunch to sandwiches. The easiest way to toast rolls and buns is in a toaster oven. However, you can also use your broiler. Simply place the sliced roll or bun, cut sides up, on the unheated rack of a broiler pan and broil 4 to 5 inches from heat for 1 to 2 minutes or until golden brown.

Tortilla: A small, thin, flat bread, popular in Mexican cooking, that is made from corn or wheat flour and usually is wrapped around a filling. To warm and soften flour tortillas, wrap a stack of 8 to 10 in foil and heat in a 350°F oven for 10 minutes.

Toss: To mix ingredients lightly by lifting and dropping them using two utensils.

Vanilla: A liquid extract made from the seed of an orchid. Imitation vanilla, an artificial flavoring, makes an inexpensive substitute for vanilla. They can be used interchangeably in our recipes.

Vanilla bean: See tip, below right.

Vegetables: For selecting and storing vegetables, see pages 529–531. For information on less-common vegetables, see pages 534–535.

Vermouth: White wine that has been fortified and flavored with herbs and spices. Dry vermouth is white and is used as a before-dinner drink or in nonsweet drinks, such as a martini. Sweet vermouth is reddish brown and can be drunk straight or used in sweet mixed drinks. Vermouth often is used as a cooking ingredient.

Vinegar: A sour liquid that is a byproduct of fermentation. Through fermentation the alcohol from grapes, grains, apples, and other sources is changed to acetic acid to create vinegar. See tip, page 472, on some of the varieties available.

Wasabi: A Japanese horseradish condiment with a distinctive, pale lime-green color and a head-clearing heat (at least if used in significant amounts). Wasabi is available as a paste in a tube or as a fine powder in a small tin or bottle. It's often used to flavor fish.

Weeping: When liquid separates out of a solid food, such as jellies, custards, and meringues.

Whip: To beat a food lightly and rapidly using a wire whisk, rotary beater, or electric mixer in order to incorporate air into the mixture and increase its volume.

Wontons, wonton wrappers: Stuffed savory Asian pastries. The wrappers, paper-thin skins used to make wontons, can be found in the produce aisle or in Asian markets. Wonton wrappers are similar to, but smaller than, egg roll skins.

Yeast: A tiny, single-celled organism that feeds on the sugar in dough, creating carbon dioxide gas that makes dough rise. Three common forms of yeast are:

Active dry yeast: This is the most popular form; these tiny, dehydrated granules are mixed with flour or dissolved in warm water before they're used.

Bread-machine yeast: This highly active yeast was developed especially for use in doughs processed in bread machines.

Quick-rising active dry yeast (sometimes called fast-rising or instant yeast): This is a more active strain of yeast than active dry yeast, and it substantially cuts down on the time it takes for dough to rise. This yeast is usually mixed with the dry ingredients before the warm liquids are added. The recipes in this book were tested using active dry yeast. For information on preparing recipes using quick-rising yeast, see page 141.

Zest: The colored outer portion of citrus fruit peel. It is rich in fruit oils and often used as a seasoning. To remove the zest, scrape a grater or fruit zester across the peel; avoid the white membrane beneath the peel because it is bitter.

Vanilla Beans

Using dried vanilla beans helps pack recipes with vanilla flavor. Here's a little know-how:

Vanilla beans are the long, thin pod of an orchid plant. The pod itself, which has been dried and cured, should not be eaten. Instead the tiny seeds inside the pod are used. They bring an intense vanilla flavor and dark brown, confetti-like flecks to dishes. Follow recipe directions for extracting the seeds from the  pod. Often the pod will be heated in a liquid mixture to make it easier to split open, but even a dry vanilla bean can be cut lengthwise with a paring knife. After it is open, scrape out the tiny seeds. Discard the pod or use it to make vanilla sugar (see Vanilla sugar, page 34).

If you can't locate vanilla beans in your area, you can generally substitute 2 teaspoons vanilla for 1 vanilla bean. Vanilla paste, which contains flecks of the vanilla bean seeds, is also available. Find it in specialty markets or through mail-order catalogs and follow package directions for using it.

Seasonings

The more you cook, the more you'll love getting to know the great variety of fresh herbs and intriguing spices and spice blends available to cooks today. Whether you're new to the world of seasonings or you're fresh out of a fresh herb and seeking a quick substitute, let this section be your guide to adding great flavor to your cooking.

Herbs

These are some of the most commonly used culinary herbs. While the photograph on page 37 shows fresh herbs, most herbs are available in fresh or dried forms. Each herb brings its own distinct flavor to recipes, but substitutions are offered when available.

Basil: This herb brings its minty, clovelike aroma to sauces, salads, and, of course, pesto. Cinnamon, lemon, and anise basil have the basil flavor, plus the flavor for which they are named. Substitute: oregano or thyme.

Bay leaves: Most commonly found in the form of whole, dried leaves, bay leaves (also called laurel leaves) bring an aromatic, woodsy note to a dish. Common in slow-simmering dishes, such as soups and stews, they should be added to the dish whole (never crumbled); always discard them before serving the dish. Turkish and California bay leaves can be used interchangeably.

Chervil: Fresh chervil has a flavor similar to parsley with a hint of tarragon. Use in soups, vegetables, and salads; keep in mind it loses flavor when boiled. Substitute: a mixture of parsley and tarragon.

Chives: Snip the mild onion-flavored leaves as you need them; just like grass, they grow back after cutting. Chives taste great sprinkled over egg dishes, in salad dressings, and on potatoes. Substitute: thinly sliced green onion tops (though use less because they're more strongly flavored than chives).

Cilantro: Also known as fresh coriander, leaf coriander, or Chinese parsley, cilantro brings an aromatic flavor to many dishes, from Asian specialties and Indian sauces to Mexican salsas. Season to taste, keeping in mind that too much can bring a harsh, soapy flavor. Substitute: parsley.

Dill: A familiar herb for peas, its delicate taste also is excellent with fish, seafood, and vegetables. Substitute: fennel leaves or tarragon.

Marjoram: Similar to oregano, but with a sweeter, milder flavor, marjoram can be used to season almost any meat and vegetable dish. Substitute: oregano (though use less).

Mint: Peppermint has a sharp, pungent flavor, while spearmint is more delicate. Both taste sweet and refreshing, with a cool aftertaste. Mint makes a great edible garnish for dessert; try mint in salads, marinades, and dressings too. Substitute: basil, marjoram, or rosemary.

Oregano: Popular as a pizza and pasta flavoring, oregano offers a robust, pungent flavor. Also try it in bean soups, sauces, and pasta salads. Substitute: marjoram, basil, or thyme.

Parsley: This herb brings a mild, fresh taste to almost any dish. Flat-leaf parsley (also called Italian parsley) has a milder flavor than the curly-leaf variety. Generally either will work in recipes that call for parsley.

Rosemary: The needlelike leaves of this herb have a bold flavor described as piney and perfumy. It's especially enjoyed in lamb, pork, and fish dishes. Substitutes: thyme, tarragon, or savory.

Sage: This subtly bitter, musty, mintlike herb is often used to season poultry, sausage, pork, and stuffing; it also complements most vegetables. Substitute: savory, marjoram, or rosemary.

Savory: This herb's thyme and mint tones provide a nice complement to soups, meats, fish, mushrooms, and bean dishes. Winter savory, which has a stronger flavor than summer savory, is great for long-simmering stews. Substitute: thyme or sage.

Tarragon: A beloved herb in French cuisine, tarragon has an aromatic, licoricelike flavor. It's excellent with poultry, most fish, and grilled meats, and in vinaigrettes. Substitute: chervil or a dash of crushed fennel seeds or a dash of crushed anise seeds.

Thyme: An old adage exclaims, "When in doubt, use thyme!" A little bit minty, a little bit lemony, thyme seasons chicken, vegetables, and sauces. Substitute: basil, marjoram, oregano, or savory.

Caring for Fresh Herbs

Fresh snipped herbs add flavor that can't be matched by dried. If you don't have an herb garden within reach, buy fresh herbs at a farmer's market or supermarket.

You can keep herbs fresh for up to 1 week by cutting ½ inch from the stems and storing them, stems submerged, in a jar of water in your refrigerator. Cover tops with a loose-fitting plastic bag. Pinch off wilting, dried out, or brown leaves as they appear. The exception is fresh basil, which may blacken in the refrigerator; instead, store it in the same way, but do not refrigerate.

If a recipe calls for snipped fresh herbs, start with clean, dry herbs (wet ones may clump together—either blot them dry with a paper towel, or for large amounts use a salad spinner to spin off excess water). With kitchen shears or scissors, simply cut the herbs into small, uniform pieces using short, quick strokes. If the stalks are tough—as is the case with rosemary—don't use the stalks. Snip herbs just before adding them to a recipe to get their maximum flavor.

If a recipe calls for dried herbs and you wish to substitute fresh, the general rule is to triple the amount of the dried herb specified. (For example, if a recipe calls for 1 teaspoon dried basil, use 1 tablespoon fresh). Generally, add fresh herbs at the end of cooking time because they lose flavor and color as they simmer. Exceptions include fresh rosemary and winter savory, which can withstand a long cooking time.

Substituting Dried Herbs for Fresh

In a pinch, dried herbs can be substituted for fresh. To do so, use one-third the amount of dried herb for the fresh herb called for in a recipe. (For example, substitute 1 teaspoon dried herb for 1 tablespoon fresh herb.) To substitute ground

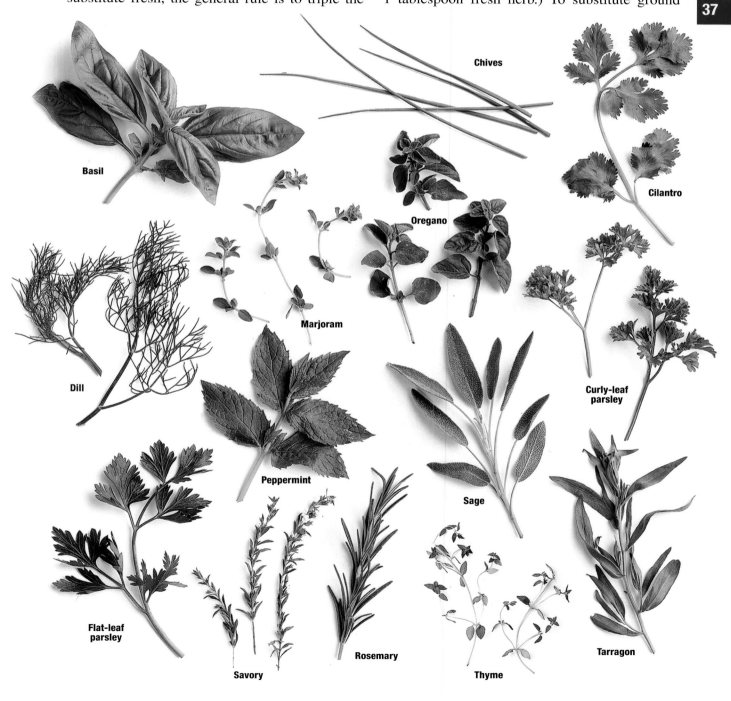

Chives

Cilantro

Basil

Oregano

Dill

Marjoram

Curly-leaf parsley

Peppermint

Sage

Flat-leaf parsley

Savory

Rosemary

Thyme

Tarragon

Spices

This spice list shows common uses and substitutions to call on in a pinch. Some substitution suggestions offer similar flavors. Others are acceptable flavor alternatives. When substituting, start with half of the amount the recipe calls for, unless directed otherwise, and add to suit your taste.

Spice	Flavor	Common Uses	Substitution
Allspice (ground)	Blend of cinnamon, nutmeg, cloves	Baked goods, jerk seasoning, stews	Ground cinnamon, nutmeg, or cloves
Anise seeds	Licoricelike flavor	Cabbage dishes, meats, fruit desserts	Fennel seeds or a few drops of anise extract
Cardamom (ground)	Spicy-sweet with peppery and gingerlike tones	Curried dishes, bean dishes, baked goods	Ground ginger
Chili powder	Hot, spicy, peppery taste and aroma	Soups, stews, marinades, meat dishes	Dash bottled hot pepper sauce plus equal measures of ground oregano and cumin
Cinnamon (ground)	Strong, spicy-sweet flavor	Meats, breads, pumpkin and fruit desserts, hot coffee, tea, chocolate	Ground nutmeg or allspice (use only $1/4$ of the amount)
Cloves (ground)	Strong, pungent, almost hot flavor	Baked beans, barbecue dishes, chili, mulled wine, fruit desserts, cakes	Ground allspice, cinnamon, or nutmeg
Cumin (ground)	Pungent, spicy, slightly bitter flavor	Indian and Mexican cooking, meats, poultry	Chili powder
Curry powder	A fragrant, mild-to-hot blend of up to 20 ground spices	Meats, sauces, stews, root vegetables; often used in Asian and Indian cooking	Combine equal parts of ground spices common in curry (such as cumin, coriander, red and black peppers, ginger, turmeric).
Fennel seeds	Mild licoricelike flavor and aroma	Meat, sausage, poultry dishes, breads, cakes, cookies, fruit desserts, coleslaw	Anise or caraway seeds
Ginger (ground)	Sweet-hot flavor, nippy aroma	Stir-fries, marinades, meats, baked goods	Ground allspice, cinnamon, mace, or nutmeg
Mustard (dry, seeds)	Seeds have hot, spicy flavor. Dry mustard attains hot flavor when mixed with water.	Mustard seeds are used in pickling, relishes, and boiled vegetables and meats. Dry mustard is used in salad dressings and egg, cheese, and meat dishes.	No substitutions for mustard seeds; to substitute prepared mustard for dry mustard in cooked mixtures, use 1 tablespoon prepared for each 1 teaspoon dry.
Nutmeg (ground)	Slightly sweet and spicy flavor and aroma	Baked goods, white sauces, custard, eggnog	Ground cinnamon, ginger, or mace
Paprika	Spanish paprika is slightly sweet and bitter. Hungarian paprika is generally more pungent, but can be labeled as sweet (mild) or hot.	Vegetables, beef, fish, chicken, salads, egg dishes	Cayenne pepper may be substituted, but use sparingly because it's much hotter.
Pepper	Black pepper is more pungent than white.	Savory foods, spiced desserts	White pepper may be substituted for black, but it's milder in flavor.
Red pepper (ground)	Hot, pungent, and smoky	Bean, meat, egg, and cheese dishes, stews, barbecue rubs and sauces	Use 2 to 3 drops bottled hot pepper sauce for $1/8$ to $1/4$ teaspoon ground red pepper.

herbs for dried leaf herbs, use about half of the amount called for.

Before adding a dried herb to a recipe, crush it between your finger and thumb to help release the flavors. To crush rosemary, use a mortar and pestle. Add dried herbs to recipes at the beginning of cooking time to allow their flavors to develop.

Spices

Spices are the seeds, bark, roots, fruit, or flowers of plants; they add flavor and color to sweet and savory dishes. For a description of the common spices of a well-stocked pantry, see the chart, page 38.

Spice Blends

Blends of herbs and spices let you add an intriguing combination of flavors with just one measure. Common blends include:

Barbecue seasoning: This zesty combination blends spices that bring a smoke-flavored heat to foods. These spices may include salt, sugar, garlic, hot red pepper, hickory smoke flavor, onion, and others. Sprinkle it onto meats before grilling, roasting, or broiling.

Bouquet garni (boo-KAY gar-NEE): This is a French term for a bundle of herbs that is either tied together or placed in a piece of cheesecloth, allowing you to remove it easily from a cooked dish. A bouquet garni is especially handy for blends that use bay leaves, which should always be removed from a dish before serving. A traditional French bouquet garni includes thyme, parsley, and bay leaf, but you can create one from just about any herbs you like. Just bundle the herbs together in several thicknesses of 100-percent-cotton cheesecloth, then tie the cheesecloth closed with kitchen string to form a bag.

Bouquet garni

Cajun seasoning: While the blends available may differ, most are peppery hot. They can include onion, garlic, and salt with the classic Cajun trio of white, black, and red peppers. Sprinkle it into crumb coatings or directly onto fish, poultry, or meat before cooking.

Dry rub: A dry rub is a blend of several different herbs and spices that is rubbed over or patted onto the surface of meat before it's cooked. Purchase dry rubs in a variety of flavor combinations from the supermarket. You can also experiment making

your own dry rubs with complementary flavorings from your spice rack.

Fines herbes (feenz ERB): This French phrase describes a mix that usually contains chervil, parsley, chives, and tarragon. Use it in place of individual herbs in gravies, sauces, creamy soups, and poultry stuffings.

Five-spice powder: Combinations may vary, but this fragrant blend usually includes cinnamon, anise seeds or star anise, fennel, black or Szechwan pepper, and cloves. To make your own five-spice powder, in a blender container combine 3 tablespoons ground cinnamon; 6 star anise or 2 teaspoons anise seeds; 1½ teaspoons fennel seeds; 1½ teaspoons whole Szechwan peppers or whole black peppercorns; and ¾ teaspoon ground cloves. Cover and blend until powdery. Store in a covered container. Makes about ⅓ cup.

Herbes de Provence: This melange of herbs, common in the South of France, usually includes basil, fennel, lavender, marjoram, rosemary, sage, savory, and thyme. Add to poultry stuffings, creamy pasta dishes, soups, and salad dressings.

Italian seasoning: Common herbs found in this mix include basil, oregano, thyme, and rosemary; sometimes garlic and red pepper are included.

Jamaican jerk seasoning: This lively mixture can include salt, sugar, allspice, thyme, cloves, ginger, cinnamon, onion, and chile pepper. It adds spice to fish, meat marinades, and salad dressings.

Lemon-pepper seasoning: This mixture, primarily salt with black pepper and grated lemon peel, adds a delicate lemon flavor to poultry and vegetables.

Mexican seasoning: This spicy blend often includes cumin, chile peppers, salt, onion, sweet peppers, garlic, oregano, and red pepper.

Storing Dried Herbs and Spices

Store dried herbs and spices in airtight containers in a dry place away from sunlight and heat. Replace them when their aroma fades. Generally, whole spices and herbs keep 1 to 2 years (whole cloves, nutmeg, and cinnamon sticks will maintain their quality slightly beyond 2 years). Ground herbs and spices maintain their quality up to 6 months. Refrigerate red spices, such as paprika, to preserve their flavor and color.

Nutrition Basics

Learning to eat healthfully is actually quite easy, especially if you follow the U.S. Department of Health and Human Services and Department of Agriculture's (USDA) Dietary Guidelines for Americans. Organized in three easy-to-follow steps, they are the ABCs of good nutrition:

Aim for Fitness
- Aim for a healthy weight
- Be physically active each day

Build a Healthy Base
- Let the Pyramid guide your food choices. See illustration, below
- Choose a variety of grains daily, especially whole grains
- Choose a variety of fruits and vegetables daily
- Keep food safe to eat

Choose Sensibly
- Choose a diet that is low in saturated fat and cholesterol and moderate in total fat
- Choose beverages and foods to moderate your intake of sugars
- Choose and prepare foods with less salt
- If you drink alcoholic beverages, do so in moderation

Healthful Eating with the Pyramid

The Pyramid contains five nutrient-rich food groups. Because each group contributes different nutrients, one food group can't replace another. To help you get all the nutrients you need for good health, let the USDA's Food Guide Pyramid guide your daily food choices. Here's how to use the Pyramid.

Understanding the Pyramid

Notice how the Food Guide Pyramid visually emphasizes which foods need to be consumed more often to enhance health and which foods should be limited. As suggested by the Pyramid's broad base, build your meals around a variety of grains (especially whole grain foods), fruits, and vegetables as a foundation for healthy eating. Add a moderate amount of low-fat foods from the milk group and the meat and beans group, but go easy on those foods at the top of the Pyramid.

The Pyramid also shows how many servings in the major groups you should strive to eat every day. People who do not need many calories (such as those who are inactive) should aim for the lower number of servings. Fats, oils, and sweets are not called a food group because there are no

Food Guide Pyramid A Guide to Daily Food Choices

Fats, Oils, and Sweets
Use Sparingly

Milk, Yogurt, and Cheese Group
2–3 Servings

Meat, Poultry, Fish, Dry Beans, Eggs, and Nuts Group
2–3 Servings

Vegetable Group
3–5 Servings

Fruit Group
2–4 Servings

Bread, Cereal, Rice, and Pasta Group
6–11 Servings

minimum requirements for these foods. They often contain mostly calories and few nutrients. Therefore a specific number of servings is not recommended—you should eat these foods sparingly. Remember that other food groups may contain fats and added sugars too.

To determine serving sizes, see tip, right. The total number of servings you need from each group depends on your age, gender, and activity level. Here are some general guidelines.

■ Children ages 2 to 6, less-active women, and some older adults should generally stick to the lower number of suggested servings, including two servings (5 ounces total) in the Meat, Poultry, Fish, Dry Beans, Eggs, and Nuts group.

■ Older children, teen girls, active women, and most men should aim for the middle of the range of suggested servings, including two servings (6 ounces total) in the Meat, Poultry, Fish, Dry Beans, Eggs, and Nuts group.

■ Teen boys and active men should aim for the higher number of suggested servings, including three servings (7 ounces total) in the Meat, Poultry, Fish, Dry Beans, Eggs, and Nuts group.

The Milk, Yogurt, and Cheese group is the exception to these guidelines. The number of servings recommended in this group depends on your age. Older children and teenagers (ages 9 to 18 years) and adults over the age of 50 need three servings daily. Everyone else needs two servings daily. The recommended number of milk group servings for pregnant or lactating women is the same as for nonpregnant women.

Consult your doctor for guidelines on feeding children younger than age 2.

Regarding Fats

If you use the Pyramid as your guide, all foods may be enjoyed as part of a healthy lifestyle. That includes fats, as long as you enjoy them in moderation. In fact, fats play an important role in nutrition because they supply energy and essential fatty acids, and they help absorb the fat-soluble vitamins A, D, E, and K, and carotenoids. They also enhance foods, making them richer and more flavorful, and—in the case of baked goods—more tender. However, keep in mind that certain kinds of fats, especially saturated fats, increase the risk for coronary heart disease by raising blood cholesterol.

Serving Sizes
What counts as a serving?

Bread, Cereal, Rice, and Pasta Group (including whole and refined grains)
- 1 slice of bread
  About 1 cup of ready-to-eat cereal
- ½ cup of cooked cereal, rice, or pasta

Vegetable Group
- 1 cup of raw leafy vegetables
- ½ cup of other vegetables, cooked or raw
- ¾ cup of vegetable juice

Fruit Group
- 1 medium apple, banana, orange, or pear
- ½ cup of chopped, cooked, or canned fruit
- ¾ cup of fruit juice

Milk, Yogurt, and Cheese Group*
- 1 cup of milk or yogurt**
- 1½ ounces of natural cheese** (such as cheddar)
- 2 ounces of processed cheese** (such as American)

Meat, Poultry, Fish, Dry Beans, Eggs, and Nuts Group
- 2 to 3 ounces of cooked lean meat, poultry, or fish
- ½ cup of cooked dry beans or ½ cup of tofu counts as 1 ounce of lean meat
- 1 2½-ounce soyburger or 1 egg counts as 1 ounce of lean meat
- ⅓ cup of nuts counts as 1 ounce of meat

A few points to consider:

■ An amount considered a serving size on a product's Nutrition Facts label may be larger than specified in the guidelines recommended above.

■ Dry beans, peas, and lentils can be counted as servings in either the meat group or the vegetable group. As a vegetable, ½ cup of cooked dry beans counts as 1 serving. As a meat substitute, 1 cup of cooked dry beans counts as 1 serving (2 ounces of meat).

*This group includes lactose-free and lactose-reduced milk products. One cup of soymilk with added calcium is an option for those who prefer a nondairy source of calcium.

**Choose fat-free or reduced-fat dairy products most often.

Source: *Nutrition and Your Health: Dietary Guidelines for Americans,* a joint publication of the U.S. Departments of Health and Human Services and Agriculture, May 30, 2000.

Reading Nutrition Labels

Today's Nutrition Facts labels, which appear on most purchased foods, can help you choose healthful foods for your family.

① Serving sizes, based on the amount of food people typically eat, are given in familiar units, such as cups or pieces.

② The Daily Values, expressed in percentages, tell how much of the recommended amount of a nutrient is in a serving of the food. Use these values to figure out how much one serving of the food will contribute to the overall daily recommended intake of particular nutrients.

③ Fat, saturated fat, cholesterol, and sodium (the nutrients shaded in blue) are listed on food labels because people tend to consume too much of these nutrients. It's OK to fall below 100 percent Daily Value each day for this group.

④ Conversely, people often do not get enough of the nutrients shaded in red. You should aim to meet 100 percent Daily Value for dietary fiber, vitamin A, vitamin C, calcium, and iron.

⑤ Daily Values are based on a 2,000 calorie-a-day intake. Depending on your age, gender, or activity level, you may require more or fewer calories per day. So for some nutrients you may also require more or less than 100 percent Daily Value.

Nutrition Facts

Serving Size 1 cup (240ml)
Servings Per Container about 16

Amount Per Serving

Calories 90   Calories from Fat 0

	% Daily Value*
Total Fat 0g	**0%**
Saturated Fat 0g	**0%**
Cholesterol 5mg	**2%**
Sodium 130mg	**5%**
Total Carbohydrate 13g	**4%**
Dietary Fiber 0g	**0%**
Sugars 12g	**15%**
Protein 9g	

Vitamin A	10%
Vitamin C	4%
Calcium	30%
Iron	0%

Percent Daily Values are based on a 2,000 calorie diet. Your Daily Values may be higher or lower depending on your calorie needs:

	Calories	2,000	2,500
Total Fat	Less than	65g	80g
Sat Fat	Less than	20g	25g
Cholesterol	Less than	300mg	300mg
Sodium	Less than	2,400mg	2,400mg
Total Carbohydrate		300g	375g
Dietary Fiber		25g	30g

Vegetarians and Nutrition

With the variety of vegetables, fruits, legumes, and grains available, vegetarian dining is more interesting and varied than ever. Keep in mind, however, that while a vegetarian diet can help you attain a low-fat, high-fiber, vitamin-rich diet, it does not necessarily ensure a healthful diet. Like everyone else, vegetarians need to keep an eye on fat, calories, and cholesterol while ensuring they also get adequate nutrients.

Some vegetarians are concerned about getting enough protein; however, because many plant foods (with the exception of fruits) are rich in protein, getting enough protein usually isn't an issue. The nutrients more likely to be lacking in a vegetarian diet include vitamin B_{12}, vitamin D, calcium, iron, and zinc. Good vegetarian sources of these nutrients include:

Vitamin B_{12}: Breakfast cereals, eggs, dairy products, soymilk products, and vegetarian burger patties fortified with vitamin B_{12}. If you eat dairy products or eggs, you'll most likely get enough B_{12}.

Vitamin D: Milk is fortified with vitamin D. If you do not drink milk, look for breakfast cereals and soymilk fortified with the nutrient.

Calcium: If you consume two to three servings of milk, cheese, and yogurt daily, your calcium intake should be adequate. If you avoid dairy products, opt for green leafy vegetables, calcium-fortified orange juice, fortified soymilk, soy cheese, and tofu.

Iron: Reach for legumes, dark-green leafy vegetables, iron-fortified cereals and bread, whole-grain products, seeds, prune juice, dried fruit, and blackstrap molasses. Keep in mind that eating a vitamin C-rich food at every meal will help your body absorb the type of iron that's found in plant sources.

Zinc: Whole grains (especially germ and bran—note that grains processed into refined flour lose zinc), whole wheat bread, legumes, tofu, seeds, and nuts are good sources for zinc.

Nutrition Information: How to Make It Work for You

With each recipe in this cookbook, you'll find useful nutrition information you easily can apply to your needs. First, read "What You Need," below, to determine your dietary requirements. Then refer to the Nutrition Facts listed with each recipe. You'll find the calorie count and the amount of fat, saturated fat, cholesterol, sodium, carbohydrates, fiber, and protein for each serving. In most cases, you will also find the amount of vitamin A, vitamin C, calcium, and iron noted as percentages of the Daily Values (see "Reading Nutrition Labels," page 42). To stay in line with the nutrition breakdown of each recipe, follow the suggested number of servings.

Analyzing the Recipes

The Better Homes and Gardens® Test Kitchen uses nutrition analysis software to determine the nutritional value of a single serving of a recipe. Here are some factors to keep in mind regarding each analysis:

■ Analyses do not include optional ingredients.
■ The first serving size listed is analyzed when a range is given. For example if a recipe makes 4 to 6 servings, the Nutrition Facts are based on 4 servings.
■ When ingredient choices (such as butter or margarine) appear in a recipe, the first one mentioned is used for analysis.
■ When milk is a recipe ingredient, the analysis is calculated using 2 percent (reduced-fat) milk.
■ The exchanges, listed for every recipe along with the Nutrition Facts, are based on the exchange list developed by the American Dietetic Association and the American Diabetes Association.

What You Need

The dietary guidelines below suggest nutrient levels that moderately active adults should strive to eat each day. There's no harm in occasionally going over or under these guidelines, but the key to good health is maintaining a balanced diet *most of the time.*

Total fat:	Less than 65 grams
Saturated fat:	Less than 20 grams
Cholesterol:	Less than 300 milligrams
Carbohydrates:	300 grams
Sodium:	Less than 2,400 milligrams
Dietary fiber:	25 grams

Low-Fat Recipes `Low Fat`

Some recipes are flagged with a low-fat symbol. To meet low-fat criteria in this cookbook, a recipe must contain 12 or fewer grams of fat for a main-dish serving. For breads and vegetables, the serving must contain 3 or fewer grams of fat. For sauces, beverages, and appetizers, the serving must contain 2 or fewer grams of fat. For cookies, each must contain 2 or fewer grams of fat. For all other side-dish recipes, each serving must contain 5 or fewer grams of fat.

Power Foods

Some foods offer added health benefits when part of a balanced and varied diet. When shopping for food and choosing recipes, keep these "power foods" in mind.

Deeply colored fruits and vegetables: These tend to have the most vitamins and minerals, so fill your shopping cart with kale, spinach, collard greens, cranberries, raisins, dried plums, carrots, cherries, and other richly colored foods.

Fish: Fatty fish, such as tuna, salmon, and mackerel, contain omega-3 fatty acids, a healthful fat that reduces the risk of heart and vascular disease. These types of fish are also among the most flavorful.

Soy: Eating soy daily can lower blood cholesterol levels. Soy is also associated with a reduced risk of some types of cancer and the maintenance or improvement of bone health. Try using textured soy protein in place of ground beef in recipes such as chili. Other good sources of soy include soymilk, tofu, edamame (green soybeans), soy flour, and tempeh (fermented soybean cake).

Tomatoes: Tomatoes offer lots of vitamin C and contain lycopene, which may help reduce the risk of prostate cancer. More good news—cooked and processed tomatoes contain up to 10 times more lycopene than fresh tomatoes, so there's no need to wait until they're in season to enjoy their benefits.

Whole grains: Whole-grain foods, such as brown rice, oatmeal, corn bran, wheat germ, and breads (those listing whole wheat as the first ingredient) contain fiber. Some types of fiber can reduce the risk of heart disease and breast and colon cancers. Refined grains, used in white bread or white flour, have minimal fiber; therefore, choose whole-grain foods when you can. To add fiber to recipes, substitute whole wheat flour for up to half of the all-purpose flour specified.

Keeping Food Safe to Eat

This section outlines some of the basic concepts of food safety, including simple steps you can take to prevent foodborne illness.

The Golden Rule of Food Safety

You'll often hear food safety experts repeat the adage "Keep hot food hot and cold food cold." The reason for this is because bacteria thrive at temperatures between 40°F and 140°F (sometimes called the "danger zone" when it comes to food safety). Therefore, cold foods need to be held at 40°F or below, and hot foods need to be served immediately or held at 140°F or above.

Basic Steps to Food Safety

While you can't see, taste, or smell the bacteria that cause foodborne illness, you can take control of keeping food safe in your kitchen by following these basic steps.

Keep It Clean!

The first step is to keep your hands and all surfaces and utensils that come into contact with food clean.

Keep hands clean: Nearly half of all cases of foodborne illness could be eliminated by proper hand washing. Remember to wash your hands:

■ Before handling food or food utensils or eating.

■ After handling food, especially raw meat, poultry, fish, shellfish, or eggs.

■ Between tasks—for example, after cutting up raw chicken and before dicing the vegetables.

■ After using the bathroom, changing diapers, playing with pets, or touching any unclean item, such as garbage, dirty dishes, cigarettes, telephones, hair, or dirty laundry.

When washing your hands, keep in mind that a quick rinse under the faucet won't do the trick. Wash your hands in hot, soapy water for at least 20 seconds (some people count this by singing "Happy Birthday" twice). Scrub thoroughly—front and back—all the way up to the wrists, over and under the fingernails, and in between fingers. Rinse your hands and use paper towels or a clean cloth to dry. If you have an open wound or cut, prevent contamination by wearing rubber gloves while handling food.

Clean fruits and vegetables: Wash raw fruit and vegetables under running water before eating or preparing them. If needed, remove surface dirt with a vegetable brush, and cut away damaged or bruised areas of produce, as they may contain bacteria.

Keep dish cloths, towels, and sponges clean: One way to eliminate the bacteria that thrive in sponges and dishcloths is to soak them in a diluted bleach solution (¾ cup bleach per 1 gallon water) three times a week. Sponges should be allowed to air-dry. Wash dish towels often using the hot cycle on your washing machine. Use paper towels to clean up spills, especially juices from raw meat, poultry, fish, and shellfish. Then immediately dispose of the paper towels.

Keep surfaces and utensils clean: Immediately after preparing raw meat, poultry, fish, shellfish, eggs, and unwashed produce, clean any utensils and surfaces that you used with hot, soapy water. Remember to do this between each separate kitchen task too.

Care for your cutting boards: After each use, cutting boards should be thoroughly washed with hot, soapy water, then rinsed and allowed to air-dry or patted dry with paper towels. Or place them in the dishwasher, provided they're dishwasher-safe. As an added measure of safety, use a sanitizing solution on cutting boards after washing them. Using a solution of 1 teaspoon of liquid chlorine bleach per quart of water, flood the surface and allow the board to stand several minutes. Rinse and air-dry or pat dry with paper towels.

Replace cutting boards whenever they have become worn or develop hard-to-clean grooves.

Wash food thermometer probes after each use with hot, soapy water and rinse before reinserting the probe into food.

In your refrigerator, wipe up spills immediately. Clean refrigerator surfaces with hot, soapy water and rinse. Once a week, throw out perishable foods that should no longer be eaten.

Keep pets off counters and away from food.

Separate, Don't Cross Contaminate

Cross contamination occurs when cooked or ready-to-eat foods pick up bacteria from other foods, hands, cutting boards, knives, or other utensils. To avoid cross contamination, it is especially important to keep raw meat, poultry, eggs, fish, and shellfish and their juices away from other foods. Follow these guidelines.

When shopping, keep raw meat, poultry, fish, and shellfish separate from other foods in your grocery cart.

Once home, store raw meat, poultry, fish, and shellfish in sealed containers or plastic bags so that the juices don't drip onto other foods. Large turkeys and roasts should be placed on a tray or pan that is large enough to catch any juices that may leak. To store eggs, see page 263.

Purchase two cutting boards, if possible, that are distinctly different from one another. Designate one for raw meat, poultry, fish, and shellfish and the other for ready-to-eat foods, such as breads and vegetables.

Follow guidelines under "Keep It Clean!" (page 44) to keep hands and any utensils and surfaces that come into contact with foods clean.

Place cooked foods on a clean plate, never on an unwashed plate that was used to hold raw meat, poultry, fish, or shellfish.

It is not necessary to wash raw poultry, beef, pork, lamb, or veal before cooking. Doing so poses a risk of cross contamination with other foods and utensils in the kitchen. Any bacteria that might be present are destroyed with proper cooking.

Marinate foods safely (see Marinate, page 27).

Cook to Proper Temperatures

Properly cooking food to a safe temperature destroys the harmful bacteria that cause food-borne illnesses. Safe temperatures vary from food to food. Follow doneness tests given with the recipes. See chart, above right, for general guidelines on checking the temperatures of foods. Leftovers should be reheated to 165°F, and reheated sauces, soups, and gravies should be brought to a rolling boil. See charts at the end of the fish and shellfish chapter for guidelines on doneness tests for those foods. For information on cooking eggs, see page 263 and Eggs, page 22.

It's essential to use a clean food thermometer to ensure that meat, poultry, casseroles, and other foods are properly cooked all the way through. See the tip on page 9 regarding the types of food thermometers available.

Chill It!

Cold temperatures keep most harmful bacteria from multiplying. Follow these steps to keep foods cold.

When shopping, buy perishable foods, including meat, poultry, eggs, fish, and shellfish, last. Take them straight home and refrigerate them promptly. Read and follow packaging labels (such as "Keep Refrigerated") for safe handling.

Refrigerate leftover foods from a meal immediately after you have finished eating. Leftovers should not stay out of the refrigerator longer than

Temperatures for Food Safety

Always use a food thermometer to ensure that food has reached a high enough temperature to destroy harmful bacteria. Here are the internal temperatures recommended by the USDA.

Food	Final Doneness Temperature
Beef, lamb, and veal steaks, chops, and roasts	
medium rare	145°F
medium	160°F
Hamburger, meat loaf, ground pork, veal, and lamb	160°F
Pork chops, ribs, and roasts	160°F
Egg dishes	160°F
Ground turkey and chicken	165°F
Stuffing and casseroles	165°F
Leftovers	165°F
Chicken and turkey breasts	170°F
Chicken and turkey whole bird, legs, thighs, and wings	180°F
Duck and goose	180°F

2 hours (1 hour if the temperature is above 80°F). To refrigerate or freeze cooked foods, see Cool It Quickly, page 47. For guidelines on storing foods properly, see pages 47–50.

Use appliance thermometers (see page 9) to ensure that your refrigerator and freezer are maintaining proper temperatures for food safety. Refrigerate at or below 40°F; freeze at or below 0°F. Because cold air needs to circulate the unit to keep foods safe, avoid packing the refrigerator too full.

Thaw Safely

Thaw frozen foods in the refrigerator—never at room temperature. A few exceptions include breads and sweets that specifically call for thawing at room temperature. Make sure that thawing foods do not drip onto other foods. Some foods may be successfully thawed in the microwave; follow your microwave manufacturer's directions and cook the food immediately after thawing. You can also thaw foods by placing the item in a leakproof plastic bag and immersing it in cold tap water in the sink. Every half hour, change the water to keep it cold and turn the food over if it's not fully submerged; cook food immediately after thawing.

Keep in Touch with Food Safety

Information on food safety is constantly emerging. For the latest information and precautions, call the USDA Meat and Poultry Hotline, 800/535-4555; the U.S. F.D.A. Center for Food Safety and Applied Nutrition Outreach Center, 888/723-3366; or consult your health-care provider. You can also get information by checking the government's food safety website at www.foodsafety.gov.

Safe Picnics

Here's how the basic steps to keeping food safe in the home—clean, separate, cook, and chill—also apply to safe outdoor eating.

Keep it clean: Clean your hands and surfaces often—bring along moist towelettes or soap and water to do the job.

Separate: To avoid cross contamination, tote plenty of plates and utensils along. Designate some for handling raw foods only and the others for handling cooked foods. Keep uncooked meats, poultry, fish, and shellfish separate from other foods—transport in tightly sealed bags or containers and pack them at the bottom of the cooler so that juices from these foods do not drip onto other foods. See Marinate, page 27, regarding safely marinating foods.

Cook properly: Use a food thermometer to make sure your foods are cooked to a safe internal temperature (follow recipe directions or see grilling charts, pages 321–328). Do not partially cook or grill food to finish cooking later.

Chill it: When toting foods, remember:

■ Keep perishable foods at a temperature of 40°F or below by packing them in a well-insulated cooler with plenty of ice or ice packs. A full cooler will maintain its cold temperature longer than a partially filled one. Thaw meat, poultry, fish, and shellfish in the refrigerator before taking it to a picnic. Wait until just before leaving home to pack perishable foods in the cooler.

■ Take two insulated coolers: one for drinks, the other for perishable foods. That way warm air won't reach the perishables each time someone grabs a chilled beverage.

■ On your way to the picnic, place coolers in the coolest part of your air-conditioned car rather than the trunk. At the picnic location, keep coolers tightly closed in a shady area and add ice often.

■ Keep foods in the coolers until you need them; remove raw food only when you're ready to put it on the grill. (If grilling in batches, keep foods not being grilled in the cooler.)

■ Discard any perishable food left outside for more than 2 hours (1 hour if the temperature is above 80°F).

Toting and Serving Hot Foods

Bacteria thrive at temperatures between 40°F and 140°F, so keeping hot foods hot is just as important as keeping cold foods cold.

■ When serving hot foods on a buffet, keep them at 140°F or higher. Use chafing dishes, crockery cookers, and warming trays to keep foods hot.

■ When toting hot foods to a party, keep the food at or above 140°F. Use heavy-duty foil, several layers of newspaper, or a heavy towel to wrap the containers well. Then, place in an insulated container.

When in Doubt, Throw It Out

One final word on food safety: If you aren't sure that food has been prepared, served, or stored safely, discard it. If a food has been improperly handled, even proper cooking cannot make it safe. Never taste food to see if it's safe to eat because contaminated food can look, smell, and taste perfectly normal, and even a small amount can make you ill.

Special Precautions

Everyone should follow steps to keep food safe; however, pregnant women, young children, older people, and people with weakened immune systems or certain chronic illnesses are especially susceptible to the risk of food-borne illness and should be extra careful to ensure the food they eat is safe.

These are some of the extra precautions persons at high risk for foodborne illness should take in addition to the guidelines outlined in this section.

■ Do not eat or drink unpasteurized juices, raw sprouts, raw (unpasteurized) milk, and products made from unpasteurized milk.

■ Do not eat raw or undercooked meat, poultry, eggs, fish, and shellfish (clams, oysters, scallops, and mussels).

Keep in mind, too, that new information on food safety is constantly emerging. People at risk for foodborne illness should stay up to date about food-safety issues. See "Keep In Touch with Food Safety," above left.

Food Storage and Make-Ahead Cooking

Make-ahead cooking—from stashing leftovers in the freezer for another meal to baking ahead for the holidays—is a great way to get the most out of time spent in the kitchen. Another key to efficient cooking is to keep your freezer, refrigerator, and cupboards well stocked with often-used foods, cutting down on trips to the grocery store.

Storage Guidelines

When you store perishable foods to be consumed later, it's important to follow the guidelines for keeping foods safe (see "Keeping Food Safe to Eat," pages 44–46). Here are additional guidelines that will help you get the best flavor and texture from the foods you store.

Cold Enough for You?

Use appliance thermometers (see page 9) to make sure your freezer and refrigerator maintain proper temperatures for safe food storage. Refrigerators should maintain a temperature of 40°F or below, and freezers should maintain a temperature of 0°F or below.

Cool It Quickly

Hot foods bound for the refrigerator or freezer must be cooled quickly for two reasons. First, it decreases the chance for harmful bacteria to grow, keeping your food safe to eat. Second, in the case of freezing, it allows the food to freeze faster, preventing the formation of large ice crystals that may ruin the flavor and texture of foods.
Here's how to cool food quickly.

■ Divide cooked foods into small portions in shallow containers. As a general rule, divide soups and stews into portions that are 2 to 3 inches deep, and stir them while cooling to speed the release of heat. Divide roasts and whole poultry into portions that are 2 to 3 inches thick. Place the small portions of hot food directly in the refrigerator. Remove stuffing from poultry and refrigerate in separate containers.

■ If the final destination is the freezer, transfer cold food from the refrigerator to the freezer. Arrange containers in a single layer in the freezer until frozen; this allows the cold air to circulate around the packages, freezing the food faster. Stack them after they are completely frozen.
Note: *Never* let perishable foods stand at room temperature to cool before they're refrigerated or frozen.

Wraps and Containers

Follow these guidelines when purchasing storage containers and food wraps for the refrigerator or freezer.
Containers: Most airtight food storage containers with tight-fitting lids—even disposables—provide adequate protection in the refrigerator. When shopping for freezer-safe containers, however, look for a phrase or an icon on the label or container bottom indicating that they are designed for freezer use.
Baking dishes: When freezing, use freezer-to-oven or freezer-to-microwave dishes and cover the surface with plastic freezer wrap or heavy-duty foil (if using foil, see note below).
Glass jars with tight-fitting lids: All major brands of canning jars are acceptable for use in the refrigerator and freezer. If freezing liquid and semiliquid foods, leave headspace in the jar so the food can expand as it freezes (see page 191).
Self-sealing storage bags and plastic wraps: Products are available for both refrigerator and freezer storage.
Regular or heavy-duty foil: When freezing food, use only heavy-duty foil.
Note: Do not use foil to wrap foods that contain acidic ingredients, such as tomatoes. Acid reacts with the foil, giving the food an off flavor. To refrigerate or freeze a casserole that contains tomatoes or another acidic ingredient, first cover the food with plastic wrap, then with foil; remove the plastic wrap before reheating.

Foods Not to Freeze

These foods lose flavor, texture, or overall quality when frozen.

■ Battered and fried foods
■ Cooked egg whites and yolks, as well as icings made with egg whites
■ Cottage and ricotta cheeses
■ Custard and cream pies or desserts with cream fillings
■ Mayonnaise
■ Soups and stews made with potatoes, which can darken and become mushy when frozen
■ Soups and stews thickened with cornstarch or flour
■ Sour cream
■ Stuffed chops or chicken breasts
■ Whole eggs in the shell, whether raw or cooked

Be Label Conscious

Always take a moment to properly label food before you freeze it. Using a wax crayon or waterproof marking pen, note on the package the name of the item or recipe; the quantity, date, and number of servings; the date it was frozen; and any special information about its use. Follow recommended storage times included in recipes (if given), or see the Storage Charts, which begin below, for additional guidelines.

Thawing and Reheating

See page 45 for important information on safely thawing foods.

Always reheat food to a safe internal temperature before serving. To do so, invest in a food thermometer (see page 9) and follow these guidelines.

■ Bring sauces, soups, and gravies to a rolling boil in a covered saucepan, stirring occasionally.

■ Heat other leftovers to 165°F.

Storage Chart for Purchased Items

By keeping the pantry, refrigerator, and freezer well stocked with commonly used ingredients, you can cut down on those last-minute trips to the store. Purchase products by "sell by" or expiration dates, and follow these guidelines for storing them.

Product:	To store:	Refrigerate (40°F) up to:	Freeze (0°F) up to:
Dairy Products			
Butter	Refrigerate in original packaging; to freeze, overwrap with moisture- and vaporproof wrap.	1 month	6 months
Buttermilk	Refrigerate in original packaging. To freeze, transfer to freezer containers; allow for headspace (see page 191).	7 days	3 months
Cheese, hard	See page 276	See page 276	See page 276
Cheese, cottage and ricotta	Refrigerate in original packaging.	Use by date on container. If no date given, use within 5 days of purchase.	Do not freeze
Sour cream	Refrigerate in original packaging.	7 days	Do not freeze
Yogurt	Refrigerate in original packaging; transfer to freezer container to freeze.	7 days	1 month
Eggs			
Hard-cooked, in shells	Refrigerate.	7 days	Do not freeze
Whites	Refrigerate in tightly covered containers; transfer to freezer container to freeze.	4 days	1 year
Whole, beaten	Beat whites and yolks together and place in freezer container.	Not applicable	1 year
Whole, in shells	Store whole eggs in carton placed in coldest part of refrigerator. Do not wash; do not store in the refrigerator door.	5 weeks after packing date (see page 263)	Do not freeze eggs in shells
Yolks	Refrigerate unbroken raw yolks covered with water in a tightly covered container.	2 days	Do not freeze
Meats, Poultry, Fish			
Bacon	Refrigerate in original wrapping; overwrap in freezer wrap to freeze.	7 days	1 month
Sausage, raw	Same as bacon, above	1 to 2 days	2 months

Product:	To store:	Refrigerate (40°F) up to:	Freeze (0°F) up to:
Meats, Poultry, Fish *(continued)*			
Sausage, smoked links/patties	Refrigerate in original wrapping; overwrap in freezer wrap to freeze.	7 days	1 month
Ham, fully cooked, whole	Wrap in appropriate refrigerator wrap or in moisture- and vaporproof wrap to freeze.	7 days	1 month
Ham, canned (labeled "keep) refrigerated")	Chill, unopened, in original can. After opening, wrap in appropriate wrap.	6 months (unopened) 3 to 5 days (opened)	1 month after opening (Do not freeze in can)
Hot dogs	Refrigerate in original wrapping. After opening, wrap in appropriate wrap.	2 weeks (unopened) 1 week (opened)	1 month
Lunch meats	Refrigerate in original wrapping. After opening, wrap in appropriate wrap.	2 weeks (unopened) 3 to 5 days (opened)	1 month
Beef, uncooked roasts and steaks	Refrigerate in original wrapping; overwrap in freezer wrap to freeze.	3 to 5 days	1 year
Lamb, uncooked roasts and chops	Refrigerate in original wrapping; overwrap in freezer wrap to freeze.	3 to 5 days	9 months
Pork, uncooked roasts and chops	Refrigerate in original wrapping; overwrap in freezer wrap to freeze.	3 to 5 days	6 months
Ground beef, lamb, pork, veal	Refrigerate in original wrapping; overwrap in freezer wrap to freeze.	1 to 2 days	4 months
Poultry (chicken or turkey), uncooked, whole	Refrigerate in original wrapping; overwrap in freezer wrap to freeze.	1 to 2 days	1 year
Poultry (chicken or turkey), uncooked, pieces	Refrigerate in original wrapping; overwrap in freezer wrap to freeze.	1 to 2 days	9 months
Ground turkey	Refrigerate in original wrapping; overwrap in freezer wrap to freeze.	1 to 2 days	4 months
Fish	Store in moisture- and vaporproof wrap in coldest part of refrigerator.	1 to 2 days	3 months

Produce *See charts, pages 529–533*

Garlic	Store in a cool, dark, dry place; do not refrigerate or freeze. Store whole bulbs up to 8 weeks; individual cloves 3 to 10 days. Discard shriveled, discolored, or dried-out cloves.

Pantry Staples

Instant chicken or beef granules	Store in a cool, dry place or refrigerate. Check package for expiration date.
Dried herbs and spices	See page 39
Olive oil	Store in a cool, dark place for up to 6 months or refrigerate up to 1 year. See page 455.
Cooking oil	Store at room temperature for up to 6 months.
Pasta and rice	Store in airtight containers in a cool, dry place. Store brown rice up to 6 months, dried pasta and long grain white rice indefinitely.

Storage Chart for Home-Cooked Foods

Below are guidelines for refrigerating and freezing home-baked and home-cooked products. Keep in mind that these are general guidelines only; specific instructions in individual recipes may vary. Follow the recipe's guidelines for best results. For appropriate wrappings and containers for freezing and refrigerating, refer to page 47.

Product:	To store:	Refrigerate (40°F) up to:	Freeze (0°F) up to:
Baked Goods/Desserts			
Bread dough	Follow recipe through mixing and kneading stages. Form dough into a ball. Wrap in moisture- and vaporproof wrap or place in self-sealing freezer bag.	Chill dough up to 24 hours. Bring to room temperature before shaping.	Up to 3 months. Thaw dough for up to 2 hours at room temperature or overnight in the refrigerator. Shape and bake according to recipe.
Breads, quick (baked)	Place in self-sealing plastic bag; seal and store at room temperature up to 3 days. To freeze, see page 127.	Not recommended	See page 127
Breads, yeast (baked)	See page 127	Not recommended	See page 127
Cakes	See page 154	See page 154	See page 154
Cheesecakes	To freeze, carefully transfer cooled cheesecake to a freezer-safe plate. Place whole cheesecake in a freezer bag. Or place individual pieces in an airtight container.	3 days	Up to 1 month (individual pieces up to 2 weeks). Thaw whole cheesecake in refrigerator overnight or pieces at room temperature 30 minutes.
Cookies, dough and baked	See page 211	See page 211	See page 211
Pies, baked and unbaked	See pages 399, 403, and 407	See pages 399, 403, and 407	See pages 399, 403, and 407
Leftovers			
Chicken nuggets, patties (cooked)	Transfer to appropriate containers. (See "Food Storage and Make-Ahead Cooking," page 47.)	1 to 2 days	3 months
Meat leftovers (cooked meat and meat dishes)	Divide into smaller portions, if appropriate. Transfer to appropriate containers. (See "Food Storage and Make-Ahead Cooking," page 47.)	3 to 4 days	3 months
Poultry dishes (cooked)	Divide into smaller portions, if appropriate. Transfer to appropriate containers. (See "Food Storage and Make-Ahead Cooking," page 47.)	3 to 4 days	4 months
Poultry pieces, plain (cooked)	Transfer to appropriate containers. (See "Food Storage and Make-Ahead Cooking," page 47.)	3 to 4 days	4 months
Soups and stews	Divide into smaller portions. Transfer to appropriate containers. (See "Food Storage and Make-Ahead Cooking," page 47.)	4 days	3 months

Planning Great Meals for Family and Friends

These days, it seems most everyone is pressed for time. Yet with a little planning and by using kitchen time wisely, sharing home-cooked meals with family and friends can still be a rewarding and meaningful part of your day.

Time-Saving Strategies

Here are some tips to help you save money and time shopping and cooking.

Shop Smart

■ Keep an ongoing list of your grocery needs. Post it somewhere in the kitchen so you can write down items as you notice they're needed.

■ Get organized before you head to the store, making a list of items you'll need for a week's worth of meals or more. Review the Food Guide Pyramid recommendations, pages 40–41, as you plan.

■ Shop during down times when the market isn't crowded. This lets you take your time to discover new foods and read facts on nutrition labels.

■ To cut down on impulse purchases, shop with a list and avoid grocery shopping when you're hungry. Do, however, keep an eye out for specials on items you routinely use—there's a difference between impulse buying and finding good bargains.

■ Check newspaper ads and inserts to take advantage of weekly specials and coupons.

Cook Smart

■ Use our prep and cook times to help you plan your time. Recipes that are designated as **Fast** can be prepared and served in 30 minutes or less. The timings assume that some steps can be performed simultaneously.

■ Read the recipe completely before you begin. This will eliminate last-minute trips to the store. Preheat your oven as you begin any recipe that needs to be baked or broiled so the oven will be ready when you are.

■ Overlap steps to accomplish two things at once. Chop vegetables, measure ingredients, open cans, or prepare sauces while waiting for water to boil, meat to brown, or appliances to preheat.

■ Clean as you go. Before you start preparation, fill the sink or dish pan with hot, soapy water.

■ Let timesaving appliances and techniques work for you. Use a food processor to chop vegetables or grate cheese. The microwave is an easy, no-mess method for melting butter or chocolate. Use a toaster oven to toast buns and rolls quickly; use kitchen shears to snip fresh herbs or dried fruit, a garlic press to crush garlic, and a mini ice cream scoop for drop cookies.

Stock Up on Shortcuts

Meals at home don't have to be entirely home-made to be nourishing and meaningful for your family. There's a middle ground between fast food and made-from-scratch food, and convenience products are often a realistic way to get there. Here are a few ideas.

■ Call on ready-made entrées such as roasted chicken from the deli and heat-and-serve meat loaf and pot roast from the meat department. Round out the meal with a recipe you've wanted to try. Or simply enjoy easygoing side dishes, such as frozen vegetables or baked potatoes.

■ Visit the supermarket deli or bakery for instant appetizers and simple side dishes or breads to add to your meal.

■ Stock up on items that take little effort from kitchen to table, such as frozen meatballs, pizza shells, pasta sauce, pasta, cheese, and eggs.

■ Purchase shortcut ingredients, such as preshredded cheeses, rice pilaf mixes, packaged salad greens, precut fruits and vegetables, and bottled roasted red sweet peppers.

Children and Mealtimes

Here are some ways to help get children involved in mealtimes and to help them develop positive attitudes about food.

■ Take the kids grocery shopping and ask them to help you choose what to buy. For example, ask them to pick three fruits and three vegetables that they'd like to eat during the week.

■ Ask each child to help plan the family meal on a designated night of the week. Encourage them to pick out the details; for example, stop at a party supply store and let them choose colorful paper napkins.

■ Remind kids that their tastes can change. Encourage them to try at least one bite of everything—call it a "no-thank-you" bite.

■ Keep trying! It takes children a while to try new things, so continue introducing them to a variety of foods. It will help if you always have some nutritious foods on hand so when their hunger (and curiosity) strike, you'll be ready.

Menu-Planning Basics

Whether you're planning a formal dinner for eight at 8 p.m. or simply looking forward to some together time around the table with your family, these guidelines will help you create a balanced and harmonious menu.

■ Combine interesting and complementary flavors, colors, and textures. Consider how flavors will work together; usually, one highly seasoned food is enough and can be rounded out by milder accompaniments (chili served with cornbread, for example). Think about how the colors and shapes of foods work together (fish, mashed potatoes, and parsnips seem dull in comparison to fish, a crisp green salad, and a wild rice pilaf mix). Think about temperature and texture too—serving foods that are soft and crisp or cold and hot alongside each other will make meals more lively and varied.

■ Use the Food Guide Pyramid and the ABCs of good nutrition on page 40 to help you plan how to eat healthfully.

■ One starchy dish (potatoes, rice, pasta, beans, or corn) is plenty with most meals. Bread can be served in addition to the one starchy dish.

■ Balance the courses: Alternate rich, highly flavored foods with simple, fresh items. For example, if you serve a rich, cheesy lasagna, dessert should be light and refreshing—perhaps a lemon sorbet with sugar cookies. Also avoid repeating flavors; even when two recipes aren't served at the same time, consider how each dish will add character to the meal.

Entertaining Thoughts

The point of entertaining is to enjoy family and friends. The more you keep stress out of the picture, the more relaxed and easygoing your event will be. Keep these tips in mind.

Stay in your comfort zone: Prepare items within your skill level and budget. Consider coming up with a list of "house specialties"—those tried-and-true favorites you can always count on to please guests. If you wish to experiment, complement your house specialties with dishes you've wanted to try.

Keep it simple: Serve the number of people you can accommodate easily. Balance make-ahead recipes with those that require a few last-minute finishing details, and round out your menu with convenience items, if you wish.

Invest a little time: Work out a schedule so you know in what order to prepare the food. Make sure your oven, refrigerator, and freezer will hold everything as needed, and that oven temperatures for oven-going foods don't conflict.

Invite guests in advance: Give them plenty of time to make arrangements. Allow 10 days for informal events, two weeks or more for formal events. For formal events, send written invitations; for informal events, call or invite guests personally. Be clear about the details—whether it's a barbecue, cocktail buffet, sit-down dinner, etc., and what time the party begins—so your guests will know what to wear and what to expect.

Serve dinner promptly: Follow the customs of your region. Allow about one hour for before-dinner appetizers and beverages, but not much more—you don't want your guests famished by the time they sit down to dinner.

Something flop? It happens to the best of cooks—the soup scorches, the soufflé falls. Make light of it and move on. If you don't let it ruin your evening, neither will your guests. Remember, entertaining isn't about perfection. Most people are happy to simply be part of the fun.

Easy Entertaining

Sure, it's a pleasure to acquire beautiful linens and eye-catching tableware, but you don't need a matching set of anything (or even a table) to gather family and friends over food. Just keep this advice in mind.

■ No tablecloth? It's absolutely optional, so go without, or use a clean sheet or light bedspread. Napkins are a must, and paper ones will do.

■ Got a drawer full of mismatched flatware and a cupboard full of mismatched china? A jumble of colors and patterns can add a cheerful and charming note—and may even lead to some interesting conversations. Use a vase of flowers or heirloom serving pieces as a focal point.

■ If you're short on table space, use your kitchen counter for a buffet line and use your coffee table and end tables for beverages.

■ No table? No problem. Make sure the food you serve can be balanced in one hand and eaten with a spoon or fork. (Chili, soups, or sandwiches, followed by cookies or brownies, are ideal.)

■ If someone volunteers to pitch in with the prep or bring a course, let them! Just be sure to return the favor when that person is hosting.

Menus for Casual Family Meals

Here are menu suggestions for family meals. The page numbers listed are for recipes in this book. For items without page numbers, either use your favorite recipe or purchase the item from the deli or supermarket. Find menu suggestions for entertaining on page 54.

Back-to-School Family Supper

Salad of torn iceberg lettuce, thin tomato wedges, and shredded mozzarella cheese drizzled with Buttermilk Dressing (page 468)

Spaghetti with Beef and Mushroom Sauce (page 383)

Italian Bread (page 150) or bakery-fresh Italian bread

One-Bowl Chocolate Cake (page 162)

Farm-Style Sunday Supper

Salad of fresh baby spinach, thinly sliced red onion, and mandarin orange sections dressed with Orange-Poppy Seed Dressing (page 469)

Ham Balls in Barbecue Sauce (page 352)

Squash, Pear, and Onion au Gratin (page 526)

Steamed greens beans drizzled with melted butter

Whole Wheat Dinner Rolls (page 140) or bakery-fresh whole wheat rolls

Red Raspberry-Cherry Pie (page 400)

Picnic in the Park

Muffuletta (page 359)

Marinated Potato Salad (page 461)

Watermelon slices

Raspberry Tea or Iced Tea (page 101)

Melt-in-Your-Mouth Sugar Cookies (page 217)

Family Game Night Feast

Caramel Corn (page 179)

Apple, pear, and/or peach slices with Sour Cream Fruit Dip (page 61)

Pulled Pork with Root Beer Sauce (page 234)

Dill pickles

Multigrain chips or potato chips

Ice cream sundaes with Hot Fudge Sauce (page 483) and assorted candy toppings

Comforting Crockery-Cooker Dinner

Salad of torn fresh spinach, sliced pears, and toasted walnut pieces served with Blue Cheese Dressing (page 467)

Pork Roast with Cherries (page 234)

Steamed broccoli drizzled with melted butter

Boston Brown Bread (page 143) or other bakery-fresh bread

Busy-Day Cake with Broiled Coconut Topping (page 158)

Fix-and-Forget Salad Supper

24-Hour Chicken Fiesta Salad (page 456)

Soft breadsticks brushed with melted butter and sprinkled with coarse salt and freshly ground pepper

Individual Caramel Flans (page 254)

Backyard Barbecue

Finger-Lickin' Barbecue Chicken (page 314)

Deli pasta salad

Marinated Cucumbers (page 459)

Sliced fresh tomatoes

Corn on the Cob with Herb Butter (page 321)

Strawberry or Peach Ice Cream (page 258)

Cool Summertime Lunch

Sliced, chilled, and grilled turkey breast half (see chart, page 322)

Apple-Rice Salad (page 462)

Bakery-fresh ciabatta rolls or other rolls

Lemon Sherbet (page 260) with gingersnap cookies

A Totable Meal of Heartwarming Foods

Makings for salad including a package of torn mixed salad greens, a red apple, honey-roasted peanuts, and a jar of Honey-Mustard Dressing (page 469)

Prosciutto, Spinach, and Pasta Casserole (page 385)

Bakery-fresh multigrain rolls or bread

Oatmeal Cake (page 157)

Hearty Weekend Breakfast

Scrambled Eggs and New Potatoes (page 266)

Cubed cantaloupe, honeydew melon, and pineapple sprinkled with Granola (page 95) and topped with plain yogurt

Toasted English Muffin Bread (page 142) or toasted English muffin halves with butter and jam

Orange, grapefruit, or cranberry juice

Light and Luscious Dinner

Fruit Salad with Cranberry Dressing (page 465)

Salmon-Veggie Bake (page 287)

Cooked linguine drizzled with olive oil and sprinkled with finely shredded lemon peel, cracked black pepper, and shredded Parmesan cheese

Sourdough rolls

Angel Food Cake (page 169)

Menus for Entertaining

The following menus will help you create memorable meals, whether you're hosting an intimate dinner for four or a houseful at the holidays. The page numbers listed are for recipes in this book. For items without page numbers, either use your favorite recipe or purchase the item from the deli or supermarket. Find menu suggestions for casual family meals on page 53.

Fireside Italian Dinner

Fruit with Prosciutto (page 71)

Salad of mixed greens, dried tart cherries, shaved Parmesan cheese, and pine nuts dressed with Balsamic Vinaigrette (page 468)

Lamb Shanks with Beans (page 356)

Focaccia (page 138) or bakery-fresh focaccia

Nut Torte (page 159)

Tex-Mex Dinner Party

Fruit Salsa (page 65) with Cinnamon Tortilla Crisps (page 64)

Arranged salad of torn romaine lettuce, orange and/or grapefruit sections, and sliced avocado drizzled with Orange Balsamic Vinaigrette (page 468)

Tortilla-Black Bean Casserole (page 84)

Mexican beer and/or Frozen Margaritas (page 109)

Sandies (page 218) or Butter-Pecan Shortbread (page 225)

Christmas Eve Dinner

Citrus Seafood Cocktail (page 76)

Salad of torn butterhead lettuce, quartered dried Calimyrna figs, thinly sliced onion, and toasted almonds drizzled with Orange Balsamic Vinaigrette (page 468)

Standing Rib Roast with Oven-Browned Potatoes (page 337)

Collard Greens with Bacon (page 517)

Assorted bakery-fresh breads and rolls

Browned Butter Tart (page 414)

Holiday Open House

Stuffed Mushrooms (page 61)

Easy Chicken Pâté (page 68)

Crostini with Tapenade (page 66)

Lemony Marinated Antipasto (page 67)

Cheese and fresh fruit platter

Cashew-Sugar Cookies (page 224)

Hazelnut-and-Cherry Caramel Clusters (page 184)

Chocolate Truffles (page 182)

Easy Party Punch (page 105) and/or other beverages

Tailgate Party

Crunchy Party Mix (page 59)

Black Bean Soup with Sausage (page 496) and/or Chili (page 492)

Corn Muffins (page 118)

Assorted vegetable dippers with ranch dressing

Peanut Butter-Oatmeal Rounds (page 213)

Spring Brunch for a Bunch

Coffee Cake Muffins (page 116) and/or Lemon Bread (page 121)

Cheese and Mushroom Brunch Eggs for 12 (page 268)

Baked ham slice

Steamed green and/or wax beans marinated in Fresh Herb Vinaigrette (page 468)

Assorted fresh berries with yogurt topping

Assorted fruit juices and/or Coffee (page 102)

Bistro-Style Dinner

Salad of torn romaine, snipped dried apricots, sliced green onions, crumbled feta cheese dressed with Apricot Vinaigrette (page 468)

Roasted Garlic Steak (page 307)

Rice and Sweet Onion Casserole (page 80)

Grilled asparagus (page 327) drizzled with olive oil and lemon juice and sprinkled with toasted pecan pieces

Artisan-Style French Bread (page 137) or bakery-fresh French bread

Lava Baby Cakes (page 254)

Hosting Vegetarian Friends

White Bean Dip (page 69) with Tortilla Crisps (page 64) and assorted vegetable dippers

Salad of mesclun, pine nuts, dried cherries, and red onion tossed with Fresh Herb Vinaigrette (page 468) made with rice vinegar

Cheese and Basil Polenta (page 89)

Steamed sugar-snap peas

Berry Fruit Pie (page 401)

Setting the Table, Setting the Scene

Getting the simple details just right is easy, and it's amazing how much pleasure it will add to your guests' overall enjoyment of a meal. Consider this a primer.

Table Setting Basics

The correct placement of flatware, plates, and glasses is more than just about tradition. Guests appreciate finding pieces in a particular spot. See Place Settings, below, for guidelines.

Tablecloths, place mats, and table runners are optional; napkins, however, are not. Generally dinner napkins are 24 inches square; luncheon and breakfast napkins are a few inches smaller. For casual and family meals, paper napkins are fine. Fold the napkin in an attractive shape and place it on the plate or to the left of the forks.

Buffet-Style Service

Serving food buffet style is an easy way to feed groups of eight or more people. Arrange the buffet table in a logical serving sequence with plates first, followed by the main dish, vegetables, salad, and bread. Arrange condiments next to the dish they accompany. Avoid objects that make it awkward to maneuver around the food, such as slender candlesticks or large centerpieces.

If guests will sit at tables, arrange napkins and flatware in settings at the tables. Place water glasses and empty wineglasses on each table before the party and have an open bottle of wine or a pitcher of water at each table. If guests are not going to be

Place Settings

Casual family meals

The knife and teaspoon go to the right of the dinner plate; the fork and napkin are placed to the left. The glass is above the knife. A soup spoon and a salad fork may be added (placed on respective sides in order of use); a cup and saucer may be placed to the right.

Informal dinners or luncheons

Arrange the knife and soup spoon to the right of the dinner plate; place dinner fork and salad fork to the left of the plate in order of use. Place dessert spoon and dessert fork above the plate, pointing left and right respectively. Arrange glasses and bread plate and bread knife as directed for formal sit-down meals, below.

Formal sit-down meals

Place knife (blade edge in) next to plate. Then place spoons to the right of the knife in order of use from outside in. Place forks to the left of the plate in order of use from the outside in. Arrange glasses above the knife. Left to right, the water goblet is first, followed by wine glasses, placed large to small. Place bread plate above forks. A butter knife may be placed across the bread plate as shown. The salad plate is placed to the left of the forks, and the cup, saucer, and coffee spoon to the right of the setting. (For formal dinners these items are usually brought to the table when served.)

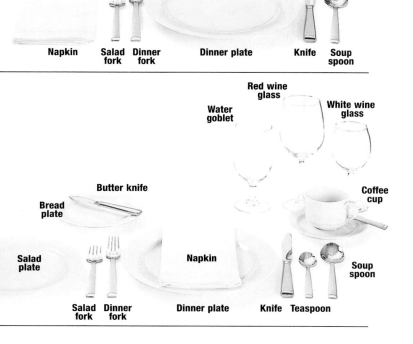

seated at tables, arrange the napkins and flatware at the end of the buffet line and set up a separate table with drinks, glasses, and coffee service. Some hosts place desserts on a separate table.

If there is no table seating for the meal, make sure guests can serve themselves, cut the foods with a fork, and eat easily while sitting with a plate in their laps.

Setting the Scene

When entertaining, a few thoughtful touches can make guests feel truly welcomed into your home.
■ Call on candles or soft lighting to create warmth; avoid scented candles that may clash with the food you serve.
■ Whether tied to the season, linked to the occasion, or an expression of your own creativity, centerpieces add a festive note. Just be sure they're not so tall that guests can't see around them.
■ Music can add to the mood. Keep it at a volume that allows guests to converse comfortably.
■ Monitor guests' comfort throughout the evening. You may have had your heart set on serving guests on the deck, for example, but if the evening turns chilly, move the party indoors.
■ If you serve alcoholic beverages, always have a nonalcoholic drink on hand, and never press a guest who declines an alcoholic beverage.

Basic Table Manners

Whether dining at home for an informal meal with family or entertaining a group, good manners help put everyone at ease. Here are a few basic customs to practice.

Flatware: As the meal begins, take silverware from the outside of the place setting for the first course and work your way in toward the plate. Never put used flatware back on the table. Generally, when not in use you may lay the knife across the back of the plate, slightly to one side, handle on the side. During the meal, lay the fork across the plate at an angle to you, with the handle on the rim.

Passing dishes (family setting): Pass to the right, from person to person. Don't pass over someone, unless it is a child who is unable to hold a large bowl or platter.

Passing dishes (formal setting): Pass to the right, and set the dishes in front of the person next to you; don't hand them directly to him or her.

Finger food? When it's not obvious whether a food should be eaten with utensils or with your fingers, watch the host, other guests, or other diners in a restaurant. If still in doubt, use utensils.

Napkins: At informal meals, put your napkin on your lap when you sit down. At formal meals, wait until after the host puts the dinner napkin in his or her lap. Leave the napkin in your lap when not in use until you leave the table. If you leave the table temporarily, place the napkin on your chair or to the left of your plate (folded to conceal soiled parts). At the end of the meal, leave the napkin loosely folded to the left of your plate; if the plate has been removed, leave the napkin in the center of your place setting.

Talking: Chew and swallow before you talk. Keep your mouth closed while you are chewing.

Smoking: As a general rule, it is not acceptable to smoke at the table.

End of the meal: Lay the knife and fork across your plate with the handles at the four o'clock position to signal you have finished eating. Remain at the table, making conversation, until everyone has finished.

Serving and clearing: Serve from a diner's left and clear from the right. The exception is beverages—wine and water are poured from the right side. Do not clear plates from guests at the table until everyone has finished eating.

Table manners and children: The best way to teach table manners to children is to eat meals with them every day and to make dinner a special, pleasant family time. When you practice good table manners yourself, your children will learn by example.

R.S.V.P. Etiquette

An invitation to dine in someone's home, whether offered in person or in writing, usually requires a prompt response. The host needs to know how many to expect at the gathering.

■ If you see "R.S.V.P" (a French acronym meaning "please respond") on an invitation, you must respond whether or not you plan to attend. If a telephone number is included, call the host promptly with your response. If a return card is offered, return it by the date requested.

■ When no R.S.V.P. is present, you need not respond; however, it is OK to do so, and chances are your host will appreciate it. If the invitation says "regrets only," you should only contact the host if you do not plan to attend.

■ If you cannot accept the invitation, or want to keep the evening open, decline politely. Once you have accepted an invitation, you are obliged to attend unless a crisis arises.

Chapter 2
Appetizers & Snacks

Appetizers & Snacks

Crunchy Party Mix

Keep some of this crispy snack mix on hand— it can be frozen for up to 4 months.

Prep: 15 minutes **Bake:** 45 minutes
Oven: 300°F **Makes:** 20 cups mix

> 5 **cups pretzel sticks**
> 4 **cups round toasted oat cereal**
> 4 **cups bite-size wheat or bran square cereal**
> 4 **cups bite-size rice or corn square cereal or bite-size shredded wheat biscuits**
> 3 **cups mixed nuts**
> 1 **cup butter or margarine**
> 3 **tablespoons Worcestershire sauce**
> ½ **teaspoon garlic powder**
> **Several drops bottled hot pepper sauce**

1. In a large roasting pan combine pretzels, oat cereal, wheat cereal, rice cereal, and mixed nuts; set aside.

2. In a small saucepan heat and stir butter, Worcestershire sauce, garlic powder, and hot pepper sauce until butter melts. Drizzle butter mixture over cereal mixture; stir gently to coat.

3. Bake in a 300° oven for 45 minutes, stirring every 15 minutes. Spread on a large piece of foil to cool. Store in an airtight container.

Cajun-Style Party Mix: Prepare as above, except substitute 3 cups pecan halves for mixed nuts and increase bottled hot pepper sauce to 1 tablespoon.

Nutrition Facts per ½ cup crunchy or Cajun variation: 171 cal., 11 g total fat (4 g sat. fat), 12 mg chol., 264 mg sodium, 16 g carbo., 2 g fiber, 3 g pro.
Daily Values: 5% vit. A, 4% vit. C, 2% calcium, 23% iron
Exchanges: 1 Starch, 2 Fat

Sweet Party Mix

Fast

Prep: 10 minutes **Bake:** 20 minutes
Oven: 300°F **Makes:** 12 cups mix

> 4 **cups bite-size corn square cereal**
> 4 **cups bite-size rice square cereal**
> 2 **cups pretzel knots**
> 1 **cup sliced almonds**
> ¾ **cup packed brown sugar**
> 6 **tablespoons butter**
> 3 **tablespoons light-colored corn syrup**
> ¼ **teaspoon baking soda**
> 1 **cup dried cranberries, blueberries, or cherries**

1. In a large roasting pan combine corn cereal, rice cereal, pretzels, and almonds; set aside.

2. In a medium saucepan combine brown sugar, butter, and corn syrup. Cook and stir over medium heat until mixture boils. Continue boiling at a moderate, steady rate, without stirring, for 5 minutes more. Remove saucepan from heat; stir in baking soda. Pour over cereal mixture; stir gently to coat.

3. Bake in a 300° oven for 15 minutes; stir cereal mixture and bake 5 minutes more. Remove from oven; stir in dried fruit. Spread on a large piece of buttered foil to cool. Break into pieces. Store in an airtight container.

Nutrition Facts per ½ cup: 157 cal., 6 g total fat (2 g sat. fat), 8 mg chol., 200 mg sodium, 25 g carbo., 1 g fiber, 2 g pro.
Daily Values: 2% vit. A, 3% vit. C, 2% calcium, 18% iron
Exchanges: 1 Starch, ½ Other Carbo., 1 Fat

Sweet Party Mix

Sweet Spiced Walnuts

Fast

Prep: 10 minutes **Bake:** 20 minutes
Oven: 325°F **Makes:** 7 cups nuts

> 1 **egg white**
> 5 **cups walnut halves or pieces**
> 1 **cup sugar**
> 1 **teaspoon ground cinnamon**
> ¼ **teaspoon ground nutmeg**
> ¼ **teaspoon ground allspice**

1. Grease a 15×10×1-inch baking pan; set aside. Combine egg white and 1 teaspoon *water.* Add nuts; toss to coat. Combine sugar, cinnamon, nutmeg, allspice, and ½ teaspoon *salt.* Sprinkle sugar mixture over nuts; toss to coat.

2. Spread the walnuts in the prepared pan. Bake in a 325° oven for 20 minutes. Spread on a piece of waxed paper; cool. Break into pieces. Store in an airtight container.

Nutrition Facts per 2 tablespoons: 84 cal., 7 g total fat
(1 g sat. fat), 0 mg chol., 22 mg sodium, 5 g carbo., 1 g fiber, 2 g pro.
Daily Values: 1% calcium, 2% iron
Exchanges: ½ Other Carbo., 1 Fat

Savory Nuts

Fast

Prep: 5 minutes **Bake:** 12 minutes
Oven: 350°F **Makes:** 2 cups nuts

> 2 **cups macadamia nuts, broken walnuts, and/or unblanched almonds**
> 2 **tablespoons white wine Worcestershire sauce**
> 1 **tablespoon olive oil**
> ½ **teaspoon dried thyme, crushed**
> ¼ **teaspoon dried rosemary, crushed**
> ⅛ **teaspoon ground red pepper**

1. Spread nuts in a 13×9×2-inch baking pan. Combine Worcestershire sauce, olive oil, thyme, rosemary, red pepper, and ¼ teaspoon *salt;* drizzle over nuts. Toss to coat.

2. Bake in a 350° oven for 12 to 15 minutes or until nuts are toasted, stirring occasionally. Spread on a piece of foil; cool. Store in an airtight container.

Nutrition Facts per 2 tablespoons: 129 cal., 14 g total fat
(2 g sat. fat), 0 mg chol., 96 mg sodium, 3 g carbo., 1 g fiber,
1 g pro.
Daily Values: 1% calcium, 3% iron
Exchanges: 3 Fat

Potato Skins

Save baking time by cooking the potatoes in the microwave on 100 percent power (high) for 15 to 20 minutes, rearranging them once.

Prep: 20 minutes **Bake:** 50 minutes
Oven: 425°F **Makes:** 24 wedges

> 6 **large baking potatoes (such as russet or long white)**
> 2 **teaspoons cooking oil**
> 1 **to 1½ teaspoons chili powder**
> **Several drops bottled hot pepper sauce**
> ⅔ **cup chopped Canadian-style bacon or 8 slices bacon or turkey bacon, crisp-cooked, drained, and crumbled**
> ⅔ **cup finely chopped tomato (1 medium)**
> 2 **tablespoons finely chopped green onion**
> 1 **cup shredded cheddar cheese (4 ounces)**
> ½ **cup dairy sour cream (optional)**

1. Scrub baking potatoes and prick with a fork. Bake in a 425° oven for 40 to 45 minutes or until tender; cool.

2. Cut each potato lengthwise into 4 wedges. Scoop out the white portion of each potato wedge (see photo, below). Cover and chill the leftover white portion for another use.

3. In a small bowl combine the oil, chili powder, and hot pepper sauce. Using a pastry brush, brush the insides of the potato wedges with the oil mixture. Place the potato wedges in a single layer on a large baking sheet. Sprinkle wedges with bacon, tomato, and green onion; top with cheese.

4. Bake about 10 minutes more or until cheese melts and potatoes wedges are heated through. If desired, serve with sour cream.

Make-ahead directions: Prepare as above through step 3. Cover; chill potato wedges for up to 24 hours. Uncover and bake as directed.

Nutrition Facts per 2 wedges: 72 cal., 5 g total fat (2 g sat. fat),
14 mg chol., 174 mg sodium, 3 g carbo., 1 g fiber, 5 g pro.
Daily Values: 5% vit. A, 7% vit. C, 8% calcium, 5% iron
Exchanges: ½ Starch, ½ Fat

Beginning at one end, use a teaspoon to carefully scrape away the inside of each potato wedge. Leave a shell about ¼ inch thick.

Stuffed Mushrooms

Prep: 25 minutes **Bake:** 8 minutes
Oven: 425°F **Makes:** 24 mushrooms

24 **large fresh mushrooms, 1½ to 2 inches in diameter**
¼ **cup sliced green onions (2)**
1 **clove garlic, minced**
¼ **cup butter or margarine**
⅔ **cup fine dry bread crumbs**
½ **cup shredded cheddar or smoked Gouda cheese or crumbled blue cheese (2 ounces)**

1. Rinse and drain mushrooms. Remove stems; reserve caps. Chop enough stems to make 1 cup.

2. In a medium saucepan cook the chopped stems, green onions, and garlic in butter until tender. Stir in bread crumbs and cheese. Spoon crumb mixture into mushroom caps. Arrange stuffed mushrooms in a 15×10×1-inch baking pan. Bake in a 425° oven 8 to 10 minutes or until heated through.

Prosciutto-Stuffed Mushrooms: Prepare as above, except omit shredded cheese. Stir ⅓ cup chopped prosciutto, ¼ cup shredded Provolone cheese, and ½ teaspoon dried Italian seasoning, crushed, into the crumb mixture.

Nutrition Facts per mushroom for cheddar or prosciutto variation: 42 cal., 3 g total fat (2 g sat. fat),7 mg chol., 97 mg sodium, 2 g carbo., 0 g fiber, 2 g pro.
Daily Values: 2% vit. A, 2% calcium, 2% iron
Exchanges: ½ Vegetable, ½ Fat

Sour Cream Fruit Dip

Prep: 10 minutes **Chill:** 1 to 24 hours
Makes: about 1 cup dip

1 **8-ounce carton dairy sour cream or light dairy sour cream**
¼ **cup apricot or peach preserves**
⅛ **teaspoon ground cinnamon, ground cardamom, pumpkin pie spice, or apple pie spice**
Apple, pear, or peach slices

1. In a small bowl stir together the sour cream, apricot preserves, and desired spice. Cover and chill for 1 to 24 hours. Serve with fruit slices.

Nutrition Facts per 1 tablespoon dip: 44 cal., 3 g total fat (2 g sat. fat), 6 mg chol., 9 mg sodium, 4 g carbo., 0 g fiber, 0 g pro.
Daily Values: 2% vit. A, 1% vit. C, 2% calcium
Exchanges: 1 Fat

Dill Dip

For colorful vegetable dippers, serve carrot or zucchini sticks, broccoli or cauliflower florets, radishes, and mushrooms.

Prep: 10 minutes **Chill:** 1 to 24 hours
Makes: about 2 cups dip

1 **8-ounce package cream cheese, softened**
1 **8-ounce carton dairy sour cream**
2 **tablespoons finely chopped green onion (1)**
2 **tablespoons snipped fresh dill or 2 teaspoons dried dill**
½ **teaspoon seasoned salt or salt**
Milk (optional)
Assorted vegetable dippers, crackers, or chips

1. In a medium mixing bowl beat cream cheese, sour cream, green onion, dill, and seasoned salt with an electric mixer on low speed until fluffy. Cover and chill for 1 to 24 hours. If the dip thickens after chilling, stir in 1 to 2 tablespoons milk. Serve with vegetable dippers, crackers, or chips.

Nutrition Facts per 1 tablespoon dip: 40 cal., 4 g total fat (2 g sat. fat), 11 mg chol., 49 mg sodium, 1 g carbo., 0 g fiber, 1 g pro.
Daily Values: 3% vit. A, 1% calcium, 1% iron
Exchanges: 1 Fat

Creamy Blue Cheese Dip: Prepare as above, except omit dill and seasoned salt or salt. Stir ½ cup crumbled blue cheese (2 ounces) and ⅓ cup finely chopped walnuts into the beaten cream cheese mixture.

Nutrition Facts per 1 tablespoon dip: 55 cal., 5 g total fat (3 g sat. fat), 12 mg chol., 50 mg sodium, 1 g carbo., 0 g fiber, 1 g pro.
Daily Values: 3% vit. A, 2% calcium, 1% iron
Exchanges: 1 Fat

How Much and How Many?

■ How many appetizers do you need per person for a party? Consider the kinds of appetizers served—if they are hearty or light—and whether or not a meal is soon to follow.

■ If a meal will be served shortly after the appetizers, allow four or five per guest. If a late meal is planned, figure six or seven per guest. When appetizers are the meal, you should plan on eight or nine per guest.

Crab Dip

Prep: 15 minutes **Chill:** 2 to 24 hours **Makes:** about 1½ cups

- ½ **cup mayonnaise or salad dressing**
- ½ **cup dairy sour cream**
- 1 **cup cooked crabmeat or one 6½-ounce can crabmeat, drained, flaked, and cartilage removed**
- 2 **tablespoons finely chopped red onion or green onion**
- 1 **tablespoon snipped fresh dill or 1 teaspoon dried dill**
- 1 **teaspoon finely shredded lemon or lime peel**
- 1 **teaspoon lemon or lime juice**
  Several dashes bottled hot pepper sauce
  Dash ground red pepper (optional)
  Assorted crackers and/or vegetable dippers

1. In a bowl combine mayonnaise, sour cream, ⅔ cup of the crabmeat, the onion, dill, lemon peel, lemon juice, hot pepper sauce, and, if desired, red pepper. Season to taste with *salt* and *black pepper*. Transfer to serving dish; sprinkle with remaining crabmeat. Cover and chill for 2 to 24 hours. Serve with crackers.

Nutrition Facts per 2 tablespoons dip: 94 cal., 9 g total fat (2 g sat. fat), 24 mg chol., 105 mg sodium, 1 g carbo., 0 g fiber, 3 g pro.
Daily Values: 2% vit. A, 1% vit. C, 2% calcium
Exchanges: ½ Very Lean Meat, 1½ Fat

Fig and Cheese Spread

Fast

Start to Finish: 30 minutes **Makes:** 8 appetizer servings

- 4 **ounces dried figs (about 8), halved or quartered**
- 1 **tablespoon butter or margarine**
- 1 **cup thinly sliced onion (1 large)**
- 1 **teaspoon snipped fresh thyme**
- 1 **tablespoon balsamic vinegar**
- 6 **ounces soft goat cheese (chèvre)**
  Assorted crackers

1. If desired, remove stems from figs. Place figs in a medium saucepan; cover with water. Bring to boiling; reduce heat. Simmer, covered, for 5 minutes. Drain well; cool slightly.

2. In a skillet melt butter over medium heat; add onion. Cook and stir about 5 minutes or until brown. Stir in drained figs and thyme. Cook, stirring gently, about 2 minutes or until slightly softened. Stir in balsamic vinegar. Cook for 2 to 3 minutes more or until glazed.

3. To serve, place the goat cheese in a serving bowl. Spoon the fig mixture over cheese. Serve with crackers.

Nutrition Facts per serving: 127 cal., 6 g total fat (4 g sat. fat), 14 mg chol., 97 mg sodium, 15 g carbo., 3 g fiber, 5 g pro.
Daily Values: 2% vit. A, 3% vit. C, 6% calcium, 5% iron
Exchanges: 1 Fruit, ½ Medium-Fat Meat, ½ Fat

Fig and Cheese Spread

Salmon and Pesto Spread

For a different shape, put this layered spread in a 3-cup mold. Don't forget to line the mold with plastic wrap for easy removal.

Prep: 30 minutes **Chill:** 6 hours **Makes:** 2 cups spread

- 1 **7½-ounce can red salmon, drained, flaked, and skin and bones removed**
- ½ **of an 8-ounce package cream cheese, softened**
- 2 **teaspoons snipped fresh dill or ½ teaspoon dried dill**
- ¼ **cup purchased basil pesto**
- 1 **8-ounce package cream cheese, softened**
- ¼ **cup butter or margarine, softened**
- 2 **tablespoons snipped fresh chives**
- ¼ **teaspoon coarsely ground black pepper**
  Fresh dill or chives (optional)
  Assorted crackers or bread

1. Line the bottom and sides of a 7½×3½×2-inch loaf pan with plastic wrap; set aside.

2. In a medium bowl stir together salmon, the 4 ounces cream cheese, and the 2 teaspoons dill. Spread salmon mixture evenly in the bottom of the prepared pan; chill for 10 minutes. Spread pesto over salmon mixture. In the same bowl combine the 8 ounces cream cheese, butter, the 2 tablespoons chives, and pepper. Drop by spoonfuls over pesto; spread over pesto. Cover and chill for at least 6 hours.

3. To serve, invert loaf pan onto a serving platter; remove plastic wrap. Let stand at room temperature for 15 minutes. If desired, garnish with additional fresh dill or chives. Serve with assorted crackers or bread.

Nutrition Facts per 2 tablespoons spread and 2 crackers:
171 cal., 15 g total fat (7 g sat. fat), 36 mg chol., 224 mg sodium,
5 g carbo., 0 g fiber, 5 g pro.
Daily Values: 9% vit. A, 7% calcium, 4% iron
Exchanges: 1 Lean Meat, 2 Fat

Baked Artichoke-Spinach Dip

Prep: 20 minutes **Bake:** 15 minutes
Oven: 350°F **Makes:** about 3 cups dip

- ½ **cup shredded mozzarella cheese**
- ½ **cup dairy sour cream**
- ½ **cup mayonnaise or salad dressing**
- ½ **cup grated Parmesan cheese**
- 1 **to 2 teaspoons Dijon-style mustard**
  Dash white pepper
- 1 **14-ounce can artichoke hearts, drained and coarsely chopped**
- 1 **cup loosely packed, coarsely chopped spinach leaves**
- ½ **cup finely chopped red onion (1 medium)**
  Pita wedges, thinly sliced French bread, and/or assorted crackers

1. In a large bowl combine mozzarella cheese, sour cream, mayonnaise, ¼ cup of the Parmesan cheese, the mustard, and pepper. Stir in artichoke hearts, spinach, and onion. Spread mixture evenly into a 9-inch pie plate. Sprinkle with the remaining ¼ cup Parmesan cheese.

2. Bake, uncovered, in a 350° oven about 15 minutes or until heated through. Serve with pita wedges, French bread, and/or crackers.

Make-ahead directions: Prepare as above through step 1. Cover and chill for up to 24 hours. Uncover and bake about 25 minutes or until heated through.

Nutrition Facts per 2 tablespoons dip: 63 cal., 6 g total fat
(2 g sat. fat), 6 mg chol., 132 mg sodium, 1 g carbo., 1 g fiber, 2 g pro.
Daily Values: 3% vit. A, 1% vit. C, 6% calcium, 3% iron
Exchanges: 1½ Fat

Salsa

No Fat

Prep: 30 minutes **Chill:** 2 hours to 2 days
Makes: about 2 cups salsa

- 4 **to 6 tomatillos, husked, rinsed, and finely chopped (about 1 cup), or one 11- to 13-ounce can tomatillos, rinsed, drained, and finely chopped**
- 2 **small tomatoes, seeded and finely chopped (¾ cup)**
- ⅓ **cup finely chopped red onion (1 small)**
- 2 **to 4 fresh serrano, habañero, or jalapeño chile peppers, seeded and finely chopped (see tip, page 64)**
- 2 **tablespoons lime juice**
- 2 **tablespoons snipped fresh cilantro**
- ¼ **teaspoon salt**
- 4 **cloves garlic, minced**

1. Stir together tomatillos, tomatoes, onion, chile peppers, lime juice, cilantro, salt, and garlic. Cover; chill for 2 hours or up to 2 days.

Tomato Salsa: Prepare as above, except omit the tomatillos and add an additional tomato, seeded and finely chopped.

Nutrition Facts per 2 tablespoons salsa or tomato variation:
6 cal., 0 g total fat (0 g sat. fat), 0 mg chol., 38 mg sodium,
1 g carbo., 0 g fiber, 0 g pro.
Daily Values: 2% vit. A, 7% vit. C, 1% iron
Exchanges: Free

Planning a Party Menu

Plan a party menu you can prepare easily and serve with confidence. Select favorite recipes you are comfortable with and try out new dishes before serving them at the party.

■ Determine how the foods will look and taste together. Balance rich, highly flavored foods with simple, fresh items. Don't forget practical matters, such as how much refrigerator space is available and how many appetizers you can keep warm at the same time. Plan one or two hot appetizers that can be made ahead and heated just before serving. Also choose appetizers you can prepare early and serve without last-minute attention.

■ When you serve appetizers buffet style, choose foods that guests can pick up easily. Too many choices that must be spooned out, sliced, or spread can cause people to bunch up around the buffet table.

Guacamole

`Fast`

Start to Finish: 15 minutes **Makes:** 1 cup dip

> 2 **medium very ripe avocados, halved, seeded, peeled, and cut up**
> ½ **of a small onion, cut up**
> ½ **of a 4-ounce can (¼ cup) diced green chile peppers, drained; 2 fresh jalapeño chile peppers, seeded and chopped (see tip, bottom right); or several drops bottled hot pepper sauce**
> 1 **tablespoon snipped fresh cilantro or parsley**
> 1 **tablespoon lemon juice or lime juice**
> 1 **clove garlic, minced**
> ⅔ **cup finely chopped, peeled, seeded tomato (1 medium) (optional)**
> **Tortilla chips**

1. In a food processor bowl or blender container combine avocados, onion, chile peppers, cilantro, lemon juice, garlic, and ¼ teaspoon *salt*. Cover and process or blend until mixture is smooth, scraping sides as necessary. If desired, stir in tomato. Serve with chips.

Make-ahead directions: Prepare as above, except do not stir in tomato, if using. Cover and chill for up to 24 hours. If desired, stir in tomato just before serving.

Nutrition Facts per 1 tablespoon dip: 40 cal., 4 g total fat, (1 g sat. fat), 0 mg chol., 49 mg sodium, 2 g carbo., 1 g fiber, 1 g pro.
Daily Values: 3% vit. A, 6% vit. C, 1% calcium, 2% iron
Exchanges: 1 Fat

Tortilla Crisps

Choose plain or Cinnamon Tortilla Crisps (see photo, page 65) to serve with salsa and other dips.

`Fast`   `Low Fat`

Prep: 10 minutes **Bake:** 15 minutes
Oven: 350°F **Makes:** 96 crisps (24 appetizer servings)

1. Cut each of twelve 7- or 8-inch flour tortillas into 8 wedges. Spread one-third of the wedges in a 15×10×1-inch baking pan. Bake in a 350° oven 5 to 10 minutes or until dry and crisp; cool. Repeat with remaining wedges. Store in an airtight container at room temperature up to 4 days or freeze up to 3 weeks.

Nutrition Facts per serving: 44 cal., 1 g total fat (0 g sat. fat), 0 mg chol., 60 mg sodium, 7 g carbo., 0 g fiber, 1 g pro.
Daily Values: 2% calcium, 3% iron
Exchanges: ½ Starch

Cinnamon Tortilla Crisps: Combine ½ cup sugar and 1 teaspoon ground cinnamon. Brush ¼ cup melted butter or margarine over twelve 7- or 8-inch flour tortillas. Sprinkle tortillas with cinnamon-sugar mixture. Cut each tortilla into 8 wedges. Bake as directed at bottom left.

Nutrition Facts per serving: 78 cal., 3 g total fat (2 g sat. fat), 5 mg chol., 80 mg sodium, 11 g carbo., 0 g fiber, 1 g pro.
Daily Values: 2% vit. A, 2% calcium, 3% iron
Exchanges: ½ Starch, ½ Fat

Nachos

You can also zap this Tex-Mex appetizer in your microwave. Microwave it on 100 percent power (high) for 2 to 3 minutes or until the cheese melts.

`Fast`

Start to Finish: 20 minutes **Oven:** 350°F
Makes: 8 appetizer servings

> 6 **cups tortilla chips**
> 1 **15-ounce can black beans or pinto beans, rinsed and drained**
> ¼ **cup thick and chunky salsa**
> 1½ **cups shredded cheddar or Colby Jack cheese (6 ounces)**
> 1 **recipe Cilantro Sour Cream (optional)**
> **Thick and chunky salsa (optional)**

1. Spread chips on an 11- or 12-inch ovenproof platter or large baking sheet.

2. Combine beans and the ¼ cup salsa; spoon over chips. Sprinkle with cheese. Bake in a 350° oven 5 to 7 minutes or until cheese melts.

3. To serve, if desired, spoon Cilantro Sour Cream over the nachos. If desired, pass additional salsa.

Cilantro Sour Cream: In a small bowl stir together ½ cup dairy sour cream and 2 tablespoons snipped fresh cilantro or parsley.

Nutrition Facts per serving: 227 cal., 13 g total fat (6 g sat. fat), 23 mg chol., 431 mg sodium, 21 g carbo., 4 g fiber, 10 g pro.
Daily Values: 7% vit. A, 2% vit. C, 20% calcium, 6% iron
Exchanges: 1½ Starch, 1 High-Fat Meat, ½ Fat

Handling Hot Chile Peppers

Because hot chile peppers, such as jalapeños, contain volatile oils that can burn your skin and eyes, avoid direct contact with chiles as much as possible. When working with chile peppers, wear plastic or rubber gloves. If your bare hands do touch the chile peppers, wash your hands well with soap and water.

Fruit Salsa

If you plan to chill this salsa for more than 6 hours, stir in the strawberries just before serving.

Low Fat

Prep: 30 minutes **Chill:** 6 to 24 hours
Makes: about 3 cups salsa

- 1 **cup finely chopped strawberries**
- 1 **medium orange, peeled and finely chopped (⅓ cup)**
- 2 **large or 3 small kiwifruit, peeled and finely chopped (⅔ cup)**
- ½ **cup finely chopped fresh pineapple or one 8-ounce can crushed pineapple (juice pack), drained**
- ¼ **cup thinly sliced green onions (2)**
- ¼ **cup finely chopped yellow or green sweet pepper**
- 1 **tablespoon lime juice or lemon juice**
- 1 **fresh jalapeño chile pepper, seeded and chopped (optional) (see tip, page 64)**
- 1 **recipe Cinnamon Tortilla Crisps (page 64)**

1. In a bowl combine strawberries, orange, kiwifruit, pineapple, green onions, sweet pepper, lime juice, and, if desired, jalapeño pepper. Cover and chill for 6 to 24 hours. Serve with Cinnamon Tortilla Crisps.

Nutrition Facts per 1 tablespoon salsa: 44 cal., 2 g total fat (1 g sat. fat), 3 mg chol., 41 mg sodium, 7 g carbo., 0 g fiber, 1 g pro.
Daily Values: 1% vit. A, 11% vit. C, 1% calcium, 2% iron
Exchanges: ½ Starch

Fruit Salsa

Mexican Eight-Layer Dip Best Loved

See photo, page 57.

Prep: 15 minutes **Chill:** 4 to 24 hours
Makes: 16 appetizer servings

- 2 **to 3 cups shredded lettuce**
- 1 **9-ounce can bean dip**
- ¼ **cup picante or taco sauce**
- 1 **6-ounce container frozen avocado dip, thawed**
- 1 **8-ounce carton dairy sour cream**
- 1 **cup shredded cheddar or taco cheese**
- ¼ **cup sliced green onions (2)**
- 2 **tablespoons sliced pitted ripe olives**
- ⅔ **cup chopped, seeded tomato (1 medium)**
- 16 **cups tortilla chips or crackers**

1. Arrange lettuce on a serving platter. Combine bean dip and picante sauce; spread over lettuce, making a layer ¼ inch thick. Next layer avocado dip and sour cream. Top with cheese, green onions, and olives. Cover and chill for 4 to 24 hours. Before serving, sprinkle with chopped tomato. Serve with chips or crackers.

Nutrition Facts per serving: 247 cal., 16 g total fat (5 g sat. fat), 14 mg chol., 331 mg sodium, 23 g carbo., 2 g fiber, 6 g pro.
Daily Values: 7% vit. A, 4% vit. C, 12% calcium, 5% iron
Exchanges: 1½ Starch, ½ High-Fat Meat, 2 Fat

Chile con Queso

Fast

Start to Finish: 30 minutes **Makes:** 1¾ cups dip

- ½ **cup finely chopped onion (1 medium)**
- 1 **tablespoon butter or margarine**
- 1⅓ **cups chopped, seeded tomatoes (2 medium)**
- 1 **4-ounce can diced green chile peppers, drained**
- 6 **ounces process cheese spread, cut into small cubes**
- 2 **ounces Monterey Jack cheese with jalapeño peppers, shredded (½ cup)**
- 1 **teaspoon cornstarch**
   Tortilla chips or corn chips

1. In a saucepan cook onion in butter until tender. Stir in tomatoes and chile peppers. Simmer, uncovered, for 10 minutes. Toss cheeses with cornstarch. Gradually add cheese mixture to saucepan, stirring until cheese is melted. Heat through. Serve with chips.

Nutrition Facts per 2 tablespoons dip: 75 cal., 5 g total fat (3 g sat. fat), 17 mg chol., 239 mg sodium, 3 g carbo., 0 g fiber, 4 g pro.
Daily Values: 9% vit. A, 11% vit. C, 10% calcium, 1% iron
Exchanges: ½ Vegetable, ½ High-Fat Meat

Quesadillas

In place of the bacon or sausage, add some chopped cooked chicken or vegetables.

`Fast`

Prep: 10 minutes **Cook:** 2 minutes per batch
Oven: 300°F **Makes:** 6 appetizer servings

- **2 cups shredded Colby Jack cheese (8 ounces)**
- **6 7- or 8-inch flour tortillas**
- **3 tablespoons canned diced green chile peppers, drained**
- **3 tablespoons chopped green onions**
- **3 slices bacon, crisp-cooked, drained, and crumbled, or 4 ounces bulk Italian sausage, cooked and drained**
  Salsa (optional)

1. Sprinkle ⅓ cup of the shredded cheese over half of each tortilla. Top with chile peppers, green onions, and bacon. Fold tortillas in half, pressing gently.

2. In a 10-inch skillet cook quesadillas, 2 at a time, over medium heat for 2 to 3 minutes or until lightly browned, turning once. Remove quesadillas from skillet; place on a baking sheet. Keep warm in a 300° oven. Repeat with remaining quesadillas. To serve, cut quesadillas into wedges. If desired, serve with salsa.

Nutrition Facts per serving: 256 cal., 16 g total fat (9 g sat. fat), 36 mg chol., 445 mg sodium, 16 g carbo., 1 g fiber, 11 g pro.
Daily Values: 6% vit. A, 4% vit. C, 31% calcium, 6% iron
Exchanges: 1 Starch, 1 High-Fat Meat, 1 Fat

Crostini with Tapenade

These classy appetizers are a blend of two European cuisines. The toasted bread, seasoned with olive oil and garlic, is Italian, while the olive-based spread originated in Southern France.

`Fast`

Start to Finish: 30 minutes **Oven:** 425°F
Makes: 24 to 30 crostini

- **1 8-ounce loaf baguette-style French bread**
- **2 to 3 tablespoons olive oil**
  Freshly ground black pepper
- **1 recipe Tapenade**

1. For crostini, cut French bread into ½-inch slices. Lightly brush both sides of each bread slice with olive oil; sprinkle with pepper. Place on an ungreased baking sheet. Bake in a 425° oven for 5 to 7 minutes or until crisp and lightly browned, turning once. Top with Tapenade. Serve immediately.

Tapenade: In a blender container or food processor bowl combine ½ cup pimiento-stuffed green olives; ½ cup kalamata olives, pitted; 1 tablespoon olive oil; 1 tablespoon Dijon-style mustard; 2 teaspoons balsamic vinegar; and 2 cloves garlic, minced. Cover and blend or process until nearly smooth, scraping down sides of container as necessary. Stir in ½ cup finely chopped, seeded tomato and 2 tablespoons thinly sliced green onion. Spread on crostini.

Nutrition Facts per crostini with tapenade: 51 cal., 3 g total fat (0 g sat. fat), 0 mg chol., 160 mg sodium, 6 g carbo., 0 g fiber, 1 g pro.
Daily Values: 1% vit. A, 2% vit. C, 1% calcium, 2% iron
Exchanges: ½ Starch, ½ Fat

Smoky Cheese Ball `Best Loved`

Prep: 30 minutes **Chill:** 4 to 24 hours **Stand:** 15 minutes
Makes: 3½ cups spread

- **2 8-ounce packages cream cheese**
- **2 cups finely shredded smoked cheddar, Swiss, or Gouda cheese**
- **½ cup butter or margarine**
- **2 tablespoons milk**
- **2 teaspoons steak sauce**
- **1 cup finely chopped nuts, toasted (see tip, page 224)**
  Assorted crackers

1. Let cream cheese, shredded cheese, and butter stand at room temperature for 30 minutes. Add milk and steak sauce; beat until fluffy. Cover and chill for 4 to 24 hours.

2. Shape mixture into a ball; roll in nuts. Let stand for 15 minutes. Serve with crackers.

Make-ahead directions: Prepare as above, except do not roll in nuts. Wrap cheese ball in moisture- and vaporproof plastic wrap. Freeze for up to 1 month. To serve, thaw the cheese ball in the refrigerator overnight. Roll in nuts. Let stand 30 minutes at room temperature before serving.

Nutrition Facts per 1 tablespoon spread: 73 cal., 7 g total fat (4 g sat. fat), 17 mg chol., 71 mg sodium, 1 g carbo., 0 g fiber, 2 g pro.
Daily Values: 5% vit. A, 4% calcium, 1% iron
Exchanges: 1½ Fat

Lemony Marinated Antipasto

Prep: 25 minutes **Cook:** 10 minutes **Chill:** 1 to 2 days
Makes: 12 to 16 appetizer servings

- 1 **pound uncooked chicken or turkey spicy Italian sausage links**
- 1 **tablespoon cooking oil**
- 1/3 **cup olive oil**
- 2 **teaspoons finely shredded lemon peel**
- 1/3 **cup lemon juice**
- 2 **tablespoons snipped fresh basil**
- 2 **teaspoons dried Italian seasoning, crushed**
- 2 **cloves garlic, minced**
- 1 **12-ounce jar roasted red sweet peppers, drained and cut into bite-size strips**
- 12 **ounces mozzarella cheese, cut into 1/2-inch cubes**
- 1 **cup pitted kalamata olives**

1. In a large skillet cook sausage links in cooking oil over medium heat about 10 minutes or until sausage is thoroughly cooked, turning frequently to brown evenly. Remove from heat; cool. Cut the cooked sausage links into 1/4-inch slices; set aside.

2. Meanwhile, for dressing, whisk together olive oil, lemon peel, lemon juice, basil, Italian seasoning, and garlic; set aside.

3. Layer cooked sausage, red pepper strips, cheese cubes, and olives in a 2-quart jar or two 1-quart jars. Pour dressing into jar(s). Cover tightly and refrigerate for 1 to 2 days. Turn jar(s) upside down occasionally to distribute the dressing.

4. Before serving, let stand at room temperature for 30 minutes. Arrange on a platter.

Nutrition Facts per serving: 200 cal., 18 g total fat (5 g sat. fat), 30 mg chol., 459 mg sodium, 4 g carbo., 1 g fiber, 12 g pro.
Daily Values: 4% vit. A, 91% vit. C, 19% calcium, 4% iron
Exchanges: 1 Vegetable, 1½ Lean Meat, 2 Fat

Cowboy Caviar

Scoop up some of this salsalike appetizer with a cracker or tortilla chip.

Prep: 15 minutes **Chill:** 12 hours **Makes:** 2 cups dip

- 1 **15-ounce can black-eyed peas, rinsed and drained**
- 1/4 **cup thinly sliced green onions (2)**
- 1/4 **cup finely chopped red sweet pepper**
- 2 **tablespoons cooking oil**
- 2 **tablespoons cider vinegar**
- 1 **to 2 fresh jalapeño chile peppers, seeded and chopped (see tip, page 64)**
- 1/4 **teaspoon cracked black pepper**
  Dash salt
- 2 **cloves garlic, minced**
  Assorted crackers or tortilla chips

1. In a bowl combine black-eyed peas, green onions, sweet pepper, oil, vinegar, jalapeño pepper, pepper, salt, and garlic. Cover and chill overnight. Serve the mixture with crackers or tortilla chips.

Nutrition Facts per 2 tablespoons dip and 2 crackers: 67 cal., 3 g total fat (0 g sat. fat), 0 mg chol., 115 mg sodium, 8 g carbo., 1 g fiber, 2 g pro.
Daily Values: 5% vit. C, 2% calcium, 3% iron
Exchanges: ½ Starch, ½ Fat

Lemony Marinated Antipasto

Easy Chicken Pâté

Purchase a 2- to 2½-pound deli-roasted chicken to use for the cooked chicken. Remove and discard the skin and bones before chopping. Or use a combination of leftover white and dark meat.

Prep: 20 minutes **Chill:** 6 to 24 hours
Makes: about 2½ cups pâté

> 3 cups chopped, cooked chicken
> ½ cup dairy sour cream
> ¼ cup snipped fresh parsley
> ¼ cup dry sherry or dry white wine
> 2 tablespoons chopped green onion
> ½ teaspoon cracked black pepper
> 1 clove garlic, minced
> 1 tablespoon snipped fresh parsley or chopped walnuts, toasted (see tip, page 224)
> Assorted crackers

1. In a food processor bowl combine chopped chicken, sour cream, the ¼ cup parsley, dry sherry, green onion, pepper, garlic, and ¼ teaspoon *salt*. Cover and process until mixture is combined and nearly smooth.

2. Line a 3-cup mold or bowl with plastic wrap; spoon in chicken mixture. Cover; chill for 6 to 24 hours. To serve, invert mold onto a platter; remove plastic wrap. Sprinkle with the 1 tablespoon parsley. Serve with crackers.

Nutrition Facts per 1 tablespoon pâté and 2 crackers: 58 cal., 3 g total fat (1 g sat. fat), 10 mg chol., 76 mg sodium, 4 g carbo., 0 g fiber, 4 g pro.
Daily Values: 1% vit. A, 1% vit. C, 1% calcium, 2% iron
Exchanges: ½ Very Lean Meat, ½ Fat

Chicken Liver Pâté

Prep: 10 minutes **Cook:** 10 minutes
Chill: 3 to 24 hours **Makes:** 1 cup pâté

> 2 slices bacon
> 8 ounces chicken livers
> ½ cup chopped onion (1 medium)
> 4 cloves garlic, minced
> 2 tablespoons dry white wine or milk
> ¼ teaspoon salt
> ¼ teaspoon black pepper
> ¼ teaspoon ground nutmeg or ⅛ teaspoon ground allspice
> 1 3-ounce package cream cheese, softened (optional)
> 2 tablespoons milk (optional)
> Snipped fresh chives (optional)
> Assorted crackers

1. In a skillet cook bacon until crisp. Remove bacon from skillet, reserving 2 tablespoons drippings. Drain and crumble bacon; set aside.

2. Add chicken livers, onion, and garlic to reserved drippings in skillet. Cook and stir over medium heat about 5 minutes or until the livers are no longer pink; cool slightly.

3. In a food processor bowl or blender container combine crumbled bacon, chicken liver mixture, wine, salt, pepper, and nutmeg. Cover and process or blend until combined (mixture will be soft). Line a 1½-cup mold or bowl with plastic wrap; spoon in liver mixture. Cover and chill for 3 to 24 hours.

4. To serve, invert mold or bowl onto a platter; remove plastic wrap. If desired, combine cream cheese and milk; spread over pâté. If desired, top with chives. Serve with crackers.

Nutrition Facts per 1 tablespoon pâté and 2 crackers: 79 cal., 5 g total fat (1 g sat. fat), 65 mg chol., 133 mg sodium, 5 g carbo., 0 g fiber, 4 g pro.
Daily Values: 47% vit. A, 7% vit. C, 1% calcium, 8% iron
Exchanges: ½ Starch, ½ Medium-Fat Meat

Swiss Fondue   Best Loved

Classic nutty-sweet Emmentaler and smooth-melting Gruyère combine with cherry-flavor kirsch in this traditional cheese fondue.

Start to Finish: 50 minutes **Oven:** 350°F
Makes: 3½ cups fondue (12 appetizer servings)

> 3 cups shredded Gruyère or Swiss cheese
> 2 cups shredded Emmentaler, Gruyère, or Swiss cheese (8 ounces)
> 3 tablespoons all-purpose flour
> 12 1-inch-thick slices herb bread or French bread, cut into 1-inch cubes, and/or broccoli or cauliflower florets
> 1½ cups dry white wine
> ¼ cup milk
> 2 tablespoons kirsch or dry sherry
> ⅛ teaspoon ground nutmeg
> ⅛ teaspoon white pepper
> Paprika (optional)

1. Let shredded cheeses stand at room temperature for 30 minutes; toss with flour. Set aside.

2. Meanwhile, to toast the bread cubes, place on a baking sheet and bake in a 350° oven for 5 to 7 minutes or until crisp and toasted; set aside. To precook broccoli or cauliflower, in a saucepan bring a small amount of water to boiling; add florets. Simmer, covered, about

3 minutes or until crisp-tender. Drain and rinse with cold water; set aside.

3. In a large saucepan heat wine over medium heat until small bubbles rise to the surface. Just before wine boils, reduce heat to low and stir in the cheese mixture, a little at a time, stirring constantly and making sure cheese is melted before adding more. Stir until the mixture bubbles gently.

4. Stir in milk, kirsch, nutmeg, and white pepper; transfer to a fondue pot. Keep mixture bubbling gently over a fondue burner. (If mixture becomes too thick, stir in a little more milk.) If desired, sprinkle with paprika. Serve with toasted bread cubes and/or florets.

Nutrition Facts per serving: 287 cal., 15 g total fat (9 g sat. fat), 48 mg chol., 299 mg sodium, 16 g carbo., 1 g fiber, 16 g pro.
Daily Values: 10% vit. A, 49% calcium, 5% iron
Exchanges: 1 Starch, 2 High-Fat Meat

White Bean Dip Best Loved

For striking presentation of this tangy, Greek-style dip, line the serving bowl with purple kale leaves or a variety lettuce such as red-tipped leaf lettuce.

Low Fat

Prep: 20 minutes **Chill:** 4 to 24 hours
Makes: about 2 cups dip

- ¼ **cup soft bread crumbs**
- 2 **tablespoons dry white wine or water**
- 1 **15- to 19-ounce can white kidney beans or Great Northern beans, rinsed and drained**
- ¼ **cup slivered almonds, toasted (see tip, page 224)**
- 2 **tablespoons lemon juice**
- 2 **tablespoons olive oil**
- ¼ **teaspoon salt**
- ⅛ **teaspoon ground red pepper**
- 3 **cloves garlic, minced**
- 2 **teaspoons snipped fresh oregano or basil or ½ teaspoon dried oregano or basil, crushed**
  Fresh basil or oregano leaves (optional)
- 1 **recipe Tortilla Crisps (page 64) and/or assorted vegetable dippers**

1. Combine bread crumbs and wine; set aside for 10 minutes to soak.

2. In a food processor bowl or blender container combine beans, almonds, lemon juice, olive oil, salt, red pepper, and garlic. Cover and process or blend until almost smooth. Add

bread crumb mixture; blend until smooth. Stir in the 2 teaspoons oregano. Cover and chill for 4 to 24 hours.

3. To serve, transfer to a serving bowl. If desired, garnish with fresh basil leaves. Serve with Tortilla Crisps and/or vegetable dippers.

Nutrition Facts per 1 tablespoon dip: 57 cal., 2 g total fat (0 g sat. fat), 0 mg chol., 86 mg sodium, 8 g carbo., 1 g fiber, 2 g pro.
Daily Values: 1% vit. C, 2% calcium, 3% iron
Exchanges: ½ Starch, ½ Fat

Sausage Bites

Here's a classic party snack with timeless appeal.

Fast

Start to Finish: 30 minutes **Makes:** 20 appetizer servings

- 1½ **cups bottled barbecue sauce**
- ⅔ **cup orange marmalade**
- ½ **teaspoon dry mustard**
- ⅛ **teaspoon ground allspice**
- 12 **ounces cooked bratwurst, cut into ½-inch slices**
- 12 **ounces cooked kielbasa, cut into ½-inch slices**
- 8 **ounces small cooked smoked sausage links**
- 1 **8-ounce can pineapple chunks, drained**

1. In a large saucepan combine barbecue sauce, orange marmalade, dry mustard, and allspice. Cook and stir until bubbly. Stir in bratwurst, kielbasa, smoked sausage links, and pineapple chunks. Cover and cook over medium-low heat about 20 minutes more or until heated through, stirring occasionally.

Crockery-cooker directions: In a 3½- or 4-quart crockery cooker combine barbecue sauce, orange marmalade, dry mustard, and allspice. Stir in bratwurst, kielbasa, and smoked sausage links. Cover and cook on high-heat setting for 2½ to 3 hours. Stir in pineapple chunks. Serve immediately or keep warm on low-heat setting for up to 2 hours.

Nutrition Facts per serving: 194 cal., 13 g total fat (5 g sat. fat), 25 mg chol., 511 mg sodium, 13 g carbo., 1 g fiber, 6 g pro.
Daily Values: 3% vit. A, 13% vit. C, 2% calcium, 4% iron
Exchanges: 1 Other Carbo., 1 High-Fat Meat, ½ Fat

Quick Pizza Breadsticks

These cheesy herb breadsticks also go great with a bowl of tomato soup.

`Fast` `Low Fat`

Prep: 10 minutes **Bake:** 10 minutes **Oven:** 425°F
Makes: 24 breadsticks

- 1 10-ounce package refrigerated pizza dough
- 2 tablespoons butter or margarine, melted
- ½ cup grated Parmesan or Romano cheese
- 2 teaspoons dried Italian seasoning, crushed
- ¼ teaspoon garlic powder
- ⅛ teaspoon ground red pepper
- 1 8-ounce can pizza sauce, warmed

1. Lightly grease a large baking sheet. Unroll pizza dough and transfer to the prepared baking sheet. Using your hands, press the dough into a 12×9-inch rectangle. Brush the dough with the melted butter.

2. In a small bowl combine Parmesan cheese, Italian seasoning, garlic powder, and red pepper; sprinkle over dough. Using a sharp knife, cut dough crosswise into twelve 1-inch strips; cut in half lengthwise to make 24 strips.

3. Bake in a 425° oven for 10 to 13 minutes or until golden brown. Serve with pizza sauce.

Nutrition Facts per breadstick: 47 cal., 2 g total fat (1 g sat. fat), 5 mg chol., 139 mg sodium, 5 g carbo., 0 g fiber, 2 g pro.
Daily Values: 1% vit. A, 2% vit. C, 3% calcium, 2% iron
Exchanges: ½ Starch

Buffalo Wings

Prep: 20 minutes **Marinate:** 30 minutes **Broil:** 20 minutes
Makes: 12 appetizer servings

- 12 chicken wings (about 2 pounds)
- 2 tablespoons butter or margarine, melted
- 3 tablespoons bottled hot pepper sauce
- 2 teaspoons paprika
- ¼ teaspoon salt
- ¼ teaspoon ground red pepper
- 1 recipe Blue Cheese Dip or Low-Fat Blue Cheese Dip
  Celery sticks (optional)

1. Cut off and discard tips of chicken wings (see photo 1, right). Cut wings at joints to form 24 pieces (see photo 2, right). Place chicken pieces in a plastic bag set in a shallow dish.

2. For marinade, stir together melted butter, hot pepper sauce, paprika, salt, and red pepper. Pour over chicken wings; seal bag. Marinate at room temperature for 30 minutes. Drain; discard the marinade.

3. Place the chicken wing pieces on the unheated rack of a broiler pan. Broil 4 to 5 inches from the heat about 10 minutes or until lightly browned. Turn chicken wings. Broil for 10 to 15 minutes more or until chicken is tender and no longer pink. Serve with Blue Cheese Dip and, if desired, celery sticks.

Blue Cheese Dip: In a blender container or food processor bowl combine ½ cup dairy sour cream, ½ cup mayonnaise or salad dressing, ½ cup crumbled blue cheese, 1 tablespoon white wine vinegar or white vinegar, and 1 clove garlic, minced. Cover and blend or process until smooth. Cover and chill for up to 1 week. If desired, top with additional crumbled blue cheese before serving. Makes 1¼ cups.

Nutrition Facts per serving: 221 cal., 19 g total fat (6 g sat. fat), 47 mg chol., 258 mg sodium, 1 g carbo., 0 g fiber, 11 g pro.
Daily Values: 11% vit. A, 1% vit. C, 5% calcium, 4% iron
Exchanges: 1½ Lean Meat, 3 Fat

Low-Fat Blue Cheese Dip Prepare as above, except substitute fat-free dairy sour cream and fat-free mayonnaise dressing or salad dressing for the regular sour cream and mayonnaise.

Nutrition Facts per serving: 149 cal., 10 g total fat (4 g sat. fat), 38 mg chol., 283 mg sodium, 3 g carbo., 0 g fiber, 11 g pro.
Daily Values: 11% vit. A, 1% vit. C, 5% calcium, 3% iron
Exchanges: 1½ Lean Meat, 1½ Fat

1. Use a sharp knife to carefully cut off the tip of each chicken wing. Discard the wing tips.

2. Spread the remaining wing portions open. With a sharp knife, carefully cut each wing at its joint into two sections.

Easy Appetizers

Assemble one or more of these tasty appetizers for last-minute entertaining and let the party begin.

Peppercorn-Cheese Melt: Remove and discard the top rind from a round of Cambozola, Camembert, or Brie cheese. Place the cheese in a shallow baking dish and sprinkle with coarsely ground mixed peppercorns and chopped, toasted walnuts or pecans. Bake in a 450°F oven for 8 to 10 minutes or until the cheese is softened and just begins to melt. Serve with slices of coarse-grain bread, crusty bread slices, or an assortment of crackers.

Fruit with Prosciutto: Wrap strips of very thinly sliced prosciutto around apple and/or pear slices or melon balls.

Roasted Garlic Spread: Peel away the dry outer layers of skin from 1 head of garlic, leaving skins and cloves intact. Cut off the pointed top portion (about ¼ inch), leaving the bulb intact but exposing the individual cloves. Place the garlic head, cut side up, in a muffin cup or custard cup. Drizzle with a little olive oil. Cover with foil and bake in a 425°F oven for 25 to 35 minutes or until the cloves feel soft when pressed. Set aside just until cool enough to handle. Squeeze out the garlic paste from individual cloves. Spread on crusty bread, toasted baguette slices, or crackers.

Pesto Roll-Ups: Separate 1 package of refrigerated crescent rolls into triangles and spread with purchased basil pesto. Cut each triangle in half, making 16 long triangles. Roll up triangles and place on an ungreased baking sheet. Bake in a 375°F oven 12 to 15 minutes or until golden.

Fruity Beef Kabobs

Low Fat

Prep: 45 minutes **Bake:** 25 minutes **Oven:** 350°F
Makes: 36 appetizer kabobs

- 1 **beaten egg**
- ¼ **cup fine dry bread crumbs**
- 2 **tablespoons snipped fresh cilantro or parsley**
- ⅛ **teaspoon ground red pepper**
- 2 **cloves garlic, minced**
- 1 **pound lean ground beef**
- ¼ **cup finely chopped peanuts**
- 1 **fresh pineapple, peeled, cored, and cut into bite-size chunks (see photo, below), or one 20-ounce can pineapple chunks (juice pack), drained**
- 1 **recipe Sweet-and-Sour Sauce (page 479) or 1¼ cups bottled sweet-and-sour sauce**

1. In a bowl combine egg, bread crumbs, cilantro, red pepper, garlic, and ¼ teaspoon *salt*. Add the beef and peanuts; mix well. Shape into 36 meatballs. Place meatballs in a 15×10×1-inch shallow baking pan. Bake in a 350° oven about 20 minutes or until done (160°F). Remove from oven; drain.

2. Thread a pineapple chunk and a meatball on a wooden toothpick. Return to the shallow baking pan. Repeat with remaining pineapple chunks and meatballs. Brush with some of the Sweet-and-Sour Sauce. Bake for 5 to 8 minutes more or until heated through.

3. Meanwhile, heat remaining sauce until bubbly; brush over meatballs and fruit before serving. Pass remaining sauce.

Make-ahead directions: Prepare as above through step 1. Cool cooked meatballs. Cover; chill up to 2 days. Assemble skewers as directed; bake 10 minutes or until heated through.

Nutrition Facts per skewer: 51 cal., 2 g total fat (1 g sat. fat), 14 mg chol., 73 mg sodium, 5 g carbo., 0 g fiber, 3 g pro.
Daily Values: 1% vit. A, 5% vit. C, 2% iron
Exchanges: ½ Starch, ½ Lean Meat

To clean a pineapple, remove the crown and cut off the top and base. Cut off wide strips of peel. Remove the eyes by cutting narrow wedge-shaped grooves diagonally around fruit, following pattern of eyes.

Rumaki

Prep: 15 minutes **Marinate:** 4 to 24 hours
Broil: 8 minutes **Makes:** 24 to 28 appetizers

- **12 ounces chicken livers (about 12 livers)**
- **¼ cup dry sherry**
- **¼ cup soy sauce**
- **2 tablespoons brown sugar**
- **2 tablespoons cooking oil**
- **¼ teaspoon garlic powder**
- **⅛ teaspoon ground ginger**
- **12 to 14 slices bacon, cut in half crosswise**
- **1 8-ounce can sliced water chestnuts, drained**

1. Cut livers in half; quarter extra-large livers. Place in a plastic bag in a deep bowl. Combine sherry, soy sauce, brown sugar, oil, garlic powder, ginger, and ¼ cup *water;* pour over livers. Refrigerate 4 to 24 hours, turning occasionally.

2. Drain livers; discard marinade. Wrap a bacon piece around a liver piece and water chestnut slice. Secure with a wooden toothpick. Place on the greased unheated rack of a broiler pan. Broil 4 inches from heat for 8 to 10 minutes or until livers are no longer pink, turning once. Serve warm.

Nutrition Facts per appetizer: 57 cal., 3 g total fat (1 g sat. fat), 65 mg chol., 141 mg sodium, 4 g carbo., 0 g fiber, 4 g pro.
Daily Values: 47% vit. A, 8% vit. C, 3% calcium, 7% iron
Exchanges: ½ Lean Meat, ½ Fat

Brie en Croûte

Prep: 30 minutes **Bake:** 20 minutes **Oven:** 400°F
Makes: 2 rounds (12 appetizer servings)

- **½ of a 17¼-ounce package frozen puff pastry, thawed (1 sheet)**
- **2 tablespoons jalapeño pepper jelly**
- **2 4½-ounce rounds Brie or Camembert cheese**
- **2 tablespoons chopped nuts, toasted**
- **1 slightly beaten egg**
  Apple and/or pear slices

1. Unfold pastry on a lightly floured surface; roll into a 16×10-inch rectangle. Cut into two 8-inch circles (see photo 1, page 73); reserve trimmings. Spread jelly over top of each cheese round. Sprinkle with nuts; press into jelly. Combine egg and 1 tablespoon *water;* set aside.

2. Place pastry circles over cheese rounds. Invert cheese and pastry. Brush pastry edges with a little egg mixture. Bring edges of pastry up and over cheese rounds (see photo 2, page 73), pleating and pinching edges to cover and seal. Trim excess pastry. Place rounds, smooth sides up, on a greased baking sheet. Brush egg mixture over tops and sides. Cut small slits for steam to escape. Using hors d'oeuvre cutters, cut shapes from reserved pastry. Brush shapes with egg mixture; place on rounds.

3. Bake in a 400° oven for 20 to 25 minutes or until pastry is deep golden brown. Let stand for 10 to 20 minutes before serving. Serve with apple and/or pear slices.

Brie en Croûte with Caramelized Onions: Prepare as on page 72, except omit jalapeño pepper jelly. For caramelized onions, cut 1 small onion into thin wedges. Cook onion in 2 teaspoons hot butter or margarine, covered, over low heat about 15 minutes or until tender and golden; stir occasionally. Meanwhile, cut up any large pieces in 2 tablespoons mango chutney; spread over top of each cheese round. Top with onions and nuts. Continue as directed.

Nutrition Facts per serving for pepper jelly or onion variation: 183 cal., 13 g total fat (4 g sat. fat), 39 mg chol., 215 mg sodium, 10 g carbo., 0 g fiber, 6 g pro.
Daily Values: 3% vit. A, 4% calcium, 1% iron
Exchanges: ½ Starch, 1 High-Fat Meat, 1 Fat

1. Using an 8-inch round cake pan as a pattern, carefully cut two circles from the dough rectangle. Reserve the trimmings to use for garnishing.

2. Gently bring the edges of the pastry up and over the cheese round, pleating and pinching to seal. Trim any excess pastry so it is not too thick.

Oysters Rockefeller

Traditionally these oysters are placed on a bed of rock salt in a shallow pan to keep them balanced as they bake. If you don't have rock salt, simply crumple a large piece of foil into the pan.

Prep: 40 minutes **Bake:** 10 minutes **Oven:** 425°F
Makes: 8 appetizer servings

  2 **cups torn spinach**
 ¼ **cup finely chopped onion**
 24 **oysters in shells**
  3 **tablespoons butter or margarine, melted**
  2 **tablespoons snipped fresh parsley**
    Several drops bottled hot pepper sauce
  1 **clove garlic, minced**
 ¼ **cup fine dry seasoned bread crumbs**
    Rock salt

1. In a saucepan cook spinach and onion in a small amount of boiling water for 2 to 3 minutes or until tender. Drain well, pressing out excess moisture.

2. Thoroughly wash oysters. Using an oyster knife or other blunt-tipped knife, open the shells (see photo 1, page 297). Remove oysters and dry (see photo 2, page 297). Discard the flat top shells; wash deep bottom shells. Place each oyster in a shell.

3. Combine spinach mixture, 2 tablespoons of the melted butter, the parsley, hot pepper sauce, garlic, and dash *black pepper.* Spoon 1 teaspoon of the spinach mixture over each oyster. Toss together the bread crumbs and the remaining 1 tablespoon butter. Sprinkle over spinach-topped oysters.

4. Line a shallow baking pan with rock salt about ½ inch deep. Arrange oysters on salt. Bake in a 425° oven for 10 to 12 minutes or until the edges of the oysters begin to curl.

Nutrition Facts per serving: 151 cal., 10 g total fat (5 g sat. fat), 39 mg chol., 498 mg sodium, 10 g carbo., 2 g fiber, 6 g pro.
Daily Values: 61% vit. A, 20% vit. C, 8% calcium, 22% iron
Exchanges: ½ Starch, 1 Lean Meat, 1 Fat

Onion Rings

Keep the fried onion rings warm in a 300°F oven while you're cooking the remaining batches.

Fast

Prep: 15 minutes **Cook:** 2 minutes per batch
Makes: 6 appetizer servings

1. For batter, in a mixing bowl combine ¾ cup all-purpose flour, ⅔ cup milk, 1 egg, 1 tablespoon cooking oil, and ¼ teaspoon salt. Using a rotary beater, beat just until smooth. In a large skillet heat 1 inch cooking oil or melted shortening for deep-fat frying to 365°F. Meanwhile, cut 4 medium-size mild yellow or white onions into ¼-inch slices; separate into rings. Using a fork, dip onion rings into batter; drain off excess batter. Fry onion rings, a few at a time, in a single layer in hot oil 2 to 3 minutes or until golden, stirring once or twice with a fork to separate rings. Remove rings from oil; drain on paper towels.

Nutrition Facts per serving: 216 cal., 13 g total fat (2 g sat. fat), 38 mg chol., 116 mg sodium, 21 g carbo., 2 g fiber, 5 g pro.
Daily Values: 7% vit. C, 4% calcium, 6% iron
Exchanges: 1 Vegetable, 1 Starch, 4 Fat

Phyllo Triangles

Prep: 30 minutes **Bake:** 15 minutes
Oven: 375°F **Makes:** 36 triangles

> 8 ounces bulk hot Italian sausage or pork sausage
> ¼ cup finely chopped onion
> ½ cup ricotta cheese
> ½ cup shredded mozzarella cheese (2 ounces)
> ½ teaspoon dried oregano, crushed
> 12 sheets frozen phyllo dough (18 x 14-inch rectangles), thawed
> ½ cup butter, melted
> 1 cup meatless spaghetti sauce, heated (optional)

1. For filling, cook sausage and onion until sausage is brown. Drain fat; pat dry with paper towels. Combine sausage mixture, ricotta cheese, mozzarella cheese, and oregano; set aside.

2. Place one sheet of phyllo dough on a cutting board or other flat surface. Lightly brush to edges of dough with some of the melted butter. Place another sheet of phyllo on top; brush with butter. (Keep remaining phyllo sheets covered with plastic wrap until needed.)

3. Cut the 2 layered phyllo sheets crosswise into 6 equal strips, each 14 inches long. Spoon 1 well-rounded teaspoon of filling about 1 inch from an end of each dough strip.

4. To fold each strip into a triangular bundle, first bring a corner over the filling so the short edge lines up with the side edge (see photo, right). Continue folding the triangular shape along the strip until the end is reached. Repeat with remaining phyllo, butter, and filling.

5. Place triangles on a baking sheet; brush with butter. Bake in a 375° oven 15 minutes or until brown. If desired, serve with spaghetti sauce.

Nutrition Facts per 2 triangles: 140 cal., 10 g total fat (5 g sat. fat), 27 mg chol., 208 mg sodium, 7 g carbo., 0 g fiber, 4 g pro.
Daily Values: 5% vit. A, 4% calcium, 3% iron
Exchanges: ½ Vegetable, ½ Starch, 1 Fat

Spinach Phyllo Triangles: Prepare Phyllo Triangles as above, except omit sausage filling and spaghetti sauce. For filling, cook one 10-ounce package frozen chopped spinach, ½ cup chopped onion, and 1 clove garlic, minced, according to spinach package directions. Drain well in a colander. Press back of spoon against mixture to force out excess moisture. Combine spinach mixture with 1½ cups finely crumbled feta cheese (6 ounces) and ½ teaspoon dried oregano, crushed. Continue as directed.

Nutrition Facts per 2 triangles: 117 cal., 8 g total fat (5 g sat. fat), 23 mg chol., 234 mg sodium, 8 g carbo., 1 g fiber, 3 g pro.
Daily Values: 29% vit. A, 4% vit. C, 7% calcium, 4% iron
Exchanges: ½ Vegetable, ½ Starch, 1 Fat

Make-ahead directions: Prepare Phyllo Triangles (and spinach variation) as at left through step 4. Place unbaked triangles in a covered freezer container; freeze for up to 2 months. Bake as directed. Do not thaw the triangles before baking.

Starting at the filling end of each strip, fold a corner over the filling to form a triangle. Continue the triangular fold for the length of the strip.

Appetizer Cheesecake

Prep: 30 minutes **Bake:** 35 minutes **Oven:** 325°F
Cool: 30 minutes **Chill:** 2 to 24 hours
Makes: 16 to 20 appetizer servings

> ½ cup fine dry bread crumbs
> 1 tablespoon butter or margarine, melted
> 1 6-ounce jar marinated artichoke hearts
> 3 8-ounce packages cream cheese, softened
> 1¼ cups crumbled feta cheese (5 ounces)
> ½ teaspoon dried oregano, crushed
> 1 clove garlic, minced
> 3 eggs
> ¼ cup sliced green onions (2)
> Assorted crackers, toasted baguette slices, and/or fresh fruit (optional)

1. For crust, combine bread crumbs and melted butter. Press the crumb mixture onto the bottom of a 9-inch springform pan; set aside.

2. Drain and chop artichoke hearts, reserving 2 tablespoons of the marinade; set aside.

3. Beat cream cheese with an electric mixer until smooth. Add feta cheese, oregano, and garlic; beat well. Add eggs; beat just until combined. Do not overbeat. Stir in artichoke hearts, reserved marinade, and green onions. Pour into crust. Bake in a 325° oven about 35 minutes or until center appears nearly set when shaken. Cool on a wire rack 30 minutes. Cover; chill at least 2 hours or up to 24 hours.

4. To serve, remove from pan and cut into wedges. Serve immediately or let stand at room temperature for 30 minutes. If desired, serve with crackers, toasted baguette slices, and/or fresh fruit.

Nutrition Facts per serving: 214 cal., 19 g total fat (11 g sat. fat), 96 mg chol., 303 mg sodium, 5 g carbo., 0 g fiber, 6 g pro.
Daily Values: 15% vit. A, 4% vit. C, 9% calcium, 6% iron
Exchanges: ½ Starch, 1 High-Fat Meat, 2 Fat

Lower-Fat Appetizer Cheesecake: Prepare as on page 74, except substitute three 8-ounce packages fat-free cream cheese for regular cream cheese.

Nutrition Facts per serving: 103 cal., 4 g total fat (2 g sat. fat), 56 mg chol., 178 mg sodium, 7 g carbo., 0 g fiber, 9 g pro.
Daily Values: 3% vit. A, 4% vit. C, 20% calcium, 3% iron
Exchanges: ½ Starch, 1 Lean Meat

Appetizer Cheesecake

Herbed Leek Tart

Prep: 20 minutes Bake: 25 minutes
Oven: 375°F Makes: 24 appetizer servings

- **9 medium leeks, thinly sliced (3 cups)**
- **4 cloves garlic, minced**
- **2 tablespoons olive oil**
- **½ cup chopped red sweet pepper**
- **2 tablespoons Dijon-style mustard**
- **1 teaspoon dried herbes de Provence or dried basil, crushed**
- **6 ounces Gruyère cheese or Swiss cheese, shredded (1½ cups)**
- **1 15-ounce package folded refrigerated unbaked piecrust (2 crusts)**
- **2 tablespoons chopped almonds or walnuts**

1. For filling, in a large skillet cook leeks and garlic in hot oil about 5 minutes or until tender. Remove from heat; stir in sweet pepper, mustard, and herbes de Provence. Cool slightly; stir in shredded cheese. Set filling aside.

2. Unfold piecrust according to package directions. On a lightly floured surface, roll one piecrust into a 12-inch circle. Transfer piecrust to a baking sheet. Spread half of the filling into the center of the piecrust, leaving a 1½-inch border. Fold border up and over filling, pleating as necessary. Sprinkle 1 tablespoon of the nuts over the filling. Repeat with remaining piecrust, filling, and nuts.

3. Bake in a 375° oven about 25 minutes or until crusts are golden. Cool 10 minutes on baking sheets. Cut each tart into 12 wedges. Serve warm or at room temperature.

Make-ahead directions: Prepare as above through step 2. Cover and chill assembled tarts up to 4 hours. Uncover and bake as directed.

Nutrition Facts per serving: 133 cal., 9 g total fat (4 g sat. fat), 11 mg chol., 100 mg sodium, 11 g carbo., 0 g fiber, 3 g pro.
Daily Values: 6% vit. A, 12% vit. C, 8% calcium, 2% iron
Exchanges: 1 Starch, 1½ Fat

Shrimp Cocktail

Low Fat

Prep: 1 hour Chill: 4 to 24 hours Makes: 6 appetizer servings

1. Thaw 1¼ pounds fresh shrimp in shells, if frozen. Peel and devein shrimp, leaving tails intact (see photos 1, 2, and 3, page 295). In a large saucepan bring 3 cups water and, if desired, 1 teaspoon salt to boiling. Add shrimp. Simmer, uncovered, for 1 to 3 minutes or until shrimp turn pink, stirring occasionally. Drain shrimp; rinse under cold water. Drain well. Chill for 4 to 24 hours. To serve, prepare 1 recipe Cocktail Sauce (page 479). Arrange the chilled shrimp in 6 lettuce-lined cocktail cups or glasses. Spoon 1 tablespoon of the sauce over each serving. If desired, serve with lemon wedges.

Nutrition Facts per serving: 105 cal., 1 g total fat (0 g sat. fat), 101 mg chol., 521 mg sodium, 9 g carbo., 2 g fiber, 14 g pro.
Daily Values: 6% vit. A, 15% vit. C, 5% calcium, 11% iron
Exchanges: 1 Vegetable, 2 Very Lean Meat

Citrus Seafood Cocktail

Prep: 30 minutes **Marinate:** 2 to 24 hours
Makes: 8 to 10 appetizer servings

- 12 ounces fresh or frozen bay scallops
- 12 ounces fresh or frozen large shrimp in shells
- 1 teaspoon finely shredded ruby red grapefruit peel
- ⅓ cup ruby red grapefruit juice
- ¼ cup salad oil
- 2 tablespoons thinly sliced green onion (1)
- 2 tablespoons finely chopped red or yellow sweet pepper
- 1 tablespoon white balsamic vinegar or white wine vinegar
- 1 tablespoon honey
- 1½ teaspoons anise seeds, crushed
- ½ teaspoon ground cinnamon
- ½ of a fresh pineapple, peeled, cored, and coarsely chopped (see photo, page 71)
- 2 ruby red grapefruit, peeled and sectioned
- 2 oranges, peeled and sectioned

1. Thaw scallops and shrimp, if frozen. Peel and devein shrimp, leaving tails intact (see photos 1, 2, and 3, page 295). Cook scallops and shrimp separately in lightly salted boiling water for 1 to 3 minutes or until scallops are opaque and shrimp turn pink, stirring occasionally. Drain; rinse under cold running water. Drain well. Place cooked scallops and shrimp in a plastic bag set in a deep bowl.

2. For marinade, combine grapefruit peel, grapefruit juice, salad oil, green onion, sweet pepper, vinegar, honey, anise seeds, cinnamon, and ½ teaspoon *salt*. Pour over seafood; seal bag. Refrigerate 2 to 24 hours; turn bag occasionally.

3. To serve, drain seafood mixture, discarding marinade. Gently combine seafood, pineapple, grapefruit sections, and orange sections. Serve in cocktail cups or glasses.

Nutrition Facts per serving: 148 cal., 5 g total fat (1 g sat. fat), 63 mg chol., 189 mg sodium, 13 g carbo., 1 g fiber, 14 g pro. Daily Values: 6% vit. A, 57% vit. C, 4% calcium, 6% iron Exchanges: 1 Fruit, 1½ Very Lean Meat, ½ Fat

Egg Rolls

Prep: 25 minutes **Cook:** 2 minutes per batch
Oven: 300°F **Makes:** 8 egg rolls

- 8 egg roll skins
- 1 recipe Pork Filling
  Shortening or cooking oil for deep-fat frying
- 1 recipe Sweet-and-Sour Sauce (page 479), 1⅓ cups bottled sweet-and-sour sauce, or ½ cup prepared Chinese-style hot mustard

1. For each egg roll, place an egg roll skin on a flat surface with a corner pointing toward you. Spoon about ¼ cup Pork Filling across and just below center of egg roll skin. Fold bottom corner over filling, tucking it under on the other side. Fold side corners over filling, forming an envelope shape. Roll egg roll toward remaining corner. Moisten top corner with *water;* press firmly to seal.

2. In a heavy saucepan or deep-fat fryer heat 2 inches melted shortening to 365°F. Fry egg rolls, a few at a time, 2 to 3 minutes or until golden; drain. Keep warm in a 300° oven while frying remainder. Serve with Sweet-and-Sour Sauce.

Pork Filling: Cook 8 ounces ground pork, 1 teaspoon grated fresh ginger, and 1 clove garlic, minced, 2 to 3 minutes or until meat is brown; drain fat. Add ½ cup finely chopped bok choy or cabbage, ½ cup chopped water chestnuts, ½ cup shredded carrot, and ¼ cup finely chopped onion. Cook and stir 2 minutes more. Combine 2 tablespoons soy sauce, 2 teaspoons cornstarch, ½ teaspoon sugar, and ¼ teaspoon salt; add to skillet. Cook and stir 1 minute. Cool slightly.

Nutrition Facts per egg roll: 240 cal., 3 g total fat (1 g sat. fat), 16 mg chol., 794 mg sodium, 44 g carbo., 1 g fiber, 9 g pro. Daily Values: 46% vit. A, 17% vit. C, 8% calcium, 10% iron Exchanges: 2 Starch, 1 Other Carbo., ½ Lean Meat

Citrus Seafood Cocktail

Beans, Rice, & Grains

Beans, Rice, & Grains

Beans, Rice, & Grains

Black beans

Black-eyed peas

Cranberry beans

**Fava beans
(broad beans)**

**Garbanzo beans
(chickpeas)**

Great Northern beans

Lima beans, baby

**Lima beans, Christmas
(calico)**

**Lima beans, large
(butter beans)**

Navy or pea beans

Pinto beans

Red beans

Red kidney beans

Soybeans (dried)

Lentils (brown)

Lentils (red)

Green split peas

Yellow split peas

Arborio rice

Basmati rice

Instant brown rice

Regular brown rice

Long grain white rice

Instant white rice

Wild rice

Barley, pearl

Buckwheat groats

Bulgur

Cornmeal (yellow)

Cracked wheat

Farina

Hominy grits

Millet

**Oats, rolled,
regular**

**Oats, rolled,
quick-cooking**

Quinoa

Rye berries

Wheat berries

Wheat bran

Wheat germ, toasted

Rice Pilaf

`Fast` `Low Fat`

Prep: 15 minutes **Cook:** 15 minutes
Makes: about 3 cups (4 side-dish servings)

- ½ **cup chopped onion (1 medium)**
- ½ **cup sliced fresh button mushrooms**
- ¼ **cup chopped celery or green sweet pepper**
- 1 **clove garlic, minced**
- 1 **tablespoon butter or margarine**
- ¾ **cup uncooked long grain rice**
- 1½ **teaspoons instant chicken, beef, or vegetable bouillon granules**
- ¼ **teaspoon black pepper**
- 2 **slices bacon, crisp-cooked, drained, and crumbled, or ¼ cup finely chopped cooked ham or Canadian bacon (optional)**

1. In a medium saucepan cook onion, mushrooms, celery, and garlic in hot butter until tender.

2. Carefully stir in rice, bouillon granules, pepper, and 1½ cups *water*. Bring to boiling; reduce heat. Simmer, covered, about 15 minutes or until the rice is tender and liquid is absorbed. If desired, stir in crumbled bacon.

Nutrition Facts per serving: 167 cal., 3 g total fat (2 g sat. fat), 8 mg chol., 367 mg sodium, 31 g carbo., 1 g fiber, 3 g pro.
Daily Values: 3% vit. A, 3% vit. C, 2% calcium, 9% iron
Exchanges: 2 Starch

Spanish Rice

`Low Fat`

Prep: 15 minutes **Cook:** 20 minutes
Makes: about 5 cups (6 to 8 side-dish servings)

- ½ **cup chopped onion (1 medium)**
- ½ **cup chopped green sweet pepper**
- 1 **clove garlic, minced**
- 1 **tablespoon cooking oil**
- 1 **teaspoon chili powder**
- 1 **28-ounce can tomatoes, undrained and cut up**
- ¾ **cup uncooked long grain rice**
- 1 **4-ounce can diced green chile peppers, undrained**
- **Several dashes bottled hot pepper sauce (optional)**
- ½ **cup shredded cheddar cheese (optional)**

1. In a large skillet cook onion, sweet pepper, and garlic in hot oil until tender. Add chili powder; cook 1 minute more. Stir in undrained tomatoes, rice, chile peppers, hot pepper sauce (if

desired), 1 cup *water*, ¼ teaspoon *salt*, and ⅛ teaspoon *black pepper*. Bring to boiling; reduce heat. Simmer, covered, about 20 minutes or until the rice is tender and most of the liquid is absorbed. If desired, sprinkle with the shredded cheese.

Nutrition Facts per serving: 144 cal., 3 g total fat (0 g sat. fat), 0 mg chol., 353 mg sodium, 27 g carbo., 2 g fiber, 4 g pro.
Daily Values: 20% vit. A, 59% vit. C, 8% calcium, 11% iron
Exchanges: 1½ Starch, ½ Fat

Rice and Sweet Onion Casserole

Prep: 45 minutes **Bake:** 30 minutes **Oven:** 325°F
Makes: 6 to 8 side-dish servings

- 1½ **cups uncooked arborio rice or short grain rice**
- ¼ **cup butter or margarine**
- 1 **cup whole fresh mushrooms, such as porcini and/or button**
- 12 **purple or white boiling onions, peeled and halved**
- 1 **medium sweet onion, such as Vidalia or Walla Walla, cut into 8 wedges**
- 2 **cloves garlic, minced**
- 1¾ **cups Vegetable Stock (see recipe, page 488) or one 14-ounce can vegetable broth**
- ¾ **cup freshly shredded Romano or Parmesan cheese**

1. In a medium saucepan combine 3 cups *water* and ½ teaspoon *salt*. Bring to boiling. Remove from heat; stir in rice. Cover and let stand for 30 minutes; drain. Rinse with cold water; drain.

2. Meanwhile, in a large skillet melt butter over medium-high heat. Add one-third of the mushrooms; cook and stir for 4 to 5 minutes or until tender. Remove mushrooms from skillet; set aside. Add the remaining mushrooms, boiling onions, sweet onion, and garlic to hot skillet. Cook and stir until vegetables are tender. Reduce heat to medium and add rice. Cook and stir for 4 to 5 minutes or until rice is golden. Carefully stir in Vegetable Stock; bring to boiling. Transfer rice mixture to a 2-quart casserole.

3. Bake, covered, in a 325° oven for 25 to 30 minutes or until rice is tender and liquid is absorbed. Fluff with a fork. Stir in ⅔ cup of the Romano cheese. Sprinkle with the remaining cheese and the reserved cooked mushrooms. Bake, uncovered, about 5 minutes more or until cheese is melted and lightly browned.

Nutrition Facts per serving: 313 cal., 12 g total fat (5 g sat. fat), 28 mg chol., 523 mg sodium, 43 g carbo., 2 g fiber, 8 g pro.
Daily Values: 7% vit. A, 3% vit. C, 11% calcium, 12% iron
Exchanges: 3 Starch, 2 Fat

Brown and Wild Rice Pilaf

Prep: 15 minutes **Cook:** 45 minutes
Makes: about 3½ cups (4 side-dish servings)

> 1 **cup sliced fresh mushrooms**
> ¼ **cup sliced green onions (2)**
> 1 **tablespoon butter or margarine**
> 1 **14-ounce can chicken broth**
> ½ **cup uncooked regular brown rice**
> ⅓ **cup uncooked wild rice, rinsed and drained**
> 1 **tablespoon snipped fresh basil or**
>   ½ **teaspoon dried basil, crushed**
> ⅛ **teaspoon black pepper**
> ½ **cup frozen peas**
> ¼ **cup shredded carrot**

1. In a medium saucepan cook mushrooms and green onions in hot butter until tender. Carefully add chicken broth; bring to boiling. Stir in brown rice; wild rice; dried basil, if using; and pepper. Return to boiling; reduce heat.

2. Simmer, covered, about 40 minutes or until the rices are tender and most of the broth is absorbed. Stir in peas, carrot, and fresh basil, if using. Simmer for 3 to 5 minutes more or until heated through, stirring occasionally.

Nutrition Facts per serving: 197 cal., 5 g total fat (2 g sat. fat), 8 mg chol., 488 mg sodium, 32 g carbo., 3 g fiber, 7 g pro.
Daily Values: 41% vit. A, 6% vit. C, 2% calcium, 6% iron
Exchanges: 2 Starch, ½ Fat

Oven-Cooked Rice

Vary this side dish by substituting ¾ cup quick-cooking barley for the rice.

Low Fat

Prep: 10 minutes **Bake:** 35 minutes **Oven:** 350°F
Makes: about 2¼ cups (4 side-dish servings)

> 1½ **cups boiling water**
> 1 **tablespoon butter or margarine**
> ¾ **cup uncooked long grain rice**
> ½ **teaspoon salt**

1. In a 1-quart casserole combine boiling water and butter; stir until butter is melted. Stir in rice and salt. Bake, covered, in a 350° oven about 35 minutes or until rice is tender and liquid is absorbed. Fluff with a fork before serving.

Nutrition Facts per serving: 152 cal., 3 g total fat (2 g sat. fat), 8 mg chol., 328 mg sodium, 28 g carbo., 0 g fiber, 3 g pro.
Daily Values: 3% vit. A, 1% calcium, 8% iron
Exchanges: 1½ Starch, ½ Fat

Oven-Cooked Rice Pilaf: Prepare as below left, except substitute boiling chicken broth for the water. Omit salt and stir ¼ cup sliced green onions, ¼ cup chopped celery, and ¼ cup chopped carrot in with the rice.

Nutrition Facts per serving: 170 cal., 4 g total fat (2 g sat. fat), 8 mg chol., 420 mg sodium, 30 g carbo., 1 g fiber, 4 g pro.
Daily Values: 42% vit. A, 3% vit. C, 2% calcium, 9% iron
Exchanges: 2 Starch

Shopper's Guide to Rice

Rice, often called "the world's leading bread," has many uses. You can serve it in casseroles, soups, salads, and even desserts. The various types and processing methods increase the grain's versatility. Here's a sampling of what's available (see photos, page 79):

White rice: Long, medium, and short grain are the three types. The shorter the grain, the more starch it contains. Because it is the starch that causes rice to stick together when cooked, long grain rice cooks up lighter and fluffier than short grain rice.

Arborio rice: This short grain white rice is preferred in risotto as it contributes to the traditional creaminess of the dish. Look for arborio rice in larger supermarkets and specialty food shops.

Instant and quick-cooking rice: Popular because of their short cooking times, instant and quick-cooking rices are partially or fully cooked before they are packaged.

Brown rice: An unpolished rice grain, it has the bran layer intact. Pleasantly chewy and nutty in flavor, brown rice requires a longer cooking time than white rice.

Converted rice: Also called parboiled rice, this white rice is steamed and pressure-cooked before it's packaged. This process helps to retain nutrients and keeps the grains from sticking together when cooked.

Aromatic rices: The aroma of basmati, Texmati, wild pecan, or jasmine rice is irresistible. Their flavors range from toasted nuts to popped corn. Look for them in food markets featuring Indian or Middle Eastern foods or in some larger supermarkets.

Wild rice: Not a grain at all, wild rice is a marsh grass. It takes three times as long to cook as white rice, but the nutlike flavor and chewy texture are worth the wait. Wash wild rice thoroughly before cooking it.

Wild Rice with Walnuts and Dates

Best Loved

Serve this pilaf-style side dish alongside broiled chicken or fish.

Prep: 15 minutes **Cook:** 1 hour
Makes: about 5 cups (6 to 8 side-dish servings)

- **1 cup chopped onion (1 large)**
- **1 tablespoon butter or margarine**
- **1 cup uncooked wild rice, rinsed and drained**
- **2 cups chopped celery (4 stalks)**
- **1 14-ounce can chicken or beef broth**
- **1 cup water**
- **½ cup pitted whole dates, snipped**
- **⅓ cup chopped walnuts, toasted (see tip, page 224)**

1. In a large skillet cook onion in hot butter about 10 minutes or until tender. Add wild rice. Cook and stir for 3 minutes more. Carefully add celery, broth, and water. Bring to boiling; reduce heat. Simmer, covered, about 40 minutes or until rice is tender and most of the liquid is absorbed.

2. Stir in dates and walnuts. Cook, uncovered, for 3 to 4 minutes more or until heated through and remaining liquid is absorbed.

Nutrition Facts per serving: 221 cal., 7 g total fat (2 g sat. fat), 5 mg chol., 347 mg sodium, 36 g carbo., 4 g fiber, 6 g pro.
Daily Values: 3% vit. A, 7% vit. C, 4% calcium, 6% iron
Exchanges: 2½ Starch, ½ Fat

Vegetable Fried Rice

Be sure the cooked rice is thoroughly chilled before you start so the rice grains won't stick together during stir-frying.

Prep: 30 minutes **Cook:** 7 minutes
Makes: about 3 cups (4 side-dish servings)

- **1 teaspoon toasted sesame oil or cooking oil**
- **1 beaten egg**
- **½ pound fresh asparagus spears, cut into 1-inch pieces (1 cup)**
- **¼ cup chopped fresh mushrooms**
- **¼ cup bias-sliced celery (½ stalk)**
- **2 tablespoons thinly sliced green onion (1)**
- **2 cloves garlic, minced**
- **1 tablespoon cooking oil**
- **3 tablespoons reduced-sodium soy sauce**
- **2 tablespoons dry white wine or water**
  Dash ground red pepper
- **2 cups chilled cooked rice**

1. In a large skillet heat the 1 teaspoon oil over medium heat. Add egg, lifting and tilting the skillet to form a thin layer (egg may not completely cover the bottom of the skillet). Cook for 1 minute or until egg is set. Invert skillet over a baking sheet to remove cooked egg; cut egg into short, narrow strips (about 3×½ inch). Set egg strips aside.

2. In the same skillet cook and stir asparagus, mushrooms, celery, green onion, and garlic in the 1 tablespoon oil about 4 minutes or until the asparagus and celery are crisp-tender. Stir in soy sauce, wine, and red pepper. Add cooked rice. Cook and stir about 2 minutes or until mixture is heated through. Stir in egg strips.

Nutrition Facts per serving: 188 cal., 6 g total fat (1 g sat. fat), 53 mg chol., 458 mg sodium, 25 g carbo., 1 g fiber, 6 g pro.
Daily Values: 4% vit. A, 16% vit. C, 3% calcium, 9% iron
Exchanges: 1½ Starch, 1 Fat

Easy Risotto

In this simplified version, the constant stirring required by more classic risotto recipes (page 83) is eliminated.

Prep: 5 minutes **Cook:** 25 minutes **Stand:** 5 minutes
Makes: about 2 cups (3 to 4 side-dish servings)

- **⅓ cup chopped onion (1 small)**
- **1 tablespoon butter or margarine**
- **⅔ cup uncooked arborio or long grain rice**
- **2 cups water**
- **1 teaspoon instant chicken bouillon granules**
  Dash black pepper
- **1 cup frozen peas (optional)**
- **¼ cup grated Parmesan or Romano cheese**

1. In a medium saucepan cook the onion in hot butter until tender; add rice. Cook and stir 2 minutes more. Carefully stir in the water, bouillon granules, and pepper. Bring to boiling; reduce heat. Simmer, covered, 20 minutes (do not lift lid).

2. Remove saucepan from heat. If desired, stir in peas. Let stand, covered, for 5 minutes. Rice should be tender but slightly firm, and mixture should be creamy. (If necessary, stir in a little water to reach desired consistency.) Stir in Parmesan cheese.

Nutrition Facts per serving: 179 cal., 6 g total fat (3 g sat. fat), 10 mg chol., 571 mg sodium, 25 g carbo., 0 g fiber, 6 g pro.
Daily Values: 5% vit. A, 2% vit. C, 12% calcium, 11% iron
Exchanges: 1½ Starch, 1 Fat

Risotto with Vegetables

Risotto (rih-SO-toh) is a classic Italian dish traditionally made with arborio rice. The finished product has a creamy consistency and a tender, but slightly firm, texture.

Prep: 20 minutes **Cook:** 30 minutes
Makes: about 4 cups (6 side-dish servings)

> 2 **cups sliced fresh mushrooms**
> ½ **cup chopped onion (1 medium)**
> 2 **cloves garlic, minced**
> 2 **tablespoons olive oil or cooking oil**
> 1 **cup uncooked arborio rice**
> 3 **cups vegetable broth or reduced-sodium chicken broth**
> ¾ **cup bite-size asparagus or broccoli pieces**
> ¾ **cup seeded and diced tomato**
> ¼ **cup shredded carrot (1 small)**
> ¼ **cup finely shredded Parmesan cheese**
> 3 **tablespoons snipped fresh basil or parsley**

1. In a large saucepan cook mushrooms, onion, and garlic in hot oil until onion is tender; add rice. Cook and stir over medium heat about 5 minutes more or until rice is golden.

2. Meanwhile, in another saucepan bring broth to boiling; reduce heat and simmer. Slowly add 1 cup of the broth to the rice mixture, stirring constantly. Continue to cook and stir over medium heat until liquid is absorbed. Add another ½ cup of the broth and the asparagus pieces to the rice mixture, stirring constantly. Continue to cook and stir until the liquid is absorbed. Add another 1 cup broth, ½ cup at a time, stirring constantly until the broth has been absorbed. (This should take about 15 minutes.)

3. Stir in the remaining ½ cup broth, the tomato, and carrot. Cook and stir until the rice is slightly creamy and just tender. Stir in the Parmesan cheese and basil.

Nutrition Facts per serving: 204 cal., 7 g total fat (2 g sat. fat), 4 mg chol., 522 mg sodium, 33 g carbo., 2 g fiber, 6 g pro.
Daily Values: 34% vit. A, 17% vit. C, 5% calcium, 12% iron
Exchanges: 1 Vegetable, 2 Starch, 1 Fat

For Bean Counters Only

How many beans do you need to buy when a recipe calls for a cup measure? Here's a guide to follow. One pound of dry beans equals 2¼ to 2½ cups uncooked beans or 6 to 7 cups cooked beans, depending on the variety. A 15-ounce can of beans contains about 1¾ cups drained beans.

Bean Salad Wraps

Specialty shops and large supermarkets carry a variety of flavored tortillas. Look for tomato-basil, pesto, fresh herb, spinach, or whole wheat.

Fast **Low Fat**

Start to Finish: 15 minutes **Oven:** 350°F
Makes: 4 main-dish servings

> 4 **8-inch flavored or plain flour tortillas**
> 1 **15-ounce can black beans, rinsed and drained (see photo, page 84)**
> ½ **cup chopped green sweet pepper or 1 fresh jalapeño chile pepper, seeded and finely chopped (see tip, page 64)**
> 2 **tablespoons snipped fresh cilantro**
> ⅓ **cup light mayonnaise dressing or salad dressing**
> 1 **tablespoon lime juice**
>   **Leaf lettuce**

1. Stack tortillas and wrap tightly in foil. Heat in a 350° oven for 10 minutes to soften.

2. Meanwhile, in a medium bowl mash black beans slightly; add sweet pepper and cilantro. Stir in light mayonnaise dressing and lime juice.

3. To serve, spread bean mixture evenly over tortillas. Top with lettuce leaves. Roll up tortillas.

Nutrition Facts per serving: 230 cal., 9 g total fat (2 g sat. fat), 7 mg chol., 504 mg sodium, 33 g carbo., 6 g fiber, 9 g pro.
Daily Values: 6% vit. A, 27% vit. C, 7% calcium, 12% iron
Exchanges: 2 Starch, ½ Very Lean Meat, 1½ Fat

Bean Salad Wraps

Tortilla-Black Bean Casserole

This Tex-Mex favorite can also be served as a side dish for 12 people.

Low Fat

Prep: 25 minutes **Bake:** 30 minutes
Oven: 350°F **Makes:** 8 main-dish servings

  2 cups chopped onion (2 large)
1½ cups chopped green sweet pepper
    (2 medium)
  1 14½-ounce can tomatoes, undrained and
    cut up
  ¾ cup bottled picante sauce or green salsa
  2 teaspoons ground cumin
  2 cloves garlic, minced
  2 15-ounce cans black beans and/or red kidney
    beans, rinsed and drained (see photo, below)
 12 6-inch corn tortillas
  8 ounces reduced-fat Monterey Jack cheese,
    shredded (2 cups)
  2 medium tomatoes, chopped (optional)
  2 cups shredded lettuce (optional)
    Sliced green onions (optional)
    Sliced pitted ripe olives (optional)
  ½ cup light dairy sour cream or plain low-fat
    yogurt (optional)

1. In a large skillet combine onion, sweet pepper, undrained tomatoes, picante sauce, cumin, and garlic. Bring to boiling; reduce heat. Simmer, uncovered, for 10 minutes. Stir in beans.

2. Spread one-third of the bean mixture over the bottom of a 3-quart rectangular baking dish. Top with 6 of the tortillas, overlapping as necessary, and 1 cup of the cheese. Add another one-third of the bean mixture; top with remaining 6 tortillas and remaining bean mixture.

3. Bake, covered, in a 350° oven 30 to 35 minutes or until heated through. Sprinkle with remaining 1 cup cheese. Let stand 10 minutes before serving. If desired, top with tomatoes, lettuce, onions, and olives, and serve with sour cream.

Nutrition Facts per serving: 295 cal., 8 g total fat (4 g sat. fat), 20 mg chol., 689 mg sodium, 46 g carbo., 8 g fiber, 18 g pro. **Daily Values:** 18% vit. A, 55% vit. C, 31% calcium, 21% iron **Exchanges:** 3 Starch, 1 Lean Meat

Canned beans may save you time, but they add salt to your dishes. You can eliminate the salty liquid by rinsing the beans in a colander under cold running water; drain well.

Two-Bean Tamale Pie   Best Loved

Prep: 25 minutes **Bake:** 25 minutes
Oven: 400°F **Makes:** 6 main-dish servings

  1 cup chopped green sweet pepper (1 large)
  ½ cup chopped onion (1 medium)
  2 cloves garlic, minced
  1 tablespoon cooking oil
  1 15-ounce can kidney beans, rinsed, drained,
    and slightly mashed (see photo, bottom left)
  1 15-ounce can pinto beans, rinsed, drained,
    and slightly mashed (see photo, bottom left)
  1 6-ounce can (⅔ cup) vegetable juice
  1 4-ounce can diced green chile peppers,
    undrained
  1 teaspoon chili powder
  ½ teaspoon ground cumin
  1 8½-ounce package corn muffin mix
  ½ cup shredded cheddar cheese (2 ounces)
  ¼ cup snipped fresh cilantro or parsley

1. Grease a 2-quart square baking dish or 10-inch quiche dish; set aside. In a medium skillet cook sweet pepper, onion, and garlic in hot oil until tender. Stir in kidney beans, pinto beans, vegetable juice, chile peppers, chili powder, and cumin; heat through. Spoon bean mixture into prepared dish.

2. Prepare corn muffin mix according to package directions; add cheese and cilantro, stirring just until combined. Spoon cornbread mixture evenly over the top of the bean mixture. Bake, uncovered, in a 400° oven about 25 minutes or until golden. If desired, serve with salsa and sour cream.

Nutrition Facts per serving: 387 cal., 13 g total fat (2 g sat. fat), 37 mg chol., 858 mg sodium, 58 g carbo., 9 g fiber, 17 g pro. **Daily Values:** 19% vit. A, 59% vit. C, 21% calcium, 16% iron **Exchanges:** 1 Vegetable, 3½ Starch, 2 Fat

Two-Bean Tamale Pie

Spaghetti Squash with Balsamic Beans

Top the golden strands of spaghetti squash with this sassy sauce of sweet-tart beans.

Fast **Low Fat**

Start to Finish: 30 minutes **Makes:** 4 main-dish servings

- ¼ cup balsamic vinegar
- 3 tablespoons olive oil
- 1 tablespoon honey mustard
- 2 cloves garlic, minced
- 1 medium spaghetti squash (2½ to 3 pounds), halved and seeded
- 1 10-ounce package frozen baby lima beans
- 1 15-ounce can red kidney beans, rinsed and drained (see photo, page 84)
- ½ of a 7-ounce jar (½ cup) roasted red sweet peppers, rinsed, drained, and cut into short strips
- ½ teaspoon salt
- Freshly ground black pepper (optional)

1. For vinaigrette, in a screw-top jar combine vinegar, oil, honey mustard, and garlic. Cover and shake well. Set vinaigrette aside.

2. Place squash halves in a large Dutch oven with about 1 inch of *water.* Bring to boiling. Cook, covered, 15 to 20 minutes or until tender.

3. Meanwhile, in a saucepan cook lima beans according to package directions, adding kidney beans during the last 3 minutes of cooking; drain and return to pan. Stir in roasted sweet peppers and salt; heat through. Pour vinaigrette over warm bean mixture; toss to coat.

4. Use a fork to scrape the squash pulp from the shells in strands. Spoon warm bean mixture over squash strands; drizzle any excess vinaigrette on top. If desired, sprinkle with pepper.

Make-ahead directions: Prepare as above through step 1. Cover and refrigerate for up to 2 days. Let vinaigrette stand at room temperature while preparing squash and beans.

Nutrition Facts per serving: 387 cal., 12 g total fat (2 g sat. fat), 0 mg chol., 563 mg sodium, 61 g carbo., 14 g fiber, 15 g pro.
Daily Values: 6% vit. A, 112% vit. C, 11% calcium, 20% iron
Exchanges: 4 Starch, 1½ Fat

Bean and Cheese Burritos

Save some fat and calories by using fat-free refried beans and reduced-fat cheese.

Fast

Prep: 15 minutes **Bake:** 10 minutes
Oven: 350°F **Makes:** 3 main-dish servings

- 6 7- or 8-inch flour tortillas
- 1 cup chopped onion (1 large)
- 1 tablespoon cooking oil
- 1 16-ounce can refried beans
- 1 cup shredded cheddar cheese (4 ounces)
- 1 cup shredded lettuce
- ⅓ cup bottled salsa

1. Stack tortillas and wrap tightly in foil. Heat in a 350° oven for 10 minutes to soften.

2. Meanwhile, for filling, in a skillet cook onion in hot oil until tender; add refried beans. Cook and stir until heated through. Spoon about ¼ cup of the filling onto each tortilla just below center. Divide cheese among tortillas. Fold bottom edge of each tortilla up and over filling (see photo 1, page 362). Fold opposite sides in and over filling (see photo 2, page 362). Roll up from the bottom. Place on a baking sheet. Bake in a 350° oven about 10 minutes or until heated through. Serve with lettuce and salsa.

Nutrition Facts per serving: 572 cal., 25 g total fat (11 g sat. fat), 40 mg chol., 1,341 mg sodium, 65 g carbo., 13 g fiber, 24 g pro.
Daily Values: 19% vit. A, 20% vit. C, 43% calcium, 32% iron
Exchanges: 1 Vegetable, 4 Starch, 1½ Medium-Fat Meat, 2 Fat

Eating Meatless

Pasta, dairy products, eggs, dry beans, lentils, tofu, rice, vegetables, and other grains are important ingredients in meatless main dishes.

■ If your meatless recipes include dairy products, watch out for the fat and calories. Some of the healthier dairy choices include fat-free milk, fat-free and low-fat yogurt, fat-free and light sour cream, reduced-fat cheeses, and low-fat cottage cheese.

■ If you are eliminating all animal products from your diet, it's critical that the foods you eat are nutritionally balanced so that you get the protein, vitamins, and minerals your body needs. If you're a strict vegetarian, you should be aware that your intake of certain nutrients, such as iron, calcium, zinc, vitamin B_{12}, and vitamin D, may end up being lower than recommended.

Mixed Bean Cassoulet

Low Fat

Prep: 1¾ hours **Cook:** 1½ hours **Bake:** 15 minutes
Oven: 350°F **Makes:** 6 main-dish servings

- ¾ **cup dry Great Northern beans**
- ¾ **cup dry pinto beans**
- ½ **cup dry garbanzo beans (chickpeas)**
- ½ **cup chopped celery (1 stalk)**
- ½ **cup chopped onion (1 medium)**
- ½ **cup chopped carrot (1 medium)**
- 1 **tablespoon olive oil**
- 3½ **cups Vegetable Stock (see recipe, page 488) or two 14-ounce cans vegetable broth***
- ¼ **cup water**
- ⅔ **cup dried porcini mushrooms**
- ¼ **cup roasted red sweet peppers, chopped**
- ¼ **cup oil-packed dried tomatoes, drained and snipped**
- 2 **tablespoons bottled roasted garlic puree**
- 1 **bay leaf**
- ¼ **teaspoon salt***
- ¼ **teaspoon dried thyme, crushed**
- ¼ **teaspoon dried oregano, crushed**
- ¼ **teaspoon black pepper**
- 2 **cups soft sourdough bread crumbs**
- 2 **tablespoons butter or margarine, melted**
- 1 **clove garlic, minced**

1. Rinse beans. In a large Dutch oven combine beans and 8 cups *water*. Bring to boiling; reduce heat. Simmer for 2 minutes. Remove from heat. Cover and let stand for 1 hour. (Or, place beans in water in Dutch oven. Cover and let soak in a cool place for 6 to 8 hours or overnight.)

2. Drain and rinse beans; set aside. In the same Dutch oven cook the celery, onion, and carrot in hot oil over medium heat about 5 minutes or until tender. Stir in the drained beans, Vegetable Stock, the ¼ cup water, and dried mushrooms. Bring to boiling; reduce heat. Simmer, covered, for 1 hour.

3. Stir in the roasted sweet peppers, dried tomatoes, garlic puree, bay leaf, salt, thyme, oregano, and pepper. Return to boiling; reduce heat. Simmer, covered, about 30 minutes more or until beans are tender and most of the liquid is absorbed. Discard bay leaf.

4. Transfer bean mixture to a 2-quart casserole. In a small bowl combine bread crumbs, melted butter, and garlic. Sprinkle over bean mixture. Bake, uncovered, in a 350° oven for 15 to 20 minutes or until bread crumbs are lightly toasted.

*Note: If using canned vegetable broth, omit salt.

Nutrition Facts per serving: 358 cal., 11 g total fat (4 g sat. fat), 10 mg chol., 435 mg sodium, 52 g carbo., 15 g fiber, 15 g pro. Daily Values: 57% vit. A, 45% vit. C, 11% calcium, 21% iron Exchanges: 3½ Starch, 1½ Lean Meat

---

Baked Bean Quintet Best Loved

Low Fat

Prep: 10 minutes **Bake:** 1 hour **Oven:** 375°F
Makes: 12 to 16 side-dish servings

- 1 **cup chopped onion (1 large)**
- 6 **slices bacon, cut up**
- 1 **clove garlic, minced**
- 1 **16-ounce can lima beans, drained**
- 1 **16-ounce can pork and beans in tomato sauce**
- 1 **15½-ounce can red kidney beans, drained**
- 1 **15-ounce can butter beans, drained**
- 1 **15-ounce can garbanzo beans (chickpeas), drained**
- ¾ **cup catsup**
- ½ **cup molasses**
- ¼ **cup packed brown sugar**
- 1 **tablespoon prepared mustard**
- 1 **tablespoon Worcestershire sauce**

1. In a skillet cook onion, bacon, and garlic until bacon is crisp and onion is tender; drain. In a bowl combine onion mixture, lima beans, pork and beans, red kidney beans, butter beans, garbanzo beans, catsup, molasses, brown sugar, mustard, and Worcestershire sauce. Transfer bean mixture to a 3-quart casserole. Bake, covered, in a 375° oven for 1 hour.

Crockery-cooker directions: Prepare the bean mixture as above. Transfer to a 3½- or 4-quart crockery cooker. Cover and cook on low-heat setting for 10 to 12 hours or on high-heat setting for 4 to 5 hours.

Nutrition Facts per serving: 245 cal., 3 g total fat (1 g sat. fat), 5 mg chol., 882 mg sodium, 47 g carbo., 9 g fiber, 10 g pro. Daily Values: 5% vit. A, 13% vit. C, 10% calcium, 22% iron Exchanges: 2 Starch, 1 Other Carbo., ½ Very Lean Meat

Old-Fashioned Baked Beans

Prep: 1 hour **Cook:** 1 hour **Bake:** 2½ hours
Oven: 300°F **Makes:** 10 to 12 side-dish servings

- **1 pound dry navy beans or dry Great Northern beans (about 2⅓ cups)**
- **¼ pound bacon or salt pork, cut up**
- **1 cup chopped onion (1 large)**
- **½ cup molasses or maple syrup**
- **¼ cup packed brown sugar**
- **1 teaspoon dry mustard**
- **½ teaspoon salt**
- **¼ teaspoon black pepper**

1. Rinse beans. In a large Dutch oven combine beans and 8 cups *water.* Bring to boiling; reduce heat. Simmer for 2 minutes. Remove from heat. Cover and let stand for 1 hour. (Or, place beans in water in Dutch oven. Cover and let soak in a cool place for 6 to 8 hours or overnight.)

2. Drain and rinse beans. Return beans to Dutch oven. Stir in 8 cups fresh *water.* Bring to boiling; reduce heat. Simmer, covered, for 1 to 1½ hours or until beans are tender, stirring occasionally. Drain beans, reserving liquid.

3. In a 2½-quart casserole combine the beans, bacon, and onion. Stir in 1 cup of the reserved bean liquid, the molasses, brown sugar, dry mustard, salt, and pepper.

4. Bake, covered, in a 300° oven about 2½ hours or to desired consistency, stirring occasionally. If necessary, add additional reserved bean liquid.

Nutrition Facts per serving: 285 cal., 7 g total fat (3 g sat. fat), 8 mg chol., 220 mg sodium, 45 g carbo., 11 g fiber, 11 g pro.
Daily Values: 4% vit. C, 12% calcium, 22% iron
Exchanges: 2 Starch, 1 Other Carbo., ½ Very Lean Meat, 1 Fat

Beans with Pesto Bulgur

Low Fat

When dinner is last minute, use one 15-ounce can of pinto beans, rinsed and drained, instead of the dry beans.

Prep: 1¼ hours **Cook:** 1¼ hours
Makes: 6 main-dish servings

- **¾ cup dry cranberry beans, dry Christmas (calico) lima beans, or dry pinto beans**
- **1⅓ cups vegetable broth or chicken broth**
- **⅔ cup bulgur**
- **¾ cup chopped red sweet pepper (1 medium)**
- **¼ cup thinly sliced green onions (2)**
- **⅓ cup refrigerated pesto sauce**

1. Rinse dry beans. In a large saucepan combine beans and 5 cups *water.* Bring to boiling; reduce heat. Simmer for 2 minutes. Remove from heat. Cover and let stand for 1 hour. (Or, place beans in water in a large saucepan. Cover and let soak in a cool place for 6 to 8 hours or overnight.)

2. Drain and rinse beans. Return beans to pan. Add 5 cup fresh *water.* Bring to boiling; reduce heat. Simmer, covered, 1¼ to 1½ hours for cranberry and pinto beans and 45 to 60 minutes for Christmas limas or until beans are tender; drain.

3. Meanwhile, in a medium saucepan bring broth to boiling; add bulgur. Return to boiling; reduce heat. Simmer, covered, about 15 minutes or until most of the liquid is absorbed. Remove from heat. Stir in sweet pepper, green onions, pesto sauce, and beans. Season with freshly ground *black pepper.*

Nutrition Facts per serving: 245 cal., 10 g total fat (0 g sat. fat), 2 mg chol., 330 mg sodium, 32 g carbo., 9 g fiber, 10 g pro.
Daily Values: 21% vit. A, 51% vit. C, 3% calcium, 10% iron
Exchanges: 2 Starch, ½ Very Lean Meat, 1½ Fat

Shortcut Baked Beans

Fast **Low Fat**

Prep: 10 minutes **Cook:** 15 minutes
Makes: 4 to 5 side-dish servings

- **1 16-ounce can pork and beans in tomato sauce**
- **1 15-ounce can red kidney beans, drained**
- **¼ cup catsup**
- **2 tablespoons brown sugar**
- **1 tablespoon cooked bacon pieces**
- **2 teaspoons dried minced onion**
- **2 teaspoons prepared mustard**

1. In a medium saucepan combine pork and beans, kidney beans, catsup, brown sugar, bacon pieces, minced onion, and mustard. Cook over low heat about 15 minutes or to desired consistency, stirring often.

Oven directions: Combine all ingredients in a 1½-quart casserole. Bake, uncovered, in a 350°F oven about 45 minutes or to desired consistency.

Crockery-cooker directions: Double all ingredients and combine in a 3½- or 4-quart crockery cooker. Cover and cook on low-heat setting for 5 to 6 hours or on high-heat setting for 2½ to 3 hours. Makes 8 to 10 side-dish servings.

Nutrition Facts per serving: 235 cal., 2 g total fat (1 g sat. fat), 9 mg chol., 894 mg sodium, 49 g carbo., 12 g fiber, 14 g pro.
Daily Values: 6% vit. A, 10% vit. C, 10% calcium, 29% iron
Exchanges: 3 Starch

Mixed Bean and Portobello Ragout

Ragout is simply a thick, savory stew of French origin. This healthy, meatless ragout features a host of legumes and meaty portobello mushrooms.

Fast   **Low Fat**

Start to Finish: 20 minutes   **Makes:** 4 main-dish servings

- 1   10-ounce package frozen baby lima beans
- 1   cup fresh green beans, cut into 1-inch pieces
- 1½ cups sliced and halved fresh portobello mushrooms or sliced button mushrooms (about 4 ounces)
- 1   tablespoon olive oil
- 1   tablespoon cold water
- 2   teaspoons cornstarch
- 1   14½-ounce can Cajun- or Italian-style stewed tomatoes, undrained
- 1   cup canned garbanzo beans (chickpeas), rinsed and drained (see photo, page 84)

1. Cook lima beans and green beans in lightly salted water according to lima bean package directions; drain.

2. Meanwhile, in a large skillet cook mushrooms in hot oil over medium heat for 5 minutes, stirring occasionally. Combine water and cornstarch; stir into mushrooms. Stir in undrained tomatoes and garbanzo beans. Cook and stir until thickened and bubbly. Cook and stir for 2 minutes more. Stir in cooked lima and green beans; heat through.

Nutrition Facts per serving: 231 cal., 4 g total fat (1 g sat. fat), 0 mg chol., 603 mg sodium, 39 g carbo., 10 g fiber, 11 g pro.
Daily Values: 6% vit. A, 24% vit. C, 8% calcium, 14% iron
Exchanges: 2 Starch, 2 Vegetable, ½ Fat

The Magic Bean

Beans are not only hearty, filling, and virtually fat-free, they're also a good way to add fiber—especially soluble fiber—to your diet. What's so important about fiber? For starters, soluble fiber can help lower blood cholesterol. Fiber also aids in digestion, and a diet low in fat and high in fiber may help reduce the risk of some types of cancer. Need more reasons to fill your pantry with the humble bean? They're also high in protein, complex carbohydrates, and iron—not to mention an inexpensive and satisfying substitute for (or way to stretch) meat.

Polenta

No Fat

Prep: 30 minutes   **Chill:** 30 minutes   **Bake:** 20 minutes
Oven: 350°F   **Makes:** 6 side-dish servings

- 1   cup cornmeal
- 1   cup cold water
- ½   teaspoon salt
     Spaghetti sauce, pizza sauce, or taco sauce (optional)
     Grated Parmesan cheese (optional)

1. In a saucepan bring 2¾ cups *water* to boiling. Meanwhile, in a bowl combine cornmeal, the 1 cup cold water, and salt.

2. Slowly add cornmeal mixture to the boiling water, stirring constantly. Cook and stir until mixture returns to boiling. Reduce heat to low. Cook 10 to 15 minutes or until mixture is very thick, stirring occasionally (see photo, below).

3. Pour hot mixture into a 9-inch pie plate, spreading into an even layer; cool. Cover and chill about 30 minutes or until firm. Bake polenta, uncovered, in a 350° oven about 20 minutes or until hot. Cut into wedges. If desired, serve with spaghetti sauce and Parmesan cheese.

Nutrition Facts per serving: 84 cal., 0 g total fat (0 g sat. fat), 0 mg chol., 199 mg sodium, 18 g carbo., 2 g fiber, 2 g pro.
Daily Values: 2% vit. A, 5% iron
Exchanges: 1 Starch

Fried Polenta: Prepare as above, except pour hot mixture into a 7½×3½×2-inch loaf pan; cool. Cover and chill for several hours or overnight. Remove from pan and cut into ½-inch slices. In a large skillet heat 3 tablespoons cooking oil, butter, or margarine over medium heat. Add 5 slices of polenta and fry for 10 to 12 minutes on each side or until brown and crisp. Repeat with remaining slices. If desired, serve with butter or margarine and honey or maple-flavored syrup. Makes 7 side-dish servings.

Nutrition Facts per serving: 124 cal., 6 g total fat (1 g sat. fat), 0 mg chol., 171 mg sodium, 15 g carbo., 1 g fiber, 2 g pro.
Daily Values: 2% vit. A, 1% calcium, 5% iron
Exchanges: 1 Starch, 1 Fat

Cook the cornmeal mixture over low heat, stirring occasionally, until the mixture is extremely thick.

Cheese and Basil Polenta

Cheese and Basil Polenta

Prep: 40 minutes **Cool:** 1 hour **Chill:** 3 to 24 hours
Bake: 40 minutes **Oven:** 350°F **Makes:** 6 main-dish servings

> 1½ **cups shredded fontina or mozzarella cheese (6 ounces)**
> ⅓ **cup grated Parmesan or Romano cheese**
> 2 **tablespoons snipped fresh basil or 2 teaspoons dried basil, crushed**
> 1 **cup yellow cornmeal**
> 1 **cup cold water**
> ½ **teaspoon salt**
> 1 **recipe Tomato-Basil Sauce**
>   **Fresh basil (optional)**

1. In a medium bowl stir together fontina cheese, Parmesan cheese, and basil. Set aside.

2. For polenta, in a medium saucepan bring 2¾ cups *water* to boiling. Meanwhile, in a bowl stir together cornmeal, the 1 cup cold water, and salt. Slowly add the cornmeal mixture to the boiling water, stirring constantly. Cook and stir until mixture returns to boiling. Reduce heat to low. Cook 10 to 15 minutes or until mixture is very thick, stirring occasionally (see photo, page 88).

3. Pour one-third of the hot mixture into a greased 2-quart square baking dish. Sprinkle with half of the cheese mixture. Repeat layers, ending with the hot mixture. Cool for 1 hour. Cover; chill several hours or overnight until firm.

4. Bake polenta, uncovered, in a 350° oven about 40 minutes or until lightly browned and heated through. Let stand for 10 minutes before serving. Serve with Tomato-Basil Sauce. If desired, garnish with additional basil.

Tomato-Basil Sauce: In a medium saucepan cook ¾ cup chopped onion and 2 cloves garlic, minced, in 2 tablespoons hot butter or margarine until onion is tender. Carefully stir in two 14½-ounce cans whole Italian-style tomatoes, undrained and cut up; half of a 6-ounce can (⅓ cup) tomato paste; ½ teaspoon sugar; ¼ teaspoon salt; and ⅛ teaspoon black pepper. Bring to boiling; reduce heat. Simmer, uncovered, about 20 minutes or to desired consistency. Stir in ¼ cup snipped fresh basil or 1 tablespoon dried basil, crushed. Cook 5 minutes more. Makes about 3⅓ cups sauce.

Nutrition Facts per serving: 310 cal., 15 g total fat (9 g sat. fat), 47 mg chol., 969 mg sodium, 29 g carbo., 4 g fiber, 14 g pro.
Daily Values: 41% vit. A, 34% vit. C, 27% calcium, 14% iron
Exchanges: 1 Vegetable, 1½ Starch, 1 Medium-Fat Meat, 1½ Fat

Baked Cheese Grits

Prep: 10 minutes **Bake:** 25 minutes
Oven: 325°F **Makes:** 4 to 5 side-dish servings

> 2 **cups water or chicken broth**
> ½ **cup quick-cooking grits**
> 1 **beaten egg**
> 1 **cup shredded American or cheddar cheese (4 ounces)**
> 1 **tablespoon butter or margarine**

1. In a saucepan bring water to boiling. Slowly add grits, stirring constantly. Gradually stir about ½ cup of the hot mixture into the beaten egg. Return egg mixture to saucepan and stir to combine. Remove saucepan from heat. Stir cheese and butter into grits until melted.

2. Spoon grits into a 1-quart casserole. Bake in a 325° oven for 25 to 30 minutes or until a knife inserted near the center comes out clean. Let stand for 5 minutes before serving.

Nutrition Facts per serving: 223 cal., 13 g total fat (8 g sat. fat), 88 mg chol., 458 mg sodium, 16 g carbo., 0 g fiber, 10 g pro.
Daily Values: 11% vit. A, 18% calcium, 6% iron
Exchanges: 1 Starch, 1 High-Fat Meat, ½ Fat

Discovering Tofu

Tofu, also referred to as bean curd, is made by curdling soy milk in a process similar to cheese-making. Although it is almost tasteless by itself, tofu acts like a sponge, easily absorbing other flavors. Tofu is rich in protein and low in sodium.

Indian Masala Tofu

Spinach-Jalapeño Tofu

Extra-Firm Silken Tofu (aseptic)

Smoked Hickory Baked Tofu

Barbecue Baked Tofu

Tomato-Basil Baked Tofu

Look for tofu in the produce section of your grocery store, although some stores sell it in the deli or dairy department. Check the "sell by" date on the package to ensure freshness. Store tofu in the refrigerator (unless it is in an aseptic package). Once opened, refrigerate tofu covered with water for up to 1 week, changing the water daily. Tofu can also be frozen for up to 5 months.

Types of Tofu

Extra-firm or firm tofu: This type is dense and keeps its shape. Use it for slicing or cubing in stir-fries, pasta dishes, or on the grill.

Soft tofu: Ideal for whipping, blending, or crumbling, use it for dressings, dips, and desserts.

Silken tofu: Sold in shelf-stable packages, it has a much finer consistency than other forms of tofu. Silken tofu is available in extra-firm, firm, soft, and reduced-fat varieties.

Flavored tofus: Available flavors include barbecue, smoked hickory, spinach-jalapeño, and tomato-basil.

Meatless Tacos

If you like lots of taco flavor, look for the taco-seasoned shredded cheese at your supermarket.

Low Fat

Prep: 10 minutes **Cook:** 35 minutes **Makes:** 8 tacos

- ½ cup water
- ¼ cup brown lentils, rinsed and drained
- ¼ cup chopped onion
- 8 taco shells
- 1 8-ounce can tomato sauce
- ½ of a 1⅛- or 1¼-ounce envelope (5 teaspoons) taco seasoning mix
- 8 ounces firm or extra-firm tub-style tofu (fresh bean curd) (see tip, left), drained and finely chopped
- 1½ cups shredded lettuce
- 1 medium tomato, chopped
- ½ cup shredded cheddar cheese (2 ounces)
- ½ cup bottled salsa (optional)

1. In a medium saucepan combine water, lentils, and onion. Bring to boiling; reduce heat. Simmer, covered, for 25 to 30 minutes or until lentils are tender and liquid is absorbed. Meanwhile, heat taco shells according to package directions.

2. Stir tomato sauce and taco seasoning mix into lentils. Bring to boiling; reduce heat. Simmer, uncovered, for 5 minutes. Stir in tofu; heat through. Spoon into taco shells. Top with lettuce, tomato, and cheese. If desired, serve with salsa.

Bulgur Tacos: Prepare as above, except increase water to ¾ cup and substitute bulgur for lentils. Simmer water, bulgur, and onion, covered, for about 15 minutes or until bulgur is tender and liquid is absorbed.

Nutrition Facts per taco for lentil or bulgur variation: 148 cal., 7 g total fat (2 g sat. fat), 7 mg chol., 460 mg sodium, 16 g carbo., 3 g fiber, 7 g pro.
Daily Values: 4% vit. A, 6% vit. C, 9% calcium, 8% iron
Exchanges: 1 Starch, ½ Lean Meat, 1 Fat

Vegetable Tacos: Prepare as above, except stir 1 cup frozen whole kernel corn and ¾ cup shredded carrot into the tomato sauce mixture. Increase number of taco shells to 12.

Nutrition Facts per taco: 133 cal., 6 g total fat (2 g sat. fat), 5 mg chol., 326 mg sodium, 17 g carbo., 3 g fiber, 6 g pro.
Daily Values: 46% vit. A, 6% vit. C, 7% calcium, 6% iron
Exchanges: 1 Starch, ½ Lean Meat, ½ Fat

Crispy Tofu and Vegetables

Low Fat

Prep: 15 minutes **Marinate:** 15 minutes
Cook: 9 minutes **Makes:** 4 main-dish servings

- 2 **cups fresh snow pea pods (8 ounces)**
- 1 **12- to 16-ounce package light, reduced-fat, or regular extra-firm tub-style tofu (fresh bean curd) (see tip, page 90), drained**
- 3 **tablespoons reduced-sodium teriyaki sauce or soy sauce**
- ¼ **cup yellow cornmeal**
- ⅛ **teaspoon ground red pepper**
- 2 **teaspoons toasted sesame oil**
- 1 **medium red sweet pepper, cut into thin strips**
- 1 **medium yellow sweet pepper, cut into thin strips**
- 8 **green onions, cut into 2-inch pieces**
- 2 **teaspoons cooking oil**
- 1 **tablespoon white or black sesame seeds, toasted (optional) (see tip, page 224)**

1. Remove strings and tips from pea pods. Set pea pods aside.

2. Cut tofu crosswise into eight ½-inch slices. Arrange slices in a single layer in a 2-quart rectangular baking dish. Pour 2 tablespoons of the teriyaki sauce over tofu; turn slices to coat. Let marinate at room temperature for 15 minutes.

3. In a shallow dish combine cornmeal and red pepper. Drain tofu, discarding marinade. Carefully dip tofu slices in cornmeal mixture; press gently to coat both sides. Set tofu slices aside.

4. Pour 1 teaspoon of the sesame oil into a large nonstick skillet. Preheat over medium-high heat. Stir-fry sweet pepper strips for 2 minutes. Add pea pods and green onions; stir-fry for 2 to 3 minutes more or until crisp-tender.

5. Remove skillet from heat; stir in remaining 1 tablespoon teriyaki sauce. Transfer vegetable mixture to a serving platter; cover and keep warm. Wipe skillet clean.

6. In the same skillet heat remaining 1 teaspoon sesame oil and the cooking oil over medium heat. Cook the coated tofu slices for 2½ to 3 minutes on each side or until crisp and golden brown, using a spatula to turn carefully. Serve tofu slices over vegetable mixture. If desired, sprinkle with sesame seeds.

Nutrition Facts per serving: 151 cal., 6 g total fat (1 g sat. fat), 0 mg chol., 473 mg sodium, 15 g carbo., 3 g fiber, 9 g pro.
Daily Values: 69% vit. A, 196% vit. C, 6% calcium, 14% iron
Exchanges: 1 Vegetable, ½ Starch, 1 Lean Meat, ½ Fat

Tofu-Vegetable Stir-Fry

Fast　**Low Fat**

Start to Finish: 30 minutes　**Makes:** 4 main-dish servings

- 1½ **cups uncooked quick-cooking brown rice**
- ½ **cup vegetable or chicken broth**
- ¼ **cup dry sherry**
- 1 **tablespoon cornstarch**
- 1 **tablespoon reduced-sodium soy sauce**
- 1 **teaspoon sugar**
- 1 **teaspoon grated fresh ginger**
- ½ **teaspoon crushed red pepper (optional)**
  Nonstick cooking spray
- 1 **cup thinly sliced carrots (2 medium)**
- 3 **cloves garlic, minced**
- 3 **cups broccoli florets**
- 6 **ounces firm or extra-firm tub-style tofu (fresh bean curd) (see tip, page 90), drained and cut into ½-inch cubes**

1. Prepare rice according to package directions; keep warm.

2. Meanwhile, for sauce, in a small bowl combine broth, sherry, cornstarch, soy sauce, sugar, ginger, and, if desired, red pepper. Set sauce aside.

3. Lightly coat an unheated wok or large skillet with cooking spray. Preheat over medium-high heat. Stir-fry carrots and garlic for 2 minutes. Add broccoli; stir-fry 3 to 4 minutes more or until vegetables are crisp-tender. Push vegetables from center of wok.

4. Stir sauce; add to center of wok. Cook and stir until thickened and bubbly. Add tofu. Stir all ingredients together to coat with sauce. Cook and stir about 1 minute more or until heated through. To serve, spoon tofu mixture over rice.

Nutrition Facts per serving: 216 cal., 3 g total fat (0 g sat. fat), 0 mg chol., 306 mg sodium, 39 g carbo., 5 g fiber, 9 g pro.
Daily Values: 173% vit. A, 92% vit. C, 6% calcium, 9% iron
Exchanges: 2 Vegetable, 2 Starch, ½ Very Lean Meat

Wheat Berry Tabbouleh

Fast

Start to Finish: 25 minutes
Makes: about 4½ cups (6 side-dish servings)

- 2⅔ **cups cooked wheat berries***
- ¾ **cup chopped tomato**
- ¾ **cup chopped cucumber**
- ½ **cup snipped fresh parsley**
- ¼ **cup thinly sliced green onions (2)**
- 1 **tablespoon snipped fresh mint**
- 3 **tablespoons cooking oil**
- 3 **tablespoons lemon juice**
- ¼ **teaspoon salt**
  Lettuce leaves
  Lemon slices (optional)

1. In a large bowl combine cooked wheat berries, tomato, cucumber, parsley, green onions, and mint.

2. For dressing, in a screw-top jar combine oil, lemon juice, and salt. Cover and shake well. Drizzle dressing over wheat berry mixture; toss to coat. Serve immediately or cover and chill up to 4 hours. Serve in a lettuce-lined bowl and, if desired, garnish with lemon slices.

*Note: To cook wheat berries, bring one 14-ounce can vegetable or chicken broth and ¼ cup water to boiling. Add 1 cup wheat berries. Return to boiling; reduce heat. Simmer, covered, for 45 to 60 minutes or until tender; drain. Cover and chill up to 3 days.

Nutrition Facts per serving: 165 cal., 8 g total fat (1 g sat. fat), 0 mg chol., 384 mg sodium, 25 g carbo., 4 g fiber, 4 g pro.
Daily Values: 9% vit. A, 28% vit. C, 2% calcium, 9% iron
Exchanges: ½ Vegetable, 1½ Starch, 1 Fat

Wheat Berry Tabbouleh

Lentil and Veggie Tostadas

The red lentils used in this hearty entrée cook in about half the time of brown lentils.

Fast　**Low Fat**

Start to Finish: 25 minutes　**Makes:** 4 main-dish servings

- 1¾ **cups water**
- ¾ **cup red lentils, rinsed and drained**
- ¼ **cup chopped onion**
- 1 **to 2 tablespoons snipped fresh cilantro**
- ½ **teaspoon salt**
- ½ **teaspoon ground cumin**
- 1 **clove garlic, minced**
- 4 **tostada shells**
- 2 **cups assorted chopped vegetables (such as broccoli, tomato, zucchini, and/or yellow summer squash)**
- ¾ **cup shredded Monterey Jack cheese (3 ounces)**

1. In a medium saucepan stir together water, lentils, onion, cilantro, salt, cumin, and garlic. Bring to boiling; reduce heat. Simmer, covered, for 12 to 15 minutes or until lentils are tender and most of the liquid is absorbed. Use a fork to mash the cooked lentils.

2. Spread lentil mixture on tostada shells; top with vegetables and cheese. Place on a large baking sheet. Broil 3 to 4 inches from the heat about 2 minutes or until cheese melts.

Nutrition Facts per serving: 285 cal., 11 g total fat (5 g sat. fat), 20 mg chol., 526 mg sodium, 33 g carbo., 8 g fiber, 16 g pro.
Daily Values: 19% vit. A, 70% vit. C, 23% calcium, 14% iron
Exchanges: 1 Vegetable, 2 Starch, 1 High-Fat Meat

Types of Lentils

In the United States, three types of lentils are commonly available: brown, which actually has a brownish-green coat and yellow interior; red; and yellow. The brown lentil is the most widely used and the one we most often call for in our recipes. More exotic varieties—green, white, or black—can be found in specialty food stores.

If you wish to substitute one type of lentil for another, you may need to adjust cooking times. Red lentils, for example, are smaller than brown, so you should reduce cooking time significantly. In the case of yellow lentils, which are the same size as brown, cooking time should remain the same. Check package labels for directions.

Lentil-Rice Patties

Low Fat

Prep: 55 minutes　**Cook:** 7 minutes per batch
Oven: 300°F　**Makes:** 12 patties (6 main-dish servings)

- 1 **14-ounce can chicken broth**
- ¾ **cup water**
- ½ **cup chopped onion (1 medium)**
- ⅓ **cup uncooked regular brown rice**
- ½ **teaspoon crushed red pepper**
- 3 **cloves garlic, minced**
- ¾ **cup brown lentils, rinsed and drained**
- 1 **15-ounce can garbanzo beans (chickpeas), rinsed and drained (see photo, page 84)**
- 1 **cup regular rolled oats**
- 2 **slightly beaten egg whites**
- ¼ **cup snipped fresh basil or 2 teaspoons dried basil, crushed**
- 1 **tablespoon Worcestershire sauce**
- ¼ **teaspoon salt**
- ½ **cup chopped walnuts or almonds, toasted (see tip, page 224)**
  Nonstick cooking spray
  Shredded lettuce, chopped tomatoes, and/or plain fat-free yogurt (optional)

1. In a medium saucepan combine chicken broth, water, onion, brown rice, red pepper, and garlic. Bring to boiling; reduce heat. Simmer, covered, for 20 minutes. Stir in lentils. Simmer, covered, about 25 minutes more or until rice and lentils are tender. Remove from heat.

2. Add garbanzo beans to saucepan; use a potato masher to mash the mixture. Stir in oats. Let stand for 5 minutes.

3. Meanwhile, combine egg whites, basil, Worcestershire sauce, and salt; add to lentil-rice mixture in pan, stirring to combine. Stir in nuts.

4. Lightly coat a 12-inch skillet with cooking spray. Heat skillet over medium heat. For each patty, place about ⅓ cup of the mixture into hot skillet; flatten to about ½ inch thick. Cook half of the patties at a time over medium heat 7 to 10 minutes or until light brown, turning once. Transfer cooked patties to a baking sheet. Keep warm in a 300° oven while cooking remaining patties.

5. If desired, serve patties on shredded lettuce topped with tomatoes and yogurt.

Nutrition Facts per serving: 357 cal., 10 g total fat (1 g sat. fat), 0 mg chol., 646 mg sodium, 53 g carbo., 13 g fiber, 17 g pro.
Daily Values: 3% vit. A, 10% vit. C, 7% calcium, 23% iron
Exchanges: 3½ Starch, 1 Lean Meat, ½ Fat

Falafel-Millet Burgers with Tomato Relish

Meet the new meatless burger! It's a tasty take on falafel, a popular street snack from the Middle East, streamlined with a mix, then customized with crunchy millet and a juicy garden relish.

`Fast` `Low Fat`

Start to Finish: 30 minutes **Makes:** 6 main-dish servings

- 2 **cups dry falafel mix**
- ¼ **cup millet**
- 1⅓ **cups cold water**
- 1¼ **cups chopped, seeded tomatoes (2 medium)**
- ½ **cup chopped green sweet pepper (1 small)**
- ½ **cup thinly sliced green onions (4)**
- 1 **tablespoon bottled balsamic vinaigrette salad dressing**
- ¼ **teaspoon black pepper**
- 1 **clove garlic, minced**
- 2 **tablespoons olive oil**
- 6 **whole grain hamburger buns, split and toasted**
- 6 **leaf lettuce leaves**

1. In a medium bowl combine falafel mix and millet; stir in water. Let stand about 10 minutes or until water is absorbed. Shape falafel mixture into six ½-inch-thick patties.

2. Meanwhile, for tomato relish, stir together tomatoes, sweet pepper, green onions, salad dressing, pepper, and garlic. Set aside.

3. In a large skillet cook 3 of the patties, uncovered, in 1 tablespoon of the hot oil over medium-high heat for 3 minutes. Turn patties over and cook for 2 to 3 minutes more or until golden brown. Remove patties from skillet and keep warm. Repeat with remaining patties and oil.

4. Serve patties on buns with lettuce. Using a slotted spoon, top each patty with some of the tomato relish.

Nutrition Facts per serving: 344 cal., 10 g total fat (2 g sat. fat), 0 mg chol., 979 mg sodium, 53 g carbo., 10 g fiber, 19 g pro.
Daily Values: 12% vit. A, 38% vit. C, 12% calcium, 34% iron
Exchanges: ½ Vegetable, 3½ Starch, ½ Lean Meat, 1 Fat

Falafel-Millet Burgers with Tomato Relish

Cajun Quinoa

Protein-packed quinoa (KEEN-wah) is an ancient grain but new to American tables. It cooks like rice and has a mild flavor and slightly chewy texture.

`Fast` `Low Fat`

Prep: 10 minutes **Cook:** 15 minutes
Makes: 5½ to 6 cups (4 main-dish servings)

- ½ **cup chopped onion (1 medium)**
- 1 **teaspoon olive oil**
- 6 **cloves garlic, minced**
- 1¼ **cups quinoa, rinsed and drained, or quick-cooking pearl barley**
- 1 **cup coarsely shredded carrots**
- 1 **teaspoon Cajun seasoning**
- 1 **medium zucchini, quartered lengthwise and sliced**
- 1 **14- to 15½-ounce can golden hominy, rinsed and drained**
- 1 **tablespoon snipped fresh thyme or oregano**

1. In a medium saucepan cook onion in hot oil over medium heat for 3 minutes. Add garlic; cook for 1 minute more. Stir in quinoa, carrots, Cajun seasoning, and 2 cups *water.* Bring to boiling; reduce heat. Simmer, covered, 10 minutes. Stir in zucchini, hominy, and thyme. Simmer, covered, about 5 minutes more or until quinoa and zucchini are tender and liquid is absorbed. Season to taste with *salt.*

Nutrition Facts per serving: 316 cal., 5 g total fat (1 g sat. fat), 0 mg chol., 427 mg sodium, 59 g carbo., 8 g fiber, 10 g pro.
Daily Values: 143% vit. A, 17% vit. C, 8% calcium, 35% iron
Exchanges: 1 Vegetable, 3½ Starch

Peppers Stuffed with Cinnamon Bulgur

Best Loved

Choose from a variety of sweet pepper colors—green, red, yellow, and orange (see photo, page 77).

Fast **Low Fat**

Start to Finish: 30 minutes **Makes:** 4 main-dish servings

- 1¾ **cups water**
- ½ **cup shredded carrot**
- ¼ **cup chopped onion**
- 1 **teaspoon instant vegetable or chicken bouillon granules**
- ⅛ **teaspoon salt**
- 3 **inches stick cinnamon or dash ground cinnamon**
- ¾ **cup bulgur**
- ⅓ **cup dried cranberries or raisins**
- 2 **large or 4 small sweet peppers**
- ¾ **cup shredded Muenster, brick, or mozzarella cheese (3 ounces)**
- ½ **cup water**
- 2 **tablespoons sliced almonds or chopped pecans, toasted (see tip, page 224)**

1. In a large skillet stir together the 1¾ cups water, carrot, onion, bouillon granules, salt, and cinnamon. Bring to boiling; reduce heat. Simmer, covered, for 5 minutes. Stir in bulgur and cranberries. Remove from heat. Cover and let stand for 5 minutes. If using stick cinnamon, remove from the bulgur mixture. Drain off excess liquid.

2. Meanwhile, halve the sweet peppers lengthwise, removing the seeds and membranes.

3. Stir cheese into bulgur mixture; spoon into sweet pepper halves. Place sweet pepper halves in skillet. Add the ½ cup water. Bring to boiling; reduce heat. Simmer, covered, 5 to 10 minutes or until peppers are crisp-tender and bulgur mixture is heated through. Sprinkle with nuts.

Nutrition Facts per serving: 253 cal., 9 g total fat (4 g sat. fat), 20 mg chol., 496 mg sodium, 36 g carbo., 8 g fiber, 10 g pro.
Daily Values: 83% vit. A, 92% vit. C, 19% calcium, 8% iron
Exchanges: 1 Vegetable, 2 Starch, 1½ Fat

Granola

Prep: 10 minutes **Bake:** 30 minutes **Oven:** 300°F
Makes: 6 cups (twelve ½-cup servings)

- 2 **cups regular rolled oats**
- 1 **cup coarsely chopped slivered or sliced almonds, chopped walnuts, or chopped peanuts**
- ½ **cup coconut (optional)**
- ½ **cup shelled sunflower seeds**
- ¼ **cup toasted wheat germ**
- ½ **cup honey or maple-flavored syrup**
- 2 **tablespoons cooking oil**

1. In a large bowl combine the oats, nuts, coconut (if desired), sunflower seeds, and wheat germ. Stir together honey and cooking oil; stir into oat mixture. Spread evenly in a greased 15×10×1-inch baking pan. Bake in a 300° oven for 30 to 35 minutes or until lightly browned, stirring after 20 minutes.

2. Spread on a large piece of foil to cool. Break into clumps. Store in an airtight container for up to 1 week. (Or, store in freezer bags and freeze for up to 2 months.)

Nutrition Facts per serving: 234 cal., 12 g total fat (1 g sat. fat), 0 mg chol., 1 mg sodium, 27 g carbo., 4 g fiber, 7 g pro.
Daily Values: 5% calcium, 9% iron
Exchanges: 1½ Starch, ½ Other Carbo., 2 Fat

Fruit Granola: Prepare as above, except immediately after removing from oven, stir in 1 cup desired dried fruit (such as raisins, snipped pitted dates, snipped apricots, cranberries, cherries, mixed dried fruit bits, or dried banana slices). Freeze mixture to store. Makes 7 cups (fourteen ½-cup servings).

Nutrition Facts per serving: 271 cal., 12 g total fat (1 g sat. fat), 0 mg chol., 3 mg sodium, 37 g carbo., 4 g fiber, 7 g pro.
Daily Values: 1% vit. C, 5% calcium, 11% iron
Exchanges: 1½ Starch, ½ Other Carbo., ½ Fruit, 2 Fat

Cranberry-Almond Cereal Mix

Keep this cereal mixture on hand and cook one or two servings at a time.

Fast

Prep: 10 minutes **Cook:** 12 minutes
Makes: about 4⅔ cups mix (14 servings)

- 1 **cup regular rolled oats**
- 1 **cup quick-cooking barley**
- 1 **cup bulgur or cracked wheat**
- 1 **cup dried cranberries, snipped dried apricots, or raisins**
- ½ **cup sliced almonds, toasted (see tip, page 224)**
- ⅓ **cup sugar**
- 1 **tablespoon ground cinnamon**
- ¼ **teaspoon salt**
  Milk (optional)

1. Combine oats, barley, bulgur, cranberries, almonds, sugar, cinnamon, and salt. Cover tightly; store at room temperature for up to 6 months.

2. For 2 breakfast servings, in a small saucepan bring 1⅓ cups *water* to boiling. Add ⅔ cup of the cereal mix to boiling water. Reduce heat. Simmer, covered, for 12 to 15 minutes or until cereal reaches desired consistency. If desired, serve with milk.

Microwave directions: For 1 breakfast serving, in a large microwave-safe cereal bowl combine ¾ cup water and ⅓ cup cereal mix. Microwave, uncovered, on 50 percent power (medium) for 8 to 11 minutes or until cereal reaches desired consistency, stirring once. Stir before serving. If desired, serve with milk.

Nutrition Facts per serving: 171 cal., 3 g total fat (0 g sat. fat), 0 mg chol., 46 mg sodium, 33 g carbo., 5 g fiber, 4 g pro.
Daily Values: 3% calcium, 6% iron
Exchanges: 2 Starch

Storing Beans and Grains

Dry beans are easy to keep and can be stored at room temperature up to 1 year or even longer in the freezer. Cooked dry beans (see chart, page 98) can be refrigerated for up to 3 days or frozen for up to 3 months.

Whole grains have a shorter storage life because they contain an oil-rich germ that can become rancid. Therefore, purchase whole grains in smaller quantities. Keep all grains in tightly covered containers.

Follow these guidelines:

Pearl and Scotch barley: Store up to 1 year in a cool, dry place. (Other forms of barley: up to 9 months in a cool, dry place.)

Buckwheat: Store up to 3 months in a cool, dry place, up to 6 months in the refrigerator, or up to 1 year in the freezer.

Bulgur: Store up to 6 months in a cool, dry place or indefinitely in the freezer.

Cornmeal: Store up to 6 months in a cool, dry place or up to 1 year in the refrigerator or freezer.

Oats: Store up to 6 months in a cool, dry place or up to 1 year in the freezer.

Rye berries: Store up to 5 months in the refrigerator or freezer.

White and wild rice: Store indefinitely in a cool, dry place.

Brown rice: Store up to 6 months in cool, dry place.

Whole or cracked wheat: Store up to 6 months in a cool, dry place or up to 1 year in the freezer.

Wheat bran: Store up to 1 month in a cool, dry place, up to 3 months in the refrigerator, or up to 1 year in the freezer.

Wheat germ: Store up to 3 months in refrigerator.

Cooking Grains

Use this chart as a guide when cooking grains. Measure the amount of water into a medium saucepan and bring to a full boil unless the chart indicates otherwise. If desired, add ¼ teaspoon salt to the water. Slowly add the grain and return to boiling; reduce heat. Simmer, covered, for the time specified or until most of the water is absorbed and the grain is tender.

Grain	Amount of Grain	Amount of Water	Cooking Directions	Yield
Barley, quick-cooking pearl	1¼ cups	2 cups	Simmer, covered, for 10 to 12 minutes. Drain, if necessary.	3 cups
Barley, regular pearl	¾ cup	3 cups	Simmer, covered, about 45 minutes. Drain, if necessary.	3 cups
Buckwheat groats or kasha	⅔ cup	1½ cups	Add to cold water. Bring to boiling. Simmer, covered, for 6 to 8 minutes.	2¼ cups
Bulgur	1 cup	2 cups	Add to cold water. Bring to boiling. Simmer, covered, about 15 minutes.	3 cups
Cornmeal	1 cup	2¾ cups	Combine cornmeal and 1 cup cold water. Add to the 2¾ cups boiling water. Simmer, uncovered, about 10 minutes, stirring occasionally.	3½ cups
Farina, quick-cooking	¾ cup	3½ cups	Simmer, uncovered, for 2 to 3 minutes, stirring constantly.	3½ cups
Hominy grits, quick-cooking	¾ cup	3 cups	Simmer, covered, about 5 minutes, stirring occasionally.	3 cups
Millet	¾ cup	2 cups	Simmer, covered, for 15 to 20 minutes. Let stand, covered, for 5 minutes.	3 cups
Oats, rolled, quick-cooking	1½ cups	3 cups	Simmer, uncovered, for 1 minute. Let stand, covered, for 3 minutes.	3 cups
Oats, rolled, regular	1⅔ cups	3 cups	Simmer, uncovered, for 5 to 7 minutes. Let stand, covered, for 3 minutes.	3 cups
Quinoa	¾ cup	1½ cups	Rinse well. Simmer, covered, about 15 minutes. Drain, if necessary.	1¾ cups
Rice, long grain white	1 cup	2 cups	Simmer, covered, about 15 minutes. Let stand, covered, for 5 minutes.	3 cups
Rice, regular brown	1 cup	2 cups	Simmer, covered, about 45 minutes. Let stand, covered, for 5 minutes.	3 cups
Rice, wild	1 cup	2 cups	Rinse well. Simmer, covered, about 40 minutes or until most of the water is absorbed. Drain, if necessary.	3 cups
Rye berries	¾ cup	2½ cups	Simmer, covered, about 1 hour; drain. (Or, soak berries in 2½ cups water in the refrigerator for 6 to 24 hours. Do not drain. Bring to boiling; reduce heat. Simmer, covered, for 30 minutes.)	2 cups
Wheat berries	¾ cup	2½ cups	Simmer, covered, for 45 to 60 minutes; drain. (Or, soak and cook as for rye berries.)	2 cups
Wheat, cracked	⅔ cup	1½ cups	Add to cold water. Bring to boiling. Simmer, covered, for 12 to 15 minutes. Let stand, covered, for 5 minutes.	1¾ cups

Cooking Dry Beans, Lentils, and Split Peas

Rinse beans, lentils, or split peas. (See special cooking instructions below for black-eyed peas, fava beans, lentils, and split peas.) In a large Dutch oven combine 1 pound beans and 8 cups cold water. Bring to boiling; reduce heat. Simmer for 2 minutes. Remove from heat. Cover and let stand for 1 hour. (Or, omit simmering; soak beans in cold water overnight in a covered Dutch oven.) Drain and rinse. In the same Dutch oven combine beans and 8 cups fresh water. Bring to boiling; reduce heat. Simmer, covered, for time listed below or until beans are tender, stirring occasionally. Cooking time depends on the dryness of the beans.

Variety	Amount	Appearance	Cooking Time	Yield
Black beans	1 pound	Small, black, oval	1 to 1½ hours	6 cups
Black-eyed peas	1 pound	Small, cream-color, oval (one side has a black oval with a cream-color dot in the center)	Do not presoak. Simmer, covered, for 45 minutes to 1 hour.	7 cups
Cranberry beans	1 pound	Small, tan-color with specks and streaks of burgundy, oval	1¼ to 1½ hours	7 cups
Fava or broad beans	1 pound	Large, brown, flat oval	Follow these soaking directions instead of those above: Bring beans to boiling; simmer, covered, 15 to 30 minutes to soften skins. Let stand 1 hour. Drain and peel. To cook, combine peeled beans and 8 cups fresh water. Bring to boiling; reduce heat. Simmer, covered, 45 to 50 minutes or until tender.	6 cups
Garbanzo beans (chickpeas)	1 pound	Medium, yellow or golden, round and irregular	1½ to 2 hours	6¼ cups
Great Northern beans	1 pound	Small to medium, white, kidney-shape	1 to 1½ hours	7 cups
Kidney beans, red	1 pound	Medium to large, brownish red, kidney-shape	1 to 1½ hours	6⅔ cups
Lentils (brown)	1 pound	Tiny, brownish green, disk-shape	Do not presoak. Use 5 cups water. Simmer, covered, about 30 minutes.	7 cups
Lima beans, baby	1 pound	Small, off-white, wide oval	45 minutes to 1 hour	6½ cups
Lima beans, Christmas (calico)	1 pound	Medium, burgundy and cream-color, wide oval	45 minutes to 1 hour	6½ cups
Lima beans, large (butter beans)	1 pound	Medium, off-white, wide oval	1 to 1¼ hours	6½ cups
Navy or pea beans	1 pound	Small, off-white, oval	1 to 1½ hours	6¼ cups
Pinto beans	1 pound	Small, tan-color with brown specks, oval	1¼ to 1½ hours	6½ cups
Red beans	1 pound	Small, dark red, oval	1 to 1½ hours	6½ cups
Soybeans	1 pound	Small, cream-color, oval	3 to 3½ hours	7 cups
Split peas	1 pound	Tiny, green or yellow, disk-shape	Do not presoak. Use 5 cups water. Simmer, covered, about 45 minutes.	5½ cups

Chapter 4
Beverages

Beverages

Tea

`Fast`　`No Fat`

Start to Finish: 15 minutes
Makes: 5 (about 6-ounce) servings

3 to 6 teaspoons loose tea or 3 to 6 tea bags
4 cups boiling water

1. Warm a teapot by filling it with boiling *water*. If using loose tea, measure tea into a tea ball. Empty teapot; add tea ball or tea bags to pot. Immediately add the 4 cups boiling water to teapot. Cover; let steep 3 to 5 minutes. Remove tea ball or tea bags; discard. Serve beverage at once.

Iced Tea: Prepare as above, except use 4 to 8 teaspoons loose tea or 4 to 8 tea bags. Steep; cool at room temperature for 2 hours. Serve over ice cubes. Store in the refrigerator. Makes 5 servings.

Refrigerator-Brewed Tea: Place 6 to 8 tea bags in a 2-quart glass container. Add 1½ quarts cold water; cover and let tea "brew" in the refrigerator about 24 hours. Remove tea bags; discard. Serve tea over ice cubes. (The refrigerator method for making iced tea is fine to use for herbal and green teas as well as black tea because refrigeration inhibits the growth of bacteria.) Makes 8 servings.

Nutrition Facts per serving: 2 cal., 0 g total fat (0 g sat. fat), 0 mg chol., 6 mg sodium, 1 g carbo., 0 g fiber, 0 g pro.
Exchanges: Free

How Sweet It Is

Sweeten iced tea with a syrup and you'll avoid undissolved sugar in the cold beverage.

To make the simple syrup, combine equal parts of water and sugar in a saucepan. Bring the mixture to boiling over medium heat, stirring until the sugar dissolves, the liquid is completely clear, and the surface is covered with bubbles. Remove from heat and cool. Transfer syrup to a covered glass pitcher or jar. Pass the syrup with iced tea or any cold beverage you wish to sweeten. Store remaining syrup, tightly covered, in the refrigerator for up to 2 weeks.

Raspberry Tea　`Best Loved`

Float extra fresh raspberries in this iced tea when berries are in season.

`No Fat`

Prep: 10 minutes　**Cool:** several hours
Makes: 6 (about 6-ounce) servings.

2 cups fresh or frozen red raspberries
4 or 5 tea bags
5 cups boiling water
Ice cubes

1. Place raspberries and tea bags in a glass bowl. Pour boiling water over raspberries and tea bags. Cover and let stand for 5 minutes. Remove tea bags; discard. Strain berries from tea; discard berries. Cool for several hours. If desired, chill. Serve tea over ice cubes.

Nutrition Facts per serving: 2 cal., 0 g total fat (0 g sat. fat), 0 mg chol., 6 mg sodium, 1 g carbo., 0 g fiber, 0 g pro.
Exchanges: Free

Cranberry Tea

Choose the garnish to suit the season—fresh mint for summer drinks and cranberries for the holidays.

`No Fat`

Prep: 15 minutes　**Chill:** 2 hours　**Makes:** 5 (8-ounce) servings

3 cups water
4 green tea bags
1 mint tea bag
2 cups cranberry juice, chilled
Ice cubes
Fresh mint leaves or fresh cranberries (optional)

1. In a medium saucepan bring water to boiling. Remove from heat. Add green and mint tea bags. Cover and let stand for 10 minutes. Remove tea bags; discard. Cover and chill for 2 hours. Transfer the tea to a pitcher; stir in the cranberry juice.

2. Serve over ice cubes. If desired, garnish with fresh mint leaves or cranberries. Chill remaining tea up to 2 days.

Nutrition Facts per serving: 58 cal., 0 g total fat (0 g sat. fat), 0 mg chol., 6 mg sodium, 15 g carbo., 0 g fiber, 0 g pro.
Daily Values: 60% vit. C, 1% calcium, 1% iron
Exchanges: 1 Fruit

Iced Green Tea

No Fat

Prep: 25 minutes **Cool:** several hours
Makes: 12 (about 8-ounce) servings

- 12 **cups water**
- ¼ **cup sugar**
- 3 **inches fresh ginger, peeled and thinly sliced**
- 12 **to 16 green tea bags**
  Strawberries (optional)
  Key limes or limes, quartered (optional)
  Orange peel strips (optional)
  Ice cubes

1. In a large saucepan combine water, sugar, and ginger. Bring to boiling; reduce heat. Simmer, covered, for 5 minutes. Remove from heat. Add tea bags; cover and let stand for 3 minutes. Remove tea bags; discard. Strain ginger from tea; discard ginger. Transfer tea to a 2-gallon pitcher or punch bowl. Cover; cool several hours. If desired, chill. If desired, alternate strawberries, lime quarters, and orange peel strips on 12-inch skewers. Serve tea over ice cubes; use fruit skewers as swizzle sticks.

Nutrition Facts per serving: 18 cal., 0 g total fat (0 g sat. fat), 0 mg chol., 7 mg sodium, 5 g carbo., 0 g fiber, 0 g pro.
Exchanges: Free

Iced Green Tea

Coffee

Fast **No Fat**

Start to Finish: 10 to 15 minutes

- 1 **to 2 tablespoons ground coffee (for each 6-ounce cup)**
- ¾ **cup cold water (for each 6-ounce cup)**

1. Drip Coffee: Measure coffee into a filter-lined coffeemaker basket. For electric drip coffeemakers, pour cold water into water compartment. Place pot on heating element; let water drip through basket. For nonelectric drip coffeemakers, pour boiling water over coffee in basket. Let water drip into pot. When dripping stops, remove basket and discard grounds.

2. Percolator Coffee: Pour cold water into a percolator. Stand stem and basket firmly in pot. Measure coffee into basket. Replace basket lid and cover the pot. Bring the water to boiling. Perk gently for 5 to 8 minutes. Let coffee stand for 1 to 2 minutes. Remove basket from pot and discard grounds.

3. French Press Coffee: Pour freshly boiled water over coffee in a French press carafe. Let stand a few minutes. Press the plunger filter through the water, trapping grounds beneath. After pouring coffee, discard grounds.

Nutrition Facts per serving: 4 cal., 0 g total fat (0 g sat. fat), 0 mg chol., 4 mg sodium, 1 g carbo., 0 g fiber, 0 g pro.
Exchanges: Free

Iced Coffee

Fast **No Fat**

Start to Finish: 10 to 15 minutes
Makes: 4 (6-ounce) servings

- ¼ **to ⅓ cup ground coffee**
- 1 **teaspoon ground cinnamon (optional)**
- 3 **cups cold water**
  Ice cubes or frozen coffee cubes

1. Measure coffee and, if desired, cinnamon into a filter-lined coffeemaker basket. Pour the cold water into water compartment. Prepare according to manufacturer's directions. Serve over ice cubes or coffee cubes.

Nutrition Facts per serving: 4 cal., 0 g total fat (0 g sat. fat), 0 mg chol., 4 mg sodium, 1 g carbo., 0 g fiber, 0 g pro.
Exchanges: Free

Dessert Coffee

`Fast` `No Fat`

Start to Finish: 10 to 15 minutes
Makes: 1 (about 6-ounce) serving

⅔ **cup hot strong coffee**
Desired coffee flavoring (see choices below)
Whipped cream (optional)
Ground cinnamon or nutmeg (optional)

1. Stir together hot coffee and desired flavoring. If desired, top with whipped cream and sprinkle with cinnamon.

Chocolate-Liqueur Dessert Coffee: Stir 1 tablespoon chocolate-flavored syrup and 1 tablespoon coffee liqueur or orange liqueur into hot coffee.

Nutrition Facts per serving: 107 cal., 0 g total fat (0 g sat. fat), 0 mg chol., 17 mg sodium, 19 g carbo., 0 g fiber, 0 g pro.
Daily Values: 2% iron
Exchanges: 1 Other Carbo., 1 Fat

Chocolate-Mint Dessert Coffee: Stir 1 tablespoon chocolate-mint liqueur into hot coffee.

Nutrition Facts per serving: 57 cal., 0 g total fat (0 g sat. fat), 0 mg chol., 5 mg sodium, 6 g carbo., 0 g fiber, 0 g pro.
Daily Values: 1% iron
Exchanges: ½ Other Carbo., ½ Fat

Espresso

`Fast` `No Fat`

Start to Finish: 10 to 15 minutes
Makes: 4 (2-ounce) servings

1. Using a drip coffeemaker, add 1 cup cold water and ⅓ cup French roast or espresso roast coffee, ground as directed for your coffeemaker. Brew according to manufacturer's directions. (If using an espresso machine, use manufacturer's suggested amounts of coffee and water.) Pour into 4 demitasse cups or small cups. Serve with sugar cubes or coarse sugar.

Nutrition Facts per serving: 1 cal., 0 g total fat (0 g sat. fat), 0 mg chol., 1 mg sodium, 0 g carbo., 0 g fiber, 0 g pro.
Exchanges: Free

Cappuccino: Prepare 1 recipe Espresso. In a small saucepan warm 1 cup low-fat milk over medium heat until hot, but not boiling. Transfer milk to a food processor bowl or blender container. Process until milk is frothy. (If using an espresso machine with a steaming nozzle, heat and froth milk according to manufacturer's directions.) Divide espresso among four 5- to 8-ounce cups. Top with frothy milk.

Sprinkle with ground cinnamon or grated chocolate. If desired, serve with sugar. Makes 4 (4-ounce) servings.

Nutrition Facts per serving: 27 cal., 1 g total fat (0 g sat. fat), 2 mg chol., 32 mg sodium, 3 g carbo., 0 g fiber, 2 g pro.
Daily Values: 3% vit. A, 1% vit. C, 8% calcium
Exchanges: Free

Café Latte: Prepare 1 recipe Cappuccino, except increase low-fat milk to 2 cups. If desired, serve with sugar. Makes 4 (6-ounce) servings.

Nutrition Facts per serving: 52 cal., 1 g total fat (1 g sat. fat), 5 mg chol., 63 mg sodium, 6 g carbo., 0 g fiber, 4 g pro.
Daily Values: 5% vit. A, 2% vit. C, 15% calcium, 1% iron
Exchanges: ½ Milk

Hot Chocolate

`Fast`

Start to Finish: 15 minutes **Makes:** 6 (about 6-ounce) servings

2 **ounces unsweetened or semisweet chocolate, coarsely chopped, or ⅓ cup semisweet chocolate pieces**
⅓ **cup sugar**
4 **cups milk**
1 **tablespoon instant coffee crystals (optional)**
Whipped cream or tiny marshmallows (optional)

1. In a medium saucepan combine chocolate, sugar, and ½ cup of the milk. Stir over medium heat until mixture just comes to boiling. Stir in remaining 3½ cups milk and, if desired, coffee crystals; heat through, but do not boil.

2. Remove from heat. If desired, beat mixture with a rotary beater until frothy. If desired, top with whipped cream or marshmallows.

Spiced Hot Chocolate: Prepare as above without coffee crystals; stir ½ teaspoon ground cinnamon and ¼ teaspoon ground nutmeg into chocolate mixture with remaining milk.

Nutrition Facts per serving for plain or spiced variation: 171 cal., 8 g total fat (5 g sat. fat), 12 mg chol., 83 mg sodium, 21 g carbo., 2 g fiber, 6 g pro.
Daily Values: 7% vit. A, 3% vit. C, 20% calcium, 4% iron
Exchanges: ½ Milk, 1 Other Carbo., 1½ Fat

Low-Fat Hot Cocoa: Prepare as above, except substitute ¼ cup unsweetened cocoa powder for the chocolate and use fat-free milk.

Nutrition Facts per serving: 113 cal., 1 g total fat (0 g sat. fat), 3 mg chol., 84 mg sodium, 20 g carbo., 0 g fiber, 6 g pro.
Daily Values: 7% vit. A, 3% vit. C, 24% calcium, 3% iron
Exchanges: ½ Milk, 1 Other Carbo.

Hot Cocoa Mix

For a no-fat version, omit nondairy creamer.

Fast **Low Fat**

Start to Finish: 15 minutes
Makes: about 5½ cups mix (16 servings)

- 3½ cups nonfat dry milk powder
- 2 cups sifted powdered sugar
- 1 cup powdered nondairy creamer
- ½ cup sifted unsweetened cocoa powder

1. In a bowl combine dry milk powder, powdered sugar, nondairy creamer, and cocoa powder. Store in an airtight container.

2. For each serving, place ⅓ cup of the mix in a mug and add ¾ cup boiling water.

Mocha Mix: Prepare mix as above, except stir ½ cup instant coffee crystals into mix. Makes about 6 cups mix (18 servings).

Nutrition Facts per serving for plain or coffee variation:
145 cal., 2 g total fat (2 g sat. fat), 3 mg chol., 84 mg sodium, 25 g carbo., 0 g fiber, 6 g pro.
Daily Values: 7% vit. A, 1% vit. C, 22% calcium, 2% iron
Exchanges: ½ Milk, 1 Other Carbo., ½ Fat

White Hot Chocolate   Best Loved

Fast

Start to Finish: about 15 minutes
Makes: 5 (6-ounce) servings

- 3 cups half-and-half or light cream
- ⅔ cup white baking pieces or chopped white chocolate baking squares
- 1 3-inch piece stick cinnamon
- ⅛ teaspoon ground nutmeg
- 1 teaspoon vanilla
- ¼ teaspoon almond extract
  Ground cinnamon (optional)

1. In a medium saucepan combine ¼ cup of the half-and-half, the baking pieces, cinnamon, and nutmeg. Stir over low heat until baking pieces are melted. Add remaining half-and-half. Cook and stir until heated through. Remove from heat. Remove and discard cinnamon. Stir in vanilla and almond extract. If desired, sprinkle with ground cinnamon.

Nutrition Facts per serving: 361 cal., 25 g total fat (18 g sat. fat), 53 mg chol., 101 mg sodium, 26 g carbo., 0 g fiber, 4 g pro.
Daily Values: 13% vit. A, 2% vit. C, 15% calcium, 1% iron
Exchanges: 2 Other Carbo., 5 Fat

Chai

Fast

Start to Finish: 15 minutes **Makes:** 2 or 3 servings

- 1 black tea bag, such as orange pekoe, English breakfast, Lapsang souchong, or Darjeeling
- 1 3-inch piece stick cinnamon
- 2 cups milk
- 2 tablespoons raw sugar or honey
- 1 teaspoon vanilla
- ⅛ teaspoon ground ginger
- ⅛ teaspoon ground cardamom

1. In a small saucepan combine tea bag, the cinnamon stick, and ½ cup *water*. Bring to boiling. Remove from heat. Cover and let stand for 5 minutes. Remove and discard tea bag and cinnamon stick. Stir the milk, sugar, vanilla, ginger, and cardamom into the tea. Cook and stir over medium heat just until mixture is heated through (do not boil). To serve, pour hot mixture into warm mugs.

Nutrition Facts per serving: 175 cal., 5 g total fat (3 g sat. fat), 18 mg chol., 124 mg sodium, 24 g carbo., 0 g fiber, 8 g pro.
Daily Values: 10% vit. A, 4% vit. C, 30% calcium, 1% iron
Exchanges: 1 Milk, 1 Other Carbo., ½ Fat

Chocolate Chai

Chocolate Chai: Prepare as on page 104, except stir 1 tablespoon unsweetened Dutch-process cocoa powder in with the milk and spices. Heat through. Serve with whipped cream. If desired, sprinkle with ground nutmeg.

Nutrition Facts per serving: 212 cal., 8 g total fat (5 g sat. fat), 29 mg chol., 127 mg sodium, 26 g carbo., 0 g fiber, 9 g pro.
Daily Values: 12% vit. A, 4% vit. C, 33% calcium, 3% iron
Exchanges: 1 Milk, 1 Other Carbo., 1½ Fat

Easy Party Punch

`Fast` `No Fat`

Prep: 10 minutes **Makes:** 25 (about 6-ounce) servings

    1 12-ounce can frozen citrus blend juice
       concentrate, thawed
    1 12-ounce can frozen berry blend juice
       concentrate, thawed
    2 2-liter bottles ginger ale, chilled
       Ice cubes or ice ring

1. In large punch bowl combine concentrates. Add ginger ale and ice. If desired, garnish with orange slices and fresh strawberries.

Nutrition Facts per serving: 101 cal., 0 g total fat (0 g sat. fat), 0 mg chol., 13 mg sodium, 26 g carbo., 0 g fiber, 0 g pro.
Daily Values: 49% vit. C, 1% calcium, 5% iron
Exchanges: ½ Fruit, 1 Other Carbo.

Hot Spiced Cider

`Fast` `No Fat`

Prep: 10 minutes **Cook:** 15 minutes
Makes: 8 (about 8-ounce) servings

    8 cups apple cider or apple juice
    ¼ cup packed brown sugar
    6 inches stick cinnamon
    1 teaspoon whole allspice
    1 teaspoon whole cloves
    1 teaspoon shredded orange peel
    8 thin orange wedges (optional)
    8 whole cloves (optional)

1. In a large saucepan combine cider and sugar. For spice bag, place cinnamon, allspice, the 1 teaspoon cloves, and the orange peel in center of a double-thick, 6-inch square of 100-percent-cotton cheesecloth. Tie closed with a clean string. Add spice bag to the saucepan with cider mixture. Bring to boiling; reduce heat. Simmer, covered, for 10 minutes. Meanwhile, if desired, stud orange wedges with cloves. Remove spice bag and discard.

Serve cider in mugs. If desired, garnish with clove-studded orange wedges.

Nutrition Facts per serving: 142 cal., 0 g total fat (0 g sat. fat), 0 mg chol., 10 mg sodium, 36 g carbo., 0 g fiber, 0 g pro.
Daily Values: 4% vit. C, 2% calcium, 6% iron
Exchanges: 2 Fruit, ½ Other Carbo.

Lemonade or Limeade Base

`No Fat`

Prep: 20 minutes **Cool:** 20 minutes **Chill:** up to 3 days
Makes: 8 (about 8-ounce servings) lemonade or limeade
(or about 4 cups of the base)

    2½ cups water
    1¼ cups sugar
     ½ teaspoon finely shredded lemon or lime peel
    1¼ cups lemon or lime juice
        Ice cubes

1. For a lemonade or limeade base, in a medium saucepan heat and stir water and sugar over medium heat until sugar is dissolved. Remove from heat; cool 20 minutes. Add citrus peel and juice to sugar mixture. Pour into a jar; cover and chill up to 3 days.

2. For each glass of lemonade, combine equal parts base and water in ice-filled glasses; stir.

Nutrition Facts per serving: 126 cal., 0 g total fat (0 g sat. fat), 0 mg chol., 6 mg sodium, 33 g carbo., 0 g fiber, 0 g pro.
Daily Values: 29% vit. C, 1% calcium
Exchanges: 2 Other Carbo.

Strawberry-Lemonade Slush: For each serving, in a blender container combine ½ cup fresh or frozen unsweetened strawberries, ⅓ cup lemonade base, and 1 tablespoon sugar. Blend until smooth. With blender running, add ½ cup ice cubes, 1 at a time, through opening in lid until beverage is slushy.

Nutrition Facts per serving: 152 cal., 0 g total fat (0 g sat. fat), 0 mg chol., 3 mg sodium, 39 g carbo., 2 g fiber, 1 g pro.
Daily Values: 88% vit. C, 1% calcium, 2% iron
Exchanges: ½ Fruit, 2 Other Carbo.

Keep It Cold

■ When making a pitcher of fruit juice or iced tea, freeze a couple of ice-cube trays with prepared juice or tea to keep from diluting the beverage.

■ For a punch bowl, freeze a shallow layer of fruit juice or some of the punch in a ring mold. If desired, arrange fruit on the frozen layer and add about 1 inch of juice to hold fruit in place. When frozen, add additional fruit juice to fill the mold. Freeze until solid. To serve, unmold and float in the punch to keep it chilled.

Slushy Punch

Slushy Punch

For a sweeter punch, use the lemon-lime carbonated beverage in lieu of the carbonated water. Double the recipe for a large party.

No Fat

Prep: 15 minutes **Freeze:** overnight
Stand: 20 minutes **Makes:** 14 (about 4-ounce) servings

  1½ **cups unsweetened pineapple juice**
    1 **ripe medium banana, cut up**
  ½ **cup sugar**
  ½ **of a 6-ounce can (⅓ cup) frozen orange juice concentrate, thawed**
    1 **tablespoon lemon juice**
    1 **1-liter bottle carbonated water or three 12-ounce cans lemon-lime carbonated beverage, chilled**
      Finely shredded orange peel (optional)

1. In a blender container combine pineapple juice, banana, sugar, orange juice concentrate, and lemon juice. Cover and blend until smooth. Stir in 1⅓ cups *water*. Transfer to a 1½- or 2-quart glass baking dish. Cover and freeze overnight.

2. To serve, let mixture stand at room temperature about 20 minutes. To form slush, scrape a large spoon across frozen mixture; spoon the slush into a punch bowl. Slowly pour carbonated water down side of bowl; stir gently to mix. If desired, garnish with orange peel

Nutrition Facts per serving: 56 cal., 0 g total fat (0 g sat. fat), 0 mg chol., 4 mg sodium, 14 g carbo., 0 g fiber, 0 g pro.
Daily Values: 27% vit. C, 1% calcium, 1% iron
Exchanges: ½ Fruit, ½ Other Carbo.

Spiked Slushy Punch: Prepare as above, except add ½ cup rum or vodka with the fruit juices. Freeze and serve as above. Makes 15 (about 4-ounce) servings.

Nutrition Facts per serving: 69 cal., 0 g total fat (0 g sat. fat), 0 mg chol., 4 mg sodium, 13 g carbo., 0 g fiber, 0 g pro.
Daily Values: 25% vit. C, 1% calcium, 1% iron
Exchanges: ½ Fruit, ½ Other Carbo.

Quantity Fruit Punch `Best Loved`

The recipe can be easily cut in half when serving a smaller group (see photo, page 99).

No Fat

Prep: 15 minutes **Chill:** 4 hours
Makes: 60 (6-ounce) servings

    8 **cups water**
    1 **12-ounce can frozen orange juice concentrate**
    1 **12-ounce can frozen lemonade concentrate**
    2 **cups sugar**
  ¼ **cup lime juice**
      Ice cubes
    2 **46-ounce cans unsweetened pineapple juice, chilled**
    2 **2-liter bottles ginger ale, chilled**
    2 **1-liter bottles carbonated water, chilled**
      Fresh strawberries, halved lengthwise (optional)
      Halved orange slices (optional)

1. In a large pitcher or bowl combine the 8 cups water, the orange juice concentrate, and the lemonade concentrate; stir to dissolve. Stir in sugar and lime juice until sugar is dissolved. Cover and chill for 4 hours.

2. To serve, pour half of the juice mixture over ice in a large punch bowl. Slowly pour in 1 can of the pineapple juice, 1 bottle of the ginger ale, and 1 bottle of the carbonated water; stir gently to combine. If desired, garnish with strawberries and orange slices. Repeat with remaining ingredients when needed.

Nutrition Facts per serving: 95 cal., 0 g total fat (0 g sat. fat), 0 mg chol., 14 mg sodium, 24 g carbo., 0 g fiber, 0 g pro.
Daily Values: 25% vit. C, 1% calcium, 2% iron
Exchanges: ½ Fruit, 1 Other Carbo.

Sangria

This version of a favorite Spanish beverage includes orange juice and lime juice.

No Fat

Prep: 10 minutes **Chill:** 3 to 24 hours
Makes: 10 (about 4-ounce) servings

　　1　cup orange juice
　¼　cup lime juice
　　1　750-milliliter bottle dry red wine
　¼　to ⅓ cup sugar
　　　Ice cubes
　　　Orange slices (optional)
　　　Lime slices (optional)

1. In a large glass or plastic pitcher stir together orange juice and lime juice. Add wine and sugar, stirring until sugar dissolves. Cover and chill for 3 to 24 hours.

2. Serve over ice. If desired, garnish each serving with orange and lime slices.

Nutrition Facts per serving: 85 cal., 0 g total fat (0 g sat. fat), 0 mg chol., 4 mg sodium, 9 g carbo., 0 g fiber, 0 g pro.
Daily Values: 1% vit. A, 24% vit. C, 1% calcium, 2% iron
Exchanges: ½ Other Carbo., 1 Fat

Glogg

Use a vegetable peeler to peel the orange, making sure to get only the outer orange part and as little as possible of the bitter white inner layer.

Low Fat

Prep: 10 minutes **Cook:** 20 minutes
Makes: 8 (about 4-ounce) servings

　　1　750-milliliter bottle dry red wine
　½　cup raisins
　½　cup gin, vodka, or aquavit
　⅓　cup sugar
　　　Peel from 1 orange
　　8　inches stick cinnamon, broken
　　6　whole cloves
　　2　cardamom pods, opened
　¼　cup blanched whole almonds

1. In a large saucepan stir together wine, raisins, gin, and sugar. For spice bag, place orange peel, cinnamon, cloves, and cardamom in center of a double-thick, 6-inch square of 100-percent-cotton cheesecloth. Bring corners of cloth together; tie closed with a clean string. Add spice bag to saucepan with wine mixture.

2. Heat mixture to simmering. Simmer, uncovered, for 10 minutes. Do not boil. Remove spice bag and discard. Just before serving, stir in almonds.

Crockery-cooker directions: In a 3½- or 4-quart crockery cooker combine ingredients as at bottom left. Cover and cook on low-heat setting for 3 hours. Remove spice bag and discard. Just before serving, stir in almonds.

Nutrition Facts per serving: 182 cal., 2 g total fat (0 g sat. fat), 0 mg chol., 6 mg sodium, 18 g carbo., 1 g fiber, 1 g pro.
Daily Values: 2% calcium, 4% iron
Exchanges: ½ Fruit, ½ Other Carbo., 2½ Fat

Raspberry Shrub

No Fat

Prep: 20 minutes **Cool:** 1 hour
Makes: about 16 (about 4-ounce) servings

　　3　12-ounce packages frozen lightly sweetened red raspberries (about 9 cups)
1½　cups honey
　　1　cup sugar
　　2　lemons
　12　inches stick cinnamon, broken
　　2　tablespoons snipped fresh rosemary or 2 to 3 teaspoons dried rosemary, crushed
　　9　or 10 whole cloves (½ teaspoon)
　⅓　to ½ cup light rum or ½ cup water
　　2　to 3 cups ice cubes
　　1　750-milliliter bottle Champagne or sparkling grape juice, chilled

1. In a 4-quart Dutch oven combine raspberries, honey, sugar, and ⅓ cup *water*. Cook and stir over medium heat until sugar dissolves.

2. Using a vegetable peeler, remove strips of peel from lemons; juice lemons (should have ½ cup). Add strips of lemon peel, lemon juice, cinnamon, rosemary, and cloves to Dutch oven. Bring mixture just to boiling; stir occasionally. Remove from heat. Cover; cool to room temperature.

3. Press mixture through a sieve; discard solids (you should have about 4 cups syrup). To serve, in a punch bowl combine syrup, rum, and ice cubes. Slowly add Champagne. Stir gently. Serve over ice in small glasses or punch cups.

Make-ahead directions: Syrup may be prepared, covered, and refrigerated up to 3 days.

Nutrition Facts per serving: 217 cal., 0 g total fat (0 g sat. fat), 0 mg chol., 2 mg sodium, 46 g carbo., 1 g fiber, 0 g pro.
Daily Values: 8% vit. C, 2% iron
Exchanges: 3 Other Carbo., 1 Fat

Milk Shakes

Fast

Start to Finish: 5 minutes **Makes:** 2 (about 8-ounce) servings

> **1 pint ice cream**
> **½ to ¾ cup milk**

1. Place ice cream and milk in a blender container. Cover; blend until smooth. Serve at once.

Nutrition Facts per serving: 296 cal., 16 g total fat (10 g sat. fat), 63 mg chol., 136 mg sodium, 34 g carbo., 0 g fiber, 7 g pro.
Daily Values: 13% vit. A, 2% vit. C, 24% calcium, 1% iron
Exchanges: 1 Milk, 1½ Other Carbo., 2½ Fat

Malts: Prepare as above, except add 2 tablespoons instant malted milk powder with milk.

Nutrition Facts per serving: 383 cal., 17 g total fat (11 g sat. fat), 67 mg chol., 240 mg sodium, 50 g carbo., 0 g fiber, 9 g pro.
Daily Values: 15% vit. A, 3% vit. C, 31% calcium, 2% iron
Exchanges: 1 Milk, 2½ Other Carbo., 3 Fat

Mocha Milk Shakes: Prepare Milk Shakes as above, except use chocolate ice cream. Add 2 teaspoons instant coffee crystals with the milk.

Nutrition Facts per serving: 320 cal., 16 g total fat (10 g sat. fat), 49 mg chol., 131 mg sodium, 41 g carbo., 2 g fiber, 7 g pro.
Daily Values: 13% vit. A, 3% vit. C, 22% calcium, 7% iron
Exchanges: 1 Milk, 2 Other Carbo., 2½ Fat

Eggnog

For a nonalcoholic version, omit the rum and bourbon and increase the milk to 2⅓ cups.

Prep: 15 minutes **Chill:** 4 to 24 hours
Makes: 7 (about 4-ounce) servings

> **4 beaten egg yolks**
> **2 cups milk**
> **⅓ cup sugar**
> **1 cup whipping cream**
> **2 tablespoons light rum**
> **2 tablespoons bourbon**
> **1 teaspoon vanilla**
> **Ground nutmeg**

1. In a large heavy saucepan combine the egg yolks, milk, and sugar. Cook and stir over medium heat until mixture just coats a metal spoon. Remove from heat. Place the pan in a sink or bowl of ice water and stir for 2 minutes. Stir in whipping cream, rum, bourbon, and vanilla. Cover and chill for 4 to 24 hours. To serve, sprinkle each serving with nutmeg.

Nutrition Facts per serving: 242 cal., 17 g total fat (10 g sat. fat), 174 mg chol., 52 mg sodium, 14 g carbo., 0 g fiber, 5 g pro.
Daily Values: 17% vit. A, 1% vit. C, 12% calcium, 2% iron
Exchanges: ½ Milk, ½ Other Carbo., 3½ Fat

Lower-Fat Eggnog: Prepare as above, except substitute 3 cups fat-free half-and-half cream for the milk and whipping cream.

Nutrition Facts per serving: 158 cal., 3 g total fat (1 g sat. fat), 122 mg chol., 107 mg sodium, 20 g carbo., 0 g fiber, 4 g pro.
Daily Values: 4% vit. A, 7% calcium, 2% iron
Exchanges: ½ Milk, 1 Other Carbo., 1 Fat

Banana-Berry Smoothies

Fast   Low Fat

Start to Finish: 10 minutes **Makes:** 3 or 4 servings

> **2 cups plain fat-free yogurt**
> **2 ripe medium bananas**
> **1 cup sliced fresh strawberries or unsweetened frozen strawberries**
> **1 cup mixed fresh berries, such as raspberries, blueberries, and/or blackberries, or unsweetened frozen mixed berries**

1. In a blender container combine yogurt and fruit. Cover and blend until pureed. If desired, top with a few fresh berries.

Nutrition Facts per serving: 199 cal., 1 g total fat (0 g sat. fat), 3 mg chol., 126 mg sodium, 39 g carbo., 3 g fiber, 11 g pro.
Daily Values: 3% vit. A, 61% vit. C, 34% calcium, 6% iron
Exchanges: 1 Milk, 1½ Fruit

Banana-Berry Smoothies

Orange Breakfast Nog

Fast **Low Fat**

Start to Finish: 5 minutes
Makes: 2 (about 10-ounce) servings

> 1½ **cups buttermilk**
> ½ **of a 6-ounce can (⅓ cup) frozen orange**
> **juice concentrate**
> 2 **tablespoons brown sugar**
> 1 **teaspoon vanilla**
> 2 or 3 **large ice cubes**

1. In a blender container combine buttermilk, orange juice concentrate, brown sugar, and vanilla. Cover; blend until smooth. With blender running, add ice cubes, 1 at a time, through opening in lid. Blend until smooth and frothy.

Nutrition Facts per serving: 182 cal., 2 g total fat (1 g sat. fat), 6 mg chol., 198 mg sodium, 34 g carbo., 0 g fiber, 7 g pro.
Daily Values: 4% vit. A, 111% vit. C, 24% calcium, 2% iron
Exchanges: 1 Milk, ½ Fruit, 1 Other Carbo.

Wine Spritzer

Fast **No Fat**

Start to Finish: 5 minutes **Makes:** 1 (8-ounce) serving

> ¾ **cup dry white, red, or rosé wine, chilled**
> ¼ **cup carbonated water or lemon-lime**
> **carbonated beverage, chilled**
> **Ice cubes**

1. Combine wine and carbonated water. Serve over ice cubes.

Nutrition Facts per serving: 120 cal., 0 g total fat (0 g sat. fat), 0 mg chol., 21 mg sodium, 1 g carbo., 0 g fiber, 0 g pro.
Daily Values: 2% calcium, 3% iron
Exchanges: 2½ Fat

Frozen Margaritas

Fast **No Fat**

Start to Finish: 10 minutes **Makes:** 8 (4-ounce) servings

> 1 **12-ounce can frozen limeade concentrate**
> ⅔ **cup tequila**
> ½ **cup orange liqueur**
> 4 **cups ice cubes**
> 1 or 2 **limes**
> **Coarse salt**

1. In a blender container combine limeade concentrate, tequila, and orange liqueur. Cover; blend until smooth. With the blender running, add ice cubes, 1 at a time, through

opening in lid until mixture becomes slushy. Cut a thick lime slice; cut slice in half. Rub slices around rims of 8 glasses. Dip rims into a dish of coarse salt. Pour mixture into prepared glasses. Slice remaining lime into 8 thin slices. Garnish glasses with lime slices.

Nutrition Facts per serving: 170 cal., 0 g total fat (0 g sat. fat), 0 mg chol., 1 mg sodium, 26 g carbo., 0 g fiber, 0 g pro.
Daily Values: 10% vit. C
Exchanges: 1½ Other Carbo., 1½ Fat

Strawberry Margaritas: Prepare as above, except blend half of the mixture at a time, adding 1 cup frozen unsweetened whole strawberries along with 2 cups of the ice cubes. Repeat with remaining mixture, additional 1 cup frozen strawberries, and remaining 2 cups ice cubes. Continue as directed, substituting sugar for the salt on glasses. If desired, garnish glasses with whole strawberries. Makes 8 (5½-ounce) servings.

Nutrition Facts per serving: 182 cal., 0 g total fat (0 g sat. fat), 0 mg chol., 1 mg sodium, 29 g carbo., 1 g fiber, 0 g pro.
Daily Values: 33% vit. C, 1% calcium, 2% iron
Exchanges: 2 Other Carbo., 1½ Fat

Lime Daiquiris

Fast **No Fat**

Start to Finish: 10 minutes **Makes:** 6 (about 4-ounce) servings

> 1 **6-ounce can frozen limeade concentrate or**
> ½ **of a 12-ounce can (¾ cup) frozen**
> **lemonade concentrate**
> ⅔ **cup rum**
> 2½ **to 3 cups ice cubes**

1. In a blender container combine limeade concentrate and rum. Cover and blend until smooth. With blender running, add ice cubes, 1 at a time, through opening in lid until slushy.

Nutrition Facts per serving: 110 cal., 0 g total fat (0 g sat. fat), 0 mg chol., 0 mg sodium, 14 g carbo., 0 g fiber, 0 g pro.
Daily Values: 6% vit. C
Exchanges: 1 Other Carbo., 1 Fat

Raspberry or Strawberry Daiquiris: Prepare as above, except use half of a 6-ounce can (⅓ cup) frozen limeade concentrate. Add one 10-ounce package frozen red raspberries or sliced strawberries and, if desired, ⅓ cup sifted powdered sugar. Makes 7 (4-ounce) servings.

Nutrition Facts per serving: 88 cal., 0 g total fat (0 g sat. fat), 0 mg chol., 0 mg sodium, 10 g carbo., 1 g fiber, 0 g pro.
Daily Values: 4% vit. C, 1% iron
Exchanges: ½ Fruit, 1 Fat

Wine

Selecting a wine to serve with a special meal can be exciting. Your exploration of wine can begin with those you know you like and branch off from there, much as you might explore the recipes in this cookbook.

While it is true that there are many rules about serving wine, you should never feel that the rules can't be broken, or at least bent. Let experience be your guide when it comes to the wines you prefer, as well as which wines you like to serve with certain foods. Rules such as "white wine with fish" are nothing more than starting points. For example, after some experimentation, you may find you prefer Pinot Noir with salmon or Beaujolais with mussels. Here are some additional starting points—not rules—to use as signposts in exploring the magical combinations of wine and food.

Wine and Food Compatibility

While there are no steadfast rules when it comes to pairing wine and food, some foods do taste better with certain wines. Generally, the fuller the food's flavor, the fuller-flavored and fuller-bodied (which refers to the wine feeling heavy or light on your tongue) the wine ought to be. Here is just a short list of wines and foods that are compatible. Note that wines can cross over between categories of light- or full-bodied depending on the winery or region they come from.

Asian foods
Chenin Blanc, Gewürztraminer, or a sparkling wine

Beef
Cabernet Sauvignon, French red Burgundy, Merlot, Pinot Noir, or red Zinfandel

Cheeses (heartier flavored)
Medium- to full-bodied Chardonnay or sparkling wine; Beaujolais-Villages or Pinot Noir; French Sauternes or port

Cheeses (mild to medium flavored)
Light-bodied Chardonnay, Pinot Grigio, Sauvignon Blanc, Vouvray, or sparkling wine

Chicken (barbecued)
Chenin Blanc, Gewürztraminer, Riesling, sparkling wine; Beaujolais, Côtes du Rhône, or red Zinfandel

Chicken (roasted)
Chablis, Chardonnay, Chenin Blanc, Johannisberg Riesling, Sauvignon Blanc; Rioja crianza or Pinot Noir

Desserts
Eiswein, Late Harvest Riesling, Muscat de Beaumes-de-Venise, or Sauternes

Duck or goose
Medium- to full-bodied red Bordeaux, Merlot, or Rioja reserva

Fish
Alsatian or Johannisberg Riesling, Chardonnay, Chenin Blanc, or Sauvignon Blanc

Game
Barolo, Hermitage, or Petite Sirah

Lamb
Cabernet Sauvignon, Merlot, Châteauneuf-du-Pape, Pinot Noir, or red Bordeaux

Pasta with tomato sauce
Barbaresco, Cabernet Sauvignon, Cabernet blends, Chianti, Merlot, red Bordeaux, red Zinfandel, Sangiovese, or Syrah

Pork (roasted)
Medium- to full-bodied Chardonnay, Mâcon-Villages, Vouvray, or sparkling wine; light-bodied Pinot Noir or Rioja crianza

Salmon
Medium- to full-bodied Chardonnay, Sauvignon Blanc, Viognier, or sparkling wine; Bardolino or Pinot Noir

Scallops, mussels, or clams
Crisp, medium- to full-bodied Chablis, Chardonnay, white Burgundy, or sparkling wine; Beaujolais-Villages or Pinot Noir

Shrimp
Chardonnay, Gewürztraminer, or sparkling wine

Steak
Barolo, Cabernet Sauvignon, Cabernet blends, Merlot, red Bordeaux, or red Zinfandel

Thai foods (spicy)
Chenin Blanc, Gewürztraminer, Riesling, or rosé Rioja

Choosing a Wine Glass

The classic rules about using the appropriate glass with various wines have merit. Most importantly, look for wine glasses that become narrower at the top—this helps concentrate the bouquet. All of the wine glasses shown below incorporate this feature. Large glasses are appropriate for red wines because they allow the wine to have more contact with air, which helps the flavor and bouquet develop. White wine glasses are smaller to help keep these wines chilled because they are usually served at cooler than room temperature.

The Pinot Noir glass is large, with a bulbous shape, to allow more flavor and aroma development for this characteristically delicate and refined wine.

The narrow, fluted glass for Champagne or sparkling wine keeps the bubbles intact and preserves the fizz.

Cabernets and Merlots are often denser and richer wines than Pinot Noirs and don't require a balloon-shaped glass.

The port glass is smaller than other wine glasses to accommodate a smaller serving. Due to the intense flavor of port, it doesn't require much room for the flavor and aroma to build.

The smaller size of the white wine glass helps keep the wine chilled. A larger surface area would cause the wine to warm to room temperature too quickly.

Removing the Cork

Removing the cork from a wine bottle should be a pleasurable experience. First, set the bottle on a firm, flat surface. Use a knife or foil cutter to cut around the foil, then remove the foil. Finally, use the spiral or prongs of a corkscrew to remove the cork. All of the corkscrews shown below are inexpensive, and most are easy to use.

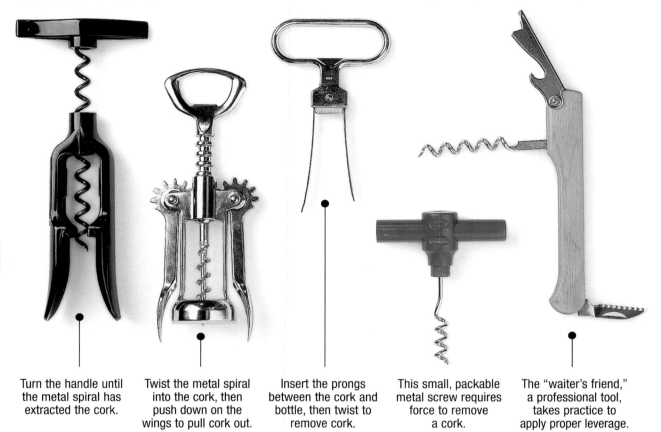

Turn the handle until the metal spiral has extracted the cork.

Twist the metal spiral into the cork, then push down on the wings to pull cork out.

Insert the prongs between the cork and bottle, then twist to remove cork.

This small, packable metal screw requires force to remove a cork.

The "waiter's friend," a professional tool, takes practice to apply proper leverage.

Serving Temperatures

If a white wine is served too cold, the true character, flavor, and aroma will be diminished. If a red wine is served too warm, it will change the balance of the flavor components and hamper the taste of the wine. The old rule about serving red wine at room temperature no longer applies because most rooms today are kept warmer than in the past. It's best if red wine is chilled ever so briefly (10 minutes in an ice bucket or 30 minutes in the refrigerator) to bring it to the correct temperature. Here are a few temperature guidelines.

Type of Wine	Serving Temperature
Champagnes and **sparkling wines**	45°F
Sauvignon Blancs and **Rieslings**	45°F to 55°F
Chardonnays	55°F to 60°F
Lighter reds (Beaujolais, Pinot Noir)	55°F to 60°F
Sauternes	58°F to 62°F
Cabernet Sauvignons and Merlots	60°F to 65°F
Ports	62°F to 65°F

Storage Temperatures

Wine will age more quickly if stored at warm temperatures (70°F or so). Fluctuations in temperature are not good for wine either. Therefore, it is best to store both red and white wines in the refrigerator, where you know they won't get warm or experience wild fluctuations in temperature. (Of course, if you have a wine cellar, you should store your wine there.) Store bottles on their sides to keep the corks from drying out.

Chapter 5
Breads

On the divider: **Artisan-Style French Bread** (see recipe, page 137)

For more recipes, visit our Recipe Center at **www.bhg.com**

Muffins

The nutty streusel topping tastes best on the plain muffins and all of the sweet variations.

Fast

Prep: 10 minutes **Bake:** 18 minutes
Oven: 400°F **Makes:** 12 muffins

  1¾ **cups all-purpose flour**
   ⅓ **cup sugar**
   2 **teaspoons baking powder**
   ¼ **teaspoon salt**
   1   **beaten egg**
   ¾ **cup milk**
   ¼ **cup cooking oil**
   1 **recipe Streusel Topping (optional)**

1. Grease twelve 2½-inch muffin cups or line with paper bake cups; set aside.

2. In a medium bowl combine flour, sugar, baking powder, and salt. Make a well in center of flour mixture; set aside.

3. In another bowl combine egg, milk, and oil. Add egg mixture all at once to flour mixture (see photo 1, right). Stir just until moistened (batter should be lumpy; see photo 2, right).

4. Spoon batter into prepared muffin cups, filling each two-thirds full (see photo 3, right). If desired, sprinkle Streusel Topping over muffin batter in cups. Bake in a 400° oven for 18 to 20 minutes or until golden and a wooden toothpick inserted in centers comes out clean. Cool in muffin cups on a wire rack for 5 minutes. Remove from muffin cups; serve warm.

Blueberry Muffins: Prepare as above, except fold ¾ cup fresh or frozen blueberries and, if desired, 1 teaspoon finely shredded lemon peel into batter.

Cranberry Muffins: Prepare as above, except combine 1 cup coarsely chopped cranberries and 2 tablespoons additional sugar; fold into batter.

Oatmeal Muffins: Prepare as above, except reduce flour to 1⅓ cups and add ¾ cup rolled oats to flour mixture.

Poppy Seed Muffins: Prepare as above, except increase sugar to ½ cup and add 1 tablespoon poppy seeds to flour mixture.

Nutrition Facts per muffin for plain, blueberry, cranberry, oatmeal, and poppy seed variations: 136 cal., 5 g total fat (1 g sat. fat), 19 mg chol., 128 mg sodium, 19 g carbo., 0 g fiber, 3 g pro.
Daily Values: 1% vit. A, 6% calcium, 5% iron
Exchanges: 1 Starch, ½ Other Carbo., ½ Fat

Banana Muffins: Prepare as at left, greasing muffin cups (do not use paper bake cups). Reduce milk to ½ cup. Stir ¾ cup mashed banana and ½ cup chopped nuts into flour mixture along with the egg mixture.

Nutrition Facts per muffin: 184 cal., 9 g total fat (1 g sat. fat), 18 mg chol., 126 mg sodium, 24 g carbo., 1 g fiber, 4 g pro.
Daily Values: 1% vit. A, 3% vit. C, 6% calcium, 6% iron
Exchanges: 1 Starch, ½ Other Carbo., 1½ Fat

Cheese Muffins: Prepare as at left, except stir ½ cup shredded cheddar cheese or Monterey Jack cheese into flour mixture.

Nutrition Facts per muffin: 155 cal., 7 g total fat (2 g sat. fat), 24 mg chol., 158 mg sodium, 19 g carbo., 0 g fiber, 4 g pro.
Daily Values: 2% vit. A, 10% calcium, 5% iron
Exchanges: 1 Starch, ½ Other Carbo., 1 Fat

Streusel Topping: Combine 3 tablespoons all-purpose flour, 3 tablespoons brown sugar, and ¼ teaspoon ground cinnamon. Cut in 2 tablespoons butter until mixture resembles coarse crumbs. Stir in 2 tablespoons chopped nuts.

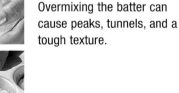

1. Use the back of a wooden spoon to make a well in the center of the flour mixture. Carefully pour all of the liquid mixture into the flour mixture.

2. Using a wooden spoon, stir the batter just until the ingredients are moistened. Overmixing the batter can cause peaks, tunnels, and a tough texture.

3. Use a spoon and a rubber spatula to add batter to each muffin cup.

Sizing Up Muffins

Muffin cups come in all shapes and sizes, from bite-size minis to standard 2½-inch cups to jumbo muffins. You'll need to adjust the baking time according to the pan you choose. Mini muffins will bake about 8 minutes less than standard-size muffins. And for jumbo muffins, lower the oven temperature to 350°F and bake about 30 minutes.

Coffee Cake Muffins

Pick a Pan for Quick Breads

One recipe of quick bread batter can be divided many ways, depending on your needs.

Sometimes you want a single large loaf; other times you may want several small loaves. Use this chart to convert the recipe to the pan size you like. The important thing to remember is that no matter what pan(s) you use, fill them only two-thirds full. If you have batter remaining, use it to make muffins.

Pan Size	Baking Time
9×5×3-inch loaf pan	1 to 1¼ hours
8×4×2-inch loaf pan	50 to 60 minutes
7½×3½×2-inch loaf pans	40 to 45 minutes
4½×2½×1½-inch loaf pans	30 to 35 minutes
2½-inch muffin cups	15 to 20 minutes

Note: These baking times are approximate and may vary with the recipe.

Coffee Cake Muffins

A rich ribbon of streusel fills the centers and decorates the tops of these muffins.

Prep: 20 minutes **Bake:** 15 minutes
Oven: 400°F **Makes:** 12 muffins

    3 tablespoons all-purpose flour
    3 tablespoons brown sugar
    ¼ teaspoon ground cinnamon
    2 tablespoons butter or margarine
    3 tablespoons chopped walnuts or pecans
 1½ cups all-purpose flour
    ½ cup granulated sugar
 1¼ teaspoons baking powder
    ½ teaspoon ground cinnamon
    ¼ teaspoon ground ginger
    ¼ teaspoon baking soda
    ¼ teaspoon salt
    ¼ cup butter or margarine
    1 beaten egg
    ½ cup buttermilk or sour milk
       (see tip, page 157)

1. Grease twelve 2½-inch muffin cups or line with paper bake cups; set aside.

2. For topping, in a small bowl stir together the 3 tablespoons flour, brown sugar, and the ¼ teaspoon cinnamon. Cut in the 2 tablespoons butter until mixture resembles coarse crumbs. Stir in nuts; set topping aside.

3. In a medium bowl stir together the 1½ cups flour, granulated sugar, baking powder, the ½ teaspoon cinnamon, ginger, baking soda, and salt. Cut in the ¼ cup butter until mixture resembles coarse crumbs.

4. In another bowl combine egg and buttermilk. Add egg mixture all at once to flour mixture (see photo 1, page 115). Stir just until moistened (batter should be lumpy; see photo 2, page 115).

5. Spoon half of the batter into the prepared muffin cups, filling each one-third full (see photo 3, page 115). Top with half of the topping, the remaining batter, and the remaining topping. Bake in a 400° oven for 15 to 18 minutes or until golden and a wooden toothpick inserted in centers comes out clean. Cool in muffin cups on a wire rack for 5 minutes. Remove from muffin cups; serve warm.

Nutrition Facts per muffin: 180 cal., 8 g total fat (4 g sat. fat), 34 mg chol., 196 mg sodium, 25 g carbo., 1 g fiber, 3 g pro.
Daily Values: 5% vit. A, 5% calcium, 6% iron
Exchanges: ½ Starch, 1 Other Carbo., 1½ Fat

Oat Bran Muffins

Low Fat

Prep: 15 minutes **Bake:** 16 minutes
Oven: 400°F **Makes:** 12 muffins

        Nonstick cooking spray
1¼ **cups oat bran**
  1 **cup all-purpose flour**
  2 **teaspoons baking powder**
  ¼ **teaspoon baking soda**
  ¼ **teaspoon salt**
  1 **beaten egg**
  ¾ **cup applesauce**
  ½ **cup fat-free milk**
  ¼ **cup honey**
  1 **tablespoon cooking oil**
  ½ **cup raisins or snipped dried fruit**

1. Lightly coat bottoms of twelve 2½-inch muffin cups with cooking spray; set aside.

2. In a medium bowl combine oat bran, flour, baking powder, baking soda, and salt. Make a well in center of flour mixture; set aside.

3. In a small bowl combine egg, applesauce, milk, honey, and oil. Add applesauce mixture all at once to flour mixture (see photo 1, page 115). Stir just until moistened (batter should be lumpy; see photo 2, page 115). Fold in raisins.

4. Divide batter evenly among prepared muffin cups (see photo 3, page 115). Bake in a 400° oven for 16 to 18 minutes or until golden and a wooden toothpick inserted in centers comes out clean. Cool in muffin cups on a wire rack for 5 minutes. Remove from muffin cups; serve warm.

Nutrition Facts per muffin: 133 cal., 2 g total fat (0 g sat. fat), 18 mg chol., 154 mg sodium, 29 g carbo., 2 g fiber, 4 g pro.
Daily Values: 1% vit. A, 1% vit. C, 7% calcium, 7% iron
Exchanges: ½ Fruit, 1½ Starch

To Sift or Not To Sift

You can skip the sifting of all-purpose flour because most of what's sold today is presifted. However, flour does settle during shipping, so it's a good idea to stir through the bag or canister just before measuring to make the flour lighter. Gently spoon it into a dry measuring cup and level it off with a spatula.

Cheddar Spoon Bread

For a punch of pepper, use Monterey Jack cheese with jalapeño peppers.

Prep: 25 minutes **Bake:** 45 minutes
Oven: 325°F **Makes:** 8 servings

1½ **cups milk**
  ½ **cup cornmeal**
  2 **cups shredded cheddar cheese or Monterey Jack cheese (8 ounces)**
  1 **tablespoon butter or margarine**
1½ **teaspoons baking powder**
  1 **teaspoon sugar**
  ¼ **teaspoon salt**
  4 **eggs**

1. In a large saucepan combine milk and cornmeal. Cook, stirring constantly, over medium-high heat until mixture is thickened and bubbly; remove from heat. Add cheese, butter, baking powder, sugar, and salt; stir until cheese melts.

2. Separate eggs. Add yolks, one at a time, to cornmeal mixture, stirring after each addition just until combined (mixture will be thick).

3. In a large mixing bowl beat egg whites with an electric mixer on high speed until stiff peaks form (tips stand straight).

4. Stir about one-third of the beaten egg whites into the cornmeal mixture. Gently fold remaining beaten egg whites into cornmeal mixture until combined. Spoon into an ungreased 2-quart casserole or soufflé dish.

5. Bake in a 325° oven for 45 to 50 minutes or until a knife inserted near the center comes out clean. Serve immediately.

Nutrition Facts per serving: 221 cal., 14 g total fat (8 g sat. fat), 143 mg chol., 393 mg sodium, 10 g carbo., 1 g fiber, 12 g pro.
Daily Values: 13% vit. A, 1% vit. C, 32% calcium, 5% iron
Exchanges: ½ Starch, 1½ High-Fat Meat

Corn Bread

Corn Bread

In the southern United States, cooks prefer baking their corn bread like this—in a skillet.

Fast

Prep: 10 minutes **Bake:** 15 minutes
Oven: 400°F **Makes:** 8 to 10 servings

　　1　**cup all-purpose flour**
　¾　**cup cornmeal**
　　2　**to 3 tablespoons sugar**
2½　**teaspoons baking powder**
　¾　**teaspoon salt**
　　1　**tablespoon butter**
　　2　**beaten eggs**
　　1　**cup milk**
　¼　**cup cooking oil or melted butter**

1. In a medium bowl stir together flour, cornmeal, sugar, baking powder, and salt; set aside.

2. Add the 1 tablespoon butter to a 10-inch cast-iron skillet or a 9×1½-inch round baking pan. Place in a 400° oven about 3 minutes or until butter melts. Remove pan from oven; swirl butter in pan to coat bottom and sides of pan.

3. Meanwhile, in a small bowl combine eggs, milk, and oil. Add egg mixture all at once to flour mixture. Stir just until moistened. Pour batter into hot skillet or pan. Bake for 15 to 20 minutes or until a wooden toothpick inserted near center comes out clean. Serve warm.

Double Corn Bread: Prepare as at left, except fold ½ cup frozen whole kernel corn, thawed, into batter.

Nutrition Facts per serving for corn bread or double corn bread variation: 219 cal., 10 g total fat (3 g sat. fat), 60 mg chol., 390 mg sodium, 26 g carbo., 1 g fiber, 5 g pro.
Daily Values: 5% vit. A, 12% calcium, 8% iron
Exchanges: 1½ Starch, 2 Fat

Green Chile Corn Bread: Prepare as at left, except fold 1 cup shredded cheddar cheese or Monterey Jack cheese and one 4-ounce can diced green chile peppers, drained, into the batter.

Nutrition Facts per serving: 279 cal., 15 g total fat (6 g sat. fat), 74 mg chol., 517 mg sodium, 26 g carbo., 1 g fiber, 9 g pro.
Daily Values: 8 vit. A, 8% vit. C, 24% calcium, 9% iron
Exchanges: 1½ Starch, ½ High-Fat Meat, 2½ Fat

Corn Muffins: Prepare as at left, except omit the 1 tablespoon butter. Spoon batter into 12 greased 2½-inch muffin cups, filling cups two-thirds full. Bake in a 400° oven about 15 minutes or until lightly browned and a wooden toothpick inserted in centers comes out clean. Makes 12 muffins.

Nutrition Facts per muffin: 137 cal., 6 g total fat (1 g sat. fat), 37 mg chol., 250 mg sodium, 17 g carbo., 1 g fiber, 3 g pro.
Daily Values: 3% vit. A, 8% calcium, 5% iron
Exchanges: 1 Starch, 1 Fat

Corn Sticks: Prepare as on page 118, except omit the 1 tablespoon butter. Generously grease corn stick pans and heat in the preheated oven for 3 minutes. Carefully fill preheated corn stick pans two-thirds full. Bake in a 400° oven about 12 minutes or until a toothpick inserted in centers comes out clean. Makes 18 to 26 corn sticks.

Nutrition Facts per corn stick: 91 cal., 4 g total fat (1 g sat. fat), 25 mg chol., 167 mg sodium, 11 g carbo., 1 g fiber, 2 g pro.
Daily Values: 2% vit. A, 5% calcium, 3% iron
Exchanges: 1 Starch

Banana Bread

Prep: 25 minutes **Bake:** 55 minutes
Oven: 350°F **Makes:** 1 loaf (16 servings)

    2 **cups all-purpose flour**
1½ **teaspoons baking powder**
 ½ **teaspoon baking soda**
 ¼ **teaspoon ground cinnamon**
 ⅛ **teaspoon ground nutmeg**
  2 **beaten eggs**
1½ **cups mashed bananas (5 medium)**
  1 **cup sugar**
 ½ **cup cooking oil or melted butter or margarine**
 ¼ **cup chopped walnuts**
  1 **recipe Streusel-Nut Topping (optional)**

1. Grease bottom and ½ inch up the sides of one 9×5×3-inch or two 7½×3½×2-inch loaf pans; set aside. Combine flour, baking powder, baking soda, cinnamon, nutmeg, and ¼ teaspoon *salt*. Make a well in center of flour mixture; set aside.

2. In a medium bowl combine eggs, bananas, sugar, and oil. Add egg mixture all at once to flour mixture (see photo 1, page 115). Stir just until moistened (batter should be lumpy; see photo 2, page 115). Fold in nuts. Spoon batter into prepared pan(s). If desired, sprinkle Streusel-Nut Topping over batter.

3. Bake in a 350° oven for 55 to 60 minutes for 9×5×3-inch pan, or 40 to 45 minutes for 7½×3½×2-inch pans, or until a wooden toothpick inserted near center comes out clean (if necessary, cover loosely with foil the last 15 minutes of baking to prevent overbrowning). Cool in pan on a wire rack for 10 minutes. Remove from pan. Cool completely on a wire rack. Wrap and store overnight before slicing.

Nutrition Facts per serving: 215 cal., 9 g total fat (1 g sat. fat), 27 mg chol., 122 mg sodium, 32 g carbo., 1 g fiber, 3 g pro.
Daily Values: 1% vit. A, 6% vit. C, 3% calcium, 5% iron
Exchanges: 1 Starch, 1 Other Carbo., 1½ Fat

Streusel-Nut Topping: In a small bowl combine ¼ cup packed brown sugar and 3 tablespoons all-purpose flour. Using a pastry blender, cut in 2 tablespoons butter until mixture resembles coarse crumbs. Stir in ⅓ cup chopped walnuts.

Zucchini Bread

Prep: 20 minutes **Bake:** 50 minutes
Oven: 350°F **Makes:** 1 loaf (16 servings)

1½ **cups all-purpose flour**
  1 **teaspoon ground cinnamon**
 ½ **teaspoon baking soda**
 ½ **teaspoon salt**
 ¼ **teaspoon baking powder**
 ¼ **teaspoon ground nutmeg**
  1 **beaten egg**
  1 **cup sugar**
  1 **cup finely shredded, unpeeled zucchini**
 ¼ **cup cooking oil**
 ½ **cup chopped walnuts or pecans, toasted (see tip, page 224)**

1. Grease the bottom and ½ inch up sides of an 8×4×2-inch loaf pan; set aside. In a medium bowl combine the flour, cinnamon, baking soda, salt, baking powder, and nutmeg. Make a well in center of flour mixture; set aside.

2. In another medium bowl combine egg, sugar, zucchini, and oil. Add zucchini mixture all at once to flour mixture (see photo 1, page 115). Stir just until moistened (batter should be lumpy; see photo 2, page 115). Fold in nuts. Spoon batter into prepared pan.

3. Bake in a 350° oven for 50 to 55 minutes or until a wooden toothpick inserted near center comes out clean. Cool in pan on a wire rack for 10 minutes. Remove from pan. Cool completely on a wire rack. Wrap and store overnight before slicing.

Apple Bread: Prepare as above, except substitute 1½ cups finely shredded, peeled apple for the shredded zucchini.

Nutrition Facts per serving for zucchini or apple variation: 147 cal., 6 g total fat (1 g sat. fat), 13 mg chol., 123 mg sodium, 21 g carbo., 1 g fiber, 2 g pro.
Daily Values: 1% vit. A, 1% vit. C, 1% calcium, 4% iron
Exchanges: ½ Starch, 1 Other Carbo., 1 Fat

Nut Bread

Prep: 20 minutes **Bake:** 50 minutes
Oven: 350°F **Makes:** 1 loaf (14 servings)

- 2 **cups all-purpose flour**
- 1 **cup sugar**
- 1 **tablespoon baking powder**
- ½ **teaspoon salt**
- 1 **beaten egg**
- 1 **cup milk**
- ¼ **cup cooking oil**
- ¾ **cup chopped almonds, pecans, or walnuts, toasted (see tip, page 224)**

1. Grease the bottom and ½ inch up sides of an 8×4×2-inch loaf pan; set aside. In a large bowl stir together flour, sugar, baking powder, and salt. Make a well in center of flour mixture; set aside.

2. In a medium bowl combine the egg, milk, and oil. Add egg mixture all at once to flour mixture (see photo 1, page 115). Stir just until moistened (batter should be lumpy; see photo 2, page 115). Fold in nuts. Spoon batter into prepared pan.

3. Bake in a 350° oven 50 to 55 minutes or until a wooden toothpick inserted near center comes out clean. Cool in pan on a wire rack for 10 minutes. Remove from pan. Cool completely on wire rack. Wrap and store overnight before slicing.

Cranberry Nut Bread: Grease the bottom and ½ inch up sides of a 9×5×3-inch loaf pan; set aside. Prepare as above, except add 2 teaspoons finely shredded orange peel to flour mixture. Substitute orange juice for the milk and fold 1 cup coarsely chopped cranberries into batter along with nuts.

Nutrition Facts per serving for nut or cranberry nut variation: 207 cal., 8 g total fat (1 g sat. fat), 16 mg chol., 183 mg sodium, 30 g carbo., 1 g fiber, 4 g pro.
Daily Values: 1% vit. A, 1% vit. C, 10% calcium, 7% iron
Exchanges: 1 Starch, 1 Other Carbo., 1½ Fat

Blueberry Nut Bread: Prepare as above, except add 1½ teaspoons finely shredded lemon peel to flour mixture. In a small bowl combine ½ cup dried blueberries with ¼ cup boiling water. Cover and let stand 10 minutes; drain, if necessary. Fold blueberries into batter along with nuts.

Nutrition Facts per serving: 231 cal., 8 g total fat (1 g sat. fat), 16 mg chol., 183 mg sodium, 35 g carbo., 1 g fiber, 5 g pro.
Daily Values: 1% vit A, 1% vit. C, 10% calcium, 7% iron
Exchanges: 1 Starch, 1½ Other Carbo., 1½ Fat

Pumpkin Bread

Prep: 20 minutes **Bake:** 55 minutes
Oven: 350°F **Makes:** 2 loaves (32 servings)

- 3 **cups sugar**
- 1 **cup cooking oil**
- 4 **eggs**
- 3⅓ **cups all-purpose flour**
- 2 **teaspoons baking soda**
- 1½ **teaspoons salt**
- 1 **teaspoon ground cinnamon**
- 1 **teaspoon ground nutmeg**
- ⅔ **cup water**
- 1 **15-ounce can pumpkin**

1. Grease the bottom and ½ inch up sides of two 9×5×3-inch, three 8×4×2-inch, or four 7½×3½-×2-inch loaf pans; set aside. In a very large mixing bowl beat sugar and oil with an electric mixer on medium speed. Add eggs and beat well; set aside.

2. In a large bowl combine flour, baking soda, salt, cinnamon, and nutmeg. Alternately add flour mixture and water to sugar mixture, beating on low speed after each addition just until combined. Beat in pumpkin. Spoon batter into prepared pans.

3. Bake in a 350° oven for 55 to 65 minutes or until a wooden toothpick inserted near centers comes out clean. Cool in pans on wire racks for 10 minutes. Remove from pans. Cool completely on wire racks. Wrap and store overnight before slicing.

Nutrition Facts per serving: 191 cal., 8 g total fat (1 g sat. fat), 27 mg chol., 197 mg sodium, 29 g carbo., 1 g fiber, 2 g pro.
Daily Values: 59% vit. A, 1% vit. C, 1% calcium, 6% iron
Exchanges: ½ Starch, 1½ Other Carbo., 1½ Fat

Raisin Nut Pumpkin Bread: Prepare as above, except fold ¾ cup raisins and ¾ cup chopped walnuts into batter after pumpkin has been added.

Nutrition Facts per serving: 220 cal., 10 g total fat (1 g sat. fat), 27 mg chol., 197 mg sodium, 32 g carbo., 1 g fiber, 8 g pro.
Daily Values: 59% vit A, 2% vit. C, 2% calcium, 6% iron
Exchanges: ½ Starch, 1½ Other Carbo., 2 Fat

Lemon Bread

If you're squeezing a fresh lemon for juice, remember to shred the lemon peel first.

Prep: 20 minutes **Bake:** 50 minutes
Oven: 350°F **Makes:** 1 loaf (16 servings)

- 1¾ **cups all-purpose flour**
- ¾ **cup sugar**
- 2 **teaspoons baking powder**
- ¼ **teaspoon salt**
- 1 **beaten egg**
- 1 **cup milk**
- ¼ **cup cooking oil or melted butter or margarine**
- 2 **teaspoons finely shredded lemon peel**
- 1 **tablespoon lemon juice**
- ½ **cup chopped almonds or walnuts**
- 2 **tablespoons lemon juice (optional)**
- 1 **tablespoon sugar (optional)**

1. Grease the bottom and ½ inch up sides of an 8×4×2-inch loaf pan; set aside. In a medium bowl stir together the flour, the ¾ cup sugar, baking powder, and salt. Make a well in center of flour mixture; set aside.

2. In another medium bowl combine the egg, milk, oil, lemon peel, and the 1 tablespoon lemon juice. Add the egg mixture all at once to the flour mixture (see photo 1, page 115). Stir just until moistened (batter should be lumpy; see photo 2, page 115). Fold in nuts. Spoon the batter into the prepared pan.

3. Bake in a 350° oven for 50 to 55 minutes or until a wooden toothpick inserted near center comes out clean. If desired, stir together the 2 tablespoons lemon juice and the 1 tablespoon sugar. While bread is still in the pan, brush lemon-sugar mixture over the top of the loaf. Cool in pan on a wire rack for 10 minutes. Remove from pan. Cool completely on a wire rack. Wrap and store overnight before serving.

Nutrition Facts per serving: 147 cal., 6 g total fat (1 g sat. fat), 14 mg chol., 98 mg sodium, 20 g carbo., 1 g fiber, 3 g pro.
Daily Values: 1% vit. A, 2% vit. C, 6% calcium, 4% iron
Exchanges: ½ Starch, 1 Other Carbo., 1 Fat

Lemon-Poppy Seed Bread: Prepare as above, except substitute 1 tablespoon poppy seeds for the almonds or walnuts.

Nutrition Facts per serving: 126 cal., 4 g total fat (1 g sat. fat), 14 mg chol., 98 mg sodium, 20 g carbo., 0 g fiber, 2 g pro.
Daily Values: 1% vit A, 2% vit. C, 6% calcium, 4% iron
Exchanges: ½ Starch, 1 Other Carbo., ½ Fat

Scones

Prep: 20 minutes **Bake:** 12 minutes
Oven: 400°F **Makes:** 8 scones

- 2½ **cups all-purpose flour**
- 2 **tablespoons sugar**
- 4 **teaspoons baking powder**
- ¼ **teaspoon salt**
- ⅓ **cup butter, cut into pieces**
- 2 **beaten eggs**
- ¾ **cup whipping cream**
- ½ **cup dried currants or snipped raisins**
  Milk
  Sugar

1. In a medium bowl combine flour, the 2 tablespoons sugar, the baking powder, and salt. Using a pastry blender, cut in butter until mixture resembles coarse crumbs. Make a well in center of flour mixture; set aside.

2. In a medium bowl combine eggs, whipping cream, and currants. Add egg mixture all at once to flour mixture. Using a fork, stir just until moistened.

3. Turn dough out onto a lightly floured surface. Knead dough by folding and gently pressing dough for 10 to 12 strokes or until dough is nearly smooth. Pat or lightly roll dough into an 8-inch circle. Cut into 8 wedges.

4. Place wedges 1 inch apart on an ungreased baking sheet. Brush wedges with milk and sprinkle with additional sugar. Bake in a 400° oven for 12 to 14 minutes or until golden. Remove scones from baking sheet; serve warm.

Nutrition Facts per scone: 353 cal., 18 g total fat (11 g sat. fat), 106 mg chol., 381 mg sodium, 42 g carbo., 2 g fiber, 7 g pro.
Daily Values: 14% vit. A, 1% vit. C, 16% calcium, 13% iron
Exchanges: ½ Fruit, 2½ Starch, 3 Fat

Scones

Dried Cherry Scones

Choose dried sweet—not dried tart—cherries for these teatime treats.

Prep: 30 minutes **Bake:** 10 minutes **Oven:** 400°F
Cool: 10 minutes **Makes:** 12 scones

- ½ **cup snipped dried sweet cherries or raisins**
- 2 **cups all-purpose flour**
- 3 **tablespoons brown sugar**
- 2 **teaspoons baking powder**
- ½ **teaspoon salt**
- ½ **teaspoon baking soda**
- ¼ **cup butter, cut into pieces**
- 1 **teaspoon finely shredded orange peel**
- 1 **beaten egg yolk**
- 1 **8-ounce carton dairy sour cream**
- 1 **recipe Orange Glaze**

1. In a small bowl pour enough boiling water over dried cherries to cover. Let stand for 5 minutes; drain well.

2. Meanwhile, in a large bowl combine flour, brown sugar, baking powder, salt, and baking soda. Using a pastry blender, cut in butter until mixture resembles coarse crumbs. Add drained cherries and orange peel; toss to coat. Make a well in the center of the flour mixture; set aside.

3. In a small bowl combine egg yolk and sour cream. Add egg mixture all at once to flour mixture. Using a fork, stir until combined (mixture may seem dry).

4. Turn dough out onto a lightly floured surface. Knead dough by folding and gently pressing dough for 10 to 12 strokes or until dough is nearly smooth. Pat or lightly roll dough into a 7-inch circle. Cut into 12 wedges.

5. Place wedges 1 inch apart on an ungreased baking sheet. Bake in a 400° oven for 10 to 12 minutes or until light brown. Remove scones from baking sheet. Cool on a wire rack for 10 minutes. Drizzle Orange Glaze over warm scones. Serve warm.

Orange Glaze: In small bowl stir together 1 cup sifted powdered sugar, 1 tablespoon orange juice, and ¼ teaspoon vanilla. Stir in enough additional orange juice, 1 teaspoon at a time, to reach drizzling consistency.

Nutrition Facts per scone: 216 cal., 9 g total fat (5 g sat. fat), 37 mg chol., 269 mg sodium, 31 g carbo., 1 g fiber, 3 g pro.
Daily Values: 7% vit. A, 2% vit. C, 7% calcium, 6% iron
Exchanges: 1 Starch, 1 Other Carbo., 1½ Fat

Cinnamon Breakfast Biscuits

Prep: 20 minutes **Bake:** 10 minutes **Oven:** 450°F
Cool: 10 minutes **Makes:** 12 biscuits

- 1¾ **cups all-purpose flour**
- ¼ **cup unprocessed wheat bran**
- 2 **tablespoons granulated sugar**
- 1 **tablespoon baking powder**
- ½ **teaspoon ground cinnamon**
- ¼ **teaspoon salt**
- ½ **cup butter or shortening**
- ⅔ **cup milk**
- ½ **cup mixed dried fruit bits**
- ½ **cup sifted powdered sugar**
- 2 **to 3 teaspoons orange juice, milk, or water**

1. In a medium bowl combine flour, wheat bran, granulated sugar, baking powder, cinnamon, and salt. Using a pastry blender, cut in butter until mixture resembles coarse crumbs. Make a well in center of flour mixture. Add milk and fruit bits all at once. Using a fork, stir just until moistened.

2. Turn dough out onto a lightly floured surface. Knead dough by folding and gently pressing dough for 10 to 12 strokes or until dough is nearly smooth. Pat or lightly roll dough until ½ inch thick (see photo 1, page 123). Cut dough with a floured 2½-inch biscuit cutter (see photo 2, page 123).

3. Place biscuits 1 inch apart on an ungreased baking sheet. Bake in a 450° oven for 10 to 12 minutes or until golden. Cool on a wire rack for 10 minutes.

4. Meanwhile, stir together powdered sugar and enough orange juice to reach drizzling consistency. Drizzle over warm biscuits. Serve warm.

Nutrition Facts per biscuit: 187 cal., 9 g total fat (5 g sat. fat), 23 mg chol., 242 mg sodium, 26 g carbo., 1 g fiber, 3 g pro.
Daily Values: 7% vit. A, 1% vit. C, 9% calcium, 6% iron
Exchanges: 1 Starch, ½ Other Carbo., 1½ Fat

Biscuits Supreme

Cut out as many biscuits as possible from a single rolling of the dough because a second rolling (and the additional flour) will result in biscuits that are a bit tougher than the first batch.

Fast

Prep: 20 minutes **Bake:** 10 minutes
Oven: 450°F **Makes:** 10 biscuits

    3 cups all-purpose flour
    4 teaspoons baking powder
    1 tablespoon sugar
    1 teaspoon salt
    ¾ teaspoon cream of tartar
    ¾ cup butter or ½ cup butter and ¼ cup shortening
    1¼ cups buttermilk or 1 cup milk

1. In a large bowl stir together the flour, baking powder, sugar, salt, and cream of tartar. Using a pastry blender, cut in butter until mixture resembles coarse crumbs. Make a well in the center of the flour mixture. Add buttermilk all at once. Using a fork, stir just until moistened.

2. Turn dough out onto a lightly floured surface. Knead dough by folding and gently pressing dough for 4 to 6 strokes or just until dough holds together. Pat or lightly roll dough until ¾ inch thick (see photo 1, right). Cut the dough with a floured 2½-inch biscuit cutter (see photo 2, right).

3. Place biscuits 1 inch apart on an ungreased baking sheet. Bake in a 450° oven for 10 to 12 minutes or until golden. Remove biscuits from baking sheet and serve immediately.

Nutrition Facts per biscuit: 273 cal., 15 g total fat (9 g sat. fat), 40 mg chol., 574 mg sodium, 29 g carbo., 1 g fiber, 5 g pro.
Daily Values: 11% vit. A, 1% vit. C, 14% calcium, 9% iron
Exchanges: 2 Starch, 2½ Fat

Drop Biscuits Supreme: Prepare as above, except add ¼ cup whipping cream with the buttermilk. Do not knead, roll, or cut dough. Drop dough by spoonfuls onto a greased baking sheet (see photo 3, right). Bake as directed. Makes 12 biscuits.

Nutrition Facts per biscuit: 293 cal., 17 g total fat (11 g sat. fat), 49 mg chol., 576 mg sodium, 29 g carbo.,1 g fiber, 5 g pro.
Daily Values: 13% vit. A, 1% vit. C, 15% calcium, 9% iron
Exchanges: 2 Starch, 3 Fat

1. On a lightly floured surface, use your hands to pat, or a rolling pin to gently roll, the dough to the thickness specified in the recipe.

2. Using a floured biscuit or metal cookie cutter, cut out the dough. Dip the cutter into flour after each use to prevent sticking.

3. For drop biscuits, push dough from a tablespoon with a rubber spatula or knife onto a greased baking sheet.

Bread Spreads

Add a zip to your breads by serving them with one of these spreads. Stir a spread together in about 5 minutes, but let it chill at least 1 hour before serving to allow flavors to blend.

Nut Butter: Combine ½ cup finely chopped almonds or walnuts; ¼ cup butter, softened; and ¼ cup apricot or peach preserves. Makes 1 cup.

Citrus Butter: Combine ½ cup butter, softened; 1 tablespoon powdered sugar; and 1 teaspoon finely shredded orange peel or lemon peel. Makes ½ cup.

Breakfast Butter: Combine ½ cup butter, softened, and 2 tablespoons honey or maple-flavored syrup. Makes ½ cup.

Onion-Parmesan Butter: Combine ½ cup butter, softened; 2 tablespoons grated Parmesan cheese; and 2 teaspoons sliced green onion. Makes ½ cup.

Herb Butter: Combine ½ cup butter, softened, and ½ teaspoon each dried thyme and marjoram, crushed, or 1 teaspoon dried basil, crushed. Makes ½ cup.

Pimiento Butter: In a blender container or food processor bowl combine one 4-ounce jar sliced pimientos, drained; 1 tablespoon anchovy paste; and 1 clove garlic, minced. Cover and blend or process until pimientos are pureed and mixture is smooth. Stir pimiento mixture into ½ cup butter, softened. Makes about 1 cup.

Buttermilk Coffee Cake [Best Loved]

Prep: 20 minutes **Bake:** 35 minutes
Oven: 350°F **Makes:** 18 servings

- 2½ cups all-purpose flour
- 1½ cups packed brown sugar
- ½ teaspoon salt
- ⅔ cup butter, margarine, or shortening
- 2 teaspoons baking powder
- ½ teaspoon baking soda
- ½ teaspoon ground cinnamon
- ½ teaspoon ground nutmeg
- 2 beaten eggs
- 1⅓ cups buttermilk or sour milk
   (see tip, page 157)
- ½ cup chopped nuts

1. Grease bottom and ½ inch up sides of a 13×9×2-inch baking pan; set aside. In a medium bowl combine flour, brown sugar, and salt. Cut in butter until mixture resembles coarse crumbs; set aside ½ cup. Stir baking powder, baking soda, cinnamon, and nutmeg into remaining crumb mixture.

2. In another bowl combine eggs and buttermilk. Add egg mixture all at once to flour mixture. Spoon batter into prepared pan. Combine reserved crumb mixture and nuts; sprinkle over batter.

3. Bake in a 350° oven for 35 to 40 minutes or until a wooden toothpick inserted near the center comes out clean. Serve warm.

Nutrition Facts per serving: 233 cal., 10 g total fat (5 g sat. fat), 44 mg chol., 250 mg sodium, 33 g carbo., 1 g fiber, 4 g pro.
Daily Values: 6% vit. A, 8% calcium, 8% iron
Exchanges: 1 Starch, 1 Other Carbo., 2 Fat

Fruit Coffee Cake [Best Loved]

Prep: 30 minutes **Bake:** 40 minutes
Oven: 350°F **Makes:** 9 servings

- 1½ to 2 cups sliced, peeled apricots or peaches; chopped, peeled apples; or blueberries or red raspberries
- ¼ cup water
- ¼ cup sugar
- 2 tablespoons cornstarch
- 1½ cups all-purpose flour
- ¾ cup sugar
- ½ teaspoon baking powder
- ¼ teaspoon baking soda
- ¼ cup butter or margarine
- 1 beaten egg
- ½ cup buttermilk or sour milk
   (see tip, page 157)
- ½ teaspoon vanilla
- ¼ cup all-purpose flour
- ¼ cup sugar
- 2 tablespoons butter or margarine

1. For filling, in a medium saucepan combine fruit and water. Bring to boiling. Reduce heat and simmer,* covered, about 5 minutes or until fruit is tender. Combine the ¼ cup sugar and cornstarch; stir into fruit. Cook and stir over medium heat until mixture is thickened and bubbly. Cook and stir 2 minutes more; set filling aside.

2. In a medium bowl combine the 1½ cups flour, the ¾ cup sugar, baking powder, and baking soda. Cut in the ¼ cup butter until mixture resembles coarse crumbs. Make a well in the center of the flour mixture; set aside.

3. In another bowl combine egg, buttermilk, and vanilla. Add the egg mixture all at once to the flour mixture. Using a wooden spoon, stir just until moistened (batter should be lumpy). Spread half of the batter into an ungreased 8×8×2-inch baking pan. Spread filling over batter. Drop remaining batter in small mounds onto filling.

4. In a small bowl stir together the ¼ cup flour and the ¼ cup sugar. Cut in the 2 tablespoons butter until mixture resembles coarse crumbs. Sprinkle over coffee cake. Bake in a 350° oven for 40 to 45 minutes or until golden. Serve warm.

*Note: Do not simmer raspberries.

Nutrition Facts per serving: 297 cal., 9 g total fat (5 g sat. fat), 46 mg chol., 162 mg sodium, 50 g carbo., 1 g fiber, 4 g pro.
Daily Values: 20% vit. A, 5% vit. C, 4% calcium, 8% iron
Exchanges: 1 Starch, 2½ Other Carbo., 1½ Fat

Fruit Coffee Cake

Rhubarb-Strawberry Coffee Cake: Prepare as on page 124, except for filling substitute ¾ cup fresh or frozen cut-up rhubarb and ¾ cup frozen unsweetened whole strawberries for fruit. Continue as directed.

Nutrition Facts per serving: 263 cal., 9 g total fat (2 g sat. fat), 46 mg chol., 162 mg sodium, 49 g carbo., 1 g fiber, 4 g pro.
Daily Values: 7% vit. A, 13% vit. C, 5% calcium, 7% iron
Exchanges: 1 Starch, 2½ Other Carbo., 1½ Fat

Blueberry Buckle

Prep: 20 minutes **Bake:** 50 minutes
Oven: 350°F **Makes:** 9 servings

    2 cups all-purpose flour
 2½ teaspoons baking powder
   ¼ teaspoon salt
   ½ cup shortening
   ¾ cup sugar
    1 egg
   ½ cup milk
    2 cups fresh or frozen blueberries
   ½ cup all-purpose flour
   ½ cup sugar
   ½ teaspoon ground cinnamon
   ¼ cup butter or margarine

1. Grease bottom and ½ inch up sides of a 9×9×2-inch or 8×8×2-inch baking pan; set aside. In a medium bowl combine the 2 cups flour, baking powder, and salt; set aside.

2. In a medium mixing bowl beat shortening with an electric mixer on medium speed 30 seconds. Add the ¾ cup sugar. Beat on medium to high speed until light and fluffy. Add egg; beat well. Alternately add flour mixture and milk to beaten egg mixture, beating until smooth after each addition.

3. Spoon batter into prepared pan. Sprinkle with blueberries. In another bowl combine the ½ cup flour, the ½ cup sugar, and cinnamon. Using a pastry blender, cut in butter until mixture resembles coarse crumbs; sprinkle over blueberries. Bake in a 350° oven for 50 to 60 minutes or until golden. Serve warm.

Raspberry Buckle: Prepare as above, except substitute fresh or frozen raspberries for blueberries.

Nutrition Facts per serving for blueberry or raspberry variation:
408 cal., 17 g total fat (6 g sat. fat), 38 mg chol., 247 mg sodium, 58 g carbo., 2 g fiber, 5 g pro.
Daily Values: 6% vit. A, 8% vit. C, 11% calcium, 11% iron
Exchanges: 1 Starch, 3 Other Carbo., 3 Fat

Double-Apple Coffee Cake

For the best results when baking with margarine, select one that contains 80 percent fat.

Prep: 20 minutes **Bake:** 25 minutes
Oven: 350°F **Makes:** 10 servings

       Nonstick cooking spray
   ⅔ cup all-purpose flour
   ½ cup whole wheat flour
    1 teaspoon baking soda
    1 teaspoon ground cinnamon
   ¼ teaspoon salt
 1½ cups finely chopped, peeled apples (2 small)
   ¼ cup refrigerated or frozen egg product, thawed
   ¾ cup granulated sugar
   ¼ cup chopped pecans or walnuts
   ¼ cup applesauce
   ¼ cup packed brown sugar
    1 tablespoon all-purpose flour
    1 tablespoon whole wheat flour
   ½ teaspoon ground cinnamon
    1 tablespoon margarine
   ¼ cup chopped pecans or walnuts

1. Lightly coat a 9-inch round baking pan with cooking spray; set aside. In a small bowl stir together the ⅔ cup all-purpose flour, the ½ cup whole wheat flour, baking soda, the 1 teaspoon cinnamon, and salt; set aside.

2. In a large bowl combine the apples and egg product; stir in granulated sugar, ¼ cup nuts, and applesauce. Stir in flour mixture. Pour batter into prepared pan.

3. For topping, stir together brown sugar, the 1 tablespoon all-purpose flour, the 1 tablespoon whole wheat flour, and the ½ teaspoon cinnamon; cut in margarine until mixture resembles coarse crumbs. Stir in ¼ cup nuts. Sprinkle topping over batter in pan.

4. Bake in a 350° oven for 25 to 30 minutes or until a wooden toothpick inserted near center comes out clean. Cool in pan for 10 minutes. Serve warm.

Nutrition Facts per serving: 203 cal., 5 g total fat (1 g sat. fat), 0 mg chol., 211 mg sodium, 38 g carbo., 3 g fiber, 3 g pro.
Daily Values: 2% vit. A, 1% vit. C, 2% calcium, 7% iron
Exchanges: ½ Starch, 2 Other Carbo., 1 Fat

Cake Doughnuts

It's best to cool the doughnuts completely if you wish to shake them in powdered sugar instead of granulated sugar. If you shake them while they're still hot, the powdered sugar will melt.

Prep: 40 minutes **Chill:** 2 hours **Fry:** 2 minutes per batch
Makes: about 15 doughnuts

> 3 **cups all-purpose flour**
> 2 **teaspoons baking powder**
> ½ **teaspoon ground cinnamon**
> ¼ **teaspoon ground nutmeg**
> ⅔ **cup milk**
> ¼ **cup butter or margarine, melted**
> 2 **beaten eggs**
> ⅔ **cup sugar**
> 1 **teaspoon vanilla**
> **Shortening or cooking oil for deep-fat frying**
> 1 **recipe Chocolate Glaze (page 163)**
> **or sugar (optional)**

1. Combine 2 cups of the flour, baking powder, cinnamon, nutmeg, and ¼ teaspoon *salt*. In a medium bowl combine milk and melted butter. In a large mixing bowl combine eggs, sugar, and vanilla; beat with an electric mixer about 3 minutes or until thick. Alternately add flour mixture and milk mixture to egg mixture, beating after each addition just until combined. Stir in remaining 1 cup flour. Cover dough; chill for 2 hours.

2. Turn dough out onto a lightly floured surface. Roll dough until ½ inch thick. Cut dough with a floured 2½-inch doughnut cutter, dipping cutter into flour between cuts. Reroll as necessary.

3. Fry doughnuts, 2 or 3 at a time, in deep, hot fat (375°F) about 1 minute on each side or until golden, turning once with a slotted spoon. Drain on paper towels. Repeat with remaining doughnuts and doughnut holes. If desired, dip tops of warm doughnuts into Chocolate Glaze or shake warm doughnuts in a bag with sugar. Cool doughnuts on wire racks.

Chocolate Cake Doughnuts: Prepare as above, except omit cinnamon and nutmeg and increase sugar to 1 cup. Reduce the amount of flour that is stirred in at the end of step 1 to ¼ cup (for a total of 2¼ cups flour) and stir in ¾ cup unsweetened cocoa powder. Continue as directed.

Nutrition Facts per doughnut for plain or chocolate variation: 253 cal.,15 g total fat (5 g sat. fat), 38 mg chol., 140 mg sodium, 27 g carbo., 1 g fiber, 4 g pro.
Daily Values: 4% vit. A, 5% calcium, 6% iron
Exchanges: 1 Starch, 1 Other Carbo., 2½ Fat

Nun's Puffs

How these light, tender morsels were named is a mystery—but they are heavenly.

Prep: 25 minutes **Bake:** 30 minutes
Oven: 375°F **Makes:** 12 puffs

> ½ **cup butter**
> 1 **cup milk**
> ¾ **cup all-purpose flour**
> 4 **eggs**
> 1 **tablespoon sugar**
> **Honey (optional)**

1. Generously grease twelve 2½-inch muffin cups, including the edge and around the top of each cup; set aside. In a medium saucepan melt butter; add milk. Bring to boiling. Add flour all at once, stirring vigorously. Cook and stir until mixture forms a ball that does not separate. Remove from heat; cool for 5 minutes.

2. Add the eggs, 1 at a time, beating for 1 minute with a wooden spoon after each addition or until smooth. Divide dough evenly among prepared muffin cups, filling cups about two-thirds full; sprinkle with sugar.

3. Bake in a 375° oven about 30 minutes or until golden brown and puffy. Remove from pan. Serve immediately. If desired, serve with honey.

Nutrition Facts per puff: 137 cal., 10 g total fat (6 g sat. fat), 94 mg chol., 114 mg sodium, 8 g carbo., 0 g fiber, 4 g pro.
Daily Values: 9% vit. A, 4% calcium, 3% iron
Exchanges: ½ Starch, 2 Fat

Nun's Puffs

Overnight Stuffed French Toast

If you prefer, serve the ruby red Raspberry Sauce on page 482 over this memorable breakfast entrée.

Prep: 40 minutes **Chill:** 10 hours **Bake:** 30 minutes
Oven: 350°F **Makes:** 6 servings

> 2 3-ounce packages cream cheese, softened
> 2 tablespoons orange marmalade or apricot preserves
> 1 teaspoon finely chopped crystallized ginger
> ⅛ teaspoon ground nutmeg
> ¼ cup chopped almonds, toasted (see tip, page 224)
> 6 1½-inch slices French bread
> 4 eggs
> 1 cup milk
> 1 teaspoon vanilla
> 1 recipe Orange Sauce

1. Generously grease a 3-quart rectangular baking dish; set aside. In a small bowl beat together cream cheese, marmalade, ginger, and nutmeg. Stir in the almonds. Cut a pocket in the top crust of each bread slice. Divide cream cheese mixture evenly among pockets. Place bread slices in prepared baking dish.

2. In a small bowl beat together the eggs, milk, and vanilla; slowly pour the egg mixture over bread slices, covering all the tops. Cover and chill overnight.

3. Bake, uncovered, in a 350° oven 30 to 35 minutes or until golden. Serve with Orange Sauce.

Orange Sauce: In a small saucepan stir together ½ teaspoon finely shredded orange peel, 1¼ cups orange juice, 2 tablespoons honey, and 4 teaspoons cornstarch. Cook and stir over medium heat until thickened and bubbly. Cook and stir 2 minutes more.

Nutrition Facts per serving: 340 cal., 18 g total fat (8 g sat. fat), 176 mg chol., 303 mg sodium, 35 g carbo., 2 g fiber, 11 g pro.
Daily Values: 16% vit. A, 45% vit. C, 13% calcium, 10% iron
Exchanges: ½ Fruit, 1½ Starch, ½ Other Carbo.,1 Medium-Fat Meat, 2 Fat

French Toast

`Fast`

Prep: 10 minutes **Cook:** 4 minutes per slice **Makes:** 4 servings

> 4 beaten eggs
> 1 cup milk
> 2 tablespoons sugar
> 2 teaspoons vanilla
> 2 teaspoons orange liqueur (optional)
> ½ teaspoon ground cinnamon (optional)
> ¼ teaspoon ground nutmeg (optional)
> 8 ½-inch slices challah bread or brioche or 8 slices dry white bread
> 2 tablespoons butter
>   Maple-flavored syrup (optional)

1. In a shallow bowl beat together eggs, milk, sugar, vanilla, and, if desired, orange liqueur and/or cinnamon and nutmeg. Dip bread slices into egg mixture, coating both sides (if using challah bread or brioche, let soak in egg mixture about 10 seconds on each side).

2. In a skillet or on a griddle melt 1 tablespoon of the butter over medium heat; add half of the bread slices and cook for 2 to 3 minutes on each side or until golden brown. Repeat with remaining butter and bread slices. Serve warm. If desired, serve with syrup.

Nutrition Facts per serving: 291 cal., 13 g total fat (6 g sat. fat), 233 mg chol., 384 mg sodium, 29 g carbo., 1 g fiber, 12 g pro.
Daily Values: 13% vit. A, 1% vit. C, 13% calcium, 10% iron
Exchanges: ½ Milk, 1½ Starch, 2 Fat

Make-Ahead Breads

Freshly baked quick breads and yeast breads are at your fingertips anytime with these freezing and reheating tips.

■ To freeze unfrosted muffins, scones, or biscuits, let them cool completely. Wrap them tightly in heavy foil or place them in a freezer container or bag; freeze up to 3 months. To reheat frozen muffins, leave them wrapped in heavy foil; heat in a 300°F oven for 15 to 18 minutes. Reheat the foil-wrapped scones or biscuits in a 300°F oven for 20 to 25 minutes.

■ To freeze quick bread loaves, place completely cooled loaves in freezer containers or bags and freeze up to 3 months. Thaw the wrapped loaves overnight in the refrigerator.

■ To freeze yeast breads, place completely cooled, unfrosted breads in a freezer container or bag; freeze up to 3 months. Thaw the wrapped bread at room temperature for 2 hours; if desired, frost after thawing.

Creamy Caramel-Pecan Rolls

Best Loved

Prep: 25 minutes **Rise:** 30 minutes **Bake:** 20 minutes
Oven: 375°F **Makes:** 24 rolls

- 1¼ **cups sifted powdered sugar**
- ⅓ **cup whipping cream**
- 1 **cup coarsely chopped pecans**
- ½ **cup packed brown sugar**
- 1 **tablespoon ground cinnamon**
- 2 **16-ounce loaves frozen white bread dough or sweet roll dough, thawed**
- 3 **tablespoons butter or margarine, melted**
- ¾ **cup raisins (optional)**

1. Grease two 9×1½-inch round baking pans; set pans aside. For topping, in a small bowl stir together powdered sugar and whipping cream; divide evenly between prepared baking pans. Sprinkle pecans evenly over sugar mixture.

2. In another small bowl stir together brown sugar and cinnamon; set aside. On a lightly floured surface, roll each loaf of dough into a 12×8-inch rectangle. Brush with melted butter; sprinkle with brown sugar-cinnamon mixture. If desired, sprinkle with raisins.

3. Roll up each rectangle starting from a long side. Seal seams. Slice each roll into 12 pieces. Place pieces, cut sides down, on topping in pans.

4. Cover; let rise in a warm place until nearly double (about 30 minutes). Break any surface bubbles with a greased toothpick.

5. Bake in a 375° oven for 20 to 25 minutes or until golden brown (if necessary, cover rolls with foil the last 10 minutes of baking to prevent over-browning). Cool in pans on a wire rack for 5 minutes. Carefully invert rolls onto a serving platter. Serve warm.

Make-ahead directions: Prepare as above through step 3. Cover with oiled waxed paper, then with plastic wrap. Refrigerate for 2 to 24 hours. Before baking, let chilled rolls stand, covered, for 30 minutes at room temperature. Uncover and bake chilled rolls for 25 to 30 minutes or until golden brown. Continue as directed.

Nutrition Facts per roll: 172 cal., 6 g total fat (2 g sat. fat),
9 mg chol., 19 mg sodium, 25 g carbo., 1 g fiber, 3 g pro.
Daily Values: 2% vit. A, 4% calcium, 2% iron
Exchanges: 1 Starch, 1 Other Carbo., 1 Fat

Creamy Caramel-Pecan Rolls

Buttermilk Pancakes

You can plan on getting about eight standard-size or 30 dollar-size pancakes from this recipe.

Fast

Prep: 10 minutes **Cook:** 4 minutes per batch
Makes: 8 servings

- 1 **cup all-purpose flour**
- 1 **tablespoon sugar**
- 1 **teaspoon baking powder**
- ¼ **teaspoon baking soda**
- ¼ **teaspoon salt**
- 1 **beaten egg**
- 1 **cup buttermilk or sour milk (see tip, page 157)**
- 2 **tablespoons cooking oil**

1. Combine the flour, sugar, baking powder, baking soda, and salt. Make a well in center of flour mixture; set aside. Combine the egg, buttermilk, and oil. Add egg mixture all at once to flour mixture. Stir just until moistened (batter should be lumpy). Add additional buttermilk to thin batter, if necessary.

2. For standard-size pancakes, pour or spread about ¼ cup batter into a 3-inch circle onto a hot, lightly greased griddle or heavy skillet. For dollar-size pancakes, pour or spread about 1 tablespoon batter into a 1-inch circle onto a hot, lightly greased griddle or heavy skillet. Cook over medium heat about 2 minutes on each side or until pancakes are golden brown, turning to second sides when pancakes have bubbly surfaces and edges are slightly dry. Serve warm.

Whole Wheat-Buttermilk Pancakes: Prepare as on page 128, except substitute whole wheat flour for all-purpose flour and brown sugar for sugar.

Pancakes: Prepare as on page 128, except substitute milk for buttermilk, increase baking powder to 2 teaspoons, and omit baking soda.

Nutrition Facts per serving for buttermilk, whole wheat, and plain variations: 114 cal., 5 g total fat (1 g sat. fat), 28 mg chol., 202 mg sodium, 15 g carbo., 0 g fiber, 3 g pro.
Daily Values: 1% vit. A, 1% vit. C, 7% calcium, 5% iron
Exchanges: 1 Starch, 1 Fat

Blueberry-Cornmeal Pancakes

Cornmeal and cinnamon are an unusual and undeniably yummy combination in these blueberry-studded pancakes.

`Fast`

Prep: 10 minutes **Cook:** 4 minutes per batch
Makes: 8 to 10 pancakes

- 1 **cup all-purpose flour**
- 2 **tablespoons cornmeal**
- 1 **tablespoon sugar**
- 1 **teaspoon baking powder**
- ½ **teaspoon baking soda**
- ¼ **teaspoon salt**
- ¼ **teaspoon ground cinnamon**
- 1 **beaten egg**
- 1 **cup buttermilk or sour milk (see tip, page 157)**
- 2 **tablespoons cooking oil**
- 1 **cup fresh or frozen blueberries**
  Maple or blueberry-flavored syrup (optional)

1. In a bowl combine flour, cornmeal, sugar, baking powder, baking soda, salt, and cinnamon. Make a well in center of flour mixture; set aside.

2. In another bowl stir together the egg, buttermilk, and oil. Add egg mixture all at once to flour mixture. Stir just until moistened (batter should be lumpy). Gently fold in blueberries.

3. For each pancake, pour or spread about ¼ cup of the batter into a 4-inch circle onto a hot, lightly greased griddle or heavy skillet. Cook over medium heat about 2 minutes on each side or until pancakes are golden brown, turning to second sides when pancakes have bubbly surfaces and edges are slightly dry. Serve warm. If desired, top with syrup.

Nutrition Facts per pancake: 133 cal., 5 g total fat (1 g sat. fat), 28 mg chol., 243 mg sodium, 19 g carbo., 1 g fiber, 4 g pro.
Daily Values: 2% vit. A, 5% vit. C, 8% calcium, 6% iron
Exchanges: 1 Starch, 1 Fat

Puffed Oven Pancake

`Fast`

Prep: 10 minutes **Bake:** 20 minutes
Oven: 400°F **Makes:** 6 servings

- 2 **tablespoons butter or margarine**
- 3 **eggs**
- ½ **cup all-purpose flour**
- ½ **cup milk**
- ¼ **teaspoon salt**
- ¼ **cup orange marmalade**
- 3 **cups sliced fresh fruit, such as strawberries, nectarines, pears, or peeled peaches**
  Powdered sugar or whipped cream (optional)

1. Place butter in a 10-inch ovenproof skillet. Place in a 400° oven for 3 to 5 minutes or until butter melts. Meanwhile, for batter, in a medium bowl use a wire whisk or rotary beater to beat eggs until combined. Add flour, milk, and salt; beat until mixture is smooth. Immediately pour batter into the hot skillet. Bake for 20 to 25 minutes or until puffed and well browned.

2. Meanwhile, in a small saucepan melt the orange marmalade over low heat. To serve, top pancake with fruit; spoon melted marmalade over fruit. If desired, sift powdered sugar over top or serve with whipped cream. Cut into wedges and serve warm.

Nutrition Facts per serving: 176 cal., 7 g total fat (4 g sat. fat), 119 mg chol., 188 mg sodium, 23 g carbo., 2 g fiber, 5 g pro.
Daily Values: 8% vit. A, 69% vit. C, 5% calcium, 6% iron
Exchanges: ½ Fruit, ½ Starch, ½ Other Carbo., 1½ Fat

Individual Puffed Oven Pancakes: Omit butter or margarine. Lightly coat six 4½-inch pie pans or 10-ounce custard cups with nonstick cooking spray; set aside. Prepare batter as above. Divide batter among prepared pans or custard cups. Bake in a 400° oven for 20 to 25 minutes or until puffed and well browned. Serve as above.

Nutrition Facts per serving: 140 cal., 3 g total fat (1 g sat. fat), 108 mg chol., 147 mg sodium, 23 g carbo., 2 g fiber, 5 g pro.
Daily Values: 5% vit. A, 69% vit. C, 5% calcium, 6% iron
Exchanges: ½ Starch, ½ Fruit, ½ Other Carbo., 1 Fat

Waffles

This batter works in regular and Belgian waffle bakers.

`Fast`

Prep: 10 minutes **Bake:** per waffle baker directions
Makes: 12 to 16 (4-inch) waffles

1¾ **cups all-purpose flour**
2 **tablespoons sugar**
1 **tablespoon baking powder**
2 **eggs**
1¾ **cups milk**
½ **cup cooking oil or butter, melted**
1 **teaspoon vanilla**

1. In a medium bowl stir together flour, sugar, baking powder, and ¼ teaspoon *salt*. Make a well in center of flour mixture; set aside.

2. In another medium bowl beat eggs slightly; stir in milk, oil, and vanilla. Add egg mixture all at once to the flour mixture. Stir just until moistened (batter should be slightly lumpy).

3. Pour 1 to 1¼ cups of batter onto grids of a preheated, lightly greased waffle baker. Close lid quickly; do not open until done. Bake according to manufacturer's directions. When done, use a fork to lift waffle off grid. Repeat with remaining batter. Serve warm.

Buttermilk Waffles: Prepare as above, except reduce baking powder to 1 teaspoon and add ½ teaspoon baking soda. Substitute 2 cups buttermilk or sour milk (see tip, page 157) for milk.

Nutrition Facts per plain or buttermilk waffle variation: 180 cal., 11 g total fat (2 g sat. fat), 38 mg chol., 177 mg sodium, 17 g carbo., 0 g fiber, 4 g pro.
Daily Values: 3% vit. A, 1% vit. C, 11% calcium, 5% iron
Exchanges: 1 Starch, 2 Fat

Cornmeal Overnight Waffles

Overnight Waffles

Prep: 10 minutes **Chill:** up to 24 hours
Bake: per waffle baker directions
Makes: about 16 (4-inch) waffles

2¼ **cups all-purpose flour**
2 **tablespoons sugar**
1 **package active dry yeast**
1 **teaspoon vanilla (optional)**
½ **teaspoon salt**
1¾ **cups milk**
2 **eggs**
⅓ **cup cooking oil or melted butter**

1. In a large bowl stir together flour, sugar, yeast, vanilla (if desired), and salt; add milk, eggs, and oil. Beat with an electric mixer until thoroughly combined. Cover batter loosely and chill overnight or up to 24 hours.

2. Stir batter. Pour about ¾ cup batter onto a preheated, lightly greased waffle baker. Close lid quickly; do not open until done. Bake according to manufacturer's directions. When done, use a fork to lift waffle off grid. Repeat with remaining batter. Serve warm. Discard any remaining batter.

Cornmeal Overnight Waffles: Prepare as above, except reduce flour to 1½ cups and add ¾ cup cornmeal.

Nutrition Facts per plain or cornmeal waffle variation: 133 cal., 6 g total fat (1 g sat. fat), 29 mg chol., 94 mg sodium, 16 g carbo., 1 g fiber, 4 g pro.
Daily Values: 2% vit. A, 1% vit. C, 4% calcium, 6% iron
Exchanges: 1 Starch, 1 Fat

Crepes

`Low Fat`

Prep: 5 minutes **Cook:** 30 minutes **Makes:** 18 crepes

1. In a bowl combine 2 beaten eggs, 1½ cups milk, 1 cup all-purpose flour, 1 tablespoon cooking oil, and ¼ teaspoon salt; beat until combined. Heat a lightly greased 6-inch skillet; remove from heat. Spoon in 2 tablespoons batter; lift and tilt skillet to spread batter. Return to heat; brown on 1 side only. (Or, cook on a crepemaker according to manufacturer's directions.) Invert over paper towels; remove crepe. Repeat with remaining batter, greasing skillet occasionally.

Nutrition Facts per crepe: 50 cal., 2 g total fat (1 g sat. fat), 25 mg chol., 50 mg sodium, 6 g carbo., 0 g fiber, 2 g pro.
Daily Values: 2% vit. A, 3% calcium, 2% iron
Exchanges: ½ Starch

Hush Puppies

For best results, fry five or six at a time and let the oil temperature return to 375°F before frying more.

Fast

Prep: 10 minutes **Fry:** 3 minutes per batch
Makes: 14 to 18 hush puppies

> 1 **cup cornmeal**
> ¼ **cup all-purpose flour**
> 2 **teaspoons sugar**
> ¾ **teaspoon baking powder**
> ¼ **teaspoon baking soda**
> ¼ **teaspoon salt**
> 1 **beaten egg**
> ½ **cup buttermilk or sour milk (see tip, page 157)**
> ¼ **cup sliced green onions (2)**
> **Shortening or cooking oil for deep-fat frying**

1. In a medium bowl combine cornmeal, flour, sugar, baking powder, baking soda, and salt. Make a well in center of flour mixture; set aside.

2. In another bowl combine egg, buttermilk, and green onions. Add egg mixture all at once to flour mixture. Stir just until moistened (batter should be lumpy).

3. Drop batter by tablespoons into deep, hot fat (375°F). Fry about 3 minutes or until golden, turning once. Drain on paper towels. Serve warm.

Nutrition Facts per hush puppy: 95 cal., 5 g total fat (1 g sat. fat), 15 mg chol., 100 mg sodium, 11 g carbo., 1 g fiber, 2 g pro.
Daily Values: 1% vit. A, 1% vit. C, 3% calcium, 4% iron
Exchanges: 1 Starch, ½ Fat

Making Better Quick Breads

These simple suggestions will help ensure successful quick-bread baking.

■ Check the bread loaves 10 to 15 minutes before the minimum baking time is reached. Cover them with foil if they're browning too fast.

■ After baking, let the loaves cool completely on a wire rack, then wrap them in foil or plastic wrap and store at room temperature. Store the bread overnight before slicing and eating to give the flavors time to mellow. It also makes the loaves easier to cut.

■ Don't be concerned about a crack down the top of the loaf. It is typical of quick breads.

Popovers

Prep: 10 minutes **Bake:** 40 minutes
Oven: 400°F **Makes:** 6 popovers

> 1 **tablespoon shortening or nonstick cooking spray**
> 2 **beaten eggs**
> 1 **cup milk**
> 1 **tablespoon cooking oil**
> 1 **cup all-purpose flour**
> ¼ **teaspoon salt**

1. Using ½ teaspoon shortening for each cup, grease the bottoms and sides of six 6-ounce custard cups or cups of a popover pan. (Or, lightly coat cups with cooking spray.) Place the custard cups on a 15×10×1-inch baking pan; set aside.

2. In a medium bowl use a wire whisk or rotary beater to beat eggs, milk, and oil until combined. Add flour and salt; beat until smooth.

3. Fill the prepared cups half full with batter. Bake in a 400° oven about 40 minutes or until very firm.

4. Immediately after removing from oven, prick each popover to let steam escape (see photo, below). For crisper popovers, turn off the oven and return popovers to oven for 5 to 10 minutes or until desired crispness is reached. Remove popovers from cups; serve immediately.

Cinnamon Popovers: Prepare as above, except add ½ teaspoon ground cinnamon with the flour. Continue as directed. If desired, serve with honey and butter or margarine.

Nutrition Facts per plain or cinnamon popover: 159 cal., 7 g total fat (2 g sat. fat), 74 mg chol., 139 mg sodium, 18 g carbo., 1 g fiber, 6 g pro.
Daily Values: 4% vit. A, 1% vit. C, 6% calcium, 7% iron
Exchanges: 1 Starch, 1½ Fat

Pierce each popover with a fork to allow the steam to escape. Steam helps popovers rise during baking, but it will make them soggy if allowed to remain inside.

White Bread

Low Fat

Prep: 30 minutes **Rise:** 1¼ hours **Bake:** 40 minutes
Oven: 375°F **Makes:** 2 loaves (24 servings)

5¾	**to 6¼ cups all-purpose flour**
1	**package active dry yeast**
2¼	**cups milk or buttermilk**
2	**tablespoons sugar**
1	**tablespoon butter, margarine, or shortening**
1½	**teaspoons salt**

1. In a large mixing bowl combine 2½ cups of the flour and the yeast; set aside. In a medium saucepan heat and stir milk, sugar, butter, and salt just until warm (120°F to 130°F) and butter almost melts. Add milk mixture to flour mixture. Beat with an electric mixer on low to medium speed for 30 seconds, scraping sides of bowl constantly. Beat on high speed for 3 minutes. Using a wooden spoon, stir in as much of the remaining flour as you can.

2. Turn dough out onto a lightly floured surface. Knead in enough of the remaining flour to make a moderately stiff dough that is smooth and elastic (6 to 8 minutes total; see photo 1, right). Shape dough into a ball. Place in a lightly greased bowl, turning once to grease surface of dough. Cover; let rise in a warm place until double in size (45 to 60 minutes; see photos 2 and 3, right).

3. Punch dough down (see photo 4, right). Turn dough out onto a lightly floured surface; divide in half. Cover; let rest 10 minutes. Meanwhile, lightly grease two 8×4×2-inch loaf pans.

4. Shape dough halves into loaves by patting or rolling. To shape by patting, gently pat and pinch, tucking edges underneath (see photo 5, right). To shape by rolling, on a lightly floured surface roll each dough half into a 12×8-inch rectangle. Roll up each rectangle, starting from a short side (see photo 6, right). Seal seams with your fingertips.

5. Place shaped dough halves in prepared pans. Cover and let rise in a warm place until nearly double in size (30 to 40 minutes).

6. Bake in a 375° oven about 40 minutes or until bread sounds hollow when lightly tapped (if necessary, cover loosely with foil the last 10 minutes of baking to prevent overbrowning). Immediately remove bread from pans. Cool on wire racks.

Nutrition Facts per serving: 130 cal., 1 g total fat (1 g sat. fat), 3 mg chol., 163 mg sodium, 25 g carbo., 1 g fiber, 4 g pro.
Daily Values: 1% vit. A, 3% calcium, 8% iron
Exchanges: 1½ Starch

1. To knead, fold dough over and push down with the heel of your hand. Turn, fold, and push down again. Repeat this process until dough is smooth and elastic (see tip, page 133).

2. Cover the dough with a clean towel. Let it rise in a warm, draft-free place, such as the upper rack of a cool oven with a bowl of warm water placed below it on the lower rack.

3. You can tell if the dough has doubled and is ready to shape by pressing two fingers ½ inch into the dough. Remove your fingers; if indentations remain, it is ready to punch down.

4. Punch down the dough by pushing your fist into its center, then using your fingers to pull the dough edges to the center.

5. To shape dough, gently pat each half into a loaf, pinching and tucking the edges beneath the loaf. Place each shaped loaf seam side down in a prepared pan.

6. Or, roll each half of dough into a 12×8-inch rectangle. Roll up tightly, starting from a short side. Pinch seams to seal. Place each loaf seam side down in a prepared pan.

Breads

132

Whole Wheat Bread

Low Fat

Prep: 30 minutes **Rise:** 1½ hours **Bake:** 35 minutes
Oven: 375°F **Makes:** 2 loaves (24 servings)

- 3 to 3½ cups all-purpose flour
- 1 package active dry yeast
- 1¾ cups water
- ⅓ cup packed brown sugar
- 3 tablespoons butter, margarine, or shortening
- 1¼ teaspoons salt
- 2 cups whole wheat flour

1. In a large mixing bowl combine 2 cups of the all-purpose flour and the yeast; set aside. In a medium saucepan heat and stir water, brown sugar, butter, and salt just until warm (120°F to 130°F) and butter almost melts. Add water mixture to flour mixture. Beat with an electric mixer on low to medium speed for 30 seconds, scraping sides of bowl constantly. Beat on high speed for 3 minutes. Using a wooden spoon, stir in whole wheat flour and as much of the remaining all-purpose flour as you can.

2. Turn dough out onto a lightly floured surface. Knead in enough of the remaining all-purpose flour to make a moderately stiff dough that is smooth and elastic (6 to 8 minutes total; see photo 1, page 132). Shape dough into a ball. Place in a lightly greased bowl, turning once to grease surface of dough. Cover; let rise in a warm place until double in size (1 to 1½ hours; see photos 2 and 3, page 132).

3. Punch dough down (see photo 4, page 132). Turn out onto a lightly floured surface; divide in half. Cover; let rest 10 minutes. Meanwhile, lightly grease two 8×4×2-inch loaf pans.

4. Shape dough halves into loaves by patting or rolling. To shape by patting, gently pat and pinch, tucking edges underneath (see photo 5, page 132). To shape by rolling, on a lightly floured surface roll each dough half into a 12×8-inch rectangle. Roll up each rectangle, starting from a short side (see photo 6, page 132). Seal seams with your fingertips.

5. Place shaped dough halves in prepared pans. Cover and let rise in a warm place until nearly double in size (30 to 45 minutes).

6. Bake in a 375° oven for 35 to 40 minutes or until bread sounds hollow when lightly tapped (if necessary, cover loosely with foil the last 10 minutes of baking to prevent overbrowning). Immediately remove bread from pans. Cool on wire racks.

Hearty Whole Wheat Bread: Prepare as at left, except reduce whole wheat flour to 1½ cups and add ½ cup toasted wheat germ.

Nutrition Facts per serving for whole wheat or hearty variation:
102 cal., 1 g total fat (1 g sat. fat), 3 mg chol., 122 mg sodium, 19 g carbo., 2 g fiber, 4 g pro.
Daily Values: 1% vit. A, 2% calcium, 6% iron
Exchanges: 1½ Starch

Oatmeal Bread: Prepare as at left, except substitute rolled oats for the whole wheat flour. Increase all-purpose flour to 4 to 4½ cups total.

Nutrition Facts per serving: 133 cal., 2 g total fat (1 g sat. fat), 4 mg chol., 139 mg sodium, 25 g carbo., 1 g fiber, 3 g pro.
Daily Values: 1% vit. A, 0% vit. C, 1% calcium, 8% iron
Exchanges: 1½ Starch

Kneading Yeast Bread

Kneading is an important part of making yeast breads. It causes a protein structure called gluten, which gives body to the finished product, to develop.

To knead, fold the dough over and push down on it with the heels of your hands, curving your fingers over the dough. Give the dough a quarter turn and repeat folding and pushing down. Continue until you have an elastic dough with the stiffness called for in the recipe. The best guide for reaching proper stiffness is to follow the timings given in the recipe. To double-check, here's a description of each of the stiffness terms used in our recipes.

Soft dough: It is very sticky and used for breads that don't need kneading.

Moderately soft dough: It is slightly sticky and is used for rich, sweet breads. This dough is kneaded on a lightly floured surface for 3 to 5 minutes.

Moderately stiff dough: It is not sticky and is slightly firm to the touch. It usually requires 6 to 8 minutes of kneading on a lightly floured surface and is used for most nonsweet breads.

Stiff dough: It is firm to the touch and will hold its shape after about 8 to 10 minutes of kneading.

Caraway-Rye Bread

Low Fat

Prep: 40 minutes **Rise:** 1½ hours **Bake:** 30 minutes
Oven: 375°F **Makes:** 2 loaves (24 servings)

- 4 to 4½ cups bread flour
- 1 package active dry yeast
- 2 cups warm water (120°F to 130°F)
- ¼ cup packed brown sugar
- 2 tablespoons cooking oil
- 1½ teaspoons salt
- 1½ cups rye flour
- 1 tablespoon caraway seeds
  Cornmeal
- 2 teaspoons milk

1. In a large mixing bowl stir together 2¾ cups of the bread flour and the yeast. Add warm water, brown sugar, oil, and salt. Beat with an electric mixer on low to medium speed for 30 seconds, scraping sides of bowl constantly. Beat on high speed for 3 minutes. Using a wooden spoon, stir in rye flour, caraway seeds, and as much of the remaining bread flour as you can.

2. Turn dough out onto a lightly floured surface. Knead in enough remaining bread flour to make a moderately stiff dough that is smooth and elastic (6 to 8 minutes total; see photo 1, page 132). Shape dough into a ball. Place in a lightly greased bowl, turning once to grease surface of dough. Cover; let rise in a warm place until double in size (about 1 hour; see photos 2 and 3, page 132).

3. Punch dough down (see photo 4, page 132). Turn dough out onto a lightly floured surface. Divide dough in half. Cover; let rest 10 minutes. Meanwhile, lightly grease a baking sheet and sprinkle with cornmeal.

4. Shape dough by gently pulling each portion into a ball, tucking edges under. Place on prepared baking sheet. Flatten each dough round slightly to about 6 inches in diameter. (Or, shape each dough half into a loaf by patting or rolling [see photos 5 and 6, page 132].) Place in two greased 8×4×2-inch loaf pans. Cover and let rise in a warm place until nearly double (30 to 45 minutes).

5. Brush tops of loaves with milk. Bake in a 375° oven for 30 to 35 minutes or until top and sides are deep golden brown and bread sounds hollow when lightly tapped. Immediately remove from baking sheet (or pans). Cool on wire racks.

Peasant Rye Bread: Prepare as at left, except reduce rye flour to 1 cup. Stir in ¼ cup whole bran cereal and ¼ cup yellow cornmeal with rye flour.

Nutrition Facts per serving for caraway-rye or peasant rye variation: 126 cal., 2 g total fat (0 g sat. fat), 0 mg chol., 148 mg sodium, 24 g carbo., 2 g fiber, 4 g pro.
Daily Values: 1% calcium, 7% iron
Exchanges: 1½ Starch

Mixed Grain Bread

Low Fat

Prep: 30 minutes **Rise:** 1½ hours **Bake:** 30 minutes
Oven: 375°F **Makes:** 2 loaves (28 servings)

- 3½ to 4 cups all-purpose flour
- 2 packages active dry yeast
- 1½ cups milk
- ¾ cup water
- ½ cup cracked wheat
- ¼ cup cornmeal
- ¼ cup packed brown sugar
- 3 tablespoons cooking oil
- 1½ teaspoons salt
- 1½ cups whole wheat flour
- ½ cup rolled oats
  Rolled oats

1. In a large mixing bowl combine 2 cups of the all-purpose flour and the yeast; set aside. In a medium saucepan combine milk, water, cracked wheat, cornmeal, brown sugar, oil, and salt. Heat and stir over medium-low heat just until warm (120°F to 130°F). Add the milk mixture to the flour mixture. Beat with an electric mixer on low to medium speed 30 seconds, scraping sides of bowl. Beat on high speed for 3 minutes. Using a wooden spoon, stir in whole wheat flour, the ½ cup rolled oats, and as much remaining all-purpose flour as you can.

2. Turn dough out onto a lightly floured surface. Knead in enough of the remaining all-purpose flour to make a moderately stiff dough that is smooth and elastic (6 to 8 minutes total; see photo 1, page 132). Shape dough into a ball. Place in a lightly greased bowl, turning once to grease surface of dough. Cover; let rise in a warm place until double in size (about 1 hour; see photos 2 and 3, page 132).

3. Punch dough down (see photo 4, page 132). Turn out onto a lightly floured surface; divide in half. Cover; let rest 10 minutes. Meanwhile, lightly grease two 8×4×2-inch loaf pans.

4. Shape dough into loaves by patting or rolling (see photos 5 and 6, page 132). Place shaped dough halves in prepared pans. Cover; let rise in a warm place until nearly double (about 30 minutes).

5. Brush tops of loaves with water; sprinkle with additional rolled oats. Bake in a 375° oven for 30 to 35 minutes or until bread sounds hollow when lightly tapped (if necessary, cover loosely with foil the last 10 minutes of baking to prevent overbrowning). Immediately remove bread from pans. Cool on wire racks.

Nutrition Facts per serving: 130 cal., 2 g total fat (0 g sat. fat), 1 mg chol., 133 mg sodium, 24 g carbo., 2 g fiber, 4 g pro.
Daily Values: 1% vit. A, 3% calcium, 8% iron
Exchanges: 1½ Starch

Marbled Loaf

Low Fat

Prep: 50 minutes **Rise:** 1½ hours **Bake:** 30 minutes
Oven: 375°F **Makes:** 1 loaf (12 servings)

   3 **to 3½ cups all-purpose flour**
   1 **package active dry yeast**
1½ **cups milk**
   2 **tablespoons sugar**
   2 **tablespoons cooking oil**
1½ **teaspoons salt**
   2 **tablespoons dark-flavored molasses**
1¼ **cups rye or whole wheat flour**

1. In a large mixing bowl combine 2 cups of the all-purpose flour and the yeast. In a saucepan heat milk, sugar, oil, and salt just until warm (120°F to 130°F). Add milk mixture to flour mixture. Beat with an electric mixer on low to medium speed for 30 seconds, scraping bowl constantly. Beat on high speed for 3 minutes.

2. Divide batter in half. To 1 portion of batter, stir in as much of the remaining all-purpose flour as you can. Turn dough out onto a floured surface. Knead in enough of the remaining all-purpose flour to make a moderately stiff dough that is smooth and elastic (6 to 8 minutes total; see photo 1, page 132). Shape into a ball. Place dough in a greased bowl, turning once to grease surface of dough.

3. To other portion of batter stir in molasses, rye flour, and as much of the remaining all-purpose flour as you can. Turn out onto a lightly floured surface. Knead in enough remaining all-purpose flour to make a moderately stiff dough that is smooth and elastic (6 to 8 minutes total; see photo 1, page 132). Shape into a ball. Place dough in a greased bowl, turning once. Cover both dough portions; let rise in a warm place until double (1 to 1¼ hours; see photos 2 and 3, page 132).

4. Punch both portions down (see photo 4, page 132). Cover; let rest 10 minutes. Meanwhile, lightly grease an 8×4×2-inch loaf pan; set aside.

5. On a lightly floured surface roll each dough portion into a 12×8-inch rectangle. Place dark dough on top of light dough. Roll up, starting from a short side (see photo 6, page 132). Place seam side down in prepared pan. Cover; let rise until nearly double (30 to 40 minutes).

6. Bake in a 375° oven for 30 to 35 minutes or until bread sounds hollow when lightly tapped (if necessary, cover loosely with foil the last 10 minutes of baking to prevent overbrowning). Immediately remove from pan. Cool on a wire rack.

Nutrition Facts per serving: 205 cal., 3 g total fat (1 g sat. fat), 2 mg chol., 308 mg sodium, 38 g carbo., 3 g fiber, 5 g pro.
Daily Values: 1% vit. A, 1% vit. C, 5% calcium, 11% iron
Exchanges: 2½ Starch

Marbled Loaf

Sourdough Starter

Prep: 10 minutes **Stand:** 5 to 10 days
Makes: about 2½ cups

>   1 **package active dry yeast**
>   2½ **cups warm water (105°F to 115°F)**
>   2 **cups all-purpose flour**
>   1 **tablespoon sugar or honey**

1. Dissolve yeast in ½ cup of the warm water. Stir in the remaining warm water, flour, and sugar. Using a wooden spoon, beat until smooth. Cover with 100-percent-cotton cheesecloth. Let stand at room temperature (75°F to 85°F) for 5 to 10 days or until the mixture has a fermented aroma and the vigorous bubbling stops, stirring two or three times a day. (Fermentation time depends on room temperature; a warmer room will hasten the fermentation process.)

2. To store, transfer Sourdough Starter to a 1-quart plastic container. Cover and chill.

3. To use, stir starter. Measure amount of cold starter called for in recipe; bring to room temperature. Replenish starter after each use by stirring ¾ cup all-purpose flour, ¾ cup water, and 1 teaspoon sugar or honey into remaining starter for each 1 cup removed. Cover with cheesecloth; let stand at room temperature 1 day or until bubbly. Cover with lid; chill for later use. If starter is not used within 10 days, stir in 1 teaspoon sugar or honey. Continue to add 1 teaspoon sugar or honey every 10 days unless starter is replenished.

How to Make Bread Without a Mixer

All of the yeast breads in this cookbook are made using an electric mixer. If you don't have an electric mixer or want a more "hands-on" approach, you can beat the dough by hand. Here's how:

Prepare the dough as directed, except when the recipe says to beat the mixture using an electric mixer, use a wooden spoon instead. When mixing by hand, be sure to beat the mixture until it is smooth (it may take longer than the 3 minutes given in most recipes). Also, note that with hand-mixed dough, you most likely will need to knead the maximum amount of flour into the dough.

Sourdough Bread

Low Fat

Prep: 45 minutes **Rise:** 1¼ hours **Bake:** 30 minutes
Oven: 375°F **Makes:** 2 loaves (24 servings)

>   1 **cup Sourdough Starter (left)**
>   5½ **to 6 cups all-purpose flour**
>   1 **package active dry yeast**
>   1½ **cups water**
>   3 **tablespoons sugar**
>   3 **tablespoons butter or margarine**
>   1½ **teaspoons salt**
>   ½ **teaspoon baking soda**

1. Measure Sourdough Starter; let stand at room temperature 30 minutes. Combine 2½ cups of the flour and the yeast; set aside. Heat and stir water, sugar, butter, and salt just until warm (120°F to 130°F) and butter almost melts; add to the flour mixture. Add Sourdough Starter. Beat with an electric mixer on low speed 30 seconds, scraping bowl. Beat on high speed for 3 minutes. Combine 2½ cups of the remaining flour and the baking soda; add to yeast mixture. Stir until combined. Stir in as much of the remaining flour as you can.

2. Turn dough out onto a lightly floured surface. Knead in enough remaining flour to make a moderately stiff dough (6 to 8 minutes total; see photo 1, page 132). Shape dough into a ball. Place in a greased bowl; turn once. Cover; let rise in a warm place until double (45 to 60 minutes; see photos 2 and 3, page 132). Punch dough down (see photo 4, page 132). Turn out onto a floured surface; divide in half. Cover; let rest 10 minutes. Meanwhile, lightly grease two baking sheets.

3. Shape dough by gently pulling each portion into a ball, tucking edges underneath. Place on prepared baking sheets. Flatten each dough round slightly to about 6 inches in diameter. Using a sharp knife, make crisscross slashes across tops of loaves. Cover; let rise in a warm place until nearly double (about 30 minutes).

4. Bake in a 375° oven for 30 to 35 minutes or until bread sounds hollow when lightly tapped (if necessary, cover loosely with foil the last 10 minutes of baking to prevent overbrowning). Immediately remove bread from baking sheets. Cool on wire racks.

Nutrition Facts per serving: 131 cal., 2 g total fat (1 g sat. fat), 4 mg chol., 189 mg sodium, 25 g carbo., 1 g fiber, 3 g pro.
Daily Values: 1% vit. A, 1% calcium, 8% iron
Exchanges: 1½ Starch

Artisan-Style French Bread

Bread bakers with some experience will find this delicious bread well worth the extra effort. Ounce measurements are included to help ensure perfect loaves. (See photo, page 113.)

No Fat

Prep: 25 minutes **Stand:** 8 to 24 hours **Rest:** 50 minutes
Rise: 2½ hours **Bake:** 15 minutes **Oven:** 450°F
Makes: 2 loaves (32 servings)

- 1 cup (8 ounces) warm water (105°F to 115°F)
- ¼ teaspoon active dry yeast
- 1 cup (4¾ ounces) bread flour
- 1 tablespoon (¼ ounce) rye flour
- ¾ cup (6 ounces) warm water (105°F to 115°F)
- 1 cup (8 ounces) warm water (105°F to 115°F)
- 3 to 3¼ cups (14¼ to 15½ ounces) bread flour
- 2 teaspoons salt
- ½ teaspoon active dry yeast
  Spray bottle filled with water

1. For the pre-ferment mixture, combine the 1 cup warm water and the ¼ teaspoon yeast; set aside for 5 minutes. Meanwhile, in a medium bowl combine the 1 cup bread flour and the rye flour.

2. Stir yeast mixture (make sure yeast has dissolved); add 1 tablespoon of the yeast mixture to the flour mixture. Discard the remaining yeast mixture. Add the ¾ cup warm water to the flour mixture, stirring until combined. Cover the pre-ferment mixture with plastic wrap and let stand at room temperature for 8 to 24 hours.

3. Add the 1 cup warm water to the pre-ferment mixture and stir until combined. In a large bowl stir together 3 cups of the bread flour, the salt, and the ½ teaspoon yeast; pour the pre-ferment mixture into the flour mixture. Using a wooden spoon, stir until combined.

4. Turn dough out onto a lightly floured surface. Knead dough only a couple of strokes (dough will be *very* sticky). Cover; let rest 20 minutes.

5. Place dough in the large mixing bowl of a freestanding electric mixer. Use the dough hook attachment to knead the dough on medium speed for 1½ minutes (see photo 1, right). (Or knead dough by hand for 3 to 5 minutes more. If dough is too sticky to work with, knead in up to ¼ cup more bread flour—dough will be wetter and softer than you may be used to.) Dough should be

smooth, but still sticky, after kneading. Place dough in a large, ungreased bowl. Cover bowl (not surface of dough) with plastic wrap; let rise until nearly double in size (2 to 2½ hours).

6. Turn dough out onto a heavily floured surface; divide dough in half (handle dough very gently, trying not to disturb air holes). Using floured hands, gently form each dough half into a small rectangular shape. Cover each with a large bowl or plastic wrap; let rest for 30 minutes.

7. Using floured hands, gently pull each piece of dough into a 12-inch baguette or a 6-inch round loaf, handling dough gently so not to disturb big bubbles inside. For baguettes, gently slide the shaped dough onto pieces of parchment paper; place parchment paper on baguette pans (see photo 2, below). For round loaves, gently place shaped dough into two greased 8×1½-inch round baking pans. Cover; let rise until double in size (for 30 to 45 minutes).

8. With a very sharp knife or clean razor blade, make 3 or 4 diagonal slashes on top of each baguette or loaf. Place pans in a 450° oven. Working quickly, mist the inside of the oven, including the bread, heavily with water. Bake about 15 minutes or until deep, golden brown and bread sounds hollow when lightly tapped (or until the internal temperature reaches 200°F). Immediately remove from pans. Cool on wire racks.

Nutrition Facts per serving: 63 cal., 0 g total fat (0 g sat. fat), 0 mg chol., 146 mg sodium, 13 g carbo., 0 g fiber, 2 g pro.
Daily Values: 4% iron
Exchanges: 1 Starch

1. Because the dough is so soft and sticky, it is much easier to let the dough hook attachment of your mixer do the kneading. Run the mixer for the 1½ minutes only—no longer.

2. Placing the shaped dough on parchment paper makes it easier to transfer to the special baguette pan. Handle the dough as little as possible so you don't disturb the air bubbles.

Potato Rolls `Best Loved`

`Low Fat`

Prep: 45 minutes **Rise:** 1½ hours **Bake:** 10 minutes
Oven: 400°F **Makes:** 24 rolls

> 4 to 4½ cups all-purpose flour
> 1 package active dry yeast
> 1 cup milk
> ¼ cup water
> ¼ cup sugar
> ¼ cup shortening
> 1½ teaspoons salt
> 1 beaten egg
> ½ cup mashed potato*

1. Combine 2 cups of the flour and the yeast. Heat and stir milk, water, sugar, shortening, and salt just until warm (120°F to 130°F) and shortening almost melts; add to flour mixture along with egg and mashed potato. Beat with an electric mixer on low speed 30 seconds, scraping bowl. Beat on high speed 3 minutes. Stir in as much of the remaining flour as you can.

2. Turn dough out onto a lightly floured surface. Knead in enough of the remaining flour to make a moderately stiff dough that is smooth and elastic (6 to 8 minutes total; see photo 1, page 132). Shape dough into a ball. Place in a lightly greased bowl, turning once to grease surface. Cover; let rise in a warm place until double (about 1 hour; see photos 2 and 3, page 132).

3. Punch dough down (see photo 4, page 132). Turn dough out onto a lightly floured surface. Divide dough in half. Cover; let rest for 10 minutes. Meanwhile, lightly grease a baking sheet. Divide each dough portion into 12 pieces. Gently pull each piece into a ball, tucking edges under to make smooth tops. Place on the prepared baking sheet. Cover; let rise in a warm place until nearly double (35 to 45 minutes).

4. Bake in a 400° oven for 10 to 12 minutes or until golden brown. Immediately remove rolls from baking sheet. Cool on wire racks.

***Note:** Peel and quarter 1 medium potato. Cook, covered, in a small amount of boiling salted water for 20 to 25 minutes or until tender; drain. Mash with a potato masher or beat with an electric mixer on low speed. Measure ½ cup.

Nutrition Facts per roll: 106 cal., 3 g total fat (1 g sat. fat), 10 mg chol., 154 mg sodium, 17 g carbo., 1 g fiber, 3 g pro.
Daily Values: 1% vit. A, 1% vit. C, 2% calcium, 6% iron
Exchanges: 1 Starch, ½ Fat

Focaccia

If you don't have a bread stone, shape the dough into a circle on a greased, unheated baking sheet and bake the focaccia on that sheet.

`Low Fat`

Prep: 30 minutes **Stand:** Overnight **Rise:** 1 hour
Rest: 30 minutes **Bake:** 15 minutes **Oven:** 475°F
Makes: 12 servings

> 4 to 4¼ cups all-purpose flour
> ½ cup warm water (105°F to 115°F)
> 1 teaspoon active dry yeast
> 1 cup warm water (105°F to 115°F)
> 2 teaspoons salt
> 1 tablespoon olive oil
> Coarse salt

1. For the sponge, in a bowl combine ½ cup of the flour, the ½ cup warm water, and the yeast. Beat with a wooden spoon until smooth. Cover loosely with plastic wrap. Let sponge stand overnight at room temperature to ferment.

2. Gradually stir in the 1 cup warm water, the 2 teaspoons salt, and just enough of the remaining flour to make a dough that pulls away from the sides of the bowl. Turn dough out onto a lightly floured surface. Knead in enough of the remaining flour to make a stiff dough that is smooth and elastic (8 to 10 minutes total; see photo 1, page 132). Place dough in a lightly greased bowl, turning once. Cover; let rise in a warm place until double (about 1 hour).

3. Turn dough out onto a well-floured baking sheet. Place an extra large bowl upside down over the dough to cover it; let rest 30 minutes. Meanwhile, preheat oven and a bread stone to 475°. Shape dough on the baking sheet into a circle about 11 inches in diameter by pulling and pressing with your fingertips. (Don't stretch dough too roughly or it will deflate; you want to keep air bubbles intact.)

4. Make ½-inch-deep indentations every 2 inches in dough (see photo, page 139). Brush dough with olive oil; sprinkle lightly with coarse salt. Carefully slide focaccia from floured baking sheet to the preheated bread stone.

5. Bake for 15 to 20 minutes or until golden, checking after 8 minutes and popping any large air bubbles with a sharp knife. Remove foccacia from bread stone with large spatulas. Cool on a wire rack about 15 minutes. Serve warm.

Focaccia

Herbed Focaccia: Prepare as on page 138, except add 2 teaspoons snipped fresh rosemary with the warm water, salt, and flour in step 2.

Nutrition Facts per serving for plain or herbed variation:
151 cal., 1 g total fat (0 g sat. fat), 0 mg chol., 583 mg sodium, 29 g carbo., 1 g fiber, 4 g pro.
Daily Values: 1% calcium, 10% iron
Exchanges: 2 Starch

Dust your fingers lightly with flour and press them ½ inch deep into the dough to make indentations. Cover dough round with indentations, spacing them about 2 inches apart.

Brioche

Prep: 1 hour **Rise:** 2¾ hours **Chill:** 6 hours
Bake: 15 minutes **Oven:** 375°F **Makes:** 24 rolls

  1 **package active dry yeast**
  ½ **cup butter or margarine**
  ⅓ **cup sugar**
  4 **cups all-purpose flour**
  ½ **cup milk**
  4 **eggs**

1. Dissolve yeast in ¼ cup warm *water* (105°F to 115°F). Let stand 5 to 10 minutes to soften. In a large mixing bowl beat butter, sugar, and ¾ tea-spoon *salt* with an electric mixer until fluffy. Add 1 cup of the flour and the milk. Separate 1 egg. Add the yolk and remaining whole eggs to beaten mixture (refrigerate egg white to use later). Add softened yeast; beat well. Stir in remaining flour until smooth. Place in a greased bowl. Cover; let rise in a warm place until double (about 2 hours). Chill dough 6 hours. (Or omit 2-hour rising time; chill dough 12 to 24 hours.)

2. Grease twenty-four 2½-inch muffin cups; set aside. Stir dough down. Turn dough out onto a lightly floured surface. Divide dough into 4 portions; set 1 portion aside. Divide each of the remaining 3 portions into 8 pieces (24 pieces total).

3. To shape, pull each piece into a ball, tucking edges under to make smooth tops. Place in prepared muffin cups, smooth sides up. Divide reserved dough portion into 24 pieces; shape into balls. With a floured finger, make an indentation in each large ball. Press a small ball into each indentation. Combine reserved egg white and 1 tablespoon *water;* brush over rolls. Cover; let rise in a warm place until double (45 to 55 minutes).

4. Bake in a 375° oven about 15 minutes or until golden, brushing again with egg white mixture after 7 minutes. Remove from pans. Cool on wire racks.

Nutrition Facts per roll: 138 cal., 5 g total fat (3 g sat. fat), 47 mg chol., 128 mg sodium, 19 g carbo., 1 g fiber, 4 g pro.
Daily Values: 4% vit. A, 1% calcium, 6% iron
Exchanges: 1 Starch, 1 Fat

Dinner Rolls

For a soft and shiny crust, brush the baked rolls with butter when you take them out of the oven. If you prefer a glossy, crisp crust, brush the shaped dough with milk or a beaten egg before baking.

Low Fat

Prep: 45 minutes **Rise:** 1½ hours **Bake:** 15 minutes
Oven: 375°F **Makes:** 24 to 32 rolls

- 3¼ to 3¾ cups all-purpose flour
- 1 package active dry yeast
- 1 cup milk
- ¼ cup sugar
- ⅓ cup butter, margarine, or shortening
- 1 beaten egg

1. Stir together 1¼ cups of the flour and the yeast. In a medium saucepan heat and stir milk, sugar, butter, and ¾ teaspoon *salt* just until warm (120°F to 130°F) and butter almost melts; add to flour mixture along with egg. Beat with an electric mixer on low speed 30 seconds, scraping bowl constantly. Beat on high speed 3 minutes. Using a wooden spoon, stir in as much remaining flour as you can.

2. Turn dough out onto a lightly floured surface. Knead in enough remaining flour to make a moderately stiff dough that is smooth and elastic (6 to 8 minutes total; see photo 1, page 132). Shape dough into a ball. Place in a greased bowl; turn once. Cover; let rise in a warm place until double (about 1 hour; see photos 2 and 3, page 132).

3. Punch dough down (see photo 4, page 132). Turn dough out onto a lightly floured surface. Divide dough in half. Cover; let rest for 10 minutes. Meanwhile, depending on what shape of roll you want to make (see photos, page 141), lightly grease a 13×9×2-inch baking pan, baking sheets, or muffin cups.

4. For dinner rolls, shape the dough into 24 balls. Place balls in prepared baking pan. (Or, shape dough into butterhorns, rosettes, Parker House rolls, or cloverleaf rolls. Place on prepared baking sheets or muffins cups.) Cover and let rise in a warm place until nearly double in size (about 30 minutes).

5. Bake in a 375° oven for 15 to 18 minutes or until rolls sound hollow when lightly tapped. Immediately remove from pan. Cool on wire racks.

Whole Wheat Dinner Rolls: Prepare as above, except substitute 1 cup whole wheat flour for 1 cup of the all-purpose flour that is stirred in at the end of step 1.

Herb-Onion Dinner Rolls: Prepare as at left, except add 1 tablespoon dried minced onion and ½ teaspoon dried basil, oregano, or Italian seasoning, crushed, to milk mixture.

Rye-Caraway Dinner Rolls: Prepare as at left, except add 2 teaspoons caraway seeds to milk mixture and substitute 1 cup rye flour for 1 cup of all-purpose flour that is stirred in at end of step 1.

Bread Machine Dinner Rolls: For a bread machine with 2-pound capacity, use ingredients at left, except use 3½ cups all-purpose flour. Add ingredients to the machine according to the manufacturer's directions. Select the dough cycle. Watch dough carefully during the first kneading. If dough looks too dry and crumbly, add milk, 1 teaspoon at a time, until one smooth ball forms. When cycle is complete, remove dough from machine. Punch down. Cover and let rest 10 minutes. Continue with step 4.

Nutrition Facts per roll for plain, whole wheat, herb-onion, rye-caraway, and bread machine variations: 97 cal., 3 g total fat (2 g sat. fat). 17 mg chol., 108 mg sodium, 15 g carbo., 0 g fiber, 2 g pro.
Daily Values: 3% vit. A, 2% calcium, 4% iron
Exchanges: 1 Starch, ½ Fat

Batter Dinner Rolls: Prepare as at left, except reduce the all-purpose flour to a total of 3 cups. Spoon batter into 18 greased 2½-inch muffin cups, filling each half full. Cover and let rise in a warm place until nearly double (about 45 minutes). Brush roll tops with milk, and, if desired, sprinkle with poppy seeds or sesame seeds. Bake in a 375° oven about 15 minutes or until golden. Makes 18 rolls.

Nutrition Facts per roll: 123 cal., 4 g total fat (3 g sat. fat), 22 g chol., 144 mg sodium, 18 g carbo., 1 g fiber, 3 g pro.
Daily Values: 4% vit. A, 2% calcium, 5% iron
Exchanges: 1 Starch, 1 Fat

Hamburger or Frankfurter Buns: Prepare as at left, except divide dough into 10 pieces. Cover; let rest 10 minutes. For hamburger buns, shape each dough portion into a circle, tucking edges under. Place on a greased baking sheet. Using your fingers, slightly flatten circles to 4 inches in diameter. For frankfurter buns, shape each dough portion into a roll about 6 inches long, tapering the ends. Place on a greased baking sheet. Bake as directed. Makes 10 buns.

Nutrition Facts per bun: 233 cal., 8 g total fat (5 g sat. fat), 40 mg chol., 259 mg sodium, 35 g carbo., 1 g fiber, 6 g pro.
Daily Values: 6% vit. A, 4% calcium, 10% iron
Exchanges: 2½ Starch, ½ Fat

Butterhorns: On a lightly floured surface, roll each portion of dough into a 12-inch circle; brush with butter or margarine. Cut each dough circle into

12 wedges. To shape, begin at the wide end of each wedge and loosely roll toward the point. Place point side down, 2 to 3 inches apart, on prepared baking sheets.

Rosettes: Divide each portion of dough into 16 pieces. On a lightly floured surface, roll each piece into a 12-inch-long rope. Tie in a loose

knot, leaving 2 long ends. Tuck top end under knot and bottom end into top center of the knot. Place 2 to 3 inches apart on prepared baking sheets.

Parker House Rolls: On a lightly floured surface, roll each portion of dough until ¼ inch thick. Cut dough with a floured 2½-inch round cutter. Brush with melted butter or margarine. Using the dull edge of a table knife, make an off-center

crease in each round. Fold each round along crease. Press folded edge firmly. Place rolls, with large half up, 2 to 3 inches apart on prepared baking sheets.

Cloverleaf Rolls: Divide each portion of dough

into 36 pieces. Shape each piece into a ball, pulling edges under to make a smooth top. Place 3 balls in each prepared muffin cup, smooth sides up.

Make-ahead directions: Prepare as on page 140 through step 4, except do not let rise. Cover shaped rolls loosely with plastic wrap, leaving room for dough to rise. Chill for 2 to 24 hours. Uncover; let stand at room temperature for 30 minutes. Bake as directed.

Dill Batter Bread

This speedy yeast bread rises just once and requires no kneading.

Prep: 15 minutes **Rise:** 50 minutes **Bake:** 25 minutes
Oven: 375°F **Makes:** 1 loaf (8 servings)

- **2 cups all-purpose flour**
- **1 package active dry yeast**
- **½ cup water**
- **½ cup cream-style cottage cheese**
- **1 tablespoon sugar**
- **1 tablespoon dillseeds or caraway seeds**
- **1 tablespoon butter or margarine**
- **1 teaspoon dried minced onion**
- **1 teaspoon salt**
- **1 beaten egg**
- **½ cup toasted wheat germ**

1. Grease a 9×1½-inch round baking pan or a 1-quart casserole; set aside. In a large mixing bowl combine 1 cup of the flour and the yeast; set aside.

2. In a medium saucepan heat and stir water, cottage cheese, sugar, dillseeds, butter, dried onion, and salt just until warm (120°F to 130°F) and butter almost melts. Add cottage cheese mixture to flour mixture along with the egg. Beat with an electric mixer on low to medium speed for 30 seconds, scraping sides of bowl constantly. Beat on high speed for 3 minutes. Using a wooden spoon, stir in the wheat germ and the remaining flour (batter will be stiff).

3. Spoon batter into the prepared pan or casserole, spreading to edges. Cover and let rise in a warm place until double in size (50 to 60 minutes).

4. Bake in a 375° oven for 25 to 30 minutes or until golden. Immediately remove from pan or casserole. Serve warm, or cool on a wire rack.

Nutrition Facts per serving: 185 cal., 4 g total fat (2 g sat. fat), 33 mg chol., 369 mg sodium, 30 g carbo., 2 g fiber, 8 g pro.
Daily Values: 3% vit. A, 1% vit. C, 3% calcium, 13% iron
Exchanges: 2 Starch, ½ Fat

For a Quick Rise

The bread recipes in this chapter were tested with active dry yeast. You can, however, prepare these recipes (except Sourdough Starter and Artisan-Style French Bread) using quick-rising active dry yeast. Follow the recipe directions, omitting the first rising time (just let the bread rest for 10 minutes). The dough should rise in about two-thirds the time given for the second rising.

Egg Bread

Low Fat

Prep: 30 minutes **Rise:** 1½ hours **Bake:** 25 minutes
Oven: 375°F **Makes:** 2 loaves (28 servings)

  4¾ to 5¼ cups all-purpose flour
  1 package active dry yeast
1⅓ cups milk
  3 tablespoons sugar
  3 tablespoons butter or margarine
  ½ teaspoon salt
  2 eggs

1. In a large mixing bowl stir together 2 cups of the flour and the yeast; set aside. In a medium saucepan heat and stir milk, sugar, butter, and salt just until warm (120°F to 130°F) and butter almost melts. Add milk mixture to flour mixture along with eggs. Beat with an electric mixer on low to medium speed for 30 seconds, scraping sides of bowl constantly. Beat on high speed for 3 minutes. Using a wooden spoon, stir in as much of the remaining flour as you can.

2. Turn dough out onto a lightly floured surface. Knead in enough of the remaining flour to make a moderately stiff dough that is smooth and elastic (6 to 8 minutes total; see photo 1, page 132). Shape dough into a ball. Place in a lightly greased bowl, turning once to grease surface of dough. Cover; let rise in a warm place until double in size (about 1 hour; see photos 2 and 3, page 132).

3. Punch dough down (see photo 4, page 132). Turn out onto a lightly floured surface; divide in half. Cover; let rest 10 minutes. Meanwhile, lightly grease two 8×4×2-inch loaf pans.

4. Shape dough into loaves by patting or rolling (see photos 5 and 6, page 132). Place shaped dough in prepared pans. Cover; let rise in a warm place until nearly double (about 30 minutes).

5. Bake in a 375° oven for 25 to 30 minutes or until bread sounds hollow when lightly tapped (if necessary, cover loosely with foil the last 10 minutes of baking to prevent overbrowning). Immediately remove bread from pans. Cool on wire racks.

Challah: Prepare dough as above, except substitute 1¼ cups water for the milk and *pareve margarine* for butter. Prepare as directed through step 2. Punch dough down; divide in thirds. Cover; let rest 10 minutes. Roll each third into an 18-inch rope. Place ropes on a large baking sheet 1 inch apart and braid. Cover; let rise until nearly double (about 30 minutes). Brush braid with 1 beaten egg yolk and sprinkle with 2 teaspoons poppy seeds. Bake as directed.

Nutrition Facts per serving for egg bread or challah variation: 106 cal., 2 g total fat (1 g sat. fat), 20 mg chol., 66 mg sodium, 18 g carbo., 1 g fiber, 3 g pro.
Daily Values: 2% vit. A, 2% calcium, 6% iron
Exchanges: 1 Starch, ½ Fat

Cinnamon Swirl Bread: Prepare dough as at left, except, on a lightly floured surface roll each portion of dough into a 12×7-inch rectangle. Brush lightly with water. Combine ½ cup sugar and 2 teaspoons ground cinnamon; sprinkle half of the sugar-cinnamon mixture over each rectangle. Roll up, starting from a short side. Pinch seam and ends to seal. Place seam side down in prepared pans. Let rise and bake as directed. If desired, drizzle warm loaves with 1 recipe Powdered Sugar Icing (page 172).

Nutrition Facts per serving: 119 cal., 2 g total fat (1 g sat. fat), 20 mg chol., 66 mg sodium, 22 g carbo., 1 g fiber, 3 g pro.
Daily Values: 2% vit. A, 2% calcium, 6% iron
Exchanges: 1 Starch, ½ Fat

English Muffin Bread

This no-knead bread makes terrific toast. Serve it for breakfast with butter.

Low Fat

Prep: 20 minutes **Rise:** 45 minutes **Bake:** 25 minutes
Oven: 400°F **Makes:** 2 loaves (32 servings)

      Cornmeal
  6 cups all-purpose flour
  2 packages active dry yeast
  ¼ teaspoon baking soda
  2 cups milk
  ½ cup water
  1 tablespoon sugar
  1 teaspoon salt

1. Grease two 8×4×2-inch loaf pans. Lightly sprinkle pans with enough cornmeal to coat bottom and sides; set pans aside.

2. In a large mixing bowl combine 3 cups of the flour, the yeast, and baking soda; set aside. In a medium saucepan heat and stir milk, water, sugar, and salt just until warm (120°F to 130°F). Using a wooden spoon, stir milk mixture into flour mixture. Stir in remaining flour.

3. Divide dough in half. Place dough in prepared pans. Sprinkle tops with cornmeal. Cover and let rise in a warm place until double in size (about 45 minutes).

4. Bake in a 400° oven about 25 minutes or until golden brown. Immediately remove bread from pans. Cool on wire racks.

Nutrition Facts per serving: 90 cal., 1 g total fat (0 g sat. fat), 1 mg chol., 91 mg sodium, 18 g carbo., 1 g fiber, 3 g pro.
Daily Values: 1% vit. A, 2% calcium, 6% iron
Exchanges: 1 Starch

English Muffin Bread

Browning Bread

If you notice your baking bread starting to get too brown, cover it with aluminum foil to reflect some of the dry heat away from the bread's surface. This prevents overbrowning while allowing the inside to finish cooking. Breads containing some sugar and butter are most likely to need this preventive measure.

Boston Brown Bread

This full-flavored bread, leavened with baking powder and baking soda, gets steamed for about 2 hours.

Low Fat

Prep: 15 minutes **Cook:** 2 hours **Makes:** 1 loaf (14 servings)

- ½ cup cornmeal
- ½ cup whole wheat flour
- ½ cup rye flour
- ½ teaspoon baking powder
- ¼ teaspoon baking soda
- ¼ teaspoon salt
- 1 cup buttermilk or sour milk (see tip, page 157)
- ⅓ cup mild-flavored molasses
- 2 tablespoons brown sugar
- 1 tablespoon cooking oil
- ⅓ cup raisins or chopped walnuts, toasted (see tip, page 224)
- Cream cheese, softened (optional)

1. Grease a 7½×3½×2-inch loaf pan well; set aside. In a large bowl combine cornmeal, whole wheat flour, rye flour, baking powder, baking soda, and salt; set aside.

2. In another bowl combine buttermilk, molasses, brown sugar, and oil. Gradually add buttermilk mixture to flour mixture, stirring just until combined. Stir in raisins. Pour into prepared pan. Grease a piece of foil. Place the foil, greased side down, over the loaf pan. Press the foil around the edges to seal.

3. Place loaf pan on a rack in a Dutch oven. Pour hot water into the Dutch oven around loaf pan until water comes up 1 inch on loaf pan. Bring the water to boiling. Reduce heat and simmer, covered, for 2 to 2¼ hours or until a wooden toothpick inserted near the center comes out clean. Add additional boiling water to the Dutch oven as needed.

4. Remove loaf pan from Dutch oven; let stand 10 minutes. Remove bread from pan. If desired, serve warm with cream cheese.

Nutrition Facts per serving: 96 cal., 1 g total fat (0 g sat. fat), 1 mg chol., 101 mg sodium, 20 g carbo., 2 g fiber, 2 g pro.
Daily Values: 1% vit. A, 5% calcium, 5% iron
Exchanges: 1 Starch, ½ Other Carbo.

Orange Bowknots [Best Loved]

Prep: 45 minutes **Rise:** 1½ hours **Bake:** 12 minutes
Oven: 400°F **Makes:** 24 rolls

- 5¼ to 5¾ **cups all-purpose flour**
- 1 **package active dry yeast**
- 1¼ **cups milk**
- ½ **cup butter, margarine, or shortening**
- ⅓ **cup sugar**
- 2 **eggs**
- 2 **tablespoons finely shredded orange peel**
- ¼ **cup orange juice**
- 1 **recipe Orange Icing**

1. Combine 2 cups of the flour and the yeast; set aside. Heat and stir the milk, butter, sugar, and ½ teaspoon *salt* just until warm (120°F to 130°F) and butter almost melts; add to flour mixture along with eggs. Beat with an electric mixer on low to medium speed 30 seconds, scraping bowl. Beat on high speed for 3 minutes. Using a wooden spoon, stir in the orange peel, orange juice, and as much of the remaining flour as you can.

2. Turn dough out onto a lightly floured surface. Knead in enough remaining flour to make a moderately soft dough that is smooth and elastic (3 to 5 minutes total; see photo 1, page 132). Shape dough into a ball. Place dough in a lightly greased bowl, turning once. Cover; let rise in a warm place until double in size (about 1 hour; see photos 2 and 3, page 132).

3. Punch dough down (see photo 4, page 132). Turn out onto a lightly floured surface. Divide in half. Cover and let rest 10 minutes. Meanwhile, lightly grease 2 baking sheets; set aside.

4. Roll each portion of the dough into a 12×7-inch rectangle. Cut each rectangle into twelve 7-inch-long strips. Tie each strip loosely in a knot. Arrange knots 2 inches apart on prepared baking sheets. Cover; let rise in a warm place until nearly double (about 30 minutes).

5. Bake in a 400° oven about 12 minutes or until golden. Immediately remove from baking sheets. Cool on wire racks. Drizzle with Orange Icing.

Orange Icing: In a bowl combine 1 cup sifted powdered sugar and 1 teaspoon finely shredded orange peel. Stir in enough orange juice (1 to 2 tablespoons) to reach drizzling consistency.

Nutrition Facts per roll: 177 cal., 5 g total fat (3 g sat. fat), 30 mg chol., 102 mg sodium, 29 g carbo., 1 g fiber, 4 g pro.
Daily Values: 4% vit. A, 4% vit. C, 2% calcium, 8% iron
Exchanges: 1 Starch, 1 Other Carbo., 1 Fat

Orange Bowknots

Cinnamon Rolls

Prep: 45 minutes **Rise:** 1 hour **Chill:** 2 to 24 hours
Stand: 30 minutes **Bake:** 20 minutes **Oven:** 375°F
Makes: 24 rolls

- 4¾ to 5¼ **cups all-purpose four**
- 1 **package active dry yeast**
- 1 **cup milk**
- ⅓ **cup butter**
- ⅓ **cup granulated sugar**
- ½ **teaspoon salt**
- 3 **eggs**
- ¾ **cup packed brown sugar**
- ¼ **cup all-purpose flour**
- 1 **tablespoon ground cinnamon**
- ⅓ **cup butter or margarine**
- ½ **cup golden raisins (optional)**
- ½ **cup chopped pecans (optional)**
- 1 **tablespoon half-and-half or light cream**
- 1 **recipe Vanilla Glaze**

1. In a large mixing bowl combine 2¼ cups of the flour and the yeast. In a saucepan heat and stir milk, ⅓ cup butter, granulated sugar, and salt just until warm (120°F to 130°F) and butter almost melts; add to flour mixture along with eggs. Beat with electric mixer on low speed for 30 seconds, scraping bowl. Beat on high speed 3 minutes. Stir in as much of the remaining flour as you can.

2. Turn dough out onto a lightly floured surface. Knead in enough of the remaining flour to make a moderately soft dough that is smooth and elastic (3 to 5 minutes total; see photo 1, page 132). Shape dough into a ball. Place in a greased bowl; turn once. Cover; let rise in a warm place until double (about 1 hour; see photos 2 and 3, page 132).

3. Punch dough down (see photo 4, page 132). Turn out onto a lightly floured surface. Divide in half. Cover; let rest for 10 minutes. Meanwhile, lightly grease two 9×1½-inch round baking pans or 2 baking sheets; set aside. For filling, stir together brown sugar, the ¼ cup flour, and cinnamon; cut in ⅓ cup butter until the mixture resembles coarse crumbs.

4. Roll each half of dough into a 12×8-inch rectangle. Sprinkle filling over dough rectangles. If desired, sprinkle with raisins and/or pecans. Roll up each rectangle starting from a long side. Seal seams. Slice each roll into 12 pieces. Place cut sides down in prepared pans or baking sheets.

5. Cover dough loosely with plastic wrap, leaving room for rolls to rise. Chill for 2 to 24 hours. Uncover; let stand at room temperature 30 minutes. (Or, to bake rolls right away, don't chill the dough. Instead, cover loosely; let dough rise in a warm place until nearly double, about 30 minutes.)

6. Break any surface bubbles with a greased toothpick. Brush dough with half-and-half. Bake in a 375° oven for 20 to 25 minutes or until light brown (if necessary, cover rolls with foil the last 5 to 10 minutes of baking to prevent overbrowning). Remove from oven. Brush again with half-and-half. Cool for 1 minute. Carefully invert rolls onto a wire rack. Cool slightly. Invert again onto a serving platter. Drizzle with Vanilla Glaze. Serve warm.

Apple-Cinnamon Rolls: Prepare as above, except substitute 1 cup finely chopped, peeled apple for the raisins and nuts.

Vanilla Glaze: In a small bowl stir together 1¼ cups sifted powdered sugar, 1 teaspoon light-colored corn syrup, and ½ teaspoon vanilla. Add enough half-and-half or light cream (1 to 2 tablespoons) to reach drizzling consistency.

Nutrition Facts per roll for plain or apple variation: 217 cal., 7 g total fat (4 g sat. fat), 42 mg chol., 120 mg sodium, 36 g carbo., 1 g fiber, 4 g pro.
Daily Values: 5% vit. A, 3% calcium, 9% iron
Exchanges: 1 Starch, 1½ Other Carbo., 1 Fat

Chocolate-Cinnamon Rolls: Prepare as at left, except substitute 1 cup semisweet chocolate pieces for the raisins and nuts.

Nutrition Facts per roll: 251 cal., 9 g total fat (5 g sat. fat), 42 mg chol., 121 mg sodium, 40 g carbo., 1 g fiber, 4 g pro.
Daily Values: 5% vit. A, 3% calcium, 10% iron
Exchanges: 1 Starch, 1½ Other Carbo., 1½ Fat

Tips for Successful Yeast Breads

■ Recipes usually give a range on the amount of flour. Start with the minimum amount and knead in as much of the remaining flour as you can.

■ When you're dissolving the yeast, check the temperature of the heated mixture with an instant-read thermometer to make sure it's just right. If it's too hot, the yeast will die and your bread won't rise. If it's too cold, the yeast won't activate and your bread won't rise either.

■ Proof (raise) yeast breads in a draft-free location between 80°F and 85°F. To use your oven for proofing, place a bowl of dough in an unheated oven with a large bowl of hot water set on the oven's lower rack.

■ Check the dough to see if it has risen enough by pressing two of your fingers ½ inch into the center. If the indentations remain after you remove your fingers, the dough has doubled in size and is ready for the next step.

■ For the second rise, don't let the dough rise above the top of the pan because the dough needs room to rise more as it bakes, a phenomenon called "oven spring."

■ You can check the doneness of a yeast bread by tapping the top of the loaf with your fingers. If it sounds hollow, the bread is done. If the sides of the loaf are pale when you remove it from the pan, put it back in the pan and bake longer. Cover top of the loaf with foil if it is getting too brown.

■ If you live at a high altitude, expect yeast dough to rise faster than it would at sea level. The higher the altitude, the faster the dough rises (see page 16 for additional information on high-altitude baking).

■ Store yeast breads at room temperature; they become stale quicker when chilled.

Stollen

Unless you have a double oven, it's best to bake only one baking sheet at a time. Place the other one in the refrigerator so the dough doesn't overrise.

Prep: 25 minutes **Rise:** 2½ hours **Bake:** 18 minutes
Oven: 375°F **Makes:** 3 loaves (36 servings)

- 4 to 4½ cups all-purpose flour
- 1 package active dry yeast
- ¼ teaspoon ground cardamom
- 1¼ cups milk
- ½ cup butter or margarine
- ¼ cup granulated sugar
- ½ teaspoon salt
- 1 egg
- 1 cup raisins or dried currants
- ¼ cup diced mixed candied fruits and peels
- ¼ cup slivered almonds
- 1 tablespoon finely shredded orange peel
- 1 tablespoon finely shredded lemon peel
- 1 cup sifted powdered sugar
- 2 tablespoons hot water
- 1 teaspoon butter or margarine

1. In a large mixing bowl combine 2 cups of the flour, the yeast, and cardamom. In a medium saucepan heat and stir milk, the ½ cup butter, granulated sugar, and salt until warm (120°F to 130°F) and butter almost melts. Add to flour mixture along with egg. Beat with an electric mixer on low speed for 30 seconds, scraping bowl constantly. Beat on high speed 3 minutes. Using a wooden spoon, stir in as much remaining flour as you can. Stir in raisins, candied fruits and peels, almonds, orange peel, and lemon peel.

2. Turn dough out onto a lightly floured surface. Knead in enough remaining flour to make a moderately soft dough (3 to 5 minutes total; see photo 1, page 132). Shape into a ball. Place in a lightly greased bowl, turning once. Cover; let rise in a warm place until double in size (about 1¾ hours; see photos 2 and 3, page 132).

3. Punch dough down (see photo 4, page 132). Turn dough out onto a lightly floured surface. Divide dough into thirds. Cover; let rest for 10 minutes. Meanwhile, grease 2 large baking sheets; set aside.

4. Roll 1 dough portion into a 10×6-inch oval. Without stretching, fold a long side over to within 1 inch of opposite side; press edges to lightly seal. Place on 1 of the prepared baking sheets. Repeat with remaining dough portions, placing them on remaining baking sheet. Cover; let rise until nearly double (45 to 60 minutes).

5. Bake in a 375° oven for 18 to 20 minutes or until golden and bread sounds hollow when lightly tapped. Remove from baking sheets. Cool 30 minutes on wire racks. In a small bowl combine powdered sugar, hot water, and the 1 teaspoon butter; brush over warm bread.

Nutrition Facts per serving: 120 cal., 4 g total fat (2 g sat. fat), 14 mg chol., 68 mg sodium, 20 g carbo., 1 g fiber, 2 g pro.
Daily Values: 3% vit. A, 2% vit. C, 2% calcium, 5% iron
Exchanges: 1 Starch, ½ Other Carbo., ½ Fat

Hot Cross Buns

Prep: 40 minutes **Rise:** 3 hours **Bake:** 15 minutes
Oven: 375°F **Makes:** 20 buns

- 4 to 4½ cups all-purpose flour
- 1 package active dry yeast
- ¾ teaspoon ground cinnamon
- ¼ teaspoon ground nutmeg
  Dash ground cloves
- ¾ cup milk
- ½ cup butter or margarine
- ⅓ cup granulated sugar
- ½ teaspoon salt
- 3 eggs
- ⅔ cup dried currants or raisins
- ¼ cup diced candied orange peel (optional)
- 1 beaten egg white
- 1 recipe Powdered Sugar Icing (page 172)

1. In a large mixing bowl combine 2 cups of the flour, the yeast, cinnamon, nutmeg, and cloves. In a saucepan heat and stir milk, butter, granulated

Stollen

sugar, and salt just until warm (120°F to 130°F) and butter almost melts. Add milk mixture to flour mixture along with the eggs. Beat with an electric mixer on low to medium speed for 30 seconds, scraping bowl constantly. Beat on high speed for 3 minutes. Using a wooden spoon, stir in currants, orange peel (if desired), and as much of the remaining flour as you can.

2. Turn dough out onto a lightly floured surface. Knead in enough remaining flour to make a moderately soft dough (3 to 5 minutes total; see photo 1, page 132). Shape into a ball. Place in a lightly greased bowl, turning once. Cover; let rise in a warm place until double (about 2 hours; see photos 2 and 3, page 132).

3. Punch dough down. Turn dough out onto a lightly floured surface. Cover; let rest 10 minutes. Meanwhile, lightly grease 2 baking sheets; set aside. Divide dough into 20 portions. Gently pull each portion into a ball, tucking edges under to make smooth tops. Place balls 1½ inches apart on prepared baking sheets. Cover; let rise until nearly double (about 1 hour).

4. Using a sharp knife, make crisscross slashes across the top of each bun. In a small bowl combine beaten egg white and 1 tablespoon *water;* brush over rolls. Bake in a 375° oven about 15 minutes or until golden brown. Immediately remove buns from baking sheets. Cool slightly on wire racks. Drizzle Powdered Sugar Icing into crisscrosses on each bun. Serve warm.

Nutrition Facts per bun: 202 cal., 6 g total fat (3 g sat. fat), 46 mg chol., 127 mg sodium, 32 g carbo., 1 g fiber, 4 g pro.
Daily Values: 5% vit. A, 3% calcium, 8% iron
Exchanges: 1 Starch, 1 Other Carbo., 1 Fat

Pizza Dough

Use this dough and your choice of toppings to make two thin-crust or pan pizzas that serve 6 each.

Prep: 20 to 50 minutes **Makes:** 2 pan or thin-crust pizzas

2¾ to 3¼ cups all-purpose flour
1 package active dry yeast
1 cup warm water (120°F to 130°F)
2 tablespoons cooking oil or olive oil

1. In a large mixing bowl combine 1¼ cups of the flour, the yeast, and ¼ teaspoon *salt;* add warm water and oil. Beat with an electric mixer on low speed for 30 seconds, scraping bowl. Beat on high speed 3 minutes. Using a wooden spoon, stir in as much of the remaining flour as you can.

2. Turn dough out onto a lightly floured surface. Knead in enough remaining flour to make a moderately stiff dough that is smooth and elastic (6 to 8 minutes total; see photo 1, page 132). Divide dough in half. Cover; let rest for 10 minutes. Use to make Pan Pizzas or Thin-Crust Pizzas.

Pan Pizzas: Grease two 11×7×1½-inch or 9×9×2-inch baking pans. If desired, sprinkle with cornmeal. With greased fingers, pat dough onto bottoms and halfway up sides of prepared pans. Cover and let rise in a warm place until nearly double (30 to 45 minutes; see photos 2 and 3, page 132). Bake in a 375°F oven for 20 to 25 minutes or until brown. Spread sauce onto hot crust; top with meat, vegetables, and cheese (see tip, below). Bake for 15 to 20 minutes more or until bubbly.

Thin-Crust Pizzas: Grease two 12-inch pizza pans or baking sheets. If desired, sprinkle with cornmeal. On a lightly floured surface, roll each dough portion into a 13-inch circle. Transfer to pans. Build up edges slightly. Do not let rise. Bake in a 425°F oven about 12 minutes or until brown. Spread sauce onto hot crust; top with meat, vegetables, and cheese (see tip, below). Bake for 10 to 15 minutes more or until bubbly.

Making Pizza

You can make delicious pizza at home. Begin by making the Pizza Dough as directed at left, selecting either pan or thin crusts. Spread one 15-ounce can pizza sauce or one 10-ounce container refrigerated Alfredo sauce over each hot, partially-baked crust.

■ For each meaty pizza, add 1 pound cooked and drained Italian sausage or ground beef, 6 ounces sliced pepperoni, or 1 cup cubed cooked ham or Canadian-style bacon.

■ Additional toppings could include 1 cup of your favorite vegetables, such as sliced green onions, sliced pitted ripe olives, sliced fresh mushrooms, and/or chopped sweet pepper for each pizza.

■ Finally, sprinkle 2 to 3 cups shredded mozzarella cheese over your toppings on each pizza. Now you're ready to finish baking your pizzas according to the directions in the Pizza Dough recipe. Enjoy!

Nutritional Facts per serving: 525 cal., 26 g total fat (10 g sat. fat), 44 mg chol., 857 mg sodium, 51 g carbo., 3 g fiber, 23 g pro.
Daily Values: 23 % vit. A, 16% vit. C, 32% calcium, 26% iron
Exchanges: 3½ Starch, 2 High-Fat Meat, 1 Fat

Adjusting Conventional Recipes for Baking in Bread Machines

To convert conventional yeast bread recipes for use in your bread machine, just follow these tips.

■ Reduce the amount of flour to only 3 cups (for a 1½-pound machine) or 4 cups (for a 2-pound machine). Reduce all ingredients by the same proportion, including the yeast (one package equals about 2¼ teaspoons). For example, for a 1½-pound bread machine, a recipe using 4½ cups flour and 1 package yeast would be decreased by one-third to 3 cups flour and 1½ teaspoons yeast.

■ If the bread uses two or more types of flour, add the flour amounts together and use that total as the basis for reducing the recipe. The total flour used should be only 3 or 4 cups, depending on the size of your machine.

■ Use bread flour instead of all-purpose flour. Rye breads usually need 1 tablespoon of gluten flour (available at health food stores and larger supermarkets) even when bread flour is used.

■ Make sure the liquid ingredients are at room temperature before starting the machine.

■ Add ingredients in the order specified by the bread machine manufacturer.

■ Do not use light-colored dried fruits, such as apricots and light raisins, because the preservatives in them inhibit yeast performance.

■ For breads containing whole wheat or rye flour, use the whole grain cycle, if available. For sweet or rich breads, use the light color setting if your machine has one.

■ When you are only making the dough in the machine, you might have to knead in a little more flour before shaping it. Knead in just enough flour to make dough easy to handle. If necessary, let dough rest for 5 minutes before shaping. Dough made in a bread machine tends to be very elastic, and letting it rest makes it easier to shape.

■ The first time you try a new bread in your machine, watch and listen carefully. Check the dough after the first 3 to 5 minutes of kneading. If your machine works excessively hard during the mixing cycle, if the dough looks dry and crumbly, or if two or more balls of dough form, add 1 to 2 tablespoons of extra liquid. If dough looks very soft and is unable to form a ball, add more flour, 1 tablespoon at a time, until a ball does form. Record how much you add so you can adjust future recipes accordingly.

Home-Style White Bread

Low Fat

Prep: 10 minutes **Bake:** per bread machine directions

For 1½-pound loaf (16 slices)

   1 cup milk
   ¼ cup water
   4 teaspoons butter, margarine, or olive oil
   3 cups bread flour
   4 teaspoons sugar
   ¾ teaspoon salt
   1 teaspoon active dry yeast or bread machine yeast

For 2-pound loaf (22 slices)

   1¼ cups milk
   ¼ cup water
   2 tablespoons butter, margarine, or olive oil
   4 cups bread flour
   2 tablespoons sugar
   1 teaspoon salt
   1¼ teaspoons active dry yeast or bread machine yeast

1. Select the loaf size you want to make. Add all the ingredients to a bread machine according to the manufacturer's directions. Select the basic white bread cycle. Remove hot bread from machine as soon as it is done. Cool on a wire rack.

Nutrition Facts per serving: 114 cal., 2 g total fat (1 g sat. fat), 4 mg chol., 128 mg sodium, 20 g carbo., 1 g fiber, 4 g pro.
Daily Values: 1% vit. A, 2% calcium, 7% iron
Exchanges: 1½ Starch

Easy Whole Wheat Bread

Low Fat

Prep: 10 minutes **Bake:** per bread machine directions

For 1½-pound loaf (16 slices)

   1 cup milk
   3 tablespoons water
   4 teaspoons honey or sugar
   1 tablespoon butter or margarine
   1½ cups whole wheat flour
   1½ cups bread flour
   ¾ teaspoon salt
   1 teaspoon active dry yeast or bread machine yeast

For 2-pound loaf (22 slices)

- 1⅓ cups milk
- ¼ cup water
- 2 tablespoons honey or sugar
- 4 teaspoons butter or margarine
- 2 cups whole wheat flour
- 2 cups bread flour
- 1 teaspoon salt
- 1¼ teaspoons active dry yeast or bread machine yeast

1. Select the loaf size you want to make. Add all the ingredients to a bread machine according to the manufacturer's directions. If available, select the whole grain cycle, or select the basic white bread cycle. Remove hot bread from machine as soon as it is done. Cool on a wire rack.

Nutrition Facts per serving: 105 cal., 1 g total fat (1 g sat. fat), 3 mg chol., 125 mg sodium, 20 g carbo., 2 g fiber, 4 g pro.
Daily Values: 1% vit. A, 2% calcium, 6% iron
Exchanges: 1½ Starch

Rye Bread

Low Fat

Prep: 10 minutes Bake: per bread machine directions

For 1½-pound loaf (16 slices)

- 1 cup water
- 2 tablespoons butter or margarine, cut up; shortening; or cooking oil
- 2 cups bread flour
- 1 cup rye flour
- 2 tablespoons gluten flour
- 2 tablespoons brown sugar
- 1½ teaspoons caraway seeds (optional)
- ¾ teaspoon salt
- 1 teaspoon active dry yeast or bread machine yeast

For 2-pound loaf (22 slices)

- 1⅓ cups water
- 3 tablespoons butter or margarine, cut up; shortening; or cooking oil
- 2⅔ cups bread flour
- 1⅓ cups rye flour
- 3 tablespoons gluten flour
- 3 tablespoons brown sugar
- 2 teaspoons caraway seeds (optional)
- 1 teaspoon salt
- 1¼ teaspoons active dry yeast or bread machine yeast

1. Select the loaf size you want to make. Add all the ingredients to a bread machine according to the manufacturer's directions. If available, select the whole grain cycle, or select the basic white bread cycle. Remove hot bread from machine as soon as it is done. Cool on a wire rack.

Nutrition Facts per serving: 106 cal., 2 g total fat (1 g sat. fat), 4 mg chol., 126 mg sodium, 19 g carbo., 1 g fiber, 3 g pro.
Daily Values: 1% vit. A, 1% calcium, 6% iron
Exchanges: 1½ Starch

Toasted Oatmeal Bread

For a tasty sandwich, layer shaved turkey, provolone cheese, lettuce, and sliced tomato between two slices of this hearty bread.

Low Fat

Prep: 25 minutes Bake: per bread machine directions

For 1½-pound loaf (16 slices)

- 1 cup quick-cooking rolled oats
- ⅔ cup milk
- ⅓ cup water
- 1 tablespoon butter, margarine, or shortening
- 2½ cups bread flour
- 3 tablespoons packed brown sugar
- ¾ teaspoon salt
- 1 teaspoon active dry yeast or bread machine yeast

For 2-pound loaf (22 slices)

- 1⅓ cups quick-cooking rolled oats
- ¾ cup milk
- ½ cup water
- 2 tablespoons butter, margarine, or shortening
- 3⅓ cups bread flour
- ¼ cup packed brown sugar
- 1 teaspoon salt
- 1¼ teaspoons active dry yeast or bread machine yeast

1. Select the loaf size you want to make. Spread the oats in a shallow baking pan. Bake in a 350°F oven for 15 to 20 minutes or until light brown, stirring occasionally; cool.

2. Add the ingredients to a bread machine according to the manufacturer's directions, adding the oats with the flour. If available, select the whole grain cycle, or select the basic white bread cycle. Remove hot bread from machine as soon as it is done. Cool on a wire rack.

Nutrition Facts per serving: 123 cal., 2 g total fat (1 g sat. fat), 3 mg chol., 124 mg sodium, 23 g carbo., 1 g fiber, 4 g pro.
Daily Values: 1% vit. A, 2% calcium, 7% iron
Exchanges: 1½ Starch

Italian Bread

When preparing this bread, your bread machine pan must have a capacity of 10 cups or more for a 1½-pound loaf and 12 cups or more for a 2-pound loaf.

`Low Fat`

Prep: 10 minutes **Bake:** per bread machine directions

For 1½-pound loaf (16 slices)

- ¾ **cup milk**
- 1 **egg**
- 3 **tablespoons water**
- 1 **tablespoon butter or margarine**
- 3 **cups bread flour**
- ½ **teaspoon salt**
- 1 **teaspoon active dry yeast or bread machine yeast**

For 2-pound loaf (22 slices)

- 1 **cup milk**
- 1 **egg**
- ¼ **cup water**
- 4 **teaspoons butter or margarine**
- 4 **cups bread flour**
- ¾ **teaspoon salt**
- 1¼ **teaspoons active dry yeast or bread machine yeast**

1. Select the loaf size you want to make. Add all the ingredients to a bread machine according to the manufacturer's directions. Select the basic white bread cycle. Remove hot bread from machine as soon as it is done. Cool on a wire rack.

Nutrition Facts per serving: 111 cal., 2 g total fat (1 g sat. fat), 16 mg chol., 91 mg sodium, 19 g carbo., 1 g fiber, 4 g pro.
Daily Values: 1% vit. A, 2% calcium, 7% iron
Exchanges: 1 Starch, ½ Fat

Cheesy Potato Bread

`Low Fat`

Prep: 25 minutes **Bake:** per bread machine directions

For 1½-pound loaf (16 slices)

- ¾ **cup water**
- ½ **cup chopped, peeled potato**
- ⅓ **cup milk**
- ⅓ **cup shredded cheddar cheese**
- 2 **teaspoons butter or margarine**
- 3 **cups bread flour**
- 1 **tablespoon sugar**
- ¾ **teaspoon onion salt**
- ¼ **teaspoon caraway seeds, crushed (optional)**
- 1 **teaspoon active dry yeast or bread machine yeast**

For 2-pound loaf (22 slices)

- 1 **cup water**
- ⅔ **cup chopped, peeled potato**
- ½ **cup milk**
- ½ **cup shredded cheddar cheese**
- 1 **tablespoon butter or margarine**
- 4 **cups bread flour**
- 4 **teaspoons sugar**
- 1 **teaspoon onion salt**
- ½ **teaspoon caraway seeds, crushed (optional)**
- 1¼ **teaspoons active dry yeast or bread machine yeast**

1. Select the loaf size you want to make. In a small saucepan combine the water and potato. Bring to boiling. Reduce heat and simmer, covered, about 10 minutes or until the potato is very tender. Do not drain. Mash potato in the water. Measure potato mixture. If necessary, add water to equal ¾ cup mixture for the 1½-pound loaf or 1 cup mixture for the 2-pound loaf; discard any excess potato mixture. Cool slightly.

2. Add the potato mixture and remaining ingredients to a bread machine according to the manufacturer's directions. Select the basic white bread cycle. Remove hot bread from machine as soon as it is done. Cool on a wire rack.

Nutrition Facts per serving: 117 cal., 2 g total fat (1 g sat. fat), 4 mg chol., 98 mg sodium, 21 g carbo., 1 g fiber, 4 g pro.
Daily Values: 1% vit. A, 1% vit. C, 3% calcium, 7% iron
Exchanges: 1½ Starch

Cheesy Potato Bread

Chapter 6

Cakes

On the divider: **Best-Ever Carrot Cake** (see recipe, page 159)

Cakes

Yellow Cake

Prep: 20 minutes **Bake:** 20 minutes **Oven:** 375°F
Cool: 1 hour **Makes:** 12 to 16 servings

- ¾ **cup butter, softened**
- 3 **eggs**
- 2½ **cups all-purpose flour**
- 2½ **teaspoons baking powder**
- ½ **teaspoon salt**
- 1¾ **cups sugar**
- 1½ **teaspoons vanilla**
- 1¼ **cups milk**

1. Allow butter and eggs to stand at room temperature for 30 minutes. Meanwhile, grease and lightly flour two 9×1½-inch or 8×1½-inch round cake pans or grease one 13×9×2-inch baking pan (see photo 1, bottom right); set pan(s) aside. In a medium bowl stir together flour, baking powder, and salt; set aside.

2. In a large mixing bowl beat butter with an electric mixer on medium to high speed for 30 seconds. Gradually add sugar, about ¼ cup at time, beating on medium speed until well combined (see photo 2, bottom right) and scraping sides of bowl. Beat on medium speed for 2 minutes more. Add eggs 1 at a time, beating after each addition (about 1 minute total). Beat in vanilla. Alternately add flour mixture and milk to butter mixture, beating on low speed after each addition just until combined. Spread batter into the prepared pan(s).

3. Bake in a 375° oven for 20 to 25 minutes for 9-inch pans, 30 to 35 minutes for 8-inch pans, 25 to 30 minutes for 13×9×2-inch pan, or until a wooden toothpick inserted near centers comes out clean. Cool cake layers in pans on wire racks for 10 minutes. Remove cake layers from pans; cool thoroughly on racks (see tip, page 156). Or, place 13×9×2-inch cake in pan on a wire rack; cool thoroughly. Frost with desired frosting.

Citrus Yellow Cake: Prepare as above, except stir 2 teaspoons finely shredded orange peel or lemon peel into batter.

Nutrition Facts per serving for yellow or citrus variation: 336 cal., 14 g total fat (8 g sat. fat), 88 mg chol., 333 mg sodium, 48 g carbo., 1 g fiber, 5 g pro.
Daily Values: 12% vit. A, 9% calcium, 7% iron
Exchanges: 3 Other Carbo., 2 Fat

Before You Start

■ Use large eggs and allow them to stand at room temperature for 30 minutes before using. Room temperature eggs provide more volume when beaten. If the eggs are to be separated, do so immediately after removing them from the refrigerator.

■ Solid fats, such as butter and shortening, hold air bubbles well, ensuring light and delicate cakes. Allow butter to stand at room temperature to soften slightly before creaming with sugar. If you prefer margarine, choose one that contains 80 percent fat. Do not use low-fat, liquid, or soft vegetable oil spreads. These products contain varying amounts of water and fat and may alter the cake's texture.

■ Allow your oven to preheat to the recommended baking temperature while you prepare the cake batter.

■ Unless specified otherwise, grease and lightly flour baking pans for butter-type layer cakes that will be removed from their pans. Use a paper towel or pastry brush to evenly spread the shortening in the pan. Add a little flour, tilt the pan, and tap it so the flour covers all the greased surfaces (see photo 1, below); tap out the excess flour. You can use cocoa powder instead of flour for chocolate cakes.

■ For butter-type cakes that will be left in their pans, grease only the bottom of the baking pan and do not coat with flour.

■ Do not grease pans for angel food, sponge, and chiffon cakes unless specified otherwise.

1. Grease and lightly flour cake pans, tilting and tapping each pan to evenly distribute the flour (see tip, above). Discard excess flour.

2. Beat the butter or shortening and sugar until they are well combined. The mixture will have a light texture.

Triple-Layer Lemon Cake `Best Loved`

Prep: 35 minutes **Bake:** 25 minutes **Oven:** 350°F
Cool: 1 hour **Makes:** 12 servings

(see tip, page 157)

- 1 **cup butter, softened**
- 4 **eggs**
- 2⅓ **cups all-purpose flour**
- 1½ **teaspoons baking powder**
- ½ **teaspoon baking soda**
- ¼ **teaspoon salt**
- 2 **cups sugar**
- 2 **teaspoons finely shredded lemon peel**
- 2 **tablespoons lemon juice**
- 1 **cup buttermilk or sour milk (see tip, page 157)**
- ½ **recipe Lemon Curd (page 260) or 1 cup purchased lemon curd**
- 1 **recipe Lemon Cream Cheese Frosting**
  Lemon peel curls (optional)

1. Allow butter and eggs to stand at room temperature for 30 minutes. Meanwhile, grease and lightly flour three 9×1½-inch round cake pans. In a medium bowl stir together flour, baking powder, baking soda, and salt. Set aside.

2. In a large mixing bowl beat butter with an electric mixer on medium to high speed for 30 seconds. Add sugar, lemon peel, and lemon juice; beat until well combined. Add eggs 1 at a time, beating well after each addition. Alternately add flour mixture and buttermilk to butter mixture, beating on low speed after each addition just until combined. Pour into prepared pans.

3. Bake in a 350° oven for 25 to 30 minutes or until a wooden toothpick inserted near centers comes out clean. Cool cake layers in pans on wire racks for 10 minutes. Remove cake layers from pans. Cool thoroughly on racks.

4. To assemble, place a cake layer on a cake plate. Spread with half of the Lemon Curd. Top with second cake layer; spread with remaining Lemon Curd. Top with the remaining cake layer. Frost top and sides with Lemon Cream Cheese Frosting. Cover and store cake in the refrigerator for up to 3 days. Let stand at room temperature for 30 minutes before serving. If desired, garnish with lemon peel curls.

Lemon Cream Cheese Frosting: Finely shred 1 teaspoon lemon peel; set aside. In a medium mixing bowl combine two 3-ounce packages cream cheese, softened; ½ cup butter, softened; and 1 teaspoon lemon juice. Beat with electric mixer on low to medium speed until light and fluffy. Gradually add 2 cups sifted powdered sugar, beating well. Gradually beat in 2½ to 2¾ cups additional sifted powdered sugar until frosting reaches spreading consistency. Stir in the lemon peel.

Nutrition Facts per serving: 730 cal., 36 g total fat (22 g sat. fat), 199 mg chol., 536 mg sodium, 96 g carbo., 1 g fiber, 8 g pro.
Daily Values: 29% vit. A, 8% vit. C, 9% calcium, 10% iron
Exchanges: 6 Other Carbo., 5½ Fat

Triple-Layer Lemon Cake

Storing and Freezing Cakes

■ Cakes filled or frosted with whipped cream should be assembled no more than 2 hours before serving to prevent them from getting soggy.

■ If your cake filling or frosting contains whipped cream, cream cheese, yogurt, or eggs, store it in the refrigerator. If you don't have a cake cover, cover the cake loosely with foil.

■ It's best to freeze a layer cake unfrosted. Place cooled layers on baking sheets and freeze just until firm. Transfer frozen layers to large freezer bags, or wrap and seal them in freezer wrap. Freeze for up to 4 months.

■ Angel food, sponge, and chiffon cakes also are best frozen unfrosted. Place them in large freezer bags and freeze for up to 3 months. The delicate sponge texture may deteriorate if stored longer. Thaw at room temperature for several hours before serving.

White Cake

You'll get a slightly whiter cake if you prepare it with shortening instead of butter.

Prep: 20 minutes **Bake:** 20 minutes **Oven:** 350°F
Cool: 1 hour **Makes:** 12 to 16 servings

- 4 egg whites
- 2 cups all-purpose flour
- 1 teaspoon baking powder
- ½ teaspoon baking soda
- ⅛ teaspoon salt
- ½ cup shortening or butter, softened
- 1¾ cups sugar
- 1 teaspoon vanilla
- 1⅓ cups buttermilk or sour milk (see tip, page 157)

1. Allow egg whites to stand at room temperature for 30 minutes. Meanwhile, grease and lightly flour two 9×1½-inch or 8×1½-inch round cake pans (see photo 1, page 153) or grease one 13×9×2-inch baking pan; set the pan(s) aside. In a medium bowl stir together flour, baking powder, baking soda, and salt; set aside.

2. In a large mixing bowl beat shortening with an electric mixer on medium to high speed for 30 seconds. Add sugar and vanilla; beat until well combined (see photo 2, page 153). Add egg whites 1 at a time, beating well after each addition. Alternately add flour mixture and buttermilk to shortening mixture, beating on low speed after each addition just until combined. Spread batter into the prepared pan(s).

3. Bake in a 350° oven for 20 to 25 minutes for 9-inch pans, 25 to 30 minutes for 8-inch pans, 30 to 35 minutes for the 13×9×2-inch pan, or until a wooden toothpick inserted near centers comes out clean. Cool cake layers in pans on wire racks for 10 minutes. Remove cake layers from pans; cool thoroughly on racks (see tip, page 156). Or, place 13×9×2-inch cake in pan on a wire rack; cool thoroughly. Frost with desired frosting.

Coconut White Cake: Prepare as above, except stir ¼ cup flaked coconut into batter.

Nutrition Facts per serving for white or coconut variation:
275 cal., 8 g total fat (2 g sat. fat), 1 mg chol., 157 mg sodium, 45 g carbo., 1 g fiber, 4 g pro.
Daily Values: 1% vit. C, 6% calcium, 6% iron
Exchanges: 3 Other Carbo., 1 Fat

Chocolate Cake `Best Loved`

Prep: 30 minutes **Bake:** 35 minutes **Oven:** 350°F
Cool: 1 hour **Makes:** 12 to 16 servings

- ¾ cup butter, softened
- 3 eggs
- 2 cups all-purpose flour
- ¾ cup unsweetened cocoa powder
- 1 teaspoon baking soda
- ¾ teaspoon baking powder
- ½ teaspoon salt
- 2 cups sugar
- 2 teaspoons vanilla
- 1½ cups milk

1. Allow butter and eggs to stand at room temperature for 30 minutes. Meanwhile, lightly grease bottoms of two 8×8×2-inch square or 9×1½-inch round cake pans. Line bottoms of pans with waxed paper. Grease and lightly flour bottoms and sides of pans. Or, grease one 13×9×2-inch baking pan. In a medium bowl stir together flour, cocoa powder, baking soda, baking powder, and salt; set aside.

2. In a large mixing bowl beat butter with an electric mixer on medium to high speed for 30 seconds. Gradually add sugar, about ¼ cup at a time, beating on medium speed until well combined (3 to 4 minutes). Scrape sides of bowl; continue beating on medium speed for 2 minutes. Add eggs 1 at a time, beating after each addition (about 1 minute total). Beat in vanilla.

3. Alternately add flour mixture and milk to butter mixture, beating on low speed after each addition just until combined. Beat on medium to high speed for 20 seconds more. Spread batter evenly into the prepared pan(s).

4. Bake in a 350° oven for 35 to 40 minutes for 8-inch pans and 13×9×2-inch pan, 30 to 35 minutes for 9-inch pans, or until a wooden toothpick inserted near centers comes out clean. Cool cake layers in pans for 10 minutes. Remove from pans. Peel off waxed paper. Cool thoroughly on racks (see tip, page 156). Or, place 13×9×2-inch cake in pan on a wire rack; cool thoroughly. Frost with desired frosting.

Nutrition Facts per serving: 360 cal., 15 g total fat (8 g sat. fat), 88 mg chol., 382 mg sodium, 51 g carbo., 1 g fiber, 6 g pro.
Daily Values: 12% vit. A, 12% calcium, 10% iron
Exchanges: 3½ Other Carbo., 3 Fat

German Chocolate Cake Best Loved

Prep: 50 minutes **Bake:** 20 minutes **Oven:** 350°F
Cool: 1 hour **Makes:** 12 to 16 servings

156

     3 **eggs**
    ⅔ **cup butter, softened**
   1½ **cups all-purpose flour**
    ¾ **teaspoon baking soda**
    ¼ **teaspoon salt**
     1 **4-ounce package sweet baking chocolate**
     1 **cup sugar**
     1 **teaspoon vanilla**
    ¾ **cup buttermilk or sour milk (see tip, page 157)**
     1 **recipe Coconut-Pecan Frosting**

1. Separate eggs. Allow egg yolks, egg whites, and butter to stand at room temperature for 30 minutes. Meanwhile, grease and lightly flour two 9×1½-inch or 8×1½-inch round cake pans (see photo 1, page 153); set pans aside. In a medium bowl stir together flour, baking soda, and salt; set aside.

2. In a small saucepan combine chocolate and ⅓ cup *water*. Cook and stir over low heat until chocolate is melted; cool.

3. In a large mixing bowl beat butter with an electric mixer on medium to high speed for 30 seconds. Gradually add sugar, beating until well combined. Scrape sides of bowl; continue beating for 2 minutes. Beat in egg yolks 1 at a time, beating well after each addition (about 1 minute total). Beat in cooled chocolate mixture and vanilla. Alternately add flour mixture and buttermilk to butter mixture; beat on low speed after each addition until combined.

4. Thoroughly wash the beaters. In a large mixing bowl beat egg whites with an electric mixer on high speed until stiff peaks form (tips stand straight; see photo 2, page 169). Gently fold egg whites into the batter. Spread batter into the prepared pans.

5. Bake in a 350° oven for 20 to 25 minutes for 9-inch pans, 25 to 30 minutes for 8-inch pans, or until a wooden toothpick inserted near centers comes out clean. Cool cake layers on wire racks for 10 minutes. Remove cake layers from pans; cool thoroughly on racks (see tip, right). Spread Coconut-Pecan Frosting over the top of each cake; stack the layers.

Coconut-Pecan Frosting: In a medium saucepan slightly beat 1 egg. Stir in one 5-ounce can (⅔ cup) evaporated milk, ⅔ cup sugar, and ¼ cup butter. Cook and stir over medium heat for 6 to 8 minutes or until thickened and bubbly. Remove from heat; stir in 1⅓ cups flaked coconut and ½ cup chopped pecans. Cover and cool thoroughly.

Nutrition Facts per serving: 484 cal., 29 g total fat (15 g sat. fat), 115 mg chol., 371 mg sodium, 52 g carbo., 2 g fiber, 7 g pro.
Daily Values: 14% vit. A, 1% vit. C, 7% calcium, 7% iron
Exchanges: 3½ Other Carbo., 5 Fat

German Chocolate Cake

Cooling Cakes

■ Before removing a butter-type layer cake from its baking pan, allow it to cool for 10 minutes on a wire rack. To remove, loosen cake edges from pan using a metal spatula or knife. Place an inverted wire rack on the cake layer, turn cake and rack over, and lift off the pan. Place a second rack on the cake layer and turn it over again so the baked cake is upright; cool completely. A butter-type cake left in its pan should cool completely on a wire rack.

■ Turn angel food, sponge, and chiffon cakes upside down immediately after baking and let them cool completely. If your cake is too high to use the built-in legs on the baking pan, invert the pan over a metal funnel or a glass bottle that has a slim neck.

Devil's Food Cake

The reaction of cocoa powder and baking soda gives this cake its characteristic reddish brown color.

Prep: 25 minutes **Bake:** 25 minutes **Oven:** 350°F
Cool: 1 hour **Makes:** 12 to 16 servings

> 3 eggs
> 2¼ cups all-purpose flour
> ½ cup unsweetened cocoa powder
> 1½ teaspoons baking soda
> ¼ teaspoon salt
> ½ cup shortening
> 1¾ cups sugar
> 1 teaspoon vanilla
> 1⅓ cups cold water

1. Allow eggs to stand at room temperature for 30 minutes. Meanwhile, grease and lightly flour two 9×1½-inch or 8×1½-inch round cake pans (see photo 1, page 153) or grease one 13×9×2-inch baking pan; set pan(s) aside. In a medium bowl stir together flour, cocoa powder, baking soda, and salt; set aside.

2. In a large mixing bowl beat shortening with an electric mixer on medium to high speed for 30 seconds. Add sugar and vanilla; beat until well combined (see photo 2, page 153). Add eggs 1 at a time, beating well after each addition. Alternately add flour mixture and water to shortening mixture, beating on low speed after each addition just until combined. Pour batter into the prepared pan(s).

3. Bake in a 350° oven for 25 to 30 minutes for 9-inch pans, 30 to 35 minutes for 8-inch and 13×9×2-inch pans, or until a wooden toothpick inserted near centers comes out clean. Cool on wire racks for 10 minutes. Remove from pans. Cool thoroughly on wire racks (see tip, page 156). Or, place 13×9×2-inch cake in pan on a wire rack; cool thoroughly. Frost with desired frosting.

Nutrition Facts per serving: 297 cal., 10 g total fat (3 g sat. fat), 53 mg chol., 223 mg sodium, 46 g carbo., 1 g fiber, 5 g pro.
Daily Values: 2% vit. A, 5% calcium, 9% iron
Exchanges: 3 Other Carbo., 1½ Fat

Making Sour Milk

If you don't have buttermilk on hand when preparing baked goods, substitute sour milk in the same amount. For each cup of sour milk needed, place 1 tablespoon lemon juice or vinegar in a glass measuring cup. Add enough milk to make 1 cup total liquid; stir. Let mixture stand for 5 minutes before using.

Oatmeal Cake

Prep: 45 minutes **Bake:** 40 minutes **Oven:** 350°F
Broil: 2 minutes **Cool:** 1⅓ hours **Makes:** 12 servings

> ½ cup butter, softened
> 2 eggs
> 1 cup rolled oats
> 2 cups all-purpose flour
> 2 teaspoons baking powder
> ¾ teaspoon ground cinnamon
> ½ teaspoon baking soda
> ¼ teaspoon ground nutmeg
> ¾ cup granulated sugar
> ½ cup packed brown sugar
> 1 teaspoon vanilla
> 1 recipe Broiled Nut Topping

1. Allow butter and eggs to stand at room temperature for 30 minutes. Meanwhile, grease and lightly flour a 9-inch springform pan; set aside. Pour 1¼ cups *boiling water* over oats. Stir until combined; let stand 20 minutes. Stir together flour, baking powder, cinnamon, baking soda, ½ teaspoon *salt*, and nutmeg; set aside.

2. In a large mixing bowl beat butter with an electric mixer on medium to high speed for 30 seconds. Add granulated sugar, brown sugar, and vanilla; beat until well combined. Add eggs 1 at a time, beating well after each addition. Alternately add flour mixture and oatmeal mixture to butter mixture, beating on low speed after each addition just until combined. Pour batter into prepared pan.

3. Bake in a 350° oven for 40 to 45 minutes or until a wooden toothpick inserted near center comes out clean. Cool cake in pan on wire rack for 20 minutes. Remove sides of pan; cool on wire rack at least 1 hour more.

4. Transfer cake to a baking sheet. Spread Broiled Nut Topping over warm cake. Broil about 4 inches from heat for 2 to 3 minutes or until topping is bubbly and golden. Cool on wire rack before serving.

Broiled Nut Topping: In a medium saucepan combine ¼ cup butter and 2 tablespoons half-and-half or milk. Cook and stir until butter melts. Add ½ cup packed brown sugar; stir until sugar dissolves. Remove from heat. Stir in ¾ cup chopped pecans or walnuts and ⅓ cup coconut.

Nutrition Facts per serving: 410 cal., 20 g total fat (10 g sat. fat), 70 mg chol., 273 mg sodium, 54 g carbo., 2 g fiber, 5 g pro.
Daily Values: 11% vit. A, 8% calcium, 11% iron
Exchanges: 3½ Other Carbo., 3 Fat

Spice Cake

Frost with Browned Butter Frosting (page 172).

Prep: 20 minutes **Bake:** 35 minutes **Oven:** 350°F
Cool: 1 hour **Makes:** 12 servings

- ¼ **cup butter**
- 2 **eggs**
- 2 **cups all-purpose flour**
- 1½ **teaspoons baking powder**
- 1 **teaspoon ground cinnamon**
- ½ **teaspoon baking soda**
- ¼ **teaspoon ground nutmeg**
- ¼ **teaspoon ground cloves**
- ¼ **teaspoon ground ginger**
- ¼ **cup shortening**
- 1½ **cups sugar**
- ½ **teaspoon vanilla**
- 1¼ **cups buttermilk or sour milk (see tip, page 157)**

1. Allow butter and eggs to stand at room temperature for 30 minutes. Meanwhile, grease a 13×9×2-inch baking pan or grease and lightly flour two 8×1½-inch round cake pans (see photo 1, page 153); set aside. In a medium bowl stir together flour, baking powder, cinnamon, baking soda, nutmeg, cloves, and ginger; set aside.

2. In a mixing bowl beat butter and shortening with an electric mixer on medium to high speed for 30 seconds. Add sugar and vanilla; beat until well combined (see photo 2, page 153). Add eggs 1 at a time, beating well after each addition. Alternately add flour mixture and buttermilk to butter mixture, beating on low speed after each addition just until combined. Pour into prepared pan(s).

3. Bake in a 350° oven for 35 to 40 minutes for the 13×9×2-inch pan, 30 to 35 minutes for the round pans, or until a wooden toothpick inserted near center comes out clean. Place 13×9×2-inch cake in pan on a wire rack; cool thoroughly. Or, cool cake layers on wire racks for 10 minutes. Remove cake layers from pans. Cool thoroughly on wire racks (see tip, page 156). Frost with desired frosting.

The Cupcake Conversion

Most butter-type cakes can be made into cupcakes. Grease and flour a muffin pan or line cups with paper bake cups; fill cups half full. Bake at same temperature called for in cake recipe, but reduce baking time by one-third to one-half. A two-layer cake usually makes 24 to 30 cupcakes.

Applesauce Spice Cake: Prepare as at left, except reduce buttermilk or sour milk to ¼ cup and combine it with 1 cup applesauce. Alternately add this mixture and flour mixture to butter mixture.

Pumpkin Spice Cake: Prepare as at left, except reduce buttermilk or sour milk to 1 cup and combine it with ½ cup canned pumpkin. Alternately add this mixture and flour mixture to butter mixture.

Nutrition Facts per serving for spice, applesauce, and pumpkin variations: 265 cal., 9 g total fat (4 g sat. fat), 47 mg chol., 182 mg sodium, 41 g carbo., 1 g fiber, 4 g pro.
Daily Values: 4% vit. A, 1% vit. C, 7% calcium, 7% iron
Exchanges: 3 Other Carbo., 1 Fat

Busy-Day Cake with Broiled Coconut Topping

Prep: 25 minutes **Bake:** 25 minutes **Oven:** 350°F
Broil: 3 minutes **Cool:** 30 minutes **Makes:** 8 servings

- 1⅓ **cups all-purpose flour**
- ⅔ **cup sugar**
- 2 **teaspoons baking powder**
- ⅔ **cup milk**
- ¼ **cup butter, softened**
- 1 **egg**
- 1 **teaspoon vanilla**
- 1 **recipe Broiled Coconut Topping**

1. Grease an 8×1½-inch round cake pan; set the pan aside.

2. In a mixing bowl combine flour, sugar, and baking powder. Add milk, butter, egg, and vanilla. Beat on low speed until combined. Beat on medium speed for 1 minute. Pour batter into prepared pan.

3. Bake in a 350° oven for 25 to 30 minutes or until a wooden toothpick inserted near center comes out clean. Spread Broiled Coconut Topping over warm cake. Broil about 4 inches from heat for 3 to 4 minutes or until golden. Cool slightly in pan on a wire rack. Serve warm.

Broiled Coconut Topping: Beat ¼ cup packed brown sugar and 2 tablespoons softened butter or margarine until combined. Stir in 1 tablespoon milk. Stir in ½ cup flaked coconut and, if desired, ¼ cup chopped nuts.

Nutrition Facts per serving: 300 cal., 13 g total fat (9 g sat. fat), 53 mg chol., 238 mg sodium, 43 g carbo., 1 g fiber, 4 g pro.
Daily Values: 9% vit. A, 10% calcium, 7% iron
Exchanges: 3 Other Carbo., 1½ Fat

Best-Ever Carrot Cake Best Loved

The appeal of this thoroughly American cake hasn't waned since it became popular in the 1960s (see photo, page 151).

Prep: 30 minutes **Bake:** 30 minutes **Oven:** 350°F
Cool: 2 hours **Makes:** 12 servings

> 4 beaten eggs
> 2 cups all-purpose flour
> 2 cups sugar
> 2 teaspoons baking powder
> 1 teaspoon ground cinnamon (optional)
> ½ teaspoon baking soda
> 3 cups finely shredded carrots* (lightly packed)
> ¾ cup cooking oil
> 1 recipe Cream Cheese Frosting (page 171)
> ½ cup finely chopped pecans, toasted (optional) (see tip, page 224)

1. Allow eggs to stand at room temperature for 30 minutes. Meanwhile, grease and flour two 9×1½-inch round cake pans (see photo 1, page 153); set pans aside. In a large mixing bowl stir together flour, sugar, baking powder, cinnamon (if desired), and baking soda.

2. In a medium bowl combine eggs, carrots, and oil. Add egg mixture to flour mixture; stir until combined. Pour batter into the prepared pans.

3. Bake in a 350° oven for 30 to 35 minutes or until a wooden toothpick inserted near centers comes out clean. Cool on wire racks for 10 minutes (see tip, page 156). Remove from pans. Cool thoroughly on racks.

4. Frost tops and sides with Cream Cheese Frosting. If desired, sprinkle chopped pecans over frosting. Store cake in the refrigerator for up to 3 days.

***Note:** The carrots need to be finely shredded or they may sink to the bottom of pan during baking.

Nutrition Facts per serving: 684 cal., 31 g total fat (12 g sat. fat), 113 mg chol., 289 mg sodium, 100 g carbo., 1 g fiber, 6 g pro.
Daily Values: 168% vit. A, 5% vit. C, 9% calcium, 10% iron
Exchanges: 6 Other Carbo., 4 Fat

Nut Torte

Prep: 15 minutes **Bake:** 20 minutes **Oven:** 350°F
Cool: 1 hour **Makes:** 12 servings

> 2 tablespoons all-purpose flour
> 1 teaspoon baking powder
> 1 teaspoon finely shredded orange peel
> 4 eggs
> ¾ cup sugar
> 2½ cups walnuts, pecans, or hazelnuts
> ½ recipe Orange Butter Frosting (page 170)

1. Grease and lightly flour two 8×1½-inch round cake pans (see photo 1, page 153); set pans aside. In a small bowl stir together the flour, baking powder, and orange peel; set aside.

2. Place eggs and sugar in a blender container or food processor bowl. Cover and blend or process until smooth. Add nuts. Cover and blend or process about 1 minute or until nearly smooth. Add flour mixture; blend or process just until combined. Spread batter evenly in the prepared pans.

3. Bake in a 350° oven about 20 minutes or until lightly browned and top springs back when lightly touched (see tip, page 160). Cool cake layers on wire racks for 10 minutes. Remove from pans. Cool thoroughly on wire racks (see tip, page 156). Frost with Orange Butter Frosting.

Nutrition Facts per serving: 442 cal., 24 g total fat (6 g sat. fat), 87 mg chol., 119 mg sodium, 53 g carbo., 2 g fiber, 7 g pro.
Daily Values: 7% vit. A, 1% vit. C, 8% calcium, 7% iron
Exchanges: 3½ Other Carbo., 4 Fat

Nut Torte

Apple Cake

Prep: 30 minutes **Bake:** 1 hour **Oven:** 350°F
Cool: 2 to 3 hours **Makes:** 12 servings

- 2 beaten eggs
- 3 cups all-purpose flour
- 2 teaspoons finely shredded lemon peel
- 1 teaspoon baking powder
- 1 teaspoon baking soda
- 1 teaspoon ground cinnamon
- ¼ teaspoon ground allspice
- ¼ teaspoon salt
- 1 cup granulated sugar
- 1 cup packed brown sugar
- 1 cup cooking oil
- 1 tablespoon vanilla
- 3 cups chopped, peeled apples
- 1 cup chopped pecans, toasted (see tip, page 224)

1. Allow eggs to stand at room temperature for 30 minutes. Meanwhile, grease and lightly flour a 10-inch tube pan; set pan aside. In a medium bowl stir together flour, lemon peel, baking powder, baking soda, cinnamon, allspice, and salt; set aside.

2. In a mixing bowl combine granulated sugar, brown sugar, oil, eggs, and vanilla. Beat with an electric mixer on medium speed for 2 minutes. Add flour mixture and beat on low speed just until combined. Fold in apples and pecans. Spoon batter into the prepared pan.

3. Bake in a 350° oven about 1 hour or until a wooden toothpick inserted near the center comes out clean. Cool cake on rack for 10 minutes. Remove from pan. Cool thoroughly on wire rack (see tip, page 156). Sprinkle with *sifted powdered sugar*. Cover; store in refrigerator.

Nutrition Facts per serving: 508 cal., 26 g total fat (4 g sat. fat), 35 mg chol., 206 mg sodium, 66 g carbo., 3 g fiber, 5 g pro.
Daily Values: 2% vit. A, 3% vit. C, 7% calcium, 14% iron
Exchanges: 4 Other Carbo., 4 Fat

Is It Done Yet?

Foam Cake: To test whether a foam cake (such as angel food, sponge, and chiffon cake) is done, touch the top lightly. If the top springs back, the cake is finished baking.

Butter-Type Cake: To test a butter-type cake for doneness, insert a wooden toothpick into cake near the center. If it comes out clean, the cake is done. If it comes out wet, bake the cake a few minutes longer, then test in another spot near the center.

Red Waldorf Cake `Best Loved`

Prep: 45 minutes **Bake:** 30 minutes **Oven:** 350°F
Cool: 1 hour **Makes:** 12 servings

- 2 eggs
- ½ cup unsweetened cocoa powder
- 2 ounces red food coloring (¼ cup)
- 2¼ cups sifted cake flour or 2 cups sifted all-purpose flour
- ½ cup shortening
- 1½ cups sugar
- 1 teaspoon vanilla
- 1 cup buttermilk or sour milk (see tip, page 157)
- 1 teaspoon baking soda
- 1 teaspoon vinegar
- 1 recipe Creamy Frosting

1. Allow eggs to stand at room temperature for 30 minutes. Meanwhile, grease and flour two 9×1½-inch round cake pans or one 13×9×2-inch baking pan. Stir together cocoa powder and food coloring; set aside. In another small bowl stir together flour and ½ teaspoon *salt*; set aside.

2. In a large mixing bowl beat shortening with an electric mixer on medium to high speed for 30 seconds. Add sugar and vanilla to shortening; beat until well combined. Add eggs 1 at a time, beating on medium speed after each addition until combined. Beat in cocoa mixture. Alternately add flour mixture and buttermilk, beating on low to medium speed after each addition just until combined. Stir together baking soda and vinegar. Add to batter, mixing until combined. Pour batter into prepared pans.

3. Bake in a 350° oven for 30 to 35 minutes for round pans, about 30 minutes for 13×9×2-inch pan, or until a wooden toothpick inserted near centers comes out clean. Cool cake layers in pans for 10 minutes. Remove cake layers from pans; cool thoroughly on wire racks. Or, place the 13×9×2-inch cake in pan on a wire rack; cool thoroughly. Frost with Creamy Frosting. Cover and store in the refrigerator for up to 3 days.

Creamy Frosting: In a medium saucepan, use a whisk to blend 1 cup milk into 3 tablespoons all-purpose flour. Cook and stir over medium heat until thickened and bubbly. Reduce heat; cook and stir 2 minutes more. Cover surface with plastic wrap. Cool to room temperature (do not stir). In a medium mixing bowl beat 1 cup softened butter, 1 cup granulated sugar, and 1 teaspoon vanilla with an electric mixer on medium speed until light and fluffy. Add cooled milk mixture to butter mixture ¼ cup at a time, beating on low speed after each addition until smooth.

Nutrition Facts per serving: 500 cal., 26 g total fat (13 g sat. fat), 81 mg chol., 410 mg sodium, 61 g carbo., 0 g fiber, 5 g pro.
Daily Values: 14% vit. A, 1% vit. C, 11% calcium, 13% iron
Exchanges: 4 Other Carbo., 4 Fat

Banana Cake

For the purist, only Cream Cheese Frosting (page 171) will do on this cake. If you use a 13×9×2-inch pan, you can reduce the frosting recipe by half.

Prep: 20 minutes **Bake:** 25 minutes **Oven:** 350°F
Cool: 2 hours **Makes:** 12 to 16 servings

   2 eggs
2¼ cups all-purpose flour
1½ cups sugar
1½ teaspoons baking powder
   1 teaspoon baking soda
  ½ teaspoon salt
   1 cup mashed ripe bananas (about 3)
  ¾ cup buttermilk or sour milk (see tip, page 157)
  ½ cup shortening
   1 teaspoon vanilla

1. Allow eggs to stand at room temperature for 30 minutes. Meanwhile, grease and lightly flour two 8×1½-inch or 9×1½-inch round cake pans (see photo 1, page 153) or grease one 13×9×2-inch baking pan; set pan(s) aside.

2. In a large mixing bowl stir together flour, sugar, baking powder, baking soda, and salt. Add bananas, buttermilk, shortening, and vanilla. Beat with an electric mixer on low speed until combined. Add eggs; beat on medium speed for 2 minutes. Pour batter into the prepared pan(s).

3. Bake in a 350° oven for 25 to 30 minutes for round pans, about 30 minutes for 13×9×2-inch pan, or until a wooden toothpick inserted near centers comes out clean. Cool cake layers in pans on wire racks for 10 minutes. Remove cake layers from pans; cool thoroughly on racks (see tip, page 156). Or, place 13×9×2-inch cake in pan on a wire rack; cool thoroughly. Frost with desired frosting.

Nutrition Facts per serving: 294 cal., 10 g total fat (3 g sat. fat), 36 mg chol., 279 mg sodium, 48 g carbo., 1 g fiber, 4 g pro.
Daily Values: 2% vit. A, 5% vit. C, 6% calcium, 7% iron
Exchanges: 3 Other Carbo., 1 Fat

Chocolate-Buttermilk Sheet Cake `Best Loved`

Known to some as Texas Sheet Cake, this sinfully rich dessert often is served as brownies.

Prep: 30 minutes **Bake:** 25 minutes **Oven:** 350°F
Cool: 1 hour **Makes:** 24 servings

   2 cups all-purpose flour
   2 cups sugar
   1 teaspoon baking soda
  ¼ teaspoon salt
   1 cup butter
  ⅓ cup unsweetened cocoa powder
   2 eggs
  ½ cup buttermilk or sour milk (see tip, page 157)
1½ teaspoons vanilla
   1 recipe Chocolate-Buttermilk Frosting

1. Grease a 15×10×1-inch or 13×9×2-inch baking pan; set aside. In a medium bowl stir together flour, sugar, baking soda, and salt; set aside.

2. In a medium saucepan combine butter, cocoa powder, and 1 cup *water*. Bring mixture just to boiling, stirring constantly. Remove from heat. Add the cocoa mixture to flour mixture and beat with an electric mixer on medium to high speed until thoroughly combined. Add eggs, buttermilk, and vanilla. Beat for 1 minute (batter will be thin). Pour batter into the prepared pan.

3. Bake in a 350° oven about 25 minutes for the 15×10-inch pan, 35 minutes for the 13×9×2-inch pan, or until a wooden toothpick comes out clean.

4. Pour warm Chocolate-Buttermilk Frosting over the warm cake, spreading evenly. Place cake in pan on a wire rack; cool thoroughly.

Chocolate-Buttermilk Frosting: In a medium saucepan combine ¼ cup butter or margarine, 3 tablespoons unsweetened cocoa powder, and 3 tablespoons buttermilk. Bring to boiling. Remove from heat. Add 2¼ cups sifted powdered sugar and ½ teaspoon vanilla. Beat until smooth. If desired, stir in ¾ cup coarsely chopped pecans.

Chocolate-Cinnamon Sheet Cake: Prepare as above, except add 1 teaspoon ground cinnamon to the flour mixture.

Nutrition Facts per serving for chocolate-buttermilk or cinnamon variation: 244 cal., 11 g total fat (6 g sat. fat), 45 mg chol., 193 mg sodium, 35 g carbo., 0 g fiber, 2 g pro.
Daily Values: 8% vit. A, 4% calcium, 5% iron
Exchanges: 2 Other Carbo., 2 Fat

Vanilla-Fudge Marble Cake

Prep: 25 minutes **Bake:** 50 minutes **Oven:** 350°F
Cool: 15 minutes **Makes:** 12 servings

- ¾ **cup butter, softened**
- 2 **eggs**
- 2¾ **cups all-purpose flour**
- 1½ **teaspoons baking powder**
- ½ **teaspoon baking soda**
- ½ **teaspoon salt**
- 1½ **cups sugar**
- 2 **teaspoons vanilla**
- 1¼ **cups buttermilk or sour milk (see tip, page 157)**
- ⅔ **cup chocolate-flavored syrup**
- 1 **recipe Semisweet Chocolate Icing**

1. Allow butter and eggs to stand at room temperature for 30 minutes. Meanwhile, grease and lightly flour a 10-inch fluted tube pan. In a medium bowl stir together flour, baking powder, baking soda, and salt. Set aside.

2. In large mixing bowl beat butter with an electric mixer on low to medium speed about 30 seconds. Add sugar and vanilla; beat until fluffy. Add eggs 1 at a time, beating on low to medium speed 1 minute after each addition and scraping bowl frequently. Alternately add flour mixture and buttermilk to butter mixture, beating on low speed after each addition just until combined. Reserve 2 cups batter. Pour remaining batter into prepared pan.

3. In a small mixing bowl combine chocolate syrup and reserved 2 cups batter. Beat on low speed until well combined. Pour chocolate batter over vanilla batter in pan. Do not mix.

4. Bake in a 350° oven about 50 minutes or until wooden toothpick inserted near center comes out clean. Cool 15 minutes on wire rack. Remove from pan; cool completely on wire rack. Drizzle cake with Semisweet Chocolate Icing.

Semisweet Chocolate Icing: In a small saucepan heat ½ cup semisweet chocolate pieces, 2 tablespoons butter, 1 tablespoon light-colored corn syrup, and ¼ teaspoon vanilla over low heat, stirring until chocolate melts and mixture is smooth. Use immediately.

Nutrition Facts per serving: 416 cal., 18 g total fat (10 g sat. fat), 75 mg chol., 400 mg sodium, 59 g carbo., 2 g fiber, 5 g pro.
Daily Values: 12% vit. A, 7% calcium, 9% iron
Exchanges: 3½ Other Carbo., 3 Fat

One-Bowl Chocolate Cake

For an elegant twist, top this cake layer with Ganache (page 170) instead of Chocolate Glaze.

Prep: 20 minutes **Bake:** 30 minutes **Oven:** 350°F
Cool: 1 hour **Makes:** 8 servings

- 1 **cup all-purpose flour**
- 1 **cup sugar**
- ½ **cup unsweetened cocoa powder**
- ½ **teaspoon baking soda**
- ¼ **teaspoon baking powder**
- ¼ **teaspoon salt**
- ¾ **cup milk**
- ⅓ **cup cooking oil**
- 1 **teaspoon vanilla**
- 1 **egg**
- 1 **recipe Chocolate Glaze**

1. Grease and lightly flour a 9×1½-inch round or 8×8×2-inch square baking pan; set pan aside.

2. In a large mixing bowl combine flour, sugar, cocoa powder, baking soda, baking powder, and salt. Add milk, oil, and vanilla. Beat with an electric mixer on low speed just until combined. Beat on medium speed for 2 minutes. Add egg and beat 2 minutes more. Pour batter into prepared pan.

3. Bake in a 350° oven for 30 to 35 minutes or until a wooden toothpick inserted near center comes out clean. Cool cake on a wire rack for 10 minutes. Remove cake from pan. Cool thoroughly on a wire rack. Spoon Chocolate Glaze over cooled cake.

Vanilla-Fudge Marble Cake

Chocolate Glaze: Melt 4 ounces coarsely chopped semisweet chocolate and 3 tablespoons butter over low heat, stirring frequently. Remove from heat. Beat in 1½ cups sifted powdered sugar and 3 tablespoons hot water until smooth. Add additional hot water, if needed, to reach drizzling consistency.

One-Bowl Mocha Cake: Prepare as on page 162, except add 2 tablespoons instant espresso coffee powder to milk; stir to dissolve. Prepare Chocolate Glaze as above, except stir 1 tablespoon instant espresso coffee powder into the hot water before beating into the chocolate mixture.

Nutrition Facts per serving for chocolate or mocha variation:
454 cal., 20 g total fat (7 g sat. fat), 41 mg chol., 230 mg sodium, 66 g carbo., 1 g fiber, 5 g pro.
Daily Values: 5% vit. A, 10% calcium, 12% iron
Exchanges: 4½ Other Carbo., 2 Fat

Gingerbread

Drizzle Vanilla Sauce (page 484) or Lemon Sauce (page 483) over wedges of warm gingerbread.

Prep: 20 minutes **Bake:** 35 minutes **Oven:** 350°F
Cool: 30 minutes **Makes:** 9 servings

- 1½ **cups all-purpose flour**
- ¾ **teaspoon ground cinnamon**
- ¾ **teaspoon ground ginger**
- ½ **teaspoon baking powder**
- ½ **teaspoon baking soda**
- ½ **cup shortening**
- ¼ **cup packed brown sugar**
- 1 **egg**
- ½ **cup mild-flavored molasses**

1. Grease a 9×1½-inch round cake pan; set aside. In a bowl stir together flour, cinnamon, ginger, baking powder, and baking soda; set aside.

2. In a large mixing bowl beat shortening with an electric mixer on medium speed for 30 seconds. Add brown sugar; beat until fluffy (see photo 2, page 153). Add egg and molasses; beat 1 minute. Alternately add flour mixture and ½ cup *water* to shortening mixture, beating on low speed after each addition until combined. Pour batter into prepared pan.

3. Bake in a 350° oven for 35 to 40 minutes or until a wooden toothpick comes out clean. Cool for 30 minutes in pan on wire rack. Serve warm.

Nutrition Facts per serving: 253 cal., 11 g total fat (3 g sat. fat), 24 mg chol., 109 mg sodium, 34 g carbo., 1 g fiber, 3 g pro.
Daily Values: 1% vit. A, 1% vit. C, 7% calcium, 13% iron
Exchanges: 2 Other Carbo., 2 Fat

Granny Cake

Prep: 20 minutes **Bake:** 70 minutes **Oven:** 325°F
Cool: 2 hours **Makes:** 12 servings

- 3 **cups all-purpose flour**
- 2 **cups granulated sugar**
- 1 **teaspoon baking soda**
- 1 **teaspoon ground nutmeg**
- ½ **teaspoon salt**
- ½ **teaspoon ground cloves**
- ¾ **cup butter, softened**
- 2 **cups mashed ripe bananas (about 6)**
- 1 **8-ounce can crushed pineapple, undrained**
- 3 **eggs**
- 2 **teaspoons vanilla**
- 1 **cup finely chopped pecans**
  Powdered sugar (optional)

1. Grease and flour a 10-inch fluted tube pan; set aside. In a medium mixing bowl stir together flour, granulated sugar, baking soda, nutmeg, salt, and cloves; set aside.

2. In large mixing bowl beat butter with an electric mixer on medium speed for 30 seconds. Add bananas, undrained pineapple, eggs, and vanilla. Beat until combined. Add flour mixture. Beat on low speed until combined. Beat on medium speed 1 minute. Fold in pecans. Spread in prepared pan.

3. Bake in a 325° oven for 70 to 75 minutes or until a wooden toothpick inserted near the center comes out clean. Cool cake in pan on a wire rack for 10 minutes. Remove cake from pan. Cool thoroughly on wire rack. If desired, sift powdered sugar over cooled cake just before serving.

Nutrition Facts per serving: 477 cal., 20 g total fat (9 g sat. fat), 86 mg chol., 343 mg sodium, 70 g carbo., 3 g fiber, 6 g pro.
Daily Values: 12% vit. A, 9% vit. C, 3% calcium, 12% iron
Exchanges: 4½ Other Carbo., 3 Fat

Perfect Pans

Bakeware is made from a range of materials that have different effects on a cake. For even baking use sturdy, single-wall aluminum pans. Shiny bakeware, including aluminum, tin, and stainless steel, reflects heat and will result in a thinner golden cake crust. Dark or dull-finish bakeware, such as tin, glass, and many nonstick pans, absorbs more heat, increasing the amount of browning. If you use a dark or dull-finish pan, follow manufacturer's directions. Most suggest reducing the oven temperature by 25°F and checking doneness 3 to 5 minutes before the minimum recommended baking time.

Fruitcake

For a larger fruitcake, double the ingredients. Pour batter into a greased and lightly floured 10-inch tube pan. Bake in a 300°F oven for 1¼ to 1½ hours or until a wooden toothpick comes out clean.

Prep: 30 minutes **Bake:** 1¼ hours **Oven:** 300°F
Cool: 2 hours **Makes:** 16 servings

- 1½ **cups all-purpose flour**
- 1 **teaspoon ground cinnamon**
- ½ **teaspoon baking powder**
- ¼ **teaspoon baking soda**
- ¼ **teaspoon ground nutmeg**
- ¼ **teaspoon ground allspice**
- ¼ **teaspoon ground cloves**
- ¾ **cup diced mixed candied fruits and peels**
- ½ **cup raisins or snipped pitted dates**
- ½ **cup candied red or green cherries, quartered**
- ½ **cup chopped pecans or walnuts**
- 2 **eggs**
- ½ **cup packed brown sugar**
- ½ **cup orange juice or apple juice**
- ⅓ **cup butter, melted**
- 2 **tablespoons mild-flavored molasses**
  Brandy or fruit juice

1. Grease and lightly flour an 8×4×2-inch loaf pan or two 5¾×3×2-inch loaf pans; set pan(s) aside. In a large bowl stir together flour, cinnamon, baking powder, baking soda, nutmeg, allspice, and cloves. Add fruits and peels, raisins, cherries, and nuts; mix ingredients well.

2. In a medium bowl beat eggs; stir in brown sugar, juice, butter, and molasses until combined. Stir into fruit mixture. Pour batter into prepared pan(s). (The smaller pans will be quite full.)

3. Bake in a 300° oven for 1¼ to 1½ hours for the 8×4×2-inch pan, 55 to 65 minutes for the 5¾×3×2-inch pans, or until a wooden toothpick inserted near center comes out clean. If necessary cover pan(s) loosely with foil the last 10 to 15 minutes of baking to prevent overbrowning. Place cake in pan(s) on wire rack; cool thoroughly.

4. Remove cake from pan(s); wrap in brandy- or fruit juice-moistened 100-percent-cotton cheesecloth. Wrap in foil. Store in the refrigerator for 2 to 8 weeks to mellow flavors. Remoisten cheesecloth with brandy weekly or as needed.

Light-Colored Fruitcake: Prepare as above, except omit nutmeg, allspice, and cloves; substitute light-colored corn syrup for the molasses. Add 1 teaspoon finely shredded lemon peel and 1 tablespoon lemon juice with the corn syrup.

Nutrition Facts per serving for fruitcake or light-colored variation: 228 cal., 7 g total fat (3 g sat. fat), 37 mg chol., 95 mg sodium, 37 g carbo., 1 g fiber, 3 g pro.
Daily Values: 4% vit. A, 7% vit. C, 4% calcium, 7% iron
Exchanges: ½ Fruit, 2 Other Carbo., 1 Fat

Pineapple Upside-Down Cake

Carefully spoon the cake batter over the fruit in the baking pan so the fruit arrangement isn't disturbed.

Prep: 20 minutes **Bake:** 30 minutes **Oven:** 350°F
Cool: 30 minutes **Makes:** 8 servings

- 2 **tablespoons butter**
- ⅓ **cup packed brown sugar**
- 1 **8-ounce can pineapple slices, drained and halved**
- 4 **maraschino cherries, halved**
- 1⅓ **cups all-purpose flour**
- ⅔ **cup granulated sugar**
- 2 **teaspoons baking powder**
- ⅔ **cup milk**
- ¼ **cup butter, softened**
- 1 **egg**
- 1 **teaspoon vanilla**

1. Melt the 2 tablespoons butter in a 9×1½-inch round cake pan. Stir in brown sugar and 1 tablespoon *water*. Arrange pineapple and cherries in the pan. Set pan aside.

2. In a medium mixing bowl stir together flour, granulated sugar, and baking powder. Add milk, the ¼ cup butter, egg, and vanilla. Beat with an electric mixer on low speed until combined. Beat on medium speed for 1 minute. Spoon batter over fruit in the prepared pan.

3. Bake in a 350° oven for 30 to 35 minutes or until a wooden toothpick inserted near center comes out clean. Cool on wire rack for 5 minutes. Loosen cake from pan; invert onto a plate. Serve warm.

Apricot Upside-Down Cake: Prepare as above, except substitute one 8½-ounce can unpeeled apricot halves, drained and halved, or peach slices, drained, for the pineapple and cherries.

Pear Upside-Down Cake: Prepare as above, except substitute one 8½-ounce can pear slices, drained, for the pineapple and cherries.

Nutrition Facts per serving for pineapple, apricot, and pear variations: 292 cal., 10 g total fat (6 g sat. fat), 53 mg chol., 216 mg sodium, 47 g carbo., 1 g fiber, 4 g pro.
Daily Values: 9% vit. A, 5% vit. C, 11% calcium, 8% iron
Exchanges: 3 Other Carbo., 1½ Fat

Orange Sponge Cake

Low Fat

Prep: 40 minutes **Bake:** 55 minutes **Oven:** 325°F
Cool: 2 hours **Makes:** 12 servings

> 6 **eggs**
> 1 **tablespoon finely shredded orange peel**
> ½ **cup orange juice or pineapple juice**
> 1 **teaspoon vanilla**
> 1 **cup sugar**
> 1¼ **cups all-purpose flour**
> ½ **teaspoon cream of tartar**
> ½ **cup sugar**

1. Separate eggs. Allow egg whites and egg yolks to stand at room temperature for 30 minutes. In a medium mixing bowl beat egg yolks with an electric mixer on high speed about 5 minutes or until thick and lemon colored (see photo, right). Add orange peel, orange juice, and vanilla; beat on low speed until combined. Gradually beat in the 1 cup sugar at low speed. Increase to medium speed; beat until mixture thickens slightly and doubles in volume (about 5 minutes total).

2. Sprinkle ¼ cup of the flour over egg yolk mixture; fold in until combined. Repeat with remaining flour, ¼ cup at a time. Set egg yolk mixture aside.

3. Thoroughly wash beaters. In a large mixing bowl beat egg whites and cream of tartar on medium speed until soft peaks form (tips curl; see photo 1, page 169). Gradually add the ½ cup sugar, beating on high speed until stiff peaks form (tips stand straight; see photo 2, page 169). Fold 1 cup of the beaten egg white mixture into the egg yolk mixture; fold egg yolk mixture into remaining egg white mixture. Pour into an ungreased 10-inch tube pan.

4. Bake in a 325° oven for 55 to 60 minutes or until cake springs back when lightly touched (see tip, page 160). Immediately invert cake (leave in pan); cool thoroughly (see tip, page 156). Loosen sides of cake from pan; remove from pan.

Lemon Sponge Cake: Prepare as above, except substitute 2 teaspoons finely shredded lemon peel for the orange peel and ¼ cup lemon juice plus ¼ cup water for the orange juice or pineapple juice.

Chocolate Sponge Cake: Prepare as above, except omit orange peel. Reduce flour to 1 cup. Stir ⅓ cup unsweetened cocoa powder into flour.

Almond Sponge Cake: Prepare as at left, except omit orange peel. Add ½ teaspoon almond extract with the juice.

Nutrition Facts per serving for plain, lemon, chocolate, and almond variations: 184 cal., 3 g total fat (1 g sat. fat), 107 mg chol., 32 mg sodium, 36 g carbo., 0 g fiber, 5 g pro.
Daily Values: 4% vit. A, 10% vit. C, 2% calcium, 6% iron
Exchanges: 2 Other Carbo., ½ Fat

Beat egg yolks until thick and the color of lemons. Lift the beaters. If the yolks are sufficiently beaten, they will flow from the beaters in a thick stream.

Hot Milk Sponge Cake

To keep this cake a low-calorie treat, dust it lightly with powdered sugar or top with fresh fruit. If you need a sweeter fix, spread Broiled Coconut Topping (page 158) over the cake and pop it under the broiler.

Low Fat

Prep: 15 minutes **Bake:** 20 minutes **Oven:** 350°F
Cool: 30 minutes **Makes:** 9 servings

> 2 **eggs**
> 1 **cup all-purpose flour**
> 1 **teaspoon baking powder**
> 1 **cup sugar**
> ½ **cup milk**
> 2 **tablespoons butter**

1. Allow eggs to stand at room temperature for 30 minutes. Meanwhile, grease a 9×9×2-inch square baking pan; set pan aside. Stir together flour and baking powder; set aside.

2. In a medium mixing bowl beat eggs with an electric mixer on high speed about 4 minutes or until thick. Gradually add sugar, beating on medium speed for 4 to 5 minutes or until light and fluffy. Add the flour mixture; beat on low to medium speed just until combined.

3. In a small saucepan heat and stir milk and butter until butter melts; add to batter, beating until combined. Pour batter into the prepared pan.

4. Bake in a 350° oven for 20 to 25 minutes or until a wooden toothpick inserted near center comes out clean. Cool cake in pan on a wire rack.

Nutrition Facts per serving: 180 cal., 4 g total fat (2 g sat. fat), 56 mg chol., 93 mg sodium, 33 g carbo., 0 g fiber, 3 g pro.
Daily Values: 4% vit. A, 5% calcium, 5% iron
Exchanges: 2 Other Carbo., ½ Fat

Jelly Roll

Filled with jelly, this cake makes an impressive low-fat dessert. Choose one of the other scrumptious fillings when you want to indulge. The Chocolate Cake Roll filled with whipped cream is shown below right.

Low Fat

Prep: 30 minutes **Bake:** 12 minutes **Oven:** 375°F
Cool: 1 hour **Makes:** 10 servings

 4 **eggs**
 ½ **cup all-purpose flour**
 1 **teaspoon baking powder**
 ½ **teaspoon vanilla**
 ⅓ **cup granulated sugar**
 ½ **cup granulated sugar**
 Sifted powdered sugar
 ½ **cup jelly or jam**

1. Separate eggs. Allow egg whites and egg yolks to stand at room temperature for 30 minutes. Meanwhile, grease and lightly flour a 15×10×1-inch jelly roll pan (see photo 1, page 153); set pan aside. In a small bowl stir together flour and baking powder; set aside.

2. In a medium mixing bowl beat egg yolks and vanilla with an electric mixer on high speed for 5 minutes or until thick and lemon colored (see photo, page 165). Gradually add the ⅓ cup granulated sugar, beating on high speed until sugar is almost dissolved.

3. Thoroughly wash the beaters. In another bowl beat egg whites on medium speed until soft peaks form (tips curl; see photo 1, page 169). Gradually add the ½ cup granulated sugar, beating until stiff peaks form (tips stand straight; see photo 2, page 169). Fold egg yolk mixture into beaten egg whites. Sprinkle flour mixture over egg mixture; fold in gently just until combined. Spread batter evenly in the prepared pan.

4. Bake in a 375° oven for 12 to 15 minutes or until cake springs back when lightly touched (see tip, page 160). Immediately loosen edges of cake from pan and turn cake out onto a towel sprinkled with powdered sugar. Roll up towel and cake into a spiral starting from one of the cake's short sides (see photo 1, right). Cool on a wire rack. Unroll cake; remove towel. Spread cake with jelly or jam to within 1 inch of edges (see photo 2, right). Roll up cake (see photo 3, right).

Ice Cream Roll: Prepare as at left, except substitute 2 cups of your favorite ice cream, softened, for the jelly. Store in the freezer.

Nutrition Facts per serving for jelly or ice cream variation:
160 cal., 2 g total fat (1 g sat. fat), 85 mg chol., 70 mg sodium, 32 g carbo., 0 g fiber, 3 g pro.
Daily Values: 3% vit. A, 4% calcium, 3% iron
Exchanges: 2 Other Carbo.

Chocolate Cake Roll: Prepare as at left, except reduce flour to ⅓ cup and omit baking powder. Add ¼ cup unsweetened cocoa powder and ¼ teaspoon baking soda to flour. Substitute 2 cups whipped cream or cooled chocolate pudding for the jelly. Roll up cake. Drizzle cake roll with half recipe Chocolate Glaze (page 163); chill up to 2 hours.

Nutrition Facts per serving: 275 cal., 15 g total fat (8 g sat. fat), 123 mg chol., 85 mg sodium, 32 g carbo., 0 g fiber, 4 g pro.
Daily Values: 11% vit. A, 5% calcium, 6% iron
Exchanges: 2 Other Carbo., 2½ Fat

Pumpkin Cake Roll: Prepare as at left, except add 2 teaspoons pumpkin pie spice to flour mixture and stir ½ cup canned pumpkin into egg yolk and sugar mixture. Substitute half recipe Cream Cheese Frosting (page 171) for the jelly. Sprinkle cake roll with additional sifted powdered sugar; chill.

Nutrition Facts per serving: 322 cal., 11 g total fat (6 g sat. fat), 110 mg chol., 150 mg sodium, 53 g carbo., 1 g fiber, 4 g pro.
Daily Values: 64% vit. A, 1% vit. C, 5% calcium, 5% iron
Exchanges: 3½ Other Carbo., 2 Fat

1. Starting from a short side, roll up the warm cake and the powdered sugar-coated towel together. Let the cake cool.

2. Carefully unroll the cooled cake and towel. Spread the desired filling over cake, leaving a 1-inch border around the edges.

3. Again, starting from a short side, roll up the cake and filling.

Banana Nut Roll Best Loved

Prep: 40 minutes **Bake:** 15 minutes **Oven:** 375°F
Cool: 1 hour **Makes:** 10 servings

         4 **eggs**
       ½ **cup all-purpose flour**
       ½ **teaspoon baking powder**
       ¼ **teaspoon baking soda**
         1 **recipe Cream Cheese Filling**
       ½ **teaspoon vanilla**
       ⅓ **cup granulated sugar**
       ½ **cup mashed ripe banana (1 large)**
       ½ **cup finely chopped walnuts or pecans**
       ½ **cup granulated sugar**
         1 **recipe Cream Cheese Icing**

1. Separate eggs. Let stand at room temperature for 30 minutes. Lightly grease a 15×10×1-inch jelly roll pan. Line bottom with waxed paper; grease the paper; set aside. For cake, stir together flour, baking powder, and baking soda; set aside.

2. Prepare Cream Cheese Filling; spread in the prepared pan. Set aside. For cake, in a small mixing bowl beat the egg yolks and vanilla with an electric mixer on high speed about 5 minutes or until thick and lemon colored (see photo, page 165). Gradually add the ⅓ cup sugar, beating on high speed until sugar is dissolved. Stir in the banana and nuts.

3. Thoroughly wash the beaters. In a large mixing bowl beat the egg whites on medium speed until soft peaks form (tips curl). Gradually add the ½ cup sugar, beating until stiff peaks form (tips stand straight). Fold yolk mixture into whites. Sprinkle flour mixture evenly over egg mixture; fold in gently just until combined. Gently spoon batter over filling in pan. Carefully spread evenly over filling.

4. Bake in a 375° oven for 15 to 20 minutes or until the cake springs back when lightly touched. Immediately loosen cake from pan and turn cake out onto a towel sprinkled with *sifted powdered sugar*. Carefully peel off waxed paper. Starting from a short side, roll cake into a spiral, using the towel as a guide; do not roll towel into cake. Cool on a wire rack. Spread top with Cream Cheese Icing. If desired, sprinkle with finely chopped *nuts*.

Cream Cheese Filling: In a mixing bowl combine one 8-ounce package and one 3-ounce package cream cheese, softened, and ½ cup sugar. Beat with mixer on medium speed until smooth. Add 1 egg and 3 tablespoons milk; beat thoroughly.

Cream Cheese Icing: In a small mixing bowl combine one 3-ounce package cream cheese, softened, and 1 teaspoon vanilla; beat with an electric mixer on medium speed until light and fluffy. Gradually beat in 2 cups sifted powdered sugar. Beat in enough milk (1 to 2 tablespoons) to reach spreading consistency.

Nutrition Facts per serving: 434 cal., 21 g total fat (10 g sat. fat), 150 mg chol., 204 mg sodium, 56 g carbo., 1 g fiber, 8 g pro.
Daily Values: 15% vit. A, 2% vit. C, 7% calcium, 7% iron
Exchanges: 3½ Other Carbo., 4 Fat

Sour Cream Pound Cake

Prep: 30 minutes **Bake:** 1 hour **Oven:** 325°F
Cool: 2 hours **Makes:** 10 servings

½ cup butter
3 eggs
½ cup dairy sour cream
1½ cups all-purpose flour
¼ teaspoon baking powder
⅛ teaspoon baking soda
1 cup sugar
½ teaspoon vanilla

1. Allow butter, eggs, and sour cream to stand at room temperature for 30 minutes. Meanwhile, grease and lightly flour an 8×4×2-inch or 9×5×3-inch loaf pan (see photo 1, page 153); set aside. In a medium bowl stir together flour, baking powder, and baking soda; set aside.

2. In a mixing bowl beat butter with an electric mixer on medium to high speed for 30 seconds. Gradually add sugar, beating about 10 minutes or until very light and fluffy. Beat in vanilla. Add eggs 1 at a time, beating 1 minute after each addition and scraping bowl frequently. Alternately add flour mixture and sour cream to butter mixture, beating on low to medium speed after each addition just until combined. Pour batter into the prepared pan.

3. Bake in a 325° oven for 60 to 75 minutes or until a wooden toothpick inserted near center comes out clean. Cool on a wire rack for 10 minutes. Remove from pan; cool.

Lemon-Poppy Seed Pound Cake: Prepare as as above, except substitute ½ cup lemon yogurt

for sour cream. Add 1 teaspoon finely shredded lemon peel, 2 tablespoons lemon juice, and 2 tablespoons poppy seeds to batter.

Orange-Rosemary Pound Cake: Prepare as at left, except stir 1¼ teaspoons finely shredded orange peel and 1 teaspoon snipped fresh rosemary into the batter.

Nutrition Facts per serving for sour cream, lemon-poppy seed, and orange-rosemary variations: 272 cal., 13 g total fat (8 g sat. fat), 94 mg chol., 149 mg sodium, 34 g carbo., 1 g fiber, 4 g pro. Daily Values: 11% vit. A, 3% calcium, 6% iron Exchanges: 2 Other Carbo., 2½ Fat

---

Chiffon Cake

Prep: 30 minutes **Bake:** 65 minutes **Oven:** 325°F
Cool: 2 hours **Makes:** 12 servings

7 eggs
2¼ cups sifted cake flour or 2 cups sifted all-purpose flour
1½ cups sugar
1 tablespoon baking powder
¼ teaspoon salt
½ cup cooking oil
2 teaspoons finely shredded orange peel
1 teaspoon finely shredded lemon peel
1 teaspoon vanilla
½ teaspoon cream of tartar

1. Separate eggs. Allow egg whites and egg yolks to stand at room temperature for 30 minutes. Meanwhile, in a large mixing bowl stir together flour, sugar, baking powder, and salt. Make a well in the center of flour mixture. Add egg yolks, oil, orange and lemon peels, vanilla, and ¾ cup *cold water*. Beat with an electric mixer on low speed until combined. Beat on high speed for 5 minutes more or until satin smooth.

2. Thoroughly wash the beaters. In a very large mixing bowl beat egg whites and cream of tartar on medium speed until stiff peaks form (tips stand straight; see photo 2, page 169). Pour batter in a thin stream over beaten egg whites; fold in gently. Pour into an ungreased 10-inch tube pan.

3. Bake in a 325° oven for 65 to 70 minutes or until top springs back when lightly touched (see tip, page 160). Immediately invert cake (leave in pan); cool thoroughly (see tip, page 156). Loosen sides of cake from pan; remove cake from pan.

Nutrition Facts per serving: 292 cal., 12 g total fat (2 g sat. fat), 124 mg chol., 186 mg sodium, 41 g carbo., 0 g fiber, 5 g pro. Daily Values: 4% vit. A, 2% vit. C, 9% calcium, 11% iron Exchanges: 2½ Other Carbo., 2 Fat

Sour Cream Pound Cake

Angel Food Cake

Loosen the cooled cake from the pan by sliding a metal spatula between the cake and pan. Constantly pressing the spatula against the pan, draw it around the pan in a continuous, not sawing, motion so you don't cut into the cake.

No Fat

Prep: 50 minutes **Bake:** 40 minutes **Oven:** 350°F
Cool: 2 hours **Makes:** 12 servings

- 1½ cups egg whites (10 to 12 large)
- 1½ cups sifted powdered sugar
- 1 cup sifted cake flour or sifted all-purpose flour
- 1½ teaspoons cream of tartar
- 1 teaspoon vanilla
- 1 cup granulated sugar

1. In a very large mixing bowl allow egg whites to stand at room temperature for 30 minutes. Meanwhile, sift powdered sugar and flour together three times; set aside.

2. Add cream of tartar and vanilla to egg whites. Beat with an electric mixer on medium speed until soft peaks form (tips curl; see photo 1, right). Gradually add granulated sugar, about 2 tablespoons at a time, beating until stiff peaks form (tips stand straight; see photo 2, right).

3. Sift one-fourth of the powdered sugar mixture over beaten egg whites (see photo 3, right); fold in gently (see photo 4, right). Repeat, folding in the remaining powdered sugar mixture by fourths. Pour into an ungreased 10-inch tube pan. Gently cut through batter to remove air pockets (see photo 5, right).

4. Bake on the lowest rack in a 350° oven for 40 to 45 minutes or until top springs back when lightly touched (see tip, page 160). Immediately invert cake; cool thoroughly in pan (see tip, page 156). Loosen cake from pan; remove cake.

Chocolate Angel Food Cake: Prepare as above, except sift ¼ cup unsweetened cocoa powder with the powdered sugar-flour mixture.

Honey Angel Food Cake: Prepare as above, except after beating egg whites to soft peaks, gradually pour ¼ cup honey in a thin stream over the egg white mixture. Continue as above, except beat only ½ cup granulated sugar into the egg whites.

Nutrition Facts per serving for plain, chocolate, and honey variations: 161 cal., 0 g total fat (0 g sat. fat), 0 mg chol., 51 mg sodium, 36 g carbo., 0 g fiber, 4 g pro.
Daily Values: 4% iron
Exchanges: 2 Other Carbo.

1. Beat egg whites, cream of tartar, and vanilla until soft peaks form. The peaks will curl when the beaters are lifted from the mixture.

2. After adding granulated sugar, beat the egg white mixture until stiff peaks form. The peaks will stand straight up when the beaters are lifted from the mixture.

3. Sift powdered sugar mixture over stiffly beaten egg white mixture. You can press the dry mixture through a sieve if you don't have a sifter.

4. To fold in, cut down through mixture with a rubber spatula; scrape across bottom of bowl and bring spatula up and over, close to surface of batter.

5. To eliminate any large air bubbles, gently cut through cake batter in the pan with a narrow metal spatula or knife.

Angel Food Cake Success

■ Separate the eggs carefully. Even a trace of yolk will deflate the beaten whites.

■ Make sure your utensils (bowls, beaters, and spatulas) are clean. The smallest amount of oil or fat on beaters or a mixing bowl will compromise the volume of the beaten egg whites.

■ Do not add the granulated sugar too late. If you begin to add the sugar when soft peaks form, you will achieve the desired volume faster.

■ Avoid overbeating the egg white mixture. Beat just until stiff peaks form (see photo 2, above) and the mixture still flows slightly when the bowl is tilted.

Butter Frosting

Start to Finish: 20 minutes   **Makes:** about 4 cups

- ¾ **cup butter, softened**
- 9 **cups sifted powdered sugar (about 2 pounds)**
- ¼ **cup milk**
- 2 **teaspoons vanilla**
   Milk
   Food coloring (optional)

1. In a very large mixing bowl beat butter until smooth. Gradually add 2 cups of the powdered sugar, beating well. Slowly beat in the ¼ cup milk and the vanilla.

2. Gradually beat in remaining powdered sugar. Beat in enough additional milk to reach spreading consistency. If desired, tint with food coloring. This frosts the tops and sides of two 8- or 9-inch cake layers. (Halve the recipe to frost a 13×9×2-inch cake.)

Chocolate Butter Frosting: Prepare as above, except beat ½ cup unsweetened cocoa powder into butter and reduce powdered sugar to a total of 8½ cups.

Lemon or Orange Butter Frosting: Prepare as above, except substitute lemon juice or orange juice for the milk and add ½ teaspoon finely shredded lemon peel or 1 teaspoon finely shredded orange peel with the juice.

Nutrition Facts per ¹⁄₁₂ of recipe for plain, chocolate, lemon and orange variations: 407 cal., 12 g total fat (8 g sat. fat), 33 mg chol., 127 mg sodium, 76 g carbo., 0 g fiber, 0 g pro.
Daily Values: 9% vit. A, 1% calcium
Exchanges: 5 Other Carbo., 1 Fat

Cake Mix Fix-Ups

You can create a special cake simply by adding one of the following to a two-layer cake mix.

■ Add ⅓ cup peanut butter to one-third of white or yellow batter. Pour plain batter into baking pans; pour peanut butter batter on top. Swirl gently. Bake and cool as directed. Frost with desired frosting and sprinkle with honey-roasted peanuts, finely chopped peanut brittle, or chopped chocolate-covered peanut butter cups.

■ Replace the oil called for in package directions of white or yellow batter with one 8½-ounce can cream of coconut. Stir ½ cup coconut into batter.

■ Add to mixed batter: ½ cup finely chopped nuts; ½ cup miniature semisweet chocolate pieces; ½ cup well-drained, chopped maraschino cherries; ⅓ cup malted milk powder; or 1 tablespoon finely shredded orange or lemon peel.

No-Cook Fudge Frosting

Start to Finish: 15 minutes   **Makes:** about 4 cups

- 9 **cups sifted powdered sugar (about 2 pounds)**
- 1 **cup unsweetened cocoa powder**
- 1 **cup butter, softened**
- ⅔ **cup boiling water**
- 2 **teaspoons vanilla**

1. In a very large bowl combine powdered sugar and cocoa powder. Add butter, boiling water, and vanilla. Beat with an electric mixer on low speed until combined. Beat for 1 minute on medium speed. If necessary, cool for 20 minutes or until mixture reaches spreading consistency. This frosts tops and sides of two 8- or 9-inch cake layers. (Halve the recipe to frost a 13×9×2-inch cake.)

Nutrition Facts per ¹⁄₁₂ of recipe: 470 cal., 17 g total fat (10 g sat. fat), 44 mg chol., 166 mg sodium, 79 g carbo., 0 g fiber, 2 g pro.
Daily Values: 12% vit. A, 8% calcium, 6% iron
Exchanges: 5 Other Carbo., 2 Fat

Ganache

Spoon this versatile chocolate icing over a single cake layer on a wire rack so the excess can drip off. Transfer the cake to a platter once Ganache sets.

Start to Finish: 35 minutes   **Makes:** a scant 2 cups

1. In a medium saucepan bring 1 cup whipping cream just to boiling over medium-high heat. Remove from heat. Add 12 ounces chopped milk chocolate, semisweet chocolate, or bittersweet chocolate (do not stir). Let stand 5 minutes. Stir until smooth. Cool for 15 minutes. Spoon evenly over desired 8- or 9-inch cake layer.

Nutrition Facts per ¹⁄₁₂ of recipe: 209 cal., 15 g total fat (9 g sat. fat), 27 mg chol., 28 mg sodium, 19 g carbo., 0 g fiber, 2 g pro.
Daily Values: 6% vit. A, 5% calcium
Exchanges: 1½ Other Carbo., 3 Fat

Truffle Frosting: Prepare Ganache as directed above, except double the ingredients and use milk chocolate only (not semisweet or bittersweet). Instead of cooling for 15 minutes, transfer to a large mixing bowl. Cover and chill mixture overnight. Beat with an electric mixer on medium speed for 30 seconds or until fluffy and of spreading consistency. This frosts the tops and sides of two 8- or 9-inch cake layers.

Nutrition Facts per ¹⁄₁₂ of recipe: 406 cal., 30 g total fat (17 g sat. fat), 55 mg chol., 53 mg sodium, 36 g carbo., 0 g fiber, 5 g pro.
Daily Values: 12% vit. A, 10% calcium
Exchanges: 2½ Other Carbo., 5 Fat

Chocolate-Sour Cream Frosting

Start to Finish: 20 minutes **Makes:** about 4½ cups

- 1 12-ounce package (2 cups) semisweet chocolate pieces
- ½ cup butter
- 1 8-ounce carton dairy sour cream
- 4½ cups sifted powdered sugar (about 1 pound)

1. In a large saucepan melt chocolate and butter over low heat, stirring frequently. Cool for 5 minutes. Stir in sour cream. Gradually add powdered sugar, beating until smooth. This frosts tops and sides of two 8- or 9-inch cake layers. (Halve the recipe to frost a 13×9×2-inch cake.) Cover and store frosted cake in the refrigerator.

Chocolate-Mint-Sour Cream Frosting: Prepare as above, except stir in ½ teaspoon mint extract with the sour cream.

Nutrition Facts per ¹⁄₁₂ of recipe for chocolate or mint variation: 400 cal., 20 g total fat (12 g sat. fat), 30 mg chol., 93 mg sodium, 48 g carbo., 4 g fiber, 1 g pro.
Daily Values: 9% vit. A, 2% calcium
Exchanges: 3 Other Carbo., 3 Fat

Cream Cheese Frosting

Start to Finish: 20 minutes **Makes:** about 4 cups

- 1 8-ounce package cream cheese, softened
- ½ cup butter or margarine, softened
- 2 teaspoons vanilla
- 5¾ to 6¼ cups sifted powdered sugar

1. Beat cream cheese, butter, and vanilla with electric mixer until light and fluffy. Gradually add 2 cups of the powdered sugar, beating well. Gradually beat in additional powdered sugar to reach spreading consistency. This frosts tops and sides of two 8- or 9-inch layers. (Halve the recipe to frost a 13×9×2-inch cake.) Cover and store frosted cake in the refrigerator.

Chocolate-Cream Cheese Frosting: Prepare frosting as above, except beat ½ cup unsweetened cocoa powder into the cream cheese mixture and reduce powdered sugar to 5¼ to 5¾ cups. Makes about 3⅔ cups.

Nutrition Facts per ¹⁄₁₂ of recipe for plain or chocolate variation: 328 cal., 15 g total fat (9 g sat. fat), 43 mg chol., 139 mg sodium, 49 g carbo., 0 g fiber, 2 g pro.
Daily Values: 12% vit. A, 2% calcium, 2% iron
Exchanges: 3 Other Carbo., 2 Fat

Creamy White Frosting

Start to Finish: 25 minutes **Makes:** about 3 cups

- 1 cup shortening
- 1½ teaspoons vanilla
- ½ teaspoon lemon extract, orange extract, or almond extract
- 4½ cups sifted powdered sugar (about 1 pound)
- 3 to 4 tablespoons milk

1. In a medium mixing bowl beat shortening, vanilla, and extract with an electric mixer on medium speed for 30 seconds. Slowly add half of the powdered sugar, beating well. Add 2 tablespoons of the milk. Gradually beat in remaining powdered sugar and enough remaining milk to reach spreading consistency. This frosts the tops and sides of two 8- or 9-inch cake layers. (Halve the recipe to frost a 13×9×2-inch cake.)

Nutrition Facts per ¹⁄₁₂ of recipe: 298 cal., 16 g total fat (4 g sat. fat), 0 mg chol., 2 mg sodium, 38 g carbo., 0 g fiber, 0 g pro.
Daily Values: 1% vit. C, 2% calcium, 1% iron
Exchanges: 2½ Other Carbo., 2 Fat

Meringue Frosting

No Fat

Start to Finish: 25 minutes **Makes:** about 5 cups

- 1½ cups granulated sugar
- ⅓ cup cold water
- 2 egg whites
- ¼ teaspoon cream of tartar
- 1 teaspoon vanilla

1. In a 2-quart top of a double boiler combine sugar, water, egg whites, and cream of tartar. Beat with an electric mixer on low speed for 30 seconds.

2. Place the pan over boiling water (upper pan should not touch the water). Cook, beating constantly with the electric mixer on high speed, for 10 to 13 minutes or until an instant-read thermometer registers 160°F when inserted in the mixture, stopping beater and quickly scraping bottom and sides of pan every 5 minutes to prevent sticking. Remove pan from the heat; add vanilla. Beat about 1 minute more or until frosting is fluffy and holds soft peaks. This frosts tops and sides of two 8- or 9-inch cake layers or one 10-inch tube cake. Store frosted cake in the refrigerator and serve the same day it is made.

Nutrition Facts per ¹⁄₁₂ of recipe: 97 cal., 0 g total fat (0 g sat. fat), 0 mg chol., 10 mg sodium, 24 g carbo., 0 g fiber, 1 g pro.
Exchanges: 1½ Other Carbo.

Browned Butter Frosting

Prep: 20 minutes   **Makes:** about 3 cups

 ¾ **cup butter**
 6 **cups sifted powdered sugar**
 3 **tablespoons milk**
 1½ **teaspoons vanilla**

1. In a small saucepan heat butter over low heat until melted. Continue heating until butter turns a delicate brown. Remove from heat. In a large bowl combine powdered sugar, milk, and vanilla. Add browned butter. Beat with an electric mixer on low speed until combined. Beat on medium to high speed, adding additional milk, if necessary, to reach spreading consistency. This frosts tops and sides of two 8- or 9-inch cake layers.

Nutrition Facts per ¹⁄₁₂ **of recipe:** 307 cal., 12 g total fat (8 g sat. fat), 33 mg chol., 126 mg sodium, 51 g carbo., 0 g fiber, 0 g pro.
Daily Values: 9% vit. A, 1% calcium
Exchanges: 3 Other Carbo., 1½ Fat

Penuche Frosting

Start to Finish: 15 minutes   **Makes:** 2 cups

1. In a saucepan melt ½ cup butter; stir in 1 cup packed brown sugar. Cook and stir until bubbly. Remove from heat. Add ¼ cup milk; beat vigorously with a wooden spoon until smooth. Add 3½ cups sifted powdered sugar; beat by hand until frosting reaches spreading consistency. Immediately frost tops of two 8- or 9-inch layers or top of one 13×9×2-inch cake.

Nutrition Facts per ¹⁄₁₂ **of recipe:** 258 cal., 8 g total fat (5 g sat. fat), 22 mg chol., 93 mg sodium, 47 g carbo., 0 g fiber, 0 g pro.
Daily Values: 6% vit. A, 2% calcium, 2% iron
Exchanges: 3 Other Carbo., 1 Fat

Powdered Sugar Icing

Start to Finish: 10 minutes
Makes: ½ cup (enough to drizzle over one 10-inch tube cake)

 1 **cup sifted powdered sugar**
 ¼ **teaspoon vanilla**
 1 **tablespoon milk or orange juice**

1. In a small bowl combine powdered sugar, vanilla, and milk. Stir in additional milk, 1 teaspoon at a time, until icing reaches drizzling consistency.

Chocolate Powdered Sugar Icing: Prepare as at left, except add 2 tablespoons unsweetened cocoa powder to the powdered sugar and only use milk, not orange juice.

Nutrition Facts per ¹⁄₁₂ **of recipe for vanilla or chocolate variation:** 34 cal., 0 g total fat (0 g sat. fat), 0 mg chol., 1 mg sodium, 8 g carbo., 0 g fiber, 0 g pro.
Exchanges: ½ Other Carbo.

Icing on the Cake

Decorating your cake can be as simple as a luscious, creamy frosting swirled attractively over the layers. Begin with these tips.

1. Get rid of loose crumbs on a cake before you frost it. Brush them off with a pastry brush or your hand.

2. To keep the plate clean, tuck strips of waxed paper under the edge of the cake before frosting it. Spread about ½ cup frosting on top of first cake layer.

3. Place the second cake layer, top side up, on top of the frosted layer. Spread a thin coating of frosting on the sides of the cake to seal in any crumbs.

4. Add a thicker coating of frosting to sides of cake. Then frost sides of cake again, swirling and building up top edge about ¼ inch above the cake.

Finally, spread the remaining frosting on top of the cake, blending the frosting at the edge. Remove the strips of waxed paper once you've finished frosting the cake. If time permits, let the cake stand about an hour before slicing to allow the frosting to set.

Chapter 7

Candies

On the divider: **Fudge** (see recipe, page 175); **Easy White Fudge** (see recipe, page 176)

Candies

Fudge

This classic candy (and other candies) can be frozen for up to 2 months (see photo, page 173).

Prep: 15 minutes **Cook:** 30 minutes **Cool:** 50 minutes
Makes: about 1¼ pounds (32 pieces)

- 2 **cups sugar**
- ¾ **cup half-and-half or light cream**
- 2 **ounces unsweetened chocolate, cut up**
- 1 **teaspoon light-colored corn syrup**
- 2 **tablespoons butter**
- 1 **teaspoon vanilla**
- ½ **cup chopped nuts (optional)**

1. Line a 9×5×3-inch loaf pan with foil, extending the foil over the edges of the pan. Butter the foil; set pan aside.

2. Butter the sides of a 2-quart heavy saucepan. In saucepan combine sugar, half-and-half, chocolate, corn syrup, and ⅛ teaspoon *salt*. Cook and stir over medium heat until mixture boils. Clip a candy thermometer to side of pan. Reduce heat to medium-low; continue boiling at a moderate, steady rate (see photo, page 181, bottom right), stirring occasionally, until thermometer registers 236°F, soft-ball stage (20 to 25 minutes). (Adjust heat as necessary to maintain a steady boil.)

3. Remove saucepan from heat. Add butter and vanilla, but do not stir. Cool, without stirring, to 110°F (50 to 60 minutes). Remove thermometer from saucepan. Beat mixture vigorously with a clean wooden spoon until it just begins to thicken. If desired, add nuts. Continue beating until fudge just starts to lose its gloss (6 to 8 minutes total).

4. Immediately spread fudge evenly in the prepared pan. Score into squares while warm. When fudge is firm, use foil to lift it out of pan. Cut fudge into squares. Store tightly covered up to 1 week.

Nutrition Facts per piece: 71 cal., 2 g total fat (1 g sat. fat), 4 mg chol., 20 mg sodium, 13 g carbo., 0 g fiber, 0 g pro.
Daily Values: 1% vit. A, 1% calcium, 1% iron
Exchanges: 1 Other Carbo., ½ Fat

It's All in the Pan

The saucepan you use when making candy has a lot to do with the success or failure of your endeavor. Most of the recipes in this chapter call for a 2-quart saucepan. When choosing a pan, select a heavy-duty one that measures 6 to 7 inches in diameter. It's also important that the pan has straight, not slanted, sides so your candy thermometer will clip on easily.

Simple Fudge `Best Loved`

Prep: 10 minutes **Cook:** 16 minutes **Chill:** 2 hours
Makes: about 2 pounds (64 pieces)

- 1½ **cups sugar**
- 1 **5-ounce can (⅔ cup) evaporated milk**
- ½ **cup butter**
- 2 **cups tiny marshmallows**
- 1 **cup semisweet chocolate pieces or chopped bittersweet chocolate**
- ½ **cup chopped walnuts**
- ½ **teaspoon vanilla**

1. Line an 8×8×2-inch baking pan with foil, extending the foil over the edges of the pan. Butter the foil; set pan aside.

2. Butter the sides of a 2-quart heavy saucepan. In saucepan combine sugar, evaporated milk, and butter. Cook and stir over medium-high heat until mixture boils (about 10 minutes). Reduce heat to medium; continue cooking, stirring constantly, for 6 minutes. Remove saucepan from heat. Add marshmallows, chocolate pieces, walnuts, and vanilla; stir until marshmallows and chocolate melt and mixture is combined. Beat by hand for 1 minute. Spread fudge evenly in the prepared pan. Score into squares while warm. Cover and chill for 2 to 3 hours or until firm. When fudge is firm, use foil to lift it out of pan. Cut fudge into squares. Store tightly covered in the refrigerator for up to 1 month.

Microwave directions: In a 2½-quart microwave-safe bowl, microwave butter, uncovered, on 100 percent power (high) for 45 to 60 seconds (for 1,000- to 1,300-watt ovens) or 60 to 75 seconds (for 600- to 800-watt ovens) or until melted. Stir in the sugar and evaporated milk. Microwave, uncovered, on high 7 minutes (for 1,000- to 1,300-watt ovens) or 10 minutes (for 600- to 800-watt ovens), stirring every 3 minutes. Carefully remove bowl from microwave oven. Add marshmallows, chocolate pieces, nuts, and vanilla, stirring until marshmallows and chocolate are melted and mixture is combined. Beat by hand for 1 minute. Pour into prepared pan; continue with step 2 as above.

Peanut Butter-Chocolate Fudge: Prepare as above, except substitute ½ cup peanut butter for the butter and, if desired, peanuts for the walnuts.

Nutrition Facts per piece for chocolate or peanut butter variation: 59 cal., 3 g total fat (2 g sat. fat), 5 mg chol., 20 mg sodium, 8 g carbo., 0 g fiber, 0 g pro.
Daily Values: 1% vit. A, 1% calcium, 1% iron
Exchanges: ½ Other Carbo., ½ Fat

Easy White Fudge

This creamy white confection has just a hint of orange flavor (see photo, page 173).

Prep: 20 minutes **Chill:** 2 hours
Makes: about 2 pounds (64 pieces)

- **3 cups white baking pieces**
- **1 14-ounce can (1¼ cups) sweetened condensed milk**
- **1 cup chopped almonds, macadamia nuts, or pecans**
- **2 teaspoons finely shredded orange peel**
- **1 teaspoon vanilla**
    Coarsely chopped almonds, macadamia nuts, or pecans (optional)

1. Line an 8×8×2-inch or 9×9×2-inch baking pan with foil, extending the foil over the edges of the pan. Butter the foil; set pan aside.

2. In a 2-quart heavy saucepan cook and stir white baking pieces and sweetened condensed milk over low heat just until pieces melt and mixture is smooth. Remove saucepan from heat. Stir in the 1 cup nuts, orange peel, and vanilla.

3. Spread fudge evenly in the prepared pan. If desired, sprinkle with additional nuts; press in lightly. Score into squares while warm. Cover and chill about 2 hours or until firm. When fudge is firm, use foil to lift it out of pan. Cut fudge into squares. Store tightly covered up to 1 week.

Nutrition Facts per piece: 92 cal., 5 g total fat (3 g sat. fat), 2 mg chol., 23 mg sodium, 11 g carbo., 0 g fiber, 1 g pro.
Daily Values: 2% calcium, 1% iron
Exchanges: 1 Other Carbo., 1 Fat

Easy Chocolate Fudge: Prepare as above, except substitute 3 cups semisweet chocolate pieces for white baking pieces. If desired, omit orange peel.

Nutrition Facts per piece: 71 cal., 4 g total fat (2 g sat. fat), 2 mg chol., 9 mg sodium, 9 g carbo., 1 g fiber, 1 g pro.
Daily Values: 3% calcium, 2% iron
Exchanges: ½ Other Carbo., 1 Fat

Lining Pans with Foil

Many candy recipes direct you to line your pan with foil. But how do you get that foil pushed into those corners without tearing it? Try this: Shape the foil around the outside of your pan, then lift it off and place it inside the pan, pressing gently into the corners.

Penuche

Prep: 15 minutes **Cook:** 20 minutes **Cool:** 40 minutes
Makes: about 1¼ pounds (32 pieces)

- **1 cup granulated sugar**
- **1 cup packed brown sugar**
- **⅔ cup half-and-half or light cream**
- **2 tablespoons butter**
- **1 teaspoon vanilla**
- **½ cup chopped pecans, walnuts, or cashews**

1. Line an 8×4×2-inch loaf pan with foil, extending the foil over the edges of the pan. Butter the foil; set pan aside.

2. Butter the sides of a 2-quart heavy saucepan. In saucepan combine granulated sugar, brown sugar, and half-and-half. Cook and stir over medium heat until mixture boils. Clip a candy thermometer to side of pan. Reduce heat to medium-low; continue boiling at a moderate, steady rate (see photo, page 181, bottom right), stirring frequently, until thermometer registers 236°F, soft-ball stage (about 15 minutes). (Adjust heat as necessary to maintain a steady boil.)

3. Remove saucepan from heat. Add butter and vanilla, but do not stir. Cool, without stirring, to 110°F (about 40 minutes).

4. Remove thermometer from saucepan. Beat mixture vigorously with a clean wooden spoon until it just begins to thicken. Add the chopped nuts. Continue beating until penuche becomes thick and just starts to lose its gloss (about 10 minutes total).

5. Immediately spread penuche evenly in the prepared pan. Score into squares while warm. When penuche is firm, use foil to lift it out of pan. Cut penuche into squares. Store tightly covered for up to 1 week.

Nutrition Facts per piece: 75 cal., 3 g total fat (1 g sat. fat), 4 mg chol., 13 mg sodium, 13 g carbo., 0 g fiber, 0 g pro.
Daily Values: 1% vit. A, 1% calcium, 1% iron
Exchanges: 1 Other Carbo., ½ Fat

Cooking and Testing Candy Mixtures

Cooking candy at the proper rate and accurately determining when it is done are two critical steps in making candy successfully.

■ Candy mixtures should boil at a moderate, steady rate over their entire surface (see photo, page 181, bottom right). To guide you, our recipes suggest range-top temperatures. However, you may need to adjust the temperature of your range in order to maintain the best rate of cooking, which ensures that the candy will cook within the recommended time. Cooking too fast or slow makes candy too hard or soft. When stirring a hot candy mixture, use a wooden spoon.

■ The most accurate way to test the stage of the hot mixture is to use a candy thermometer. Be sure to check the accuracy of your thermometer every time you use it. To test it, place the thermometer in a saucepan of boiling water for a few minutes, then read the temperature. If the thermometer reads above or below 212°F, add or subtract the same number of degrees from the temperature specified in the recipe and cook to that temperature. And don't forget to add or subtract that same number of degrees from the cooling temperature in recipes where candy mixtures need to cool.

■ If a candy thermometer is not available, use the corresponding cold-water test described below. Start testing the candy shortly before it reaches the minimum cooking time.

Cold-Water Test

For the cold-water test, spoon a few drops of the hot candy mixture into a cup of very cold (but not icy) water. Using your fingers, form the drops into a ball. Remove the ball from the water; the firmness will indicate the temperature of the candy mixture. If the mixture has not reached the correct stage, continue cooking and retesting, using fresh water and a clean spoon each time.

Thread stage (230° to 233°F)
When a teaspoon is dipped into the hot mixture, then removed, the candy falls off the spoon in a 2-inch-long, fine, thin thread.

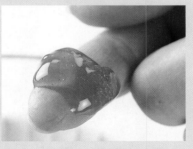

Soft-ball stage (234° to 240°F)
When the ball of candy is removed from the cold water, the candy instantly flattens and runs over your finger.

Firm-ball stage (244° to 248°F)
When the ball of candy is removed from the cold water, it is firm enough to hold its shape, but quickly flattens.

Hard-ball stage (250° to 266°F)
When the ball of candy is removed from the cold water, it can be deformed by pressure, but it doesn't flatten until pressed.

Soft-crack stage (270° to 290°F)
When dropped into the cold water, the candy separates into hard, but pliable and elastic, threads.

Hard-crack stage (295° to 310°F)
When dropped into the cold water, the candy separates into hard, brittle threads that snap easily.

Pralines

Prep: 15 minutes **Cook:** 21 minutes
Cool: 30 minutes **Makes:** about 36 pieces

  1½ **cups granulated sugar**
  1½ **cups packed brown sugar**
    1 **cup half-and-half or light cream**
    3 **tablespoons butter**
    2 **cups pecan halves**

1. Butter the sides of a 2-quart heavy saucepan. In saucepan combine granulated sugar, brown sugar, and half-and-half. Cook and stir over medium-high heat until mixture boils. Clip a candy thermometer to side of pan. Reduce heat to medium-low; continue boiling at a moderate, steady rate (see photo, page 181, bottom right), stirring occasionally, until thermometer registers 234°F, soft-ball stage (16 to 18 minutes). (Adjust heat as necessary to maintain a steady boil.)

2. Remove saucepan from heat. Add butter, but do not stir. Cool, without stirring, to 150°F (about 30 minutes).

3. Remove thermometer from saucepan. Stir in pecans. Beat vigorously with a clean wooden spoon until mixture just begins to thicken but is still glossy (about 3 minutes).

4. Working quickly, drop candy by spoonfuls onto waxed paper. Let stand until firm. Store tightly covered for up to 1 week.

Chocolate Pralines: Prepare as above, except add 2 ounces unsweetened chocolate, finely chopped, with the butter.

Nutrition Facts per piece for plain or chocolate variation:
125 cal., 6 g total fat (1 g sat. fat), 5 mg chol., 17 mg sodium,
18 g carbo.,1 g fiber, 1 g pro.
Daily Values: 1% vit. A, 2% calcium, 2% iron
Exchanges: 1 Other Carbo., 1½ Fat

Divinity

No Fat

Prep: 15 minutes **Cook:** 20 minutes **Makes:** about 40 pieces

  2½ **cups sugar**
   ½ **cup water**
   ½ **cup light-colored corn syrup**
    2 **egg whites**
    1 **teaspoon vanilla**
    1 **or 2 drops food coloring (optional)**
   ½ **cup chopped candied fruit or nuts**

1. In a 2-quart heavy saucepan combine sugar, water, and corn syrup. Cook and stir over medium-high heat until mixture boils. Clip a candy thermometer to side of pan. Reduce heat to medium; continue cooking, without stirring, until the thermometer registers 260°F, hard-ball stage (10 to 15 minutes). (Adjust heat as necessary to maintain a steady boil.)

2. Remove saucepan from heat; remove thermometer. In a large mixing bowl beat egg whites with a freestanding electric mixer on medium speed until stiff peaks form (tips stand straight). Gradually pour hot mixture in a thin stream over egg whites, beating on high speed about 3 minutes; scrape sides of bowl occasionally. Add vanilla and, if desired, food coloring. Continue beating on high just until candy mixture starts to lose its gloss (5 to 6 minutes). When beaters are lifted, candy mixture should fall in a ribbon that mounds on itself (see photo 1, below).

3. Drop a spoonful of candy mixture onto waxed paper. If it stays mounded, the mixture has been beaten sufficiently. If mixture flattens, beat ½ to 1 minute more; check again. If mixture is too stiff to spoon, beat in a few drops hot water until mixture is a softer consistency. Immediately stir in candied fruit. Quickly drop remaining mixture onto waxed paper (see photo 2, below). Store tightly covered for up to 1 week.

Nutrition Facts per piece: 67 cal., 0 g total fat (0 g sat. fat), 0 mg chol., 10 mg sodium, 17 g carbo., 0 g fiber, 0 g pro.
Exchanges: 1 Other Carbo.

1. When candy mixture just starts to lose its gloss, lift beaters. The mixture should fall in a ribbon, mound on itself, and not disappear into what remains in the bowl.

2. With two teaspoons, quickly drop mounds of the candy mixture onto waxed paper.

Caramels

Prep: 15 minutes **Cook:** 55 minutes
Makes: about 2 pounds (64 pieces)

- 1 **cup chopped walnuts (optional)**
- 1 **cup butter**
- 1 **16-ounce package (2¼ cups) packed brown sugar**
- 2 **cups half-and-half or light cream**
- 1 **cup light-colored corn syrup**
- 1 **teaspoon vanilla**

1. Line an 8×8×2-inch or 9×9×2-inch baking pan with foil, extending foil over edges of pan. Butter the foil. If desired, sprinkle walnuts over bottom of pan. Set pan aside.

2. In a 3-quart heavy saucepan melt butter over low heat. Add brown sugar, half-and-half, and corn syrup; mix well. Cook and stir over medium-high heat until mixture boils. Clip a candy thermometer to side of pan. Reduce heat to medium; continue boiling at a moderate, steady rate (see photo, page 181, bottom right), stirring frequently, until the thermometer registers 248°F, firm-ball stage (45 to 60 minutes). (Adjust heat as necessary to maintain a steady boil.)

3. Remove saucepan from heat; remove thermometer. Stir in vanilla. Quickly pour mixture into prepared pan. When firm, use foil to lift it out of pan. Use a buttered knife to cut into 1-inch squares. Wrap each piece in plastic wrap. Store up to 2 weeks.

Shortcut Caramels: Prepare as above, except substitute one 14-ounce can (1¼ cups) sweetened condensed milk for the half-and-half. This mixture will take less time to reach 248°F (about 15 to 20 minutes instead of 45 to 60 minutes).

Nutrition Facts per piece for plain or shortcut variation: 80 cal., 4 g total fat (2 g sat. fat), 11 mg chol., 43 mg sodium, 12 g carbo., 0 g fiber, 0 g pro.
Daily Values: 3% vit. A, 2% calcium, 1% iron
Exchanges: 1 Other Carbo., ½ Fat

Caramel Corn `Best Loved`

Prep: 10 minutes **Cook:** 10 minutes **Bake:** 20 minutes
Oven: 300°F **Makes:** 7 to 8 cups (7 servings)

- 7 **to 8 cups popped popcorn**
- ¾ **cup packed brown sugar**
- 6 **tablespoons butter**
- 3 **tablespoons light-colored corn syrup**
- ¼ **teaspoon baking soda**
- ¼ **teaspoon vanilla**

1. Remove all unpopped kernels from popped popcorn. Put popcorn into a 17×12×2-inch baking or roasting pan. Keep popcorn warm in a 300° oven while making caramel mixture.

2. For caramel mixture, in a medium saucepan combine brown sugar, butter, and corn syrup. Cook and stir over medium heat until mixture boils. Continue boiling at a moderate, steady rate, without stirring, for 5 minutes more.

3. Remove saucepan from heat. Stir in baking soda and vanilla. Pour caramel mixture over popcorn; stir gently to coat. Bake in a 300° oven for 15 minutes. Stir mixture; bake 5 minutes more. Spread caramel corn on a large piece of buttered foil to cool. Store tightly covered for 1 week.

Nutrition Facts per serving: 236 cal., 11 g total fat (7 g sat. fat), 28 mg chol., 171 mg sodium, 36 g carbo., 1 g fiber, 1 g pro.
Daily Values: 8% vit. A, 2% calcium, 4% iron
Exchanges: 2 Other Carbo., 2 Fat

Weather Makes a Difference

Many candies, especially divinity, won't turn out on a day when the humidity is higher than 60 percent. A dry day is best for candymaking.

Caramel Corn

Toffee Butter Crunch

Prep: 15 minutes **Cook:** 20 minutes **Chill:** 20 minutes
Makes: about 1½ pounds (48 servings)

- **1 cup butter**
- **1 cup sugar**
- **3 tablespoons water**
- **1 tablespoon light-colored corn syrup**
- **1 cup semisweet chocolate pieces**
- **½ cup finely chopped pecans or almonds, toasted (see tip, page 224)**

1. Line a 15×10×1-inch baking pan with foil, extending foil over edges of pan; set pan aside.

2. Butter the sides of a 2-quart heavy saucepan. In saucepan melt butter; add sugar, water, and corn syrup. Cook and stir over medium-high heat until mixture boils. Clip a candy thermometer to side of pan. Reduce heat to medium; continue boiling at a moderate, steady rate (see photo, page 181, bottom right), stirring frequently, until thermometer registers 290°F, soft-crack stage (about 15 minutes). (Adjust heat as necessary to maintain a steady boil.) Watch carefully after 280°F to prevent scorching. Remove saucepan from heat; remove thermometer. Pour candy into the prepared pan, spreading quickly.

3. Let candy stand about 2 minutes or until set; sprinkle with chocolate pieces. Let stand 1 to 2 minutes. When chocolate has softened, spread over candy. Sprinkle with nuts. Chill about 20 minutes or until firm. When firm, use foil to lift it out of pan; break into pieces. Store tightly covered in the refrigerator for up to 3 weeks.

Nutrition Facts per serving: 78 cal., 6 g total fat (3 g sat. fat), 11 mg chol., 42 mg sodium, 6 g carbo., 1 g fiber, 0 g pro.
Daily Values: 3% vit. A
Exchanges: ½ Other Carbo., 1 Fat

Cool Down

Many candy recipes require the candy mixture to cool down before it's beaten. For this step, it's important that the bulb of the candy thermometer be totally immersed in the candy mixture so you get an accurate reading. As soon as you remove your saucepan from the heat, tilt the pan slightly by propping one side up with a hot pad. Don't touch the pan at all as it cools because even the slightest disturbance will result in a grainy final product.

Toffee Butter Crunch

Candied Nuts

Try sprinkling some of these sweetened nuts over a salad in place of croutons.

Fast

Start to Finish: 20 minutes
Makes: about 10 ounces (12 servings)

- **1½ cups raw or roasted cashews, peanuts, whole almonds, and/or pecan halves**
- **½ cup sugar**
- **2 tablespoons butter**
- **½ teaspoon vanilla**

1. Line a baking sheet with foil. Butter the foil; set baking sheet aside. In a 10-inch heavy skillet combine nuts, sugar, butter, and vanilla. Cook over medium-high heat, shaking skillet occasionally, until sugar begins to melt. Do not stir.

2. Reduce heat to low. Continue cooking until sugar is golden brown, stirring occasionally. Remove skillet from heat. Pour nut mixture onto the prepared baking sheet. Cool completely. Break into clusters. Store tightly covered in the refrigerator for up to 3 weeks.

Nutrition Facts per serving: 148 cal., 10 g total fat (3 g sat. fat), 5 mg chol., 23 mg sodium, 14 g carbo., 1 g fiber, 3 g pro.
Daily Values: 2% vit. A, 1% calcium, 6% iron
Exchanges: 1 Other Carbo., 2 Fat

Peanut Brittle

Change this classic candy to feature cashews, if you like. Just be sure to use raw cashew pieces or they'll end up with a scorched flavor.

Prep: 10 minutes **Cook:** 50 minutes
Makes: about 2¼ pounds (72 servings)

> 2 **cups sugar**
> 1 **cup light-colored corn syrup**
> ¼ **cup butter**
> 2½ **cups raw peanuts**
> 1½ **teaspoons baking soda, sifted**

1. Butter 2 large baking sheets; set aside. Butter the sides of a 3-quart heavy saucepan. In saucepan combine sugar, corn syrup, butter, and ½ cup *water*. Cook and stir over medium-high heat until mixture boils. Clip a candy thermometer to side of pan. Reduce heat to medium-low; continue boiling at a moderate, steady rate (see photo, below right), stirring occasionally, until the thermometer registers 275°F, soft-crack stage (about 30 minutes). (Adjust heat as necessary to maintain a steady boil.)

2. Stir in nuts; continue cooking over medium-low heat, stirring frequently, until thermometer registers 295°F, hard-crack stage (15 to 20 minutes more). Remove saucepan from heat; remove thermometer. Quickly sprinkle baking soda over mixture, stirring constantly (see photo 1, below). Immediately pour onto prepared baking sheets. Use 2 forks to lift and pull candy as it cools (see photo 2, below). Cool completely; break into pieces. Store tightly covered for up to 1 week.

Nutrition Facts per serving: 68 cal., 3 g total fat (1 g sat. fat), 2 mg chol., 39 mg sodium, 10 g carbo., 0 g fiber, 1 g pro.
Daily Values: 1% vit. A, 1% calcium, 1% iron
Exchanges: ½ Other Carbo., ½ Fat

1. Stir constantly as you sprinkle baking soda over the candy mixture. The mixture will foam as it reacts chemically to the soda. This makes the brittle porous.

2. As the candy cools, stretch it into a thin sheet by gently lifting and pulling with two forks. Stretching it helps make the brittle crisp.

Popcorn Balls

No time to shape the coated popcorn into balls? Spread it out on buttered foil to cool, then break it into clusters.

No Fat

Prep: 10 minutes **Cook:** 26 minutes
Oven: 300°F **Makes:** about 20 popcorn balls

> 18 **cups popped popcorn**
> 2 **cups sugar**
> 1 **cup water**
> ½ **cup light-colored corn syrup**
> 1 **teaspoon vinegar**
> ½ **teaspoon salt**
> 1 **tablespoon vanilla**

1. Remove all unpopped kernels from popped popcorn. Put popcorn in a greased 17×12×2-inch baking or roasting pan. Keep popcorn warm in a 300° oven while making syrup.

2. For syrup, butter the sides of a 2-quart heavy saucepan. In saucepan combine sugar, water, corn syrup, vinegar, and salt. Cook and stir over medium-high heat until mixture boils, stirring to dissolve sugar (about 6 minutes). Clip a candy thermometer to side of pan. Reduce heat to medium; continue boiling at a moderate, steady rate (see photo, below), stirring occasionally, until thermometer registers 250°F, hard-ball stage (about 20 minutes). (Adjust heat as necessary to maintain a steady boil.)

3. Remove saucepan from heat; remove thermometer. Stir in vanilla. Pour syrup over the hot popcorn; stir gently to coat. Cool until the coated popcorn is easy to handle. With buttered hands, quickly shape the coated popcorn into 2½-inch-diameter balls. Wrap each popcorn ball in plastic wrap. Store up to 1 week.

Nutrition Facts per ball: 126 cal., 0 g total fat (0 g sat. fat), 0 mg chol., 69 mg sodium, 31 g carbo., 1 g fiber, 1 g pro.
Daily Values: 1% iron
Exchanges: 2 Other Carbo.

Boil all candy mixtures at a moderate, steady rate over the entire surface. For accurate readings, be sure the bulb of the candy thermometer is completely covered by the candy mixture.

Chocolate-Covered Cherries

Buy three 10-ounce jars of cherries with stems to make sure you have enough for this recipe.

Drain cherries: 2 hours **Prep:** 1¼ hours
Chill: 1 hour **Makes:** 60 pieces

- 60 **maraschino cherries with stems**
- 3 **tablespoons butter, softened**
- 3 **tablespoons light-colored corn syrup**
- 2 **cups sifted powdered sugar**
- 1 **pound chocolate-flavored candy coating, cut up**

1. Let cherries stand on paper towels for 2 hours to drain thoroughly. Line a baking sheet with waxed paper; set baking sheet aside.

2. In a medium bowl combine butter and corn syrup; stir in powdered sugar. Knead mixture until smooth (chill if mixture is too soft to handle). Shape about ½ teaspoon powdered sugar mixture around each cherry. Place coated cherries, stem sides up, on the prepared baking sheet. Chill for 1 to 4 hours or until firm.

3. In a heavy saucepan melt candy coating over low heat, stirring constantly until smooth. Line another baking sheet with waxed paper. Holding cherries by stems, dip one at a time into coating; if necessary, spoon coating over cherries to cover completely. (Be sure to completely seal cherries in coating to prevent juice from leaking.) Let excess coating drip off. Place coated cherries, stem sides up, on prepared baking sheet.

4. Let cherries stand until the coating is set. Store tightly covered in a cool, dry place for 1 to 2 weeks before serving. (This allows the powdered sugar mixture around the cherries to soften and liquefy.)

Nutrition Facts per piece: 66 cal., 3 g total fat (2 g sat. fat), 2 mg chol., 9 mg sodium, 10 g carbo., 0 g fiber, 0 g pro.
Exchanges: ½ Other Carbo., ½ Fat

Butter Makes Candy Better

There are a couple of good reasons to use butter, not substitutes, when you're making candy. First of all, margarine blends and spreads that resemble margarine are soft and contain too much water and varying amounts of fat to result in good candy. And second, when you take the time and go to the trouble of making candy, you want the absolute best flavor—the flavor only butter can provide.

Chocolate Truffles

If you prefer, roll these truffles in ½ cup ground, toasted almonds or hazelnuts instead of dipping them in candy coating.

Prep: 1 hour **Chill:** 20 minutes **Freeze:** 30 minutes
Stand: 30 minutes **Makes:** about 24 pieces

- 1 **12-ounce package semisweet chocolate pieces or one 11½-ounce package milk chocolate pieces**
- ⅓ **cup whipping cream**
- ½ **teaspoon vanilla**
- 12 **ounces chocolate-flavored candy coating, cut up**
- ½ **cup white baking pieces**
- 2 **teaspoons shortening**

1. Line a baking sheet with waxed paper; set aside. In a medium heavy saucepan combine chocolate pieces and whipping cream. Cook and stir constantly over low heat until chocolate melts. Remove saucepan from heat; cool slightly. Stir in vanilla. Beat truffle mixture with an electric mixer on low speed until smooth. Drop truffle mixture by teaspoons onto prepared baking sheet. Chill about 20 minutes or until firm.

2. Shape chilled truffle mixture into balls; freeze for 30 minutes. Meanwhile, in a heavy saucepan melt candy coating over low heat, stirring constantly until smooth. Using a fork, quickly dip truffles, one at a time, into coating. Draw the fork across the rim of the saucepan to remove excess coating. Return truffles to baking sheet. Let stand about 30 minutes or until coating is set.

3. In a small saucepan combine the white baking pieces and shortening. Cook and stir over low heat until melted and smooth; decoratively drizzle over tops of chocolate-covered truffles. Let stand until set. Store truffles tightly covered in the refrigerator for up to 2 weeks. Let stand at room temperature about 30 minutes before serving.

Nutrition Facts per piece: 163 cal., 10 g total fat (7 g sat. fat), 5 mg chol., 9 mg sodium, 18 g carbo., 1 g fiber, 1 g pro.
Daily Values: 1% vit. A, 1% calcium, 3% iron
Exchanges: 1 Other Carbo., 2 Fat

Easy Candy-Bar Treats Best Loved

Prep: 10 minutes **Cook:** 7¾ minutes **Chill:** 2 hours
Makes: about 2¾ pounds (64 pieces)

 ½ **cup butter**
 ⅓ **cup unsweetened cocoa powder**
 ¼ **cup packed brown sugar**
 ¼ **cup milk**
 3½ **cups sifted powdered sugar**
 1 **teaspoon vanilla**
 30 **vanilla caramels, unwrapped**
 1 **tablespoon water**
 2 **cups unsalted peanuts**
 ½ **cup semisweet chocolate pieces**
 ½ **cup milk chocolate pieces**

1. Line a 9×9×2-inch or 11×7×1½-inch baking pan with foil, extending the foil over the edges of the pan. Butter the foil; set pan aside.

2. In a large microwave-safe bowl, microwave the butter, uncovered, on 100 percent power (high) for 1 to 1½ minutes or until melted. Stir in cocoa powder, brown sugar, and milk. Microwave, uncovered, on high for 1 to 2 minutes or until mixture comes to a boil, stirring once. Stir again; microwave for 30 seconds more. Stir in powdered sugar and vanilla until smooth. Spread mixture in prepared pan.

3. In a medium microwave-safe bowl, combine caramels and water. Microwave, uncovered, on 50 percent power (medium) for 2½ to 3 minutes or until caramels are melted, stirring once. Stir in peanuts. Microwave, uncovered, on medium for 45 to 60 seconds more or until mixture is softened. Gently and quickly spread peanut mixture over fudge layer in pan.

4. In a 2-cup microwave-safe glass measure, combine semisweet and milk chocolate pieces. Microwave, uncovered, on 50 percent power (medium) for 2 to 3 minutes or until melted, stirring once or twice. Spread over peanut layer. Score into pieces while warm. Cover and chill for 2 to 3 hours or until bottom is firm. Use foil to lift candy out of pan. Cut into pieces. Store tightly covered in the refrigerator for up to 3 weeks.

Stove-top directions: In a medium saucepan melt butter over medium heat. Stir in cocoa powder, brown sugar, and milk. Bring to boiling. Remove from heat; stir in powdered sugar and vanilla. Spread in prepared pan. In another saucepan melt caramels with water over low heat; stir in peanuts. Gently and quickly spread over fudge layer in pan. In a small saucepan melt semisweet and milk chocolate pieces over low heat, stirring constantly. Spread over peanut layer. Continue as directed in step 4.

Nutrition Facts per piece: 100 cal., 5 g total fat (2 g sat. fat), 5 mg chol., 29 mg sodium, 12 g carbo., 0 g fiber, 2 g pro.
Daily Values: 1% vit. A, 2% calcium, 1% iron
Exchanges: 1 Other Carbo., 1 Fat

Peanut Butter Balls

Start to Finish: 1 hour **Makes:** about 30 pieces

 ½ **cup peanut butter**
 3 **tablespoons butter, softened**
 1 **cup sifted powdered sugar**
 8 **ounces chocolate-flavored candy coating, cut up**

1. In a bowl stir together peanut butter and butter. Gradually add powdered sugar, stirring until combined. Shape mixture into 1-inch balls; place on waxed paper. Let stand for 20 minutes.

2. In a heavy saucepan melt candy coating over low heat, stirring constantly until smooth. Cool slightly. Dip balls, one at a time, into coating. Let excess coating drip off peanut butter balls. Place on waxed paper; let stand until firm. Store tightly covered in the refrigerator up to 3 weeks.

Nutrition Facts per piece: 92 cal., 6 g total fat (3 g sat. fat), 3 mg chol., 32 mg sodium, 9 g carbo., 0 g fiber, 1 g pro.
Daily Values: 1% vit. A, 1% iron
Exchanges: ½ Other Carbo., 1½ Fat

Easy Candy-Bar Treats

Cream Cheese Mints

Start to Finish: 50 minutes **Stand:** Overnight
Makes: 48 to 60 pieces

> 1 **3-ounce package cream cheese, softened**
> ½ **teaspoon peppermint extract**
> 3 **cups sifted powdered sugar**
>   **Few drops desired food coloring**
>   **Granulated sugar**

1. Combine softened cream cheese and peppermint extract. Gradually add powdered sugar, stirring until mixture is smooth. (Knead in the last of the powdered sugar with your hands.) Add food coloring; knead until evenly distributed.

2. Form cream cheese mixture into ¾-inch balls. Roll each ball in granulated sugar; place on waxed paper. Flatten each ball with the bottom of a juice glass or with the tines of a fork. (Or, sprinkle small candy molds lightly with sugar. Press ¾ to 1 teaspoon cream cheese mixture into each mold. Remove from molds.) Cover the mints with paper towels and let stand overnight. Store mints tightly covered in the refrigerator or freeze for up to 1 month.

Nutrition Facts per piece: 33 cal., 1 g total fat (0 g sat. fat), 2 mg chol., 5 mg sodium, 7 g carbo., 0 g fiber, 0 g pro.
Daily Values: 1% vit. A
Exchanges: ½ Other Carbo.

White Chocolate Cereal Drops

Start to Finish: 30 minutes **Stand:** 1 hour
Makes: about 60 pieces

> 1½ **cups tiny marshmallows**
> 1½ **cups peanut butter cereal or puffed corn cereal**
> 1½ **cups crisp rice cereal**
> 1½ **cups mixed nuts**
> 1¼ **pounds vanilla-flavored candy coating, cut up**

1. Line 2 baking sheets with waxed paper; set aside. In a large bowl combine marshmallows, peanut butter cereal, rice cereal, and nuts; set cereal mixture aside. In a 2-quart heavy saucepan melt candy coating over low heat, stirring constantly until smooth. Remove from heat; pour over cereal mixture. Stir gently to coat. Drop by rounded teaspoons onto prepared baking sheets. Let stand about 1 hour or until set. Store tightly covered for up to 3 days.

Nutrition Facts per piece: 84 cal., 5 g total fat (3 g sat. fat), 0 mg chol., 15 mg sodium, 10 g carbo., 0 g fiber, 1 g pro.
Daily Values: 1% vit. C, 1% calcium, 2% iron
Exchanges: ½ Other Carbo., 1 Fat

Hazelnut-and-Cherry Caramel Clusters `Best Loved`

Start to Finish: 30 minutes
Stand: 1 hour 10 minutes **Makes:** 18 pieces

> 4 **ounces white chocolate or white chocolate baking squares, chopped**
> 1 **tablespoon shortening**
> 1½ **cups coarsely chopped hazelnuts (filberts) or almonds, toasted (see tip, page 224)**
> ⅓ **cup dried tart red cherries or dried cranberries**
> 12 **vanilla caramels, unwrapped**
> 2 **teaspoons butter**

1. Line a baking sheet with foil. Butter the foil; set baking sheet aside.

2. In a small heavy saucepan melt white chocolate and shortening over low heat, stirring constantly until smooth. Remove from heat; stir in hazelnuts and cherries. Let stand for 10 minutes to allow mixture to set up slightly. Drop by a rounded tablespoon onto prepared baking sheet.

3. In another small heavy saucepan combine caramels and butter. Cook and stir over low heat until melted and smooth (if mixture is too thick to drizzle, stir in 2 teaspoons hot water). Remove from heat; drizzle caramel mixture over the candy clusters. Let stand about 1 hour or until firm. Store tightly covered for up to 3 days.

Nutrition Facts per piece: 146 cal., 10 g total fat (2 g sat. fat), 4 mg chol., 27 mg sodium, 11 g carbo., 1 g fiber, 2 g pro.
Daily Values: 1% vit. C, 3% calcium, 3% iron
Exchanges: 1 Other Carbo., 2 Fat

Hazelnut-and-Cherry Caramel Clusters

Canning & Freezing

Jellies and Jams

Ingredients: *Fruits* should be at their peak of freshness for best flavor and color. Canned or frozen unsweetened fruit or juice can be used. *Pectin* is necessary for jelling. It is naturally present in some fruits or can be added in a powdered or liquid form. Do not substitute one form of pectin for another; add pectin exactly as specified in the recipe. Using less pectin than the recipe suggests is likely to produce a syrup rather than a jelly or jam. Be sure to use the pectin by the date indicated on its package. *Sugar* acts as a preservative, develops the flavor, and aids in jelling. Always use the amount of sugar specified in a recipe. *Acid* is needed for proper jelling and for flavor. When fruits are low in acid, recipes call for adding lemon juice or citric acid.

Procedures: Prepare only one batch at a time. Do not try to double the recipe.

Vigorous boiling is part of jellymaking. A full rolling boil is one so rapid that you can't stir it down (see top photo). To prevent it from boiling over, fill a pan no more than one-third full.

A mixture will sheet off a spoon when it has reached its jelling point. To test it, dip a metal spoon into the boiling mixture, then hold it over the kettle. If mixture is done, two drops will hang off edge of spoon, then run together in a sheetlike action (see middle photo). You also can use a candy thermometer to find when the jelling point is reached (8°F above the boiling point of water—or 220°F at sea level).

Foam is a natural result of boiling. Quickly skim it off with a large metal spoon (see bottom photo) before ladling jelly into sterilized jars (see tip, page 188). Process jellies and jams in a boiling-water canner (see instructions on pages 200–201). For locations with altitudes below 1,000 feet above sea level, process for 5 minutes. Add 1 minute for each additional 1,000 feet.

After processing, let jellies and jams sit for 12 to 24 hours or until set. Use within 6 months.

Grape Jam

No Fat

Prep: 65 minutes **Process:** 5 minutes **Makes:** about 6 half-pints

- 3½ **pounds Concord grapes**
- 2 **cups water**
- 4½ **cups sugar**

1. Wash and stem grapes. Measure 8 cups. Remove skins from half of the grapes; set grape skins aside.

2. In an 8- to 10-quart heavy kettle combine the skinned and unskinned grapes. Cover and cook 10 minutes or until very soft. Press grapes through a sieve; discard seeds and cooked skins. Measure 3 cups of strained pulp; return to kettle. Stir in the uncooked grape skins and water. Cook, covered, for 10 minutes. Uncover; stir in sugar. Bring mixture to a full rolling boil, stirring often (see top photo, left). Boil, uncovered, about 12 minutes or until mixture sheets off a metal spoon (see middle photo, left).

3. Remove kettle from heat; quickly skim off foam with a metal spoon (see bottom photo, left).

4. Ladle at once into hot, sterilized half-pint canning jars (see tip, page 188), leaving a ¼-inch headspace (see tip, page 191). Wipe jar rims; adjust lids. Process in a boiling-water canner for 5 minutes (start timing when water returns to boil). Remove jars and cool on racks until set.

Nutrition Facts per 1 tablespoon: 46 cal., 0 g total fat (0 g sat. fat), 0 mg chol., 0 mg sodium, 12 g carbo., 0 g fiber, 0 g pro.
Daily Values: 1% vit. C
Exchanges: 1 Other Carbo.

Important Safety Reminder

■ Always inspect a home-canned jar of food carefully before serving its contents. If the jar has leaked, shows patches of mold, or has a swollen lid, or if the food has a foamy or murky appearance, discard the food and the jar where it will not be consumed by people or pets.

■ The odor from an opened jar should be pleasant. If food does not look or smell right, don't use it.

■ Always boil all home-canned vegetables before tasting or using them. Bring the food to a boil and boil for 10 minutes if you live less than 1,000 feet above sea level. If you live more than 1,000 feet above sea level, add an additional minute for each 1,000 feet of elevation. Add water, if needed, to prevent sticking. If you smell an unnatural odor as the food heats, discard the food.

Orange Marmalade **Best Loved**

Allow this sweet-tart marmalade to set up for 2 weeks before sampling it.

No Fat

Prep: 55 minutes **Process:** 5 minutes **Makes:** 6 half-pints

> 4 **medium oranges**
> 1 **medium lemon**
> 1½ **cups water**
> ⅛ **teaspoon baking soda**
> 5 **cups sugar**
> ½ **of a 6-ounce package (1 foil pouch) liquid fruit pectin**

1. Score orange and lemon peels into 4 lengthwise sections; remove the peels with your fingers. Scrape off the bitter white portions of peels with a sharp knife and discard; cut peels into thin strips. Bring peels, water, and baking soda to boiling. Cover; simmer for 20 minutes. Do not drain. Section fruits, reserving juices; discard seeds. Add fruits and juices to peel mixture; return to boiling. Cover and simmer 10 minutes. Measure 3 cups.

2. In an 8- to 10-quart heavy kettle combine fruit mixture and sugar. Bring to a full rolling boil, stirring constantly (see top photo, page 187). Quickly stir in pectin. Return to a full rolling boil; boil for 1 minute, stirring constantly. Remove from heat; skim off foam with a metal spoon (see bottom photo, page 187).

3. Ladle into hot, sterilized half-pint canning jars (see tip, below), leaving a ¼-inch headspace (see tip, page 191). Wipe jar rims; adjust lids. Process in a boiling-water canner for 5 minutes (start timing when water returns to boil). Remove jars; cool on racks.

Nutrition Facts per 1 tablespoon: 46 cal., 0 g total fat (0 g sat. fat), 0 mg chol., 2 mg sodium, 12 g carbo., 0 g fiber, 0 g pro.
Daily Values: 5% vit. C
Exchanges: 1 Other Carbo.

Orange Marmalade

Sterilizing Jars

Jars for canning foods that will be processed in a water-bath canner for 10 minutes or less, such as jams and jellies, must be sterilized.

To sterilize empty canning jars, wash them in hot, soapy water. Rinse thoroughly. Place in boiling water for 10 minutes if you live less than 1,000 feet above sea level. If you live more than 1,000 feet above sea level, add an additional 1 minute for each 1,000 feet of elevation.

Blueberry-Orange Jam

No Fat

Prep: 30 minutes **Process:** 5 minutes **Makes:** 6 half-pints

> 3 **pints blueberries, stems removed**
> 1 **tablespoon finely shredded orange peel**
> ¼ **cup orange juice**
> 1 **1¾-ounce package regular powdered fruit pectin**
> ½ **teaspoon butter or margarine**
> 4 **cups sugar**

1. Place 1 cup of berries in a 6- to 8-quart heavy kettle. Use a potato masher to crush berries. Continue adding berries and crushing until you have 4 cups crushed berries. Stir in orange peel, orange juice, pectin, and butter. Heat on high, stirring constantly, until mixture comes to full rolling boil (see top photo, page 187). Add sugar all at once. Return to boiling; boil 1 minute, stirring constantly. Remove from heat; quickly skim off foam (see bottom photo, page 187).

2. Ladle at once into hot, sterilized half-pint canning jars (see tip, left), leaving a ¼-inch headspace (see tip, page 191). Wipe jar rims; adjust lids. Process in a boiling-water canner for 5 minutes (start timing when water returns to boil). Remove jars and cool on racks until set.

Nutrition Facts per 1 tablespoon: 44 cal., 0 g total fat (0 g sat. fat), 0 mg chol., 2 mg sodium, 11 g carbo., 0 g fiber, 0 g pro.
Daily Values: 3% vit. C
Exchanges: 1 Other Carbo.

Berry Freezer Jam

No Fat

Prep: 30 minutes **Stand:** 24 hours **Makes:** about 5 half-pints

- **4 cups blackberries, raspberries, or hulled strawberries**
- **4 cups sugar**
- **½ teaspoon finely shredded lemon peel**
- **1 1¾-ounce package regular powdered fruit pectin**
- **¾ cup water**

1. In a bowl use a potato masher to crush the berries until you have 2 cups. Mix berries, sugar, and lemon peel. Let stand for 10 minutes, stirring occasionally. In a small saucepan combine pectin and water. Bring to boiling over high heat; boil 1 minute, stirring constantly. Remove from heat and add to berry mixture; stir for 3 minutes or until sugar is dissolved and mixture is no longer grainy.

2. Ladle into half-pint freezer containers, leaving a ½-inch headspace (see tip, page 191). Seal and label. Let stand at room temperature 24 hours or until set. Store up to 3 weeks in the refrigerator or for up to 1 year in the freezer.

Nutrition Facts per 1 tablespoon: 49 cal., 0 g total fat (0 g sat. fat), 0 mg chol., 1 mg sodium, 13 g carbo., 0 g fiber, 0 g pro.
Daily Values: 3% vit. C
Exchanges: 1 Other Carbo.

Strawberry Jam **Best Loved**

No Fat

Prep: 35 minutes **Process:** 5 minutes **Makes:** 8 half-pints

- **2 quarts fresh strawberries, hulled**
- **1 1¾-ounce package regular powdered fruit pectin**
- **½ teaspoon butter or margarine**
- **7 cups sugar**

1. Place 1 cup of berries in an 8-quart heavy kettle. Crush berries. Continue adding berries and crushing until you have 5 cups crushed berries. Stir in pectin and butter. Heat on high, stirring constantly, until mixture comes to a full rolling boil (see top photo, page 187). Add sugar all at once. Return to boiling; boil 1 minute, stirring constantly. Remove from heat; quickly skim off foam with a metal spoon (see bottom photo, page 187).

2. Ladle at once into hot, sterilized half-pint canning jars (see tip, page 188), leaving a ¼-inch headspace (see tip, page 191). Wipe jar rims; adjust lids. Process in a boiling-water canner for 5 minutes (start timing when water returns to boil). Remove jars; cool on racks.

Nutrition Facts per 1 tablespoon: 51 cal., 0 g total fat (0 g sat. fat), 0 mg chol., 1 mg sodium, 13 g carbo., 0 g fiber, 0 g pro.
Daily Values: 10% vit. C
Exchanges: 1 Other Carbo.

Rhubarb-Raspberry Jam

No Fat

Prep: 50 minutes **Makes:** 5 half-pints

- **6 cups fresh or frozen unsweetened sliced rhubarb**
- **4 cups sugar**
- **2 cups raspberries or one 12-ounce package frozen lightly sweetened red raspberries**
- **1 3-ounce package raspberry-flavored gelatin (not sugar-free)**

1. In a large heavy kettle combine rhubarb and sugar. Let stand 15 to 20 minutes or until sugar is moistened. Bring to boiling. Boil, uncovered, for 10 minutes, stirring often. Add berries; return to boiling. Boil hard 5 to 6 minutes or until thick, stirring often. Remove from heat. Add gelatin and stir until dissolved.

2. Ladle into half-pint freezer containers, leaving a ½-inch headspace (see tip, page 191). Seal; label. Let stand at room temperature until set. Store the jam up to 3 weeks in the refrigerator or 1 year in the freezer.

Nutrition Facts per 1 tablespoon: 51 cal., 0 g total fat (0 g sat. fat), 0 mg chol., 5 mg sodium, 13 g carbo., 0 g fiber, 0 g pro.
Daily Values: 3% vit. C, 1% calcium
Exchanges: 1 Other Carbo.

Rhubarb-Raspberry Jam

Altitude Adjustments

Times given in this chapter are for altitudes up to 1,000 feet above sea level. Because water boils at a lower temperature at higher altitudes, make the following changes:

Blanching: Add 1 minute if you live 5,000 feet or more above sea level.

Boiling-water canning: Use a longer processing time. Call your county extension service agent for detailed instructions.

Jellies and jams: Add 1 minute to processing time for each additional 1,000 feet.

Pressure canning: Times remain the same, but different pressures must be used. For dial-gauge pressure canners, use 11 pounds of pressure if you live up to 2,000 feet above sea level; use 12 pounds pressure for 2,001 to 4,000 feet; use 13 pounds pressure for 4,001 to 6,000 feet; and use 14 pounds pressure for 6,001 to 8,000 feet.

For weighted-gauge canners, use 10 pounds of pressure if you live up to 1,000 feet above sea level. Use 15 pounds of pressure above 1,000 feet.

Sterilizing jars: Boil the jars 1 additional minute for each additional 1,000 feet.

Pepper Jelly

No Fat

Prep: 50 minutes **Process:** 5 minutes **Makes:** 5 half-pints

- 1½ **cups cranberry juice (not low-calorie)**
- 1 **cup vinegar**
- 2 **to 4 fresh jalapeño chile peppers, halved (see tip, page 64)**
- 5 **cups sugar**
- ½ **of a 6-ounce package (1 foil pouch) liquid fruit pectin**

1. In a medium stainless-steel, enamel, or non-stick saucepan combine cranberry juice, vinegar, and jalapeño peppers. Bring to boiling; reduce heat. Simmer, covered, for 10 minutes. Strain mixture through a sieve, pressing with the back of a spoon to remove all the liquid; measure 2 cups and set aside. Discard pulp.

2. In a 6-quart heavy kettle combine the 2 cups liquid and the sugar. Bring to a full rolling boil over high heat, stirring constantly (see top photo, page 187). Quickly stir in pectin. Return to a full rolling boil; boil for 1 minute, stirring constantly. Remove from heat. Skim off foam (see bottom photo, page 187).

3. Ladle at once into hot, sterilized half-pint canning jars (see tip, page 188), leaving a ¼-inch headspace (see tip, page 191). Wipe jar rims; adjust lids. Process in a boiling-water canner for 5 minutes (start timing when water returns to boil). Remove jars and cool on a wire rack until set (2 to 3 days).

Nutrition Facts per 1 tablespoon: 57 cal., 0 g total fat (0 g sat. fat), 0 mg chol., 0 mg sodium, 15 g carbo., 0 g fiber, 0 g pro.
Daily Values: 3% vit. C
Exchanges: 1 Other Carbo.

Fruit Juice Jelly

Because this jelly starts with fruit juice, it goes together quickly and easily, yet has the great taste of homemade jelly. If you'd like, substitute other 100 percent fruit juice blends for suggested juices.

No Fat

Prep: 25 minutes **Process:** 5 minutes **Makes:** 5 half-pints

- 4 **cups cranberry juice (not low-calorie) or unsweetened apple, grape, or orange juice**
- ¼ **cup lemon juice**
- 1 **1¾-ounce package regular powdered fruit pectin**
- 4½ **cups sugar**

1. Pour desired fruit juice and lemon juice into a 6- to 8-quart heavy kettle. Sprinkle with pectin. Let stand for 1 to 2 minutes; stir to dissolve. Bring to a full rolling boil over medium-high heat, stirring frequently (see top photo, page 187). Stir in sugar. Return to a full rolling boil, stirring often. Boil hard 1 minute, stirring constantly. Remove from heat; quickly skim off foam with a metal spoon (see bottom photo, page 187).

2. Ladle at once into hot, sterilized half-pint canning jars (see tip, page 188), leaving a ¼-inch headspace (see tip, page 191). Wipe jar rims and adjust lids. Process in a boiling-water canner for 5 minutes (start timing when water returns to boil). Remove jars and cool on racks until set.

Nutrition Facts per 1 tablespoon: 68 cal., 0 g total fat (0 g sat. fat), 0 mg chol., 2 mg sodium, 18 g carbo., 0 g fiber, 0 g pro.
Daily Values: 11% vit. C
Exchanges: 1 Other Carbo.

Apple Butter

No Fat

Prep: 3 hours **Process:** 5 minutes **Makes:** 8 half-pints

- 4½ **pounds tart cooking apples, cored and quartered (about 14 medium)**
- 3 **cups apple cider or apple juice**
- 2 **cups sugar**
- 1½ **teaspoons ground cinnamon**
- ½ **teaspoon ground cloves**
- ½ **teaspoon ground allspice**

1. In an 8- to 10-quart heavy kettle combine apples and cider. Bring to boiling; reduce heat. Simmer, covered, for 30 minutes, stirring occasionally. Press through a food mill or sieve until you have 8½ cups pulp. Return pulp to kettle.

2. Stir in sugar, cinnamon, cloves, and allspice. Bring to boiling; reduce heat. Cook, uncovered, over very low heat 1½ hours or until very thick and mixture mounds on a spoon, stirring often.

Boiling-Water Canning: Ladle hot apple butter into hot, sterilized half-pint canning jars (see tip, page 188), leaving a ¼-inch headspace (see tip, right). Wipe jar rims; adjust lids. Process in a boiling-water canner for 5 minutes (start timing when water returns to boil). Remove jars and cool on racks.

Freezing: Place kettle of apple butter in a sink filled with ice water; stir mixture to cool. Ladle into wide-top freezer containers, leaving a ½-inch headspace (see tip, right). Seal, label, and freeze up to 10 months. Apple butter may darken slightly on freezing.

Nutrition Facts per 1 tablespoon: 25 cal., 0 g total fat (0 g sat. fat), 0 mg chol., 0 mg sodium, 7 g carbo., 0 g fiber, 0 g pro.
Daily Values: 1% vit. C
Exchanges: ½ Other Carbo.

Applesauce

Use apples with red skins for a rosy color.

Low Fat

Prep: 1½ hours **Process:** 15 minutes **Makes:** 6 pints

- 8 **pounds cooking apples, cored and quartered (24 cups)**
- 2 **cups water**
- 10 **inches stick cinnamon (optional)**
- ¾ **to 1¼ cups sugar**

1. In an 8- to 10-quart heavy kettle combine apples, water, and, if desired, cinnamon sticks. Bring to boiling; reduce heat. Simmer, covered, for 25 to 35 minutes until very tender, stirring often.

2. Remove cinnamon, if used. Press apples through a food mill or sieve. Return pulp to kettle. Stir in sugar to taste. If necessary, add ½ to 1 cup water for desired consistency. Bring to boiling.

Boiling-Water Canning: Ladle hot applesauce into hot, clean canning jars, leaving ½-inch headspace (see tip, below). Wipe jar rims; adjust lids. Process in a boiling-water canner for 15 minutes for pints and 20 minutes for quarts (start timing when water returns to boil). Remove jars; cool on racks.

Freezing: Place kettle of applesauce in a sink filled with ice water; stir mixture to cool. Ladle into wide-top freezer containers, leaving ½-inch headspace (see tip, below). Seal, label, and freeze up to 8 months.

Nutrition Facts per ½-cup serving: 112 cal., 1 g total fat (0 g sat. fat), 0 mg chol., 1 mg sodium, 29 g carbo., 4 g fiber, 0 g pro.
Daily Values: 1% vit. A, 10% vit. C, 1% calcium, 2% iron
Exchanges: 2 Fruit

Allow for Headspace

The amount of space between the top of the food and the rim of its container is called headspace. Leaving the correct amount is essential when canning and freezing.

Canning: Headspace is necessary for a vacuum to form and for the jar to seal. Use the amount of headspace specified in recipes and for each food  in charts on pages 194–199. After the food and liquid are added, measure with a ruler (see photo) to be sure you have maintained the correct headspace.

Freezing: Headspace allows room for the food to expand without breaking the container or causing the lid to pop off. When using unsweetened or dry pack (no sugar or liquid added), leave a ½-inch headspace unless otherwise directed. When using sugar, sugar-syrup, or water pack and wide-top containers with straight or slightly flared sides, leave a ½-inch headspace for pints and a 1-inch headspace for quarts. For narrow-top containers and freezing jars, leave a ¾-inch headspace for pints and a 1½-inch headspace for quarts.

Pickles and Relishes

The best homemade pickles and relishes start with high-quality ingredients and are prepared according to tested recipes. Follow these general guidelines when making them.

Ingredients: Cucumbers identified as pickling types will make crunchier pickles than table or slicing varieties. Select top-quality, unwaxed cucumbers. Use them as soon as possible after harvest (within 24 hours). Otherwise, refrigerate cucumbers or spread them in a cool, well-ventilated area. Just before using, remove the blossoms and slice off the blossom ends. Wash well, especially around the stems.

Granulated pickling or canning salt should be used instead of table salt, which may cause the pickles to darken or make the brine cloudy.

Cider vinegar is most often used for pickles and relishes, but white vinegar can be used for a lighter-colored product. Never dilute the vinegar more than is indicated in the recipe.

Spices should be as fresh as possible. If a recipe calls for a whole spice, don't substitute the ground alternative; it may cause the product to be dark and cloudy. Hard water may prevent brined pickles from curing properly; for best results, use soft or distilled water.

Procedures: Use stoneware, glass, enamelware, stainless-steel, or nonstick pans and food-grade plastic containers and utensils. Do not use aluminum, brass, copper, zinc, galvanized, or iron pans or utensils. Process pickles and relishes in a boiling-water canner (see instructions on pages 200–201) to destroy yeasts, molds, and bacteria.

Dill Pickles

If using fresh dill with small heads, add the maximum amount of dill to each jar.

No Fat

Prep: 30 minutes **Process:** 10 minutes
Makes: 6 pints (36 servings)

> 3 **pounds 4-inch pickling cucumbers (about 36)***
> 3¾ **cups water**
> 3¾ **cups cider vinegar**
> ¼ **cup pickling salt**
> 12 **to 18 heads fresh dill or**
>   6 **tablespoons dillseeds**
> 1 **tablespoon mustard seeds**

1. Thoroughly rinse cucumbers. Remove stems; cut off a slice from blossom ends. In a large stainless-steel, enameled, or nonstick saucepan combine water, vinegar, and salt. Bring to boiling.

2. Pack cucumbers loosely into hot, sterilized pint canning jars (see tip, page 188), leaving a ½-inch headspace. Add 2 to 3 heads of dill or 1 tablespoon dillseeds and ½ teaspoon mustard seeds to each jar. Pour hot vinegar mixture over cucumbers, leaving a ½-inch headspace (see tip, page 191). Wipe jar rims and adjust lids.

3. Process in a boiling-water canner for 10 minutes (start timing when water returns to boil). Remove jars and cool on racks. Let stand 1 week.

Kosher-Style Dill Pickles: Prepare as above, except omit the mustard seeds and add 1 clove garlic, halved, to each jar (6 garlic cloves total).

*Note: If pickling cucumbers are not available, cut regular cucumbers into 4-inch spears.

Nutrition Facts per serving plain or kosher pickle: 7 cal., 0 g total fat (0 g sat. fat), 0 mg chol., 474 mg sodium, 2 g carbo., 0 g fiber, 0 g pro.
Daily Values: 2% vit. A, 1% vit. C, 1% iron
Exchanges: Free

Bread and Butter Pickles

Cut the cucumbers into ⅛-inch slices.

No Fat

Prep: 40 minutes **Chill:** 3 to 12 hours
Process: 10 minutes **Makes:** 7 pints (70 servings)

> 4 **quarts (16 cups) sliced medium cucumbers**
> 8 **medium white onions, sliced**
> ⅓ **cup pickling salt**
> 3 **cloves garlic, halved**
>   **Cracked ice**
> 4 **cups sugar**
> 3 **cups cider vinegar**
> 2 **tablespoons mustard seeds**
> 1½ **teaspoons ground turmeric**
> 1½ **teaspoons celery seeds**

1. In a 6- to 8-quart stainless-steel, enameled, or nonstick kettle combine cucumbers, onions, pickling salt, and garlic. Add 2 inches of cracked ice. Cover with lid and refrigerate for 3 to 12 hours. Remove any remaining ice. Drain mixture well in a large colander. Remove garlic.

2. In the kettle combine sugar, vinegar, mustard seeds, turmeric, and celery seeds. Heat to boiling. Add cucumber mixture. Return to boiling.

3. Pack hot cucumber mixture and liquid into hot, sterilized pint canning jars (see tip, page 188), leaving a 1/2-inch headspace (see tip, page 191). Wipe jar rims; adjust lids. Process in a boiling-water canner for 10 minutes (start timing when water returns to boil). Remove jars and cool on racks.

Nutrition Facts per serving: 33 cal., 0 g total fat (0 g sat. fat), 0 mg chol., 266 mg sodium, 9 g carbo., 0 g fiber, 0 g pro.
Daily Values: 1% vit. A, 1% vit. C, 1% iron
Exchanges: 1/2 Other Carbo.

Chunky Salsa Best Loved

Use vine-ripened tomatoes for this recipe—they provide the high acidity needed for safe boiling-water canning. Avoid using tomatoes from dead or frost-killed vines. If in doubt, store the salsa in the refrigerator (see photo, page 185).

No Fat

Prep: 2 1/2 hours **Stand:** 30 minutes
Process: 15 minutes **Makes:** 5 pints

    7 pounds ripe tomatoes (20 medium)
   10 fresh Anaheim or poblano chile peppers, seeded and chopped (about 3 cups) (see tip, page 64)
   1/3 cup seeded and chopped fresh jalapeño chile peppers (3 large) (see tip, page 64)
    2 cups chopped onions (2 large)
   1/2 cup snipped fresh cilantro
    1 cup vinegar
   1/2 of a 6-ounce can (1/3 cup) tomato paste
    5 cloves garlic, minced
    1 teaspoon salt
    1 teaspoon black pepper

1. Seed, core, and coarsely chop tomatoes (you should have about 14 cups). Place tomatoes in a large colander. Let drain 30 minutes.

2. Place drained tomatoes in an 8-quart stainless-steel, enameled, or nonstick heavy kettle. Bring to boiling; reduce heat. Simmer, uncovered, about 1 1/4 hours or until thickened, stirring frequently. Add chile peppers, onions, cilantro, vinegar, tomato paste, garlic, salt, and pepper. Return mixture to boiling; reduce heat. Simmer, uncovered, for 10 minutes. Remove from heat.

3. Ladle hot salsa into hot, clean pint canning jars, leaving a 1/2-inch headspace (see tip, page 191). Wipe jar rims; adjust lids. Process in a boiling-water canner for 15 minutes (start timing when water returns to boil). Remove jars and cool on racks.

Note: If desired, for fresh flavor stir 1 tablespoon snipped fresh cilantro into each pint of processed salsa before serving.

Nutrition Facts per 2 tablespoons: 15 cal., 0 g total fat (0 g sat. fat), 0 mg chol., 41 mg sodium, 3 g carbo., 1 g fiber, 1 g pro.
Daily Values: 7% vit. A, 61% vit. C, 1% calcium, 3% iron
Exchanges: Free

Corn Relish

No Fat

Prep: 1 1/2 hours **Process:** 15 minutes **Makes:** 7 pints

   16 to 18 fresh ears of corn
    2 cups water
    3 cups chopped celery (6 stalks)
   1 1/2 cups chopped red sweet peppers (2 medium)
   1 1/2 cups chopped green sweet peppers
    1 cup chopped onions (2 medium)
    3 cups vinegar
    2 cups sugar
    4 teaspoons dry mustard
    2 teaspoons pickling salt
    2 teaspoons celery seeds
    1 teaspoon ground turmeric
    3 tablespoons cornstarch
    2 tablespoons cold water

1. Cut corn from cobs (do not scrape cobs). Measure 8 cups corn. In an 8- to 10-quart stainless-steel, enameled, or nonstick heavy kettle combine corn and the 2 cups water. Bring to boiling; reduce heat. Simmer, covered, for 4 to 5 minutes or until corn is nearly tender; drain.

2. In the same kettle combine corn, celery, red and green sweet peppers, and onions. Stir in vinegar, sugar, mustard, pickling salt, celery seeds, and turmeric. Bring to boiling. Boil gently, uncovered, for 5 minutes, stirring occasionally. Combine cornstarch and the 2 tablespoons cold water; add to corn mixture. Cook and stir until bubbly; cook and stir for 2 minutes more.

3. Ladle hot relish into hot, clean pint canning jars, leaving a 1/2-inch headspace (see tip, page 191). Wipe jar rims and adjust lids. Process in a boiling-water canner for 15 minutes (start timing when water returns to boil). Remove jars; cool on racks.

Nutrition Facts per 1/4-cup serving: 64 cal., 0 g total fat (0 g sat. fat), 0 mg chol., 103 mg sodium, 16 g carbo., 1 g fiber, 1 g pro.
Daily Values: 6% vit. A, 21% vit. C, 1% calcium, 2% iron
Exchanges: 1 Starch

Canning and Freezing Fruits

Read canning and freezing information on pages 200–202. Wash fresh fruits with cool, clear tap water, but do not soak them; drain. Follow preparation directions below. If you choose to can or freeze fruits with syrup, select the syrup that best suits the fruit and your taste. Generally, heavier syrups are used with sour fruits, and lighter syrups are recommended for mild-flavored fruits. To prepare the syrup, place the specified amounts of sugar and water in a large saucepan. Heat until

Food	Preparation	Boiling-Water Canning, Raw Pack
Apples	Allow $2\frac{1}{2}$ to 3 pounds per quart. Select varieties that are crisp, not mealy, in texture. Peel and core; halve, quarter, or slice. Dip into ascorbic-acid color-keeper solution; drain.	Not recommended.
Apricots	Allow 2 to $2\frac{1}{2}$ pounds per quart. If desired, peel as for peaches, below. Prepare as for peaches.	See peaches, below.
Berries	Allow $\frac{3}{4}$ to 1 pound per pint. Can or freeze blackberries, blueberries, currants, elderberries, gooseberries, huckleberries, loganberries, mulberries, and raspberries. Freeze (do not can) boysenberries and strawberries.	Fill jars with blackberries, loganberries, mulberries, or raspberries. Shake down gently. Add boiling syrup, leaving a $\frac{1}{2}$-inch headspace.* Process pints for 15 minutes and quarts for 20 minutes.
Cherries	Allow 2 to 3 pounds per quart. If desired, treat with ascorbic-acid color-keeper solution; drain. If unpitted, prick skin on opposite sides to prevent splitting.	Fill jars, shaking down gently. Add boiling syrup or water, leaving a $\frac{1}{2}$-inch headspace.* Process pints and quarts for 25 minutes.
Melons	Allow about 4 pounds per quart for honeydew, cantaloupe, and watermelon.	Not recommended.
Nectarines, Peaches	Allow 2 to 3 pounds per quart. To peel peaches, immerse in boiling water for 20 to 30 seconds or until skins start to crack; remove and plunge into cold water. (Peeling nectarines is not necessary.) Halve and pit. If desired, slice. Treat with ascorbic-acid color-keeper solution; drain.	Fill jars, placing cut sides down. Add boiling syrup or water, leaving a $\frac{1}{2}$-inch headspace.* Process pints for 25 minutes and quarts for 30 minutes. (Note: The hot-pack method generally results in a better product.)
Pears	Allow 2 to 3 pounds per quart. Peel, halve, and core. Treat with ascorbic-acid color-keeper solution; drain.	Not recommended.
Plums	Allow 2 pounds per quart. Prick skin on two sides. Freestone varieties may be halved and pitted.	Pack firmly into jars. Add boiling syrup, leaving a $\frac{1}{2}$-inch headspace.* Process pints for 20 minutes and quarts for 25 minutes.
Rhubarb	Allow $1\frac{1}{2}$ pounds per quart. Discard leaves and woody ends. Cut into $\frac{1}{2}$- to 1-inch pieces.	Not recommended.

*See "Allow for Headspace," page 191.

the sugar dissolves. **Skim off foam, if necessary. Use the syrup hot for canned fruits and chilled for frozen fruits. Allow ½ to ⅔ cup syrup for each 2 cups of fruit. For *very thin syrup*, use 1 cup sugar and 4 cups water to yield 4 cups syrup. For *thin syrup*, use 1⅔ cups sugar and 4 cups water to yield 4¼ cups syrup. For *medium syrup*, use 2⅔ cups sugar and 4 cups water to yield 4⅔ cups syrup. For *heavy syrup*, use 4 cups sugar and 4 cups water to yield 5¾ cups syrup.**

	Boiling-Water Canning, Hot Pack	Freezing
	Simmer in syrup for 5 minutes, stirring occasionally. Fill jars with fruit and syrup, leaving a ½-inch headspace.* Process pints and quarts for 20 minutes.	Use a syrup, sugar, or dry pack (see step 3, page 202), leaving the recommended headspace.*
	See peaches, below.	Peel as for peaches, below. Use a syrup, sugar, or water pack (see step 3, page 202), leaving the recommended headspace.*
	Simmer blueberries, currants, elderberries, gooseberries, and huckleberries in water for 30 seconds; drain. Fill jars with berries and hot syrup, leaving a ½-inch headspace.* Process pints and quarts for 15 minutes.	Slice strawberries, if desired. Use a syrup, sugar, or dry pack (see step 3, page 202), leaving the recommended headspace.*
	Add cherries to hot syrup; bring to boiling. Fill jars with fruit and syrup, leaving a ½-inch headspace.* Process pints for 15 minutes and quarts for 20 minutes.	Use a syrup, sugar, or dry pack (see step 3, page 202), leaving the recommended headspace.*
	Not recommended.	Use a syrup or dry pack (see step 3, page 202), leaving the recommended headspace.*
	Add fruit to hot syrup; bring to boiling. Fill jars with fruit (placing cut sides down) and syrup, leaving a ½-inch headspace.* Process pints for 20 minutes and quarts for 25 minutes.	Use a syrup, sugar, or water pack (see step 3, page 202), leaving the recommended headspace.*
	Simmer fruit in syrup for 5 minutes. Fill jars with fruit and syrup, leaving a ½-inch headspace.* Process pints for 20 minutes and quarts for 25 minutes.	Not recommended.
	Simmer in water or syrup for 2 minutes. Remove from heat. Let stand, covered, for 20 to 30 minutes. Fill jars with fruit and cooking liquid or syrup, leaving a ½-inch headspace.* Process pints for 20 minutes and quarts for 25 minutes.	Halve and pit. Treat with ascorbic-acid color-keeper solution; drain well. Use a syrup pack (see step 3, page 202), leaving the recommended headspace.*
	In a saucepan sprinkle ½ cup sugar over each 4 cups fruit; mix well. Let stand until juice appears. Bring slowly to boiling, stirring gently. Fill jars with hot fruit and juice, leaving a ½-inch headspace.* Process pints and quarts for 15 minutes.	Blanch for 1 minute; cool quickly and drain. Use a syrup or dry pack (see step 3, page 202), leaving the recommended headspace.* Or use a sugar pack of ½ cup sugar to 3 cups fruit.

Canning and Freezing Vegetables

Read canning and freezing information on pages 200–202. Wash fresh vegetables with cool, clear tap water; scrub firm vegetables with a clean produce brush to remove any dirt.

Vegetable	Preparation	Pressure Canning, Raw Pack*
Asparagus	Allow 2$\frac{1}{2}$ to 4$\frac{1}{2}$ pounds per quart. Wash; scrape off scales. Break off woody bases where spears snap easily. Wash again. Sort by thickness. Leave whole or cut into 1-inch lengths.	Not recommended.
Beans: butter, lima, or pinto	Allow 3 to 5 pounds unshelled beans per quart. Wash, shell, rinse, drain, and sort beans by size.	Fill jars with beans; do not shake down.** Add boiling water, leaving a 1-inch headspace for pints, 1$\frac{1}{4}$-inch for large beans in quarts, and 1$\frac{1}{2}$-inch for small beans in quarts. Process pints for 40 minutes and quarts for 50 minutes.
Beans: green, Italian, snap, or wax	Allow 1$\frac{1}{2}$ to 2$\frac{1}{2}$ pounds per quart. Wash; remove ends and strings. Leave whole or cut into 1-inch pieces.	Pack tightly in jars;** add boiling water, leaving a 1-inch headspace. Process pints for 20 minutes and quarts for 25 minutes.
Beets	Allow 3 pounds (without tops) per quart. Trim off beet tops, leaving an inch of stem and roots to reduce bleeding of color. Scrub well. Cover with boiling water. Boil about 15 minutes or until skins slip off easily; cool. Peel; remove stem and root ends. Leave baby beets whole. Cut medium or large beets into $\frac{1}{2}$-inch cubes or slices. Halve or quarter large slices.	Not recommended.
Carrots	Use 1- to 1$\frac{1}{4}$-inch diameter carrots (larger carrots may be too fibrous). Allow 2 to 3 pounds per quart. Wash, trim, peel, and rinse again. Leave tiny ones whole; slice or dice the remainder.	Fill jar tightly with raw carrots;** leave 1-inch headspace. Add boiling water, leaving a 1-inch headspace. Remove air bubbles. Process pints for 25 minutes and quarts for 30 minutes.
Corn, cream-style	Allow 2 to 3 pounds per pint. Remove husks. Scrub with a vegetable brush to remove silks. Wash and drain.	Not recommended.
Corn, whole kernel	Allow 4 to 5 pounds per quart. Remove husks. Scrub with a vegetable brush to remove silks. Wash and drain.	Cover ears with boiling water; boil 3 minutes. Cut corn from cobs at three-quarters depth of kernels; do not scrape. Pack loosely in jars; do not shake or press down.** Add boiling water, leaving a 1-inch headspace. Process pints for 55 minutes; quarts for 85 minutes.
Peas, edible pods	Wash Chinese, snow, sugar, or sugar snap peas. Remove stems, blossom ends, and any strings.	Not recommended.

* For a dial-gauge canner, use 11 pounds of pressure; for a weighted-gauge canner, use 10 pounds of pressure. At altitudes above 1,000 feet, see tip, page 190.
** Add salt, if desired: $\frac{1}{4}$ to $\frac{1}{2}$ teaspoon for pints and $\frac{1}{2}$ to 1 teaspoon for quarts.

Pressure Canning, Hot Pack*	Freezing
Not recommended.	Blanch small spears for 2 minutes, medium for 3 minutes, and large for 4 minutes; cool quickly. Fill containers; shake down, leaving no headspace.
Cover beans with boiling water; return to boiling. Boil for 3 minutes. Fill jars loosely with beans and cooking liquid,** leaving a 1-inch headspace. Process pints for 40 minutes and quarts for 50 minutes.	Blanch small beans for 2 minutes, medium beans for 3 minutes, and large beans for 4 minutes; cool quickly. Fill containers loosely, leaving a $1/2$-inch headspace.
Cover beans with boiling water; return water to boiling. Boil for 5 minutes. Loosely fill jars with beans and cooking liquid,** leaving a 1-inch headspace. Process pints for 20 minutes and quarts for 25 minutes.	Blanch for 3 minutes; cool quickly. Fill containers; shake down, leaving a $1/2$-inch headspace.
Pack into hot jars, leaving 1-inch headspace.** Fill jars to 1 inch from top with boiling water. Process pints for 30 minutes and quarts for 35 minutes.	Cook unpeeled beets in boiling water until tender. (Allow 25 to 30 minutes for small beets; 45 to 50 minutes for medium beets.) Cool quickly in cold water. Peel; remove stem and root ends. Cut into slices or cubes. Fill containers, leaving a $1/2$-inch headspace.
Cover carrots with boiling water; return water to boiling. Reduce heat; simmer for 5 minutes. Fill jars with carrots and cooking liquid,** leaving a 1-inch headspace. Process pints for 25 minutes and quarts for 30 minutes.	Blanch tiny whole carrots for 5 minutes and cut-up carrots for 2 minutes; cool quickly. Pack tightly into containers, leaving a $1/2$-inch headspace.
Cover ears with boiling water; return to boiling and boil for 4 minutes. Use a sharp knife to cut off just the kernel tips, then scrape cob with a dull knife. Bring to boiling 1 cup water for each 2 cups corn. Add corn; simmer 3 minutes. Fill pint jars loosely,** leaving a 1-inch headspace. Process pints 85 minutes; do not use quart jars.	Cover ears with boiling water; return to boiling and boil 4 minutes. Cool quickly; drain. Use a sharp knife to cut off just the kernel tips, then scrape corn with a dull knife. Fill containers, leaving a $1/2$-inch headspace.
Cover ears with boiling water; return to boiling and boil 3 minutes. Cut corn from cobs at three-quarters depth of kernels; do not scrape. Bring to boiling 1 cup water for each 4 cups corn. Add corn; simmer 5 minutes. Fill jars with corn and liquid,** leaving a 1-inch headspace. Process pints for 55 minutes and quarts for 85 minutes.	Cover ears with boiling water; return to boiling and boil 4 minutes. Cool quickly; drain. Cut corn from cobs at two-thirds depth of kernels; do not scrape. Fill containers, leaving a $1/2$-inch headspace.
Not recommended.	Blanch small flat pods $1/2$ minutes or large flat pods 2 minutes. (If peas have started to develop, blanch 3 minutes. If peas are already developed, shell and follow directions for green peas.) Cool, drain, and fill containers, leaving a $1/2$-inch headspace.

Canning and Freezing Vegetables *(continued)*

Vegetable	Preparation	Pressure Canning, Raw Pack*
Peas: English or green	Allow 2 to 2½ pounds per pint. Wash, shell, rinse, and drain.	Pack loosely in jars; do not shake or press down.** Add boiling water, leaving a 1-inch headspace. Process pints and quarts for 40 minutes.
Peppers, hot	Select firm jalapeño or other chile peppers; wash. Halve large peppers. Remove stems, seeds, and membranes (see tip, page 64). Place cut sides down on a foil-lined baking sheet. Bake in a 425°F oven for 20 to 25 minutes or until skins are bubbly and browned. Cover peppers or wrap in foil and let stand about 15 minutes or until cool. Pull the skins off gently and slowly using a paring knife.	Not recommended.
Peppers, sweet	Select firm green, bright red, or yellow peppers; wash. Remove stems, seeds, and membranes. Place cut sides down on a foil-lined baking sheet. Bake in a 425°F oven for 20 to 25 minutes or until skins are bubbly and browned. Cover peppers or wrap in foil and let stand about 15 minutes or until cool. Pull the skins off gently and slowly using a paring knife.	Not recommended.

*For a dial-gauge canner, use 11 pounds of pressure; for a weighted-gauge canner, use 10 pounds of pressure.
At altitudes above 1,000 feet, see tip, page 190.
**Add salt, if desired: ¼ to ½ teaspoon for pints and ½ to 1 teaspoon for quarts.

Canning and Freezing Tomatoes

Allow 2½ to 3½ pounds unblemished tomatoes per quart. Wash tomatoes. To peel, dip tomatoes in boiling water for 30 seconds or until skins start to split. Dip in cold water; core and skin. Continue as directed below.

Tomatoes	Preparation	Boiling-Water Canning
Crushed	Cut into quarters; add enough to a large pan to cover bottom. Crush with a wooden spoon. Heat and stir until boiling. Slowly add remaining pieces, stirring constantly. Simmer for 5 minutes. Fill jars. Add bottled lemon juice: 1 tablespoon for pints, 2 tablespoons for quarts. Add salt, if desired: ¼ to ½ teaspoon for pints, ½ to 1 teaspoon for quarts. Leave a ½-inch headspace.	Process pints for 35 minutes and quarts for 45 minutes.
Whole or halved, no added liquid	Fill jars with whole or halved tomatoes, pressing to fill spaces with juice. Add bottled lemon juice: 1 tablespoon for pints, 2 tablespoons for quarts. Add salt, if desired: ¼ to ½ teaspoon for pints, ½ to 1 teaspoon for quarts. Leave a ½-inch headspace.	Process pints and quarts for 85 minutes.
Whole or halved, water-packed	Fill jars with whole or halved tomatoes. Add bottled lemon juice: 1 tablespoon for pints, 2 tablespoons for quarts. Add salt, if desired: ¼ to ½ teaspoon for pints, ½ to 1 teaspoon for quarts. Add boiling water, leaving a ½-inch headspace. Or, heat tomatoes in a saucepan with enough water to cover; simmer 5 minutes. Fill jars with tomatoes and cooking liquid. Add bottled lemon juice: 1 tablespoon for pints, 2 tablespoons for quarts. Add salt, if desired: ¼ to ½ teaspoon for pints, ½ to 1 teaspoon for quarts. Leave a ½-inch headspace.	Process pints for 40 minutes and quarts for 45 minutes.

*For a dial-gauge canner, use 11 pounds of pressure; for a weighted-gauge canner, use 10 pounds of pressure.
At altitudes above 1,000 feet, see tip, page 190.

Pressure Canning, Hot Pack*	Freezing
Cover with water; heat to boiling and boil for 2 minutes. Fill jars loosely with peas and cooking liquid,** leaving a 1-inch headspace. Process pints and quarts for 40 minutes.	Blanch 1½ minutes; chill quickly. Fill containers, shaking down and leaving a ½-inch headspace.
Pack in pint jars.** Add boiling water, leaving a 1-inch headspace. Process pints for 35 minutes.	Package in freezer containers, leaving no headspace.
Quarter large pepper pieces or cut into strips. Pack pepper pieces loosely in pint jars,** leaving 1-inch head space. Add boiling water, leaving a 1-inch headspace. Process pints for 35 minutes.	Quarter large pepper pieces or cut into strips. Fill containers, leaving a ½-inch headspace. Or, spread peppers in a single layer on a baking sheet; freeze until firm. Fill container, shaking to pack tightly and leaving no headspace.

Pressure Canning*	Freezing
Process pints and quarts for 15 minutes.	Set pan of tomatoes in ice water to cool. Fill containers, leaving a 1-inch headspace.
Process pints and quarts for 25 minutes.	Fill freezer containers, leaving a 1-inch headspace. (Use only for cooking due to texture changes from freezing.)
Process pints and quarts for 10 minutes.	If heated, set pan of tomatoes in cold water to cool. Fill containers, leaving a 1-inch headspace.

Canning

Reaching for a jar of home-canned fruits or vegetables is a satisfying experience. To make it a reality, you'll need a knowledge of canning basics, some top-quality food, and the right equipment. Plant fruit and vegetable varieties that are recommended for canning (check seed catalogs or ask a county extension service agent). Select only top-quality fruits and vegetables that are fresh, young, and tender. For best results, can food within 12 hours of harvest. Wash produce under running water or dip in several changes of clean water. If you live more than 1,000 feet above sea level, read "Altitude Adjustments," page 190, before beginning.

Equipment

Canner: Choose one of two types, depending on the kind of food you are canning. A boiling-water (or water-bath) canner is used for fruits, tomatoes, pickles, relishes, jams, and jellies. It is a large kettle with a lid and a rack designed to hold canning jars. Any large cooking pot can be used if it has a rack and tight-fitting lid and is deep enough for briskly boiling water to cover tops of jars by 1 inch.

A pressure canner must be used for vegetables and other low-acid foods. It is a large heavy pot with a rack and a tight-fitting lid that has a vent or petcock, a dial or weighted pressure gauge, and a safety fuse. It may or may not have a gasket. Pressure canners allow foods to be heated to 240°F and to be held at that temperature as long as necessary. Each type of pressure canner is different; always refer to the manufacturer's instructions specific to your canner.

Jars: Use only standard canning jars. These are tempered to withstand the heat inside a canner, and their mouths are specially threaded for sealing canning lids. Inspect all jars before using them; discard any that are cracked or have chipped rims. To remove mineral deposits or hard-water film, soak the empty jars in a solution of 1 cup vinegar per gallon of water. To avoid mineral deposits during processing, add ¼ cup vinegar per gallon of water in the canner.

Lids: Use screw bands and flat metal lids with a built-in sealing compound. Prepare them according to the manufacturer's directions. The flat lids are designed for one-time use only. Screw bands can be reused if they are not bent or rusty.

Other useful pieces of equipment include a kitchen scale, wide-mouth funnel, jar lifter, and food mill, colander, or sieve.

General Canning Steps

Follow these steps whether using a boiling-water canner or a pressure canner and review them before you harvest or buy the produce. Allow sufficient time to follow all directions exactly (see charts, pages 194–199), and try to choose a time when you can work with few or no interruptions.

Foods are packed into canning jars by the raw-pack (cold-pack) or the hot-pack method. In raw packing, uncooked food is packed into the canning jar and covered with boiling water, juice, or syrup (see chart introduction, pages 194–195, for syrup information). In hot packing, food is partially cooked, packed into jars, and covered with cooking liquid. The following guidelines apply to both methods.

1. Wash empty canning jars in hot, soapy water. Rinse thoroughly. Pour boiling water over jars and let them stand in the hot water until you're ready to fill them. Sterilize jars that will be processed for 10 minutes or less (see tip, page 188). Prepare lids and screw bands according to the manufacturer's directions.

2. Start heating water in the canner.

3. Prepare only as much food as needed to fill the maximum number of jars your canner will hold at one time. Work quickly, preparing the food as specified. Keep the work area clean.

4. Place the hot jars on cloth towels to prevent them from slipping during packing.

5. Pack the food into the jars, keeping in mind the recommended headspace.

6. Ladle or pour boiling liquid over the food, leaving the specified headspace (see tip, page 191).

7. Release trapped air bubbles in the jars by gently working a narrow rubber scraper or nonmetal utensil down the jars' sides. Add liquid, if needed, to maintain the necessary headspace.

8. Wipe jar rims with a clean, damp cloth. Food on the rims prevents a perfect seal.

9. Place prepared lids on jars; add screw bands, tightening according to manufacturer's directions.

10. Set each jar into the canner as it is filled. Jars should not touch each other (see photo, page 201).

As you fill each jar, add it to the canner. Leave space between the filled jars so that they don't touch.

11. Process filled jars, following the recipe's procedures and timings exactly.

12. Remove jars and place them on a rack or dry towels to cool. Leave at least 1 inch of space between the jars to allow air to circulate, but keep the area free of drafts.

13. After the jars are completely cooled (12 to 24 hours), press the center of each lid to check the seal. If the dip in the lid holds, the jar is sealed. If the lid bounces up and down, the jar isn't sealed.

Check unsealed jars for flaws. The contents can be refrigerated and used within 2 to 3 days, frozen, or reprocessed within 24 hours. To reprocess, use a clean jar and a new lid; process for the full length of time specified. Mark the label so you can use any recanned jars first.

If jars have lost liquid but are still sealed, the contents are safe. However, any food not covered by liquid will discolor, so use these jars first.

14. Wipe the jars and lids. Remove, wash, and dry the screw bands; store for future use. Label jars with contents and date; include a batch number if you are doing more than one canner load per day (if one jar spoils, you can easily identify others from that same load). Store jars in a cool (50°F to 70°F), dry, dark place. Use within 1 year.

Boiling-Water Canning

Set the canner and rack on the range top. Fill the canner half full with water. Cover and heat over high heat. Heat additional water in another kettle.

Prepare syrup (see chart introduction, pages 194–195, for syrup information), if needed; keep it warm but not boiling. Prepare the food. When the water in the canner is hot, fill each jar and place it on the rack in the canner. Replace the canner cover each time you add a jar. After the last jar has been added, pour additional boiling water into the canner until jars are 1 inch below the water line. Cover; heat to a brisk, rolling boil. Now begin the processing timing. Keep the water boiling gently during processing, adding more boiling water if the level drops. If the water stops boiling when you add more, stop counting the

time, turn up the heat, and wait for a full boil before resuming counting. At the end of the processing time, turn off the heat and remove the jars. Cool on a rack or dry towels. When jars are completely cool (12 to 24 hours), check the seals.

Pressure Canning

Read the manufacturer's instructions before attempting to use the pressure canner. Make sure all parts are clean and work properly.

If your canner has a dial gauge, have it checked yearly for accuracy. (Contact your county extension service office for the nearest testing location.) Weighted-gauge canners remain accurate from year to year.

When you are ready to start canning, check to see that the steam vent is clear. Set the canner and rack on the range top. Add 2 to 3 inches of hot water (or the amount specified by the canner manufacturer). Turn the heat to low.

Next, prepare enough food for one canner load. Fill each jar and place it in the canner. When the last jar is added, cover and lock the canner. Turn the heat to high. When steam comes out the vent, reduce the heat until the steam flows freely at a moderate rate. Let the steam flow steadily for 10 minutes or more to release all the air from inside the canner. Close the vent, or place the weighted gauge over the vent according to your canner's instructions. Start the timing when the recommended pressure is reached. Adjust the heat to maintain a constant pressure.

When the processing time is up, carefully remove the canner from the heat and set it away from drafts on a rack or a wooden board. If the canner is too heavy to move, simply turn off the heat. Let the pressure return to normal (allow 30 to 60 minutes). Do not lift the weight, open the vent, or run water over the canner.

Follow the manufacturer's instructions for opening the canner. Be sure to lift the cover away from you to avoid a blast of steam. If the food is still boiling vigorously in the jars, wait a few minutes before removing the jars from the canner. Cool the jars 2 to 3 inches apart on a rack or dry towels in a draft-free area. Do not tighten the lids. When the jars are completely cool (12 to 24 hours), check the seals.

Freezing

Freezing is an easy way to preserve fruits and vegetables. For best results, start with garden-fresh products that are top quality. Prepare, package, and store them as recommended and use within the suggested storage time.

Equipment

An accurate freezer thermometer will help you regulate your freezer temperature at 0°F or below. Higher temperatures will cause food to deteriorate faster. When freezing vegetables and fruits you will need a colander plus a large kettle, or a saucepan with a wire basket.

A variety of freezer containers and materials are available. Whatever you choose should be moistureproof and vaporproof, able to withstand temperatures of 0°F or below, and capable of being tightly sealed. For liquid or semiliquid foods, use rigid plastic freezer containers, freezer bags, or wide-top jars specifically designed for freezing. Regular jars are seldom tempered to withstand freezer temperatures. For solid or dry-pack foods, use freezer bags, heavy foil, plastic wrap for the freezer, or laminated freezer wrap.

General Freezing Steps

1. Select only the best-quality fruits and vegetables that are at their peak of maturity. Fruits should be firm yet ripe. Vegetables should be young, tender, unwilted, and garden fresh. Hold produce in the refrigerator if it can't be frozen immediately. Rinse and drain small quantities through several changes of cold water. Lift fruits and vegetables out of the water; do not let them soak. Prepare cleaned produce as specified in the charts on pages 194–199.

2. Blanch vegetables (and fruits when directed) by scalding them in boiling water for a short time. This stops or slows the enzymes that cause loss of flavor and color, and toughen the food. Blanching in the microwave is not recommended because some enzymes may not be inactivated. Timings vary according to vegetable type and size.

Blanching is a heat-and-cool process. First, fill a large pot with water using 1 gallon of water per pound of prepared vegetables. Heat to boiling. Add prepared food to the boiling water (or place it in a wire basket and lower it into the water); cover. Start timing immediately. Cook over high heat for the time specified in the charts. (Add

1 minute if you live 5,000 feet above sea level or higher.) Near the end of the time, fill your sink or a large container with ice water. As soon as the blanching time is complete, use a slotted spoon to transfer the food from the boiling water to a colander (or lift the wire basket out of the water). Immediately plunge the food into the ice water. Chill for the same amount of time it was boiled; drain well.

3. Package the cooled, drained food into freezer containers, leaving the specified headspace (see "Allow for Headspace," page 191).

Fruits often are frozen with added sugar or liquid for better texture and flavor. Refer to the directions in the chart introduction on pages 194–195.

Unsweetened or dry pack: Add no sugar or liquid to the fruit; simply pack in a container. This works well for small whole fruits, such as berries.

Water pack: Cover the fruit with water. Do not use glass jars. Maintain the recommended headspace. Unsweetened fruit juice also can be used.

Sugar pack: Place a small amount of fruit in the container and sprinkle lightly with sugar; repeat layering. Cover and let stand about 15 minutes or until juicy; seal.

Syrup pack: Cover fruit with a syrup of sugar and water (see chart introduction, pages 194–195, for syrup information).

4. Wipe container rims. Seal according to the manufacturer's directions, pressing out as much air as possible. If necessary, use freezer tape around the edges of the lids to ensure a tight seal.

5. Label each container with its contents, the amount, and the date.

6. Add packages to the freezer in batches to make sure that food freezes quickly and solidly. Leave some space between the packages so air can circulate around them. When frozen solid, the packages can be placed closer together.

7. Use frozen fruits and vegetables within 8 to 10 months. Vegetables are best cooked from a frozen state, without thawing them first. Thaw fruits in their containers either in the refrigerator or in a bowl of cool water.

Chapter 9
Cookies

On the divider: **Chocolate-Caramel Bars** (see recipe, page 207);
Melt-in-Your-Mouth Sugar Cookies (see recipe, page 217); **Cashew-Sugar Cookies** (see recipe, page 224)

For more recipes, visit our Recipe Center at **www.bhg.com**

Fruit-Filled Oatmeal Bars

Choose your favorite filling for these treasured lunch-box treats.

Prep: 20 minutes **Bake:** 30 minutes
Oven: 350°F **Makes:** 25 bars

> 1 cup all-purpose flour
> 1 cup quick-cooking rolled oats
> ⅔ cup packed brown sugar
> ¼ teaspoon baking soda
> ½ cup butter
> 1 recipe Apricot Filling, Apple-Cranberry Filling, Easy Filling, or Raisin Filling

1. In a medium bowl combine flour, oats, brown sugar, and baking soda. Using a pastry blender, cut in butter until the mixture resembles coarse crumbs. Reserve ½ cup of the crumb mixture.

2. Press remaining crumb mixture into bottom of an ungreased 9×9×2-inch or 11×7×1½-inch baking pan. Spread with desired filling. Sprinkle with reserved crumb mixture. Bake in a 350° oven for 30 to 35 minutes or until the top is golden. Cool on a wire rack. Cut into bars.

Apricot Filling: In a medium saucepan combine 1 cup snipped dried apricots and ¾ cup water. Bring to boiling; reduce heat. Simmer, covered, for 5 minutes. Meanwhile, combine ¼ cup sugar and 1 tablespoon all-purpose flour; stir into apricot mixture. Cook and stir about 1 minute more or until thickened and bubbly.

Apple-Cranberry Filling: Combine 1 cup chunky applesauce, ⅔ cup dried cranberries or blueberries, ½ teaspoon ground cinnamon, and dash ground cloves.

Easy Filling: Use 1½ cups canned mincemeat or one 21-ounce can cherry or peach pie filling.

Raisin Filling: In a medium saucepan combine ¾ cup water, 2 tablespoons sugar, and 2 teaspoons cornstarch. Add 1¼ cups golden raisins. Cook and stir until thickened and bubbly.

Nutrition Facts per bar for all variations: 111 cal., 4 g total fat (2 g sat. fat), 11 mg chol., 55 mg sodium, 18 g carbo., 1 g fiber, 1 g pro.
Daily Values: 11% vit. A, 1% calcium, 4% iron
Exchanges: 1 Other Carbo., 1 Fat

Fruit-Filled Oatmeal Bars with Easy Filling

Luscious Lemon Bars `Best Loved`

It's easy to lift the bars out of the pan for cutting if you first line your baking pan with foil, then grease the foil.

Prep: 25 minutes **Bake:** 33 minutes
Oven: 350°F **Makes:** 36 bars

> 2 cups all-purpose flour
> ½ cup sifted powdered sugar
> 2 tablespoons cornstarch
> ¼ teaspoon salt
> ¾ cup butter
> 4 slightly beaten eggs
> 1½ cups granulated sugar
> 3 tablespoons all-purpose flour
> 1 teaspoon finely shredded lemon peel
> ¾ cup lemon juice
> ¼ cup half-and-half, light cream, or milk
> Powdered sugar

1. In a large bowl combine the 2 cups flour, the ½ cup powdered sugar, cornstarch, and salt. Using a pastry blender, cut in butter until the mixture resembles coarse crumbs. Press mixture into the bottom of a greased 13×9×2-inch baking pan. Bake in a 350° oven for 18 to 20 minutes or until edges are golden.

2. Meanwhile, for the filling, in a medium bowl stir together the eggs, granulated sugar, the 3 tablespoons flour, lemon peel, lemon juice, and half-and-half. Pour filling over hot crust.

3. Bake for 15 to 20 minutes more or until center is set. Cool on a wire rack. Sift powdered sugar over top. Cut into bars. Cover and store in the refrigerator.

Nutrition Facts per bar: 114 cal., 5 g total fat (3 g sat. fat), 35 mg chol., 65 mg sodium, 16 g carbo., 0 g fiber, 2 g pro.
Daily Values: 4% vit. A, 4% vit. C, 1% calcium, 3% iron
Exchanges: 1 Other Carbo., 1 Fat

Pumpkin Bars

Prep: 35 minutes **Bake:** 25 minutes
Oven: 350°F **Cool:** 2 hours **Makes:** 48 bars

   2 **cups all-purpose flour**
1½ **cups sugar**
   2 **teaspoons baking powder**
   2 **teaspoons ground cinnamon**
   1 **teaspoon baking soda**
 ¼ **teaspoon salt**
 ¼ **teaspoon ground cloves**
   4 **beaten eggs**
   1 **15-ounce can pumpkin**
   1 **cup cooking oil**
 ½ **recipe Cream Cheese Frosting (page 171)**

1. In a large bowl stir together the flour, sugar, baking powder, cinnamon, baking soda, salt, and cloves. Stir in the eggs, pumpkin, and oil until combined. Spread in an ungreased 15×10×1-inch baking pan.

2. Bake in a 350° oven for 25 to 30 minutes or until a wooden toothpick inserted near the center comes out clean. Cool for 2 hours on a wire rack. Spread with Cream Cheese Frosting. Cut into bars.

Applesauce Bars: Prepare as above, except substitute one 15-ounce jar applesauce for the pumpkin.

Nutrition Facts per bar for pumpkin or applesauce variation:
133 cal., 7 g total fat (2 g sat. fat), 23 mg chol., 78 mg sodium, 17 g carbo., 0 g fiber, 1 g pro.
Daily Values: 44% vit. A, 1% vit. C, 2% calcium, 3% iron
Exchanges: 1 Other Carbo., 1½ Fat

Brandied Cranberry-Apricot Bars

Brandied Cranberry-Apricot Bars

Prep: 1 hour **Bake:** 1 hour **Oven:** 350°F **Makes:** 16 bars

 ⅔ **cup golden and/or dark raisins**
 ⅓ **cup dried cranberries**
 ⅓ **cup snipped dried apricots**
 ⅓ **cup brandy or water**
1⅓ **cups all-purpose flour**
1⅓ **cups packed brown sugar**
 ⅓ **cup butter**
   2 **eggs**
   1 **teaspoon vanilla**
 ⅓ **cup chopped pecans**
    Powdered sugar

1. In a saucepan combine the raisins, cranberries, apricots, and brandy. Bring to boiling. Remove from heat. Let stand for 20 minutes; drain.

2. In a medium bowl stir together 1 cup of the flour and ⅓ cup of the brown sugar. Using a pastry blender, cut in butter until mixture resembles coarse crumbs. Press mixture into an ungreased 8×8×2-inch baking pan. Bake in a 350° oven about 20 minutes or until golden.

3. Meanwhile, for filling, in a medium mixing bowl beat the eggs with an electric mixer on low speed for 4 minutes. Stir in the remaining ⅓ cup flour, the remaining 1 cup brown sugar, and the vanilla until combined. Stir in the drained fruit and the pecans. Pour filling over hot crust, spreading evenly.

4. Bake about 40 minutes more or until a wooden toothpick inserted near the center comes out clean. (If necessary, cover loosely with foil the last 10 minutes of baking to prevent overbrowning.) Cool on a wire rack. Sift powdered sugar over top. Cut into bars.

Nutrition Facts per bar: 216 cal., 6 g total fat (3 g sat. fat), 37 mg chol., 58 mg sodium, 36 g carbo., 1 g fiber, 2 g pro.
Daily Values: 8% vit. A, 3% calcium, 7% iron
Exchanges: ½ Fruit, 2 Other Carbo., 1 Fat

Chocolate Revel Bars `Best Loved`

Prep: 30 minutes **Bake:** 25 minutes
Oven: 350°F **Makes:** 60 bars

- 1 **cup butter, softened**
- 2 **cups packed brown sugar**
- 1 **teaspoon baking soda**
- 2 **eggs**
- 2 **teaspoons vanilla**
- 2½ **cups all-purpose flour**
- 3 **cups quick-cooking rolled oats**
- 1½ **cups semisweet chocolate pieces**
- 1 **14-ounce can (1¼ cups) sweetened condensed milk or low-fat sweetened condensed milk**
- ½ **cup chopped walnuts or pecans**
- 2 **teaspoons vanilla**

1. Set aside 2 tablespoons of the butter. In a large mixing bowl beat the remaining butter with an electric mixer on medium to high speed for 30 seconds. Add the brown sugar and baking soda. Beat until combined, scraping sides of bowl occasionally. Beat in eggs and 2 teaspoons vanilla until combined. Beat in as much of the flour as you can with the mixer. Stir in any remaining flour. Stir in the rolled oats.

2. For filling, in a medium saucepan combine the reserved 2 tablespoons butter, chocolate pieces, and sweetened condensed milk. Cook over low heat until chocolate melts, stirring occasionally. Remove from heat. Stir in the nuts and 2 teaspoons vanilla.

3. Press two-thirds (about 3⅓ cups) of the rolled oats mixture into the bottom of an ungreased 15×10×1-inch baking pan. Spread filling evenly over the oats mixture. Dot remaining rolled oats mixture on filling (see photo, top right).

4. Bake in a 350° oven about 25 minutes or until top is lightly browned (chocolate filling will still look moist). Cool on a wire rack. Cut into bars.

Peanut Butter-Chocolate Revel Bars: Prepare as above, except substitute ½ cup peanut butter for the 2 tablespoons butter when making the filling and substitute peanuts for the walnuts or pecans.

Whole Wheat-Chocolate Revel Bars: Prepare as above, except reduce the all-purpose flour to 1½ cups and add 1 cup whole wheat flour.

Nutrition Facts per bar for chocolate, peanut butter, and whole wheat variations: 146 cal., 6 g total fat (3 g sat. fat), 18 mg chol., 68 mg sodium, 21 g carbo., 1 g fiber, 2 g pro.
Daily Values: 3% vit. A, 3% calcium, 4% iron
Exchanges: 1½ Other Carbo., 1 Fat

Use your fingers to work the remaining oat mixture into flat pieces of various sizes; place them on the chocolate filling. Or drop the dough from two teaspoons.

Chocolate-Caramel Bars

These bars feature all kinds of goodies—pecans, coconut, caramels, and milk chocolate—piled on a buttery shortbread crust (see photo, page 203).

Prep: 20 minutes **Bake:** 40 minutes **Oven:** 350°F
Cool: 10 minutes **Makes:** 48 bars

- 1 **cup all-purpose flour**
- ½ **cup packed brown sugar**
- ½ **cup butter**
- 2 **cups coarsely chopped pecans**
- 1 **cup flaked coconut**
- 1 **14-ounce can (1¼ cups) sweetened condensed milk**
- 2 **teaspoons vanilla**
- 20 **vanilla caramels, unwrapped**
- 2 **tablespoons milk**
- 1 **cup milk chocolate pieces or semisweet chocolate pieces**

1. For crust, in a medium bowl stir together the flour and brown sugar. Using a pastry blender, cut in the butter until the mixture resembles coarse crumbs. Press crumb mixture into the bottom of an ungreased 13×9×2-inch baking pan. Bake in a 350° oven for 15 minutes. Sprinkle pecans and coconut over hot crust.

2. For filling, combine sweetened condensed milk and vanilla; pour over pecans and coconut. Bake for 25 to 30 minutes more or until the filling is set. Cool on a wire rack for 10 minutes.

3. Meanwhile, in a small saucepan combine caramels and milk. Cook and stir over medium-low heat just until caramels melt. Drizzle caramel mixture over filling. Sprinkle with chocolate pieces. Cool completely. Cut into bars.

Nutrition Facts per bar: 142 cal., 8 g total fat (3 g sat. fat), 10 mg chol., 46 mg sodium, 16 g carbo., 1 g fiber, 2 g pro.
Daily Values: 2% vit. A, 4% calcium, 2% iron
Exchanges: 1 Other Carbo., 1½ Fat

Double-Cherry Streusel Bars

The season for fresh cherries is brief, but you can enjoy this very cherry bar any time of the year, thanks to dried tart cherries and cherry preserves.

Prep: 20 minutes **Bake:** 32 minutes **Oven:** 350°F
Cool: 2 hours **Makes:** 48 bars

>   2 **cups water**
>   1 **cup dried tart cherries or dried cranberries, snipped**
>   2 **cups quick-cooking rolled oats**
> 1½ **cups all-purpose flour**
> 1½ **cups packed brown sugar**
>   1 **teaspoon baking powder**
>   ½ **teaspoon baking soda**
>   1 **cup butter**
>   ½ **cup coarsely chopped slivered almonds**
>   2 **12-ounce jars cherry preserves**
>   1 **teaspoon finely shredded lemon peel**
>   ½ **cup semisweet chocolate pieces**
>   1 **teaspoon shortening**

1. In a small saucepan bring water to boiling; remove from heat. Add dried cherries and let stand about 10 minutes or until softened. Drain and set aside.

2. For crust, in a large bowl combine oats, flour, brown sugar, baking powder, and baking soda. Using a pastry blender, cut in the butter until mixture resembles coarse crumbs. Reserve 1 cup of the crumb mixture. Stir the almonds into the reserved crumb mixture; set aside. Press remaining crumb mixture into the bottom of an ungreased 15×10×1-inch baking pan. Bake in a 350° oven for 12 minutes.

3. Meanwhile, for filling, stir together the drained cherries, cherry preserves, and lemon peel. Spread the filling evenly over hot crust; sprinkle with reserved crumb mixture. Bake for 20 to 25 minutes more or until top is golden brown. Cool on a wire rack for 2 hours.

4. In a small saucepan combine the chocolate pieces and shortening. Cook and stir over medium-low heat until chocolate melts; drizzle over top. Cut into bars.

Nutrition Facts per bar: 157 cal., 6 g total fat (3 g sat. fat),
11 mg chol., 70 mg sodium, 26 g carbo., 1 g fiber, 2 g pro.
Daily Values: 3% vit. A, 2% vit. C, 2% calcium, 4% iron
Exchanges: 1½ Other Carbo., 1 Fat

Terrific Toffee Bars

Prep: 15 minutes **Bake:** 15 minutes **Oven:** 350°F
Stand: 2 minutes **Makes:** 36 bars

>   ½ **cup butter, softened**
>   ¾ **cup packed brown sugar**
>   1 **egg**
>   ½ **teaspoon vanilla**
>   1 **cup all-purpose flour**
>   ⅛ **teaspoon salt**
>   ¾ **cup semisweet chocolate pieces**
>   ⅓ **cup chopped walnuts or pecans**
>   ⅓ **cup chocolate-covered toffee pieces**

1. In a large mixing bowl beat butter with an electric mixer on medium to high speed for 30 seconds. Add brown sugar, egg, and vanilla. Beat until combined, scraping the sides of the bowl occasionally. Beat in the flour and the salt until combined.

2. Spread evenly in an ungreased 13×9×2-inch baking pan. Bake in a 350° oven about 15 minutes or until edges begin to brown and surface is dry. Remove from oven and immediately sprinkle with chocolate pieces. Let stand about 2 minutes or until chocolate is softened; spread evenly. Sprinkle with nuts and toffee pieces. Immediately cut into bars. Cool on a wire rack.

Nutrition Facts per bar: 88 cal., 5 g total fat (2 g sat. fat),
14 mg chol., 46 mg sodium, 9 g carbo., 1 g fiber, 1 g pro.
Daily Values: 2% vit. A, 1% calcium, 2% iron
Exchanges: ½ Other Carbo., 1 Fat

Beyond Squares

There's more than one way to cut bars and brownies. Shapes other than squares make for an interesting presentation.

■ Make triangles by cutting bars or brownies into 2- or 2½-inch squares. Then cut each square in half diagonally.

■ For diamonds, first cut straight lines 1 or 1½ inches apart down the length of the pan. Then cut straight lines 1 to 1½ inches apart diagonally across the pan.

Spiced Apricot Bars

Looking for a low-fat treat? These bars are a good choice because using applesauce reduces the amount of oil needed.

Low Fat

Prep: 15 minutes **Bake:** 20 minutes   **Oven:** 350°F
Cool: 2 hours **Makes:** 24 bars

     1 **cup all-purpose flour**
    ½ **teaspoon baking powder**
    ¼ **teaspoon baking soda**
    ¼ **teaspoon ground cardamom or ⅛ teaspoon ground nutmeg**
     1 **slightly beaten egg**
    ½ **cup packed brown sugar**
    ½ **cup apricot nectar or orange juice**
    ¼ **cup unsweetened applesauce**
     2 **tablespoons cooking oil**
    ½ **cup finely snipped dried apricots**
     1 **recipe Apricot Icing**

1. In a medium bowl stir together the flour, baking powder, baking soda, and cardamom; set aside. In another bowl stir together the egg, brown sugar, apricot nectar, applesauce, and oil until combined. Add egg mixture to flour mixture, stirring just until combined. Stir in the apricots.

2. Spread batter in an ungreased 11×7×1½-inch baking pan. Bake in a 350° oven for 20 to 25 minutes or until a wooden toothpick inserted near the center comes out clean. Cool on a wire rack for 2 hours. Drizzle with Apricot Icing. Cut into bars.

Apricot Icing: In a small bowl stir together ½ cup sifted powdered sugar and enough apricot nectar or orange juice (2 to 3 teaspoons) to make icing of drizzling consistency.

Nutrition Facts per bar: 67 cal., 1 g total fat (0 g sat. fat),
9 mg chol., 26 mg sodium, 13 g carbo., 0 g fiber, 1 g pro.
Daily Values: 6% vit. A, 1% calcium, 3% iron
Exchanges: 1 Other Carbo.

Cake Brownies

These one-bowl brownies make cleanup a snap because you prepare the batter in the same bowl or pan used for melting the butter.

Prep: 30 minutes **Bake:** 15 minutes   **Oven:** 350°F
Cool: 2 hours   **Makes:** 48 brownies

    ¾ **cup butter**
   1¼ **cups sugar**
    ½ **cup unsweetened cocoa powder**
     2 **eggs**
     1 **teaspoon vanilla**
   1½ **cups all-purpose flour**
     1 **teaspoon baking powder**
    ¼ **teaspoon baking soda**
     1 **cup milk**
     1 **cup chopped walnuts or pecans**
    ½ **recipe No-Cook Fudge Frosting (page 170)**

1. Grease a 15×10×1-inch baking pan; set aside. In a large microwave-safe bowl microwave butter on 100 percent power (high) for 1½ to 2 minutes or until melted. (Or, melt butter in a medium saucepan over medium heat; remove saucepan from heat.) Stir in sugar and cocoa powder until combined. Add eggs and vanilla. Using a wooden spoon, beat lightly just until combined.

2. In a small bowl combine flour, baking powder, and baking soda. Add flour mixture and milk alternately to chocolate mixture, beating after each addition. Stir in nuts.

3. Pour batter into prepared baking pan. Bake in a 350° oven for 15 to 18 minutes or until a wooden toothpick inserted near the center comes out clean. Cool 2 hours on a wire rack. Frost with No-Cook Fudge Frosting. Cut into bars.

Nutrition Facts per brownie: 146 cal., 7 g total fat (3 g sat. fat),
23 mg chol., 72 mg sodium, 19 g carbo., 0 g fiber, 2 g pro.
Daily Values: 4% vit. A, 4% calcium, 3% iron
Exchanges: 1 Other Carbo., 1½ Fat

Spiced Apricot Bars

Fudgy Brownies   Best Loved

Prep: 20 minutes **Bake:** 30 minutes
Oven: 350°F **Makes:** 16 brownies

- ½ **cup butter**
- 3 **ounces unsweetened chocolate, coarsely chopped**
- 1 **cup sugar**
- 2 **eggs**
- 1 **teaspoon vanilla**
- ⅔ **cup all-purpose flour**
- ¼ **teaspoon baking soda**
- ½ **cup chopped nuts (optional)**
- 1 **recipe Chocolate-Cream Cheese Frosting (optional)**

1. In a medium saucepan melt butter and unsweetened chocolate over low heat, stirring constantly. Remove from heat; cool.

2. Meanwhile, grease an 8×8×2-inch or 9×9×2-inch baking pan; set aside. Stir sugar into cooled chocolate mixture in saucepan. Add the eggs, 1 at a time, beating with a wooden spoon after each addition just until combined. Stir in the vanilla.

3. In a small bowl stir together the flour and baking soda. Add flour mixture to chocolate mixture; stir just until combined. If desired, stir in nuts. Spread the batter in the prepared pan.

4. Bake in a 350° oven for 30 minutes for 8-inch pan or 25 minutes for 9-inch pan. Cool on a wire rack. If desired, frost with Chocolate-Cream Cheese Frosting. Cut into bars.

Nutrition Facts per brownie: 157 cal., 10 g total fat (6 g sat. fat), 43 mg chol., 90 mg sodium, 18 g carbo., 1 g fiber, 2 g pro.
Daily Values: 5% vit. A, 1% calcium, 4% iron
Exchanges: 1 Other Carbo., 2 Fat

Chocolate-Cream Cheese Frosting: In a saucepan melt 1 cup semisweet chocolate pieces over low heat, stirring constantly. Remove from heat; cool. In a small bowl stir together two 3-ounce packages softened cream cheese and ½ cup sifted powdered sugar. Stir in melted chocolate until smooth.

Cream Cheese Brownies

Prep: 30 minutes **Bake:** 45 minutes **Oven:** 350°F
Cool: 2 hours **Chill:** 1 hour **Makes:** 32 brownies

- 8 **ounces semisweet chocolate, chopped**
- 3 **tablespoons butter**
- 4 **eggs**
- 1¼ **cups sugar**
- ⅓ **cup water**
- 2 **teaspoons vanilla**
- 1 **cup all-purpose flour**
- ¾ **cup chopped macadamia nuts, toasted (see tip, page 224)**
- 1 **teaspoon baking powder**
- ¼ **teaspoon salt**
- 1 **8-ounce package cream cheese, softened**
- ⅔ **cup sugar**
- 2 **tablespoons all-purpose flour**
- 1 **tablespoon lemon juice**
- 1 **recipe Chocolate Glaze**

1. Line a 13×9×2-inch baking pan with foil, extending foil over edges of pan. Grease foil; set pan aside. In a large heavy saucepan cook and stir the chocolate and butter over low heat until chocolate melts. Remove from heat; cool.

2. In a large mixing bowl beat 2 of the eggs with an electric mixer on medium speed until foamy. Add the 1¼ cups sugar, the water, and 1 teaspoon of the vanilla; beat about 5 minutes or until mixture is thick and lemon-colored. Beat in cooled chocolate mixture. Stir in the 1 cup flour, nuts, baking powder, and salt. Spread half of the batter in prepared baking pan; set pan and remaining batter aside.

Fudgy Brownies

3. In a medium mixing bowl beat the remaining 2 eggs, the remaining 1 teaspoon vanilla, the cream cheese, the ⅔ cup sugar, the 2 tablespoons flour, and the lemon juice with an electric mixer until smooth. Spread evenly over batter in pan. Spoon remaining batter evenly over cream cheese mixture. Swirl batter with a knife to marble. Bake in a 350° oven for 45 minutes. Cool on a wire rack for 2 hours. Frost with Chocolate Glaze. Chill about 1 hour or until glaze is set. Cut into bars.

Chocolate Glaze: In a small saucepan cook and stir ⅓ cup whipping cream and 6 ounces finely chopped semisweet chocolate over low heat until chocolate melts.

Nutrition Facts per brownie: 199 cal., 12 g total fat (6 g sat. fat), 41 mg chol., 72 mg sodium, 23 g carbo., 1 g fiber, 3 g pro.
Daily Values: 4% vit. A, 2% calcium, 6% iron
Exchanges: 1½ Other Carbo., 2 Fat

Blondies

A Southern cook's preference for brown sugar over granulated sugar resulted in these butterscotch bar cookies many years ago.

Prep: 20 minutes **Bake:** 25 minutes
Oven: 350°F **Makes:** 36 bars

- 2 **cups packed brown sugar**
- ⅔ **cup butter**
- 2 **eggs**
- 2 **teaspoons vanilla**
- 2 **cups all-purpose flour**
- 1 **teaspoon baking powder**
- ¼ **teaspoon baking soda**
- 1 **cup semisweet chocolate pieces**
- 1 **cup chopped nuts**

1. Grease a 13×9×2-inch baking pan; set aside. In a medium saucepan heat brown sugar and butter over medium heat until butter melts and the mixture is smooth, stirring constantly. Cool slightly. Stir in eggs 1 at a time; stir in vanilla. Stir in flour, baking powder, and baking soda.

2. Spread batter in prepared baking pan. Sprinkle with chocolate pieces and nuts. Bake in a 350° oven for 25 to 30 minutes or until a wooden toothpick inserted near center comes out clean (avoid chocolate pieces). Cool slightly on a wire rack. Cut into bars while warm.

Nutrition Facts per bar: 157 cal., 8 g total fat (4 g sat. fat), 21 mg chol., 65 mg sodium, 21 g carbo., 1 g fiber, 2 g pro.
Daily Values: 3% vit. A, 2% calcium, 5% iron
Exchanges: 1½ Other Carbo., 1½ Fat

Fudge Ecstasies `Best Loved`

If you like brownies, you'll love these oh-so-chocolaty cookies studded with nuts.

Prep: 20 minutes **Bake:** 8 minutes per batch
Oven: 350°F **Makes:** about 36 cookies

- 1 **12-ounce package (2 cups) semisweet chocolate pieces**
- 2 **ounces unsweetened chocolate, chopped**
- 2 **tablespoons butter**
- 2 **eggs**
- ⅔ **cup sugar**
- ¼ **cup all-purpose flour**
- 1 **teaspoon vanilla**
- ¼ **teaspoon baking powder**
- 1 **cup chopped nuts**

1. Grease a cookie sheet; set aside. In a heavy medium saucepan cook and stir 1 cup of the chocolate pieces, the unsweetened chocolate, and butter until melted. Remove from heat; add the eggs, sugar, flour, vanilla, and baking powder. Beat until combined, scraping sides of pan. Stir in remaining 1 cup chocolate pieces and nuts.

2. Drop dough by rounded teaspoons 2 inches apart onto the prepared cookie sheet (see photo, page 212). Bake in a 350° oven for 8 to 10 minutes or until edges are firm and surfaces are dull and crackled. Transfer to a wire rack and let cool.

Nutrition Facts per cookie: 103 cal., 7 g total fat (3 g sat. fat), 14 mg chol., 15 mg sodium, 11 g carbo., 1 g fiber, 2 g pro.
Daily Values: 1% vit. A, 1% calcium, 3% iron
Exchanges: 1 Other Carbo., 1 Fat

Make-Ahead Tips

To store dough for dropped or shaped cookies: Place in an airtight container; chill up to 1 week. Or, place in a freezer container; freeze up to 6 months. To use, thaw in the refrigerator.

To store dough for sliced cookies: Wrap rolls of dough in plastic wrap. Place in an airtight container; chill up to 1 week. Or, place in a freezer container; freeze up to 6 months. To use, thaw in the refrigerator just until soft enough to slice.

To store baked cookies: Cool the cookies completely. If freezing, do not frost. In an airtight or freezer container, arrange cookies in a single layer; cover with a sheet of waxed paper. Repeat layers, leaving enough airspace to close container easily. Store at room temperature up to 3 days (refrigerate cookies frosted with cream cheese or yogurt icing). Or freeze cookies up to 3 months.

Chocolate Chip Cookies

Prep: 25 minutes **Bake:** 8 minutes per batch
Oven: 375°F **Makes:** about 60 cookies

- ½ **cup shortening**
- ½ **cup butter, softened**
- 1 **cup packed brown sugar**
- ½ **cup granulated sugar**
- ½ **teaspoon baking soda**
- 2 **eggs**
- 1 **teaspoon vanilla**
- 2½ **cups all-purpose flour**
- 1 **12-ounce package (2 cups) semisweet chocolate pieces or miniature candy-coated semisweet chocolate pieces**
- 1½ **cups chopped walnuts, pecans, or hazelnuts (filberts) (optional)**

1. In a large mixing bowl beat shortening and butter with an electric mixer on medium to high speed for 30 seconds. Add brown sugar, granulated sugar, and baking soda. Beat until mixture is combined, scraping sides of bowl occasionally. Beat in eggs and vanilla until combined. Beat in as much of the flour as you can with the mixer. Stir in any remaining flour. Stir in chocolate pieces and, if desired, nuts.

2. Drop dough by rounded teaspoons 2 inches apart onto an ungreased cookie sheet (see photo, right). Bake in a 375° oven for 8 to 10 minutes or until edges are lightly browned. Transfer to a wire rack and let cool.

Macadamia Nut and White Chocolate Chip Cookies: Prepare as above, except substitute white baking pieces for the semisweet chocolate pieces. Stir in one 3½-ounce jar macadamia nuts, chopped, with the baking pieces.

Nutrition Facts per cookie for plain or macadamia nut variation:
98 cal., 5 g total fat (2 g sat. fat), 11 mg chol., 31 mg sodium, 13 g carbo., 0 g fiber, 1 g pro.
Daily Values: 1% vit. A, 1% calcium, 3% iron
Exchanges: 1 Other Carbo., 1 Fat

Chocolate Chip Cookie Bars: Prepare as above, except press dough into an ungreased 15×10×1-inch baking pan. Bake in a 375° oven for 15 to 20 minutes or until golden. Cool on a wire rack. Cut into bars. Makes 48 bars.

Nutrition Facts per bar: 122 cal., 6 g total fat (3 g sat. fat), 14 mg chol., 39 mg sodium, 16 g carbo., 1 g fiber, 1 g pro.
Daily Values: 2% vit. A, 1% calcium, 4% iron
Exchanges: 1 Other Carbo., 1 Fat

Big Chocolate Chip Cookies: Prepare as at left, except use a ¼-cup measure or scoop to drop mounds of dough about 4 inches apart onto an ungreased cookie sheet. Bake in a 375° oven for 11 to 13 minutes or until edges are lightly browned. Makes about 20 cookies.

Nutrition Facts per cookie: 293 cal., 15 g total fat (7 g sat. fat), 34 mg chol., 94 mg sodium, 38 g carbo., 1 g fiber, 3 g pro.
Daily Values: 4% vit. A, 3% calcium, 9% iron
Exchanges: 2½ Other Carbo., 3 Fat

Chocolate Chip Cookie Pizzas: Prepare as at left, except do not stir in chocolate pieces and nuts. Press half of the dough into an ungreased 12-inch pizza pan. Sprinkle half of the chocolate pieces and half of the nuts over the top, pressing in lightly. Repeat with a second ungreased 12-inch pizza pan and the remaining dough and toppings. Bake in a 375° oven about 15 minutes or until golden. Frost as desired. Cut each pizza into 8 wedges, then cut a circle through wedges halfway between the center and the edge of the pan. Makes 32 pieces total.

Nutrition Facts per piece: 183 cal., 10 g total fat (5 g sat. fat), 21 mg chol., 59 mg sodium, 24 g carbo., 1 g fiber, 2 g pro.
Daily Values: 3% vit. A, 2% calcium, 6% iron
Exchanges: 1½ Other Carbo., 2 Fat

Using two teaspoons, one to scoop the dough and the other to push it off in a mound, drop dough onto a cookie sheet.

Ranger Cookies

Prep: 25 minutes **Bake:** 8 minutes per batch
Oven: 375°F **Makes:** about 48 cookies

- ½ **cup butter, softened**
- ½ **cup granulated sugar**
- ½ **cup packed brown sugar**
- ½ **teaspoon baking powder**
- ¼ **teaspoon baking soda**
- 1 **egg**
- 1 **teaspoon vanilla**
- 1¼ **cups all-purpose flour**
- 1 **cup quick-cooking rolled oats**
- 1 **cup coconut**
- 1 **cup raisins, dried cherries, dried cranberries, or mixed dried fruit bits**

1. In a large mixing bowl beat butter with electric mixer on medium to high speed for 30 seconds. Add granulated sugar, brown sugar, baking powder, and baking soda. Beat until combined, scraping sides of bowl occasionally. Beat in egg and vanilla until combined. Beat in as much of the flour as you can with the mixer. Stir in any remaining flour. Stir in rolled oats, coconut, and raisins.

2. Drop dough by rounded teaspoons 2 inches apart onto an ungreased cookie sheet (see photo, page 212). Bake in a 375° oven about 8 minutes or until edges are golden. Cool on cookie sheet 1 minute. Transfer to a wire rack and let cool.

Nutrition Facts per cookie: 71 cal., 3 g total fat (2 g sat. fat), 10 mg chol., 34 mg sodium, 11 g carbo., 0 g fiber, 1 g pro.
Daily Values: 2% vit. A, 1% calcium, 2% iron
Exchanges: 1 Other Carbo., ½ Fat

Jumbo Ranger Cookies: Prepare as above, except use a ⅓-cup measure or scoop to drop mounds of dough 2 inches apart on an ungreased cookie sheet. Press into 4-inch circles. Bake in a 375° oven 8 to 10 minutes or until edges are golden. Cool on cookie sheet 1 minute. Transfer to a wire rack and let cool. Makes about 10 cookies.

Nutrition Facts per cookie: 341 cal., 14 g total fat (9 g sat. fat) 48 mg chol., 165 mg sodium, 53 g carbo., 2 g fiber, 4 g pro.
Daily Values: 8% vit. A, 1% vit. C, 4% calcium, 10% iron
Exchanges: 3½ Other Carbo., 2½ Fat

Peanut Butter-Oatmeal Rounds

Prep: 30 minutes **Bake:** 10 minutes per batch
Oven: 375°F **Makes:** about 48 cookies

- ¾ **cup butter, softened**
- ½ **cup peanut butter**
- 1 **cup granulated sugar**
- ½ **cup packed brown sugar**
- 1 **teaspoon baking powder**
- ½ **teaspoon baking soda**
- 2 **eggs**
- 1 **teaspoon vanilla**
- 1¼ **cups all-purpose flour**
- 2 **cups rolled oats**
- 1 **cup chopped cocktail peanuts or semisweet chocolate pieces**

1. In a large mixing bowl beat butter and peanut butter with an electric mixer on medium to high speed about 30 seconds or until combined. Add granulated sugar, brown sugar, baking powder, and baking soda. Beat until combined, scraping

sides of bowl occasionally. Beat in eggs and vanilla until combined. Beat in as much of the flour as you can with the mixer. Stir in any remaining flour. Stir in rolled oats and peanuts.

2. Drop dough by rounded teaspoons 2 inches apart onto an ungreased cookie sheet (see photo, page 212). Bake in a 375° oven about 10 minutes or until edges are lightly browned. Transfer cookies to wire rack and let cool.

Chocolate-Peanut Butter-Oatmeal Rounds: Prepare as above, except melt and cool 3 ounces unsweetened chocolate. After beating in eggs and vanilla, stir in chocolate. Bake in a 375° oven about 10 minutes or until edges are set.

Nutrition Facts per cookie for regular or chocolate variation: 114 cal., 6 g total fat (2 g sat. fat), 17 mg chol., 82 mg sodium, 12 g carbo., 1 g fiber, 3 g pro.
Daily Values: 3% vit. A, 2% calcium, 3% iron
Exchanges: 1 Other Carbo., 1 Fat

Peanut Butter-Oatmeal Rounds

Oatmeal Cookies

Prep: 25 minutes **Bake:** 8 minutes per batch
Oven: 375°F **Makes:** about 48 cookies

> ¾ **cup butter, softened**
> 1 **cup packed brown sugar**
> ½ **cup granulated sugar**
> 1 **teaspoon baking powder**
> ¼ **teaspoon baking soda**
> ½ **teaspoon ground cinnamon (optional)**
> ¼ **teaspoon ground cloves (optional)**
> 2 **eggs**
> 1 **teaspoon vanilla**
> 1¾ **cups all-purpose flour**
> 2 **cups rolled oats**

1. In a large mixing bowl beat butter with an electric mixer on medium to high speed for 30 seconds. Add brown sugar, granulated sugar, baking powder, baking soda, and, if desired, cinnamon and cloves. Beat until combined, scraping sides of bowl occasionally. Beat in eggs and vanilla until combined. Beat in as much of the flour as you can with the mixer. Stir in any remaining flour. Stir in rolled oats.

2. Drop dough by rounded teaspoons 2 inches apart onto an ungreased cookie sheet (see photo, page 212). Bake in a 375° oven for 8 to 10 minutes or until edges are golden. Cool on cookie sheet for 1 minute. Transfer to a wire rack and let cool.

Oatmeal-Raisin Cookies: Prepare as above, except after stirring in oats, stir in 1 cup raisins or snipped dried tart cherries. Makes about 54 cookies.

Oatmeal-Chip Cookies: Prepare as above, except after stirring in oats, stir in 1 cup semisweet chocolate, butterscotch-flavored, or peanut butter-flavored pieces and ½ cup chopped walnuts or pecans. Makes about 54 cookies.

Nutrition Facts per cookie for regular, raisin, and chip variations: 86 cal., 4 g total fat (2 g sat. fat), 17 mg chol., 51 mg sodium, 12 g carbo., 1 g fiber, 1 g pro.
Daily Values: 3% vit. A, 1% calcium, 2% iron
Exchanges: 1 Other Carbo., ½ Fat

Oversize Oatmeal Cookies: Prepare as above, except use a ¼-cup measure or scoop to drop mounds of dough 2 inches apart onto an ungreased cookie sheet. Press into 3-inch circles. Bake in a 375° oven 8 to 10 minutes or until edges are golden. Cool on cookie sheet 1 minute. Transfer to wire rack and let cool. Makes 10 cookies.

Nutrition Facts per cookie: 415 cal., 17 g total fat (10 g sat. fat), 82 mg chol., 242 mg sodium, 60 g carbo., 3 g fiber, 6 g pro.
Daily Values: 12% vit. A, 7% calcium, 12% iron
Exchanges: 4 Other Carbo., 3 Fat

Coconut Macaroons

Low Fat

It's thoughtful to include lighter cookies such as these in your holiday assortment. Anyone watching fat intake will appreciate having the choice.

Prep: 15 minutes **Bake:** 20 minutes per batch
Oven: 325°F **Makes:** about 30 cookies

> 2 **egg whites**
> ½ **teaspoon vanilla**
> ⅔ **cup sugar**
> 1 **3½-ounce can (1⅓ cups) flaked coconut**

1. Lightly grease a cookie sheet; set aside. In a medium mixing bowl beat egg whites and vanilla with an electric mixer on high speed until soft peaks form (tips curl; see photo 1, page 169). Gradually add sugar, about 1 tablespoon at a time, beating until stiff peaks form (tips stand straight; see photo 2, page 169). Fold in coconut.

2. Drop mixture by rounded teaspoons 2 inches apart onto the prepared cookie sheet (see photo, page 212). Bake in 325° oven about 20 minutes or until edges are lightly browned. Transfer to a wire rack and let cool.

Lemon Macaroons: Prepare as above, except substitute 1 tablespoon lemon juice for the vanilla and add 1 teaspoon finely shredded lemon peel.

Nutrition Facts per cookie for plain or lemon variation: 32 cal., 1 g total fat (1 g sat. fat), 0 mg chol., 4 mg sodium, 6 g carbo., 0 g fiber, 0 g pro.
Exchanges: ½ Other Carbo.

Almond Macaroons: Prepare as above, except substitute one 8-ounce can almond paste (made without syrup or liquid glucose) for the coconut. Stir ½ cup of the beaten egg whites into crumbled almond paste; fold this mixture into the remaining egg whites. Continue as directed.

Nutrition Facts per cookie: 52 cal., 2 g total fat (0 g sat. fat), 0 mg chol., 4 mg sodium, 8 g carbo., 0 g fiber, 1 g pro.
Daily Values: 1% calcium, 1% iron
Exchanges: ½ Other Carbo., ½ Fat

Giant Ginger Cookies

Chewy and delicious, these cookies are giants in both size and snappy ginger flavor.

Prep: 20 minutes **Bake:** 11 minutes per batch
Oven: 350°F **Makes:** about 24 cookies

- 4½ **cups all-purpose flour**
- 4 **teaspoons ground ginger**
- 2 **teaspoons baking soda**
- 1½ **teaspoons ground cinnamon**
- 1 **teaspoon ground cloves**
- ¼ **teaspoon salt**
- 1½ **cups shortening**
- 2 **cups sugar**
- 2 **eggs**
- ½ **cup molasses**
- ¾ **cup sugar**

1. In a medium bowl stir together flour, ginger, baking soda, cinnamon, cloves, and salt; set aside. In a large mixing bowl beat shortening with an electric mixer on low speed for 30 seconds. Add the 2 cups sugar. Beat until combined, scraping sides of bowl occasionally. Beat in eggs and molasses until combined. Beat in as much of the flour mixture as you can with the mixer. Stir in any remaining flour mixture.

2. Shape dough into 2-inch balls using a ¼-cup measure or scoop. Roll balls in the ¾ cup sugar. Place 2½ inches apart on an ungreased cookie sheet.

3. Bake in a 350° oven for 11 to 13 minutes or until bottoms are lightly browned and tops are puffed (do not overbake). Cool on cookie sheet 2 minutes. Transfer to a wire rack and let cool.

Nutrition Facts per cookie: 306 cal., 13 g total fat (3 g sat. fat), 18 mg chol., 138 mg sodium, 45 g carbo., 1 g fiber, 3 g pro.
Daily Values: 1% vit. A, 1% vit. C, 3% calcium, 10% iron
Exchanges: 3 Other Carbo., 2½ Fat

Ginger Cookies: Prepare as above, except shape dough into 1-inch balls; roll in sugar. Place 1½ inches apart on an ungreased cookie sheet. Bake in a 350° oven for 8 to 9 minutes or until bottoms are lightly browned and tops are puffed (do not overbake). Cool on cookie sheet for 1 minute. Transfer to a wire rack and let cool. Makes about 120 cookies.

Nutrition Facts per cookie: 61 cal., 3 g total fat (1 g sat. fat), 4 mg chol., 28 mg sodium, 9 g carbo., 0 g fiber, 1 g pro.
Daily Values: 1% calcium, 2% iron
Exchanges: ½ Other Carbo., ½ Fat

Chocolate Crinkles

Prep: 25 minutes **Chill:** 1 to 2 hours
Bake: 8 minutes per batch **Oven:** 375°F
Makes: about 48 cookies

- 3 **eggs**
- 1½ **cups granulated sugar**
- 4 **ounces unsweetened chocolate, melted**
- ½ **cup cooking oil**
- 2 **teaspoons baking powder**
- 2 **teaspoons vanilla**
- 2 **cups all-purpose flour**
  Sifted powdered sugar

1. In a large mixing bowl beat eggs, granulated sugar, chocolate, oil, baking powder, and vanilla with an electric mixer until combined. Beat in as much of the flour as you can with the mixer. Stir in any remaining flour. Cover and chill dough for 1 to 2 hours or until easy to handle.

2. Shape dough into 1-inch balls. Roll balls in powdered sugar to coat generously. Place balls 1 inch apart on an ungreased cookie sheet. Bake in a 375° oven for 8 to 10 minutes or until edges are set and tops are crackled. Transfer to a wire rack and let cool. If desired, sprinkle with additional powdered sugar.

Nutrition Facts per cookie: 81 cal., 4 g total fat (1 g sat. fat), 13 mg chol., 21 mg sodium, 11 g carbo., 1 g fiber, 1 g pro.
Daily Values: 2% calcium, 3% iron
Exchanges: ½ Other Carbo., 1 Fat

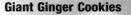

Giant Ginger Cookies

Buried Cherry Cookies

Prep: 30 minutes **Bake:** 10 minutes per batch
Oven: 350°F **Makes:** 42 to 48 cookies

- 1 **10-ounce jar maraschino cherries (42 to 48)**
- ½ **cup butter, softened**
- 1 **cup sugar**
- ¼ **teaspoon baking powder**
- ¼ **teaspoon baking soda**
- 1 **egg**
- 1½ **teaspoons vanilla**
- ½ **cup unsweetened cocoa powder**
- 1½ **cups all-purpose flour**
- 1 **cup semisweet chocolate pieces***
- ½ **cup sweetened condensed milk or low-fat sweetened condensed milk**

1. Drain cherries, reserving juice. Halve any large cherries. Beat butter with an electric mixer on medium to high speed for 30 seconds. Add the sugar, baking powder, baking soda, and ¼ teaspoon *salt*. Beat until combined, scraping bowl. Beat in egg and vanilla until combined. Beat in cocoa powder and as much of the flour as you can with the mixer. Stir in any remaining flour.

2. Shape dough into 1-inch balls. Place balls about 2 inches apart on an ungreased cookie sheet. Press your thumb into the center of each ball. Place a cherry in each center.

3. For frosting, in a small saucepan combine chocolate pieces and sweetened condensed milk. Cook and stir over low heat until chocolate melts. Stir in 4 teaspoons reserved cherry juice. Spoon 1 teaspoon frosting over each cherry, spreading to cover (see photo, below). (If necessary, frosting may be thinned with additional cherry juice.)

4. Bake in a 350° oven about 10 minutes or until edges are firm. Cool on cookie sheet 1 minute. Transfer to a wire rack and let cool.

*Note: Do not substitute imitation chocolate pieces for semisweet chocolate pieces.

Nutrition Facts per cookie: 97 cal., 4 g total fat (2 g sat. fat), 13 mg chol., 56 mg sodium, 14 g carbo., 0 g fiber, 1 g pro.
Daily Values: 2% vit. A, 3% calcium, 3% iron
Exchanges: 1 Other Carbo., 1 Fat

Carefully spoon about 1 teaspoon of the frosting over each cherry. Using the back of a spoon, spread the frosting so it completely covers the cherry.

Snickerdoodles

Cinnamon and sugar coat these old-fashioned crackled-top goodies.

Prep: 25 minutes **Chill:** 1 hour **Bake:** 10 minutes per batch
Oven: 375°F **Makes:** about 36 cookies

- ½ **cup butter, softened**
- 1 **cup sugar**
- ¼ **teaspoon baking soda**
- ¼ **teaspoon cream of tartar**
- 1 **egg**
- ½ **teaspoon vanilla**
- 1½ **cups all-purpose flour**
- 2 **tablespoons sugar**
- 1 **teaspoon ground cinnamon**

1. In a medium mixing bowl beat butter with an electric mixer on medium to high speed for 30 seconds. Add the 1 cup sugar, baking soda, and cream of tartar. Beat until combined, scraping sides of bowl occasionally. Beat in egg and vanilla until combined. Beat in as much of the flour as you can with the mixer. Stir in any remaining flour. Cover and chill dough about 1 hour or until easy to handle.

2. Combine the 2 tablespoons sugar and the cinnamon. Shape dough into 1-inch balls. Roll balls in sugar-cinnamon mixture to coat. Place 2 inches apart on an ungreased cookie sheet. Bake in a 375° oven for 10 to 11 minutes or until edges are golden. Transfer to a wire rack and let cool.

Nutrition Facts per cookie: 69 cal., 3 g total fat (2 g sat. fat), 13 mg chol., 38 mg sodium, 10 g carbo., 0 g fiber, 1 g pro.
Daily Values: 2% vit. A, 2% iron
Exchanges: ½ Other Carbo., ½ Fat

Jam Thumbprints

Instead of jam, fill the centers with spoonfuls of your favorite frosting.

Prep: 25 minutes **Chill:** 1 hour **Bake:** 10 minutes per batch
Oven: 375°F **Makes:** about 42 cookies

- ⅔ **cup butter, softened**
- ½ **cup sugar**
- 2 **egg yolks**
- 1 **teaspoon vanilla**
- 1½ **cups all-purpose flour**
- 2 **slightly beaten egg whites**
- 1 **cup finely chopped walnuts**
- ⅓ **to ½ cup strawberry, cherry, or apricot jam or preserves**

1. Beat butter with an electric mixer on medium to high speed 30 seconds. Add sugar. Beat until combined, scraping bowl. Beat in egg yolks and vanilla until combined. Beat in as much flour as you can. Stir in any remaining flour. Cover and chill dough about 1 hour or until easy to handle.

2. Grease a cookie sheet; set aside. Shape dough into 1-inch balls. Roll balls in egg whites, then in walnuts. Place 1 inch apart on the prepared cookie sheet. Press your thumb into the center of each ball. Bake in a 375° oven for 10 to 12 minutes or until edges are lightly browned. Transfer to a wire rack and let cool. Just before serving, fill centers with jam.

Nutrition Facts per cookie: 82 cal., 5 g total fat (2 g sat. fat), 18 mg chol., 35 mg sodium, 8 g carbo., 0 g fiber, 1 g pro.
Daily Values: 3% vit. A, 1% calcium, 2% iron
Exchanges: ½ Other Carbo., 1 Fat

Fudgy Cappuccino Crinkles

Low Fat

Prep: 15 minutes **Chill:** 3 hours **Bake:** 8 minutes per batch
Oven: 350°F **Makes:** about 40 cookies

- ⅓ **cup butter, softened**
- 1 **cup packed brown sugar**
- ⅔ **cup unsweetened cocoa powder**
- 1 **tablespoon instant coffee granules**
- 1 **teaspoon baking soda**
- 1 **teaspoon ground cinnamon**
- 2 **egg whites**
- ⅓ **cup vanilla low-fat yogurt**
- 1½ **cups all-purpose flour**
- ¼ **to ½ cup granulated sugar or sifted powdered sugar**

1. Lightly grease a cookie sheet; set aside. Beat butter with an electric mixer on medium speed 30 seconds. Add brown sugar, cocoa powder, coffee granules, baking soda, and cinnamon. Beat until combined, scraping bowl. Beat in egg whites and yogurt until combined. Beat in as much flour as you can. Stir in any remaining flour. Cover and chill dough 3 hours or until easy to handle.

2. Place the sugar in a small bowl. Drop dough by a teaspoon into sugar and roll into balls. Place 2 inches apart on the prepared cookie sheet. Bake in a 350° oven for 8 to 10 minutes or until edges are firm. Transfer to a wire rack and let cool.

Nutrition Facts per cookie: 66 cal., 2 g total fat (1 g sat. fat), 4 mg chol., 54 mg sodium, 11 g carbo., 0 g fiber, 1 g pro.
Daily Values: 1% vit. A, 3% calcium, 3% iron
Exchanges: ½ Other Carbo., ½ Fat

Melt-in-Your-Mouth Sugar Cookies

See photo, page 203.

Prep: 20 minutes **Bake:** 15 minutes per batch
Oven: 300°F **Makes:** about 60 cookies

- ½ **cup butter, softened**
- ½ **cup shortening**
- 2 **cups sugar**
- 1 **teaspoon baking soda**
- 1 **teaspoon cream of tartar**
- ⅛ **teaspoon salt**
- 3 **egg yolks**
- ½ **teaspoon vanilla**
- 1¾ **cups all-purpose flour**

1. In a large mixing bowl beat butter and shortening with an electric mixer on medium to high speed for 30 seconds. Add sugar, baking soda, cream of tartar, and salt. Beat until combined, scraping sides of bowl occasionally. Beat in egg yolks and vanilla until combined. Beat in as much flour as you can. Stir in remaining flour.

2. Shape dough into 1-inch balls. Place 2 inches apart on an ungreased cookie sheet. Bake in a 300° oven about 15 minutes or until sides are set (do not let edges brown). Cool on cookie sheet for 1 minute. Transfer to a wire rack and let cool.

Nutrition Facts per cookie: 70 cal., 4 g total fat (1 g sat. fat), 15 mg chol., 43 mg sodium, 9 g carbo., 0 g fiber, 1 g pro.
Daily Values: 2% vit. A, 1% iron
Exchanges: ½ Other Carbo., ½ Fat

Chilling Out

Many cookie recipes call for chilling the dough in the refrigerator before shaping, slicing, or rolling. This helps to stiffen the butter or shortening and makes the dough more manageable. It also makes the finished product better because chilled dough needs to be worked less than an unchilled dough.

■ Chill all cookie doughs made with butter or shortening in the refrigerator for the time recommended in the recipe. If you're using margarine for shaped or sliced cookies (see tip, page 222), you should quick-chill the dough in the freezer for about one-third of the refrigerator chilling time. Do not quick-chill cookie dough made with butter or shortening in the freezer; it will become too firm.

■ For rolled cookies made with margarine, refrigerate the dough at least 5 hours or freeze for 2 hours before rolling.

Peanut Butter Cookies

Add a new look to this classic favorite by decorating the tops of cooled cookies with drizzles of melted semisweet chocolate pieces.

Prep: 25 minutes **Bake:** 7 minutes per batch
Oven: 375°F **Makes:** about 36 cookies

   ½ **cup butter, softened**
   ½ **cup peanut butter**
   ½ **cup granulated sugar**
   ½ **cup packed brown sugar or ¼ cup honey**
   ½ **teaspoon baking soda**
   ½ **teaspoon baking powder**
   1 **egg**
   ½ **teaspoon vanilla**
  1¼ **cups all-purpose flour**
     Granulated sugar

1. In a large mixing bowl beat butter and peanut butter with an electric mixer on medium to high speed for 30 seconds. Add the granulated sugar, brown sugar, baking soda, and baking powder. Beat until combined, scraping sides of bowl occasionally. Beat in egg and vanilla until combined. Beat in as much of the flour as you can with the mixer. Stir in any remaining flour. If necessary, cover and chill dough until easy to handle.

2. Shape dough into 1-inch balls. Roll in additional granulated sugar to coat. Place 2 inches apart on an ungreased cookie sheet. Flatten by making crisscross marks with the tines of a fork. Bake in a 375° oven for 7 to 9 minutes or until bottoms are lightly browned. Transfer to a wire rack and let cool.

Nutrition Facts per cookie: 87 cal., 5 g total fat (2 g sat. fat), 13 mg chol., 70 mg sodium, 10 g carbo., 0 g fiber, 2 g pro.
Daily Values: 2% vit. A, 1% calcium, 2% iron
Exchanges: ½ Other Carbo., 1 Fat

Sandies

Prep: 25 minutes **Bake:** 15 minutes per batch
Oven: 325°F **Makes:** about 48 cookies

   1 **cup butter, softened**
   ½ **cup sifted powdered sugar**
   1 **tablespoon water**
   1 **teaspoon vanilla**
   2 **cups all-purpose flour**
  1½ **cups finely chopped pecans**
   1 **cup sifted powdered sugar**

1. Beat butter with an electric mixer on medium speed 30 seconds. Add the ½ cup powdered sugar. Beat until combined, scraping bowl. Beat in water and vanilla. Beat in as much flour as you can. Stir in any remaining flour. Stir in pecans.

2. Shape dough into 1-inch balls or 2×½-inch logs. Place 1 inch apart on an ungreased cookie sheet. Bake in a 325° oven about 15 minutes or until bottoms are lightly browned. Transfer to a wire rack; let cool. Gently shake cooled cookies in a plastic bag with the 1 cup powdered sugar.

Cocoa Sandies: Prepare as above, except add ¼ cup unsweetened cocoa powder with the flour.

Nutrition Facts per cookie for plain or cocoa variation: 91 cal., 7 g total fat (3 g sat. fat), 11 mg chol., 41 mg sodium, 8 g carbo., 0 g fiber, 1 g pro.
Daily Values: 3% vit. A, 2% iron
Exchanges: ½ Other Carbo., 1½ Fat

Peanut Butter Blossoms

Prep: 25 minutes **Bake:** 10 minutes per batch
Oven: 350°F **Makes:** about 54 cookies

   ½ **cup shortening**
   ½ **cup peanut butter**
   ½ **cup granulated sugar**
   ½ **cup packed brown sugar**
   1 **teaspoon baking powder**
   ⅛ **teaspoon baking soda**
   1 **egg**
   2 **tablespoons milk**
   1 **teaspoon vanilla**
  1¾ **cups all-purpose flour**
   ¼ **cup granulated sugar**
     Milk chocolate kisses or stars

1. Beat shortening and peanut butter with an electric mixer 30 seconds. Add the ½ cup granulated sugar, brown sugar, baking powder, and baking soda. Beat until combined, scraping bowl. Beat in egg, milk, and vanilla. Beat in as much flour as you can. Stir in any remaining flour.

2. Shape dough into 1-inch balls. Roll balls in the ¼ cup granulated sugar. Place 2 inches apart on an ungreased cookie sheet. Bake in a 350° oven for 10 to 12 minutes or until edges are firm and bottoms are lightly browned. Immediately press a chocolate kiss into each cookie's center. Transfer to a wire rack and let cool.

Nutrition Facts per cookie: 94 cal., 5 g total fat (2 g sat. fat), 5 mg chol., 28 mg sodium, 11 g carbo., 0 g fiber, 2 g pro.
Daily Values: 2% calcium, 2% iron
Exchanges: 1 Other Carbo., 1 Fat

Cranberry-Orange Pinwheels

Fresh cranberries give these pleasingly soft cookies a tangy taste and bright color.

Prep: 25 minutes **Chill:** 5 to 24 hours
Bake: 8 minutes per batch **Oven:** 375°F
Makes: about 60 cookies

> 1 **cup cranberries**
> 1 **cup pecans**
> ¼ **cup packed brown sugar**
> 1 **cup butter, softened**
> 1½ **cups granulated sugar**
> ½ **teaspoon baking powder**
> ½ **teaspoon salt**
> 2 **eggs**
> 2 **teaspoons finely shredded orange peel**
> 3 **cups all-purpose flour**

1. For filling, in a blender container or food processor bowl combine cranberries, pecans, and brown sugar. Cover; blend or process until cranberries and nuts are finely chopped; set aside.

2. In a large mixing bowl beat butter with an electric mixer on medium to high speed for 30 seconds. Add granulated sugar, baking powder, and salt. Beat until combined, scraping sides of bowl occasionally. Beat in eggs and orange peel until combined. Beat in as much of the flour as you can with the mixer. Stir in any remaining flour. Divide dough in half. Cover and chill dough about 1 hour or until easy to handle.

3. Roll half of the dough between pieces of waxed paper into a 10-inch square. Spread half of the filling over dough square to within ½ inch of edges; roll up dough (see photo 1, page 220). Moisten edges; pinch to seal. Wrap in waxed paper or plastic wrap. Repeat with remaining dough and filling. Chill for 4 to 24 hours.

4. Cut rolls into ¼-inch slices (see photo 2, page 220). Place slices 2 inches apart on an ungreased cookie sheet. Bake in a 375° oven for 8 to 10 minutes or until edges are firm and bottoms are lightly browned. Cool on cookie sheet for 1 minute. Transfer to a wire rack and let cool.

Nutrition Facts per cookie: 89 cal., 5 g total fat (2 g sat. fat), 16 mg chol., 58 mg sodium, 11 g carbo., 0 g fiber, 1 g pro.
Daily Values: 3% vit. A, 1% vit. C, 1% calcium, 2% iron
Exchanges: ½ Other Carbo., 1 Fat

Cranberry-Orange Pinwheels

Cookie Sheet Clues

The sweet success of freshly baked cookies lies partly in choosing the right cookie sheet.

■ Opt for heavy-gauge aluminum with low sides or no sides at all.

■ Invest in lighter-colored cookie sheets. If they are too dark, cookies may overbrown.

■ For most cookies, select sheets with a dull finish so cookie bottoms brown more evenly.

■ Use shiny sheets for cookies that should not brown on bottoms, such as shortbread.

■ Choose nonstick cookie sheets if you prefer to skip the greasing step. However, the dough may not spread as much, resulting in thicker cookies with smooth bottoms.

■ Use insulated cookie sheets selectively. They are fine if you want pale drop cookies with soft-set centers. You may have trouble using them for cookies high in butter, shaped cookies, and some drop cookies because the butter may start to melt, leaking out before dough is set. And because dough spreads before it sets, cookies may have thin edges.

Date Pinwheels

Prep: 40 minutes **Chill:** 3 to 24 hours
Bake: 8 minutes per batch **Oven:** 375°F
Makes: about 64 cookies

    1 8-ounce package (1⅓ cups) pitted whole
       dates, finely snipped
    ½ cup water
    ⅓ cup granulated sugar
    2 tablespoons lemon juice
    ½ teaspoon vanilla
    ½ cup shortening
    ½ cup butter, softened
    ½ cup granulated sugar
    ½ cup packed brown sugar
    ½ teaspoon baking soda
    ¼ teaspoon salt
    1 egg
    3 tablespoons milk
    1 teaspoon vanilla
    3 cups all-purpose flour

1. For filling, combine dates, water, and the ⅓ cup granulated sugar. Bring to boiling; reduce heat. Cook and stir about 2 minutes or until thick. Stir in lemon juice and the ½ teaspoon vanilla; set filling aside to cool.

2. In a large mixing bowl beat shortening and butter with an electric mixer on medium to high speed for 30 seconds. Add the ½ cup granulated sugar, the brown sugar, baking soda, and salt. Beat until combined, scraping sides of bowl occasionally. Beat in egg, milk, and the 1 teaspoon vanilla until combined. Beat in as much of the flour as you can with the mixer. Stir in any remaining flour. Divide dough in half. Cover and chill dough about 1 hour or until easy to handle.

3. Roll half the dough between pieces of waxed paper into a 12×10-inch rectangle. Spread with half of the filling; roll up dough (see photo 1, top right). Moisten edges; pinch to seal. Wrap in waxed paper or plastic wrap. Repeat with remaining dough and filling. Chill 2 to 24 hours.

4. Grease a cookie sheet; set aside. Cut rolls into ¼-inch slices (see photo 2, top right). Place slices 1 inch apart on prepared cookie sheet. Bake in a 375° oven 8 to 10 minutes or until edges are lightly browned. Transfer to a wire rack; let cool.

Nutrition Facts per cookie: 76 cal., 3 g total fat (1 g sat. fat), 7 mg chol., 37 mg sodium, 11 g carbo., 0 g fiber, 1 g pro.
Daily Values: 1% vit. A, 1% vit. C, 1% calcium, 2% iron
Exchanges: 1 Other Carbo., ½ Fat

1. Beginning with a long side, carefully roll up the dough and filling, using the waxed paper to lift and guide the roll.

2. Cut each chilled roll into ¼-inch slices with a thin, sharp knife, wiping the knife occasionally with a clean paper towel. Turn the roll frequently to avoid creating flat sides.

Double Chocolate Biscotti

Prep: 30 minutes **Bake:** 35 minutes **Oven:** 375°F
Cool: 1 hour **Makes:** about 24 cookies

    ½ cup butter, softened
    ⅔ cup sugar
    ¼ cup unsweetened cocoa powder
    2 teaspoons baking powder
    2 eggs
  1¾ cups all-purpose flour
    ¾ cup white baking pieces
    ½ cup large semisweet chocolate pieces or
       regular chocolate pieces

1. Lightly grease a cookie sheet; set aside. In a large mixing bowl beat butter with an electric mixer on medium to high speed for 30 seconds. Add sugar, cocoa powder, and baking powder. Beat until combined, scraping sides of bowl occasionally. Beat in eggs until combined. Beat in as much of the flour as you can with the mixer. Stir in any remaining flour. Stir in white baking pieces and chocolate pieces.

2. Shape dough into two 9-inch-long rolls. Place rolls on prepared cookie sheet; flatten slightly until about 2 inches wide (see photo 1, page 221).

3. Bake in a 375° oven for 20 to 25 minutes or until a wooden toothpick inserted near center comes out clean. Cool on cookie sheet for 1 hour. (If desired, wrap cooled rolls in plastic wrap and let stand overnight at room temperature.)

4. Use a serrated knife to cut each roll diagonally into ½-inch slices (see photo 2, page 221). Place slices, cut sides down, on an ungreased cookie sheet. Bake in a 325° oven for 8 minutes.

Turn slices over and bake for 7 to 9 minutes more or until dry and crisp (do not overbake). Transfer to a wire rack and let cool.

Nutrition Facts per cookie: 157 cal., 8 g total fat (5 g sat. fat), 29 mg chol., 91 mg sodium, 19 g carbo., 0 g fiber, 2 g pro.
Daily Values: 4% vit. A, 4% calcium, 4% iron
Exchanges: 1½ Other Carbo., 1½ Fat

Lemon-Pistachio Biscotti

Prep: 35 minutes **Bake:** 36 minutes **Oven:** 375°F
Cool: 30 minutes **Makes:** about 36 cookies

- ⅓ **cup butter, softened**
- ⅔ **cup sugar**
- 2 **teaspoons baking powder**
- ½ **teaspoon salt**
- 2 **eggs**
- 1 **teaspoon vanilla**
- 2 **cups all-purpose flour**
- 4 **teaspoons finely shredded lemon peel**
- 1¼ **cups pistachio nuts**
- 1 **recipe Lemon Icing**

1. Lightly grease 2 cookie sheets; set aside. In a large mixing bowl beat butter with an electric mixer on medium to high speed for 30 seconds. Add sugar, baking powder, and salt. Beat until combined, scraping sides of bowl occasionally. Beat in eggs and vanilla until combined. Beat in as much of the flour as you can with the mixer. Stir in any remaining flour and lemon peel. Stir in the pistachio nuts.

2. Divide dough into 3 equal portions. Shape each portion into an 8-inch-long roll. Place at least 3 inches apart on prepared cookie sheets; flatten slightly until about 2½ inches wide (see photo 1, right).

3. Bake in a 375° oven for 20 to 25 minutes or until golden brown and tops are cracked (loaves will spread slightly). Cool on cookie sheet for 30 minutes.

4. Use a serrated knife to cut each roll diagonally into ½-inch slices (see photo 2, right). Place slices, cut sides down, on ungreased cookie sheets. Bake

in a 325° oven for 8 minutes. Turn slices over and bake for 8 to 10 minutes more or until dry and crisp (do not overbake). Transfer to a wire rack and let cool. Dip ends into or drizzle with Lemon Icing.

Lemon Icing: In a small bowl stir together 1 cup sifted powdered sugar and 1 teaspoon finely shredded lemon peel. Stir in enough milk or lemon juice (1 to 2 tablespoons) to make icing of drizzling consistency.

Nutrition Facts per cookie: 95 cal., 4 g total fat (1 g sat. fat), 17 mg chol., 76 mg sodium, 13 g carbo., 1 g fiber, 2 g pro.
Daily Values: 2% vit. A, 1% vit. C, 2% calcium, 3% iron
Exchanges: 1 Other Carbo., 1 Fat

1. Place rolls about 3 inches apart on a lightly greased cookie sheet. Use your fingers to slightly flatten each roll.

2. Carefully transfer the cooled rolls to a cutting board. Using a sharp knife, diagonally cut the rolls into ½-inch slices.

Lemon-Pistachio Biscotti

Santa's Whiskers Best Loved

Prep: 20 minutes **Chill:** 2 to 24 hours
Bake: 10 minutes per batch **Oven:** 375°F
Makes: about 60 cookies

- ¾ **cup butter, softened**
- ¾ **cup sugar**
- 1 **tablespoon milk**
- 1 **teaspoon vanilla**
- 2 **cups all-purpose flour**
- ¾ **cup finely chopped candied red or green cherries**
- ⅓ **cup finely chopped pecans**
- ¾ **cup shredded coconut**

1. Beat butter with an electric mixer on medium speed 30 seconds. Add sugar. Beat until combined, scraping bowl. Beat in milk and vanilla until combined. Beat in as much flour as you can. Stir in remaining flour. Stir in cherries and pecans.

2. Divide dough in half. Shape each half into an 8-inch-long roll; roll in coconut. Wrap in plastic wrap or waxed paper. Chill for 2 to 24 hours or until firm enough to slice.

3. Cut rolls into ¼-inch slices (see photo 2, page 220). Place slices 1 inch apart on an ungreased cookie sheet. Bake in a 375° oven for 10 to 12 minutes or until edges are golden. Transfer to a wire rack and let cool.

Nutrition Facts per cookie: 65 cal., 3 g total fat (2 g sat. fat), 7 mg chol., 30 mg sodium, 8 g carbo., 0 g fiber, 1 g pro.
Daily Values: 2% vit. A, 1% iron
Exchanges: ½ Other Carbo., ½ Fat

Best Bet: Butter

All of the cookie recipes in this book call for butter rather than margarine. In cookies, butter gives a wonderful flavor and ensures the best results. Although cookies made with margarine can be satisfactory, choosing the right product can be tricky.

■ If you choose to use margarine instead of butter, select a stick margarine that contains 80 percent fat. Stick margarines may produce a softer dough, so you may need to chill the dough longer than directed in the recipe or even freeze it (see tip, page 217).

■ Low-fat, liquid, and soft vegetable oil spreads are for table use—not for baking. Their lower fat content can cause cookie dough to spread.

Brown Sugar-Hazelnut Rounds

Prep: 25 minutes **Chill:** 4 to 48 hours
Bake: 7 minutes per batch **Oven:** 375°F
Makes: about 60 cookies

- ½ **cup shortening**
- ½ **cup butter, softened**
- 1¼ **cups packed brown sugar**
- ½ **teaspoon baking soda**
- ¼ **teaspoon salt**
- 1 **egg**
- 1 **teaspoon vanilla**
- 2½ **cups all-purpose flour**
- ¾ **cup ground hazelnuts (filberts) or pecans, toasted (see tip, page 224)**
- 1 **recipe Browned Butter Icing (optional)**

1. In a large mixing bowl beat shortening and butter with an electric mixer on medium to high speed for 30 seconds. Add brown sugar, baking soda, and salt. Beat until combined, scraping sides of bowl occasionally. Beat in egg and vanilla until combined. Beat in as much of the flour as you can with the mixer. Stir in any remaining flour. Stir in nuts.

2. Divide the dough in half. Shape each half into a 10-inch-long roll. Wrap dough in plastic wrap or waxed paper. Chill for 4 to 48 hours or until firm enough to slice.

3. Cut rolls into ¼-inch slices (see photo 2, page 220). Place slices 1 inch apart on an ungreased cookie sheet. Bake in a 375° oven for 7 to 8 minutes or until edges are firm and slightly golden. Transfer cookies to a wire rack; let cool. If desired, drizzle cookies with Browned Butter Icing.

Nutrition Facts per cookie: 76 cal., 4 g total fat (2 g sat. fat), 8 mg chol., 40 mg sodium, 8 g carbo., 0 g fiber, 1 g pro.
Daily Values: 1% vit. A, 1% calcium, 2% iron
Exchanges: ½ Other Carbo., 1 Fat

Browned Butter Icing: In a small saucepan heat 2 tablespoons butter over medium heat until butter turns the color of light brown sugar, stirring frequently. Remove from heat. Slowly beat in 1½ cups sifted powdered sugar, 1 teaspoon vanilla, and enough milk (1 to 2 tablespoons) to make of drizzling consistency.

Sugar Cookie Cutouts

Prep: 30 to 45 minutes **Chill:** 30 minutes (if necessary)
Bake: 7 minutes per batch **Oven:** 375°F
Makes: about 36 cookies

- ⅔ **cup butter, softened**
- ¾ **cup granulated sugar**
- 1 **teaspoon baking powder**
- ¼ **teaspoon salt**
- 1 **egg**
- 1 **tablespoon milk**
- 1 **teaspoon vanilla**
- 2 **cups all-purpose flour**
- 1 **recipe Powdered Sugar Icing
  (page 172) (optional)**

1. In a large mixing bowl beat butter with an electric mixer on medium to high speed for 30 seconds. Add granulated sugar, baking powder, and salt. Beat until combined, scraping sides of bowl occasionally. Beat in egg, milk, and vanilla until combined. Beat in as much of the flour as you can with mixer. Stir in any remaining flour. Divide dough in half. If necessary, cover and chill dough 30 minutes or until easy to handle.

2. On a lightly floured surface, roll half the dough at a time until ⅛ inch thick (see photo, right). Using a 2½-inch cookie cutter, cut dough into desired shapes. Place 1 inch apart on an ungreased cookie sheet.

3. Bake in a 375° oven for 7 to 8 minutes or until edges are firm and bottoms are very lightly browned. Transfer to a wire rack and let cool. If desired, frost with Powdered Sugar Icing.

Candy Windowpane Cutouts: Prepare as above, except place cutout dough on a foil-lined cookie sheet. Cut small shapes out of cookie centers. Finely crush 3 ounces hard candy (about ½ cup). Fill each center cutout with some of the candy. When baked, cool cookies on foil. Store tightly covered.

Nutrition Facts per cookie for plain or candy cutout variation:
73 cal., 4 g total fat (2 g sat. fat), 16 mg chol., 66 mg sodium, 9 g carbo., 0 g fiber, 1 g pro.
Daily Values: 3% vit. A, 1% calcium, 2% iron
Exchanges: ½ Other Carbo., 1 Fat

Sugar Cookie Squares: Prepare dough as at left, except increase milk to 2 tablespoons. Pat dough into an ungreased 15×10×1-inch baking pan (chilling the dough is not necessary, but may make it easier to handle). Bake in a 375° oven for 10 to 12 minutes or until edges are firm but not brown. Cool on a wire rack. Carefully spread ¼ recipe Cream Cheese Frosting (page 171) or Butter Frosting (page 170) over cookie. Decorate with candy-coated milk chocolate pieces or other candies. Cut into squares. Makes 40 squares.

Nutrition Facts per square: 102 cal., 5 g total fat (3 g sat. fat), 18 mg chol., 72 mg sodium, 13 g carbo., 0 g fiber, 1 g pro.
Daily Values: 4% vit. A, 1% calcium, 2% iron
Exchanges: 1 Other Carbo., 1 Fat

On either a lightly floured surface or a pasty cloth, roll dough until it is the desired thickness, using a ruler to ensure accuracy.

Sugar Cookie Cutouts

Gingerbread Cutouts

Prep: 35 minutes **Chill:** 3 hours **Bake:** 5 minutes per batch
Oven: 375°F **Makes:** 36 to 48 cookies

- ½ **cup shortening**
- ½ **cup granulated sugar**
- 1 **teaspoon baking powder**
- 1 **teaspoon ground ginger**
- ½ **teaspoon baking soda**
- ½ **teaspoon ground cinnamon**
- ½ **teaspoon ground cloves**
- ½ **cup molasses**
- 1 **egg**
- 1 **tablespoon vinegar**
- 2½ **cups all-purpose flour**
- 1 **recipe Powdered Sugar Icing (page 172) (optional)**
  Decorative candies (optional)

1. In a mixing bowl beat shortening with an electric mixer on medium to high speed for 30 seconds. Add granulated sugar, baking powder, ginger, baking soda, cinnamon, and cloves. Beat until combined, scraping sides of bowl occasionally. Beat in molasses, egg, and vinegar until combined. Beat in as much of the flour as you can with the mixer. Stir in any remaining flour. Divide dough in half. Cover and chill dough about 3 hours or until easy to handle.

2. Grease a cookie sheet; set aside. On a lightly floured surface, roll half of the dough at a time until ⅛ inch thick (see photo, page 223). Using a 2½-inch cookie cutter, cut into desired shapes. Place 1 inch apart on prepared cookie sheet.

3. Bake in a 375° oven for 5 to 6 minutes or until edges are lightly browned. Cool on cookie sheet 1 minute. Transfer to a wire rack and let cool. If desired, decorate cookies with Powdered Sugar Icing and candies.

Nutrition Facts per cookie: 81 cal., 3 g total fat (1 g sat. fat), 6 mg chol., 32 mg sodium, 12 g carbo., 0 g fiber, 1 g pro.
Daily Values: 2% calcium, 4% iron
Exchanges: 1 Other Carbo., ½ Fat

Gingerbread People Cutouts: Prepare as above, except roll dough until ¼ inch thick. Cut with 4½- to 6-inch people-shape cookie cutters. Bake in a 375° oven 6 to 8 minutes or until edges are lightly browned. Makes about 18 cookies.

Nutrition Facts per cookie: 161 cal., 6 g total fat (1 g sat. fat), 12 mg chol., 65 mg sodium, 25 g carbo., 1 g fiber, 2 g pro.
Daily Values: 1% vit. C, 4% calcium, 8% iron
Exchanges: 1½ Other Carbo., 1 Fat

Cashew-Sugar Cookies

These shortbread-style sweets are perfect with a cup of afternoon tea (see photo, page 203).

Prep: 35 minutes **Bake:** 8 minutes per batch
Oven: 375°F **Makes:** about 42 cookies

- 1¼ **cups all-purpose flour**
- ½ **cup ground lightly salted cashews or ground almonds**
- ¼ **cup granulated sugar**
- ¼ **cup packed brown sugar**
- ½ **cup butter**
  Granulated or coarse sugar
  Whole cashews or blanched whole almonds, toasted (see tip, below)

1. In a medium bowl combine flour, ground nuts, the ¼ cup granulated sugar, and the brown sugar. Using a pastry blender, cut in butter until mixture resembles fine crumbs. Form mixture into a ball and knead gently until smooth.

2. On a lightly floured surface, roll dough until ¼ inch thick (see photo, page 223). Using a 1½-inch cookie cutter, cut into desired shapes. Place 1 inch apart on an ungreased cookie sheet. Lightly sprinkle with additional granulated sugar. Lightly press a whole nut in center of each cookie.

3. Bake in a 375° oven for 8 to 10 minutes or until lightly browned. Transfer cookies to a wire rack and let cool.

Nutrition Facts per cookie: 65 cal., 4 g total fat (2 g sat. fat), 6 mg chol., 28 mg sodium, 7 g carbo., 0 g fiber, 1 g pro.
Daily Values: 2% vit. A, 2% iron
Exchanges: ½ Other Carbo., 1 Fat

Toasting Nuts, Seeds, and Coconut

Toasting heightens the flavor of nuts, seeds, and coconut. To toast, spread the food in a single layer in a shallow baking pan. Bake in a 350°F oven for 5 to 10 minutes or until light golden brown, watching carefully and stirring once or twice so the food doesn't burn.

Shortbread

Prep: 15 minutes **Bake:** 25 minutes
Oven: 325°F **Makes:** 16 wedges

> 1¼ **cups all-purpose flour**
> 3 **tablespoons granulated sugar**
> ½ **cup butter**

1. Combine flour and sugar; cut in butter until mixture resembles fine crumbs and starts to cling. Form mixture into a ball; knead until smooth.

2. To make shortbread wedges, on an ungreased cookie sheet pat or roll the dough into an 8-inch circle. Make a scalloped edge (see photo 1, right). Cut circle into 16 wedges (see photo 2, right). Leave wedges in the circle. Bake in a 325° oven for 25 to 30 minutes or until bottom just starts to brown and center is set. Cut circle into wedges again while warm. Cool on the cookie sheet for 5 minutes. Transfer to a wire rack and let cool.

To make shortbread rounds: On a lightly floured surface roll dough until ½ inch thick (see photo, page 223). Using a 1½-inch cookie cutter, cut into 24 rounds. Place 1 inch apart on an ungreased cookie sheet. Bake for 20 to 25 minutes.

To make shortbread strips: On a lightly floured surface roll dough into an 8×6-inch rectangle about ½ inch thick. Using a knife, cut into twenty-four 2×1-inch strips (see photo 3, top right). Place 1 inch apart on an ungreased baking sheet. Bake for 20 to 25 minutes.

Butter-Pecan Shortbread: Prepare as above, except substitute brown sugar for the granulated sugar. After cutting in butter, stir in 2 tablespoons finely chopped pecans. Sprinkle mixture with ½ teaspoon vanilla before kneading.

Lemon-Poppy Seed Shortbread: Prepare as above, except stir 1 tablespoon poppy seeds into flour mixture and add 1 teaspoon finely shredded lemon peel with the butter.

Oatmeal Shortbread: Prepare as above, except reduce flour to 1 cup. After cutting in butter, stir in ⅓ cup quick-cooking rolled oats.

Spiced Shortbread: Prepare as above, except substitute brown sugar for the granulated sugar and stir ½ teaspoon ground cinnamon, ¼ teaspoon ground ginger, and ⅛ teaspoon ground cloves into the flour mixture.

Nutrition Facts per wedge for all variations: 98 cal., 6 g total fat (4 g sat. fat), 16 mg chol., 62 mg sodium, 10 g carbo., 0 g fiber, 1 g pro.
Daily Values: 5% vit. A, 3% iron
Exchanges: ½ Starch, 1 Fat

1. Using your thumb on one hand and your thumb and index finger on the other, carefully crimp the edge of the dough circle.

2. Before baking, use a long, sharp knife to cut the dough circle into 16 wedges of equal size. This keeps the shortbread from breaking when you cut it after it's baked.

3. To cut same-size strips, mark the long sides of the rectangle at 1-inch intervals and the short sides at 2-inch intervals. Use a sharp knife or pizza cutter to do the cutting.

Cookie Gadgets

Several gadgets make life easy for the serious cookie baker. If your cupboards don't already contain these gadgets, you might want to consider purchasing them.

Offset spatulas: Available in several sizes, these utensils are great for spreading frosting on bars and brownies. Your hands stay above the frosting, so it's easy to get into the corners, and you don't have to worry about scraping your fingers in the frosting.

Cookie scoops: Found in many sizes, the scoops guarantee your drop cookies will be uniform in size and shape.

Cookie press: This gadget is most often used for making spritz cookies. The dough is forced out either by a trigger pump or by twisting the handle. Cookie presses come with several different templates that allow you to make various shapes.

Spritz

When making spritz, observe these two rules: Use only butter and do not chill the dough.

Prep: 25 minutes **Bake:** 8 minutes per batch
Oven: 375°F **Makes:** about 84 cookies

- 1½ **cups butter, softened**
- 1 **cup granulated sugar**
- 1 **teaspoon baking powder**
- 1 **egg**
- 1 **teaspoon vanilla**
- ¼ **teaspoon almond extract (optional)**
- 3½ **cups all-purpose flour**
- 1 **recipe Powdered Sugar Icing (page 172) (optional)**

1. In a large mixing bowl beat butter with an electric mixer on medium to high speed for 30 seconds. Add granulated sugar and baking powder. Beat until combined, scraping sides of bowl occasionally. Beat in egg, vanilla, and, if desired, almond extract until combined. Beat in as much of the flour as you can with mixer. Stir in any remaining flour.

2. Force unchilled dough through a cookie press onto an ungreased cookie sheet. Bake in a 375° oven 8 to 10 minutes or until edges are firm but not brown. Transfer to a wire rack and let cool. If desired, dip tops into Powdered Sugar Icing.

Chocolate Spritz: Prepare as above, except reduce flour to 3¼ cups and add ¼ cup unsweetened cocoa powder with the sugar.

Nutty Spritz: Prepare as above, except reduce sugar to ⅔ cup and flour to 3¼ cups. After adding flour, stir in 1 cup finely ground, toasted almonds or hazelnuts (filberts) (see tip, page 224).

Nutrition Facts per cookie for plain, chocolate, and nut variations: 60 cal., 4 g total fat (2 g sat. fat), 12 mg chol., 41 mg sodium, 6 g carbo., 0 g fiber, 1 g pro.
Daily Values: 3% vit. A, 1% iron
Exchanges: ½ Starch, ½ Fat

Pecan Tassies

Prep: 30 minutes **Bake:** 25 minutes
Oven: 325°F **Makes:** 24 cookies

- ½ **cup butter, softened**
- 1 **3-ounce package cream cheese, softened**
- 1 **cup all-purpose flour**
- 1 **egg**
- ¾ **cup packed brown sugar**
- 1 **tablespoon butter, melted**
- ⅔ **cup coarsely chopped pecans**

1. For pastry, in a mixing bowl beat the ½ cup butter and cream cheese until combined. Stir in the flour. Press a rounded teaspoon of pastry evenly into the bottom and up the sides of 24 ungreased 1¾-inch muffin cups.

2. For pecan filling, in bowl beat egg, brown sugar, and the 1 tablespoon melted butter until combined. Stir in pecans. Spoon about 1 heaping teaspoon of filling into each pastry-lined muffin cup. Bake in a 325° oven for 25 to 30 minutes or until pastry is golden and filling is puffed. Cool slightly in pan. Carefully transfer to a wire rack and let cool.

Nutrition Facts per cookie: 120 cal., 8 g total fat (4 g sat. fat), 25 mg chol., 62 mg sodium, 11 g carbo., 0 g fiber, 1 g pro.
Daily Values: 5% vit. A, 1% calcium, 3% iron
Exchanges: ½ Other Carbo., 1½ Fat

Fudge Brownie Tassies: Prepare as above, except instead of pecan filling, in a small saucepan heat and stir ½ cup semisweet chocolate pieces and 2 tablespoons butter or margarine over low heat until melted; remove from heat. Stir in ⅓ cup sugar, 1 beaten egg, and 1 teaspoon vanilla. If desired, place 1 hazelnut (filbert), almond, macadamia nut, or walnut piece in each pastry-lined muffin cup. Spoon about 1 teaspoon of the chocolate mixture into each pastry-lined muffin cup. Bake in a 325° oven for 20 to 25 minutes or until pastry is golden and filling is puffed. Continue as directed.

Nutrition Facts per cookie: 106 cal., 8 g total fat (5 g sat. fat), 26 mg chol., 65 mg sodium, 8 g carbo., 1 g fiber, 1 g pro.
Daily Values: 5% vit. A, 1% calcium, 2% iron
Exchanges: ½ Other Carbo., 1½ Fat

Pecan Tassies and Fudge Brownie Tassies

Chapter 10
Crockery Cooking

Crockery Cooking

Beef Brisket with Barbecue Sauce

Prep: 25 minutes **Cook:** 10 to 12 hours
Makes: 6 to 8 servings

- ¾ **cup water**
- ¼ **cup Worcestershire sauce**
- 1 **tablespoon vinegar**
- 1 **teaspoon instant beef bouillon granules**
- ½ **teaspoon dry mustard**
- ½ **teaspoon chili powder**
- ¼ **teaspoon ground red pepper**
- 2 **cloves garlic, minced**
- 1 **2½-pound fresh beef brisket**
- ½ **cup catsup**
- 2 **tablespoons brown sugar**
- 2 **tablespoons butter or margarine**

1. For cooking liquid, in a bowl combine water, Worcestershire sauce, vinegar, bouillon granules, dry mustard, chili powder, red pepper, and garlic. Reserve ½ cup liquid for sauce; set aside in the refrigerator. Trim fat from meat. If necessary, cut brisket to fit into a 3½- or 4-quart crockery cooker. Place meat in cooker. Pour remaining liquid over brisket.

2. Cover and cook on low-heat setting for 10 to 12 hours or on high-heat setting for 5 to 6 hours. For sauce, in a small saucepan combine the ½ cup reserved liquid, catsup, brown sugar, and butter. Heat and pass sauce with meat.

For a 5- or 6-quart crockery cooker: Double the cooking liquid ingredients, reserving ½ cup for sauce. Leave all other ingredient amounts the same. Prepare as above. Makes 6 to 8 servings.

Nutrition Facts per serving: 488 cal., 33 g total fat (13 g sat. fat), 131 mg chol., 672 mg sodium, 11 g carbo., 0 g fiber, 35 g pro.
Daily Values: 10% vit. A, 8% vit. C, 4% calcium, 23% iron
Exchanges: ½ Other Carbo., 5 Medium-Fat Meat, 2 Fat

Beef and Brats

The addition of spicy bratwurst brings a new flavor dimension to this American classic.

Prep: 15 minutes **Cook:** 10 to 12 hours **Makes:** 4 servings

- 1 **pound boneless beef round steak, cut 1 inch thick**
- 4 **ounces uncooked spicy bratwurst or other sausage, cut into ¾-inch slices**
- 1 **tablespoon cooking oil**
- 1 **small onion, sliced and separated into rings**
- 2 **tablespoons quick-cooking tapioca**

Types of Slow Cooking Appliances

Continuous slow cooker/crockery cooker: This type of electric cooker cooks foods at a very low wattage. The heating coils or elements wrap around the sides of the cooker and remain on continuously. This type of appliance has two fixed settings—low (about 200°F) and high (about 300°F), and in some models, automatic (cooker shifts from high to low automatically). The ceramic liner may or may not be removable. All crockery recipes in this book were tested in this type of appliance.

Intermittent slow cooker: This type of cooker has the heating element or coil located below the food container. It cycles on and off during operation and has a dial indicating temperatures in degrees. Because the recipes in this book need continuous slow cooking, they will not cook properly in this type of appliance.

- 1 **teaspoon dried thyme, crushed**
- ¼ **teaspoon salt**
- ¼ **teaspoon black pepper**
- 1 **14½-ounce can chunky tomatoes with garlic and spices, undrained**
- 2 **cups hot cooked noodles or rice**

1. Trim fat from beef. Cut beef into 4 serving-size pieces. In a large skillet brown beef and bratwurst on all sides in hot oil. Drain off fat.

2. In a 3½- or 4-quart crockery cooker place onion. Sprinkle with tapioca, thyme, salt, and pepper. Pour undrained tomatoes over onion in cooker. Add beef and bratwurst.

3. Cover and cook on low-heat setting for 10 to 12 hours. Serve with noodles or rice.

Nutrition Facts per serving: 429 cal., 18 g total fat (5 g sat. fat), 99 mg chol., 883 mg sodium, 35 g carbo., 3 g fiber, 32 g pro.
Daily Values: 10% vit. A, 14% vit. C, 5% calcium, 26% iron
Exchanges: 1 Vegetable, 2 Starch, 3 Medium-Fat Meat

Pepper Steak

If you can't find Italian-style stewed tomatoes and tomato paste at your supermarket, purchase regular tomato products and add 1 teaspoon dried Italian seasoning, crushed (see photo, page 227).

Prep: 15 minutes **Cook:** 10 to 12 hours **Makes:** 4 servings

- 1 **pound boneless beef round steak, cut ¾ to 1 inch thick**
- **Salt**
- **Black pepper**
- 1 **tablespoon cooking oil**
- 1 **14½-ounce can Italian-style stewed tomatoes, undrained**
- 3 **tablespoons Italian-style tomato paste**
- 1 **teaspoon Worcestershire sauce**
- 1 **16-ounce package frozen pepper stir-fry vegetables (yellow, green, and red sweet peppers and onion)**

1. Trim fat from meat. Cut meat into 4 serving-size pieces; sprinkle lightly with salt and pepper. In a large skillet brown meat on both sides in hot oil. Transfer meat to a 3½- or 4-quart crockery cooker. In a medium bowl stir together undrained tomatoes, tomato paste, and Worcestershire sauce; pour over meat in cooker. Top with frozen stir-fry vegetables.

2. Cover and cook on low-heat setting for 10 to 12 hours or on high-heat setting for 5 to 6 hours or until meat and vegetables are tender.

Nutrition Facts per serving: 344 cal., 18 g total fat (6 g sat. fat), 71 mg chol., 496 mg sodium, 17 g carbo., 4 g fiber, 25 g pro.
Daily Values: 42% vit. A, 34% vit. C, 6% calcium, 20% iron
Exchanges: 3 Vegetable, 2½ Medium-Fat Meat, 1 Fat

Gingersnap Pot Roast

Round out the meal with dark rye bread and a salad.

Prep: 25 minutes **Cook:** 10 to 12 hours **Makes:** 6 servings

- 1 **2- to 2½-pound beef chuck pot roast**
- 1 **tablespoon cooking oil**
- 1 **cup water**
- 8 **gingersnaps, crumbled (about ⅔ cup)**
- 2 **tablespoons red wine vinegar**
- 1 **teaspoon instant beef bouillon granules**
- ⅛ **teaspoon ground red pepper**
- 3 **medium sweet potatoes, peeled and quartered**
- 3 **medium carrots or 2 medium parsnips, peeled and cut into bite-size chunks**
- 1 **bay leaf**

1. Trim fat from meat. If necessary, cut roast to fit into a 3½- or 4-quart crockery cooker. In a large skillet brown roast on all sides in hot oil. Meanwhile, in a small bowl combine water, gingersnaps, vinegar, bouillon granules, and red pepper. Place sweet potatoes, carrots, and bay leaf in cooker. Place meat on top of vegetables. Pour gingersnap mixture over meat.

2. Cover and cook on low-heat setting for 10 to 12 hours or on high-heat setting for 5 to 6 hours.

3. Transfer meat and vegetables to a platter. Remove bay leaf. Skim fat from gravy. Stir gravy to combine; ladle over roast and vegetables.

Nutrition Facts per serving: 523 cal., 31 g total fat (12 g sat. fat), 103 mg chol., 316 mg sodium, 29 g carbo., 3 g fiber, 30 g pro.
Daily Values: 427% vit. A, 24% vit. C, 4% calcium, 25% iron
Exchanges: 1½ Starch, 1 Vegetable, 3½ Medium-Fat Meat, 2½ Fat

For a 5- or 6-quart crockery cooker: Use one 2½- to 3-pound beef chuck pot roast. Increase the sweet potatoes to 4 medium and carrots to 4 medium, sliced. Prepare meat and vegetables as above. Makes 8 servings.

Vegetable-Beef Soup

Low Fat

Prep: 25 minutes **Cook:** 8 to 10 hours **Makes:** 6 servings

- 1 **pound lean boneless beef chuck pot roast, cut into ¾-inch pieces**
- 1 **tablespoon cooking oil**
- 4 **cups water**
- 1 **14½-ounce can diced tomatoes, undrained**
- 2 **cups frozen mixed vegetables**
- 2 **cups frozen loose-pack hash brown potatoes or 2 medium potatoes, peeled and chopped**
- 1 **1-ounce envelope onion soup mix (½ of a 2-ounce package)**
- 1 **teaspoon instant beef bouillon granules**
- 1 **clove garlic, minced, or ⅛ teaspoon garlic powder**
- ⅛ **teaspoon black pepper**

1. In a large skillet brown beef pieces, about half at a time, in hot oil. Drain off fat. In a 3½- or 4-quart crockery cooker combine beef and remaining ingredients.

2. Cover and cook on low-heat setting for 8 to 10 hours or on high-heat setting for 4 to 5 hours.

Nutrition Facts per serving: 289 cal., 12 g total fat (4 g sat. fat), 48 mg chol., 519 mg sodium, 26 g carbo., 3 g fiber, 19 g pro.
Daily Values: 49% vit. A, 28% vit. C, 6% calcium, 19% iron
Exchanges: 2 Vegetable, 1 Starch, 1½ Very Lean Meat, 1 Fat

Beef and Chipotle Burritos

Beef and Chipotle Burritos

Chipotle peppers are smoked jalapeños that lend a great smoky flavor to foods.

Prep: 20 minutes **Cook:** 8 to 10 hours **Makes:** 6 servings

 1½ **pounds boneless beef round steak, cut ¾ inch thick**
 1 **14½-ounce can diced tomatoes, undrained**
 ⅓ **cup chopped onion (1 small)**
 1 **to 2 canned chipotle peppers in adobo sauce, chopped (see tip, page 64)**
 1 **teaspoon dried oregano, crushed**
 ¼ **teaspoon ground cumin**
 1 **clove garlic, minced**
 6 **9- to 10-inch tomato-flavored or plain flour tortillas, warmed***
 ¾ **cup shredded sharp cheddar cheese (3 ounces)**
 1 **recipe Pico de Gallo Salsa**
   Shredded jicama or radishes (optional)
   Dairy sour cream (optional)

1. Trim fat from meat. Cut meat into 6 pieces. In a 3½- or 4-quart crockery cooker place meat, undrained tomatoes, onion, chipotle peppers, oregano, cumin, and garlic.

2. Cover and cook on low-heat setting for 8 to 10 hours or on high-heat setting for 4 to 5 hours. Remove meat from cooker. Using 2 forks, pull meat apart into shreds. Place meat in a large bowl. Stir in cooking liquid to reach desired consistency. Divide meat among warm tortillas, spooning it just below the center. Top with cheese, Pico de Gallo Salsa, and, if desired, jicama and sour cream. Roll up tortillas.

*Note: To warm tortillas, wrap a stack in foil. Heat in a 350°F oven for 10 minutes to soften.

Pico de Gallo Salsa: In bowl combine 2 medium finely chopped tomatoes; 2 tablespoons finely chopped onion; 2 tablespoons snipped fresh cilantro; 1 fresh serrano chile pepper, seeded and finely chopped (see tip, page 64); and dash sugar. Cover; chill several hours.

Nutrition Facts per serving: 361 cal., 13 g total fat (5 g sat. fat), 71 mg chol., 433 mg sodium, 29 g carbo., 2 g fiber, 30 g pro.
Daily Values: 11% vit. A, 30% vit. C, 19% calcium, 26% iron
Exchanges: 1 Vegetable, 1½ Starch, ½ Medium-Fat Meat

Shredded-Beef Sandwiches

Shred tender meat and pile it on French rolls for a great meal in a bun.

Prep: 15 minutes **Cook:** 11 to 12 hours **Makes:** 8 servings

- 1 3-pound beef chuck pot roast
- 1 large onion, cut up
- 3 bay leaves
- ½ teaspoon salt
- ¼ teaspoon garlic powder
- ⅛ teaspoon ground cloves
- ⅓ cup vinegar
- 8 French rolls, split (toasted, if desired)
  Spinach or lettuce leaves (optional)

1. Trim fat from meat. If necessary, cut meat to fit into a 3½- or 4-quart crockery cooker. Place meat and onion in cooker. Add bay leaves, salt, garlic powder, and cloves; pour vinegar over meat and onion.

2. Cover and cook on low-heat setting for 11 to 12 hours or on high-heat setting for 5½ to 6 hours. Remove meat from cooker. Discard bay leaves. Using 2 forks, pull meat apart into shreds, discarding bones and fat. Strain juices; skim off fat.

3. If desired, line rolls with spinach or lettuce leaves. Place shredded meat on rolls. Drizzle meat with some of the reserved juices. Serve remaining juices with sandwiches for dipping.

Nutrition Facts per serving: 449 cal., 23 g total fat (9 g sat. fat), 109 mg chol., 480 mg sodium, 22 g carbo., 2 g fiber, 36 g pro.
Daily Values: 2% vit. C, 5% calcium, 27% iron
Exchanges: 1½ Starch, 4½ Medium-Fat Meat

Meatball and Vegetable Stew

Add frozen meatballs straight from the package because they're already cooked.

Prep: 10 minutes **Cook:** 6 to 8 hours **Makes:** 4 servings

- 1 16- to 18-ounce package frozen cooked meatballs
- ½ of a 16-ounce package (about 2 cups) loose-pack frozen broccoli, corn, and red sweet peppers, or other mixed vegetables
- 1 14½-ounce can diced tomatoes with onion and garlic, or stewed tomatoes, undrained
- 1 12-ounce jar mushroom gravy
- ⅓ cup water
- 1½ teaspoons dried basil, crushed

1. In a 3½- or 4-quart crockery cooker place cooked meatballs and mixed vegetables. In a bowl stir together tomatoes, gravy, water, and basil; pour over meatballs and vegetables.

2. Cover and cook on low-heat setting for 6 to 8 hours or on high-heat setting for 3 to 4 hours.

For a 5- or 6-quart crockery cooker: Double all ingredients. Makes 8 servings.

Nutrition Facts per serving: 458 cal., 32 g total fat (14 g sat. fat), 87 mg chol., 2,003 mg sodium, 23 g carbo., 5 g fiber, 21 g pro.
Daily Values: 69% vit. A, 31% vit. C, 9% calcium, 20% iron
Exchanges: 1½ Vegetable, 1 Starch, 2 Medium-Fat Meat, 4 Fat

Meatball and Vegetable Stew

Spaghetti Sauce Italiano

Prep: 25 minutes **Cook:** 8 to 10 hours **Makes:** 4 servings

- 8 ounces bulk Italian sausage
- 4 ounces ground beef
- ½ cup chopped onion (1 medium)
- 1 clove garlic, minced
- 1 14½- or 16-ounce can tomatoes, undrained and cut up
- 1 8-ounce can tomato sauce
- 1 4-ounce can mushroom stems and pieces, drained
- ½ cup chopped green sweet pepper
- 2 tablespoons quick-cooking tapioca
- 1 bay leaf
- 1 teaspoon dried Italian seasoning, crushed
- ⅛ teaspoon black pepper
  Dash salt
- 8 ounces spaghetti, cooked and drained

1. In a skillet cook sausage, ground beef, onion, and garlic until meat is brown and onion is tender; drain off fat.

2. Meanwhile, in a 3½- or 4-quart crockery cooker combine undrained tomatoes, tomato sauce, mushrooms, sweet pepper, tapioca, bay leaf, Italian seasoning, black pepper, and salt. Stir in meat mixture.

3. Cover and cook on low-heat setting for 8 to 10 hours or on high-heat setting for 4 to 5 hours. Discard bay leaf. Serve over hot spaghetti.

For a 5- or 6-quart crockery cooker: Double all ingredients. Prepare as above. Makes 8 to 10 servings.

Nutrition Facts per serving: 504 cal., 17 g total fat (7 g sat. fat), 56 mg chol., 897 mg sodium, 60 g carbo., 4 g fiber, 23 g pro.
Daily Values: 15% vit. A, 51% vit. C, 7% calcium, 23% iron
Exchanges: 3 Vegetable, 3 Starch, 1 Medium-Fat Meat, 2 Fat

Tomato-Sauced Pork Ribs

Prep: 20 minutes **Cook:** 8 to 10 hours **Makes:** 6 servings

- 1 28-ounce can crushed tomatoes, undrained
- 1 cup chopped celery (2 stalks)
- ¾ cup chopped green sweet pepper (1 medium)
- ½ cup chopped onion (1 medium)
- 2 tablespoons quick-cooking tapioca
- 1½ teaspoons sugar
- 1½ teaspoons snipped fresh basil or ½ teaspoon dried basil, crushed
- ½ teaspoon salt
- ¼ teaspoon black pepper
- ¼ teaspoon bottled hot pepper sauce
- 1 clove garlic, minced
- 2 pounds boneless pork country-style ribs
- 3 cups hot cooked noodles

1. For sauce, in a 3½- or 4-quart crockery cooker combine undrained tomatoes, celery, sweet pepper, onion, tapioca, sugar, dried basil (if using), salt, black pepper, hot pepper sauce, and garlic. Add ribs; stir to coat ribs with sauce.

2. Cover and cook on low-heat setting for 8 to 10 hours or on high-heat setting for 4 to 5 hours.

3. Transfer ribs to a serving platter. Skim fat from sauce. If using, stir fresh basil into sauce. Spoon some of the sauce over ribs. Serve with hot cooked noodles. Pass remaining sauce.

Nutrition Facts per serving: 413 cal., 13 g total fat (4 g sat. fat), 122 mg chol., 640 mg sodium, 36 g carbo., 4 g fiber, 35 g pro.
Daily Values: 3% vit. A, 50% vit. C, 9% calcium, 20% iron
Exchanges: 2 Vegetable, 1½ Starch, 3 Medium-Fat Meat

Ribs with Apples and Sauerkraut

Browning the ribs before putting them in the cooker helps to seal in the natural juices.

Prep: 30 minutes **Cook:** 8 to 10 hours **Makes:** 4 servings

- 2½ pounds pork country-style ribs, cut crosswise in half and cut into 1- to 2-rib portions
- 1 tablespoon cooking oil
- 2 medium potatoes, cut into ½-inch slices
- 2 medium carrots, cut into ¼-inch slices
- 1 medium onion, thinly sliced
- 1 8-ounce can sauerkraut, rinsed and drained
- ½ cup apple cider or apple juice
- 2 teaspoons caraway seeds or fennel seeds
- ⅛ teaspoon ground cloves
- 2 tablespoons cold water
- 1 tablespoon all-purpose flour
- ½ of a large apple, cored and thinly sliced
  Salt (optional)
  Black pepper (optional)
- 1 tablespoon snipped fresh parsley

1. In a large skillet brown pork ribs on both sides in hot oil over medium-high heat. In a 3½- or 4-quart crockery cooker place potatoes, carrots, and onion. Add browned pork ribs and sauerkraut. In a bowl combine apple cider, caraway seeds, and cloves. Pour over sauerkraut.

2. Cover and cook on low-heat setting for 8 to 10 hours or on high-heat setting for 4 to 5 hours. Transfer meat and vegetables to a serving platter, reserving juices; cover meat and keep warm.

3. For gravy, strain cooking juices into a glass measuring cup. Skim off fat. Measure 1 cup juices, adding water, if necessary. Pour into a saucepan. In a small bowl stir the 2 tablespoons cold water into the flour until smooth; stir into the juices in saucepan. Cook and stir over medium heat until thickened and bubbly. Stir in the apple. Cook and stir for 1 minute more or until heated through. If desired, season to taste with salt and pepper. Stir in parsley just before serving. Serve gravy with ribs and vegetables.

Nutrition Facts per serving: 473 cal., 19 g total fat (6 g sat. fat), 87 mg chol., 455 mg sodium, 29 g carbo., 5 g fiber, 45 g pro.
Daily Values: 191% vit. A, 43% vit. C, 7% calcium, 20% iron
Exchanges: 1½ Vegetable, 1½ Starch, 5 Lean Meat, ½ Fat

Pulled Pork with Root Beer Sauce `Best Loved`

Look for root beer concentrate in the spice section.

`Low Fat`

Prep: 15 minutes **Cook:** 8 to 10 hours
Makes: 8 to 10 servings

- 1 2½- to 3-pound pork sirloin roast
- ½ teaspoon salt
- ½ teaspoon black pepper
- 1 tablespoon cooking oil
- 2 medium onions, cut into thin wedges
- 1 cup root beer*
- 2 tablespoons minced garlic
- 3 cups root beer (two 12-ounce cans or bottles)*
- 1 cup bottled chili sauce
- ¼ teaspoon root beer concentrate (optional)
   Several dashes bottled hot pepper sauce (optional)
- 8 to 10 hamburger buns, split (toasted, if desired)
   Lettuce leaves (optional)
   Tomato slices (optional)

1. Trim fat from meat. If necessary, cut meat to fit into a 3½- to 5-quart crockery cooker. Sprinkle meat with salt and pepper. In a large skillet brown meat on all sides in hot oil. Drain off fat. Transfer meat to cooker. Add onions, the 1 cup root beer, and garlic.

2. Cover and cook on low-heat setting for 8 to 10 hours or on high-heat setting for 4 to 5 hours.

3. Meanwhile, for sauce, in a medium saucepan combine the 3 cups root beer and the chili sauce. Bring to boiling; reduce heat. Boil gently, uncovered, stirring occasionally, about 30 minutes or until mixture is reduced to 2 cups. If desired, add root beer concentrate and hot pepper sauce.

4. Transfer meat to a cutting board or serving platter. Using a slotted spoon, remove onions from cooking juices and place on a serving platter. Discard juices. Using 2 forks, pull meat apart into shreds. To serve, if desired, line buns with lettuce leaves and tomato slices. Add meat and onions; spoon on sauce.

*Note: Do not use diet root beer.

Nutrition Facts per serving: 433 cal., 12 g total fat (3 g sat. fat), 89 mg chol., 877 mg sodium, 45 g carbo., 3 g fiber, 35 g pro.
Daily Values: 4% vit. A, 14% vit. C, 10% calcium, 17% iron
Exchanges: 2 Starch, 1 Other Carbo., 4 Lean Meat

Pork Roast with Cherries

If you like, substitute other dried fruits, such as coarsely chopped cranberries, apricots, golden raisins, or dried mixed fruit, for the cherries.

Prep: 20 minutes **Cook:** 7 to 9 hours **Makes:** 6 to 8 servings

- 1 2- to 2½-pound boneless pork shoulder roast
- 2 tablespoons cooking oil
- 1 tablespoon quick-cooking tapioca
- 1 tablespoon snipped fresh thyme or 1 teaspoon dried thyme, crushed
- ½ teaspoon black pepper
- 1 medium onion, sliced
- 1 cup dried cherries
- ½ cup apple juice or apple cider
- 3 to 4 cups hot cooked rice or noodles

1. Trim fat from meat. If necessary, cut meat to fit into a 3½- or 4-quart crockery cooker. In a large skillet brown meat on all sides in hot oil. Drain off fat. Transfer meat to cooker. Sprinkle tapioca, dried thyme (if using), and pepper over meat. Add onion and dried cherries. Pour apple juice over all.

2. Cover and cook on low-heat setting for 7 to 9 hours or on high-heat setting for 3½ to 4½ hours. Transfer meat to a serving platter; cover to keep warm.

3. For sauce, skim fat from cooking juices. If using, stir fresh thyme into juices. Serve meat and cooking juices with rice or noodles.

Nutrition Facts per serving: 431 cal., 13 g total fat (4 g sat. fat), 101 mg chol., 117 mg sodium, 44 g carbo., 2 g fiber, 33 g pro.
Daily Values: 1% vit. A, 4% vit. C, 4% calcium, 17% iron
Exchanges: 1 Fruit, 2 Starch, 3½ Lean Meat

For Make-Ahead Convenience

If you chop vegetables or do other preparations ahead of time, wrap and store the items in separate containers in the refrigerator overnight until you are ready to start the cooker. It's OK to brown ground beef and ground poultry the night before if you cook it completely. However, wait to brown meat cubes, poultry pieces, and roasts until just before cooking because browning does not cook these items through.

Pork and Sweet Potato Stew

Here's a great way to use one of the best bargains you can find at the meat counter—pork shoulder.

Low Fat

Prep: 25 minutes **Cook:** 6 hours **Makes:** 6 servings

- 1 **pound boneless pork shoulder roast, cut into 1-inch cubes**
- 1 **tablespoon cooking oil**
- 6 **medium sweet potatoes, peeled and cut into 1-inch pieces (about 2 pounds)**
- 1 **cup coarsely chopped onion (1 large)**
- ⅓ **cup dried apples, coarsely chopped**
- 1 **tablespoon quick-cooking tapioca**
- 1 **clove garlic, minced**
- 2 **teaspoons snipped fresh sage or ½ teaspoon dried sage, crushed**
- ¼ **teaspoon ground cardamom**
- ¼ **teaspoon black pepper**
- 2 **cups chicken broth**
- 1 **cup apple juice or apple cider**

1. In a large skillet brown meat, half at a time, in hot oil. Drain off fat. In a 3½- or 4-quart crockery cooker place sweet potatoes, onion, and dried apples. Add meat. Sprinkle with tapioca, garlic, dried sage (if using), cardamom, and pepper. Pour broth and apple juice over all.

2. Cover and cook on low-heat setting for 6 hours or on high-heat setting for 3 hours. If using, stir fresh sage into juices.

Nutrition Facts per serving: 356 cal., 9 g total fat (3 g sat. fat), 51 mg chol., 337 mg sodium, 49 g carbo., 6 g fiber, 19 g pro.
Daily Values: 546% vit. A, 45% vit. C, 6% calcium, 13% iron
Exchanges: 3 Starch, 1½ Medium-Fat Meat

Spicy Fruited Lamb

Ask the butcher to cut the lamb shanks in half crosswise if you can't find them that way at the meat counter.

Prep: 25 minutes **Cook:** 9 to 10 hours
Makes: 6 servings

- 3½ **pounds lamb shanks, halved crosswise (3 to 4 shanks)**
- **Salt and black pepper**
- ¼ **cup all-purpose flour**
- 2 **tablespoons cooking oil**
- ½ **cup dried apricots**
- ½ **cup pitted dried plums (prunes), halved**
- ½ **cup raisins**
- ¾ **cup beef broth**
- 2 **tablespoons sugar**
- 2 **tablespoons vinegar**
- 2 **tablespoons lemon juice**
- ½ **teaspoon ground allspice**
- ½ **teaspoon ground cinnamon**
- 1 **tablespoon cornstarch**
- 1 **tablespoon cold water**
- 4 **cups hot cooked rice**

1. Sprinkle lamb shanks with salt and pepper. Coat with flour. In a large skillet brown shanks on all sides in hot oil. Drain off fat. In a 3½- or 4-quart crockery cooker combine apricots, plums, raisins, broth, sugar, vinegar, lemon juice, allspice, and cinnamon. Add lamb shanks.

2. Cover; cook on low-heat setting 9 to 10 hours or on high-heat setting for 4½ to 5 hours or until lamb is tender. Remove shanks; keep warm.

3. For gravy, strain cooking juices into a glass measuring cup, reserving fruit. Skim off fat from juices. Measure juices, adding enough water, if necessary, to equal 1½ cups. Pour into a medium saucepan. Combine cornstarch and the 1 tablespoon cold water; stir into juices in saucepan. Cook and stir over medium heat until thickened and bubbly; cook and stir for 2 minutes more. Stir in reserved fruit. Heat through. Serve gravy over lamb shanks and rice.

Nutrition Facts per serving: 543 cal., 13 g total fat (4 g sat. fat), 116 mg chol., 241 mg sodium, 65 g carbo., 3 g fiber, 42 g pro.
Daily Values: 22% vit. A, 6% vit. C, 4% calcium, 34% iron
Exchanges: 1 Fruit, 3 Starch, 4½ Lean Meat

Spicy Fruited Lamb

Lamb with Sausage and Beans

Prep: 25 minutes **Stand:** 1 hour
Cook: 8 to 10 hours plus 30 minutes **Makes:** 6 servings

- 1 cup dry Great Northern beans or navy beans
- 12 ounces lamb stew meat, cut into 1-inch cubes
- 1 tablespoon cooking oil
- 2 cups beef broth
- 8 ounces cooked kielbasa, cut into ¼-inch slices
- 1 tablespoon snipped fresh thyme or 1 teaspoon dried thyme, crushed
- 3 cloves garlic, minced
- ¼ teaspoon whole black peppercorns
- 1 bay leaf
- 1 small eggplant, peeled and chopped
- 1 cup coarsely chopped green or red sweet pepper (1 large)
- 1 6-ounce can tomato paste
  Salt and black pepper
- 3 cups hot cooked couscous

1. Rinse beans; place in a large saucepan. Add enough water to cover beans by 2 inches. Bring to boiling; reduce heat. Simmer, uncovered, for 10 minutes. Remove from heat. Cover; let stand for 1 hour. Drain and rinse beans.

2. In a large skillet brown lamb in hot oil. Drain off fat. In a 3½- or 4-quart crockery cooker combine beans, lamb, broth, kielbasa, dried thyme (if using), garlic, peppercorns, and bay leaf.

3. Cover and cook on low-heat setting for 8 to 10 hours or on high-heat setting for 4 to 5 hours. If using low-heat setting, turn to high-heat setting. Stir in the eggplant, sweet pepper, and tomato paste. Cover and cook for 30 minutes more on high-heat setting. Discard bay leaf. Stir in fresh thyme (if using). Season to taste with salt and black pepper. Serve over couscous.

Nutrition Facts per serving: 473 cal., 18 g total fat (6 g sat. fat), 62 mg chol., 701 mg sodium, 50 g carbo., 10 g fiber, 29 g pro.
Daily Values: 4% vit. A, 46% vit. C, 7% calcium, 21% iron
Exchanges: 1 Vegetable, 3 Starch, 1½ Medium-Fat Meat, 1½ Fat

Cooking Dry Beans

■ Dry beans cook more slowly in a crockery cooker than in a saucepan. Therefore, the beans must be precooked for 10 minutes.

■ Soaking dry beans overnight does not work for crockery cooker recipes because the beans never become tender.

Irish Stew

Prep: 30 minutes **Cook:** 10 to 12 hours
Makes: 4 or 5 servings

- 1 pound lean boneless lamb
- 1 tablespoon cooking oil
- 2½ cups peeled turnips cut into ½-inch pieces (2 medium)
- 1½ cups carrots cut into ½-inch pieces (3 medium)
- 1½ cups peeled potatoes cut into ½-inch pieces (2 medium)
- 2 medium onions, cut into wedges
- ¼ cup quick-cooking tapioca
- ½ teaspoon salt
- ¼ teaspoon black pepper
- ¼ teaspoon dried thyme, crushed
- 3 cups beef broth

1. Cut lamb into 1-inch pieces. In a large skillet brown lamb, half at a time, in hot oil. Drain off fat. In a 3½- or 4-quart crockery cooker combine turnips, carrots, potatoes, onions, tapioca, salt, pepper, and thyme. Stir in browned lamb and beef broth.

2. Cover and cook on low-heat setting for 10 to 12 hours or on high-heat setting for 5 to 6 hours.

Nutrition Facts per serving: 442 cal., 22 g total fat (9 g sat. fat), 75 mg chol., 1,037 mg sodium, 35 g carbo., 5 g fiber, 25 g pro.
Daily Values: 231% vit. A, 45% vit. C, 6% calcium, 19% iron
Exchanges: 1 Vegetable, 2 Starch, 2½ Lean Meat, 2 Fat

Plum-Sauced Chicken in Tortillas

Hoisin sauce is a reddish-brown Chinese condiment that adds a sweet-and-spicy flavor to the chicken.

Low Fat

Prep: 15 minutes **Cook:** 4 to 5 hours **Makes:** 6 servings

- 1 16-ounce can whole, unpitted purple plums, drained
- 1 cup hot-style vegetable juice
- ¼ cup hoisin sauce
- 4½ teaspoons quick-cooking tapioca
- 2 teaspoons grated fresh ginger
- ½ teaspoon five-spice powder
- 1 pound skinless, boneless chicken thighs
- 6 7- to 8-inch flour tortillas, warmed*
- 2 cups packaged shredded broccoli (broccoli slaw mix) or packaged shredded cabbage with carrot (coleslaw mix)

1. Remove pits from plums. Place plums in a blender container or food processor bowl. Cover and blend or process until smooth. Transfer plum puree to a 3½- or 4-quart crockery cooker. Stir in vegetable juice, hoisin sauce, tapioca, ginger, and five-spice powder. Cut chicken into strips. Stir chicken into crockery cooker.

2. Cover and cook on low-heat setting for 4 to 5 hours or on high-heat setting for 2 to 2½ hours. Remove chicken from cooker, reserving juices.

3. Spoon about ⅓ cup of the chicken mixture onto each warm tortilla just below the center. Drizzle with the reserved juices. Top each with ⅓ cup shredded slaw mix. Roll up tortillas.

*Note: To warm tortillas, wrap a stack in foil. Heat in a 350°F oven for 10 minutes to soften.

Nutrition Facts per serving: 276 cal., 4 g total fat (1 g sat. fat), 44 mg chol., 510 mg sodium, 38 g carbo., 2 g fiber, 21 g pro.
Daily Values: 31% vit. A, 60% vit. C, 7% calcium, 12% iron
Exchanges: ½ Fruit, 2 Starch, 2 Very Lean Meat

Chicken and Sausage Paella

If you don't have saffron, one of the world's most expensive spices, substitute turmeric, an economical and equally delicious alternative.

Low Fat

Prep: 30 minutes **Cook:** 7 to 8 hours
Stand: 5 minutes **Makes:** 6 servings

2½ to 3 pounds meaty chicken pieces (breasts, thighs, and drumsticks), skinned
1 tablespoon cooking oil
8 ounces cooked smoked turkey sausage, halved lengthwise and sliced
1 large onion, sliced
3 cloves garlic, minced
2 tablespoons snipped fresh thyme or 2 teaspoons dried thyme, crushed
¼ teaspoon black pepper
⅛ teaspoon thread saffron or ¼ teaspoon ground turmeric
1 14-ounce can reduced-sodium chicken broth
½ cup water
2 cups chopped tomatoes
2 medium yellow or green sweet peppers, cut into thin bite-size strips (1½ cups)
1 cup frozen peas
3 cups hot cooked rice or one 5-ounce package saffron-flavored yellow rice mix, cooked according to package directions

Tips for Crockery Cooking
■ Thaw raw meat or poultry completely in the refrigerator before adding it to the cooker.

■ Do not cook large pieces of meat in a crockery cooker. Cut in half any roasts that are larger than 2½ pounds.

■ For best results, a crockery cooker must be at least half full and no more than two-thirds full.

■ If you are using an automatic timer to start the cooker, make sure it is set to start cooking within 2 hours of adding ingredients and that food is thoroughly chilled when it is placed in the cooker.

■ Resist peeking into the pot during cooking. Because a crockery cooker works at low temperatures, lost heat is not quickly recovered. If you must lift the lid to stir or add ingredients, replace it as quickly as possible, especially when cooking on the low-heat setting.

■ Transfer any leftovers from the crockery cooker to storage containers as quickly as possible. Cover and refrigerate or freeze. If you store warm food in the crockery liner in the refrigerator, the food may not cool down quickly enough to be safe to eat as leftovers.

1. In a large skillet brown chicken pieces, half at a time, in hot oil. Drain off fat. In a 3½- or 4-quart crockery cooker place chicken pieces, turkey sausage, and onion. Sprinkle with garlic, dried thyme (if using), black pepper, and saffron. Pour broth and water over all.

2. Cover and cook on low-heat setting for 7 to 8 hours or on high-heat setting for 3½ to 4 hours. Add the tomatoes, sweet peppers, peas, and fresh thyme (if using) to the cooker. Cover and let stand for 5 minutes. Serve over rice.

Nutrition Facts per serving: 394 cal., 12 g total fat (3 g sat. fat), 99 mg chol., 609 mg sodium, 36 g carbo., 3 g fiber, 36 g pro.
Daily Values: 15% vit. A, 190% vit. C, 5% calcium, 19% iron
Exchanges: 1 Vegetable, 2 Starch, 4 Lean Meat

Chicken and Sausage Paella

Creamy Chicken and Noodles

Low Fat

Prep: 25 minutes **Cook:** 8 to 9 hours **Makes:** 6 servings

  2 **cups sliced carrots (4 medium)**
1½ **cups chopped onion (3 medium)**
  1 **cup sliced celery (2 stalks)**
  2 **tablespoons snipped fresh parsley**
  1 **bay leaf**
  3 **medium chicken legs (drumstick-thigh portion) (about 2 pounds), skinned**
  2 **10¾-ounce cans reduced-fat and reduced-sodium condensed cream of chicken soup**
  ½ **cup water**
  1 **teaspoon dried thyme, crushed**
  ¼ **teaspoon black pepper**
 10 **ounces dried wide noodles (about 5 cups)**
  1 **cup frozen peas**
    Salt (optional)
    Black pepper (optional)

1. In a 3½- or 4-quart crockery cooker place carrots, onion, celery, parsley, and bay leaf. Place chicken on top of vegetables. In a bowl stir together soup, water, thyme, and the ¼ teaspoon pepper. Pour over chicken and vegetables.

2. Cover and cook on low-heat setting for 8 to 9 hours or on high-heat setting for 4 to 4½ hours. Remove chicken from cooker; cool slightly. Remove and discard bay leaf.

3. Meanwhile, cook noodles according to package directions; drain. Stir peas into soup mixture in cooker. Remove chicken from bones; discard bones. Cut meat into bite-size pieces; stir into

mixture in cooker. To serve, pour chicken mixture over noodles; toss gently to combine. If desired, season to taste with salt and pepper.

Nutrition Facts per serving: 396 cal., 7 g total fat (1 g sat. fat), 114 mg chol., 554 mg sodium, 56 g carbo., 5 g fiber, 26 g pro. **Daily Values:** 213% vit. A, 21% vit. C, 6% calcium, 20% iron **Exchanges:** 1 Vegetable, 3½ Starch, 2 Very Lean Meat

---

Chicken and Sausage Gumbo   **Best Loved**

Save time by making the roux ahead of time. When cooked, the roux should be a coppery color, similar to that of a tarnished penny.

Prep: 40 minutes **Cook:** 6 to 7 hours **Makes:** 5 servings

  ⅓ **cup all-purpose flour**
  ⅓ **cup cooking oil**
  3 **cups water**
 12 **ounces cooked smoked sausage links, quartered and sliced lengthwise**
1½ **cups chopped cooked chicken or 12 ounces skinless, boneless chicken breasts or thighs, cut into ¾-inch pieces**
  2 **cups sliced okra or one 10-ounce package frozen whole okra, partially thawed and cut into ½-inch slices**
  1 **cup chopped onion (1 large)**
  ½ **cup chopped green sweet pepper**
  ½ **cup chopped celery (1 stalk)**
  4 **cloves garlic, minced**
  ½ **teaspoon salt**
  ½ **teaspoon black pepper**
  ¼ **teaspoon ground red pepper**
  3 **cups hot cooked rice**

1. For roux, in a medium heavy saucepan stir together flour and oil until smooth. Cook over medium-high heat for 5 minutes, stirring constantly. Reduce heat to medium. Cook and stir constantly about 15 minutes more or until a dark, reddish-brown color is reached; cool.

2. Place water in a 3½- or 4-quart crockery cooker. Stir in roux. Add sausage, chicken, okra, onion, sweet pepper, celery, garlic, salt, black pepper, and red pepper.

3. Cover and cook on low-heat setting for 6 to 7 hours or on high-heat setting for 3 to 3½ hours. Skim off fat. Serve over hot cooked rice.

Nutrition Facts per serving: 665 cal., 40 g total fat (11 g sat. fat), 84 mg chol., 1,307 mg sodium, 44 g carbo., 3 g fiber, 33 g pro. **Daily Values:** 11% vit. A, 44% vit. C, 10% calcium, 19% iron **Exchanges:** 2 Vegetable, 2 Starch, 3 Medium-Fat Meat, 4 Fat

Chicken and Sausage Gumbo

Garlic Chicken with Artichokes

Twelve cloves of garlic may sound like a lot, but garlic's flavor mellows as it slowly cooks.

Low Fat

Prep: 20 minutes **Cook:** 6 to 7 hours **Makes:** 6 servings

- 12 cloves garlic, minced
- ½ cup chopped onion (1 medium)
- 1 tablespoon olive oil or cooking oil
- 1 8- or 9-ounce package frozen artichoke hearts
- 1 red sweet pepper, cut into strips
- ½ cup chicken broth
- 1 tablespoon quick-cooking tapioca
- 2 teaspoons dried rosemary, crushed
- 1 teaspoon finely shredded lemon peel
- ½ teaspoon black pepper
- 1½ pounds skinless, boneless chicken breast halves or thighs
- 4 cups hot cooked brown rice

1. In a small skillet cook garlic and onion in hot oil over medium heat, stirring occasionally, about 5 minutes or until tender. In a 3½- or 4-quart crockery cooker combine the garlic mixture, frozen artichoke hearts, sweet pepper, chicken broth, tapioca, rosemary, lemon peel, and black pepper. Add chicken; spoon some of the garlic mixture over chicken.

2. Cover and cook on low-heat setting for 6 to 7 hours or on high-heat setting for 3 to 3½ hours. Serve with rice.

Nutrition Facts per serving: 341 cal., 6 g total fat (1 g sat. fat), 66 mg chol., 159 mg sodium, 39 g carbo., 6 g fiber, 32 g pro. **Daily Values:** 22% vit. A, 62% vit. C, 7% calcium, 10% iron **Exchanges:** 1 Vegetable, 2½ Starch, 3 Lean Meat

---

Chicken and Corn Bread Stuffing

Prep: 15 minutes **Cook:** 5 to 6 hours **Makes:** 6 servings

- 1 10¾-ounce can reduced-fat and reduced-sodium condensed cream of chicken soup or cream of mushroom soup
- ¼ cup butter or margarine, melted
- ¼ cup water
- 1 16-ounce package loose-pack frozen broccoli, corn, and red sweet peppers
- 2½ cups cubed cooked chicken
- 1 8-ounce package corn bread stuffing mix

1. In a very large bowl stir together soup, butter, and water. Add frozen vegetables, chicken, and stuffing mix; stir until combined. Transfer mixture to a 3½- or 4-quart crockery cooker.

2. Cover and cook on low-heat setting for 5 to 6 hours or on high-heat setting for 2½ to 3 hours.

Nutrition Facts per serving: 393 cal., 14 g total fat (6 g sat. fat), 76 mg chol., 1,041 mg sodium, 40 g carbo., 3 g fiber, 24 g pro. **Daily Values:** 30% vit. A, 52% vit. C, 5% calcium, 11% iron **Exchanges:** 1 Vegetable, 2½ Starch, 2 Lean Meat, 1 Fat

---

Scalloped Potatoes and Beans

Kidney and black beans elevate scalloped potatoes from a supporting role to a meal's main dish.

Low Fat

Prep: 15 minutes **Cook:** 8 to 10 hours **Makes:** 5 servings

- 1 15-ounce can red kidney beans, rinsed and drained
- 1 15-ounce can black beans, rinsed and drained
- 1 cup chopped onion (1 large)
- 1 cup sliced celery (2 stalks)
- 1 cup frozen peas
- 1 cup chopped green sweet pepper (1 large)
- 1 10¾-ounce can condensed cheddar cheese, cream of potato, or cream of mushroom soup
- 4 cloves garlic, minced
- 1 teaspoon dried thyme, crushed
- ¼ teaspoon black pepper
- 3 medium potatoes, cut into ¼-inch slices (1 pound)
- 1 cup shredded cheddar cheese (4 ounces) (optional)

1. In a large bowl combine kidney beans, black beans, onion, celery, peas, sweet pepper, condensed soup, garlic, thyme, and black pepper. Spoon half of the bean mixture into a 3½- or 4-quart crockery cooker. Top with the potatoes and remaining bean mixture.

2. Cover and cook on low-heat setting for 8 to 10 hours or on high-heat setting for 4 to 5 hours. If desired, top individual servings with the shredded cheddar cheese.

Nutrition Facts per serving: 315 cal., 6 g total fat (3 g sat. fat), 14 mg chol., 851 mg sodium, 55 g carbo., 14 g fiber, 19 g pro. **Daily Values:** 20% vit. A, 69% vit. C, 16% calcium, 22% iron **Exchanges:** 1 Vegetable, 3 Starch, 1 Very Lean Meat, ½ Fat

White Chili Soup

To cook chicken for this soup, poach 3 or 4 skinned and boned chicken breast halves in boiling water or chicken broth, covered, for 12 to 14 minutes or until no pink remains (170°F). Drain, cool the chicken slightly, then chop.

Low Fat

Prep: 25 minutes **Cook:** 8 to 10 hours **Makes:** 6 servings

> 3 15- to 15½-ounce cans Great Northern, pinto, or white kidney (cannellini) beans, rinsed and drained
> 2½ cups chopped cooked chicken
> 1 cup chopped onion (1 large)
> 1½ cups chopped red, green, and/or yellow sweet pepper (2 medium)
> 2 fresh jalapeño chile peppers, seeded and chopped (see tip, page 64)
> 2 cloves garlic, minced
> 2 teaspoons ground cumin
> ½ teaspoon salt
> ½ teaspoon dried oregano, crushed
> 3½ cups chicken broth
> Shredded Monterey Jack cheese (optional)
> Broken tortilla chips (optional)

1. In a 3½- or 4-quart crockery cooker combine the drained beans, chicken, onion, sweet pepper, jalapeño peppers, garlic, cumin, salt, and oregano. Stir in chicken broth.

2. Cover and cook on low-heat setting for 8 to 10 hours or on high-heat setting for 4 to 5 hours. Ladle soup into bowls. If desired, top each serving with some of the cheese and tortilla chips.

Nutrition Facts per serving: 422 cal., 6 g total fat (2 g sat. fat), 52 mg chol., 709 mg sodium, 54 g carbo., 13 g fiber, 38 g pro. **Daily Values:** 42% vit. A, 112% vit. C, 16% calcium, 28% iron **Exchanges:** ½ Vegetable, 3½ Starch, 4 Very Lean Meat

Black Bean and Corn Soup

Low Fat

Prep: 20 minutes **Stand:** 1 hour
Cook: 8 to 10 hours **Makes:** 6 servings

> 2¼ cups dry black beans (1 pound)
> 1 10-ounce package frozen whole kernel corn
> 1 cup chopped onion (1 large)
> 4 cloves garlic, minced
> 1 tablespoon ground cumin
> 1 teaspoon salt
> 1 teaspoon ground coriander
> ¼ to ½ teaspoon bottled hot pepper sauce

> 4 cups boiling water
> 1 14½-ounce can Mexican-style stewed tomatoes, undrained
> 1 recipe Pepper Salsa

1. Rinse beans; place in a large saucepan. Add enough water to cover beans by 2 inches. Bring to boiling; reduce heat. Simmer, uncovered, for 10 minutes. Remove from heat. Cover; let stand for 1 hour. Drain and rinse beans.

2. In a 3½- or 4-quart crockery cooker combine the beans, corn, onion, garlic, cumin, salt, coriander, and hot pepper sauce. Pour boiling water over all.

3. Cover and cook on low-heat setting for 8 to 10 hours or on high-heat setting for 4 to 5 hours. To serve, mash beans slightly to thicken. Stir in undrained tomatoes. Serve with Pepper Salsa.

Pepper Salsa: In a bowl combine 1½ cups finely chopped yellow and/or green sweet peppers; 1 finely chopped small fresh jalapeño chile pepper (see tip, page 64); ⅓ cup chopped, seeded tomato; and 1 tablespoon snipped fresh cilantro. Cover and chill up to 24 hours.

Nutrition Facts per serving: 359 cal., 2 g total fat (0 g sat. fat), 0 mg chol., 639 mg sodium, 70 g carbo., 14 g fiber, 20 g pro. **Daily Values:** 7% vit. A, 220% vit. C, 14% calcium, 26% iron **Exchanges:** 2 Vegetable, 4 Starch

Adapting Recipe Favorites

Use these tips when preparing your favorite main dishes in a crockery cooker.

■ Use recipes that call for less tender meat cuts. They benefit from long, slow cooking.

■ Find a similar recipe in this chapter and use it as a guide for approximate quantities, piece sizes, liquid levels, and cooking time.

■ Cut vegetables into uniform, bite-size pieces so they'll cook evenly and be easy to eat. If using larger pieces of meat, place the meat on top of the vegetables to ensure the vegetables will be tender when the meat is done.

■ Trim the meat. Brown meat, if desired. Cut a roast as necessary to fit in your crockery cooker

■ Unless your dish contains long grain rice, reduce the liquids in the recipe you are adapting by about half.

Chapter 11
Desserts

Desserts

For more recipes, visit our Recipe Center at **www.bhg.com**

Polenta-Pecan Apple Cobbler

Polenta, made from cornmeal, makes an updated topping for this pecan-studded apple cobbler.

Prep: 30 minutes **Bake:** 30 minutes
Oven: 375°F **Makes:** 6 servings

- ½ **cup all-purpose flour**
- ⅓ **cup quick-cooking polenta mix or yellow cornmeal**
- 2 **tablespoons granulated sugar**
- 1 **teaspoon baking powder**
- ⅛ **teaspoon salt**
- 3 **tablespoons butter**
- ½ **cup chopped pecans**
- 2 **tablespoons brown sugar**
- ½ **teaspoon ground cinnamon**
- 8 **cups cubed, peeled cooking apples (8 medium)**
- ½ **cup dried tart cherries (optional)**
- ⅓ **cup packed brown sugar**
- 1 **tablespoon lemon juice**
- ¼ **cup cold water**
- 1 **tablespoon cornstarch**
- ⅓ **cup half-and-half or light cream**
  Vanilla ice cream (optional)

1. For topping, in a small bowl stir together flour, polenta mix, granulated sugar, baking powder, and salt. Using a pastry blender or two knives, cut in butter until mixture resembles coarse crumbs; set aside.

2. In another small bowl combine the pecans, the 2 tablespoons brown sugar, and ¼ teaspoon of the cinnamon; set aside.

3. For filling, in a large saucepan combine the remaining ¼ teaspoon cinnamon, the apples, dried cherries (if desired), the ⅓ cup brown sugar, and the lemon juice. Bring to boiling, stirring constantly; reduce heat. Simmer, covered, about 5 minutes or until apples are almost tender, stirring occasionally. Combine the cold water and cornstarch; add to saucepan. Cook and stir until thickened and bubbly. Keep hot.

4. Add the half-and-half to the topping mixture, stirring just until moistened. Transfer filling to a 2-quart square baking dish set in a shallow baking pan. Using a spoon, immediately drop topping into small mounds onto filling. Sprinkle with pecan mixture.

5. Bake in a 375° oven for 30 to 35 minutes or until a toothpick inserted into the topping comes out clean. If desired, serve with ice cream.

Nutrition Facts per serving: 431 cal., 15 g total fat (5 g sat. fat), 21 mg chol., 191 mg sodium, 75 g carbo., 9 g fiber, 4 g pro.
Daily Values: 8% vit. A, 4% vit. C, 9% calcium, 9% iron
Exchanges: 1 Fruit, 4 Other Carbo., 1 Fat

Polenta-Pecan Peach Cobbler: Prepare as at left, except substitute 8 cups sliced, peeled peaches for the apples.

Nutrition Facts per serving: 402 cal., 14 g total fat (5 g sat. fat), 21 mg chol., 189 mg sodium, 67 g carbo., 7 g fiber, 5 g pro.
Daily Values: 30% vit. A, 27% vit. C, 9% calcium, 8% iron
Exchanges: 1 Fruit, 3½ Other Carbo., 1½ Fat

Polenta-Pecan Blueberry Cobbler: Prepare as at left, except substitute 8 cups blueberries for the apples; increase cornstarch to 2 tablespoons.

Polenta-Pecan Rhubarb Cobbler: Prepare as at left, except substitute 8 cups chopped rhubarb for the apples; increase brown sugar in filling to ⅔ cup and increase cornstarch to 2 tablespoons.

Nutrition Facts per serving for blueberry or rhubarb variations: 389 cal., 15 g total fat (5 g sat. fat), 21 mg chol., 200 mg sodium, 62 g carbo., 6 g fiber, 5 g pro.
Daily Values: 9% vit. A, 24% vit. C, 23% calcium, 10% iron
Exchanges: 1 Fruit, 3 Other Carbo., 1½ Fat

Baked Apples

Low Fat

Prep: 15 minutes **Bake:** 40 minutes
Oven: 350°F **Makes:** 4 servings

- 4 **medium cooking apples, such as Rome Beauty, Granny Smith, or Jonathan**
- ½ **cup raisins, snipped pitted whole dates, or mixed dried fruit bits**
- 2 **tablespoons brown sugar**
- ½ **teaspoon ground cinnamon**
- ¼ **teaspoon ground nutmeg**
- ⅓ **cup apple juice or water**
  Ice cream or half-and-half (optional)

1. Core apples; peel a strip from the top of each. Place apples in a 2-quart casserole. Combine the raisins, brown sugar, cinnamon, and nutmeg; spoon into centers of apples. Pour apple juice into casserole. Bake apples in a 350° oven for 40 to 45 minutes or until the apples are tender, basting occasionally. If desired, serve warm with ice cream.

Nutrition Facts per serving: 164 cal., 1 g total fat (0 g sat. fat), 0 mg chol., 5 mg sodium, 42 g carbo., 5 g fiber, 1 g pro.
Daily Values: 1% vit. A, 12% vit. C, 3% calcium, 5% iron
Exchanges: 1½ Fruit, 1 Other Carbo.

Saucy Apple Dumplings [Best Loved]

These dumplings have a luscious sauce that bakes along with the apples.

Prep: 45 minutes **Bake:** 1 hour
Oven: 350°F **Makes:** 6 servings

   2 cups water
1¼ cups sugar
   1 teaspoon ground cinnamon
   ¼ cup butter or margarine
   2 cups all-purpose flour
   ½ teaspoon salt
   ⅔ cup shortening
   ⅓ to ½ cup half-and-half, light cream, or whole milk
   2 tablespoons chopped golden raisins or raisins
   2 tablespoons chopped walnuts
   1 tablespoon honey
   2 tablespoons sugar
   6 small cooking apples (about 1½ pounds), such as Granny Smith or Rome Beauty
   1 tablespoon butter or margarine

1. For sauce, in a medium saucepan combine the water, the 1¼ cups sugar, and ½ teaspoon of the cinnamon. Bring to boiling; reduce heat. Simmer, uncovered, for 5 minutes. Add the ¼ cup butter or margarine. Set aside.

2. Meanwhile, for pastry, in a medium bowl combine the flour and salt. Using a pastry blender, cut in shortening until pieces are pea-size. Sprinkle 1 tablespoon of the half-and-half over part of the mixture; gently toss with a fork. Push moistened dough to the side of the bowl. Repeat, using 1 tablespoon of the half-and-half at a time, until all of the dough is moistened. Form dough into a ball. On a lightly floured surface, roll dough into an 18×12-inch rectangle.* Using a pastry wheel or sharp knife, cut into six 6-inch squares.

3. In a small bowl combine the raisins, walnuts, and honey. In another small bowl stir together the remaining ½ teaspoon cinnamon and the 2 tablespoons sugar. Set aside.

4. Peel and core the apples (see photo 1, below). Place an apple on each pastry square. Fill centers of apples with raisin mixture. Sprinkle with sugar-cinnamon mixture; dot with the 1 tablespoon butter or margarine. Moisten edges of each pastry square with water; fold corners to center over apple (see photo 2, below). Pinch to seal seams. Place dumplings in a 13×9×2-inch baking pan. Reheat sauce to boiling and pour over dumplings. Bake, uncovered, in a 350° oven about 1 hour or until apples are tender and pastry is golden. To serve, spoon sauce over dumplings.

*Note: If desired, roll pastry slightly larger and use excess pastry to make pastry leaves for garnishing. Cut the 6-inch squares, then reroll scraps and cut them into leaf shapes. Moisten underside of leaf shapes with water; place on top of dumplings, pressing slightly to adhere.

Nutrition Facts per serving: 586 cal., 36 g total fat (18 g sat. fat), 32 mg chol., 306 mg sodium, 68 g carbo., 4 g fiber, 1 g pro.
Daily Values: 10% vit. A, 9% vit. C, 4% calcium, 3% iron
Exchanges: 1 Fruit, 3½ Other Carbo., 5 Fat

1. Carefully insert an apple corer firmly into the stem end of the apple. Twist and pull to remove the core.

2. After brushing the edges of the pastry with water, gather all four corners of the pastry square at the top of the apple and pinch the edges firmly together to form a tight seal.

Saucy Apple Dumplings

Caramel Apple Crepes

If you're in a hurry, use purchased crepes rather than making your own.

Prep: 15 minutes **Cook:** 20 minutes **Makes:** 6 servings

- ¾ **cup all-purpose flour**
- ⅓ **cup milk**
- 2 **eggs**
- 2 **tablespoons sugar**
- 4 **teaspoons walnut oil or cooking oil**
- 1 **recipe Caramel Apple Sauce**
- ½ **recipe Candied Nuts (page 180; use pecans)**
  Vanilla ice cream (optional)

1. For crepes, in a blender container combine flour, ⅓ cup *water,* milk, eggs, sugar, and oil. Cover and blend until smooth, stopping and scraping the sides of container as necessary.

2. Heat a lightly greased 6-inch skillet over medium heat; remove from heat. Spoon 2 tablespoons batter into skillet; lift and tilt skillet to spread the batter evenly. Return skillet to heat; brown crepe on 1 side only. Invert pan over paper towels; remove crepe from pan. Repeat with remaining batter, making 12 crepes total.

3. Prepare Caramel Apple Sauce.

4. Fold the crepes in half, browned side out. Fold in half again, forming a triangle. Place 2 crepes on each of 6 dessert plates.

5. To serve, pour warm Caramel Apple Sauce over crepes. Sprinkle with Candied Nuts. If desired, serve with vanilla ice cream.

Caramel Apple Sauce: In a large saucepan stir together 1 cup packed brown sugar and 4 teaspoons cornstarch. Stir in 1 cup whipping cream; 2 tablespoons apple brandy, brandy, or apple juice; 1 tablespoon butter or margarine. Add 2 cups thinly sliced apples. Cook and stir over medium heat until thickened and bubbly. Cook and stir for 2 minutes more.

Make-ahead directions: Prepare crepes as above through step 2. Layer cooled crepes with sheets of waxed paper in an airtight container; freeze up to 4 months. Thaw at room temperature for 1 hour before using.

Nutrition Facts per serving: 386 cal., 21 g total fat (11 g sat. fat), 114 mg chol., 67 mg sodium, 45 g carbo., 2 g fiber, 4 g pro.
Daily Values: 16% vit. A, 5% vit. C, 7% calcium, 7% iron
Exchanges: ½ Fruit, 2½ Other Carbo., 3½ Fat

Caramel Apple Pudding Cake

Prep: 25 minutes **Bake:** 35 minutes
Oven: 350°F **Makes:** 12 servings

- 2 **cups thinly sliced, peeled tart cooking apples, such as Granny Smith or Rome Beauty**
- 3 **tablespoons lemon juice**
- ½ **teaspoon ground cinnamon**
- ⅛ **teaspoon ground nutmeg**
- ¼ **cup raisins or dried cherries**
- 1 **cup all-purpose flour**
- ¾ **cup packed brown sugar**
- 1 **teaspoon baking powder**
- ¼ **teaspoon baking soda**
- ½ **cup milk**
- 2 **tablespoons butter, melted**
- 1 **teaspoon vanilla**
- ½ **cup chopped pecans or walnuts**
- ¾ **cup caramel ice cream topping**
- ½ **cup water**
- 1 **tablespoon butter or margarine**
  Vanilla ice cream (optional)

1. Grease a 2-quart square baking dish. Arrange apple slices in the bottom of dish; sprinkle with lemon juice, cinnamon, and nutmeg. Top evenly with raisins.

2. In a large bowl combine flour, brown sugar, baking powder, and baking soda. Add milk, the 2 tablespoons melted butter, and vanilla; mix well. Stir in pecans. Spread the batter evenly over the apple mixture.

3. In a small saucepan combine the caramel topping, water, and the 1 tablespoon butter; bring to boiling. Pour mixture over batter in baking dish.

4. Bake in a 350° oven about 35 minutes or until center is set. While warm, spoon cake, apples, and caramel mixture from bottom of dish into dessert bowls. If desired, serve with ice cream.

Nutrition Facts per serving: 240 cal., 7 g total fat (2 g sat. fat), 9 mg chol., 157 mg sodium, 44 g carbo., 2 g fiber, 2 g pro.
Daily Values: 3% vit. A, 6% vit. C, 7% calcium, 5% iron
Exchanges: 3 Other Carbo., ½ Fat

Fruit Crisp

Prep: 30 minutes **Bake:** 30 minutes
Oven: 375°F **Makes:** 6 servings

> 5 **cups sliced, peeled cooking apples, pears, peaches, or apricots, or frozen unsweetened peach slices**
> 2 **to 4 tablespoons granulated sugar**
> ½ **cup regular rolled oats**
> ½ **cup packed brown sugar**
> ¼ **cup all-purpose flour**
> ¼ **teaspoon ground nutmeg, ginger, or cinnamon**
> ¼ **cup butter or margarine**
> ¼ **cup chopped nuts or coconut**
> **Vanilla ice cream (optional)**

1. For fruit filling, thaw fruit if frozen. Do not drain. Place fruit in a 2-quart square baking dish. Stir in the granulated sugar.

2. For topping, in a medium bowl combine the oats, brown sugar, flour, and nutmeg. Cut in butter until mixture resembles coarse crumbs. Stir in the nuts. Sprinkle topping over fruit.

3. Bake in a 375° oven for 30 to 35 minutes (40 minutes for thawed fruit) or until fruit is tender and topping is golden. If desired, serve warm with ice cream.

Microwave directions: Prepare fruit filling as in recipe above. Microwave fruit, covered with vented plastic wrap, on 100 percent power (high) for 4 to 6 minutes or until fruit is tender, stirring twice. Prepare topping as in step 2, above. Sprinkle over filling. Cook, uncovered, on high for 2 to 4 minutes or until topping is heated through, giving the dish a half-turn once.

Blueberry Crisp: Prepare filling as at left, except use 5 cups fresh or frozen blueberries for the fruit. Use 4 tablespoons granulated sugar and add 3 tablespoons all-purpose flour.

Nutrition Facts per serving for fruit or blueberry variation:
319 cal., 13 g total fat (6 g sat. fat), 22 mg chol., 92 mg sodium, 53 g carbo., 5 g fiber, 3 g pro.
Daily Values: 7% vit. A, 1% vit. C, 4% calcium, 7% iron
Exchanges: 1 Fruit, 2½ Other Carbo., 1½ Fat

Cherry Crisp: Prepare filling as at left, except use 5 cups fresh or frozen unsweetened pitted tart red cherries for the fruit. Increase granulated sugar to ½ cup and add 3 tablespoons all-purpose flour.

Rhubarb Crisp: Prepare filling as at left, except use 5 cups fresh or frozen* unsweetened sliced rhubarb for the fruit. Increase granulated sugar to ¾ cup and add 3 tablespoons all-purpose flour.

***Note:** If rhubarb is frozen, thaw but do not drain.

Nutrition Facts per serving for cherry or rhubarb variations:
360 cal., 13 g total fat (6 g sat. fat), 22 mg chol., 92 mg sodium, 61 g carbo., 4 g fiber, 4 g pro.
Daily Values: 8% vit. A, 12% vit. C, 12% calcium, 8% iron
Exchanges: 1 Fruit, 3 Other Carbo., 1½ Fat

Strawberry Shortcake

For variety, substitute sliced peaches for the berries.

Prep: 25 minutes **Bake:** 15 minutes **Oven:** 450°F
Cool: 10 minutes **Makes:** 8 servings

> 6 **cups sliced strawberries**
> ½ **cup sugar**
> 2 **cups all-purpose flour**
> 2 **teaspoons baking powder**
> ½ **cup butter**
> 1 **beaten egg**
> ⅔ **cup milk**
> 1 **cup whipping cream, whipped**

1. In a small bowl stir together the strawberries and ¼ cup of the sugar; set aside. Stir together remaining sugar, the flour, and baking powder. Cut in butter until mixture resembles coarse crumbs. Combine egg and milk; add to flour mixture. Stir just to moisten. Spread the dough in a greased 8×1½-inch round baking pan.

2. Bake in a 450° oven for 15 to 18 minutes or until a wooden toothpick inserted near the center comes out clean. Cool in pan for 10 minutes. Remove from pan. Split into 2 layers. Spoon half

Fruit Crisp

of the whipped cream and strawberries over bottom layer. Replace the top layer. Top with remaining berries and whipped cream. Cut into wedges to serve.

Individual Shortcakes: Drop dough into 8 mounds on an ungreased baking sheet; flatten each mound with the back of a spoon until about ¾ inch thick. Bake in a 450° oven about 10 minutes or until golden. Cool on a wire rack about 10 minutes. Cut shortcakes in half horizontally. Spoon half of berries and whipped cream over bottom layers. Replace top layers. Top with remaining strawberries and whipped cream.

Nutrition Facts per serving: 423 cal., 25 g total fat (15 g sat. fat), 102 mg chol., 255 mg sodium, 45 g carbo., 3 g fiber, 6 g pro.
Daily Values: 20% vit. A, 103% vit. C, 13% calcium, 11% iron
Exchanges: 1 Fruit, 2 Other Carbo., 4 Fat

Gingered Fruit Compote

Low Fat

Prep: 25 minutes **Bake:** 40 minutes
Oven: 375°F **Makes:** 6 servings

- ½ **cup dried tart cherries, dried blueberries, raisins, or currants**
- ½ **teaspoon finely shredded orange peel**
- ½ **cup white grape juice**
- 2 **tablespoons orange liqueur or white grape juice**
- ¼ **cup packed brown sugar**
- 2 **tablespoons finely chopped crystallized ginger**
- 4 **cups thinly sliced, peeled peaches, nectarines, apples, and/or pears**
- 1 **tablespoon butter or margarine, cut up**

1. In a 1½-quart casserole combine dried cherries, orange peel, white grape juice, liqueur, brown sugar, and ginger. Stir in the peaches; dot with butter.

2. Bake, covered, in a 375° oven for 40 to 45 minutes or until fruit is tender, stirring after 30 minutes. Serve warm.

Tropical Fruit Compote: Prepare as above, except substitute 4 cups cubed pineapple, papaya, and/or mango for the peaches.

Nutrition Facts per serving for gingered compote or tropical fruit variation: 171 cal., 2 g total fat (1 g sat. fat), 5 mg chol., 24 mg sodium, 36 g carbo., 2 g fiber, 1 g pro.
Daily Values: 2% vit. A, 37% vit. C, 1% calcium, 5% iron
Exchanges: 1½ Fruit, 1 Other Carbo.

Fresh Fruit Compote with Basil

No Fat

Prep: 25 minutes **Stand:** 1 hour **Makes:** 6 servings

- ½ **cup sugar**
- ½ **cup water**
- ¼ **cup honey**
- 1 **vanilla bean, split lengthwise, or 1 teaspoon vanilla**
- 2 **teaspoons cornstarch**
- 1 **tablespoon cold water**
- 2 **tablespoons crème de cassis, almond or strawberry liqueur, or orange juice**
- 4 **cups assorted fresh fruit, such as blackberries, raspberries, or blueberries; pitted sweet cherries; and/or sliced bananas,* strawberries, peaches, or pears**
- ⅓ **cup shredded fresh basil**
  Lemon sherbet or vanilla ice cream (optional)

1. In a small saucepan combine sugar, the ½ cup water, honey, and, if using, vanilla bean. Bring to boiling, stirring to dissolve sugar; reduce heat. Simmer, uncovered, for 5 minutes. Stir together cornstarch and the 1 tablespoon cold water; add to saucepan. Cook and stir until thickened and bubbly. Cook and stir for 2 minutes more. Cool mixture slightly.

2. Remove vanilla bean, if using. Add liqueur and, if using, the vanilla. Place fruit and basil in a large bowl. Add honey mixture to bowl; stir fruit gently. Cover; let stand about 1 hour or until cooled to room temperature, or chill several hours, stirring once or twice. If desired, serve with a small scoop of lemon sherbet.

*Note: If using bananas, slice and add to compote just before serving.

Nutrition Facts per serving: 187 cal., 0 g total fat (0 g sat. fat), 0 mg chol., 2 mg sodium, 45 g carbo., 4 g fiber, 1 g pro.
Daily Values: 9% vit. A, 40% vit. C, 2% calcium, 3% iron
Exchanges: 3 Fruit

Blueberry Rolls Best Loved

From the 1939 Better Homes and Gardens New Cook Book, *this recipe is a family favorite.*

Prep: 25 minutes **Bake:** 20 minutes
Oven: 425°F **Makes:** 9 servings

　1　16½-ounce can blueberries
　1　recipe Rich Shortcake
　1　tablespoon butter or margarine, melted
　2　tablespoons sugar
　½　teaspoon ground cinnamon
　¼　cup sugar
　2　tablespoons all-purpose flour
　2　teaspoons lemon juice
　　　Vanilla ice cream (optional)

1. Drain blueberries, reserving juice; set aside. Grease a 2-quart square baking dish; set aside. Prepare Rich Shortcake dough. On a lightly floured surface, roll dough into an 11×9-inch rectangle. Brush dough with melted butter. Combine the 2 tablespoons sugar with the cinnamon; sprinkle over dough. Sprinkle 1 cup of the drained blueberries over dough. Roll up, starting from a short side; pinch to seal seam. Set aside.

2. In a small saucepan combine the ¼ cup sugar and the flour. Add remaining blueberries and reserved juice. Cook and stir over medium heat until thickened and bubbly. Remove from heat; stir in lemon juice. Pour blueberry mixture into prepared dish. Cut roll into 9 equal slices. Place slices, cut side down, on top of blueberry mixture. Bake in a 425° oven for 20 minutes or until rolls are golden. If desired, serve warm with vanilla ice cream.

Rich Shortcake: In a medium mixing bowl combine 2 cups all-purpose flour, 4 teaspoons baking powder, 1 tablespoon sugar, and ½ teaspoon salt. Using a pastry blender, cut in ⅓ cup shortening until mixture resembles coarse crumbs. Make a well in the center of mixture. Add ⅔ cup milk and 1 beaten egg all at once. Stir just until dough clings together. On a heavily floured surface, coat the dough lightly with flour. Knead the dough gently for 10 to 12 strokes.

Nutrition Facts per serving: 283 cal., 10 g total fat (3 g sat. fat), 29 mg chol., 339 mg sodium, 44 g carbo., 2 g fiber, 5 g pro.
Daily Values: 3% vit. A, 3% vit. C, 15% calcium, 10% iron
Exchanges: 1 Fruit, 2 Other Carbo., 1½ Fat

Bananas Foster

　Fast

Start to Finish: 15 minutes **Makes:** 4 servings

　⅓　cup butter
　⅓　cup packed brown sugar
　3　ripe bananas, bias-sliced (2 cups)
　¼　teaspoon ground cinnamon
　2　tablespoons crème de cacao or banana liqueur
　¼　cup rum
　2　cups vanilla ice cream

1. In a large skillet melt butter; stir in brown sugar until melted. Add bananas. Cook and gently stir over medium heat about 2 minutes or until heated through. Sprinkle with cinnamon. Stir in crème de cacao.

2. In a saucepan heat rum until it almost simmers. Ignite rum with a long match (see photo, below). Pour over bananas; stir gently to coat. Spoon sauce over ice cream; serve immediately.

Nutrition Facts per serving: 483 cal., 24 g total fat (15 g sat. fat), 72 mg chol., 225 mg sodium, 57 g carbo., 2 g fiber, 3 g pro.
Daily Values: 19% vit. A, 14% vit. C, 11% calcium, 4% iron
Exchanges: 1 Fruit, 2½ Other Carbo., 5 Fat

Use a long match to ignite the rum while it's in the saucepan. Carefully pour the flaming sauce over the bananas. Serve over ice cream when the flame dies.

Cheesecake Supreme

Prep: 30 minutes **Bake:** 40 minutes **Oven:** 375°F
Cool: 2 hours **Chill:** 4 hours **Makes:** 12 to 16 servings

　1½　cups finely crushed graham crackers
　¼　cup finely chopped walnuts
　1　tablespoon sugar
　½　teaspoon ground cinnamon (optional)
　½　cup butter, melted
　3　8-ounce packages cream cheese, softened
　1　cup sugar
　2　tablespoons all-purpose flour
　1　teaspoon vanilla
　¼　cup milk
　3　slightly beaten eggs
　½　teaspoon finely shredded lemon peel (optional)
　1　recipe Raspberry Sauce (page 482) (optional)

1. For crust, in a bowl combine graham crackers, walnuts, the 1 tablespoon sugar, and, if desired, cinnamon. Stir in melted butter. Press crumb mixture onto the bottom and 2 inches up the sides of an 8- or 9-inch springform pan. Set aside.

2. For filling, in a large mixing bowl beat cream cheese, the 1 cup sugar, flour, and vanilla with an electric mixer until combined. Beat in milk until smooth. Stir in eggs and, if desired, lemon peel.

3. Pour filling into crust-lined pan. Place pan in a shallow baking pan. Bake in a 375° oven 40 to 45 minutes for an 8-inch pan, about 35 minutes for a 9-inch pan, or until a 2½-inch area around the outside edge appears set when gently shaken.

4. Cool in pan on a wire rack for 15 minutes. Using a sharp small knife, loosen the crust from sides of pan; cool for 30 minutes more. Remove the sides of the pan; cool cheesecake completely on rack. Cover and chill at least 4 hours before serving. If desired, serve with Raspberry Sauce.

Sour Cream Cheesecake: Prepare Cheesecake Supreme as above, except reduce cream cheese to 2 packages. Omit milk; substitute two 8-ounce cartons dairy sour cream. Bake 40 to 45 minutes for an 8-inch pan or 45 to 50 minutes for a 9-inch pan.

Nutrition Facts per serving for supreme cheesecake or sour cream variation: 426 cal., 32 g total fat (18 g sat. fat), 138 mg chol., 326 mg sodium, 29 g carbo., 1 g fiber, 7 g pro.
Daily Values: 24% vit. A, 7% calcium, 8% iron
Exchanges: 2 Other Carbo., 6 Fat

Chocolate Marble Cheesecake: Prepare Cheesecake Supreme as at left, except omit lemon peel. Melt 4 ounces semisweet chocolate. Stir the melted chocolate into half of the filling. Pour plain filling into the crust; pour chocolate filling into the crust. Use a narrow metal spatula to gently swirl the fillings. If desired, garnish with strawberries and chocolate curls.

Nutrition Facts per serving: 474 cal., 35 g total fat (20 g sat. fat), 138 mg chol., 34 carbo., 326 mg sodium, 1 g fiber, 8 g pro.
Daily Values: 24% vit. A, 7% calcium, 11% iron
Exchanges: 2 Other Carbo., 7 Fat

Low-Fat Cheesecake: Prepare Cheesecake Supreme as at left, except reduce crushed graham crackers to ⅓ cup. Omit the walnuts, the 1 tablespoon sugar, cinnamon, and butter. Sprinkle crushed graham crackers on bottom and sides of a well-buttered 8- or 9-inch springform pan. Substitute three 8-ounce packages nonfat cream cheese for the regular cream cheese and ½ cup refrigerated or frozen egg product, thawed, for the eggs. Bake in a 375° oven for 40 to 45 minutes for an 8-inch pan, 30 to 35 minutes for a 9-inch pan, or until the center appears nearly set when shaken. Continue as directed in step 4. If desired, serve with strawberries, raspberries, blueberries, and/or kiwifruit.

Nutrition Facts per serving: 135 cal., 0 g total fat (0 g sat. fat), 9 mg chol., 32 mg sodium, 23 g carbo., 0 g fiber, 8 g pro.
Daily Values: 1% vit. A, 0% vit. C, 20% calcium, 2% iron
Exchanges: 1½ Other Carbo.

Tiramisu

Tiramisu (tih ruh mee SOO) is an Italian dessert.

Prep: 40 minutes **Cook:** 5 minutes **Chill:** at least 4 hours
Makes: 16 servings

- 1 **recipe Hot Milk Sponge Cake (page 165)**
- ⅓ **cup granulated sugar**
- 2 **tablespoons instant espresso coffee powder or instant coffee crystals**
- 2 **tablespoons rum**
- 2 **8-ounce cartons mascarpone cheese or two 8-ounce packages cream cheese, softened**
- ½ **cup sifted powdered sugar**
- 1 **teaspoon vanilla**
- 2 **ounces semisweet chocolate, grated**
- 1 **cup whipping cream**
- 2 **tablespoons coffee liqueur or strong coffee**
- ½ **ounce semisweet chocolate, grated**

1. Chill a medium mixing bowl and the beaters of an electric mixer.

2. Prepare Hot Milk Sponge Cake as directed, except grease and flour the baking pan. Cool for 10 minutes in pan; remove cake from pan. Cool cake completely on a wire rack.

3. Meanwhile, for syrup, in a small saucepan combine granulated sugar, espresso coffee powder, and ⅓ cup *water.* Cook over medium heat until boiling. Boil for 1 minute. Remove from heat; stir in rum. Cool completely.

4. For filling, in a medium bowl stir together the mascarpone, powdered sugar, and vanilla. Stir in the 2 ounces grated chocolate.

5. To assemble, evenly cut the cake horizontally into 3 layers. Return a cake layer to the baking pan. Brush layer with one-third of the syrup and spread with half of the filling. Add the second cake layer; top with one-third of the syrup and the remaining filling. Top with third cake layer; brush with remaining syrup.

6. In the chilled mixing bowl combine whipping cream and liqueur. Beat with the chilled beaters on medium speed until soft peaks form. Spread whipped cream over top cake layer; sprinkle with the ½ ounce grated chocolate. Cover and chill at least 4 hours before serving. To serve, cut into squares; use a spatula to remove cake from pan.

Nutrition Facts per serving: 340 cal., 22 g total fat (13 g sat. fat), 88 mg chol., 75 mg sodium, 31 g carbo., 1 g fiber, 8 g pro.
Daily Values: 7% vit. A, 4% calcium, 4% iron
Exchanges: 2 Other Carbo., 4 Fat

Quick Tiramisu: Prepare as at left, except substitute two 3-ounce packages ladyfingers, split, for the Hot Milk Sponge Cake. To assemble, place one-third of the ladyfinger halves in the bottom of a 9×9×2-inch baking pan. Brush ladyfinger halves with one-third of the syrup and spread with half of the filling. Add one-third more ladyfinger halves, and top with one-third of the syrup and the remaining filling. Top with remaining ladyfinger halves; brush with remaining syrup. Continue as directed in step 6.

Nutrition facts per serving: 277 cal., 21 g total fat (12 g sat. fat), 95 mg chol., 38 mg sodium, 19 g carbo., 0 fiber, 8 g pro.
Daily Values: 6% vit. A, 1% vit. C, 2% calcium, 4% iron
Exchanges: 1½ Other Carbo., 3½ Fat

Honey Cheese Blintzes

Prep: 40 minutes **Cook:** 1 to 2 minutes per wrapper
Makes: 6 servings (12 blintzes)

- 1 **8-ounce carton mascarpone cheese or one 8-ounce package cream cheese, softened**
- 1 **tablespoon honey**
- 1 **tablespoon milk**
- 2 **teaspoons finely shredded orange peel**
- ¼ **teaspoon anise seeds, crushed (optional)**
- 2 **eggs**
- 1⅓ **cups milk**
- ¾ **cup all-purpose flour**
- 1 **tablespoon walnut oil or hazelnut oil**
- 1½ **teaspoons sugar**
- ½ **teaspoon vanilla**
- 1½ **cups Cherry Sauce (page 482) or Raspberry Sauce (page 482)**

1. For filling, in a medium mixing bowl beat together mascarpone cheese, honey, the 1 tablespoon milk, orange peel, and, if desired, anise seeds. Cover; set aside.

2. For wrappers, in a medium bowl using a wire whisk or rotary beater whisk or beat the eggs, the 1⅓ cups milk, flour, oil, sugar, and vanilla until well combined.

3. Heat a lightly oiled 6-inch heavy skillet over medium heat; remove skillet from heat. Spoon 2 tablespoons batter into skillet; lift and tilt skillet to spread batter evenly. Return to heat; brown wrapper on 1 side only for 1 to 2 minutes. To remove wrapper, invert pan over clean white paper towels. Repeat with remaining batter, lightly oiling skillet, if necessary. Separate wrappers with dry paper towels. Keep wrappers covered.

4. To serve, spoon 1 slightly rounded tablespoon of the filling across each wrapper just below the center. Fold bottom of wrapper over filling. Fold in sides; roll up. Arrange blintzes, seam sides down, on dessert plates or a serving platter. Serve immediately or at room temperature with Cherry or Raspberry Sauce.

Make-ahead directions: Prepare wrappers as on page 250, steps 2 and 3. To freeze, alternately stack wrappers with 2 layers of waxed paper. Wrap stack in a moisture- and vaporproof sealable plastic bag. Freeze up to 4 months. Thaw wrappers at room temperature 1 hour before using.

Nutrition Facts per serving: 311 cal., 22 g total fat (11 g sat. fat), 123 mg chol., 71 mg sodium, 21 g carbo., 1 g fiber, 13 g pro. Daily Values: 4% vit. A, 2% vit. C, 8% calcium, 6% iron Exchanges: 1½ Other Carbo., 1 Medium-Fat Meat, 2½ Fat

---

Cream Puffs

Prep: 30 minutes **Cool:** 10 minutes **Bake:** 30 minutes
Oven: 400°F **Makes:** 12 cream puffs

> 1 **cup water**
> ½ **cup butter**
> ⅛ **teaspoon salt**
> 1 **cup all-purpose flour**
> 4 **eggs**
> 3 **cups whipped cream, pudding, or ice cream**
> **Powdered sugar (optional)**

1. In a medium saucepan combine water, butter, and salt. Bring to boiling. Add flour all at once, stirring vigorously. Cook and stir until mixture forms a ball (see photo 1, above right). Remove from heat. Cool for 10 minutes. Add eggs, 1 at a time, beating well with a wooden spoon after each addition (see photo 2, above right).

2. Drop 12 heaping tablespoons of dough onto a greased baking sheet. Bake in a 400° oven for 30 to 35 minutes or until golden. Transfer cream puffs to a wire rack; cool.

3. Cut tops from puffs; remove soft dough from inside (see photo 3, above right). Fill with whipped cream. Replace tops. If desired, sift powdered sugar over tops.

Nutrition Facts per cream puff: 238 cal., 21 g total fat (12 g sat. fat), 134 mg chol., 140 mg sodium, 9 g carbo., 0 g fiber, 4 g pro. Daily Values: 17% vit. A, 3% calcium, 4% iron Exchanges: ½ Other Carbo., 4 Fat

Éclairs: Prepare as above, except spoon dough into a decorating bag fitted with a large plain round tip (about ½-inch opening). Pipe 12 strips of dough, 3 inches apart, onto a greased baking sheet, making each strip 4 inches long, 1 inch wide, and ¾ inch high. Bake, cool, and split as in steps 2 and 3. Fill éclairs with whipped cream or pudding. Frost with 1 recipe Chocolate Glaze (page 163). Makes 12 éclairs.

Nutrition Facts per éclair: 361 cal., 27 g total fat (16 g sat. fat), 142 mg chol., 27 g carbo., 171 mg sodium, 1 g fiber, 5 g pro. Daily Values: 19% vit. A, 3% calcium, 7% iron Exchanges: 1½ Other Carbo., 5 Fat

1. Add the flour to the butter mixture all at once. Cook and stir the dough vigorously until the mixture forms a ball that doesn't separate.

2. After cooling the dough for 10 minutes, add the eggs one at a time. After each addition, use a wooden spoon to beat the dough until it is smooth.

3. When the baked cream puffs are cool enough to handle, cut off the top one-third of each. Carefully remove any soft dough inside the cream puffs with a fork or spoon.

Perfect Cream Puffs

Crisp, tender, and beautifully puffed are characteristics of perfect cream puffs or éclairs. Follow these tips to ensure yours are stellar:

■ Measure the water accurately, using a glass liquid measure. Too much or too little water can make a difference in the outcome.

■ Add the flour as soon as the butter has melted and the mixture is boiling so that the liquid doesn't boil away.

■ Use large eggs. Add them one at a time, stirring until each is incorporated before adding the next one.

■ Remove the baked cream puffs from the oven only when they are golden brown, firm, and dry.

■ To keep the bottoms from getting soggy, fill the cream puff shells just before serving, or fill and chill the puffs for no more than 2 hours.

■ For mini appetizer puffs, drop dough by rounded teaspoons. Bake in a 400°F oven about 18 minutes.

Bread Pudding

To dry bread cubes, place them in a large, shallow baking pan and bake in a 350°F oven about 10 minutes, stirring twice.

Low Fat

Prep: 30 minutes (includes time to dry bread)
Bake: 40 minutes **Oven:** 350°F **Makes:** 8 servings

>   4 beaten eggs
> 2¼ cups milk
>   ½ cup sugar
>   1 tablespoon vanilla
>   1 teaspoon finely shredded orange peel (optional)
>   ½ teaspoon ground cinnamon
>   4 cups dry French bread cubes or regular bread cubes (6 to 7 slices bread)
>   ⅓ cup dried cherries or cranberries, or raisins
>   1 recipe Caramel Sauce (page 484) or Bourbon Sauce (page 484) (optional)

1. In a large bowl beat together eggs, milk, sugar, vanilla, orange peel (if desired), and cinnamon. In an ungreased 2-quart square baking dish toss together bread cubes and dried fruit; pour egg mixture evenly over bread mixture. Press mixture lightly with back of a large spoon.

2. Bake, uncovered, in a 350° oven for 40 to 45 minutes or until puffed and a knife inserted near the center comes out clean. Cool slightly. If desired, serve warm with Caramel Sauce or Bourbon Sauce.

Pear-Ginger Bread Pudding: Prepare as above, except substitute snipped dried pears for the dried cherries or raisins. Stir orange peel into the milk mixture. Substitute 1 tablespoon finely chopped crystallized ginger for the cinnamon. If desired, serve with whipped cream, Caramel Sauce, or Bourbon Sauce.

Nutrition Facts per serving for bread pudding or pear variation: 191 cal., 4 g total fat (2 g sat. fat), 111 mg chol., 180 mg sodium, 30 g carbo., 1 g fiber, 7 g pro.
Daily Values: 6% vit. A, 1% vit. C, 11% calcium, 5% iron
Exchanges: 2 Other Carbo., ½ Fat

Chocolate Chip Bread Pudding: Prepare as at left, except substitute chocolate milk for milk and semisweet chocolate pieces for the dried cherries or raisins. Add ½ cup chopped pecans. Omit optional orange peel. If desired, serve with vanilla ice cream.

Nutrition Facts per serving: 271 cal., 11 g total fat (3 g sat. fat), 111 mg chol., 189 mg sodium, 35 g carbo., 2 g fiber, 8 g pro.
Daily Values: 6% vit. A, 1% vit. C, 11% calcium, 8% iron
Exchanges: 2½ Other Carbo., 1½ Fat

Brownie Pudding   **Best Loved**

This classic cake comes from the pages of the January 1944 issue of Better Homes and Gardens *magazine.*

Prep: 15 minutes **Bake:** 40 minutes
Oven: 350°F **Cool:** 45 minutes **Makes:** 6 to 8 servings

>   1 cup all-purpose flour
>   ¾ cup granulated sugar
>   2 tablespoons unsweetened cocoa powder
>   2 teaspoons baking powder
>   ¼ teaspoon salt
>   ½ cup milk
>   2 tablespoons cooking oil
>   1 teaspoon vanilla
>   ½ cup chopped walnuts
>   ¾ cup packed brown sugar
>   ¼ cup unsweetened cocoa powder
> 1½ cups boiling water
>   Vanilla ice cream (optional)

1. Grease an 8×8×2-inch baking pan; set aside. In a medium bowl stir together the flour, granulated sugar, the 2 tablespoons cocoa powder, the baking powder, and salt. Stir in the milk, oil, and vanilla. Stir in the walnuts.

2. Pour batter into prepared baking pan. In a small bowl stir together the brown sugar and the ¼ cup cocoa powder; stir in the boiling water. Slowly pour water mixture over batter.

3. Bake in a 350° oven for 40 minutes. Cool on a wire rack for 45 to 60 minutes. Serve warm. Spoon cake into dessert bowls; spoon sauce over cake. If desired, serve with vanilla ice cream.

Nutrition Facts per serving: 412 cal., 13 g total fat (2 g sat. fat), 2 mg chol., 254 mg sodium, 71 g carbo., 1 g fiber, 6 g pro.
Daily Values: 1% vit. A, 1% vit. C, 21% calcium, 14% iron
Exchanges: 4 Other Carbo., 2 Fat

Chocolate Truffle Torte

Prep: 40 minutes **Bake:** 45 minutes **Oven:** 325°F
Cool: 4⅓ hours **Makes:** 16 servings

> 1 **cup pecans, toasted (see tip, page 224) and coarsely ground**
> 1 **cup graham cracker crumbs**
> ¼ **cup butter or margarine, melted**
> 2 **tablespoons sugar**
> 2 **8-ounce packages semisweet chocolate, cut up**
> 1 **cup whipping cream**
> 6 **beaten eggs**
> ¾ **cup sugar**
> ⅓ **cup all-purpose flour**
> **Whipped cream (optional)**

1. For crust, in a medium bowl combine pecans, cracker crumbs, melted butter, and the 2 tablespoons sugar. Press onto bottom and about 1½ inches up sides of a greased 9-inch springform pan. Set pan aside.

2. In a large saucepan cook and stir chocolate and whipping cream over low heat until the chocolate melts. Transfer the chocolate mixture to a medium bowl. Set aside.

3. In a large mixing bowl combine eggs, the ¾ cup sugar, and flour; beat for 10 minutes or until thick and lemon colored. Fold one-fourth of the egg mixture into the chocolate mixture; fold mixture into remaining egg mixture. Pour batter into crust-lined pan.

4. Bake cake in a 325° oven about 45 minutes or until puffed around edge and halfway to center (the center will be slightly soft). Cool in pan on a wire rack for 20 minutes. Remove sides of pan. Cool for 4 hours. If desired, serve with whipped cream. Store in the refrigerator.

Orange-Chocolate Truffle Torte: Prepare Truffle Cake as above, except stir 2 teaspoons finely shredded orange peel into the egg mixture after beating.

Nutrition Facts per serving for truffle cake or orange-chocolate variation: 369 cal., 25 g total fat (12 g sat. fat), 108 mg chol., 89 mg sodium, 35 g carbo., 3 g fiber, 6 g pro.
Daily Values: 9% vit. A, 3% calcium, 13% iron
Exchanges: 2 Other Carbo., 4½ Fat

Chocolate Pot de Crème

Prep: 10 minutes **Cook:** 10 minutes
Chill: 4 hours **Makes:** 8 servings

> 2 **cups whipping cream**
> 6 **ounces semisweet chocolate, coarsely chopped**
> ⅓ **cup sugar**
> 4 **beaten egg yolks**
> 1 **teaspoon vanilla**
> **White chocolate curls (optional)**

1. In a medium heavy saucepan combine the whipping cream, chocolate, and sugar. Cook and stir over medium heat about 10 minutes or until mixture comes to a full boil and thickens. (If chocolate flecks remain, use a rotary beater or wire whisk to beat mixture until blended.)

2. Gradually stir all of the hot mixture into the beaten egg yolks; stir in vanilla. Divide chocolate mixture evenly into 8 sake cups, small cups, pot de crème cups, or 3-ounce ramekins. Cover and chill for 4 to 24 hours before serving. If desired, garnish with white chocolate curls.

Mocha Pot de Crème: Prepare as above, except add 1 tablespoon instant espresso coffee powder or 2 tablespoons instant coffee crystals to whipping cream mixture before heating.

Nutrition Facts per serving for chocolate or mocha variation: 375 cal., 32 g total fat (18 g sat. fat), 189 mg chol., 26 mg sodium, 22 g carbo., 2 g fiber, 4 g pro.
Daily Values: 21% vit. A, 1% vit. C, 5% calcium, 8% iron
Exchanges: 1½ Other Carbo., 6½ Fat

Chocolate Pot de Crème

Lava Baby Cakes

See photo, page 241.

Prep: 15 minutes **Bake:** 13 minutes **Oven:** 400°F
Chill: 45 minutes **Makes:** 6 servings

> 1¾ cups (10½ ounces) semisweet chocolate
>   pieces
>   2 tablespoons whipping cream
> ¾ cup butter
>   3 eggs
>   3 egg yolks
> ⅓ cup granulated sugar
> 1½ teaspoons vanilla
> ⅓ cup all-purpose flour
>   3 tablespoons unsweetened cocoa powder
>   Powdered sugar (optional)
>   Raspberries (optional)

1. For filling, in a small heavy saucepan combine ¾ cup of the chocolate pieces and whipping cream. Cook and stir over low heat until chocolate melts. Remove from heat. Cool, stirring occasionally. Cover; chill about 45 minutes or until firm.

2. Meanwhile, in a medium heavy saucepan cook and stir the remaining 1 cup chocolate pieces and the butter over low heat until melted. Remove from heat; cool.

3. Form filling into 6 equal-size balls; set aside. Lightly grease and flour six ¾-cup soufflé dishes or six 6-ounce custard cups. Place dishes or cups in a 15×10×1-inch baking pan; set aside.

4. In a mixing bowl beat eggs, egg yolks, granulated sugar, and vanilla with an electric mixer on high speed for 5 minutes or until lemon colored. Beat in cooled chocolate mixture on medium speed. Sift flour and cocoa powder over mixture; beat on low speed just until combined. Spoon ⅓ cup batter into dishes. Place 1 ball of filling into each dish. Spoon remaining batter into dishes.

5. Bake in a 400° oven about 13 minutes or until cakes feel firm at edges. Cool in dishes for 2 to 3 minutes. Using a knife, loosen cakes from sides of dishes. Invert onto dessert plates. If desired, dust with powdered sugar and garnish with raspberries. Serve immediately.

Make-ahead directions: Prepare as above through step 4. Cover and chill until ready to bake or up to 4 hours. Let stand at room temperature for 30 minutes before baking as directed.

Nutrition Facts per serving: 621 cal., 47 g total fat (27 g sat. fat), 285 mg chol., 291 mg sodium, 50 g carbo., 3 g fiber, 8 g pro.
Daily Values: 26% vit. A, 8% calcium, 16% iron
Exchanges: 3 Other Carbo., 8 Fat

Individual Caramel Flans

Prep: 25 minutes **Bake:** 30 minutes
Oven: 325°F **Makes:** 4 servings

> ⅓ cup sugar
> 3 beaten eggs
> 1½ cups milk
> ⅓ cup sugar
> 1 teaspoon vanilla
>   Ground nutmeg or cinnamon (optional)

1. To caramelize sugar, in an 8-inch heavy skillet cook ⅓ cup sugar over medium-high heat until sugar begins to melt, shaking skillet occasionally to heat sugar evenly. Do not stir (see photo 1, below). Once the sugar starts to melt, reduce heat to low. Cook about 5 minutes more or until all of the sugar is melted and golden, stirring as needed with a wooden spoon. Immediately divide caramelized sugar among four 6-ounce custard cups; tilt cups to coat bottoms evenly. Let stand for 10 minutes.

2. Meanwhile, combine eggs, milk, the ⅓ cup sugar, and vanilla. Beat until well combined but not foamy. Place custard cups in a 2-quart square baking dish. Divide egg mixture among custard cups. If desired, sprinkle with nutmeg. Place baking dish on oven rack. Pour boiling water into the baking dish around custard cups to a depth of 1 inch. Bake in a 325° oven for 30 to 45 minutes or until a knife inserted near the center of each flan comes out clean (see photo 2, below).

1. Before the sugar begins to melt, shake the pan occasionally; do not stir until the melting begins. Sugar is caramelized when it is syrupy and golden.

2. To test the custards for doneness, insert the tip of a table knife into the center of each custard. The knife will come out clean if the custards are fully cooked.

3. Remove cups from water. Cool slightly on a wire rack. (Or cool completely in cups. Cover and chill until serving time.) To unmold, loosen edges of flans with a knife, slipping point between flans and side of custard cups. Invert a dessert plate over each flan; turn plate and custard cup over together. Remove cups from flans.

Nutrition Facts per serving: 227 cal., 6 g total fat (2 g sat. fat), 166 mg chol., 93 mg sodium, 37 g carbo., 0 g fiber, 8 g pro.
Daily Values: 9% vit. A, 1% vit. C, 13% calcium, 3% iron
Exchanges: ½ Milk, 2 Other Carbo., ½ Fat

Baked Custard: Prepare as on page 254, except omit the ⅓ cup sugar that is caramelized in step 1. Divide egg mixture among custard cups or one 3½-cup soufflé dish. Bake custards as directed, or bake in soufflé dish for 50 to 60 minutes. Serve custard warm or chilled.

Nutrition Facts per serving: 166 cal., 6 g total fat (2 g sat. fat), 166 mg chol., 93 mg sodium, 0 g fiber, 8 g pro.
Daily Values: 9% vit. A, 1% vit. C, 13% calcium, 3% iron
Exchanges: 1 Other Carbo., ½ Milk, 1 Fat

Vanilla Pudding

Prep: 20 minutes **Chill:** 4 hours **Makes:** 4 servings

  ¾ **cup sugar**
  3 **tablespoons cornstarch**
  3 **cups milk**
  4 **beaten egg yolks**
  1 **tablespoon butter or margarine**
1½ **teaspoons vanilla**

1. In a medium heavy saucepan combine sugar and cornstarch. Stir in milk. Cook and stir mixture over medium heat until thickened and bubbly. Cook and stir for 2 minutes more. Remove pan from heat. Gradually stir 1 cup of milk mixture into egg yolks. Add egg mixture to milk mixture in pan. Bring milk mixture to a gentle boil; reduce heat. Cook and stir for 2 minutes more.

2. Remove pan from heat. Stir in butter and vanilla. Pour pudding into a bowl. Cover surface of pudding with plastic wrap. Serve warm or cold (do not stir during chilling).

Chocolate Pudding: Prepare as above, except add ⅓ cup Dutch process unsweetened cocoa powder or unsweetened cocoa powder along with the sugar; decrease the cornstarch to 2 tablespoons and the milk to 2⅔ cups.

Nutrition Facts per serving for vanilla or chocolate pudding:
342 cal., 11 g total fat (5 g sat. fat), 234 mg chol., 133 mg sodium, 51 g carbo., 0 g fiber, 9 g pro.
Daily Values: 16% vit. A, 3% vit. C, 25% calcium, 4% iron
Exchanges: 3 Other Carbo., 1½ Fat

Baked Rice Pudding

Low Fat

Prep: 10 minutes **Bake:** 45 minutes
Oven: 325°F **Makes:** 6 servings

  3 **beaten eggs**
1½ **cups milk**
  ⅓ **cup sugar**
  1 **teaspoon vanilla**
  1 **cup cooked rice**
  ½ **cup raisins**
     Ground nutmeg or cinnamon (optional)

1. In a bowl combine eggs, milk, sugar, and vanilla. Beat until combined but not foamy. Stir in rice and raisins. Pour egg mixture into a 1½-quart casserole. If desired, sprinkle with nutmeg. Place casserole in a 2-quart square baking dish on an oven rack. Pour boiling water into baking dish around casserole to a depth of 1 inch.

2. Bake in a 325° oven for 45 to 55 minutes or until a knife inserted near the center comes out clean, stirring after 30 minutes. Serve warm or cold. To store, cover and chill.

Nutrition Facts per serving: 181 cal., 4 g total fat (2 g sat. fat), 111 mg chol., 64 mg sodium, 31 g carbo., 1 g fiber, 6 g pro.
Daily Values: 6% vit. A, 2% vit. C, 10% calcium, 5% iron
Exchanges: 2 Other Carbo., ½ Fat

Secrets to Successful Custard

■ Ensure a smooth baked custard by beating the eggs just until the yolks and whites are combined. Don't beat the eggs until foamy or the custard surface will have bubbles.

■ Use a hot-water bath when baking custard. It helps even out the heat so the edges won't overcook before the center is done. Don't be tempted to omit this step.

■ Place baking dish with filled custard cups in the oven. Pull the oven rack out slightly. Fill the baking dish with enough boiling water to come about halfway up the sides of the custard cups. Carefully push rack back into place.

■ Test each baked custard with a knife to see if it is done (see photo 2, page 254). Bake it a few more minutes if any custard clings to the knife.

■ Remove each custard from the hot water bath immediately when it tests done. If it remains in the bath, it will continue to cook.

Saucepan Rice Pudding

Low Fat

Prep: 10 minutes **Cook:** 30 minutes **Makes:** 6 servings

> 3 **cups milk**
> ⅓ **cup uncooked long grain rice**
> ⅓ **cup raisins or mixed dried fruit bits**
> ¼ **cup sugar**
> 1 **teaspoon vanilla**
> ¼ **teaspoon ground nutmeg**

1. In a medium heavy saucepan bring milk just to boiling; stir in uncooked rice and raisins. Cook, covered, over low heat for 30 to 40 minutes or until most of the milk is absorbed, stirring occasionally. (Mixture may appear curdled.)

2. Remove saucepan from heat. Stir in sugar and vanilla. Spoon into dessert dishes. Sprinkle with nutmeg. Serve warm or chilled.

Nutrition Facts per serving: 155 cal., 2 g total fat (2 g sat. fat), 9 mg chol., 63 mg sodium, 28 g carbo., 0 g fiber, 5 g pro.
Daily Values: 5% vit. A, 2% vit. C, 16% calcium, 4% iron
Exchanges: ½ Milk, 1½ Other Carbo.

Crème Brûlée

Caramelized sugar is drizzled over the chilled custards to create a contrast of crunch to the smooth custard.

Prep: 10 minutes **Bake:** 30 minutes **Oven:** 325°F
Chill: 1 to 8 hours **Stand:** 20 minutes **Makes:** 6 servings

> 2 **cups half-and-half or light cream**
> 5 **slightly beaten egg yolks**
> ⅓ **cup sugar**
> 1 **teaspoon vanilla**
> ⅛ **teaspoon salt**
> ¼ **cup sugar**

1. In a small heavy saucepan heat half-and-half over medium-low heat just until bubbly. Remove from heat; set aside.

2. Meanwhile, in a medium bowl combine egg yolks, the ⅓ cup sugar, vanilla, and salt. Beat with a wire whisk or rotary beater just until combined. Slowly whisk the hot half-and-half into the egg mixture.

3. Place six ¾-cup soufflé dishes or 6-ounce custard cups in a 3-quart baking dish. Divide custard mixture evenly among the soufflé dishes or cups. Place baking dish on oven rack. Pour enough boiling water into the baking dish to reach halfway up the sides of the soufflé dishes.

4. Bake in a 325° oven for 30 to 40 minutes or until a knife inserted near the center of each custard comes out clean (see photo 2, page 254). Remove dishes from water; cool on a wire rack. Cover and chill for at least 1 hour or for up to 8 hours.

5. Before serving, let custards stand at room temperature for 20 minutes. Meanwhile, in an 8-inch heavy skillet heat the ¼ cup sugar over medium-high heat until sugar begins to melt, shaking skillet occasionally to heat sugar evenly. Do not stir (see photo 1, page 254). Once sugar starts to melt, reduce heat to low; cook about 5 minutes more or until all of the sugar is melted and golden, stirring as needed with a wooden spoon.

6. Quickly drizzle caramelized sugar over the custards. (If sugar starts to harden in the skillet, return to heat, stirring until melted.) Serve custards immediately.

Crème Brûlée with Liqueur: Prepare Crème Brûlée as above, except decrease half-and-half to 1¾ cups. Stir 2 tablespoons amaretto, crème de cacao, or coffee liqueur into the egg yolk mixture.

Nutrition Facts per serving for plain or liqueur variation: 228 cal., 13 g total fat (7 g sat. fat), 207 mg chol., 87 mg sodium, 22 g carbo., 0 g fiber, 5 g pro.
Daily Values: 12% vit. A, 1% vit. C, 10% calcium, 3% iron
Exchanges: 1½ Other Carbo., 2 Fat

Mango Mousse

Prep: 30 minutes **Chill:** 4 hours **Makes:** 6 servings

> 3 **ripe mangoes, seeded, peeled, and cut up (3 cups)**
> ⅓ **cup sugar**
> 1 **teaspoon unflavored gelatin**
> 1 **cup whipping cream**
> ¼ **teaspoon coconut extract**
> 2 **kiwifruits, peeled and sliced**
> ¼ **cup coconut, toasted (see tip, page 224)**

1. Chill a medium mixing bowl and the beaters of an electric mixer.

2. In a food processor bowl or blender container place 2 cups of the mangoes. Cover and process or blend until smooth. You should have 1 cup of puree; set aside.

3. In a saucepan combine sugar and gelatin. Stir in ¼ cup *cold water*. Cook and stir over low heat just until gelatin dissolves. Remove from heat. Stir in mango puree; cool mixture to room temperature.

4. In the chilled bowl beat whipping cream and coconut extract with an electric mixer on low speed until soft peaks form (tips curl). Using a rubber spatula, fold mango mixture into whipped cream. Chill until mixture mounds when spooned.

5. Divide half of the mango mixture among 6 dessert bowls or dishes. Divide kiwifruit slices and remaining cut-up mango among each serving. Top with remaining mango mixture; sprinkle with toasted coconut. Cover and chill for 4 hours or until set.

Nutrition Facts per serving: 273 cal., 17 g total fat (11 g sat. fat), 55 mg chol., 34 mg sodium, 31 g carbo., 3 g fiber, 2 g pro.
Daily Values: 77% vit. A, 80% vit. C, 4% calcium, 1% iron
Exchanges: 1 Fruit, 1 Other Carbo., 3 Fat

Hazelnut Meringues with Coffee Cream

Prep: 45 minutes Bake: 35 minutes Oven: 300°F
Stand: 1 hour Cool: 2 hours Chill: 2 to 24 hours
Makes: 8 servings

> 4 **egg whites**
> 1 **teaspoon vanilla**
> ¼ **teaspoon cream of tartar**
> 1⅓ **cups sugar**
> 1 **cup ground hazelnuts (filberts)**
> 1 **3-ounce package cream cheese, softened**
> 3 **tablespoons butter or margarine, softened**
> ⅓ **cup sugar**
> 1 **cup whipping cream**
> 3 **tablespoons coffee liqueur or strong coffee**
> 2 **ounces semisweet chocolate**
>   **Coarsely chopped hazelnuts (filberts) (optional)**
> 1 **recipe Chocolate Shapes (optional)**

1. Allow egg whites to stand at room temperature for 30 minutes. Cover a large cookie sheet with parchment paper or foil. Draw eight 3-inch circles, 3 inches apart, on paper or foil; set aside.

2. For meringue, in a large mixing bowl combine egg whites, vanilla, and cream of tartar. Beat with an electric mixer on medium speed until soft peaks form (tips curl; see photo 1, page 169). Gradually add the 1⅓ cups sugar, 1 tablespoon at a time, beating about 4 minutes on high speed until stiff peaks form (tips stand straight; see photo 2, page 169) and sugar is almost dissolved. Gently fold in ground hazelnuts.

3. Transfer meringue to a pastry bag fitted with a large round tip. Pipe meringue onto the circles on the paper or foil, building up the sides to form shells. (Or spread meringue onto circles using the back of a spoon.) Bake in a 300° oven for 35 minutes. Turn oven off. Let meringues dry in oven, with door closed, for 1 hour. Remove from oven; cool completely on cookie sheet.

4. In a medium mixing bowl beat cream cheese with 2 tablespoons of the butter until smooth; beat in the ⅓ cup sugar. Add the whipping cream and liqueur. Beat on low speed until combined; beat on medium speed just until soft peaks form.

5. Remove meringues from paper or foil. Place meringues on a platter. Fill shells with whipped cream mixture. Cover loosely; chill 2 to 24 hours.

6. Just before assembling, in a small saucepan melt the remaining 1 tablespoon butter and the chocolate over low heat, stirring constantly. Cool slightly. To serve, drizzle 8 dessert plates with melted chocolate. Place filled meringue shells on top of chocolate. If desired, sprinkle with chopped nuts and garnish with chocolate shapes.

Chocolate Shapes: Melt 1 ounce semisweet chocolate. Drizzle melted chocolate into 8 desired shapes onto a sheet of waxed paper. Allow to set before removing from waxed paper. (Or to set quickly, place shapes in the freezer for 1 to 2 minutes.)

Nutrition Facts per serving: 504 cal., 32 g total fat (14 g sat. fat), 65 mg chol., 121 mg sodium, 50 g carbo., 2 g fiber, 6 g pro.
Daily Values: 16% vit. A, 2% vit. C, 5% calcium, 7% iron
Exchanges: 3 Other Carbo., 5½ Fat

Hazelnut Meringues with Coffee Cream

Chocolate Soufflé

Prep: 25 minutes **Bake:** 40 minutes **Oven:** 350°F
Makes: 6 servings

> Butter
> Sugar
> 2 tablespoons butter or margarine
> 3 tablespoons all-purpose flour
> ¾ cup milk
> ½ cup semisweet chocolate pieces
> 4 beaten egg yolks
> 4 egg whites
> ½ teaspoon vanilla
> ¼ cup sugar
> Whipped cream (optional)

1. Butter the sides of a 1½-quart soufflé dish. For a collar on the soufflé dish, measure enough foil to wrap around the top of the dish and add 3 inches. Fold foil into thirds lengthwise. Lightly grease 1 side with butter; sprinkle with sugar. Place foil, sugar side in, around the outside of the dish so it extends about 2 inches above edges of dish. Tape ends of foil together. Sprinkle the inside of dish with sugar; set dish aside.

2. In a small saucepan melt the 2 tablespoons butter. Stir in flour. Add milk all at once. Cook and stir until thickened and bubbly. Add chocolate; stir until melted. Remove from heat. Gradually stir chocolate mixture into beaten egg yolks. Set aside.

3. Beat egg whites and vanilla until soft peaks form (tips curl). Gradually add the sugar, beating until stiff peaks form (tips stand straight). Fold about 1 cup of the beaten egg whites into chocolate mixture. Fold chocolate mixture into remaining beaten whites. Transfer to prepared dish.

4. Bake in a 350° oven for 40 to 45 minutes or until a knife inserted near the center comes out clean. Serve immediately. To serve, insert two forks back to back; gently pull soufflé apart into serving-size wedges. Use a large spoon to transfer to plates. If desired, top with whipped cream.

Make-ahead directions: Prepare the soufflé as above through step 3, omitting the collar on the dish because it is not necessary. Cover and chill for up to 2 hours. Bake as above for 45 to 50 minutes or until the soufflé tests done.

Nutrition Facts per serving: 216 cal., 12 g total fat (6 g sat. fat), 155 mg chol., 100 mg sodium, 22 g carbo., 1 g fiber, 6 g pro.
Daily Values: 9% vit. A, 6% calcium, 6% iron
Exchanges: 1½ Other Carbo., 2 Fat

Vanilla Ice Cream

This will ripen to soft-serve consistency.

Prep: 5 minutes **Freeze:** per manufacturer's directions
Ripen: 4 hours (optional) **Makes:** 2 quarts (16 servings)

> 4 cups half-and-half, light cream, or milk
> 1½ cups sugar
> 1 tablespoon vanilla
> 2 cups whipping cream

1. In a large bowl combine half-and-half, sugar, and vanilla. Stir until sugar dissolves. Stir in whipping cream. Freeze ice cream mixture in a 4- or 5-quart ice cream freezer according to the manufacturer's directions. Ripen 4 hours (see tip, page 259).

Strawberry or Peach Ice Cream: Prepare as above, except in a blender container blend 4 cups fresh strawberries; frozen unsweetened strawberries, thawed; or cut-up, peeled peaches until nearly smooth (you should have 2 cups). Stir fruit into ice cream mixture before freezing.

Coffee Ice Cream: Prepare as above, except dissolve 2 to 3 tablespoons instant coffee crystals in the half-and-half mixture. If desired, stir ½ cup miniature semisweet chocolate pieces into ice cream mixture before freezing.

Nutrition Facts per serving for vanilla, strawberry, peach, and coffee variations: 253 cal., 18 g total fat (11 g sat. fat), 63 mg chol., 36 mg sodium, 22 g carbo., 0 g fiber, 2 g pro.
Daily Values: 14% vit. A, 1% vit. C, 8% calcium
Exchanges: 1½ Other Carbo., 3 Fat

Chocolate-Almond Ice Cream: Prepare as above, except reduce sugar to 1 cup. Stir one 16-ounce can (1½ cups) chocolate-flavored syrup and ½ cup chopped almonds, toasted (see tip, page 224), into ice cream mixture before freezing.

Nutrition Facts per serving: 327 cal., 20 g total fat (11 g sat. fat), 63 mg chol., 54 mg sodium, 34 g carbo., 1 g fiber, 4 g pro.
Daily Values: 14% vit. A, 1% vit. C, 9% calcium, 3% iron
Exchanges: 2 Other Carbo., 3 Fat

Pecan-Praline Ice Cream: Prepare as above, except in a heavy skillet cook ½ cup chopped pecans, ¼ cup sugar, and 1 tablespoon butter or margarine over medium-high heat until sugar begins to melt, shaking skillet occasionally. Do not stir. Reduce heat to low and cook until sugar turns golden, stirring frequently. Immediately spread on a baking sheet lined with greased foil. Cool; break into chunks. Stir nut mixture into ice cream mixture before freezing.

Nutrition Facts per serving: 295 cal., 21 g total fat (12 g sat. fat), 65 mg chol., 44 mg sodium, 25 g carbo., 0 g fiber, 3 g pro.
Daily Values: 15% vit. A, 1% vit. C, 9% calcium, 1% iron
Exchanges: 1½ Other Carbo., 3 Fat

Custard Cream Gelato

Prep: 30 minutes   **Chill:** several hours or overnight
Freeze: per manufacturer's directions   **Ripen:** 4 hours (optional)
Makes: about 1½ quarts (12 servings)

> 1 **medium lemon or orange**
> 4 **cups whole milk**
> 1⅓ **cups sugar**
> 12 **beaten egg yolks**

1. Use a vegetable peeler to remove long strips of peel from the lemon; set peels aside.

2. In a large saucepan combine the milk, sugar, and egg yolks. Add lemon peels to saucepan. Cook and stir over medium heat until the mixture just coats a metal spoon. Remove from the heat.

3. Cover surface of custard mixture with plastic wrap. Chill several hours or overnight until completely chilled. (Or, to chill quickly, transfer custard to a bowl. Place bowl in a sink of ice water, stirring occasionally, for 30 minutes to 1 hour.)

4. Remove peels from mixture. Freeze custard mixture in a 4- or 5-quart ice cream freezer according to the manufacturer's directions. If desired, ripen for 4 hours.

Berry Gelato: Prepare as above, except omit lemon or orange peels. In a blender container or food processor bowl place 3 cups fresh raspberries or cut-up strawberries. Cover and blend or process until smooth (you should have about 2 cups puree). (If desired, sieve berries and discard seeds; there should be about 1 cup sieved puree.) Stir puree and, if desired, several drops of red food coloring into the custard mixture. Chill thoroughly; freeze in ice cream freezer as directed.

Nutrition Facts per serving for custard cream or berry variation:
192 cal., 8 g total fat (3 g sat. fat), 224 mg chol., 47 mg sodium, 25 g carbo., 0 g fiber, 5 g pro.
Daily Values: 9% vit. A, 2% vit. C, 12% calcium, 4% iron
Exchanges: 1½ Other Carbo., 1½ Fat

Amaretti Gelato: Prepare as above, except omit lemon or orange peels. Stir ¼ cup amaretto into the custard mixture. Chill thoroughly; freeze in ice cream freezer as directed. Stir ¾ cup toasted slivered almonds into gelato before ripening. If desired, sprinkle each serving with crumbled macaroons or coarsely crushed amaretti cookies.

Chocolate Gelato: Prepare as above, except omit the lemon or orange peels. Melt 12 ounces bittersweet or semisweet chocolate; add to the custard mixture. Stir with a wire whisk or beat with a rotary beater until smooth. Chill thoroughly. Freeze in ice cream freezer as directed. If desired, chop 6 ounces semisweet chocolate (about 1 cup) and stir into gelato before ripening. Makes about 2 quarts (16 servings).

Nutrition Facts per serving for amaretti or chocolate variation:
254 calories, 12 g total fat (4 g sat. fat), 334 mg chol., 47 g sodium, 28 g carbo., 1 g fiber, 7 g pro.
Daily Values: 9% vit. A, 1% vit. C, 14% calcium, 6% iron
Exchanges: 2 Other Carbo., 2 Fat

Berry Gelato and Chocolate Gelato

Ripening Frozen Desserts

Ripening or hardening homemade ice cream, sorbets, sherbets, or gelato isn't a requirement, but it improves the texture and helps to keep them from melting too quickly during eating.

■ To ripen in a traditional-style ice cream freezer, after churning, remove the lid and dasher and cover the top of the freezer can with waxed paper or foil. Plug the hole in the lid with a small piece of cloth; replace the lid. Pack the outer freezer bucket with enough ice and rock salt to cover the top of the freezer can (use 4 cups ice to 1 cup salt). Ripen about 4 hours.

■ When using an ice cream freezer with an insulated freezer bowl, transfer the ice cream to a covered freezer-proof container and ripen in your regular freezer about 4 hours (or check the manufacturer's recommendations).

Orange Sherbet

Low Fat

Prep: 20 minutes **Ripen:** 4 hours (optional)
Freeze: per manufacturer's directions
Makes: 1½ quarts (12 servings)

> 1½ **cups sugar**
> 1 **envelope unflavored gelatin**
> 3¾ **cups orange juice**
> 1 **cup milk**
> 1 **teaspoon grated orange peel**
>   **Few drops orange food coloring (optional)**

1. In a medium saucepan combine sugar and gelatin. Stir in 2 cups of the orange juice. Cook and stir until sugar and gelatin dissolve. Remove from heat. Stir in the remaining 1¾ cups orange juice, the milk, orange peel, and, if desired, food coloring. (Mixture may appear curdled.)

2. Transfer mixture to a 4-quart ice cream freezer; freeze according to manufacturer's directions. Ripen 4 hours. (Or transfer the mixture to a 13×9×2-inch baking pan. Cover; freeze several hours or until almost firm. Break mixture into small chunks; transfer to a large chilled bowl. Beat with an electric mixer until smooth but not melted. Return to pan. Cover; freeze until firm.)

Lemon Sherbet: In a saucepan combine 1½ cups sugar and 1 envelope unflavored gelatin. Stir in 1½ cups water. Cook and stir until sugar and gelatin dissolve. Remove from heat. Stir in 1½ cups cold water, 1 cup milk, 1 teaspoon grated lemon peel, ¾ cup lemon juice, and, if desired, a few drops yellow food coloring. (Mixture may appear curdled.) Continue with step 2, above.

Nutrition Facts per serving for orange or lemon sherbet variation: 140 cal., 1 g total fat (0 g sat. fat), 2 mg chol., 12 mg sodium, 33 g carbo., 0 g fiber, 2 g pro.
Daily Values: 4% vit. A, 65% vit. C, 3% calcium, 1% iron
Exchanges: ½ Milk, 1½ Other Carbo.

Lemon Curd

Prep: 5 minutes **Cook:** 8 minutes
Chill: 1 to 48 hours **Makes:** 2 cups

> 1 **cup sugar**
> 2 **tablespoons cornstarch**
> 3 **teaspoons finely shredded lemon peel**
> 6 **tablespoons lemon juice**
> 6 **tablespoons water**
> 6 **beaten egg yolks**
> ½ **cup butter or margarine, cut up**

1. In a medium saucepan stir together sugar and cornstarch. Stir in lemon peel, lemon juice, and water. Cook and stir over medium heat until thickened and bubbly. Stir half of the lemon mixture into egg yolks. Return the egg yolk mixture to the saucepan. Cook and stir over medium heat until mixture comes to a gentle boil. Cook and stir for 2 minutes more. Remove from heat.

2. Add butter pieces, stirring until melted. Cover surface of the curd with plastic wrap. Chill at least 1 hour or for up to 48 hours. Store covered in the refrigerator for up to 1 week. Or transfer to a freezer container; freeze for up to 2 months. Thaw in the refrigerator before serving.

Nutrition Facts per 2 tablespoons: 128 cal., 8 g total fat (4 g sat. fat), 96 mg chol., 65 mg sodium, 14 g carbo., 0 g fiber, 1 g pro.
Daily Values: 7% vit. A, 5% vit. C, 1% calcium, 1% iron
Exchanges: 1 Other Carbo., 1½ Fat

Orange Curd: Prepare as above, except decrease sugar to ¾ cup; substitute orange peel for the lemon peel and ¾ cup orange juice for the lemon juice and water. Makes about 1½ cups.

Nutrition Facts per 2 tablespoons: 160 cal., 11 g total fat (6 g sat. fat), 128 mg chol., 87 mg sodium, 15 g carbo., 0 g fiber, 2 g pro.
Daily Values: 10% vit. A, 14% vit. C, 2% calcium, 2% iron
Exchanges: 1 Other Carbo., 2 Fat

Whipped Cream

Fast

Start to Finish: 10 minutes **Makes:** 2 cups

> 1 **cup whipping cream**
> 2 **tablespoons sugar**
> ½ **teaspoon vanilla**

1. Chill a medium mixing bowl and the beaters of an electric mixer.

2. In chilled bowl beat whipping cream, sugar, and vanilla with an electric mixer on medium speed until soft peaks form (see photo 1, page 169). Serve on pie or hot cocoa or in cream puffs.

Flavored Whipped Cream: Prepare as above, except add one of the following: 2 tablespoons unsweetened cocoa powder plus 1 tablespoon additional sugar; 2 tablespoons amaretto or coffee, hazelnut, orange, or praline liqueur; 1 teaspoon instant coffee crystals; ½ teaspoon almond extract; ½ teaspoon finely shredded lemon, orange, or lime peel; or ¼ teaspoon ground cinnamon, nutmeg, or ginger.

Nutrition Facts per 1 tablespoon plain or flavored variation: 29 cal., 3 g total fat (2 g sat. fat), 10 mg chol., 3 mg sodium, 1 g carbo., 0 g fiber, 0 g pro.
Daily Values: 2% vit. A
Exchanges: ½ Fat

Chapter 12
Eggs & Cheese

On the divider: Cheese Soufflé (see recipe, page 272)

Eggs & Cheese

For more recipes, visit our Recipe Center at **www.bhg.com**

Soft-Cooked Eggs

 **Fast** **Low Fat**

Start to Finish: 10 minutes **Makes:** 4 soft-cooked eggs

> **4 eggs**
> **Cold water**

1. Place eggs in a single layer in a medium saucepan. Add enough cold water to just cover the eggs. Bring to a rapid boil over high heat (water will have large rapidly breaking bubbles). Remove from heat, cover, and let stand for 3 to 4 minutes; drain.

2. Run cold water over the eggs or place them in ice water just until cool enough to handle; drain. Cut off tops and serve in egg cups. Or cut the eggs in half and use a spoon to scoop the eggs into serving dishes.

Nutrition Facts per egg: 78 cal., 5 g total fat (2 g sat. fat), 212 mg chol., 62 mg sodium, 1 g carbo., 0 g fiber, 6 g pro.
Daily Values: 6% vit. A, 3% calcium, 3% iron
Exchanges: 1 Medium-Fat Meat

Hard-Cooked Eggs

Sometimes hard-cooked eggs have an unattractive, but harmless, greenish ring around the yolk. To minimize the chances of a ring forming, time the cooking carefully. Cool hard-cooked eggs in ice water.

Fast **Low Fat**

Start to Finish: 25 minutes **Makes:** 4 hard-cooked eggs

> **4 eggs**
> **Cold water**

1. Place eggs in a single layer in a medium saucepan. Add enough cold water to just cover the eggs. Bring to a rapid boil over high heat (water will have large rapidly breaking bubbles). Remove from heat, cover, and let stand for 15 minutes; drain.

2. Run cold water over the eggs or place them in ice water until cool enough to handle; drain.

3. To peel eggs, gently tap each egg on the countertop. Roll the egg between the palms of your hands. Peel off eggshell, starting at the large end.

Nutrition Facts per egg: 78 cal., 5 g total fat (2 g sat. fat), 212 mg chol., 62 mg sodium, 1 g carbo., 0 g fiber, 6 g pro.
Daily Values: 6% vit. A, 3% calcium, 3% iron
Exchanges: 1 Medium-Fat Meat

Using Eggs Safely

Tasty egg dishes depend on eggs that are in top condition. Here are some egg-handling pointers to remember. For additional information, see page 22.

■ Select clean, fresh eggs from refrigerated display cases. Don't use dirty, cracked, or leaking eggs. They may have become contaminated with harmful bacteria.

■ When you arrive home from the grocery store, promptly refrigerate the eggs with the large ends up. Store them in their cartons because eggs easily absorb refrigerator odors. Fresh eggs can be refrigerated for up to 5 weeks after the packing date (a number stamped on the carton from 1 to 365 with 1 representing January 1 and 365 representing December 31) or about 3 weeks after you bring them home.

■ When cracking eggs, avoid getting any eggshell in the raw eggs. Also, when separating eggs, don't pass the yolk from shell half to shell half. Instead, use an egg separator so that if bacteria is present on shell, it won't contaminate either the yolk or the white.

■ To store raw egg whites, refrigerate them in a tightly covered container for up to 4 days. Or, place them in a freezer container and freeze for up to 1 year. Although you can refrigerate unbroken raw yolks covered with water in a tightly covered container for up to 2 days, you should not freeze them. To freeze whole eggs, beat the whites and yolks together, place in a freezer container, and freeze for up to 1 year. Refrigerate hard-cooked eggs in their shells for up to 7 days.

■ Be sure to wash your hands, utensils, and countertop after working with eggs.

■ Serve hot egg dishes as soon as they're cooked. Chill leftovers promptly and reheat thoroughly before serving. Refrigerate cold egg dishes immediately.

■ For more information on handling eggs safely, call the U.S. Department of Agriculture's Meat and Poultry Hotline at 800/535-4555 (202/720-3333 in the Washington, D.C., area).

Eggs Benedict Best Loved

The popularity of this classic recipe inspired chefs and home cooks to create new versions. Here you'll find the classic recipe as well as crab and vegetable-topped varieties.

Start to Finish: 35 minutes **Makes:** 4 servings

- 4 **eggs**
- 1 **recipe Hollandaise Sauce (page 476)**
- 2 **English muffins, split**
- 4 **slices Canadian-style bacon**
  Paprika (optional)

1. Lightly grease a medium skillet. Half fill the skillet with *water*. Bring water to boiling; reduce heat to simmering (bubbles should begin to break the surface of the water). Break one of the eggs into a measuring cup. Carefully slide egg into simmering water, holding the lip of the cup as close to the water as possible (see photo 1, page 265). Repeat with remaining eggs, allowing each egg an equal amount of space.

2. Simmer eggs, uncovered, for 3 to 5 minutes or until the whites are completely set and yolks begin to thicken but are not hard. Remove eggs with a slotted spoon and place them in a large pan of warm water to keep them warm. Prepare the Hollandaise Sauce.

3. Meanwhile, place muffin halves, cut sides up, on a baking sheet. Broil 3 to 4 inches from the heat about 2 minutes or until toasted. Top each muffin half with a slice of Canadian-style bacon; broil about 1 minute more or until meat is heated.

4. To serve, top each bacon-topped muffin half with an egg; spoon Hollandaise Sauce over eggs. If desired, sprinkle with paprika.

Crab Benedict: Prepare as above, except substitute one 6½-ounce can crabmeat, drained, flaked, and with the cartilage removed, for the Canadian-style bacon.

Nutrition Facts per serving for bacon or crab variation: 442 cal., 36 g total fat (19 g sat. fat), 451 mg chol., 836 mg sodium, 14 g carbo., 1 g fiber, 16 g pro.
Daily Values: 30% vit. A, 3% vit. C, 10% calcium, 12% iron
Exchanges: 1 Starch, 2 Medium-Fat Meat, 4½ Fat

Make-ahead directions: Prepare the eggs and toast English muffins as above. Place muffin halves in a greased 8×8×2-inch baking pan. Top each muffin half with a slice of Canadian-style bacon and 1 cooked egg. Cover and chill for up to 24 hours. To serve, prepare 1 recipe Mock Hollandaise Sauce (page 476); spoon sauce over eggs. Bake, covered, in a 350°F oven about 25 minutes or until heated through.

Nutrition Facts per serving: 335 cal., 22 g total fat (6 g sat. fat), 239 mg chol., 640 mg sodium, 14 g carbo., 1 g fiber, 15 g pro.
Daily Values: 9% vit. A, 1% vit. C, 9% calcium, 9% iron
Exchanges: 1 Starch, 1½ Medium-Fat Meat, 2 Fat

Deluxe Eggs Benedict: Prepare as at left, except in a skillet cook 1 medium red or green sweet pepper, seeded and sliced into rings, and 1 small onion, sliced and separated into rings, in 1 tablespoon melted butter or margarine until crisp-tender. After broiling bacon-topped English muffin halves, top with cooked vegetable mixture. To serve, add an egg to each muffin half; spoon Hollandaise Sauce over eggs. If desired, sprinkle with paprika.

Nutrition Facts per serving: 481 cal., 39 g total fat (21 g sat. fat), 459 mg chol., 868 mg sodium, 17 g carbo., 2 g fiber, 17 g pro.
Daily Values: 62% vit. A, 79% vit. C, 10% calcium, 13% iron
Exchanges: 1 Starch, 2 Medium-Fat Meat, 5½ Fat

Eggs Benedict

Poached Eggs

Fast   Low Fat

Start to Finish: 10 minutes

- 1 **to 2 teaspoons instant chicken bouillon granules (optional)**
  Eggs

1. If desired, lightly grease a medium skillet (for 3 or 4 eggs) or a 1-quart saucepan (for 1 or 2 eggs) with cooking oil or shortening. Half fill the skillet with *water*. If desired, stir in chicken bouillon granules. Bring the water to boiling; reduce heat to simmering (bubbles should begin to break surface).

2. Break 1 egg into a measuring cup. Carefully slide egg into simmering water, holding the lip of the cup as close to the water as possible (see photo 1, below). Repeat with remaining eggs, allowing each egg an equal amount of space.

3. Simmer eggs, uncovered, 3 to 5 minutes or until whites are completely set and yolks begin to thicken but are not hard. Remove eggs with a slotted spoon. Season with *salt* and *black pepper*.

Poaching-pan directions: Lightly grease each cup of an egg-poaching pan. Place poacher cups over the pan of boiling water (water should not touch bottoms of cups); reduce heat to simmering. Break an egg into a measuring cup. Carefully slide egg into a poacher cup. Repeat with remaining eggs (see photo 2, below). Cover and cook 4 to 6 minutes or until the whites are completely set and yolks begin to thicken but are not hard. Run a knife around edges to loosen eggs. Invert poacher cups to remove eggs.

Nutrition Facts per egg: 78 cal., 5 g total fat (2 g sat. fat), 212 mg chol., 62 mg sodium, 1 g carbo., 0 g fiber, 6 g pro.
Daily Values: 6% vit. A, 3% calcium, 3% iron
Exchanges: 1 Medium-Fat Meat

1. Using a measuring cup with a handle, gently slide each egg into the simmering water, taking care not to break the egg.

2. When using an egg-poaching pan, gently slide each egg from a measuring cup into a greased poacher cup.

Egg Substitutes

Refrigerated or frozen egg products are easy to use, readily available, and enable anyone on a cholesterol-restricted diet to enjoy great-tasting egg dishes. These products are based mostly on egg whites and contain less fat than whole eggs and no cholesterol. Use ¼ cup of either refrigerated or frozen egg product for each whole egg in scrambled egg dishes, omelets, quiches, and stratas. To replace hard-cooked eggs in salads and other recipes, cook the egg product as you would cook an omelet and cut it up.

Huevos Rancheros

This egg dish serves up a meal on its own because it includes something from the four basic food groups—eggs, a bit of cheese, bread in the form of tortillas, and vegetables.

Start to Finish: 40 minutes **Oven:** 300°F **Makes:** 4 servings

- 3 **tablespoons olive oil or cooking oil**
- 5 **6-inch corn tortillas**
- ½ **cup chopped onion (1 medium)**
- 2 **cloves garlic, minced**
- 1 **14½-ounce can tomatoes, drained and cut up**
- 1 **or 2 chipotle peppers in adobo sauce, chopped (see tip, page 64), or half of a 4-ounce can diced green chile peppers, drained**
- 2 **tablespoons snipped fresh cilantro**
- ¼ **teaspoon ground cumin**
- 8 **eggs**
- 1 **tablespoon water**
- ½ **cup shredded Monterey Jack cheese or crumbled queso fresco (2 ounces)**
  Cilantro or parsley sprigs (optional)

1. In a 12-inch skillet heat 2 tablespoons of the oil. Dip each tortilla, one at a time, into the oil just until hot. Drain tortillas on paper towels (do not stack), reserving oil in skillet. Keep 4 of the tortillas warm on a baking sheet in a 300° oven. Reserve remaining tortilla.

2. Meanwhile, for salsa, in the oil remaining in the skillet cook onion and garlic for 2 to 3 minutes or until tender. Stir in drained tomatoes, chile peppers, cilantro, and cumin. Bring to boiling; reduce heat. Simmer, uncovered, for 5 minutes. Transfer mixture to a blender container or food processor bowl. Tear reserved tortilla into pieces and add to blender or food processor. Cover and blend or process until a coarse puree. Keep warm.

3. In the skillet heat remaining 1 tablespoon oil over medium heat. Carefully break eggs into skillet. When whites are set, add water. Cover skillet and cook eggs to desired doneness (3 to 4 minutes for soft-set yolks or 4 to 5 minutes for firm-set yolks).

4. Place a warm tortilla on each of 4 dinner plates. Top each with 2 fried eggs. Spoon the warm salsa over the eggs. Sprinkle with cheese. If desired, garnish with cilantro sprigs.

Nutrition Facts per serving: 413 cal., 26 g total fat (7 g sat. fat), 437 mg chol., 397 mg sodium, 27 g carbo., 3 g fiber, 20 g pro.
Daily Values: 31% vit. A, 29% vit. C, 23% calcium, 22% iron
Exchanges: ½ Vegetable, 1½ Starch, 2 Medium-Fat Meat, ½ High-Fat Meat, 2 Fat

Fried Eggs

This simple method produces an egg similar to one cooked over easy, but you don't need to flip it and you use less fat.

Fast

Start to Finish: 10 minutes **Makes:** 4 fried eggs

> 2 teaspoons butter, margarine, or nonstick cooking spray
> 4 eggs
> 1 to 2 teaspoons water

1. In a large skillet melt butter over medium heat. (Or coat an unheated skillet with nonstick cooking spray before heating.) Break eggs into skillet. When whites are set, add water. Cover skillet and cook eggs for 3 to 4 minutes or until yolks begin to thicken but are not hard.

Nutrition Facts per egg: 92 cal., 7 g total fat (3 g sat. fat), 218 mg chol., 84 mg sodium, 1 g carbo., 0 g fiber, 6 g pro.
Daily Values: 8% vit. A, 3% calcium, 4% iron
Exchanges: 1 Medium-Fat Meat, ½ Fat

Baked Eggs

Baked eggs sometimes are referred to as shirred (SHERD) eggs.

Low Fat

Prep: 10 minutes **Bake:** 25 minutes **Oven:** 325°F
Makes: 3 servings

> Butter or margarine
> 6 eggs
> Snipped fresh chives or desired herb
> 6 tablespoons shredded cheddar, Swiss, or Monterey Jack cheese (optional)

1. Generously grease three 10-ounce casseroles with butter. Carefully break 2 eggs into each casserole; sprinkle with chives, *salt,* and *black pepper.* Set casseroles in a 13×9×2-inch baking pan; place on an oven rack. Pour *hot water* around casseroles in pan to a depth of 1 inch.

2. Bake in a 325° oven about 25 minutes or until the eggs are firm and the whites are opaque. If desired, after 20 minutes of baking, sprinkle shredded cheese on eggs. Bake for 5 to 10 minutes more or until eggs are cooked and cheese melts.

Nutrition Facts per serving: 167 cal., 12 g total fat (4 g sat. fat), 430 mg chol., 147 mg sodium, 1 g carbo., 0 g fiber, 13 g pro.
Daily Values: 15% vit. A, 5% calcium, 8% iron
Exchanges: 2 Medium-Fat Meat, ½ Fat

Deviled Eggs

Start to Finish: 35 minutes **Makes:** 12 servings

> 6 Hard-Cooked Eggs (page 263)
> ¼ cup mayonnaise or salad dressing
> 1 teaspoon prepared mustard
> 1 teaspoon vinegar
> Paprika or parsley sprigs (optional)

1. Halve hard-cooked eggs lengthwise and remove yolks. Set whites aside. Place yolks in a bowl; mash with a fork. Add mayonnaise, mustard, and vinegar; mix well. If desired, season with *salt* and *black pepper.* Stuff egg white halves with yolk mixture. If desired, garnish with paprika or parsley.

Italian-Style Deviled Eggs: Prepare as above, except omit mayonnaise, mustard, and vinegar. Stir ¼ cup bottled creamy Italian salad dressing and 2 tablespoons grated Parmesan cheese into mashed yolks; mix well.

Greek-Style Deviled Eggs: Prepare as above, except fold 2 tablespoons feta cheese, 1 tablespoon finely chopped pitted kalamata olives or other pitted ripe olives, and 2 teaspoons snipped fresh oregano into yolk mixture. If desired, season with *black pepper.*

Nutrition Facts per serving for plain, Italian, and Greek variations: 72 cal., 6 g total fat (1 g sat. fat), 109 mg chol., 62 mg sodium, 0 g carbo., 0 g fiber, 3 g pro.
Daily Values: 3% vit. A, 1% calcium, 2% iron
Exchanges: ½ Medium-Fat Meat, 1 Fat

Scrambled Eggs and New Potatoes

Instead of chopping your own potatoes, use 1½ cups loose-pack frozen or refrigerated hash browns in this hearty dish.

Fast

Start to Finish: 30 minutes **Makes:** 4 servings

> 2 cups coarsely chopped tiny new potatoes or round red potatoes
> ½ cup chopped onion (1 medium)
> ½ cup chopped green or red sweet pepper
> 2 tablespoons butter or margarine
> 6 eggs
> ¼ cup milk
> 1 cup diced cooked ham or Polish sausage
> ½ cup shredded cheddar cheese (2 ounces)

1. In a large nonstick or well-seasoned skillet cook the potatoes, onion, and sweet pepper in hot butter, covered, over medium-low heat for 10 to 15 minutes or until tender, stirring occasionally.

2. Meanwhile, in a medium bowl beat together eggs, milk, ¼ teaspoon *black pepper,* and ⅛ teaspoon *salt* with a rotary beater; stir in ham. Pour egg mixture over potato mixture. Cook, without stirring, until mixture begins to set on the bottom and around edge. With a spatula or a large spoon, lift and fold the partially cooked egg mixture so that the uncooked portion flows underneath. Continue cooking 4 minutes more or until mixture is cooked through but is still slightly moist.

3. Remove from heat; sprinkle with cheese. Cover and let stand for 1 to 2 minutes or until cheese melts.

Nutrition Facts per serving: 361 cal., 22 g total fat (10 g sat. fat), 372 mg chol., 853 mg sodium, 17 g carbo., 2 g fiber, 24 g pro.
Daily Values: 20% vit. A, 43% vit. C, 18% calcium, 13% iron
Exchanges: 1 Starch, 3 Medium-Fat Meat, 1 Fat

Scrambled Eggs

`Fast`

Start to Finish: 10 minutes **Makes:** 3 servings

> **6 eggs**
> **⅓ cup milk, half-and-half, or light cream**
> **¼ teaspoon salt**
> **Dash black pepper**
> **1 tablespoon butter or margarine**

1. In a medium bowl beat together eggs, milk, salt, and pepper with a rotary beater. In a large skillet melt butter over medium heat; pour in egg mixture. Cook over medium heat, without stirring, until mixture begins to set on the bottom and around edge.

2. With a spatula or a large spoon, lift and fold the partially cooked egg mixture so that the uncooked portion flows underneath (see photo 1, right). Continue cooking over medium heat for 2 to 3 minutes or until egg mixture is cooked through but is still glossy and moist (see photo 2, right). Remove from heat immediately.

Nutrition Facts per serving: 198 cal., 15 g total fat (6 g sat. fat), 438 mg chol., 375 mg sodium, 3 g carbo., 0 g fiber, 13 g pro.
Daily Values: 17% vit. A, 8% calcium, 8% iron
Exchanges: 2 Medium-Fat Meat, 1 Fat

Cheese-and-Onion Scrambled Eggs: Prepare as above, except cook 1 sliced green onion in the

butter for 30 seconds; add egg mixture and continue as directed. Fold in ½ cup shredded American cheese after the eggs begin to set.

Nutrition Facts per serving: 271 cal., 21 g total fat (10 g sat. fat), 456 mg chol., 646 mg sodium, 3 g carbo., 0 g fiber, 18 g pro.
Daily Values: 22% vit. A, 2% vit. C, 20% calcium, 9% iron
Exchanges: 2½ Medium-Fat Meat, 2 Fat

Mushroom Scrambled Eggs: Prepare as at left, except increase the butter to 2 tablespoons. Cook ½ cup sliced fresh mushrooms and 1 tablespoon chopped onion in the butter. Add 1 tablespoon snipped fresh parsley, ½ teaspoon dry mustard, and ¼ teaspoon Worcestershire sauce to beaten egg mixture. Add egg mixture to skillet and continue as directed.

Nutrition Facts per serving: 242 cal., 19 g total fat (9 g sat. fat), 449 mg chol., 422 mg sodium, 3 g carbo., 0 g fiber, 14 g pro.
Daily Values: 21% vit. A, 4% vit. C, 9% calcium, 9% iron
Exchanges: 2 Medium-Fat Meat, 2 Fat

Denver Scrambled Eggs: Prepare as at left, except omit salt and increase the butter to 2 tablespoons. Cook ⅓ cup diced cooked ham; ¼ cup chopped onion; one 2-ounce can mushroom stems and pieces, drained; and 2 tablespoons finely chopped green sweet pepper in butter. Add egg mixture to skillet and continue as directed.

Nutrition Facts per serving: 273 cal., 20 g total fat (9 g sat. fat), 458 mg chol., 534 mg sodium, 5 g carbo., 1 g fiber, 18 g pro.
Daily Values: 21% vit. A, 10% vit. C, 9% calcium, 11% iron
Exchanges: 1 Vegetable, 2½ Medium-Fat Meat, 1½ Fat

Low-Fat Scrambled Eggs: Prepare as at left, except substitute 3 whole eggs and 5 eggs whites for the 6 whole eggs. Substitute fat-free milk for the milk. Omit the butter and coat a nonstick skillet with nonstick cooking spray before cooking the egg mixture.

Nutrition Facts per serving: 112 cal., 5 g total fat (2 g sat. fat), 213 mg chol., 362 mg sodium, 3 g carbo., 0 g fiber, 13 g pro.
Daily Values: 7% vit. A, 6% calcium, 4% iron
Exchanges: 2 Lean Meat

1. As the egg mixture begins to set, lift and fold it, allowing the uncooked egg mixture to flow underneath the cooked mixture.

2. The egg mixture is done when it is set but still looks glossy and moist. Overcooking eggs makes them dry and rubbery.

Cheese and Mushroom Brunch Eggs

Use fat-free milk and refrigerated or frozen egg product for a lower-fat version.

Prep: 30 minutes **Bake:** 15 minutes **Oven:** 350°F
Stand: 10 minutes **Makes:** 6 servings

- 2 tablespoons butter or margarine
- 2 tablespoons all-purpose flour
- 1⅓ cups milk or fat-free milk
- ½ cup shredded Swiss or Gruyère cheese (2 ounces)
- ¼ cup grated Parmesan cheese
- ⅛ teaspoon salt
- ⅛ teaspoon ground nutmeg
  Nonstick cooking spray
- 1½ cups sliced fresh mushrooms, such as button, shiitake, or crimini
- ¼ cup thinly sliced green onions (2)
- 1 tablespoon butter
- 12 beaten eggs or 3 cups refrigerated or frozen egg product, thawed
  Tomato slices, cut in half

1. For sauce, in a medium saucepan melt the 2 tablespoons butter. Stir in flour. Cook and stir for 1 minute. Add milk all at once. Cook and stir over medium heat until thickened and bubbly. Stir in Swiss cheese, Parmesan cheese, salt, and nutmeg. Cook and stir over medium heat until cheeses melt. Remove from heat; set aside.

2. Coat an unheated large nonstick skillet with cooking spray. Heat skillet over medium heat. Cook mushrooms and green onions in skillet until tender. Transfer mushroom mixture to a small bowl; set aside.

3. For scrambled eggs, in the same skillet melt the 1 tablespoon butter. Add eggs. Cook over medium heat without stirring until eggs begin to set on the bottom and around the edge. Using a large spatula, lift and fold the partially cooked eggs so that the uncooked portion flows underneath (see photo 1, page 267). Continue cooking until the eggs are cooked through but are still glossy and moist (see photo 2, page 267).

4. Transfer half of the scrambled eggs to a 2-quart square baking dish. Spread half of the mushroom mixture over the eggs in the baking dish. Drizzle about half of the sauce over mushroom mixture. Repeat layers.

5. Bake, uncovered, in a 350° oven for 15 to 20 minutes or until heated through. Top with tomato. Let stand 10 minutes before serving.

Cheese and Mushroom Brunch Eggs for 12: Prepare as at left, except double all ingredients and use a 12-inch nonstick skillet. To scramble eggs, melt 1 tablespoon of the butter in the skillet. Beat 12 eggs together at one time and add them to butter in skillet. Cook as in step 3. Transfer scrambled eggs to a 3-quart rectangular baking dish. Scramble remaining 12 beaten eggs using remaining butter. Spread half of the mushroom mixture over eggs in baking dish; top with half of the sauce. Top with remaining eggs, mushroom mixture, and sauce. Bake, uncovered, about 25 minutes or until heated through. Top with tomato slices. Let stand 10 minutes before serving. Makes 12 servings.

Nutrition Facts per serving: 306 cal., 22 g total fat (10 g sat. fat), 458 mg chol., 369 mg sodium, 8 g carbo., 1 g fiber, 20 g pro.
Daily Values: 24% vit. A, 8% vit. C, 27% calcium, 11% iron
Exchanges: ½ Starch, 2½ Medium-Fat Meat, 1½ Fat

Scrambled Egg Pizza [Best Loved]

To give the pizza crust a decorative edge, make little cuts around the edge of the dough with kitchen scissors before baking.

Start to Finish: 45 minutes **Oven:** 375°F **Makes:** 10 servings

- 1 16-ounce loaf frozen whole wheat bread dough, thawed
- 1 cup chopped zucchini or green sweet pepper
- 1 cup sliced fresh mushrooms
- ¼ teaspoon crushed red pepper
- 1 tablespoon cooking oil
- 8 eggs
- ½ cup milk
- 1 tablespoon butter or margarine
- ¾ cup shredded mozzarella cheese (3 ounces)
- 2 slices bacon, crisp-cooked, drained, and crumbled

1. On a lightly floured surface, roll bread dough into a 14-inch circle. Transfer dough to a greased 13-inch pizza pan. Build up edges slightly. Prick dough generously with a fork. Bake in a 375° oven 15 to 20 minutes or until light brown.

2. Meanwhile, in a large skillet cook zucchini, mushrooms, and crushed red pepper in hot oil about 5 minutes or until vegetables are almost tender. Remove zucchini mixture and drain.

3. In a medium bowl beat together eggs and milk. In the same skillet melt butter over medium heat; pour in egg mixture. Cook, without stirring, until mixture begins to set on the bottom and around edge. Using a large spatula, lift and fold partially cooked egg mixture so that the uncooked portion flows underneath (see photo 1, page 267). Continue cooking over medium heat for 2 to 3 minutes or until egg mixture is cooked through but is still glossy and moist (see photo 2, page 267). Remove from heat.

4. Sprinkle half of the shredded cheese over the hot crust. Top with scrambled eggs, zucchini mixture, bacon, and remaining cheese. Bake for 5 to 8 minutes more or until cheese melts.

Nutrition Facts per serving: 238 cal., 11 g total fat (3 g sat. fat), 180 mg chol., 381 mg sodium, 24 g carbo., 2 g fiber, 14 g pro.
Daily Values: 8% vit. A, 2% vit. C, 9% calcium, 5% iron
Exchanges: 1½ Starch, 1½ Medium-Fat Meat

Puffy Omelet

Puffy omelets are cooked on the range top until they swell up and are set on the bottom. They're transferred to the oven to brown and set the top. Fill them with a combination of shredded cheese, strips of ham or chicken, and cooked vegetables.

`Fast`

Start to Finish: 30 minutes **Oven:** 325°F **Makes:** 2 servings

- 4 **egg whites**
- 2 **tablespoons water**
- 4 **beaten egg yolks**
- ¼ **teaspoon salt**
- ⅛ **teaspoon white pepper (optional)**
- 1 **tablespoon butter or margarine**

1. In a medium mixing bowl beat egg whites with an electric mixer on medium to high speed until frothy. Add water; continue beating about 1½ minutes or until stiff peaks form (tips stand straight). Fold in egg yolks, salt, and, if desired, white pepper.

2. In a large ovenproof skillet heat butter until a drop of water sizzles. Pour in egg mixture, mounding it slightly at the sides (see photo 1, right). Cook over low heat about 6 minutes or until puffed and set on the bottom. Bake in a 325° oven 10 to 12 minutes or until a knife inserted near the center comes out clean.

3. Loosen the omelet from the sides of the skillet with a metal spatula. Make a shallow cut slightly off-center across the omelet (see photo 2, below). Add filling ingredients as desired to larger side. Fold smaller side of omelet over larger side. Cut omelet in half. Serve immediately.

Nutrition Facts per serving unfilled omelet: 203 cal., 16 g total fat (7 g sat. fat), 441 mg chol., 479 mg sodium, 1 g carbo., 0 g fiber, 13 g pro.
Daily Values: 17% vit. A, 5% calcium, 8% iron
Exchanges: 2 Medium-Fat Meat, 1 Fat

1. Use a metal spatula to spread the egg mixture in the skillet. Mound the mixture slightly around the edge.

2. To fold the cooked omelet, make a slightly off-center shallow cut across the middle so that one portion is larger than the other.

Denver Omelet `Best Loved`

Chopped ham, mushrooms, green sweet pepper, and green onions fill this classic dish.

Start to Finish: 35 minutes **Oven:** 325°F **Makes:** 3 servings

- 1 **recipe Puffy Omelet**
- 1 **tablespoon butter or margarine**
- 1 **cup sliced fresh mushrooms**
- ¾ **cup chopped green sweet pepper (1 medium)**
- ½ **cup bias-sliced green onions (4)**
- ¼ **teaspoon dried basil, crushed**
- ½ **cup cooked ham, cut into julienne strips**
- ½ **cup cherry tomatoes, quartered**

1. Prepare Puffy Omelet as directed. While omelet is baking, prepare filling.

2. For filling, melt butter in a skillet. Add mushrooms, sweet pepper, green onions, and basil; cook and stir until tender but not brown. Stir in ham and cherry tomatoes; heat through.

3. Spoon filling over larger side of omelet. Fold smaller side over larger side. Cut into 3 portions. Serve immediately.

Nutrition Facts per serving: 244 cal., 18 g total fat (8 g sat. fat), 319 mg chol., 719 mg sodium, 7 g carbo., 2 g fiber, 16 g pro.
Daily Values: 24% vit. A, 62% vit. C, 6% calcium, 12% iron
Exchanges: 1½ Vegetable, 2 Medium-Fat Meat, 1½ Fat

French Omelet

French Omelet

`Fast`

Start to Finish: 10 minutes **Makes:** 1 serving

　　2 **eggs**
　　2 **tablespoons water**
　⅛ **teaspoon salt**
　　　Dash black pepper
　　1 **tablespoon butter**

1. In a small bowl combine eggs, water, salt, and pepper. Beat until combined but not frothy with a fork. Heat an 8-inch nonstick skillet with flared sides over medium-high heat until skillet is hot.

2. Add butter to skillet. When butter has melted, add egg mixture to skillet; lower heat to medium. Immediately begin stirring egg mixture gently but continuously with a wooden or plastic spatula until mixture resembles small pieces of cooked egg surrounded by liquid egg (see photo 1, right). Stop stirring. Cook 30 to 60 seconds more or until egg mixture is set but shiny.

3. If desired, spoon filling across center. With a spatula lift and fold an edge of the omelet about a third of the way toward the center (see photo

2, below). Remove from heat. Fold the opposite edge toward the center; transfer to a warm plate.

Nutrition Facts per serving without filling: 257 cal., 22 g total fat (11 g sat. fat), 458 mg chol., 541 mg sodium, 1 g carbo., 0 g fiber, 13 g pro.
Daily Values: 22% vit. A, 5% calcium, 8% iron
Exchanges: 2 Medium-Fat Meat, 2½ Fat

Lower-Cholesterol Omelet: Prepare as at left, except substitute 1 whole egg and 2 egg whites.

Nutrition Facts per serving: 215 cal., 17 g total fat (9 g sat. fat), 245 mg chol., 588 mg sodium, 1 g carbo., 0 g fiber, 13 g pro.
Daily Values: 16% vit. A, 3% calcium, 4% iron
Exchanges: 1 Very Lean Meat, 1 Medium-Fat Meat, 2½ Fat

Mushroom Omelet: For filling, in the 8-inch skillet cook ⅓ cup sliced fresh mushrooms in 1 teaspoon butter until tender. Remove from skillet; keep warm. Prepare omelet as at left, adding filling in step 3.

Nutrition Facts per serving: 301 cal., 27 g total fat (13 g sat. fat), 469 mg chol., 584 mg sodium, 2 g carbo., 0 g fiber, 14 g pro.
Daily Values: 25% vit. A, 6% calcium, 9% iron
Exchanges: ½ Vegetable, 2 Medium-Fat Meat, 3 Fat

Cheese Omelet: Prepare as at left, except omit salt. In step 3, sprinkle ¼ cup shredded cheddar, Swiss, or Monterey Jack cheese across center of omelet for filling.

Nutrition Facts per serving: 370 cal., 32 g total fat (17 g sat. fat), 487 mg chol., 426 mg sodium, 2 g carbo., 0 g fiber, 20 g pro.
Daily Values: 28% vit. A, 26% calcium, 9% iron
Exchanges: 2 Medium-Fat Meat, 1 High-Fat Meat, 2½ Fat

Fruit Omelet: Prepare as at left. In step 3, spread 2 tablespoons dairy sour cream or plain yogurt across center for filling. Fold in sides. Top with ¼ cup halved strawberries; sliced, peeled peaches; or blueberries. Sprinkle with 1 tablespoon brown sugar.

Nutrition Facts per serving: 352 cal., 27 g total fat (14 g sat. fat), 468 mg chol., 558 mg sodium, 14 g carbo., 1 g fiber, 14 g pro.
Daily Values: 26% vit. A, 34% vit. C, 9% calcium, 10% iron
Exchanges: 2 Medium-Fat Meat, 3½ Fat

1. As the egg mixture cooks, use a wooden or plastic spatula to stir it gently but continuously until it resembles small pieces of cooked egg surrounded by liquid egg.

2. When egg mixture is set but still looks shiny, spoon desired filling across the center. Loosen edges. Fold one edge, then the other, over filling, allowing edges to overlap.

Oven Omelet

`Fast`

Start to Finish: 25 minutes **Oven:** 400°F **Makes:** 6 servings

　　　Nonstick cooking spray
10　eggs
¼　cup water
½　teaspoon salt
⅛　teaspoon white or black pepper
1　recipe Ham and Vegetable Filling
1　cup shredded cheddar, Swiss, mozzarella, or Monterey Jack cheese (4 ounces)

1. Lightly coat a 15×10×1-inch baking pan with cooking spray; set aside. In a medium bowl beat together eggs, water, salt, and pepper with a fork or a rotary beater until combined but not frothy.

2. Place the prepared pan on an oven rack. Carefully pour the egg mixture into the pan. Bake in a 400° oven about 7 minutes or until egg mixture is set but still has a glossy surface.

3. Meanwhile, prepare Ham and Vegetable Filling; keep warm. Cut the baked egg mixture into six 5-inch square omelets. Remove each omelet using a large spatula. Invert omelets onto warm serving plates.

4. Divide Ham and Vegetable Filling among omelets, spooning over half of each square. Sprinkle with desired cheese. Fold the other omelet half over the filled half, forming a triangle or rectangle. Serve immediately.

Ham and Vegetable Filling: Stir together 2 cups of your favorite hot cooked vegetables (such as broccoli, zucchini, and/or red sweet peppers) and 1 cup hot chopped cooked ham.

Nutrition Facts per serving: 385 cal., 25 g total fat (11 g sat. fat), 582 mg chol., 1,170 mg sodium, 6 g carbo., 2 g fiber, 33 g pro.
Daily Values: 44% vit. A, 97% vit. C, 31% calcium, 17% iron
Exchanges: 1 Vegetable, 4 Medium-Fat Meat, 1 Fat

Oven Omelet with Tomato-Basil Filling: Prepare as above through step 3, except don't make filling. In a medium skillet heat 1 teaspoon olive oil; add 2 cups chopped plum tomatoes. Cook and stir over medium heat for 2 to 3 minutes or until heated through; remove from heat. Stir in 1 tablespoon snipped fresh basil. Proceed with step 4 using Tomato-Basil Filling.

Nutrition Facts per serving: 330 cal., 23 g total fat (10 g sat. fat), 561 mg chol., 633 mg sodium, 6 g carbo., 1 g fiber, 23 g pro.
Daily Values; 34% vit. A, 29% vit. C, 27% calcium, 14% iron
Exchanges: 1 Vegetable, 3 Medium-Fat Meat, 1½ Fat

Corn Frittata with Cheese

`Fast`

Start to Finish: 25 minutes **Makes:** 4 servings

8　slightly beaten eggs
1　tablespoon snipped fresh basil or 1 teaspoon dried basil, crushed
2　tablespoons olive oil
1　cup frozen whole kernel corn or cut fresh corn
½　cup chopped zucchini
⅓　cup thinly sliced green onions (3)
¾　cup chopped plum tomatoes (2)
½　cup shredded cheddar cheese (2 ounces)

1. In a medium bowl combine eggs and basil; set aside. Heat oil in a large broilerproof skillet; add corn, zucchini, and green onions. Cook and stir for 3 minutes; add tomatoes. Cook, uncovered, over medium heat about 5 minutes or until vegetables are crisp-tender, stirring occasionally.

2. Pour egg mixture over vegetables in skillet. Cook over medium heat. As mixture sets, run a spatula around edge of skillet, lifting egg mixture so uncooked portion flows underneath (see photo 1, page 267). Continue cooking and lifting edges until egg mixture is almost set (surface will be moist). Sprinkle with cheese.

3. Place the skillet under broiler 4 to 5 inches from heat. Broil for 1 to 2 minutes or until the top is just set and cheese is melted.

Nutrition Facts per serving: 313 cal., 22 g total fat (7 g sat. fat), 440 mg chol., 220 mg sodium, 13 g carbo., 2 g fiber, 18 g pro.
Daily Values: 22% vit. A, 19% vit. C, 16% calcium, 12% iron
Exchanges: 1 Vegetable, ½ Starch, 2 Medium-Fat Meat, 2 Fat

Corn Frittata with Cheese

Cheese Soufflé `Best Loved`

Using a combination of cheeses makes this light and airy soufflé taste even better (see photo, page 261).

Prep: 50 minutes **Bake:** 40 minutes
Oven: 350°F **Makes:** 4 servings

- 4 **egg yolks**
- 4 **egg whites**
- ¼ **cup butter or margarine**
- ¼ **cup all-purpose flour**
- ¼ **teaspoon dry mustard**
- **Dash ground red pepper**
- 1 **cup milk**
- 2 **cups shredded cheddar, colby, Havarti, and/or process Swiss cheese (8 ounces)**

1. Allow the egg yolks and egg whites to stand at room temperature for 30 minutes.

2. For cheese sauce, in a medium saucepan melt butter; stir in flour, dry mustard, and red pepper. Add milk all at once. Cook and stir over medium heat until thickened and bubbly. Remove from heat. Add cheese, a little at a time, stirring until melted. In a medium bowl beat egg yolks with a fork until combined. Slowly add cheese sauce to egg yolks, stirring constantly. Cool slightly.

3. In a large mixing bowl beat egg whites with an electric mixer on medium to high speed until stiff peaks form (tips stand straight). Gently fold about 1 cup of the stiffly beaten egg whites into cheese sauce (see photo, below).

4. Gradually pour cheese sauce over remaining stiffly beaten egg whites, folding to combine. Pour into an ungreased 1½-quart soufflé dish.

5. Bake in a 350° oven about 40 minutes or until a knife inserted near center comes out clean. Serve immediately (see tip, top right).

Nutrition Facts per serving: 469 cal., 37 g total fat (22 g sat. fat), 309 mg chol., 568 mg sodium, 10 g carbo., 0 g fiber, 23 g pro.
Daily Values: 30% vit. A, 1% vit. C, 51% calcium, 9% iron
Exchanges: ½ Starch, 3 High-Fat Meat, 2½ Fat

To fold some of the egg whites into the cheese sauce, use a spatula to cut down through the mixture, scrape across the bottom of the bowl, and come up to the surface.

Serving a Soufflé

A soufflé makes a great entrée when you're entertaining because it bakes for 40 minutes, giving you time to socialize.

■ Just make the salad and side dishes ahead, then pop the soufflé in the oven when your guests arrive. Just before the soufflé finishes baking, gather everyone around the table and wait for the oohs and ahs.

■ To cut your soufflé for serving, insert two forks back to back and gently pull it apart. Create serving-size wedges in this manner. Use a large serving spoon to transfer the soufflé portions to individual plates.

Farmer's Casserole

Here is a homey breakfast-style dish that is delicious for supper too.

`Low Fat`

Prep: 25 minutes **Bake:** 40 minutes
Oven: 350°F **Stand:** 5 minutes **Makes:** 6 servings

- **Nonstick cooking spray**
- 3 **cups frozen shredded hash brown potatoes**
- ¾ **cup shredded Monterey Jack cheese with jalapeño peppers or shredded cheddar cheese (3 ounces)**
- 1 **cup diced cooked ham or Canadian-style bacon**
- ¼ **cup sliced green onions (2)**
- 4 **beaten eggs or 1 cup refrigerated or frozen egg product, thawed**
- 1½ **cups milk or one 12-ounce can evaporated milk or evaporated fat-free milk**
- ⅛ **teaspoon salt**
- ⅛ **teaspoon black pepper**

1. Coat a 2-quart square baking dish with nonstick cooking spray. Arrange potatoes evenly in the bottom of the dish. Sprinkle with cheese, ham, and green onions.

2. In a bowl combine eggs, milk, salt, and pepper. Pour egg mixture over potato mixture.

3. Bake, uncovered, in a 350° oven 40 to 45 minutes or until a knife inserted near the center comes out clean. Let stand 5 minutes before serving.

Farmer's Casserole for 12: Prepare as above, except double all ingredients and use a 3-quart rectangular baking dish. Bake casserole, uncovered, for 45 to 55 minutes or until a knife inserted near center comes out clean. Let stand 5 minutes before serving. Makes 12 servings.

Make-ahead directions: Prepare as on page 272 through step 2. Cover; chill up to 24 hours. Bake, uncovered, in a 350° oven for 50 to 55 minutes or until a knife inserted near the center comes out clean. Let stand 5 minutes before serving.

Nutrition Facts per serving: 265 cal., 12 g total fat (6 g sat. fat), 175 mg chol., 590 mg sodium, 23 g carbo., 2 g fiber, 17 g pro. Daily Values: 11% vit. A, 13% vit. C, 21% calcium, 11% iron Exchanges: 1½ Starch, 2 Medium-Fat Meat

Ham-Asparagus Strata

Ham-Asparagus Strata `Best Loved`

Prep: 25 minutes **Chill:** 2 to 24 hours **Bake:** 1 hour
Oven: 325°F **Stand:** 10 minutes **Makes:** 6 servings

> 4 **English muffins, torn or cut into bite-size pieces (4 cups)**
> 2 **cups cubed cooked ham or chicken (10 ounces)**
> 1 **10-ounce package frozen cut asparagus or frozen cut broccoli, thawed and well drained, or 2 cups cut-up fresh cooked asparagus or broccoli**
> 4 **ounces process Swiss cheese, torn, or process Gruyère cheese, cut up**
> 4 **beaten eggs**
> ¼ **cup dairy sour cream**
> 1¼ **cups milk**
> 2 **tablespoons finely chopped onion**
> 1 **tablespoon Dijon-style mustard**

1. In a greased 2-quart square baking dish spread half of the English muffin pieces. Top with ham, asparagus, and cheese. Top with the remaining English muffin pieces.

2. In a bowl whisk together eggs and sour cream. Stir in milk, onion, mustard, and ⅛ teaspoon *black pepper.** Pour evenly over layers in dish. Cover and chill 2 to 24 hours.

3. Bake, uncovered, in a 325° oven for 60 to 65 minutes or until the internal temperature registers 170° on an instant-read thermometer. Let stand for 10 minutes before serving.

*Note: If using chicken, add ¼ teaspoon salt.

Nutrition Facts per serving: 349 cal., 16 g total fat (7 g sat. fat), 193 mg chol., 1,224 mg sodium, 25 g carbo., 2 g fiber, 26 g pro. Daily Values: 20% vit. A, 26% vit. C, 32% calcium, 15% iron Exchanges: ½ Vegetable, 1½ Starch, 3 Lean Meat, 2 Fat

Dijon Chicken Strata

This cheesy strata makes a wonderful brunch dish because you can assemble it the night before and bake it in the morning.

Prep: 25 minutes **Chill:** 2 to 24 hours **Bake:** 40 minutes
Oven: 325°F **Stand:** 10 minutes **Makes:** 10 to 12 servings

> 1 **8-ounce loaf French bread, cut into 1-inch cubes (8 cups)**
> 2 **cups chopped cooked chicken or turkey**
> 1 **4½-ounce jar sliced mushrooms, drained**
> ½ **cup sliced green onions (4)**
> 3 **cups shredded Colby Jack cheese or American cheese (12 ounces)**
> 5 **beaten eggs**
> 2½ **cups milk**
> 3 **tablespoons Dijon-style mustard**
> ¼ **teaspoon black pepper**

1. Place bread cubes in a greased 3-quart rectangular baking dish. Layer chicken, mushrooms, and green onions over bread; sprinkle with cheese.

2. In a large bowl whisk together eggs, milk, mustard, and pepper. Carefully pour over layers in dish. Cover and chill for 2 to 24 hours.

3. Bake, uncovered, in a 325° oven about 40 minutes or until a knife inserted near the center comes out clean. Let stand for 10 minutes before serving.

Nutrition Facts per serving: 327 cal., 18 g total fat (10 g sat. fat), 166 mg chol., 536 mg sodium, 17 g carbo., 1 g fiber, 23 g pro. Daily Values: 11% vit. A, 3% vit. C, 36% calcium, 9% iron Exchanges: 2 Starch, 2 Lean Meat, 1½ Fat

Quiche

This recipe offers several cheese options and allows you to select from ham, chicken, or crabmeat.

Prep: 25 minutes **Bake:** 52 minutes **Oven:** 450°/325°F
Stand: 10 minutes **Makes:** 6 servings

- 1 recipe Pastry for Single-Crust Pie (page 416)
- 4 beaten eggs
- 1½ cups half-and-half, light cream, or milk
- ¼ cup sliced green onions (2)
- ¼ teaspoon salt
- ⅛ teaspoon black pepper
  Dash ground nutmeg
- ¾ cup chopped cooked ham, chicken, or crabmeat (about 3½ ounces)
- 1½ cups shredded Swiss, cheddar, Monterey Jack, and/or Havarti cheese (6 ounces)
- 1 tablespoon all-purpose flour

1. Prepare and roll out Pastry for Single-Crust Pie. Line a 9-inch pie plate with pastry. Trim; crimp edge as desired. Line unpricked pastry with a double thickness of foil. Bake in a 450° oven for 8 minutes. Remove foil. Bake for 4 to 5 minutes more or until pastry is set and dry. Remove from oven. Reduce the oven temperature to 325°.

2. Meanwhile, in medium bowl stir together eggs, half-and-half, green onions, salt, pepper, and nutmeg. Stir in ham. In a small bowl toss together the cheese and flour. Add to egg mixture; mix well.

3. Pour egg mixture into hot, baked pastry shell. Bake in the 325° oven for 40 to 45 minutes or

until knife inserted near center comes out clean. Let stand 10 minutes before serving.

Vegetarian Quiche: Prepare as at left, except omit the ham and add ½ cup shredded carrot to the egg mixture.

Nutrition Facts per serving for ham or vegetarian variation: 411 cal., 28 g total fat (13 g sat. fat), 200 mg chol., 573 mg sodium, 19 g carbo., 1 g fiber, 20 g pro.
Daily Values: 15% vit. A, 2% vit. C, 36% calcium, 10% iron
Exchanges: 1 Starch, 2½ Medium-Fat Meat, 3 Fat

Spinach Quiche   Best Loved

Prep: 25 minutes **Bake:** 57 minutes **Oven:** 450°/325°F
Stand: 10 minutes **Makes:** 6 to 8 servings

- 1 recipe Pastry for Single-Crust Pie (page 416)
- ½ cup chopped onion (1 medium)
- 6 slices bacon, chopped
- 8 beaten eggs
- ½ cup dairy sour cream
- ½ cup half-and-half, light cream, or milk
- ¼ teaspoon salt
- ⅛ teaspoon white pepper
  Dash ground nutmeg (optional)
- 3 cups lightly packed chopped fresh spinach
- ⅔ cup shredded mozzarella cheese
- ½ cup shredded Swiss cheese (2 ounces)
  Cherry tomatoes, cut up (optional)

1. Prepare and roll out Pastry for Single-Crust Pie. Line a 9-inch pie plate with the pastry. Trim; crimp edge as desired. Line unpricked pastry shell with a double thickness of foil. Bake in a 450° oven for 8 minutes. Remove foil. Bake for 4 to 5 minutes more or until pastry is set and dry. Reduce oven temperature to 325°.

2. Meanwhile, in a large skillet cook onion and bacon until onion is tender and bacon is crisp. Drain on paper towels.

3. In a bowl stir together eggs, sour cream, half-and-half, salt, pepper, and, if desired, nutmeg. Stir in onion mixture, spinach, and cheeses.

4. Pour egg mixture into hot, baked pastry shell. Bake in the 325° oven 45 to 50 minutes or until a knife inserted near center comes out clean. If necessary, cover edge of crust with foil to prevent overbrowning. Let stand for 10 minutes before serving. If desired, garnish with cherry tomatoes.

Nutrition Facts per serving: 465 cal., 32 g total fat (13 g sat. fat), 320 mg chol., 479 mg sodium, 23 g carbo., 1 g fiber, 20 g pro.
Daily Values: 37% vit. A, 8% vit. C, 27% calcium, 15% iron
Exchanges: 1 Vegetable, 1 Starch, 2 Medium-Fat Meat, 4 Fat

Spinach Quiche

Cheesy Brunch Roll-Ups

To prevent tortillas from cracking as they are rolled, wrap the unfilled tortillas in foil and heat in a 350°F oven for 10 minutes.

Prep: 40 minutes **Bake:** 30 minutes **Oven:** 350°F
Stand: 10 minutes **Makes:** 4 servings

- 1½ **cups sliced fresh mushrooms**
- ½ **cup sliced green onions (4)**
- ½ **cup chopped fresh poblano chile pepper (see tip, page 64)**
- 2 **tablespoons butter or margarine**
- 8 **6-inch corn tortillas**
- 1½ **cups shredded cheddar cheese (6 ounces)**
- 4 **beaten eggs**
- 2 **cups milk**
- 1 **tablespoon all-purpose flour**
- ¼ **teaspoon garlic powder**
  Few drops bottled hot pepper sauce
- ½ **cup shredded cheddar cheese (2 ounces)**
  Sliced green onions (optional)
  Salsa (optional)

1. In a large skillet cook mushrooms, the ½ cup green onions, and chile pepper in butter until tender; drain. Divide mushroom mixture evenly among tortillas, spooning it along center of each one. Divide the 1½ cups cheese evenly among tortillas. Roll up tortillas. Place tortillas, seam sides down, in a greased 2-quart rectangular baking dish.

2. In a bowl combine eggs, milk, flour, garlic powder, and hot pepper sauce. Pour egg mixture over tortillas.

3. Bake, uncovered, in a 350° oven about 30 minutes or until edges are set and tortillas are golden (center may not be completely set until after standing time). Sprinkle the ½ cup cheese over top. Let stand 10 minutes. If desired, sprinkle with additional sliced green onions and serve with salsa.

Make-ahead directions: Prepare as above through step 2. Cover and chill for 2 to 24 hours. Bake, uncovered, in a 350° oven 30 to 35 minutes or until edges are set and tortillas are golden (center may not be completely set until after standing time). Sprinkle the ½ cup cheese over top. Let stand 10 minutes. If desired, sprinkle with additional sliced green onions and serve with salsa.

Nutrition Facts per serving: 583 cal., 34 g total fat (19 g sat. fat), 298 mg chol., 546 mg sodium, 41 g carbo., 3 g fiber, 30 g pro.
Daily Values: 32% vit. A, 97% vit. C, 65% calcium, 27% iron
Exchanges: ½ Milk, 1 Vegetable, 2 Starch, 4 Fat

Chile Rellenos Casserole Best Loved

Poblano peppers are either red or dark green in color and vary in strength from medium to hot. The red peppers are slightly sweeter than the green ones.

Prep: 20 minutes **Bake:** 15 minutes
Oven: 450°F **Stand:** 5 minutes **Makes:** 4 servings

- 2 **large fresh poblano chile peppers, fresh anaheim chile peppers, or green sweet peppers (8 ounces)**
- 1½ **cups shredded Monterey Jack cheese with jalapeño peppers or Mexican-blend cheese (6 ounces)**
- 3 **beaten eggs**
- ¼ **cup milk**
- ⅓ **cup all-purpose flour**
- ½ **teaspoon baking powder**
- ¼ **teaspoon ground red pepper**
  Picante sauce (optional)
  Dairy sour cream (optional)

1. Quarter the peppers and remove seeds, stems, and veins (see tip, page 64). Immerse peppers into boiling water for 3 minutes; drain. Invert peppers on paper towels to drain well. Place the peppers in a well-greased 2-quart square baking dish. Top with 1 cup of the cheese.

2. In a bowl combine eggs and milk. Add flour, baking powder, ground red pepper, and ⅛ teaspoon *salt*. Beat until smooth with a rotary beater. Pour egg mixture over peppers and cheese.

3. Bake, uncovered, in a 450° oven about 15 minutes or until a knife inserted into the egg mixture comes out clean. Sprinkle with the remaining ½ cup cheese. Let stand about 5 minutes or until cheese melts. If desired, serve with picante sauce and sour cream.

Nutrition Facts per serving: 286 cal., 18 g total fat (10 g sat. fat), 206 mg chol., 466 mg sodium, 14 g carbo., 0 g fiber, 18 g pro.
Daily Values: 26% vit. A, 207% vit. C, 38% calcium, 13% iron
Exchanges: 1 Vegetable, ½ Starch, 2 High-Fat Meat

Low-Fat Chile Rellenos Casserole: Prepare as above, except use reduced-fat Monterey Jack cheese with jalapeño peppers (or reduced-fat plain Monterey Jack cheese plus 2 teaspoons chopped jalapeño peppers) or reduced-fat Mexican-blend cheese. Substitute ¾ cup refrigerated or frozen egg product (thawed) for the eggs and fat-free milk for the milk.

Nutrition Facts per serving: 207 calories, 9 g total fat (6 g sat. fat), 30 mg chol., 569 mg sodium, 15 g carbo., 1 g fiber, 18 g pro.
Daily Values: 25% vit. A, 213% vit. C, 38% calcium, 15% iron
Exchanges: 1 Vegetable, ½ Starch, 2 Lean Meat

Cheese

In addition to its role as an important cooking ingredient, cheese complements almost any meal or makes a meal itself. Serve a cheese course—after the main course and before dessert—and let its worldly flavors and sumptuous textures transform a good meal into a special memory to savor. Or make cheese the basis of a simple get-together, serving it with fruit, bread, and wine. Best of all, there is a variety of cheese from which to choose, and no matter how full you are, there is always room for another little nibble of cheese!

Selecting and Serving Cheese

■ Cheese is made from the milk of cows, goats, and sheep, or a combination of any of these. The type of milk used greatly affects the flavor of the cheese, so try them all to find your favorites.

■ Aging enhances the flavor of cheese. The older the cheese, the stronger and sharper the flavor. The texture also gets harder as cheese ages.

■ For a cheese platter, choose three to five types. Select cheeses of different textures, flavor intensities, and milk sources. Fruit, bread, and wine are natural accompaniments.

■ Cheese should be served at room temperature. Colder temperatures mute the flavor and aroma, and also affect texture. For instance, the texture of a creamy style of cheese, such as St. André or Camembert, will be somewhat tough and rubbery when the cheese is cold. At room temperature, the same cheese will develop its characteristically smooth, rich texture.

■ Buy quality. When you use high-quality cheese as an ingredient, it will add more flavor to your dish than a mass-produced variety would. Although better cheeses are often more expensive, you can use smaller quantities. For a cheese tray, where the cheeses alone are the stars, seek out handcrafted cheese from small producers; the flavor difference can be dramatic. These cheeses are often found at specialty stores and farmers' markets. A locally made cheese can be as good or better than an imported, well-known variety.

■ Pairing wine with cheese is not difficult. The key is to match the wine's flavor intensity and mouth feel with that of the cheese. For instance, creamy-textured cheeses often pair well with heavy, dessert-type wines because they both have a thick, rich feel on the tongue. Tangy, fresh goat cheeses, on the other hand, often taste best with crisp white wines, such as Sauvignon Blanc and Pinot Grigio. The sharp, acidic flavors and light textures of these cheeses and wines complement each other perfectly.

■ Ask for a sample at the cheese counter, especially if you have the opportunity to sample different versions of the same style of cheese. This "head-to-head" sampling offers the best opportunity to compare quality.

Storing Cheese

Airtight packaging is the key to proper cheese storage. If the cheese has a rind, leave it on to keep the cheese fresh. Wrap unused cheese tightly in foil or plastic wrap, then seal it in a plastic bag or a container with a tight-fitting lid. Store the cheese in the refrigerator.

Most cheese comes stamped with a "sell by" date on the package. In general, the softer the cheese, the shorter the storage life. If there is no date on the container, soft cheeses, such as cottage and ricotta, should be stored no longer than 5 days after purchase. Firm and hard cheeses have less moisture and can be stored for longer periods. For instance, sharp cheddar may keep for weeks in your refrigerator, if properly wrapped. For longer storage, cheese can be frozen, but expect a quality compromise. Freezing usually destroys the texture and affects the flavor and aroma. For instance, semisoft and hard cheeses will be more crumbly, and soft cheeses may separate slightly. Because of these changes, it's best to reserve cheeses that have been frozen for use as ingredients—in casseroles, for example.

As cheese ages, it naturally develops more flavor and may develop surface mold. Most surface mold looks unappealing but is harmless. For firm cheese, cut away at least 1 inch around the moldy area and use the remaining cheese. Discard soft cheeses, such as cottage cheese, ricotta, and cream cheese, that have mold.

Manchego
Firm texture; mellow, buttery flavor; sheep's milk; Spain

Monterey Jack, dry
Hard texture; full-bodied, tangy flavor; cow's milk; United States (California)

Parmigiano-Reggiano
Hard texture; nutty, yet tangy flavor; cow's milk; Italy

Stilton
Soft, slightly crumbly texture; assertive flavor; cow's milk; England

Havarti
Soft texture; very mild flavor; cow's milk; Denmark, United States

Mozzarella, fresh
Soft texture; extremely mild flavor; traditionally made from buffalo milk, cow's milk more common; Italy, United States

Camembert
Soft texture; rich, mild flavor; cow's milk; France

Saint André
Soft texture; very rich, creamy, mild flavor; cow's milk (triple cream); France

Chèvre
Soft, spreadable texture; mild, slightly tangy flavor; goat's milk; France, United States

Gruyère
Firm texture; mild, nutty flavor; cow's milk; Switzerland, France

Gouda, aged
Firm to hard (depending on age); nutty, caramel-sweet flavor; cow's milk; Holland

Maytag blue
Soft and crumbly to slightly creamy texture; assertive, somewhat peppery flavor; cow's milk; United States (Iowa)

Swiss
Firm texture; mild flavor; cow's milk; Switzerland, United States

Asiago
Firm to hard texture; somewhat sharp flavor; cow's milk; Italy

White cheddar
Firm to crumbly texture; sharp flavor; cow's milk; United States

Feta
Firm to crumbly texture; sharp, tangy, and salty flavor; traditionally made from sheep's milk, but may also be made from goat's milk or cow's milk; Greece, United States

Pecorino Romano
Hard texture; sharp flavor; sheep's milk; Italy

French goat cheese
(*Crottin* or *Chabichou*)
Soft to firm texture (depending on age); mild to slightly sharp flavor; goat's milk; France

Chapter 13
Fish & Shellfish

On the divider: Veracruz-Style Red Snapper (see recipe, page 289)

Crispy Oven-Fried Fish

Fast **Low Fat**

Prep: 20 minutes **Bake:** 4 to 6 minutes per ½-inch thickness
Oven: 450°F **Makes:** 4 servings

 1 **pound fresh or frozen skinless cod, orange roughy, or catfish fillets**
 ¼ **cup milk**
 ⅓ **cup all-purpose flour**
 ⅓ **cup fine dry bread crumbs**
 ¼ **cup grated Parmesan cheese**
 ½ **teaspoon dried dill**
 ⅛ **teaspoon black pepper**
 2 **tablespoons butter or margarine, melted**

1. Thaw fish, if frozen. Rinse fish; pat dry with paper towels. Cut into 4 serving-size pieces, if necessary. Measure the thickness of each piece. Place milk in a shallow dish. Place flour in another shallow dish. In a third shallow dish combine bread crumbs, Parmesan cheese, dill, and pepper. Add melted butter; stir until combined.

2. Dip fish in the milk; coat with flour. Dip again in the milk, then in the bread crumb mixture. Place fish on a greased baking sheet. Bake, uncovered, in a 450° oven for 4 to 6 minutes per ½-inch thickness or until fish flakes easily when tested with a fork.

Nutrition Facts per serving: 242 cal., 9 g total fat (5 g sat. fat), 71 mg chol., 423 mg sodium, 13 g carbo., 1 g fiber, 25 g pro.
Daily Values: 7% vit. A, 2% vit. C, 14% calcium, 8% iron
Exchanges: 1 Starch, 3 Very Lean Meat, 1 Fat

Dijon Mustard Fillets

Fast **Low Fat**

Start to Finish: 15 minutes **Makes:** 4 servings

 1 **pound fresh or frozen fish fillets, ½ to 1 inch thick**
 ½ **teaspoon lemon-pepper seasoning**
 ¼ **cup dairy sour cream**
 1 **tablespoon milk**
 1 **tablespoon Dijon-style mustard**
 2 **teaspoons snipped fresh chives or chopped green onion tops**
 2 **to 3 teaspoons capers, drained (optional)**

1. Thaw fish, if frozen. Rinse fish; pat dry with paper towels. Cut into 4 serving-size pieces, if necessary. Measure thickness of fish. Place fish on the greased unheated rack of a broiler pan. Turn any thin portions under to make uniform thickness. Sprinkle with lemon-pepper seasoning.

2. Broil 4 inches from the heat until fish flakes easily when tested with a fork (allow 4 to 6 minutes per ½-inch thickness of fish). (If fillets are 1 inch thick, turn once halfway through broiling.)

3. Meanwhile, in a small saucepan stir together sour cream, milk, mustard, and chives. Cook and stir over low heat until heated through (do not boil). Spoon sauce over fish to serve. Sprinkle with capers, if desired.

Nutrition Facts per serving: 112 cal., 4 g total fat (2 g sat. fat), 28 mg chol., 237 mg sodium, 1 g carbo., 0 g fiber, 17 g pro.
Daily Values: 4% vit. A, 1% vit. C, 6% calcium, 2% iron
Exchanges: 2½ Very Lean Meat, ½ Fat

Selecting Fish

Freshness First
Trust your eyes and nose when shopping for fish. Look for fish with:

■ Clear, bright bulging eyes with black pupils
■ Shiny, taut, bright skin
■ Red gills that are not slippery
■ Flesh that feels firm, elastic, and tight to bone
■ Moist, cleanly cut fillets and steaks

What to Avoid:

■ Strong "fishy" odor
■ Dull, bloody, or sunken eyes
■ Fading skin with bruises, red spots, or browning or yellowing at edges of flesh
■ Ragged-cut fillets and steaks

Frozen Fish
Flesh should be solidly frozen and glossy without dry papery edges. Avoid packages that have torn wrappers, frost, or blood visible inside or out.

Common Fish Forms
Whole or round: as it comes from the water
Drawn: whole fish with internal organs removed; may or may not be scaled
Dressed: ready to cook; organs, scales, gills, and fins have been removed (pan-dressed fish have heads and tails removed)
Steak: ready to cook; crosscut slice (½ to 1 inch thick) from a large, dressed fish
Fillet: ready to cook; boneless piece cut from the side and away from the backbone; may or may not be skinned

Questions?
Call the U.S. Food and Drug Administration's Center for Food Safety and Applied Nutrition Outreach Center, 888/723-3366, weekdays from 10 a.m. to 4 p.m. (Eastern Standard Time).

Baked Fish with Mushrooms

Almost any fish will taste delicious in this dish. Choose your favorite fillets. If you're undecided, see Guide to Fish Types, page 302.

Fast **Low Fat**

Prep: 15 minutes **Bake:** 12 minutes
Oven: 450°F **Makes:** 4 servings

- **1 pound fresh or frozen fish fillets, ½ to ¾ inch thick**
- **2 tablespoons butter or margarine**
- **1½ cups sliced fresh mushrooms**
- **¼ cup sliced green onions (2)**
- **1 teaspoon snipped fresh tarragon or thyme, or ¼ teaspoon dried tarragon or thyme, crushed**

1. Thaw fish, if frozen. Rinse fish; pat dry with paper towels. Cut into 4 serving-size pieces, if necessary. Arrange fish in a 2-quart rectangular baking dish, turning under thin edges. Sprinkle with *salt*.

2. In a small saucepan melt butter; add mushrooms, green onions, and dried tarragon, if using. Cook over medium heat until mushrooms and green onions are tender. Spoon mushroom mixture over fish; sprinkle with fresh tarragon, if using. Bake, covered, in a 450° oven for 12 to 18 minutes or until fish flakes easily when tested with a fork.

Nutrition Facts per serving: 159 cal., 8 g total fat (4 g sat. fat), 71 mg chol., 104 mg sodium, 1 g carbo., 0 g fiber, 22 g pro.
Daily Values: 5% vit. A, 2% vit. C, 1% calcium, 2% iron
Exchanges: 3 Very Lean Meat, 1 Fat

What is a serving?

Fish and shellfish come in many shapes and sizes. Use the following guidelines to determine portion sizes.

One-serving-size equivalents:
- 12 ounces to 1 pound of whole fish
- 8 ounces of drawn or dressed fish
- 4 to 5 ounces of steaks or fillets
- 1 pound live crabs
- 3 to 4 ounces of shelled shrimp
- One 1- to 1½-pound whole lobster, one 8-ounce lobster tail, or 4 to 5 ounces of cooked lobster meat

Red Snapper with Orange-Ginger Sauce

Fast **Low Fat**

Prep: 20 minutes **Cook:** 4 to 6 minutes per ½-inch thickness
Makes: 4 servings

- **1 pound fresh or frozen skinless red snapper or whitefish fillets, ½ to 1 inch thick**
- **¼ teaspoon salt**
- **⅛ teaspoon black pepper**
- **½ cup chicken broth**
- **½ cup water**
- **¼ cup sliced green onions (2)**
- **3 tablespoons frozen orange juice concentrate, thawed**
- **3 tablespoons water**
- **2 tablespoons reduced-sodium soy sauce**
- **1 tablespoon honey**
- **1 teaspoon toasted sesame oil**
- **½ teaspoon grated fresh ginger or ¼ teaspoon ground ginger**
- **6 cups torn mixed greens, such as spinach, Swiss chard, and/or mustard, beet, or collard greens**

1. Thaw fish, if frozen. Rinse fish; pat dry with paper towels. Cut fish into 4 serving-size pieces, if necessary. Sprinkle with salt and pepper. In a large skillet, combine the chicken broth, the ½ cup water, and green onions. Bring to boiling; add fish. Return to boiling; reduce heat. Simmer, covered, for 4 to 6 minutes per ½-inch thickness of fish or until fish flakes easily when tested with a fork. Remove fish; set aside and keep warm.

2. Meanwhile, for sauce, in a small bowl combine orange juice concentrate, the 3 tablespoons water, soy sauce, honey, sesame oil, and ginger.

3. Discard cooking liquid from skillet. Add the orange juice concentrate mixture to the skillet; bring to boiling. Boil gently, uncovered, for 1 minute, stirring once. Remove from heat. Place the greens in a large bowl. Pour half of the sauce over mixed greens, tossing to coat.

4. To serve, arrange greens on a platter. Place fish on top of greens; drizzle with remaining sauce.

Nutrition Facts per serving: 181 cal., 4 g total fat (1 g sat. fat), 41 mg chol., 493 mg sodium, 11 g carbo., 1 g fiber, 26 g pro.
Daily Values: 64% vit. A, 55% vit. C, 8% calcium, 11% iron
Exchanges: 2 Vegetable, 3½ Very Lean Meat

Fish Fillets and Baby Spinach with Balsamic Vinaigrette

`Fast` `Low Fat`

Start to Finish: 30 minutes **Makes:** 4 servings

- 1 **pound fresh or frozen skinless cod or orange roughy fillets, ¾ to 1 inch thick**
- 4 **cups baby spinach leaves, trimmed**
- 1 **medium onion, cut into thin wedges**
- 3 **tablespoons olive oil or cooking oil**
- 1 **medium red or yellow sweet pepper, cut into thin strips**
- 2 **tablespoons balsamic vinegar**
- 1 **tablespoon honey**

1. Thaw fish, if frozen. Rinse fish; pat dry with paper towels. Cut fish into 4 serving-size pieces, if necessary. Set aside. Place spinach in a large bowl; set aside. In a large skillet cook onion in 1 tablespoon of the oil over medium heat for 5 to 6 minutes or until tender and slightly golden. Add sweet pepper; cook and stir 1 minute more. Remove from heat. Stir onion mixture into spinach; transfer to a serving platter. Set aside.

2. Meanwhile, sprinkle fish fillets with ⅛ teaspoon *salt* and ⅛ teaspoon *black pepper*. In same large skillet heat the remaining 2 tablespoons oil over medium-high heat. Add fish; cook 4 minutes. Carefully turn fish. Reduce heat to medium; cook 3 minutes more or until fish flakes easily when tested with a fork. Place fish fillets on top of wilted spinach; cover to keep warm.

3. In a small bowl stir together the balsamic vinegar and honey. Add to skillet. Cook and stir until heated through, scraping up any browned bits. To serve, spoon balsamic vinaigrette over fish and spinach.

Nutrition Facts per serving: 225 cal., 11 g total fat (2 g sat. fat), 49 mg chol., 159 mg sodium, 10 g carbo., 2 g fiber, 22 g pro.
Daily Values: 71% vit. A, 93% vit. C, 6% calcium, 8% iron
Exchanges: 2 Vegetable, 2½ Very Lean Meat, 2 Fat

Fish Tacos `Best Loved`

`Fast`

Start to Finish: 20 minutes **Oven:** 450°F **Makes:** 4 servings

- 1 **pound fresh or frozen skinless cod, orange roughy, or other fish fillets**
- 2 **tablespoons butter or margarine, melted**
- ¼ **teaspoon ground cumin**
- ⅛ **teaspoon garlic powder**
- 3 **tablespoons mayonnaise or salad dressing**
- 1 **teaspoon lime juice**
- 1½ **cups packaged shredded cabbage with carrot (coleslaw mix) or shredded cabbage**
- 8 **corn taco shells, warmed according to package directions**
- 1 **recipe Mango Salsa (page 291)**

1. Thaw fish, if frozen. Rinse fish and pat dry with paper towels. Cut fish crosswise into ¾-inch slices. Place fish in single layer in greased shallow baking pan. Combine butter, cumin, and garlic powder. Brush over fish. Bake in a 450° oven for 4 to 6 minutes or until fish flakes easily when tested with a fork.

2. Meanwhile, in a medium bowl stir together mayonnaise and lime juice. Add cabbage; toss to coat. Spoon some of the coleslaw mixture into each taco shell; add fish slices. Top with Mango Salsa.

Nutrition Facts per serving: 435 cal., 25 g total fat (7 g sat. fat), 71 mg chol., 433 mg sodium, 32 g carbo., 5 g fiber, 23 g pro.
Daily Values: 87% vit. A, 140% vit. C, 9% calcium, 9% iron
Exchanges: ½ Vegetable, ½ Fruit, 1½ Starch, 2½ Very Lean Meat, 4 Fat

Fish Tacos

Fish Fillet Muffuletta

Fast

Start to Finish: 25 minutes **Makes:** 4 sandwiches

- **4 frozen battered or breaded fish fillets**
- **3 tablespoons mayonnaise or salad dressing**
- **1 teaspoon finely shredded lime peel**
- **2 teaspoons lime juice**
- **1 cup packaged shredded cabbage with carrot (coleslaw mix) or shredded cabbage**
- **4 3½- to 4-inch French-style or club rolls, split**
- **½ cup bottled salsa**
- **½ cup sliced pitted kalamata olives**
- **2 tablespoons capers, drained**

1. Cook fish according to package directions. Meanwhile, in a medium bowl stir together mayonnaise, lime peel, and lime juice. Add cabbage; stir until combined. Set aside. Hollow out the inside of top halves of each roll, leaving a ½-inch-thick shell. Place a fish fillet on the bottom half of each roll. Top with cabbage mixture and salsa. Sprinkle with olives and capers. Add roll tops.

Nutrition Facts per sandwich: 383 cal., 22 g total fat (3 g sat. fat), 26 mg chol., 1,165 mg sodium, 37 g carbo., 3 g fiber, 12 g pro.
Daily Values: 43% vit. A, 16% vit. C, 7% calcium, 15% iron
Exchanges: 1 Vegetable, 2 Starch, 1 Very Lean Meat, 3½ Fat

Marinated Fish Steaks

Low Fat

Prep: 15 minutes **Marinate:** 30 minutes
Broil: 8 minutes **Makes:** 4 servings

- **1 pound fresh or frozen salmon, swordfish, or halibut steaks, 1 inch thick**
- **2 tablespoons lime juice or lemon juice**
- **1 tablespoon snipped fresh oregano or thyme, or ½ teaspoon dried oregano or thyme, crushed**
- **2 teaspoons olive oil**
- **2 cloves garlic, minced**
- **1 teaspoon lemon-pepper seasoning**
- **4 lime wedges**

1. Thaw fish, if frozen. Rinse fish steaks; pat dry with paper towels. Cut into 4 serving-size pieces, if necessary. For marinade, in a shallow dish combine lime juice, oregano, oil, garlic, and lemon-pepper seasoning. Add fish; turn to coat with marinade. Cover and marinate in refrigerator for 30 minutes to 1½ hours, turning steaks occasionally.

2. Drain fish, reserving marinade. Place fish on the greased unheated rack of a broiler pan. Broil 4 inches from the heat for 8 to 12 minutes or until fish flakes easily when tested with a fork, turning once and brushing with reserved marinade halfway through cooking. Discard any remaining marinade. Before serving, squeeze the juice from 1 lime wedge over each steak.

Nutrition Facts per serving: 158 cal., 6 g total fat (1 g sat. fat), 59 mg chol., 348 mg sodium, 2 g carbo., 0 g fiber, 23 g pro.
Daily Values: 3% vit. A, 7% vit. C, 2% calcium, 5% iron
Exchanges: 3 Lean Meat

Poached Fish with Dill Sauce

Low Fat

Prep: 25 minutes **Cook:** 15 minutes **Makes:** 6 servings

- **1 2- to 2½-pound fresh or frozen dressed or pan-dressed fish (see tip, page 281)**
- **3 lemon slices**
- **1 bay leaf**
- **½ teaspoon salt**
- **2 tablespoons butter or margarine**
- **4 teaspoons all-purpose flour**
- **½ teaspoon sugar**
- **2 teaspoons snipped fresh dill or ½ teaspoon dried dill**
- **Dash salt**
- **1 slightly beaten egg yolk**

1. Thaw fish, if frozen. Rinse fish; pat dry with paper towels. In a fish poacher or a large roasting pan that has a wire rack with handles, add enough water to almost reach the rack. Remove and grease rack; set aside. To water in pan add lemon slices, bay leaf, and the ½ teaspoon salt. Place pan over two burners on range top. Bring to boiling; reduce heat. Place fish on rack and lower into pan. Simmer, covered, for 15 to 20 minutes or until fish flakes easily when tested with a fork. Remove fish; keep warm while preparing sauce.

2. For dill sauce, strain cooking liquid, reserving 1 cup. In a small saucepan melt butter; stir in flour, sugar, dill, and the dash salt. Add reserved 1 cup liquid. Cook and stir until thickened and bubbly. Gradually stir about ½ cup of the hot butter mixture into beaten egg yolk; return egg yolk mixture to saucepan. Cook and stir 1 minute more. Pass dill sauce with fish.

Nutrition Facts per serving: 190 cal., 7 g total fat (3 g sat. fat), 118 mg chol., 285 mg sodium, 2 g carbo., 0 g fiber, 29 g pro.
Daily Values: 5% vit. A, 4% vit. C, 3% calcium, 4% iron
Exchanges: 4 Very Lean Meat, 1 Fat

Orange Roughy with Lemon Sauce

Fast **Low Fat**

Start to Finish: 20 minutes **Makes:** 4 servings

- 1 **pound fresh or frozen orange roughy or red snapper fillets, about ½ inch thick**
- 1 **pound asparagus spears**
- 1 **14-ounce can reduced-sodium chicken broth**
- 2 **teaspoons finely shredded lemon peel**
- ⅛ **teaspoon black pepper**
- 1 **medium yellow sweet pepper, cut into strips**
- 4 **teaspoons cornstarch**
- 2 **tablespoons snipped fresh chives**
- 2 **cups hot cooked couscous or rice**

1. Thaw fish, if frozen. Rinse fish; pat dry. Cut fish into 4 serving-size pieces, if necessary; set aside. Snap off and discard woody bases from asparagus. Cut asparagus in half; set aside.

2. In a large skillet combine 1 cup of the broth, the lemon peel, and black pepper. Bring to boiling; reduce heat. Carefully add fish and asparagus. Cook, covered, over medium-low heat for 4 minutes. Add sweet pepper strips. Cook, covered, 2 minutes more or until fish flakes easily when tested with a fork. Using a slotted spatula, transfer fish and vegetables to a serving platter, reserving liquid in skillet. Keep fish and vegetables warm while preparing sauce.

3. For sauce, stir together remaining broth and cornstarch. Stir into liquid in skillet. Cook and stir until thickened and bubbly. Cook and stir for 2 minutes more. Stir in chives. Arrange fish and vegetables on couscous; spoon sauce over top.

Nutrition Facts per serving: 209 cal., 1 g total fat (0 g sat. fat), 23 mg chol., 345 mg sodium, 25 g carbo., 2 g fiber, 23 g pro.
Daily Values: 6% vit. A, 108% vit. C, 6% calcium, 6% iron
Exchanges: 2 Vegetable, 1 Starch, 3 Very Lean Meat

Thawing Fish

Your best bet for safety and quality is to thaw fish or shellfish slowly in the refrigerator. Place the unopened package of fish or shellfish in a container in the refrigerator, allowing overnight thawing for a 1-pound package. If necessary, you can place the wrapped package under cold running water for 1 to 2 minutes to hasten thawing. Don't thaw fish or shellfish in warm water or at room temperature and do not refreeze fish; it is unsafe.

Orange Roughy with Lemon Sauce

Salmon with Pesto Mayo

Fast

Start to Finish: 20 minutes **Makes:** 4 servings

- 4 **5- to 6-ounce fresh or frozen skinless salmon fillets**
- 2 **tablespoons crumbled firm-textured bread**
- ¼ **cup mayonnaise or salad dressing**
- 3 **tablespoons purchased basil pesto**
- 1 **tablespoon grated Parmesan cheese**

1. Thaw fish, if frozen. Rinse fish; pat dry with paper towels. Set aside. Place crumbled bread in a shallow baking pan. Broil 4 inches from heat for 1 to 2 minutes or until bread crumbs are lightly toasted, stirring once. Set bread crumbs aside.

2. Measure thickness of fish. Place fish on the greased unheated rack of broiler pan, tucking under any thin edges. Broil 4 inches from heat for 4 to 6 minutes per ½-inch thickness or until fish flakes easily when tested with a fork. (If fillets are 1 inch thick, turn once halfway through broiling.)

3. Meanwhile, in a small bowl stir together mayonnaise and pesto; set aside. Combine toasted bread crumbs and Parmesan cheese. Spoon mayonnaise mixture over fillets. Sprinkle with crumb mixture. Broil 1 to 2 minutes more or until crumbs are lightly browned.

Nutrition Facts per serving: 354 cal., 24 g total fat (3 g sat. fat), 84 mg chol., 291 mg sodium, 3 g carbo., 0 g fiber, 30 g pro.
Daily Values: 4% vit. A, 4% calcium, 7% iron
Exchanges: 4½ Lean Meat, 2½ Fat

Sea Bass with Fruited Tomatillo Salsa

Low Fat

Prep: 25 minutes **Bake:** 15 minutes
Oven: 450°F **Makes:** 4 servings

  4 fresh or frozen sea bass steaks, 1 inch thick
  1 cup chopped pineapple
  ½ cup chopped, peeled peaches or nectarines
  ½ cup chopped tomatillos
  2 tablespoons snipped fresh cilantro
  1 tablespoon finely chopped green onion
  1 fresh serrano chile pepper, seeded and chopped (see tip, page 64)
  1 teaspoon finely shredded lime peel
  1 tablespoon lime juice
  2 teaspoons honey
  1 cup quick-cooking couscous

1. Thaw fish, if frozen. Rinse fish; pat dry with paper towels. Set aside. For salsa, combine pineapple, peaches, tomatillos, cilantro, green onion, and chile pepper. Stir in lime peel, lime juice, and honey; set aside. Combine the couscous, 1 cup boiling *water*, and ¼ teaspoon *salt*.

2. Spread couscous evenly in a greased 2-quart rectangular baking dish. Arrange fish over couscous. Spoon salsa over fish. Loosely cover and bake in a 450° oven for 15 to 18 minutes or until fish flakes easily when tested with a fork.

Nutrition Facts per serving: 357 cal., 3 g total fat (1 g sat. fat), 58 mg chol., 250 mg sodium, 47 g carbo., 4 g fiber, 33 g pro.
Daily Values: 18% vit. A, 72% vit. C, 3% calcium, 7% iron
Exchanges: 1 Fruit, 2 Starch, 4 Very Lean Meat

Fennel and Fish au Gratin

Bulb shaped with feathery, dill-like leaves, fennel has a mild licorice flavor and a celerylike texture. Cooking makes the flavor more delicate.

Low Fat

Prep: 45 minutes **Bake:** 8 minutes
Oven: 425°F **Makes:** 4 servings

  1 pound fresh or frozen skinless orange roughy, salmon, or other fish fillets, ½ to ¾ inch thick
  2 large fennel bulbs with leaves
  1½ cups coarsely shredded carrot
  1¼ cups milk
  3 tablespoons all-purpose flour
  ¼ teaspoon salt
  ⅛ teaspoon black pepper
  3 tablespoons fine dry bread crumbs
  2 tablespoons grated Parmesan cheese
  1 tablespoon butter or margarine, melted

1. Thaw fish, if frozen. Rinse fish; pat dry with paper towels. Cut into 4 serving-size pieces, if necessary. Set aside.

2. Remove upper stalks from fennel, including feathery leaves; reserve leaves and discard stalks. Discard any wilted outer layers on fennel bulbs; cut off a thin slice from each base. Wash fennel and pat dry. Quarter each fennel bulb lengthwise and remove core; slice each portion crosswise (should have about 3 cups sliced fennel). Chop enough of the reserved fennel leaves to make ¼ cup; set aside.

3. In a large covered saucepan cook sliced fennel in a small amount of lightly salted boiling water for 8 to 10 minutes or until tender, adding the carrots the last 1 minute of cooking; drain. Transfer vegetables to a 2-quart square or rectangular baking dish. Rinse saucepan.

4. Meanwhile, in a large skillet cook the fish, covered, in a small amount of lightly salted simmering water until fish flakes easily when tested with a fork (allow 4 to 6 minutes per ½-inch thickness of fish); drain. Arrange fish on top of vegetables in baking dish.

5. For sauce, in the large saucepan combine the milk and flour with a whisk. Cook and stir over medium heat until thickened and bubbly. Stir in the chopped fennel leaves, salt, and pepper. Pour sauce over fish and vegetables. Combine bread crumbs, Parmesan cheese, and butter; sprinkle over the sauce. Bake, uncovered, in a 425° oven for 8 to 10 minutes or until crumbs are browned and crisp.

Nutrition Facts per serving: 228 cal., 7 g total fat (3 g sat. fat), 38 mg chol., 475 mg sodium, 20 g carbo., 19 g fiber, 23 g pro.
Daily Values: 263% vit. A, 21% vit. C, 22% calcium, 5% iron
Exchanges: 2½ Vegetable, ½ Starch, 2½ Very Lean Meat, 1 Fat

Storing Fish

Sooner is better when it comes to cooking fish. When that's not possible, wrap fresh fish loosely in plastic wrap, store in the coldest part of the refrigerator, and use within 2 days. Cover and refrigerate any leftover cooked fish and use within 2 days.

If you purchase frozen fish, keep it in a freezer set at 0°F or lower for up to 3 months. If you cut your own fillets or steaks, put them in self-sealing freezer bags or wrap in moisture- and vaporproof wrap before freezing.

Salmon-Veggie Bake

Salmon-Veggie Bake

The packets will be extremely hot when they come out of the oven. Transfer the contents of each to a dinner plate. For casual dining leave the meal in the packet, grab a fork, and dig in.

Low Fat

Prep: 30 minutes **Bake:** 30 minutes
Oven: 350°F **Makes:** 4 servings

- 1 **pound fresh or frozen skinless salmon, orange roughy, cod, flounder, or sea bass fillets, about ¾ inch thick**
- 2 **cups thinly sliced carrots (4)**
- 2 **cups sliced fresh mushrooms**
- ½ **cup sliced green onions (4)**
- 2 **teaspoons finely shredded orange peel**
- 2 **teaspoons snipped fresh oregano or ½ teaspoon dried oregano, crushed**
- 4 **cloves garlic, halved**
- ¼ **teaspoon salt**
- ¼ **teaspoon black pepper**
- 4 **teaspoons olive oil**
  Salt and black pepper
- 2 **medium oranges, thinly sliced**
- 4 **sprigs fresh oregano (optional)**

1. Thaw fish, if frozen. Rinse fish; pat dry with paper towels. Cut into 4 serving-size pieces, if necessary. Set aside. In a small saucepan cook carrots, covered, in a small amount of boiling water for 2 minutes. Drain and set aside. Tear off four 24-inch pieces of 18-inch-wide heavy foil. Fold each in half to make four 18×12-inch pieces.

2. In a large bowl combine carrots, mushrooms, green onions, orange peel, oregano, garlic, the ¼ teaspoon salt, and the ¼ teaspoon pepper; toss gently to combine.

3. Divide vegetables among the 4 pieces of foil, placing vegetables in center of each piece. Place 1 piece of salmon on top of each portion of vegetables. Drizzle 1 teaspoon of the oil over each piece of salmon. Sprinkle each lightly with additional salt and pepper; top with orange slices and, if desired, a sprig of oregano. Bring together 2 opposite edges of foil and seal with a double fold. Fold remaining ends to completely enclose the food, allowing space for steam to build. Place the foil packets in a single layer on a baking pan.

4. Bake in a 350° oven about 30 minutes or until carrots are tender and fish flakes easily when tested with a fork. Open slowly to allow steam to escape. Transfer the packets to individual plates.

Nutrition Facts per serving: 252 cal., 10 g total fat (1 g sat. fat), 59 mg chol., 393 mg sodium, 18 g carbo., 4 g fiber, 26 g pro.
Daily Values: 314% vit. A, 73% vit. C, 8% calcium, 10% iron
Exchanges: 2 Vegetable, ½ Fruit, 3 Lean Meat

Orange Halibut

`Fast` `Low Fat`

Start to Finish: 30 minutes **Makes:** 4 servings

- 1 **pound fresh or frozen halibut steaks, ¾ inch thick**
- ⅓ **cup finely chopped onion (1 small)**
- 1 **clove garlic, minced**
- 1 **tablespoon butter or margarine**
- ½ **teaspoon finely shredded orange peel**
- ¼ **cup orange juice**
- ¼ **teaspoon salt**
- ⅛ **teaspoon black pepper**
- 2 **tablespoons snipped fresh parsley**
  Thin orange slices (optional)

1. Thaw fish, if frozen. Rinse fish; pat dry with paper towels. Measure thickness of fish. Cut into 4 serving-size pieces, if necessary.

2. In a large skillet cook onion and garlic in butter until tender. Carefully add orange peel, orange juice, salt, and pepper to skillet. Add fish. Bring just to boiling; reduce heat. Simmer, uncovered, for 4 to 6 minutes per ½-inch thickness of fish or until fish flakes easily when tested with a fork.

3. Transfer fish to a serving platter. Spoon pan juices over fish; sprinkle with parsley. If desired, garnish with orange slices.

Nutrition Facts per serving: 165 cal., 6 g total fat (2 g sat. fat), 44 mg chol., 239 mg sodium, 3 g carbo., 0 g fiber, 24 g pro. **Daily Values:** 8% vit. A, 19% vit. C, 6% calcium, 7% iron **Exchanges:** 3 Very Lean Meat, 1 Fat

Crunchy Catfish

`Fast`

Prep: 20 minutes **Cook:** 6 minutes **Makes:** 4 servings

- 1 **pound fresh or frozen catfish fillets, about ½ inch thick**
- 1 **beaten egg**
- 3 **tablespoons Dijon-style mustard**
- 1 **tablespoon milk**
- ¼ **teaspoon black pepper**
- ¼ **cup all-purpose flour**
- 1 **cup coarsely crushed pretzels (about 2 cups pretzels)**
- 2 **tablespoons cooking oil**
  Thin lemon slices (optional)

1. Thaw fish, if frozen. Rinse fish; pat dry with paper towels. Cut into 4 serving-size pieces, if necessary. In a shallow dish combine the egg, mustard, milk, and pepper, beating with a whisk or fork until smooth. Place flour in another shallow dish. In a third shallow dish place the coarsely crushed pretzels. Coat both sides of fillets with flour. Dip fillets in the mustard mixture; coat with crushed pretzels.

2. In a large skillet cook fish in hot oil over medium heat for 3 to 4 minutes per side or until golden and fish flakes easily when tested with a fork. (Reduce heat as necessary to prevent burning.) If desired, serve with lemon slices.

Nutrition Facts per serving: 364 cal., 18 g total fat (4 g sat. fat), 106 mg chol., 504 mg sodium, 26 g carbo., 1 g fiber, 23 g pro. **Daily Values:** 3% vit. A, 2% vit. C, 5% calcium, 11% iron **Exchanges:** 1½ Starch, 3 Very Lean Meat, 3 Fat

Fish 'n' Chips `Best Loved`

Start to Finish: 50 minutes **Makes:** 4 servings

- 1 **pound fresh or frozen skinless perch, cod, haddock, or halibut fillets, about ½ inch thick**
- 1¼ **pounds medium potatoes (about 4)**
  Shortening or cooking oil for deep-fat frying
- 1 **cup all-purpose flour**
- 1 **cup beer**
- 2 **eggs**
- ½ **teaspoon baking powder**
- ½ **teaspoon salt**
- ½ **teaspoon black pepper**
  Coarse salt (optional)
  Tartar Sauce (page 479) (optional)
  Malt vinegar or cider vinegar (optional)

1. Thaw fish, if frozen; cut into 3×2-inch pieces. Rinse fish; pat dry with paper towels. Cover and refrigerate until needed.

2. For chips, cut the potatoes lengthwise into about ⅜-inch-wide wedges. Pat dry with paper towels. In a 3-quart saucepan or deep-fat fryer heat 2 inches of shortening or cooking oil to 375°F. Fry potatoes, one-fourth at a time, for 4 to 6 minutes or until lightly browned. Remove potatoes and drain on paper towels. Sprinkle lightly with *salt*. Transfer potatoes to a wire rack on a baking sheet, arranging them in a single layer. Keep warm in a 300°F oven.

3. Meanwhile, for batter, in a medium mixing bowl combine flour, beer, eggs, baking powder, the ½ teaspoon salt, and the black pepper. Beat with a rotary beater or wire whisk until smooth.

Dip fish into batter. Fry fish in the hot (375°F) fat, 1 or 2 pieces at a time, until coating is golden brown and fish flakes easily when tested with a fork, turning once (about 3 to 4 minutes). Drain cooked fish on paper towels, transfer to another baking sheet, and keep warm in the 300°F oven while frying remaining fish. To serve, if desired, sprinkle coarse salt over fish and chips and serve with Tartar Sauce or vinegar.

Nutrition Facts per serving: 721 cal., 40 g total fat (10 g sat. fat), 208 mg chol., 454 mg sodium, 52 g carbo., 3 g fiber, 31 g pro.
Daily Values: 4% vit. A, 38% vit. C, 18% calcium, 25% iron
Exchanges: 3½ Starch, 3 Very Lean Meat, 7 Fat

Trout Amandine

This recipe lets you easily substitute your favorite fillets for the pan-dressed fish. Prepare recipe as directed but cook fillets 3 to 4 minutes on each side per ½-inch thickness.

Prep: 15 minutes **Cook:** 16 minutes **Makes:** 4 servings

> 4 fresh or frozen boned pan-dressed trout or other pan-dressed fish (about 8 ounces each)
> 1 beaten egg
> ¼ cup milk
> 1 cup all-purpose flour
> ½ teaspoon salt
> ¼ cup cooking oil
> ¼ cup sliced almonds
> 2 tablespoons butter or margarine
> 2 tablespoons lemon juice

1. Thaw fish, if frozen. Rinse fish; pat dry with paper towels. Spread fish open. In a shallow dish combine egg and milk. In another shallow dish stir together flour and salt. Coat fish with flour mixture, dip into egg mixture, then coat again with flour mixture. In a 12-inch skillet heat the oil. Fry half of the fish in hot oil, skin side up, for 3 to 4 minutes or until browned. Turn fish and cook 3 to 4 minutes more or until fish flakes easily when tested with a fork. Keep cooked fish warm in a 300°F oven while frying remaining fish.

2. In a medium skillet cook sliced almonds in butter until golden. Remove from heat; stir in lemon juice. To serve, place fish, skin side down, on a serving platter and spoon almond mixture over the fish.

Nutrition Facts per serving: 603 cal., 35 g total fat (9 g sat. fat), 171 mg chol., 436 mg sodium, 27 g carbo., 2 g fiber, 43 g pro.
Daily Values: 15% vit. A, 13% vit. C, 17% calcium, 14% iron
Exchanges: 2 Starch, 5 Very Lean Meat, 4½ Fat

Veracruz-Style Red Snapper

One bite and you'll know why this is one of Mexico's best known recipes (see photo, page 279).

Low Fat

Start to Finish: 45 minutes **Makes:** 6 servings

> 1½ pounds fresh or frozen skinless red snapper or other fish fillets
> ⅓ cup all-purpose flour
> ¼ teaspoon salt
> ⅛ teaspoon black pepper
> 2 tablespoons olive oil
> 1 large onion, sliced and separated into rings
> 1 teaspoon bottled minced garlic or 2 cloves garlic, minced
> 2 large tomatoes, chopped (2 cups)
> ¼ cup sliced pimiento-stuffed olives
> 2 tablespoons lime juice
> 2 tablespoons capers, drained
> 1 to 2 fresh jalapeño or serrano chile peppers, seeded and chopped (see tip, page 64); or 1 to 2 canned jalapeño chile peppers, rinsed, drained, seeded, and chopped
> ½ teaspoon sugar
> 1 tablespoon snipped fresh oregano
> Snipped fresh oregano (optional)
> Hot cooked rice (optional)

1. Thaw fish, if frozen. Rinse fish; pat dry with paper towels. Measure thickness of fish. Cut fish into 6 serving-size pieces, if necessary. In a shallow dish combine flour, salt, and black pepper. Coat fish with flour mixture.

2. In a 12-inch skillet cook fish in 1 tablespoon of the hot oil until golden, adding additional oil to skillet during cooking if necessary. Allow 3 to 4 minutes per side for ½-inch-thick fillets (5 to 6 minutes per side for 1-inch-thick fillets). Transfer to a serving platter; cover and keep warm.

3. Meanwhile, for sauce, in a medium saucepan heat the remaining 1 tablespoon oil; cook onion and garlic in oil until onion is tender. Stir in tomatoes, olives, lime juice, capers, chile peppers, and sugar. Bring to boiling; reduce heat. Simmer, uncovered, about 5 minutes or until desired consistency. Stir in the 1 tablespoon oregano.

4. To serve, spoon sauce over fish. If desired, sprinkle with additional fresh oregano and serve with hot cooked rice.

Nutrition Facts per serving: 216 cal., 8 g total fat (1 g sat. fat), 40 mg chol., 411 mg sodium, 12 g carbo., 2 g fiber, 25 g pro.
Daily Values: 11% vit. A, 28% vit. C, 4% calcium, 9% iron
Exchanges: 1 Vegetable, ½ Starch, 3 Very Lean Meat, 1 Fat

Pan-Fried Fish

`Fast`

Prep: 10 minutes **Cook:** 6 minutes per batch
Makes: 4 servings

- **1 pound fresh or frozen fish fillets,
  ½ to 1 inch thick**
- **1 beaten egg**
- **⅔ cup cornmeal or fine dry bread crumbs**
- **½ teaspoon salt**
- **Dash black pepper**
- **Shortening or cooking oil for frying**

1. Thaw fish, if frozen. Rinse fish and pat dry with paper towels. Cut into 4 serving-size pieces, if necessary. Measure thickness of fish. In a shallow dish combine egg and 2 tablespoons *water*. In another shallow dish stir together cornmeal, salt, and pepper. Dip fish into egg mixture; coat fish with cornmeal mixture (see photo 1, right).

2. In a large skillet heat ¼ inch melted shortening or oil. Add half of the fish in a single layer, frying on 1 side until golden. (If fillets have skin, fry skin side last.) Turn carefully (see photo 2, right); fry until second side is golden and fish flakes easily when tested with a fork. Allow 3 to 4 minutes per side for ½-inch-thick fillets (5 to 6 minutes per side for 1-inch-thick fillets). Drain on paper towels; keep warm in a 300°F oven while frying remaining fish.

Spicy Hot Pan-Fried Fish: Prepare as above, except omit pepper. Reduce cornmeal to ¼ cup and combine it with ¼ cup all-purpose flour, ¾ teaspoon ground red pepper, ½ teaspoon chili powder, ½ teaspoon garlic powder, and ½ teaspoon paprika.

Nutrition Facts per serving for plain or spicy fish variation:
277 cal., 11 g total fat (3 g sat. fat), 102 mg chol., 369 mg sodium, 18 g carbo., 2 g fiber, 24 g pro.
Daily Values: 4% vit. A, 2% vit. C, 3% calcium, 9% iron
Exchanges: 1 Starch, 3 Very Lean Meat, 2 Fat

Potato Chip Pan-Fried Fish: Prepare as above, except substitute 1⅓ cups finely crushed potato chips (about 4 cups of chips) or saltine crackers for the cornmeal and omit salt.

Nutrition Facts per serving: 303 cal., 18 g total fat (4 g sat. fat), 102 mg chol., 185 mg sodium, 10 g carbo., 1 g fiber, 23 g pro.
Daily Values 2% vit. A, 22% vit. C, 4% calcium, 6% iron
Exchanges: ½ Starch, 3 Very Lean Meat, 3½ Fat

Curried Pan-Fried Fish: Prepare as above, except add 1 tablespoon lime or lemon juice to egg mixture and add 2 teaspoons curry powder to cornmeal. Serve with chutney.

Nutrition Facts per serving: 335 cal., 12 g total fat (3 g sat. fat), 102 mg chol., 386 mg sodium, 33 g carbo., 3 g fiber, 24 g pro.
Daily Values: 18% vit. A, 18% vit. C, 4% calcium, 12% iron
Exchanges: 1 Starch, 1 Other Carbo., 3 Very Lean Meat, 2 Fat

1. After dipping the fish in the egg mixture, roll it in the cornmeal mixture. Turn the fish to coat all sides.

2. When the fish is golden, carefully lift it with a wide metal spatula underneath and a thin metal spatula on top. Turn the fish over and cook the second side.

Seared Tuna with Grapefruit-Orange Relish

Tweak the seared tuna topping to suit your family's taste. Try any of the salsas or sauces in tip, page 291.

`Fast` `Low Fat`

Prep: 20 minutes **Cook:** 6 minutes **Makes:** 4 servings

- **4 fresh or frozen tuna steaks, ¾ inch thick**
- **2 teaspoons sherry vinegar or white wine vinegar**
- **2 teaspoons soy sauce**
- **½ teaspoon grated fresh ginger**
- **1 tablespoon olive oil**
- **1 medium grapefruit, peeled and sectioned**
- **1 medium orange, peeled and sectioned**
- **2 tablespoons finely chopped red onion**
- **2 tablespoons snipped fresh cilantro**
- **2 teaspoons olive oil**
- **Fresh cilantro sprigs (optional)**

1. Thaw fish, if frozen. For relish, in a small bowl combine vinegar, soy sauce, and ginger. Whisk in the 1 tablespoon oil. Cut grapefruit sections into thirds and orange sections in half. Stir fruit pieces, red onion, and the 2 tablespoons cilantro into vinegar mixture. Set aside.

2. Rinse fish; pat dry. In a large skillet heat the 2 teaspoons oil over medium-high heat. Add fish; cook for 6 to 9 minutes or until fish flakes easily when tested with a fork, turning once. Sprinkle with *salt* and *black pepper*. Serve the fish with relish. If desired, garnish with cilantro sprigs.

Nutrition Facts per serving: 210 cal., 7 g total fat (1 g sat. fat), 51 mg chol., 253 mg sodium, 9 g carbo., 2 g fiber, 27 g pro.
Daily Values: 9% vit. A, 71% vit. C, 4% calcium, 6% iron
Exchanges: ½ Fruit, 4 Very Lean Meat, 1 Fat

Spinach-Stuffed Sole with Lemon-Chive Sauce Best Loved

Prep: 20 minutes **Bake:** 30 minutes
Oven: 350°F **Makes:** 4 servings

- 4 4-ounce fresh or frozen skinless sole, flounder, or other fish fillets, about ¼ inch thick
-    Salt and black pepper
- 1 10-ounce package frozen chopped spinach, thawed
- 1 beaten egg
- 1 cup herb-seasoned stuffing mix, slightly crushed
- 2 tablespoons slivered almonds, toasted (see tip, page 224)
- ⅓ cup dairy sour cream
- ⅓ cup mayonnaise or salad dressing
- 1 tablespoon snipped fresh thyme or 1 teaspoon dried thyme, crushed
- 1 teaspoon finely shredded lemon peel
- ½ teaspoon prepared mustard
- ¼ cup whipping cream
- 1 tablespoon snipped fresh chives
-    Snipped fresh chives or thinly sliced green onion (optional)

1. Thaw fish, if frozen. Rinse fish; pat dry with paper towels. Season with salt and pepper; set aside. For filling, drain spinach; squeeze out excess liquid. In a medium bowl combine spinach, egg, stuffing mix, and almonds.

2. Spoon one-fourth of the filling onto the widest end of each fillet. Roll up, securing rolls with wooden toothpicks. Place fish in a greased 2-quart square baking dish. Bake, covered, in a 350° oven for 30 to 35 minutes or until fish flakes easily when tested with a fork and filling is heated through.

3. Meanwhile, for sauce, in a small saucepan combine sour cream, mayonnaise, thyme, lemon peel, and mustard. Cook and stir over low heat until heated through (do not boil). Remove from heat. In a medium mixing bowl beat whipping cream with an electric mixer on low speed until soft peaks form (tips curl). Fold whipped cream and the 1 tablespoon chives into sour cream mixture. Serve immediately over fish. If desired, sprinkle with additional snipped chives or thinly sliced green onions.

Nutrition Facts per serving: 427 cal., 29 g total fat (8 g sat. fat), 143 mg chol., 702 mg sodium, 14 g carbo., 3 g fiber, 26 g pro.
Daily Values: 217% vit. A, 12% vit. C, 13% calcium, 13% iron
Exchanges: 1 Starch, 3½ Very Lean Meat, 5 Fat

Saucy Solutions

Pair one of these stir-together toppings with fish fillets or steaks prepared as you like them (see chart, page 301).

Avocado Salsa: In a medium bowl combine 1 large tomato, seeded and chopped; 1 avocado, halved, seeded, peeled, and chopped; half of a small onion, chopped; 1 tablespoon snipped fresh cilantro; 1 tablespoon lemon or lime juice; 1 clove garlic, minced; a few dashes bottled hot pepper sauce; and a dash salt. Cover and chill for 2 to 6 hours. Makes 2½ cups.

Lemon Mayonnaise: In a small bowl stir together ½ cup mayonnaise or salad dressing, ¼ cup regular or light dairy sour cream, 2 tablespoons snipped fresh flat-leaf parsley, 2 teaspoons finely shredded lemon peel, 2 teaspoons lemon juice, and ¼ teaspoon coarsely cracked black pepper. Cover and chill until serving time. Makes ⅔ cup.

Mango Salsa: In a medium bowl combine 1½ cups chopped, peeled mangoes or peaches; 1 medium red sweet pepper, seeded and finely chopped; ¼ cup thinly sliced green onions; 1 jalapeño chile pepper, seeded and finely chopped (see tip, page 64); 1 tablespoon olive oil; ½ teaspoon finely shredded lime peel; 1 tablespoon lime juice; 1 tablespoon vinegar; ¼ teaspoon salt; and ¼ teaspoon black pepper. Makes 2 cups.

Pineapple Salsa: In a small bowl stir together 1 cup bottled chunky salsa; one 8-ounce can crushed pineapple (juice pack), drained; and ¼ teaspoon grated fresh ginger or dash ground ginger. Cover and chill until serving time; bring to room temperature to serve. Makes 1½ cups.

Spinach-Stuffed Sole with Lemon-Chive Sauce

Flavored Butters

Add a flavor boost to steamed, baked, or broiled fish fillets or steaks. Store butters in the refrigerator up to 2 weeks or freeze up to 1 month.

Herb Butter: Stir together ¼ cup softened butter and 1 tablespoon snipped fresh tarragon or dill or ¼ teaspoon dried tarragon, crushed, or dried dill.

Tomato-Pepper Butter: Stir together ¼ cup softened butter; 2 tablespoons finely snipped, drained dried tomatoes (oil pack); and ¼ teaspoon cracked black pepper.

Ginger-Garlic Butter: Stir together ¼ cup softened butter, 2 tablespoons snipped flat-leaf parsley, 2 teaspoons grated fresh ginger, and 1 clove garlic, minced.

Vermouth-Shallot Butter: With an electric mixer beat together ¼ cup softened butter, 1 tablespoon finely chopped shallot, and 2 teaspoons vermouth.

Mustard-Sage Butter: Stir together ¼ cup softened butter; 1 tablespoon snipped fresh sage or ½ teaspoon dried sage, crushed; and 1 teaspoon Dijon-style mustard.

Steamed Orange Roughy

`Fast`   `Low Fat`

Start to Finish: 20 minutes **Makes:** 4 servings

> 1 to 1¼ pounds fresh or frozen orange roughy fillets
> 1 medium onion, sliced
> ¼ teaspoon garlic salt
> 4 celery stalks, leafy ends only
> 1 recipe desired Flavored Butter (above) or desired salsa (page 291)

1. Thaw fish, if frozen. Rinse fish; pat dry with paper towels. Cut fish into 4 serving-size pieces, if necessary. Measure thickness of fish; set aside. Fill a large skillet with water to a depth of 1 inch. Bring water to boiling; reduce heat.

2. Meanwhile, arrange onion slices in the bottom of a steamer basket. Place fish on top of onions; sprinkle with garlic salt and a dash of *black pepper*. Place steamer over simmering water. Place celery on fish. Cover; simmer gently until fish flakes easily when tested with a fork. Allow 4 to 6 minutes per ½-inch thickness of fish. Discard vegetables. Serve fish with your favorite flavored butter or salsa.

Nutrition Facts per serving without butter or salsa: 92 cal., 1 g total fat (0 g sat. fat), 23 mg chol., 160 mg sodium, 3 g carbo., 1 g fiber, 17 g pro.
Daily Values: 2% vit. A, 6% vit. C, 5% calcium, 2% iron
Exchanges: 2½ Very Lean Meat

Salmon Patties

`Fast`   `Low Fat`

Start to Finish: 30 minutes **Makes:** 4 servings

> 1 beaten egg
> ¼ cup milk
> ¼ cup chopped green onions (2)
> 1 tablespoon snipped fresh dill or 1 teaspoon dried dill
> ¼ teaspoon black pepper
> 1 14¾-ounce can salmon, drained, flaked, and skin and bones removed
> ¼ cup fine dry bread crumbs
> 1 tablespoon cooking oil
> 1 recipe Honey Mustard Sauce or Tartar Sauce (page 479) (optional)

1. In a medium bowl combine the egg, milk, green onions, dill, and pepper. Add salmon and bread crumbs; mix well. Form mixture into eight ½-inch-thick patties. In a large skillet cook patties in hot oil over medium-low heat about 6 minutes or until golden brown, turning once. If desired, serve with Honey Mustard Sauce or Tartar Sauce.

Nutrition Facts per serving: 231 cal., 12 g total fat (3 g sat. fat), 112 mg chol., 656 mg sodium, 6 g carbo., 0 g fiber, 24 g pro.
Daily Values: 4% vit. A, 2% vit. C, 26% calcium, 9% iron
Exchanges: ½ Starch, 3 Very Lean Meat, 1½ Fat

Honey Mustard Sauce: In a small bowl stir together ¼ cup mayonnaise or salad dressing and 1 tablespoon honey mustard. Cover and chill until serving time.

Salmon in Phyllo `Best Loved`

Start to Finish: 45 minutes **Oven:** 375°F **Makes:** 4 servings

> 1 pound fresh or frozen skinless salmon fillets, about ½ inch thick
> ⅓ cup butter or margarine, melted
> 2 tablespoons snipped fresh dill or 1 teaspoon dried dill
> Dash salt
> Dash black pepper
> 8 sheets frozen phyllo dough (18×14-inch rectangles), thawed
> 1 recipe Mustard Cream Sauce

1. Thaw salmon, if frozen. Rinse salmon; pat dry with paper towels. Cut salmon into 4 serving-size pieces, if necessary. Brush some of the melted butter over each salmon portion. Sprinkle with dill, salt, and pepper. Set aside.

2. Unfold phyllo dough; cover with plastic wrap. Lay 1 sheet of phyllo dough flat; brush with some of the melted butter. Top with another sheet of phyllo dough. Brush with more melted butter. Add 6 more sheets of dough (a total of 8 sheets), brushing each sheet with butter. Cut into four 9×7-inch rectangles. Place a salmon fillet, buttered side down, in the middle of a dough rectangle. Fold a long side of the dough over salmon; repeat with the other long side, brushing dough with butter and pressing lightly. Fold up ends (see photo, below). Repeat with remaining rectangles, butter, and salmon. Arrange bundles, seam sides down, on a baking sheet. Brush with butter.

3. Bake in a 375° oven for 15 to 18 minutes or until phyllo dough is golden and fish flakes easily when tested with a fork. Serve with Mustard Cream Sauce.

Mustard Cream Sauce: Combine ⅓ cup dry white wine and 3 tablespoons finely chopped shallots in a small saucepan. Bring to boiling; reduce heat. Simmer, uncovered, about 5 minutes or until the liquid is reduced to about 3 tablespoons, stirring occasionally. Stir 1 cup half-and-half or light cream into 4 teaspoons all-purpose flour. Stir into wine mixture with ⅛ teaspoon white or black pepper. Cook and stir over medium heat until thickened and bubbly (sauce may look curdled). Stir in 1 tablespoon Dijon-style mustard. Cook and stir for 1 minute more.

Nutrition Facts per serving: 498 cal., 29 g total fat (15 g sat. fat), 124 mg chol., 507 mg sodium, 26 g carbo., 1 g fiber, 28 g pro.
Daily Values: 22% vit. A, 2% vit. C, 10% calcium, 14% iron
Exchanges: 1½ Starch, 3½ Lean Meat, 4 Fat

Fold the long edges of the phyllo dough over the fillets. Brush the dough with butter and press the edges lightly to seal. Fold up the ends to complete the bundles.

Bread Crumbs

Use a blender or food processor to make fluffy soft bread crumbs. One slice yields ¾ cup crumbs.

For fine dry bread crumbs, arrange ½-inch bread cubes in a single layer on a baking pan. Bake in a 300°F oven for 10 to 15 minutes or until dry, stirring twice. Let cool. Place in a food processor or blender; cover and process or blend into fine crumbs. One slice yields ¼ cup fine dry crumbs.

Tuna-Noodle Casserole Best Loved

For a faster version, substitute a 10¾-ounce can condensed cream of mushroom soup mixed with ¾ cup milk for the sauce.

Prep: 25 minutes **Bake:** 20 minutes
Oven: 375°F **Makes:** 4 servings

> 3 cups medium noodles (4 ounces) or 1 cup elbow macaroni (3½ ounces)
> ½ cup soft bread crumbs (see tip, below)
> 1 tablespoon butter or margarine, melted
> 1 cup chopped celery
> ¼ cup chopped onion
> ¼ cup butter or margarine
> ¼ cup all-purpose flour
> ½ teaspoon salt
> ½ teaspoon dry mustard
> ¼ teaspoon black pepper
> 2 cups milk
> 1 9- or 9¼-ounce can tuna, drained and broken into chunks, or two 6-ounce cans skinless, boneless salmon, drained
> 1 cup cheddar cheese cubes (4 ounces)
> ¼ cup chopped roasted red sweet pepper or pimiento

1. Cook noodles according to package directions. Drain and set aside. Meanwhile, combine bread crumbs and the 1 tablespoon melted butter; set aside.

2. For sauce, in a medium saucepan cook celery and onion in the ¼ cup butter until tender. Stir in flour, salt, dry mustard, and black pepper. Add milk all at once; cook and stir until slightly thickened and bubbly. Combine sauce, tuna, cheese, roasted sweet pepper, and cooked noodles. Transfer to a 1½-quart casserole. Sprinkle with crumb mixture. Bake, uncovered, in a 375° oven for 20 to 25 minutes or until bubbly and crumb topping is golden.

Nutrition Facts per serving: 588 cal., 34 g total fat (18 g sat. fat), 127 mg chol., 986 mg sodium, 37 g carbo., 2 g fiber, 34 g pro.
Daily Values: 24% vit. A, 47% vit. C, 39% calcium, 13% iron
Exchanges: 2½ Starch, 4 Very Lean Meat, 5 Fat

Vegetable Tuna-Noodle Casserole: Prepare as above, except add 1 cup frozen vegetables, thawed, with the tuna; bake in a 2-quart casserole.

Nutrition Facts per serving: 615 cal., 34 g total fat, (18 g sat. fat), 127 mg chol., 43 g carbo., 4 g fiber, 35 g pro.
Daily Values: 63% vit. A, 50% vit. C, 40% calcium, 16% iron
Exchanges: 3 Starch, 4 Very Lean Meat, 5 Fat

Baked Coconut Shrimp with Curried Apricot Sauce

Prep: 30 minutes **Bake:** 10 minutes
Oven: 400°F **Makes:** 6 servings

- 24 **fresh or frozen jumbo shrimp in shells**
- 1 **cup mayonnaise or salad dressing**
- 3 **tablespoons apricot preserves**
- 1 **teaspoon curry powder**
- 2 **tablespoons cooking oil**
- 1½ **cups shredded unsweetened coconut, toasted (see tip, page 224)**
- ¼ **cup cornstarch**
- 1 **tablespoon sugar**
- ½ **teaspoon salt**
- 3 **slightly beaten egg whites**

1. Thaw shrimp, if frozen. Peel and devein shrimp (see photos 1, 2, and 3, page 295), leaving tails intact. Rinse shrimp; pat dry with paper towels. Set aside.

2. For sauce, in a small bowl stir together mayonnaise, apricot preserves, and curry powder. Cover and chill until ready to serve.

3. Spread the oil on the bottom of a 15×10×1-inch baking pan; set pan aside. In a large shallow dish combine the coconut, cornstarch, sugar, and salt. In another small shallow dish place the egg whites. Dip shrimp into the egg whites; coat with coconut mixture, pressing the mixture firmly onto the shrimp. Arrange shrimp in prepared pan. Bake in a 400° oven about 10 minutes or until shrimp are opaque and coconut is golden, turning once. Serve with sauce.

Nutrition Facts per serving: 545 cal., 42 g total fat (11 g sat. fat), 172 mg chol., 585 mg sodium, 19 g carbo., 2 g fiber, 23 g pro.
Daily Values: 5% vit. A, 6% vit. C, 7% calcium, 17% iron
Exchanges: 1 Other Carbo., 3 Very Lean Meat, 5 Fat

Shrimp Creole Best Loved

Low Fat

Prep: 20 minutes **Cook:** 25 minutes **Makes:** 4 servings

- 1 **pound fresh or frozen medium shrimp in shells**
- 1 **medium onion, chopped (½ cup)**
- 1 **stalk celery, chopped (½ cup)**
- ½ **cup chopped green sweet pepper**
- 2 **cloves garlic, minced**
- 2 **tablespoons butter or margarine**
- 1 **14½-ounce can diced tomatoes, undrained**
- 2 **tablespoons snipped fresh parsley**
- ½ **teaspoon paprika**
- ⅛ **to ¼ teaspoon ground red pepper**
- 1 **bay leaf**
- ⅓ **cup cold water**
- 2 **teaspoons cornstarch**
- 2 **cups hot cooked rice**

1. Thaw shrimp, if frozen. Peel and devein shrimp, removing tails (see photos 1, 2, and 3, page 295). Rinse shrimp; pat dry with paper towels. Set aside.

2. In a large skillet cook onion, celery, sweet pepper, and garlic in butter over medium heat about 5 minutes or until tender. Stir in undrained tomatoes, parsley, ½ teaspoon *salt*, paprika, ground red pepper, and bay leaf. Bring to boiling; reduce heat. Simmer, covered, for 15 minutes.

3. Remove bay leaf. In a small bowl stir together cold water and cornstarch. Stir cornstarch mixture and shrimp into tomato mixture. Cook and stir until thickened and bubbly; cook and stir for 2 minutes more or until shrimp turn opaque. Serve over rice.

Fish Creole: Prepare as above, except substitute 12 ounces fresh or frozen fish fillets for the shrimp. Thaw fish, if frozen. Rinse fish; cut into 1-inch pieces. Add fish to the

Baked Coconut Shrimp with Curried Apricot Sauce

tomato mixture after mixture is thickened and bubbly. Cook and stir about 3 minutes more or until fish flakes easily when tested with a fork.

Nutrition Facts per serving of shrimp or fish creole: 261 cal., 7 g total fat (4 g sat. fat), 136 mg chol., 659 mg sodium, 32 g carbo., 2 g fiber, 17 g pro.
Daily Values: 28% vit. A, 59% vit. C, 8% calcium, 21% iron
Exchanges: 2 Vegetable, 1½ Starch, 1½ Very Lean Meat, 1 Fat

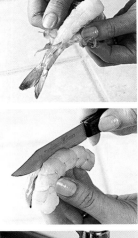

1. To peel a shrimp, open the shell lengthwise down the body. Start at the head end and peel back the shell. If desired, gently pull on the tail to remove it.

2. To devein a shrimp, use a sharp knife to make a shallow slit along the back from the head to the tail end. Locate the black vein.

3. If the vein is visible, hold the shrimp under cold running water to rinse it away. Or, remove the vein using the tip of a knife, then rinse the shrimp.

Spiced Shrimp with Rice

Low Fat

Start to Finish: 45 minutes   **Makes:** 4 servings

- 1 pound fresh or frozen medium shrimp in shells
- 1 teaspoon grated fresh ginger
- 1 teaspoon ground coriander
- ½ teaspoon five-spice powder or Homemade Five-Spice Powder
- ½ teaspoon paprika
- ¼ teaspoon ground cumin
- ¼ teaspoon ground turmeric
- ¼ cup finely chopped onion
- 3 cloves garlic, minced
- 1 fresh Anaheim chile pepper, seeded and chopped (see tip, page 64), or 3 tablespoons canned diced green chile peppers
- 3 tablespoons butter or margarine
- 1½ cups uncooked long grain rice
- 3¼ cups water or chicken broth
- 1 teaspoon salt*
- 2 tablespoons sliced green onion (1)

1. Thaw shrimp, if frozen. Peel and devein shrimp, removing tails (see photos 1, 2, and 3, at left). Rinse shrimp; pat dry with paper towels. Set aside. In a large bowl stir together ginger, coriander, five-spice powder, paprika, cumin, and turmeric. Add shrimp; toss to coat. Cover and let stand at room temperature for up to 30 minutes.

2. Meanwhile, in a large saucepan cook onion, garlic, and chile pepper in hot butter about 5 minutes or until onion is tender. Add rice. Stir in water and salt or chicken broth (*omit salt if using chicken broth). Bring to boiling; reduce heat. Simmer, covered, for 10 minutes (rice will not be done).

3. Stir in shrimp mixture. Cook, covered, about 5 minutes more or until shrimp are opaque and rice is tender. Sprinkle each serving with green onions.

Nutrition Facts per serving: 411 cal., 11 g total fat (6 g sat. fat), 144 mg chol., 823 mg sodium, 59 g carbo., 2 g fiber, 19 g pro.
Daily Values: 14% vit. A, 34% vit. C, 7% calcium, 29% iron
Exchanges: 4 Starch, 2 Very Lean Meat, ½ Fat

Homemade Five-Spice Powder: In a blender container combine 3 tablespoons ground cinnamon, 6 star anise or 2 teaspoons anise seeds, 1½ teaspoons fennel seeds, 1½ teaspoons whole Szechwan peppers or whole black peppercorns, and ¾ teaspoon ground cloves. Cover and blend to a fine powder. Store in a tightly covered container for up to 6 months. Makes ⅓ cup.

Shrimp Facts

Raw or "green" shrimp in the shell are available fresh or frozen and are sold by the pound. Use the list below as a shopping reference for market names and the corresponding number per pound.

Market Name	Number/Pound
Colossal	less than 15
Extra jumbo	16 to 20
Jumbo	20 to 21
Extra large	26 to 30
Large	31 to 40
Medium large	36 to 40
Medium	41 to 50
Small	51 to 60
Extra small	61 to 70

Shrimp Equivalents: 12 ounces of raw shrimp in the shell is equal to 8 ounces of raw, shelled shrimp, one 4½-ounce can shrimp, or 1 cup cooked, shelled shrimp

Stir-Fried Shrimp and Broccoli

Low Fat

Start to Finish: 45 minutes **Makes:** 4 servings

- 1 **pound fresh or frozen medium shrimp in shells or 12 ounces fresh or frozen scallops**
- ⅓ **cup water**
- ¼ **cup soy sauce**
- 2 **tablespoons rice vinegar**
- 1 **tablespoon cornstarch**
- 1½ **teaspoons sugar**
- 1 **tablespoon cooking oil**
- 2 **cloves garlic, minced**
- 2 **cups broccoli florets**
- 1 **cup thinly bias-sliced carrots**
- 1 **small onion, halved lengthwise and sliced**
- 1 **cup sliced fresh mushrooms**
- 2 **cups hot cooked rice or 8 ounces packaged dried vermicelli or fusilli, cooked and drained**
- ¼ **cup cashews or sliced almonds, toasted (see tip, page 224)**

1. Thaw shrimp or scallops, if frozen. If using shrimp, peel and devein shrimp, leaving tails intact (see photos 1, 2, and 3, page 295). If using scallops, cut any large scallops in half. Rinse shrimp or scallops; pat dry with paper towels. Set aside. In a small bowl combine water, soy sauce, vinegar, cornstarch, and sugar; set aside.

2. Heat oil in a wok or a 12-inch skillet over medium-high heat. (Add more oil as necessary

during cooking.) Cook and stir the garlic in the hot oil for 15 seconds. Add the broccoli, carrots, and onion; cook and stir for 3 minutes. Add the mushrooms; cook and stir for 1 to 2 minutes more or until vegetables are crisp-tender. Remove vegetables from wok with slotted spoon. Stir soy sauce mixture. Add to wok; cook and stir until slightly thickened and bubbly. Add shrimp or scallops; cook about 3 minutes or until shrimp or scallops are opaque. Stir in vegetables; heat through. Serve with rice or pasta and sprinkle with cashews.

Nutrition Facts per serving: 446 cal., 10 g total fat (2 g sat. fat), 129 mg chol., 1,075 mg sodium, 57 g carbo., 4 g fiber, 31 g pro.
Daily Values: 186% vit. A, 67% vit. C, 9% calcium, 28% iron
Exchanges: 2 Vegetable, 3 Starch, 2½ Very Lean Meat, 1½ Fat

Seared Scallops in Garlic Butter

Fast **Low Fat**

Start to Finish: 20 minutes **Makes:** 4 servings

- 1 **pound fresh or frozen sea scallops**
- 2 **tablespoons butter or margarine**
- 3 **cloves garlic, minced**
- 2 **tablespoons dry white wine**
- 1 **tablespoon snipped fresh chives or parsley**
- ⅛ **teaspoon salt**

1. Thaw scallops, if frozen. Rinse scallops; pat dry with paper towels.

2. Heat a 12-inch skillet over medium-high heat. Add 1 tablespoon of the butter and the garlic; cook and stir until butter is melted. Add the scallops. Cook, stirring frequently, for 2 to 3 minutes or until scallops turn opaque. Remove from skillet and transfer to a serving platter. Add remaining 1 tablespoon butter and wine to the skillet. Cook and stir to loosen any browned bits. Pour over scallops; sprinkle with chives and salt.

Shrimp in Garlic Butter: Prepare as above, except substitute 1½ pounds fresh or frozen medium shrimp in shells for the scallops. Thaw shrimp, if frozen. Peel and devein shrimp, leaving tails intact (see photos 1, 2, and 3, page 295). Rinse shrimp; pat dry with paper towels. Cook shrimp in the butter and garlic for 1 to 3 minutes or until shrimp turn opaque. Continue as above.

Nutrition Facts per serving of scallops or shrimp: 183 cal., 8 g total fat (4 g sat. fat), 189 mg chol., 303 mg sodium, 2 g carbo., 0 g fiber, 23 g pro.
Daily Values: 9% vit. A, 5% vit. C, 7% calcium, 14% iron
Exchanges: 3 Very Lean Meat, 1½ Fat

Stir-Fried Shrimp and Broccoli

Oysters au Gratin

Prep: 30 minutes **Bake:** 10 minutes
Oven: 400°F **Makes:** 4 servings

- 2 **pints shucked oysters (see photos 1 and 2, below)**
- 3 **tablespoons butter or margarine**
- 1 **cup sliced fresh mushrooms**
- 1 **clove garlic, minced**
- 2 **tablespoons all-purpose flour**
- ¾ **cup milk**
- ¼ **cup dry white wine**
- 2 **tablespoons snipped fresh parsley**
- ½ **teaspoon Worcestershire sauce**
- ¾ **cup soft bread crumbs (see tip, page 293)**
- ¼ **cup grated Parmesan cheese**
- 1 **tablespoon butter or margarine, melted**

1. Rinse oysters; pat dry with paper towels. In a large skillet cook and stir oysters in 1 tablespoon of the butter for 3 to 4 minutes or until oyster edges curl; drain. Divide oysters among four 8- to 10-ounce casseroles or four 10-ounce custard cups.

2. For sauce, in the same skillet cook mushrooms and garlic in remaining 2 tablespoons butter until tender. Stir in flour. Add milk all at once. Cook and stir until thickened and bubbly. Stir in wine, parsley, and Worcestershire sauce. Spoon over oysters. In a small bowl toss together the bread crumbs, Parmesan cheese, and the 1 tablespoon melted butter. Sprinkle over casseroles. Bake in a 400° oven about 10 minutes or until crumbs are brown.

Nutrition Facts per serving: 345 cal., 19 g total fat (10 g sat. fat), 98 mg chol., 722 mg sodium, 23 g carbo., 1 g fiber, 18 g pro.
Daily Values: 15% vit. A, 24% vit. C, 26% calcium, 78% iron
Exchanges: 1½ Starch, 2 Very Lean Meat, 3½ Fat

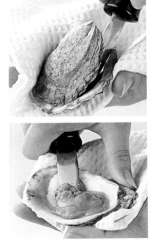

1. Hold oyster in a heavy towel or mitt. Insert an oyster knife tip into the hinge between the shells. Move blade along the inside of the upper shell to free muscle, twisting to pry it open.

2. Slide the knife under the oyster to sever the muscle from the bottom shell.

Selecting and Storing Shellfish

The quality of the shellfish that you purchase can make or break the recipe.

When purchasing live crabs and lobsters look for:

- ■ Hard shells (except for soft-shell crabs)
- ■ Vigorous activity (the lobster's or crab's legs should move when the body is touched)
- ■ Lobster tails should curl under the body when the lobster is lifted

To store: Lobsters should be cooked live or killed immediately before cooking. Ideally, live lobsters and crabs should be cooked on the day they are purchased. Otherwise, place them on a tray and refrigerate them covered with a damp towel. Or place them on damp newspapers in an insulated cooler half filled with ice. Cook within 1 day.

When purchasing live clams, mussels, and oysters look for:

- ■ Tightly closed shells (mussels may gape slightly but should close when tapped; oysters should always be tightly closed)
- ■ Clean, unbroken, moist shells (mussels should have beards)
- ■ Fresh scent (not a strong fishy odor)

To store: Refrigerate live clams, mussels, and oysters covered with a moist cloth in an open container for up to 5 days.

When purchasing shucked clams, oysters, and scallops look for:

- ■ Plump meats in clear liquor (juices) without shell particles or grit (liquor should not exceed 10 percent of total volume)
- ■ Fresh oceanlike scent (not sour or sulfurlike)
- ■ Scallops that are firm and moist, retaining their shape when touched

To store: Refrigerate shucked clams, oysters, and scallops covered in their liquor for up to 5 days or freeze for up to 3 months.

When purchasing shrimp look for:

- ■ Firm meat
- ■ Translucent, moist shells without black spots
- ■ Fresh scent (ammonia indicates spoilage)
- ■ Absence of vein, if peeled and deveined

To store: Refrigerate fresh shrimp in a covered container for up to 2 days. Keep frozen shrimp in the freezer for up to 6 months.

Boiled Lobster

Although considered a delicacy by some lobster lovers, food safety experts suggest you pass on the green tomalley, or liver, of the lobster.

Prep: 35 minutes **Cook:** 20 minutes **Makes:** 2 servings

- **8 quarts water**
- **2 teaspoons salt**
- **2 1- to 1½-pound live lobsters**
- **1 recipe Clarified Butter**

1. In a 12-quart kettle bring water and salt to boiling. Grasp lobsters just behind the eyes; rinse them under cold running water. Quickly plunge lobsters headfirst into the boiling water. Return to boiling; reduce heat. Simmer, covered, for 20 minutes. Drain lobsters; remove bands or pegs on large claws.

2. When cool enough to handle, place each lobster on its back. Separate the lobster tail from the body (see photo 1, below). Cut away the tail membrane to expose the meat (see photo 2, below). Remove and discard the black vein running through the tail. Remove meat from tail. Twist the large claws away from the body (see photo 3, right). Using a nutcracker, break open the claws (see photo 4, right). Remove the meat from the claws. Crack the shell on remaining part of the body; remove meat with a small fork. Discard the green tomalley (liver) and the coral roe (found in female lobsters). Serve lobster meat with Clarified Butter.

Clarified Butter: Melt ¼ cup butter over low heat without stirring; cool slightly. Pour off clear top layer; discard milky bottom layer.

Nutrition Facts per serving: 340 cal., 25 g total fat (15 g sat. fat), 158 mg chol., 1,023 mg sodium, 2 g carbo., 0 g fiber, 26 g pro.
Daily Values: 21% vit. A, 9% calcium, 3% iron
Exchanges: 4 Very Lean Meat, 4½ Fat

1. Remove the tail from a lobster by twisting the tail and body in opposite directions.

2. Using kitchen shears, cut away the membrane from the tail to expose the meat. Discard the intestinal vein that runs through the tail.

3. Twist off the large claws where they join the body.

4. Pull the small pincer off each claw and discard. Using a nutcracker, break open the claws. Use a seafood fork to remove the meat.

Fried Soft-Shell Crabs

Live soft-shell blue crabs are available mid-May through September, but frozen soft-shells can be purchased year-round. As an added bonus, the frozen variety is cleaned before packaging.

Fast

Start to Finish: 30 minutes **Makes:** 4 servings

- **4 large or 8 small live soft-shell blue crabs**
- **1 beaten egg**
- **¼ cup milk**
- **½ cup all-purpose flour**
- **¼ teaspoon salt**
- **⅛ teaspoon ground red pepper**
- **Shortening or cooking oil for frying**

1. Immerse crabs in ice water. (This numbs them, making them easier to handle.) To clean each soft-shell crab, hold the crab between the back legs. Insert a knife into brain at top of skull to kill it. Using kitchen scissors, remove head by cutting horizontally across the body ½ inch behind the eyes. Lift one pointed side of the soft top shell to expose the gills (spongy projectiles). Using your fingers, push up on the gills and pull off. Replace the soft top shell over the body. Repeat on the other side. Turn crab over. Fold back the tail flap (or apron); twist off and discard. Thoroughly rinse crabs under cold running water. Pat crabs dry with paper towels.

2. In a shallow dish combine egg and milk. In another dish combine flour, salt, and red pepper. Dip crabs in egg mixture; roll in flour mixture, coating evenly.

3. In a medium or large skillet heat ½ inch shortening or cooking oil over medium heat for 15 to 20 minutes (oil should be 365°F). Carefully add

2 or 3 crabs, back sides down. Fry for 1½ to 2 minutes or until golden. Turn carefully. Fry for 1 to 2 minutes more or until crabs are crisp and golden. Drain on paper towels. Keep warm in a 300°F oven while frying remaining crabs.

Nutrition Facts per serving: 169 cal., 9 g total fat (2 g sat. fat), 104 mg chol., 375 mg sodium, 13 g carbo., 0 g fiber, 9 g pro.
Daily Values: 5% vit. A, 1% vit. C, 19% calcium, 9% iron
Exchanges: 1 Starch, 1 Very Lean Meat, 1½ Fat

Broiled Crab Legs

If you don't have unsalted butter, use Clarified Butter (page 298) for this recipe.

`Fast` `Low Fat`

Start to Finish: 15 minutes   Makes: 4 servings

- 1½ **pounds fresh or frozen crab legs, split***
- 3 **tablespoons unsalted butter, melted**
- 1 **tablespoon snipped fresh basil or 1 teaspoon dried basil, crushed**
- ½ **teaspoon finely shredded lemon peel**
- 1 **tablespoon lemon juice**

1. Thaw crab legs, if frozen. Rinse crab; pat dry with paper towels. Place crab legs, cut sides up, on the greased unheated rack of a broiler pan. Stir together butter, basil, lemon peel, and lemon juice. Brush crab legs with butter mixture. Broil 4 to 6 inches from the heat for 3 to 4 minutes or until heated through.

***Note:** If split crab legs are unavailable from your grocer, purchase whole legs. Using kitchen shears cut through the lighter colored underside of each leg. Lay partially split legs on a cutting board. Cut through each hard shell with a sharp knife, completely splitting the legs.

Nutrition Facts per serving: 154 cal., 10 g total fat (6 g sat. fat), 64 mg chol., 799 mg sodium, 0 g carbo., 0 g fiber, 15 g pro.
Daily Values: 8% vit. A, 13% vit. C, 5% calcium, 3% iron
Exchanges: 2 Very Lean Meat, 2 Fat

Crab Cakes   `Best Loved`

Prep: 20 minutes Bake: 12 minutes
Oven: 450°F Makes: 4 servings

- 1 **beaten egg**
- 1 **cup soft bread crumbs (see tip, page 293)**
- 3 **tablespoons mayonnaise or salad dressing**
- 2 **tablespoons thinly sliced green onion (1)**
- 1 **tablespoon snipped fresh dill or 1 teaspoon dried dill**
- 1 **teaspoon seafood seasoning**
- ¼ **teaspoon black pepper**

- 1 **16-ounce can pasteurized crabmeat or two 6½-ounce cans crabmeat, drained, flaked, and cartilage removed**
- 3 **tablespoons fine dry bread crumbs**
- 2 **teaspoons cooking oil**
- 1 **recipe Red Pepper Relish, 1 recipe Lemon Mayonnaise (page 291), or Dijon-style mustard (optional)**

1. In a medium mixing bowl combine egg, soft bread crumbs, mayonnaise, green onion, dill, seafood seasoning, and pepper. Stir in flaked crabmeat. Divide mixture into 8 portions. Moisten hands and form each portion into a 2½-inch patty.

2. Place crab cakes in a greased shallow baking pan. Combine the dry bread crumbs and oil. Sprinkle over crab cakes, pressing to adhere. Bake, uncovered, in a 450° oven for 12 to 15 minutes or until light brown. (To pan fry, do not place in baking pan. Coat with crumbs as above. In an extra large skillet cook patties in 2 tablespoons hot oil over medium-high heat for 5 to 6 minutes or until brown, turning halfway through cooking. Add additional oil, if necessary. Drain on paper towels.) If desired, serve crab cakes with Red Pepper Relish, Lemon Mayonnaise, or mustard.

Make-ahead directions: Prepare as above through step 1. Cover and chill for up to 24 hours. Bake or fry as directed.

Nutrition Facts per serving: 219 cal., 13 g total fat (2 g sat. fat), 149 mg chol., 690 mg sodium, 9 g carbo., 1 g fiber, 16 g pro.
Daily Values: 2% vit. A, 1% vit. C, 9% calcium, 5% iron
Exchanges: ½ Starch, 2 Very Lean Meat, 2½ Fat

Red Pepper Relish: In a small bowl combine half of a 7-ounce jar roasted red sweet peppers, drained and chopped (½ cup); 1 tablespoon drained and chopped oil-packed dried tomatoes; and ¼ teaspoon seafood seasoning. Makes about ½ cup.

Crab Cakes

Cooking Shellfish

Refer to these directions for cooking fresh shellfish. Many types of shellfish are available partially prepared or even cooked. Ask at the fish and shellfish counter for additional information when making purchases.

Shellfish Type	Amount Per Serving	Preparing	Cooking
Clams	6 clams in the shell	Scrub live clams under cold running water. For 24 clams in shells, in an 8-quart kettle combine 4 quarts of cold water and ⅓ cup salt. Add clams and soak for 1 hour; drain and rinse. Discard water.	For 24 clams in shells, add ½ inch water to an 8-quart kettle; bring to boiling. Place clams in a steamer basket. Steam, covered, 5 to 7 minutes or until clams open. Discard any that do not open.
Crabs, hard-shell	1 pound live crabs	Grasp live crabs from behind, firmly holding the back two legs on each side. Rinse under cold running water.	To boil 3 pounds live hard-shell blue crabs, in a 12- to 16-quart kettle bring 8 quarts water and 2 teaspoons salt to boiling. Add crabs. Simmer, covered, for 10 minutes or until crabs turn pink; drain. (To crack and eat, see tip, page 301.)
Crawfish	1 pound live crawfish	Rinse live crawfish under cold running water. For 4 pounds crawfish, in a 12- to 16-quart kettle combine 8 quarts cold water and ⅓ cup salt. Add crawfish. Soak for 15 minutes; rinse and drain.	For 4 pounds live crawfish, in a 12- to 16-quart kettle bring 8 quarts water and 2 teaspoons salt to boiling. Add crawfish. Simmer, covered, 5 to 8 minutes or until shells turn red; drain.
Lobster tails	One 8-ounce frozen lobster tail	Thaw frozen lobster tails in the refrigerator.	For four 8-ounce lobster tails, in a 3-quart saucepan bring 6 cups water and 1½ teaspoons salt to boiling. Add tails; simmer, uncovered, for 8 to 12 minutes or until shells turn bright red and meat is tender; drain. (For boiling live lobster, see page 298.)
Mussels	12 mussels in shells	Scrub live mussels under cold running water. Using your fingers, pull out the beards that are visible between the shells. Soak as for clams, above.	For 24 mussels, add ½ inch water to an 8-quart kettle; bring to boiling. Place mussels in a steamer basket. Steam, covered, for 5 to 7 minutes or until shells open. Discard any that do not open.
Oysters	6 oysters in shells	Scrub live oysters under cold running water. For easier shucking, chill them first. Shuck, reserving bottom shells, if desired (see photos, page 297).	See Oysters Au Gratin, page 297; Oysters Rockefeller, page 73; Oyster Stuffing, page 441.
Shrimp	6 ounces shrimp in shells or 3 to 4 ounces peeled, deveined shrimp	To peel shrimp, open the shell down the underside. Starting at the head end, pull back the shell. Gently pull on the tail to remove. Use a sharp knife to remove the black vein that runs along the center of the back. Rinse under cold running water (see photos, page 295).	For 1 pound shrimp, in a 3-quart saucepan bring 4 cups water and 1 teaspoon salt to boiling. Add shrimp. Simmer, uncovered, for 1 to 3 minutes or until shrimp turn opaque, stirring occasionally. Rinse under cold running water; drain and chill, if desired.

Cracking and Cleaning Cooked Crab

Cracking and cleaning hard-shell crabs, such as the Atlantic blue crab or the Pacific Dungeness (shown below), may be intimidating to the inexperienced, but the reward is well worth the effort. The rich, flavorful meat is delicious simply dipped in butter, chilled, and tossed in salads, or as an added surprise to soups or stews. Follow these simple steps to get every last bit of the sweet-tasting meat.

1. Turn the crab on its back. Using your thumb, fold back the tail flap (or apron), twist off, and discard.

2. Holding the crab with the top shell in one hand, grasp the bottom shell at the point where the apron was removed. Pull the top shell away from the body of the crab and discard.

3. Discard the crab's internal organs, mouth, and appendages at the front; rinse crab. Using a small knife remove the spongy gills from each side of the top of the crab.

4. Twist off the claws and legs. Use a nutcracker to crack each joint, then pick out the meat. Cut the crab body into quarters. Use a small fork to remove the meat.

Cooking Fish

Minutes count when cooking fish. Weigh dressed fish or use a ruler to measure the thickness of fillets and steaks in order to better estimate when to check for doneness. Properly cooked fish is opaque, flakes easily when tested with a fork, and comes away from the bones readily; the juices should be milky white.

Cooking Method	Preparation	Fresh or Thawed Fillets or Steaks	Dressed
Bake	Place in a single layer in a greased shallow baking pan. For fillets, tuck under any thin edges. Brush with melted butter or margarine.	Bake, uncovered, in a 450°F oven for 4 to 6 minutes per $\frac{1}{2}$-inch thickness.	Bake, uncovered, in a 350°F oven for 6 to 9 minutes per 8 ounces.
Broil	Preheat broiler. Place fish on greased unheated rack of a broiler pan. For fillets, tuck under any thin edges. Brush with melted butter or margarine.	Broil 4 inches from the heat for 4 to 6 minutes per $\frac{1}{2}$-inch thickness. If fish is 1 inch or more thick, turn once halfway through broiling.	Not recommended.
Microwave	Arrange fish in a single layer in a shallow baking dish. For fillets, tuck under any thin edges. Cover with vented plastic wrap.	Cook on 100 percent power (high). For $\frac{1}{2}$ pound of $\frac{1}{2}$-inch-thick fillets, allow $1\frac{1}{2}$ to 2 minutes; for 1 pound of $\frac{1}{2}$-inch-thick fillets, allow $2\frac{1}{2}$ to 4 minutes. For 1 pound of $\frac{3}{4}$- to 1-inch-thick steaks, allow 3 to 5 minutes.	Not recommended.
Poach	Add $1\frac{1}{2}$ cups water, broth, or wine to a large skillet. Bring to boiling. Add fish. Return to boiling; reduce heat.	Simmer, uncovered, for 4 to 6 minutes per $\frac{1}{2}$-inch thickness.	Simmer, covered, for 6 to 9 minutes per 8 ounces.

Guide to Fish Types

Use this guide to become acquainted with various types of fish. Note that the flavors range from delicate to pronounced. This list of fish makes it easy to substitute one type of fish for another.

Types	Market Forms	Texture	Flavor	Substitutions
Freshwater Fish				
Catfish	Whole, fillets, steaks	Firm	Mild	Grouper, rockfish, sea bass, tilapia
Lake trout (North American char)	Whole, fillets, steaks	Slightly firm	Moderate	Pike, seatrout, whitefish
Rainbow trout	Fillets	Slightly firm	Delicate	Salmon, seatrout
Tilapia	Whole, dressed, fillets	Slightly firm	Delicate	Catfish, flounder, orange roughy
Whitefish	Whole, fillets	Moderately firm	Delicate	Cod, lake trout, salmon, sea bass
Saltwater Fish				
Atlantic ocean perch (redfish)	Whole, fillets	Slightly firm	Mild	Orange roughy, rockfish, snapper
Cod	Fillets, steaks	Moderately firm	Delicate	Flounder, haddock, pollack
Flounder	Whole, fillets	Fine	Delicate to mild	Cod, orange roughy, seatrout, sole, whitefish, whiting
Grouper	Whole, dressed, fillets	Moderately firm	Mild	Mahi mahi, sea bass
Haddock	Fillets	Moderately firm	Delicate	Cod, grouper, halibut, lake trout, sole, whitefish, whiting
Halibut*	Fillets, steaks	Firm	Delicate	Cod, grouper, sea bass, red snapper
Mackerel*	Whole	Delicate	Pronounced	Mahi mahi, swordfish, tuna
Mahi mahi (dolphinfish)	Whole, fillets	Firm	Mild to moderate	Grouper, orange roughy, red snapper
Orange roughy	Fillets	Moderately firm	Delicate	Cod, flounder, haddock, ocean perch, sea bass, sole
Red snapper	Whole, fillets	Moderately firm	Mild to moderate	Grouper, lake trout, ocean perch, rockfish, whitefish
Rockfish	Whole, fillets	Slightly firm	Mild to moderate	Cod, grouper, ocean perch, red snapper
Salmon*	Whole, fillets, steaks	Moderately firm	Mild to moderate	Rainbow trout, swordfish, tuna
Shark (mako)	Fillets, steaks	Firm, dense	Moderate	Swordfish, tuna
Sole	Fillets	Fine	Delicate	Flounder, halibut, haddock, pollack
Swordfish*	Loins, steaks	Firm, dense	Mild to moderate	Halibut, shark, tuna
Tuna*	Loins, steaks	Firm	Mild to moderate	Mackerel, salmon, shark, swordfish

*Good source of Omega-3 fatty acids

Chapter 14
Grilling

On the divider: Glazed Country Ribs (see recipe, page 312);
Corn on the Cob with Herb Butter (see recipe, page 321)

Grilling

Grilling Basics

Reliable equipment and an appropriate fire are the basic needs for successful grilling. The recipes in this chapter are suitable for gas or charcoal grills and include directions for both. The chart on page 328 gives suggested timings for cooking foods on indoor electric grills.

Sparking the Fire

If you have a gas or electric grill, follow the directions in your owner's manual for lighting and preheating it.

When building a charcoal fire, start with enough coals on the bottom grate to cover an area about 3 inches larger on all sides than the size of the food you plan to cook. Add a few more briquettes if the weather is humid or windy. Mound the briquettes or put them in a chimney starter (see photo 1, below) and ignite them, leaving the grill's lid off. After lighting the coals, leave them in a pile or in the starter until they're glowing red (about 20 minutes), then spread them over the grate in a single layer. Let the coals burn for 5 to 10 minutes more or until they are covered with gray ash before putting the food on the grill.

1. Light charcoal briquettes: Arrange briquettes in a mound in the center of the bottom grate. Placing them close together helps the fire to ignite.

Instant-lighting briquettes, which ash over in about 20 minutes, are saturated with a petroleum product that lights easily with a match. Besides electric starters and liquid lighter fluids, fire-starter gels and paraffin fire starters are both environmentally safe ways to make the job of starting a charcoal fire easier. Wait about 1 minute after adding a liquid, gel, or wax starter before igniting the briquettes. Never use gasoline or kerosene as a fire starter.

Direct vs. Indirect Grilling

Before arranging the coals, know whether you're going to grill directly or indirectly. Any grill can be used for direct grilling, including braziers (the basic shallow firebox on legs) and hibachis. For indirect grilling, you need a grill that has a cover. These grills can be either kettle- or wagon-shaped and have gas, electric, or charcoal heat sources.

With direct grilling, the food goes on the grill rack directly over the heat. Direct grilling is best-suited to foods that are tender, small, or thin and can be cooked in less than 30 minutes, which include steaks, burgers, kabobs, hot dogs, boneless poultry, fish, and most vegetables. For a charcoal grill, use long-handled tongs to spread the hot coals evenly in a single layer (see photo 2, below). To set up a gas grill for direct grilling, preheat it, then adjust the gas flow settings to the desired heat level.

2. Direct grilling with charcoal: Rake out the glowing coals evenly directly under the section of the grill rack where food will go. To test the temperature, count as directed on page 306.

Indirect grilling means placing the food over an area on the grill with no direct heat source and the grill is covered during cooking. Indirect grilling is the choice for cooking whole birds, ribs, large roasts, and whole fish.

To set up a charcoal grill for indirect cooking, use long-handled tongs to arrange the hot coals around a drip pan (see photo 3, below), which collects the fat drippings from the foods, minimizing flare-ups. Use a disposable foil roasting pan or make one out of heavy-duty foil.

3. Indirect grilling with charcoal: Move the coals to accommodate a drip pan; rearrange the coals as needed. To test the temperature, count as directed on page 306.

For indirect grilling on a gas grill, light the grill according to your owner's manual. Turn the setting to high and let preheat for 10 to 15 minutes. If your grill has two burners, reduce the heat on one burner to desired temperature and turn the other burner off. With a three burner gas grill, turn the center burner off. Place food over the unlit burner. Adjust the gas flow to the burner that's on to maintain the desired temperature. Most gas grills have a built-in drip pan under the fire box, so generally no drip pan is needed. We recommend placing whole birds and roasts on a rack in a roasting pan and placing the roasting pan directly on the grill over the unlit burner.

When indirect grilling, resist lifting the cover to peek. Every time you uncover the grill you let heat escape and add as much as 15 minutes to the grilling time. Let the foods cook the minimum time specified in the recipe or chart before checking for doneness.

Refueling the Fire

When charcoal grilling for a long period, use tongs to replenish the coals, adding 8 to 10 fresh coals every 30 to 45 minutes. The amount of coals needed depends on weather conditions. With strong winds or very cold temperatures, you may need more coals. Never use lighter fluid on or near burning coals. If you are using presoaked wood chips, add them whenever you refuel your grill.

Safety First

■ Allow coals to burn completely and let the ashes cool for 48 hours before disposing of them.

■ Let your grill completely cool down before covering or storing it.

■ Use charcoal or gas grills outside only—never in a garage, porch, or enclosed area.

■ Test your gas grill for leaks periodically and clean the venturi tubes regularly according to the manufacturer's directions.

■ Don't use lighter fluid, an electric starter, or a chimney starter with instant-lighting briquettes.

■ Never leave a grill unattended or try to move it while it's in use or hot.

It's Hot, Hot, Hot (or Not)

One key to successful grilling is determining when the charcoal or gas grill has obtained the ideal cooking temperature. No matter what type of grill, you can judge the temperature the same way.

Hold your hand, palm side down, at cooking level and time how long you can comfortably keep it there (see photos 2 and 3, page 305). A hot fire allows a 2-second hand count. A medium-hot fire is considered a 3-second hand count. A medium fire equals a hand count of 4 seconds. And a low fire is considered a 5-second count. When grilling indirectly, hot coals will provide medium-hot heat and medium-hot coals will provide medium heat.

BBQ Burgers

To toast the buns, place them on the grill rack for 1 to 2 minutes while your burgers finish grilling.

Prep: 15 minutes **Grill:** 14 minutes **Makes:** 4 servings

- ¼ cup catsup
- 2 tablespoons steak sauce
- 1 tablespoon water
- 1 teaspoon sugar
- 1 teaspoon vinegar
- 1 clove garlic, minced
  Few dashes bottled hot pepper sauce (optional)
- 1 pound lean ground beef
- ¼ teaspoon salt
- ¼ teaspoon black pepper
- 4 hamburger buns, split and toasted
  American cheese slices, lettuce leaves, tomato slices, onion slices, pickle slices (optional)

1. For sauce, in a small saucepan combine catsup, steak sauce, water, sugar, vinegar, garlic, and, if desired, hot pepper sauce. Bring to boiling; reduce heat. Simmer, uncovered, for 3 minutes. Remove from heat; set aside.

2. In a medium bowl combine ground beef, salt, and pepper. Shape meat mixture into four ¾-inch-thick patties.

3. For a charcoal grill, grill patties on the rack of an uncovered grill directly over medium coals (see photo 2, page 305) for 14 to 18 minutes or until meat is done (160°F), turning once halfway through grilling and brushing once or twice with sauce during the last 5 minutes. (For a gas grill, preheat grill. Reduce heat to medium. Place patties on grill rack over heat. Cover and grill as above.)

4. Serve burgers on buns. Spoon any remaining sauce over burgers. If desired, serve burgers with cheese, lettuce, tomato, onion, and pickles.

Nutrition Facts per serving: 372 cal., 17 g total fat (6 g sat. fat), 61 mg chol., 734 mg sodium, 28 g carbo., 2 g fiber, 25 g pro.
Daily Values: 4% vit. A, 6% vit. C, 7% calcium, 21% iron
Exchanges: 1½ Starch, 3 Medium-Fat Meat, ½ Fat

Roasted Garlic Steak

Low Fat

Prep: 15 minutes **Grill:** 30 minutes **Makes:** 6 servings

> 1 or 2 whole garlic bulb(s)
> 3 to 4 teaspoons snipped fresh basil or 1 teaspoon dried basil, crushed
> 1 tablespoon snipped fresh rosemary or 1 teaspoon dried rosemary, crushed
> 2 tablespoons olive oil or cooking oil
> 1½ pounds boneless beef ribeye steaks or sirloin steak, cut 1 inch thick

1. With a sharp knife, cut off the top ½ inch from each garlic bulb to expose the ends of the individual cloves. Leaving garlic bulb(s) whole, remove any loose, papery outer layers.

2. Fold a 20×18-inch piece of heavy foil in half crosswise. Trim into a 10-inch square. Place garlic bulb(s), cut sides up, in center of foil square. Sprinkle the garlic with basil and rosemary and drizzle with oil. Bring up opposite edges of foil and seal with a double fold. Fold remaining edges together to completely enclose garlic, leaving space for steam to build.

3. For a charcoal grill, grill garlic on the rack of an uncovered grill directly over medium coals (see photo 2, page 305) about 30 minutes or until garlic feels soft when packet is squeezed, turning garlic occasionally.

4. Meanwhile, trim fat from steaks. Sprinkle 1 to 2 teaspoons cracked *black pepper* and ½ teaspoon *salt* evenly over both sides of steaks; rub in with your fingers. While garlic is grilling, add steaks to grill. Grill to desired doneness, turning once halfway through grilling. For ribeye steaks, allow 11 to 15 minutes for medium rare (145°F) and 14 to 18 minutes for medium (160°F). For sirloin steak, allow 14 to 18 minutes for medium rare (145°F) and 18 to 22 minutes for medium (160°F). (For a gas grill, preheat grill. Reduce heat to medium. Place garlic, then steaks on grill rack over heat. Cover and grill as above.)

5. To serve, cut steaks into 6 serving-size pieces. Remove garlic from foil, reserving the oil mixture. Squeeze garlic pulp from each clove onto steaks. Mash pulp slightly with a fork; spread over steaks. Drizzle with the reserved oil mixture.

Nutrition Facts per serving: 189 cal., 9 g total fat (2 g sat. fat), 52 mg chol., 139 mg sodium, 4 g carbo., 0 g fiber, 22 g pro.
Daily Values: 1% vit. A, 6% vit. C, 3% calcium, 14% iron
Exchanges: 3 Lean Meat, ½ Fat

Lemony London Broil `Best Loved`

Low Fat

Prep: 15 minutes **Marinate:** 2 to 24 hours
Grill: 17 minutes **Makes:** 6 servings

> 1 1½-pound beef flank steak
> 1 teaspoon finely shredded lemon peel
> ½ cup lemon juice
> 2 tablespoons sugar
> 2 tablespoons soy sauce
> 2 teaspoons snipped fresh oregano or ½ teaspoon dried oregano, crushed
> ⅛ teaspoon black pepper

1. Trim fat from steak. Score steak on both sides by making shallow cuts at 1-inch intervals in a diamond pattern. Place steak in a plastic bag set in a shallow dish. For marinade, combine the lemon peel, lemon juice, sugar, soy sauce, oregano, and pepper. Pour over steak; seal bag. Marinate in the refrigerator for 2 to 24 hours, turning bag occasionally.

2. Drain steak, reserving marinade. For a charcoal grill, grill steak on the rack of an uncovered grill directly over medium coals (see photo 2, page 305) for 17 to 21 minutes for medium (160°F), turning and brushing once with marinade halfway through grilling. (For a gas grill, preheat grill. Reduce heat to medium. Place steak on grill rack over heat. Cover and grill as above.) To serve, thinly slice steak diagonally across the grain.

Nutrition Facts per serving: 191 cal., 7 g total fat (3 g sat. fat), 43 mg chol., 364 mg sodium, 6 g carbo., 0 g fiber, 24 g pro.
Daily Values: 16% vit. C, 1% calcium, 10% iron
Exchanges: 3 Lean Meat, ½ Other Carbo.

Controlling Flare-Ups

Fat and meat juices dripping onto hot coals may cause sudden small blazes, called flare-ups, which can make your meat taste charred. To control flare-ups, just raise the grill rack, cover the grill, space the hot coals farther apart, or remove a few coals. As a last resort, remove the food from the grill and mist the fire with water from a spray bottle. When the flame subsides, return the food to the grill.

To prevent flare-ups on a gas grill, after each use turn the grill setting to high for 10 to 15 minutes with the lid closed. Use a brass bristle brush to remove any baked-on food from the grill rack. This will also burn off some of the residue on the lava rock or ceramic briquettes.

Spicy Grilled Brisket Best Loved

Low Fat

Prep: 25 minutes **Grill:** 3 hours
Stand: 10 minutes **Makes:** 15 servings

- 4 **to 6 cups mesquite wood chips**
- 1 **4- to 5-pound fresh beef brisket**
- 1 **tablespoon cooking oil**
- 2 **tablespoons paprika**
- 1 **tablespoon coarse salt or coarse kosher salt**
- 1 **tablespoon black pepper**
- 1 **teaspoon ground red pepper**
- 1 **teaspoon dried thyme, crushed**
- 1 **recipe Sweet and Hot Barbecue Sauce or 3 cups bottled barbecue sauce**

1. At least 1 hour before grilling, soak wood chips in enough water to cover.

2. Trim fat from brisket. Brush brisket with oil. In a bowl stir together paprika, salt, black pepper, red pepper, and thyme. Sprinkle mixture evenly over both sides of meat; rub in with your fingers.

3. Drain wood chips. For a charcoal grill, arrange medium-low coals around a drip pan. Test for low heat above pan (see photo 3, page 305). Sprinkle some of the drained wood chips over the coals. Place brisket on grill rack over drip pan. Cover and grill for 3 to 3¾ hours or until meat is tender. Add more wood chips about every 30 minutes. (For a gas grill, preheat grill. Reduce heat to low. Adjust for indirect cooking. Add wood chips according to manufacturer's directions. Place meat on a rack in a roasting pan, place on grill rack, and grill as above.)

4. Meanwhile, prepare Sweet and Hot Barbecue Sauce or warm bottled barbecue sauce in a saucepan over low heat. Let meat stand for 10 minutes. To serve, slice meat thinly across the grain. Serve with barbecue sauce.

Sweet and Hot Barbecue Sauce: In a large saucepan cook ½ cup chopped onion; 6 fresh jalapeño chile peppers, seeded and chopped (see tip, page 64); and 2 cloves garlic, minced, in 1 tablespoon hot cooking oil until onion is tender. Stir in 2 cups catsup, ¼ cup packed brown sugar, ¼ cup white wine vinegar, ¼ cup orange juice, 3 tablespoons Worcestershire sauce, and 1 teaspoon dry mustard. Bring to boiling; reduce heat. Simmer, uncovered, for 10 to 15 minutes or to desired consistency. Makes about 3 cups.

Nutrition Facts per serving: 253 cal., 9 g total fat (2 g sat. fat), 71 mg chol., 956 mg sodium, 15 g carbo., 1 g fiber, 27 g pro.
Daily Values: 19% vit. A, 19% vit. C, 3% calcium, 18% iron
Exchanges: 1 Other Carbo., 3½ Lean Meat

Apple-Glazed Lamb Chops

Lamb chops make an elegant quick-to-fix dish, and these cinnamon- and apple-spiced chops are the ultimate company fare.

Fast Low Fat

Prep: 15 minutes **Grill:** 12 minutes **Makes:** 4 servings

- 3 **tablespoons apple jelly**
- 1 **green onion, thinly sliced**
- 1 **tablespoon soy sauce**
- 2 **teaspoons lemon juice**
- ⅛ **teaspoon curry powder**
  Dash ground cinnamon
  Dash ground red pepper
- 2 **small red and/or green apples, cut crosswise into ¼-inch slices**
  Lemon juice
- 8 **lamb loin chops, cut 1 inch thick (about 2 pounds)**
  Hot cooked couscous (optional)
- 1 **tablespoon snipped fresh mint**

1. For glaze, in a small saucepan cook and stir apple jelly, green onion, soy sauce, lemon juice, curry powder, cinnamon, and red pepper over medium heat until bubbly; remove from heat. Remove seeds from apple slices; brush apple slices with lemon juice. Set aside.

Spicy Grilled Brisket

2. Trim fat from chops. For a charcoal grill, grill chops on the rack of an uncovered grill directly over medium coals (see photo 2, page 305) to desired doneness, turning and brushing once with glaze halfway through grilling. Allow 12 to 14 minutes for medium rare (145°F) and 15 to 17 minutes for medium (160°F). Place apple slices on grill rack next to chops the last 5 minutes of grilling, turning and brushing once with glaze halfway through grilling. (For a gas grill, preheat grill. Reduce heat to medium. Place chops, then apple slices on grill rack over heat. Cover and grill as above.) Serve chops with grilled apples and, if desired, couscous. Sprinkle with mint.

Nutrition Facts per serving: 248 cal., 7 g total fat (2 g sat. fat), 80 mg chol., 306 mg sodium, 19 g carbo., 2 g fiber, 26 g pro.
Daily Values: 1% vit. A, 11% vit. C, 2% calcium, 15% iron
Exchanges: ½ Other Carbo., 3½ Very Lean Meat, 1 Fat

Smoked Leg of Lamb

Low Fat

Prep: 15 minutes **Grill:** 1¾ hours **Stand:** 15 minutes
Makes: 12 to 14 servings

>   4 **cups apple or cherry wood chips**
>   1 **5- to 6-pound whole leg of lamb (with bone)**
>   ½ **cup whipping cream**
>   1 **tablespoon Dijon-style mustard**
>   1 **teaspoon snipped fresh rosemary**
>   **Cracked black pepper (optional)**

1. At least 1 hour before grilling, soak wood chips in enough water to cover.

2. Trim fat from meat. Drain wood chips. For a charcoal grill, arrange medium coals around a drip pan. Test for medium-low heat above the pan (see photo 3, page 305). Sprinkle half of the drained wood chips over the coals. Place meat on grill rack over drip pan. Cover and grill until done. Allow 1¾ to 2¼ hours for medium rare (140°F) and 2¼ to 2¾ hours for medium (155°F). Add remaining wood chips halfway through grilling. (For a gas grill, preheat grill. Reduce heat to medium-low. Adjust for indirect cooking. Place meat on a rack in a roasting pan, place on grill rack, and grill as above.)

3. Remove meat from grill; cover with foil and let stand for 15 minutes. The temperature of the meat after standing should be 145°F for medium rare and 160°F for medium.

4. Meanwhile, in a small mixing bowl, beat whipping cream with a rotary beater or wire whisk until slightly thickened and starts to mound; stir in mustard and rosemary. Serve immediately over lamb slices. If desired, sprinkle with pepper.

Nutrition Facts per serving: 185 cal., 9 g total fat (4 g sat. fat), 90 mg chol.,67 mg sodium, 0 g carbo., 0 g fiber, 25 g pro.
Daily Values: 3% vit. A, 2% calcium, 12% iron
Exchanges: 3½ Lean Meat

Marinades, Rubs, and Sauces

Add a zesty marinade, rub, or sauce to a quality piece of meat, poultry, or seafood, and you transform it from just another good dinner into a memorable event.

Asian-Flavored Marinade: Combine ¼ cup soy sauce, 1 tablespoon finely shredded orange peel, ¼ cup orange juice, 1 tablespoon finely shredded lemon peel, 3 tablespoons lemon juice, 1 tablespoon brown sugar, 2 teaspoons toasted sesame oil, and 3 cloves garlic, minced. Pour over chicken, fish, or seafood in a plastic bag set in a dish. Marinate in the refrigerator for 1 to 2 hours, turning bag occasionally. Drain, discarding marinade. Makes ¾ cup.

Jamaican Jerk Rub: Combine 2 teaspoons sugar; 1½ teaspoons onion powder; 1½ teaspoons dried thyme, crushed; 1 teaspoon ground allspice; 1 teaspoon black pepper; ½ to 1 teaspoon ground red pepper; ½ teaspoon salt; ¼ teaspoon ground nutmeg; and ⅛ teaspoon ground cloves. Sprinkle mixture evenly over pork, chicken, or seafood; rub in with your fingers. Makes enough for about 4 pounds meat.

Herb Rub: In a blender container combine 2 teaspoons dried rosemary, 2 teaspoons dried thyme, 2 teaspoons dried minced onion, 2 teaspoons dried minced garlic, 1 teaspoon coarse salt, and ¾ teaspoon black pepper. Cover and blend until coarsely ground. Sprinkle mixture evenly over beef, pork, chicken, or seafood; rub in with your fingers. Makes enough for about 5 pounds meat.

Cranberry-Chipotle Sauce: In a small saucepan combine one 8-ounce can jellied cranberry sauce, ⅓ cup apricot or peach preserves, ¼ cup chopped onion, 1 tablespoon lemon juice or cider vinegar, and 1 canned chipotle pepper in adobo sauce or 1 fresh jalapeño chile pepper, seeded and chopped (see tip, page 64). Bring to boiling, stirring constantly; reduce heat. Simmer, uncovered, for 5 minutes, stirring occasionally. Brush sauce over pork or chicken during the last 10 minutes of grilling. Makes about 1½ cups.

Lemon-Rosemary Lamb Kabobs   `Best Loved` ♥

Prep: 15 minutes **Marinate:** 2 to 6 hours
Grill: 12 minutes **Makes:** 4 servings

- 1 **pound lean boneless leg of lamb**
- ¼ **cup olive oil**
- 1 **teaspoon finely shredded lemon peel**
- 3 **tablespoons lemon juice**
- 1 **tablespoon snipped fresh rosemary**
- ½ **teaspoon ground cumin**
- ½ **teaspoon freshly ground black pepper**
- 2 **cloves garlic, minced**
- 2 **small red onions, each cut lengthwise into 8 wedges**
- **Hot cooked couscous (optional)**

1. Trim fat from meat. Cut meat into 1½-inch pieces. Place meat in a plastic bag set in a shallow dish. For marinade, combine oil, lemon peel, lemon juice, rosemary, cumin, pepper, garlic, and ¼ teaspoon *salt*. Pour over meat; seal bag. Marinate in refrigerator 2 to 6 hours, turning occasionally.

2. In a medium saucepan cook onions, covered, in a small amount of boiling water for 3 minutes; drain. Drain meat, reserving marinade. On 8 long metal skewers, alternately thread the meat and onion wedges, leaving about a ¼-inch space between pieces. Brush onion wedges with some of the marinade.

**Lemon-Rosemary
Lamb Kabobs**

3. For a charcoal grill, place kabobs on grill rack directly over medium coals (see photo 2, page 305). Cover and grill for 12 to 16 minutes for medium (160°F), turning and brushing once with marinade halfway through grilling. (For a gas grill, preheat grill. Reduce heat to medium. Place kabobs on grill rack over heat. Cover and grill as above.) If desired, serve with couscous.

Nutrition Facts per serving: 277 cal., 18 g total fat (4 g sat. fat), 72 mg chol., 200 mg sodium, 4 g carbo., 1 g fiber, 24 g pro.
Daily Values: 13% vit. C, 2% calcium, 13% iron
Exchanges: 3½ Lean Meat, 1½ Fat

Apricot-Mustard Pork Chops

If you want to use chops that are ¾ to 1 inch thick, reduce the grilling time to 22 to 25 minutes.

Prep: 10 minutes **Grill:** 35 minutes **Makes:** 4 servings

- ⅓ **cup apricot spreadable fruit or peach preserves**
- 1 **tablespoon prepared mustard**
- ⅛ **teaspoon ground ginger or ground cinnamon**
- 4 **pork loin chops, cut 1¼ inches thick**

1. For glaze, combine spreadable fruit, mustard, and ginger; set aside. Trim fat from chops. If desired, season meat with *salt* and *black pepper*.

2. For a charcoal grill, arrange medium-hot coals around a drip pan. Test for medium heat above drip pan (see photo 3, page 305). Place chops on the grill rack over drip pan. Cover and grill for 35 to 40 minutes or until done (160°F), turning once halfway through grilling and brushing frequently with the glaze during the last 10 minutes of grilling. (For a gas grill, preheat grill. Reduce heat to medium. Adjust for indirect cooking. Grill as above.)

Nutrition Facts per serving: 444 cal., 14 g total fat (5 g sat. fat), 152 mg chol., 142 mg sodium, 16 g carbo., 0 g fiber, 61 g pro.
Daily Values: 1% vit. C, 6% calcium, 12% iron
Exchanges: 1 Other Carbo., 8½ Very Lean Meat, 2 Fat

Cleaning Your Grill

Soak the grill rack of your charcoal grill in hot, sudsy water after every use to loosen cooked-on grime. If the rack is too large for your sink, let it stand for about 1 hour wrapped in wet paper towels or newspaper, then wipe it clean. If necessary, use a stiff brush to remove stubborn burned-on food.

For gas grills, follow the steps suggested in "Controlling Flare-Ups," page 307.

Hickory-Smoked Pork Loin

Tossing wood chips on a grill gives foods a wood-smoked aroma and flavor. Good choices for wood chips include mesquite, hickory, oak, and sweet fruitwoods, such as apple, cherry, and peach. Supermarkets that stock charcoal usually carry wood chips as well.

Low Fat

Prep: 10 minutes **Stand:** 30 minutes **Grill:** 1 hour
Stand: 15 minutes **Makes:** 6 to 8 servings

- 3 cups hickory or oak wood chips
- 1 2- to 2½-pound boneless pork top loin roast (single loin)
- 2 tablespoons brown sugar
- 1 teaspoon finely shredded orange peel
- 1 teaspoon ground coriander
- 1 teaspoon paprika
- ½ teaspoon salt
- ½ teaspoon ground ginger
- ¼ teaspoon black pepper

1. At least 1 hour before grilling, soak wood chips in enough water to cover.

2. Meanwhile, trim fat from meat. Place meat in a shallow dish. In a small bowl stir together brown sugar, orange peel, coriander, paprika, salt, ginger, and pepper. Sprinkle mixture evenly over all sides of meat; rub in with your fingers. Cover and let stand at room temperature for 30 minutes or in the refrigerator for 2 to 4 hours.

3. Drain wood chips. For a charcoal grill, arrange medium coals around a drip pan. Test for medium-low heat above the pan (see photo 3, page 305). Sprinkle half of the drained wood chips over the coals. Place meat on grill rack over drip pan. Cover and grill for 1 to 1½ hours or until 155°F. Add remaining wood chips halfway through grilling. (For a gas grill, preheat grill. Reduce heat to medium-low. Adjust for indirect cooking. Place meat on a rack in a roasting pan, place on grill rack, and grill as above.)

4. Remove meat from grill; cover with foil and let stand for 15 minutes. The temperature of the meat after standing should be 160°F.

Nutrition Facts per serving: 224 cal., 7 g total fat (3 g sat. fat), 83 mg chol., 250 mg sodium, 3 g carbo., 0 g fiber, 33 g pro.
Daily Values: 4% vit. A, 2% vit. C, 4% calcium, 7% iron
Exchanges: 4½ Lean Meat

Tangy Peanut-Sauced Ribs

Peanut butter, ginger, and crushed red pepper combine to give these ribs an exotic Asian flavor.

Prep: 20 minutes **Grill:** 1½ hours **Makes:** 4 to 6 servings

- 4 pounds meaty pork spareribs or pork loin back ribs
- ¼ cup hot water
- ¼ cup peanut butter
- 2 tablespoons lime juice
- 2 tablespoons sliced green onion (1)
- ½ teaspoon grated fresh ginger or ¼ teaspoon ground ginger
- ¼ teaspoon ground red pepper

1. Trim fat from ribs. Cut ribs into 4 to 6 serving-size pieces (see photo, below). For a charcoal grill, arrange medium-hot coals around a drip pan. Test for medium heat above pan (see photo 3, page 305). Place ribs, bone sides down, on grill rack over drip pan. (Or, place ribs in a rib rack; place on grill rack.) Cover and grill for 1½ to 1¾ hours or until tender. (For a gas grill, preheat grill. Reduce heat to medium. Adjust for indirect cooking. Place ribs in a roasting pan, place on grill rack, and grill as above.)

2. Meanwhile, for sauce, in a small saucepan gradually stir hot water into peanut butter (mixture will stiffen at first). Stir in lime juice, green onion, ginger, and red pepper. Cook and stir over low heat until heated through. Spoon sauce over ribs.

Nutrition Facts per serving: 802 cal., 62 g total fat (21 g sat. fat), 214 mg chol., 241 mg sodium, 4 g carbo., 1 g fiber, 56 g pro.
Daily Values: 2% vit. A, 6% vit. C, 10% calcium, 21% iron
Exchanges: 8 High-Fat Meat

With a sharp boning knife, cut between the bones to separate the ribs into serving-size portions of two or three ribs each.

Glazed Country Ribs `Best Loved`

Get out knives, forks, and plenty of napkins when you serve these unforgettable ribs glazed with a rich, tart-sweet sauce (see photo, page 303).

Prep: 15 minutes **Grill:** 1½ hours **Makes:** 4 servings

> 1 **cup catsup**
> ¼ **cup finely chopped onion**
> ¼ **cup cider vinegar or wine vinegar**
> ¼ **cup mild-flavored molasses**
> 2 **tablespoons Worcestershire sauce**
> 2 **teaspoons chili powder**
> 2 **cloves garlic, minced**
> 2½ **to 3 pounds pork country-style ribs**

1. For sauce, in a medium saucepan combine catsup, onion, vinegar, molasses, Worcestershire sauce, chili powder, garlic, and ½ cup *water*. Bring to boiling; reduce heat. Simmer, uncovered, for 10 to 15 minutes or to desired consistency, stirring often.

2. Trim fat from ribs. For a charcoal grill, arrange medium-hot coals around a drip pan. Test for medium heat above pan (see photo 3, page 305). Place ribs, bone sides down, on grill rack over pan. (Or, place ribs in a rib rack; place on grill rack.) Cover and grill for 1½ to 2 hours or until tender, brushing occasionally with sauce during the last 10 minutes of grilling. (For a gas grill, preheat grill. Reduce heat to medium. Adjust for indirect cooking. Place ribs in a roasting pan, place on grill rack, and grill as above.) Pass remaining sauce with ribs.

Nutrition Facts per serving: 431 cal., 18 g total fat (6 g sat. fat), 112 mg chol., 852 mg sodium, 34 g carbo., 1 g fiber, 33 g pro.
Daily Values: 22% vit. A, 21% vit. C, 11% calcium, 20% iron
Exchanges: 2 Other Carbo., 4 Medium-Fat Meat

Adjusting the Heat

■ If the coals are too hot, raise the grill rack, spread the coals apart, close the air vents halfway, or remove some briquettes. For a gas or electric grill, adjust the burner to a lower setting.

■ If the coals are too cool, use long-handled tongs to tap ashes off the burning coals, move the coals together, add briquettes, lower the rack, or open the vents. For a gas or electric grill, adjust the burner to a higher setting.

■ Not everyone judges the temperature of coals exactly alike. Therefore, the time ranges in our recipes are recommendations. For perfectly done food, use our timings as guides and watch all foods on the grill closely.

Mojo Pork

The word "mojo" (moe-hoe) comes from the Spanish word mojado, *which means "wet." Found predominantly in Spanish and Cuban cuisine, mojos are used as sauces or marinades.*

`Low Fat`

Prep: 20 minutes **Marinate:** 2 hours
Grill: 40 minutes **Makes:** 6 servings

> 2 **12- to 16-ounce pork tenderloins**
> 4 **canned chipotle peppers in adobo sauce**
> ½ **cup orange juice**
> ¼ **cup coarsely chopped onion**
> 2 **tablespoons snipped fresh oregano or**
>   2 **teaspoons dried oregano, crushed**
> 2 **tablespoons lime juice**
> 1 **tablespoon honey**
> 1 **tablespoon cooking oil**
> ½ **teaspoon salt**
> 3 **cloves garlic, minced**

1. Trim fat from meat. Place meat in a plastic bag set in a shallow dish. For marinade, remove any stems from chipotle peppers. In a food processor bowl or blender container combine chipotle peppers and adobo sauce, orange juice, onion, oregano, lime juice, honey, oil, salt, and garlic. Cover and process or blend until nearly smooth. Pour over meat; seal bag. Marinate in the refrigerator for 2 hours, turning bag occasionally. (Do not marinate more than 2 hours because the citrus juices cause the meat to become mushy.) Drain meat, discarding marinade.

2. For a charcoal grill, arrange hot coals around a drip pan. Test for medium-hot heat above pan (see photo 3, page 305). Place meat on grill rack over the drip pan. Cover and grill for 40 to 50 minutes or until done (160°F). (For a gas grill, preheat grill. Reduce heat to medium-high. Adjust for indirect cooking. Place the meat on a rack in a roasting pan, place on grill rack, and grill as above.)

Nutrition Facts per serving: 157 cal., 4 g total fat (1 g sat. fat), 73 mg chol., 154 mg sodium, 3 g carbo., 0 g fiber, 24 g pro.
Daily Values: 1% vit. A, 12% vit. C, 1% calcium, 8% iron
Exchanges: 3½ Very Lean Meat, ½ Fat

Barbecued Pork Sandwiches

Barbecued Pork Sandwiches

Double the recipe and use two grills to cook up a feast for 24 people.

Prep: 40 minutes **Grill:** 4 hours
Stand: 30 minutes **Makes:** 12 to 16 servings

- 1 4½- to 5-pound boneless pork shoulder roast
- ½ teaspoon salt
- ½ teaspoon black pepper
- ¼ teaspoon celery seeds
- ⅛ teaspoon onion powder
- ⅛ teaspoon garlic powder
- ⅛ teaspoon ground cloves
- Dash ground red pepper
- 1 8-ounce can tomato sauce
- 1 cup catsup
- 1 cup chopped onion (1 large)
- ½ cup chopped green sweet pepper
- ¼ cup vinegar
- 2 tablespoons brown sugar
- 2 tablespoons Worcestershire sauce
- 1 tablespoon prepared mustard
- 2 teaspoons chili powder
- 2 cloves garlic, minced
- 12 to 16 French-style rolls, split and toasted

1. Trim fat from meat. In a bowl combine salt, pepper, celery seeds, onion powder, garlic powder, cloves, and red pepper. Sprinkle mixture evenly over all sides of meat; rub in with your fingers.

2. For a charcoal grill, arrange medium-hot coals around a drip pan. Test for medium heat above pan (see photo 3, page 305). Place meat on grill rack over drip pan. Cover and grill about 4 hours or until meat is very tender. (For a gas grill, preheat grill. Reduce heat to medium. Adjust heat for indirect cooking. Place meat on a rack in a roasting pan, place on grill rack, and grill as above.) Remove meat from grill; cover with foil and let stand for 30 minutes.

3. Meanwhile, for sauce, in a large saucepan combine tomato sauce, catsup, onion, sweet pepper, vinegar, brown sugar, Worcestershire sauce, mustard, chili powder, and garlic. Bring to boiling; reduce heat. Simmer, covered for 15 minutes.

4. Shred pork with forks (see photo, below). Stir shredded pork into sauce; heat through. Spoon pork onto toasted rolls.

Nutrition Facts per serving: 405 cal., 14 g total fat (5 g sat. fat), 114 mg chol., 823 mg sodium, 30 g carbo., 2 g fiber, 37 g pro.
Daily Values: 12% vit. A, 22% vit. C, 9% calcium, 21% iron
Exchanges: 2 Starch, 4½ Lean Meat

When the pork roast has been grilled until it's extremely tender, use two forks to gently separate the meat into long, thin strands.

Finger-Lickin' Barbecue Chicken

Best Loved

Prep: 45 minutes **Marinate:** 2 to 4 hours
Grill: 50 minutes **Makes:** 6 servings

3 to 4 pounds meaty chicken pieces (breast halves, thighs, and drumsticks)
1½ cups dry sherry
1 cup finely chopped onion (1 large)
¼ cup lemon juice
2 bay leaves
6 cloves garlic, minced
1 15-ounce can tomato puree
¼ cup honey
3 tablespoons mild-flavored molasses
1 teaspoon salt
½ teaspoon dried thyme, crushed
¼ to ½ teaspoon ground red pepper
¼ teaspoon black pepper
2 tablespoons white vinegar

1. Place chicken in a plastic bag set in a shallow dish. For marinade, in a medium bowl combine sherry, onion, lemon juice, bay leaves, and garlic. Pour over chicken; seal bag. Marinate in the refrigerator for 2 to 4 hours, turning bag occasionally. Drain chicken, reserving marinade. Cover and chill chicken until ready to grill.

2. For sauce, in a large saucepan combine the reserved marinade, the tomato puree, honey, molasses, salt, thyme, red pepper, and black pepper. Bring to boiling; reduce heat. Simmer, uncovered, about 30 minutes or until reduced to 2 cups. Remove from heat; remove bay leaves. Stir in vinegar.

3. For a charcoal grill, arrange medium-hot coals around a drip pan. Test for medium heat above the pan (see photo 3, page 305). Place chicken pieces, bone sides down, on grill rack over drip pan. Cover and grill for 50 to 60 minutes or until chicken is no longer pink (170°F for breasts, 180°F for thighs and drumsticks), brushing with some of the sauce during the last 15 minutes of grilling. (For a gas grill, preheat grill. Reduce heat to medium. Adjust for indirect cooking. Grill as above.) To serve, reheat and pass the remaining sauce with chicken.

Nutrition Facts per serving: 503 cal., 18 g total fat (5 g sat. fat), 129 mg chol., 779 mg sodium, 35 g carbo., 2 g fiber, 35 g pro.
Daily Values: 22% vit. A, 29% vit. C, 7% calcium, 18% iron
Exchanges: 1 Vegetable, 2 Other Carbo., 5 Lean Meat, 2 Fat

Herb-Mustard Chicken Quarters

Another time, brush this oregano-infused sauce on pork chops.

Prep: 15 minutes **Grill:** 50 minutes **Makes:** 4 servings

2 tablespoons creamy Dijon-style mustard blend
1 tablespoon snipped fresh parsley
1 tablespoon snipped fresh oregano or 1 teaspoon dried oregano, crushed
1 tablespoon water
⅛ teaspoon ground red pepper
1 3- to 3½-pound whole broiler-fryer chicken, cut into quarters

1. For sauce, in a small bowl combine mustard blend, parsley, oregano, water, and red pepper. Cover and chill until ready to use.

2. If desired, remove skin from chicken. For a charcoal grill, arrange medium-hot coals around a drip pan. Test for medium heat above the pan (see photo 3, page 305). Place chicken, bone sides down, on grill rack over the drip pan. Cover and grill for 50 to 60 minutes or until chicken is no longer pink (170°F for breasts, 180°F for dark meat), brushing occasionally with sauce during the last 10 minutes of grilling. (For a gas grill, preheat grill. Reduce heat to medium. Adjust heat for indirect cooking. Grill as above.)

Nutrition Facts per serving: 288 cal., 16 g total fat (4 g sat. fat), 102 mg chol., 201 mg sodium, 2 g carbo., 0 g fiber, 32 g pro.
Daily Values: 6% vit. A, 3% vit. C, 3% calcium, 10% iron
Exchanges: 4 Medium-Fat Meat

Herb-Mustard Chicken Quarters

Sesame-Ginger Barbecued Chicken

This Asian-style barbecue sauce—spiked with Oriental chili sauce—is so good you'll definitely want to warm the extra and pass it at the table with the chicken.

Fast **Low Fat**

Prep: 15 minutes **Grill:** 12 minutes **Makes:** 6 servings

- ⅓ cup bottled plum sauce or bottled sweet and sour sauce
- ¼ cup water
- 3 tablespoons hoisin sauce
- 1½ teaspoons sesame seeds (toasted, if desired; see tip, page 224)
- 1 teaspoon grated fresh ginger or ¼ teaspoon ground ginger
- ¼ to ½ teaspoon Oriental chili sauce or several dashes bottled hot pepper sauce
- 1 clove garlic, minced
- 6 skinless, boneless chicken breast halves and/or skinless, boneless chicken thighs

1. For sauce, in a small saucepan combine plum sauce, water, hoisin sauce, sesame seeds, ginger, Oriental chili sauce, and garlic. Bring to boiling over medium heat, stirring frequently; reduce heat. Simmer, covered, for 3 minutes. Remove saucepan from heat.

2. For a charcoal grill, grill chicken on the rack of an uncovered grill directly over medium coals (see photo 2, page 305) for 12 to 15 minutes or until chicken is no longer pink (170°F for breasts, 180°F for thighs), turning once and brushing with some of the sauce during the last 5 minutes of grilling. (For a gas grill, preheat grill. Reduce heat to medium. Place chicken on grill rack over heat. Cover and grill as above.) Reheat and pass remaining sauce.

Nutrition Facts per serving: 177 cal., 2 g total fat (0 g sat. fat), 66 mg chol., 222 mg sodium, 11 g carbo., 0 g fiber, 27 g pro.
Daily Values: 1% vit. A, 3% vit. C, 2% calcium, 6% iron
Exchanges: ½ Other Carbo., 4 Very Lean Meat

Chicken Breasts with Firecracker Barbecue Sauce

Resist the temptation to slather the sauce onto the chicken too early. To prevent overbrowning or burning, it's best to brush on a sweet or tomato-based barbecue sauce during the last few minutes of grilling.

Low Fat

Prep: 25 minutes **Grill:** 12 minutes **Makes:** 6 servings

- ¼ cup chipotle peppers in adobo sauce
  Nonstick cooking spray
- ⅓ cup finely chopped onion (1 small)
- 3 cloves garlic, minced
- 1 cup catsup
- 3 tablespoons white wine vinegar
- 3 tablespoons full-flavored molasses or sorghum
- 1 tablespoon Worcestershire sauce
- 6 skinless, boneless chicken breast halves

1. For sauce, remove any stems from chipotle peppers. Place peppers and adobo sauce in a blender container. Cover and blend until smooth. Set aside.

2. Lightly coat an unheated medium saucepan with nonstick cooking spray. Cook onion and garlic in saucepan until tender. Stir in chipotle pepper mixture, catsup, vinegar, molasses, and Worcestershire sauce. Bring to boiling; reduce heat. Simmer, uncovered, about 10 minutes or until sauce is slightly thickened.

3. For a charcoal grill, grill chicken on the rack of an uncovered grill directly over medium coals (see photo 2, page 305) for 12 to 15 minutes or until chicken is no longer pink (170°F), turning once halfway through grilling and brushing with sauce during the last 5 minutes of grilling. (For a gas grill, preheat grill. Reduce heat to medium. Place chicken on grill rack over heat. Cover and grill as above.) Bring remaining sauce to boiling; pass with chicken.

Nutrition Facts per serving: 207 cal., 2 g total fat (0 g sat. fat), 66 mg chol., 612 mg sodium, 20 g carbo., 1 g fiber, 27 g pro.
Daily Values: 11% vit. A, 14% vit. C, 5% calcium, 10% iron
Exchanges: 1½ Other Carbo., 3½ Very Lean Meat

Five-Spice Chicken Kabobs

Metal skewers are easier to use than wooden skewers, which will burn if not soaked first.

`Fast` `Low Fat`

Prep: 15 minutes **Grill:** 12 minutes **Makes:** 6 servings

- ¼ cup frozen orange juice concentrate, thawed
- 2 tablespoons honey
- 1 tablespoon soy sauce
- ¼ teaspoon five-spice powder
  Dash ground ginger
- 1 pound skinless, boneless chicken breast halves or skinless, boneless chicken thighs
- 1 cup fresh pineapple chunks or one 8-ounce can pineapple chunks (juice pack), drained
- 1 medium green sweet pepper, cut into 1-inch pieces
- 1 medium red sweet pepper, cut into 1-inch pieces
- 2 cups hot cooked rice

1. For glaze, in a small bowl combine orange juice concentrate, honey, soy sauce, five-spice powder, and ginger. Set aside.

2. Cut chicken into 1-inch pieces. On 6 long metal skewers, alternately thread chicken, pineapple, green sweet pepper, and red sweet pepper, leaving a ¼-inch space between pieces.

3. For a charcoal grill, grill kabobs on the rack of an uncovered grill directly over medium coals (see photo 2, page 305) for 12 to 14 minutes or until no longer pink, turning and brushing once with glaze up to the last 5 minutes of grilling. (For

a gas grill, preheat grill. Reduce heat to medium. Place kabobs on grill rack over heat. Cover and grill as above.) Serve with hot cooked rice.

Nutrition Facts per serving: 216 cal., 1 g total fat (0 g sat. fat), 44 mg chol., 251 mg sodium, 31 g carbo., 1 g fiber, 20 g pro.
Daily Values: 25% vit. A, 116% vit. C, 2% calcium, 8% iron
Exchanges: 1 Vegetable, ½ Fruit, 1 Starch, 2 Very Lean Meat

Glazed Turkey Burgers `Best Loved`

A glaze of mustard and fruit preserves gives these burgers a sweet-sour taste.

Prep: 20 minutes **Grill:** 14 minutes **Makes:** 4 servings

- 1 tablespoon prepared mustard
- 1 tablespoon cherry, apricot, peach, or pineapple preserves
- 1 beaten egg
- ¼ cup quick-cooking rolled oats
- ¼ cup finely chopped celery
- 3 tablespoons snipped dried tart cherries or dried apricots (optional)
- ¼ teaspoon salt
- ⅛ teaspoon black pepper
- 1 pound uncooked ground turkey or chicken
- 4 kaiser rolls or hamburger buns, split and toasted
  Mayonnaise or salad dressing, lettuce leaves, and/or tomato slices (optional)

1. For glaze, stir together mustard and preserves; set aside.

2. In a medium bowl combine egg, rolled oats, celery, dried cherries (if desired), salt, and pepper. Add ground turkey; mix well. Shape turkey mixture into four ¾-inch-thick patties.

3. For a charcoal grill, grill patties on the rack of an uncovered grill directly over medium coals (see photo 2, page 305) for 14 to 18 minutes or until no longer pink (165°F), turning once halfway through grilling and brushing with glaze during the last minute of grilling. (For a gas grill, preheat grill. Reduce heat to medium. Place burgers on the grill rack over heat. Cover and grill as above.)

4. Serve burgers on toasted buns. Brush any remaining glaze over burgers. If desired, serve burgers with mayonnaise, lettuce, and tomato.

Nutrition Facts per serving: 397 cal., 14 g total fat (3 g sat. fat), 143 mg chol., 599 mg sodium, 38 g carbo., 2 g fiber, 28 g pro.
Daily Values: 2% vit. A, 2% vit. C, 9% calcium, 21% iron
Exchanges: 2½ Starch, 2½ Medium-Fat Meat

Glazed Turkey Burgers

Turkey Tenders with Sweet Pepper-Citrus Salsa

Precut turkey breast tenderloin steaks are available in most areas. If you find only large whole tenderloins, slice them horizontally into ½-inch-thick steaks.

Prep: 15 minutes **Marinate:** 2 to 4 hours
Grill: 12 minutes **Makes:** 6 servings

6 ½-inch-thick turkey breast tenderloin steaks (about 1½ pounds)
⅓ cup olive oil
¼ cup lemon juice
1 teaspoon finely shredded orange peel
¼ cup orange juice
¼ teaspoon salt
¼ teaspoon black pepper
4 cloves garlic, minced
1 recipe Sweet Pepper-Citrus Salsa

1. Place turkey in a plastic bag set in a shallow bowl. For marinade, in a small bowl combine oil, lemon juice, orange peel, orange juice, salt, pepper, and garlic. Pour over turkey; seal bag. Marinate in the refrigerator for 2 to 4 hours, turning bag occasionally.

2. Drain turkey, reserving marinade. For a charcoal grill, grill turkey on the rack of an uncovered grill directly over medium coals (see photo 2, page 305) for 12 to 15 minutes or until no longer pink (170°F), turning once halfway through grilling and brushing with marinade during the first 6 minutes of grilling. (For a gas grill, preheat grill. Reduce heat to medium. Place turkey on grill rack over heat. Cover and grill as above.) Serve with Sweet Pepper-Citrus Salsa.

Sweet Pepper-Citrus Salsa: In a small bowl combine one 7-ounce jar roasted red sweet peppers, drained and chopped; 1 orange, peeled, seeded, and cut up; 2 green onions, sliced; 2 tablespoons balsamic vinegar; and 1 tablespoon snipped fresh basil or 1 teaspoon dried basil, crushed. Cover and chill until serving time. Makes 1½ cups salsa.

Nutrition Facts per serving: 262 cal., 13 g total fat (2 g sat. fat), 70 mg chol., 141 mg sodium, 8 g carbo., 1 g fiber, 29 g pro.
Daily Values: 2% vit. A, 138% vit. C, 3% calcium, 10% iron
Exchanges: 1 Vegetable, 4 Very Lean Meat, 2 Fat

Caramelized Salmon with Orange-Pineapple Salsa

This do-ahead recipe is especially impressive because the orange-scented sugar rub turns a rich golden brown during grilling.

Low Fat

Prep: 20 minutes **Marinate:** 8 to 24 hours
Grill: 14 minutes **Makes:** 4 servings

1 1½-pound fresh or frozen salmon fillet (with skin), cut 1 inch thick
2 tablespoons sugar
2½ teaspoons finely shredded orange peel
2 oranges, peeled, sectioned, and coarsely chopped
1 cup chopped fresh pineapple or canned crushed pineapple, drained
2 tablespoons snipped fresh cilantro
1 tablespoon finely chopped shallot
1 fresh jalapeño chile pepper, seeded and finely chopped (see tip, page 64)

1. Thaw fish, if frozen. Rinse fish; pat dry. Place fish, skin side down, in a shallow dish. In a small bowl stir together sugar, 1½ teaspoons of the orange peel, 1 teaspoon *salt,* and ¼ teaspoon freshly ground *black pepper.* Sprinkle mixture evenly over fish (not on skin side); rub in with your fingers. Cover and marinate in the refrigerator for 8 to 24 hours.

2. Meanwhile, for salsa, in a small bowl stir together the remaining 1 teaspoon orange peel, the oranges, pineapple, cilantro, shallot, and jalapeño pepper. Cover and chill until ready to serve or up to 24 hours.

3. Drain fish, discarding any liquid. For a charcoal grill, arrange medium-hot coals around a drip pan. Test for medium heat above the pan (see photo 3, page 305). Place fish, skin side down, on greased grill rack over drip pan. Cover and grill for 14 to 18 minutes or until fish flakes easily when tested with a fork. (For a gas grill, preheat grill. Reduce heat to medium. Adjust for indirect cooking. Grill as above.)

4. To serve, cut fish into 4 serving-size pieces, cutting up to but not through the skin. Carefully slip a metal spatula between fish and skin, lifting fish up and away from skin. Serve fish with salsa.

Nutrition Facts per serving: 258 cal., 6 g total fat (1 g sat. fat), 81 mg chol., 688 mg sodium, 20 g carbo., 2 g fiber, 32 g pro.
Daily Values: 10% vit. A, 75% vit. C, 6% calcium, 9% iron
Exchanges: 1½ Fruit, 4½ Very Lean Meat

Mustard-Glazed Halibut Steaks

Fast **Low Fat**

Prep: 10 minutes **Grill:** 8 minutes **Makes:** 4 servings

- **4 6-ounce fresh or frozen halibut steaks, cut 1 inch thick**
- **2 tablespoons butter or margarine**
- **2 tablespoons lemon juice**
- **1 tablespoon Dijon-style mustard**
- **2 teaspoons snipped fresh basil or ½ teaspoon dried basil, crushed**

1. Thaw fish, if frozen. Rinse fish; pat dry. In a small saucepan heat butter, lemon juice, mustard, and basil over low heat until melted. Brush both sides of steaks with mustard mixture.

2. For a charcoal grill, grill fish on the greased rack of an uncovered grill directly over medium coals (see photo 2, page 305) for 8 to 12 minutes or until fish flakes easily when tested with a fork, gently turning once halfway through grilling and brushing occasionally with mustard mixture. (For a gas grill, preheat grill. Reduce heat to medium. Place fish on greased grill rack over heat. Cover and grill as above.)

Nutrition Facts per serving: 247 cal., 10 g total fat (4 g sat. fat), 71 mg chol., 175 mg sodium, 1 g carbo., 0 g fiber, 36 g pro.
Daily Values: 10% vit. A, 6% vit. C, 9% calcium, 9% iron
Exchanges: 5 Very Lean Meat, 1½ Fat

Rosemary Trout with Lemon Butter

Fast **Low Fat**

Prep: 15 minutes **Grill:** 6 minutes **Makes:** 4 servings

- **2 8- to 10-ounce fresh or frozen dressed, boned rainbow trout or other dressed fish**
- **1 tablespoon snipped fresh rosemary**
- **1 tablespoon finely chopped shallot or onion**
- **1 teaspoon finely shredded lemon peel (set aside)**
- **1 tablespoon lemon juice**
- **2 teaspoons olive oil**
- **4 teaspoons butter, softened**
- **2 medium tomatoes, halved crosswise**
- **1 tablespoon snipped fresh parsley**

1. Thaw fish, if frozen. Rinse fish; pat dry. Spread each fish open, skin side down. Rub the rosemary and half of the shallot over fish; sprinkle with *salt* and *black pepper*. Drizzle with the lemon juice and oil. Set aside.

2. For lemon butter, in a small bowl stir together the remaining shallot, the lemon peel, and butter. Sprinkle with *salt* and *black pepper*. Dot each tomato half with ¼ teaspoon of the butter mixture.

3. For a charcoal grill, grill fish, skin sides down, and tomatoes on the greased rack of an uncovered grill directly over medium coals (see photo 2, page 305) until fish flakes easily when tested with a fork and tomatoes are heated through. Allow 6 to 9 minutes for fish and about 5 minutes for tomatoes. (For a gas grill, preheat grill. Reduce heat to medium. Place fish, skin sides down, and tomatoes on greased grill rack over heat. Cover and grill as above.)

4. To serve, in a small saucepan melt remaining butter mixture. Cut each fish in half lengthwise; sprinkle with parsley. Drizzle butter mixture over fish and tomatoes.

Nutrition Facts per serving: 210 cal., 12 g total fat (4 g sat. fat), 69 mg chol., 301 mg sodium, 4 g carbo., 1 g fiber, 21 g pro.
Daily Values: 18% vit. A, 30% vit. C, 8% calcium, 4% iron
Exchanges: 1 Vegetable, 3 Very Lean Meat, 2 Fat

Rosemary Trout with Lemon Butter

Tuna with Roasted Pepper Sauce

Prep: 30 minutes **Grill:** 8 minutes **Makes:** 4 servings

> 4 5- to 6-ounce fresh or frozen tuna or halibut steaks, cut 1 inch thick
> 1 tablespoon olive oil or cooking oil
> 2 roasted red sweet peppers (see tip, page 519)
> 2 tablespoons lime juice
> 2 tablespoons water
> 2 teaspoons snipped fresh thyme or dill, or ½ teaspoon dried thyme, crushed, or dried dill
> ¼ teaspoon salt
> ⅛ teaspoon black pepper
> 1 tablespoon butter or margarine

1. Thaw fish, if frozen. Rinse fish; pat dry. Brush some of the oil over both sides of fish. For a charcoal grill, grill fish on the greased rack of an uncovered grill directly over medium coals (see photo 2, page 305) for 8 to 12 minutes or until fish flakes easily when tested with a fork, gently turning once and brushing once with remaining oil halfway through grilling. (For a gas grill, preheat grill. Reduce heat to medium. Place fish on greased grill rack over heat. Cover and grill as above.)

2. For sauce, in a blender container or food processor bowl combine roasted peppers, lime juice, water, thyme, salt, and pepper. Cover and blend or process until smooth. Pour into a small saucepan. Cook and stir over low heat until heated through. Stir in butter.

3. To serve, pour warm pepper sauce onto 4 serving plates. Top with fish steaks.

Nutrition Facts per serving: 278 cal., 13 g total fat (4 g sat. fat), 62 mg chol., 233 mg sodium, 4 g carbo., 1 g fiber, 34 g pro. **Daily Values:** 119% vit. A, 155% vit. C, 2% calcium, 10% iron **Exchanges:** 1 Vegetable, 4½ Lean Meat

Orange and Dill Sea Bass Best Loved

Fast   Low Fat

Prep: 15 minutes **Grill:** 6 minutes **Makes:** 4 servings

> 4 5- to 6-ounce fresh or frozen sea bass or orange roughy fillets, cut ¾ inch thick
> 2 tablespoons snipped fresh dill
> 2 tablespoons olive oil
> ¼ teaspoon salt
> ¼ teaspoon white pepper
> 4 large oranges, cut into ¼-inch slices
> 1 orange, cut into wedges

1. Thaw fish, if frozen. Rinse fish; pat dry. In a small bowl stir together dill, oil, salt, and pepper. Brush both sides of fish fillets with dill mixture.

2. For a charcoal grill, arrange a bed of orange slices on greased grill rack directly over medium coals (see photo 2, page 305). Arrange fish on orange slices. Cover and grill for 6 to 9 minutes or until fish flakes easily when tested with a fork (do not turn fish). (For a gas grill, preheat grill. Reduce heat to medium. Arrange orange slices and fish on greased grill rack over heat. Cover and grill as above.)

3. To serve, use a spatula to transfer fish and grilled orange slices to a serving platter. Squeeze the juice from orange wedges over fish.

Nutrition Facts per serving: 268 cal., 10 g total fat (2 g sat. fat), 58 mg chol., 242 mg sodium, 18 g carbo., 3 g fiber, 28 g pro. **Daily Values:** 11% vit. A, 133% vit. C, 7% calcium, 4% iron **Exchanges:** 1 Fruit, 4 Very Lean Meat, 1½ Fat

Are Grilled Foods Safe?

You may have heard of possible health risks associated with cooking over high heat. Grilling, broiling, and smoking have all been implicated. These cooking methods can produce small amounts of harmful substances when fat from meat drips over hot coals, resulting in flare-ups. Although the risk is low, you may want to take some precautions.

■ Minimize flare-ups by choosing lean cuts of meat and trimming visible fat before grilling.

■ During a flare-up, rescue food from scorching by moving it to a cooler area and temporarily covering the grill to extinguish the fire.

■ Use minimal oil on foods and grill racks, and grill fatty foods or skin-on poultry indirectly.

■ It is best to apply sugary sauces with a light hand toward the end of grilling to prevent burning.

■ Most important, always clean the grill of charred food debris before grilling again.

If you're still concerned about possible risks, grill foods over indirect heat (see page 305). Consult the charts at the end of this chapter for indirect grilling times and techniques.

Shrimp and Tropical Fruit

Low Fat

Prep: 25 minutes **Grill:** 10 minutes **Makes:** 6 servings

- 1¼ **pounds fresh or frozen jumbo shrimp in shells**
- 1 **cup bottled barbecue sauce**
- ⅔ **cup unsweetened pineapple juice**
- 2 **tablespoons cooking oil**
- 4 **teaspoons grated fresh ginger or** 1½ **teaspoons ground ginger**
- ¼ **of a fresh pineapple, sliced crosswise**
- 1 **medium papaya, peeled, seeded, and cut up**
- 3 **medium kiwifruit, peeled and cut up**

1. Thaw shrimp, if frozen. Peel and devein shrimp, leaving tails intact (see photos, page 295). Rinse shrimp; pat dry. Thread shrimp onto 6 long metal skewers. For sauce, in a medium bowl stir together barbecue sauce, pineapple juice, oil, and ginger; brush sauce over shrimp.

2. For a charcoal grill, grill kabobs and pineapple slices on the greased rack of an uncovered grill directly over medium coals (see photo 2, page 305) until shrimp are opaque and pineapple is heated through, turning once and brushing occasionally with some of the sauce up to the last 5 minutes of grilling. Allow 10 to 12 minutes for shrimp and about 5 minutes for pineapple. (For a gas grill, preheat grill. Reduce heat to medium. Place kabobs and pineapple slices on greased grill rack over heat. Cover and grill as above.)

3. In a small saucepan bring remaining sauce to boiling. Boil gently, uncovered, for 1 minute; cool slightly. Pass sauce for dipping. Serve shrimp and pineapple with papaya and kiwifruit.

Nutrition Facts per serving: 231 cal., 6 g total fat (1 g sat. fat), 96 mg chol., 640 mg sodium, 29 g carbo., 3 g fiber, 14 g pro.
Daily Values: 8% vit. A, 126% vit. C, 7% calcium, 10% iron
Exchanges: 2 Fruit, 2 Very Lean Meat, 1 Fat

Vegetable Pizzas **Best Loved**

Prep: 25 minutes **Grill:** 11 minutes **Makes:** 4 servings

- 1 **medium zucchini, quartered lengthwise**
- 1 **small yellow summer squash, quartered lengthwise**
- 1 **small red sweet pepper, quartered lengthwise**
- 2 **tablespoons olive oil**
- 1 **teaspoon black pepper**
- ½ **teaspoon salt**
- 1 **large ripe tomato, seeded and chopped**
- ¼ **cup mayonnaise or salad dressing**
- 2 **tablespoons purchased basil pesto**
- 1 **tablespoon snipped fresh basil**
- 1 **tablespoon snipped fresh oregano**
- 4 **6- to 7-inch flour tortillas**
- 1 **cup shredded mozzarella or smoked provolone cheese**

1. Brush zucchini, summer squash, and sweet pepper with oil; sprinkle with pepper and salt. For a charcoal grill, grill vegetables on the rack of an uncovered grill directly over medium coals (see photo 2, page 305) until crisp-tender, turning once halfway through grilling. Allow 8 to 10 minutes for sweet pepper and 5 to 6 minutes for zucchini and summer squash. Remove vegetables from grill.

2. Chop grilled vegetables. In a medium bowl combine chopped vegetables, tomato, mayonnaise, pesto, basil, and oregano. Place tortillas on grill rack directly over heat. Cover and grill for 1 to 2 minutes or until lightly toasted on one side. Turn tortillas over and spread the vegetable mixture over the toasted sides of tortillas. Sprinkle with shredded cheese. Cover and grill for 2 to 3 minutes more or until tortillas are lightly toasted, vegetables are just heated, and cheese begins to melt. Carefully remove from grill. (For a gas grill, preheat grill. Reduce heat to medium. Cover and grill vegetables and tortillas as above.)

Nutrition Facts per serving: 426 cal., 31 g total fat (7 g sat. fat), 24 mg chol., 737 mg sodium, 27 g carbo., 3 g fiber, 12 g pro.
Daily Values: 38% vit. A, 78% vit. C, 27% calcium, 11% iron
Exchanges: 1 Vegetable, 1½ Starch, 1 Medium-Fat Meat, 4½ Fat

Vegetable Pizzas

Corn on the Cob with Herb Butter

Buy the freshest ears you can find for grilling. Yellow, white, or yellow-and-white corn varieties are all excellent for grilling (see photo, page 303).

Prep: 20 minutes **Grill:** 25 minutes **Makes:** 6 servings

  6 **fresh ears corn (with husks)**
  6 **tablespoons butter or margarine, softened**
 36 **sprigs or leaves of cilantro or basil**
    100-percent-cotton kitchen string
    Lime or lemon wedges (optional)

1. Carefully peel back corn husks, but do not remove. Remove and discard the silks. Gently rinse corn; pat dry. Spread softened butter over each ear of corn. Space 6 sprigs or leaves evenly around cob, gently pressing herbs into butter. Carefully fold husks back around cobs. Tie husk tops with string.

2. For a charcoal grill, grill corn on the rack of an uncovered grill directly over medium coals (see photo 2, page 305) for 25 to 30 minutes or until corn kernels are tender, turning and rearranging occasionally. (For a gas grill, preheat grill. Reduce heat to medium. Place corn on grill rack over heat. Cover and grill as above.)

3. To serve, remove string from corn; peel back husks. If desired, squeeze lime juice over corn.

Nutrition Facts per serving: 185 cal., 13 g total fat (8 g sat. fat), 33 mg chol., 138 mg sodium, 17 g carbo., 2 g fiber, 3 g pro.
Daily Values: 15% vit. A, 9% vit. C, 1% calcium, 3% iron
Exchanges: 1 Starch, 2½ Fat

Direct-Grilling Poultry

If desired, remove skin from poultry. For a charcoal grill, place poultry on grill rack, bone side up, directly over medium coals (see photo 2, page 305). Grill, uncovered, for the time given below or until the proper temperature is reached and meat is no longer pink, turning once halfway through grilling. For a gas grill, preheat grill. Reduce heat to medium. Place poultry on grill rack, bone side down, over heat. Cover and grill.

Test for doneness using a meat thermometer (use an instant-read thermometer to test smaller portions). Thermometer should register 180°F, except in breast meat when thermometer should register 170°F. Poultry should be tender and no longer pink. If desired, during last 5 to 10 minutes of grilling, brush often with a sauce.

Type of Bird	Weight	Grilling Temperature	Approximate Direct-Grilling Time	Doneness
Chicken				
Chicken, broiler-fryer, half or quarters	1½- to 1¾-pound half or 12- to 14-ounce quarters	Medium	40 to 50 minutes	180°F
Chicken breast half, skinned and boned	4 to 5 ounces	Medium	12 to 15 minutes	170°F
Chicken thigh, skinned and boned	4 to 5 ounces	Medium	12 to 15 minutes	180°F
Meaty chicken pieces (breast halves, thighs, and drumsticks)	2½ to 3 pounds total	Medium	35 to 45 minutes	180°F
Turkey				
Turkey breast tenderloin steak	4 to 6 ounces	Medium	12 to 15 minutes	170°F

All cooking times are based on poultry removed directly from refrigerator.

Indirect-Grilling Poultry

If desired, remove skin from poultry. Rinse whole birds; pat dry. For a charcoal grill, arrange medium-hot coals around a drip pan. Test for medium heat above the pan (see photo 3, page 305). Place unstuffed poultry, breast side up, on grill rack over drip pan. Cover and grill for the time given below or until the proper temperature is reached and meat is no longer pink, adding more charcoal to maintain heat as necessary. For large poultry cuts and whole birds, we suggest placing the poultry on a rack in a roasting pan and omitting the drip pan. For a gas grill, preheat grill. Reduce heat to medium. Adjust heat for indirect cooking (see page 305).

Test for doneness using a meat thermometer (use an instant-read thermometer to test smaller portions). For whole birds, insert thermometer into the center of the inside thigh muscle, not touching bone (see photo 5, page 441). Thermometer should register 180°F, except in breast meat when thermometer should register 170°F. Poultry should be tender and no longer pink. (Note: Birds vary in size and shape. Use these times as general guides.)

Type of Bird	Weight	Grilling Temperature	Approximate Indirect-Grilling Time	Doneness
Chicken				
Chicken, whole	2½ to 3 pounds 3½ to 4 pounds 4½ to 5 pounds	Medium Medium Medium	1 to 1¼ hours 1¼ to 1¾ hours 1¾ to 2 hours	180°F 180°F 180°F
Chicken breast half, skinned and boned	4 to 5 ounces	Medium	15 to 18 minutes	170°F
Chicken, broiler-fryer, half	1½ to 1¾ pounds	Medium	1 to 1¼ hours	180°F
Chicken, broiler-fryer, quarters	12 to 14 ounces each	Medium	50 to 60 minutes	180°F
Chicken thigh, skinned and boned	4 to 5 ounces	Medium	15 to 18 minutes	180°F
Meaty chicken pieces (breast halves, thighs, and drumsticks)	2½ to 3 pounds total	Medium	50 to 60 minutes	180°F
Game				
Cornish game hen, whole	1¼ to 1½ pounds	Medium	50 to 60 minutes	180°F
Pheasant, whole	2 to 3 pounds	Medium	1 to 1½ hours	180°F
Quail, semiboneless	3 to 4 ounces	Medium	15 to 20 minutes	180°F
Squab	12 to 16 ounces	Medium	¾ to 1 hour	180°F
Turkey				
Turkey, whole	6 to 8 pounds 8 to 12 pounds 12 to 16 pounds	Medium Medium Medium	1¾ to 2¼ hours 2½ to 3½ hours 3 to 4 hours	180°F 180°F 180°F
Turkey breast, half	2 to 2½ pounds	Medium	1¼ to 2 hours	170°F
Turkey breast, whole	4 to 6 pounds 6 to 8 pounds	Medium Medium	1¾ to 2¼ hours 2½ to 3½ hours	170°F 170°F
Turkey breast tenderloin steak	4 to 6 ounces	Medium	15 to 18 minutes	170°F
Turkey drumstick	½ to 1 pound	Medium	¾ to 1¼ hours	180°F
Turkey tenderloin	8 to 10 ounces (¾ to 1 inch thick)	Medium	25 to 30 minutes	170°F
Turkey thigh	1 to 1½ pounds	Medium	50 to 60 minutes	180°F

Direct-Grilling Meat

For a charcoal grill, place meat on grill rack directly over medium coals (see photo 2, page 305). Grill, uncovered, for the time given below or to desired doneness, turning once halfway through grilling. For a gas grill, preheat grill. Reduce heat to medium. Place meat on grill rack over heat. Cover the grill. Test for doneness using a meat thermometer.

Cut	Thickness/ Weight	Grilling Temperature	Approximate Direct-Grilling Time	Doneness
Beef				
Boneless steak (ribeye, tenderloin, top loin)	1 inch	Medium	11 to 15 minutes	145°F medium rare
			14 to 18 minutes	160°F medium
	1½ inches	Medium	15 to 19 minutes	145°F medium rare
			18 to 23 minutes	160°F medium
Boneless top sirloin steak	1 inch	Medium	14 to 18 minutes	145°F medium rare
			18 to 22 minutes	160°F medium
	1½ inches	Medium	20 to 24 minutes	145°F medium rare
			24 to 28 minutes	160°F medium
Boneless tri-tip steak (bottom sirloin)	¾ inch	Medium	9 to 11 minutes	145°F medium rare
			11 to 13 minutes	160°F medium
	1 inch	Medium	13 to 15 minutes	145°F medium rare
			15 to 17 minutes	160°F medium
Flank steak	1¼ to 1¾ pounds	Medium	17 to 21 minutes	160°F medium
Steak with bone (porterhouse, rib, T-bone)	1 inch	Medium	11 to 14 minutes	145°F medium rare
			13 to 16 minutes	160°F medium
	1½ inches	Medium	18 to 21 minutes	145°F medium rare
			22 to 25 minutes	160°F medium
Ground Meat				
Patties (beef, lamb, pork, or veal)	½ inch	Medium	10 to 13 minutes	160°F medium
	¾ inch	Medium	14 to 18 minutes	160°F medium
Lamb				
Chop (loin or rib)	1 inch	Medium	12 to 14 minutes	145°F medium rare
			15 to 17 minutes	160°F medium
Chop (sirloin)	¾ to 1 inch	Medium	14 to 17 minutes	160°F medium
Pork				
Chop with bone (loin or rib)	¾ to 1 inch	Medium	11 to 14 minutes	160°F medium
	1¼ to 1½ inches	Medium	18 to 22 minutes	160°F medium
Chop (boneless top loin)	¾ to 1 inch	Medium	12 to 15 minutes	160°F medium
	1¼ to 1½ inches	Medium	17 to 21 minutes	160°F medium
Sausages, cooked (frankfurters, smoked bratwurst, etc.)		Medium	3 to 7 minutes	Heated through
Veal				
Chop (loin or rib)	1 inch	Medium	12 to 15 minutes	160°F medium

All cooking times are based on meat removed directly from refrigerator.

Indirect-Grilling Meat

For a charcoal grill, arrange medium-hot coals around a drip pan. Test for medium heat above pan, unless chart says otherwise (see photo 3, page 305). Place meat, fat side up, on grill rack over drip pan. Cover and grill for the time given below or to desired temperature, adding more charcoal to maintain heat as necessary. For a gas grill, preheat grill. Reduce heat to medium. Adjust heat for indirect cooking (see page 305).

   To test for doneness, insert a meat thermometer (see tip, page 331), using an instant-read thermometer to test smaller portions. Thermometer should register the "final grilling temperature." Remove meat from grill. For larger cuts, such as roasts, cover with foil and let stand 15 minutes before carving. The meat's temperature will rise 5°F to 10°F during the time it stands. Thinner cuts, such as steaks, do not have to stand.

Cut	Thickness/ Weight	Approximate Indirect-Grilling Time	Final Grilling Temperature (when to remove from grill)	Final Doneness Temperature (after 15 minutes standing)
Beef				
Boneless top sirloin steak	1 inch 1½ inches	22 to 26 minutes 26 to 30 minutes 32 to 36 minutes 36 to 40 minutes	145°F medium rare 160°F medium 145°F medium rare 160°F medium	No standing time No standing time No standing time No standing time
Boneless tri-tip roast (bottom sirloin)	1½ to 2 pounds	35 to 40 minutes 40 to 45 minutes	140°F 155°F	145°F medium rare 160°F medium
Flank steak	1¼ to 1¾ pounds	23 to 28 minutes	160°F medium	No standing time
Ribeye roast (medium-low heat)	4 to 6 pounds	1¼ to 1¾ hours 1½ to 2¼ hours	135°F 150°F	145°F medium rare 160°F medium
Rib roast (chine bone removed) (medium-low heat)	4 to 6 pounds	2 to 2¾ hours 2½ to 3¼ hours	135°F 150°F	145°F medium rare 160°F medium
Steak (porterhouse, rib, ribeye, T-bone, tenderloin, top loin)	1 inch 1½ inches	16 to 20 minutes 20 to 24 minutes 22 to 25 minutes 25 to 28 minutes	145°F medium rare 160°F medium 145°F medium rare 160°F medium	No standing time No standing time No standing time No standing time
Tenderloin roast (medium-high heat)	2 to 3 pounds 4 to 5 pounds	¾ to 1 hour 1 to 1¼ hours	135°F 135°F	145°F medium rare 145°F medium rare
Ground Meat				
Patties (beef, lamb, pork, or veal)	½ inch ¾ inch	15 to 18 minutes 20 to 24 minutes	160°F medium 160°F medium	No standing time No standing time
Lamb				
Boneless leg roast (medium-low heat)	3 to 4 pounds 4 to 6 pounds	1½ to 2¼ hours 1¾ to 2½ hours 1¾ to 2½ hours 2 to 2¾ hours	140°F 155°F 140°F 155°F	145°F medium rare 160°F medium 145°F medium rare 160°F medium
Boneless sirloin roast (medium-low heat)	1½ to 2 pounds	1 to 1¼ hours 1¼ to 1½ hours	140°F 155°F	145°F medium rare 160°F medium

Cut	Thickness/ Weight	Approximate Indirect-Grilling Time	Final Grilling Temperature (when to remove from grill)	Final Doneness Temperature (after 15 minutes standing)
Lamb (continued)				
Chop (loin or rib)	1 inch 1 inch	16 to 18 minutes 18 to 20 minutes	145°F medium rare 160°F medium	No standing time No standing time
Leg of lamb (with bone) (medium-low heat)	5 to 7 pounds	$1\frac{3}{4}$ to $2\frac{1}{4}$ hours $2\frac{1}{4}$ to $2\frac{3}{4}$ hours	140°F 155°F	145°F medium rare 160°F medium
Pork				
Boneless sirloin roast (medium-low heat)	$1\frac{1}{2}$ to 2 pounds	1 to $1\frac{1}{2}$ hours	155°F	160°F medium
Boneless top loin roast (medium-low heat)	2 to 3 pounds (single loin) 3 to 5 pounds (double loin, tied)	1 to $1\frac{1}{2}$ hours $1\frac{1}{2}$ to $2\frac{1}{4}$ hours	155°F 155°F	160°F medium 160°F medium
Chop (boneless top loin)	$\frac{3}{4}$ to 1 inch $1\frac{1}{4}$ to $1\frac{1}{2}$ inches	20 to 24 minutes 30 to 35 minutes	160°F medium 160°F medium	No standing time No standing time
Chop (loin or rib)	$\frac{3}{4}$ to 1 inch $1\frac{1}{4}$ to $1\frac{1}{2}$ inches	22 to 25 minutes 35 to 40 minutes	160°F medium 160°F medium	No standing time No standing time
Country-style ribs		$1\frac{1}{2}$ to 2 hours	Tender	No standing time
Ham, cooked (boneless) (medium-low heat)	3 to 5 pounds 6 to 8 pounds	$1\frac{1}{4}$ to 2 hours 2 to $2\frac{3}{4}$ hours	140°F 140°F	No standing time No standing time
Ham, cooked (slice) (medium-high heat)	1 inch	20 to 24 minutes	140°F	No standing time
Loin back ribs or spareribs		$1\frac{1}{2}$ to $1\frac{3}{4}$ hours	Tender	No standing time
Loin center rib roast (backbone loosened) (medium-low heat)	3 to 4 pounds 4 to 6 pounds	$1\frac{1}{4}$ to 2 hours 2 to $2\frac{3}{4}$ hours	155°F 155°F	160°F medium 160°F medium
Sausages, uncooked (bratwurst, Polish or Italian sausage links)	about 4 per pound	20 to 30 minutes	160°F medium	No standing time
Smoked shoulder picnic (with bone), cooked (medium-low heat)	4 to 6 pounds	$1\frac{1}{2}$ to $2\frac{1}{4}$ hours	140°F	No standing time
Tenderloin (medium-high heat)	$\frac{3}{4}$ to 1 pound	30 to 35 minutes	155°F	160°F medium
Veal				
Chop (loin or rib)	1 inch	19 to 23 minutes	160°F medium	No standing time

All cooking times are based on meat removed directly from refrigerator.

Direct-Grilling Fish and Seafood

Thaw fish or seafood, if frozen. Place fish fillets in a well-greased grill basket. For fish steaks and whole fish, grease grill rack. Thread scallops or shrimp on skewers, leaving a ¼-inch space between pieces. For a charcoal grill, place fish on grill rack directly over medium coals (see photo 2, page 305). Grill, uncovered, for the time given below or until fish flakes easily when tested with a fork (seafood should look opaque), turning once halfway through grilling. For a gas grill, preheat grill. Reduce heat to medium. Place fish on grill rack over heat. Cover the grill. If desired, brush fish with melted butter or margarine after turning.

Form of Fish	Thickness, Weight, or Size	Grilling Temperature	Approximate Direct-Grilling Time	Doneness
Dressed whole fish	½ to 1½ pounds	Medium	6 to 9 minutes per 8 ounces	Flakes
Fillets, steaks, cubes (for kabobs)	½ to 1 inch thick	Medium	4 to 6 minutes per ½-inch thickness	Flakes
Lobster tails	6 ounces 8 ounces	Medium Medium	10 to 12 minutes 12 to 15 minutes	Opaque Opaque
Sea scallops (for kabobs)	12 to 15 per pound	Medium	5 to 8 minutes	Opaque
Shrimp (for kabobs)	Medium (20 per pound) Jumbo (12 to 15 per pound)	Medium Medium	5 to 8 minutes 7 to 9 minutes	Opaque Opaque

Indirect-Grilling Fish and Seafood

Thaw fish or seafood, if frozen. Place fish fillets in a well-greased grill basket. For fish steaks and whole fish, grease grill rack. Thread scallops or shrimp on skewers, leaving a ¼-inch space between pieces. For a charcoal grill, arrange medium-hot coals around a drip pan. Test for medium heat above the pan (see photo 3, page 305). Place fish on grill rack over drip pan. Cover and grill for the time given below or until fish flakes easily when tested with a fork (seafood should look opaque), turning once halfway through grilling, if desired. For a gas grill, preheat grill. Reduce heat to medium. Adjust heat for indirect cooking (see page 305). If desired, brush with melted butter or margarine halfway through grilling.

Form of Fish	Thickness, Weight, or Size	Grilling Temperature	Approximate Indirect-Grilling Time	Doneness
Dressed fish	½ to 1½ pounds	Medium	15 to 20 minutes per 8 ounces	Flakes
Fillets, steaks, cubes (for kabobs)	½ to 1 inch thick	Medium	7 to 9 minutes per ½-inch thickness	Flakes
Sea scallops (for kabobs)	12 to 15 per pound	Medium	11 to 14 minutes	Opaque
Shrimp (for kabobs)	Medium (20 per pound) Jumbo (12 to 15 per pound)	Medium Medium	8 to10 minutes 9 to 11 minutes	Opaque Opaque

All cooking times are based on fish or seafood removed directly from refrigerator.

Direct-Grilling Vegetables

Before grilling, rinse, trim, cut up, and precook vegetables as directed below. To precook vegetables, bring a small amount of water to boiling in a saucepan; add desired vegetable and simmer, covered, for the time specified in the chart. Drain well. Generously brush vegetables with olive oil, butter, or margarine before grilling to prevent vegetables from sticking to the grill rack. Place vegetables on a piece of heavy foil or directly on grill rack. (If putting vegetables directly on grill rack, lay them perpendicular to wires of the rack so they won't fall into the coals.) For a charcoal grill, place vegetables directly over medium coals (see photo 2, page 305). Grill, uncovered, for the time given below or until crisp-tender, turning occasionally. For a gas grill, preheat grill. Reduce heat to medium. Place vegetables on grill rack directly over heat. Cover the grill. Monitor grilling closely so vegetables don't char.

Vegetable	Preparation	Precooking Time	Approximate Direct-Grilling Time
Asparagus	Snap off and discard tough bases of stems. Precook, then tie asparagus in bundles with strips of cooked green onion tops.	3 minutes	3 to 5 minutes
Baby carrots, fresh	Cut off carrot tops. Wash and peel carrots.	3 to 5 minutes	3 to 5 minutes
Corn on the cob	Peel back corn husks, but do not remove. Remove corn silks. Rinse corn; pat dry. Fold husks back around cobs. Tie husk tops with 100-percent-cotton kitchen string.	Do not precook.	25 to 30 minutes
Eggplant	Cut off top and blossom ends; cut crosswise into 1-inch slices.	Do not precook.	8 minutes
Fennel	Snip off feathery leaves; cut off stems.	10 minutes; then cut into 6 to 8 wedges	8 minutes
Leeks	Cut off green tops; trim bulb roots and remove 1 or 2 layers of white skin.	10 minutes or until almost tender; halve lengthwise	5 minutes
New potatoes	Halve potatoes.	10 minutes or until almost tender	10 to 12 minutes
Potatoes	Scrub potatoes; prick with a fork. Wrap individually in a double thickness of foil.	Do not precook.	1 to 2 hours
Sweet peppers	Remove stems. Halve peppers lengthwise; remove seeds and membranes. Cut into 1-inch-wide strips.	Do not precook.	8 to 10 minutes
Tomatoes	Remove cores; cut in half crosswise.	Do not precook.	5 minutes
Zucchini or yellow summer squash	Wash; cut off ends. Quarter lengthwise.	Do not precook.	5 to 6 minutes

Indoor Electric Grills

If grilling poultry, fish, or seafood, lightly grease the rack of an indoor electric grill or lightly coat with cooking spray. Preheat grill. Place meat, poultry, fish, or seafood on grill rack. (For fish fillets, tuck under any thin edges.) If using a grill with a cover, close the lid. Grill for the time given below or until done. If using a grill without a cover, turn food once halfway through grilling. The following timings should be used as general guidelines. Test for doneness using a meat thermometer. Refer to your owner's manual for preheating directions, suggested cuts, and recommended grilling times.

Cut or Type	Thickness, Weight, or Size	Covered Grilling Time	Uncovered Grilling Time	Doneness
Beef				
Boneless steak (ribeye, tenderloin, top loin)	1 inch	4 to 6 minutes 6 to 8 minutes	8 to 12 minutes 12 to 15 minutes	145°F medium rare 160°F medium
Boneless top sirloin steak	1 inch	5 to 7 minutes 7 to 9 minutes	12 to 15 minutes 15 to 18 minutes	145°F medium rare 160°F medium
Flank steak		7 to 9 minutes	12 to 14 minutes	160°F medium
Ground meat patties	½ to ¾ inch	5 to 7 minutes	14 to 18 minutes	160°F medium
Sausages, cooked (frankfurters, smoked bratwurst, etc.)	6 per pound	2½ to 3 minutes	5 to 6 minutes	140°F heated through
Steak with bone (porterhouse, rib, T-bone)	1 inch	Not recommended Not recommended	8 to 12 minutes 12 to 15 minutes	145°F medium rare 160°F medium
Lamb				
Chop (loin or rib)	1 inch	6 to 8 minutes	12 to 15 minutes	160°F medium
Pork				
Chop (boneless top loin)	¾ inch	6 to 8 minutes	12 to 15 minutes	160°F medium
Veal				
Chop (boneless loin)	¾ inch	4 to 5 minutes	7 to 9 minutes	160°F medium
Poultry				
Chicken breast half, skinned and boned	4 to 5 ounces	4 to 6 minutes	12 to 15 minutes	170°F
Turkey breast tenderloin steak	4 to 6 ounces	4 to 6 minutes	8 to 12 minutes	170°F
Fish and Seafood				
Fillets or steaks	½ to 1 inch	2 to 3 minutes per ½-inch thickness	4 to 6 minutes per ½-inch thickness	Flakes
Sea scallops	15 to 20 per pound	2½ to 4 minutes	6 to 8 minutes	Opaque
Shrimp	Medium (20 per pound)	2½ to 4 minutes	6 to 8 minutes	Opaque

Meat

Meat

For more recipes, visit our Recipe Center at **www.bhg.com**

Steak with Sweet Pepper Sauce

Fast   **Low Fat**

Start to Finish: 30 minutes   **Makes:** 4 servings

> 2 medium green and/or red sweet peppers, cut into thin strips
>
> ½ cup chopped onion (1 medium)
>
> 2 cloves garlic, minced
>
> 1 tablespoon cooking oil
>
> 1 pound beef ribeye steak, cut ½ to ¾ inch thick, or 1 pound beef top sirloin steak, cut ½ to ¾ inch thick
>
> Salt
>
> Black pepper
>
> ½ cup beef broth
>
> 1 tablespoon snipped fresh oregano or basil or 1 teaspoon dried oregano or basil, crushed
>
> 1 cup chopped, seeded tomatoes (2 medium)
>
> Hot cooked rice (optional)

1. In a large skillet cook sweet peppers, onion, and garlic in hot oil about 4 minutes or until vegetables are crisp-tender. Remove vegetables from skillet with a slotted spoon.

2. Season meat with salt and pepper. Place meat in the skillet. (Add more oil, if necessary.) Cook over medium-high heat about 4 minutes on each side or until desired doneness (145°F for medium rare to 160°F for medium). Transfer the meat to a serving platter, reserving drippings in the skillet. Keep warm.

3. For sauce, carefully add beef broth and oregano to reserved drippings. Bring to boiling. Boil gently, uncovered, over medium heat for 2 to 3 minutes or until broth is reduced to ¼ cup, scraping up crusty browned bits in pan. Stir in the cooked vegetables and tomatoes. Heat through. Spoon over meat. If desired, serve with hot cooked rice.

Nutrition Facts per serving: 212 cal., 8 g total fat (2 g sat. fat), 53 mg chol., 223 mg sodium, 9 g carbo., 2 g fiber, 26 g pro.
Daily Values: 15% vit. A, 94% vit. C, 4% calcium, 17% iron
Exchanges: 2 Vegetable, 3 Lean Meat

Using a Meat Thermometer

To ensure perfectly cooked meat, check the doneness with a meat thermometer. Final doneness temperatures are listed in recipes or in the cooking charts on pages 371–374.

Dial oven-going meat thermometer: For larger meat cuts, such as a roast, insert the thermometer before roasting or grilling begins. Insert it at least 2 inches into the center of the largest muscle or thickest portion of the uncooked meat (see photo). The thermometer should not touch any fat or bone or the pan. This type of thermometer can remain in the meat while roasting in

the oven or cooking on the grill. When the meat reaches the desired final roasting temperature, push in the thermometer a little farther. If the temperature drops, continue cooking the meat. If it stays the same, remove the meat from the oven or grill. Cover meat with foil and let it stand about 15 minutes before carving. Its temperature will rise 5°F to 10°F during the standing time.

Dial instant-read thermometer: The stem of the thermometer needs to be inserted at least 2 inches into the food. For thinner foods, such as

burgers and chops, insert the stem through the side of the meat cut to get an accurate reading (see photo). The thermometer will register the temperature in 15 to 20 seconds. This type of meat thermometer should not be left in food while it's cooking.

Digital instant-read thermometer: The thermometer's probe should be placed at least ½ inch into the food (see photo) and will register

the temperature in about 10 seconds. This type of thermometer can be used to check the doneness of larger cuts as well as thinner foods, such as burgers, steaks, and chops. The thermometer should not be left in the food while it is cooking.

Bistro Beef and Mushrooms

Bistro Beef and Mushrooms

Fast

Start to Finish: 20 minutes **Makes:** 4 servings

- 4 beef tenderloin steaks, cut ¾ inch thick (1 pound)
- 1 tablespoon Dijon-style mustard or coarse-grain brown mustard
- 2 tablespoons olive oil or roasted garlic olive oil
- 2 4-ounce packages sliced crimini, shiitake, or portobello mushrooms or one 8-ounce package sliced button mushrooms (3 cups)
- ⅓ cup dry red wine or sherry
- 1 tablespoon white wine Worcestershire sauce
- 2 teaspoons snipped fresh thyme

1. Trim fat from steaks. Spread mustard evenly over both sides of steaks. In a large skillet heat 1 tablespoon of the oil over medium-high heat. Add steaks; reduce heat to medium. Cook to desired doneness, turning once. Allow 7 to 9 minutes for medium rare (145°F) to medium (160°F). Transfer steaks to a serving platter; keep warm.

2. Add remaining 1 tablespoon oil to drippings in skillet. Add mushrooms; cook and stir for 4 minutes. Stir in wine, Worcestershire sauce, and thyme. Simmer, uncovered, for 3 minutes. Spoon over steaks.

Nutrition Facts per serving: 231 cal., 13 g total fat (3 g sat. fat), 52 mg chol., 115 mg sodium, 3 g carbo., 1 g fiber, 21 g pro.
Daily Values: 2% vit. C, 2% calcium, 17% iron
Exchanges: ½ Vegetable, 3 Lean Meat, 1 Fat

Steak au Poivre   Best Loved

Top loin steaks are also called strip steaks, New York strip, or Kansas City steaks.

Fast

Start to Finish: 30 minutes **Makes:** 4 servings

- 1 tablespoon cracked black pepper
- 4 beef tenderloin steaks or 2 beef top loin steaks, cut 1 inch thick (1 pound)
- 2 tablespoons butter or margarine
- ¼ cup brandy or beef broth
- ¼ cup beef broth
- ½ cup whipping cream
- 2 teaspoons Dijon-style mustard

1. Use your fingers to press the pepper onto both sides of the steaks. If using top loin steaks, cut each steak in half crosswise. In a large skillet cook steaks in hot butter over medium heat to desired doneness, turning once. For tenderloin steaks, allow 10 to 13 minutes for medium rare (145°F) to medium (160°F). For top loin steaks, allow 12 to 15 minutes for medium rare to medium. Transfer steaks to a serving platter, reserving the drippings in the skillet. Keep warm. Remove skillet from burner and allow to stand 1 minute.

2. For sauce, combine brandy and beef broth (or all beef broth); carefully stir into drippings in skillet, scraping up crusty browned bits. Stir in whipping cream and mustard. Bring to boiling. Boil gently, uncovered, over medium heat for 5 to 6 minutes or until mixture is reduced to ½ cup, stirring occasionally. Spoon sauce over steaks to serve.

Nutrition Facts per serving: 370 cal., 25 g total fat (13 g sat. fat), 114 mg chol., 192 mg sodium, 2 g carbo., 0 g fiber, 25 g pro.
Daily Values: 13% vit. A, 1% vit. C, 4% calcium, 20% iron
Exchanges: 3½ Lean Meat, 4 Fat

USDA Hotline

Have a meat or poultry food safety question? The United States Department of Agriculture Meat and Poultry Hotline is ready to help. Call weekdays from 10 a.m. to 4 p.m. (Eastern Standard Time). The toll free number is 800/535-4555 (in Washington, D.C., area, 202/720-3333).

Top Sirloin with Onions and Carrots

If you don't have a 12-inch skillet, brown the onions in two batches in a 9- or 10-inch skillet.

Low Fat

Start to Finish: 1 hour **Makes:** 4 servings

- 4 slices bacon
- 4 small onions, peeled and cut into 1-inch slices
- 8 small white or orange carrots, halved lengthwise
- 4 small red potatoes, cut up (1 pound)
- ½ cup beef broth
- ¼ cup beer, dark beer, or beef broth
- 1 tablespoon brown sugar
- 1 teaspoon dried thyme, crushed
- 1¼ pounds boneless beef top sirloin steak, cut 1½ to 2 inches thick
- ¼ teaspoon salt
- ¼ teaspoon black pepper
- Snipped fresh thyme (optional)

1. In a 12-inch skillet cook bacon over medium heat until crisp. Remove from skillet; drain bacon on paper towels. Drain all but about 1 tablespoon of the drippings from the skillet.

2. In the skillet brown onions on both sides, about 3 minutes per side. Remove onions; set aside. Add carrots to skillet; cook about 5 minutes or until light brown, turning occasionally. Remove skillet from heat. Carefully add potatoes, broth, beer, brown sugar, and half of the dried thyme. Return onions to skillet. Return skillet to range top. Bring to boiling; reduce heat. Simmer, covered, for 30 to 35 minutes or until vegetables are tender.

3. Meanwhile, preheat broiler. Season beef with remaining dried thyme, salt, and pepper. Place meat on the unheated rack of a broiler pan. Broil 4 to 5 inches from heat for 25 to 27 minutes for medium rare (145°F) or 30 to 32 minutes for medium (160°F), turning once halfway through broiling. Cut into 4 pieces.

4. Remove vegetables from skillet with a slotted spoon. Gently boil juices, uncovered, 1 to 2 minutes or until slightly thickened. Divide steak, vegetables, and bacon among 4 dinner plates. Spoon juices over. If desired, sprinkle with fresh thyme.

Nutrition Facts per serving: 396 cal., 12 g total fat (4 g sat. fat), 94 mg chol., 451 mg sodium, 33 g carbo., 5 g fiber, 36 g pro.
Daily Values: 309% vit. A, 38% vit. C, 6% calcium, 34% iron
Exchanges: 1 Vegetable, 2 Starch, 4 Lean Meat

Orange-Beef Stir-Fry

This version of the classic Szechwan recipe is less pungent than you might find at a Chinese restaurant. Spinach and water chestnuts add extra color and crunch.

Low Fat

Prep: 30 minutes **Cook:** 6 minutes **Makes:** 4 servings

- 12 ounces beef top round steak
- 1 teaspoon finely shredded orange peel
- ½ cup orange juice
- 1 tablespoon cornstarch
- 1 tablespoon soy sauce
- 1 teaspoon sugar
- 1 teaspoon instant beef bouillon granules
- 2 tablespoons cooking oil
- 4 green onions, bias-sliced into 1-inch pieces
- 1 clove garlic, minced
- 5 cups coarsely shredded fresh spinach (5 to 6 ounces)
- ½ of an 8-ounce can sliced water chestnuts, drained
- 3 cups hot cooked rice

1. If desired, partially freeze beef for easier slicing. Trim fat from beef. Thinly slice beef across the grain into bite-size strips (see photo, page 334). Set aside. For sauce, in a small bowl stir together orange peel, orange juice, cornstarch, soy sauce, sugar, and bouillon granules. Set aside.

2. In a wok or large skillet heat 1 tablespoon of the oil over medium-high heat. Add green onions and garlic; cook and stir in hot oil for 1 minute. Remove green onion mixture from wok using a slotted spoon. Add remaining 1 tablespoon oil to wok or skillet. Add beef to hot wok. (Add more oil as necessary during cooking.) Cook and stir for 2 to 3 minutes or to desired doneness. Push beef from center of wok.

3. Stir sauce. Add sauce to center of wok. Cook and stir until thickened and bubbly. Return green onion mixture to wok. Add spinach and water chestnuts. Stir all ingredients together to coat with sauce. Cover and cook for 1 minute more or until heated through. Serve immediately over hot cooked rice.

Nutrition Facts per serving: 364 cal., 9 g total fat (2 g sat. fat), 37 mg chol., 562 mg sodium, 44 g carbo., 2 g fiber, 25 g pro.
Daily Values: 50% vit. A, 48% vit. C, 8% calcium, 25% iron
Exchanges: 1½ Vegetable, 2½ Starch, 2 Very Lean Meat, 1½ Fat

Fajitas ♥ Best Loved

While fajitas are traditionally made with beef skirt steak, flank steak makes a good substitute and is easier to find at the meat counter.

Prep: 30 minutes **Chill:** 30 minutes
Oven: 350°F **Makes:** 4 to 6 servings

- 12 ounces beef flank steak or bite-size strips of chicken or turkey
- 1 tablespoon purchased or Homemade Fajita Seasoning
- 4 to 6 8-inch flour tortillas
- 2 tablespoons cooking oil
- 1 cup thin strips of red or green sweet pepper (1 medium)
- ½ cup thinly sliced onion, separated into rings (1 medium)
- ¾ cup chopped tomato (1 medium)
- 1 tablespoon lime juice
  Guacamole (page 64) (optional)
  Bottled salsa (optional)
  Dairy sour cream (optional)
  Lime wedges

1. If desired, partially freeze beef for easier slicing. If using steak, trim fat from meat and thinly slice steak across the grain into bite-size strips (see photo, bottom right). Place meat strips in a deep bowl. Sprinkle with 2 teaspoons of the fajita seasoning. Cover and chill 30 minutes.

2. Wrap tortillas tightly in foil. Heat in a 350° oven about 10 minutes or until heated through. Meanwhile, in a 12-inch skillet heat 1 tablespoon of the oil over medium-high heat. Add sweet pepper, onion, and remaining 1 teaspoon seasoning. Cook and stir about 3 minutes or until crisp-tender. Remove onion mixture from skillet.

3. Add remaining 1 tablespoon oil and the meat to the skillet. Cook and stir for 2 to 3 minutes until desired doneness for steak or until chicken or turkey strips are no longer pink. Drain well. Return onion mixture to skillet. Stir in tomato. Cook and stir 1 minute or until heated through. Remove skillet from heat; stir in lime juice.

4. To serve, fill warm tortillas with meat mixture. If desired, top meat mixture with guacamole, salsa, and sour cream. Roll up tortillas. Serve with lime wedges.

Homemade Fajita Seasoning: In a small bowl combine 1½ teaspoons ground cumin; ½ teaspoon dried oregano, crushed; ¼ teaspoon salt; ¼ teaspoon ground red pepper; ¼ teaspoon ground black pepper; ⅛ teaspoon garlic powder; and ⅛ teaspoon onion powder.

Nutrition Facts per serving: 312 cal., 15 g total fat (4 g sat. fat), 34 mg chol., 319 mg sodium, 21 g carbo., 2 g fiber, 21 g pro.
Daily Values: 34% vit. A, 90% vit. C, 4% calcium, 15% iron
Exchanges: 1 Vegetable, 1 Starch, 2½ Lean Meat, 1½ Fat

Beef Stroganoff

Fast

Prep: 20 minutes **Cook:** 10 minutes **Makes:** 4 servings

- 12 ounces boneless beef sirloin steak
- 1 8-ounce carton dairy sour cream
- 2 tablespoons all-purpose flour
- 2 teaspoons instant beef bouillon granules
- 2 cups sliced fresh mushrooms
- ½ cup chopped onion (1 medium)
- 1 clove garlic, minced
- 2 tablespoons butter or margarine
- 2 cups hot cooked noodles

1. If desired, partially freeze beef for easier slicing. Trim fat from meat. Thinly slice meat across the grain into bite-size strips (see photo, below). In a small bowl stir together sour cream and flour. Stir in bouillon granules, ½ cup *water*, and ¼ teaspoon *black pepper*; set aside.

2. In a large skillet cook and stir the meat, mushrooms, onion, and garlic in hot butter over medium-high heat for 5 minutes or until desired doneness. Drain off fat.

3. Stir sour cream mixture into skillet. Cook and stir until thickened and bubbly. Cook and stir for 1 minute more. Serve over noodles.

Mustard-Seasoned Stroganoff: Prepare as above, except add 2 tablespoons tomato paste, 4 teaspoons Dijon-style mustard, 4 teaspoons Worcestershire sauce, and, if desired, 1 teaspoon caraway seeds to the sour cream mixture.

Nutrition Facts per serving for plain or mustard variation:
427 cal., 23 g total fat (13 g sat. fat), 119 mg chol., 575 mg sodium, 29 g carbo., 2 g fiber, 26 g pro.
Daily Values: 14% vit. A, 3% vit. C, 9% calcium, 23% iron
Exchanges: 2 Starch, 3 Lean Meat, 2 Fat

Partially freezing meat makes it easier to slice. And slicing it as thinly as possible across the grain results in a more tender final product.

Fajita-Style Steak

You serve up lots of flavor because the meat is marinated in lime, garlic, and cinnamon, then glazed with a sauce of sweet peppers, honey, mustard, and more garlic.

Prep: 15 minutes **Marinate:** up to 6 hours
Broil: 15 minutes **Makes:** 4 servings

> 4 **boneless beef top sirloin steaks (2 pounds)**
> **Salt and black pepper**
> ⅓ **cup lime juice**
> ¼ **cup cooking oil**
> 2 **cloves garlic, minced**
> 2 **teaspoons ground cinnamon**
> ½ **of a 7-ounce jar (about ½ cup) roasted red sweet peppers, minced**
> ¼ **cup honey**
> ¼ **cup Dijon-style mustard**
> 2 or 3 **cloves garlic, minced**

1. Sprinkle meat with salt and pepper. Place in a plastic bag set in a shallow dish. For marinade, in a small bowl stir together lime juice, oil, the 2 cloves garlic, and cinnamon. Pour over meat; close bag. Marinate in refrigerator up to 6 hours.

2. For glaze, in a small saucepan stir together sweet peppers, honey, mustard, and the 2 or 3 cloves garlic. Bring to boiling; reduce heat. Simmer, uncovered, for 5 to 7 minutes or until slightly thickened and reduced to ¾ cup. Remove from heat; set aside.

3. Drain meat. Discard marinade. Preheat broiler. Place steaks on the unheated rack of a broiler pan. Broil 3 to 4 inches from the heat to desired doneness, turning meat over once and brushing several times with glaze during last half of broiling. For 1-inch-thick steaks, allow 15 to 17 minutes for medium rare (145°F) or 20 to 22 minutes for medium (160°F).

Nutrition Facts per serving: 422 cal., 15 g total fat (4 g sat. fat), 138 mg chol., 344 mg sodium, 22 g carbo., 1 g fiber, 50 g pro.
Daily Values: 91% vit. C, 5% calcium, 37% iron
Exchanges: 1 Vegetable, 1 Other Carbo., 6 Lean Meat

Beef with Cucumber Raita

Raita (RYE-tah), a simple, cooling salad of yogurt and chopped vegetables or fruits, provides a soothing counterpoint to highly seasoned dishes.

Fast **Low Fat**

Start to Finish: 25 minutes **Makes:** 4 servings

> 1 **8-ounce carton plain fat-free or low-fat yogurt**
> ¼ **cup coarsely shredded unpeeled cucumber**
> 1 **tablespoon finely chopped red or sweet onion**
> 1 **tablespoon snipped fresh mint**
> ¼ **teaspoon sugar**
> **Salt and black pepper**
> 1 **pound boneless beef sirloin steak, cut 1 inch thick**
> ½ **teaspoon lemon-pepper seasoning**
> **Fresh mint leaves (optional)**

1. Preheat broiler. For raita, in a small bowl combine yogurt, cucumber, onion, snipped mint, and sugar. Season yogurt mixture to taste with salt and pepper; set aside.

2. Trim fat from meat. Sprinkle meat with lemon-pepper seasoning. Place meat on the unheated rack of a broiler pan. Broil 3 to 4 inches from the heat, turning meat over after half of the broiling time. Allow 15 to 17 minutes for medium rare (145°F) or 20 to 22 minutes for medium (160°F).

3. Cut steak across the grain into thin slices. If desired, garnish steak slices with mint leaves. Serve with raita.

Nutrition Facts per serving: 176 cal., 4 g total fat (1 g sat. fat), 55 mg chol., 312 mg sodium, 5 g carbo., 0 g fiber, 28 g pro.
Daily Values: 3% vit. C, 14% calcium, 15% iron
Exchanges: 4 Very Lean Meat, 1 Fat

Beef with Cucumber Raita

Chicken Fried Steak

Fresh basil or oregano adds a flavor twist to this country-style classic.

Prep: 20 minutes **Cook:** 1 hour **Makes:** 4 servings

- 1 **pound boneless beef top round steak, cut ½ inch thick**
- ¾ **cup fine dry bread crumbs**
- 1½ **teaspoons snipped fresh basil or oregano or ½ teaspoon dried basil or oregano, crushed**
- ½ **teaspoon salt**
- ¼ **teaspoon black pepper**
- 1 **beaten egg**
- 1 **tablespoon milk**
- 2 **tablespoons cooking oil**
- 1 **small onion, sliced and separated into rings**
- 2 **tablespoons all-purpose flour**
- 1⅓ **cups milk**
    Salt and black pepper (optional)

1. Trim fat from meat. Cut meat into 4 serving-size pieces. Place each piece of meat between 2 pieces of plastic wrap. Working from center to edges, pound meat lightly with the flat side of a meat mallet to ¼-inch thickness. Remove plastic wrap.

2. In a shallow dish or on waxed paper combine bread crumbs, basil, the ½ teaspoon salt, and the ¼ teaspoon pepper. In another shallow dish combine egg and the 1 tablespoon milk. Dip meat pieces into egg mixture, then coat with the bread crumb mixture.

3. In a 12-inch skillet cook meat, half at time, in hot oil over medium heat about 6 minutes or until brown, turning once. (Add more oil, if necessary.) Return all meat to skillet. Reduce heat to medium-low. Cover and cook for 45 to 60 minutes more or until meat is tender. Transfer meat to a serving platter, reserving drippings in skillet. Keep warm.

4. For gravy, cook onion in reserved drippings until tender but not brown. (Add more oil, if necessary.) Stir in flour. Gradually stir in the 1⅓ cups milk. Cook and stir over medium heat until thickened and bubbly. Cook and stir for 1 minute more. If desired, season to taste with additional salt and pepper. Serve gravy with meat.

Nutrition Facts per serving: 351 cal., 13 g total fat (3 g sat. fat), 108 mg chol., 578 mg sodium, 23 g carbo., 1 g fiber, 34 g pro.
Daily Values: 5% vit. A, 3% vit. C, 17% calcium, 21% iron
Exchanges: 1½ Starch, 4 Lean Meat

Cubed Steaks Paprika

Fast

Start to Finish: 30 minutes **Makes:** 4 servings

- 1 **tablespoon butter or margarine**
- 4 **4- to 6-ounce beef cubed steaks**
- 1 **cup sliced fresh mushrooms**
- ½ **cup chopped onion (1 medium)**
- 1 **clove garlic, minced**
- 2 **teaspoons paprika**
- ¼ **teaspoon black pepper**
- 1 **cup beef broth**
- ½ **cup dairy sour cream**
- 2 **tablespoons all-purpose flour**
- 2 **cups hot cooked noodles**

1. In a 12-inch skillet melt butter over medium-high heat until butter sizzles. Add steaks; reduce heat to medium and cook for 5 to 8 minutes or until done (160°F), turning once. Remove meat, reserving drippings in skillet. For sauce, cook mushrooms, onion, garlic, paprika, and pepper in reserved drippings in skillet until mushrooms are tender. Stir in broth. Stir together sour cream and flour; stir into skillet. Cook and stir over medium heat until thickened and bubbly. Cook and stir 1 minute more. Return steaks to skillet with sauce; heat through. Serve with noodles.

Nutrition Facts per serving: 392 cal., 16 g total fat (7 g sat. fat), 94 mg chol., 312 mg sodium, 27 g carbo., 2 g fiber, 35 g pro.
Daily Values: 19% vit. A, 4% vit. C, 5% calcium, 21% iron
Exchanges: 2 Starch, 4 Lean Meat, ½ Fat

Freezing Meats

To store meat for longer than 1 or 2 days, freeze it according to the following guidelines:

■ If you plan to use the meat within a week after buying it, freeze it in the plastic film-wrapped retail packaging. For longer storage, rewrap or overwrap the meat with moisture- and vapor-proof wrap, such as freezer paper, heavy-duty aluminum foil, or freezer bags.

■ Freeze the meat quickly and maintain your freezer's temperature at 0°F or below. For best quality, freeze beef roasts and steaks up to 12 months; lamb roasts and chops up to 9 months; pork roasts and chops up to 6 months; ground beef and lamb up to 4 months; and pork sausage up to 2 months.

■ Thaw the frozen meat in the refrigerator on a plate or in a pan to catch any juices. Do not thaw meat on the counter at room temperature.

Standing Rib Roast

Horseradish Sauce, right, makes a peppy topping for this bone-in roast.

Prep: 10 minutes **Roast:** 1¾ hours **Oven:** 350°F
Stand: 15 minutes **Makes:** 12 to 16 servings

> 1 **4- to 6-pound beef rib roast**
>   **Salt and black pepper**
> 1 **recipe Oven-Browned Potatoes or Yorkshire Pudding (see below)**

1. Season meat with salt and pepper. Place meat, fat side up, in a 15½×10½×2-inch roasting pan. Insert an oven-going meat thermometer into center of roast (see tip, page 331), making sure it doesn't touch bone. Roast, uncovered, in a 350° oven. For medium rare, roast for 1¾ to 2¼ hours or until meat thermometer registers 135°F. Cover with foil; let stand 15 minutes. Temperature of meat after standing should be 145°F. (For medium, roast for 2¼ to 2¾ hours or until the meat thermometer registers 150°F. Cover and let stand 15 minutes. Temperature of the meat after standing should be 160°F.)

2. Meanwhile, prepare Oven-Browned Potatoes or Yorkshire Pudding.

Nutrition Facts per serving meat: 354 cal., 29 g total fat (12 g sat. fat), 88 mg chol., 83 mg sodium, 0 g carbo., 0 g fiber, 22 g pro.
Daily Values: 1% calcium, 13% iron
Exchanges: 3½ High-Fat Meat

Oven-Browned Potatoes: Peel 4 pounds medium potatoes; cut into quarters. Cook in boiling salted water for 10 minutes; drain. About 30 to 40 minutes before roast is done (the roast temperature should be about 100°F), arrange potatoes around roast, turning to coat them in drippings. Serve potatoes with the roast.

Nutrition Facts per serving potatoes: 110 cal., 0 g total fat (0 g sat. fat), 0 mg chol., 4 mg sodium, 23 g carbo., 3 g fiber, 4 g pro.
Daily Values: 34% vit. C, 1% calcium, 7% iron
Exchanges: 1½ Starch

Yorkshire Pudding: After removing meat from the oven, increase oven temperature to 450°F. Measure pan drippings. If necessary, add enough cooking oil to drippings to equal ¼ cup; return to pan. In a mixing bowl combine 4 eggs and 2 cups milk. Add 2 cups all-purpose flour and ¼ teaspoon salt. Beat with an electric mixer or rotary beater until smooth. Stir into drippings in roasting pan. Bake for 20 to 25 minutes or until puffy and golden. Cut into squares. Serve at once with roast.

Nutrition Facts per serving pudding: 154 cal., 7 g total fat (3 g sat. fat), 79 mg chol., 90 mg sodium, 17 g carbo., 1 g fiber, 5 g pro.
Daily Values: 4% vit. A, 1% vit. C, 6% calcium, 6% iron
Exchanges: 1 Starch, 1½ Fat

Horseradish Sauce

Fast

Start to Finish: 10 minutes **Makes:** 1 cup sauce

> 1 **cup whipping cream**
> 4 **to 5 tablespoons prepared horseradish**

1. In a mixing bowl beat whipping cream until soft peaks form. Fold in horseradish. Cover and store in the refrigerator for up to 24 hours. Serve with beef or pork.

Nutrition Facts per tablespoon: 27 cal., 3 g total fat (2 g sat. fat), 10 mg chol., 5 mg sodium, 0 g carbo., 0 g fiber, 0 g pro.
Daily Values: 2% vit. A, 1% calcium
Exchanges: ½ Fat

Southwestern Tri-Tip Roast

Dried chipotle peppers spice the beef rub.

Low Fat

Prep: 15 minutes **Chill:** 6 to 24 hours **Roast:** 30 minutes
Oven: 425°F **Stand:** 15 minutes **Makes:** 6 to 8 servings

> 1 **tablespoon dried chipotle chile peppers, seeded and finely chopped (about 2 teaspoons) (see tip, page 64)**
> 1 **tablespoon snipped fresh oregano or 1 teaspoon dried oregano, crushed**
> 1 **tablespoon olive oil**
> 1 **teaspoon ground cumin**
> ½ **teaspoon salt**
> 2 **cloves garlic, minced**
> 1 **1½- to 2-pound boneless beef tri-tip roast (bottom sirloin)**

1. For rub, combine chipotle peppers, oregano, oil, cumin, salt, and garlic. Spread over surface of meat, rubbing in with glove-covered hands. Cover and chill for 6 to 24 hours.

2. Place meat on a rack in a shallow roasting pan. Insert an oven-going meat thermometer into center of meat (see tip, page 331). Roast in a 425° oven. For medium rare, roast for 30 to 35 minutes or until meat thermometer registers 140°F. Cover with foil and let stand 15 minutes. The temperature of the meat after standing should be 145°F. (For medium, roast for 40 to 45 minutes or until meat thermometer registers 155°F. Cover and let stand 15 minutes. The temperature of meat after standing should be 160°F.)

Nutrition Facts per serving: 156 cal., 7 g total fat (2 g sat. fat), 45 mg chol., 248 mg sodium, 1 g carbo., 0 g fiber, 21 g pro.
Daily Values: 2% vit. A, 1% vit. C, 1% calcium, 11% iron
Exchanges: 3 Lean Meat

Tenderizing Meats

Less tender cuts of meat, such as beef flank steak, round steak, and chuck roast, can be tenderized in several ways before cooking.

Pounding: Use the flat side of a meat mallet to pound the meat from the center to the edges to break up connective tissue.

Scoring: Use a sharp knife to make shallow diagonal cuts across the surface of a steak.

Marinating: Pour a marinade mixture containing an acidic food ingredient, such as lemon juice, tomatoes, vinegar, or wine, over the meat. Refrigerate the meat according to recipe directions. Marinades add more flavor than tenderness.

Moist-heat cooking: Cook meat in liquid for a long time at a low, simmering temperature.

Meat tenderizer: Use a commercial tenderizing product to help break up the connective tissue that makes meat chewy.

Pan Gravy for Roasted Meat

If you don't get ¼ cup fat from the roast, add enough cooking oil to equal that amount.

`Fast`

Start to Finish: 10 minutes **Makes:** 2 cups

　　　Drippings from roasted meat
　　　Beef broth or water
¼　cup all-purpose flour
　　　Salt and black pepper (optional)

1. After removing roasted meat from pan, pour drippings into a large measuring cup, scraping out the crusty browned bits. Skim fat from drippings (see photo, page 444); reserve ¼ cup of the fat. Measure remaining drippings. Add enough beef broth or water to equal 2 cups.

2. In a medium saucepan combine reserved fat and flour. Gradually stir the 2 cups drippings into flour mixture. Cook and stir over medium heat until thickened and bubbly. Cook and stir for 1 minute more. If desired, season to taste with salt and pepper.

Nutrition Facts per ¼-cup serving: 71 cal., 6 g total fat (3 g sat. fat), 6 mg chol., 94 mg sodium, 3 g carbo., 0 g fiber, 0 g pro.
Daily Values: 1% iron
Exchanges: 1½ Fat

Beef and Noodles

`Low Fat`

Prep: 30 minutes **Cook:** 1¾ hours **Makes:** 4 servings

1　pound boneless beef round steak or chuck roast
¼　cup all-purpose flour
1　tablespoon cooking oil
½　cup chopped onion (1 medium)
2　cloves garlic, minced
3　cups beef broth
1　teaspoon dried marjoram or basil, crushed
¼　teaspoon black pepper
8　ounces frozen noodles
2　tablespoons snipped fresh parsley

1. Trim fat from meat. Cut meat into ¾-inch cubes. Coat meat with the flour. In a large saucepan brown half of the coated meat in hot oil. Remove from saucepan. Brown the remaining meat with the onion and garlic, adding more oil if necessary. Drain off fat. Return all meat to the saucepan.

2. Stir in the broth, marjoram, and pepper. Bring to boiling; reduce heat. Simmer, covered, for 1¼ to 1½ hours or until meat is tender.

3. Stir noodles into broth mixture. Bring to boiling; reduce heat. Cook, uncovered, for 25 to 30 minutes or until noodles are tender. To serve, sprinkle with parsley.

Nutrition Facts per serving: 351 cal., 12 g total fat (3 g sat. fat), 94 mg chol., 677 mg sodium, 29 g carbo., 1 g fiber, 31 g pro.
Daily Values: 3% vit. A, 7% vit. C, 3% calcium, 25% iron
Exchanges: 2 Starch, 3½ Lean Meat

Beef Pot Roast

Long, moist cooking tenderizes chuck pot roast.

`Low Fat`

Prep: 20 minutes **Cook:** 1¾ hours **Makes:** 8 to 10 servings

1　2½- to 3-pound boneless beef chuck pot roast
2　tablespoons cooking oil
¾　cup water
1　tablespoon Worcestershire sauce
1　teaspoon instant beef bouillon granules
1　teaspoon dried basil, crushed
¼　teaspoon salt
12　ounces tiny new potatoes or 2 medium potatoes or sweet potatoes

1 **pound carrots or 6 medium parsnips, peeled and cut into 2-inch pieces**
2 **small onions, cut into wedges**
2 **stalks celery, bias-sliced into 1-inch pieces**
½ **cup cold water**
¼ **cup all-purpose flour**
  Black pepper (optional)

1. Trim fat from meat. In a 4- to 6-quart Dutch oven brown roast on all sides in hot oil. Drain off fat. Combine the ¾ cup water, Worcestershire sauce, bouillon granules, basil, and salt. Pour over roast. Bring to boiling; reduce heat. Simmer, covered, for 1 hour.

2. Meanwhile, if using new potatoes, peel a strip of skin from center of each. If using medium potatoes or sweet potatoes, peel and quarter. Add potatoes, carrots, onions, and celery to meat. Return to boiling; reduce heat. Simmer, covered, for 45 to 60 minutes more or until tender, adding water if necessary. Transfer meat and vegetables to a platter, reserving juices in Dutch oven. Keep warm.

3. For gravy, measure juices; skim fat (see photo, page 444). If necessary, add enough water to juices to equal 1½ cups. Return to Dutch oven. In a small bowl stir the ½ cup cold water into the flour. Stir into juices in pan. Cook and stir over medium heat until thickened and bubbly. Cook and stir for 1 minute more. If desired, season with pepper. Serve gravy with meat and vegetables.

Oven directions: Trim fat from meat. Brown roast as directed above. Combine the ¾ cup water, Worcestershire sauce, bouillon granules, basil, and salt. Pour over meat. Bake, covered, in a 325°F oven for 1 hour. Prepare potatoes as directed. Add vegetables to meat. Cover and bake for 45 to 60 minutes more or until tender. Prepare gravy in a saucepan as directed above.

Crockery-cooker directions: Trim fat from meat. Thinly slice vegetables; place vegetables in a 4- or 5-quart crockery cooker. Cut roast to fit; place on top of vegetables. Combine the ¾ cup water, Worcestershire sauce, bouillon granules, basil, and salt. Add to cooker. Cover and cook on low-heat setting for 10 to 12 hours or on high-heat setting for 5 to 6 hours. Prepare gravy in a medium saucepan on the range top as in step 3 above. Serve gravy with meat and vegetables.

Nutrition Facts per serving: 307 cal., 10 g total fat (3 g sat. fat), 100 mg chol., 298 mg sodium, 17 g carbo., 3 g fiber, 35 g pro.
Daily Values: 288% vit. A, 19% vit. C, 4% calcium, 27% iron
Exchanges: 2 Vegetable, ½ Starch, 4 Lean Meat

Winter Pot Roast

See photo page 329.

Prep: 30 minutes **Cook:** 2 hours **Makes:** 6 to 8 servings

1 **2½- to 3-pound boneless beef chuck arm or shoulder pot roast**
1 **tablespoon cooking oil**
1 **14-ounce can beef broth**
1 **tablespoon finely shredded lemon peel**
2 **teaspoons dried oregano, crushed**
2 **cloves garlic, minced**
½ **teaspoon salt**
¼ **teaspoon black pepper**
6 **to 8 medium carrots and/or parsnips, peeled and cut into 1½-inch pieces**
1 **large onion, cut into wedges**
1 **cup pitted dried plums (prunes), halved**
½ **cup dried apricots, halved**
⅓ **cup cold water**
¼ **cup all-purpose flour**
3 **to 4 cups hot cooked noodles**

1. Trim fat from meat. In a 4- to 6-quart Dutch oven brown meat in hot oil. Combine broth, lemon peel, oregano, garlic, salt, and pepper. Pour over meat. Bring to boiling; reduce heat. Simmer, covered, for 1½ hours.

2. Add carrots, onion, plums, and apricots. Return to boiling; reduce heat. Simmer, covered, 30 to 40 minutes more or until meat is tender. Transfer meat, vegetables, and fruit to a platter, reserving juices in Dutch oven; keep warm.

3. For gravy, measure juices; skim fat (see photo, page 444). If necessary, add enough water to juices to equal 2½ cups. Return to Dutch oven. Stir cold water into flour until smooth. Stir into juices. Cook and stir until thickened and bubbly. Cook and stir for 1 minute more. Season to taste. Serve with meat, vegetables, fruit, and noodles.

Oven directions: Trim fat from meat. Brown roast as directed above. Combine the broth, lemon peel, oregano, garlic, salt, and pepper. Pour over roast. Bake, covered, in a 325°F oven for 1½ hours. Add carrots, onion, plums, and apricots. Cover and bake for 30 to 40 minutes more or until tender. Transfer meat, vegetables, and fruit to a platter, reserving juices; keep warm. Prepare gravy in a saucepan and serve as directed above.

Nutrition Facts per serving: 604 cal., 23 g total fat (8 g sat. fat), 140 mg chol., 476 mg sodium, 58 g carbo., 7 g fiber, 42 g pro.
Daily Values: 335% vit. A, 15% vit. C, 8% calcium, 41% iron
Exchanges: 1 Vegetable, 1½ Fruit, 2 Starch, 5 Lean Meat, 1 Fat

Swiss Steak `Best Loved`

`Low Fat`

Prep: 25 minutes **Cook:** 1¼ hours **Makes:** 4 servings

- 1 **pound boneless beef round steak, cut ¾ inch thick**
- 2 **tablespoons all-purpose flour**
- ¼ **teaspoon salt**
- ¼ **teaspoon black pepper**
- 1 **tablespoon cooking oil**
- 1 **14½-ounce can diced tomatoes with basil, oregano, and garlic, undrained**
- 1 **small onion, sliced and separated into rings**
- ½ **cup sliced celery (1 stalk)**
- ½ **cup sliced carrot (1 medium)**
- 2 **cups hot cooked noodles or mashed potatoes**

1. Trim fat from meat. Cut into 4 serving-size pieces. Combine the flour, salt, and pepper. With the notched side of a meat mallet, pound flour mixture into meat.

2. In a large skillet brown meat on both sides in hot oil. Drain off fat. Add undrained tomatoes, onion, celery, and carrot. Bring to boiling; reduce heat. Simmer, covered, about 1¼ hours or until meat is tender. Skim off fat. Serve with noodles or mashed potatoes.

Oven directions: Prepare and brown meat in skillet as above. Transfer meat to a 2-quart square baking dish. In the same skillet combine undrained tomatoes, onion, celery, and carrot. Bring to boiling, scraping up any browned bits. Pour over meat. Cover and bake in a 350°F oven about 1 hour or until tender. Serve as above.

Nutrition Facts per serving: 340 cal., 9 g total fat (2 g sat. fat), 82 mg chol., 459 mg sodium, 35 g carbo., 3 g fiber, 28 g pro.
Daily Values: 78% vit. A, 26% vit. C, 7% calcium, 26% iron
Exchanges: 1 Vegetable, 2 Starch, 3 Lean Meat

Oven-Barbecued Beef Brisket

`Low Fat`

Prep: 15 minutes **Roast:** 3 hours
Oven: 325°F **Makes:** 10 to 12 servings

- 1 **3- to 3½-pound fresh beef brisket**
- ¾ **cup water**
- ½ **cup chopped onion (1 medium)**
- 3 **tablespoons Worcestershire sauce**
- 2 **tablespoons cider vinegar or white wine vinegar**
- 1 **tablespoon chili powder**
- 1 **teaspoon instant beef bouillon granules**

- ⅛ **teaspoon ground red pepper**
- 2 **cloves garlic, minced**
- 1½ **cups bottled barbecue sauce or Barbecue Sauce (page 478)**

1. Trim fat from meat. Place meat in a 13×9×2-inch baking pan. In a small bowl stir together water, onion, Worcestershire sauce, vinegar, chili powder, bouillon granules, red pepper, and garlic. Pour over meat. Cover with foil. Bake in a 325° oven about 3 hours or until tender, turning once. Remove meat; discard juices. Thinly slice meat across the grain. Place on a serving platter. Serve with barbecue sauce.

Nutrition Facts per serving: 244 cal., 7 g total fat (2 g sat. fat), 78 mg chol., 735 mg sodium, 13 g carbo., 0 g fiber, 29 g pro.
Daily Values: 8% vit. A, 3% vit. C, 2% calcium, 17% iron
Exchanges: 1 Other Carbo., 3½ Lean Meat

New England Boiled Dinner

Prep: 20 minutes **Cook:** 2½ hours **Makes:** 6 servings

- 1 **2- to 2½-pound corned beef brisket**
- 1 **teaspoon whole black pepper***
- 2 **bay leaves***
- 2 **medium potatoes, peeled and quartered**
- 3 **medium carrots, quartered**
- 2 **medium parsnips or 1 medium rutabaga, peeled and cut into chunks**
- 1 **medium onion, cut into 6 wedges**
- 1 **small cabbage, cut into 6 wedges**
  Prepared horseradish or mustard (optional)

1. Trim fat from meat. Place in a 4- to 6-quart Dutch oven; add juices and spices from package of corned beef. (*Add pepper and bay leaves if your brisket doesn't come with an additional packet of spices.) Add enough *water* to cover meat. Bring to boiling; reduce heat. Simmer, covered, about 2 hours or until almost tender.

2. Add potatoes, carrots, parsnips, and onion to meat. Return to boiling; reduce heat. Simmer, covered, for 10 minutes. Add cabbage. Cover and cook for 15 to 20 minutes more or until tender. Discard bay leaves. Thinly slice meat across the grain. Transfer meat and vegetables to a serving platter. If desired, season to taste with *salt* and *black pepper* and serve with prepared horseradish or mustard.

Nutrition Facts per serving: 357 cal., 18 g total fat (5 g sat. fat), 77 mg chol., 131 mg sodium, 23 g carbo., 5 g fiber, 25 g pro.
Daily Values: 193% vit. A, 104% vit. C, 6% calcium, 21% iron
Exchanges: 1½ Vegetable, 1 Starch, 2½ Medium-Fat Meat, 1 Fat

Corned Beef and Cabbage: Prepare as on page 340, except omit potatoes, carrots, and parsnips.

Nutrition Facts per serving: 279 cal., 18 g total fat (5 g sat. fat), 77 mg chol., 112 mg sodium, 5 g carbo., 2 g fiber, 23 g pro.
Daily Values 2% vit. A, 82% vit. C, 4% calcium, 17% iron
Exchanges 1 Vegetable, 3 Medium-Fat Meat, ½ Fat

Zesty Short Ribs

Prep: 20 minutes **Cook:** 1½ hours
Broil: 10 minutes **Makes:** 4 servings

   3 to 4 pounds beef short ribs, cut into
      serving-size pieces
   ⅓ cup catsup
   ⅓ cup bottled chili sauce
   ¼ cup molasses
   3 tablespoons lemon juice
   2 tablespoons prepared mustard
   ¼ teaspoon ground red pepper

1. Trim fat from meat. Place meat in a 4- to 6-quart Dutch oven. Add enough water to cover meat. Bring to boiling; reduce heat. Simmer, covered, for 1½ to 2 hours or until meat is tender; drain.

2. For sauce, combine catsup, chili sauce, molasses, lemon juice, mustard, and red pepper. Place ribs on the unheated rack of a broiler pan. Brush with some of the sauce. Broil 4 to 5 inches from the heat for 10 to 15 minutes or until heated through, turning often and brushing with sauce. Heat any remaining sauce and pass with ribs.

Nutrition Facts per serving: 489 cal., 23 g total fat (9 g sat. fat), 106 mg chol., 1,048 mg sodium, 27 g carbo., 1 g fiber, 43 g pro.
Daily Values: 19% vit. A, 17% vit. C, 9% calcium, 28% iron
Exchanges: 2 Other Carbo., 5 Medium-Fat Meat

Osso Buco

Ask the butcher to cut shanks into crosswise slices.

Low Fat

Prep: 15 minutes **Cook:** 1¼ hours **Makes:** 6 servings

   2 to 2½ pounds veal shanks, cut crosswise
      into 2- to 2½-inch-thick slices
   2 tablespoons all-purpose flour
   ¼ teaspoon lemon-pepper seasoning
   2 tablespoons olive oil or cooking oil
   1 14½-ounce can diced tomatoes with basil,
      oregano, and garlic, undrained
   1 cup chopped onion (1 large)
   ½ cup chopped celery (1 stalk)
   ½ cup chopped carrot (1 medium)
   ½ cup water

   ¼ cup dry white wine or water
   ½ teaspoon finely shredded orange peel
   ½ teaspoon instant beef bouillon granules
   ½ teaspoon dried Italian seasoning, crushed
   1 clove garlic, minced
   1 teaspoon anchovy paste (optional)
   3 cups hot cooked rice
   1 tablespoon snipped fresh parsley

1. Trim fat from meat. In a shallow dish stir together the flour and lemon-pepper seasoning. Dip meat slices into flour mixture, coating well on all sides. In a 4-quart Dutch oven brown meat in hot oil over medium-high heat.

2. Add undrained tomatoes, onion, celery, carrot, water, wine, orange peel, bouillon granules, Italian seasoning, garlic, and anchovy paste (if desired) to Dutch oven; stir to combine. Bring to boiling; reduce heat. Simmer, covered, for 1¼ to 1½ hours or until veal is tender. Remove meat and bones, reserving vegetable mixture. If desired, remove meat from bones. Keep warm.

3. Boil vegetable mixture gently, uncovered, about 10 minutes or until desired consistency. Toss rice with parsley; place rice in a serving dish. Arrange meat on top of rice. Spoon the vegetable mixture over meat and rice.

Nutrition Facts per serving: 335 cal., 8 g total fat (2 g sat. fat), 89 mg chol., 343 mg sodium, 34 g carbo., 2 g fiber, 28 g pro.
Daily Values: 52% vit. A, 20% vit. C, 6% calcium, 14% iron
Exchanges: 1 Vegetable, 2 Starch, 3 Lean Meat

Osso Buco

Veal Parmigiana

Prep: 30 minutes **Cook:** 25 minutes **Makes:** 4 servings

 ⅓ **cup chopped onion**
 1 **clove garlic, minced**
 1 **tablespoon butter or margarine**
 1 **14½-ounce can diced tomatoes, undrained**
 ½ **teaspoon sugar**
 ⅛ **teaspoon salt**
   Dash black pepper
 3 **tablespoons whipping cream, half-and-half, or light cream**
 1 **pound boneless veal sirloin steak or boneless veal leg round steak, cut ½ inch thick**
 ⅓ **cup seasoned fine dry bread crumbs**
 3 **tablespoons grated Parmesan cheese**
 ½ **teaspoon dried oregano, crushed**
 1 **beaten egg**
 2 **tablespoons milk**
 3 **tablespoons olive oil or cooking oil**
 ¼ **cup shredded mozzarella cheese (1 ounce)**
 1 **tablespoon grated Parmesan cheese**

1. For sauce, in a medium saucepan cook onion and garlic in hot butter until onion is tender. Carefully stir in the undrained tomatoes, sugar, salt, and pepper. Bring to boiling; reduce heat. Simmer, uncovered, for 10 minutes or until desired consistency, stirring occasionally. Slowly add whipping cream, stirring constantly. Cook and stir for 3 minutes more.

2. Meanwhile, cut veal into 4 serving-size pieces. With a meat mallet, pound pieces of veal between 2 pieces of plastic wrap to ⅛-inch thickness.

3. In a shallow dish stir together bread crumbs, the 3 tablespoons Parmesan cheese, and oregano. In another bowl stir together the egg and milk. Dip veal pieces in egg mixture, then in crumb mixture to coat. In a 12-inch skillet cook meat in hot oil over medium heat for 2 to 3 minutes on each side or until golden. Transfer veal to a serving platter.

4. Spoon sauce over veal. Top with shredded mozzarella and 1 tablespoon Parmesan cheese. Let stand about 2 minutes or until cheese melts.

Nutrition Facts per serving: 411 cal., 24 g total fat (9 g sat. fat), 173 mg chol., 748 mg sodium, 15 g carbo., 1 g fiber, 32 g pro. **Daily Values:** 10% vit. A, 23% vit. C, 21% calcium, 11% iron **Exchanges:** 1½ Vegetable, ½ Starch, 4 Lean Meat, 2½ Fat

Veal Chops with Mushroom Sauce

Perfect with veal or pork, the mushroom sauce also dresses up noodles or rice.

Fast

Start to Finish: 25 minutes **Makes:** 4 servings

 4 **veal loin chops or pork loin chops, cut ¾ inch thick (about 1¾ pounds)**
   Salt and black pepper
 ¾ **cup sliced fresh mushrooms**
 2 **tablespoons sliced green onion (1)**
 1 **tablespoon butter or margarine**
 1 **tablespoon all-purpose flour**
 2 **teaspoons snipped fresh thyme or ¼ teaspoon dried thyme, crushed**
 1 **cup half-and-half, light cream, or milk**
 2 **tablespoons dry white wine or 1 tablespoon water plus 2 teaspoons white wine Worcestershire sauce**

1. Preheat broiler. Place chops on the unheated rack of a broiler pan. Sprinkle lightly with salt and pepper. Broil 3 to 4 inches from the heat until done (160°F), turning meat over after half of the broiling time. For veal, allow 14 to 16 minutes; for pork allow 9 to 12 minutes.

2. Meanwhile, for sauce, in a medium saucepan cook mushrooms and green onion in hot butter until tender. Stir in flour and, if using, dried thyme. Add half-and-half all at once. Cook and stir until thickened and bubbly. Cook and stir for 1 minute more. Stir in wine and, if using, fresh thyme. If desired, season sauce with *salt* and *black pepper*. Transfer chops to a serving platter. Spoon some of the sauce over the chops. Pass any remaining sauce.

Nutrition Facts per serving: 219 cal., 13 g total fat (7 g sat. fat), 97 mg chol., 267 mg sodium, 5 g carbo., 0 g fiber, 19 g pro. **Daily Values:** 8% vit. A, 3% vit. C, 8% calcium, 5% iron **Exchanges:** 1 Vegetable, 2½ Very Lean Meat, 2½ Fat

Pork Doneness

Pork cooked with foods such as bacon, spinach, or tomatoes sometimes remains pink even when well done. The same is true of grilled and smoked pork. In those cases, rely on a meat thermometer to determine doneness.

Pork Pot Roast in Cider

Prep: 15 minutes **Cook:** 1½ hours **Makes:** 4 servings

> 1 1½- to 2-pound boneless pork blade or sirloin roast
> 2 tablespoons cooking oil
> 1¼ cups apple cider or apple juice
> 2 teaspoons instant beef bouillon granules
> ½ teaspoon dry mustard
> ¼ teaspoon black pepper
> 3 medium red potatoes or round white potatoes, peeled (if desired) and quartered
> 3 medium carrots, cut into 2-inch pieces
> 3 medium parsnips, peeled and cut into 2-inch pieces
> 1 large onion, cut into wedges
> ⅓ cup cold water
> ¼ cup all-purpose flour

1. Trim fat from meat. In a 4- to 6-quart Dutch oven brown meat on all sides in hot oil. Drain off fat. Stir together apple cider, bouillon granules, mustard, and pepper. Pour over meat. Bring to boiling; reduce heat. Simmer, covered, for 1 hour.

2. Add potatoes, carrots, parsnips, and onion. Simmer, covered, for 30 to 40 minutes more or until meat and vegetables are tender. Transfer meat and vegetables to a serving platter, reserving juices in Dutch oven. Keep warm.

3. For gravy, measure juices; skim fat (see photo, page 444). If necessary, add enough water to juices to equal 1½ cups. Return to Dutch oven. Stir cold water into flour. Stir into juices in pan. Cook and stir over medium heat until thickened and bubbly. Cook and stir for 1 minute more. To serve, remove string from meat, if present. Slice meat and serve with vegetables and gravy.

Crockery-cooker directions: Trim fat from meat. Brown meat as directed above. Place potatoes, carrots, parsnips, and onion in a 3½- or 4-quart crockery cooker. Cut meat to fit in cooker and place on top of vegetables. Stir together apple cider, bouillon granules, mustard, and pepper. Pour over meat and vegetables. Cover and cook on low-heat setting for 8 to 10 hours or on high-heat setting for 4 to 5 hours or until tender. Transfer meat and vegetables to a serving platter; keep warm. Prepare gravy in a medium saucepan on the range top as in step 3. Serve as above.

Nutrition Facts per serving: 538 cal., 17 g total fat (5 g sat. fat), 110 mg chol., 608 mg sodium, 56 g carbo., 7 g fiber, 39 g pro.
Daily Values: 287% vit. A, 53% vit. C, 7% calcium, 24% iron
Exchanges: 2 Vegetable, 3 Starch, 3½ Lean Meat, 1 Fat

Rhubarb-Glazed Pork Best Loved

Low Fat

Prep: 25 minutes **Roast:** 1¼ hours **Oven:** 325°F
Stand: 15 minutes **Makes:** 6 to 8 servings

> 1 2- to 3-pound boneless pork top loin roast (single loin)
> 4 cups fresh or frozen sliced rhubarb
> ½ of a 12-ounce can frozen cranberry-apple juice concentrate
> 2 tablespoons cornstarch
> 2 tablespoons cold water
> ⅓ cup honey
> 2 tablespoons Dijon-style mustard
> 1 tablespoon wine vinegar

1. Place roast on a rack in a shallow roasting pan. Insert an oven-going meat thermometer into center of roast (see tip, page 331). Roast in a 325° oven for 1¼ hours to 1¾ hours or until the thermometer registers 155°F.

2. Meanwhile, prepare the rhubarb glaze. In a 2-quart saucepan combine rhubarb and cranberry-apple juice concentrate. Bring to boiling; reduce heat. Simmer, covered, for 10 to 15 minutes or until rhubarb is very tender. Strain mixture into a 2-cup liquid measure, pressing out liquid with the back of a spoon; discard pulp. If necessary, add enough water to liquid to equal 1¼ cups. In the saucepan stir together cornstarch and the cold water. Stir in rhubarb liquid. Cook and stir over medium heat until thickened and bubbly. Cook and stir for 2 minutes more. Stir in honey, mustard, and vinegar. Heat through.

3. Brush some of the glaze onto the meat for the last 30 minutes of roasting. Cover meat with foil and let stand 15 minutes. The temperature of the meat after standing should be 160°F. Reheat remaining glaze; serve with meat.

Nutrition Facts per serving: 336 cal., 8 g total fat (3 g sat. fat), 83 mg chol., 85 mg sodium, 32 g carbo., 0 g fiber, 33 g pro.
Daily Values: 38% vit. C, 4% calcium, 8% iron
Exchanges: 2 Other Carbo., 4 Lean Meat

Apricot-Glazed Pork: Prepare roast as above, except substitute apricot glaze for rhubarb glaze. For apricot glaze, in a small saucepan combine ⅔ cup apricot preserves, 4 teaspoons lime juice, 2 teaspoons soy sauce, ¼ teaspoon grated fresh ginger or ⅛ teaspoon ground ginger, and dash ground red pepper. Cook and stir until bubbly.

Nutrition Facts per serving: 309 cal., 7 g total fat (3 g sat. fat), 83 mg chol., 168 mg sodium, 25 g carbo., 0 g fiber, 33 g pro.
Daily Values: 7% vit. C, 4% calcium, 7% iron
Exchanges: 1½ Other Carbo., 4 Lean Meat

Festive Pork Roast

Handling Meat Safely

It's important to handle meat properly in the kitchen. Follow these food safety tips:

■ Keep clean everything that the meat touches, including hands, utensils, countertops, and cutting boards.

■ Always wash your hands with hot, soapy water before and after touching raw meat.

■ If you use a knife or any other utensil or plate for raw meat, don't use it for other foods without first washing it in hot, soapy water.

■ Reserve one cutting board just for raw meats. Designate another for all other foods.

■ Cook ground beef, pork, veal, and lamb to 160°F. The color of the cooked meat is not a good indication of doneness. Cook other cuts of beef to at least 145°F (medium rare) and pork to at least 160°F (medium). (All recipes in this cookbook provide directions to ensure reaching these minimum temperatures.)

■ To use a marinade as a sauce, before serving, bring marinade to a rolling boil to destroy any bacteria that may be present.

■ Don't cook any meat, poultry, or fish in stages (partially cooking it to save time, then finishing it later). Even if you store it in the refrigerator between cooking periods, safe temperatures may not be maintained.

Festive Pork Roast Best Loved

Low Fat

Prep: 15 minutes **Marinate:** 6 to 24 hours **Roast:** 2¼ hours
Oven: 325°F **Stand:** 15 minutes **Makes:** 15 servings

- 1 **5-pound boneless pork top loin roast (double loin, tied)**
- ¾ **cup dry red wine**
- ⅓ **cup packed brown sugar**
- ¼ **cup vinegar**
- ¼ **cup catsup**
- ¼ **cup water**
- 2 **tablespoons cooking oil**
- 1 **tablespoon soy sauce**
- 1 **clove garlic, minced**
- 1 **teaspoon curry powder**
- ½ **teaspoon ground ginger**
- ¼ **teaspoon black pepper**
- 2 **teaspoons cornstarch**

1. Place roast in a large plastic bag set in a large, deep bowl. For marinade, combine wine, brown sugar, vinegar, catsup, water, oil, soy sauce, garlic, curry powder, ginger, and pepper. Pour marinade over meat; seal bag. Marinate in the refrigerator for 6 to 8 hours or overnight, turning bag several times. Drain meat, reserving 1¼ cups marinade; cover marinade and chill. Pat meat dry with paper towels.

2. Place the meat on a rack in a shallow roasting pan. Insert an oven-going meat thermometer into center of roast (see tip, page 331). Roast in a 325° oven for $2\frac{1}{4}$ to $2\frac{1}{2}$ hours or until meat thermometer registers 155°F.

3. About 25 minutes before the meat is done, prepare the sauce. In a small saucepan stir cornstarch into the reserved marinade. Cook and stir until thickened and bubbly. Cook and stir for 2 minutes more. Brush meat frequently with sauce during the last 15 minutes of roasting. Cover meat with foil; let stand 15 minutes. The temperature of the meat after standing should be 160°F. Bring remaining sauce to boiling and pass with meat.

Nutrition Facts per serving: 203 cal., 6 g total fat (2 g sat. fat), 84 mg chol., 129 mg sodium, 4 g carbo., 0 g fiber, 29 g pro.
Daily Values: 1% vit. A, 2% vit. C, 2% calcium, 8% iron
Exchanges: 4 Very Lean Meat, $1\frac{1}{2}$ Fat

Shredded Savory Pork

This well-seasoned pork filling is used to prepare tacos or hearty sandwiches.

Low Fat

Prep: 15 minutes **Roast:** $2\frac{1}{2}$ hours **Oven:** 325°F
Makes: 12 servings (about 5 cups cooked meat)

> 1 3-pound boneless pork shoulder blade roast
> 8 cloves garlic, minced
> 2 teaspoons ground coriander
> 2 teaspoons ground cumin
> 2 teaspoons dried oregano, crushed
> 1 teaspoon onion powder
> ½ teaspoon salt
> ½ teaspoon ground black pepper
> ½ teaspoon ground red pepper
> 1 cup beef broth
> Hamburger buns or kaiser rolls, split and toasted (optional)

1. Trim fat from meat. In a small bowl combine garlic, coriander, cumin, oregano, onion powder, salt, black pepper, and red pepper; rub into the meat. Place meat in a roasting pan that has a cover; add beef broth. Cover and roast in a 325° oven for $2\frac{1}{2}$ to 3 hours or until very tender.

2. Remove meat from liquid with a slotted spoon; discard excess fat from cooking liquid, reserving the liquid. When meat is cool enough to handle, shred it using 2 forks to pull through it in opposite directions (see photo, page 313). Stir

in $\frac{1}{4}$ cup of the reserved cooking liquid to use as taco filling. Or, stir in enough cooking liquid to moisten; reheat in a saucepan over medium heat, stirring frequently, and serve on toasted buns.

Crockery-cooker directions: Prepare meat as at left. Place meat in a $3\frac{1}{2}$- to 5-quart crockery cooker; add beef broth. Cover and cook on low-heat setting for 8 to 10 hours or on high-heat setting for 4 to 5 hours. Continue as at left.

Nutrition Facts per serving meat: 182 cal., 9 g total fat (3 g sat. fat), 77 mg chol., 246 mg sodium, 1 g carbo., 0 g fiber, 22 g pro.
Daily Values: 1% vit. A, 2% vit. C, 4% calcium, 9% iron
Exchanges: 3 Lean Meat

Shredded Pork Tacos

This recipe is truer to Mexican tacos than the ones often eaten in the United States, which are made with ground meat.

Fast   Low Fat

Start to Finish: 25 minutes **Oven:** 350°F **Makes:** 8 tacos

> 2 cups Shredded Savory Pork (left)
> 8 taco shells or four 6- to 8-inch flour tortillas
> ¾ cup bottled salsa
> 2 cups shredded lettuce
> ½ cup finely shredded anejo enchilado cheese or Monterey Jack cheese (2 ounces)
> ¼ cup sliced pitted ripe olives
> Dairy sour cream (optional)
> 1 medium avocado, halved, seeded, peeled, and chopped (optional)

1. Prepare Shredded Savory Pork. Place taco shells on a baking sheet and heat in a 350° oven for 5 to 7 minutes or until heated through. (Or, wrap tortillas tightly in foil. Heat in a 350° oven about 10 minutes or until heated through.)

2. Meanwhile, in a medium saucepan combine Shredded Savory Pork and salsa; heat through (add additional salsa, if necessary, to moisten).

3. To assemble tacos, place pork mixture in warm taco shells. Top with lettuce, cheese, and olives. If desired, serve with sour cream and avocado. (If using flour tortillas, place pork mixture in center of warm tortillas and add remaining ingredients as directed; fold tortillas in half.)

Nutrition Facts per taco: 208 cal., 11 g total fat (4 g sat. fat), 53 mg chol., 365 mg sodium, 11 g carbo., 2 g fiber, 16 g pro.
Daily Values: 10% vit. A, 10% vit. C, 10% calcium, 10% iron
Exchanges: ½ Vegetable, ½ Starch, 2 Lean Meat, 1 Fat

Apricot-Sauced Pork Medallions

Let the tangy apricot sauce enhance the pork tenderloin's mild flavor.

`Fast` `Low Fat`

Start to Finish: 20 minutes **Makes:** 4 servings

>   1 **cup uncooked instant rice**
> 12 **ounces pork tenderloin**
>   1 **tablespoon butter or margarine**
>   1 **16-ounce can unpeeled apricot halves in light syrup**
>   1 **tablespoon cornstarch**
> ¼ **cup red plum jam or currant jelly**
>   2 **tablespoons white wine vinegar**
> ¼ **cup sliced green onions (2)**

1. Cook rice according to package directions. Meanwhile, trim fat from pork. Cut pork into ¾-inch-thick slices. Place each slice of pork between 2 pieces of plastic wrap. Working from center to edges, use the flat side of a meat mallet to lightly pound each slice into a ½-inch-thick medallion. Remove plastic wrap.

2. In a large skillet melt butter over medium-high heat until butter sizzles. Add pork; reduce heat to medium and cook for 4 to 8 minutes or until done (160°F), turning once. Remove pork from skillet. Keep warm.

3. Meanwhile, for sauce, drain apricots, reserving ⅔ cup of the syrup. Set syrup aside. Slice apricot halves. In a small saucepan stir together reserved apricot syrup and cornstarch. Stir in jam and vinegar. Cook and stir over medium heat until thickened and bubbly. Cook and stir for 2 minutes more. Stir in apricots. Heat through. Divide rice among 4 dinner plates. Top with pork medallions. Spoon sauce over pork. Sprinkle with green onions.

Nutrition Facts per serving: 357 cal., 6 g total fat (3 g sat. fat), 63 mg chol., 88 mg sodium, 55 g carbo., 2 g fiber, 20 g pro.
Daily Values: 33% vit. A, 11% vit. C, 3% calcium, 15% iron
Exchanges: 1 Fruit, 1½ Starch, 1 Other Carbo., 2 Lean Meat

Pork with Fennel and Pancetta

`Fast`

Start to Finish: 30 minutes **Makes:** 4 servings

> 12 **ounces pork tenderloin**
> ¼ **cup all-purpose flour**
>   **Dash salt**
>   **Dash black pepper**
>   2 **tablespoons olive oil**
>   2 **ounces pancetta (Italian bacon) or bacon, finely chopped**
>   2 **fennel bulbs, trimmed and cut crosswise into ¼-inch slices**
>   1 **small onion, thinly sliced**
>   2 **cloves garlic, minced**
>   2 **tablespoons lemon juice**
> ½ **cup whipping cream**

1. Trim fat from meat. Cut meat crosswise into 1-inch-thick slices. Place each slice between 2 pieces of plastic wrap. Use the flat side of a meat mallet to lightly pound each slice into a ¼-inch-thick medallion. Remove plastic wrap.

2. In a shallow bowl combine flour, salt, and pepper; coat meat with flour mixture. In a large heavy skillet heat oil over medium-high heat. Add meat, half at a time, and cook for 2 to 3 minutes or until meat is slightly pink in center, turning once. (Add more oil, if necessary.) Remove from skillet.

3. In the same skillet cook pancetta over medium-high heat until crisp. Add fennel, onion, and garlic. Cook for 3 to 5 minutes or until crisp-tender. Add lemon juice; stir in whipping cream. Bring to boiling; return meat to pan. Cook until meat is heated through and sauce is slightly thickened. Transfer the meat to a serving platter. Spoon the sauce over the meat.

Nutrition Facts per serving: 417 cal., 29 g total fat (12 g sat. fat), 106 mg chol., 256 mg sodium, 18 g carbo., 4 g fiber, 22 g pro.
Daily Values: 12% vit. A, 33% vit. C, 9% calcium, 14% iron
Exchanges: 2 Vegetable, ½ Starch, 2½ Lean Meat, 4 Fat

Pork with Fennel and Pancetta

Cashew Pork and Pea Pods

Start to Finish: 45 minutes **Makes:** 4 servings

- 1 **pound lean boneless pork**
- ½ **cup orange juice**
- ¼ **cup orange marmalade**
- 2 **tablespoons soy sauce**
- 1 **tablespoon cornstarch**
- 1 **teaspoon grated fresh ginger or ½ teaspoon ground ginger**
- 1 **tablespoon cooking oil**
- 2 **cups fresh pea pods or one 6-ounce package frozen pea pods, thawed**
- 2 **medium peaches or nectarines or 1½ cups cubed papaya or frozen peach slices, thawed**
- ½ **cup cashews or peanuts**
- 2 **cups hot cooked rice**

1. If desired, partially freeze meat for easier slicing. Trim fat from meat. Thinly slice meat across the grain into bite-size strips (see photo, page 334). For sauce, in a bowl stir together orange juice, marmalade, soy sauce, cornstarch, and ginger. Set aside.

2. Pour oil into a wok or large skillet. (Add more oil as necessary during cooking.) Preheat over medium-high heat. Add half of the pork. Cook and stir for 2 to 3 minutes or until juices run clear; remove from pan. Add remaining pork; cook and stir for 2 to 3 minutes. Return all meat to wok. Stir in pea pods and fruit. Push ingredients from center of wok.

3. Stir sauce; pour into center of wok. Cook and stir sauce until thickened and bubbly. Stir in meat mixture to coat with sauce. Cook and stir for 2 minutes. Stir in nuts. Serve with rice.

Nutrition Facts per serving: 497 cal., 17 g total fat (4 g sat. fat), 62 mg chol., 520 mg sodium, 54 g carbo., 4 g fiber, 32 g pro.
Daily Values: 8% vit. A, 69% vit. C, 7% calcium, 16% iron
Exchanges: 1 Fruit, 1½ Starch, 1 Other Carbo., 4 Lean Meat, 1 Fat

Stir-Frying Hints

■ If you don't have a wok, use a large, deep skillet or saute pan.

■ Prepare ingredients before starting to stir-fry. Some ingredients may need precooking.

■ When you add oil, lift and tilt wok to distribute it evenly over the bottom. Preheat wok over medium-high heat 1 minute. To test oil's hotness, add a vegetable piece; if it sizzles, start frying.

■ Don't overload your wok or skillet. When too much food is added at once, the food stews.

Pork Chop Suey

For Pork Chow Mein, substitute chow mein noodles for the hot cooked rice.

Low Fat

Prep: 30 minutes **Cook:** 15 minutes **Makes:** 4 to 6 servings

- 1 **pound lean boneless pork**
- ¾ **cup water**
- 3 **tablespoons reduced-sodium soy sauce**
- 2 **tablespoons cornstarch**
- 2 **tablespoons dry sherry or water**
- 1 **teaspoon instant chicken bouillon granules**
- ¼ **teaspoon black pepper**
- 1 **tablespoon cooking oil**
- 2 **teaspoons grated fresh ginger**
- 1 **cup thinly bias-sliced celery (2 stalks)**
- 2 **cups sliced fresh mushrooms**
- 2 **cups fresh bean sprouts or one 16-ounce can bean sprouts, rinsed and drained**
- 10 **green onions, bias-sliced into 1-inch pieces**
- 1 **8-ounce can sliced water chestnuts or bamboo shoots, drained**
- 2 to 3 **cups hot cooked rice**

1. If desired, partially freeze meat for easier slicing. Trim fat from meat. Thinly slice pork across the grain into bite-size strips (see photo, page 334). For sauce, in a bowl stir together water, soy sauce, cornstarch, sherry, bouillon granules, and pepper. Set aside.

2. Pour oil into a wok or 12-inch skillet. (Add more oil as necessary during cooking.) Preheat over medium-high heat. Cook and stir ginger in hot oil for 15 seconds. Add celery; cook and stir for 2 minutes. Add mushrooms, fresh bean sprouts (if using), and green onions. Cook and stir for 1 to 2 minutes or until the celery is crisp-tender. Remove vegetables from wok.

3. Add half of the pork to hot wok. Cook and stir for 2 to 3 minutes or until juices run clear. Remove from wok. Repeat with remaining pork. Return all meat to wok. Push from center of wok.

4. Stir sauce; add to center of wok. Cook and stir until thickened and bubbly. Add cooked vegetables, water chestnuts, and, if using, canned bean sprouts. Cook and stir until heated through. Serve with hot cooked rice.

Nutrition Facts per serving: 379 cal., 7 g total fat (2 g sat. fat), 66 mg chol., 788 mg sodium, 43 g carbo., 4 g fiber, 35 g pro.
Daily Values: 4% vit. A, 25% vit. C, 7% calcium, 25% iron
Exchanges: 2½ Vegetable, 2 Starch, 3 Lean Meat

Sweet-and-Sour Pork Best Loved

Start to Finish: 45 minutes **Makes:** 4 servings

- **12 ounces lean boneless pork**
- **2 tablespoons mirin or dry sherry**
- **2 tablespoons soy sauce**
- **1 teaspoon sesame oil**
- **1 cup chicken broth**
- **⅓ cup sugar**
- **⅓ cup rice vinegar**
- **4 teaspoons cornstarch**
- **1 tablespoon soy sauce**
- **Cooking oil or shortening for deep-fat frying**
- **1 beaten egg**
- **½ cup cornstarch**
- **½ cup all-purpose flour**
- **½ cup chicken broth**
- **1 tablespoon cooking oil**
- **1 clove garlic, minced**
- **3 medium carrots, thinly bias sliced (1½ cups)**
- **1 medium green sweet pepper, cut into 1-inch pieces (¾ cup)**
- **1 medium red sweet pepper, cut into 1-inch pieces (¾ cup)**
- **3 green onions, bias sliced into 1-inch pieces**
- **1 8-ounce can pineapple chunks (juice pack), drained**
- **3 cups hot cooked rice**

1. Trim fat from pork. Cut pork into ¾-inch cubes; place in a bowl. For marinade, stir together mirin, the 2 tablespoons soy sauce, and sesame oil. Pour over pork. Toss to coat. Cover; let stand at room temperature for 20 minutes.

2. For sauce, stir together the 1 cup broth, sugar, vinegar, the 4 teaspoons cornstarch, and the 1 tablespoon soy sauce. Set aside. In a wok or large saucepan heat 1½ to 2 inches of cooking oil or shortening to 365°F. Meanwhile, for batter, in a bowl stir together egg, the ½ cup cornstarch, flour, and the ½ cup broth until smooth.

3. Drain pork; pat dry. Dip pork into batter, swirling to coat. Fry a few pieces of pork at a time in hot oil for 4 to 5 minutes or until golden and no pink remains. Remove from oil. Drain on paper towels. Keep pork warm in a 300°F oven while frying remaining pork.

4. Pour the 1 tablespoon oil into a large skillet. (Add more oil as needed during cooking.) Preheat over medium-high heat. Cook and stir garlic in hot oil 15 seconds. Add carrots, sweet peppers, and green onions; cook and stir 4 to 5 minutes or until crisp-tender. Remove vegetables from skillet. Stir sauce; add to skillet. Cook and stir until bubbly. Cook and stir for 2 minutes more. Stir in pineapple and cooked vegetables. Cook and stir about 1 minute or until hot. Stir in pork. Serve over rice.

Nutrition Facts per serving: 754 cal., 24 g total fat (5 g sat. fat), 100 mg chol., 829 mg sodium, 102 g carbo., 4 g fiber, 29 g pro.
Daily Values: 267% vit. A, 130% vit. C, 7% calcium, 23% iron
Exchanges: 2 Vegetable, 5 Starch, 1 Other Carbo., 2 Lean Meat, 3 Fat

Sweet-and-Sour Pork

Oven-Fried Pork Chops

Fast

Prep: 10 minutes **Bake:** 20 minutes
Oven: 425°F **Makes:** 4 servings

- **4 pork loin chops, cut ¾ inch thick**
- **2 tablespoons butter, melted**
- **1 beaten egg**
- **2 tablespoons milk**
- **¼ teaspoon black pepper**
- **1 cup herb-seasoned stuffing mix, finely crushed**

1. Trim fat from meat. Pour butter into a 13×9×2-inch baking pan, tilting pan to coat the bottom. In a shallow dish combine egg, milk, and pepper. Place stuffing mix in another shallow dish. Dip chops into egg mixture. Coat both sides with stuffing mix. Place in prepared pan.

2. Bake, uncovered, in a 425° oven for 10 minutes. Turn chops. Bake for 10 to 15 minutes more or until done (160°F) and juices run clear.

Nutrition Facts per serving: 289 cal., 13 g total fat (6 g sat. fat), 141 mg chol., 342 mg sodium, 12 g carbo., 1 g fiber, 29 g pro.
Daily Values: 7% vit. A, 2% vit. C, 5% calcium, 10% iron
Exchanges: 1 Starch, 3½ Lean Meat

Pesto-Stuffed Pork Chops

Prep: 20 minutes **Bake:** 35 minutes
Oven: 375°F **Makes:** 4 servings

> **3** tablespoons crumbled feta cheese
> **2** tablespoons refrigerated basil pesto
> **1** tablespoon pine nuts, toasted (see tip, page 224)
> **4** pork loin chops or boneless pork loin chops, cut 1¼ inches thick
> **1** teaspoon freshly ground black pepper
> **1** teaspoon dried oregano, crushed
> **1** teaspoon bottled minced garlic
> **¼** teaspoon crushed red pepper
> **¼** teaspoon dried thyme, crushed
> **1** tablespoon balsamic vinegar

1. For filling, stir together cheese, pesto, and nuts. Set aside. Trim fat from meat. Make a pocket in each chop by cutting horizontally from the fat side almost to the bone or the opposite side (see photo, below). Divide filling among pockets in chops. If necessary, secure opening with a wooden toothpick.

2. For rub, in a small bowl combine black pepper, oregano, garlic, red pepper, and thyme. Rub evenly onto all sides of meat. Place chops on a rack in a shallow roasting pan. Bake in a 375° oven for 35 to 45 minutes or until done (160°F) and juices run clear. Brush vinegar onto chops during the last 5 minutes of baking. Before serving, discard toothpicks.

Nutrition Facts per serving: 358 cal., 18 g total fat (5 g sat. fat), 104 mg chol., 201 mg sodium, 4 g carbo., 0 g fiber, 41 g pro.
Daily Values: 2% vit. A, 2% vit. C, 6% calcium, 11% iron
Exchanges: 6 Lean Meat, ½ Fat

To create a pocket in thick chops, use a sharp knife to make a 2-inch-wide slit in fatty side. Work knife through chop; cut almost to other side, keeping original slit as narrow as possible.

Rosemary Pork Chop Skillet

Low Fat

Start to Finish: 35 minutes **Makes:** 4 servings

> **1** pound boneless pork sirloin chops, cut ½ inch thick
> **1** tablespoon olive oil
> **2** cups peeled and cubed (1 inch) winter squash, such as butternut, banana, spaghetti, and/or acorn
> **1** medium onion, cut into thin wedges
> **2** teaspoons snipped fresh rosemary
> **¼** cup chicken broth
> **¼** cup orange juice
> **2** medium zucchini, quartered lengthwise and cut into 1-inch pieces
> **1** teaspoon snipped fresh sage

1. Trim fat from pork. Sprinkle chops with ½ teaspoon *salt* and ½ teaspoon *black pepper*. In a 12-inch skillet heat oil over medium-high heat. Brown chops about 4 minutes, turning once. Combine squash, onion, and rosemary; spoon squash mixture over chops. Pour broth and juice over squash mixture and chops. Bring to boiling; reduce heat. Simmer, covered, for 10 minutes.

2. Add zucchini and sage. Cook, covered, about 5 minutes more or until chops are done (160°F). Using a slotted spoon, transfer chops and vegetables to a serving platter. Cover; keep warm.

3. Bring reserved juices in skillet to boiling; reduce heat. Simmer, uncovered, about 5 minutes or until liquid is reduced to about ¼ cup. Spoon over chops and vegetables.

Nutrition Facts per serving: 220 cal., 8 g total fat (2 g sat. fat), 63 mg chol., 411 mg sodium, 15 g carbo., 2 g fiber, 24 g pro.
Daily Values: 111% vit. A, 49% vit. C, 7% calcium, 11% iron
Exchanges: 1 Starch, 3 Very Lean Meat, 1 Fat

Pork Chops with Black Bean Salsa

Fast

Start to Finish: 25 minutes **Makes:** 4 servings

> **4** pork loin chops, cut 1¼ inches thick
> **1** teaspoon Jamaican jerk or Cajun seasoning
> **⅔** cup corn relish
> **½** of a 15-ounce can black beans, rinsed and drained
> **1½** teaspoons lime juice
> **¼** teaspoon ground cumin

1. Preheat broiler. Trim fat from meat. Rub seasoning and ⅛ teaspoon *black pepper* onto both sides of chops. Place pork chops on the unheated rack of a broiler pan. Broil 3 to 4 inches from the heat for 16 to 20 minutes or until done (160°F), turning meat over after half the broiling time.

2. Meanwhile, for salsa, combine corn relish, beans, lime juice, and cumin. Serve chops with salsa and, if desired, dairy sour cream.

Nutrition Facts per serving: 470 cal., 13 g total fat (5 g sat. fat), 152 mg chol., 425 mg sodium, 21 g carbo., 3 g fiber, 64 g pro.
Daily Values: 2% vit. C, 6% calcium, 13% iron
Exchanges: 1½ Starch, 8½ Very Lean Meat, 1 Fat

Oven-Roasted
Honey-and-Apple Ribs

Prep: 40 minutes **Bake:** 1¾ hours
Oven: 350°F **Makes:** 4 servings

   3 pounds pork country-style ribs
  ½ cup chopped onion (1 medium)
   2 cloves garlic, minced
   1 tablespoon cooking oil
  ¾ cup bottled chili sauce
  ½ cup apple juice or apple cider
  ¼ cup honey
   2 tablespoons Worcestershire sauce
  ½ teaspoon dry mustard

1. Place ribs in a shallow roasting pan. Bake, uncovered, in a 350° oven for 1 hour. Drain off fat.

2. Meanwhile, for sauce, in a medium saucepan cook onion and garlic in hot oil until tender. Stir in chili sauce, apple juice, honey, Worcestershire sauce, and dry mustard. Bring to boiling; reduce heat. Simmer, uncovered, for 20 minutes. (You should have about 1½ cups sauce.)

3. Spoon ⅓ cup of the sauce over the ribs. Bake, covered, for 45 to 60 minutes more or until tender, turning ribs and spooning ⅓ cup more of the sauce over ribs after 25 minutes. Heat remaining sauce and pass with ribs.

Nutrition Facts per serving: 529 cal., 25 g total fat (8 g sat. fat), 135 mg chol., 730 mg sodium, 36 g carbo., 3 g fiber, 40 g pro. Daily Values: 7% vit. A, 18% vit. C, 7% calcium, 16% iron Exchanges: 2½ Other Carbo., 5 Medium-Fat Meat

Barbecued Ribs   Best Loved

Prep: 25 minutes **Bake:** 1½ hours
Oven: 350°F **Makes:** 6 servings

   3 to 4 pounds pork loin back ribs
  ¾ cup catsup
  ¾ cup water
   2 tablespoons vinegar
   2 tablespoons Worcestershire sauce
   1 teaspoon paprika
   1 teaspoon chili powder
  ½ teaspoon black pepper
  ¼ teaspoon salt
  ¼ to ½ teaspoon ground red pepper
   1 cup finely chopped onion (1 large)

1. If desired, cut ribs into serving-size pieces. In a large shallow roasting pan place the ribs with the bone sides down. Bake, covered, in a 350° oven for 1 hour. Carefully drain off liquid in roasting pan.

2. Meanwhile, in a medium bowl combine the catsup, water, vinegar, Worcestershire sauce, paprika, chili powder, black pepper, salt, and red pepper. Stir in onion. Pour mixture over ribs. Bake, uncovered, for 30 minutes more or until ribs are tender, basting once with sauce. Pass sauce with ribs.

Nutrition Facts per serving: 298 cal., 15 g total fat (5 g sat. fat), 67 mg chol., 579 mg sodium, 12 g carbo., 1 g fiber, 29 g pro. Daily Values: 14% vit. A, 13% vit. C, 3% calcium, 9% iron Exchanges: 1 Other Carbo., 3½ Medium-Fat Meat

Oven-Roasted Oriental-
Style Pork Ribs

Boiling the ribs before they're baked reduces the total cooking time.

Prep: 40 minutes **Bake:** 15 minutes
Oven: 350°F **Makes:** 4 servings

   3 pounds pork loin back ribs or pork spareribs
   3 tablespoons pineapple, peach, or apricot preserves
  ⅓ cup catsup
   2 tablespoons soy sauce
   1 teaspoon grated fresh ginger or ¼ teaspoon ground ginger
   1 clove garlic, minced

1. Cut ribs into serving-size pieces. Place ribs in a 4- to 6-quart Dutch oven. Add enough water to cover. Bring to boiling; reduce heat. Simmer, covered, for 20 to 30 minutes or until ribs are tender; drain.

2. Meanwhile, for sauce, cut up any large pieces of fruit in the preserves. In a bowl stir together preserves, catsup, soy sauce, ginger, and garlic.

3. Brush some sauce over both sides of the ribs. Place ribs, bone sides down, in a shallow roasting pan. Bake, uncovered, in a 350° oven for 15 to 20 minutes or until glazed and heated through. Brush with remaining sauce before serving.

Nutrition Facts per serving: 442 cal., 22 g total fat (7 g sat. fat), 101 mg chol., 797 mg sodium, 16 g carbo., 1 g fiber, 43 g pro. Daily Values: 4% vit. A, 8% vit. C, 3% calcium, 8% iron Exchanges: 1 Other Carbo., 5½ Medium-Fat Meat

Smoked Pork Chops with Curried Fruit

Fast

Start to Finish: 20 minutes **Makes:** 4 servings

> 4 **cooked smoked pork chops, cut ¾ inch thick**
> 1 **tablespoon cooking oil**
> 1 **8-ounce can pineapple chunks (juice pack)**
> ⅓ **cup chopped onion (1 small)**
> 1 **tablespoon butter or margarine**
> 1½ **teaspoons curry powder**
> ¾ **cup orange juice**
> 1 **tablespoon cornstarch**
> 1 **cup cranberries**
> 1 **11-ounce can mandarin orange sections, drained**
> 2 **cups hot cooked couscous or basmati rice (optional)**

1. Trim fat from meat. In a 12-inch skillet cook chops in hot oil for 8 to 10 minutes or until hot, turning once.

2. Meanwhile, for sauce, drain pineapple, reserving juice. In a medium saucepan cook onion in hot butter until tender. Stir in curry powder. Cook and stir for 1 minute. Stir together reserved pineapple juice, orange juice, and cornstarch. Stir into saucepan. Add cranberries. Cook and stir over medium heat until thickened and bubbly. Cook and stir for 2 minutes more. Gently stir in pineapple and mandarin oranges; heat through. Serve sauce over pork chops. If desired, serve with couscous or rice.

Nutrition Facts per serving: 422 cal., 20 g total fat (7 g sat. fat), 92 mg chol., 2,162 mg sodium, 28 g carbo., 3 g fiber, 33 g pro.
Daily Values: 18% vit. A, 100% vit. C, 4% calcium, 15% iron
Exchanges: 2 Fruit, 4½ Lean Meat, 1 Fat

Glazed Ham

Low Fat

Prep: 15 minutes **Roast:** 1½ hours
Oven: 325°F **Makes:** 16 to 20 servings

> 1 **5- to 6-pound cooked ham (rump half or shank portion)**
> 24 **whole cloves (optional)**
> 1 **recipe Orange Glaze, Chutney Glaze, or Raspberry-Chipotle Glaze**

1. Score ham by making diagonal cuts in a diamond pattern. If desired, stud ham with cloves. Place ham on a rack in a shallow roasting pan. Insert an oven-going meat thermometer into center of ham (see tip, page 331). The thermometer should not touch the bone. Bake in a 325° oven for 1½ to 2¼ hours or until thermometer registers 140°F. Brush ham with some of the desired glaze during the last 20 minutes of baking. Serve with remaining glaze.

Orange Glaze: In a medium saucepan combine 2 teaspoons finely shredded orange peel, 1 cup orange juice, ½ cup packed brown sugar, 4 teaspoons cornstarch, and 1½ teaspoons dry mustard. Cook and stir over medium heat until thickened and bubbly. Cook and stir for 2 minutes more. Makes 1¼ cups glaze.

Chutney Glaze: In a food processor bowl or blender container combine one 9-ounce jar mango chutney, ¼ cup maple syrup, and 2 teaspoons stone-ground mustard. Cover and process or blend until smooth. Makes 1¼ cups glaze.

Nutrition Facts per serving with orange or chutney glaze:
166 cal., 5 g total fat (2 g sat. fat), 47 mg chol., 1,078 mg sodium, 10 g carbo., 0 g fiber, 19 g pro.
Daily Values: 1% vit. A, 14% vit. C, 2% calcium, 8% iron
Exchanges: ½ Other Carbo., 3 Very Lean Meat, ½ Fat

Raspberry-Chipotle Glaze: In a medium saucepan combine 1½ cups seedless raspberry preserves; 2 tablespoons vinegar; 2 or 3 canned chipotle peppers in adobo sauce, drained and chopped (see tip, page 64); and 3 cloves garlic, minced. Cook and stir just until boiling. Reduce heat. Cook, uncovered, 10 minutes more. Makes 1½ cups glaze.

Nutrition Facts per serving: 216 cal., 5 g total fat (2 g sat. fat), 47 mg chol., 1,104 mg sodium, 23 g carbo., 0 g fiber, 19 g pro.
Daily Values: 5% vit. C, 2% calcium, 8% iron
Exchanges: 1½ Other Carbo., 3 Very Lean Meat, ½ Fat

Hams: To Cook or Not to Cook

Fully cooked ham: This is the most popular kind of ham. It's ready to eat when you buy it. To serve the ham hot, heat it to an internal temperature of 140°F (see chart, page 373).

"Cook before eating" ham: Hams labeled like this are not completely cooked during processing and should be cooked to 160°F. If you are unsure whether the ham you've purchased is fully cooked, heat it to an internal temperature of 160°F.

Country or country-style ham: These hams are distinctively flavored and specially processed. They are cured, may or may not be smoked, and usually are aged. Country hams generally are saltier than other hams and often are named for the city where they are processed. Follow package directions for these hams.

Guide to Sausages

Several types of sausage are available in supermarkets. Fresh sausage comes in bulk, link, or patty form. Other sausage types come in links, rings, chunks, or slices.

Fresh (Uncooked): Made from fresh meat. Because fresh sausage is neither cooked nor cured, cook it well before eating.

Uncooked and Smoked: Made with fresh or cured meat. This sausage is smoked but not cooked. Cook it well before serving.

Cooked: Usually made from fresh meat that is cured during processing and fully cooked. Although these sausages are ready to eat, you can heat them before serving.

Cooked and Smoked: Made from fresh meat that is cured, smoked, and fully cooked. Serve these ready-to-eat sausages cold or hot.

Dry and Semidry: Made from fresh meat that is cured and dried during processing. Dry and semidry sausages may be smoked during processing. Most dry sausages are salamis (highly seasoned with a characteristic fermented flavor). Most semidry sausages are a type of summer sausage (mildly seasoned and easy to store). These are ready to eat and require no cooking.

Cooking Sausages

Different forms of sausage require different preparation methods. Here are some cooking suggestions:

Uncooked Patties: Place ½-inch-thick sausage patties in an unheated skillet and cook over medium-low heat for 10 to 12 minutes or until juices run clear, turning once (an instant-read thermometer inserted into the patty should register 160°F). Drain well. Or, arrange patties on a rack in a shallow baking pan. Bake in a 400°F oven about 15 minutes or until juices run clear and internal temperature reaches 160°F.

Uncooked Links: Place 1- to 1½-inch-diameter sausage links in an unheated skillet. Add ½ inch of water. Bring to boiling; reduce heat. Cover and simmer about 15 minutes or until juices run clear; drain. Cook 1 to 2 minutes more or until browned, turning often.

Fully Cooked Links: Place sausage links in a saucepan. Cover with cold water. Bring to boiling; reduce heat. Simmer for 5 to 10 minutes or until heated through.

Cooking Bacon

Fast

Start to Finish: 20 minutes

To bake: Place pork or turkey bacon slices side by side on a rack in a shallow baking pan with sides. Bake in a 400°F oven for 15 to 18 minutes or until crisp-cooked. Drain well on paper towels.

To cook in skillet: Place pork or turkey bacon slices in an unheated skillet (if using an electric range, preheat the element for 2 to 4 minutes). Cook over medium heat for 8 to 10 minutes, turning occasionally. If bacon browns too quickly, reduce heat slightly. Drain well on paper towels.

To microwave: Place bacon slices on a microwave-safe rack or a plate lined with microwave-safe paper towels. Cover with a paper towel. Microwave on 100 percent power (high) to desired doneness, rearranging bacon once. Allow 2 to 3 minutes for 2 slices; 3 to 4½ minutes for 4 slices; and 4 to 5 minutes for 6 slices.

Nutrition Facts per slice: 36 cal., 3 g total fat (1 g sat. fat), 5 mg chol., 101 mg sodium, 0 g carbo., 0 g fiber, 2 g pro.
Daily Values: 1% iron
Exchanges: 1 Fat

Ham Balls in Barbecue Sauce

Best Loved

Prep: 20 minutes **Bake:** 35 minutes
Oven: 350°F **Makes:** 6 servings

- 2 beaten eggs
- 1½ cups soft bread crumbs (see tip, page 293)
- ½ cup finely chopped onion (1 medium)
- 2 tablespoons milk
- 1 teaspoon dry mustard
- ¼ teaspoon black pepper
- 12 ounces ground cooked ham
- 12 ounces ground pork or ground beef
- ¾ cup packed brown sugar
- ½ cup catsup
- 2 tablespoons vinegar
- 1 teaspoon dry mustard

1. In a large bowl combine eggs, bread crumbs, onion, milk, 1 teaspoon mustard, and pepper. Add ground ham and ground pork; mix well. Shape into 12 balls, using about ⅓ cup mixture for each ball. Place ham balls in a lightly greased 2-quart rectangular baking dish.

2. In a bowl combine brown sugar, catsup, vinegar, and 1 teaspoon mustard. Stir until brown sugar is dissolved. Pour over meatballs.

3. Bake, uncovered, in a 350° oven about 35 minutes or until done (an instant-read thermometer inserted into meatballs should register 160°F). Transfer meatballs to a serving platter. Stir sauce in dish. Spoon sauce over meatballs to serve.

Nutrition Facts per serving: 439 cal., 20 g total fat (7 g sat. fat), 144 mg chol., 1,111 mg sodium, 42 g carbo., 1 g fiber, 23 g pro. Daily Values: 6% vit. A, 7% vit. C, 7% calcium, 14% iron Exchanges: 1 Starch, 2 Other Carbo., 2½ High-Fat Meat

---

Ham with Five-Spice Vegetables

`Fast` `Low Fat`

Start to Finish: 20 minutes **Makes:** 4 servings

> 2 **cups sliced carrots (4 medium)**
> 1 **cup fresh or frozen sugar snap peas**
> 1 **cup packaged shredded broccoli (broccoli slaw mix)**
> 1 **to 1½ pound cooked center-cut ham slice**
> 1 **teaspoon cooking oil**
> ½ **teaspoon five-spice powder**
> 1 **tablespoon honey**
> 1 **tablespoon reduced-sodium soy sauce**

1. In a covered medium saucepan cook carrots in a small amount of boiling water for 5 minutes. Add snap peas and broccoli; return to boiling. Cook, covered, 2 minutes more or until vegetables are crisp-tender; drain.

2. Meanwhile, trim fat from ham. Cut ham into 4 serving-size pieces. In a large skillet cook ham in hot oil over medium heat until heated through, turning once. Transfer ham to a serving platter; keep warm. Stir five-spice powder into drippings in skillet. Stir in honey and soy sauce. Bring to boiling. Gently stir in cooked vegetables; heat through. Spoon vegetable mixture over ham.

Nutrition Facts per serving: 222 cal., 7 g total fat (2 g sat. fat), 53 mg chol., 1,465 mg sodium, 16 g carbo., 4 g fiber, 24 g pro. Daily Values: 328% vit. A, 39% vit. C, 6% calcium, 10% iron Exchanges: 3 Vegetable, 3 Lean Meat

Lamb Chops with Mint Pesto

`Fast`

Prep: 15 minutes **Broil:** 10 minutes **Makes:** 4 servings

> 1 **cup lightly packed fresh mint leaves with stems removed**
> 1 **clove garlic**
> 3 **tablespoons olive oil or cooking oil**
> 1 **tablespoon white wine vinegar**
> ¼ **cup grated Parmesan cheese**
> 2 **tablespoons slivered almonds**
> ⅛ **teaspoon salt**
> ⅛ **teaspoon black pepper**
> 8 **lamb rib or loin chops, cut 1 inch thick**
> ¼ **cup apple jelly, melted**
> **Fresh mint leaves (optional)**

1. Preheat broiler. For pesto, in a food processor bowl or blender container place mint, garlic, oil, vinegar, Parmesan cheese, almonds, salt, and pepper. Cover and process or blend until nearly smooth, stopping to scrape sides as necessary. Set aside.

2. Trim fat from meat. Place chops on the unheated rack of a broiler pan. Sprinkle with additional *salt* and *black pepper*. Broil 3 to 4 inches from heat for 10 to 15 minutes for medium (160°F), turning and brushing chops with melted apple jelly about halfway through cooking. Serve chops with pesto. If desired, garnish with fresh mint leaves.

Nutrition Facts per serving: 363 cal., 23 g total fat (6 g sat. fat), 69 mg chol., 256 mg sodium, 15 g carbo., 1 g fiber, 23 g pro. Daily Values: 1% vit. A, 23% vit. C, 13% calcium, 31% iron Exchanges: 1 Other Carbo., 3½ Lean Meat, 2½ Fat

Ham with Five-Spice Vegetables

Lamb and Peppers

Fast **Low Fat**

Start to Finish: 25 minutes **Makes:** 4 servings

- 8 **lamb rib or loin chops, cut 1 inch thick**
- 3 **small green, red, and/or yellow sweet peppers, cut into 1-inch pieces**
- 2 **cloves garlic, minced**
- 1 **tablespoon snipped fresh oregano**
- 1 **tablespoon olive oil or cooking oil**
- ¼ **cup sliced pitted green or ripe olives**

1. Preheat broiler. Place chops on the unheated rack of a broiler pan. Broil 3 to 4 inches from heat for 10 to 15 minutes for medium (160°F), turning meat over after half of the broiling time. Transfer to a serving platter.

2. Meanwhile, in a large skillet cook sweet peppers, garlic, and oregano in hot oil for 8 to 10 minutes or until sweet peppers are crisp-tender. Add olives. Cook and stir until heated through. Spoon over chops.

Nutrition Facts per serving: 186 cal., 10 g total fat (2 g sat. fat), 60 mg chol., 257 mg sodium, 4 g carbo., 1 g fiber, 20 g pro.
Daily Values: 7% vit. A, 72% vit. C, 3% calcium, 12% iron
Exchanges: 1 Vegetable, 2½ Lean Meat, ½ Fat

Lamb Chops with Sweet Potato Chutney

Best Loved

Fast **Low Fat**

Prep: 20 minutes **Cook:** 10 minutes **Makes:** 4 servings

- 8 **lamb rib or loin chops, cut 1 inch thick**
- ⅓ **cup finely chopped shallots**
- ¼ **teaspoon crushed red pepper**
- ¼ **cup packed brown sugar**
- ¼ **cup vinegar**
- 2 **tablespoons dried cranberries or currants**
- ½ **teaspoon grated fresh ginger**
- 1 **medium sweet potato, peeled and coarsely chopped**

1. Preheat broiler. Trim fat from chops. In a small bowl combine shallots and pepper; reserve 2 tablespoons shallot mixture for chutney. Rub both sides of chops with remaining shallot mixture. Place chops on unheated rack of broiler pan; set aside.

2. For chutney, in a medium saucepan combine reserved shallot mixture, the brown sugar, vinegar, cranberries, and ginger. Stir in sweet potato. Bring to boiling; reduce heat. Simmer, covered, for 10 minutes, stirring occasionally.

3. Broil chops 3 to 4 inches from heat for 10 to 15 minutes for medium (160°F), turning meat over after half of the broiling time. Serve chops with the chutney.

Nutrition Facts per serving: 229 cal., 7 g total fat (2 g sat. fat), 48 mg chol., 56 mg sodium, 27 g carbo., 1 g fiber, 16 g pro.
Daily Values: 121% vit. A, 10% vit. C, 3% calcium, 10% iron
Exchanges: 1 Starch, 1 Other Carbo., 2 Lean Meat

Lamb Chops with Sweet Potato Chutney

Tuscan Lamb Chop Skillet

This dish illustrates the simple freshness of Tuscan-style cooking. Serve it with Italian bread and a salad of mixed baby greens.

Fast **Low Fat**

Start to Finish: 20 minutes **Makes:** 4 servings

- 8 **lamb rib chops, cut 1 inch thick**
- 2 **teaspoons olive oil**
- 3 **cloves garlic, minced**
- 1 **19-ounce can white kidney beans (cannellini), rinsed and drained**
- 1 **8-ounce can Italian-style stewed tomatoes, undrained**
- 1 **tablespoon balsamic vinegar**
- 2 **teaspoons snipped fresh rosemary**
  Fresh rosemary sprigs (optional)

1. Trim fat from chops. In a large skillet cook chops in hot oil over medium heat for 9 to 11 minutes for medium (160°F), turning once. Transfer chops to a plate; keep warm.

2. Stir garlic into drippings in skillet. Cook and stir for 1 minute. Stir in beans, undrained tomatoes, vinegar, and snipped rosemary. Bring to boiling; reduce heat. Simmer, uncovered, for 3 minutes. Spoon bean mixture onto 4 dinner plates; arrange 2 chops on each plate. If desired, garnish with rosemary sprigs.

Nutrition Facts per serving: 245 cal., 9 g total fat (3 g sat. fat), 48 mg chol., 374 mg sodium, 23 g carbo., 7 g fiber, 23 g pro.
Daily Values: 2% vit. C, 6% calcium, 16% iron
Exchanges: 1½ Starch, 2½ Lean Meat

1. Use a paring knife to cut ½-inch-wide slits about 1 inch deep into the leg of lamb. These slits allow flavors of the seasonings to better penetrate the meat.

Herb-Rubbed Leg of Lamb

If your grocery store doesn't regularly carry this cut, order it from the butcher a few days early.

Low Fat

Prep: 30 minutes **Roast:** 1¾ hours **Oven:** 325°F
Stand: 15 minutes **Makes:** 12 to 16 servings

1	5- to 7-pound whole leg of lamb (with bone)
	Lemon juice
2	tablespoons snipped fresh parsley
1	tablespoon snipped fresh mint or basil or 1 teaspoon dried mint or basil, crushed
1	tablespoon snipped fresh rosemary or ½ teaspoon dried rosemary, crushed
½	teaspoon onion salt
¼	teaspoon black pepper
1	or 2 cloves garlic, slivered
	Mint jelly (optional)
1	recipe Creamy Mustard Sauce (page 477) (optional)

1. Trim fat from meat. Cut slits into roast (see photo 1, top right). Drizzle lemon juice over meat's surface and into the slits. Stir together parsley, mint, rosemary, onion salt, and pepper. Rub parsley mixture onto meat and into slits. Insert garlic slivers (see photo 2, top right).

2. Place meat, fat side up, on a rack in a shallow roasting pan. Insert an oven-going meat thermometer into center of roast (see tip, page 331). The thermometer should not touch bone. Roast in a 325° oven. For medium rare, roast for 1¾ to 2¼ hours until meat thermometer registers 140°F. Cover with foil and let stand 15 minutes. The temperature of the meat after standing should be 145°F. (For medium, roast for 2¼ to 2¾ hours or until meat thermometer registers 155°F. Cover; let stand 15 minutes. The temperature of the meat after standing should be 160°F.) If desired, serve with mint jelly or Creamy Mustard Sauce.

Nutrition Facts per serving: 150 cal., 5 g total fat (2 g sat. fat), 77 mg chol., 123 mg sodium, 0 g carbo., 0 g fiber, 25 g pro.
Daily Values: 1% vit. A, 3% vit. C, 1% calcium, 13% iron
Exchanges: 3½ Very Lean Meat, ½ Fat

2. Rub the seasoning mixture over the meat's surface and into the slits. Push garlic slivers into the slits in the meat.

Roast Rack of Lamb with Peach-Ginger Chutney

Low Fat

Prep: 20 minutes **Roast:** 45 minutes **Oven:** 325°F
Stand: 15 minutes **Makes:** 6 servings

2	1- to 1½-pound lamb rib roasts (6 to 8 ribs each), with or without backbone
3	tablespoons Dijon-style mustard
3	tablespoons lemon juice
1	tablespoon snipped fresh rosemary or thyme
½	teaspoon salt
¾	cup soft bread crumbs (see tip, page 293)
1	tablespoon butter or margarine, melted
1	recipe Peach-Ginger Chutney (page 481)

1. Trim fat from meat. Stir together mustard, juice, rosemary, and salt. Rub onto meat. Toss together crumbs and butter. Sprinkle onto meat.

2. Place meat on a rack in a shallow roasting pan. Insert an oven-going meat thermometer (see tip, page 331). The thermometer should not touch bone. Roast, uncovered, in a 325° oven. For medium rare, roast for ¾ to 1 hour or until meat thermometer registers 140°F. Cover with foil and let stand 15 minutes. The temperature of the meat after standing should be 145°F. (For medium, roast for 1 to 1½ hours or until meat thermometer registers 155°F. Cover; let stand 15 minutes. The temperature of the meat after standing should be 160°F.) Serve with warm Peach-Ginger Chutney.

Nutrition Facts per serving: 299 cal., 9 g total fat (3 g sat. fat), 50 mg chol., 332 mg sodium, 41 g carbo., 3 g fiber, 16 g pro.
Daily Values: 11% vit. A, 16% vit. C, 5% calcium, 12% iron
Exchanges: 1 Fruit, 1½ Other Carbo., 2 Lean Meat, ½ Fat

Lamb Shanks with Beans

Choose meaty lamb pieces cut from the foreshank. Ask the butcher to cut the lamb shanks for you.

Low Fat

Prep: 30 minutes **Stand:** 1 hour
Cook: 1¾ hours **Makes:** 6 servings

- 1¼ **cups dry navy beans**
- 4 **cups water**
- 1 **tablespoon cooking oil**
- 4 **meaty lamb shanks (about 4 pounds), cut into 3- to 4-inch pieces, or meaty veal shank cross cuts (about 3 pounds)**
- 1 **medium onion, sliced and separated into rings**
- 2 **cloves garlic, minced**
- 2 **cups chicken broth**
- 1 **teaspoon dried thyme, crushed**
- ½ **teaspoon salt**
- ¼ **teaspoon black pepper**
- 1 **7½-ounce can tomatoes, undrained and cut up**
- ½ **cup dry white wine (optional)**

1. Rinse beans. In a 4- to 6-quart Dutch oven combine the beans and the water. Bring to boiling; reduce heat. Simmer, uncovered, for 2 minutes. Remove from heat. Do not drain. Cover and let stand for 1 hour. (Or, add water to cover beans. Cover and let stand overnight.)

2. Drain and rinse beans. In the same pan heat the oil. Add lamb shanks and brown on all sides; remove from pan. Add onion and garlic to pan and cook until tender. Carefully stir in beans, shanks, chicken broth, thyme, salt, and pepper. Bring to boiling; reduce heat. Simmer, covered, for 1½ to 2 hours or until meat and beans are tender. (If necessary, add more chicken broth to keep mixture moist.)

3. If desired, remove meat from pan. Cool slightly. When cool enough to handle, cut meat off bones and coarsely chop. Discard fat and bones. Skim fat from the top of the bean mixture. Stir in the meat (if necessary), undrained tomatoes, and, if desired, wine. Bring to boiling; reduce heat. Simmer, covered, for 10 to 15 minutes or until heated through.

Nutrition Facts per serving: 426 cal., 10 g total fat (3 g sat. fat), 131 mg chol., 817 mg sodium, 28 g carbo., 11 g fiber, 53 g pro.
Daily Values: 1% vit. A, 12% vit. C, 9% calcium, 34% iron
Exchanges: 2 Starch, 6½ Very Lean Meat, 1 Fat

Curried Lamb `Best Loved`

If you like, toast the coconut before serving it as one of the accompaniments.

Low Fat

Prep: 25 minutes **Cook:** 30 minutes **Makes:** 4 servings

- 12 **ounces lean boneless lamb or skinless, boneless chicken breast halves**
- 1 **cup coarsely chopped onion (1 large)**
- 2 to 3 **teaspoons curry powder**
- 2 **cloves garlic, minced**
- 1 **tablespoon cooking oil**
- 1 **cup water**
- 1 **teaspoon instant chicken bouillon granules**
- 2 **medium apples, cored and cut into chunks (about 2 cups)**
- ¼ **cup cold water**
- 1 **tablespoon cornstarch**
- 3 **tablespoons chutney**
  Salt (optional)
  Black pepper (optional)
- 2 **cups hot cooked rice**
  Chutney, sliced green onions, raisins, shredded coconut, and/or chopped peanuts (optional)

1. Trim fat from lamb. Cut lamb or chicken into ¾-inch cubes. In a large saucepan brown meat or chicken with onion, curry powder, and garlic in hot oil over medium heat until onion is tender but not brown.

2. Stir in the 1 cup water and bouillon granules. Bring to boiling; reduce heat. Simmer, covered, for 25 minutes for lamb or 15 minutes for chicken. Stir in apple chunks. Cover; cook 5 minutes more or until meat is tender.

3. In a small bowl stir the ¼ cup water into cornstarch; stir into mixture in saucepan. Cook and stir over medium heat until thickened and bubbly. Cook and stir for 2 minutes more. Cut up any large pieces of chutney; stir into meat mixture. If desired, season to taste with salt and pepper. Serve over hot cooked rice. If desired, pass additional chutney, green onions, raisins, coconut, and/or peanuts as accompaniments.

Nutrition Facts per serving: 332 cal., 8 g total fat (2 g sat. fat), 55 mg chol., 342 mg sodium, 45 g carbo., 4 g fiber, 20 g pro.
Daily Values: 11% vit. A, 19% vit. C, 4% calcium, 15% iron
Exchanges: 1 Fruit, 2 Starch, 2 Lean Meat

Braised Venison with Gravy

Low Fat

Prep: 25 minutes **Cook:** 1½ hours **Makes:** 6 to 8 servings

- 1 2- to 3-pound boneless venison shoulder or rump roast
- 1 tablespoon cooking oil
- 1 6-ounce can (⅔ cup) tomato juice
- ½ cup finely chopped onion (1 medium)
- ½ cup finely chopped carrot (1 medium)
- 1 teaspoon instant beef bouillon granules
- 3 tablespoons all-purpose flour
- ½ cup dairy sour cream
  Salt (optional)
  Black pepper (optional)
  Hot cooked noodles or mashed potatoes (optional)

1. Trim fat from meat. In a 4- to 6-quart Dutch oven brown meat in hot oil. Drain off fat. Add tomato juice, onion, carrot, and bouillon granules. Bring to boiling; reduce heat. Simmer, covered, for 1½ to 2 hours or until meat is tender. Transfer meat to a platter. Keep warm.

2. For gravy, measure vegetable mixture; skim fat. If necessary, add enough water to vegetable mixture to equal 2 cups. Return to Dutch oven. Stir flour into sour cream. Stir into vegetable mixture in pan. Cook and stir over medium heat until thickened and bubbly. Cook and stir for 1 minute more. If desired, season to taste with salt and black pepper. Serve gravy with meat and, if desired, noodles or mashed potatoes.

Crockery-cooker directions: Trim fat from meat and brown as above. Place onion and carrot in a 3½- or 4-quart crockery cooker. Cut meat to fit in cooker; place on top of vegetables. Combine tomato juice and bouillon granules. Add to cooker. Cover and cook on low-heat setting for 10 to 12 hours or on high-heat setting for 5 to 6 hours. Transfer meat to a serving platter; keep warm. Prepare gravy in a saucepan on the range top as in step 2. Serve as above.

Nutrition Facts per serving: 211 cal., 8 g total fat (3 g sat. fat), 98 mg chol., 463 mg sodium, 7 g carbo., 1 g fiber, 26 g pro.
Daily Values: 57% vit. A, 11% vit. C, 3% calcium, 23% iron
Exchanges: 1 Vegetable, 3½ Very Lean Meat, 1½ Fat

Marinated Venison Chops

Low Fat

Prep: 12 minutes **Marinate:** 2 to 4 hours
Broil: 10 minutes **Makes:** 4 servings

- 4 8-ounce venison rib chops, cut 1 inch thick
- ¼ cup finely chopped green onions (2)
- 2 tablespoons lime juice
- 2 tablespoons soy sauce
- 2 tablespoons grated fresh ginger
- 1 tablespoon brown sugar
- 1 fresh jalapeño chile pepper, seeded and finely chopped (see tip, page 64)
- 2 cloves garlic, minced

1. Place chops in a plastic bag set in a shallow dish. For marinade, in a small bowl combine remaining ingredients. Pour marinade over chops; seal bag. Marinate in the refrigerator for 2 to 4 hours, turning bag occasionally. Drain chops, discarding marinade. Preheat broiler. Place chops on the unheated rack of a broiler pan. Broil 3 to 4 inches from the heat for 10 to 12 minutes for medium (160°F), turning meat over after half of the broiling time.

Nutrition Facts per serving: 214 cal., 4 g total fat (1 g sat. fat), 144 mg chol., 306 mg sodium, 2 g carbo., 0 g fiber, 40 g pro.
Daily Values: 1% vit. A, 9% vit. C, 2% calcium, 33% iron
Exchanges: 6 Very Lean Meat

Liver and Onions

Fast **Low Fat**

Prep: 10 minutes **Cook:** 10 minutes **Makes:** 4 servings

- 1 pound sliced beef liver
- 2 medium onions, sliced and separated into rings
- 2 tablespoons butter or margarine
- 2 teaspoons lemon juice
- 1 teaspoon Worcestershire sauce

1. Pat liver dry with paper towels; set aside. In a large skillet cook onions in hot butter over medium heat until tender. Remove onions from skillet. Add liver to skillet. Sprinkle with *salt* and *black pepper*. Cook over medium heat for 3 minutes; turn. Return onions to skillet. Cook for 2 to 3 minutes more or until liver is slightly pink in center. Remove liver and onions from skillet. Stir in 2 teaspoons *water*, lemon juice, and Worcestershire sauce. Heat through. Pour over liver and onions.

Nutrition Facts per serving: 233 cal., 11 g total fat (5 g sat. fat), 418 mg chol., 197 mg sodium, 11 g carbo., 1 g fiber, 23 g pro.
Daily Values: 646% vit. A, 39% vit. C, 2% calcium, 44% iron
Exchanges: ½ Vegetable, ½ Starch, 3 Lean Meat, ½ Fat

Sausage and Pepper Sandwiches Best Loved

If you like, after topping sausage sandwiches with the vegetable mixture, add mozzarella cheese slices. Broil for 1 to 2 minutes to melt cheese. Add top of bun and serve.

`Fast`

Prep: 5 minutes **Cook:** 25 minutes **Makes:** 4 sandwiches

- **4 uncooked sweet (mild) Italian sausage links (about 1 pound)**
- **½ cup water**
- **1 tablespoon cooking oil**
- **1 cup green sweet pepper strips (1 medium)**
- **1 cup red sweet pepper strips (1 medium)**
- **1 large onion, sliced and separated into rings**
- **¼ cup bottled Italian salad dressing**
- **1 tablespoon Dijon-style mustard**
- **4 French-style rolls or hoagie buns, split***

1. In a large skillet cook sausage links over medium heat about 5 minutes or until brown, turning frequently. Carefully add water. Bring to boiling; reduce heat. Simmer, covered, for 5 minutes. Uncover and cook sausages, turning frequently until liquid evaporates and sausages are cooked through (160°F). Watch carefully so that sausages do not burn. Drain sausages on paper towels. Wipe out skillet, if necessary.

2. In the same skillet add the oil, green and red sweet peppers, and onion. Cook and stir about 5 minutes or until vegetables are crisp-tender.

Return sausage links to skillet. Combine the salad dressing and mustard. Stir into mixture in skillet. Heat through.

3. To serve, hollow out bottoms of rolls or buns. If desired, toast roll halves 4 inches from the heat of the broiler for 2 to 3 minutes. Place sausages on roll bottoms. Top with sweet pepper mixture and roll tops. (*If desired, do not split rolls. Instead cut unsplit rolls through the top and almost to the bottom. Add cooked sausages and vegetable mixture.)

Nutrition Facts per sandwich: 567 cal., 38 g total fat (12 g sat. fat), 77 mg chol., 993 mg sodium, 29 g carbo., 3 g fiber, 21 g pro. **Daily Values:** 34% vit. A, 116% vit. C, 7% calcium, 13% iron **Exchanges:** 1 Vegetable, 1½ Starch, 2½ High-Fat Meat, 4 Fat

---

Reuben Sandwiches

`Fast`

Prep: 10 minutes **Cook:** 8 minutes **Makes:** 4 sandwiches

- **3 tablespoons butter or margarine, softened**
- **8 slices dark rye or pumpernickel bread**
- **3 tablespoons bottled Thousand Island or Russian salad dressing**
- **6 ounces thinly sliced cooked corned beef, beef, pork, or ham**
- **4 slices Swiss cheese (3 ounces)**
- **1 cup sauerkraut, well drained**

1. Spread butter on 1 side of each bread slice and salad dressing on the other. With the buttered side down, top 4 slices with meat, cheese, and sauerkraut. Top with remaining bread slices, dressing side down.

2. Preheat a large skillet over medium heat. Reduce heat to medium-low. Cook 2 of the sandwiches at a time over medium-low heat for 4 to 6 minutes or until the bread is toasted and the cheese is melted, turning once. Repeat with the remaining sandwiches.

Nutrition Facts per sandwich: 487 cal., 29 g total fat (13 g sat. fat), 89 mg chol., 1,509 mg sodium, 36 g carbo., 5 g fiber, 20 g pro. **Daily Values:** 11% vit. A, 14% vit. C, 27% calcium, 20% iron **Exchanges:** 2½ Starch, 1½ Medium-Fat Meat, 3½ Fat

Sausage and Pepper Sandwiches

Beef and Sweet Onion Sandwiches

Fast **Low Fat**

Start to Finish: 20 minutes **Makes:** 4 sandwiches

> 12 ounces boneless beef sirloin or top round steak, cut 1 inch thick
>
> ½ teaspoon coarsely ground black pepper
>
> 2 teaspoons cooking oil
>
> 1 medium sweet onion, such as Vidalia or Walla Walla, sliced
>
> 2 tablespoons Dijon-style mustard
>
> ½ of a 7-ounce jar (about ½ cup) roasted red sweet peppers, drained
>
> 8 1-inch slices sourdough or marbled rye bread
>
> 1½ cups prewashed spinach or other salad greens, shredded

1. Trim fat from steak. Sprinkle both sides of steak with pepper; press in lightly. In a large skillet cook steak in hot oil over medium heat for 12 to 15 minutes or to desired doneness (145°F for medium rare and 160°F for medium), turning once. Remove from skillet; keep warm.

2. Add onion to drippings in skillet. (Add more oil, if necessary.) Cook and stir about 5 minutes or until onion is crisp-tender. Stir in mustard; remove from heat.

3. Meanwhile, cut roasted sweet peppers into ½-inch-wide strips. If desired, toast bread. To serve, cut steak into bite-size strips. Top 4 bread slices with spinach, steak strips, roasted pepper strips, onion mixture, and remaining bread slices.

Nutrition Facts per sandwich: 390 cal., 6 g total fat (1 g sat. fat), 40 mg chol., 600 mg sodium, 54 g carbo., 1 g fiber, 28 g pro.
Daily Values: 15% vit. A, 92% vit. C, 4% calcium, 27% iron
Exchanges: 1 Vegetable, 3 Starch, 2½ Lean Meat

French Dip Sandwiches

Fast

Start to Finish: 30 minutes **Makes:** 4 sandwiches

> 1 large onion, sliced and separated into rings
>
> 1 clove garlic, minced
>
> 1 tablespoon butter or margarine
>
> 1 14-ounce can beef broth
>
> ½ teaspoon dried thyme, marjoram, or oregano, crushed
>
> ¼ teaspoon black pepper
>
> 12 ounces thinly sliced cooked beef
>
> 4 French-style rolls, split

1. In a saucepan cook onion and garlic in hot butter until tender. Stir in broth, thyme, and pepper. Bring to boiling; reduce heat. Simmer, uncovered, for 10 minutes. Add beef. Return to boiling; reduce heat. Simmer, uncovered, 5 minutes more or until beef is heated through.

2. If desired, toast rolls. Remove beef slices and onion rings from liquid. Arrange on rolls. Serve with individual dishes of broth mixture for dipping.

Nutrition Facts per sandwich: 358 cal., 15 g total fat (7 g sat. fat), 76 mg chol., 596 mg sodium, 24 g carbo., 2 g fiber, 29 g pro.
Daily Values: 3% vit. A, 5% vit. C, 6% calcium, 22% iron
Exchanges: 1½ Starch, 3 Medium-Fat Meat

Muffuletta

Fast

Prep: 25 minutes **Makes:** 6 servings

> 1 16-ounce jar pickled mixed vegetables (1½ cups)
>
> ¼ cup chopped pimiento-stuffed green olives and/or pitted ripe olives
>
> 1 clove garlic, minced
>
> 1 tablespoon olive oil
>
> 1 16-ounce loaf unsliced French bread
>
> 6 lettuce leaves
>
> 6 ounces thinly sliced salami, pepperoni, summer sausage, cooked ham, prosciutto, or a combination
>
> 6 ounces thinly sliced provolone, Swiss, or mozzarella cheese
>
> 1 to 2 medium tomatoes, thinly sliced
>
> ⅛ teaspoon coarsely ground pepper

1. Drain vegetables, reserving 2 tablespoons liquid. Chop vegetables. Combine reserved liquid, vegetables, olives, garlic, and oil.

2. Horizontally split loaf of bread. Hollow out inside of the top half, leaving a ¾-inch-thick shell.

3. Top the bottom bread half with lettuce, desired meats, desired cheese, and tomato slices. Sprinkle tomato slices with pepper. Stir vegetable mixture. Mound on top of tomato slices. Top with hollowed-out bread half. Slice into 6 portions.

Nutrition Facts per serving: 425 cal., 22 g total fat (9 g sat. fat), 42 mg chol., 1,823 mg sodium, 36 g carbo., 2 g fiber, 19 g pro.
Daily Values: 52% vit. A, 14% vit. C, 27% calcium, 14% iron
Exchanges: 1 Vegetable, 2 Starch, 2 High-Fat Meat, 1 Fat

Tostada Pizza

Tostada Pizza Best Loved

Start to Finish: 40 minutes **Oven:** 400°F **Makes:** 6 servings

- 1 **pound lean ground beef**
- 1 **4-ounce can diced green chile peppers, drained**
- ½ **of a 1½-ounce envelope (about 2 tablespoons) taco seasoning mix**
- 1 **teaspoon chili powder**
- 1 **tablespoon cornmeal**
- 1 **10-ounce package refrigerated pizza dough**
- 1 **15-ounce can pinto beans with jalapeño peppers, rinsed and drained**
- 1 **cup shredded cheddar or Monterey Jack cheese (4 ounces)**
- 1 **cup shredded lettuce**
- 1 **medium tomato, chopped**
- ½ **cup thinly sliced green onions (4)**
   Bottled taco sauce (optional)

1. In a large skillet cook meat until brown. Drain off fat. Stir in ¾ cup *water*, chile peppers, taco seasoning mix, and chili powder. Bring to boiling; reduce heat. Simmer, uncovered, 15 to 20 minutes or until most of the liquid is gone.

2. Meanwhile, grease a baking sheet and sprinkle with the cornmeal. Pat pizza dough into a 12×8-inch rectangle on the baking sheet. Bake in a 400° oven for 5 minutes.

3. In a bowl mash beans with a fork; spread over partially baked dough to within ½ inch of edges. Spoon meat mixture over beans. Bake, uncovered, 10 minutes more or until crust is just golden. Sprinkle with cheese. Bake 1 to 2 minutes more or until cheese melts. Top with lettuce, tomato, and onions. If desired, serve with taco sauce.

Nutrition Facts per serving: 384 cal., 17 g total fat (7 g sat. fat), 67 mg chol., 882 mg sodium, 34 g carbo., 5 g fiber, 27 g pro. **Daily Values:** 15% vit. A, 24% vit. C, 20% calcium, 21% iron **Exchanges:** 2 Starch, 3 Medium-Fat Meat

Chili-Pasta Skillet

Prep: 10 minutes **Cook:** 25 minutes **Makes:** 6 servings

- 1 **pound ground beef**
- ¾ **cup chopped onion**
- 1 **15½-ounce can red kidney beans, rinsed and drained**
- 1 **14½-ounce can diced tomatoes, undrained**
- 1 **8-ounce can tomato sauce**
- ½ **cup dried elbow macaroni (2 ounces)**
- 1 **4-ounce can diced green chile peppers, drained**
- 2 **to 3 teaspoons chili powder**
- ½ **teaspoon garlic salt**
- ½ **cup shredded Monterey Jack or cheddar cheese (2 ounces)**

1. In a large skillet cook meat and onion until meat is brown and onion is tender. Drain off fat.

2. Stir in beans, undrained tomatoes, tomato sauce, uncooked macaroni, chile peppers, chili powder, and garlic salt. Bring to boiling; reduce heat. Simmer, covered, about 20 minutes or until macaroni is tender, stirring often. Remove skillet from heat; sprinkle mixture with cheese. Cover and let stand about 2 minutes or until cheese is melted.

Nutrition Facts per serving: 311 cal., 13 g total fat (5 g sat. fat), 56 mg chol., 634 mg sodium, 27 g carbo., 5 g fiber, 24 g pro.
Daily Values: 8% vit. A, 27% vit. C, 15% calcium, 18% iron
Exchanges: 1 Vegetable, 1½ Starch, 2½ Medium-Fat Meat

Meat Loaf   Best Loved

Another time, top loaf with ⅓ cup barbecue sauce.

Prep: 20 minutes **Bake:** 1 hour 10 minutes **Oven:** 350°F
Stand: 10 minutes **Makes:** 8 servings

  2 **beaten eggs**
  ¾ **cup milk**
  ⅔ **cup fine dry bread crumbs or 2 cups soft bread crumbs (see tip, page 293)**
  ¼ **cup finely chopped onion**
  2 **tablespoons snipped fresh parsley**
  1 **teaspoon salt**
  ½ **teaspoon dried leaf sage, basil, or oregano, crushed**
  1½ **pounds ground beef, lamb, or pork**
  ¼ **cup catsup**
  2 **tablespoons brown sugar**
  1 **teaspoon dry mustard**

1. In a bowl combine eggs and milk; stir in bread crumbs, onion, parsley, salt, sage, and ⅛ teaspoon *black pepper*. Add meat; mix well. Lightly pat mixture into an 8×4×2-inch loaf pan.

2. Bake in a 350° oven for 1 to 1¼ hours or until internal temperature registers 160°F. Spoon off fat. In a bowl combine catsup, sugar, and mustard; spread over meat. Bake for 10 minutes more. Let stand for 10 minutes before serving.

Ham Loaf: Prepare as above, except use soft bread crumbs. Substitute ½ teaspoon dry mustard for the sage, basil, or oregano and omit the salt. Substitute 12 ounces ground beef or pork and 12 ounces ground cooked ham for the 1½ pounds ground beef, lamb, or pork. Bake as above.

Nutrition Facts per serving for plain or ham variation: 243 cal., 13 g total fat (5 g sat. fat), 108 mg chol., 631 mg sodium, 12 g carbo., 1 g fiber, 20 g pro.
Daily Values: 5% vit. A, 5% vit. C, 6% calcium, 13% iron
Exchanges: ½ Starch, 2½ Medium-Fat Meat

Garden Beef Burgers

Fast

Prep: 15 minutes **Broil:** 11 minutes **Makes:** 4 servings

  1 **beaten egg**
  1 **tablespoon catsup**
  ½ **teaspoon dried basil, crushed**
  ½ **teaspoon onion salt**
  ¼ **teaspoon black pepper**
  1 **cup frozen loose-pack chopped broccoli, thawed, or shredded carrot**
  ¼ **cup soft bread crumbs (see tip, page 293)**
  1 **pound ground beef or pork**
     Catsup or bottled barbecue sauce
  4 **hamburger buns, split and toasted**
     Mayonnaise or salad dressing
     Leaf lettuce

1. Preheat broiler. In a large bowl combine egg, the 1 tablespoon catsup, basil, onion salt, and pepper. Stir in broccoli and bread crumbs. Add ground meat; mix well. Shape into four ½-inch-thick patties.

2. Place patties on the unheated rack of a broiler pan. Broil 3 to 4 inches from the heat for 11 to 13 minutes or until done (160°F), turning meat after half of the broiling time, then brushing once with additional catsup. Brush again with catsup before serving. Serve patties on buns with mayonnaise and lettuce.

Nutrition Facts per serving: 446 cal., 23 g total fat (7 g sat. fat), 127 mg chol., 715 mg sodium, 30 g carbo., 3 g fiber, 29 g pro.
Daily Values: 29% vit. A, 40% vit. C, 12% calcium, 24% iron
Exchanges: 2 Starch, 3 Medium-Fat Meat, 1 Fat

Doneness of Burgers

The internal color of the meat is not a reliable doneness indicator when cooking ground meat patties. Regardless of color, a beef, lamb, pork, or veal burger cooked to an internal temperature of 160°F is safe to eat. (Ground turkey and chicken burgers must be cooked to 165°F.) Sometimes ground beef has lost its pink color before it reaches the safe internal temperature of 160°F. Use an instant-read thermometer to check for doneness (see tip, page 331). If using a dial instant-read thermometer, insert it through the side of the burger to a depth of 2 to 3 inches to get an accurate temperature reading.

Super Burritos

Prep: 40 minutes **Bake:** 20 minutes
Oven: 350°F **Makes:** 8 servings

- 1 **pound ground beef or uncooked bulk chorizo sausage**
- 1 **cup chopped onion (1 large)**
- ½ **cup chopped green sweet pepper (1 small)**
- 1 **clove garlic, minced**
- ¼ **cup water**
- 1 **tablespoon medium or hot chili powder**
- ¼ **teaspoon ground cumin**
- 1 **cup cooked rice**
- 1 **4-ounce can diced green chile peppers, drained**
- 8 **10-inch flour tortillas**
- 1½ **cups shredded Monterey Jack or cheddar cheese (6 ounces)**
- ⅔ **cup chopped tomato (1 medium)**
- 2 **cups shredded lettuce**
- 1 **recipe Guacamole (page 64) or frozen avocado dip (guacamole), thawed**
  Bottled salsa (optional)

1. For filling, in a large skillet cook ground beef, onion, sweet pepper, and garlic until meat is brown and onion is tender. Drain off fat. Stir in water, chili powder, and cumin. Cook about 5 minutes or until most of the water has evaporated. Remove from heat. Stir in cooked rice and chile peppers.

2. Meanwhile, wrap tortillas tightly in foil. Heat in a 350° oven for 10 minutes to soften. (When ready to fill tortillas, remove only half of them at a time, keeping remaining tortillas warm in the oven.)

3. Spoon about ½ cup filling onto each tortilla just below the center. Top filling with cheese and tomato. Fold bottom edge of each tortilla up and over filling (see photo 1, top right). Fold opposite sides in and over filling (see photo 2, top right). Roll up from the bottom. Secure them with wooden toothpicks.

4. Arrange burritos on a baking sheet, seam sides down. Bake in a 350° oven for 10 to 12 minutes or until heated through. Remove and discard toothpicks. Serve warm burritos on lettuce with Guacamole and, if desired, salsa.

Nutrition Facts per serving: 492 cal., 31 g total fat (11 g sat. fat), 68 mg chol., 506 mg sodium, 36 g carbo., 5 g fiber, 19 g pro.
Daily Values: 28% vit. A, 42% vit. C, 25% calcium, 20% iron
Exchanges: ½ Vegetable, 2 Starch, 1½ High-Fat Meat, 3½ Fat

1. To shape a burrito, first fold the bottom edge of a softened tortilla up and over the filling.

2. While holding the bottom of the tortilla over the filling, fold in the sides. Then, starting from the folded bottom edge, roll up the tortilla to encase the filling.

Swedish Meatballs

Start to Finish: 50 minutes **Makes:** 5 or 6 servings

- 1 **beaten egg**
- ¼ **cup milk**
- ¾ **cup soft bread crumbs (see tip, page 293)**
- ½ **cup finely chopped onion (1 medium)**
- ¼ **cup snipped fresh parsley**
- ¼ **teaspoon black pepper**
- ⅛ **teaspoon ground allspice or nutmeg**
- 8 **ounces ground beef or ground veal**
- 8 **ounces ground pork or ground lamb**
- 1 **tablespoon butter or margarine**
- 2 **tablespoons all-purpose flour**
- 2 **teaspoons instant beef bouillon granules**
- ⅛ **teaspoon black pepper**
- 2 **cups milk**
- 3 **cups hot cooked noodles**
  Snipped fresh parsley (optional)

1. In a large bowl combine egg and the ¼ cup milk. Stir in bread crumbs, onion, the ¼ cup parsley, the ¼ teaspoon pepper, and allspice. Add beef and pork. Mix well. Shape into 30 meatballs.

2. In a large skillet cook half the meatballs at a time in hot butter over medium heat about 10 minutes or until done (an instant-read thermometer inserted into meatballs should register 160°F), turning to brown evenly. Remove meatballs from skillet, reserving drippings; drain meatballs on paper towels. Measure 2 tablespoons drippings; if necessary, add *cooking oil* to make the 2 tablespoons.

3. Stir flour, bouillon granules, and the ⅛ teaspoon pepper into drippings. Gradually stir in the

2 cups milk. Cook and stir over medium heat until thickened and bubbly. Cook and stir for 1 minute more. Return meatballs to skillet. Heat through. Serve over noodles. If desired, sprinkle with additional snipped parsley.

Nutrition Facts per serving: 518 cal., 29 g total fat (12 g sat. fat), 160 mg chol., 602 mg sodium, 37 g carbo., 2 g fiber, 26 g pro. Daily Values: 11% vit. A, 11% vit. C, 18% calcium, 20% iron Exchanges: 2½ Starch, 2½ High-Fat Meat, 1½ Fat

---

Sloppy Joes

To keep this sandwich low in fat, use lean ground beef. Ground pork will mean a higher fat content.

`Fast`

Start to Finish: 25 minutes **Makes:** 6 sandwiches

 1 **pound lean ground beef or ground pork**
½ **cup chopped onion (1 medium)**
½ **cup chopped green sweet pepper (1 small)**
 1 **8-ounce can tomato sauce**
 2 **tablespoons water**
 1 **to 1½ teaspoons chili powder**
 1 **teaspoon Worcestershire sauce**
½ **teaspoon garlic salt**
   Dash bottled hot pepper sauce
 6 **kaiser rolls or hamburger buns, split and toasted**

1. In a large skillet cook ground beef, onion, and sweet pepper until meat is brown and vegetables are tender. Drain off fat. Stir in tomato sauce, water, chili powder, Worcestershire sauce, garlic salt, and hot pepper sauce. Bring to boiling; reduce heat. Simmer, uncovered, for 5 minutes. Serve on toasted rolls.

Sloppy Joes for a Crowd: In a 4- to 6-quart Dutch oven cook 3 pounds lean ground beef or pork, 1½ cups chopped onion, and 1½ cups chopped green sweet pepper until meat is brown and vegetables are tender. Drain off fat. Stir in one 15-ounce can tomato sauce, one 8-ounce can tomato sauce, ¼ cup water, 3 to 4 teaspoons chili powder, 1 tablespoon Worcestershire sauce, 1½ teaspoons garlic salt, and ¼ teaspoon bottled hot pepper sauce. Bring to boiling; reduce heat. Simmer, uncovered, for 10 minutes. Split and toast 18 kaiser rolls or hamburger buns. Serve mixture on toasted rolls. Makes 18 sandwiches.

Nutrition Facts per sandwich: 369 cal., 16 g total fat (6 g sat. fat), 54 mg chol., 678 mg sodium, 35 g carbo., 2 g fiber, 20 g pro. Daily Values: 12% vit. A, 26% vit. C, 7% calcium, 20% iron Exchanges: 2½ Starch, 2 Medium-Fat Meat, ½ Fat

---

Stuffed Cabbage Rolls

Prep: 30 minutes **Bake:** 35 minutes **Oven:** 350°F **Makes:** 4 servings

12 **ounces ground beef, ground pork, ground lamb, or bulk pork sausage**
⅓ **cup chopped onion (1 small)**
 1 **7½-ounce can tomatoes, undrained and cut up**
½ **cup water**
⅓ **cup uncooked long grain rice**
½ **teaspoon dried oregano or thyme, crushed**
 8 **medium to large cabbage leaves**
¼ **cup shredded Swiss cheese (1 ounce)**
 1 **15-ounce can tomato sauce**
 1 **teaspoon sugar**
½ **teaspoon dried oregano or thyme, crushed**
¼ **cup shredded Swiss cheese (1 ounce)**

1. In a large skillet cook meat and onion until meat is brown and onion is tender. Drain off fat. Stir in undrained tomatoes, water, uncooked rice, ½ teaspoon oregano, and ¼ teaspoon *black pepper*. Bring to boiling; reduce heat. Simmer, covered, for 20 minutes or until the rice is tender.

2. Trim veins from cabbage leaves (see photo, below). Immerse leaves, 4 at a time, into boiling water for 2 to 3 minutes or until just limp.

3. Stir the ¼ cup Swiss cheese into the meat mixture. Place about ⅓ cup of the meat mixture on each cabbage leaf. Fold in sides. Starting at an unfolded edge, carefully roll up each leaf, making sure folded sides are included in the roll.

4. For sauce, in a small bowl stir together tomato sauce, sugar, and ½ teaspoon oregano. Pour half of the tomato mixture into a 2-quart square baking dish. Arrange cabbage rolls on the tomato mixture. Spoon remaining tomato mixture over cabbage rolls. Bake, covered, in a 350° oven for 35 to 40 minutes or until heated through. Sprinkle with remaining ¼ cup cheese. Let stand about 2 minutes or until cheese is melted.

Nutrition Facts per serving: 353 cal., 16 g total fat (7 g sat. fat), 63 mg chol., 827 mg sodium, 28 g carbo., 4 g fiber, 25 g pro. Daily Values: 31% vit. A, 57% vit. C, 21% calcium, 22% iron Exchanges: 2½ Vegetable, 1 Starch, 2½ Medium-Fat Meat, ½ Fat

To ensure easy rolling of the cabbage leaves, trim the heavy vein off the back of each one so that it's even with the rest of the leaf.

Corned Beef Hash

`Fast`

Prep: 20 minutes **Cook:** 10 minutes **Makes:** 4 servings

- 2 **tablespoons butter or margarine**
- 2 **cups finely chopped cooked potatoes or loose-pack frozen diced hash brown potatoes, thawed**
- 1½ **cups finely chopped cooked corned beef**
- ½ **cup chopped onion (1 medium)**
- 2 **tablespoons snipped fresh parsley**
- 1 **to 2 teaspoons Worcestershire sauce**
- ⅛ **teaspoon black pepper**
- 2 **tablespoons milk**

1. In a large skillet melt butter over medium heat. Stir in potatoes, beef, onion, parsley, Worcestershire sauce, and pepper. Spread in an even layer in the skillet. Cook over medium heat about 10 minutes or until potatoes are browned, turning occasionally. Stir in milk; heat through.

Nutrition Facts per serving: 277 cal., 17 g total fat (7 g sat. fat), 73 mg chol., 727 mg sodium, 18 g carbo., 2 g fiber, 12 g pro.
Daily Values: 7% vit. A, 23% vit. C, 3% calcium, 9% iron
Exchanges: 1 Starch, 1½ Medium-Fat Meat, 1½ Fat

Pan Sauce with Steak

Another time, try substituting dry white wine and reduced-sodium chicken broth for the red wine and beef broth and serve with sauteed chicken breasts.

`Fast`

Start to Finish: 20 minutes **Makes:** 2 servings

- 5 **tablespoons cold unsalted butter**
- 2 **beef steaks, such as top loin, ribeye, or tenderloin, cut about ¾ inch thick**
- ⅓ **cup dry red wine**
- ¼ **cup reduced-sodium beef broth**
- 2 **tablespoons finely chopped shallots or 1 clove garlic, minced**
- 1 **tablespoon whipping cream (no substitutes)**

1. Heat a large skillet over medium-high heat (if possible do not use a nonstick skillet). Add 1 tablespoon of the butter; reduce heat to medium. Cook steaks about 3 minutes per side or until medium rare (145°F). Transfer steaks to a platter; cover with foil to keep warm (steaks will continue to cook as they stand). Drain fat from skillet.

2. Add wine, broth, and shallots to the hot skillet. Using a wire whisk, stir and scrape the bottom of pan to remove browned bits (see photo 1, right).

Continue to cook over medium heat about 3 to 4 minutes or until liquid is reduced to about 2 tablespoons. Reduce heat to medium low.

3. Stir in whipping cream, then remaining butter, 1 tablespoon at a time (see photo 2, below), whisking until butter is melted and sauce has thickened slightly (see photo 3, below). Season to taste with *salt* and *white pepper*. Serve sauce at once over meat. Makes about ¼ cup sauce.

Nutrition Facts per serving: 654 cal., 45 g total fat (25 g sat. fat), 199 mg chol., 325 mg sodium, 3 g carbo., 0 g fiber, 53 g pro.
Daily Values: 28% vit. A, 1% vit. C, 4% calcium, 25% iron
Exchanges: 7 Lean Meat, 6 Fat

Pan Sauce Flavor Variations:

■ Stir in 1 teaspoon snipped fresh thyme, tarragon, or oregano with the shallots.

■ Stir in ½ teaspoon Dijon-style mustard with the shallots.

■ Stir ½ teaspoon balsamic vinegar into the finished sauce.

■ Stir ½ teaspoon capers into the finished sauce.

1. After removing meat from skillet, drain off fat. Add the wine, broth, and shallots. Using a wire whisk, scrape the pan to remove any browned bits.

2. Stir cream into the reduced sauce. Add the butter, 1 tablespoon at a time, while using a wire whisk to incorporate it into the sauce.

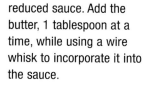

3. The sauce should be slightly thickened and have a sheen to it, as shown, when the sauce has been properly cooked.

Meat Buying Guidelines

Boneless roasts: Plan on 4 or 5 servings per pound. A rolled and tied roast is an example.

Bone-in meat cuts: Plan on 2 to 3 servings per pound. Examples include a leg of lamb, rib roast with bone, and bone-in ham.

Bony cuts: Plan on about 1 serving per pound. Cuts include beef shanks and pork ribs.

Veal

The drawing below illustrates wholesale veal cuts. The photos on this page are of retail veal cuts; the numbers in parentheses refer to the drawing. The best ways to cook each cut also are listed.

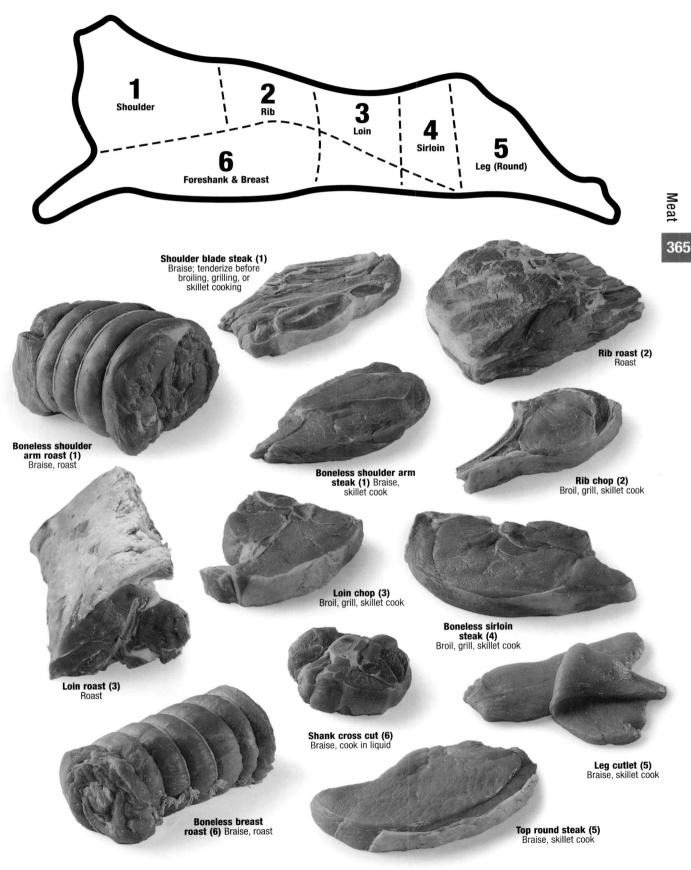

1 Shoulder

2 Rib

3 Loin

4 Sirloin

5 Leg (Round)

6 Foreshank & Breast

Shoulder blade steak (1)
Braise; tenderize before broiling, grilling, or skillet cooking

Rib roast (2)
Roast

Boneless shoulder arm roast (1)
Braise, roast

Boneless shoulder arm steak (1) Braise, skillet cook

Rib chop (2)
Broil, grill, skillet cook

Loin chop (3)
Broil, grill, skillet cook

Boneless sirloin steak (4)
Broil, grill, skillet cook

Loin roast (3)
Roast

Shank cross cut (6)
Braise, cook in liquid

Leg cutlet (5)
Braise, skillet cook

Boneless breast roast (6) Braise, roast

Top round steak (5)
Braise, skillet cook

Beef

The drawing below illustrates wholesale beef cuts. The photos on these two pages are of retail beef cuts; the numbers in parentheses refer to the drawing. The best ways to cook each cut also are listed.

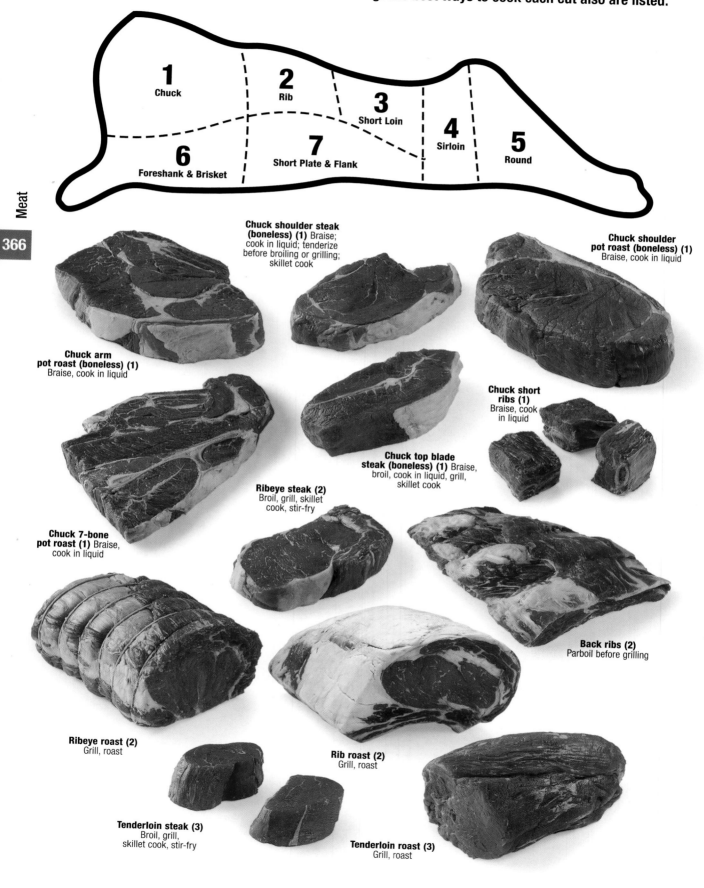

1 Chuck

2 Rib

3 Short Loin

4 Sirloin

5 Round

6 Foreshank & Brisket

7 Short Plate & Flank

Chuck shoulder steak (boneless) (1) Braise; cook in liquid; tenderize before broiling or grilling; skillet cook

Chuck shoulder pot roast (boneless) (1) Braise, cook in liquid

Chuck arm pot roast (boneless) (1) Braise, cook in liquid

Chuck short ribs (1) Braise, cook in liquid

Chuck top blade steak (boneless) (1) Braise, broil, cook in liquid, grill, skillet cook

Chuck 7-bone pot roast (1) Braise, cook in liquid

Ribeye steak (2) Broil, grill, skillet cook, stir-fry

Back ribs (2) Parboil before grilling

Ribeye roast (2) Grill, roast

Rib roast (2) Grill, roast

Tenderloin steak (3) Broil, grill, skillet cook, stir-fry

Tenderloin roast (3) Grill, roast

Top loin (strip) steak (3)
Broil, grill, skillet cook, stir-fry

T-bone/porterhouse steak (3)
Broil, grill, skillet cook

Tri-tip steak (4)
Broil, grill, skillet cook, stir-fry

Top sirloin steak (boneless) (4)
Broil, grill, skillet cook, stir-fry

Top round steak (5)
Tenderize before broiling, grilling, or skillet cooking; stir-fry

Tri-tip roast (4)
Grill, roast

Meat

367

Round tip steak (5)
Skillet cook, stir-fry

Eye round steak (5)
Braise, tenderize before grilling or skillet cooking

Bottom round steak (5) Braise

Round tip roast (5)
Roast

Bottom round roast (5)
Braise, roast

Eye round roast (5)
Braise, roast

Skirt steak (7)
Braise; tenderize before broiling, grilling, or skillet cooking

Top round roast (5) Roast

Boneless round rump roast (5) Braise, roast

Shank cross cut (6)
Braise, cook in liquid

Brisket (6)
Braise, cook in liquid

Flank steak (7) Braise, tenderize before broiling or grilling; stir-fry

Pork

The drawing below illustrates wholesale pork cuts. The photos on these two pages are of retail pork cuts; the numbers in parentheses refer to the drawing. The best ways to cook each cut also are listed.

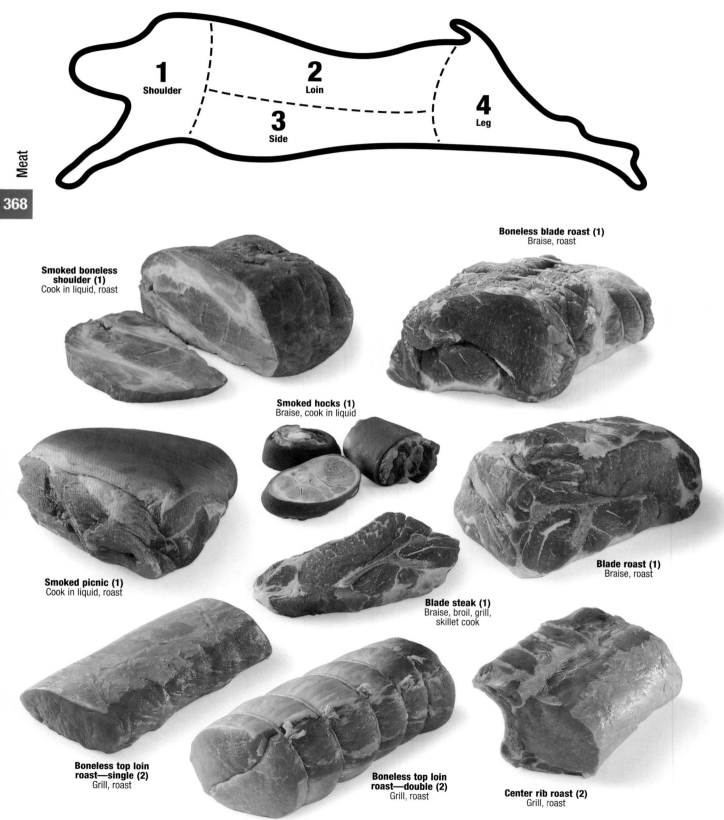

Smoked boneless shoulder (1)
Cook in liquid, roast

Boneless blade roast (1)
Braise, roast

Smoked hocks (1)
Braise, cook in liquid

Smoked picnic (1)
Cook in liquid, roast

Blade steak (1)
Braise, broil, grill, skillet cook

Blade roast (1)
Braise, roast

Boneless top loin roast—single (2)
Grill, roast

Boneless top loin roast—double (2)
Grill, roast

Center rib roast (2)
Grill, roast

Loin back ribs (2)
Braise, broil,
cook in liquid, roast

Country-style ribs (2)
Braise, broil,
cook in liquid, roast

Top loin chop (2)
Broil, grill, skillet cook

Butterfly chop (2)
Broil, grill,
skillet cook

Crown roast (2) Roast

Tenderloin (2)
Grill, roast

Rib chop (2)
Broil, grill, skillet cook

**Boneless sirloin
chop (2)** Braise, broil,
grill, skillet cook

Loin chop (2)
Broil, grill,
skillet cook

Sirloin chop (2)
Braise, broil, grill,
skillet cook

Canadian-style bacon (2)
Broil, skillet cook, roast

**Smoked loin
chop (2)** Broil, skillet
cook, roast

Spareribs (3)
Braise, broil,
cook in liquid,
roast

Bacon (3)
Bake, broil,
skillet cook

**Boneless cooked ham—
whole muscle (4)**
Grill, roast

**Ham
(shank half) (4)**
Grill, roast

**Center-cut ham
slice (4)** Broil, grill,
roast, skillet cook

**Boneless cooked ham—
sectioned and formed (4)**
Grill, roast

Lamb

The drawing below illustrates wholesale lamb cuts. The photos on this page are of retail lamb cuts; the numbers in parentheses refer to the drawing. The best ways to cook each cut also are listed.

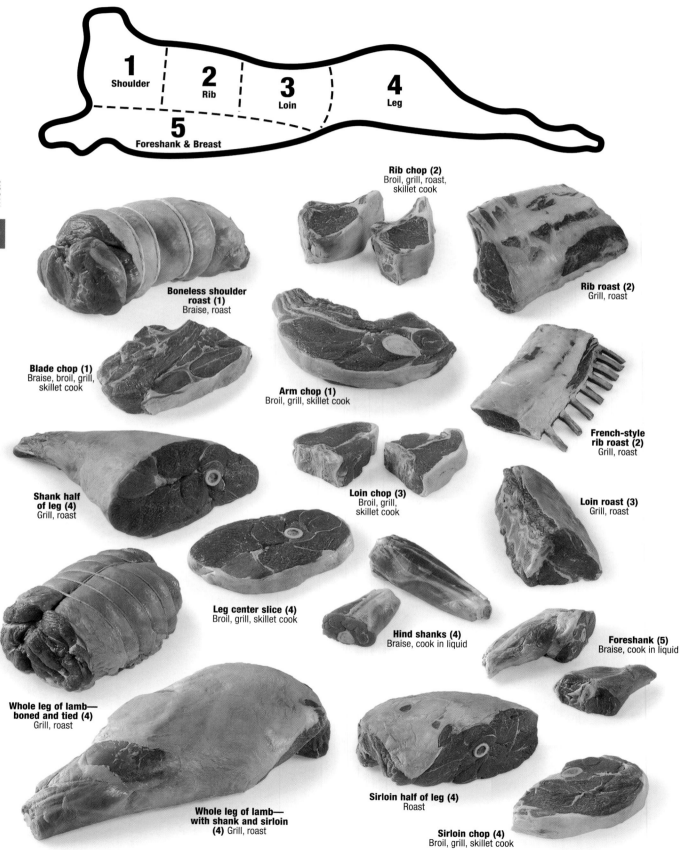

1 Shoulder

2 Rib

3 Loin

4 Leg

5 Foreshank & Breast

Rib chop (2)
Broil, grill, roast, skillet cook

Boneless shoulder roast (1)
Braise, roast

Rib roast (2)
Grill, roast

Blade chop (1)
Braise, broil, grill, skillet cook

Arm chop (1)
Broil, grill, skillet cook

French-style rib roast (2)
Grill, roast

Shank half of leg (4)
Grill, roast

Loin chop (3)
Broil, grill, skillet cook

Loin roast (3)
Grill, roast

Leg center slice (4)
Broil, grill, skillet cook

Hind shanks (4)
Braise, cook in liquid

Foreshank (5)
Braise, cook in liquid

Whole leg of lamb—boned and tied (4)
Grill, roast

Whole leg of lamb—with shank and sirloin (4) Grill, roast

Sirloin half of leg (4)
Roast

Sirloin chop (4)
Broil, grill, skillet cook

Broiling Meat

Preheat broiler. Place meat on the unheated rack of a broiler pan. For cuts less than 1½ inches thick, broil 3 to 4 inches from the heat. For 1½-inch-thick cuts, broil 4 to 5 inches from the heat. Broil for the time given or until done, turning meat over after half of the broiling time.

Cut	Thickness/Weight	Approximate Time	Doneness
Beef			
Boneless steak (ribeye, tenderloin, top loin)	1 inch 1½ inches	12 to 14 minutes 15 to 18 minutes 18 to 21 minutes 22 to 27 minutes	145°F medium rare 160°F medium 145°F medium rare 160°F medium
Boneless top sirloin steak	1 inch 1½ inches	15 to 17 minutes 20 to 22 minutes 25 to 27 minutes 30 to 32 minutes	145°F medium rare 160°F medium 145°F medium rare 160°F medium
Boneless tri-tip steak (bottom sirloin)	¾ inch 1 inch	6 to 7 minutes 8 to 9 minutes 9 to 10 minutes 11 to 12 minutes	145°F medium rare 160°F medium 145°F medium rare 160°F medium
Flank steak	1¼ to 1¾ pounds	15 to 18 minutes	160°F medium
Steak with bone (porterhouse, rib, T-bone)	1 inch 1½ inches	12 to 15 minutes 15 to 20 minutes 20 to 25 minutes 25 to 30 minutes	145°F medium rare 160°F medium 145°F medium rare 160°F medium
Ground Meat			
Patties (beef, lamb, pork, or veal)	½ inch ¾ inch	10 to 12 minutes 12 to 14 minutes	160°F medium 160°F medium
Lamb			
Chop (loin or rib)	1 inch	10 to 15 minutes	160°F medium
Chop (sirloin)	1 inch	12 to 15 minutes	160°F medium
Pork			
Chop with bone (loin or rib)	¾ to 1 inch 1¼ to 1½ inches	9 to 12 minutes 16 to 20 minutes	160°F medium 160°F medium
Chop with bone (sirloin)	¾ to 1 inch	10 to 13 minutes	160°F medium
Chop (boneless top loin)	¾ to 1 inch 1¼ to 1½ inches	9 to 11 minutes 15 to 18 minutes	160°F medium 160°F medium
Ham slice, cooked	1 inch	12 to 15 minutes	140°F heated through
Sausages			
Frankfurters and sausage links, cooked		3 to 7 minutes	140°F heated through
Veal			
Chop (loin or rib)	¾ to 1 inch 1½ inches	14 to 16 minutes 21 to 25 minutes	160°F medium 160°F medium

All cooking times are based on meat removed directly from refrigerator.

Roasting Meat

Place meat, fat side up, on a rack in a shallow roasting pan. (Roasts with a bone do not need a rack.) Insert a meat thermometer (see tip, page 331). Do not add water or liquid, and do not cover. Roast in a 325°F oven (unless chart says otherwise) for the time given and until the thermometer registers the "final roasting temperature." (This will be 5°F to 10°F below the "final doneness temperature.") Remove the roast from the oven; cover with foil and let it stand 15 minutes before carving. The meat's temperature will rise 5°F to 10°F during the time it stands.

Cut	Weight	Approximate Roasting Time	Final Roasting Temperature (when to remove from oven)	Final Doneness Temperature (after 15 minutes standing)
Beef				
Boneless tri-tip roast (bottom sirloin) Roast at 425°F	1½ to 2 pounds	30 to 35 minutes 40 to 45 minutes	140°F 155°F	145°F medium rare 160°F medium
Eye round roast Roasting past medium rare is not recommended.	2 to 3 pounds	1½ to 1¾ hours	135°F	145°F medium rare
Ribeye roast Roast at 350°F	3 to 4 pounds 4 to 6 pounds 6 to 8 pounds	1½ to 1¾ hours 1¾ hours to 2 hours 1¾ hours to 2 hours 2 to 2½ hours 2 to 2¼ hours 2½ to 2¾ hours	135°F 150°F 135°F 150°F 135°F 150°F	145°F medium rare 160°F medium 145°F medium rare 160°F medium 145°F medium rare 160°F medium
Rib roast (chine bone removed) Roast at 350°F	4 to 6 pounds 6 to 8 pounds 8 to 10 pounds*	1¾ to 2¼ hours 2¼ to 2¾ hours 2¼ to 2½ hours 2¾ to 3 hours 2½ to 3 hours 3 to 3½ hours	135°F 150°F 135°F 150°F 135°F 150°F	145°F medium rare 160°F medium 145°F medium rare 160°F medium 145°F medium rare 160°F medium
Round tip roast	3 to 4 pounds 4 to 6 pounds 6 to 8 pounds	1¾ to 2 hours 2¼ to 2½ hours 2 to 2½ hours 2½ to 3 hours 2½ to 3 hours 3 to 3½ hours	140°F 155°F 140°F 155°F 140°F 155°F	145°F medium rare 160°F medium 145°F medium rare 160°F medium 145°F medium rare 160°F medium
Tenderloin roast Roast at 425°F	2 to 3 pounds 4 to 5 pounds	35 to 40 minutes 45 to 50 minutes 50 to 60 minutes 60 to 70 minutes	135°F 150°F 135°F 150°F	145°F medium rare 160°F medium 145°F medium rare 160°F medium
Top round roast Roasting past medium rare is not recommended.	4 to 6 pounds 6 to 8 pounds	1¾ to 2½ hours 2½ to 3 hours	135°F 135°F	145°F medium rare 145°F medium rare
Lamb				
Boneless shoulder roast	3 to 4 pounds 4 to 5 pounds	1½ to 2 hours 1¾ to 2¼ hours 2 to 2½ hours 2¼ to 3 hours	140°F 155°F 140°F 155°F	145°F medium rare 160°F medium 145°F medium rare 160°F medium
Boneless sirloin roast	1½ to 2 pounds	1 to 1¼ hours 1¼ to 1½ hours	140°F 155°F	145°F medium rare 160°F medium

Cut	Weight	Approximate Roasting Time	Final Roasting Temperature (when to remove from oven)	Final Doneness Temperature (after 15 minutes standing)
Lamb (continued)				
Boneless leg roast	4 to 5 pounds	1³/₄ to 2¹/₄ hours 2 to 2¹/₂ hours	140°F 155°F	145°F medium rare 160°F medium
	5 to 6 pounds	2 to 2¹/₂ hours 2¹/₂ to 3 hours	140°F 155°F	145°F medium rare 160°F medium
Leg of lamb (with bone)	5 to 7 pounds	1³/₄ to 2¹/₄ hours 2¹/₄ to 2³/₄ hours	140°F 155°F	145°F medium rare 160°F medium
	7 to 8 pounds	2¹/₄ to 2³/₄ hours 2¹/₂ to 3 hours	140°F 155°F	145°F medium rare 160°F medium
Leg of lamb, shank half (with bone)	3 to 4 pounds	1³/₄ to 2¹/₄ hours 2 to 2¹/₂ hours	140°F 155°F	145°F medium rare 160°F medium
Leg of lamb, sirloin half (with bone)	3 to 4 pounds	1¹/₂ to 2 hours 1³/₄ to 2¹/₄ hours	140°F 155°F	145°F medium rare 160°F medium
Pork				
Boneless sirloin roast	1¹/₂ to 2 pounds	³/₄ to 1¹/₄ hours	155°F	160°F medium
Boneless top loin roast (double loin)	3 to 4 pounds 4 to 5 pounds	1¹/₂ to 2¹/₄ hours 2 to 2¹/₂ hours	155°F 155°F	160°F medium 160°F medium
Boneless top loin roast (single loin)	2 to 3 pounds	1¹/₄ to 1³/₄ hours	155°F	160°F medium
Loin center rib roast (backbone loosened)	3 to 4 pounds 4 to 6 pounds	1¹/₄ to 1³/₄ hours 1³/₄ to 2¹/₂ hours	155°F 155°F	160°F medium 160°F medium
Loin back ribs or spareribs		1¹/₂ to 1³/₄ hours	Tender	No standing time
Country-style ribs Roast at 350°F		1¹/₂ to 2 hours	Tender	No standing time
Crown roast	6 to 8 pounds	2¹/₂ to 3¹/₄ hours	155°F	160°F medium
Tenderloin Roast at 425°F	³/₄ to 1 pound	25 to 35 minutes	155°F	160°F medium
Ham, cooked (boneless)	1¹/₂ to 3 pounds 3 to 5 pounds 6 to 8 pounds 8 to 10 pounds*	³/₄ to 1¹/₄ hours 1 to 1³/₄ hours 1³/₄ to 2¹/₂ hours 2¹/₄ to 2³/₄ hours	140°F 140°F 140°F 140°F	No standing time No standing time No standing time No standing time
Ham, cooked (with bone) (half or whole)	6 to 8 pounds 14 to 16 pounds*	1¹/₂ to 2¹/₄ hours 2³/₄ to 3³/₄ hours	140°F 140°F	No standing time No standing time
Ham, cook-before-eating (with bone)	3 to 5 pounds 7 to 8 pounds 14 to 16 pounds*	1³/₄ to 3 hours 2¹/₂ to 3¹/₄ hours 4 to 5¹/₄ hours	155°F 155°F 155°F	160°F medium 160°F medium 160°F medium
Smoked shoulder picnic, cooked (with bone)	4 to 6 pounds	1¹/₄ to 2 hours	140°F	No standing time
Veal				
Loin roast (with bone)	3 to 4 pounds	1³/₄ to 2¹/₄ hours	155°F	160°F medium
Rib roast (chine bone removed)	4 to 5 pounds	1¹/₂ to 2¹/₄ hours	155°F	160°F medium

All cooking times are based on meat removed directly from refrigerator.
*Roasts weighing more than 8 pounds should be loosely covered with foil halfway through roasting.

Skillet Cooking Meat

Select a skillet that is the correct size for the amount of meat you are cooking. (If the skillet is too large, the pan juices can burn.) Lightly coat a heavy skillet with nonstick cooking spray. (Or use a heavy nonstick skillet.) Preheat skillet over medium-high heat until very hot. Add meat. Do not add any liquid and do not cover the skillet. Reduce heat to medium and cook for the time given or until done, turning meat occasionally. If meat browns too quickly, reduce heat to medium-low.

Cut	Thickness	Approximate Cooking Time	Doneness
Beef			
Boneless chuck eye steak	¾ inch 1 inch	9 to 11 minutes 12 to 15 minutes	145°F med. rare to 160°F medium 145°F med. rare to 160°F medium
Boneless top sirloin steak	¾ inch 1 inch	10 to 13 minutes 15 to 20 minutes	145°F med. rare to 160°F medium 145°F med. rare to 160°F medium
Boneless tri-tip steak (bottom sirloin)	¾ inch 1 inch	6 to 9 minutes 9 to 12 minutes	145°F med. rare to 160°F medium 145°F med. rare to 160°F medium
Cubed steak	½ inch	5 to 8 minutes	160°F medium
Porterhouse or T-bone steak	¾ inch 1 inch	11 to 13 minutes 14 to 17 minutes	145°F med. rare to 160°F medium 145°F med. rare to 160°F medium
Ribeye steak	¾ inch 1 inch	8 to 10 minutes 12 to 15 minutes	145°F med. rare to 160°F medium 145°F med. rare to 160°F medium
Tenderloin steak	¾ inch 1 inch	7 to 9 minutes 10 to 13 minutes	145°F med. rare to 160°F medium 145°F med. rare to 160°F medium
Top loin steak	¾ inch 1 inch	10 to 12 minutes 12 to 15 minutes	145°F med. rare to 160°F medium 145°F med. rare to 160°F medium
Ground Meat			
Patties (beef, lamb, pork, or veal)	½ inch ¾ inch	9 to 12 minutes 12 to 15 minutes	160°F medium 160°F medium
Lamb			
Chop (loin or rib)	1 inch	9 to 11 minutes	160°F medium
Pork			
Canadian-style bacon	¼ inch	3 to 4 minutes	Heated through
Chop (loin or rib) (with bone or boneless)	¾ to 1 inch	8 to 12 minutes	160°F medium
Cutlet	¼ inch	3 to 4 minutes	160°F medium
Ham slice, cooked	1 inch	14 to 16 minutes	140°F heated through
Tenderloin medallions	¼ to ½ inch	4 to 8 minutes	160°F medium
Veal			
Chop (loin or rib)	¾ to 1 inch	10 to 14 minutes	160°F medium
Cutlet	⅛ inch ¼ inch	2 to 4 minutes 4 to 6 minutes	160°F medium 160°F medium

All cooking times are based on meat removed directly from refrigerator.

Chapter 16
Pasta

Pasta

375

Pasta

Homemade Pasta

Low Fat

Prep: 1 hour **Cook:** see chart, below right
Makes: 5 main-dish servings (about 1 pound pasta)

> 2⅓ **cups all-purpose flour**
>   1 **teaspoon dried basil, marjoram, or sage, crushed (optional)**
>   ½ **teaspoon salt**
>   2 **beaten eggs**
>   ⅓ **cup water**
>   1 **teaspoon cooking oil or olive oil**

1. In a large bowl stir together 2 cups of the flour, the basil (if desired), and salt. Make a well in the center of the flour mixture. In a small bowl combine eggs, water, and oil. Add egg mixture to flour mixture; stir to combine.

2. Sprinkle a clean kneading surface with the remaining ⅓ cup flour. Turn dough out onto floured surface. Knead until dough is smooth and elastic (8 to 10 minutes total). Cover and let the dough rest for 10 minutes.

3. Divide the dough into 4 equal portions. On lightly floured kneading surface, roll each dough portion into a 12-inch square (about ⅟₁₆ inch thick). Let stand, uncovered, about 20 minutes. Cut as desired (see photos 1 and 2, above right). If using a pasta machine, pass each portion through machine according to manufacturer's directions until dough is ⅟₁₆ inch thick. Let stand; cut as desired.

4. To serve pasta immediately, cook pasta according to the chart at right.

5. To store cut pasta, hang it from a pasta-drying rack or clothes hanger, or spread it on a wire cooling rack. Let pasta dry overnight or until completely dry. Place in an airtight container and chill for up to 3 days. Or dry the pasta for at least 1 hour; place it in a freezer bag or freezer container and freeze for up to 8 months.

Food processor directions: Place steel blade in food processor bowl. Add flour, basil (if desired), salt, and eggs to bowl. Cover and process until mixture forms fine crumbs (about the consistency of cornmeal). With the processor running, slowly pour the water and oil through the feed tube. Continue processing just until the dough forms a ball. Transfer dough to a lightly floured surface. Cover; let dough rest for 10 minutes. Continue as directed in step 3.

Nutrition Facts per serving: 250 cal., 4 g total fat (1 g sat. fat), 85 mg chol., 259 mg sodium, 45 g carbo., 2 g fiber, 9 g pro.
Daily Values: 2% calcium, 17% iron
Exchanges: 3 Starch

1. For linguine, fettuccine, or noodles, loosely roll up dough; cut into ⅛-inch strips for linguine or ¼-inch strips for fettuccine or noodles. Separate strips; cut strips into 12-inch lengths.

2. For lasagna noodles, use a fluted pastry wheel or a sharp knife to cut dough into 2½-inch-wide strips. Cut strips into desired lengths.

Cooking Homemade Pasta

In a large saucepan or kettle bring water (3 quarts of water for 4 to 8 ounces pasta) to boiling. If desired, add 1 teaspoon salt and 1 tablespoon olive oil or cooking oil to the water to prevent pasta from sticking together. Add pasta a little at a time so the water does not stop boiling. Reduce heat slightly and boil, uncovered, stirring occasionally, for the time specified below or until the pasta is al dente (see tip, page 393). Test often for doneness near the end of the cooking time. Drain in a colander. (To cook purchased dried pasta, check the package directions because brands vary.)

Homemade Pasta	Cooking Time*
Bow ties, large or tiny	2 to 3 min.
Fettuccine	1½ to 2 min.
Lasagna	2 to 3 min.
Linguine	1½ to 2 min.
Noodles	1½ to 2 min.
Ravioli	7 to 9 min.
Tortellini	7 to 9 min.

*If homemade pasta is dried or frozen, allow 1 to 2 minutes more.

Pasta

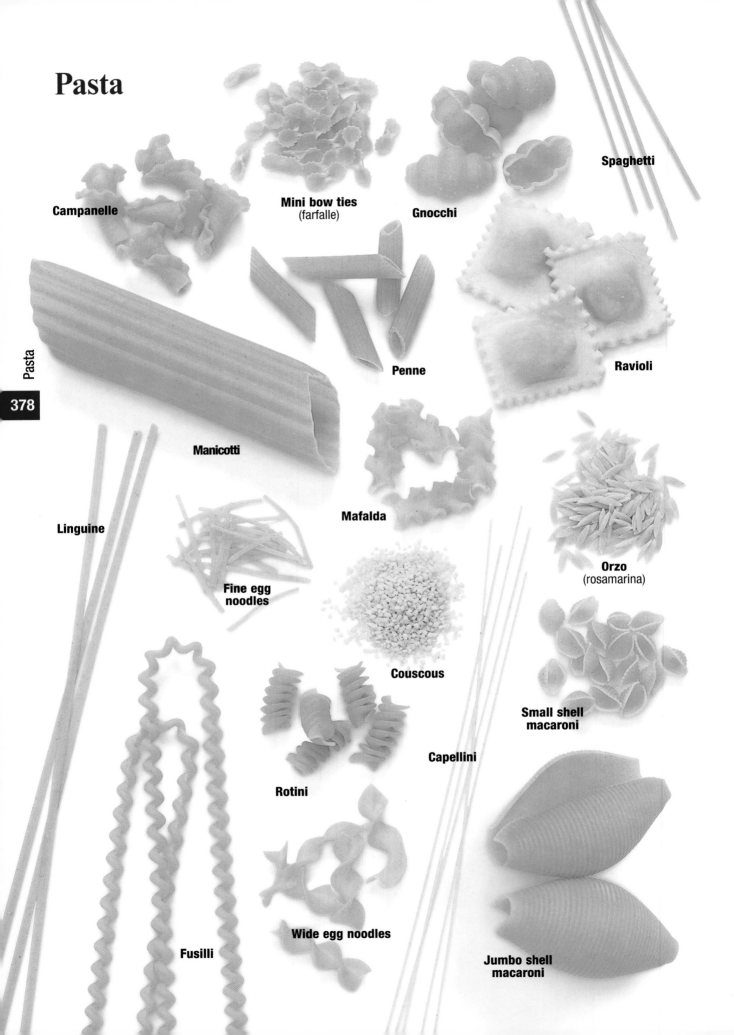

Campanelle

Mini bow ties
(farfalle)

Gnocchi

Spaghetti

Manicotti

Penne

Ravioli

Linguine

Mafalda

Orzo
(rosamarina)

Fine egg
noodles

Couscous

Small shell
macaroni

Rotini

Capellini

Wide egg noodles

Fusilli

Jumbo shell
macaroni

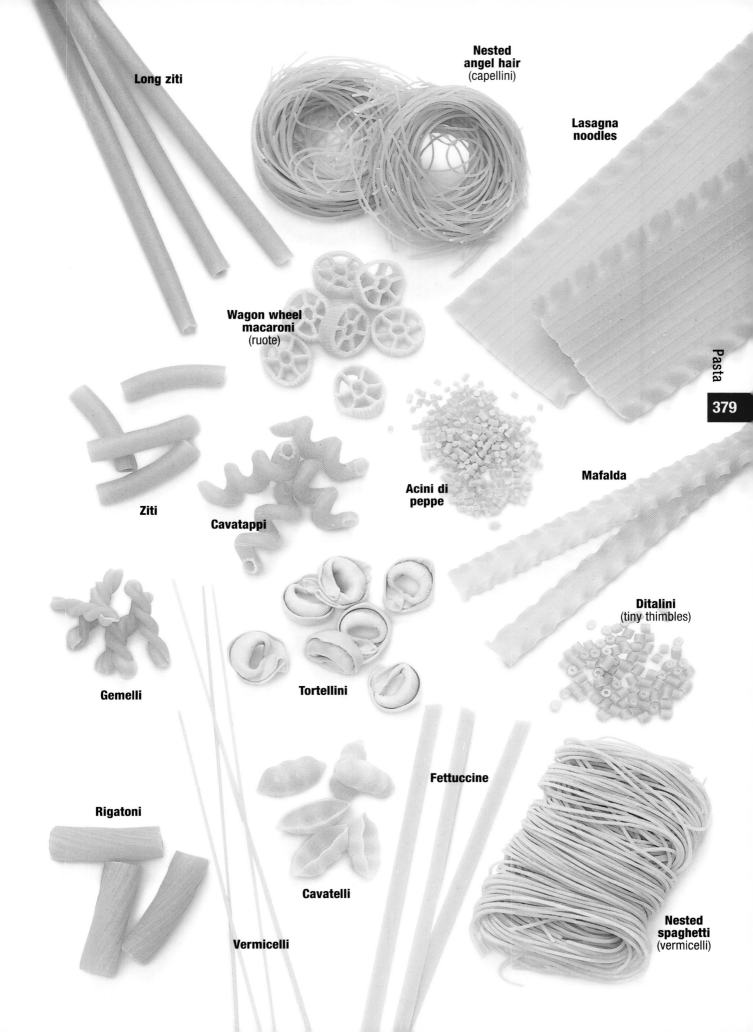

Long ziti

Nested
angel hair
(capellini)

Lasagna
noodles

Wagon wheel
macaroni
(ruote)

Acini di
peppe

Mafalda

Ziti

Cavatappi

Ditalini
(tiny thimbles)

Gemelli

Tortellini

Fettuccine

Rigatoni

Cavatelli

Nested
spaghetti
(vermicelli)

Vermicelli

Spinach Pasta

Low Fat

Prep: 1 hour **Cook:** see chart, page 377
Makes: 6 main-dish servings (about 1¼ pounds pasta)

    2¾ cups all-purpose flour
    ½   teaspoon salt
    2   beaten eggs
    ¼   cup water
    ¼   cup cooked spinach, well drained and finely
          chopped
    1   teaspoon cooking oil or olive oil

1. In a large bowl stir together 2 cups of the flour and the salt. Make a well in the center of the flour mixture. In a small bowl combine eggs, water, spinach, and oil. Add to flour mixture; mix well.

2. Sprinkle a clean kneading surface with the remaining ¾ cup flour. Turn dough out onto floured surface. Knead dough until smooth and elastic (8 to 10 minutes total). Cover and let dough rest for 10 minutes.

3. Divide dough into 4 equal portions. On lightly floured surface, roll each portion into a 12-inch square (about ¹⁄₁₆ inch thick). If using a pasta machine, pass each portion through the machine according to the manufacturer's directions until dough is ¹⁄₁₆ inch thick. Let stand, uncovered, about 20 minutes. Cut as desired (see photos 1 and 2, page 377).

4. To serve pasta immediately, cook according to the chart on page 377.

5. To store cut pasta, hang it from a pasta-drying rack or clothes hanger, or spread it on a wire cooling rack. Let pasta dry overnight or until completely dry. Place in an airtight container; chill for up to 3 days. Or dry pasta for at least 1 hour and place in a freezer bag or freezer container; freeze for up to 8 months.

Nutrition Facts per serving: 242 cal., 3 g total fat (1 g sat. fat), 71 mg chol., 221 mg sodium, 44 g carbo., 2 g fiber, 8 g pro.
Daily Values: 14% vit. A, 1% vit. C, 3% calcium, 18% iron
Exchanges: 3 Starch

Noodles

Low Fat

Prep: 1 hour **Cook:** 1½ minutes
Makes: 5 main-dish servings (about 1 pound noodles)

    2   cups all-purpose flour
    ½   teaspoon salt
    2   beaten egg yolks
    1   beaten egg
    ⅓   cup water
    1   teaspoon cooking oil or olive oil

1. In a large bowl stir together 1¾ cups of the flour and the salt. Make a well in the center of the flour mixture. In a small bowl stir together egg yolks, whole egg, water, and oil. Add egg mixture to flour mixture; mix well.

2. Sprinkle kneading surface with the remaining ¼ cup flour. Turn dough out onto floured surface. Knead until dough is smooth and elastic (8 to 10 minutes total). Cover and let dough rest for 10 minutes.

3. Divide dough into 4 equal portions. On a lightly floured surface, roll each portion of dough into a 12×9-inch rectangle (about ¹⁄₁₆ inch thick). (If using a pasta machine, pass each portion of dough through machine according to manufacturer's directions until dough is ¹⁄₁₆ inch thick.) Let stand, uncovered, for 20 minutes. Lightly dust dough with flour. Loosely roll dough into a spiral; cut into ¼-inch-wide strips (see photo 1, page 377). Shake the strands to separate; cut into 2- to 3-inch lengths.

4. To serve immediately, cook for 1½ to 2 minutes or until tender but still firm, allowing 1 to 2 more minutes for dried or frozen noodles. Drain.

5. To store cut noodles, spread them on a wire cooling rack. Let noodles dry overnight or until completely dry. Place in an airtight container and refrigerate for up to 3 days. Or dry noodles for at least 1 hour and place them in a freezer bag or freezer container; freeze for up to 8 months.

Nutrition Facts per serving: 229 cal., 4 g total fat (1 g sat. fat), 128 mg chol., 249 mg sodium, 38 g carbo., 1 g fiber, 8 g pro.
Daily Values: 4% vit. A, 2% calcium, 15% iron
Exchanges: 2½ Starch, ½ Fat

Yolkless Noodles: Prepare as above, except substitute 2 beaten egg whites for the 2 beaten egg yolks and 1 beaten egg. Increase the oil to 2 teaspoons.

Nutrition Facts per serving: 204 cal., 2 g total fat (0 g sat. fat), 0 mg chol., 256 mg sodium, 38 g carbo., 1 g fiber, 7 g pro.
Daily Values: 1% calcium, 13% iron
Exchanges: 2½ Starch

Spaghetti Sauce

Low Fat

Prep: 20 minutes **Cook:** 40 minutes **Makes:** 4 servings

    1   cup chopped onion (1 large)
    ½   cup chopped green sweet pepper
    ¼   cup chopped celery
    2   cloves garlic, minced
    1   tablespoon cooking oil
    4   cups chopped, peeled tomatoes (6 large) or
        two 14½-ounce cans tomatoes, undrained
        and cut up
    1   6-ounce can tomato paste
    2   tablespoons snipped fresh parsley
    1   tablespoon snipped fresh basil or
        1 teaspoon dried basil, crushed
    1   tablespoon snipped fresh oregano or
        1 teaspoon dried oregano, crushed
    2   teaspoons snipped fresh marjoram or
        ½ teaspoon dried marjoram, crushed
    1   teaspoon sugar
    ½   teaspoon salt
    ¼   teaspoon black pepper
    8   ounces dried spaghetti or linguine
        Finely shredded Parmesan cheese (optional)

1. In a Dutch oven cook onion, sweet pepper, celery, and garlic in hot oil until vegetables are tender.

2. Stir in ⅓ cup *water*, tomatoes, tomato paste, parsley, dried herbs (if using), sugar, salt, and black pepper. Bring to boiling; reduce heat. Simmer, covered, for 30 minutes. Uncover; simmer for 10 to 15 minutes more or to desired consistency, stirring occasionally. Stir in fresh herbs, if using.

3. Meanwhile, cook pasta according to package directions. Serve sauce over hot cooked pasta. If desired, sprinkle with Parmesan cheese.

Nutrition Facts per serving: 325 cal., 5 g total fat (1 g sat. fat), 0 mg chol., 342 mg sodium, 62 g carbo., 7 g fiber, 12 g pro.
Daily Values: 28% vit. A, 104% vit. C, 5% calcium, 22% iron
Exchanges: 2 Vegetable, 3 Starch, 1 Fat

Spaghetti Sauce with Ground Beef or Sausage: Prepare as above, except omit the oil. In a large saucepan or Dutch oven cook 12 ounces ground beef or pork sausage with the onion, sweet pepper, celery, and garlic until meat is brown. Drain. Continue as in step 2.

Nutrition Facts per serving: 459 cal., 12 g total fat (4 g sat. fat), 53 mg chol., 386 mg sodium, 62 g carbo., 7 g fiber, 28 g pro.
Daily Values: 28% vit. A, 104% vit. C, 5% calcium, 31% iron
Exchanges: 2 Vegetable, 3½ Starch, 2 Medium-Fat Meat, 1 Fat

Hot Pasta

Pasta continues to cook even after you've removed it from the cooking liquid. Therefore, use cooked pasta immediately or it will become too soft. To keep pasta warm for a few minutes before serving, use one of the following suggestions:

■ Return the cooked and drained pasta to the warm cooking pan. Stir in any additional ingredients, or toss plain pasta with a little butter, margarine, or oil to help prevent it from sticking together. (If you add oil to the cooking water, it is not necessary to add more oil.) Cover the pan and let the pasta stand for no more than 15 minutes.

■ Use a warmed serving bowl. Warm a bowl by filling it with hot water and allowing it to stand for a few minutes. Empty and dry the bowl; add the hot pasta. Serve the pasta within 5 minutes.

Spaghetti Sauce with Meatballs: Prepare sauce as at left. Meanwhile, in a large bowl combine 1 egg; ¾ cup soft bread crumbs (1 slice); ¼ cup finely chopped onion; 2 tablespoons finely chopped green sweet pepper; ¼ teaspoon dried oregano, crushed; and ¼ teaspoon salt. Add 12 ounces ground beef or bulk pork sausage; mix well. Shape into 24 meatballs. Arrange meatballs in a 15×10×1-inch baking pan. Bake in a 350°F oven for 15 to 20 minutes or until done (160°F). Drain. Serve with sauce and hot pasta.

Nutrition Facts per serving: 535 cal., 17 g total fat (5 g sat. fat), 107 mg chol., 593 mg sodium, 67 g carbo., 7 g fiber, 31 g pro.
Daily Values: 30% vit. A, 112% vit. C, 7% calcium, 34% iron
Exchanges: 2 Vegetable, 3½ Starch, 2 Medium-Fat Meat, 1 Fat

Spaghetti Sauce with Meatballs

One-Pot Spaghetti

This easy spaghetti lets you cook the pasta right in the tomato sauce, so there's one less saucepan to wash.

Start to Finish: 40 minutes **Makes:** 4 servings

- 8 **ounces ground beef or bulk pork sausage**
- 1 **cup sliced fresh mushrooms or one 6-ounce jar sliced mushrooms, drained**
- ½ **cup chopped onion (1 medium)**
- 1 **clove garlic, minced, or ⅛ teaspoon garlic powder**
- 1 **14-ounce can chicken broth or beef broth**
- 1¾ **cups water**
- 1 **6-ounce can tomato paste**
- 1 **teaspoon dried oregano, crushed**
- ½ **teaspoon dried basil or marjoram, crushed**
- ¼ **teaspoon black pepper**
- 6 **ounces dried spaghetti, broken**
- ¼ **cup grated Parmesan cheese**

1. In a large saucepan cook the ground beef, fresh mushrooms (if using), onion, and garlic until meat is brown and onion is tender. Drain.

2. Stir in the canned mushrooms (if using), broth, water, tomato paste, oregano, basil, and pepper. Bring to boiling. Add the broken spaghetti, a little at a time, stirring constantly. Return to boiling; reduce heat. Boil gently, uncovered, for 17 to 20 minutes or until spaghetti is tender and sauce is of the desired consistency, stirring frequently. Serve with Parmesan cheese.

Nutrition Facts per serving: 394 cal., 15 g total fat (6 g sat. fat), 39 mg chol., 926 mg sodium, 44 g carbo., 4 g fiber, 22 g pro.
Daily Values: 23% vit. A, 33% vit. C, 13% calcium, 20% iron
Exchanges: 1 Vegetable, 2½ Starch, 2 Medium-Fat Meat, ½ Fat

Pasta Pizza

If you like, sprinkle pepperoni, thinly sliced green sweet pepper, black olives, sliced mushrooms, or other favorites over the top along with the cheese.

Low Fat

Prep: 30 minutes **Bake:** 30 minutes
Oven: 350°F **Makes:** 6 servings

- 5 **ounces dried rotini (2 cups)**
- 1 **beaten egg**
- ¼ **cup milk**
- 2 **tablespoons grated Parmesan cheese**
- 8 **ounces ground beef**
- 1½ **cups chunky garden-style pasta sauce**
- 1 **cup shredded mozzarella cheese (4 ounces)**

1. Cook rotini according to package directions. Drain; rinse with cold water. Drain well.

2. For pasta crust, in a large bowl combine egg, milk, and Parmesan cheese. Stir in drained rotini. Spread rotini mixture evenly in a greased 12-inch pizza pan. Bake in a 350° oven for 20 minutes.

3. Meanwhile, in a large skillet cook ground beef until brown. Drain. Stir in pasta sauce. Spoon meat mixture over baked rotini crust. Sprinkle with mozzarella cheese.

4. Bake in the 350° oven for 10 to 12 minutes more or until heated through and cheese is melted. To serve, cut into wedges.

Nutrition Facts per serving: 288 cal., 11 g total fat (4 g sat. fat), 72 mg chol., 414 mg sodium, 28 g carbo., 2 g fiber, 18 g pro.
Daily Values: 9% vit. A, 5% vit. C, 19% calcium, 12% iron
Exchanges: 1 Vegetable, 1½ Starch, 1½ Lean Meat, 1 Fat

Spaghetti Pie Best Loved

When forming the crust, use a large wooden spoon or rubber spatula to press the spaghetti onto the bottom and up the sides of the pie plate.

Low Fat

Prep: 30 minutes **Bake:** 20 minutes
Oven: 350°F **Makes:** 6 servings

- 4 **ounces dried spaghetti**
- 1 **tablespoon butter or margarine**
- 1 **beaten egg**
- ¼ **cup grated Parmesan cheese**
- 8 **ounces ground beef**
- ½ **cup chopped onion (1 medium)**
- ½ **cup chopped green sweet pepper**
- 1 **clove garlic, minced**
- ½ **teaspoon fennel seeds, crushed**
- 1 **8-ounce can tomato sauce**
- 1 **teaspoon dried oregano, crushed**
  Nonstick cooking spray
- 1 **cup low-fat cottage cheese, drained**
- ½ **cup shredded part-skim mozzarella cheese**

1. Cook spaghetti according to package directions. Drain.

2. Return spaghetti to warm saucepan. Stir butter into hot pasta until melted. Stir in egg and Parmesan cheese; set aside.

3. Meanwhile, in a medium skillet cook ground beef, onion, sweet pepper, garlic, and fennel seeds until meat is brown and onion is tender. Drain. Stir in tomato sauce and oregano; heat through.

4. Coat a 9-inch pie plate with nonstick cooking spray. Press spaghetti mixture onto bottom and up sides of pie plate, forming a crust. Spread cottage cheese on the top and up the sides of pasta crust. Spread meat mixture over cottage cheese. Sprinkle with shredded mozzarella cheese.

5. Bake in a 350° oven for 20 to 25 minutes or until bubbly and heated through. To serve, cut into wedges.

Nutrition Facts per serving: 270 cal., 11 g total fat (6 g sat. fat), 76 mg chol., 500 mg sodium, 20 g carbo., 1 g fiber, 21 g pro.
Daily Values: 7% vit. A, 17% vit. C, 16% calcium, 11% iron
Exchanges: ½ Vegetable, 1 Starch, 2½ Medium-Fat Meat

Spaghetti with Beef and Mushroom Sauce
Best Loved

This recipe originally ran in the 1953 edition of the Better Homes and Gardens New Cook Book. *It relies on canned soups as the base for the sauce.*

Prep: 15 minutes **Cook:** 20 minutes **Makes:** 6 servings

  1 **pound ground beef**
  ½ **cup chopped onion**
  1 **10¾-ounce can condensed cream of mushroom soup**
  1 **10¾-ounce can condensed tomato soup**
  1 **4-ounce can sliced mushrooms, drained (optional)**
  ½ **teaspoon dried Italian seasoning, crushed**
  ½ **teaspoon chili powder**
  ¼ **teaspoon black pepper**
  ¼ **teaspoon bottled hot pepper sauce (optional)**
  12 **ounces dried spaghetti**
    Grated Parmesan cheese (optional)

1. In a large saucepan or a Dutch oven cook ground beef and onion until meat is brown and onion is tender. Drain. Stir in mushroom soup, tomato soup, mushrooms (if desired), Italian seasoning, chili powder, black pepper, and, if desired, hot pepper sauce. Bring sauce to boiling; reduce heat. Simmer, covered, for 20 minutes, stirring occasionally.

2. Meanwhile, cook spaghetti according to package directions. Drain. Serve sauce over hot spaghetti. If desired, sprinkle each serving with Parmesan cheese.

Nutrition Facts per serving: 512 cal., 22 g total fat (8 g sat. fat), 50 mg chol., 709 mg sodium, 55 g carbo., 3 g fiber, 22 g pro.
Daily Values: 6% vit. A, 4% vit. C, 4% calcium, 20% iron
Exchanges: 3½ Starch, 1½ Medium-Fat Meat, 2 Fat

Saucy Stuffed Shells

You'll like the meat filling of these shells if you like sausage. Fennel seeds are the secret to the flavor.

Prep: 35 minutes **Bake:** 35 minutes
Oven: 375°F **Makes:** 4 servings

  12 **dried jumbo shell macaroni**
  12 **ounces ground beef or ground pork**
  1 **medium onion, chopped (½ cup)**
  ½ **cup chopped green sweet pepper**
  1 **clove garlic, minced**
  1 **beaten egg**
  ¼ **cup fine dry bread crumbs**
  ¼ **teaspoon fennel seeds, crushed**
  ¼ **teaspoon salt**
  ¼ **teaspoon black pepper**
  1 **15½-ounce jar meatless spaghetti sauce**
  ¼ **cup finely shredded or grated Parmesan cheese**

1. Cook macaroni according to package directions. Drain; rinse with cold water. Drain again.

2. Meanwhile, in a large skillet cook ground meat, onion, sweet pepper, and garlic until meat is brown. Drain.

3. In a medium bowl combine egg, bread crumbs, fennel seeds, salt, and black pepper. Add the meat mixture and ¼ cup of the spaghetti sauce; mix well. Spoon about 2 tablespoons of the meat mixture into each macaroni shell. Arrange the filled shells in a 2-quart square baking dish. Pour the remaining sauce over the filled shells. Cover the dish with foil.

4. Bake in a 375° oven for 35 to 40 minutes or until heated through. Sprinkle with Parmesan cheese before serving.

Nutrition Facts per serving: 548 cal., 27 g total fat (11 g sat. fat), 115 mg chol., 978 mg sodium, 49 g carbo., 4 g fiber, 24 g pro.
Daily Values: 24% vit. A, 40% vit. C, 13% calcium, 24% iron
Exchanges: 1 Vegetable, 3 Starch, 2 High-Fat Meat, 1½ Fat

Using Refrigerated Fresh Pasta

When buying refrigerated fresh pasta, plan on 3 ounces for each main-dish serving and 1½ to 2 ounces for each side-dish serving. To use fresh pasta instead of dried pasta in a recipe, substitute 6 to 8 ounces of refrigerated fresh pasta for 4 ounces of dried pasta.

Turkey and Pasta with Peanut Sauce

For this Thai-style dish, there's no stir-frying to do or complicated sauces to compose. Just heat, mix, and serve.

Fast **Low Fat**

Start to Finish: 30 minutes **Makes:** 4 servings

- 6 **ounces dried fettuccine or linguine**
- 2 **cups fresh pea pods, tips trimmed, or one 6-ounce package frozen pea pods**
- 1 **cup cooked turkey or chicken strips**
- 1 **cup coarsely chopped fresh pineapple or one 8-ounce can pineapple chunks, drained**
- ¼ **cup reduced-sodium chicken broth**
- 2 **tablespoons creamy peanut butter**
- 1 **tablespoon reduced-sodium soy sauce**
- 1 **tablespoon lime juice or lemon juice**
- ¼ **teaspoon crushed red pepper**
- 1 **clove garlic, minced**

1. Cook pasta according to package directions. Meanwhile, halve the fresh pea pods diagonally. Place pea pods and turkey in a large colander. Pour hot cooking liquid from pasta over pea pods and turkey in colander; drain well. Return the pasta, pea pods, and turkey to the hot pan. Add the pineapple.

2. Meanwhile, for sauce, in a small saucepan stir chicken broth into peanut butter. Heat and stir with a whisk until peanut butter melts. Stir in soy sauce, lime juice, red pepper, and garlic; heat through.

3. Add sauce to the pasta mixture. Gently stir to coat pasta with sauce.

Nutrition Facts per serving: 317 cal., 7 g total fat (2 g sat. fat), 30 mg chol., 254 mg sodium, 44 g carbo., 3 g fiber, 21 g pro.
Daily Values: 3% vit. A, 56% vit. C, 5% calcium, 15% iron
Exchanges: 1 Vegetable, 2½ Starch, 1½ Lean Meat

Pasta Math

Here are some basic guidelines for cooking the right amount of pasta for a specific number of people (estimate that the average person will eat about 1 cup cooked pasta):

- 8 ounces uncooked small to medium pasta (rotini, wagon wheels, bow ties, penne, ziti, elbow macaroni) = 4 cups cooked
- 8 ounces uncooked long pasta (spaghetti, angel hair, linguine, fettuccine) = 1½-inch diameter bunch = 4 cups cooked
- 8 ounces uncooked egg noodles = 2½ cups cooked

Turkey and Pasta with Peanut Sauce

White Bean and Sausage Rigatoni

Reminiscent of a baked Italian casserole, this dish is made on the stove top instead of the oven, which means it's ready to serve in less than half the time.

Fast **Low Fat**

Start to Finish: 20 minutes **Makes:** 4 servings

- 8 **ounces dried rigatoni (2 cups)**
- 1 **15-ounce can white kidney (cannellini), Great Northern, or navy beans, rinsed and drained**
- 1 **14½-ounce can Italian-style stewed tomatoes, undrained**
- 6 **ounces cooked smoked turkey sausage, cut into ½-inch slices**
- ⅓ **cup snipped fresh basil**
- ¼ **cup finely shredded Asiago or Parmesan cheese (1 ounce)**

1. Cook pasta according to package directions. Drain; return pasta to saucepan.

2. Meanwhile, in a large saucepan combine beans, undrained tomatoes, and sausage. Cook and stir until heated through. Add bean mixture and basil to pasta; stir gently to combine. To serve, sprinkle each serving with Asiago cheese.

Nutrition Facts per serving: 399 cal., 8 g total fat (3 g sat. fat), 36 mg chol., 813 mg sodium, 64 g carbo., 7 g fiber, 23 g pro.
Daily Values: 12% vit. A, 4% vit. C, 11% calcium, 21% iron
Exchanges: 1 Vegetable, 4 Starch, 1 Lean Meat

Prosciutto, Spinach, and Pasta Casserole

Prosciutto (proh-SHOO-toh), a product of Italy, is a spicy, cured ham. You can substitute cooked lean ham if you like. Anise seeds give this dish an interesting flavor—don't be tempted to skip them. You'll find them at the supermarket next to other herbs and spices.

Low Fat

Prep: 25 minutes **Bake:** 25 minutes **Oven:** 350°F
Stand: 5 minutes **Makes:** 6 servings

- 8 ounces dried orecchiette, mostaccioli, or ziti (2⅔ cups)
- 2 medium onions, cut into thin wedges, or 5 medium leeks, sliced
- 2 cloves garlic, minced
- 1 tablespoon butter or margarine
- ¼ cup all-purpose flour
- ½ teaspoon anise seeds, crushed
- 1¾ cups milk
- 1½ cups chicken broth
- ¼ cup grated Parmesan cheese
- 1 10-ounce package frozen chopped spinach, thawed and well drained
- 2 ounces prosciutto, cut into thin bite-size strips
- 1 medium tomato, seeded and chopped

1. Cook pasta according to package directions. Drain; rinse pasta with cold water. Drain again.

2. In a large saucepan cook onions and garlic, covered, in hot butter about 5 minutes or until onions are tender, stirring occasionally. Stir in flour and anise seeds. Add milk and chicken broth all at once. Cook and stir until slightly thickened and bubbly. Stir in Parmesan cheese. Stir in the cooked pasta, spinach, and prosciutto. Spoon mixture into a 2-quart casserole.

3. Bake, covered, in a 350° oven for 25 to 30 minutes or until heated through. Let stand about 5 minutes. To serve, stir gently and top with chopped tomato.

Nutrition Facts per serving: 288 cal., 7 g total fat (3 g sat. fat), 21 mg chol., 627 mg sodium, 42 g carbo., 3 g fiber, 15 g pro.
Daily Values: 81% vit. A, 20% vit. C, 23% calcium, 14% iron
Exchanges: 1 Vegetable, 2½ Starch, ½ Medium-Fat Meat

Fettuccine with Vegetables and Prosciutto

Fast   **Low Fat**

Start to Finish: 25 minutes **Makes:** 4 servings

- 8 ounces dried fettuccine, broken
- 1 pound fresh asparagus, bias-sliced into 1½-inch pieces
- 1 tablespoon olive oil or cooking oil
- 4 roma tomatoes, chopped
- 3 ounces prosciutto or cooked ham, cut into thin strips (½ cup)
- ⅓ cup grated Parmesan cheese

1. Cook fettuccine according to package directions. Drain; keep warm.

2. Meanwhile, in a large skillet cook and stir asparagus in hot oil for 4 minutes or until nearly tender. Add tomatoes and prosciutto; cook about 2 minutes more or until heated through. Add asparagus mixture to fettuccine; stir gently to combine. Sprinkle with Parmesan cheese. Season to taste with *salt* and *black pepper*.

Nutrition Facts per serving: 350 cal., 9 g total fat (3 g sat. fat), 21 mg chol., 744 mg sodium, 47 g carbo., 3 g fiber, 19 g pro.
Daily Values: 11% vit. A, 46% vit. C, 14% calcium, 15% iron
Exchanges: 1 Vegetable, 2½ Starch, 1½ Medium-Fat Meat

How Much Pasta?

When your recipe calls for 8 ounces of a type of dried pasta and your 16-ounce package has only a portion left, how do you know how much to use? Here's a measuring chart for quick reference. All weights are for a 1-cup measure of the uncooked type of pasta:

Type of Pasta	Amount
Bow ties, large or small	2 ounces
Cavatelli	3 ounces
Ditalini	4½ ounces
Macaroni, elbow or rings	4 ounces
Mostaccioli	3 ounces
Noodles, all sizes	2 ounces
Orecchiette	3 ounces
Penne	3 ounces
Rigatoni	2½ ounces
Rotini	2½ ounces
Shells, medium	3 ounces
Wagon wheels	3 ounces
Ziti	3 ounces

Thai Pork and Vegetable Curry

Many supermarkets now stock coconut milk and curry paste, two classic Thai ingredients. Sold in cans in regular and reduced-fat versions, coconut milk is a creamy puree of fresh coconut meat and water. Bottled curry paste blends herbs, spices, and chile peppers.

Fast

Start to Finish: 30 minutes **Makes:** 4 servings

- 1⅓ **cups dried orzo (about 8 ounces)**
- 2 **tablespoons cooking oil**
- 12 **ounces pork tenderloin or lean boneless pork, cut into bite-size pieces**
- 8 **ounces green beans, bias-sliced into 1½-inch pieces (2 cups)***
- 1 **red sweet pepper, cut into thin bite-size strips**
- 2 **green onions, bias-sliced into ¼-inch pieces**
- 1 **14-ounce can reduced-fat unsweetened coconut milk**
- 4 **teaspoons bottled curry paste**
- 2 **teaspoons sugar**
- 2 **tablespoons lime juice**

1. Cook orzo according to package directions. Drain. Keep warm.

2. Meanwhile, pour 1 tablespoon of the oil into a large nonstick skillet. Preheat over medium-high heat. Add pork; cook and stir about 4 minutes or until no pink remains. Remove from skillet.

3. Add the remaining 1 tablespoon of the oil to the skillet. Add green beans; cook and stir for 3 minutes. Add sweet pepper and green onions; cook and stir about 2 minutes more or until vegetables are crisp-tender. Add coconut milk, curry paste, and sugar. Reduce heat to low, stirring until combined. Stir in cooked pork and lime juice; heat through. Serve over hot orzo.

*Note: A 9-ounce package of frozen cut green beans, thawed, can be substituted for the fresh beans. Add them to the skillet along with the sweet pepper and onions; cook as directed.

Nutrition Facts per serving: 502 cal., 17 g total fat (5 g sat. fat), 50 mg chol., 447 mg sodium, 57 g carbo., 4 g fiber, 29 g pro.
Daily Values: 50% vit. A, 153% vit. C, 4% calcium, 26% iron
Exchanges: 2 Vegetable, 3 Starch, 2 Lean Meat, 2 Fat

Thai Pork and Vegetable Curry

Salmon-Sauced Mostaccioli

Prep: 20 minutes **Cook:** 20 minutes **Makes:** 4 servings

- 8 **ounces dried mostaccioli or rigatoni (about 3 cups)**
- 1 **small green or red sweet pepper, cut into bite-size strips**
- ½ **cup chopped onion (1 medium)**
- 2 **tablespoons butter or margarine**
- 1½ **cups chicken broth**
- 2 **teaspoons snipped fresh dill or ½ teaspoon dried dill**
- ½ **cup plain low-fat yogurt**
- 3 **tablespoons all-purpose flour**
- 1 **15½-ounce can salmon, drained, broken into large chunks, and skin and bones removed**
- 2 **tablespoons snipped fresh parsley**

1. Cook pasta according to package directions. Drain; keep warm.

2. Meanwhile, for sauce, in a medium saucepan cook sweet pepper and onion in hot butter until tender but not brown. Stir in 1 cup of the broth and the dill. Bring to boiling; reduce heat. Stir together the remaining ½ cup broth, the yogurt, and flour. Add yogurt mixture to saucepan. Cook and stir until thickened and bubbly. Cook and stir for 1 minute more. Gently stir in salmon; heat through. Serve sauce over hot pasta. Sprinkle with parsley.

Nutrition Facts per serving: 471 cal., 13 g total fat (6 g sat. fat), 78 mg chol., 964 mg sodium, 53 g carbo., 2 g fiber, 30 g pro.
Daily Values: 9% vit. A, 30% vit. C, 9% calcium, 20% iron
Exchanges: 3½ Starch, 3 Lean Meat, ½ Fat

Pasta with Scallops

A white wine sauce makes this pasta dish elegant enough for company.

Fast **Low Fat**

Start to Finish: 30 minutes **Makes:** 4 servings

- 1 pound fresh or frozen sea scallops
- 8 ounces dried bow ties (4 cups)
- 1 tablespoon butter or margarine
- 1 tablespoon cooking oil
- 2 to 3 cloves garlic, minced
- 1½ cups thinly bias-sliced carrots (3 medium)
- 2 cups sugar snap peas
- ⅓ cup sliced green onions
- ⅔ cup chicken broth
- ½ cup dry white wine
- 1 tablespoon snipped fresh dill, thyme, or basil, or 1 teaspoon dried dill, thyme, or basil, crushed
- ¼ teaspoon salt
- 2 tablespoons cornstarch
- 2 tablespoons cold water
- ¼ cup finely shredded Parmesan cheese

1. Thaw sea scallops, if frozen. Halve any large scallops.

2. Cook pasta according to package directions. Drain; toss with butter or margarine. Keep warm.

3. Meanwhile, pour oil into a wok or large skillet. Preheat over medium-high heat. Cook and stir garlic in hot oil for 15 seconds. Add carrots; cook and stir for 4 minutes. Add sugar snap peas and green onions. Cook and stir for 2 to 3 minutes more or until vegetables are crisp-tender. Remove vegetables from wok.

4. Carefully add broth, wine, desired herb, and salt to wok; bring to boiling. Add scallops; reduce heat. Simmer, uncovered, for 1 to 2 minutes or until scallops are opaque, stirring occasionally.

5. Stir together cornstarch and water; add to wok. Cook and stir until thickened and bubbly. Return vegetables to wok. Add cooked pasta, stirring to coat; heat through. Sprinkle with Parmesan cheese.

Nutrition Facts per serving: 498 cal., 10 g total fat (4 g sat. fat), 52 mg chol., 693 mg sodium, 63 g carbo., 5 g fiber, 32 g pro. **Daily Values:** 262% vit. A, 24% vit. C, 17% calcium, 20% iron **Exchanges:** 2 Vegetable, 3½ Starch, 2½ Very Lean Meat, 1 Fat

Pasta with White Clam Sauce

Fast

Start to Finish: 30 minutes **Makes:** 4 servings

- 10 ounces dried linguine or fettuccine
- 2 6½-ounce cans chopped or minced clams
- 1¾ cups half-and-half, light cream, or milk
- ½ cup chopped onion (1 medium)
- 2 cloves garlic, minced
- 2 tablespoons butter or margarine
- ¼ cup all-purpose flour
- 2 teaspoons snipped fresh oregano or ½ teaspoon dried oregano, crushed
- ¼ teaspoon salt
- ⅛ teaspoon black pepper
- ¼ cup snipped fresh parsley
- ¼ cup dry white wine or nonalcoholic dry white wine
- ¼ cup finely shredded or grated Parmesan cheese

1. Cook pasta according to package directions. Drain; keep warm. Meanwhile, drain canned clams, reserving the juice from one of the cans (you should have about ⅓ cup). Add enough of the half-and-half to the reserved clam juice to equal 2 cups liquid. Set clams and clam juice mixture aside.

2. In a medium saucepan cook onion and garlic in hot butter over medium heat until tender but not brown. Stir in flour, dried oregano (if using), salt, and pepper. Add clam juice mixture all at once. Cook and stir until thickened and bubbly. Cook and stir for 1 minute more. Stir in clams, fresh oregano (if using), parsley, and wine. Heat through. Serve over hot pasta. Sprinkle with Parmesan cheese.

Nutrition Facts per serving: 636 cal., 21 g total fat (12 g sat. fat), 113 mg chol., 421 mg sodium, 70 g carbo., 2 g fiber, 37 g pro. **Daily Values:** 28% vit. A, 44% vit. C, 27% calcium, 148% iron **Exchanges:** 4½ Starch, 3 Very Lean Meat, 2 Fat

Matching Sauces to Pasta

Here are a few guidelines for choosing the best type of pasta to complement your sauce.

■ Light, thin sauces are best paired with thin, delicate pastas such as angel hair (capellini) or thin spaghetti (vermicelli).

■ Chunky sauces are best partnered with pastas that have holes or ridges, such as mostaccioli, ziti, rotini, or radiatore.

■ Heavy pasta sauces complement thicker pasta shapes, such as fettuccine.

Citrus Shrimp with Penne

`Fast` `Low Fat`

Start to Finish: 30 minutes **Makes:** 4 servings

- 12 **ounces fresh or frozen peeled and deveined medium shrimp**
- 8 **ounces dried penne or bow ties (4 cups)**
- 1 **teaspoon finely shredded orange peel (set aside)**
- 2 **oranges**
  - **Orange juice**
- ½ **cup water**
- 1 **tablespoon cornstarch**
- 1 **teaspoon instant chicken bouillon granules**
- 1 **teaspoon toasted sesame oil**
- ¼ **teaspoon salt**
- ⅛ **teaspoon ground red pepper**
- 1 **red or green sweet pepper, cut into ¾-inch squares (about 1 cup)**
- 1 **tablespoon cooking oil**
- 1½ **cups fresh pea pods, ends trimmed and halved diagonally, or one 6-ounce package frozen pea pods, thawed and halved diagonally**

1. Thaw shrimp, if frozen. Cook pasta according to package directions. Drain; keep warm.

2. Meanwhile, after shredding peel from oranges, remove remaining peels. Section the oranges over a bowl to catch the juice; set oranges aside. Add enough orange juice to the juice in the bowl to equal ½ cup. In a small bowl combine orange peel, orange juice, water, cornstarch, bouillon granules, sesame oil, salt, and ground red pepper; set aside.

3. In a large skillet cook sweet pepper in hot oil over medium-high heat for 1 to 2 minutes or until crisp-tender. Remove sweet pepper from skillet. Add shrimp to skillet; cook and stir about 2 minutes or until shrimp turn opaque. Remove shrimp from skillet.

4. Stir orange juice mixture; add to skillet. Cook and stir until thickened and bubbly. Return shrimp and sweet pepper to skillet; stir in pea pods. Cook and stir for 2 minutes more. Gently stir in orange sections. Gently toss shrimp mixture with pasta.

Nutrition Facts per serving: 384 cal., 7 g total fat (1 g sat. fat), 129 mg chol., 492 mg sodium, 53 g carbo., 2 g fiber, 26 g pro.
Daily Values: 45% vit. A, 115% vit. C, 8% calcium, 22% iron
Exchanges: 3½ Starch, 2 Very Lean Meat, 1 Fat

Citrus Shrimp with Penne

Pasta with Bolognese Sauce

Bolognese (boh-luh-NEEZ) sauce is a hearty Italian meat and vegetable sauce flavored with red wine and cream.

Prep: 40 minutes **Cook:** 45 minutes **Makes:** 5 to 6 servings

- 12 **ounces bulk sweet Italian sausage or ground beef**
- 1 **cup chopped onion (1 large)**
- ½ **cup chopped green sweet pepper**
- ¼ **cup chopped celery**
- 4 **cloves garlic, minced**
- 3 **pounds roma tomatoes, peeled, seeded, and chopped (about 4 cups), or two 14½-ounce cans tomatoes, undrained and cut up**
- 1 **6-ounce can tomato paste**
- ½ **cup dry red wine or beef broth**
- 2 **tablespoons snipped fresh basil or 1½ teaspoons dried basil, crushed**
- 1 **tablespoon snipped fresh oregano or 1 teaspoon dried oregano, crushed**
- 2 **teaspoons snipped fresh marjoram or ½ teaspoon dried marjoram, crushed**
- ½ **teaspoon salt**
- ¼ **teaspoon black pepper**
- ¼ **cup whipping cream**
- 2 **tablespoons snipped fresh parsley**
- 10 **ounces dried pasta, such as spaghetti, linguine, or penne**

1. In a large saucepan or Dutch oven cook the sausage, onion, sweet pepper, celery, and garlic until meat is brown and onion is tender. Drain.

2. Carefully stir in tomatoes, tomato paste, wine, dried herbs (if using), salt, and black pepper. Bring to boiling; reduce heat. Simmer, covered, for 30 minutes. Uncover; simmer 10 to 15 minutes more or to desired consistency, stirring occasionally. Stir in whipping cream, parsley, and fresh herbs (if using); heat through.

3. Meanwhile, cook pasta according to package directions. Drain. Serve sauce over hot pasta.

Nutrition Facts per serving: 549 cal., 21 g total fat (9 g sat. fat), 62 mg chol., 653 mg sodium, 61 g carbo., 5 g fiber, 21 g pro.
Daily Values: 26% vit. A, 85% vit. C, 6% calcium, 22% iron
Exchanges: 2 Vegetable, 3½ Starch, 1 High-Fat Meat, 2 Fat

Baked Cavatelli `Best Loved`

Prep: 25 minutes **Bake:** 30 minutes
Oven: 375°F **Makes:** 5 to 6 servings

- **7 ounces dried cavatelli or wagon wheel macaroni (about 2⅓ cups)**
- **12 ounces uncooked Italian sausage links, sliced ½ inch thick, or lean ground beef**
- **¾ cup chopped onion (1 medium)**
- **2 cloves garlic, minced**
- **1 26-ounce jar pasta sauce**
- **1 cup shredded mozzarella cheese (4 ounces)**
- **¼ teaspoon black pepper**

1. Cook pasta according to package directions. Drain; set aside.

2. In a large skillet cook the sausage, onion, and garlic until sausage is brown; remove from skillet. Drain.

3. In a large bowl stir together pasta sauce, ¾ cup of the mozzarella cheese, and the pepper. Add the cooked pasta and the sausage mixture. Stir gently to combine. Spoon the mixture into a 2-quart casserole.*

4. Bake, covered, in a 375° oven for 25 to 30 minutes or until nearly heated through. Uncover; sprinkle with the remaining ¼ cup mozzarella cheese. Bake about 5 minutes more or until cheese is melted.

***Note:** For individual portions, spoon the mixture into 5 or 6 individual (8- to 10-ounce) casseroles. Place the casseroles on a large baking sheet. Cover the casseroles with foil and bake for 15 to 20 minutes or until nearly heated through. Uncover, sprinkle with remaining ¼ cup cheese, and bake about 5 minutes more or until cheese is melted.

Nutrition Facts per serving: 503 cal., 24 g total fat (9 g sat. fat), 58 mg chol., 1,464 mg sodium, 43 g carbo., 4 g fiber, 23 g pro.
Daily Values: 14% vit. A, 13% vit. C, 23% calcium, 15% iron
Exchanges: 1 Vegetable, 2½ Starch, 1 Fat

Baked Cavatelli

Bow Ties with Sausage and Sweet Peppers

`Fast`

Start to Finish: 25 minutes **Makes:** 4 servings

- **8 ounces dried large bow ties (about 4 cups)**
- **12 ounces spicy Italian sausage links**
- **2 medium red sweet peppers, cut into ¾-inch pieces**
- **½ cup vegetable broth or beef broth**
- **¼ teaspoon coarsely ground black pepper**
- **¼ cup snipped fresh flat-leaf parsley**

1. Cook pasta according to package directions. Drain; keep warm.

2. Meanwhile, cut the sausage into 1-inch pieces. In a large skillet cook sausage and sweet peppers over medium-high heat until sausage is brown. Drain.

3. Add the broth and black pepper to sausage in skillet. Bring to boiling; reduce heat. Simmer, uncovered, for 5 minutes. Remove from heat. Pour over pasta; add parsley. Stir gently to coat.

Nutrition Facts per serving: 476 cal., 20 g total fat (8 g sat. fat), 57 mg chol., 597 mg sodium, 47 g carbo., 3 g fiber, 20 g pro.
Daily Values: 62% vit. A, 151% vit. C, 3% calcium, 16% iron
Exchanges: 1 Vegetable, 3 Starch, 2 High-Fat Meat

Lasagna Best Loved

In a hurry? Try the Quick Lasagna, right. It uses a jar of pasta sauce for convenience.

Prep: 45 minutes **Bake:** 30 minutes **Oven:** 375°F
Stand: 10 minutes **Makes:** 8 servings

- 12 ounces bulk Italian or pork sausage or ground beef
- 1 cup chopped onion (1 large)
- 2 cloves garlic, minced
- 1 14½-ounce can diced tomatoes, undrained
- 1 8-ounce can tomato sauce
- 1 tablespoon dried Italian seasoning, crushed
- 1 teaspoon fennel seeds, crushed (optional)
- ¼ teaspoon black pepper
- 6 dried lasagna noodles
- 1 beaten egg
- 1 15-ounce container ricotta cheese or 2 cups cream-style cottage cheese, drained
- ¼ cup grated Parmesan cheese
- 6 ounces shredded mozzarella cheese
  Grated Parmesan cheese (optional)

1. For sauce, in a large saucepan cook sausage, onion, and garlic until meat is brown. Drain.

2. Stir in undrained tomatoes, tomato sauce, Italian seasoning, fennel seeds (if desired), and pepper into meat mixture. Bring to boiling; reduce heat. Simmer, covered, for 15 minutes, stirring occasionally.

3. Meanwhile, cook noodles for 10 to 12 minutes or until tender but still firm. Drain noodles; rinse with cold water. Drain well; set aside.

4. For filling, combine egg, ricotta, and the ¼ cup Parmesan cheese. Set aside.

5. Spread about ½ cup of the sauce over the bottom of a 2-quart rectangular baking dish. Layer half of the cooked noodles in the bottom of the dish, trimming or overlapping as necessary to fit. Spread with half of the filling. Top with half of the remaining sauce and half of the mozzarella cheese. Repeat layers. If desired, sprinkle additional Parmesan cheese over top.

6. Place baking dish on a baking sheet. Bake in a 375° oven for 30 to 35 minutes or until heated through. Let stand for 10 minutes before serving.

Make-ahead directions: Prepare as above through step 5. Cover unbaked lasagna; chill for up to 24 hours. To serve, bake, covered, in a 375° oven

for 40 minutes. Uncover; bake about 20 minutes more or until heated through. Let stand for 10 minutes before serving.

Nutrition Facts per serving: 441 cal., 22 g total fat (11 g sat. fat), 97 mg chol., 658 mg sodium, 33 g carbo., 2 g fiber, 24 g pro.
Daily Values: 9% vit. A, 14% vit. C, 34% calcium, 13% iron
Exchanges: 1 Vegetable, 2 Starch, 2 High-Fat Meat, 1 Fat

Quick Lasagna: Substitute 6 no-boil lasagna noodles (one-third of a 9-ounce package) for regular lasagna noodles and skip step 3. Omit tomatoes, tomato sauce, and Italian seasoning, fennel seeds, and pepper. For sauce, stir a 26-ounce jar pasta sauce into the browned meat mixture. Do not simmer. Continue as directed in step 4.

Nutrition Facts per serving: 391 cal., 24 g total fat (11 g sat. fat), 97 mg chol., 1,047 mg sodium, 18 g carbo., 2 g fiber, 22 g pro.
Daily Values: 15% vit. A, 9% vit. C, 33% calcium, 8% iron
Exchanges: 1 Starch, 1 Vegetable, 2½ High-Fat Meat, 1 Fat

Vegetable Lasagna

This lasagna can be prepared up to 48 hours ahead (see photo, page 375).

Prep: 40 minutes **Bake:** 35 minutes **Oven:** 350°F
Stand: 10 minutes **Makes:** 12 servings

- 8 ounces dried lasagna noodles (9 or 10 noodles)
- 2 beaten eggs
- 2 cups cream-style cottage cheese
- 1 15-ounce carton ricotta cheese
- 2 teaspoons dried Italian seasoning, crushed
- 2 cups sliced fresh mushrooms
- 1 cup chopped onion (1 large)
- 4 cloves garlic, minced
- 2 tablespoons olive oil or cooking oil
- 2 tablespoons all-purpose flour
- ½ to 1 teaspoon black pepper
- 1¼ cups milk
- 1 10-ounce package frozen chopped spinach, thawed and thoroughly drained
- 1 10-ounce package frozen chopped broccoli, thawed and thoroughly drained
- 1 cup shredded carrot
- ¾ cup shredded Parmesan cheese (3 ounces)
- 1 8-ounce package shredded mozzarella cheese

1. Cook lasagna noodles according to package directions. Drain; set aside.

2. In a bowl combine eggs, cottage cheese, ricotta cheese, and Italian seasoning. Set aside.

3. In a large skillet cook the mushrooms, onion, and garlic in hot oil until tender. Stir in flour and pepper; add milk all at once. Cook and stir until slightly thickened and bubbly. Remove from heat. Stir in the spinach, broccoli, carrot, and ½ cup of the Parmesan cheese.

4. To assemble, in a greased 3-quart rectangular baking dish, layer one-third of the noodles, folding or cutting to fit, if necessary. Spread with one-third of the cottage cheese mixture, then one-third of the vegetable mixture. Sprinkle with one-third of the mozzarella. Repeat the layers twice. Sprinkle with the remaining ¼ cup Parmesan cheese.

5. Bake, uncovered, in a 350° oven for 35 minutes or until heated through. Let stand for 10 minutes before serving.

No-Boil Lasagna: Substitute 6 ounces no-boil lasagna noodles (12) for the dried lasagna noodles. Increase milk to 2 cups. Spread ½ cup of the vegetable mixture in the bottom of the dish before adding the first layer of noodles. Continue as directed above.

Make-ahead directions: Prepare as above through step 4. Cover the unbaked lasagna with foil and chill for up to 48 hours. Bake, covered, in a 350° oven for 30 minutes. Uncover; bake for 30 to 35 minutes more or until heated through. Let stand for 10 minutes before serving.

Nutrition Facts per serving: 322 cal., 15 g total fat (8 g sat. fat), 78 mg chol., 388 mg sodium, 25 g carbo., 3 g fiber, 22 g pro.
Daily Values: 107% vit. A, 24% vit. C, 37% calcium, 10% iron
Exchanges: 2 Vegetable, 1 Starch, 2 Medium-Fat Meat, 1 Fat

Trattoria-Style Spinach Fettuccine

This dish is the kind that small, neighborhood Italian restaurants serve. It features an intensely flavored double-tomato sauce with tangy feta cheese.

Fast   **Low Fat**

Start to Finish: 18 minutes   **Makes:** 4 servings

   1 **9-ounce package refrigerated spinach fettuccine**
   2 **tablespoons chopped shallot or green onion**
   1 **tablespoon olive oil**
   4 **red and/or yellow tomatoes, chopped (2 cups)**
   1 **medium carrot, finely chopped**
   ¼ **cup oil-packed dried tomatoes, drained and snipped**
   ½ **cup crumbled garlic and herb feta cheese or peppercorn feta cheese (2 ounces)**

1. Using kitchen shears, cut fettuccine in half crosswise. Cook the pasta according to package directions. Drain; return pasta to hot pan.

2. Meanwhile, in a large skillet cook shallot in hot oil over medium heat for 30 seconds. Stir in fresh tomatoes, carrot, and dried tomatoes. Cook, covered, for 5 minutes, stirring once. Spoon tomato mixture over cooked pasta; toss gently. Sprinkle each serving with feta cheese.

Nutrition Facts per serving: 318 cal., 12 g total fat (4 g sat. fat), 77 mg chol., 294 mg sodium, 43 g carbo., 2 g fiber, 13 g pro.
Daily Values: 93% vit. A, 44% vit. C, 15% calcium, 20% iron
Exchanges: 1½ Vegetable, 2½ Starch, 2 Fat

Mushroom Stroganoff

Beef stroganoff, a classic pasta recipe, gets a makeover with wild mushrooms replacing beef.

Low Fat

Start to Finish: 35 minutes   **Makes:** 4 servings

   8 **ounces dried fettuccine**
   1 **8-ounce carton light dairy sour cream**
   2 **tablespoons all-purpose flour**
   ¾ **cup water**
   1 **vegetable bouillon cube, crumbled**
   ¼ **teaspoon black pepper**
   2 **medium onions, cut into thin wedges**
   2 **tablespoons butter or margarine**
   4½ **cups (about 12 ounces) sliced mushrooms (such as shiitake, button, and/or crimini)**
   1 **clove garlic, minced**
     Snipped fresh chives

1. Cook fettuccine according to package directions. Drain; keep warm. In a small bowl stir together the sour cream and flour. Stir in the water, bouillon, and pepper. Set aside.

2. In a large skillet cook onions in hot butter about 5 minutes or until onions are tender, stirring frequently. Stir in mushrooms and garlic. Cook and stir about 5 minutes more or until the vegetables are tender. Remove mushroom mixture from skillet and add to drained pasta; keep warm.

3. Wipe out skillet. Stir the sour cream mixture into the skillet. Cook and stir until thickened and bubbly. Cook and stir for 1 minute more. Pour the sour cream mixture over the pasta mixture, stirring gently to coat. Sprinkle with chives.

Nutrition Facts per serving: 459 cal., 12 g total fat (7 g sat. fat), 35 mg chol., 355 mg sodium, 76 g carbo., 6 g fiber, 14 g pro.
Daily Values: 13% vit. A, 5% vit. C, 14% calcium, 15% iron
Exchanges: 2 Vegetable, 4 Starch, 1½ Fat

Creamy Herbed Pasta

Fast

Start to Finish: 30 minutes **Makes:** 4 servings

- **10 ounces dried rigatoni or rotini (about 4 cups)**
- **¼ cup snipped fresh basil or 4 teaspoons dried basil, crushed**
- **4 cloves garlic, minced**
- **1 tablespoon olive oil or cooking oil**
- **½ of an 8-ounce package reduced-fat cream cheese (Neufchâtel)**
- **½ cup low-fat cottage cheese**
- **⅓ cup grated Parmesan cheese**
- **½ cup water**
- **¼ cup snipped fresh parsley**
- **2 tablespoons dry white wine**

1. Cook pasta according to package directions. Drain; keep warm.

2. Meanwhile, for sauce, in a medium heavy saucepan cook basil and garlic in hot oil about 30 seconds. Reduce heat. Add cream cheese, cottage cheese, and Parmesan cheese. Heat and stir until nearly smooth. Stir in water, parsley, and wine. Bring to a gentle boil; reduce heat. Cook and stir 2 to 3 minutes until slightly thickened. Serve sauce over hot pasta.

Nutrition Facts per serving: 441 cal., 14 g total fat (7 g sat. fat), 30 mg chol., 387 mg sodium, 57 g carbo., 2 g fiber, 20 g pro.
Daily Values: 14% vit. A, 11% vit. C, 18% calcium, 15% iron
Exchanges: 3½ Starch, 1½ Lean Meat, 1 Fat

Macaroni and Cheese Best Loved

If you prefer a milder flavor, use only American cheese.

Prep: 25 minutes **Bake:** 25 minutes **Oven:** 350°F
Stand: 10 minutes **Makes:** 4 servings

- **8 ounces dried elbow macaroni (2 cups)**
- **½ cup chopped onion (1 medium)**
- **2 tablespoons butter or margarine**
- **2 tablespoons all-purpose flour**
- **⅛ teaspoon black pepper**
- **2½ cups milk**
- **1½ cups shredded cheddar cheese (6 ounces)**
- **1½ cups shredded American cheese (6 ounces)**

1. Cook macaroni according to package directions. Drain; set aside.

2. Meanwhile, for cheese sauce, in a medium saucepan cook onion in hot butter until tender but not brown. Stir in flour and pepper. Add milk all at once. Cook and stir over medium heat until

slightly thickened and bubbly. Add cheeses, stirring until melted. Stir in cooked macaroni. Transfer mixture to a 2-quart casserole.

3. Bake, uncovered, in a 350° oven for 25 to 30 minutes or until bubbly and heated through. Let stand for 10 minutes before serving.

Nutrition Facts per serving: 692 cal., 37 g total fat (23 g sat. fat), 112 mg chol., 1,012 mg sodium, 56 g carbo., 2 g fiber, 33 g pro.
Daily Values: 30% vit. A, 4% vit. C, 77% calcium, 14% iron
Exchanges: 3½ Starch, 3 High-Fat Meat, 2 Fat

Saucepan Macaroni and Cheese: Prepare as above, except reduce milk to 2 cups. After draining macaroni, immediately return macaroni to the saucepan. Pour cheese sauce over macaroni; stir to coat macaroni with sauce. Cook over low heat for 2 to 3 minutes or until heated through, stirring frequently. Let stand for 10 minutes before serving.

Nutrition Facts per serving: 677 cal., 37 g total fat (23 g sat. fat), 110 mg chol., 997 mg sodium, 54 g carbo., 2 g fiber, 32 g pro.
Daily Values: 29% vit. A, 4% vit. C, 73% calcium, 13% iron
Exchanges: 3½ Starch, 3 High-Fat Meat, 2½ Fat

Roasted Red Pepper Sauce over Tortellini

When you take advantage of ready-to-use roasted red peppers and refrigerated tortellini, dinner is ready in 20 minutes. The sauce is equally good spooned over chicken or fish.

Fast   **Low Fat**

Start to Finish: 20 minutes **Makes:** 6 servings

- **2 9-ounce packages refrigerated meat- or cheese-filled tortellini**
- **2 12-ounce jars roasted red sweet peppers, drained**
- **1 cup chopped onion (1 large)**
- **4 cloves garlic, minced**
- **2 tablespoons butter or margarine**
- **1 tablespoon snipped fresh thyme or 1 teaspoon dried thyme, crushed**
- **1 tablespoon snipped fresh oregano or ½ teaspoon dried oregano, crushed**
- **2 teaspoons sugar**

1. Cook tortellini according to package directions; drain. Return to saucepan.

2. Meanwhile, place roasted sweet peppers in a food processor bowl. Cover and process until smooth. Set aside.

3. For sauce, in a medium saucepan cook the onion and garlic in hot butter until tender. Add pureed peppers, thyme, oregano, and sugar. Cook and stir until heated through. Pour sauce over tortellini; toss to coat.

Nutrition Facts per serving: 330 cal., 12 g total fat (6 g sat. fat), 30 mg chol., 474 mg sodium, 46 g carbo., 3 g fiber, 12 g pro.
Daily Values: 5% vit. A, 232% vit. C, 7% calcium, 14% iron
Exchanges: 2 Vegetable, 2½ Starch, ½ Very Lean Meat, 1 Fat

Rotini and Sweet Pepper Primavera

Primavera *means "springtime" in Italian. This creamy pasta, brimming with tender asparagus, crisp sweet pepper, and tiny baby squash, is the essence of that welcome season.*

`Fast` `Low Fat`

Start to Finish: 20 minutes **Makes:** 4 servings

- 14 ounces asparagus spears
- 8 ounces dried rotini or gemelli (about 2½ cups)
- 1 large red or yellow sweet pepper, cut into 1-inch pieces
- 1 cup halved baby pattypan squash or sliced yellow summer squash
- 1 10-ounce container refrigerated light Alfredo sauce
- 2 tablespoons snipped fresh tarragon or thyme
- ¼ teaspoon crushed red pepper
  Fresh tarragon (optional)

1. Snap off and discard woody bases from asparagus spears. Bias-slice asparagus into 1-inch pieces.

2. Cook pasta according to package directions, adding asparagus, sweet pepper, and squash to pasta the last 3 minutes of cooking. Drain. Return pasta and vegetable mixture to hot saucepan.

3. Meanwhile, for sauce, in a small saucepan combine Alfredo sauce, the 2 tablespoons tarragon, and red pepper. Cook and stir over medium heat about 5 minutes or until heated through. Pour sauce over pasta and vegetable mixture; stir gently to coat. If desired, garnish with fresh tarragon.

Nutrition Facts per serving: 353 cal., 9 g total fat (4 g sat. fat), 23 mg chol., 326 mg sodium, 55 g carbo., 4 g fiber, 11 g pro.
Daily Values: 47% vit. A, 107% vit. C, 18% calcium, 13% iron
Exchanges: 2 Vegetable, 3 Starch, 1½ Fat

Perfect Pasta

To get the best flavor from your pasta, cook it only until it is al dente (al-DEN-tay), or firm and somewhat chewy. In Italian, al dente means "to the tooth" and describes the doneness of pasta and other foods, such as vegetables. For the best results, follow the cooking directions on the package of dried or fresh pasta carefully.

Tortellini with Rosemary-Tomato Sauce

`Fast` `Low Fat`

Start to Finish: 15 minutes **Makes:** 6 servings

- 2 9-ounce packages refrigerated cheese- or meat-filled tortellini
- 2 14½-ounce cans pasta-style tomatoes, undrained
- ¼ cup tomato paste
- 1 tablespoon snipped fresh rosemary or 1 teaspoon dried rosemary, crushed
- ½ cup sliced pitted ripe olives

1. Cook tortellini according to package directions. Drain; keep warm.

2. Meanwhile, for sauce, in a medium saucepan stir together undrained tomatoes, tomato paste, and rosemary. Bring to boiling; reduce heat. Simmer, uncovered, for 2 to 3 minutes or until of desired consistency. Stir in olives; heat through. Spoon sauce over tortellini.

Nutrition Facts per serving: 333 cal., 7 g total fat (3 g sat. fat), 45 mg chol., 1,035 mg sodium, 54 g carbo., 6 g fiber, 15 g pro.
Daily Values: 1% vit. A, 12% vit. C, 18% calcium, 15% iron
Exchanges: 2 Vegetable, 3 Starch, ½ Fat

Rotini and Sweet Pepper Primavera

Fresh Tomato and Arugula Pasta

Quick-cook fresh tomatoes with peppery arugula and top them with Gorgonzola cheese.

Fast **Low Fat**

Start to Finish: 30 minutes **Makes:** 4 servings

  8 **ounces dried ziti or mostaccioli (about 2⅔ cups)**
  1 **medium onion, thinly sliced**
  2 **cloves garlic, minced**
  1 **tablespoon olive oil**
  4 to 6 **medium tomatoes, seeded and coarsely chopped (3 cups)**
  1 **teaspoon salt**
  ½ **teaspoon black pepper**
  ¼ **teaspoon crushed red pepper (optional)**
  3 **cups arugula and/or spinach, coarsely chopped**
  ¼ **cup pine nuts or slivered almonds, toasted**
  2 **tablespoons crumbled Gorgonzola or other blue cheese**

1. Cook pasta according to package directions. Drain; keep warm.

2. Meanwhile, in a large skillet cook onion and garlic in hot oil over medium heat until onion is tender. Add tomatoes, salt, black pepper, and, if desired, red pepper. Cook and stir over medium-high heat about 2 minutes or until the tomatoes are warm and release some of their juices. Stir in arugula and/or spinach; heat just until greens are wilted.

3. To serve, top pasta with tomato mixture; sprinkle with toasted pine nuts and cheese.

Nutrition Facts per serving: 349 cal., 11 g total fat (2 g sat. fat), 3 mg chol., 659 mg sodium, 53 g carbo., 4 g fiber, 12 g pro.
Daily Values: 25% vit. A, 49% vit. C, 7% calcium, 20% iron
Exchanges: 1½ Vegetable, 3 Starch, 1½ Fat

Storing Pasta

Dried uncooked pasta: Keeps indefinitely if kept in an airtight container in a cool, dry place.

Refrigerated fresh pasta: Keeps up to 5 days if kept in its original packaging. If frozen, it will keep up to 8 months.

Cooked pasta: Can be kept refrigerated for 1 to 2 days if it is sealed in an airtight container. Reheat the pasta in a sauce or clear broth.

Note: Freezing prepared pasta dishes is not recommended because the pasta will become soft and mushy once it's thawed and baked.

Rigatoni and Eggplant with Dried Tomato Pesto

Dried Tomato Pesto makes more than you'll need for this recipe. You can refrigerate or freeze the additional pesto for another time. It's also great as a spread for slices of Italian bread.

Start to Finish: 35 minutes **Bake:** 25 minutes **Oven:** 425°F
Makes: 4 servings

  1 **medium onion, cut into 8 wedges**
  2 **tablespoons olive oil**
  1 **medium eggplant (about 1 pound), halved lengthwise**
  6 **ounces dried rigatoni, penne, or fusilli**
  ⅓ **recipe Dried Tomato Pesto**
  ¼ **teaspoon coarsely ground black pepper**
  2 **tablespoons crumbled goat cheese or feta cheese (optional)**

1. Place onion wedges in a large shallow baking pan; brush with 1 tablespoon of the olive oil. Roast onion in a 425° oven for 10 minutes; stir. Brush eggplant halves with the remaining 1 tablespoon oil. Place eggplant in pan, cut sides down. Roast 15 minutes more or until onion is golden brown and eggplant is tender.

2. Meanwhile, cook pasta according to package directions. Drain. Add Dried Tomato Pesto and pepper to pasta; stir gently to coat. Transfer pasta to a warm serving dish; keep warm.

3. Cut eggplant into ½-inch-thick slices. Gently stir onion and eggplant into pasta; season to taste with *salt*. If desired, top with goat cheese.

Dried Tomato Pesto: Drain ¾ cup oil-packed dried tomatoes, reserving oil. Add enough olive oil to make ½ cup; set aside. Place tomatoes, ¼ cup pine nuts or slivered almonds, ¼ cup snipped fresh basil, ½ teaspoon salt, and 8 cloves garlic, chopped, in a food processor bowl. Cover; process until finely chopped. With machine running, gradually add the ½ cup oil, processing until almost smooth. Divide pesto into thirds. Chill (up to 2 days) or freeze (up to 3 months) unused portions. Makes approximately three ⅓-cup portions.

Nutrition Facts per serving: 370 cal., 19 g total fat (3 g sat. fat), 0 mg chol., 121 mg sodium, 43 g carbo., 5 g fiber, 8 g pro.
Daily Values: 4% vit. A, 18% vit. C, 3% calcium, 12% iron
Exchanges: 2½ Vegetable, 2 Starch, 3½ Fat

Spinach Manicotti

Three different cheeses—Swiss, ricotta, and Parmesan—plus spinach are the major ingredients in this tasty meatless main dish.

Prep: 40 minutes **Bake:** 30 minutes **Oven:** 350°F
Stand: 10 minutes **Makes:** 4 servings

- 8 **dried manicotti shells**
- ¼ **cup sliced green onions (2)**
- 1 **clove garlic, minced**
- 2 **tablespoons butter or margarine**
- 2 **tablespoons all-purpose flour**
- 1⅓ **cups milk**
- 3 **ounces process Swiss cheese, torn**
- ⅓ **cup chicken broth**
- 1 **beaten egg**
- 1 **10-ounce package frozen chopped spinach, thawed and well drained**
- ¾ **cup ricotta cheese**
- ½ **cup grated Parmesan cheese**
- ¼ **teaspoon finely shredded lemon peel**

1. Cook manicotti according to package directions. Drain. Cool manicotti in a single layer on a piece of greased foil.

2. Meanwhile, for sauce, in a medium saucepan cook green onions and garlic in butter until tender. Stir in flour. Add milk all at once. Cook and stir until thickened and bubbly. Add Swiss cheese and broth, stirring until cheese melts.

3. For filling, in a medium bowl stir together egg, spinach, ricotta cheese, Parmesan cheese, and lemon peel. Use a small spoon to fill manicotti shells with filling. Arrange filled shells in a 2-quart rectangular baking dish. Pour sauce over filled shells.

4. Bake, covered, in a 350° oven 30 to 35 minutes or until heated through. Let stand for 10 minutes before serving.

Nutrition Facts per serving: 487 cal., 25 g total fat (15 g sat. fat), 128 mg chol., 572 mg sodium, 38 g carbo., 3 g fiber, 28 g pro.
Daily Values: 130% vit. A, 18% vit. C, 69% calcium, 16% iron
Exchanges: 1 Vegetable, 2 Starch, 3 Medium-Fat Meat, 1½ Fat

Lemon Cream-Sauced Pasta with Asparagus and Squash

Delicate asparagus and succulent baby squash nestle with pasta in a low-fuss, lemon-infused cream sauce.

`Fast`

Start to Finish: 25 minutes **Makes:** 4 servings

- 8 **ounces dried mafalda or rotini**
- 2 **cups asparagus cut into 2-inch pieces**
- 8 **baby sunburst squash and/or pattypan squash, halved (4 ounces)***
- 2 **cloves garlic, minced**
- 1 **tablespoon butter or margarine**
- ½ **cup whipping cream**
- 2 **teaspoons finely shredded lemon peel**

1. Cook pasta according to package directions. Drain; keep warm.

2. Meanwhile, in a large skillet cook asparagus, squash, and garlic in hot butter for 2 to 3 minutes or until vegetables are crisp-tender, stirring frequently. Remove vegetables from skillet with a slotted spoon; add to pasta.

3. Combine whipping cream and lemon peel in skillet; bring to boiling. Boil for 2 to 3 minutes or until reduced to ⅓ cup. To serve, pour cream mixture over pasta mixture; stir gently to coat.

*Note: One medium zucchini or yellow summer squash cut into 8 pieces can be substituted for the baby sunburst squash and/or pattypan squash.

Nutrition Facts per serving: 256 cal., 14 g total fat (8 g sat. fat), 47 mg chol., 35 mg sodium, 48 g carbo., 3 g fiber, 10 g pro.
Daily Values: 19% vit. A, 18% vit. C, 5% calcium, 13% iron
Exchanges: 2 Vegetable, 2½ Starch, 2½ Fat

Pasta

395

Lemon Cream-Sauced Pasta with Asparagus and Squash

Fettuccine alla Carbonara

Substitute pancetta for bacon if you like.

`Fast`

Start to Finish: 25 minutes **Makes:** 4 servings

- 6 slices bacon, cut into 1-inch pieces
- 6 ounces dried fettuccine or linguine
- 1 beaten egg
- 1 cup half-and-half, light cream, or milk
- 2 tablespoons butter or margarine
- ½ cup grated Parmesan or Romano cheese
- ¼ cup snipped fresh parsley
  Coarsely ground black pepper

1. Cook bacon until crisp. Drain.

2. Cook pasta according to package directions. Drain; keep warm.

3. Meanwhile, for sauce, in a saucepan combine egg, half-and-half, and butter. Cook and stir over medium heat until egg mixture just coats a metal spoon (about 6 minutes); do not boil. Immediately pour sauce over pasta; stir gently to coat.

4. Add cooked bacon, Parmesan cheese, and parsley; stir gently to combine. Season with pepper. Serve immediately.

Nutrition Facts per serving: 422 cal., 23 g total fat (13 g sat. fat), 110 mg chol., 489 mg sodium, 35 g carbo., 1 g fiber, 17 g pro.
Daily Values: 17% vit. A, 9% vit. C, 26% calcium, 11% iron
Exchanges: 2½ Starch, 1½ Medium-Fat Meat, 2½ Fat

Fettuccine Alfredo

Start to Finish: 35 minutes **Makes:** 4 servings

- ½ cup half-and-half, light cream, or whipping cream
- 1 tablespoon butter or margarine
- 6 ounces dried fettuccine or spinach fettuccine
- ¾ cup grated Parmesan cheese
  Cracked black pepper

1. Allow half-and-half and butter to stand at room temperature for 30 minutes.

2. Meanwhile, cook fettuccine according to package directions. Drain. Return fettuccine to saucepan; add half-and-half, butter, and Parmesan cheese. Stir gently until fettuccine is well coated. Transfer to a warm serving dish. Sprinkle with pepper. Serve immediately.

Lemony Fettuccine Alfredo with Asparagus: Prepare as at left, except add 1 cup fresh or frozen asparagus, cut into 1-inch pieces, to the fettuccine the last 5 minutes of cooking. Drain. Return fettuccine and asparagus to saucepan. Gently stir in ½ teaspoon finely shredded lemon peel along with half-and-half, butter, and Parmesan cheese. To serve, sprinkle with pepper and, if desired, ¼ cup broken pecans or walnuts.

Nutrition Facts per serving for plain or lemon variation: 309 cal., 13 g total fat (8 g sat. fat), 34 mg chol., 411 mg sodium, 34 g carbo., 2 g fiber, 14 g pro.
Daily Values: 8% vit. A, 32% calcium, 9% iron
Exchanges: 2½ Starch, 1 Lean Meat, 1 Fat

Homemade Pesto `Best Loved`

This recipe makes enough to chill or freeze for another time. In addition to tossing it with hot pasta, pesto can be spread on Italian bread slices or crackers, spooned onto baked potatoes, or stirred into mayonnaise for a stellar chicken or pasta salad.

`Fast` `Low Fat`

Start to Finish: 15 minutes **Makes:** enough pesto for 18 side-dish servings (about ¾ cup pesto total)

- ¼ cup olive oil or cooking oil
- ½ cup chopped walnuts and/or pine nuts
- 2 cups firmly packed fresh basil leaves
- ½ cup grated Parmesan or Romano cheese
- 4 cloves garlic, peeled and quartered
- ¼ teaspoon salt
  Black pepper

1. In a food processor bowl or blender container combine oil, nuts, basil, cheese, garlic, and salt. Cover and process or blend until nearly smooth, stopping and scraping sides as necessary. Add pepper to taste. If you're not serving the pesto immediately, divide it into 3 portions. Place each portion in a small airtight container and chill for 1 to 2 days or freeze for up to 3 months.

Note: For 6 side-dish servings, cook 6 ounces dried pasta, such as spaghetti, linguine, or fettuccine, according to package directions. Toss with one portion (¼ cup) of the pesto.

Nutrition Facts per serving pesto with pasta: 166 cal., 6 g total fat (1 g sat. fat), 2 mg chol., 74 mg sodium, 22 g carbo., 1 g fiber, 5 g pro.
Daily Values: 4% vit. A, 2% vit. C, 5% calcium, 6% iron
Exchanges: 1½ Starch, 1 Fat

Chapter 17
Pies & Tarts

On the divider: Berry Fruit Pie (see recipe, page 401)

For more recipes, visit our Recipe Center at **www.bhg.com**

Apple Pie `Best Loved`

Choose an apple variety that will stand up to the heat. Granny Smith apples are favored among tart apple-lovers; if you prefer a sweeter cooking apple, choose from Cortland, Golden Delicious, Jonathan, Newtown Pippin, Rome Beauty, Winesap, or York Imperial and add the lemon juice.

Prep: 30 minutes **Bake:** 1 hour
Oven: 375°F **Makes:** 8 servings

- 1 **recipe Pastry for Double-Crust Pie (page 417)**
- 6 **cups thinly sliced, peeled cooking apples (about 2¼ pounds)**
- 1 **tablespoon lemon juice (optional)**
- ¾ **cup sugar**
- 2 **tablespoons all-purpose flour**
- ½ **teaspoon ground cinnamon**
- ⅛ **teaspoon ground nutmeg**
- ⅓ **cup dried cranberries (optional)**
  Milk (optional)
  Sugar (optional)

1. Prepare and roll out Pastry for Double-Crust Pie. Line a 9-inch pie plate with half of the pastry (see photo 2, page 417).

2. If desired, sprinkle apples with lemon juice. In a large bowl stir together the ¾ cup sugar, the flour, cinnamon, and nutmeg. Add apple slices and, if desired, cranberries. Gently toss until coated.

3. Transfer apple mixture to the pastry-lined pie plate. Trim bottom pastry to edge of pie plate. Cut slits in remaining pastry; place on filling and seal (see photo 4, page 417). Crimp edge as desired (see photos 5, 6, and 7, page 417).

4. If desired, brush top pastry with milk and sprinkle with additional sugar. To prevent overbrowning, cover edge of pie with foil (see photo, above right). Bake in a 375° oven for 40 minutes. Remove foil. Bake 20 minutes more or until fruit is tender and filling is bubbly. Cool on a wire rack.

Apple Crumb Pie: Prepare as above, except substitute 1 recipe Pastry for Single-Crust Pie (page 416) for Pastry for Double-Crust Pie. Fill pastry-lined pie plate as above. Prepare Crumb Topping (page 400). Sprinkle over apple mixture. Do not brush top with milk or sprinkle with sugar. Bake as directed above.

Nutrition Facts per serving for apple or apple crumb variation:
395 cal., 18 g total fat (4 g sat. fat), 0 mg chol., 219 mg sodium, 57 g carbo., 3 g fiber, 4 g pro.
Daily Values: 1% vit. A, 6% vit. C, 1% calcium, 10% iron
Exchanges: 1 Fruit, 3 Other Carbo., 3½ Fat

To protect the edges of the pie from overbrowning, fold a 12-inch square of foil into quarters. Cut a 7-inch circle out of the center. Unfold and loosely mold the foil over the pie's edge.

Making and Storing Fruit Pies

■ For a two-crust pie, be sure to use either a double-crust or lattice-top as the recipe specifies. Some fruit fillings require the venting that a lattice-top provides; others, such as apples, benefit from steaming under a top crust.

■ Make several slits in the top of a double-crust pie before baking to allow steam to escape and to prevent excessive bubbling. Or use a small cutter to cut a few decorative shapes from near the center of the top pastry.

■ For an attractive glazed crust, brush the top pastry with milk, then sprinkle with granulated or coarse sugar before baking.

■ Place a pizza pan or baking sheet under a double-crust pie when you put it in the oven to catch any filling that may bubble over.

■ Fruit pies should bubble in the center to be properly cooked—otherwise, the thickener (cornstarch, flour, or tapioca) won't be clear and the filling will be too thin. To see if a double-crust pie is done, look for bubbling around the slits in the top crust.

■ So the pieces don't fall apart when you cut the pie, let fruit pies cool at least 2 hours before serving. Fruit pies may stand at room temperature for 24 hours. Cover and refrigerate for longer storage.

■ To freeze a baked fruit pie, let it cool completely. Place it in a freezer bag; seal, label, and freeze for up to 4 months. To serve, thaw the pie, covered, at room temperature. If desired, reheat pie, covered, in a 325°F oven until warm.

■ To freeze unbaked fruit pies, treat any light-colored fruit with ascorbic-acid color-keeper. Assemble the pie in a metal or freezer-to-oven pie pan or pie plate. Place in a freezer bag; seal, label, and freeze for up to 4 months. To bake a frozen pie, unwrap it and cover with foil. Bake in a 450°F oven for 15 minutes; reduce temperature to 375°F; bake 15 minutes more. Uncover and continue baking for 55 to 60 minutes more or until crust is golden and filling is bubbly.

Cherry Pie Best Loved

Tart pie cherries, such as Montmorency, Early Richmond, and English Morello, generally are available in June and July.

Prep: 30 minutes **Bake:** 55 minutes
Oven: 375°F **Makes:** 8 servings

1¼ cups granulated sugar
3 tablespoons cornstarch or quick-cooking tapioca
5½ cups fresh or frozen unsweetened pitted tart red cherries
1 recipe Pastry for Double-Crust Pie (page 417)
Milk (optional)
Granulated or coarse sugar (optional)

1. In a large bowl stir together the 1¼ cups sugar and cornstarch; add cherries. Gently toss until coated. Let mixture stand about 15 minutes or until a syrup forms, stirring occasionally. (If using frozen cherries, let cherry mixture stand 45 minutes or until fruit is partially thawed but still icy.)

2. Meanwhile, prepare and roll out Pastry for Double-Crust Pie. Line a 9-inch pie plate with half of the pastry (see photo 2, page 417).

3. Stir cherry mixture; transfer to pastry-lined pie plate. Trim bottom pastry to edge of pie plate. Cut slits in remaining pastry; place on filling and seal (see photo 4, page 417). Crimp edge as desired (see photos 5, 6, and 7, page 417). If desired, brush top with milk and sprinkle with additional sugar.

4. Place pie on a baking sheet. To prevent over-browning, cover edge of the pie with foil (see photo, page 399). Bake in a 375° oven for 30 minutes (or 50 minutes for frozen fruit). Remove foil. Bake for 25 to 30 minutes more or until filling in center is bubbly and pastry is golden. Cool on a wire rack.

Lattice Cherry Pie: Prepare as above, except follow directions for Pastry for Lattice-Top Pie (page 417).

Nutrition Facts per serving: 446 cal., 18 g total fat (4 g sat. fat), 0 mg chol., 221 mg sodium, 69 g carbo., 3 g fiber, 4 g pro.
Daily Values: 19% vit. A, 3% vit. C, 2% calcium, 11% iron
Exchanges: ½ Fruit, 4 Other Carbo., 3½ Fat

Red Raspberry-Cherry Pie: Prepare as above, except use 3 cups fresh or frozen unsweetened pitted tart red cherries and 2 cups fresh or frozen lightly sweetened raspberries.

Nutrition Facts per serving: 488 cal., 18 g total fat (4 g sat. fat), 0 mg chol., 221 mg sodium, 80 g carbo., 5 g fiber, 4 g pro.
Daily Values: 11% vit. A, 19% vit. C, 2% calcium, 12% iron
Exchanges: ½ Fruit, 5 Other Carbo., 3½ Fat

Rhubarb Pie

Prep: 30 minutes **Bake:** 45 minutes
Oven: 375°F **Makes:** 8 servings

1 recipe Pastry for Single-Crust Pie (page 416)
1 recipe Crumb Topping
¾ cup sugar
⅓ cup all-purpose flour
½ teaspoon ground cinnamon (optional)
6 cups fresh or frozen unsweetened, sliced rhubarb

1. Prepare and roll out Pastry for Single-Crust Pie. Line a 9-inch pie plate with the pastry (see photo 2, page 417). Trim (see photo 3, page 417) and crimp edge as desired (see photos 5, 6, and 7, page 417). Prepare Crumb Topping; set aside.

2. In a large bowl stir together sugar, flour, and, if desired, cinnamon. Add rhubarb. Gently toss until coated. (If using frozen fruit, let mixture stand for 45 minutes or until fruit is partially thawed but still icy.)

3. Transfer rhubarb mixture to the pastry-lined pie plate. Sprinkle Crumb Topping over filling.

4. To prevent overbrowning, cover edge of the pie with foil (see photo, page 399). Bake in a 375° oven for 25 minutes (or 60 minutes for frozen fruit). Remove foil. Bake for 20 to 30 minutes more or until topping is golden and filling in center is bubbly. Cool on a wire rack.

Crumb Topping: Stir together ½ cup all-purpose flour and ½ cup packed brown sugar. Using a pastry blender, cut in 3 tablespoons butter until mixture resembles coarse crumbs.

Double-Crust Rhubarb Pie: Prepare as above, except omit Crumb Topping. Substitute 1 recipe Pastry for Double-Crust Pie (page 417) for the Pastry for Single-Crust Pie. Follow directions for Pastry for Double-Crust Pie. If desired, brush top of pie with *milk* and sprinkle with additional *sugar* before baking. Bake as directed above. Cool on a wire rack.

Nutrition Facts per serving for pie with crumb topping or double-crust variation: 365 cal., 13 g total fat (5 g sat. fat), 12 mg chol., 129 mg sodium, 58 g carbo., 2 fiber, 4 g pro.
Daily Values: 5% vit. A, 10% vit. C, 10% calcium, 10% iron
Exchanges: 1 Fruit, 3 Other Carbo., 2½ Fat

Berry Fruit Pie [Best Loved]

Choose your favorite berry pie filling from the chart below (see photo, page 397).

Prep: 30 minutes **Bake:** 50 minutes
Oven: 375°F **Makes:** 8 servings

- 1 **recipe Pastry for Double-Crust Pie (page 417)**
- 1 **recipe filling for blackberries, blueberries, raspberries, or mixed berries (see below)**
- 2 **teaspoons finely shredded lemon peel or ½ teaspoon ground cinnamon**

1. Prepare and roll out Pastry for Double-Crust Pie. Line a 9-inch pie plate with half of the pastry.

2. In a large bowl combine the sugar and thickener for desired berries, according to the amounts given below. Stir in berries and lemon peel. Gently toss berries until coated. (If using frozen fruit, let mixture stand for 45 minutes or until fruit is partially thawed but still icy.)

3. Transfer berry mixture to the pastry-lined pie plate. Trim bottom pastry to edge of pie plate. Cut slits in remaining pastry; place on filling and seal (see photo 4, page 417). Crimp edge as desired (see photos 5, 6, and 7, page 417).

4. If desired, brush top pastry with *milk* and sprinkle with additional *sugar*. To prevent over-browning, cover edge of pie with foil (see photo, page 399). Bake in a 375° oven for 25 minutes (or 50 minutes for frozen fruit). Remove foil. Bake pie for 25 to 30 minutes more or until filling is bubbly and pastry is golden. Cool on a wire rack.

Lattice Berry Fruit Pie: Prepare as above, except follow directions for Lattice-Top Pie (page 417).

Nutrition Facts per serving for double-crust or lattice-top variation: 373 cal., 18 g total fat (4 g sat. fat), 0 mg chol., 222 mg sodium, 50 g carbo., 4 g fiber, 5 g pro.
Daily Values: 2% vit. A, 49% vit. C, 2% calcium, 11% iron
Exchanges: 1 Fruit, 2½ Other Carbo., 3½ Fat

Berry Glacé Pie

Prep: 1 hour **Chill:** 1 to 2 hours **Makes:** 8 servings

- 1 **recipe Baked Pastry Shell (page 416)**
- 8 **cups medium fresh strawberries**
- ⅔ **cup sugar**
- 2 **tablespoons cornstarch**
  Several drops red food coloring (optional)

1. Prepare Baked Pastry Shell; set aside. Meanwhile, remove stems from strawberries. Cut any large strawberries in half lengthwise; set aside.

2. For glaze, in a blender container or food processor bowl combine 1 cup of the strawberries and ⅔ cup *water*. Cover and blend or process until smooth. Add enough additional *water* to the mixture to equal 1½ cups. In a medium saucepan combine sugar and cornstarch; stir in blended berry mixture. Cook and stir over medium heat until mixture is thickened and bubbly. Cook and stir 2 minutes more. If desired, stir in red food coloring. Cool for 10 minutes without stirring.

3. Spread about ¼ cup of the glaze over bottom and sides of Baked Pastry Shell. Arrange half of the remaining strawberries, stem ends down, in pastry.

4. Carefully spoon half of the remaining glaze over berries, making sure all berries are covered. Arrange remaining berries over first layer. Spoon remaining glaze over berries, covering each. Chill for 1 to 2 hours. (After 2 hours, filling may begin to water out.) If desired, garnish with *whipped cream*.

Peach Glacé Pie: Prepare as above, except substitute 6 cups sliced, peeled peaches for the strawberries and omit the food coloring.

Nutrition Facts per serving for strawberry or peach variation: 253 cal., 9 g total fat (2 g sat. fat), 0 mg chol., 75 mg sodium, 42 g carbo., 4 g fiber, 3 g pro.
Daily Values: 1% vit. A, 136% vit. C, 2% calcium, 8% iron
Exchanges: 1 Fruit, 2 Other Carbo., 1½ Fat

Berry Fruit Pie Filling

Whether you have an abundance of fresh berries from the farmer's market or frozen berries tucked away in your freezer, the chart below will guarantee a perfect berry pie every time.

Berries	Amount	Sugar	Thickener
Blackberries, fresh or frozen	5 cups	¾ to 1 cup	⅓ cup all-purpose flour
Blueberries, fresh or frozen	5 cups	⅔ to ¾ cup	3 tablespoons all-purpose flour
Raspberries, fresh or frozen	5 cups	¾ to 1 cup	⅓ cup all-purpose flour
Mixed Berries (2 cups blueberries, 2 cups halved strawberries, and 1 cup blackberries or raspberries)	5 cups	½ to ⅔ cup	⅓ cup all-purpose flour

Festive Cranberry-Apricot Pie

Best Loved

If you don't have small cutters, follow the directions for a Lattice-Top Pie (page 417), brushing the strips with the egg mixture and sprinkling half of the strips with the sugar mixture.

Prep: 30 minutes **Bake:** 50 minutes
Oven: 375°F **Makes:** 8 servings

> 1 recipe Pastry for Double-Crust Pie (page 417)
> ½ cup sugar
> 3 tablespoons cornstarch
> 1½ teaspoons pumpkin pie spice
> ¼ teaspoon salt
> 3 15¼-ounce cans apricot halves, drained and cut into quarters
> ½ cup dried cranberries, snipped
> 1 egg white
> 1 tablespoon milk
> 1 tablespoon sugar
> ¼ teaspoon pumpkin pie spice

1. Prepare and roll out Pastry for Double-Crust Pie. Line a 9-inch pie plate with half of pastry (see photo 2, page 417); trim (see photo 3, page 417).

2. In a large bowl combine the ½ cup sugar, the cornstarch, the 1½ teaspoons pumpkin pie spice, and the salt. Stir in apricots and cranberries. Spoon fruit mixture into pastry-lined pie plate.

3. Roll remaining dough into a circle about 12 inches in diameter. Using a 1- to 1½-inch leaf-shaped cutter or other desired cutter, cut 36 to 40 shapes from the dough. In a small bowl stir together egg white and milk. Brush egg white mixture over pastry shapes; reserve remaining egg white mixture. Stir together the 1 tablespoon sugar and the ¼ teaspoon pumpkin pie spice. Sprinkle half of the pastry shapes with the sugar mixture. Arrange 10 to 12 of the shapes, alternating brushed and sprinkled shapes, in a circle in center of the top of pie filling. Brush edge of crust with remaining egg white mixture. Evenly distribute the remaining pastry shapes around edge of crust.

4. To prevent overbrowning, cover edge of pie lightly with foil (see photo, page 399). Bake in a 375° oven for 35 minutes. Remove foil. Bake for 15 minutes more. Cool on a wire rack.

Nutrition Facts per serving: 437 cal., 18 g total fat (4 g sat. fat), 0 mg chol., 308 mg sodium, 67 g carbo., 4 g fiber, 5 g pro.
Daily Values: 55% vit. A, 13% vit. C, 3% calcium, 12% iron
Exchanges: 2 Fruit, 2½ Other Carbo., 2½ Fat

Festive Cranberry-Apricot Pie

Peach Pie with Candied Pecan Topping

Best Loved

Prep: 35 minutes **Stand:** 20 minutes **Bake:** 55 minutes
Oven: 375°F **Makes:** 8 servings

> ½ to ⅔ cup granulated sugar
> 2 tablespoons quick-cooking tapioca
> ¼ teaspoon ground cinnamon
> ¼ teaspoon ground nutmeg
> 6 cups thinly sliced, peeled peaches or frozen unsweetened peach slices
> 1 recipe Pastry for Double-Crust Pie (page 417)
> ⅓ cup packed brown sugar
> 2 tablespoons butter
> 1 tablespoon water
> 1 teaspoon cornstarch
> ¾ cup chopped pecans

1. For filling, in a large bowl stir together granulated sugar, tapioca, cinnamon, and nutmeg. Add peaches. Gently toss until coated. Let mixture stand for 20 minutes, stirring occasionally. (If using frozen peaches, let stand 45 minutes.)

2. Meanwhile, prepare and roll out Pastry for Double-Crust Pie. Line a 9-inch pie plate with half of the pastry (see photo 2, page 417).

3. Stir peach mixture. Transfer peach mixture to the pastry-lined pie plate. Trim bottom pastry to edge of pie plate. Cut slits in the remaining pastry; place on filling and seal (see photo 4, page 417). Crimp edge as desired (see photos 5, 6, and 7, page 417).

4. Place pie plate on a baking sheet. To prevent overbrowning, cover edge of pie with foil (see photo, page 399). Bake in a 375° oven for 25 minutes (or 50 minutes for frozen fruit). Remove foil. Bake 25 to 30 minutes more or until pastry is golden and filling is bubbly.

5. Meanwhile, for pecan topping, in small saucepan combine brown sugar, butter, water, and cornstarch. Cook and stir over medium heat until bubbly. Stir in pecans. Spread warm pecan mixture over hot crust. Bake for 5 minutes more. Cool pie on a wire rack. Cover and refrigerate any leftovers.

Nutrition Facts per serving: 500 cal., 28 g total fat (7 g sat. fat), 8 mg chol., 169 mg sodium, 61 g carbo., 4 g fiber, 5 g pro.
Daily Values: 16% vit. A, 14% vit. C, 3% calcium, 11% iron
Exchanges: 1 Fruit, 3 Other Carbo., 5 Fat

Peach Pie: Prepare as at left, except omit the pecan topping.

Nutrition Facts per serving: 381 cal., 17 g total fat (4 g sat. fat), 0 mg chol., 219 mg sodium, 54 g carbo., 3 g fiber, 4 g pro.
Daily Values: 14% vit. A, 14% vit. C, 1% calcium, 9% iron
Exchanges: 1 Fruit, 2½ Other Carbo., 3 Fat

Custard Pie

Prep: 25 minutes **Bake:** 52 minutes
Oven: 450°/350°F **Makes:** 8 servings

- 1 **recipe Pastry for Single-Crust Pie (page 416)**
- 4 **eggs**
- ½ **cup sugar**
- 2 **teaspoons vanilla**
- ⅛ **teaspoon salt**
- ⅛ **teaspoon ground nutmeg**
- 2 **cups half-and-half, light cream, or milk**

1. Prepare and roll out Pastry for Single-Crust Pie. Line a 9-inch pie plate with pastry (see photo 2, page 417), trim (see photo 3, page 417), and crimp edge as desired (see photos 5, 6, and 7, page 417). Line pastry with a double thickness of foil (see photo, above right). Bake in a 450° oven for 8 minutes. Remove foil. Bake 4 to 5 minutes more or until set and dry. Remove crust from oven; reduce the oven temperature to 350°.

2. Meanwhile, for filling, in a medium mixing bowl slightly beat eggs with a rotary beater or fork. Stir in sugar, vanilla, salt, and nutmeg. Gradually stir in half-and-half until mixture is thoroughly combined.

3. Place partially baked pastry shell on the oven rack. Carefully pour filling into the pastry shell.

4. To prevent overbrowning, cover edge of pie with foil (see photo, page 399). Bake in a 350° oven for 25 minutes. Remove foil. Bake for 15 to 20 minutes more or until a knife inserted near the center comes out clean. Cool on a wire rack. Serve warm (cool on wire rack for 1 hour) or chilled (refrigerate within 2 hours). Cover and refrigerate any remaining pie.

Nutrition Facts per serving: 305 cal., 18 g total fat (7 g sat. fat), 128 mg chol., 166 mg sodium, 29 g carbo., 0 g fiber, 7 g pro.
Daily Values: 8% vit. A, 1% vit. C, 8% calcium, 7% iron
Exchanges: 2 Other Carbo., 3½ Fat

Coconut Custard Pie: Prepare as above, except stir in ½ cup toasted coconut with the half-and-half.

Nutrition Facts per serving: 340 cal., 21 g total fat (10 g sat. fat), 128 mg chol., 188 mg sodium, 32 g carbo., 1 g fiber, 7 g pro.
Daily Values: 8% vit. A, 1% vit. C, 8% calcium, 7% iron
Exchanges: 2 Other Carbo., 4 Fat

When partially baking a crust, first line it with a double thickness of foil or a single layer of heavy foil. The foil prevents the crust from shrinking.

Making and Storing Custard Pie

To make a smooth, velvety custard pie, follow these tips.

■ Don't skip partially baking the pastry shell. The delicate custard can't bake at the higher temperature that is required to make a golden brown, flaky crust.

■ To avoid spills, place the partially baked pastry shell on the oven rack before adding the custard filling. Carefully pour filling into the pastry shell.

■ Because the filling continues to set after it is removed from the oven, a custard pie is done if the amount of liquid in the center is smaller than a quarter. Another way to test doneness is to insert a knife near the pie's center. If it comes out clean, the pie is done. (The knife test may cause the filling to crack.) Overbaking a custard pie may cause the filling to weep.

■ Cool pie on a wire rack for 1 hour. Cover with plastic wrap and refrigerate up to 2 days. Custard pies don't maintain a smooth, creamy texture if frozen.

Caramel-Pecan Pumpkin Pie `Best Loved`

Prep: 25 minutes **Bake:** 45 minutes
Oven: 375°F **Makes:** 8 servings

> 1 **recipe Pastry for Single-Crust Pie (page 416)**
> 2 **slightly beaten eggs**
> 1 **15-ounce can pumpkin**
> ¼ **cup half-and-half, light cream, or milk**
> ¾ **cup granulated sugar**
> 1 **tablespoon all-purpose flour**
> 1 **teaspoon finely shredded lemon peel**
> ½ **teaspoon vanilla**
> ¼ **teaspoon salt**
> ¼ **teaspoon ground cinnamon**
> ¼ **teaspoon ground nutmeg**
> ⅛ **teaspoon ground allspice**
> ½ **cup packed brown sugar**
> ½ **cup chopped pecans**
> 2 **tablespoons butter, softened**

1. Prepare and roll out Pastry for Single-Crust Pie. Line a 9-inch pie plate with pastry (see photo 2, page 417). Trim (see photo 3, page 417); crimp edge as desired (see photos 5, 6, and 7, page 417). In a large bowl stir together eggs, pumpkin, and half-and-half. Stir in the granulated sugar, flour, lemon peel, vanilla, salt, cinnamon, nutmeg, and allspice. Pour pumpkin mixture into pastry-lined pie plate. To prevent overbrowning, cover edge of pie with foil (see photo, page 399). Bake in a 375° oven for 25 minutes.

2. Meanwhile, in a medium bowl stir together the brown sugar, pecans, and butter until combined. Remove foil. Sprinkle brown sugar mixture over top of pie. Bake for 20 minutes more or until a knife inserted near the center comes out clean and topping is golden and bubbly. Cool on a wire rack. Cover and refrigerate within 2 hours.

Nutrition Facts per serving: 386 cal., 19 g total fat (5 g sat. fat), 64 mg chol., 204 mg sodium, 52 g carbo., 3 g fiber, 5 g pro.
Daily Values: 239% vit. A, 5% vit. C, 5% calcium, 12% iron
Exchanges: 3½ Other Carbo., 3½ Fat

Pumpkin Pie `Best Loved`

Rather than measuring individual spices, you can use 1½ teaspoons pumpkin pie spice instead.

Prep: 30 minutes **Bake:** 50 minutes
Oven: 375°F **Makes:** 8 servings

> 1 **recipe Pastry for Single-Crust Pie (page 416)**
> 1 **15-ounce can pumpkin**
> ½ **cup sugar**
> 1 **teaspoon ground cinnamon**
> ½ **teaspoon ground ginger**
> ¼ **teaspoon ground nutmeg**
> 2 **slightly beaten eggs**
> ¾ **cup half-and-half, light cream, or milk**

1. Prepare and roll out Pastry for Single-Crust Pie. Line a 9-inch pie plate with the pastry (see photo 2, page 417). Trim (see photo 3, page 417); crimp edge as desired (see photos 5, 6, and 7, page 417).

2. For filling, in a medium bowl combine pumpkin, sugar, cinnamon, ginger, and nutmeg. Add eggs; beat lightly with a fork just until combined. Gradually add half-and-half; stir until combined.

3. Place the pastry-lined pie plate on the oven rack. Carefully pour filling into the pastry shell.

4. To prevent overbrowning, cover edge of the pie with foil (see photo, page 399). Bake in a 375° oven for 25 minutes. Remove foil. Bake about 25 minutes more or until a knife inserted near the center comes out clean. Cool on a wire rack. Cover and refrigerate within 2 hours.

Nutrition Facts per serving: 255 cal., 13 g total fat (4 g sat. fat), 61 mg chol., 94 mg sodium, 31 g carbo., 2 g fiber, 5 g pro.
Daily Values: 238% vit. A, 4% vit. C, 5% calcium, 11% iron
Exchanges: 2 Other Carbo., 2½ Fat

Caramel-Pecan Pumpkin Pie

Sweet Potato Pie

This Southern classic is similar in appearance to pumpkin pie; it just tastes slightly less sweet.

Prep: 45 minutes **Bake:** 35 minutes **Oven:** 375°F
Cool: 30 minutes **Makes:** 8 servings

- 1 recipe Baked Pastry Shell (page 416)
- 2 cups cooked, mashed sweet potatoes* or one 17-ounce can sweet potatoes, drained and mashed
- ½ cup sugar
- ½ teaspoon ground cinnamon
- ¼ teaspoon ground allspice
- ¼ teaspoon ground nutmeg
- ⅛ teaspoon salt
- 3 slightly beaten eggs
- 1 cup buttermilk or dairy sour cream
  Whipped cream (optional)

1. Prepare Baked Pastry Shell; set aside.

2. Meanwhile, for filling, in a large bowl stir together sweet potatoes, sugar, cinnamon, allspice, nutmeg, and salt. Add eggs. Beat lightly with a fork just until combined. Gradually stir in buttermilk until thoroughly combined.

3. Place the Baked Pastry Shell on the oven rack. Carefully pour filling into pastry shell.

4. To prevent overbrowning, cover edge of pie with foil. Bake in a 375° oven for 35 to 40 minutes or until a knife inserted near the center comes out clean and edges are puffed. If necessary, remove foil the last 5 to 10 minutes to allow pastry to brown. Cool on a wire rack for 30 minutes. Cover and refrigerate within 2 hours. If desired, serve with whipped cream.

*Note: To cook sweet potatoes, see page 544.

Nutrition Facts per serving: 315 cal., 11 g total fat (3 g sat. fat), 81 mg chol., 176 mg sodium, 48 g carbo., 2 g fiber, 7 g pro.
Daily Values: 285% vit. A, 24% vit. C, 7% calcium, 9% iron
Exchanges: 1 Starch, 2 Other Carbo., 2 Fat

Pecan Pie Best Loved

Prep: 25 minutes **Bake:** 45 minutes
Oven: 350°F **Makes:** 8 servings

- 1 recipe Pastry for Single-Crust Pie (page 416)
- 3 slightly beaten eggs
- 1 cup corn syrup
- ⅔ cup sugar
- ⅓ cup butter or margarine, melted
- 1 teaspoon vanilla
- 1¼ cups pecan halves or chopped macadamia nuts

1. Prepare and roll out pastry for Single-Crust Pie. Line a 9-inch pie plate with the pastry (see photo 2, page 417). Trim (see photo 3, page 417); crimp edge as desired (see photos 5, 6, and 7, page 417).

2. For filling, combine eggs, corn syrup, sugar, butter, and vanilla. Mix well; stir in pecan halves.

3. Place the pastry-lined pie plate on the oven rack. Carefully pour the filling into pastry shell.

4. To prevent overbrowning, cover edge of the pie with foil (see photo, page 399). Bake in a 350° oven for 25 minutes. Remove foil. Bake for 20 to 25 minutes more or until a knife inserted near the center comes out clean. Cool on a wire rack. Cover and refrigerate within 2 hours.

Nutrition Facts per serving: 532 cal., 31 g total fat (9 g sat. fat), 101 mg chol., 227 mg sodium, 63 g carbo., 2 g fiber, 6 g pro.
Daily Values: 9% vit. A, 3% calcium, 9% iron
Exchanges: 4 Other Carbo., 6 Fat

Pie Pans and Pie Plates

Because glass pie plates and dull metal pie pans absorb and retain heat evenly, they are ideal choices for beautifully browned piecrusts. Ceramic and clay pie plates also have these desirable qualities. Shiny metal pie pans—which work well for crumb crusts—can cause the bottom pastry crust to turn out soggy because they absorb the heat more slowly.

Check the size of your pie plates. Standard pie plates come in 8-, 9- and 10-inch sizes. The most common pie plate is 9 inches in diameter (measure pie plate from the inside top rim to the opposite side), 1½ inches deep, and will hold about 3¾ cups of liquid. If your pie plate holds less liquid, you may need to adjust the amount of filling and baking time given in these recipes.

Disposable foil pans usually are smaller than standard pie plates, although foil deep-dish pie pans are closer to the standard.

Tart Pans

Tart pans guarantee beautifully scalloped pastry edges—with little effort or skill. Tart pans come two ways: with a fixed bottom or with a removable bottom. Both forms come in shiny tinned steel, blue or black steel, and nonstick finishes. Although all three finishes produce even, well-browned crusts, the blue steel may brown the crust more rapidly, so it may require reducing the oven temperature. The tinned steel variety is the most common and widely available.

Lemon Meringue Pie Best Loved

Prep: 40 minutes **Bake:** 15 minutes **Oven:** 350°F
Cool: 1 hour **Chill:** 3 hours **Makes:** 8 servings

> 1 **recipe Baked Pastry Shell (page 416)**
> 3 **eggs**
> 1½ **cups sugar**
> 3 **tablespoons all-purpose flour**
> 3 **tablespoons cornstarch**
> 2 **tablespoons butter or margarine**
> 1 **to 2 teaspoons finely shredded lemon peel**
> ⅓ **cup lemon juice**
> 1 **recipe Meringue for Pie (page 418)**

1. Prepare Baked Pastry Shell; set aside. Separate egg yolks from whites; set whites aside for meringue.

2. For filling, in a medium saucepan combine sugar, flour, cornstarch, and dash *salt*. Gradually stir in 1½ cups *water*. Cook and stir over medium-high heat until mixture is thickened and bubbly: reduce heat. Cook and stir for 2 minutes more. Remove from heat. Slightly beat egg yolks with a rotary beater or fork. Gradually stir about 1 cup of the hot filling into yolks. Return egg yolk mixture to saucepan. Bring to a gentle boil. Reduce heat; cook and stir 2 minutes more. Remove from heat. Stir in butter and lemon peel. Gently stir in lemon juice. Keep filling warm; prepare Meringue for Pie.

3. Pour warm filling into Baked Pastry Shell. Spread meringue over warm filling; seal to edge (see photo, below). Bake in a 350° oven for 15 minutes. Cool on wire rack 1 hour. Chill for 3 to 6 hours before serving; cover for longer storage (see tip, page 407).

Nutrition Facts per serving: 395 cal., 14 g total fat (5 g sat. fat), 88 mg chol., 182 mg sodium, 65 g carbo., 1 g fiber, 5 g pro.
Daily Values: 5% vit. A, 8% vit. C, 2% calcium, 7% iron
Exchanges: 4½ Other Carbo., 2½ Fat

Spread meringue over warm pie filling, carefully pushing the meringue to the crimped pastry edge to seal well and prevent shrinking.

Key Lime Pie Best Loved

Key limes grow only in Florida and the Caribbean; Persian limes grow in many locales and are available in most markets.

Prep: 25 minutes **Bake:** 30 minutes **Oven:** 325°/350°F
Cool: 1 hour **Chill:** 3 hours **Makes:** 8 servings

> 1 **recipe Baked Pastry Shell (page 416)**
> 3 **eggs**
> 1 **14-ounce can (1¼ cups) sweetened condensed milk**
> ½ **cup lime juice (10 to 12 Key limes or 4 to 6 Persian limes) or bottled Key lime juice**
> 3 **tablespoons water**
> **Few drops green food coloring (optional)**
> 1 **recipe Meringue for Pie (page 418)**

1. Prepare Baked Pastry Shell; set aside. Separate egg yolks from whites; set whites aside for meringue.

2. For filling, in a medium bowl beat egg yolks with a wire whisk or fork. Gradually whisk or stir in sweetened condensed milk; add lime juice, water, and, if desired, food coloring. Mix well (mixture will thicken).

3. Spoon thickened filling into Baked Pastry Shell. Bake in a 325° oven for 15 minutes. Meanwhile, prepare Meringue for Pie. Remove pie from oven. Increase the oven temperature to 350°. Spread meringue over hot filling; seal to edge (see photo, left). Bake in 350° oven for 15 minutes. Cool on a wire rack for 1 hour. Chill for 3 to 6 hours before serving; cover for longer storage.

Nutrition Facts per serving: 368 cal., 15 g total fat (5 g sat. fat), 97 mg chol., 160 mg sodium, 51 g carbo., 1 g fiber, 8 g pro.
Daily Values: 6% vit. A, 10% vit. C, 15% calcium, 6% iron
Exchanges: 1 Starch, 3 Fat

Key Lime Pie with Whipped Cream Topping:

Prepare as above, except omit meringue; set aside the 3 egg whites for another use. Spoon filling into Baked Pastry Shell. Bake in a 350° oven for 25 minutes. Cool on a wire rack for 1 hour. Cover and chill pie for 3 to 4 hours. Meanwhile, prepare 1 recipe Whipped Cream (page 260). Spread over chilled pie.

Nutrition Facts per serving: 442 cal., 26 g total fat (12 g sat. fat), 138 mg chol., 151 mg sodium, 46 g carbo., 0 g fiber, 8 g pro.
Daily Values: 15% vit. A, 10% vit. C, 17% calcium, 6% iron
Exchanges: 3 Other Carbo., 5 Fat

Vanilla Cream Pie

If you wish, skip the meringue and top the chilled pie with Whipped Cream (page 260).

Prep: 45 minutes **Bake:** 30 minutes **Oven:** 325°F
Cool: 1 hour **Chill:** 3 hours **Makes:** 8 servings

- 1 **recipe Baked Pastry Shell (page 416)**
- 4 **eggs**
- ¾ **cup sugar**
- ¼ **cup cornstarch**
- 2½ **cups half-and-half, light cream, or milk**
- 1 **tablespoon butter or margarine**
- 1½ **teaspoons vanilla**
- 1 **recipe Four Egg White Meringue (page 418)**

1. Prepare Baked Pastry Shell. Separate egg yolks from whites; set whites aside for meringue.

2. For filling, in a medium saucepan combine sugar and cornstarch. Gradually stir in half-and-half. Cook and stir over medium-high heat until thickened and bubbly; reduce heat. Cook and stir for 2 minutes more. Remove from heat. Slightly beat egg yolks with a rotary beater or fork. Gradually stir about 1 cup of the hot filling into yolks. Add egg yolk mixture to filling in saucepan. Bring to a gentle boil; reduce heat. Cook and stir for 2 minutes more. Remove from heat. Stir in butter and vanilla. Keep filling warm; prepare meringue.

3. Pour warm filling into Baked Pastry Shell. Spread meringue over warm filling; seal to edge (see photo, page 406). Bake in a 325° oven for 30 minutes. Cool on a wire rack 1 hour. Chill 3 to 6 hours before serving; cover for longer storage.

Microwave directions: Prepare as above through step 1. For filling, in a 1½-quart microwave-safe casserole combine sugar and cornstarch. Stir in half-and-half. Microwave, uncovered, on 100 percent power (high) for 7 to 9 minutes or until thickened and bubbly, stirring every 2 minutes until slightly thickened, then every 30 seconds. Microwave, uncovered, 1 minute more, stirring once. In a bowl beat egg yolks with a rotary beater or fork. Gradually stir 1 cup of the hot mixture into beaten egg yolks. Add egg yolk mixture to hot mixture in casserole. Microwave, uncovered, 1 to 2 minutes more or until edges are bubbly, stirring every 30 seconds. Microwave 30 seconds more. Stir in butter and vanilla. Keep filling warm; prepare meringue. Continue with step 3 above.

Nutrition Facts per serving: 425 cal., 21 g total fat (9 g sat. fat), 138 mg chol., 151 mg sodium, 51 g carbo., 1 g fiber, 7 g pro.
Daily Values: 11% vit. A, 1% vit. C, 10% calcium, 7% iron
Exchanges: 3½ Other Carbo., 4 Fat

Coconut Cream Pie: Prepare as at left, except stir in 1 cup flaked coconut with butter and vanilla. Sprinkle another ⅓ cup flaked coconut over meringue before baking.

Nutrition Facts per serving: 482 cal., 25 g total fat (13 g sat. fat), 138 mg chol., 154 mg sodium, 56 g carbo., 1 g fiber, 8 g pro.
Daily Values: 11% vit. A, 1% vit. C, 10% calcium, 8% iron
Exchanges: 4 Other Carbo., 5 Fat

Banana Cream Pie: Prepare as at left, except before adding filling, arrange 3 medium bananas, sliced (about 2¼ cups), over bottom of shell.

Nutrition Facts per serving: 466 cal., 22 g total fat (9 g sat. fat), 138 mg chol., 151 mg sodium, 62 g carbo., 2 g fiber, 8 g pro.
Daily Values: 12% vit. A, 8% vit. C, 10% calcium, 7% iron
Exchanges: ½ Fruit, 3½ Other Carbo., 4 Fat

Dark Chocolate Cream Pie: Prepare as at left, except increase the sugar to 1 cup. Stir in 3 ounces chopped unsweetened chocolate with the half-and-half.

Sour Cream-Raisin Pie: Prepare as at left, except decrease sugar to ⅔ cup and increase the cornstarch to ⅓ cup. Fold in 1 cup raisins and ½ cup dairy sour cream with the butter and vanilla. Heat filling mixture through (do not boil).

Nutrition Facts per serving for chocolate or raisin variation:
504 cal., 27 g total fat (13 g sat. fat), 138 mg chol., 153 mg sodium, 60 g carbo., 2 g fiber, 8 g pro.
Daily Values: 11% vit. A, 1% vit. C, 10% calcium, 10% iron
Exchanges: 4 Other Carbo., 5½ Fat

Storing and Serving Cream Pies

Storing pies topped with meringue or whipped cream can be tricky. Here's the scoop for making sure your pie comes out of the refrigerator as beautifully as it went in.

■ To store a meringue-topped cream pie, let it cool 1 hour, then refrigerate. Chill it for 3 to 6 hours before serving; there's no need to cover it unless you're going to store it longer.

■ For longer storage, insert wooden toothpicks into meringue halfway between the center and edge of the pie; loosely drape clear plastic wrap over the toothpicks. Refrigerate for up to 2 days. Refrigerate whipped cream-topped pies for up to 4 hours. Do not freeze cream pies.

■ To easily cut a meringue-topped cream pie, dip the knife in water (don't dry it off) before cutting each slice of pie. This prevents the meringue from clinging to the knife.

Strawberry Chiffon Pie

Prep: 30 minutes **Chill:** 4 hours **Makes:** 8 servings

 1 recipe Baked Pastry Shell (page 416)
 1 envelope unflavored gelatin
 ⅓ cup cold water
 ¾ to 1 cup sugar
 3 egg yolks
 3 tablespoons lemon juice
 Dash salt
 2½ cups fresh strawberries, crushed (about 1½ cups after crushing)
 Dried egg whites equivalent to 3 fresh egg whites (see tip, below) or 1 cup whipping cream

1. Prepare Baked Pastry Shell; set aside. In a small saucepan stir gelatin into cold water. Let stand 1 minute. Add sugar, egg yolks, lemon juice, and salt. Cook mixture over medium heat, stirring constantly, until mixture begins to boil; remove from heat. Transfer gelatin mixture to a medium bowl; stir in crushed strawberries. Cover and chill until mixture mounds when spooned, stirring occasionally.

2. In a medium mixing bowl prepare and beat dried egg white product to stiff peaks according to package directions, or whip the cream to soft peaks. With a wooden spoon or rubber spatula, gently fold egg white mixture or whipped cream into strawberry mixture. Spoon filling into cooled crust. Cover and refrigerate at least 4 hours or until filling is firm. If desired, garnish with halved *strawberries* and *strawberry* or *mint leaves*.

Nutrition Facts per serving: 252 cal., 11 g total fat (3 g sat. fat), 80 mg chol., 103 mg sodium, 35 g carbo., 2 g fiber, 4 g pro.
Daily Values: 3% vit. A, 47% vit. C, 2% calcium, 7% iron
Exchanges: 2½ Other Carbo., 2 Fat

Egg White Products

Dried and liquid egg whites: Use these pasteurized products in dessert recipes requiring little or no baking because the pasteurization process makes them safe to eat. Have patience when beating; it takes more time to reach desired volume and consistency. Check the dairy case for liquid whites and the baking supply section for dried whites.

Meringue powder: Pasteurized dried egg whites, sugar, and edible gums compose this powder. Just add additional sugar and water and beat for a fluffy meringue. The added gums make the meringue more stable. It's available in bakers' catalogs and specialty stores.

Chocolate and Peanut Butter Pie

Prep: 25 minutes **Chill:** 2 hours **Makes:** 10 servings

 1 recipe Chocolate Wafer Crust (page 418)
 1 8-ounce package cream cheese, softened
 ¾ cup peanut butter
 1 cup sifted powdered sugar
 2 tablespoons milk
 1 teaspoon vanilla
 1 cup whipping cream
 2 tablespoons sifted powdered sugar
 ¾ cup miniature semisweet chocolate pieces
 Coarsely chopped peanuts (optional)

1. Prepare Chocolate Wafer Crust; set aside. Chill a medium mixing bowl and beaters.

2. For filling, beat cream cheese and peanut butter until smooth. Add the 1 cup powdered sugar, milk, and vanilla; beat until combined.

3. In the chilled mixing bowl beat whipping cream and the 2 tablespoons powdered sugar until soft peaks form. Gently fold about one-third of the whipped cream into the peanut butter mixture. Fold remaining whipped cream and miniature chocolate pieces into peanut butter mixture. Spoon into Chocolate Wafer Crust. If desired, sprinkle with peanuts. Cover and chill about 2 hours or until set.

Nutrition Facts per serving: 512 cal., 39 g total fat (18 g sat. fat), 77 mg chol., 343 mg sodium, 32 g carbo., 3 g fiber, 8 g pro.
Daily Values: 18% vit. A, 5% calcium, 5% iron
Exchanges: 2 Other Carbo., 8 Fat

French Silk Pie Best Loved

Prep: 40 minutes **Chill:** 5 hours **Makes:** 8 servings

 1 recipe Baked Pastry Shell (page 416)
 1 cup whipping cream
 1 cup semisweet chocolate pieces (6 ounces)
 ⅓ cup butter
 ⅓ cup sugar
 2 beaten egg yolks
 3 tablespoons crème de cacao or whipping cream
 1 cup whipped cream
 Chocolate curls (optional)

1. Prepare Baked Pastry Shell; set aside. Meanwhile, in a medium heavy saucepan combine the 1 cup whipping cream, the chocolate pieces, butter, and sugar. Cook over low heat, stirring constantly, until chocolate is melted (about 10 minutes). Remove from heat.

Gradually stir half of the chocolate mixture into beaten egg yolks. Return egg mixture to chocolate mixture in saucepan. Cook over medium-low heat, stirring constantly, until mixture is slightly thickened and begins to bubble (about 5 minutes). Remove from heat. (Mixture may appear to separate.) Stir in the crème de cacao. Place the saucepan in a bowl of ice water, stirring occasionally, until the mixture stiffens and becomes hard to stir (about 20 minutes). Transfer chocolate mixture to a medium mixing bowl.

2. Beat cooled chocolate mixture with an electric mixer on medium to high speed for 2 to 3 minutes or until light and fluffy. Spread filling in the Baked Pastry Shell. Cover and refrigerate pie for 5 to 24 hours. To serve, top with whipped cream. If desired, garnish with chocolate curls.

Nutrition Facts per serving: 533 cal., 41 g total fat (21 g sat. fat), 137 mg chol., 168 mg sodium, 31 g carbo., 3 g fiber, 4 g pro.
Daily Values: 21% vit. A, 4% calcium, 6% iron
Exchanges: 2 Other Carbo., 8 Fat

Chocolate Bar Pie Best Loved

Prep: 45 minutes **Bake:** 10 minutes **Oven:** 325°F
Freeze: 5 hours **Stand:** 10 minutes **Makes:** 8 servings

> 6 1- to 1½-ounce bars milk chocolate with almonds, chopped
> 15 large marshmallows or 1½ cups tiny marshmallows
> ½ cup milk
> 1 recipe Walnut Crust
> 1 cup whipping cream
> ½ teaspoon vanilla
>   Whipped cream (optional)
>   Coarsely chopped milk chocolate bars with almonds (optional)

1. Chill a large mixing bowl and beaters. Meanwhile, for filling, in a medium saucepan combine the 6 chopped chocolate bars, the marshmallows, and milk. Cook and stir over medium-low heat until chocolate is melted. Remove from heat. Let the chocolate mixture stand until cooled to room temperature.

2. Prepare Walnut Crust; set aside.

3. In the chilled mixing bowl beat the 1 cup cream and the vanilla with an electric mixer on medium speed until soft peaks form (tips curl). Fold whipped cream mixture into cooled chocolate mixture. Spoon chocolate mixture into crust. Freeze about 5 hours or until firm.

4. To serve, remove from the freezer and let stand about 10 minutes before cutting into wedges.* If desired, garnish with additional whipped cream and chopped chocolate bars.

Walnut Crust: In a medium bowl combine 1½ cups coarsely ground walnuts (6 ounces), 3 tablespoons melted butter or margarine, and 2 tablespoons sugar. Press onto the bottom and sides of a 9-inch pie plate. Bake in a 325° oven about 10 minutes or until edge is golden brown. Cool on a wire rack.

*Note: For easier serving, set the pie on a warm, damp towel for a few minutes.

Nutrition Facts per serving: 455 cal., 35 g total fat (14 g sat. fat), 57 mg chol., 90 mg sodium, 29 g carbo., 2 g fiber, 9 g pro.
Daily Values: 14% vit. A, 2% vit. C, 9% calcium, 6% iron
Exchanges: 2 Other Carbo., 7 Fat

Brownie-Walnut Pie

Prep: 40 minutes **Bake:** 50 minutes
Oven: 350°F **Makes:** 8 servings

> ½ cup butter or margarine
> 3 ounces unsweetened chocolate, cut up
> 1 recipe Pastry for Single-Crust Pie (page 416)
> 3 beaten eggs
> 1½ cups sugar
> ½ cup all-purpose flour
> 1 teaspoon vanilla
> 1 cup chopped walnuts
> 1 recipe Hot Fudge Sauce (page 483) or fresh fruit, such as raspberries, sliced strawberries, or sliced peaches (optional)

1. For filling, in a small heavy saucepan melt butter and chocolate over low heat, stirring frequently. Cool 20 minutes.

2. Meanwhile, prepare and roll out Pastry for Single-Crust Pie. Line a 9-inch pie plate with the pastry (see photo 2, page 417). Trim (see photo 3, page 417), and crimp edge as desired (see photos 5, 6, and 7, page 417).

3. In a bowl combine eggs, sugar, flour, and vanilla; stir in the cooled chocolate mixture and nuts.

4. Pour filling into the pastry-lined pie plate. Bake in a 350° oven for 50 to 55 minutes or until a knife inserted near the center comes out clean. Cool on a wire rack. If desired, serve with Hot Fudge Sauce or fresh fruit.

Nutrition Facts per serving: 597 cal., 38 g total fat (15 g sat. fat), 113 mg chol., 223 mg sodium, 61 g carbo., 3 g fiber, 8 g pro.
Daily Values: 12% vit. A, 4% calcium, 14% iron
Exchanges: 4 Other Carbo., 7½ Fat

Fudge Ribbon Pie Best Loved

If you're short on time, streamline this recipe by using purchased fudge ice cream topping and replacing the meringue topping with Whipped Cream (page 260).

Prep: 50 minutes **Freeze:** several hours **Bake:** 3 minutes
Oven: 475°F **Makes:** 8 servings

- 1 recipe Baked Pastry Shell (page 416)
- 1 cup sugar
- 1 5-ounce can (⅔ cup) evaporated milk
- 2 tablespoons butter or margarine
- 2 ounces unsweetened chocolate, cut up
- 1 teaspoon vanilla
- 2 pints (4 cups) peppermint ice cream
- ¾ cup sugar
- ½ cup boiling water
- ¼ cup meringue powder (see tip, page 408)
- ¼ cup crushed peppermint-stick candy

1. Prepare Baked Pastry Shell; set aside. For fudge sauce, in a small saucepan combine the 1 cup sugar, the evaporated milk, butter, and chocolate. Cook and stir over medium heat until bubbly. Reduce heat and boil gently for 4 to 5 minutes, stirring occasionally, until mixture is thickened and reduced to 1½ cups. Remove from heat; stir in vanilla. If necessary, beat until smooth with wire whisk or rotary beater. Set aside to cool completely.

2. In a chilled bowl, stir 1 pint of the ice cream until softened. Spread into cooled Baked Pastry Shell. Cover with half of the cooled fudge sauce. Freeze until nearly firm. Repeat with remaining ice cream and fudge sauce. Return to freezer while preparing meringue.

3. In a medium mixing bowl dissolve the ¾ cup sugar in the boiling water. Cool to room temperature. Add the meringue powder. Beat on low speed until combined; beat on high speed until stiff peaks form (tips stand straight). By hand, fold 3 tablespoons of the crushed candy into the meringue. Spread meringue over chocolate sauce layer, sealing to edge. Sprinkle top with remaining crushed candy. Freeze until firm (several hours or overnight). Bake in a 475° oven for 3 to 4 minutes or just until meringue is lightly browned. Cover loosely and return to freezer for a few hours or overnight before serving.

Nutrition Facts per serving: 564 cal., 24 g total fat (12 g sat. fat), 43 mg chol., 198 mg sodium, 83 g carbo., 2 g fiber, 6 g pro.
Daily Values: 3% vit. A, 1% vit. C, 10% calcium, 7% iron
Exchanges: 5½ Other Carbo., 4½ Fat

Peanutty Ice Cream Pie

Prep: 30 minutes **Freeze:** 6 hours **Makes:** 8 servings

- 1½ cups coarsely ground peanuts
- 3 tablespoons butter or margarine, melted
- 2 tablespoons sugar
- ¼ cup flaked coconut
- ¼ cup light-colored corn syrup
- ¼ cup peanut butter
- 3 tablespoons chopped peanuts
- 1 quart vanilla ice cream
  Chopped candy-coated milk chocolate pieces or peanuts (optional)

1. Lightly grease a 9-inch pie plate. In a medium bowl combine ground peanuts, butter, and sugar. Press mixture firmly onto bottom and up sides of the prepared pie plate. Chill for 15 minutes.

2. Meanwhile, for filling, in a small bowl stir together coconut, corn syrup, peanut butter, and the 3 tablespoons chopped peanuts. Place ice cream in a large chilled bowl; stir ice cream just to soften. Stir in the coconut mixture just until combined. Spoon into chilled crust. If desired, sprinkle chopped chocolate pieces or peanuts over pie. Cover; freeze about 6 hours or until firm. Remove from freezer and place the pie on a warm, damp towel for a few minutes before cutting into wedges.

Nutrition Facts per serving: 493 cal., 36 g total fat (14 g sat. fat), 57 mg chol., 269 mg sodium, 36 g carbo., 3 g fiber, 13 g pro.
Daily Values: 13% vit. A, 1% vit. C, 12% calcium, 4% iron
Exchanges: 2½ Other Carbo., 7 Fat

Fudge Ribbon Pie

Country Peach Tart

Prep: 30 minutes **Bake:** 35 minutes **Oven:** 375°F
Cool: 30 minutes **Makes:** 8 servings

   1 **recipe Pastry for Single-Crust Pie (page 416)**
  ¼ **cup granulated sugar**
   4 **teaspoons all-purpose flour**
  ¼ **teaspoon ground nutmeg**
   3 **cups sliced, peeled peaches or nectarines (1½ pounds)**
   1 **tablespoon lemon juice**
   1 **tablespoon sliced almonds**
     Milk
     Sifted powdered sugar
     Whipped cream (optional)

1. Prepare pastry for Single-Crust Pie; set aside. Line a baking sheet with foil; sprinkle lightly with flour. Roll pastry to a 13-inch circle on prepared baking sheet.

2. In a large bowl stir together granulated sugar, the 4 teaspoons flour, and nutmeg. Add peaches and lemon juice; toss gently until coated. Mound peach mixture in center of pastry, leaving a 2-inch border. Fold border up over peaches (see photo, right). Sprinkle center with sliced almonds. Lightly brush top and sides of the crust with milk.

3. Bake in a 375° oven for 35 to 40 minutes or until crust is golden and filling is bubbly. If necessary, cover edge with foil the last 5 to 10 minutes of baking to prevent overbrowning (see photo, page 399). Cool 30 minutes on the baking sheet. Dust edges with powdered sugar. If desired, serve with whipped cream.

Country Pear Tart: Prepare 1 recipe Browned Butter Pastry (page 416). Prepare filling as above, except substitute 4 cups sliced, peeled pears (1½ pounds) for the peaches and 1 tablespoon finely chopped crystallized ginger or ¼ teaspoon ground ginger for the nutmeg. Assemble tart as above, except after brushing pastry edges with milk, sprinkle with additional granulated or coarse sugar. Bake as directed. Do not dust with powdered sugar.

Nutrition Facts per serving for peach or pear variation: 205 cal., 9 g total fat (2 g sat. fat), 0 mg chol., 74 mg sodium, 29 g carbo., 2 g fiber, 3 g pro.
Daily Values: 7% vit. A, 8% vit. C, 1% calcium, 5% iron
Exchanges: 1 Fruit, 1 Other Carbo., 1½ Fat

Using your fingers, carefully fold the pastry border up and over the peaches, pleating the pastry as necessary to lie flat against the filling.

Raspberry-Lemon Tartlets

Prep: 35 minutes **Bake:** 15 minutes **Oven:** 375°F
Chill: 1½ hours **Makes:** 4 servings

     Nonstick cooking spray
   1 **recipe Poppy Seed Pastry**
  ¼ **cup apple jelly**
   2 **teaspoons water**
  ½ **recipe Lemon Curd (page 260) or 1 cup purchased lemon curd**
   2 **to 2½ cups fresh raspberries or blueberries**

1. Coat four 4- to 4¼-inch tart pans with nonstick cooking spray. Prepare Poppy Seed Pastry; divide into 4 equal portions. Wrap and chill 3 portions. Press remaining portion of pastry onto bottom and up the sides of a prepared tart pan. Repeat with remaining pastry. Generously prick bottom and sides of pastry in each tart pan.

2. Bake in a 375° oven for 15 to 17 minutes or until golden. Cool completely on a wire rack.

3. In a small saucepan combine jelly and water. Cook and stir until jelly is melted; cool slightly. Spread Lemon Curd into pastry shells. Top with berries; brush gently with jelly. Cover and chill in refrigerator for 1 to 4 hours before serving.

Poppy Seed Pastry: In a medium bowl stir together 1¼ cups all-purpose flour and ¼ cup sugar. Using a pastry blender, cut in ½ cup cold butter until pieces are pea-size. In a small bowl combine 2 beaten egg yolks, 1 tablespoon water, and 1 teaspoon poppy seeds. Gradually stir the egg yolk mixture into flour mixture. (Dough will not be completely moistened.) Using your fingers, gently knead the dough in bowl just until a ball forms. Cover dough with plastic wrap and chill for 30 to 60 minutes or until dough is easy to handle.

Nutrition Facts per serving: 716 cal., 31 g total fat (18 g sat. fat), 217 mg chol., 303 mg sodium, 108 g carbo., 11 g fiber, 6 g pro.
Daily Values: 23% vit. A, 26% vit. C, 5% calcium, 15% iron
Exchanges: ½ Fruit, 6½ Other Carbo., 6 Fat

Harvest Fruit Tart

Prep: 35 minutes **Bake:** 45 minutes
Oven: 375°F **Makes:** 12 servings

>   1 **recipe Pastry for Lattice-Top Pie (page 417)**
> 1⅔ **cups apple juice or apple cider**
>   ¾ **cup snipped dried apricots or peaches**
>   ¾ **cup snipped dried pitted plums (prunes)**
>   ½ **cup dried tart cherries or raisins**
>   ⅓ **cup packed brown sugar**
>   ¼ **cup all-purpose flour**
>   ¼ **teaspoon ground nutmeg**
>   1 **cup chopped, peeled cooking apple or pear**
>   ½ **cup broken walnuts**

1. Prepare and roll out Pastry for Lattice-Top Pie. Line a 10- or 11-inch tart pan with a removable bottom with the bottom pastry. Press pastry into fluted sides of tart pan and trim edges. Set aside remaining pastry for lattice top.

2. For filling, in a medium saucepan combine apple juice, apricots, plums, and cherries. Bring to boiling; reduce heat. Simmer, covered, for 10 minutes. Remove from heat. Meanwhile, in a large bowl stir together brown sugar, flour, and nutmeg; add apple and walnuts. Gradually stir dried fruit mixture into apple mixture.

3. Transfer filling to the pastry-lined tart pan. Top with pastry strips in a lattice pattern (see photos 1 through 4). If desired, brush pastry strips with *milk* and sprinkle with *granulated sugar*. Bake in 375° oven about 45 minutes or until fruit is bubbly and pastry is golden. Cool on a wire rack. To serve, remove sides of tart pan.

Nutrition Facts per serving: 333 cal., 15 g total fat (3 g sat. fat), 0 mg chol., 152 mg sodium, 47 g carbo., 3 g fiber, 4 g pro.
Daily Values: 16% vit. A, 2% vit. C, 3% calcium, 12% iron
Exchanges: 1½ Fruit, 1½ Other Carbo., 3 Fat

1. For a lattice top, lay half of the pastry strips on top of the filling at 1-inch intervals.

2. Fold alternate pastry strips back halfway. Place a pastry strip in the center of the tart across the strips already in place.

3. Unfold the folded strips; fold back remaining strips. Place another pastry strip across the first set of strips parallel to strip in the center. Repeat the weaving steps until lattice covers the filling.

4. Use your fingers and the edge of the tart pan to trim the pastry strips even with the pan. Press strips against the pan to seal.

Fresh Fruit and Cream Tarts `Best Loved`

Use the fruits suggested or mix fruits in a variety of colors and shapes for your own combination.

Prep: 40 minutes **Bake:** 13 minutes **Oven:** 450°F
Chill: 4 hours **Makes:** 8 servings

>   1 **recipe Rich Tart Pastry (page 415)**
>   1 **recipe Pastry Cream (page 413)**
>   2 **cups fresh fruit, such as sliced strawberries; raspberries; blackberries; peeled, sliced papaya; and/or peeled, sliced kiwifruit**

1. Prepare Rich Tart Pastry through step 1; divide dough into 8 portions. On a floured surface, use your hands to slightly flatten 1 portion. Roll dough from center to edges into a circle about 5 inches in diameter. Line a 4-inch tart pan with a removable bottom with pastry. Press pastry into fluted sides of tart pan; trim edges. Prick bottom and sides of pastry. Repeat with remaining 7 portions of pastry. Line pastry with a double thickness of foil (see photo, page 403). Bake in a 450° oven for 8 minutes. Remove foil. Bake for 5 to 6 minutes more or until pastry shells are golden. Cool pastry shells on a wire rack.

2. Meanwhile, prepare Pastry Cream. Cover surface with plastic wrap; chill about 4 hours or until cold (do not stir).

3. Divide the chilled Pastry Cream evenly among the pastry shells. Arrange desired fresh fruit on top of each tart. To serve, remove sides of tart pans. Tarts can be assembled and chilled up to 4 hours before serving.

Pastry Cream: In a medium heavy saucepan combine ½ cup sugar, 4 teaspoons cornstarch, and ¼ teaspoon salt. Gradually stir in 2 cups half-and-half or light cream. If desired, add 1 vanilla bean, split lengthwise. Cook and stir over medium heat until thickened and bubbly. Cook and stir 1 minute more. Gradually stir half of the hot mixture into 4 beaten egg yolks. Return all of egg yolk mixture to saucepan. Bring to a gentle boil; reduce heat. Cook and stir 2 minutes. Remove from heat. Remove vanilla bean. Strain into a bowl. If not using vanilla bean, stir in 1 teaspoon liquid vanilla. Place bowl of pastry cream in a bowl of ice water; chill for 5 minutes, stirring occasionally. Cover surface with plastic wrap. Chill in refrigerator until serving time; do not stir. Makes 2 cups.

Nutrition Facts per serving: 388 cal., 23 g total fat (13 g sat. fat), 214 mg chol., 227 mg sodium, 40 g carbo., 1 g fiber, 6 g pro.
Daily Values: 19% vit. A, 35% vit. C, 9% calcium, 9% iron
Exchanges: 2½ Other Carbo., 4½ Fat

Peaches and Cream Tart

Prep: 25 minutes **Bake:** 15 minutes **Oven:** 350°F
Chill: 2 hours **Makes:** 10 to 12 servings

    9 soft coconut macaroon cookies,
       crumbled (2 cups)
    1 cup (4 ounces) ground pecans*
    3 tablespoons butter or margarine, softened
    ½ cup whipping cream
    1 8-ounce package cream cheese, softened
    ⅓ cup sugar
    2 teaspoons dark rum or orange juice
    1 teaspoon vanilla
    ¼ teaspoon almond extract
    2 to 4 medium peaches, peeled, pitted,
       and thinly sliced (1½ to 3 cups)
    2 tablespoons lemon juice
    ½ cup fresh raspberries
    ¼ cup apricot preserves
    2 teaspoons honey

1. Chill a medium mixing bowl and the beaters of an electric mixer. Meanwhile, for crust, in a bowl stir together cookie crumbs, pecans, and butter. Press mixture onto bottom and up sides of a 10- to 11-inch tart pan with a removable bottom or into a 12-inch pizza pan. Bake in a 350° oven until golden, allowing 15 to 18 minutes for tart pan and 12 to 15 minutes for pizza pan. Cool on a wire rack.

2. For filling, in the chilled bowl beat whipping cream with a mixer on medium speed until soft peaks form; set aside.

3. In a small mixing bowl beat cream cheese and sugar with an electric mixer on medium speed until fluffy. Add rum, vanilla, and almond extract; beat until smooth. Gently fold in whipped cream. Spoon mixture into cooled crust; spread evenly. Cover and chill for 2 to 4 hours.

4. Before serving, toss peach slices with lemon juice. Arrange peaches and raspberries on filling.

5. For glaze, in small saucepan combine preserves and honey; heat and stir just until melted. Snip any large pieces of fruit in the glaze. Strain glaze, if desired. Carefully brush or spoon the glaze over the fruit.

6. To serve, remove side of tart pan. Transfer tart to serving platter. Cut into wedges.

*Note: To grind pecans, process or blend the nuts, ½ cup at a time, in a food processor or blender until very finely chopped. Be careful not to overprocess or the nuts will form a paste.

Nutrition Facts per serving: 388 cal., 27 g total fat (13 g sat. fat), 51 mg chol., 165 mg sodium, 35 g carbo., 3 g fiber, 4 g pro.
Daily Values: 16% vit. A, 9% vit. C, 4% calcium, 5% iron
Exchanges: 2½ Other Carbo., 5½ Fat

Peaches and Cream Tart

Browned Butter Tart `Best Loved`

A generous spoonful of honeyed fresh fruit brings out the best in each wedge of this buttery tart.

Prep: 40 minutes **Bake:** 35 minutes **Oven:** 350°F
Cool: 1 hour **Makes:** 12 to 16 servings

    1 recipe Rich Tart Pastry (page 415)
    3 eggs
 1¼ cups sugar
   ½ cup all-purpose flour
    1 vanilla bean, split lengthwise, or
         1 teaspoon vanilla
   ¾ cup butter
   ⅓ cup orange juice
    2 tablespoons honey
    1 tablespoon orange liqueur or orange juice
    3 cups assorted mixed berries or assorted
         cut-up fresh fruit

1. Prepare and roll out Rich Tart Pastry. Line a 10-inch tart pan with a removable bottom with pastry. Ease pastry into pan without stretching it (see photo 2, page 417). Press pastry into fluted sides of tart pan and trim edges. Set aside.

2. For filling, in a large bowl slightly beat eggs with a rotary beater or a fork. Stir in sugar, flour, and, if using, liquid vanilla; set aside.

3. In a medium heavy saucepan combine the vanilla bean, if using, and butter. Cook over medium-high heat until the butter turns the color of light brown sugar. Remove from heat. Remove and discard vanilla bean. Slowly add the browned butter to the egg mixture, stirring until combined. Pour into the pastry-lined tart pan.

4. Bake in a 350° oven about 35 minutes or until the top is crisp and golden. Cool 1 to 2 hours in pan on a wire rack. Refrigerate within 2 hours; cover for longer storage.

5. Meanwhile, in a medium mixing bowl stir together the orange juice, honey, and orange liqueur. Stir in the fruit. Let fruit mixture stand up to 1 hour.

6. To serve, remove sides of the tart pan. Cut tart into wedges. Place wedges on individual dessert plates. Using a slotted spoon, spoon some of the fruit mixture beside each tart wedge.

Nutrition Facts per serving: 395 cal., 23 g total fat (13 g sat. fat), 143 mg chol., 224 mg sodium, 45 g carbo., 2 g fiber, 4 g pro.
Daily Values: 19% vit. A, 26% vit. C, 3% calcium, 7% iron
Exchanges: 3 Other Carbo., 4½ Fat

Candy Crème Tart

Imagine all your favorite candies from childhood embedded in every creamy bite.

Prep: 25 minutes **Bake:** 40 minutes **Oven:** 350°F
Cool: 1 hour **Chill:** 4 hours **Makes:** 12 servings

   ¾ cup finely crushed shortbread cookies
         (about 12 cookies)
   ¼ cup finely crushed graham crackers
    1 tablespoon butter, melted
    1 8-ounce package cream cheese, softened
    3 tablespoons butter, softened
   ½ cup half-and-half or light cream
    3 eggs
   ¼ cup sugar
    1 teaspoon vanilla
    3 1.4-ounce bars chocolate-covered English
         toffee, coarsely chopped
    1 1.5-ounce bar white chocolate with
         chocolate cookie bits, coarsely chopped
  15 malted milk balls, coarsely chopped

1. For crust, stir together the crushed cookies, crushed graham crackers, and the 1 tablespoon melted butter. Press crumb mixture onto the bottom and up the sides of a 9-inch tart pan with a removable bottom. Bake in a 350° oven for 10 minutes or until lightly brown. Cool on a wire rack.

2. For filling, in a blender container or food processor bowl combine the cream cheese, the 3 tablespoons softened butter, half-and-half, eggs, sugar, and vanilla. Cover and blend or process until smooth. Transfer cream cheese mixture to a large bowl; stir in chopped candies. Pour filling into baked crust. Place tart pan in a shallow baking pan to catch any drips.

3. Bake about 30 minutes or until center appears nearly set when shaken. Cool on a wire rack for 1 hour. Cover and chill at least 4 hours before serving.

Nutrition Facts per serving: 268 cal., 19 g total fat (10 g sat. fat), 94 mg chol., 191 mg sodium, 20 g carbo., 0 g fiber, 4 g pro.
Daily Values: 11% vit. A, 4% calcium, 3% iron
Exchanges: 1½ Other Carbo., 4 Fat

Nut and Chocolate Chip Tart

The addition of chocolate to a pecan pie filling creates a splendid dessert you won't soon forget.

Prep: 30 minutes **Bake:** 40 minutes
Oven: 350°F **Makes:** 8 to 10 servings

> 1 **recipe Pastry for Single-Crust Pie (page 416)**
> 3 **eggs**
> 1 **cup light-colored corn syrup**
> ½ **cup packed brown sugar**
> ⅓ **cup butter, melted and cooled**
> 1 **teaspoon vanilla**
> 1 **cup coarsely chopped salted mixed nuts**
> ½ **cup miniature semisweet chocolate pieces**
> ⅓ **cup miniature semisweet chocolate pieces (optional)**
> 1 **tablespoon shortening (optional)**

1. Prepare and roll out Pastry for Single-Crust Pie. Line an 11-inch tart pan with a removable bottom with pastry. Press pastry into fluted sides of tart pan and trim edges. Do not prick pastry.

2. For filling, in a large bowl beat eggs slightly with a fork. Stir in corn syrup. Add brown sugar, melted butter, and vanilla, stirring until sugar is dissolved. Stir in nuts and the ½ cup chocolate pieces. Place pastry-lined tart pan on a baking sheet; place baking sheet on the oven rack. Carefully pour filling into tart pan. Bake in a 350° oven about 40 minutes or until a knife inserted near the center comes out clean; cool on a wire rack.

3. To serve, remove sides of tart pan. Cut tart into wedges; transfer to dessert plates. If desired, in a small heavy saucepan melt the ⅓ cup chocolate pieces and shortening over very low heat. Immediately remove from heat; stir until smooth. Cool slightly. Transfer cooled chocolate to a small, heavy plastic bag. Snip a small hole in one corner of the bag; drizzle chocolate mixture over each serving. Cover and chill remaining tart for up to 2 days.

Nutrition Facts per serving: 548 cal., 30 g total fat (10 g sat. fat), 101 mg chol., 287 mg sodium, 64 g carbo., 3 g fiber, 7 g pro.
Daily Values: 9% vit. A, 1% vit. C, 4% calcium, 10% iron
Exchanges: 4 Other Carbo., 6 Fat

Nut and Chocolate Chip Tart

Rich Tart Pastry

Prep: 15 minutes **Chill:** 30 minutes
Makes: 8 to 10 servings (1 tart crust)

> 1¼ **cups all-purpose flour**
> ¼ **cup sugar**
> ½ **cup cold butter**
> 2 **beaten egg yolks**
> 1 **tablespoon ice water**

1. In a medium bowl stir together flour and sugar. Using a pastry blender, cut butter into flour until pieces are pea-size (see photo 1, page 417). In a small bowl stir together egg yolks and ice water. Gradually stir egg yolk mixture into flour mixture. Using your fingers, gently knead the dough just until a ball forms. Cover dough with plastic wrap and refrigerate for 30 to 60 minutes or until dough is easy to handle.

2. On a floured surface, use your hands to slightly flatten the dough. Roll dough from center to edges into a circle 12 inches in diameter.

3. To transfer pastry, wrap it around the rolling pin. Unroll pastry into a 10-inch tart pan with a removable bottom. Ease pastry into pan without stretching it (see photo 2, page 417). Press pastry into fluted sides of tart pan and trim edges. Do not prick pastry. Bake as directed in individual recipes.

Nutrition Facts per serving: 217 cal., 14 g total fat (8 g sat. fat), 86 mg chol., 126 mg sodium, 21 g carbo., 1 g fiber, 3 g pro.
Daily Values: 11% vit. A, 1% calcium, 6% iron

Pastry for Single-Crust Pie

Butter-flavored shortening also works well in this basic recipe.

Prep: 10 minutes **Makes:** 8 servings (1 piecrust)

>   1¼ **cups all-purpose flour**
>   ¼ **teaspoon salt**
>   ⅓ **cup shortening**
>   4 **to 5 tablespoons cold water**

1. In a medium bowl stir together flour and salt. Using a pastry blender, cut in shortening until pieces are pea-size (see photo 1, page 417).

2. Sprinkle 1 tablespoon of the water over part of the flour mixture; gently toss with a fork. Push moistened dough to the side of the bowl. Repeat moistening flour mixture, using 1 tablespoon of the water at a time, until all the flour mixture is moistened. Form dough into a ball.

3. On a lightly floured surface, use your hands to slightly flatten dough. Roll dough from center to edges into a circle about 12 inches in diameter.

4. To transfer pastry, wrap it around the rolling pin. Unroll pastry into a 9-inch pie plate. Ease pastry into pie plate without stretching it (see photo 2, page 417).

5. Trim pastry to ½ inch beyond edge of pie plate. Fold under extra pastry (see photo 3, page 417). Crimp edge as desired (see photos 5, 6, and 7, page 417). Do not prick pastry. Bake as directed in individual recipes.

Browned Butter Pastry: Prepare as above, except in a small saucepan melt ¼ cup butter over medium heat until butter turns the color of light brown sugar. Cover and chill browned butter until solid, about 45 minutes. Add 1 tablespoon sugar to flour mixture. Using a pastry blender, cut in browned butter and 2 tablespoons shortening. Continue with step 2 above.

Food processor directions: Place a steel blade in food processor bowl. Add flour, shortening, and salt. Cover and process with on/off turns until most of mixture resembles cornmeal but a few larger pieces remain. With food processor running, quickly add 3 tablespoons water through the feed tube. Stop processor as soon as all water is added; scrape down sides. Process with 2 on/off turns (mixture may not all be moistened). Remove dough from bowl; shape into a ball. Continue with step 3 above.

Baked Pastry Shell: Prepare as at left, except prick bottom and sides of pastry with a fork. Line pastry with a double thickness of foil (see photo, page 403). Bake in a 450°F oven for 8 minutes. Remove foil. Bake 5 to 6 minutes more or until golden. Cool on a wire rack.

Nutrition Facts per serving: 140 cal., 9 g total fat (2 g sat. fat), 0 mg chol., 73 mg sodium, 14 g carbo., 0 g fiber, 2 g pro.
Daily Values: 4% iron

Easy Oil Pastry

Just stir together and press pastry into the pie plate.

Prep: 10 minutes **Makes:** 8 servings (1 piecrust)

>   1¼ **cups all-purpose flour**
>   1 **tablespoon sugar**
>   ¼ **teaspoon salt**
>   ¼ **cup cooking oil**
>   3 **tablespoons milk**

1. In a medium bowl stir together flour, sugar, and salt. Add oil and milk all at once to flour mixture. Stir lightly with a fork. Form into a ball. Press dough firmly onto bottom and up sides of a 9-inch pie plate. Fill and bake as directed.

Nutrition Facts per serving: 140 cal., 7 g total fat (1 g sat. fat), 0 mg chol., 76 mg sodium, 17 g carbo., 1 g fiber, 2 g pro.
Daily Values: 1% vit. C, 1% calcium, 6% iron

Pastry Pointers

Make tender, flaky pastry every time with these simple tips.

■ Measure your ingredients accurately. Too much flour makes pastry tough, too much shortening makes it crumble, and too much water makes it tough.

■ Stir together the flour and salt, then cut in shortening until the mixture resembles coarse crumbs. If you overwork the mixture, your pastry may not be flaky.

■ Add water gradually to the flour mixture, then gently toss it together just until it's evenly moist.

■ To roll out dough with little sticking, use a rolling pin with a cotton knit cover and a pastry cloth. Lightly flour both the rolling pin cover and pastry cloth.

■ Roll pastry to an even thickness. Try not to stretch it as you're transferring it to the pie plate.

■ Use a glass pie plate or dull metal pie pan so the pastry browns evenly (see tip, page 405).

■ Check that your oven temperature is accurate. If it's too low, the bottom crust will be soggy.

Pastry for Double-Crust Pie

Prep: 15 minutes **Makes:** 8 servings (2 piecrusts)

- 2¼ **cups all-purpose flour**
- ¾ **teaspoon salt**
- ⅔ **cup shortening**
- 8 **to 10 tablespoons cold water**

1. In a medium bowl stir together flour and salt. Using a pastry blender, cut in shortening until pieces are pea-size (see photo 1, right).

2. Sprinkle 1 tablespoon of the water over part of flour mixture; gently toss with a fork. Push moistened dough to side of bowl. Repeat, using 1 tablespoon water at a time, until all the flour mixture is moistened. Divide in half; form each half into a ball.

3. On a lightly floured surface, use your hands to slightly flatten 1 dough ball. Roll dough from center to edges into a circle 12 inches in diameter.

4. To transfer pastry, wrap it around the rolling pin; unroll into a 9-inch pie plate. Ease pastry into pie plate without stretching it (see photo 2, right). Trim pastry even with rim of pie plate. Transfer filling to pastry-lined pie plate.

5. Roll remaining dough ball into a circle about 12 inches in diameter. Cut slits to allow steam to escape. Place pastry on filling; trim to ½ inch beyond edge of plate. Fold top pastry under bottom pastry (see photo 4, right). Crimp edge as desired (see photos 5, 6, and 7, right). Bake as directed in individual recipes.

Food processor directions: Place a steel blade in food processor bowl. Add flour, shortening, and salt. Cover; process with on/off turns until most of mixture resembles cornmeal but a few larger pieces remain. With the processor running, quickly add 6 tablespoons water through feed tube. Stop processor when all water is added; scrape down sides. Process with 2 on/off turns. Remove dough from bowl; shape into a ball. Divide in half. Continue with step 3 above.

Pastry for Lattice-Top Pie: Prepare as above, except trim bottom pastry to ½ inch beyond edge of pie plate. Cut remaining pastry circle into ½-inch-wide strips. Fill pastry-lined pie plate with desired filling. Weave strips over filling in a lattice pattern (see photos 1, 2, and 3, page 412). Press ends of strips into bottom pastry rim. Fold bottom pastry over strip ends; seal and crimp edge. Bake as directed.

Nutrition Facts per serving: 269 cal., 17 g total fat (4 g sat. fat), 0 mg chol., 219 mg sodium, 25 g carbo., 1 g fiber, 3 g pro.
Daily Values: 1% calcium, 8% iron

1. Use a pastry blender to cut the shortening into the flour mixture until the pieces are the size of small peas.

2. Wrap pastry around rolling pin. Starting at one side, unroll pastry over a pie plate. Ease pastry into the plate without stretching it; stretching pastry causes it to shrink while baking.

3. For a single-crust pie, trim pastry to ½ inch beyond the edge of the pie plate. Fold the extra pastry under, even with the plate's rim, to build up the edge.

4. For a double-crust pie, trim bottom pastry; add filling. Place top pastry on the filling. Lift bottom pastry edge away from plate and fold excess top pastry under it.

5. For a fluted edge, place your thumb on the inside of the pastry and your other thumb and index finger on the outside; press together.

6. For a rope edge, pinch the pastry, pushing forward on a slant with your bent index finger and pulling back with your thumb.

7. For a petal edge, flute the pastry as directed in photo 5. Press the tines of a fork lightly into the center of each flute.

Graham Cracker Crust

Prep: 10 minutes **Chill:** 1 hour **Makes:** 8 servings (1 crust)

⅓ **cup butter**

¼ **cup sugar**

1¼ **cups finely crushed graham crackers (about 18)**

1. Melt butter; stir in sugar. Add crushed crackers; toss to mix well. Spread evenly into a 9-inch pie plate. Press onto bottom and sides to form an even crust. Chill about 1 hour or until firm. (Or, bake in a 375° oven for 4 to 5 minutes or until edge is lightly browned. Cool on a wire rack before filling.)

Chocolate Wafer Crust: Prepare as above, except omit sugar and substitute 1½ cups finely crushed chocolate wafers (about 25) for the graham crackers. Do not bake.

Gingersnap Crust: Prepare as above, except omit the sugar and substitute 1¼ cups finely crushed gingersnaps (20 to 22) for the graham crackers.

Vanilla Wafer Crust: Prepare as above, except omit sugar and substitute 1½ cups finely crushed vanilla wafers (about 44) for the graham crackers.

Nutrition Facts per serving for graham cracker, chocolate wafer, gingersnap, and vanilla wafer variations: 154 cal., 9 g total fat (5 g sat. fat), 22 mg chol., 154 mg sodium, 17 g carbo., 0 g fiber, 1 g pro. **Daily Values:** 6% vit. A, 1% calcium, 3% iron

---

Meringue for Pie

Prep: 10 minutes **Stand:** 30 minutes
Makes: 8 servings (enough to top one 9-inch pie)

3 **egg whites**

½ **teaspoon vanilla**

¼ **teaspoon cream of tartar**

6 **tablespoons sugar**

1. Allow egg whites to stand at room temperature for 30 minutes. In a large mixing bowl combine egg whites, vanilla, and cream of tartar. Beat with an electric mixer on medium speed about 1 minute or until soft peaks form (tips curl; see photo 1, page 169).

2. Gradually add the sugar, 1 tablespoon at a time, beating on high speed about 4 minutes more or until mixture forms stiff, glossy peaks (tips stand straight; see photo 2, page 169) and sugar dissolves.

3. Immediately spread meringue over hot pie filling, carefully sealing to edge of pastry to prevent shrinkage (see photo, page 406). Bake as directed in individual recipes.

Nutrition Facts per serving: 42 cal., 0 g total fat (0 g sat. fat), 0 mg chol., 21 mg sodium, 9 g carbo., 0 g fiber, 1 g pro.

Four Egg White Meringue: Prepare as above, except use 4 egg whites, 1 teaspoon vanilla, ½ teaspoon cream of tartar, and ½ cup sugar. Beat about 5 minutes or until stiff, glossy peaks form. Continue as directed in step 3.

Nutrition Facts per serving: 57 cal., 0 g total fat (0 g sat. fat), 0 mg chol., 28 mg sodium, 12 g carbo., 0 g fiber, 2 g pro.

Making a Perfect Meringue

■ Let the egg whites stand at room temperature for 30 minutes before beating to ensure a meringue with great volume.

■ Be sure to use the size bowl called for in your recipe. Copper, stainless-steel, and glass bowls work best. Also make sure your electric mixer beaters are clean.

■ Begin to gradually add the sugar as soon as soft peaks form (tips bend over slightly).

■ After adding all of the sugar, continue beating until stiff peaks form and sugar is completely dissolved (rub a little of the meringue between your fingers; it should feel completely smooth). Underbeaten whites may cause meringue to shrink.

■ To prevent beading (the fine drops of moisture that form on the meringue surface), avoid overbaking the meringue.

■ To prevent weeping (the watery layer that forms between the meringue and filling), spoon meringue onto piping hot filling to help the underside of the meringue cook at the same rate as the top surface. Don't underbake meringue.

Chapter 18
Poultry

On the divider: **Oven-Barbecued Chicken** (see recipe, page 422)

Poultry

Lemon-Mustard Chicken

Low Fat

Prep: 10 minutes **Broil:** 25 minutes **Makes:** 6 servings

2½ to 3 pounds meaty chicken pieces (breast halves, thighs, and drumsticks)
2 tablespoons cooking oil
1 tablespoon Dijon-style mustard
1 tablespoon lemon juice
1½ teaspoons lemon-pepper seasoning
1 teaspoon dried oregano or basil, crushed
⅛ teaspoon ground red pepper

1. Skin chicken. Place chicken pieces, bone side up, on the unheated rack of a broiler pan. Broil 4 to 5 inches from the heat about 20 minutes or until light brown.

2. Meanwhile, in a bowl stir together oil, mustard, lemon juice, lemon-pepper seasoning, oregano, and red pepper. Brush mustard mixture onto chicken. Turn chicken; brush with remaining mixture. Broil for 5 to 15 minutes more or until chicken is no longer pink (170°F for breasts; 180°F for thighs and drumsticks).

Nutrition Facts per serving: 207 cal., 11 g total fat (2 g sat. fat), 77 mg chol., 355 mg sodium, 1 g carbo., 0 g fiber, 25 g pro. Daily Values: 1% vit. A, 2% vit. C, 2% calcium, 7% iron Exchanges: 3½ Medium-Fat Meat, ½ Fat

---

Pepper-Lime Chicken

Prep: 10 minutes **Broil:** 25 minutes **Makes:** 6 servings

2½ to 3 pounds meaty chicken pieces (breast halves, thighs, and drumsticks)
1 teaspoon finely shredded lime peel
¼ cup lime juice
1 tablespoon cooking oil
2 cloves garlic, minced
1 teaspoon dried thyme or basil, crushed
½ to 1 teaspoon black pepper
¼ teaspoon salt

1. If desired, skin chicken. Place chicken pieces, bone side up, on the unheated rack of a broiler pan. Broil 4 to 5 inches from the heat about 20 minutes or until light brown.

2. Meanwhile, for glaze, in a small bowl stir together lime peel, lime juice, oil, garlic, thyme, pepper, and salt. Brush chicken with glaze. Turn chicken; brush with more glaze. Broil for 5 to 15 minutes more or until chicken is no longer pink (170°F for breasts; 180°F for thighs and drumsticks), brushing often with glaze during the last 5 minutes of cooking time.

Nutrition Facts per serving: 242 cal., 13 g total fat (3 g sat. fat), 86 mg chol., 173 mg sodium, 2 g carbo., 0 g fiber, 28 g pro. Daily Values: 1% vit. A, 6% vit. C, 2% calcium, 8% iron Exchanges: 4 Medium-Fat Meat, ½ Fat

---

Oven-Fried Chicken

Prep: 15 minutes **Bake:** 45 minutes **Oven:** 375°F **Makes:** 6 servings

1 beaten egg
3 tablespoons milk
1¼ cups finely crushed saltine crackers or rich round crackers (about 35)
1 teaspoon dried thyme, crushed
½ teaspoon paprika
⅛ teaspoon black pepper
2½ to 3 pounds meaty chicken pieces (breast halves, thighs, and drumsticks)
2 tablespoons butter or margarine, melted

1. In a small bowl combine egg and milk. In a shallow dish combine crushed crackers, thyme, paprika, and pepper. Set aside. Skin chicken. Dip chicken pieces, 1 at a time, into egg mixture; coat with crumb mixture.

2. In a greased 15×10×1-inch baking pan, arrange the chicken, bone side down, so the pieces aren't touching. Drizzle chicken with the melted butter.

3. Bake, uncovered, in a 375° oven for 45 to 55 minutes or until chicken is no longer pink (170°F for breasts; 180°F for thighs and drumsticks). Do not turn chicken pieces while baking.

Oven-Fried Parmesan Chicken: Prepare as above, except omit thyme and reduce crushed crackers to ½ cup. Combine crushed crackers, ½ cup grated Parmesan cheese, and 1 teaspoon dried oregano, crushed, with the paprika and pepper. Continue as above.

Nutrition Facts per serving for regular or Parmesan variation: 345 cal., 18 g total fat (6 g sat. fat), 133 mg chol., 360 mg sodium, 13 g carbo., 1 g fiber, 31 g pro. Daily Values: 8% vit. A, 5% calcium, 13% iron Exchanges: 1 Starch, 4 Medium-Fat Meat

Coq au Vin

The name of this classic French recipe means chicken cooked in wine. Serve the chicken over noodles to soak up all of the delicious sauce.

Prep: 35 minutes **Cook:** 35 minutes **Makes:** 6 servings

- 2½ to 3 pounds meaty chicken pieces (breast halves, thighs, and drumsticks)
- 2 tablespoons cooking oil
- 12 to 18 pearl onions or shallots, peeled
- 1¼ cups Pinot Noir or Burgundy
- ¼ cup chicken broth or water
- 1 cup whole fresh mushrooms
- 1 cup thinly sliced carrots (2 medium)
- 1 tablespoon snipped fresh parsley
- 2 cloves garlic, minced
- 1½ teaspoons snipped fresh marjoram or ½ teaspoon dried marjoram, crushed
- 1½ teaspoons snipped fresh thyme or ½ teaspoon dried thyme, crushed
- 1 bay leaf
- 2 tablespoons all-purpose flour
- 2 tablespoons butter or margarine, softened
- 2 slices bacon, crisp-cooked, drained, and crumbled
  Snipped fresh parsley (optional)
  Hot cooked noodles (optional)

1. Skin chicken. In a 12-inch skillet cook chicken in hot oil about 15 minutes or until light brown, turning to brown evenly. Drain fat. Season chicken with *salt* and *black pepper*. Add onions, wine, broth, mushrooms, carrots, the 1 tablespoon parsley, garlic, dried marjoram (if using), dried thyme (if using), and bay leaf. Bring to boiling; reduce heat. Simmer, covered, for 35 to 40 minutes or until chicken is no longer pink (170°F for breasts; 180°F for thighs and drumsticks). Add fresh marjoram and thyme, if using. Transfer chicken and vegetables to a serving platter; keep warm. Discard the bay leaf.

2. In a small bowl stir together the flour and softened butter to make a smooth paste. Stir into wine mixture in skillet. Cook and stir until thickened and bubbly. Cook and stir for 1 minute more. Season to taste with *salt* and *black pepper.*

3. Pour sauce over chicken and vegetables. Sprinkle with bacon. If desired, top with additional parsley and serve with hot cooked noodles.

Nutrition Facts per serving: 318 cal., 16 g total fat (5 g sat. fat), 89 mg chol., 211 mg sodium, 7 g carbo., 1 g fiber, 27 g pro.
Daily Values: 107% vit. A, 6% vit. C, 3% calcium, 10% iron
Exchanges: 1 Vegetable, 3½ Medium-Fat Meat

Coq au Vin

Oven-Barbecued Chicken

See photo, page 419.

Low Fat

Prep: 10 minutes **Bake:** 45 minutes
Oven: 375°F **Makes:** 6 servings

- 2½ to 3 pounds meaty chicken pieces (breast halves, thighs, and drumsticks)
- ½ cup chopped onion (1 medium)
- 1 clove garlic, minced
- 1 tablespoon cooking oil
- ¾ cup bottled chili sauce
- 2 tablespoons honey
- 2 tablespoons soy sauce
- 1 tablespoon prepared mustard
- ½ teaspoon prepared horseradish
- ¼ teaspoon crushed red pepper

1. Skin chicken. Arrange chicken pieces, bone side up, in a 15×10×1-inch baking pan. Bake in a 375° oven for 25 minutes.

2. Meanwhile, for sauce, in a saucepan cook onion and garlic in hot oil until tender but not brown. Stir in chili sauce, honey, soy sauce, mustard, horseradish, and red pepper; heat through.

3. Turn chicken bone side down. Brush half of the sauce over chicken. Bake for 20 to 30 minutes more or until chicken is no longer pink (170°F for breasts; 180°F for thighs and drumsticks). Reheat remaining sauce; pass with the chicken.

Nutrition Facts per serving: 244 cal., 9 g total fat (2 g sat. fat), 77 mg chol., 807 mg sodium, 15 g carbo., 2 g fiber, 26 g pro.
Daily Values: 4% vit. A, 10% vit. C, 2% calcium, 8% iron
Exchanges: 1 Other Carbo., 3½ Medium-Fat Meat

Chicken and Dumplings Best Loved

Low Fat

Prep: 30 minutes **Cook:** 47 minutes **Makes:** 6 servings

- 2½ to 3 pounds meaty chicken pieces (breast halves, thighs, and drumsticks)
- 1 medium onion, cut into wedges
- ½ teaspoon dried sage or marjoram, crushed
- 1 bay leaf
- 1 cup sliced celery (2 stalks)
- 1 cup thinly sliced carrots (2 medium)
- 1 cup sliced fresh mushrooms
- 1 recipe Dumplings
- ¼ cup all-purpose flour

1. Skin chicken. In a 4-quart Dutch oven combine the chicken, onion, sage, bay leaf, ¾ teaspoon *salt,* ¼ teaspoon *black pepper,* and 3 cups *water.* Bring to boiling; reduce heat. Simmer, covered, for 25 minutes. Add celery, carrots, and mushrooms. Return mixture to boiling; reduce heat. Simmer, covered, about 10 minutes more or until vegetables are tender and chicken is no longer pink (170°F for breasts; 180°F for thighs and drumsticks). Discard bay leaf. Using tongs, rearrange the chicken pieces so they rest on top of the vegetables.

2. Meanwhile, prepare Dumplings. Spoon the dumpling batter into 6 mounds on top of the chicken. (Do not spoon the batter into the cooking liquid.) Return to boiling; reduce heat. Simmer, covered, for 12 to 15 minutes or until a wooden toothpick inserted into a dumpling comes out clean. Do not lift cover while simmering. With a slotted spoon transfer chicken, dumplings, and vegetables to a serving platter; keep warm.

3. For gravy, pour 2 cups of cooking liquid into a large measuring cup. Skim fat from liquid (see photo, page 444); discard fat. Pour liquid into the Dutch oven. Stir ½ cup *cold water* into the ¼ cup flour; stir into the liquid in Dutch oven. Cook and stir over medium heat until mixture is thickened and bubbly. Cook and stir for 1 minute more. Serve gravy over chicken, vegetables, and dumplings.

Dumplings: In a medium bowl combine 1 cup all-purpose flour, 1 teaspoon baking powder, and ½ teaspoon salt. Cut in 2 tablespoons shortening until mixture resembles coarse crumbs. Add ½ cup buttermilk, stirring just until moistened.

Nutrition Facts per serving: 322 cal., 11 g total fat (3 g sat. fat), 77 mg chol., 672 mg sodium, 25 g carbo., 2 g fiber, 29 g pro.
Daily Values: 103% vit. A, 6% vit. C, 10% calcium, 15% iron
Exchanges: 1 Vegetable, 1½ Starch, 3 Medium-Fat Meat

Spicy Chicken and Rice Bake

Low Fat

Prep: 20 minutes **Bake:** 45 minutes
Oven: 375°F **Makes:** 6 servings

- 2½ to 3 pounds meaty chicken pieces (breast halves, thighs, and drumsticks)
- ½ cup chopped onion (1 medium)
- ½ cup chopped green sweet pepper
- 2 cloves garlic, minced
- 1 tablespoon cooking oil
- 1 15-ounce can black beans, rinsed and drained
- 1 14½-ounce can diced tomatoes, undrained
- 1 cup tomato juice
- 1 cup frozen whole kernel corn
- ⅔ cup uncooked long grain rice
- 1 teaspoon chili powder
- ⅛ to ¼ teaspoon ground red pepper
  Paprika

1. Skin chicken; set aside.

2. In a large saucepan cook onion, sweet pepper, and garlic in hot oil until vegetables are tender. Stir in black beans, undrained tomatoes, tomato juice, corn, uncooked rice, chili powder, red pepper, and ½ teaspoon *salt.* Bring to boiling. Transfer rice mixture to a 3-quart rectangular baking dish. Arrange chicken pieces on top of rice mixture. Sprinkle chicken with paprika.

3. Bake, covered, in a 375° oven for 45 to 50 minutes or until chicken is no longer pink (170°F for breasts; 180°F for thighs and drumsticks) and rice is tender.

Nutrition Facts per serving: 355 cal., 9 g total fat (2 g sat. fat), 77 mg chol., 728 mg sodium, 39 g carbo., 6 g fiber, 33 g pro.
Daily Values: 10% vit. A, 41% vit. C, 6% calcium, 18% iron
Exchanges: ½ Vegetable, 2½ Starch, 3½ Medium-Fat Meat

Spicy Chicken and Rice Bake

Maryland Fried Chicken `Best Loved`

What sets this fried chicken apart from other recipes is that milk is added after partially cooking the chicken so the pieces simmer rather than fry.

Prep: 20 minutes **Cook:** 55 minutes **Makes:** 6 servings

- 1 beaten egg
- 3 tablespoons milk
- 1 cup finely crushed saltine crackers (28 crackers)
- 1 teaspoon dried thyme, crushed
- ½ teaspoon paprika
- ⅛ teaspoon black pepper
- 2½ to 3 pounds meaty chicken pieces (breasts, thighs, and drumsticks)
- 2 to 3 tablespoons cooking oil
- 1 cup milk
- 1 recipe Gravy
  Mashed Potatoes (page 525) (optional)

1. In a small bowl combine the egg and the 3 tablespoons milk. In a shallow bowl combine crushed crackers, thyme, paprika, and pepper. Dip chicken pieces, 1 at a time, into egg mixture; roll in cracker mixture.

2. In a large skillet heat oil over medium heat. Add chicken. Cook, uncovered, for 10 to 15 minutes, turning occasionally to brown evenly. Drain well.

3. Add the 1 cup milk to skillet. Reduce heat to medium-low; cover tightly. Cook for 35 minutes. Uncover; cook about 10 minutes more or until chicken is no longer pink (170°F for breasts; 180°F for thighs and drumsticks). Transfer chicken to a serving platter, reserving drippings for gravy. Cover chicken and keep warm. Prepare Gravy. If desired, serve with Mashed Potatoes.

Gravy: Skim fat from drippings. Reserve 3 tablespoons of the drippings in skillet. In a screw-top jar combine ¾ cup milk, 3 tablespoons all-purpose flour, ¼ teaspoon salt, and ⅛ teaspoon black pepper; cover and shake until well combined. Add to skillet. Stir in an additional ¾ cup milk. Cook over medium heat, stirring constantly, until thickened and bubbly. Cook and stir for 1 minute more. (If desired, thin with additional milk.) Makes about 1½ cups.

Nutrition Facts per serving: 383 cal., 19 g total fat (5 g sat. fat), 127 mg chol., 404 mg sodium, 17 g carbo., 1 g fiber, 33 g pro.
Daily Values: 7% vit. A, 2% vit. C, 13% calcium, 14% iron
Exchanges: 1 Starch, 4 Medium-Fat Meat

Fried Chicken with Creamy Gravy

Prep: 25 minutes **Cook:** 40 minutes **Makes:** 6 servings

- ⅓ cup all-purpose flour
- 1½ teaspoons poultry seasoning or paprika; dried basil or marjoram, crushed; or ½ teaspoon garlic powder or onion powder
- ½ teaspoon salt
- 2½ to 3 pounds meaty chicken pieces (breasts halves, thighs, and drumsticks)
  Cooking oil
- 1 recipe Creamy Gravy
  Mashed Potatoes (page 525) (optional)

1. In a plastic bag combine flour, poultry seasoning, salt, and ¼ teaspoon *black pepper.* Add chicken pieces, a few at a time, shaking to coat.

2. Add oil to a 12-inch heavy skillet to a depth of ¼ to ½ inch. Heat over medium-high heat until hot enough to sizzle a drop of water. Reduce heat. Add chicken to skillet. (Do not crowd chicken. If necessary, use 2 skillets.) Cook, uncovered, over medium heat for 15 minutes, turning to brown evenly. Reduce heat; cover tightly. Cook for 15 minutes. Uncover and cook for 5 to 10 minutes more or until chicken is no longer pink (170°F for breasts; 180°F for thighs and drumsticks). Drain on paper towels, reserving drippings for gravy. Transfer chicken to a serving platter; keep warm. Prepare Creamy Gravy. If desired, serve with Mashed Potatoes.

Oven directions: Coat chicken pieces as above. Brown chicken in a 12-inch ovenproof skillet. (Or brown chicken in a regular skillet; transfer to a 15×10×1-inch baking pan, arranging bone side down.) Bake, uncovered, in a 375°F oven for 35 to 40 minutes or until chicken is no longer pink. Do not turn.

Creamy Gravy: Pour off drippings in skillet, reserving 2 tablespoons. Return reserved drippings to skillet. Add 2 tablespoons all-purpose flour, ⅛ teaspoon black pepper, and, if desired, 1 teaspoon instant chicken bouillon granules, stirring until smooth. Add 1⅔ cups milk all at once. Cook and stir over medium heat until thickened and bubbly. Cook and stir for 1 minute more. (If necessary, thin with a little additional milk.) Makes 1⅔ cups.

Nutrition Facts per serving: 315 cal., 17 g total fat (4 g sat. fat), 91 mg chol., 304 mg sodium, 9 g carbo., 0 g fiber, 31 g pro.
Daily Values: 7% vit. A, 2% vit. C, 10% calcium, 9% iron
Exchanges: ½ Starch, 4 Medium-Fat Meat

Buttermilk-Brined Fried Chicken

Don't be surprised by the amount of salt in the buttermilk brine. It gives the chicken great flavor.

Prep: 30 minutes **Chill:** 2 to 4 hours
Cook: 12 minutes per batch **Makes:** 6 servings

> 3 cups buttermilk
> ⅓ cup coarse salt
> 2 tablespoons sugar
> 2½ to 3 pounds meaty chicken pieces (breast halves, thighs, and drumsticks)
> 2 cups all-purpose flour
> ¼ teaspoon salt
> ¼ teaspoon black pepper
> ¾ cup buttermilk
> Cooking oil

1. For brine, in a plastic bag set in a bowl, combine the 3 cups buttermilk, coarse salt, and sugar. Cut chicken breasts in half crosswise. Add all chicken pieces to bag; close bag. Chill 2 to 4 hours; remove chicken from brine. Drain; pat dry with paper towels. Discard brine.

2. In a large bowl combine flour, salt, and pepper. Coat chicken with flour mixture. Dip in the ¾ cup buttermilk; coat again with flour mixture.

3. Meanwhile, in a deep, heavy Dutch oven or kettle, or a deep-fat fryer, heat 1½ inches oil to 350°F. Using tongs carefully add chicken to Dutch oven (oil temperature will drop; maintain temperature at 325°F). Fry chicken, a few pieces at a time, in hot oil for 12 to 15 minutes or until an instant-read thermometer inserted into the thickest portion of the chicken piece registers 170°F for breasts, 180°F for thighs or drumsticks, and coating is golden, turning once. Drain on paper towels. Keep fried chicken warm in a 300°F oven while frying remaining chicken.

Spicy Buttermilk-Brined Fried Chicken: Prepare as above, except add 1½ teaspoons ground red pepper to flour mixture.

Nutrition Facts per serving plain or spicy variation: 549 cal., 30 g total fat (6 g sat. fat), 88 mg chol., 1,191 mg sodium, 35 g carbo., 1 g fiber, 34 g pro.
Daily Values: 2% vit. C, 9% calcium, 19% iron
Exchanges: 2½ Starch, 3½ Medium-Fat Meat, 2 Fat

Pecan Buttermilk-Brined Fried Chicken: Prepare as above, except reduce all-purpose flour to 1¼ cups; add ¾ cup finely ground pecans to flour mixture.

Nutrition Facts per serving: 585 cal., 40 g total fat (7 g sat. fat), 88 mg chol., 1,191 mg sodium, 25 g carbo., 2 g fiber, 33 g pro.
Daily Values: 1% vit. A, 2% vit. C, 10% calcium, 17% iron
Exchanges: 1½ Starch, 3½ Medium-Fat Meat, 4 Fat

Chicken Marsala

Low Fat

Start to Finish: 35 minutes **Makes:** 4 servings

> ¼ cup all-purpose flour
> ½ teaspoon dried marjoram, crushed
> 4 skinless, boneless chicken breast halves
> 2 cups sliced fresh mushrooms
> ¼ cup sliced green onions (2)
> 3 tablespoons butter or margarine
> ½ cup chicken broth
> ½ cup dry Marsala or dry sherry
> Hot cooked pasta, such as capellini or linguine (optional)

1. In a shallow bowl stir together flour, marjoram, ⅛ teaspoon *salt,* and ⅛ teaspoon *black pepper.* Place a chicken breast half between 2 pieces of plastic wrap. Using the flat side of a meat mallet, pound chicken lightly to about ¼ inch thick (see photo 2, page 437). Remove plastic wrap. Repeat with remaining chicken breast halves. Lightly coat chicken pieces on both sides with flour mixture; shake off excess.

2. In a 12-inch skillet cook mushrooms and green onions in 1 tablespoon of the butter over medium-high heat until tender; remove from skillet. In the same skillet cook chicken in remaining 2 tablespoons butter for 5 to 6 minutes, turning to brown evenly.

3. Remove skillet from heat. Return mushrooms and green onions to skillet. Carefully add broth and Marsala to skillet. Bring mixture to boiling; reduce heat. Simmer, uncovered, for 2 minutes, stirring occasionally. Season sauce to taste with additional *salt* and *pepper.* Transfer chicken to a serving platter. Spoon mushroom mixture over chicken. If desired, serve over pasta.

Nutrition Facts per serving: 298 cal., 12 g total fat (6 g sat. fat), 90 mg chol., 329 mg sodium, 10 g carbo., 1 g fiber, 30 g pro.
Daily Values: 8% vit. A, 4% vit. C, 3% calcium, 10% iron
Exchanges: 1½ Vegetable, 3½ Very Lean Meat, 3 Fat

Veal Marsala: Prepare as directed above, except substitute 12 ounces veal scallopini for chicken. Cook veal in the 2 tablespoons hot butter for 2 to 3 minutes or until light brown, tuning once halfway through cooking time. If necessary, cook half of veal at a time. Continue as directed in step 3.

Nutrition Facts per serving: 260 cal., 12 g total fat (6 g sat. fat), 91 mg chol., 313 mg sodium, 10 g carbo., 1 g fiber, 21 g pro.
Daily Values: 7% vit. A, 2% vit. C, 2% calcium, 9% iron
Exchanges: 1½ Vegetable, 2½ Very Lean Meat, 3 Fat

Chicken Cacciatore

Low Fat

Start to Finish: 1 hour **Makes:** 6 servings

- 2½ **to 3 pounds meaty chicken pieces (breast halves, thighs, and drumsticks)**
- 2 **tablespoons olive oil**
- 1½ **cups sliced fresh mushrooms**
- 1 **medium onion, sliced**
- 1 **clove garlic, minced**
- 1 **14½-ounce can diced tomatoes, undrained**
- 1 **6-ounce can tomato paste**
- ¾ **cup dry white wine**
- 1 **teaspoon sugar**
- ½ **teaspoon salt**
- ½ **teaspoon dried rosemary, crushed**
- ½ **teaspoon dried thyme, crushed**
- ¼ **teaspoon dried oregano, crushed**
- ⅛ **teaspoon black pepper**
- 1 **tablespoon snipped fresh parsley**
  Hot cooked fettuccine or linguine (optional)

1. Skin chicken. In a 12-inch skillet cook chicken in hot oil about 15 minutes or until light brown, turning to brown evenly. Remove chicken from skillet, reserving drippings in skillet; set chicken aside.

2. Add mushrooms, onion, and garlic to drippings in skillet. Cook and stir about 5 minutes or until vegetables are just tender. Return chicken to skillet.

3. Meanwhile, in a medium bowl combine undrained tomatoes, tomato paste, wine, sugar, salt, rosemary, thyme, oregano, and pepper. Pour over chicken in skillet. Bring to boiling; reduce heat. Simmer, covered, for 30 to 35 minutes or until chicken is no longer pink (170°F for breasts; 180°F for thighs and drumsticks), turning once during cooking. Sprinkle with parsley. If desired, serve over hot cooked pasta.

Nutrition Facts per serving: 280 cal., 11 g total fat (2 g sat. fat), 77 mg chol., 396 mg sodium, 12 g carbo., 2 g fiber, 28 g pro.
Daily Values: 1% vit. A, 26% vit. C, 5% calcium, 13% iron
Exchanges: 2 Vegetable, 3½ Medium-Fat Meat, 2½ Fat

Chicken Breasts with Tomatillo Salsa

Although tomatillos look like tiny green tomatoes, their acidic flavor hints of lemon and apple. They're commonly used in Southwest-inspired cooking. For a speedier dinner, omit the tomatillo salsa and substitute 1½ cups purchased green salsa.

Fast **Low Fat**

Start to Finish: 25 minutes **Makes:** 4 servings

- 2 **tablespoons yellow cornmeal**
- 2 **tablespoons all-purpose flour**
- 1 **tablespoon chili powder**
- ½ **teaspoon salt**
- ¼ **teaspoon black pepper**
- 4 **skinless, boneless chicken breast halves**
- 2 **tablespoons cooking oil**
- 1 **13-ounce can tomatillos**
- 3 **tablespoons snipped fresh cilantro**
- 3 **tablespoons finely chopped onion**
- 2 **tablespoons lime juice**
- 1 **fresh jalapeño pepper, seeded and finely chopped (see tip, page 64)**

1. In a plastic bag combine cornmeal, flour, chili powder, salt, and black pepper. Add chicken pieces, a few at a time, shaking to coat.

2. In a large skillet cook chicken in hot oil for 8 to 10 minutes or until chicken is no longer pink (170°F), turning once.

3. Meanwhile, for salsa, drain, rinse, and coarsely chop tomatillos (you should have about 1 cup). In a small bowl combine tomatillos, cilantro, onion, lime juice, and jalapeño pepper. Serve salsa over chicken.

Nutrition Facts per serving: 258 cal., 9 g total fat (1 g sat. fat), 66 mg chol., 1,065 mg sodium, 16 g carbo., 3 g fiber, 27 g pro.
Daily Values: 22% vit. A, 15% vit. C, 4% calcium, 20% iron
Exchanges: 1½ Vegetable, ½ Starch, 3 Very Lean Meat, 1½ Fat

Chicken Cacciatore

Chicken and Artichokes with Wine Sauce

Fast

Start to Finish: 30 minutes **Makes:** 4 servings

- ¼ **cup all-purpose flour**
- ½ **teaspoon dried sage, crushed**
- ¼ **teaspoon salt**
- ⅛ **teaspoon black pepper**
- 4 **skinless, boneless chicken breast halves**
- 2 **tablespoons cooking oil**
- 2 **cups sliced fresh mushrooms**
- 1 **8- or 9-ounce package frozen artichoke hearts, thawed and halved lengthwise**
- 1 **tablespoon butter or margarine**
- ⅓ **cup dry white wine**
- ⅓ **cup chicken broth**
- ⅛ **teaspoon salt**
- 2 **tablespoons grated Parmesan or Romano cheese**
- 2 **tablespoons snipped fresh parsley**

1. In a shallow dish stir together flour, sage, the ¼ teaspoon salt, and pepper; reserve 1 tablespoon of the flour mixture. Coat chicken with remaining flour mixture.

2. In a large skillet cook chicken in hot oil over medium-high heat for 8 to 10 minutes or until no longer pink (170°F), turning once. Remove chicken from skillet; cover and keep warm. Drain off any excess oil in skillet.

3. In the same skillet, cook mushrooms and artichoke hearts in hot butter over medium heat for 3 minutes or until artichokes are tender.

4. In a small bowl stir together reserved flour mixture, wine, broth, and the ⅛ teaspoon salt until smooth. Add wine mixture to skillet. Cook and stir until thickened and bubbly. Cook and stir for 1 minute more. Pour sauce over chicken. Sprinkle with cheese and parsley.

Nutrition Facts per serving: 310 cal., 14 g total fat (4 g sat. fat), 76 mg chol., 462 mg sodium, 12 g carbo., 4 g fiber, 32 g pro.
Daily Values: 7% vit. A, 13% vit. C, 8% calcium, 11% iron
Exchanges: 2 Vegetable, 4 Very Lean Meat, 2½ Fat

Basil Chicken in Coconut-Curry Sauce

To reduce the fat and calories use light coconut milk. You'll save about 14 grams fat and 130 calories per serving.

Prep: 25 minutes **Chill:** 1 to 2 hours **Cook:** 15 minutes
Makes: 4 servings

- 4 **skinless, boneless chicken breast halves**
- 2 **teaspoons curry powder**
- ½ **teaspoon salt**
- ½ **teaspoon cracked black pepper**
- ¼ **teaspoon chili powder**
- 1 **large red onion, chopped (1 cup)**
- 5 **cloves garlic, minced**
- 2 **fresh jalapeño peppers, seeded and finely chopped (see tip, page 64)**
- 1 **tablespoon olive oil**
- 1 **13½- or 14-ounce can unsweetened coconut milk**
- 1 **tablespoon cornstarch**
- 3 **tablespoons snipped fresh basil**
- 1 **teaspoon grated fresh ginger**
- 3 **cups hot cooked rice**

1. Cut chicken into 1-inch pieces. Place chicken in a medium bowl. In a small bowl stir together the curry powder, salt, black pepper, and chili powder. Sprinkle spice mixture over chicken, tossing to coat evenly. Cover and chill for 1 to 2 hours to allow spices to penetrate meat.

2. In a large nonstick wok or skillet cook and stir onion, garlic, and jalapeño peppers in hot oil over medium-high heat for 2 minutes. Remove onion mixture from wok. Add half of the chicken to wok. Cook and stir for 3 to 4 minutes or until chicken is no longer pink. Remove chicken from wok. (If necessary, add additional oil.) Cook remaining chicken as above; remove from wok.

3. Combine coconut milk and cornstarch. Carefully add to wok. Cook and stir until slightly thickened and bubbly. Return chicken and onion mixture to wok. Stir in basil and ginger. Cook and stir about 2 minutes more or until heated through. Serve over hot rice.

Nutrition Facts per serving: 495 cal., 26 g total fat (19 g sat. fat), 66 mg chol., 370 mg sodium, 36 g carbo., 2 g fiber, 32 g pro.
Daily Values: 4% vit. A, 14% vit. C, 6% calcium, 30% iron
Exchanges: 2½ Starch, 3½ Very Lean Meat, 4 Fat

Pacific Rim Stir-Fry

and stir for 2 minutes more. Add sweet pepper; cook and stir for 1½ to 2 minutes more or until vegetables are crisp-tender. Remove vegetables from wok. Add chicken to wok; cook and stir for 2 to 3 minutes or until no longer pink. Push chicken from center of wok. Stir sauce; add to center of wok. Cook and stir until thickened and bubbly. Return vegetables to wok; add fresh basil (if using). Cook and stir for 2 minutes or until heated through. Serve over rice sticks; sprinkle with cashews.

Nutrition Facts per serving: 313 cal., 13 g total fat (2 g sat. fat), 70 mg chol., 703 mg sodium, 30 g carbo., 3 g fiber, 22 g pro.
Daily Values: 201% vit. A, 146% vit. C, 5% calcium, 13% iron
Exchanges: 1½ Vegetable, 1½ Starch, 2 Lean Meat, 1 Fat

Pacific Rim Stir-Fry

Prep: 25 minutes **Cook:** 15 minutes **Makes:** 4 servings

>   3 **ounces rice sticks or rice noodles or thin vermicelli, broken**
>   12 **ounces skinless, boneless chicken thighs or breast halves**
>   ½ **cup chicken broth**
>   2 **tablespoons soy sauce**
>   2 **tablespoons snipped fresh basil or 2 teaspoons dried basil, crushed**
>   2 **teaspoons cornstarch**
>   1 **teaspoon chile oil or ½ teaspoon crushed red pepper**
>   ½ **teaspoon ground turmeric**
>   1 **tablespoon cooking oil**
>   2 **medium carrots, cut into short strips or thinly sliced (1 cup)**
>   2 **cups broccoli florets**
>   1 **red or green sweet pepper, cut into 1-inch strips (½ cup)**
>   ¼ **cup cashew halves or peanuts**

1. In a saucepan cook rice sticks or rice noodles in boiling water for 3 minutes. (Or cook vermicelli according to package directions.) Drain; set aside and keep warm.

2. Cut chicken into thin, bite-size strips. For sauce, combine broth, soy sauce, dried basil (if using), cornstarch, chile oil, and turmeric; set aside.

3. Pour cooking oil into a wok or large skillet. (If necessary, add more oil during cooking.) Heat over medium-high heat. Add carrots to wok; cook and stir for 1 minute. Add broccoli; cook

Honey-Glazed Chicken Stir-Fry

Use stir-fry vegetables from the produce section to help prepare the meal more quickly.

`Fast` `Low Fat`

Start to Finish: 25 minutes **Makes:** 4 servings

>   12 **ounces skinless, boneless chicken breast halves or thighs**
>   2 **tablespoons honey**
>   2 **tablespoons vinegar**
>   2 **tablespoons orange juice**
>   4 **teaspoons soy sauce**
>   1½ **teaspoons cornstarch**
>   2 **tablespoons cooking oil**
>   4 **cups cut-up vegetables, such as broccoli, sweet pepper, onion, and/or mushrooms**
>   2 **cups hot cooked rice**

1. Cut chicken into bite-size strips; set aside. For sauce, in a small bowl stir together honey, vinegar, orange juice, soy sauce, and cornstarch; set aside.

2. Pour oil into a wok or large skillet. (If necessary, add more oil during cooking.) Heat over medium-high heat. Add vegetables to wok; cook and stir for 3 to 4 minutes or until vegetables are crisp-tender. Remove vegetables from wok. Add chicken; cook and stir for 3 to 4 minutes or until chicken is no longer pink. Push chicken from the center of the wok. Stir sauce; add to center of the wok. Cook and stir until thickened and bubbly.

3. Return cooked vegetables to wok. Cook and stir about 1 minute more or until heated through. Serve over rice.

Nutrition Facts per serving: 324 cal., 9 g total fat (1 g sat. fat), 49 mg chol., 376 mg sodium, 38 g carbo., 3 g fiber, 25 g pro.
Daily Values: 26% vit. A, 125% vit. C, 7% calcium, 14% iron
Exchanges: 1½ Vegetable, 2 Starch, 2½ Very Lean Meat, 1 Fat

Garlic Chicken Stir-Fry

Low Fat

Prep: 20 minutes **Marinate:** 30 minutes **Cook:** 6 minutes
Makes: 4 servings

- 12 **ounces skinless, boneless chicken breast halves**
- 1 **cup water**
- 3 **tablespoons reduced-sodium soy sauce**
- 2 **tablespoons dry white wine**
- 1 **tablespoon cornstarch**
- 2 **tablespoons cooking oil**
- 10 **green onions, bias-sliced into 1-inch pieces**
- 1 **cup thinly sliced fresh mushrooms**
- 12 **cloves garlic, peeled and finely chopped, or 2 tablespoons bottled minced garlic**
- ½ **cup sliced water chestnuts**
  Hot cooked white rice (optional)

1. Cut chicken into ½-inch pieces. Place chicken in a plastic bag set in a shallow bowl.

2. For marinade, combine water, soy sauce, and white wine; pour marinade over chicken in bag. Marinate in the refrigerator for 30 minutes. Drain chicken, reserving the marinade. Stir cornstarch into the reserved marinade; set aside.

3. Pour oil into a wok or large skillet. (If necessary, add more oil during cooking.) Heat over medium-high heat. Add green onions, mushrooms, and garlic to wok; cook and stir for 1 to 2 minutes or until tender. Remove vegetables from wok. Add chicken to wok; cook and stir for 2 to 3 minutes or until no longer pink. Push chicken from the center of wok. Stir marinade mixture; add to center of wok. Cook and stir until thickened and bubbly.

4. Return cooked vegetables to wok; add water chestnuts. Cook and stir about 1 minute more or until heated through. If desired, serve with hot cooked rice.

Nutrition Facts per serving: 226 cal., 9 g total fat (1 g sat. fat), 49 mg chol., 491 mg sodium, 13 g carbo., 2 g fiber, 23 g pro.
Daily Values: 4% vit. A, 19% vit. C, 6% calcium, 10% iron
Exchanges: 2 Vegetable, 3 Very Lean Meat, 1½ Fat

Garlic Chicken Stir-Fry with Cashews: Prepare

as above, except stir ½ teaspoon crushed red pepper into marinade. Stir in 1 cup cashews with water chestnuts.

Nutrition Facts per serving: 422 cal., 25 g total fat (5 g sat. fat), 49 mg chol., 497 mg sodium, 25 g carbo., 3 g fiber, 28 g pro.
Daily Values: 5% vit. A, 19% vit. C, 8% calcium, 22% iron
Exchanges: 1 Starch, 3 Very Lean Meat, 2 Vegetable, 4 Fat

Thai Chicken Stir-Fry

Low Fat

Start to Finish: 35 minutes **Makes:** 4 servings

- 12 **ounces skinless, boneless chicken breast halves**
- 3 **tablespoons dry sherry**
- 2 **tablespoons reduced-sodium soy sauce**
- 1 **tablespoon fish sauce (optional)**
- 1 **tablespoon water**
- 1 **teaspoon cornstarch**
- ½ **teaspoon crushed red pepper**
- 1 **tablespoon cooking oil**
- 1 **teaspoon grated fresh ginger**
- 2 **cloves garlic, minced**
- 1 **cup bias-sliced carrots**
- 2 **cups fresh pea pods, tips and strings removed, or one 6-ounce package frozen pea pods, thawed**
- 4 **green onions, bias-sliced into 1-inch pieces (½ cup)**
- ⅓ **cup dry roasted peanuts**
  Hot cooked rice (optional)

1. Cut chicken into 1-inch pieces; set aside.

2. For sauce, in a small bowl stir together the sherry, soy sauce, fish sauce (if using), water, cornstarch, and red pepper. Set aside.

3. Pour oil into a wok or large skillet. (If necessary, add more oil during cooking.) Heat over medium-high heat. Add ginger and garlic to wok; cook and stir for 15 seconds. Add carrots; cook and stir for 2 minutes. Add pea pods and green onions; cook and stir for 2 to 3 minutes more or until vegetables are crisp-tender. Remove vegetables from wok.

4. Add chicken to wok; cook and stir for 3 to 4 minutes or until chicken is no longer pink. Push chicken from center of wok. Stir sauce; add to center of wok. Cook and stir until thickened and bubbly. Return vegetables to wok. Stir in peanuts. Cook and stir for 1 to 2 minutes more or until heated through. If desired, serve with rice.

Nutrition Facts per serving: 263 cal., 11 g total fat (2 g sat. fat), 49 mg chol., 351 mg sodium, 12 g carbo., 3 g fiber, 25 g pro.
Daily Values: 158% vit. A, 14% vit. C, 6% calcium, 10% iron
Exchanges: 2½ Vegetable, 3 Very Lean Meat, 2 Fat

Chicken and Noodles `Best Loved`

This homey dish is full of noodles, vegetables, and chicken. It's a perfect one-dish meal, needing only a small salad or dinner rolls to complete it.

`Low Fat`

Prep: 20 minutes **Cook:** 40 minutes **Makes:** 6 servings

- 3 chicken legs (thigh-drumstick piece) (about 2 pounds)
- 3 cups water
- 2 bay leaves
- 1 teaspoon dried thyme, crushed
- ½ teaspoon salt
- ¼ teaspoon black pepper
- 1½ cups chopped onions (3 medium)
- 2 cups sliced carrots (4 medium)
- 1 cup sliced celery (2 stalks)
- 3 cups wide noodles (6 ounces)
- 1 cup loose-pack frozen peas
- 2 cups milk
- ½ teaspoon salt
- 3 tablespoons all-purpose flour

1. Skin chicken. In a 4½-quart Dutch oven combine chicken, water, bay leaves, thyme, the ½ teaspoon salt, and the pepper. Add onions, carrots, and celery. Bring to boiling; reduce heat. Simmer, covered, for 20 to 30 minutes or until chicken is tender and no longer pink. Discard the bay leaves. Remove chicken from Dutch oven; cool slightly. Remove meat from bones; discard bones. Chop chicken; set aside.

2. Bring broth mixture to boiling. Add noodles; cook for 5 minutes. Stir in frozen peas, 1½ cups of the milk, and the ½ teaspoon salt.

3. In a screw-top jar combine the remaining ½ cup milk and the flour. Cover and shake until smooth; stir into noodle mixture. Cook and stir until thickened and bubbly. Stir in chopped chicken. Cook and stir for 1 to 2 minutes more or until mixture is heated through.

Nutrition Facts per serving: 311 cal., 6 g total fat (2 g sat. fat), 93 mg chol., 550 mg sodium, 39 g carbo., 5 g fiber, 25 g pro.
Daily Values: 214% vit. A, 19% vit. C, 15% calcium, 16% iron
Exchanges: 2 Vegetable, 2 Starch, 2 Lean Meat

Southwest-Style Chicken Burgers `Best Loved`

Prep: 20 minutes **Broil:** 15 minutes **Makes:** 4 servings

- 1 slightly beaten egg
- ¼ cup finely crushed nacho-flavor or plain tortilla chips
- 3 tablespoons finely chopped green sweet pepper
- ¾ teaspoon chili powder
- ¼ teaspoon salt
- ¼ teaspoon black pepper
- 1 pound uncooked ground chicken
- 2 ounces Monterey Jack cheese with jalapeño peppers, sliced
- 4 kaiser rolls or hamburger buns, split and toasted
- 1 avocado, halved, seeded, peeled, and sliced
- 4 lettuce leaves
- ¼ cup bottled salsa

1. In a medium bowl combine egg, tortilla chips, sweet pepper, chili powder, salt, and black pepper. Add chicken; mix well. (Mixture will be wet.) Shape chicken mixture into four ¾-inch-thick round patties.

2. Place patties on the unheated rack of a broiler pan. Broil 4 inches from the heat 14 to 18 minutes or until no longer pink and an instant-read thermometer registers 165°F, turning once halfway through broiling time. Top burgers with cheese. Broil for 1 minute more or until cheese melts.

3. Serve burgers on toasted rolls; top with avocado, lettuce, and salsa.

Nutrition Facts per serving: 522 cal., 26 g total fat (5 g sat. fat), 66 mg chol., 698 mg sodium, 39 g carbo., 4 g fiber, 32 g pro.
Daily Values: 16% vit. A, 19% vit. C, 21% calcium, 23% iron
Exchanges: 2½ Starch, 3½ Medium-Fat Meat, 1½ Fat

Buying and Storing Poultry

Poultry is highly perishable and should be purchased and stored carefully. Check the "sell by" date on the package label. That is the last day the product should be sold. (If properly refrigerated, poultry will retain its freshness for a couple of days after that date.)

Store fresh poultry in the coldest part of your refrigerator as soon as you get it home. Plan to use it within 1 to 2 days. Poultry that's packaged in supermarket trays can be refrigerated in its original wrapping.

Greek-Style Turkey Burgers

A cucumber, olive, and tomato salsa top these flavorful ground poultry burgers. Feta cheese adds a Greek influence.

Prep: 20 minutes **Broil:** 11 minutes **Makes:** 4 servings

- ⅓ **cup fine dry bread crumbs or 1 cup soft whole wheat bread crumbs**
- 1 **slightly beaten egg white**
- 1 **tablespoon milk**
- 1 **0.7-ounce envelope Italian salad dressing mix (5 teaspoons)**
- 1 **pound lean uncooked ground turkey or chicken**
- 4 **pita bread rounds, toasted, or 4 whole wheat hamburger buns, split and toasted**
- 1 **recipe Greek Salsa**
- ¼ **cup crumbled feta cheese**

1. In a medium bowl combine bread crumbs, egg white, milk, and half of the salad dressing mix. (Reserve the remaining half of salad dressing mix for Greek Salsa.) Add turkey; mix well. Shape turkey mixture into four 6-inch-long × ½-inch-thick oval patties.

2. Place patties on the unheated rack of a broiler pan. Broil 4 to 5 inches from the heat for 11 to 13 minutes or until no longer pink (165°F), turning once halfway through broiling time.

3. Serve the burgers in pita bread rounds. Top with Greek Salsa and sprinkle with feta cheese.

Greek Salsa: In a small bowl stir together 2 tablespoons white wine vinegar, 2 teaspoons olive oil, and the remaining half of the salad dressing mix. Stir in 1 cup finely chopped tomato, ¼ cup finely chopped cucumber, and ¼ cup finely chopped, pitted kalamata or ripe olives. Makes about 1⅓ cups.

Nutrition Facts per serving: 403 cal., 18 g total fat (5 g sat. fat), 96 mg chol., 1,177 mg sodium, 32 g carbo., 3 g fiber, 28 g pro.
Daily Values: 7% vit. A, 15% vit. C, 10% calcium, 20% iron
Exchanges: 2 Starch, 3 Medium-Fat Meat, ½ Fat

Pulled Chicken Sandwiches

This convenient recipe uses a deli-roasted chicken. The sauce goes together quickly and cooks in just 7 minutes.

Low Fat

Prep: 25 minutes **Cook:** 7 minutes **Makes:** 4 sandwiches

- 1 **1¾- to 2-pound purchased roasted chicken**
- 1 **medium onion, cut into ¼-inch slices**
- 1 **tablespoon olive oil**
- ⅓ **cup apple cider vinegar or white wine vinegar**
- ½ **cup tomato sauce**
- 3 **to 4 tablespoons seeded and finely chopped fresh red and/or green serrano peppers (see tip, page 64)**
- 2 **tablespoons snipped fresh thyme**
- 2 **tablespoons molasses**
- ½ **teaspoon salt**
- 4 **kaiser rolls or hamburger buns, split**
  Bread-and-butter pickle slices or sweet pickle slices

1. Cut the meat from the chicken, discarding skin and bones. Use 2 forks or your fingers to pull meat into shreds.

2. In a large skillet cook onion in hot oil over medium heat about 5 minutes or until tender, stirring occasionally to separate slices into rings. Add vinegar. Cook and stir for 1 minute more.

3. Stir in tomato sauce, serrano peppers, thyme, molasses, 2 tablespoons *water,* and salt. Bring to boiling. Add the chicken; stirring gently to coat. Heat through. Serve on split rolls with pickle slices.

Nutrition Facts per sandwich: 668 cal., 18 g total fat (4 g sat. fat), 126 mg chol., 1,485 mg sodium, 76 g carbo., 3 g fiber, 50 g pro.
Daily Values: 9% vit. A, 19% vit. C, 14% calcium, 26% iron
Exchanges: 5 Starch, 5 Lean Meat

Greek-Style Turkey Burgers

Deep-Dish Chicken Pie

Prep: 50 minutes **Bake:** 30 minutes **Oven:** 400°F
Stand: 20 minutes **Makes:** 6 servings

- 1 **recipe Pastry Topper**
- 3 **medium leeks or 1 large onion, chopped**
- 1 **cup sliced fresh mushrooms**
- ¾ **cup sliced celery**
- ½ **cup chopped red sweet pepper**
- 2 **tablespoons butter or margarine**
- ⅓ **cup all-purpose flour**
- 1 **teaspoon poultry seasoning**
- ¼ **teaspoon black pepper**
- 1½ **cups chicken broth**
- 1 **cup half-and-half, light cream, or milk**
- 2½ **cups chopped cooked chicken (see tip, page 437)**
- 1 **cup loose-pack frozen peas**
- 1 **beaten egg**

1. Prepare Pastry Topper; set aside.

2. In a large saucepan cook leeks, mushrooms, celery, and sweet pepper in hot butter over medium heat for 4 to 5 minutes or until vegetables are tender. Stir in flour, poultry seasoning, pepper, and ¼ teaspoon *salt*. Add broth and half-and-half all at once. Cook and stir until thickened and bubbly. Stir in chicken and peas. Pour into a 2-quart rectangular baking dish.

3. Place pastry over chicken mixture in dish. Turn edges of pastry under; flute to edges of dish. Brush pastry with some of the egg.

4. Bake, uncovered, in a 400° oven for 30 to 35 minutes or until crust is golden brown. Let stand about 20 minutes before serving.

Pastry Topper: In a medium bowl stir together 1¼ cups all-purpose flour and ¼ teaspoon salt. Using a pastry blender, cut in ⅓ cup shortening until dough pieces are pea-size. Sprinkle 1 tablespoon cold water over part of the mixture; gently toss with a fork. Push moistened dough to side of bowl. Sprinkle an additional 3 to 4 tablespoons cold water over remaining flour mixture, 1 tablespoon at a time, tossing with a fork until all dough is moistened. Form into a ball. On a lightly floured surface, roll dough into a 13×9-inch rectangle. Using a sharp knife, cut slits in pastry to allow steam to escape.

Nutrition Facts per serving: 471 cal., 26 g total fat (10 g sat. fat), 113 mg chol., 543 mg sodium, 33 g carbo., 3 g fiber, 26 g pro.
Daily Values: 26% vit. A, 42% vit. C, 9% calcium, 19% iron
Exchanges: 2 Vegetable, 1½ Starch, 2½ Lean Meat, 3½ Fat

Chicken Tetrazzini

This classic favorite was named for an opera singer.

Prep: 30 minutes **Bake:** 15 minutes
Oven: 350°F **Makes:** 6 servings

- 8 **ounces dried spaghetti or linguine**
- 2 **cups sliced fresh mushrooms**
- ½ **cup sliced green onions (4)**
- 2 **tablespoons butter or margarine**
- ¼ **cup all-purpose flour**
- ⅛ **teaspoon black pepper**
- ⅛ **teaspoon ground nutmeg**
- 1¼ **cups chicken broth**
- 1¼ **cups milk, half-and-half, or light cream**
- 2 **cups chopped cooked chicken or turkey (see tip, page 437)**
- 2 **tablespoons dry sherry (optional)**
- ¼ **cup grated Parmesan cheese**
- ¼ **cup sliced almonds, toasted (see tip, page 224)**
- 2 **tablespoons snipped fresh parsley (optional)**

1. Cook spaghetti or linguine according to package directions; drain.

2. Meanwhile, in a large saucepan cook mushrooms and green onions in hot butter until tender. Stir in flour, pepper, and nutmeg. Add broth and milk all at once. Cook and stir until thickened and bubbly. Stir in chicken, sherry (if using), and half of the Parmesan cheese. Add cooked spaghetti; stir gently to coat.

3. Transfer pasta mixture to a 2-quart rectangular baking dish. Sprinkle with the remaining Parmesan cheese and the almonds. Bake in a 350° oven, uncovered, for 15 minutes. If desired, sprinkle with parsley before serving.

Nutrition Facts per serving: 379 cal., 14 g total fat (5 g sat. fat), 60 mg chol., 397 mg sodium, 38 g carbo., 2 g fiber, 25 g pro.
Daily Values: 7% vit. A, 3% vit. C, 16% calcium, 14% iron
Exchanges: 2½ Starch, 2½ Lean Meat, 1 Fat

Chicken Burritos Best Loved

Prep: 20 minutes **Bake:** 30 minutes
Oven: 350°F **Makes:** 8 servings

- 8 8- to 10-inch flour tortillas
- 1½ cups shredded cooked chicken, beef, or pork
- 1 cup bottled salsa
- 1 3⅛-ounce can jalapeño-flavored bean dip
- 1 teaspoon fajita seasoning
- 8 ounces Monterey Jack cheese or cheddar cheese, cut into eight 5×½-inch sticks
  - Shredded lettuce (optional)
  - Dairy sour cream (optional)
  - Bottled salsa (optional)

1. Wrap tortillas in foil; heat in a 350° oven for 10 minutes or until heated through.

2. Meanwhile, in a large bowl combine chicken, the 1 cup salsa, the bean dip, and fajita seasoning.

3. To assemble, spoon ⅓ cup meat mixture onto each tortilla near one edge. Top meat mixture with a stick of cheese. Fold in sides and roll up, starting from edge with the filling. Place filled tortillas, seam sides down, in a greased 3-quart rectangular baking dish.

4. Bake, uncovered, in a 350° oven about 30 minutes or until heated through. If desired, serve with lettuce, sour cream, and additional salsa.

Nutrition Facts per serving: 261 cal., 13 g total fat (6 g sat. fat), 48 mg chol., 441 mg sodium, 18 g carbo., 1 g fiber, 17 g pro.
Daily Values: 8% vit. A, 4% vit. C, 25% calcium, 9% iron
Exchanges: 1 Starch, 2 Lean Meat, 1½ Fat

Chicken Enchiladas Best Loved

If you prefer a red sauce on your enchiladas, omit the soup, sour cream, and 1 cup milk. Stir the reserved chile peppers into 2½ cups of canned or homemade enchilada sauce. Bake as directed.

Prep: 30 minutes **Bake:** 40 minutes
Oven: 350°F **Makes:** 6 servings

- ¼ cup slivered almonds
- ¼ cup chopped onion
- 2 tablespoons butter or margarine
- 1 4-ounce can diced green chile peppers, drained
- 1 3-ounce package cream cheese, softened
- 1 tablespoon milk
- ¼ teaspoon ground cumin
- 2 cups chopped cooked chicken (see tip, page 437)
- 12 7-inch flour tortillas or 6-inch corn tortillas
- 1 10¾-ounce can condensed cream of chicken or cream of mushroom soup
- 1 8-ounce carton dairy sour cream
- 1 cup milk
- ¾ cup shredded Monterey Jack or cheddar cheese (3 ounces)
- 2 tablespoons slivered almonds

1. In a medium skillet cook the ¼ cup almonds and the onion in hot butter over medium heat until onion is tender and nuts are lightly toasted. Remove skillet from heat. Stir in 1 tablespoon of the green chile peppers; reserve remaining peppers for sauce.

2. In a medium bowl combine cream cheese, the 1 tablespoon milk, and cumin; add nut mixture and chicken. Stir until combined. Spoon about 3 tablespoons of the chicken mixture onto each tortilla near one edge; roll up. Place filled tortillas, seam side down, in a greased 3-quart rectangular baking dish. Set aside.

3. For sauce, in a medium bowl combine the reserved chile peppers, soup, sour cream, and the 1 cup milk. Pour evenly over the tortillas in the baking dish. Cover with foil. Bake in a 350° oven about 35 minutes or until heated through. Remove foil. Sprinkle enchiladas with cheese and the 2 tablespoons almonds. Return to oven; bake about 5 minutes more or until cheese melts.

Nutrition Facts per serving: 610 cal., 38 g total fat (17 g sat. fat), 105 mg chol., 932 mg sodium, 40 g carbo., 2 g fiber, 28 g pro.
Daily Values: 23% vit. A, 12% vit. C, 34% calcium, 19% iron
Exchanges: 2½ Starch, 3 Lean Meat, 5½ Fat

Healthful Chicken Enchiladas: Prepare as above, except use fat-free cream cheese (4 ounces), reduced-sodium condensed soup, fat-free or light dairy sour cream, fat-free milk, and reduced-fat Monterey Jack cheese. Omit the 2 tablespoons slivered almonds. Top the baked enchiladas with ½ cup chopped tomatoes.

Nutrition Facts per serving: 476 cal., 19 g total fat (6 g sat. fat), 74 mg chol., 762 mg sodium, 47 g carbo., 2 g fiber, 29 g pro.
Daily Values: 12% vit. A, 16% vit. C, 38% calcium, 17% iron
Exchanges: 3 Starch, 3 Lean Meat, 1½ Fat

Poultry Hotline

For answers to your questions about safely handling meat and poultry, call the U.S. Department of Agriculture's Meat and Poultry Hotline, 800/535-4555 (202/720-3333 in the Washington, D.C., area). The hotline's food safety specialists answer calls from 10 a.m. to 4 p.m. weekdays (Eastern Standard Time).

Turkey and Phyllo Pie

Turkey and Phyllo Pie Best Loved

Prep: 20 minutes **Bake:** 45 minutes **Oven:** 375°F
Stand: 10 minutes **Makes:** 8 servings

- 2 **medium leeks, thinly sliced**
- 1 **clove garlic, minced**
- 1 **tablespoon butter or margarine**
- 3 **slightly beaten eggs**
- 1 **10-ounce package frozen chopped spinach, thawed and well drained**
- 1 **cup shredded mozzarella cheese (4 ounces)**
- ⅔ **cup milk**
- 2 **tablespoons grated Parmesan cheese**
- ¼ **teaspoon black pepper**
- 2 **cups chopped cooked turkey**
- 4 **sheets frozen phyllo dough (18×14-inch rectangles), thawed**
- 3 **tablespoons butter or margarine, melted**

1. In a medium skillet cook leeks and garlic in 1 tablespoon hot butter until leeks are tender. In a large bowl combine leek mixture, eggs, spinach, mozzarella cheese, milk, Parmesan cheese, and pepper. Stir in turkey; set aside.

2. Lightly brush 1 sheet of phyllo with some of the melted butter; fold in half crosswise. (Cover remaining phyllo with plastic wrap and a damp kitchen towel to prevent drying.) Gently press folded phyllo into a 9-inch pie plate; allow ends to hang

over edge. Repeat with remaining sheets of phyllo and remaining butter, staggering phyllo in pie plate so the bottom and sides are evenly covered.

3. Spoon turkey filling into phyllo crust. Fold ends of the phyllo toward the center. Bake, uncovered, in a 375° oven for 45 to 50 minutes or until a knife inserted near the center comes out clean. Let stand for 10 minutes before serving. Cut into wedges to serve.

Nutrition Facts per serving: 244 cal., 13 g total fat (7 g sat. fat), 133 mg chol., 308 mg sodium, 11 g carbo., 1 g fiber, 19 g pro.
Daily Values: 113% vit. A, 9% vit. C, 19% calcium, 11% iron
Exchanges: 1 Vegetable, ½ Starch, 2 Lean Meat, 1½ Fat

Artichoke-Turkey Casserole

Low Fat

Prep: 20 minutes **Bake:** 40 minutes **Oven:** 350°F
Stand: 10 minutes **Makes:** 6 servings

- ½ **cup chopped carrot (1)**
- ½ **cup chopped red sweet pepper**
- ¼ **cup sliced green onions (2)**
- 1 **tablespoon butter or margarine**
- 1 **10¾-ounce can condensed cream of chicken soup**
- 1 **8- or 9-ounce package frozen artichoke hearts, thawed and cut up**
- 1½ **cups chopped cooked turkey or chicken (see tip, page 437)**

1 **cup hot cooked long grain rice or wild rice**

½ **cup shredded mozzarella cheese (2 ounces)**

⅔ **cup milk**

½ **teaspoon dried thyme, crushed**

2 **slices bacon, crisp-cooked, drained, and crumbled**

3 **tablespoons grated Parmesan cheese**

1. In a large skillet cook carrot, sweet pepper, and green onions in hot butter until the carrot is crisp-tender. Remove from heat. Stir in chicken soup, artichoke hearts, turkey, rice, mozzarella cheese, milk, thyme, and bacon. Transfer turkey mixture to a 2-quart rectangular baking dish. Sprinkle with Parmesan cheese.

2. Bake, covered, in a 350° oven for 20 minutes. Uncover and bake about 20 minutes more or until bubbly. Let stand for 10 minutes before serving.

Make-ahead directions: Prepare as above through step 1. Cover and refrigerate for up to 24 hours. Bake, covered, in a 350° oven for 30 minutes. Uncover and bake about 20 minutes more or until bubbly.

Nutrition Facts per serving: 248 cal., 11 g total fat (5 g sat. fat), 47 mg chol., 611 mg sodium, 18 g carbo., 3 g fiber, 18 g pro.
Daily Values: 75% vit. A, 41% vit. C, 18% calcium, 9% iron
Exchanges: ½ Vegetable, 1 Starch, 2 Lean Meat, 1 Fat

Cheese-Stuffed Chicken Breasts

If you like, serve these cheese-stuffed chicken breasts draped with warmed pasta sauce.

Prep: 20 minutes **Bake:** 45 minutes
Oven: 375°F **Makes:** 6 servings

6 **medium chicken breast halves (about 3 pounds)**

½ **cup ricotta cheese**

½ **cup shredded fontina or mozzarella cheese**

⅓ **cup grated Parmesan or Romano cheese**

2 **teaspoons snipped fresh basil or ½ teaspoon dried basil, crushed**

1 **teaspoon snipped fresh oregano or ¼ teaspoon dried oregano, crushed**

¼ **teaspoon lemon-pepper seasoning**

2 **tablespoons butter or margarine, melted**

1. Using your fingers, gently separate the chicken skin from the meat of the breasts along rib edge (see photo, above right).

2. For stuffing, in a bowl combine cheeses, basil, oregano, and lemon-pepper seasoning. Spoon a rounded tablespoon of stuffing between the skin

and meat of each breast. Place chicken, bone side down, in a 3-quart rectangular baking dish. Brush chicken with butter. Bake in a 375° oven for 45 to 55 minutes or until no longer pink (170°F).

Nutrition Facts per serving: 346 cal., 22 g total fat (10 g sat. fat), 116 mg chol., 356 mg sodium, 1 g carbo., 0 g fiber, 35 g pro.
Daily Values: 10% vit. A, 2% vit. C, 20% calcium, 6% iron
Exchanges: 5 Lean Meat, 1½ Fat

To form a pocket for the stuffing, use your fingers to gently separate the skin from the meat of a chicken breast along the rib edge; leave the skin attached at the breast bone.

Handling Poultry Safely

Follow these simple guidelines to safely handle fresh poultry (see also "Poultry Hotline," page 433).

■ Always wash your hands, work surfaces, and utensils in hot soapy water after handling raw poultry to prevent spreading bacteria to other foods.

■ When cutting raw poultry, use a plastic cutting board because it's easier to clean and disinfect than a wooden one.

■ If you're planning to stuff the bird, you can rinse the inside cavity, let it drain well, and pat the bird dry with paper towels. Thoroughly clean the kitchen sink and any surfaces the poultry has been in contact with.

■ Washing raw poultry is not necessary because any bacteria will be destroyed by cooking to the proper temperatures. The less you handle poultry, the safer it remains.

■ Never use the same plate for uncooked and cooked poultry.

■ Always marinate poultry in the refrigerator.

■ Heat any marinade or basting sauce that has been in contact with the raw poultry if it is to be served with the cooked poultry. Juices from the uncooked poultry may contain bacteria. Or, before you start basting, set some of the sauce aside to serve with the poultry.

■ Serve poultry immediately after cooking it. Don't let it stand at room temperature longer than 2 hours or bacteria will multiply rapidly—especially in warm weather. Refrigerate leftovers as soon as possible.

■ Heat leftover gravy to a rolling boil in a covered saucepan, stirring occasionally, for food safety assurance.

Baked Chicken Chiles Rellenos

Expect lots of compliments when you serve these chicken rolls; each has cheese and chile peppers nestled inside.

Low Fat

Prep: 35 minutes   **Bake:** 25 minutes   **Oven:** 375°F
Makes: 6 servings

- **6 skinless, boneless chicken breast halves**
- **⅓ cup all-purpose flour**
- **3 tablespoons cornmeal**
- **¼ teaspoon ground red pepper**
- **1 egg**
- **1 tablespoon water**
- **1 4-ounce can whole green chile peppers, rinsed, seeded, and cut in half lengthwise (6 pieces total) (see tip, page 64)**
- **2 ounces Monterey Jack cheese, cut into six 2×½-inch sticks**
- **2 tablespoons snipped fresh cilantro or fresh parsley**
- **¼ teaspoon black pepper**
- **2 tablespoons butter or margarine, melted**
- **1 8-ounce jar green or red salsa**

1. Place a chicken breast half between 2 pieces of plastic wrap. Using the flat side of a meat mallet, pound meat lightly into a rectangle about ⅛ inch thick (see photo 2, page 437). Remove plastic wrap. Repeat with remaining chicken breast halves.

2. In a shallow dish combine the flour, cornmeal, and red pepper. Place egg in another shallow dish; add water and beat lightly to combine.

3. For each roll, place a chile pepper half on a chicken piece near an edge. Place a stick of cheese on the chile pepper near an edge. Sprinkle with some of the cilantro and black pepper. Fold in sides; roll up, starting from edge with cheese and chile pepper (see photo 3, page 437). Secure with wooden toothpicks.

4. Dip chicken rolls in egg mixture; coat with cornmeal mixture. Place rolls, seam side down, in a shallow baking pan. Drizzle with butter.

5. Bake, uncovered, in a 375° oven for 25 to 30 minutes or until chicken is no longer pink (170°F). Remove toothpicks. Meanwhile, heat salsa; serve over chicken.

Nutrition Facts per serving: 260 cal., 10 g total fat (5 g sat. fat), 120 mg chol., 381 mg sodium, 10 g carbo., 1 g fiber, 31 g pro.
Daily Values: 14% vit. A, 22% vit. C, 13% calcium, 10% iron
Exchanges: ½ Vegetable, ½ Starch, 4 Lean Meat

Baked Chicken Chiles Rellenos

Chicken Cordon Bleu

Cordon bleu refers to chicken or veal that has been pounded thin, layered with Swiss cheese and ham, rolled, breaded, and sauteed until golden brown. This version leaves the breading behind.

Prep: 20 minutes   **Cook:** 20 minutes   **Makes:** 4 servings

- **4 skinless, boneless chicken breast halves**
- **4 slices prosciutto or cooked ham**
- **4 slices Swiss cheese (3 ounces)**
- **1 tablespoon butter or margarine**

1. Place a chicken breast half between 2 pieces of plastic wrap. Using the flat side of a meat mallet, pound meat lightly into a rectangle about ⅛ inch thick (see photo 2, page 437). Remove plastic wrap. Repeat with remaining chicken.

2. Place a slice of prosciutto and a slice of cheese on each chicken piece. Fold in the bottom and sides; roll up (see photo 3, page 437). Secure with wooden toothpicks.

3. In a 10-inch skillet cook rolls in hot butter over medium-low heat for 20 to 25 minutes or until no longer pink (170°F), turning to brown evenly. To serve, remove toothpicks.

Nutrition Facts per serving: 290 cal., 13 g total fat (7 g sat. fat), 113 mg chol., 911 mg sodium, 1 g carbo., 0 g fiber, 40 g pro.
Daily Values: 6% vit. A, 2% vit. C, 22% calcium, 6% iron
Exchanges: 5½ Lean Meat

Chicken Kiev

Prep: 20 minutes **Chill:** 1 to 24 hours **Bake:** 15 minutes
Oven: 400°F **Makes:** 4 servings

> 1 tablespoon chopped green onion
> 1 tablespoon snipped fresh parsley
> 1 clove garlic, minced
> ½ of a ¼-pound stick of butter, chilled
> 1 beaten egg
> 1 tablespoon water
> ¼ cup all-purpose flour
> ½ cup fine dry bread crumbs
> 4 skinless, boneless chicken breast halves
> 1 tablespoon butter
> 1 tablespoon cooking oil

1. In a small bowl combine green onion, parsley, and garlic; set aside. Cut chilled butter into four 2½×½-inch sticks (see photo 1, right). In a shallow bowl stir together egg and water. Place flour in another shallow bowl. Place bread crumbs in another shallow bowl. Set aside.

2. Place a chicken breast half between 2 pieces of plastic wrap. Using the flat side of a meat mallet, pound chicken lightly into a rectangle about ⅛ inch thick (see photo 2, right). Remove plastic wrap. Sprinkle with *salt* and *black pepper.* Sprinkle with one-fourth of the green onion mixture. Place a butter piece in center of chicken piece. Fold in sides; roll up, pressing edges to seal (see photo 3, right). Repeat with remaining chicken.

3. Coat chicken rolls with flour. Dip in egg mixture; coat with bread crumbs. Dip in egg mixture again; coat with additional bread crumbs. (Coat ends well to seal in the butter.) Place coated chicken rolls in a 2-quart rectangular baking dish. Cover and chill for 1 to 24 hours.

4. In a large skillet melt the 1 tablespoon butter; add oil. Add chilled chicken rolls. Cook over medium-high heat about 5 minutes or until golden brown, turning to brown all sides. Place in the 2-quart rectangular baking dish.

5. Bake in a 400° oven for 15 to 18 minutes or until chicken is no longer pink (170°F). Spoon any drippings over rolls.

Nutrition Facts per serving: 377 cal., 22 g total fat (11 g sat. fat), 160 mg chol., 499 mg sodium, 13 g carbo., 1 g fiber, 30 g pro.
Daily Values: 15% vit. A, 5% vit. C, 5% calcium, 11% iron
Exchanges: 1 Starch, 4 Lean Meat, 2 Fat

Cheesy Chicken Rolls: Prepare as at left, except substitute 2½×½-inch sticks of caraway, blue cheese, Gruyère, or cheddar for the butter. Omit parsley if using caraway or blue cheese. Substitute 2 teaspoons snipped fresh tarragon for the parsley if using Gruyère cheese. Substitute 2 teaspoons snipped fresh thyme for the parsley if using cheddar cheese.

Nutrition Facts per serving: 328 cal., 15 g total fat (6 g sat. fat), 142 mg chol., 479 mg sodium, 13 g carbo., 1 g fiber, 33 g pro.
Daily Values: 9% vit. A, 5% vit. C, 15% calcium, 12% iron
Exchanges: 1 Starch, 4 Lean Meat, ½ Fat

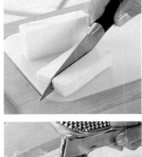

1. For the Chicken Kiev filling, cut the half stick of chilled butter lengthwise into 4 sticks, each measuring 2½×½ inches.

2. Lightly pound skinless, boneless chicken breast halves using the flat side of a meat mallet. Work from the center to the edges until an even thickness is achieved.

3. Fold in the sides of the chicken breast half and roll up. Press all edges firmly to seal in the filling.

Quick-Cooked Poultry

If your recipe calls for cooked poultry and you don't have any leftovers to use, purchase a deli-roasted chicken. A roasted chicken will yield 1½ to 2 cups boneless chopped meat.

Another option is to poach chicken breasts. In a large skillet place 12 ounces skinless, boneless chicken breasts and 1½ cups water. Bring to boiling; reduce heat. Simmer, covered, for 12 to 14 minutes or until chicken is no longer pink (170°F). Drain well. Cut up chicken as recipe directs. The 12 ounces boneless breasts will yield about 2 cups cubed, cooked chicken.

If your recipe calls for chilled chicken or turkey, cover the cut-up cooked chicken or turkey meat and refrigerate it for at least 2 hours or freeze it for 30 minutes or until thoroughly chilled.

Glazed Chicken and Vegetables

Prep: 15 minutes **Roast:** 1¼ hours
Oven: 375°F **Makes:** 4 servings

> 1 3- to 3½-pound whole broiler-fryer chicken
> Cooking oil
> 3 medium potatoes, quartered (about 1 pound)
> 6 carrots, bias-sliced ½ inch thick (about 1 pound)
> ½ cup honey
> ¼ cup prepared mustard
> 2 tablespoons butter or margarine
> 2 tablespoons finely chopped onion
> 2 teaspoons curry powder
> ½ teaspoon garlic salt
> ¼ teaspoon crushed red pepper
> ¼ teaspoon ground ginger
> 2 medium apples, cored and cut into wedges

1. Rinse inside of chicken; pat dry with paper towels. Skewer neck skin of chicken to back (see photo 2, page 441); tie legs to tail. Twist wing tips under back (see photo 4, page 441). Place chicken, breast side up, on a rack in a shallow roasting pan. Brush with oil. If desired, insert a meat thermometer into center of an inside thigh muscle, not touching bone (see photo 5, page 441). Roast, uncovered, in a 375° oven for 45 minutes.

2. Meanwhile, cook potatoes and carrots in boiling water for 15 to 20 minutes or until nearly tender; drain.

3. For glaze, in a saucepan combine honey, mustard, butter, onion, curry powder, garlic salt, red pepper, and ginger. Bring to boiling, stirring constantly. Remove from heat; set glaze aside.

4. Discard drippings in roasting pan. Arrange potatoes, carrots, and apple wedges around chicken in pan. Spoon glaze over poultry, vegetables, and apples. Roast, uncovered, for 30 to 40 minutes more or until the drumsticks move easily in their sockets and chicken is no longer pink (180°F). Serve any cooking juices over chicken and vegetables.

Nutrition Facts per serving: 728 cal., 28 g total fat (10 g sat. fat), 148 mg chol., 517 mg sodium, 78 g carbo., 8 g fiber, 45 g pro.
Daily Values: 522% vit. A, 47% vit. C, 8% calcium, 23% iron
Exchanges: 2 Vegetable, ½ Fruit, 2 Starch, 2 Other Carbo., 5 Medium-Fat Meat

Herb-Roasted Chicken

Prep: 15 minutes **Roast:** 1¼ hours **Oven:** 375°F
Stand: 10 minutes **Makes:** 4 servings

> 1 3- to 3½-pound whole broiler-fryer chicken
> 2 tablespoons butter or margarine, melted
> 2 cloves garlic, minced
> 1 teaspoon dried basil, crushed
> ½ teaspoon salt
> ½ teaspoon ground sage
> ½ teaspoon dried thyme, crushed
> ¼ teaspoon lemon-pepper seasoning or black pepper

1. Rinse inside of chicken; pat dry with paper towels. Skewer neck skin of chicken to back (see photo 2, page 441); tie legs to tail. Twist wing tips under back (see photo 4, page 441). Place chicken, breast side up, on a rack in a shallow roasting pan. Brush with melted butter; rub garlic over chicken.

2. In a small bowl stir together basil, salt, sage, thyme, and lemon-pepper seasoning; rub onto chicken. If desired, insert a meat thermometer into center of an inside thigh muscle (see photo 5, page 441), not touching bone.

3. Roast, uncovered, in a 375° oven for 1¼ to 1½ hours or until drumsticks move easily in their sockets and chicken is no longer pink (180°F). Remove chicken from oven. Cover; let stand for 10 minutes before carving.

Nutrition Facts per serving: 417 cal., 26 g total fat (9 g sat. fat), 148 mg chol., 544 mg sodium, 1 g carbo., 0 g fiber, 41 g pro.
Daily Values: 11% vit. A, 1% vit. C, 4% calcium, 12% iron
Exchanges: 5½ Medium-Fat Meat

Honey Mustard-Glazed Turkey Breast

Low Fat

Prep: 15 minutes **Roast:** 1¼ hours **Oven:** 325°F
Stand: 10 minutes **Makes:** 6 servings

> 1 1¾- to 2-pound turkey breast portion with bone
> 1 tablespoon cooking oil
> ¼ teaspoon salt
> ⅛ teaspoon black pepper
> 1 recipe Honey-Mustard Glaze

1. Place turkey, bone side down, on a rack in a shallow roasting pan. Brush with oil; sprinkle with salt and pepper. Insert a meat thermometer into thickest part of the breast. The thermometer should not touch the bone.

2. Roast turkey, uncovered, in a 325° oven for 1¼ to 1½ hours or until juices run clear and turkey is no longer pink (170°F), brushing with Honey-Mustard Glaze several times during the last 15 minutes of roasting. Transfer turkey to a cutting board; let stand 10 to 15 minutes before carving. Heat any remaining glaze. Serve warm glaze with turkey.

Honey-Mustard Glaze: In a bowl stir together ¼ cup honey, 1 tablespoon Dijon-style mustard, 1 tablespoon white wine Worcestershire sauce, and 1 tablespoon butter or margarine, melted.

Nutrition Facts per serving: 218 cal., 10 g total fat (3 g sat. fat), 58 mg chol., 198 mg sodium, 12 g carbo., 0 g fiber, 20 g pro.
Daily Values: 2% vit. A, 1% vit. C, 2% calcium, 7% iron
Exchanges: 1 Other Carbo., 3 Lean Meat

Maple-Brined Turkey Best Loved

Low Fat

Prep: 20 minutes **Marinate:** 12 to 24 hours **Oven:** 325°F
Roast: 2¾ hours **Stand:** 15 minutes **Makes:** 12 servings

  1½ **gallons water**
  1½ **cups pure maple syrup or maple-flavored syrup**
  1 **cup coarse salt**
  ¾ **cup packed brown sugar**
  1 **10-pound turkey (not a self-basting type)**
   Cooking oil

1. For brine, in a 10-quart kettle combine water, syrup, salt, and brown sugar; stir to dissolve sugar and salt. Set aside.

2. Rinse turkey; remove any excess fat from cavity. Add turkey to brine in kettle. Cover; marinate in the refrigerator for 12 to 24 hours.

3. Remove turkey from brine. Drain turkey; pat dry with paper towels. Place turkey, breast side up, on a rack in a shallow roasting pan. Tuck ends of drumsticks under the band of skin across the tail. If there is no band of skin, tie drumsticks securely to tail. Twist wing tips under the back (see photo 4, page 441). Brush with oil. If desired, insert a meat thermometer into the center of an inside thigh muscle (see photo 5, page 441). The thermometer should not touch bone. Cover turkey loosely with foil.

4. Roast turkey in a 325° oven for 2¼ hours; cut band of skin or string between drumsticks so thighs cook evenly; remove foil. Continue roasting 30 to 45 minutes more or until drumsticks move easily in their sockets and turkey is no longer pink (180°F).

5. Remove turkey from oven. Cover and let stand for 15 to 20 minutes before carving.

Nutrition Facts per serving: 280 cal., 11 g total fat (3 g sat. fat), 101 mg chol., 1,250 mg sodium, 7 g carbo., 0 g fiber, 36 g pro.
Daily Values: 4% calcium, 13% iron
Exchanges: ½ Other Carbo., 4½ Lean Meat

Deep-Frying Turkey Safely

Deep-frying, a popular technique for cooking turkey, requires these safety precautions.

■ Use a pot, basket, and burner designed for deep-frying. Carefully follow any instructions that accompany the equipment. The vessel should be large enough to hold the turkey and enough oil to completely cover the turkey. (It can take up to 5 gallons of oil.)

■ Do not overfill the fryer with oil. To estimate how much oil you need, before unwrapping the frozen bird, put it in the fryer; add water until the turkey is submerged. Remove the turkey; note the water level. This is the level the oil should be.

■ Have on hand thermometers for taking oil and meat temperatures, and long oven mitts. Keep a fire extinguisher (appropriate for grease fires) nearby.

■ Find a level dirt or grassy area on which to position the fryer. (Wooden decks are not appropriate; they can catch fire. Oil will stain concrete.) Do not fry your turkey indoors or in a garage or other attached structure.

■ Only fry a turkey that weighs less than 12 pounds.

■ Thaw the turkey completely.

■ Do not stuff the bird.

■ Remove any plastic pieces from the turkey, such as a plastic tie to hold the legs together or the piece that pops up when the turkey is done. These plastics will melt in hot oil.

■ Heating the oil can take up to 1 hour.

■ Estimate cooking time to take about 3 minutes per pound at an oil temperature of 350°F (the skin and wings will turn black).

■ The turkey is done when a meat thermometer inserted into the thigh muscle registers 180°F.

■ Keep children and pets away from the cooking area and do not leave the hot oil unattended.

■ Allow oil to cool completely after use. Discard oil by pouring it back into the original container using a funnel. If you plan to reuse the oil, strain it through 100-percent-cotton cheesecloth. Store in a covered container in the refrigerator. Reuse the oil once or twice; discard after 1 month.

For more information, visit the National Turkey Federation web site at www.eatturkey.com or call 202/898-0100 or call the USDA Meat and Poultry Hotline at 800/535-4555.

Roast Turkey

Fill the turkey with any of the stuffings listed on pages 441 to 444. Check roasting times for various size turkeys on pages 448 and 449.

Low Fat

Prep: 15 minutes **Roast:** 2¾ hours **Oven:** 325°F
Stand: 15 minutes **Makes:** 12 to 14 servings

> 1 8- to 12-pound turkey
> Stuffing (optional)
> Cooking oil

1. Rinse the inside of turkey; pat dry with paper towels. If desired, season body cavity with *salt.* Spoon stuffing, if using, loosely into neck and body cavities (see photo 1, page 441). Pull neck skin to the back; fasten with a skewer (see photo 2, page 441). Tuck the ends of the drumsticks under the band of skin across the tail (see photo 3, page 441). If there is no band of skin, tie the drumsticks securely to the tail. Twist wing tips under the back (see photo 4, page 441).

2. Place turkey, breast side up, on a rack in a shallow roasting pan. Brush with oil. If desired, insert a meat thermometer into the center of an inside thigh muscle (see photo 5, page 441). (See page 331 for tips on thermometers.) The thermometer should not touch bone. Cover turkey loosely with foil.

3. Place turkey in a 325° oven. Roast for 2¾ to 3 hours (3¼ to 3½ hours, if stuffed). During the last 45 minutes of roasting, remove foil. Cut band of skin or string between drumsticks so thighs cook evenly. Roast until the thermometer registers 180°F and the center of the stuffing (if using) is 165°F. (The juices should run clear and the drumsticks should move easily in their sockets.)

4. Remove turkey from oven. Cover; let stand for 15 to 20 minutes before carving (see tips for carving, below).

Nutrition Facts per serving: 255 cal., 12 g total fat (3 g sat. fat), 101 mg chol., 83 mg sodium, 0 g carbo., 0 g fiber, 35 g pro.
Daily Values: 3% calcium, 12% iron
Exchanges: 5 Lean Meat

Carving a Roasted Bird

To carve poultry with confidence, use a sharp knife and follow these directions.

1. When the bird is done roasting, remove it from the oven and cover it with foil. Let it stand for 15 to 20 minutes before carving. Standing allows the bird's flesh to firm up, which helps the carved slices hold together.

2. Place the bird on a cutting board. Remove the stuffing. Grasp the tip of one drumstick and pull it away from the body. Cut through the skin and meat between the thigh and the body (see first photo, below). Repeat on the other side.

3. With the tip of the knife, separate the thighbone from the backbone by cutting through the joint. Repeat on the other side.

4. To separate the thighs and drumsticks, cut through the joints where the drumstick bones and thighbones meet.

5. To carve the meat from the drumsticks, hold each drumstick vertically by the tip with the large end resting on the cutting board. Slice the meat parallel to the bone and under some tendons, turning the leg to get even slices. Slice the thigh meat the same way.

6. To carve breast meat, make a deep horizontal cut into the breast above each wing (see second photo, below). This cut marks the end of each breast meat slice. Beginning at the outer top edge of each breast, cut the slices from the top down to the horizontal cut (see third photo, below). Cut the final smaller slices following the curve of the breastbone.

7. Remove wings by cutting through the joints where the wing bones and backbone meet.

1. Lightly spoon some of the stuffing into the neck cavity. Do not pack stuffing tightly or it won't be thoroughly cooked when the turkey is done. Use no more than ¾ cup stuffing per pound.

2. After adding stuffing to the neck cavity, pull the neck skin over the stuffing onto the back of the turkey; secure with a small skewer.

3. Loosely fill body cavity with stuffing, again packing it lightly. Tuck the legs under the band of skin, if there is one, or tie legs to tail with kitchen string.

4. To prevent the wing tips from overbrowning and for a neater appearance, twist the wing tips under the back of the turkey.

5. Insert a thermometer into the center of an inside thigh muscle. The tip should not touch bone. After roasting, use an instant-read thermometer to check the stuffing and thigh in several places.

Classic Giblet Stuffing

Prep: 35 minutes **Bake:** 35 minutes
Oven: 325°F **Makes:** 10 to 12 servings (7½ cups)

Turkey giblets
1 cup finely chopped celery
½ cup chopped onion (1 medium)
½ cup butter or margarine
1 tablespoon snipped fresh sage or 1 teaspoon poultry seasoning or ground sage
¼ teaspoon black pepper
8 cups dry bread cubes (see tip, page 443)
1 to 1⅓ cups chicken broth or water

1. Rinse giblets. Refrigerate liver until needed. In a small saucepan cook the remaining giblets, covered, in enough boiling water to cover for 1 hour. Add liver. Simmer, covered, 20 to 30 minutes more or until tender. Drain* and chop giblets; set aside.

2. In the small saucepan cook celery and onion in butter until tender but not brown; remove from heat. Stir in giblets, sage, pepper, and ⅛ teaspoon *salt*. Place dry bread cubes in a very large bowl; add the onion mixture. Drizzle with enough broth to moisten, tossing lightly to combine. Use to stuff one 8- to 10-pound turkey. (See tip, page 443, and roasting chart, page 449, for doneness temperatures and roasting times.) Place any remaining stuffing in a 1-quart casserole. (If necessary, to moisten, add more liquid to stuffing in casserole.) Cover and chill.

3. Bake stuffing in casserole alongside turkey about the last 35 to 40 minutes of roasting time or until heated through. Or place all of the stuffing in a 2-quart casserole. Bake, covered, in a 325° oven for 35 to 40 minutes or until heated through.

*Note: If desired, use the giblet cooking broth instead of the chicken broth or water for a flavorful substitute.

Oyster Stuffing: Prepare as above, except omit the giblets and use a medium saucepan. Add 1 pint shucked oysters, drained and chopped, to the cooked vegetables. Cook and stir 2 minutes more. Stir in seasonings. Continue as above, except reduce broth to ¼ cup.

Nutrition Facts per serving for plain or oyster variation:
189 cal., 11 g total fat (6 g sat. fat), 62 mg chol., 379 mg sodium, 16 g carbo., 1 g fiber, 5 g pro.
Daily Values: 18% vit. A, 2% vit. C, 4% calcium, 9% iron
Exchanges: 1 Starch, 2½ Fat

Chestnut Stuffing: Prepare as above, except omit the giblets. With a knife, cut an X in the shells of 1 pound fresh chestnuts (3 cups). Spread chestnuts on a large baking sheet. Roast chestnuts in a 400°F oven for 15 minutes; cool. Peel and coarsely chop chestnuts. (Or use one 8-ounce jar or one 10-ounce can whole, peeled chestnuts, drained and chopped.) Add chestnuts with seasonings. Use ¾ cup to 1 cup broth or water.

Nutrition Facts per serving: 271 cal., 12 g total fat (6 g sat. fat), 27 mg chol., 376 mg sodium, 37 g carbo., 5 g fiber, 4 g pro.
Daily Values: 8% vit. A, 34% vit. C, 6% calcium, 8% iron
Exchanges: 2½ Starch, 2 Fat

Old-Fashioned Bread Stuffing `Best Loved`

Prep: 15 minutes **Bake:** 30 minutes **Oven:** 325°F
Makes: 12 to 14 servings (about 8 cups)

1½	cups chopped celery (3 stalks)
1	cup chopped onion (1 large)
½	cup butter or margarine
1	tablespoon snipped fresh sage or 1 teaspoon poultry seasoning or ground sage
¼	teaspoon black pepper
12	cups dry bread cubes (see tip, page 443)
1	to 1¼ cup chicken broth

1. In a large skillet cook celery and onion in hot butter until tender but not brown. Remove from heat. Stir in sage and pepper. Place dry bread cubes in a large bowl; add onion mixture. Drizzle with enough chicken broth to moisten, tossing lightly to combine.

2. Place stuffing in a 2-quart casserole. Bake, covered, in a 325° oven for 30 to 45 minutes or until heated through. (See stuffing tips, page 443.) Or use to stuff one 10- to 12-pound turkey; prepare as above, except use ¾ cup to 1 cup chicken broth instead of 1 to 1¼ cups broth. (For doneness and roasting temperatures for turkey and stuffing, see roasting chart, page 449.)

Nutrition Facts per serving: 181 cal., 10 g total fat (5 g sat. fat), 22 mg chol., 342 mg sodium, 20 g carbo., 1 g fiber, 4 g pro.
Daily Values: 6% vit. A, 2% vit. C, 5% calcium, 7% iron
Exchanges: 1½ Starch, 1½ Fat

Harvest Stuffing

Prep: 20 minutes **Bake:** 40 minutes **Oven:** 325°F
Makes: 12 to 14 servings (about 11 cups)

1	cup shredded carrots (2 medium)
1	cup chopped celery (2 stalks)
½	cup chopped onion (1 medium)
½	cup butter or margarine
¼	teaspoon salt
¼	teaspoon ground nutmeg
¼	teaspoon black pepper
8	cups dry bread cubes (see tip, page 443)
3	cups chopped peeled apples
½	cup chopped walnuts
¼	cup toasted wheat germ
½	to 1 cup chicken broth

1. In a large skillet cook carrots, celery, and onion in hot butter about 5 minutes or until tender. Stir in salt, nutmeg, and pepper.

2. In a large bowl combine bread cubes, apples, walnuts, and wheat germ; add carrot mixture. Drizzle with enough broth to moisten, tossing lightly to combine.

3. Place stuffing in a 3-quart casserole. Bake, covered, in a 325° oven alongside turkey for 40 to 45 minutes or until heated through. (See stuffing tips, page 443.) Or use to stuff one 10- to 12-pound turkey. (For doneness and roasting temperatures for turkey and stuffing, see roasting chart, page 449.)

Make-ahead directions: Place stuffing in a 3-quart casserole. Cover and chill up to 24 hours. Bake, covered, in a 325°F oven for 50 to 55 minutes or until heated through. (For safety reasons, do not make stuffing ahead if planning to use for stuffing a turkey.)

Nutrition Facts per serving: 210 cal., 13 g total fat (6 g sat. fat), 22 mg chol., 308 mg sodium, 21 g carbo., 3 g fiber, 4 g pro.
Daily Values: 58% vit. A, 6% vit. C, 5% calcium, 7% iron
Exchanges: 1 Vegetable, 1 Starch, 2½ Fat

Mediterranean-Style Stuffing `Best Loved`

Prep: 30 minutes **Bake:** 40 minutes **Oven:** 325°F
Makes: 6 to 8 servings (5 cups)

8	cups Italian bread cubes (about 8 ounces)
¾	cup chopped red or yellow sweet pepper
½	cup chopped onion (1 medium)
3	cloves garlic, minced
¼	cup olive oil
1	tablespoon lemon juice
1	teaspoon dried rosemary, crushed
⅛	teaspoon ground red pepper
¼	cup snipped fresh parsley
1	to 1¼ cups chicken broth

1. Place bread cubes in a single layer in a 15×10×1-inch baking pan. Bake in a 375° oven 10 minutes or until golden, stirring once or twice; set aside. Reduce oven temperature to 325°.

2. In a medium skillet cook the sweet pepper, onion, and garlic in hot oil about 4 minutes or until vegetables are tender; remove from heat. Stir in the lemon juice, rosemary, and red pepper. In a large bowl toss together the bread cubes, onion mixture, and parsley. Drizzle with enough broth to moisten, tossing lightly to combine. Transfer mixture to a 1½-quart casserole. Or use to stuff one 8-pound turkey. (For doneness and roasting temperatures for turkey and stuffing, see roasting chart, page 449.)

3. Bake, covered, for 20 minutes. Uncover; bake about 20 minutes more or until heated through.

Nutrition Facts per serving: 202 cal., 11 g total fat (2 g sat. fat), 0 mg chol., 390 mg sodium, 22 g carbo., 2 g fiber, 4 g pro.
Daily Values: 23% vit. A, 60% vit. C, 4% calcium, 8% iron
Exchanges: 1½ Starch, 2 Fat

Wild Rice Stuffing

Low Fat

Prep: 15 minutes **Cook:** 45 minutes
Makes: 6 servings (2½ cups)

¼	**cup wild rice**
1¾	**cups water**
¼	**cup brown rice**
1	**teaspoon instant chicken bouillon granules**
⅛ to ¼	**teaspoon ground sage or nutmeg**
2	**cups sliced fresh mushrooms**
½	**cup sliced celery (1 stalk)**
3	**green onions, sliced**
¼	**cup sliced almonds or pine nuts, toasted (see tip, page 224) (optional)**

1. Rinse uncooked wild rice in a strainer under cold water about 1 minute. In a medium saucepan combine wild rice, the 1¾ cups water, uncooked brown rice, bouillon granules, and sage. Bring to boiling; reduce heat. Simmer, covered, for 20 minutes.

2. Add mushrooms, celery, and green onions. Cook, covered, over medium-low heat for 25 minutes more or until vegetables are just tender, stirring frequently. If desired, stir in almonds. Use to stuff a 3½- to 4-pound broiler-fryer chicken or serve immediately.

Make-ahead directions: Place stuffing in a 1-quart casserole and chill for up to 24 hours. Stir in ¼ cup water. Bake, covered, in a 375°F oven about 30 minutes or until heated through.

Nutrition Facts per serving: 66 cal., 1 g total fat (0 g sat. fat), 0 mg chol., 155 mg sodium, 13 g carbo., 1 g fiber, 3 g pro.
Daily Values: 1% vit. A, 3% vit. C, 1% calcium, 3% iron
Exchanges: 1 Vegetable, ½ Starch

Stuffing Tips

■ To make dry bread for stuffing, cut fresh bread into ½-inch cubes. (You'll need 12 to 14 slices of bread to make 8 cups of dry cubes.) Spread cubes in a 15½×10½×2-inch baking pan. Bake in a 300°F oven for 10 to 15 minutes or until bread cubes are dry, stirring twice; cool. (Bread will continue to dry and crisp as it cools.) Or let bread stand, loosely covered, at room temperature for 8 to 12 hours.

■ Never stuff a turkey or other poultry until just before you roast it.

■ You'll need no more than ¾ cup stuffing for each pound of turkey.

■ Spoon the stuffing into the turkey loosely to allow room for expansion during roasting. If the stuffing is too tightly packed, it will not reach a safe temperature by the time the turkey is done. Place remaining stuffing in a casserole; heat thoroughly.

■ Stuffing temperature should reach at least 165°F. Use a meat thermometer to test for doneness. Insert it through the body cavity into the thickest part of the stuffing and let it stand for 5 minutes. Or after removing the stuffed bird from the oven, use a dial or digital instant-read thermometer to check the temperature in the center of the stuffing.

■ If you wish, bake an entire recipe of stuffing in a casserole instead of using it to stuff a bird. Bake the casserole, covered, in a 325°F oven for 30 to 45 minutes or until heated through.

Wild Rice Stuffing

Sausage Stuffing

For the corn bread needed in this stuffing, make Corn Bread on page 118 or prepare one 8-ounce package corn muffin mix.

Prep: 30 minutes **Bake:** 30 minutes **Oven:** 325°F
Makes: 10 to 12 servings (8 cups)

- 12 ounces bulk pork sausage
- ¾ cup finely chopped onion
- ½ cup chopped green sweet pepper
- ½ cup chopped celery
- ½ cup butter or margarine
- 5 cups dry white bread cubes (see tip, page 443)
- 4½ cups crumbled corn bread
- 1 teaspoon poultry seasoning
- ⅛ teaspoon black pepper
- ¾ cup chopped pecans, toasted (see tip, page 224) (optional)
- 1¼ to 1½ cups chicken broth

1. In a large skillet cook sausage until brown. Drain; set aside.

2. In the same skillet cook onion, sweet pepper, and celery in hot butter until tender; set aside.

3. In a large bowl combine bread cubes and corn bread. Add cooked sausage, onion mixture, poultry seasoning, pepper, and, if desired, pecans. Drizzle with enough broth to moisten (about 1 cup), tossing lightly to combine.

4. Place all the stuffing in a 2-quart casserole. Baked, covered, in a 325° oven for 30 to 45 minutes or until heated through. (See stuffing tips, page 443.) Or use to stuff one 10- to 12-pound turkey. Place any remaining stuffing in a casserole; drizzle with enough of the remaining chicken broth (¼ to ½ cup) to make a stuffing of desired moistness. Cover and chill until ready to bake. Bake, covered, in a 325° oven alongside turkey for 40 to 45 minutes or until heated through. (For doneness and roasting temperatures for turkey and stuffing, see roasting chart, page 449.)

Quick Sausage Stuffing: Prepare as above, except omit the crumbled corn bread and substitute 3 cups corn bread stuffing mix (one 8-ounce package). Reduce poultry seasoning to ½ teaspoon; omit black pepper. Use water in place of the chicken broth.

Nutrition Facts per serving for both stuffings: 373 cal., 24 g total fat (10 g sat. fat), 62 mg chol., 686 mg sodium, 29 g carbo., 1 g fiber, 8 g pro.
Daily Values: 8% vit. A, 12% vit. C, 7% calcium, 8% iron
Exchanges: 2 Starch, ½ High-Fat Meat, 3½ Fat

Pan Gravy

To make gravy for other roasted meats, follow these same steps, substituting meat drippings and beef broth for the poultry drippings and chicken broth.

Start to Finish: 15 minutes **Makes:** 2 cups (8 to 10 servings)

- **Pan drippings from roasted poultry**
- ¼ cup all-purpose flour
- **Chicken broth**

1. After roasting, transfer roasted poultry to a serving platter. Pour pan drippings into a large measuring cup. Scrape the browned bits from the pan into the cup. Skim and reserve fat from the drippings (see photo, below).

2. Pour ¼ cup of the fat* into a medium saucepan (discard remaining fat). Stir in flour. Add enough broth to remaining drippings in the measuring cup to equal 2 cups; add broth mixture all at once to flour mixture in saucepan. Cook and stir over medium heat until thickened and bubbly. Cook and stir for 1 minute more. Season to taste with *salt* and *black pepper.*

***Note:** If there is no fat, use ¼ cup melted butter.

Nutrition Facts per ¼-cup serving: 77 cal., 6 g total fat (4 g sat. fat), 16 mg chol., 256 mg sodium, 3 g carbo., 0 g fiber, 2 g pro.
Daily Values: 5% vit. A, 2% iron
Exchanges: 1½ Fat

To skim off the fat from poultry or meat drippings, tip the container and use a metal spoon to remove the oily liquid (fat) that rises to the top.

Giblet Gravy

Giblets are poultry's edible internal organs—the liver, heart, and gizzard.

Prep: 15 minutes **Cook:** 1½ hours
Makes: 2½ cups (8 to 10 servings)

- **Whole turkey or chicken**
- 4 ounces turkey or chicken giblets plus the neck
- 1 stalk celery with leaves, cut up
- ½ small onion, cut up
- **Pan drippings from roasted turkey or chicken, or ¼ cup butter, melted**
- ¼ cup all-purpose flour
- ¼ teaspoon salt
- ⅛ teaspoon black pepper

1. Prepare turkey or chicken according to roasting chart on pages 448 and 449. Rinse giblets and neck. Refrigerate liver until needed. In a medium saucepan combine remaining giblets, neck, celery, onion, and enough lightly *salted water* (3½ to 4 cups) to cover the mixture. Bring to boiling; reduce heat. Simmer, covered, for 1 hour. Add liver. Simmer, covered, for 20 to 30 minutes more for turkey (5 to 10 minutes more for chicken) or until tender. Remove giblets and finely chop. Discard neck. Strain broth (see photo, page 487). Discard vegetables. Cover and chill giblets and broth while turkey or chicken roasts.

2. Transfer turkey or chicken to a serving platter; pour pan drippings into a large measuring cup. Skim and reserve fat from drippings (see photo, page 444). Pour ¼ cup of the fat into a medium saucepan (discard remaining fat).

3. Add enough of the reserved broth to drippings in measuring cup to equal 2 cups. Stir flour, salt, and pepper into fat in saucepan. Add drippings mixture all at once to flour mixture. Cook and stir over medium heat until thickened and bubbly. Cook and stir for 1 minute more. Stir in chopped giblets. Heat through.

Nutrition Facts per ⅓-cup serving: 85 cal., 7 g total fat (4 g sat. fat), 56 mg chol., 150 mg sodium, 3 g carbo., 0 g fiber, 3 g pro.
Daily Values: 22% vit. A, 1% vit. C, 1% calcium, 6% iron
Exchanges: ½ Very Lean Meat, 1½ Fat

Cornish Game Hens with Artichokes and Potatoes

Prep: 20 minutes **Oven:** 450°F **Roast:** 50 minutes
Makes: 4 servings

> 2 **tablespoons lemon juice**
> 3 **cloves garlic, minced**
> 2 **teaspoons olive oil**
> 1 **tablespoon snipped fresh oregano**
> 1 **teaspoon snipped fresh thyme**
> ½ **teaspoon salt**
> 1 **8- or 9-ounce package frozen artichoke hearts, thawed**
> 8 **ounces small potatoes or tiny new potatoes, quartered**
> 2 **1¼- to 1½-pound Cornish game hens**

1. In a large bowl combine lemon juice, garlic, oil, oregano, thyme, salt, and ¼ teaspoon *black pepper*. Add artichoke hearts and potatoes; toss to coat. Using a slotted spoon, transfer artichoke hearts and potatoes to another bowl, reserving garlic mixture.

Freezing and Thawing Tips

To freeze: If you can't use purchased fresh poultry within 2 days, freeze it. It can be frozen in its original package or repackaged. If freezing for longer than 2 months, leave the poultry in its original packaging and wrap it with heavy foil or freezer paper, or place in a freezer bag. If wrapped and frozen at 0°F or below, uncooked whole turkeys or chickens should retain their best flavor and texture for up to 1 year and frozen uncooked turkey or chicken pieces for up to 9 months. Never freeze stuffed poultry.

To thaw: Never thaw poultry on your kitchen countertop. Bacteria that can cause food poisoning multiply rapidly at room temperature. The refrigerator is the best place to thaw poultry. Be sure to put the poultry on a tray before setting it in your refrigerator. Plan on 1 day for every 5 pounds, not counting the day you'll be roasting it. Err on the side of extra time just to be safe.

Cold-water thawing is another safe way to defrost poultry. Place poultry in its leak-proof freezer wrapping in a sink or large bowl of cold water. Allow about 30 minutes of thawing time for every pound of poultry, changing the water every 30 minutes with additional cold water. Poultry defrosted by the cold-water method should be cooked as soon as possible.

2. Brush hens with some of the reserved garlic mixture. Arrange hens on one side of the rack of a large roasting pan. Twist wing tips under the backs. Arrange artichoke hearts and potatoes on the opposite side of rack. Drizzle hens and vegetables with the remaining garlic mixture.

3. Place roasting pan on middle rack of oven. Roast, uncovered, in a 450° oven about 50 minutes or until the vegetables are tender and an instant-read meat thermometer inserted into the thigh of each hen registers 180°F. (The thermometer should not touch bone.)

4. To serve, using kitchen shears or a long heavy knife, carefully cut hens in half lengthwise. Remove vegetables from roasting pan with a slotted spoon. Serve vegetables with the hens.

Nutrition Facts per serving: 443 cal., 25 g total fat (5 g sat. fat), 120 mg chol., 427 mg sodium, 16 g carbo., 5 g fiber, 39 g pro.
Daily Values: 2% vit. A, 29% vit. C, 5% calcium, 7% iron
Exchanges: 1 Starch, 5 Medium-Fat Meat

Roast Duckling with Wild Mushroom Sauce

Look for domestic duckling in your supermarket's freezer case. Thaw it in the refrigerator for 24 hours before roasting.

Prep: 25 minutes **Cook:** 35 minutes **Oven:** 350°F
Roast: 1½ hours **Stand:** 15 minutes
Makes: 4 servings

- 1 4- to 6-pound domestic duckling
- ¼ cup broken dried mushrooms
- 1 cup frozen small whole onions, thawed
- 2 tablespoons butter or margarine
- 2 teaspoons sugar
- 4 teaspoons all-purpose flour
- 1½ cups beef broth
- 1 tablespoon tomato paste
- ½ teaspoon dried savory, sage, or thyme, crushed
- ½ teaspoon Worcestershire sauce

1. Rinse inside of duckling; pat dry with paper towels. Pull neck skin to back; fasten with a skewer. Tie legs to tail. Twist wing tips under back. Place duckling, breast side up, on a rack in a shallow roasting pan. Using a fork, prick skin generously. Roast in a 350° oven for 1½ to 2 hours or until the drumsticks move easily in their sockets (180°F). Cover and let stand for 15 minutes before carving.

2. Meanwhile, for sauce, pour enough boiling water over dried mushrooms to cover. Let stand for 30 minutes; drain.

3. In a saucepan cook mushrooms and onions in hot butter about 15 minutes or until tender. Stir in sugar. Cook and stir for 5 to 7 minutes or until vegetables are glazed. Stir in flour. Cook and stir for 3 to 5 minutes more or until flour is browned.

4. Add beef broth, tomato paste, savory, and Worcestershire sauce. Bring to boiling; reduce heat. Simmer, uncovered, for 10 to 15 minutes or until sauce is reduced to about 1⅔ cups.

5. To carve duckling, if desired, remove the skin. Using a sharp knife, cut duckling along the backbone. Cut downward, cutting the meat from the ribs. Cut the wings and legs from the duckling. Slice breast meat. Serve meat with the mushroom sauce.

Nutrition Facts per serving: 452 cal., 24 g total fat (9 g sat. fat), 232 mg chol., 473 mg sodium, 11 g carbo., 1 g fiber, 45 g pro.
Daily Values: 7% vit. A, 12% vit. C, 3% calcium, 31% iron
Exchanges: 1 Vegetable, ½ Starch, 6 Lean Meat, 1 Fat

Roast Duckling with Raspberry Sauce Best Loved

Prep: 15 minutes **Oven:** 350°F **Roast:** 1½ hours
Stand: 15 minutes **Makes:** 4 servings

- 1 4- to 6-pound domestic duckling
- ⅓ cup orange juice
- ¼ cup chicken broth
- 2 tablespoons blackberry brandy or orange juice
- 1 cup fresh or frozen lightly sweetened raspberries
- ⅓ cup seedless raspberry preserves
- ¼ teaspoon ground ginger
- ⅛ teaspoon ground allspice
- 1 tablespoon butter or margarine
- ¼ cup coarsely chopped toasted walnuts
- 1 teaspoon snipped fresh sage

1. Rinse inside of duckling; pat dry with paper towels. Pull neck skin to back; fasten with a skewer. Tie legs to tail. Twist wing tips under back. Place duckling, breast side up, on a rack in a shallow roasting pan. Using a fork, prick skin generously. Sprinkle with *salt* and *black pepper.*

2. Roast in a 350° oven for 1½ to 2 hours or until the drumsticks move easily in their sockets (180°F). Cover and let stand for 15 minutes before carving.

3. Meanwhile, for sauce, in a small saucepan combine orange juice, broth, and brandy. Bring to boiling. Cook, uncovered, over medium-high heat about 8 minutes or until sauce is reduced to ¼ cup. Stir in ¼ cup of the raspberries, the raspberry preserves, ginger, allspice, and dash *salt.* Simmer, uncovered, about 5 minutes, stirring occasionally. Remove saucepan from heat; stir in butter until melted. Stir in remaining raspberries, the walnuts, and sage. (If using frozen raspberries, heat sauce until raspberries are thawed and sauce is heated through.)

4. To carve duckling, if desired, remove the skin. Using a sharp knife, cut duckling along the backbone. Cut downward, removing meat from ribs. Cut the wings and legs from the duckling. Slice breast meat. Serve with raspberry sauce.

Nutrition Facts per serving: 537 cal., 27 g total fat (7 g sat. fat), 224 mg chol., 275 mg sodium, 25 g carbo., 3 g fiber, 44 g pro.
Daily Values: 6% vit. A, 41% vit. C, 4% calcium, 30% iron
Exchanges: 1½ Other Carbo., 6 Lean Meat, 2 Fat

Pheasant Marsala

Look for domestic pheasant near the frozen turkeys in large supermarkets or specialty stores.

Prep: 25 minutes **Bake:** 40 minutes **Oven:** 325°F
Makes: 4 servings

- 1 2- to 2½-pound pheasant or broiler-fryer chicken, cut up
- 2 tablespoons cooking oil
- 2 tablespoons butter or margarine
   Salt
   Black pepper
- 3 cups sliced fresh mushrooms (8 ounces)
- 1 medium onion, cut into wedges
- 2 cloves garlic, minced
- ½ cup chicken broth
- ¼ cup dry Marsala
- ½ teaspoon finely shredded orange peel
- 1 8-ounce carton dairy sour cream
- 2 tablespoons all-purpose flour
- ¼ teaspoon salt

1. Remove skin from pheasant. (If using chicken, skin if desired.) In a large skillet cook pheasant in hot oil and butter until brown, turning once. Place in a 2-quart rectangular baking dish. Sprinkle with salt and pepper. Add mushrooms, onion, and garlic to skillet. Cook and stir over medium heat for 2 to 3 minutes or until onion is tender. Stir in broth, Marsala, and orange peel. Pour broth mixture evenly over pheasant in baking dish.

2. Bake, covered, in a 325° oven about 40 minutes or until an instant-read thermometer inserted into the breast registers 170°F.

3. Using a slotted spoon, transfer pheasant and vegetables to a serving platter. Cover and keep warm.

4. Pour cooking juices into a medium saucepan. In a small bowl stir together sour cream, flour, and the ¼ teaspoon salt. Whisk sour cream mixture into the pan juices until smooth. Cook and stir until thickened and bubbly. Cook and stir for 1 minute more. Spoon some of the sour cream mixture over pheasant and vegetables; pass remaining sauce.

Nutrition Facts per serving: 534 cal., 33 g total fat (15 g sat. fat), 155 mg chol., 577 mg sodium, 12 g carbo., 1 g fiber, 46 g pro.
Daily Values: 18% vit. A, 20% vit. C, 11% calcium, 16% iron
Exchanges: ½ Starch, 1 Vegetable, 6 Very Lean Meat, 6 Fat

Wine-Marinated Pheasant

Prep: 35 minutes **Marinate:** 6 to 24 hours **Roast:** 1¼ hours
Oven: 350°F **Makes:** 4 servings

- 1 small onion, thinly sliced
- ¾ cup dry white wine
- ¼ cup lime juice or lemon juice
- 2 tablespoons cooking oil
- ½ teaspoon dried savory, crushed
- ¼ teaspoon salt
- ¼ teaspoon bottled hot pepper sauce
- 1 2- to 2½-pound pheasant
- 1 tablespoon butter or margarine
- 4 teaspoons all-purpose flour
- ½ cup chicken broth
- 2 tablespoons snipped fresh flat-leaf parsley

1. For marinade, in a small bowl combine onion, wine, lime juice, oil, savory, salt, and hot pepper sauce. Set aside.

2. Place pheasant in a large plastic bag set into a deep bowl. Pour marinade over pheasant in bag. Close bag; turn pheasant to coat well. Marinate in the refrigerator for 6 to 24 hours, turning bag occasionally. Remove pheasant from bag, reserving marinade.

3. Tie legs to tail. Twist wing tips under back. Place pheasant, breast side up, on a rack in a shallow roasting pan. Cover pheasant with foil, leaving air space between bird and foil. Lightly press the foil to the ends of drumsticks and neck to enclose bird. Roast in a 350° oven for 1¼ to 1½ hours. After about 1 hour of roasting, remove foil and cut the string between drumsticks.

4. Continue roasting until drumsticks move easily in their sockets and juices run clear (180°F). (Check temperature of thigh in several places with a meat thermometer.)

5. Meanwhile, strain marinade, reserving ½ cup. In a medium saucepan melt butter; stir in flour. Add the reserved ½ cup marinade and the chicken broth. Cook and stir until thickened and bubbly; cook and stir for 1 minute more. Stir in parsley. Season to taste with *black pepper.*

Nutrition Facts per serving: 480 cal., 27 g total fat (8 g sat. fat), 146 mg chol., 341 mg sodium, 3 g carbo., 0 g fiber, 45 g pro.
Daily Values: 10% vit. A, 22% vit. C, 3% calcium, 14% iron
Exchanges: 6½ Lean Meat, 2½ Fat

Roasting Poultry

To prepare a bird for roasting, follow the steps below. Because birds vary in size and shape, use the times as general guides. To stuff a bird, see the photos on page 441.

1. If desired, rinse a whole bird thoroughly on outside as well as inside the body and neck cavities. Pat dry with paper towels. If desired, sprinkle inside of the body cavity with salt.

2. For an unstuffed bird, if desired, place quartered onions and celery in body cavity. Pull neck skin to back and fasten with a skewer. If a band of skin crosses tail, tuck drumsticks under band. If there is no band, tie drumsticks to tail. Twist wing tips under the back. To stuff a bird (do not stuff duckling or goose), just before cooking spoon some stuffing loosely into the neck and body cavities (see tip, page 443). Fasten neck skin and secure the drumsticks and wings as for an unstuffed bird.

3. Place bird, breast side up, on a rack in a shallow roasting pan; brush with cooking oil and, if desired, sprinkle with a crushed dried herb, such as thyme or oregano. (When cooking a domestic duckling or goose, use a fork to prick skin generously all over and omit cooking oil.) For large birds,

insert a meat thermometer into center of one of the inside thigh muscles. The thermometer should not touch the bone.

4. Cover Cornish game hen, pheasant, squab, and whole turkey with foil, leaving air space between bird and foil. Lightly press the foil to the ends of drumsticks and neck to enclose bird. Leave all other types of poultry uncovered.

5. Roast in an uncovered pan. Two-thirds through roasting time, cut band of skin or string between drumsticks. Uncover bird the last 45 minutes of roasting for larger birds or the last 30 minutes of roasting for smaller birds. Continue roasting until the meat thermometer registers 180°F in thigh muscle (check temperature of thigh in several places) or until drumsticks move easily in their sockets and juices run clear. Center of stuffing should register 165°F. (For a whole or half turkey breast, thermometer should register 170°F.) Remove bird from oven; cover. Allow whole birds and turkey portions to stand for 15 minutes before carving.

Type of Bird	Weight	Oven Temperature	Roasting Time
Chicken			
Capon	5 to 7 pounds	325°F	1¾ to 2½ hours
Meaty pieces (breast halves, drumsticks, and thighs with bone)	2½ to 3 pounds total	375°F	45 to 55 minutes
Whole	2½ to 3 pounds 3 to 3½ pounds 3½ to 4 pounds 4½ to 5 pounds	375°F 375°F 375°F 375°F	1 to 1¼ hours 1¼ to 1½ hours 1¼ to 1¾ hours 1½ to 2 hours
Game			
Cornish game hen	1¼ to 1½ pounds	375°F	1 to 1¼ hours
Duckling, domestic	4 to 6 pounds	350°F	1½ to 2 hours
Goose, domestic	7 to 8 pounds 8 to 10 pounds	350°F 350°F	2 to 2½ hours 2½ to 3 hours
Pheasant	2 to 3 pounds	350°F	1¼ to 1½ hours
Squab, domestic	12 to 16 ounces	375°F	45 to 60 minutes
Turkey			
Boneless whole	2½ to 3½ pounds 4 to 6 pounds	325°F 325°F	2 to 2½ hours 2½ to 3½ hours
Breast, whole	4 to 6 pounds 6 to 8 pounds	325°F 325°F	1½ to 2¼ hours 2¼ to 3¼ hours

Type of Bird	Weight	Oven Temperature	Roasting Time
Turkey *(continued)*			
Drumstick	1 to 1½ pounds	325°F	1¼ to 1¾ hours
Thigh	1½ to 1¾ pounds	325°F	1½ to 1¾ hours
Whole (unstuffed)*	8 to 12 pounds 12 to 14 pounds 14 to 18 pounds 18 to 20 pounds 20 to 24 pounds	325°F 325°F 325°F 325°F 325°F	2¾ to 3 hours 3 to 3¾ hours 3¾ to 4¼ hours 4¼ to 4½ hours 4½ to 5 hours

*Stuffed birds generally require 15 to 45 minutes more roasting time than unstuffed birds. Always verify doneness of poultry and stuffing with a meat thermometer.

Broiling Poultry

If desired, remove the skin from the poultry; sprinkle with salt and black pepper. Remove broiler pan from the oven and preheat the broiler for 5 to 10 minutes. Arrange the poultry on the unheated rack of the broiler pan with the bone side up. If desired, brush poultry with cooking oil. Place the pan under the broiler so the surface of the poultry is 4 to 5 inches from the heat; chicken and Cornish game hen halves should be 5 to 6 inches from the heat. Turn the pieces over when browned on one side, usually after half of the broiling time. Chicken halves and quarters and meaty pieces should be turned after 20 minutes. Brush again with oil. The poultry is done when the meat is no longer pink and the juices run clear. If desired, brush with a sauce the last 5 minutes of cooking.

Type of Bird	Thickness/Weight	Broiling Time
Chicken		
Broiler-fryer, half	1¼ to 1½ pounds each	28 to 32 minutes
Broiler-fryer, quarter	10 to 12 ounces	28 to 32 minutes
Kabobs (boneless breast, cut into 2×½-inch strips and threaded loosely onto skewers)		8 to 10 minutes
Meaty pieces (breast halves, drumsticks, and thighs with bone)	2½ to 3 pounds total	25 to 35 minutes
Skinless, boneless breast halves	4 to 5 ounces	12 to 15 minutes
Game		
Cornish game hen, half	10 to 12 ounces	25 to 35 minutes
Turkey		
Breast steak or slice	2 ounces	6 to 8 minutes
Breast tenderloin steak	4 to 6 ounces	8 to 10 minutes
Patties (ground raw turkey)	¾ inch thick ½ inch thick	14 to 18 minutes 11 to 13 minutes

Microwaving Poultry

Arrange bone-in pieces in a microwave-safe baking dish with meaty portions toward edges of dish, tucking under thin boneless portions. Do not crowd the pieces in the dish. Cover with waxed paper. (Or, for skinless poultry, cover with a lid or vented plastic wrap.) Microwave on 100 percent power (high) for the time given or until no longer pink, rearranging and turning pieces over after half of the cooking time.

Type of Bird	Amount	Power Level	Cooking Time
Chicken			
Breast halves	Two 6-ounce	100% (high)	6 to 9 minutes
	Two 8-ounce	100% (high)	8 to 11 minutes
Drumsticks	2 drumsticks	100% (high)	3½ to 5 minutes
	6 drumsticks	100% (high)	6 to 10 minutes
Meaty pieces (breast halves, drumsticks, and thighs with bone)	2½ to 3 pounds	100% (high)	9 to 17 minutes
Skinless, boneless breast halves	Two 4- to 5-ounces	100% (high)	4 to 7 minutes
	Four 4- to 5-ounces	100% (high)	5 to 8 minutes
Game			
Cornish game hen, halved	1¼ to 1½ pounds	100% (high)	7 to 10 minutes
Turkey			
Breast tenderloin steaks	Four 4-ounce	100% (high)	5 to 8 minutes
Breast tenderloins	Two 8- to 10-ounce	100% (high)	8 to 12 minutes

Chapter 19
Salads & Dressings

Salads & Dressings

For more recipes, visit our Recipe Center at **www.bhg.com**

Chef's Salad

Give this timeless classic a new look every time you make it by choosing different greens, meats, cheeses, and dressings.

Fast

Start to Finish: 30 minutes   **Makes:** 4 main-dish servings

- 4 **cups torn iceberg or leaf lettuce (see photo, page 470)**
- 4 **cups torn romaine or fresh spinach (see photo, page 470)**
- 4 **ounces cooked ham, chicken, turkey, beef, pork, or lamb, cut into bite-size strips**
- 1 **cup cubed Swiss, cheddar, American, provolone, or Gruyère cheese, or ½ cup crumbled blue cheese (4 ounces)**
- 2 **Hard-Cooked Eggs, sliced (page 263)**
- 2 **medium tomatoes, cut into wedges, or 8 cherry tomatoes, halved**
- 1 **small green or red sweet pepper, cut into bite-size strips**
- 1 **cup Parmesan Croutons (page 457) or purchased croutons (optional)**
- ½ **cup Creamy French Dressing (page 467), Buttermilk Dressing (page 468), Creamy Italian Dressing (page 468), or other salad dressing**

1. In a large salad bowl toss together greens. Divide among 4 large salad plates. Arrange meat, cheese, eggs, tomatoes, and sweet pepper strips on top of the greens. If desired, sprinkle with Parmesan Croutons. Drizzle desired salad dressing over all, passing any remaining dressing.

Nutrition Facts per serving: 472 cal., 40 g total fat (10 g sat. fat), 145 mg chol., 621 mg sodium, 13 g carbo., 3 g fiber, 19 g pro. **Daily Values:** 59% vit. A, 74% vit. C, 32% calcium, 11% iron **Exchanges:** 2½ Vegetable, 2 Medium-Fat Meat, 6 Fat

---

Taco Salad

If you're short on time, omit the Tortilla Cups and serve the salad on coarsely crushed tortilla chips.

Prep: 30 minutes   **Bake:** 15 minutes
Oven: 350°F   **Makes:** 6 main-dish servings

- 1 **recipe Tortilla Cups**
- 8 **ounces lean ground beef or uncooked ground turkey**
- 3 **cloves garlic, minced**
- 1 **15-ounce can dark red kidney beans, rinsed and drained**
- 1 **8-ounce jar taco sauce**
- ¾ **cup frozen whole kernel corn, thawed (optional)**

- 6 **cups shredded leaf or iceberg lettuce**
- 2 **medium tomatoes, chopped**
- 1 **large green sweet pepper, chopped**
- ½ **cup thinly sliced green onions (4)**
- 1 **medium avocado, pitted, peeled, and chopped**
- ¾ **cup shredded sharp cheddar cheese (3 ounces)**
  Dairy sour cream (optional)

1. Prepare Tortilla Cups; set aside. In a medium saucepan cook ground beef and garlic until beef is brown. Drain off fat. Stir in kidney beans, taco sauce, and, if desired, corn. Bring to boiling; reduce heat. Simmer, covered, for 10 minutes.

2. Meanwhile, in a very large bowl combine lettuce, tomatoes, sweet pepper, and green onions. To serve, divide lettuce mixture among the Tortilla Cups. Top each serving with some of the meat mixture and avocado. Sprinkle with cheese. If desired, serve with sour cream.

Tortilla Cups: Lightly brush 1 side of six 9- or 10-inch flour tortillas with a small amount of water or lightly coat with nonstick cooking spray. Coat six small oven-safe bowls or six 16-ounce individual casseroles with nonstick cooking spray. Press tortillas, coated sides up, into prepared bowls or casseroles (see photo, below). Place a ball of foil in each tortilla cup. Bake in a 350° oven for 15 to 20 minutes or until light brown. Remove the foil; let Tortilla Cups cool. Remove cups from the bowls. Serve immediately or store in an airtight container for up to 5 days.

Nutrition Facts per serving: 412 cal., 18 g total fat (6 g sat. fat), 35 mg chol., 632 mg sodium, 45 g carbo., 8 g fiber, 21 g pro. **Daily Values:** 37% vit. A, 74% vit. C, 22% calcium, 26% iron **Exchanges:** 3 Starch, 2 Medium-Fat Meat, ½ Fat

With the coated side up, fit the tortilla into an individual bowl or casserole, creating loose pleats. Place a ball of foil in the cupped tortilla so it holds its shape as it bakes.

Salad Niçoise

You can cook and chill the beans and potatoes for this French salad a day before serving.

Prep: 35 minutes   **Chill:** 2 to 24 hours
Makes: 4 main-dish servings

- **8 ounces fresh green beans**
- **12 ounces tiny new potatoes, scrubbed and sliced**
- **1 recipe Niçoise Dressing**
  Boston or Bibb lettuce leaves
- **1½ cups flaked cooked tuna or salmon (8 ounces) or one 9¼-ounce can chunk white tuna (water-pack), drained and broken into chunks**
- **2 medium tomatoes, cut into wedges**
- **2 Hard-Cooked Eggs, sliced (page 263)**
- **½ cup pitted ripe olives (optional)**
- **¼ cup thinly sliced green onions (2)**
- **4 anchovy fillets, drained, rinsed, and patted dry (optional)**
  Fresh tarragon (optional)

1. Wash green beans; remove ends and strings. In a large saucepan cook green beans and potatoes, covered, in a small amount of lightly salted boiling water for 10 to 15 minutes or just until tender. Drain; place vegetables in a medium bowl. Cover and chill for 2 to 24 hours.

2. Prepare Niçoise Dressing. To serve, line 4 salad plates with lettuce leaves. Arrange green beans, potatoes, tuna, tomatoes, eggs, and, if desired, olives on the lettuce-lined plates. Sprinkle each serving with green onions. If desired, top each salad with an anchovy fillet and garnish with tarragon. Shake dressing; drizzle over each salad.

Salad Niçoise

Niçoise Dressing: In a screw-top jar combine ¼ cup olive or salad oil; ¼ cup white wine vinegar or white vinegar; 1 teaspoon honey; 1 teaspoon snipped fresh tarragon or ¼ teaspoon dried tarragon, crushed; 1 teaspoon Dijon-style mustard; ¼ teaspoon salt; and dash black pepper. Cover and shake well. Makes about ½ cup.

Nutrition Facts per serving: 348 cal., 17 g total fat (3 g sat. fat), 139 mg chol., 228 mg sodium, 24 g carbo., 4 g fiber, 24 g pro.
Daily Values: 26% vit. A, 56% vit. C, 8% calcium, 17% iron
Exchanges: 2 Vegetable, 1 Starch, 2½ Lean Meat, 2 Fat

Chicken Salad

Serve this salad over mixed greens for a light lunch or on your favorite bread for a satisfying sandwich.

Prep: 20 minutes   **Chill:** 1 to 4 hours   **Makes:** 4 servings

- **1½ cups chopped cooked chicken or turkey**
- **½ cup chopped celery (1 stalk)**
- **½ cup chopped cucumber**
- **¼ cup thinly sliced green onions (2)**
- **⅓ cup mayonnaise or salad dressing**
- **1 tablespoon lemon juice**
- **1 teaspoon snipped fresh tarragon or basil, or ¼ teaspoon dried tarragon or basil, crushed**

1. In a medium bowl combine chicken, celery, cucumber, and green onions. For dressing, stir together mayonnaise, lemon juice, tarragon, and ¼ teaspoon *salt*. Pour over chicken mixture; toss to coat. Cover and chill for 1 to 4 hours.

Curried Chicken Salad: Prepare as above, except reduce mayonnaise to ¼ cup, add 2 tablespoons chutney, and 1 teaspoon curry powder; substitute basil for tarragon. Before serving, stir in 2 tablespoons toasted cashews or almonds.

Ham Salad: Prepare as above, except substitute finely chopped cooked ham for the chicken. Omit cucumber and salt; substitute basil for the tarragon.

Nutrition Facts per serving for chicken, curried chicken, and ham salad variations: 245 cal., 19 g total fat (3 g sat. fat), 57 mg chol., 315 mg sodium, 4 g carbo., 1 g fiber, 16 g pro.
Daily Values: 13% vit. A, 14% vit. C, 4% calcium, 7% iron
Exchanges: 1 Vegetable, 2 Lean Meat, 2½ Fat

Tuna or Salmon Salad: Prepare as above, except substitute two 6-ounce cans tuna, drained and broken into chunks, or two 7½-ounce cans salmon, drained, flaked, skin and bones removed, for chicken. Add 2 teaspoons snipped fresh dill or ½ teaspoon dried dill instead of basil or tarragon.

Nutrition Facts per serving: 283 cal., 19 g total fat (3 g sat. fat), 69 mg chol., 756 mg sodium, 5 g carbo., 1 g fiber, 20 g pro.
Daily Values: 13% vit. A, 14% vit. C, 5% calcium, 10% iron
Exchanges: 1 Vegetable, 2½ Lean Meat, 2½ Fat

Thai Chicken and Nectarine Salad Best Loved

Low Fat

Start to Finish: 40 minutes **Makes:** 4 main-dish servings

- ¼ cup reduced-sodium chicken broth
- 3 tablespoons reduced-sodium soy sauce
- 2 tablespoons bottled hoisin sauce
- 1 tablespoon sugar
- 1 tablespoon salad oil or olive oil
- 2 teaspoons toasted sesame oil
- 3 cloves garlic, minced
- 1½ teaspoons grated fresh ginger
- 1 teaspoon crushed red pepper
- ⅛ teaspoon ground black pepper
- 12 ounces skinless, boneless chicken breast halves
- 4 ounces dried angel hair pasta
- 3 medium nectarines, plums, or peeled peaches, pitted and sliced
- 2 cups shredded bok choy
- ¼ cup thinly sliced green onions (2)

1. For dressing, in a screw-top jar combine broth, soy sauce, hoisin sauce, sugar, salad oil, sesame oil, garlic, ginger, red pepper, and black pepper. Cover and shake well; set aside.

2. In a large skillet cook chicken, covered, in a small amount of boiling water for 12 to 15 minutes or until chicken is tender and no longer pink (170°F); drain. Cool slightly; cut into cubes. Cook pasta according to package directions; drain.

3. In a large bowl toss pasta with 3 tablespoons of the dressing. Divide pasta mixture among 4 dinner plates. Top with the chicken, fruit, bok choy, and green onions. Drizzle with remaining dressing.

Nutrition Facts per serving: 349 cal., 8 g total fat (1 g sat. fat), 50 mg chol., 669 mg sodium, 43 g carbo., 3 g fiber, 26 g pro.
Daily Values: 39% vit. A, 41% vit. C, 8% calcium, 12% iron
Exchanges: 1 Vegetable, 1 Fruit, 1½ Starch, 3 Very Lean Meat, 1 Fat

---

Chicken Cabbage Salad Best Loved

Fast

Prep: 20 minutes **Bake:** 5 minutes
Oven: 350°F **Makes:** 4 main-dish servings

- 1 3-ounce package ramen noodles
- ¼ cup slivered or sliced almonds
- 2 tablespoons sesame seeds
- 3 cups shredded Napa or green cabbage (about ½ of a 1-pound head) (see photo, page 470)
- 2 cups chopped cooked chicken or turkey
- 1 cup pea pods, halved crosswise
- ¼ cup thinly sliced green onions (2)
- ¼ cup chopped red sweet pepper (optional)
- 3 tablespoons salad oil
- 2 tablespoons white wine vinegar or rice vinegar
- 2 tablespoons soy sauce
- 1 teaspoon sugar
- ½ teaspoon toasted sesame oil (optional)

1. Save seasoning packet from noodles for another use. Break up noodles; place in a 15×10×1-inch baking pan with the almonds and sesame seeds. Bake in a 350° oven for 5 to 8 minutes or until golden, stirring once. Set aside.

2. In large salad bowl place cabbage, chicken, pea pods, green onions, and, if desired, red sweet pepper; toss to combine.

3. For dressing, in a screw-top jar combine salad oil, vinegar, soy sauce, sugar, and, if desired, sesame oil. Cover and shake well. Pour over cabbage mixture. Add toasted noodle mixture; toss to coat. Serve immediately.

Nutrition Facts per serving: 435 cal., 27 g total fat (4 g sat. fat), 63 mg chol., 517 mg sodium, 21 g carbo., 4 g fiber, 28 g pro.
Daily Values: 16% vit. A, 31% vit. C, 14% calcium, 14% iron
Exchanges: 1 Vegetable, 1 Starch, 3 Lean Meat, 3½ Fat

Salad Oil Glossary

Nut oils: Almond oil is pale in color with a delicate, sweet flavor. Other nut oils, such as hazelnut and walnut, are golden with rich aromas and pronounced nut flavors. Refrigerate to store.

Olive oil: This versatile oil is made from pressed olives. Extra-virgin olive oil, made from the first pressing of olives, is considered the finest type. With the most robust olive flavor and aroma, it has a rich golden-to-green hue. It's also the most expensive. Products labeled "olive oil" (once called pure olive oil) are usually lighter in color and have a more delicate taste. Store in a cool, dark place for up to 6 months or refrigerate up to 1 year. Chilled olive oil becomes thick and cloudy; let it stand at room temperature until it becomes liquid and clear.

Salad oils or vegetable oils: The most common varieties are made from soybeans, sunflowers, corn, peanuts, canola, and safflower. All are light yellow and have a neutral flavor. Store at room temperature and use within 6 months.

Sesame oil: This pale yellow oil is made from untoasted sesame seeds and has a mild sesame flavor. **Toasted sesame oil,** also called Oriental sesame oil, is made from toasted sesame seeds. It is a rich brown color with a concentrated flavor. Refrigerate both varieties to delay rancidity.

Layered Vegetable Salad

Prep: 35 minutes **Chill:** 4 to 24 hours
Makes: 8 to 10 side-dish servings

- 6 **cups torn mixed salad greens**
- 1 **15-ounce can garbanzo beans, rinsed and drained, or one 10-ounce package frozen peas, thawed**
- 1 **cup cherry tomatoes, quartered or halved**
- 1 **cup thinly sliced fennel bulb or broccoli florets**
- 1 **cup chopped yellow and/or red sweet pepper (1 large)**
- 1 **cup diced cooked ham (6 ounces)**
- ¼ **cup thinly sliced green onions (2)**
- 1 **cup Mayonnaise (page 467) or light mayonnaise dressing or salad dressing**
- 2 **tablespoons milk**
- 1 **tablespoon snipped fennel tops (optional)**
- ⅛ **teaspoon ground white pepper or black pepper**
- ¾ **cup shredded smoked cheddar cheese or cheddar cheese (3 ounces)**

1. Place mixed greens in the bottom of a 3-quart clear salad bowl. Layer in the following order: garbanzo beans, tomatoes, sliced fennel, sweet pepper, ham, and green onions.

2. For dressing, stir together mayonnaise, milk, snipped fennel tops (if desired), and white pepper. Spoon dressing over salad. Cover tightly with plastic wrap. Chill for 4 to 24 hours.

3. Before serving, top salad with shredded cheese; toss lightly to coat evenly.

Nutrition Facts per serving: 352 cal., 29 g total fat (6 g sat. fat), 34 mg chol., 676 mg sodium, 13 g carbo., 6 g fiber, 10 g pro.
Daily Values: 9% vit. A, 84% vit. C, 12% calcium, 7% iron
Exchanges: 1 Vegetable, ½ Starch, 1 Lean Meat, 5 Fat

Layered Vegetable Salad

24-Hour Chicken Fiesta Salad

Chilling the salad for up to 24 hours allows the flavors to blend. Layer the ingredients one evening and have a ready-to-serve meal the next.

Prep: 30 minutes **Chill:** 4 to 24 hours
Makes: 4 main-dish servings

- 4 **cups torn iceberg, Boston, or Bibb lettuce**
- ½ **cup shredded Monterey Jack cheese with jalapeño peppers (2 ounces)**
- 1 **8-ounce can red kidney beans, rinsed and drained, or ½ of a 15-ounce can garbanzo beans, rinsed and drained (1 cup)**
- 1½ **cups chopped cooked chicken or turkey (about 8 ounces) (see tip, page 437)**
- 2 **small tomatoes, cut into thin wedges**
- ½ **of a small jicama (about 4 ounces), cut into bite-size strips (1 cup), or 1 cup shredded carrot**
- ½ **cup sliced pitted ripe olives (optional)**
- 1 **recipe Chile Dressing**
- ¾ **cup crushed tortilla chips (optional)**

1. Place the lettuce in a large (2-quart) salad bowl. Layer ingredients in the following order: cheese, beans, chicken, tomatoes, jicama, and, if desired, olives. Spread Chile Dressing evenly over salad, sealing to edge of bowl. Cover salad tightly with plastic wrap. Chill for 4 to 24 hours. To serve, toss lightly to coat evenly. If desired, sprinkle with crushed tortilla chips.

Chile Dressing: In a small bowl stir together ½ cup mayonnaise or salad dressing, one 4-ounce can chopped canned green chile peppers, 1½ teaspoons chili powder, and 1 clove garlic, minced. Makes about ¾ cup.

Nutrition Facts per serving: 444 cal., 32 g total fat (7 g sat. fat), 73 mg chol., 460 mg sodium, 17 g carbo., 5 g fiber, 26 g pro.
Daily Values: 21% vit. A, 50% vit. C, 18% calcium, 14% iron
Exchanges: 2 Vegetable, ½ Starch, 2½ Lean Meat, 4½ Fat

Packaged Greens

If you're running short on time, choose a packaged salad mix from the produce section. Available in a wide assortment, not only will these handy mixes shave minutes from your prep time, they allow you to add variety to any green salad. Because they are packaged in a specially designed wrapper that allows the greens to "breathe," store any leftovers in the original bag. If refrigerated immediately, unopened packages will keep for up to 14 days.

Caesar Salad `Best Loved`

Traditional Caesar Salad contains raw eggs, which may be unsafe to eat. Our cooked-egg version puts this classic back on the menu.

Prep: 30 minutes **Chill:** 2 to 24 hours **Bake:** 20 minutes
Oven: 300°F **Makes:** 6 side-dish servings

- 3 **cloves garlic**
- 3 **anchovy fillets**
- 3 **tablespoons lemon juice**
- 3 **tablespoons olive oil**
- 1 **tablespoon Dijon-style mustard**
- ½ **teaspoon Worcestershire sauce**
- 1 **hard-cooked egg yolk**
- 1 **clove garlic, halved**
- 10 **cups torn romaine (see photo, page 470)**
- 1 **recipe Parmesan Croutons or 2 cups purchased garlic or Parmesan croutons**
- ¼ **cup grated Parmesan cheese or ½ cup Parmesan curls**
  Freshly ground black pepper

1. For dressing, in a blender container or food processor bowl combine the 3 garlic cloves, anchovy fillets, and lemon juice. Cover and blend or process until mixture is nearly smooth, stopping to scrape down sides as needed. Add oil, mustard, Worcestershire sauce, and cooked egg yolk. Cover; blend or process until smooth. Cover surface with plastic wrap; chill for 2 to 24 hours.

2. To serve, rub inside of a wooden salad bowl with cut edges of halved garlic clove; discard garlic clove. Add romaine and croutons to bowl. Pour dressing over salad; toss lightly to coat. Sprinkle Parmesan cheese over top; toss gently. To serve, divide salad among 6 salad plates; sprinkle pepper over each salad.

Parmesan Croutons: Cut four ½-inch-thick slices French bread into ¾-inch cubes; set aside. In a large skillet melt ¼ cup butter or margarine. Remove from heat. Stir in 3 tablespoons grated Parmesan cheese and ⅛ teaspoon garlic powder. Add bread cubes, stirring until cubes are coated with butter mixture. Spread bread cubes in a single layer in a shallow baking pan. Bake in a 300° oven for 10 minutes; stir. Bake about 10 minutes more or until bread cubes are crisp and golden. Cool completely; store in an airtight container for up to 1 week. Makes about 2 cups.

Nutrition Facts per serving: 243 cal., 19 g total fat (8 g sat. fat), 64 mg chol., 409 mg sodium, 13 g carbo., 2 g fiber, 7 g pro.
Daily Values: 57% vit. A, 44% vit. C, 16% calcium, 10% iron
Exchanges: 1 Vegetable, ½ Starch, 4 Fat

Chicken Caesar Salad: Prepare as at left, except add 2 cups chopped cooked chicken with the romaine. Makes 6 main-dish servings.

Nutrition Facts per serving: 331 cal., 22 g total fat (9 g sat. fat), 106 mg chol., 450 mg sodium, 13 g carbo., 2 g fiber, 21 g pro.
Daily Values: 57% vit. A, 44% vit. C, 16% calcium, 14% iron
Exchanges: 1 Vegetable, ½ Starch, 2½ Very Lean Meat, 4 Fat

Before tearing romaine, cut the fibrous rib from the larger leaves by placing each leaf on a cutting board and slicing along both sides of the rib with a small, sharp knife.

Tips Before You Toss

Handling greens properly, from the time you buy them until the time you're ready to toss them, ensures crisp and flavorful salads.

■ Before washing and storing greens, remove and discard discolored or wilted outer greens. Take off any rubber or metal bands that hold the greens together. (See chart for specific washing instructions, page 471.)

■ Any water that clings to the greens will dilute the flavor and consistency of the dressing and will make the salad soggy. After draining greens in a colander, place them on a clean kitchen towel or several layers of paper towels. Gently pat dry with paper towels. Alternately, greens may be dried in a salad spinner. Fill spinner one-half to two-thirds full to avoid bruising greens.

■ Wrap washed greens in a clean, dry kitchen towel or paper towels, and refrigerate them in a resealable plastic bag or airtight container for 30 minutes or up to several hours to crisp. If you are not using the greens right away, place washed and dried greens in the vegetable storage bins of your refrigerator. (See chart for specific storage directions, page 471.)

■ To avoid bruising the leaves or causing them to brown, tear, rather than cut, salad greens into bite-size pieces. Tearing greens also exposes more of the insides of the leaves so they absorb more dressing.

■ Dress the salad just before serving to prevent wilted, soggy greens. Add enough dressing to lightly coat the greens, then toss with salad servers or two spoons. Gently push downward to the bottom of a deep bowl with the servers and lift upward so the greens at the top fall to the bottom. For arranged salads, drizzle or pass the dressing; do not toss.

Mesclun with Pears and Blue Cheese [Best Loved]

Candied Nuts dress up this salad (see photo, page 451).

[Fast]

Start to Finish: 25 minutes **Makes:** 8 side-dish servings

  10 cups mesclun (see tip, below) or torn
      romaine (see photo, page 470)
   3 medium red and/or green pears, cored
      and thinly sliced
 ¼ cup pear nectar
   2 tablespoons walnut oil or salad oil
   2 tablespoons white wine vinegar
   1 teaspoon Dijon-style mustard
 ⅛ teaspoon ground ginger
 ⅛ teaspoon black pepper
 ½ cup broken walnuts, toasted (see tip, page
      224) or 1 recipe Candied Nuts (page 180)
 ½ cup crumbled blue cheese

1. In a large salad bowl place mesclun and pear slices. Toss lightly to combine.

2. For dressing, in a screw-top jar combine pear nectar, oil, vinegar, mustard, ginger, and pepper. Cover and shake well. Pour dressing over salad; toss lightly to coat.

3. Divide salad among 8 salad plates. Sprinkle each serving with nuts and blue cheese.

Nutrition Facts per serving: 152 cal., 11 g total fat (2 g sat. fat), 5 mg chol., 110 mg sodium, 13 g carbo., 3 g fiber, 4 g pro.
Daily Values: 6% vit. A, 10% vit. C, 7% calcium, 4% iron
Exchanges: 1 Vegetable, ½ Fruit, 2 Fat

Balsamic-Dressed Mesclun with Pears: Prepare as directed above, except omit dressing. Toss salad with ½ cup Balsamic Vinaigrette (page 468) or bottled balsamic vinaigrette.

Nutrition Facts per serving: 183 cal., 13 g total fat (3 g sat. fat), 5 mg chol., 107 mg sodium, 15 g carbo., 3 g fiber, 4 g pro.
Daily Values: 6% vit. A, 10% vit. C, 7% calcium, 5% iron
Exchanges: 1 Vegetable, ½ Fruit, 2½ Fat

Mesclun

Mesclun is a mixture of young, small salad greens. The mixture varies depending on the source, but usually includes arugula, dandelion, frisée, mâche, mizuna, oak leaf lettuce, radicchio, and sorrel. Mesclun may be available packaged or in bulk. Look for crisp leaves without signs of wilting. Before serving, wash in cold water, drain in a colander, and pat dry with paper towels. Store in a plastic bag lined with paper towels for up to 5 days.

Cranberry-Raspberry Spinach Salad

Prep: 35 minutes **Chill:** 1 hour **Makes:** 6 side-dish servings

   1 10-ounce package frozen red raspberries in
      syrup, thawed
 ¼ cup sugar
   2 teaspoons cornstarch
 ½ cup cranberry-raspberry drink
 ¼ cup red wine vinegar
 ¼ teaspoon celery seeds
 ¼ teaspoon ground cinnamon
 ⅛ teaspoon ground cloves
   1 10-ounce package fresh spinach, stems
      removed and torn (8 cups)
 ½ cup broken walnuts
 ⅓ cup dried cranberries
 ¼ cup sunflower seeds
   3 green onions, thinly sliced

1. For dressing, place raspberries and syrup in a blender container or food processor bowl. Cover and blend or process until smooth; strain through a sieve to remove seeds. Discard seeds.

2. In a medium saucepan combine sugar and cornstarch; stir in strained raspberries, the berry drink, vinegar, celery seeds, cinnamon, and cloves. Cook and stir over medium heat until thickened and bubbly; cook and stir for 2 minutes more. Transfer to a nonmetal container. Cover and chill at least 1 hour.

3. To serve, place spinach, walnuts, cranberries, sunflower seeds, and green onions in a large bowl; toss to combine. Drizzle with some of the dressing; toss to coat evenly. Pass remaining dressing.

Nutrition Facts per serving: 195 cal., 10 g total fat (1 g sat. fat), 0 mg chol., 48 mg sodium, 25 g carbo., 4 g fiber, 4 g pro.
Daily Values: 64% vit. A, 32% vit. C, 7% calcium, 14% iron
Exchanges: 1 Vegetable, ½ Fruit, 1 Other Carbo., 2 Fat

Wilted Spinach Salad [Best Loved]

[Fast]

Start to Finish: 25 minutes **Makes:** 4 side-dish servings

   6 cups torn fresh spinach
   1 cup sliced fresh mushrooms
 ¼ cup thinly sliced green onions (2)
      Dash black pepper (optional)
   3 slices bacon
 ¼ cup vinegar
   2 teaspoons sugar
 ½ teaspoon dry mustard
   1 Hard-Cooked Egg, chopped (page 263)

1. In a large bowl combine spinach, mushrooms, and green onions. If desired, sprinkle with pepper; set aside.

2. For dressing, in a 12-inch skillet cook bacon until crisp. Remove bacon, reserving 2 tablespoons drippings in skillet (add *salad oil*, if necessary). Or, if desired, substitute 2 tablespoons *salad oil* for bacon drippings. Crumble bacon; set aside. Stir vinegar, sugar, and dry mustard into drippings. Bring to boiling; remove from heat. Add the spinach mixture. Toss mixture in skillet for 30 to 60 seconds or until spinach is just wilted.

3. Transfer mixture to a serving dish. Add chopped egg and crumbled bacon; toss to combine. Serve immediately.

Nutrition Facts per serving: 128 cal., 11 g total fat (4 g sat. fat), 63 mg chol., 150 mg sodium, 4 g carbo., 4 g fiber, 5 g pro.
Daily Values: 53% vit. A, 21% vit. C, 5% calcium, 21% iron
Exchanges: 1 Vegetable, 2½ Fat

White Corn and Baby Pea Salad Best Loved

Low Fat

Prep: 15 minutes **Chill:** 1 to 2 hours
Makes: 10 to 12 side-dish servings

- 1 16-ounce package frozen white whole kernel corn (shoe peg), thawed
- 1 16-ounce package frozen baby peas, thawed
- 1 cup chopped, peeled jicama
- ⅔ cup sliced celery
- ½ cup thinly sliced green onions (4)
- ¼ cup chopped red and/or orange sweet pepper
- ½ cup seasoned rice vinegar
- 2 tablespoons brown sugar
- 1 tablespoon snipped fresh parsley
- ½ teaspoon salt
- ¼ teaspoon ground white pepper or black pepper
- 1 tablespoon snipped fresh mint

1. In a large bowl combine corn, peas, jicama, celery, green onions, and sweet pepper.

2. For dressing, in a screw-top jar combine vinegar, brown sugar, parsley, salt, and white pepper. Cover and shake well. Pour dressing over vegetable mixture; toss to coat. Stir in mint. Cover and chill for 1 to 2 hours.

Nutrition Facts per serving: 95 cal., 1 g total fat (0 g sat. fat), 0 mg chol., 298 mg sodium, 21 g carbo., 4 g fiber, 4 g pro.
Daily Values: 12% vit. A, 39% vit. C, 2% calcium, 7% iron
Exchanges: 1 Vegetable, 1 Starch

Marinated Cucumbers

No Fat

Prep: 15 minutes **Chill:** 4 hours to 5 days
Makes: 6 side-dish servings

- ¼ cup vinegar or lemon juice
- 1 to 2 tablespoons sugar
- ½ teaspoon salt
- ¼ teaspoon celery seeds
- 1 large cucumber, halved lengthwise and thinly sliced (3 cups)
- ⅓ cup thinly sliced onion (1 small)

1. For marinade, in a covered container combine vinegar, sugar, salt, and celery seeds. Add cucumber and onion; toss to coat. Cover and chill for 4 hours or up to 5 days, stirring occasionally.

Nutrition Facts per serving: 20 cal., 0 g total fat (0 g sat. fat), 0 mg chol., 195 mg sodium, 5 g carbo., 1 g fiber, 0 g pro.
Daily Values: 2% vit. A, 6% vit. C, 1% calcium, 1% iron
Exchanges: 1 Vegetable

Creamy Cucumbers: Prepare recipe as above, except omit marinade ingredients (vinegar, sugar, salt, and celery seeds). In a medium bowl stir together ½ cup dairy sour cream or plain yogurt, 1 tablespoon vinegar, 1 teaspoon sugar, ½ teaspoon salt, ¼ teaspoon dried dill, and a dash of black pepper. Add cucumber and onion; toss to coat. Cover and chill for 4 to 24 hours, stirring often. Stir before serving. Makes 6 side-dish servings.

Nutrition Facts per serving: 48 cal., 3 g total fat (2 g sat. fat), 7 mg chol., 204 mg sodium, 4 g carbo., 1 g fiber, 1 g pro.
Daily Values: 5% vit. A, 6% vit. C, 3% calcium, 1% iron
Exchanges: 1 Vegetable, ½ Fat

White Corn and Baby Pea Salad

Greek Salad

`Fast`

Start to Finish: 15 minutes **Makes:** 4 side-dish servings

> 3 **medium tomatoes, cut into wedges**
> 1 **medium cucumber, halved lengthwise and thinly sliced**
> 1 **small red onion, cut into thin wedges**
> 1 **recipe Greek Vinaigrette**
> 8 **to 10 pitted kalamata olives**
> ½ **cup crumbled feta cheese (2 ounces)**

1. In a salad bowl combine the tomatoes, cucumber, and red onion. Add Greek Vinaigrette; toss to coat. Sprinkle with olives and cheese.

Greek Vinaigrette: In a screw-top jar combine 2 tablespoons olive oil or salad oil; 2 tablespoons lemon juice; 2 teaspoons snipped fresh oregano or ½ teaspoon dried oregano, crushed; ⅛ teaspoon salt; and ⅛ teaspoon black pepper. Cover and shake well.

Nutrition Facts per serving: 154 cal., 12 g total fat (4 g sat. fat), 17 mg chol., 369 mg sodium, 9 g carbo., 2 g fiber, 4 g pro.
Daily Values: 17% vit. A, 43% vit. C, 12% calcium, 6% iron
Exchanges: 2 Vegetable, 2½ Fat

Mango-Broccoli Salad

`Fast`

Start to Finish: 20 minutes **Makes:** 8 side-dish servings

> 4 **cups chopped fresh broccoli**
> 1 **large ripe mango, seeded, peeled, and diced**
> ½ **cup cashews**
> 1 **small red onion, cut into thin wedges**
> ½ **cup bottled buttermilk ranch salad dressing**
> 2 **tablespoons orange juice**
> 1 **tablespoon prepared horseradish**
> 1 **11-ounce can mandarin orange sections, drained**

1. In a large salad bowl combine broccoli, mango, cashews, and onion. For dressing, in a small bowl stir together ranch dressing, orange juice, and horseradish. Pour over broccoli mixture; toss to coat. Gently stir in mandarin orange sections. Serve immediately or cover and chill up to 2 hours.

Nutrition Facts per serving: 175 cal., 12 g total fat (2 g sat. fat), 1 mg chol., 195 mg sodium, 16 g carbo., 3 g fiber, 3 g pro.
Daily Values: 46% vit. A, 109% vit. C, 4% calcium, 6% iron
Exchanges: 1½ Vegetable, ½ Fruit, 2½ Fat

Tangy Vegetable Salad

Canned cut green beans can be used instead of fresh green beans. Drain them and add to other vegetables with the zucchini.

`Low Fat`

Prep: 25 minutes **Cook:** 5 minutes **Chill:** 4 to 24 hours
Makes: 8 side-dish servings

> 2 **cups small cauliflower florets**
> 2 **cups green beans, bias-sliced into 1-inch pieces**
> 1 **cup thinly sliced carrots (2 medium)**
> 1 **cup coarsely chopped red or green sweet pepper (1 medium)**
> 1 **medium onion, sliced and separated into rings**
> 1 **small zucchini, halved lengthwise and thinly sliced (1 cup)**
> ¼ **cup halved pitted ripe olives (optional)**
> ⅓ **cup white wine vinegar or ½ cup cider vinegar**
> ¼ **cup salad oil**
> 1 **tablespoon sugar**
> 1 **tablespoon snipped fresh oregano or 1 teaspoon dried oregano, crushed**
> ½ **teaspoon salt**
> ¼ **teaspoon black pepper**

1. In a large saucepan cook cauliflower, green beans, carrots, sweet pepper, and onion, covered, in a small amount of boiling water for 5 minutes. Drain; transfer to a large bowl. Stir in zucchini and, if desired, olives.

2. For marinade, in a screw-top jar combine vinegar, oil, sugar, oregano, salt, and pepper. Cover and shake well. Pour marinade over vegetables; stir gently. Cover and chill for 4 to 24 hours, stirring occasionally. Serve with a slotted spoon.

Nutrition Facts per serving: 72 cal., 4 g total fat (1 g sat. fat), 0 mg chol., 162 mg sodium, 9 g carbo., 3 g fiber, 2 g pro.
Daily Values: 111% vit. A, 92% vit. C, 3% calcium, 4% iron
Exchanges: 2 Vegetable, ½ Fat

Mango-Broccoli Salad

Vinaigrette Coleslaw

Low Fat

Prep: 20 minutes **Chill:** 2 to 24 hours
Makes: 6 side-dish servings

- 3 tablespoons vinegar
- 2 tablespoons sugar
- 2 tablespoons salad oil
- ½ teaspoon caraway seeds (optional)
- ¼ teaspoon dry mustard
- ¼ teaspoon salt
- ⅛ to ¼ teaspoon black pepper
- 3 cups shredded green cabbage
- 1 cup shredded red or green cabbage
- 1 cup shredded carrots (2 medium)
- ¼ cup thinly sliced green onions (2)

1. For vinaigrette, in a screw-top jar combine vinegar, sugar, oil, caraway seeds (if desired), mustard, salt, and pepper. Cover; shake well. In a large bowl combine cabbages, carrots, and green onions. Pour vinaigrette over cabbage mixture. Toss lightly to coat. Cover and chill for 2 to 24 hours.

Nutrition Facts per serving: 79 cal., 5 g total fat (1 g sat. fat),
0 mg chol., 112 mg sodium, 10 g carbo., 2 g fiber, 1 g pro.
Daily Values: 115% vit. A, 35% vit. C, 3% calcium, 3% iron
Exchanges: 1½ Vegetable, 1 Fat

Creamy Coleslaw: Prepare as above, except omit vinaigrette (vinegar, sugar, salad oil, caraway seeds, dry mustard, salt, and pepper). In a small bowl stir together ½ cup mayonnaise or salad dressing, 1 tablespoon vinegar, 1 to 2 teaspoons sugar, ½ teaspoon celery seeds, and ¼ teaspoon salt. Pour mayonnaise mixture over cabbage mixture. Toss lightly to coat. Cover and chill for 2 to 24 hours. Makes 6 side-dish servings.

Nutrition Facts per serving: 159 cal., 15 g total fat (2 g sat. fat),
7 mg chol., 213 mg sodium, 6 g carbo., 2 g fiber, 1 g pro.
Daily Values: 115% vit. A, 35% vit. C, 3% calcium, 3% iron
Exchanges: 1½ Vegetable, 3 Fat

Three-Bean Salad

Low Fat

Prep: 15 minutes **Chill:** 4 to 24 hours
Makes: 6 side-dish servings

- 1 16-ounce can cut wax beans, black beans, or garbanzo beans, rinsed and drained
- 1 8-ounce can cut green beans or lima beans, rinsed and drained
- 1 8-ounce can red kidney beans, rinsed and drained
- ½ cup chopped green sweet pepper
- ⅓ cup chopped red onion (1 small)

- ¼ cup vinegar
- 2 tablespoons sugar
- 2 tablespoons salad oil
- ½ teaspoon celery seeds
- ½ teaspoon dry mustard
- 1 clove garlic, minced

1. In a large bowl combine wax beans, green beans, kidney beans, sweet pepper, and onion.

2. For dressing, in a screw-top jar combine the vinegar, sugar, oil, celery seeds, dry mustard, and garlic. Cover and shake well. Pour over vegetables; stir lightly. Cover and chill for 4 to 24 hours, stirring often.

Nutrition Facts per serving: 120 cal., 5 g total fat (1 g sat. fat),
0 mg chol., 419 mg sodium, 17 g carbo., 5 g fiber, 4 g pro.
Daily Values: 6% vit. A, 30% vit. C, 5% calcium, 10% iron
Exchanges: 2 Vegetable, ½ Starch, 1 Fat

Marinated Potato Salad

Prep: 30 minutes **Chill:** 4 to 24 hours
Makes: 6 side-dish servings

- 1 pound tiny new potatoes
- 1 8- or 9-ounce package frozen artichoke hearts, thawed, drained, and halved
- 1 small green sweet pepper, seeded and cut into bite-size strips
- 6 cherry tomatoes, halved
- ½ of a small red onion, sliced and separated into rings
- ¼ cup halved pitted olives (such as ripe, kalamata, or green)
- ¼ cup snipped fresh parsley
- ½ cup Fresh Herb Vinaigrette (page 468) or bottled oil-and-vinegar or flavored vinaigrette salad dressing

1. In a medium saucepan place potatoes, ¼ teaspoon *salt*, and enough water to cover. Bring to boiling; reduce heat. Simmer, covered, for 15 to 20 minutes or until just tender. Drain well; cool.

2. Cut potatoes into quarters and place in a large serving bowl. Add artichoke hearts, sweet pepper, tomatoes, onion, olives, and parsley. Pour the vinaigrette over potato mixture; toss gently to combine. Cover and chill for 4 to 24 hours, stirring salad occasionally.

Nutrition Facts per serving: 164 cal., 9 g total fat (1 g sat. fat),
0 mg chol., 79 mg sodium, 18 g carbo., 4 g fiber, 3 g pro.
Daily Values: 8% vit. A, 52% vit. C, 4% calcium, 8% iron
Exchanges: ½ Vegetable, 1 Starch, 1½ Fat

Classic Potato Salad Best Loved

Boiling potatoes in their skins prevents them from absorbing too much water during cooking and ensures firm potatoes for salads.

Prep: 40 minutes **Chill:** 6 to 24 hours
Makes: 12 side-dish servings

6 medium potatoes (2 pounds) (see tip, below)
1¼ cups mayonnaise or salad dressing
1 tablespoon prepared mustard
½ teaspoon salt
¼ teaspoon black pepper
1 cup thinly sliced celery (2 stalks)
⅓ cup chopped onion (1 small)
½ cup chopped sweet or dill pickles or sweet or dill pickle relish
6 Hard-Cooked Eggs, coarsely chopped (page 263)
Lettuce leaves (optional)
Paprika (optional)

1. In a medium saucepan place potatoes, ¼ teaspoon *salt*, and enough water to cover. Bring to boiling; reduce heat. Simmer, covered, for 20 to 25 minutes or until just tender. Drain well; cool slightly. Peel and cube the potatoes.

2. Meanwhile, for dressing, in a large bowl combine the mayonnaise, mustard, the ½ teaspoon salt, and pepper.

3. Stir in the celery, onion, and pickles. Add the potatoes and eggs. Toss lightly to coat. Cover and chill for 6 to 24 hours.

4. To serve, if desired, line a salad bowl with lettuce leaves. Transfer the potato salad to the bowl. If desired, sprinkle with paprika.

Nutrition Facts per serving: 277 cal., 21 g total fat (4 g sat. fat), 120 mg chol., 337 mg sodium, 18 g carbo., 2 g fiber, 5 g pro.
Daily Values: 5% vit. A, 17% vit. C, 3% calcium, 4% iron
Exchanges: 1 Starch, 4 Fat

Salad Spuds

When buying potatoes to use in potato salad, it's important to select a variety that keeps its shape when cooked. Potatoes classified as waxy, such as long whites and round reds, have a moist, smooth texture and perform well for this purpose. New potatoes are not a type of potato but are just young, small potatoes—often the round red variety—making them another good choice for salads.

German-Style Potato Salad

Start to Finish: 45 minutes **Makes:** 4 to 6 side-dish servings

1¼ pounds red or white potatoes (see tip, below)
4 slices bacon
½ cup chopped onion (1 medium)
1 tablespoon all-purpose flour
1 tablespoon sugar
½ teaspoon salt
½ teaspoon celery seeds
½ teaspoon dry mustard
⅛ to ¼ teaspoon black pepper
⅔ cup water
¼ cup vinegar
Snipped fresh parsley (optional)

1. In a medium saucepan place potatoes, ¼ teaspoon *salt*, and enough water to cover. Bring to boiling; reduce heat. Simmer, covered, for 20 to 25 minutes or until just tender. Drain well; cool slightly. Halve, peel, and cut potatoes into ¼-inch slices. Set aside.

2. For dressing, in a large skillet cook bacon over medium heat until crisp. Remove bacon, reserving 2 tablespoons drippings in skillet. Drain bacon on paper towels. Crumble the bacon and set aside.

3. Add onion to the reserved drippings. Cook over medium heat until tender. Stir in the flour, sugar, the ½ teaspoon salt, celery seeds, dry mustard, and pepper. Stir in the ⅔ cup water and vinegar. Cook and stir until thickened and bubbly. Gently stir in the potatoes and bacon. Cook, stirring gently, for 1 to 2 minutes more or until heated through. Transfer to a serving bowl. If desired, sprinkle with parsley.

Nutrition Facts per serving: 235 cal., 10 g total fat (4 g sat. fat), 11 mg chol., 402 mg sodium, 33 g carbo., 3 g fiber, 5 g pro.
Daily Values: 35% vit. C, 2% calcium, 8% iron
Exchanges: 2 Starch, 1½ Fat

Apple-Rice Salad

Prep: 50 minutes **Chill:** 2 to 6 hours
Makes: 6 side-dish servings

⅓ cup uncooked brown rice
⅓ cup uncooked wild rice, rinsed and drained
2 cups chopped apple (about 2 medium)
1 cup thinly sliced celery (2 stalks)
¼ cup shelled sunflower seeds
¼ cup dried currants or dried cranberries
2 tablespoons balsamic vinegar

1 tablespoon olive oil
2 teaspoons honey
2 teaspoons brown or Dijon-style mustard
2 teaspoons finely shredded orange peel
1 clove garlic, minced
¼ teaspoon salt
  Lettuce leaves (optional)

1. In a medium saucepan place the brown rice and wild rice. Add 1¾ cups *water*. Bring to boiling; reduce heat. Simmer, covered, for 40 to 45 minutes or until rice is tender; drain. Transfer to a large bowl; cover and chill for 2 hours.

2. Add apple, celery, sunflower seeds, and currants to the chilled rice mixture; stir to combine. For dressing, in a screw-top jar combine the vinegar, oil, honey, mustard, orange peel, garlic, and salt. Cover and shake well. Pour over rice mixture; toss gently to coat. Serve immediately on lettuce leaves, if desired. Or cover and chill for up to 4 hours.

Nutrition Facts per serving: 191 cal., 6 g total fat (1 g sat. fat), 0 mg chol., 143 mg sodium, 32 g carbo., 4 g fiber, 4 g pro.
Daily Values: 5% vit. A, 12% vit. C, 3% calcium, 7% iron
Exchanges: 1 Fruit, 1 Starch, 1 Fat

Tabbouleh

Bulgur is the result of soaking, cooking, drying, and cracking whole wheat kernels. There is no need to cook the bulgur further for this salad—the dressing softens the wheat while the salad chills.

Prep: 25 minutes **Chill:** 4 to 24 hours
Makes: 4 to 6 side-dish servings

¾ cup bulgur
1 small cucumber, peeled, seeded, and chopped
3 tablespoons snipped fresh parsley
2 tablespoons snipped fresh mint or
  2 teaspoons dried mint, crushed
2 tablespoons thinly sliced green onion (1)
¼ cup olive oil or salad oil
3 tablespoons lemon juice
2 tablespoons water
¼ teaspoon salt
⅛ teaspoon black pepper
½ cup chopped, seeded tomato (1 small)

1. Place bulgur in a colander; rinse with cold water and drain. In a medium bowl combine bulgur, cucumber, parsley, mint, and green onion.

2. For dressing, in a screw-top jar combine the oil, lemon juice, water, salt, and pepper. Cover and shake well. Pour dressing over the bulgur mixture. Toss lightly to coat. Cover and chill for 4 to 24 hours. Bring to room temperature before serving. Stir tomato into the bulgur mixture just before serving.

Nutrition Facts per serving: 228 cal., 14 g total fat (2 g sat. fat), 0 mg chol., 156 mg sodium, 24 g carbo., 6 g fiber, 4 g pro.
Daily Values: 8% vit. A, 31% vit. C, 3% calcium, 9% iron
Exchanges: ½ Vegetable, 1½ Starch, 2 Fat

Macaroni Salad

Prep: 30 minutes **Chill:** 4 to 24 hours
Makes: 6 side-dish servings

1 cup elbow macaroni or wagon wheel macaroni (3 ounces)
¾ cup cubed cheddar or American cheese (3 ounces)
½ cup thinly sliced celery (1 stalk)
½ cup frozen peas
½ cup thinly sliced radishes
2 tablespoons thinly sliced green onion or chopped onion
½ cup mayonnaise or salad dressing
¼ cup sweet or dill pickle relish, or chopped sweet or dill pickles
2 tablespoons milk
2 tablespoons horseradish mustard (optional)
¼ teaspoon salt
  Dash black pepper
2 Hard-Cooked Eggs, coarsely chopped (page 263)

1. Cook pasta according to package directions; drain. Rinse with cold water; drain again. In a large bowl combine cooked pasta, cheese, celery, peas, radishes, and green onion.

2. For dressing, in a small bowl stir together the mayonnaise, pickle relish, milk, mustard (if desired), salt, and pepper.

3. Pour dressing over pasta mixture. Add chopped eggs. Toss lightly to coat. Cover and chill for 4 to 24 hours. Before serving, if necessary, stir in additional milk to moisten.

Nutrition Facts per serving: 311 cal., 22 g total fat (6 g sat. fat), 97 mg chol., 411 mg sodium, 20 g carbo., 1 g fiber, 9 g pro.
Daily Values: 8% vit. A, 9% vit. C, 13% calcium, 7% iron
Exchanges: 1½ Starch, 1 High-Fat Meat, 2 Fat

Tortellini-Asparagus Salad

Prep: 25 minutes **Chill:** 2 to 8 hours
Makes: 10 side-dish servings

- 2 9-ounce packages refrigerated cheese-filled tortellini
- 1 pound fresh asparagus spears (about 16 spears), trimmed and cut into 1-inch pieces
- 1 large yellow sweet pepper, cut into ½-inch pieces
- 1 to 1½ teaspoons finely shredded lemon peel
- ⅓ cup lemon juice
- ¼ cup olive oil or salad oil
- 1 tablespoon Dijon-style mustard
- 1 teaspoon sugar
- ¼ teaspoon salt
- 1 clove garlic, minced
- ½ cup finely shredded Parmesan cheese
- ½ cup sliced green onions (4)
- ¼ cup pine nuts or chopped almonds, toasted (see tip, page 224)

1. In a 4-quart Dutch oven cook tortellini according to package directions, adding asparagus and sweet pepper the last minute of cooking; drain. Rinse tortellini and vegetables with cold water; drain again.

2. For dressing, in a screw-top jar combine lemon peel, lemon juice, oil, mustard, sugar, salt, and garlic. Cover and shake well.

3. In a very large bowl place tortellini and vegetables. Add dressing; toss to coat. Cover and chill for 2 to 8 hours. Just before serving, stir in cheese, green onions, and nuts. Let stand 10 minutes before serving.

Nutrition Facts per serving: 263 cal., 12 g total fat (3 g sat. fat), 30 mg chol., 329 mg sodium, 29 g carbo., 3 g fiber, 11 g pro.
Daily Values: 4% vit. A, 84% vit. C, 15% calcium, 11% iron
Exchanges: 1 Vegetable, 1½ Starch, ½ Lean Meat, 2 Fat

Potluck Pasta Salad Best Loved

Prep: 30 minutes **Chill:** 2 to 24 hours
Makes: 16 side-dish servings

- 3 cups dried wagon wheel macaroni, rotini, or other desired pasta (8 ounces)
- 1 medium yellow summer squash or zucchini, halved lengthwise and sliced (2 cups)
- 1 cup frozen peas, thawed; shelled fresh peas, cooked and cooled (page 543); or frozen whole kernel corn, thawed
- 1 medium red sweet pepper, cut into strips
- 8 ounces smoked cheddar cheese or cheddar cheese, cubed
- 1 6-ounce can pitted ripe olives, drained and coarsely chopped
- 1 cup cherry tomatoes, halved
- ½ cup chopped red onion
- 2 tablespoons snipped fresh oregano or basil or 2 teaspoons dried oregano or basil, crushed
- 1 cup bottled balsamic vinaigrette or red wine vinaigrette salad dressing

1. Cook pasta according to package directions; drain. Rinse with cold water; drain again.

2. In a large bowl combine pasta, squash, peas, sweet pepper, cheese, olives, tomatoes, onion, and oregano. Add dressing to pasta mixture; toss gently to coat. Cover and chill for 2 to 24 hours.

Nutrition Facts per serving: 182 cal., 11 g total fat (4 g sat. fat), 15 mg chol., 368 mg sodium, 16 g carbo., 2 g fiber, 6 g pro.
Daily Values: 15% vit. A, 31% vit. C, 12% calcium, 6% iron
Exchanges: 1 Vegetable, 1 Starch, ½ High-Fat Meat, 2 Fat

Fruit and Pasta Salad

Prep: 30 minutes **Chill:** 4 to 24 hours
Makes: 6 side-dish servings

- 1 cup dried bow-tie pasta or ⅔ cup orecchiette or medium shell macaroni (about 2 ounces)
- 1 cup sliced, peeled peaches, orange sections, and/or cubed cantaloupe or honeydew melon
- ½ cup sliced celery (1 stalk)
- ½ recipe Orange-Poppy Seed Dressing (page 469)
- 1 cup sliced strawberries
- 1 kiwifruit, peeled and sliced

1. Cook pasta according to package directions; drain. Rinse with cold water; drain again. Combine the cooked pasta, peaches, and celery. Add dressing; toss to coat. Cover; chill for 4 to 24 hours. Before serving, stir in strawberries and kiwifruit.

Nutrition Facts per serving: 145 cal., 6 g total fat (1 g sat. fat), 0 mg chol., 10 mg sodium, 21 g carbo., 3 g fiber, 2 g pro.
Daily Values: 7% vit. A, 54% vit. C, 2% calcium, 3% iron
Exchanges: 1 Fruit, ½ Starch, 1 Fat

Tortellini-Asparagus Salad

Honey-Mustard Dressing

[Fast]

Start to Finish: 10 minutes **Makes:** about 1 cup

1. In a a screw-top jar combine ¼ to ⅓ cup coarse grain mustard, ¼ cup olive or salad oil, ¼ cup lemon juice, ¼ cup honey, and 2 cloves garlic, minced. Cover and shake well. Serve immediately or cover and store in refrigerator for up to 2 weeks. Shake before serving.

Nutrition Facts per tablespoon: 51 cal., 4 g total fat (0 g sat. fat), 0 mg chol., 52 mg sodium, 5 g carbo., 0 g fiber, 0 g pro.
Daily Values: 3% vit. C
Exchanges: 1 Fat

Thousand Island Dressing

[Fast]

Start to Finish: 15 minutes **Makes:** 1½ cups

1. In a small bowl combine 1 cup mayonnaise or salad dressing and ¼ cup chili sauce. Stir in 2 tablespoons sweet pickle relish, 2 tablespoons finely chopped green or red sweet pepper, 2 tablespoons finely chopped onion, and 1 teaspoon Worcestershire sauce or prepared horseradish.

2. Serve immediately or cover and store in refrigerator for up to 1 week. Before serving, if necessary, stir in 1 to 2 tablespoons milk until dressing reaches desired consistency.

Nutrition Facts per tablespoon: 70 cal., 7 g total fat (1 g sat. fat), 5 mg chol., 97 mg sodium, 1 g carbo., 0 g fiber, 0 g pro.
Daily Values: 1% vit. A, 2% vit. C
Exchanges: 1½ Fat

Russian Dressing

[Fast]

Start to Finish: 10 minutes **Makes:** ⅔ cup

- ¼ cup salad oil
- ¼ cup catsup
- 1 tablespoon sugar
- 1 tablespoon white wine vinegar or vinegar
- 1 tablespoon lemon juice
- 1 teaspoon Worcestershire sauce
- ½ teaspoon paprika
- ¼ teaspoon salt
- ⅛ teaspoon black pepper

1. In a screw-top jar combine oil, catsup, sugar, vinegar, lemon juice, Worcestershire sauce, paprika, salt, and pepper. Cover; shake well.

2. Serve immediately or cover and store in refrigerator for up to 2 weeks. Shake before serving.

Nutrition Facts per tablespoon: 61 cal., 6 g total fat (1 g sat. fat), 0 mg chol., 135 mg sodium, 3 g carbo., 0 g fiber, 0 g pro.
Daily Values: 3% vit. A, 3% vit. C, 1% calcium, 1% iron
Exchanges: 1 Fat

Orange-Poppy Seed Dressing

[Fast]

Start to Finish: 10 minutes **Makes:** ⅔ cup

- 3 tablespoons sugar
- 1½ teaspoons finely shredded orange peel
- 2 tablespoons orange juice
- 2 tablespoons vinegar
- 1 tablespoon finely chopped onion
  Dash black pepper
- ⅓ cup salad oil
- 1 teaspoon poppy seeds

1. In a food processor bowl or blender container combine sugar, orange peel, orange juice, vinegar, onion, and pepper. Cover and process or blend until combined. With processor or blender running, slowly add ⅓ cup salad oil in a steady stream until mixture is thickened. Stir in poppy seeds. Serve immediately or cover and store in refrigerator for up to 1 week. Shake well before serving.

Nutrition Facts per tablespoon: 81 cal., 7 g total fat (1 g sat. fat), 0 mg chol., 0 mg sodium, 4 g carbo., 0 g fiber, 0 g pro.
Daily Values: 3% vit. C, 1% calcium
Exchanges: 1½ Fat

Orange-Poppy Seed Dressing

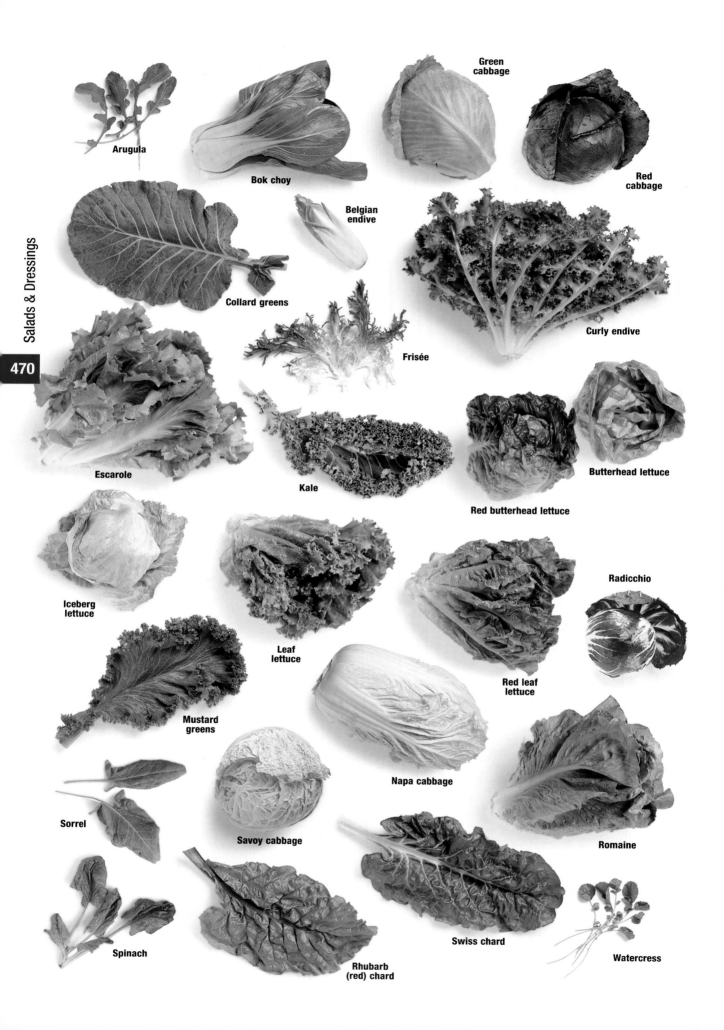

Arugula

Bok choy

Green cabbage

Red cabbage

Collard greens

Belgian endive

Curly endive

Frisée

Escarole

Kale

Red butterhead lettuce

Butterhead lettuce

Iceberg lettuce

Leaf lettuce

Radicchio

Red leaf lettuce

Mustard greens

Sorrel

Savoy cabbage

Napa cabbage

Romaine

Spinach

Rhubarb (red) chard

Swiss chard

Watercress

Guide to Greens

Type/Description	Weight As Purchased	Amount After Preparation	Preparation and Storage
Arugula	1 ounce	1 cup torn	Rinse thoroughly in cold water to remove all sand; pat dry. Refrigerate in plastic bag for up to 2 days.
Bok choy	1¼ pounds (1 head)	7 cups sliced stems and shredded leaves	Trim base; pull stalks apart. Rinse in cold water; pat dry. Refrigerate in plastic bag for up to 3 days.
Cabbage	2 pounds (1 head)	12 cups shredded or 10 cups coarsely chopped	Rinse in cold water just before using; pat dry. Refrigerate in a plastic bag for up to 5 days.
Collard greens	8 ounces	6 cups torn, stems removed	Wash in cold water; pat dry. Refrigerate in plastic bag for up to 5 days.
Endive, Belgian	4 ounces (1 head)	20 leaves	Cut off bottom core. Rinse in cold water; pat dry. Refrigerate in plastic bag; use within 1 day.
Endive, curly	12 ounces (1 head)	14 cups torn	Rinse in cold water; pat dry. Refrigerate, tightly wrapped, for up to 3 days.
Escarole	8 ounces (1 head)	7 cups torn	Rinse in cold water; pat dry. Refrigerate, tightly wrapped, for up to 3 days.
Frisée	8 ounces	7 cups torn	Rinse in cold water; pat dry. Refrigerate in plastic bag for up to 3 days.
Kale	8 ounces	7 cups torn, heavy vein removed	Wash in cold water; pat dry. Refrigerate in plastic bag for up to 3 days; longer storage increases bitterness.
Lettuce, butterhead (Bibb or Boston)	8 ounces (1 head)	6 cups torn	Cut off bottom core. Rinse in cold water; pat dry. Refrigerate in plastic bag for up to 5 days.
Lettuce, iceberg	1¼ pounds (1 head)	10 cups torn or 12 cups shredded	Remove core. Rinse (core side up) under cold running water; invert to drain. Refrigerate in plastic bag for up to 5 days.
Lettuce, leaf	12 ounces (1 head)	10 cups torn	Cut off bottom core. Rinse in cold water; pat dry. Refrigerate in plastic bag for up to 5 days.
Mustard greens	8 ounces	8 cups torn	Refrigerate in plastic bag for up to 3 days. Wash in cold water just before using; pat dry.
Napa cabbage	2 pounds (1 head)	12 cups sliced stems and shredded leaves	Cut off bottom core. Rinse in cold water; pat dry. Refrigerate in plastic bag for up to 3 days.
Radicchio	8 ounces (1 head)	5½ cups torn	Rinse in cold water; pat dry. Refrigerate in plastic bag for up to 1 week.
Romaine	1 pound (1 head)	10 cups torn	Cut off bottom core. Rinse leaves in cold water; pat dry. Refrigerate in plastic bag for up to 5 days. Before using, remove fibrous rib from each leaf (see photo, page 457).
Savoy cabbage	1¾ pounds (1 head)	12 cups coarsely shredded	Rinse in cold water just before using; pat dry. Refrigerate in a plastic bag for up to 5 days.
Sorrel	1 ounce	1 cup torn	Rinse in cold water; pat dry. Refrigerate in plastic bag for up to 3 days.
Spinach	1 pound	12 cups torn, stems removed	Rinse thoroughly in cold water to remove all sand; pat dry. Refrigerate in plastic bag for up to 3 days.
Swiss chard	1 pound	12 cups	Rinse in cold water; pat dry. Refrigerate in plastic bag for up to 3 days.
Watercress	4 ounces	2⅓ cups, stems removed	Rinse in cold water. Wrap in damp paper towels; refrigerate in plastic bag for up to 2 days.

Note: Always choose the freshest-looking greens. To store, line a plastic bag or airtight container with a paper towel. Discard leaves that are bruised, discolored, or wilted.

Fruit Vinegar

Fruit vinegar makes a perfect gift. Simply pour any one of these beautifully colored flavored vinegars into a decorative bottle and tie with a ribbon.

No Fat

Prep: 15 minutes **Stand:** 2 weeks **Makes:** about 1½ cups

> 1 cup fresh or frozen unsweetened tart red cherries, blueberries, or raspberries
>
> 2 cups white wine vinegar

1. Thaw fruit, if frozen. In a small stainless-steel or enamel saucepan combine fruit and vinegar. Bring to boiling; reduce heat. Boil gently, uncovered, for 3 minutes. Remove from heat and cover loosely with 100-percent-cotton cheesecloth; cool.

2. Pour mixture into a clean 1-quart jar. Cover jar tightly with a nonmetallic lid (or cover with plastic wrap and tightly seal with a metal lid). Let stand in a cool, dark place for 2 weeks.

3. Line a colander with several layers of 100-percent-cotton cheesecloth. Pour vinegar mixture through the colander and let it drain into a bowl. Discard the fruit.

4. Transfer strained vinegar to a clean 1-pint jar or bottle. If desired, add a few pieces of fresh fruit to the jar or bottle (the fruit must be completely submerged in the vinegar). Cover the jar or bottle tightly with a nonmetallic lid (or cover with plastic wrap and tightly seal with a metal lid).

5. Store vinegar in a cool, dark place for up to 6 months.

Nutrition Facts per tablespoon: 7 cal., 0 g total fat (0 g sat. fat), 0 mg chol., 1 mg sodium, 0 g carbo., 0 g fiber, 0 g pro.
Daily Values: 1% iron
Exchanges: Free

Herb Vinegar

Allow 2 weeks between preparation and use of this flavorful alternative to plain vinegar.

No Fat

Prep: 15 minutes **Stand:** 2 weeks **Makes:** about 2 cups

> ½ cup tightly packed fresh tarragon, thyme, mint, rosemary, or basil leaves
>
> 2 cups white wine vinegar or cider vinegar

1. Wash desired herbs; pat dry with paper towels. In a small stainless-steel or enamel saucepan combine the herbs and vinegar. Bring almost to boiling. Remove from heat and cover loosely with 100-percent-cotton cheesecloth; cool. Pour mix-ture into a clean 1-quart jar, making sure herbs are completely submerged in the vinegar. Cover jar tightly with a nonmetallic lid (or cover the jar with plastic wrap and tightly seal with a metal lid). Let stand in a cool, dark place for 2 weeks.

2. Line a colander with several layers of 100-percent-cotton cheesecloth. Pour vinegar mixture through the colander and let it drain into a bowl. Discard herbs.

3. Transfer strained vinegar to a clean 1½-pint jar or bottle. If desired, add a small sprig (2 to 3 inches long) of fresh herb to the jar (the sprig must be completely submerged in the vinegar). Cover jar with a nonmetallic lid (or cover with plastic wrap and tightly seal with a metal lid). Store vinegar in a cool, dark place for up to 6 months.

Nutrition Facts per tablespoon: 5 cal., 0 g total fat (0 g sat. fat), 0 mg chol., 1 mg sodium, 0 g carbo., 0 g fiber, 0 g pro.
Exchanges: Free

Vinegar

Due to its acidity, vinegar can be stored at room temperature almost indefinitely. Use different vinegars to vary the flavor of your favorite vinaigrette.

Balsamic vinegar gets its sweetness and dark color from aging in barrels. According to Italian law, balsamic vinegars labeled as *aceto balsamico tradizionale* cannot contain any wine vinegar and must be aged at least 12 years.

Cider vinegar is made from fermented apple cider. It is golden brown with a strong bite and a faint apple flavor.

Fruit vinegar is made by steeping berries or other fruits in cider or white wine vinegar (see recipe at left).

Herb vinegar is made by infusing tarragon, basil, dill, or other herbs in white wine vinegar or cider vinegar (see recipe at left).

Rice vinegar is clear to pale gold and made from rice wine or sake. It has a subtle tang, mildly sweet flavor, and is available plain or seasoned.

White or distilled vinegar is colorless and made from grain alcohol; its flavor is the strongest and sharpest of all vinegars.

Wine vinegar reflects the color and flavor of the source: red, white, or rosé wine; Champagne; or sherry.

Chapter 20
Sauces & Relishes

Sauces & Relishes

White Sauce

White sauce provides the base for numerous recipes. The recipe below is considered a white sauce with a medium consistency because of the proportions of flour to milk. It is used for scalloped dishes and creamed dishes as well as many sauces.

A thin white sauce is necessary for cream soups and creamed vegetables. To make a thin sauce, prepare the recipe below using 2 cups milk. Use the tips below to ensure a sauce free of lumps.

1. Use a small heavy saucepan and a wooden spoon. Cook and stir flour and seasonings into melted fat over low heat until evenly combined, making a roux.

2. After fat and flour are combined with no lumps, slowly add all the milk. Stir constantly with a wooden spoon or wire whisk to evenly blend fat-flour mixture and milk.

3. Stir the sauce over medium heat until the mixture bubbles across the entire surface. Cook and stir 1 minute more to completely cook the flour in the sauce.

White Sauce

`Fast`

Start to Finish: 15 minutes **Makes:** 1½ cups sauce

 2 **tablespoons butter or margarine**
 2 **tablespoons all-purpose flour**
 ¼ **teaspoon salt**
  Dash black pepper
 1½ **cups milk**

1. In a small saucepan melt butter. Stir in flour, salt, and pepper (see photo 1, above). Stir in milk (see photo 2, above). Cook and stir over medium heat until thickened and bubbly (see photo 3, above). Cook and stir for 1 minute more.

Curry Sauce: Prepare as above, except cook 1 teaspoon curry powder in the melted butter for 1 minute before adding the flour. Stir 2 tablespoons chopped chutney into the cooked sauce. Serve with fish or poultry.

Herb-Garlic Sauce: Prepare as at bottom left, except cook 2 cloves garlic, minced, in the melted butter for 30 seconds. Stir in ½ teaspoon caraway seeds; celery seeds; or dried basil, oregano, or sage, crushed, with the flour. Serve with vegetables or poultry.

Lemon-Chive Sauce: Prepare as at bottom left, except stir in 2 tablespoons snipped fresh chives and 1 teaspoon finely shredded lemon peel with the flour. Serve with vegetables, poultry, or fish.

Nutrition Facts per 2 tablespoons for plain, curry, herb-garlic, and lemon-chive variations: 38 cal., 3 g total fat (2 g sat. fat), 8 mg chol., 84 mg sodium, 2 g carbo., 0 g fiber, 1 g pro.
Daily Values: 3% vit. A, 4% calcium
Exchanges: ½ Fat

Cheese Sauce: Prepare as at bottom left, except omit salt. Over low heat, stir 1½ cups shredded process Swiss, American, or Gruyère cheese; ½ cup crumbled blue cheese; or ¾ cup grated Parmesan cheese into the cooked sauce until melted. Serve with vegetables. Makes about 2 cups sauce.

Nutrition Facts per 2 tablespoons: 85 cal., 6 g total fat (4 g sat. fat), 20 mg chol., 230 mg sodium, 3 g carbo., 0 g fiber, 5 g pro.
Daily Values: 5% vit. A, 15% calcium, 1% iron
Exchanges: ½ High-Fat Meat, ½ Fat

Creamy Mushroom Sauce

`Fast`

Start to Finish: 20 minutes **Makes:** about 1½ cups sauce

 1 **cup sliced fresh mushrooms**
 ¼ **cup chopped onion**
 1 **tablespoon butter or margarine**
 1 **tablespoon all-purpose flour**
 ⅛ **teaspoon salt**
  Dash black pepper
 ⅔ **cup milk**
 ½ **cup dairy sour cream**

1. In a medium saucepan cook mushrooms and onion in hot butter until tender. Stir in flour, salt, and pepper (see photo 1, above left). Stir in milk all at once (see photo 2, above left). Cook and stir over medium heat until thickened and bubbly. Cook and stir for 1 minute more (see photo 3, above left). Stir in sour cream; heat through (do not boil). Serve with beef or poultry.

Nutrition Facts per 2 tablespoons: 39 cal., 3 g total fat (2 g sat. fat), 7 mg chol., 46 mg sodium, 2 g carbo., 0 g fiber, 1 g pro.
Daily Values: 3% vit. A, 1% vit. C, 3% calcium, 1% iron
Exchanges: ½ Fat

Hollandaise Sauce

Well-known for its role in classic Eggs Benedict (see recipe, page 264), this sauce is best made in a double boiler to prevent overheating.

Prep: 50 minutes **Cook:** 10 minutes **Makes:** ¾ cup sauce

> ½ **cup unsalted butter**
> 3 **beaten egg yolks**
> 1 **tablespoon lemon juice**
> 1 **tablespoon water**
> **Salt**
> **White pepper**

1. Cut the butter into thirds and bring it to room temperature; allow about 45 minutes.

2. In the top of a double boiler combine egg yolks, lemon juice, and water. Add a piece of the butter. Place over gently boiling water (upper pan should not touch water). Cook, stirring rapidly with a whisk, until butter melts and sauce begins to thicken (see photo 1, below). (Sauce may appear to curdle at this point, but will smooth out when remaining butter is added.) Add the remaining butter, a piece at a time, stirring constantly until melted. Continue to cook and stir for 2 to 2½ minutes more or until sauce thickens (see photo 2, below). Immediately remove from heat. If sauce is too thick or curdles, immediately whisk in 1 to 2 tablespoons *hot water.* Season to taste with salt and pepper. Serve with cooked vegetables, poultry, fish, or eggs.

Nutrition Facts per 2 tablespoons: 174 cal., 19 g total fat (11 g sat. fat), 150 mg chol., 54 mg sodium, 0 g carbo., 0 g fiber, 2 g pro.
Daily Values: 15% vit. A, 2% vit. C, 2% calcium, 2% iron
Exchanges: 4 Fat

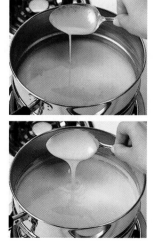

1. After adding one piece of butter, cook and stir the sauce until it starts to thinly coat a spoon.

2. Continue cooking over boiling water, adding remaining butter pieces and stirring with a whisk until the butter melts and sauce becomes thicker.

Mock Hollandaise Sauce

Fast

Start to Finish: 10 minutes **Makes:** ½ cup sauce

> ¼ **cup dairy sour cream**
> ¼ **cup mayonnaise or salad dressing**
> 1 **teaspoon lemon juice**
> ½ **teaspoon prepared mustard**
> **Milk (optional)**

1. In a small saucepan combine sour cream, mayonnaise, lemon juice, and mustard. Cook and stir over medium-low heat until hot. If desired, thin with a little milk. Serve with vegetables, poultry, fish, or eggs.

Nutrition Facts per 2 tablespoons: 125 cal., 13 g total fat (3 g sat. fat), 13 mg chol., 92 mg sodium, 1 g carbo., 0 g fiber, 1 g pro.
Daily Values: 3% vit. A, 1% vit. C, 2% calcium
Exchanges: 2½ Fat

Béarnaise Sauce   Best Loved

Fast

Start to Finish: 15 minutes **Makes:** about 1 cup sauce

> 3 **tablespoons white wine vinegar**
> 1 **teaspoon finely chopped green onion**
> 1 **teaspoon snipped fresh tarragon or**
>   ¼ **teaspoon dried tarragon, crushed**
> ¼ **teaspoon snipped fresh chervil or dash dried chervil, crushed**
> 4 **beaten egg yolks**
> ½ **cup butter, cut into thirds and softened**

1. In a small saucepan combine vinegar, green onion, tarragon, chervil, and ⅛ teaspoon *white pepper.* Bring to boiling. Boil, uncovered, about 2 minutes or until reduced by about half.

2. In the top of a double boiler combine vinegar mixture, egg yolks, and 1 tablespoon *water.* Add a piece of the butter. Place over boiling water (upper pan should not touch water). Cook, stirring rapidly with a whisk, until butter melts and sauce begins to thicken (see photo 1, left). Add remaining butter, a piece at a time, stirring constantly until melted. Continue to cook and stir 1 to 2 minutes more or until sauce is thickened (see photo 2, left). Immediately remove from heat. If sauce is too thick or curdles, whisk in 1 to 2 tablespoons *hot water.* Serve with beef, pork, or poultry.

Nutrition Facts per 2 tablespoons: 139 cal., 15 g total fat (8 g sat. fat), 139 mg chol., 128 mg sodium, 0 g carbo., 0 g fiber, 2 g pro.
Daily Values: 12% vit. A, 2% calcium, 2% iron
Exchanges: 3 Fat

Beurre Blanc

For a silky, smooth sauce, take your time and make sure each piece of butter is melted before adding the next (see photo, page 473).

Fast

Start to Finish: 30 minutes
Makes: 1¾ cups unstrained sauce

½	**cup dry white wine**
⅓	**cup finely chopped shallots**
2	**tablespoons white wine vinegar**
3	**tablespoons whipping cream (no substitutes)**
1½	**cups (3 sticks) cold unsalted butter, cut into 2-tablespoon pieces**
	Salt and white pepper

1. In a medium saucepan* combine the wine, shallots, and vinegar. Bring to boiling; reduce heat to medium. Boil gently, uncovered, for 7 to 9 minutes or until mixture is reduced to ¼ cup.

2. Using a wire whisk, stir in the cream, then the butter, 1 piece at a time, allowing each piece to melt before adding the next. Allow about 10 minutes (see photos 1 and 2, right). Strain sauce, if desired. Season to taste with salt and white pepper. Serve immediately over sauteed fish or cooked vegetables.

*Note: Because vinegar may react with aluminum and cause curdling, be sure to use a stainless-steel saucepan and wire whisk.

Lemony Beurre Blanc: Prepare as above, except substitute lemon juice for the vinegar. If desired, garnish with finely shredded lemon peel.

Successful Sauces

For a perfect sauce every time, follow the recipe directions and remember these tips:

■ Prevent lumps in sauces thickened with cornstarch or flour by stirring constantly. If lumps do form, beat the sauce briskly with a wire whisk or a rotary beater.

■ Cook sauces over low to medium heat unless the recipe says otherwise. Cook your sauces no longer than the time specified. High heat and lengthy cooking can cause sauces to curdle or break down.

■ If it's necessary to leave the sauce during cooking, remove it from the heat.

Creamy Mustard Sauce: Prepare as at left, except whisk in 2 teaspoons Dijon-style mustard before serving.

Nutrition Facts per 2 tablespoons for plain, lemony, and mustard variations: 195 cal., 21 g total fat (13 g sat. fat), 58 mg chol., 26 mg sodium, 1 g carbo., 0 g fiber, 0 g pro.
Daily Values: 17% vit. A, 1% vit. C, 1% calcium, 1% iron
Exchanges: 4 Fat

1. Using a stainless-steel wire whisk, stir in the butter, 1 piece at a time, allowing each piece to melt before adding the next.

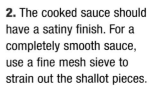

2. The cooked sauce should have a satiny finish. For a completely smooth sauce, use a fine mesh sieve to strain out the shallot pieces.

Sauce Provençal Best Loved

Tomatoes, garlic, and olive oil imbue this versatile sauce with the taste of Provence, France.

Fast   **Low Fat**

Start to Finish: 25 minutes **Makes:** 1¾ cups sauce

2	**tablespoons olive oil**
¼	**cup finely chopped onion**
1	**clove garlic, minced**
¼	**cup dry white wine**
¼	**cup chicken broth**
3	**medium tomatoes, peeled, seeded, and chopped (about 1 pound)**
1	**tablespoon snipped fresh parsley**
2	**teaspoons snipped fresh thyme**
¼	**teaspoon salt**

1. In a medium saucepan heat oil over medium-high heat. Add onion and garlic; cook and stir until tender but not brown. Stir in the wine and broth. Bring to boiling; reduce heat. Boil gently, uncovered, about 8 minutes or until reduced to ¼ cup. Stir in tomatoes, parsley, thyme, and salt; heat through. Serve over fish, chicken, couscous, or pasta.

Nutrition Facts per 2 tablespoons: 29 cal., 2 g total fat (0 g sat. fat), 0 mg chol., 59 mg sodium, 2 g carbo., 0 g fiber, 0 g pro.
Daily Values: 4% vit. A, 12% vit. C, 1% iron
Exchanges: ½ Fat

Barbecue Sauce

Low Fat

Start to Finish: 40 minutes **Makes:** about 1⅓ cups sauce

- ½ cup finely chopped onion
- 2 cloves garlic, minced
- 1 tablespoon olive oil or cooking oil
- ¾ cup apple juice
- ½ of a 6-ounce can (⅓ cup) tomato paste
- ¼ cup vinegar
- 2 tablespoons brown sugar
- 2 tablespoons molasses
- 1 tablespoon paprika
- 1 tablespoon prepared horseradish
- 1 tablespoon Worcestershire sauce
- 1 teaspoon salt
- ½ teaspoon black pepper

1. In a medium saucepan cook onion and garlic in hot oil until onion is tender. Stir in apple juice, tomato paste, vinegar, brown sugar, molasses, paprika, horseradish, Worcestershire sauce, salt, and pepper. Bring to boiling; reduce heat. Simmer, uncovered, about 30 minutes or until desired consistency, stirring occasionally.

2. To use, brush chicken, pork, or beef with some of the sauce during the last 10 minutes of grilling. If desired, reheat and pass additional sauce. (Cover and chill any leftovers for up to 3 days.)

Nutrition Facts per 2 tablespoons: 52 cal., 2 g total fat (0 g sat. fat), 1 mg chol., 238 mg sodium, 9 g carbo., 1 g fiber, 1 g pro.
Daily Values: 7% vit. A, 5% vit. C, 2% calcium, 4% iron
Exchanges: ½ Other Carbo., ½ Fat

What Is a Reduction?

Reduction is aptly named. It's a technique that involves decreasing the volume of a liquid by boiling rapidly to cause evaporation. As some of the liquid evaporates, the rest thickens and intensifies in flavor. You can make a quick sauce for meats and roasted vegetables by reducing stock or broth, wine, vinegar, or another liquid.

■ The amount of reduction needed in a recipe usually is specified in one of two ways. A recipe may tell you to reduce a liquid by a general amount—one-third or one-half, for example. Or it may say to keep boiling until the liquid has reached a specific volume, such as ½ cup or 3 tablespoons.

■ The size of the pan you use will affect the time it takes to reduce a liquid. A bigger pan has a larger surface area and results in faster evaporation. Be sure to use the pan size recommended in the recipe.

Bordelaise Sauce

Start to Finish: 40 minutes **Makes:** about 1 cup sauce

- 1¼ cups reduced-sodium beef broth
- ¾ cup dry red wine
- 2 tablespoons finely chopped shallot or onion
- 3 tablespoons butter or margarine, softened
- 1 tablespoon all-purpose flour
- 1 tablespoon snipped fresh parsley (optional)

1. In a medium saucepan combine beef broth, red wine, and shallot. Bring just to boiling; reduce heat. Simmer, uncovered, skimming the surface often with a spoon, for 25 to 30 minutes or until reduced to 1 cup.

2. With a fork, stir together butter and flour. Stir butter mixture into wine mixture, 1 teaspoon at a time, stirring constantly. Continue cooking and stirring until mixture is slightly thickened; cook and stir for 1 minute more. If desired, stir in parsley. Serve with broiled or grilled beef or lamb.

Nutrition Facts per 2 tablespoons: 63 cal., 5 g total fat (3 g sat. fat), 12 mg chol., 117 mg sodium, 2 g carbo., 0 g fiber, 1 g pro.
Daily Values: 5% vit. A, 1% vit. C, 1% iron
Exchanges: 1½ Fat

Bordelaise Sauce

Plum Sauce

Use this glistening dipping sauce for egg rolls or wontons. Or stir 2 tablespoons of it into your favorite stir-fry recipe.

Fast　**No Fat**

Start to Finish: 15 minutes　**Makes:** ⅔ cup sauce

- ½ **cup red plum jam**
- ¼ **cup sliced green onions (2)**
- 2 **teaspoons cornstarch**
- 2 **tablespoons soy sauce**
- 1 **tablespoon dry sherry**
- 1 **tablespoon vinegar**
- ⅛ **teaspoon crushed red pepper (optional)**

1. In a small saucepan stir together jam, green onions, and cornstarch. Stir in soy sauce, sherry, vinegar, and, if desired, crushed red pepper. Cook and stir until thickened and bubbly. Cook and stir for 2 minutes more. Serve warm.

Nutrition Facts per 2 tablespoons: 103 cal., 0 g total fat (0 g sat. fat), 0 mg chol., 379 mg sodium, 24 g carbo., 0 g fiber, 1 g pro.
Daily Values: 6% vit. C, 1% calcium, 1% iron
Exchanges: 1½ Other Carbo.

Sweet-and-Sour Sauce

Fast　**No Fat**

Start to Finish: 20 minutes　**Makes:** 1½ cups sauce

- ½ **cup packed brown sugar**
- 4 **teaspoons cornstarch**
- ½ **cup chicken broth**
- ⅓ **cup red wine vinegar**
- ¼ **cup finely chopped green sweet pepper**
- 2 **tablespoons chopped pimiento**
- 2 **tablespoons corn syrup**
- 2 **tablespoons soy sauce**
- 1½ **teaspoons grated fresh ginger**
- 1 **clove garlic, minced**

1. In a small saucepan combine brown sugar and cornstarch. Stir in chicken broth, vinegar, sweet pepper, pimiento, corn syrup, soy sauce, ginger, and garlic. Cook and stir until thickened and bubbly. Cook and stir for 2 minutes more. Serve warm with egg rolls and wontons or use in recipes calling for sweet-and-sour sauce. (Cover and chill any leftovers for up to 3 days.)

Nutrition Facts per 2 tablespoons: 52 cal., 0 g total fat (0 g sat. fat), 0 mg chol., 213 mg sodium, 13 g carbo., 0 g fiber, 0 g pro.
Daily Values: 1% vit. A, 8% vit. C, 1% calcium, 2% iron
Exchanges: 1 Other Carbo.

Cocktail Sauce

Because this sauce stores nicely for a couple of weeks, you can prepare it ahead of time.

Fast　**No Fat**

Start to Finish: 10 minutes　**Makes:** about 1 cup sauce

- ¾ **cup bottled chili sauce**
- 2 **tablespoons lemon juice**
- 2 **tablespoons thinly sliced green onion (1)**
- 1 **tablespoon prepared horseradish**
- 2 **teaspoons Worcestershire sauce**
  Several dashes bottled hot pepper sauce

1. In a small bowl combine chili sauce, lemon juice, green onion, horseradish, Worcestershire sauce, and hot pepper sauce. Transfer to a storage container. Cover and chill for up to 2 weeks. Serve with fish or seafood.

Nutrition Facts per 2 tablespoons: 30 cal., 0 g total fat (0 g sat. fat), 1 mg chol., 321 mg sodium, 6 g carbo., 1 g fiber, 1 g pro.
Daily Values: 4% vit. A, 10% vit. C, 1% calcium, 2% iron
Exchanges: ½ Other Carbo.

Tartar Sauce

If you prefer a sweet tartar sauce, use the sweet pickle relish option.

Prep: 10 minutes　**Chill:** 2 hours　**Makes:** 1 cup sauce

- ¾ **cup mayonnaise or salad dressing**
- ¼ **cup drained dill or sweet pickle relish**
- 2 **tablespoons finely chopped onion**
- 1 **tablespoon snipped fresh parsley**
- 2 **teaspoons capers, drained (optional)**

1. In a small bowl stir together the mayonnaise, pickle relish, onion, parsley, and, if desired, capers. Cover and chill for at least 2 hours before serving. Serve with fish or seafood. (Cover and chill any leftovers for up to 1 week.)

Nutrition Facts per 2 tablespoons: 159 cal., 17 g total fat (2 g sat. fat), 8 mg chol., 168 mg sodium, 2 g carbo., 0 g fiber, 0 g pro.
Daily Values: 1% vit. C
Exchanges: 3½ Fat

Low-Fat Tartar Sauce: Prepare as above, except replace the ¾ cup mayonnaise or salad dressing with ½ cup light mayonnaise dressing or salad dressing and ¼ cup plain low-fat yogurt.

Nutrition Facts per 2 tablespoons: 63 cal., 5 g total fat (1 g sat. fat), 5 mg chol., 151 mg sodium, 5 g carbo., 0 g fiber, 0 g pro.
Daily Values: 1% vit. A, 1% vit. C, 2% calcium
Exchanges: 1 Fat

Yogurt-Dill Sauce

Fast   **Low Fat**

Start to Finish: 5 minutes **Makes:** 1 cup sauce

1. In a small bowl combine one 8-ounce carton plain yogurt; 1 tablespoon snipped fresh dill or 1 teaspoon dried dill; ¼ teaspoon finely shredded lemon peel; 1 small clove garlic, minced; and ¼ teaspoon black pepper. Cover and chill until serving time. Serve with fish or seafood.

Yogurt-Cucumber-Mint Sauce: Prepare as above, except omit dill and lemon peel. Stir ⅓ cup finely chopped cucumber into yogurt mixture along with 1 teaspoon snipped fresh mint. Serve with lamb or fish.

Nutrition Facts per 2 tablespoons for dill or cucumber-mint variation: 18 cal., 1 g total fat (1 g sat. fat), 4 mg chol., 13 mg sodium, 1 g carbo., 0 g fiber, 1 g pro.
Daily Values: 1% vit. A, 1% vit. C, 4% calcium
Exchanges: Free

Cranberry Sauce

Fast   **No Fat**

Start to Finish: 20 minutes **Makes:** about 2 cups sauce

1. In a medium saucepan combine 1 cup sugar and 1 cup water. Bring to boiling, stirring to dissolve sugar. Boil rapidly for 5 minutes. Add 2 cups cranberries. Return to boiling; reduce heat. Boil gently, uncovered, over medium-high heat for 3 to 4 minutes or until skins pop, stirring occasionally. Remove from heat. Serve warm or chilled with poultry or pork.

Nutrition Facts per 2 tablespoons: 53 cal., 0 g total fat (0 g sat. fat), 0 mg chol., 1 mg sodium, 14 g carbo., 1 g fiber, 0 g pro.
Daily Values: 3% vit. C
Exchanges: 1 Other Carbo.

Refrigerator Corn Relish

No Fat

Prep: 25 minutes **Cook:** 10 minutes
Makes: about 2¼ cups relish

> **4** ears of fresh corn or one 10-ounce package frozen whole kernel corn (2 cups)
> **⅓** cup sugar
> **1** tablespoon cornstarch
> **⅓** cup vinegar
> **¼** cup chopped celery
> **¼** cup chopped green or red sweet pepper
> **¼** cup chopped onion
> **2** tablespoons chopped pimiento
> **1** teaspoon ground turmeric
> **½** teaspoon dry mustard

1. Remove husks from fresh ears of corn; scrub with a stiff brush to remove silks and rinse. Cut kernels from cob. Cook kernels, covered, in a small amount of boiling salted water for 4 minutes. Or cook frozen corn according to package directions. Drain corn.

2. In a medium saucepan combine sugar and cornstarch; stir in vinegar and ⅓ cup *cold water.* Stir in corn, celery, sweet pepper, onion, pimiento, turmeric, mustard, and ¼ teaspoon *salt.* Cook and stir over medium heat until thickened and bubbly. Cook and stir 2 minutes more. Let cool. Transfer to a storage container. Cover and chill up to 2 weeks. Serve with pork, beef, or poultry.

Nutrition Facts per ¼ cup: 71 cal., 0 g total fat (0 g sat. fat), 0 mg chol., 69 mg sodium, 18 g carbo., 1 g fiber, 1 g pro.
Daily Values: 4% vit. A, 14% vit. C, 3% iron
Exchanges: ½ Starch, ½ Other Carbo.

Mango-Ginger Chutney

No Fat

Prep: 20 minutes **Cook:** 15 minutes
Makes: about 2½ cups chutney

- ½ **cup packed brown sugar**
- ½ **cup dried tart red cherries or raisins**
- ⅓ **cup vinegar**
- ¼ **cup chopped onion**
- 1 **teaspoon grated fresh ginger**
- ¼ **teaspoon crushed red pepper**
- 3 **cups chopped, peeled mangoes (about 3 mangoes*)**

1. In a medium saucepan combine brown sugar, cherries, vinegar, onion, ginger, and red pepper. Bring to boiling; reduce heat. Simmer, uncovered, 15 minutes, stirring occasionally. Stir in mangoes; heat through. Let cool. Transfer to a container. Cover; chill up to 4 weeks. Or freeze up to 12 months. Serve with beef, lamb, pork, or poultry.

*Note: To prepare a mango, slide a sharp knife next to the seed along 1 side, cutting through the fruit. Repeat on the other side of the seed, dividing the mango into 2 large pieces. Cut away the meat that remains around the seed. Remove the peel and chop all the meat.

Peach-Ginger Chutney: Prepare as above, except substitute 3 cups chopped, peeled fresh peaches or frozen peach slices, thawed and chopped, for the mangoes.

Nutrition Facts per ¼ cup for mango or peach variation: 104 cal., 0 g total fat (0 g sat. fat), 0 mg chol., 6 mg sodium, 27 g carbo., 1 g fiber, 1 g pro.
Daily Values: 48% vit. A, 29% vit. C, 2% calcium, 2% iron
Exchanges: 1 Fruit, 1 Other Carbo.

Cantaloupe Relish

Allowing the flavors to mingle for as long as 24 hours lets the cantaloupe and pear absorb a whole palette of flavors.

No Fat

Prep: 20 minutes **Chill:** 1 hour **Makes:** about 3 cups relish

- 1 **cup chopped cantaloupe**
- 1 **cup chopped Asian pear or chopped, peeled jicama**
- 1 **cup chopped, peeled papaya or mango**
- ¼ **cup thinly sliced green onions (2)**
- 3 **tablespoons lemon juice**
- 1 **teaspoon snipped fresh lemon thyme or thyme**
- 1 **teaspoon olive oil**

1. In a medium bowl stir together cantaloupe, Asian pear, papaya, green onions, lemon juice, thyme, and oil. Cover and chill for 1 to 24 hours before serving. Serve with grilled or roasted chicken or pork.

Nutrition Facts per ¼ cup: 18 cal., 0 g total fat (0 g sat. fat), 0 mg chol., 2 mg sodium, 4 g carbo., 1 g fiber, 0 g pro.
Daily Values: 9% vit. A, 26% vit. C, 1% calcium
Exchanges: Free

Cranberry Relish Best Loved

Low Fat

Prep: 15 minutes **Chill:** 2 hours
Makes: about 2½ cups relish

- ¾ **cup apple juice or orange juice**
- ½ **to ⅔ cup sugar**
- ¼ **teaspoon ground cinnamon**
- ¼ **teaspoon ground nutmeg**
  Dash ground cloves
- 1 **12-ounce package (3 cups) cranberries**
- ½ **cup golden raisins**
- ½ **cup chopped pecans**

1. In a medium saucepan combine apple juice, sugar, cinnamon, nutmeg, and cloves. Cook and stir over medium heat until sugar is dissolved. Add the cranberries and raisins. Bring to boiling; reduce heat. Cook and stir for 3 to 4 minutes or until cranberries pop. Remove from heat. Stir in pecans. Cover and chill for at least 2 hours before serving. Serve with poultry, pork, or ham. (Cover and chill any leftovers for up to 2 days.)

Nutrition Facts per 2 tablespoons: 63 cal., 2 g total fat (0 g sat. fat), 0 mg chol., 2 mg sodium, 12 g carbo., 1 g fiber, 0 g pro.
Daily Values: 4% vit. C, 1% calcium, 1% iron
Exchanges: 1 Other Carbo.

Raspberry Sauce `Best Loved`

`No Fat`

Prep: 20 minutes **Chill:** 1 hour **Makes:** about 1 cup sauce

>   **3 cups fresh or frozen slightly sweetened raspberries**
>   **⅓ cup sugar**
>   **1 teaspoon cornstarch**

1. Thaw berries, if frozen. Do not drain. Place half of the berries in a blender container or food processor bowl. Cover and blend until berries are smooth. Press berries through a fine-mesh sieve; discard seeds. Repeat with remaining berries. (You should have about 1¼ cups sieved puree.)

2. In a small saucepan combine sugar and cornstarch. Add sieved berries. Cook and stir over medium heat until thickened and bubbly. Cook and stir for 2 minutes more. Transfer to a bowl. Cover and chill for at least 1 hour. Serve over angel food cake, cheesecake, or ice cream.

Nutrition Facts per 2 tablespoons: 55 cal., 0 g total fat (0 g sat. fat), 0 mg chol., 0 mg sodium, 14 g carbo., 3 g fiber, 0 g pro.
Daily Values: 1% vit. A, 19% vit. C, 1% calcium, 1% iron
Exchanges: 1 Other Carbo.

Strawberry Sauce: Prepare as above, except substitute 3 cups fresh strawberries or one 16-ounce package frozen unsweetened whole strawberries, thawed, for raspberries and do not sieve; use a medium saucepan and reduce sugar to ¼ cup. (You should have 1¾ to 2 cups puree.) Makes 2 cups.

Nutrition Facts per 2 tablespoons: 20 cal., 0 g total fat (0 g sat. fat), 0 mg chol., 0 mg sodium, 5 g carbo., 1 g fiber, 0 g pro.
Daily Values: 26% vit. C, 1% iron
Exchanges: ½ Other Carbo.

Raspberry Sauce

Cherry Sauce

Spoon this luscious topping over a bowl of frozen vanilla yogurt or use it as a filling in Cream Puffs (page 251).

`Fast`   `No Fat`

Start to Finish: 15 minutes **Makes:** 2 cups sauce

>   **½ cup sugar**
>   **2 tablespoons cornstarch**
>   **½ cup water**
>   **2 cups fresh or frozen pitted tart cherries**
>   **1 tablespoon orange or cherry liqueur, cherry brandy, or orange juice**
>   **Few drops red food coloring (optional)**

1. In a medium saucepan stir together sugar and cornstarch; stir in water. Add cherries. Cook and stir over medium heat until thickened and bubbly. Cook and stir for 2 minutes more. Remove saucepan from heat.

2. Stir in liqueur and, if desired, food coloring. Serve warm or cooled to room temperature. (Cover and chill any leftovers for up to 3 days.)

Nutrition Facts per 2 tablespoons: 39 cal., 0 g total fat (0 g sat. fat), 0 mg chol., 1 mg sodium, 10 g carbo., 0 g fiber, 0 g pro.
Daily Values: 5% vit. A, 3% vit. C
Exchanges: ½ Other Carbo.

Rhubarb Sauce

You'll need about 1 pound of rhubarb to make 3 cups of sliced fruit.

`Fast`   `No Fat`

Start to Finish: 20 minutes **Makes:** 2 cups sauce

>   **½ to ⅔ cup sugar**
>   **¼ cup water**
>   **1 strip orange peel (optional)**
>   **3 cups sliced rhubarb**

1. In a medium saucepan stir together sugar, water, and, if desired, orange peel. Bring to boiling; stir in rhubarb. Return to boiling; reduce heat. Cover and simmer about 5 minutes or until rhubarb is tender. Remove the orange peel, if using. Serve warm over cake or ice cream. (Cover and chill any leftovers for up to 3 days.)

Nutrition Facts per 2 tablespoons: 28 cal., 0 g total fat (0 g sat. fat), 0 mg chol., 1 mg sodium, 7 g carbo., 0 g fiber, 0 g pro.
Daily Values: 3% vit. C, 2% calcium
Exchanges: ½ Other Carbo.

Lemon Sauce

Serve this sauce over freshly baked gingerbread or a bowl of fresh berries.

Fast

Start to Finish: 20 minutes **Makes:** 1⅓ cups sauce

- ⅔ **cup sugar**
- 4 **teaspoons cornstarch**
- ¼ **cup water**
- 2 **teaspoons finely shredded lemon peel**
- ¼ **cup lemon juice**
- 2 **beaten egg yolks**
- 6 **tablespoons butter, cut up**
- ¼ **cup half-and-half, light cream, or milk**

1. In a small saucepan stir together the sugar and cornstarch. Stir in the water, lemon peel, and lemon juice. Cook and stir over medium heat until mixture is slightly thickened and bubbly. Cook and stir for 1 minute more.

2. Gradually stir hot mixture into egg yolks. Return mixture to saucepan. Cook and stir for 2 minutes more. Gradually stir in butter until melted. Stir in half-and-half. Serve warm. (Cover and chill any leftovers for up to 3 days.)

Orange Sauce: Prepare as above, except omit water, lemon peel, and lemon juice and add 2 teaspoons finely shredded orange peel and ½ cup orange juice to the sugar mixture.

Nutrition Facts per 2 tablespoons for lemon or orange variation: 126 cal., 8 g total fat (5 g sat. fat), 59 mg chol., 72 mg sodium, 13 g carbo., 0 g fiber, 1 g pro.
Daily Values: 7% vit. A, 5% vit. C, 1% calcium, 1% iron
Exchanges: 1 Other Carbo., 1½ Fat

Custard Sauce Best Loved

This delicate sauce is also commonly known as crème anglaise.

Low Fat

Prep: 15 minutes **Chill:** 2 hours **Makes:** about 2 cups sauce

- 5 **beaten egg yolks**
- 1½ **cups milk**
- ¼ **cup sugar**
- 1½ **teaspoons vanilla**

1. In a medium heavy saucepan stir together egg yolks, milk, and sugar. Cook and stir continuously with a wooden spoon or heatproof rubber spatula over medium heat until mixture just coats the back of a clean metal spoon. Remove pan from heat. Stir in vanilla. Quickly cool mixture by placing saucepan in a large bowl of ice water for 1 to 2 minutes, stirring constantly.

2. Pour mixture into a bowl. Cover the surface with plastic wrap to prevent a skin from forming. Chill at least 2 hours before serving. Do not stir. Serve over fresh fruit, baked fruit tarts, or dessert soufflés. (Cover and chill any leftovers for up to 3 days.)

Chocolate Custard Sauce: Prepare as at bottom left, except add ¼ cup Dutch process unsweetened cocoa powder or unsweetened cocoa powder and, if desired, a dash ground cinnamon along with the sugar (use a whisk, if necessary, to combine ingredients).

Liqueur Custard Sauce: Prepare as at bottom left, except add 1 to 2 tablespoons liqueur after removing from heat. Try cinnamon, orange, amaretto, or raspberry liqueur.

Nutrition Facts per 2 tablespoons for plain, chocolate, and liqueur variations: 43 cal., 2 g total fat (1 g sat. fat), 68 mg chol., 14 mg sodium, 4 g carbo., 0 g fiber, 2 g pro.
Daily Values: 3% vit. A, 3% calcium, 1% iron
Exchanges: ½ Other Carbo., ½ Medium-Fat Meat, ½ Fat

Hot Fudge Sauce Best Loved

To reheat this rich sauce in your microwave oven, allow 15 to 30 seconds on high power.

Fast

Start to Finish: 15 minutes **Makes:** 1½ cups sauce

- ¾ **cup semisweet chocolate pieces**
- ¼ **cup butter**
- ⅔ **cup sugar**
- 1 **5-ounce can (⅔ cup) evaporated milk**

1. In a small heavy saucepan melt the chocolate and butter. Add the sugar; gradually stir in the evaporated milk. Bring mixture to boiling; reduce heat. Boil gently over low heat for 8 minutes, stirring frequently. Remove pan from heat. Cool slightly. Serve warm over ice cream. (Cover and chill any leftovers for up to 3 days.)

Peanut Butter-Fudge Sauce: Prepare as above, except after gently boiling for 8 minutes, stir in ¼ cup peanut butter. Makes 1¾ cups sauce.

Nutrition Facts per 2 tablespoons for plain or peanut butter variation: 146 cal., 8 g total fat (5 g sat. fat), 14 mg chol., 54 mg sodium, 15 g carbo., 2 g fiber, 1 g pro.
Daily Values: 4% vit. A, 3% calcium
Exchanges: 1 Other Carbo., 1½ Fat

Vanilla Sauce

`Fast` `Low Fat`

Start to Finish: 10 minutes **Makes:** 1¼ cups sauce

- ½ **cup sugar**
- 1 **tablespoon cornstarch**
- 1 **cup boiling water**
- 2 **tablespoons butter**
- 1 **teaspoon vanilla paste or vanilla extract**
  Dash salt

1. In a medium saucepan stir together sugar and cornstarch. Slowly stir in water. Cook over medium heat until mixture is gently boiling. Boil for 5 minutes; remove from heat. Stir in butter, vanilla, and salt. Serve over gingerbread, apple dumplings, or your favorite berry pie. (Cover and chill any leftovers for up to 3 days.)

Nutrition Facts per 2 tablespoons: 63 cal., 2 g total fat (2 g sat. fat), 7 mg chol., 40 mg sodium, 10 g carbo., 0 g fiber, 0 g pro.
Daily Values: 2% vit. A
Exchanges: ½ Other Carbo., ½ Fat

Caramel Sauce

`Fast`

Start to Finish: 10 minutes **Makes:** ¾ cup sauce

- ½ **cup packed brown sugar**
- 1 **tablespoon cornstarch**
- ⅓ **cup half-and-half or light cream**
- 2 **tablespoons light-colored corn syrup**
- 1 **tablespoon butter**
- ½ **teaspoon vanilla**

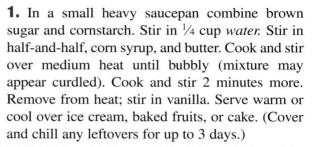

Caramel Sauce

1. In a small heavy saucepan combine brown sugar and cornstarch. Stir in ¼ cup *water.* Stir in half-and-half, corn syrup, and butter. Cook and stir over medium heat until bubbly (mixture may appear curdled). Cook and stir 2 minutes more. Remove from heat; stir in vanilla. Serve warm or cool over ice cream, baked fruits, or cake. (Cover and chill any leftovers for up to 3 days.)

Nutrition Facts per 2 tablespoons: 129 cal., 4 g total fat (2 g sat. fat), 10 mg chol., 42 mg sodium, 25 g carbo., 0 g fiber, 0 g pro.
Daily Values: 3% vit. A, 3% calcium, 2% iron
Exchanges: 1½ Other Carbo., 1 Fat

Hard Sauce

Prep: 10 minutes **Chill:** 30 minutes **Makes:** ⅔ cup sauce

- ¼ **cup butter, softened**
- 1 **cup sifted powdered sugar**
- ½ **teaspoon vanilla or 1 tablespoon brandy or rum**

1. In a small mixing bowl beat together butter and powdered sugar with an electric mixer on medium speed for 3 to 5 minutes or until mixture is combined. Beat in vanilla. Spoon into a serving bowl. Cover; chill 30 minutes before serving.

Orange Hard Sauce: Prepare as above, except substitute ¼ teaspoon grated orange peel and 1 tablespoon orange juice or liqueur for vanilla.

Nutrition Facts per 1 tablespoon for plain or orange variation: 83 cal., 5 g total fat (3 g sat. fat), 13 mg chol., 50 mg sodium, 10 g carbo., 0 g fiber, 0 g pro.
Daily Values: 4% vit. A
Exchanges: ½ Other Carbo., 1 Fat

Bourbon Sauce

`Fast`

Start to Finish: 10 minutes **Makes:** ⅔ cup sauce

- ¼ **cup butter**
- ½ **cup sugar**
- 1 **beaten egg yolk**
- 2 **tablespoons water**
- 1 **to 2 tablespoons bourbon**

1. In a small saucepan melt the butter. Stir in the sugar, egg yolk, and water. Cook and stir mixture over medium-low heat 5 to 6 minutes or until sugar dissolves and mixture boils. Remove from heat; stir in bourbon. Serve warm over bread pudding.

Nutrition Facts per 2 tablespoons: 180 cal., 11 g total fat (6 g sat. fat), 69 mg chol., 101 mg sodium, 119 g carbo., 0 g fiber, 1 g pro.
Daily Values: 9% vit. A, 1% calcium, 1% iron
Exchanges: 1½ Other Carbo., 2 Fat

Chapter 21
Soups & Stews

On the divider: Turkey Frame Soup (see recipe, page 497)

For more recipes, visit our Recipe Center at **www.bhg.com**

Beef Broth

Depending on the meatiness of the soup bones, they'll yield 3 to 4 cups of meat. Add the cooked meat to soups, stews, or casseroles.

Prep: 30 minutes **Bake:** 30 minutes **Oven:** 450°F
Cook: 3½ hours **Makes:** 8 to 9 cups broth

- 4 **pounds meaty beef soup bones (beef shank cross cuts or short ribs)**
- ½ **cup water**
- 3 **carrots, cut up**
- 2 **medium onions, unpeeled and cut up**
- 2 **stalks celery with leaves, cut up**
- 1 **tablespoon dried basil or thyme, crushed**
- 1½ **teaspoons salt**
- 10 **whole black peppercorns**
- 8 **sprigs fresh parsley**
- 4 **bay leaves**
- 2 **cloves garlic, unpeeled and halved**
- 10 **cups water**

1. Place soup bones in a large shallow roasting pan. Bake in a 450° oven about 30 minutes or until well browned, turning once. Place soup bones in a large kettle. Pour the ½ cup water into the roasting pan and scrape up browned bits; add water mixture to kettle. Stir in carrots, onions, celery, basil, salt, peppercorns, parsley, bay leaves, and garlic. Add the 10 cups water. Bring to boiling; reduce heat. Simmer, covered, for 3½ hours. Remove soup bones.

2. Strain broth (see photo, right). Discard vegetables and seasonings. If desired, clarify broth (see Note, right). If using the broth while hot, skim fat (see tip, page 491). Or chill broth; lift off fat. If desired, when bones are cool enough to handle, remove meat; reserve meat for another use. Discard bones. Place broth and reserved meat in separate containers. Cover and chill for up to 3 days or freeze for up to 6 months.

Nutrition Facts per 1 cup: 20 cal., 1 g total fat (1 g sat. fat),
5 mg chol., 409 mg sodium, 1 g carbo., 0 g fiber, 2 g pro.
Daily Values: 1% calcium, 1% iron
Exchanges: Free

Chicken Broth

Prep: 25 minutes **Cook:** 2½ hours
Makes: about 6 cups broth

- 3 **pounds bony chicken pieces (wings, backs, and/or necks)**
- 3 **stalks celery with leaves, cut up**
- 2 **carrots, cut up**
- 1 **large onion, unpeeled and cut up**
- 1 **teaspoon salt**
- 1 **teaspoon dried thyme, sage, or basil, crushed**
- ½ **teaspoon whole black peppercorns or** ¼ **teaspoon ground black pepper**
- 4 **sprigs fresh parsley**
- 2 **bay leaves**
- 2 **garlic cloves, unpeeled and halved**
- 6 **cups cold water**

1. If using wings, cut each wing at joints into 3 pieces. Place chicken pieces in a 6-quart kettle. Add celery, carrots, onion, salt, thyme, peppercorns, parsley, bay leaves, garlic, and water. Bring to boiling; reduce heat. Simmer, covered, for 2½ hours. Remove chicken pieces from broth.

2. Strain broth (see photo, below). Discard vegetables and seasonings. If desired, clarify broth (see Note, below). If using the broth while hot, skim fat (see tip, page 491). Or chill broth; lift off fat. If desired, when bones are cool enough to handle, remove meat; reserve meat for another use. Discard bones. Place broth and reserved meat in separate containers. Cover and chill for up to 3 days or freeze for up to 6 months.

Note: To clarify hot, strained broth, return the broth to the kettle. Combine ¼ cup cold water and 1 beaten egg white. Stir water mixture into broth. Bring to boiling. Remove from heat; let stand for 5 minutes and strain (see photo, below).

Nutrition Facts per 1 cup: 30 cal., 2 g total fat (1 g sat. fat),
5 mg chol., 435 mg sodium, 1 g carbo., 0 g fiber, 2 g pro.
Daily Values: 1% calcium, 1% iron
Exchanges: ½ Fat

Line a large colander or sieve with 2 layers of 100-percent-cotton cheesecloth. Set colander in a large heatproof bowl; carefully pour broth mixture into the lined colander.

Roasted Mushroom Stock

Prep: 20 minutes **Bake:** 30 minutes **Oven:** 450°F
Cook: 2 hours **Makes:** about 4 cups stock

> 4 **medium onions, quartered and unpeeled**
> 4 **stalks celery with leaves, cut up**
> 2 **carrots, cut up**
> 6 **cloves garlic, halved**
> 1 **teaspoon salt**
> ¼ **teaspoon whole black peppercorns**
> 2 **pounds fresh button or other mushrooms**
> 2 **sprigs fresh thyme**
> 2 **sprigs fresh marjoram**
> 2 **sprigs fresh parsley**

1. Place onions, celery, carrots, and garlic in a shallow roasting pan. Sprinkle with salt and peppercorns. Bake, uncovered, in a 450° oven for 15 minutes. Stir in mushrooms; bake for 15 minutes more. Remove from oven; stir 1 cup *cold water* into vegetable mixture.

2. Transfer vegetable mixture to a 6- to 8-quart Dutch oven. Stir in 6 cups *cold water.* Bring to boiling over high heat; reduce heat. Simmer, uncovered, for 1½ hours. Stir in thyme, marjoram, and parsley. Simmer, uncovered, for 30 minutes more. Strain stock (see photo, page 487). Discard vegetable mixture. Place stock in a storage container; cover. Chill for up to 1 week or freeze for up to 6 months.

Nutrition Facts per 1 cup: 50 cal., 1 g total fat (0 g sat. fat), 0 mg chol., 561 mg sodium, 11 g carbo., 0 g fiber, 3 g pro. **Daily Values:** 42% vit. A, 19% vit. C, 3% calcium, 14% iron **Exchanges:** 2 Vegetable

Vegetable Stock

Prep: 30 minutes **Cook:** 2 hours **Makes:** about 7 cups stock

> 4 **medium yellow onions, unpeeled**
> 4 **medium carrots**
> 3 **medium potatoes**
> 2 **medium parsnips, turnips, or rutabagas**
> 1 **small head cabbage**
> 1 **tablespoon olive oil**
> 8 **cups water**
> 1 **teaspoon salt**
> ½ **teaspoon dried dill, basil, rosemary, or marjoram, crushed**
> ¼ **teaspoon black pepper**

1. Scrub all vegetables; cut off root and stem ends. Do not peel vegetables unless coated with wax. Cut onions into wedges. Cut carrots, potatoes, parsnips, and cabbage into 2-inch pieces.

2. In a 6-quart Dutch oven heat oil over medium heat. Add vegetables. Cook and stir about 10 minutes or until vegetables start to brown. Stir in water, salt, dill, and pepper. Bring to boiling; reduce heat. Simmer, covered, for 2 hours.

3. Strain stock (see photo, page 487). Discard vegetable mixture. Place stock in a storage container; cover. Chill for up to 3 days or freeze for up to 6 months.

Nutrition Facts per 1 cup: 17 cal., 2 g total fat (0 g sat. fat), 0 mg chol., 313 mg sodium, 0 g carbo., 0 g fiber, 0 g pro. **Exchanges:** Free

Old-Fashioned Beef Stew

You can substitute pork stew meat or boneless lamb for the beef in this hearty stew. For pork, simmer only 30 minutes in step 1. If using crockery-cooker directions, prepare as directed for any type of meat.

Prep: 20 minutes **Cook:** 1½ hours
Makes: 5 servings (about 7 cups)

> 2 **tablespoons all-purpose flour**
> 12 **ounces beef stew meat, cut into ¾-inch cubes**
> 2 **tablespoons cooking oil**
> 3 **cups vegetable juice**
> 1 **cup water**
> 1 **medium onion, cut into thin wedges**
> 1 **tablespoon Worcestershire sauce**
> 1½ **teaspoons instant beef bouillon granules**
> 1 **teaspoon dried oregano, crushed**
> ½ **teaspoon dried marjoram, crushed**
> ¼ **teaspoon black pepper**
> 1 **bay leaf**
> 3 **cups cubed potatoes (about 3 medium)**
> 1½ **cups frozen cut green beans**
> 1 **cup frozen whole kernel corn**
> 1 **cup sliced carrots (2 medium)**

1. Place flour in a plastic bag. Add meat cubes, a few at a time, shaking to coat. In a large saucepan or Dutch oven brown meat in hot oil; drain fat. Stir in vegetable juice, water, onion, Worcestershire sauce, bouillon granules, oregano, marjoram, pepper, and bay leaf. Bring to boiling; reduce heat. Simmer, covered, for 1 to 1¼ hours or until meat is nearly tender.

2. Stir in potatoes, green beans, corn, and carrots. Return to boiling; reduce heat. Simmer, covered, about 30 minutes more or until meat and vegetables are tender. Discard bay leaf.

Crockery-cooker directions: Prepare and brown meat as in step 1 on page 488. In a 3½- or 4-quart crockery cooker layer meat, onion, potatoes, green beans, corn, and carrots. Decrease vegetable juice to 2 cups. Combine vegetable juice, water, Worcestershire sauce, bouillon granules, oregano, marjoram, pepper, and bay leaf. Pour over meat and vegetables in crockery cooker. Cover and cook on low-heat setting for 10 to 12 hours or on high-heat setting for 5 to 6 hours or until meat and vegetables are tender.

Nutrition Facts per serving: 331 cal., 13 g total fat (4 g sat. fat), 43 mg chol., 744 mg sodium, 36 g carbo., 6 g fiber, 18 g pro.
Daily Values: 162% vit. A, 97% vit. C, 6% calcium, 21% iron
Exchanges: 1 Vegetable, 2 Starch, 1½ Medium-Fat Meat, ½ Fat

Polenta Beef Stew `Best Loved`

Prep: 25 minutes **Cook:** 2 hours
Makes: 8 servings (7 cups)

- ¼ **cup all-purpose flour**
- 1 **teaspoon garlic powder**
- 1 **teaspoon dried thyme, crushed**
- 1 **teaspoon dried basil, crushed**
- 2 **pounds boneless beef chuck steak, cut into 1-inch pieces**
- 2 **tablespoons olive oil**
- ½ **cup chopped onion (1 medium)**
- 1 **teaspoon snipped fresh rosemary or ¼ teaspoon dried rosemary, crushed**
- 6 **cloves garlic, minced**
- 1 **14-ounce can beef broth**
- 1½ **cups dry red wine**
- 8 **ounces boiling onions**
- 5 **medium carrots, cut into 1-inch chunks**
- 1 **recipe Polenta**
- ½ **cup snipped fresh flat-leaf parsley**
- ¼ **cup tomato paste**
- **Fresh rosemary sprigs (optional)**

1. Place flour, garlic powder, thyme, basil, ½ teaspoon *salt*, and ½ teaspoon *black pepper* in a plastic bag. Add meat pieces, a few at a time, shaking to coat. In a Dutch oven brown meat, half at a time, in hot oil; drain fat. Return all meat to Dutch oven; add chopped onion, dried rosemary (if using), and garlic. Cook and stir until onion is tender. Stir in broth and wine. Bring to boiling; reduce heat. Simmer, covered, for 1½ hours.

2. Stir in boiling onions and carrots. Bring to boiling; reduce heat. Simmer, covered, about 30 minutes more or until meat and vegetables are tender. Meanwhile, prepare Polenta.

3. Just before serving, stir the 1 teaspoon fresh rosemary (if using), parsley, and tomato paste into the stew. Serve stew with Polenta. If desired, garnish with rosemary sprigs.

Polenta: In a large saucepan bring 3 cups milk just to a simmer over medium heat. In a medium bowl combine 1 cup cornmeal, 1 cup water, and 1 teaspoon salt. Stir cornmeal mixture slowly into hot milk. Cook and stir until mixture comes to a boil. Reduce heat to low. Cook for 10 to 15 minutes or until mixture is thick, stirring occasionally. (If mixture is too thick, stir in additional milk.) Stir in 2 tablespoons butter or margarine until melted.

Nutrition Facts per serving: 508 cal., 26 g total fat (10 g sat. fat), 88 mg chol., 736 mg sodium, 32 g carbo., 4 g fiber, 29 g pro.
Daily Values: 205% vit. A, 22% vit. C, 16% calcium, 25% iron
Exchanges: 1 Vegetable, 2 Starch, 3 Lean Meat, 3 Fat

Broth Substitutions

When a recipe calls for chicken or beef broths or vegetable stock, you can make your own using one of the recipes on pages 487 to 488. Or choose a store-bought variety, below.

Canned Broths: Canned chicken and beef broth are ready to use straight from the can (low-sodium versions are available too).

Bouillon: Instant bouillon granules or cubes can be purchased in beef, chicken, or vegetable flavors. One teaspoon of granules, or 1 cube, mixed with 1 cup water makes an easy broth.

Condensed Broths: Cans of condensed chicken or beef broth also can be used, but remember to dilute them according to the label directions.

Polenta Beef Stew

Barley-Beef Soup

If desired, substitute ½ cup regular barley for quick-cooking barley; add it with the water.

Low Fat

Prep: 25 minutes **Cook:** 1¼ hours
Makes: 6 servings (about 8 cups)

- **12** ounces beef or lamb stew meat, cut into 1-inch cubes
- **1** tablespoon cooking oil
- **4** cups water
- **1** cup chopped onion (1 large)
- **½** cup chopped celery (1 stalk)
- **2** teaspoons instant beef bouillon granules
- **1** teaspoon dried oregano or basil, crushed
- **¼** teaspoon black pepper
- **2** cloves garlic, minced
- **1** bay leaf
- **1** cup frozen mixed vegetables
- **1** 14½-ounce can diced tomatoes, undrained
- **1** cup parsnips cut into ½-inch slices, or peeled potatoes cut into ½-inch cubes
- **½** cup quick-cooking barley

1. In a large saucepan brown meat in hot oil. Stir in water, onion, celery, bouillon granules, oregano, pepper, garlic, and bay leaf. Bring to boiling; reduce heat. Simmer, covered, for 1 hour for beef (45 minutes for lamb).

2. Stir in frozen vegetables, undrained tomatoes, parsnips, and barley. Return to boiling; reduce heat. Simmer, covered, about 15 minutes more or until meat and vegetables are tender. Discard bay leaf.

Nutrition Facts per serving: 210 cal., 6 g total fat (1 g sat. fat), 27 mg chol., 515 mg sodium, 23 g carbo., 4 g fiber, 16 g pro.
Daily Values: 24% vit. A, 27% vit. C, 7% calcium, 13% iron
Exchanges: ½ Vegetable, 1½ Starch, 1½ Lean Meat

Beef Bourguignon

Prep: 30 minutes **Cook:** 1¼ hours
Makes: 6 servings (about 6 cups)

- **1** pound boneless beef chuck roast, cut into ¾-inch cubes
- **1** tablespoon cooking oil
- **1½** cups chopped onion
- **2** cloves garlic, minced
- **1½** cups Pinot Noir or Burgundy wine
- **¾** cup beef broth
- **1** teaspoon dried thyme, crushed
- **¾** teaspoon dried marjoram, crushed
- **½** teaspoon salt
- **¼** teaspoon black pepper
- **2** bay leaves
- **3** cups whole fresh mushrooms
- **4** medium carrots, cut into ¾-inch pieces
- **1** cup pearl onions, peeled,* or frozen small whole onions
- **2** tablespoons all-purpose flour
- **2** tablespoons butter or margarine, softened
- **2** slices bacon, crisp-cooked, drained, and crumbled
- **3** cups hot cooked noodles or 1 recipe Mashed Potatoes (see page 525)

1. In a 4-quart Dutch oven brown half of the meat in the hot oil; remove meat from Dutch oven. Add remaining meat, chopped onion, and garlic to Dutch oven. Cook and stir until meat is brown and onion is tender. Return all meat to Dutch oven.

2. Stir in wine, broth, thyme, marjoram, salt, pepper, and bay leaves. Bring to boiling; reduce heat. Simmer, covered, for 45 minutes. Add mushrooms, carrots, and pearl onions. Return to boiling; reduce heat. Cook, covered, for 25 to 30 minutes more or until meat and vegetables are tender. Discard bay leaves.

3. In a small bowl stir together flour and butter until smooth; stir into meat mixture. Cook and stir until thickened and bubbly. Cook and stir for 1 minute more. Stir in crumbled bacon. Serve with hot noodles.

Crockery-cooker directions: Brown meat, chopped onion, and garlic in hot oil as above. In a 3½- or 4-quart crockery cooker layer mushrooms, carrots, and pearl onions. Omit the flour and butter or margarine. Sprinkle vegetables with 3 tablespoons *quick-cooking tapioca*. Place meat mixture on top of vegetables. Add thyme, marjoram, salt, pepper, and bay leaves. Decrease wine to 1¼ cups and beef broth to ½ cup; pour over meat. Cover; cook on low-heat setting for 10 to 12 hours or on high-heat setting for 5 to 6 hours or until meat and vegetables are tender. Discard bay leaves. Stir in bacon.

*Note: To peel pearl onions, place them in boiling water for 30 seconds; drain and rinse with cold water. Cut off the root end and squeeze from the other end.

Nutrition Facts per serving: 395 cal., 14 g total fat (5 g sat. fat), 87 mg chol., 436 mg sodium, 35 g carbo., 4 g fiber, 23 g pro.
Daily Values: 210% vit. A, 12% vit. C, 6% calcium, 25% iron
Exchanges: 2 Vegetable, 1½ Starch, 2 Lean Meat, 2½ Fat

Vegetable-Beef Soup

Low Fat

Prep: 25 minutes **Cook:** 1½ hours
Makes: 8 servings (about 12 cups)

- 1½ pounds boneless beef chuck roast, cubed, or beef stew meat
- 1 tablespoon cooking oil
- 4 cups water
- 3 10½-ounce cans condensed beef broth
- 1 teaspoon dried oregano, crushed
- ½ teaspoon dried marjoram, crushed
- ¼ teaspoon black pepper
- 2 bay leaves
- 2 cups chopped, peeled tomatoes (2 large) or one 14½-ounce can diced tomatoes, undrained
- 1 10-ounce package frozen whole kernel corn
- 1½ cups cubed, peeled potatoes
- 1 cup frozen cut green beans
- 1 cup sliced carrots (2 medium)
- 1 cup sliced celery (2 stalks)
- ½ cup chopped onion (1 medium)

1. In a 6- to 8-quart Dutch oven brown meat, half at a time, in hot oil; drain fat. (Add more oil, if necessary.) Return all meat to Dutch oven. Stir in water, beef broth, oregano, marjoram, pepper, and bay leaves. Bring to boiling; reduce heat. Simmer, covered, for 1 hour. Discard bay leaves. If necessary, skim fat (see tip, right).

2. Stir in tomatoes, corn, potatoes, green beans, carrots, celery, and onion. Return to boiling; reduce heat. Simmer, covered, about 30 minutes more or until vegetables are tender.

Nutrition Facts per serving: 235 cal., 7 g total fat (2 g sat. fat), 40 mg chol., 921 mg sodium, 20 g carbo., 3 g fiber, 24 g pro.
Daily Values: 84% vit. A, 30% vit. C, 4% calcium, 16% iron
Exchanges: 1 Vegetable, 1 Starch, 2½ Lean Meat

Hamburger-Vegetable Soup

Can't find a package of frozen succotash? Use 1 cup each frozen corn and frozen lima beans.

Fast **Low Fat**

Prep: 20 minutes **Cook:** 10 minutes
Makes: 6 servings (about 9½ cups)

- 1 pound lean ground beef or pork
- ½ cup chopped onion (1 medium)
- ½ cup chopped green sweet pepper
- 4 cups beef broth
- 1 14½-ounce can diced tomatoes, undrained
- 1 10-ounce package frozen succotash
- ½ cup chopped, peeled potato or ½ cup frozen loose-pack diced hash brown potatoes
- ½ cup purchased shredded carrot or 1 medium carrot, cut into short thin strips
- 1 teaspoon dried basil, crushed
- 1 teaspoon Worcestershire sauce
- ⅛ teaspoon black pepper

1. In a large saucepan cook ground beef, onion, and sweet pepper until meat is brown and onion is tender; drain fat. Stir in beef broth, undrained tomatoes, succotash, potato, carrot, basil, Worcestershire sauce, and pepper. Bring to boiling; reduce heat. Simmer, covered, for 10 to 15 minutes or until vegetables are tender.

Nutrition Facts per serving: 227 cal., 8 g total fat (3 g sat. fat), 48 mg chol., 613 mg sodium, 19 g carbo., 3 g fiber, 20 g pro.
Daily Values: 55% vit. A, 43% vit. C, 6% calcium, 16% iron
Exchanges: 2 Vegetable, ½ Starch, 2 Medium-Fat Meat

Skimming Fat from Broth

Make your homemade soups as low-fat and low-calorie as possible by skimming off extra fat with these techniques.

■ To remove fat from hot soup or broth, use a large metal spoon and skim off the fat that rises to the top (see top photo).

■ You also can cover and refrigerate the soup or broth for 6 to 8 hours or until the fat solidifies on the surface. Then use a spoon to lift off the hardened fat (see middle photo).

■ A fat-separating pitcher (see bottom photo) also is useful. It has a spout near the bottom. Broth is poured into the pitcher and allowed to stand for a few minutes. Because fat rises to the top, the broth can be poured off and the fat will remain in the pitcher.

■ Another tool to try is a fat-skimming ladle. Slots near the upper edge catch the fat, which stays in the ladle.

Meatball Soup

Accompany this hearty meat and pasta soup with a fresh fruit salad.

Low Fat

Prep: 35 minutes (includes meatballs) **Cook:** 11 minutes
Makes: 5 servings (about 7 cups)

- **1 beaten egg white**
- **½ cup soft bread crumbs**
- **¼ cup finely chopped onion**
- **⅛ teaspoon garlic powder**
- **⅛ teaspoon black pepper**
- **8 ounces lean ground beef**
- **Nonstick cooking spray**
- **2 14-ounce cans (3½ cups) reduced-sodium beef broth**
- **1 14½-ounce can diced tomatoes with Italian herbs, undrained**
- **1 15-ounce can garbanzo beans (chickpeas), rinsed and drained**
- **1 cup sliced fresh mushrooms**
- **½ cup water**
- **½ cup dried small bow tie pasta**
- **3 cups torn fresh spinach or ½ of a 10-ounce package frozen chopped spinach, thawed and well drained**

1. In a medium bowl combine egg white, bread crumbs, onion, garlic powder, and pepper. Add ground beef; mix well. Shape meat mixture into thirty-six ¾-inch meatballs.

2. Lightly coat a large skillet with cooking spray. Cook meatballs over medium heat about 8 minutes or until no pink remains, turning occasionally to brown evenly. Set meatballs aside.

3. Meanwhile, in a large saucepan stir together broth, undrained tomatoes, garbanzo beans, mushrooms, and water. Bring to boiling; add pasta. Return to boiling; reduce heat. Simmer, covered, for 10 to 12 minutes or until pasta is tender. Stir in meatballs and spinach. Cook for 1 to 2 minutes more or just until fresh spinach wilts or frozen spinach is heated through.

Nutrition Facts per serving: 235 cal., 6 g total fat (2 g sat. fat), 34 mg chol., 853 mg sodium, 27 g carbo., 6 g fiber, 18 g pro.
Daily Values: 20% vit. A, 25% vit. C, 9% calcium, 21% iron
Exchanges: 1 Vegetable, 1½ Starch, 1½ Lean Meat

Meatball Soup

Chili

Prep: 20 minutes **Cook:** 20 minutes
Makes: 4 servings (about 5 cups)

- **12 ounces lean ground beef**
- **1 cup chopped onion (1 large)**
- **½ cup chopped green sweet pepper**
- **2 cloves garlic, minced**
- **1 15-ounce can dark red kidney beans, rinsed and drained**
- **1 14½-ounce can diced tomatoes, undrained**
- **1 8-ounce can tomato sauce**
- **2 to 3 teaspoons chili powder**
- **½ teaspoon dried basil, crushed**

1. In a large saucepan cook ground beef, onion, sweet pepper, and garlic until meat is brown and onion is tender; drain fat. Stir in kidney beans, undrained tomatoes, tomato sauce, chili powder, basil, and ¼ teaspoon *black pepper.* Bring to boiling; reduce heat. Simmer, covered, for 20 minutes.

Crockery-cooker directions: In a Dutch oven cook 1½ pounds lean ground beef, 2 cups chopped onions, 1 cup chopped green sweet pepper, and 2 cloves minced garlic, half at a time, as above. Drain fat. In a 3½- or 4-quart crockery cooker combine meat mixture; two 15-ounce cans dark red kidney beans, rinsed and drained; one 15-ounce can tomato sauce; two 14½-ounce cans diced tomatoes, undrained; 4 to 6 teaspoons chili powder; 1 teaspoon dried basil, crushed; and ½ teaspoon black pepper. Cover; cook on low-heat setting for 8 to 10 hours or on high-heat setting for 4 to 5 hours. Makes 8 servings (about 9½ cups).

Nutrition Facts per serving regular or crockery chili:
355 cal., 16 g total fat (6 g sat. fat), 61 mg chol., 751 mg sodium, 33 g carbo., 9 g fiber, 25 g pro.
Daily Values: 23% vit. A, 63% vit. C, 10% calcium, 23% iron
Exchanges: 2 Vegetable, 1½ Starch, 2 High-Fat Meat

Steak Chili: Prepare as on page 492, except substitute 12 ounces boneless beef top round steak for the ground beef. Partially freeze meat; thinly slice meat across the grain into bite-size strips. In a Dutch oven brown meat in 1 tablespoon hot cooking oil. Remove meat, reserving drippings in pan. Cook onion, sweet pepper, and garlic in drippings until tender; drain. Return meat to Dutch oven; add ½ cup *water*. Continue as directed, except simmer, covered, about 40 minutes or until meat is tender. Makes 4 servings (about 5 cups).

Nutrition Facts per serving: 281 cal., 6 g total fat (1g sat. fat), 37 mg chol., 741 mg sodium, 33 g carbo., 7 g fiber, 29 g pro.
Daily Values: 23% vit. A, 63% vit. C, 10% calcium, 24% iron
Exchanges: 2 Vegetable, 1½ Starch, 3 Very Lean Meat, ½ Fat

Pork and Hominy Stew

Fast   **Low Fat**

Start to Finish: 30 minutes **Makes:** 4 servings (about 6 cups)

- 12 ounces boneless pork strips for stir-frying
- 1 cup chopped onion (1 large)
- 2 cloves garlic, minced
- 1 tablespoon cooking oil
- 4 cups chicken broth
- 1 cup thinly sliced carrots (2 medium)
- ¼ teaspoon ground cumin
- ¼ teaspoon crushed red pepper
- 1 14½-ounce can hominy, drained
- 3 tablespoons snipped fresh cilantro
- ¼ cup shredded radishes

1. In a large saucepan cook pork, onion, and garlic in hot oil until pork is no longer pink. Remove pork mixture from saucepan; set aside. Add chicken broth, carrots, cumin, and red pepper to saucepan. Bring to boiling; reduce heat. Simmer, covered, for 7 to 9 minutes or until carrots are crisp-tender. Stir in pork mixture, hominy, and cilantro. Cook and stir until heated through. Top each serving with radishes.

Nutrition Facts per serving: 294 cal., 10 g total fat (3 g sat. fat), 47 mg chol., 1,045 mg sodium, 23 g carbo., 4 g fiber, 26 g pro.
Daily Values: 156% vit. A, 12% vit. C, 6% calcium, 12% iron
Exchanges: ½ Vegetable, 1½ Starch, 3 Lean Meat

Ham and Bean Soup with Vegetables

Next time you cook a whole ham with the bone, save the bone to use in this classic soup.

Low Fat

Prep: 1¾ hours **Cook:** 1¼ hours
Makes: 5 servings (about 8 cups)

- 1 cup dry navy beans
- 1 to 1½ pounds meaty smoked pork hocks or one 1- to 1½-pound meaty ham bone
- 1 tablespoon butter or margarine
- 1½ cups sliced celery (3 stalks)
- 1½ cups chopped onion
- ¾ teaspoon dried thyme, crushed
- ¼ to ½ teaspoon salt
- ¼ teaspoon black pepper
- 1 bay leaf
- 2 cups sliced carrots (4 medium)
- 2 cups sliced parsnips or chopped, peeled rutabaga

1. Rinse beans. In a 4-quart Dutch oven combine beans and 4 cups *water*. Bring to boiling; reduce heat. Simmer for 2 minutes. Remove from heat. Cover and let stand for 1 hour. (Or place beans in water in Dutch oven. Cover and let soak in a cool place for 6 to 8 hours or overnight.) Drain and rinse beans; set aside.

2. In the same Dutch oven brown pork hocks on all sides in hot butter over medium heat. Add the celery and onion. Cook and stir until softened. Stir in beans, thyme, salt, pepper, bay leaf, and 4 cups fresh *water*. Bring to boiling; reduce heat. Simmer, covered, for 1 to 1½ hours or until beans are tender. Remove pork hocks. When cool enough to handle, cut meat off bones; coarsely chop meat. Discard bones and bay leaf. Slightly mash beans in Dutch oven.

3. Stir in carrots and parsnips. Return to boiling; reduce heat. Simmer, covered, about 15 minutes more or until vegetables are tender. Stir in chopped meat; heat through. Season to taste with additional salt and pepper.

Nutrition Facts per serving: 276 cal., 6 g total fat (3 g sat. fat), 18 mg chol., 273 mg sodium, 44 g carbo., 15 g fiber, 14 g pro.
Daily Values: 250% vit. A, 28% vit. C, 13% calcium, 21% iron
Exchanges: 1 Vegetable, 2½ Starch, 1 Lean Meat

Split Pea Soup

Low Fat

Prep: 20 minutes **Cook:** 1⅓ hours
Makes: 4 servings (about 5 cups)

2¾	**cups water**
1½	**cups dry split peas, rinsed and drained**
1	**14-ounce can reduced-sodium chicken broth**
1 to 1½	**pounds meaty smoked pork hocks or one 1- to 1½-pound meaty ham bone**
¼	**teaspoon dried marjoram, crushed**
	Dash black pepper
1	**bay leaf**
½	**cup chopped carrot (1 medium)**
½	**cup chopped celery (1 stalk)**
½	**cup chopped onion (1 medium)**

1. In a large saucepan combine water, split peas, chicken broth, pork hocks, marjoram, pepper, and bay leaf. Bring to boiling; reduce heat. Simmer, covered, for 1 hour, stirring occasionally. Remove pork hocks. When cool enough to handle, cut meat off bones; coarsely chop meat. Discard bones. Return meat to saucepan. Stir in carrot, celery, and onion. Return to boiling; reduce heat. Simmer, covered, for 20 to 30 minutes more or until vegetables are tender. Discard bay leaf.

Crockery-cooker directions: In a 3½- or 4-quart crockery cooker combine split peas, pork hocks, marjoram, pepper, bay leaf, carrot, celery, and onion. Pour water and chicken broth over all. Cover and cook on low-heat setting for 8 to 10 hours or on high-heat setting for 4 to 5 hours. Discard bay leaf. Remove pork hocks; coarsely chop meat. Stir meat into soup.

Nutrition Facts per serving: 303 cal., 3 g total fat (1 g sat. fat), 13 mg chol., 605 mg sodium, 47 g carbo., 19 g fiber, 24 g pro. **Daily Values:** 79% vit. A, 6% vit. C, 5% calcium, 18% iron **Exchanges:** 3 Starch, 2 Very Lean Meat

---

Lamb and Orzo Soup

Low Fat

Prep: 15 minutes **Cook:** 1½ hours
Makes: 6 servings (about 10 cups)

2½	**pounds lamb shanks**
4	**cups water**
4	**cups chicken broth or vegetable broth**
2	**bay leaves**
1	**tablespoon snipped fresh oregano or 1 teaspoon dried oregano, crushed**
1½	**teaspoons snipped fresh marjoram or ½ teaspoon dried marjoram, crushed**
¼	**teaspoon black pepper**
2	**medium carrots, peeled into thin ribbons or cut into short thin strips (1 cup)**
1	**cup sliced celery (2 stalks)**
¾	**cup dried orzo**
3	**cups torn fresh spinach or ½ of a 10-ounce package frozen chopped spinach, thawed and well drained**
	Finely shredded Parmesan cheese (optional)

1. In a large Dutch oven combine lamb shanks, water, broth, bay leaves, oregano, marjoram, and pepper. Bring to boiling; reduce heat. Simmer, covered, for 1¼ to 1½ hours or until meat is tender.

2. Remove shanks from Dutch oven. When cool enough to handle, cut meat off bones; coarsely chop meat. Discard bones. Strain broth (see photo, page 487); discard bay leaves and herbs. Skim fat (see tip, page 491); return broth to Dutch oven.

3. Stir chopped meat, carrots, celery, and orzo into Dutch oven. Return to boiling; reduce heat. Simmer, covered, about 15 minutes or until vegetables and orzo are tender. Stir in spinach. Cook for 1 to 2 minutes more or just until fresh spinach wilts or frozen spinach is heated through. If desired, serve with Parmesan cheese.

Nutrition Facts per serving: 240 cal., 9 g total fat (4 g sat. fat), 54 mg chol., 513 mg sodium, 19 g carbo., 3 g fiber, 20 g pro. **Daily Values:** 120% vit. A, 10% vit. C, 4% calcium, 18% iron **Exchanges:** 1 Vegetable, 1 Starch, 2 Lean Meat, ½ Fat

Lamb and Orzo Soup

Lamb and Vegetable Stew

Low Fat

Prep: 30 minutes **Cook:** 50 minutes
Makes: 4 to 5 servings (about 8 cups)

- 1 **pound lean boneless lamb, cut into ¾-inch cubes**
- 1 **tablespoon cooking oil**
- 1 **14-ounce can beef broth**
- 1 **cup dry red wine or beef broth**
- 1 **tablespoon snipped fresh thyme or 1 teaspoon dried thyme, crushed**
- 2 **cloves garlic, minced**
- 1 **bay leaf**
- 2 **cups cubed, peeled butternut squash**
- 1 **cup parsnips cut into ½-inch slices**
- 1 **cup chopped, peeled sweet potatoes**
- 1 **cup sliced celery (2 stalks)**
- 1 **medium onion, cut into thin wedges**
- ½ **cup plain low-fat yogurt or dairy sour cream**
- 3 **tablespoons all-purpose flour**

1. In a large saucepan brown meat, half at a time, in hot oil; drain fat. Return all meat to pan. Stir in broth, wine, dried thyme (if using), garlic, and bay leaf. Bring to boiling; reduce heat. Simmer, covered, for 20 minutes.

2. Stir in squash, parsnips, sweet potatoes, celery, and onion. Return to boiling; reduce heat. Simmer, covered, about 30 minutes more or until meat and vegetables are tender. Discard bay leaf.

3. In a small bowl combine yogurt, fresh thyme (if using), and flour. Stir ½ cup of the hot liquid into the yogurt mixture. Add yogurt mixture to saucepan. Cook and stir until thickened and bubbly. Cook and stir for 1 minute more. Season to taste with *salt* and *black pepper*.

Nutrition Facts per serving: 365 cal., 9 g total fat (2 g sat. fat), 75 mg chol., 397 mg sodium, 32 g carbo., 4 g fiber, 30 g pro.
Daily Values: 166% vit. A, 35% vit. C, 13% calcium, 22% iron
Exchanges: ½ Vegetable, 2 Starch, 3½ Lean Meat

Lamb Cassoulet Best Loved

Low Fat

Soak: 1 hour **Prep:** ½ hour **Cook:** 1½ hours
Makes: 8 servings (about 8 cups)

- 2 **cups dry navy beans**
- 1 **pound boneless lamb, cut into 1-inch cubes**
- 1 **tablespoon cooking oil**
- 1 **cup chopped carrots (2 medium)**
- ½ **cup chopped green sweet pepper**
- ½ **cup chopped onion (1 medium)**
- 1 **tablespoon instant beef bouillon granules**
- 1 **tablespoon Worcestershire sauce**
- 2 **teaspoons snipped fresh thyme or 1 teaspoon dried thyme, crushed**
- 3 **cloves garlic, minced**
- 2 **bay leaves**
- 8 **ounces skinless, boneless chicken thighs, cut into 1-inch pieces**
- 1 **14½-ounce can diced tomatoes, undrained**

1. Rinse beans. In a large Dutch oven combine beans and 8 cups *water*. Bring to boiling; reduce heat. Simmer for 2 minutes. Remove from heat. Cover and let stand for 1 hour. (Or place beans in water in Dutch oven. Cover and let soak in a cool place for 6 to 8 hours or overnight.) Drain and rinse beans. Return beans to Dutch oven.

2. Meanwhile, in a large skillet brown lamb, half at a time, in hot oil; drain fat. Add lamb, carrots, sweet pepper, onion, bouillon granules, Worcestershire sauce, dried thyme (if using), garlic, and bay leaves to beans in Dutch oven. Add 4 cups fresh *water*. Bring to boiling; reduce heat. Simmer, covered, for 1 to 1½ hours or until beans are tender.

3. Stir in fresh thyme (if using), chicken, undrained tomatoes, and ½ teaspoon *salt*. Return to boiling; reduce heat. Simmer, covered, for 30 minutes more. Discard bay leaves. Skim fat.

Nutrition Facts per serving: 313 cal., 6 g total fat (1 g sat. fat), 60 mg chol., 693 mg sodium, 37 g carbo., 14 g fiber, 29 g pro.
Daily Values: 85% vit. A, 31% vit. C, 10% calcium, 24% iron
Exchanges: 1 Vegetable, 2 Starch, 3 Very Lean Meat, ½ Fat

Sodium Sense

Even sodium sleuths may need a refresher on the meaning of certain terms used on food labels. Here are the legal definitions for lower-sodium foods.

Sodium-free: 5 mg or less of sodium per serving.

Very-low sodium: 35 mg or less of sodium per serving.

Low-sodium: 140 mg or less of sodium per serving.

Reduced-sodium: The product contains at least 25 percent less sodium than the original version of the product. Some reduced-sodium foods, such as broth, canned soups, and soy sauce, may still contain a lot of sodium. Check the nutrition information.

No added salt or unsalted: No salt is added during processing, but this does not guarantee the product is sodium-free.

Italian Sausage-Navy Bean Stew

Prep: 1½ hours **Cook:** 1¾ hours
Makes: 8 servings (about 10½ cups)

- 2⅓ **cups dry navy beans**
- 1 **pound uncooked Italian sausage links, cut into ½-inch slices**
- 1 **cup chopped onion (1 large)**
- 1 **clove garlic, minced**
- 3½ **cups beef broth**
- 1 **teaspoon dried oregano, crushed**
- 2 **bay leaves**
- 3 **cups chopped cabbage**
- 1 **14½-ounce can diced tomatoes, undrained**

1. Rinse beans. In a 4-quart Dutch oven combine beans and 6 cups *water*. Bring to boiling; reduce heat. Simmer for 2 minutes. Remove from heat. Cover and let stand for 1 hour. (Or place beans in water in Dutch oven. Cover and let soak in a cool place for 6 to 8 hours or overnight.) Drain and rinse beans; set aside.

2. In the same Dutch oven cook sausage, onion, and garlic over medium-high heat until meat is brown and onion is tender; drain fat. Stir in beans, beef broth, oregano, bay leaves, and ¾ cup *water*. Bring to boiling; reduce heat. Simmer, covered, for 1 to 1½ hours or until beans are tender, stirring occasionally. Stir in cabbage and undrained tomatoes. Return to boiling; reduce heat. Simmer, covered, about 15 minutes more or until cabbage is tender. Discard bay leaves. Skim off fat (see tip, page 491). Season to taste with *salt* and *black pepper*.

Nutrition Facts per serving: 391 cal., 14 g total fat (6 g sat. fat), 38 mg chol., 840 mg sodium, 41 g carbo., 15 g fiber, 22 g pro. Daily Values: 1% vit. A, 27% vit. C, 12% calcium, 22% iron Exchanges: 1 Vegetable, 2½ Starch, 2 Medium-Fat Meat, ½ Fat

Lentil and Sausage Soup

Low Fat

Prep: 20 minutes **Cook:** 25 minutes
Makes: 5 servings (about 7 cups)

- 2 **14-ounce cans reduced-sodium chicken broth**
- 1½ **cups water**
- 1 **cup brown lentils, rinsed and drained**
- 1 **cup sliced celery (2 stalks)**
- 1 **cup sliced carrots (2 medium)**
- ½ **cup chopped onion (1 medium)**
- 1 **teaspoon snipped fresh thyme or ½ teaspoon dried thyme, crushed**
- ⅛ **teaspoon ground red pepper**
- 2 **cloves garlic, minced**
- 6 **ounces cooked, smoked sausage links, quartered lengthwise and sliced**

1. In a large saucepan combine chicken broth, water, lentils, celery, carrots, onion, dried thyme (if using), red pepper, and garlic. Bring to boiling; reduce heat. Simmer, covered, for 20 to 25 minutes or until vegetables and lentils are tender. Stir in fresh thyme, if using, and sausage. Heat through.

Nutrition Facts per serving: 294 cal., 11 g total fat (4 g sat. fat), 23 mg chol., 962 mg sodium, 28 g carbo., 13 g fiber, 21 g pro. Daily Values: 124% vit. A, 11% vit. C, 5% calcium, 20% iron Exchanges: 1 Vegetable, 1½ Starch, 2 Medium-Fat Meat

Black Bean Soup with Sausage

Low Fat

Prep: 1½ hours **Cook:** 1¼ hours
Makes: 6 servings (about 7½ cups)

- 1 **cup dry black beans**
- 2 **cups chicken broth**
- 1 **cup chopped onion (1 large)**
- 1 **cup chopped celery (2 stalks)**
- 1 **teaspoon ground coriander**
- ¼ **teaspoon salt**
- ⅛ to ¼ **teaspoon ground red pepper**
- 4 **cloves garlic, minced**
- 8 **ounces cooked, smoked turkey sausage or Polish sausage, chopped**
   Dairy sour cream or shredded Monterey Jack cheese (optional)
   Snipped fresh cilantro (optional)

1. Rinse beans. In a large saucepan or Dutch oven combine beans and 6 cups *water*. Bring to boiling; reduce heat. Simmer for 2 minutes. Remove from heat. Cover; let stand for 1 hour. (Or place beans and water in pan. Cover; let soak in a cool place for 6 to 8 hours or overnight.) Drain and rinse beans.

2. Return beans to saucepan. Stir in 2 cups *water*, the broth, onion, celery, coriander, salt, red pepper, and garlic. Bring to boiling; reduce heat. Simmer, covered, for 1 to 1½ hours or until beans are tender.

3. If desired, mash beans slightly. Stir in sausage; heat through. If desired, serve topped with sour cream and cilantro.

Crockery-cooker directions: Prepare as above through step 1. In a 3½- or 4-quart crockery cooker combine chicken broth, 2 cups water, onion, celery, coriander, salt, red pepper, and garlic. Stir in beans. Cover and cook on high-heat setting for 5 to 6 hours. If desired, mash beans slightly. Stir in sausage. Cover and cook for 30 minutes more.

Nutrition Facts per serving: 198 cal., 6 g total fat (2 g sat. fat), 29 mg chol., 682 mg sodium, 24 g carbo., 6 g fiber, 14 g pro.
Daily Values: 1% vit. A, 5% vit. C, 8% calcium, 13% iron
Exchanges: ½ Vegetable, 1½ Starch, 1 Lean Meat

Shortcut Black Bean Soup with Sausage: Prepare as on page 496, except omit dry black beans and the 6 cups soaking water. Decrease chicken broth to 1½ cups. Rinse and drain two 15-ounce cans black beans. In a large saucepan combine beans, broth, 2 cups water, onion, celery, coriander, salt, red pepper, and garlic. Bring to boiling; reduce heat. Simmer, covered, about 15 minutes or until vegetables are tender. Stir in sausage; heat through. Makes 4 servings (about 6½ cups).

Nutrition Facts per serving: 268 cal., 8 g total fat (2 g sat. fat), 1,421 mg sodium, 35 carbo., 11 g fiber, 25 g pro.
Daily Values: 1% vit. A, 8% vit. C, 13% calcium, 19% iron
Exchanges: 1 Vegetable, 2 Starch, 2 Lean Meat

Turkey Frame Soup

This soup takes advantage of any leftover meat and the bones from a turkey dinner (see photo, page 485).

Low Fat

Prep: 30 minutes **Cook:** 1¾ hours
Makes: 6 servings (about 11 cups)

- 1 meaty turkey frame
- 2 large onions, quartered
- 2 stalks celery, sliced
- 1 tablespoon instant chicken bouillon granules
- 3 cloves garlic, minced
  Chopped cooked turkey
- 1 14½-ounce can diced tomatoes, undrained
- 1½ teaspoons dried oregano, basil, marjoram, or thyme, crushed
- 3 cups (any combination) sliced celery, carrots, parsnips, or mushrooms; chopped onion or rutabagas; or broccoli or cauliflower florets
- 1½ cups dried medium noodles

1. Break turkey frame or cut in half with kitchen shears. Place in an 8- to 10-quart kettle or Dutch oven. Add 8 cups *water,* onions, celery, bouillon granules, and garlic. Bring to boiling; reduce heat. Simmer, covered, for 1½ hours.

2. Remove turkey frame. When cool enough to handle, remove meat from bones. Discard bones. Coarsely chop meat. If necessary, add enough turkey to equal 2 cups; set turkey aside.

3. Strain broth, discarding solids (see photo, page 487). Skim fat from broth (see tip, page 491). Return broth to kettle. Stir in undrained tomatoes, oregano, and ¼ teaspoon *black pepper.* Stir in vegetables. Return to boiling; reduce heat. Simmer, covered, for 10 minutes. Stir in noodles. Simmer for 8 to 10 minutes more or until noodles are tender but still firm and vegetables are tender. Stir in turkey; heat through.

Nutrition Facts per serving: 182 cal., 4 g total fat (1 g sat. fat), 52 mg chol., 608 mg sodium, 17 g carbo., 2 g fiber, 20 g pro.
Daily Values: 54% vit. A, 30% vit. C, 8% calcium, 13% iron
Exchanges: 1 Vegetable, 1 Starch, 2 Very Lean Meat

Old-Fashioned Chicken Noodle Soup   Best Loved

Stewing chickens are from 10 to 18 months old and weigh about 3 to 6 pounds. They have more flavor than younger birds but are less tender. Moist heat cooking, such as stewing, makes them tender.

Low Fat

Prep: 20 minutes **Cook:** 2¼ hours
Makes: 8 servings (about 9¼ cups)

- 1 4- to 5-pound stewing chicken, cut up
- 6 cups water
- ½ cup chopped onion (1 medium)
- 2 teaspoons salt
- ¼ teaspoon black pepper
- 1 bay leaf
- 1½ cups dried medium noodles
- 1 cup chopped carrots (2 medium)
- 1 cup chopped celery (2 stalks)
- 2 tablespoons snipped fresh parsley

1. In a large Dutch oven or kettle combine chicken, water, onion, salt, pepper, and bay leaf. Bring to boiling; reduce heat. Simmer, covered, about 2 hours or until chicken is tender.

2. Remove chicken from broth. When cool enough to handle, remove meat from bones. Discard bones. Cut meat into bite-size pieces; set aside. Discard bay leaf. Skim fat from broth (see tip, page 491).

3. Bring broth to boiling. Stir in the noodles, carrots, and celery. Simmer, covered, about 8 minutes or until noodles are tender but still firm. Stir in chicken and parsley; heat through.

Nutrition Facts per serving: 210 cal., 6 g total fat (2 g sat. fat), 84 mg chol., 665 mg sodium, 10 g carbo., 1 g fiber, 26 g pro.
Daily Values: 79% vit. A, 6% vit. C, 3% calcium, 9% iron
Exchanges: ½ Vegetable, ½ Starch, 3½ Very Lean Meat, 1 Fat

Chicken Stew with Cornmeal Dumplings

Best Loved

Start to Finish: 40 minutes
Makes: 4 servings (about 6 cups)

Soups & Stews

498

- 1 14-ounce can chicken broth
- 1 10-ounce package frozen mixed vegetables
- 1 cup frozen small whole onions
- ½ cup water
- 2 teaspoons snipped fresh basil, oregano, or dill, or ½ teaspoon dried basil, oregano, or dill, crushed
- ½ teaspoon salt
- ⅛ teaspoon garlic powder
- ⅛ teaspoon black pepper
- 1 cup milk
- ⅓ cup all-purpose flour
- 2 cups cubed cooked chicken or turkey (see tip, page 437) or two 5-ounce cans chunk-style chicken or turkey
- 1 recipe Cornmeal Dumplings

1. In a large saucepan combine broth, frozen vegetables, onions, water, dried herb (if using), salt, garlic powder, and pepper. Bring to boiling.

2. Meanwhile, in a small bowl combine milk and flour; stir into vegetable mixture. Stir in chicken. Cook and stir until thickened and bubbly. Stir in fresh herb, if using.

3. Drop dumpling dough from a tablespoon into 4 to 8 mounds on top of the bubbling stew. Simmer, covered (do not lift cover), over low heat for 10 to 12 minutes or until a wooden toothpick inserted in a dumpling comes out clean.

Cornmeal Dumplings: In a medium bowl stir together ½ cup all-purpose flour, ½ cup shredded cheddar cheese, ⅓ cup yellow cornmeal, 1 teaspoon baking powder, and dash black pepper. In a small bowl combine 1 beaten egg, 2 tablespoons milk, and 2 tablespoons cooking oil; add to flour mixture, stirring with a fork just until combined.

Nutrition Facts per serving: 510 cal., 21 g total fat (7 g sat. fat), 135 mg chol., 1,045 mg sodium, 46 g carbo., 5 g fiber, 35 g pro.
Daily Values: 81% vit. A, 17% vit. C, 33% calcium, 20% iron
Exchanges: 1½ Vegetable, 2½ Starch, 3½ Lean Meat, 1½ Fat

Chipotle Pepper and Chicken Soup

Low Fat

Start to Finish: 35 minutes
Makes: 3 servings (about 4 cups)

- 1 cup chopped onion (1 large)
- 4 cloves garlic, minced
- 1 tablespoon olive oil or cooking oil
- 12 ounces skinless, boneless chicken breast halves, cut into bite-size pieces
- 1 14-ounce can chicken broth
- 2 teaspoons chopped canned chipotle peppers in adobo sauce
- ½ teaspoon sugar
- 2 cups chopped tomatoes (2 large) or one 14½-ounce can low-sodium diced tomatoes, undrained
- ¼ cup snipped fresh cilantro

1. In a Dutch oven cook onion and garlic in hot oil over medium-high heat about 4 minutes or until tender. Add chicken; cook and stir for 2 minutes more. Stir in broth, chipotle peppers, sugar, and ¼ teaspoon *salt*. Bring to boiling; reduce heat. Simmer, uncovered, for 15 minutes. Remove from heat; stir in tomatoes and cilantro.

Nutrition Facts per serving: 249 cal., 8 g total fat (1 g sat. fat), 66 mg chol., 729 mg sodium, 14 g carbo., 3 g fiber, 31 g pro.
Daily Values: 23% vit. A, 51% vit. C, 5% calcium, 11% iron
Exchanges: 2½ Vegetable, 4 Very Lean Meat, 1 Fat

Jambalaya   Best Loved

Prep: 25 minutes   **Cook:** 20 minutes
Makes: 6 servings (about 7 cups)

- 1 pound fresh or frozen peeled and deveined shrimp
- ½ cup chopped onion (1 medium)
- ⅓ cup chopped celery
- ¼ cup chopped green sweet pepper
- 2 cloves garlic, minced
- 2 tablespoons cooking oil
- 2 cups chicken broth
- 1 14½-ounce can diced tomatoes, undrained
- 8 ounces andouille or kielbasa sausage, halved lengthwise and cut into ½-inch slices
- ¾ cup uncooked long grain rice
- 1 teaspoon dried thyme, crushed
- ½ teaspoon dried basil, crushed
- ¼ teaspoon ground red pepper
- 1 bay leaf
- 1 cup cubed cooked ham

Spiced Pumpkin and Shrimp Soup

1. Thaw shrimp, if frozen; set aside. In a 12-inch skillet cook onion, celery, sweet pepper, and garlic in hot oil until tender. Stir in chicken broth, undrained tomatoes, sausage, rice, thyme, basil, ¼ teaspoon *black pepper,* red pepper, and bay leaf. Bring to boiling; reduce heat. Simmer, covered, for 15 minutes.

2. Stir in shrimp. Return to boiling. Simmer, covered, about 5 minutes more or until shrimp turn opaque and rice is tender. Stir in ham; heat through. Discard bay leaf.

Nutrition Facts per serving: 416 cal., 20 g total fat (6 g sat. fat), 154 mg chol., 1,199 mg sodium, 27 g carbo., 1 g fiber, 30 g pro.
Daily Values: 5% vit. A, 29% vit. C, 9% calcium, 22% iron
Exchanges: 1 Vegetable, 1½ Starch, 3½ Medium-Fat Meat

Spiced Pumpkin and Shrimp Soup

`Fast` `Low Fat`

Start to Finish: 30 minutes
Makes: 4 servings (about 5¾ cups)

   2 **medium onions, sliced**
   2 **medium carrots, sliced (1 cup)**
   1 **tablespoon snipped fresh cilantro**
   2 **teaspoons grated fresh ginger**
   ½ **teaspoon ground allspice**
   2 **cloves garlic, minced**

   2 **tablespoons butter or margarine**
   1 **14-ounce can chicken broth**
   1 **15-ounce can pumpkin**
   1 **cup milk**
   1 **8-ounce package frozen peeled and deveined cooked shrimp, thawed**
     Plain yogurt or dairy sour cream (optional)
     Snipped fresh chives (optional)

1. In a large saucepan cook onions, carrots, cilantro, ginger, allspice, and garlic in hot butter, covered, for 10 to 12 minutes or until vegetables are tender, stirring once or twice.

2. Transfer vegetable mixture to a blender container or food processor bowl. Add ½ cup of the chicken broth. Cover and blend or process until nearly smooth.

3. In the same saucepan combine the remaining 1¼ cups broth, the pumpkin, and milk. Stir in blended vegetable mixture and shrimp; heat through. If desired, serve topped with plain yogurt and chives.

Nutrition Facts per serving: 247 cal., 10 g total fat (5 g sat. fat), 134 mg chol., 537 mg sodium, 20 g carbo., 5 g fiber, 21 g pro.
Daily Values: 634% vit. A, 20% vit. C, 17% calcium, 21% iron
Exchanges: 1 Vegetable, 1 Starch, 2 Very Lean Meat, 1½ Fat

Hot-and-Sour Soup with Shrimp

Low Fat

Start to Finish: 35 minutes
Makes: 4 servings (about 6 cups)

> 8 ounces fresh or frozen peeled and deveined shrimp
> 3½ cups chicken broth
> ½ of a 15-ounce jar whole straw mushrooms, drained, or one 6-ounce jar sliced mushrooms, drained
> ¼ cup rice vinegar or white vinegar
> 2 tablespoons soy sauce
> 1 teaspoon sugar
> 1 teaspoon grated fresh ginger
> ½ teaspoon black pepper
> 4 ounces firm, silken-style tofu (fresh bean curd), drained and cut into bite-size pieces
> 1 tablespoon cornstarch
> 1 tablespoon cold water
> ½ cup frozen peas
> ½ cup shredded carrot
> 2 tablespoons thinly sliced green onion (1)
> 1 beaten egg

1. Thaw shrimp, if frozen; set aside. In a large saucepan combine chicken broth, mushrooms, vinegar, soy sauce, sugar, ginger, and pepper. Bring to boiling; reduce heat. Simmer, covered, for 2 minutes. Stir in shrimp and tofu. Return to boiling; reduce heat. Simmer, covered, for 1 minute more.

2. Stir together cornstarch and cold water; stir into chicken broth mixture. Cook and stir until slightly thickened and bubbly. Cook and stir for 2 minutes more. Stir in peas, carrot, and green onion. Pour egg into the soup in a steady stream, stirring a few times to create shreds.

Nutrition Facts per serving: 195 cal., 6 g total fat (1 g sat. fat), 139 mg chol., 1,703 mg sodium, 11 g carbo., 3 g fiber, 22 g pro.
Daily Values: 76% vit. A, 10% vit. C, 9% calcium, 17% iron
Exchanges: ½ Vegetable, ½ Starch, 3 Very Lean Meat, 1 Fat

Quick Cioppino

This version of the classic Italian fish stew is easy to make.

Fast **Low Fat**

Start to Finish: 20 minutes
Makes: 4 servings (about 5½ cups)

> 6 ounces fresh or frozen cod fillets
> 6 ounces fresh or frozen peeled and deveined shrimp
> 1 medium green sweet pepper, cut into thin bite-size strips
> 1 cup chopped onion (1 large)
> 2 cloves garlic, minced
> 1 tablespoon olive oil or cooking oil
> 2 14½-ounce cans Italian-style stewed tomatoes, undrained
> ½ cup water
> 3 tablespoons snipped fresh basil

1. Thaw cod and shrimp, if frozen. Cut cod into 1-inch pieces; set aside. In a large saucepan cook sweet pepper, onion, and garlic in hot oil until tender. Stir in undrained tomatoes and water. Bring to boiling. Stir in cod and shrimp. Return to boiling; reduce heat. Simmer, covered, for 2 to 3 minutes or until cod flakes easily when tested with a fork and shrimp turn opaque. Stir in basil.

Nutrition Facts per serving: 222 cal., 6 g total fat (1 g sat. fat), 85 mg chol., 538 mg sodium, 19 g carbo., 3 g fiber, 19 g pro.
Daily Values: 7% vit. A, 45% vit. C, 10% calcium, 13% iron
Exchanges: 4 Vegetable, 2 Very Lean Meat, 1 Fat

Oyster Stew

Fast

Start to Finish: 20 minutes
Makes: 4 servings (about 5 cups)

> ¼ cup finely chopped shallot or onion
> 1 tablespoon butter or margarine
> 1 pint shucked oysters, undrained
> ½ teaspoon salt
> 2 cups half-and-half or light cream
> 1 cup milk
> 1 tablespoon snipped fresh parsley
> ¼ teaspoon white pepper
> Butter or margarine (optional)

1. In a large saucepan cook shallot in hot butter until tender. Stir in undrained oysters and salt. Bring to boiling; reduce heat to medium. Cook for 3 to 5 minutes or until oysters curl around the edges, stirring occasionally.

2. Stir in half-and-half, milk, parsley, and pepper; heat through. If desired, top each serving with additional butter.

Nutrition Facts per serving: 273 cal., 20 g total fat (12 g sat. fat), 100 mg chol., 573 mg sodium, 12 g carbo., 0 g fiber, 11 g pro.
Daily Values: 18% vit. A, 10% vit. C, 24% calcium, 28% iron
Exchanges: 1 Lean Meat, 3 Fat

Roasted Corn and Crab Soup

You can also serve this soup as an appetizer for 12.

Low Fat

Start to Finish: 1 hour Oven: 450°F
Makes: 6 servings (about 8½ cups)

1	16-ounce package frozen whole kernel corn
2	cups chopped onions (2 large)
1½	cups coarsely chopped red sweet peppers
1	tablespoon cooking oil
4	14-ounce cans chicken broth
½	teaspoon dried thyme, crushed
⅛ to ¼	teaspoon ground red pepper
⅓	cup all-purpose flour
½	cup half-and-half or light cream
4	ounces cooked crabmeat, cut into bite-size pieces (⅔ cup)

1. Thaw frozen corn and pat dry with paper towels. Line a 15×10×1-inch baking pan with foil; lightly grease the foil. Spread corn in prepared pan. Bake in a 450° oven for 10 minutes; stir. Bake about 10 minutes more until golden brown, stirring once or twice. Remove from oven; set aside.

2. In a 4-quart Dutch oven cook onions and sweet peppers in hot oil over medium heat for 3 to 4 minutes or until nearly tender. Add roasted corn, 3 cans of the broth, thyme, and red pepper. Bring to boiling; reduce heat. Simmer, uncovered, for 15 minutes.

3. In a large screw-top jar combine remaining 1 can broth and the flour. Cover and shake well; stir into soup. Cook and stir until slightly thickened and bubbly. Cook and stir 1 minute more. Stir in half-and-half; heat through. To serve, ladle soup into bowls; divide crabmeat among bowls.

Make-ahead directions: Prepare as above, except do not add crabmeat. Cool soup; cover and chill for up to 2 days. To serve, reheat soup. Ladle into bowls and divide crabmeat among servings.

Nutrition Facts per serving: 229 cal., 7 g total fat (2 g sat. fat), 26 mg chol., 907 mg sodium, 30 g carbo., 4 g fiber, 14 g pro.
Daily Values: 43% vit. A, 113% vit. C, 7% calcium, 9% iron
Exchanges: 1 Vegetable, 1½ Starch, 1 Very Lean Meat, 1 Fat

New England Clam Chowder

To retain more nutrients and fiber, don't peel the potatoes. Wash and scrub them well with a vegetable brush before chopping.

Start to Finish: 45 minutes Makes: 4 servings (about 6 cups)

1	pint shucked clams or two 6½-ounce cans minced clams
2	slices bacon, halved
2½	cups chopped, peeled potatoes (3 medium)
1	cup chopped onion (1 large)
1	teaspoon instant chicken bouillon granules
1	teaspoon Worcestershire sauce
¼	teaspoon dried thyme, crushed
⅛	teaspoon black pepper
2	cups milk
1	cup half-and-half or light cream
2	tablespoons all-purpose flour

1. Chop fresh clams, if using, reserving juice; set clams aside. Strain clam juice to remove bits of shell. (Or drain canned clams, reserving juice.) If necessary, add enough water to reserved clam juice to equal 1 cup. Set juice aside.

2. In a large saucepan cook bacon until crisp. Remove bacon, reserving 1 tablespoon drippings in pan. Drain bacon on paper towels; crumble bacon and set aside.

3. Stir the reserved 1 cup clam juice, potatoes, onion, bouillon granules, Worcestershire sauce, thyme, and pepper into saucepan. Bring to boiling; reduce heat. Simmer, covered, about 15 minutes or until potatoes are tender. With the back of a fork, mash potatoes slightly against the side of the pan.

4. Stir together milk, half-and-half, and flour; add to potato mixture. Cook and stir until slightly thickened and bubbly. Stir in clams. Return to boiling; reduce heat. Cook for 1 to 2 minutes more or until heated through. Sprinkle each serving with crumbled bacon.

Nutrition Facts per serving: 376 cal., 15 g total fat (8 g sat. fat), 76 mg chol., 495 mg sodium, 35 g carbo., 2 g fiber, 24 g pro.
Daily Values: 17% vit. A, 49% vit. C, 28% calcium, 86% iron
Exchanges: 2½ Starch, 2½ Very Lean Meat, 2 Fat

Manhattan Clam Chowder

Low Fat

Start to Finish: 40 minutes
Makes: 4 servings (about 6½ cups)

- 1 pint shucked clams or two 6½-ounce cans minced clams
- 1 cup chopped celery (2 stalks)
- ¼ cup chopped carrot (1 small)
- ⅓ cup chopped onion (1 small)
- 2 tablespoons olive oil or cooking oil
- 1 8-ounce bottle clam juice or 1 cup chicken broth
- 2 cups cubed, unpeeled red potatoes
- 1 teaspoon dried thyme, crushed
- ⅛ teaspoon ground red pepper
- ⅛ teaspoon black pepper
- 1 14½-ounce can diced tomatoes, undrained
- 2 tablespoons purchased cooked bacon pieces or cooked crumbled bacon*

1. Chop fresh clams, if using, reserving juice; set clams aside. Strain clam juice to remove bits of shell. (Or drain canned clams, reserving juice.) If necessary, add enough water to reserved clam juice to equal 1½ cups. Set juice aside.

2. In a large saucepan cook celery, carrot, and onion in hot oil until tender. Stir in the reserved 1½ cups clam juice and the 8 ounces clam juice. Stir in potatoes, thyme, red pepper, and black pepper. Bring to boiling; reduce heat. Simmer, covered, for 10 minutes. Stir in the clams, undrained tomatoes, and bacon. Return to boiling; reduce heat. Cook for 1 to 2 minutes more or until heated through.

*Note: If using bacon, cook 2 slices, reserving 2 tablespoons drippings. Omit oil and cook the celery, carrot, and onion in the reserved drippings.

Nutrition Facts per serving: 254 cal., 9 g total fat (1 g sat. fat), 41 mg chol., 507 mg sodium, 24 g carbo., 3 g fiber, 19 g pro.
Daily Values: 47% vit. A, 61% vit. C, 12% calcium, 90% iron
Exchanges: 2 Vegetable, 1 Starch, 2 Very Lean Meat, 1½ Fat

Manhattan Clam Chowder

Salmon Chowder

Low Fat

Start to Finish: 35 minutes **Makes:** 6 servings (7 cups)

- 8 ounces fresh or frozen skinless salmon fillets, cut into ¾-inch cubes
- ½ cup thinly sliced celery (1 stalk)
- ½ cup chopped onion (1 medium)
- 1 tablespoon olive oil
- 4 cups milk
- 1 10¾-ounce can condensed cream of celery soup
- 1 tablespoon snipped fresh dill or 1 teaspoon dried dill, crushed
- ¼ teaspoon caraway seeds
- ¼ teaspoon black pepper
- 1⅓ cups cubed, peeled potato (1 large)

1. Thaw salmon, if frozen; set aside. In a large saucepan cook celery and onion in hot oil over medium-high heat about 4 minutes or until tender. Stir in milk, soup, dill, caraway seeds, pepper, and ⅛ teaspoon *salt*. Stir in potato. Bring to boiling; reduce heat. Simmer, covered, for 10 to 15 minutes or until potato is tender. Stir in salmon. Simmer, uncovered, for 2 to 3 minutes more or until salmon flakes easily with a fork.

Nutrition Facts per serving: 215 cal., 9 g total fat (3 g sat. fat), 37 mg chol., 547 mg sodium, 19 g carbo., 1 g fiber, 15 g pro.
Daily Values: 10% vit. A, 13% vit. C, 23% calcium, 6% iron
Exchanges: ½ Milk, 1 Starch, 1 Lean Meat, 1 Fat

Wild Rice-Mushroom Soup

To rinse wild rice, place it in a pan of warm water, stir, and remove particles that float to the top. Drain and rinse again; drain before using.

Prep: 15 minutes **Cook:** 50 minutes
Makes: 4 side-dish servings (about 3½ cups)

- **3 cups chicken broth**
- **⅓ cup uncooked wild rice, rinsed and drained**
- **½ cup thinly sliced green onions (4)**
- **1 cup half-and-half or light cream**
- **2 tablespoons all-purpose flour**
- **1 teaspoon snipped fresh thyme or ¼ teaspoon dried thyme, crushed**
- **⅛ teaspoon black pepper**
- **1½ cups sliced fresh mushrooms**
- **1 tablespoon dry sherry**

1. In a medium saucepan combine broth and wild rice. Bring to boiling; reduce heat. Simmer, covered, for 40 minutes. Stir in green onions; cook for 5 to 10 minutes more or until rice is tender.

2. In a small bowl combine half-and-half, flour, thyme, and pepper; stir into rice mixture along with mushrooms. Cook and stir until thickened and bubbly. Cook and stir for 1 minute more. Stir in sherry; heat through.

Nutrition Facts per serving: 182 cal., 9 g total fat (5 g sat. fat), 22 mg chol., 779 mg sodium, 19 g carbo., 2 g fiber, 7 g pro.
Daily Values: 6% vit. A, 5% vit. C, 8% calcium, 5% iron
Exchanges: ½ Vegetable, 1 Starch, 2 Fat

Cream of Vegetable Soup

`Fast`

Start to Finish: 25 minutes
Makes: 4 side-dish servings (about 4½ cups)

- **Desired vegetable (see variations)**
- **1½ cups chicken broth or vegetable stock**
- **1 tablespoon butter or margarine**
- **1 tablespoon all-purpose flour**
- **Seasoning (see variations)**
- **¼ teaspoon salt**
- **Dash black pepper**
- **1 cup milk, half-and-half, or light cream**

1. In a large saucepan cook desired vegetable, covered, in a large amount of boiling water according to directions in each variation. Drain well. Reserve 1 cup cooked vegetables.

2. In a food processor bowl combine remaining cooked vegetables and ¾ cup of the broth. Cover; process about 1 minute or until smooth. Set aside.

3. In the same saucepan melt butter. Stir in flour, seasoning, salt, and pepper. Add milk all at once. Cook and stir until slightly thickened and bubbly. Cook and stir for 1 minute more.

4. Stir in the reserved 1 cup cooked vegetables, blended vegetable mixture, and remaining ¾ cup broth. Cook and stir until heated through. If necessary, stir in additional milk to reach desired consistency. If desired, season to taste with additional salt and pepper.

Cream of Potato Soup: Cook 5 medium potatoes, peeled and cubed, and ½ cup chopped onion as directed in step 1 about 15 minutes or until tender; drain. Reserve 1 cup of the potato-onion mixture. Blend remaining mixture as directed in step 2, except use all of the broth. For the seasoning in step 3, use ¼ teaspoon dried dill or basil, crushed.

Nutrition Facts per serving: 236 cal., 5 g total fat (3 g sat. fat), 13 mg chol., 509 mg sodium, 40 g carbo., 3 g fiber, 8 g pro.
Daily Values: 5% vit. A, 47% vit. C, 10% calcium, 10% iron
Exchanges: 2½ Starch, ½ Fat

Cream of Cauliflower Soup: Cook 4 cups fresh or loose-pack frozen cauliflower florets as directed in step 1 for 8 to 10 minutes or until tender; drain. Reserve 1 cup cauliflower florets. Blend remaining cauliflower florets as directed in step 2. For the seasoning in step 3, use ½ teaspoon celery seeds. Stir in ½ cup shredded American cheese along with the blended vegetable mixture in step 4. If desired, top each serving with additional shredded American cheese.

Cream of Broccoli Soup: Cook 4 cups fresh or loose-pack frozen chopped broccoli as directed in step 1 for 8 to 10 minutes or until tender; drain. Reserve 1 cup of broccoli. Blend remaining broccoli as directed in step 2. For the seasoning in step 3, use ¼ teaspoon lemon-pepper seasoning. Stir in ½ cup shredded American cheese with the blended vegetable mixture in step 4. If desired, top each serving with additional shredded American cheese.

Nutrition Facts per serving for cauliflower or broccoli variation: 158 cal., 9 g total fat (6 g sat. fat), 26 mg chol., 729 mg sodium, 10 g carbo., 3 g fiber, 9 g pro.
Daily Values: 9% vit. A, 63% vit. C, 19% calcium, 5% iron
Exchanges: 2 Vegetable, ½ High-Fat Meat, 1½ Fat

French Onion Soup Best Loved

Although the sherry is optional, it lends sweetness to the soup and rounds out the flavor.

Fast

Start to Finish: 30 minutes
Makes: 6 side-dish servings (about 5 cups)

> 2 tablespoons butter or margarine
> 2 cups thinly sliced yellow onions (2 large)
> 4 cups beef broth
> 2 tablespoons dry sherry or dry white wine (optional)
> 1 teaspoon Worcestershire sauce
>   Dash black pepper
> 6 slices French bread, toasted
> 1 cup shredded Swiss, Gruyère, or Jarlsberg cheese (4 ounces)

1. In a large saucepan melt butter; add onions. Cook, covered, over medium-low heat for 8 to 10 minutes or until onions are tender and golden, stirring occasionally. Stir in broth, sherry (if desired), Worcestershire sauce, and pepper. Bring to boiling; reduce heat. Simmer, covered, for 10 minutes.

2. Meanwhile, sprinkle toasted bread with shredded cheese. Place bread under broiler until cheese melts and turns light brown. To serve, ladle soup into bowls and top with bread.

Nutrition Facts per serving: 212 cal., 11 g total fat (6 g sat. fat), 31 mg chol., 778 mg sodium, 18 g carbo., 2 g fiber, 10 g pro.
Daily Values: 7% vit. A, 5% vit. C, 20% calcium, 6% iron
Exchanges: ½ Vegetable, 1 Starch, 1 High-Fat Meat, ½ Fat

Cheese Chowder

Fast

Start to Finish: 30 minutes
Makes: 6 to 8 side-dish servings (about 5 cups)

> 1 cup water
> ½ cup chopped carrot (1 medium)
> ½ cup sliced celery (1 stalk)
> ½ cup chopped red sweet pepper
> ¼ cup thinly sliced green onions (2)
> 3 cups milk
> ¼ cup all-purpose flour
> ½ teaspoon instant chicken bouillon granules
> ¼ teaspoon white pepper
> 1½ cups shredded sharp cheddar cheese (6 ounces)
> 1½ cups shredded American cheese (6 ounces)

1. In a large saucepan bring water to boiling; add carrot, celery, sweet pepper, and green onions. Cook, covered, about 5 minutes or until vegetables are tender. Do not drain.

2. In a small bowl gradually stir about 1 cup of the milk into the flour; stir into cooked vegetables in saucepan. Add the remaining milk, the bouillon granules, and white pepper.

3. Cook and stir over medium heat until thickened and bubbly. Cook and stir for 1 minute more. Add cheddar cheese and American cheese, stirring until melted.

Quick Cheese Chowder: Prepare as above, except omit celery, sweet pepper, and green onions. In a large saucepan combine the water, carrot, and one 10-ounce package frozen cauliflower or frozen cut broccoli. Bring to boiling; reduce heat. Simmer, covered, about 4 minutes or just until vegetables are crisp-tender. Do not drain. Cut up any large pieces of cauliflower or broccoli. Continue as directed in step 2. Makes 6 to 8 side-dish servings (about 6 cups).

Beer-Cheese Chowder: Prepare as above, except add ¾ cup beer to the cooked vegetables along with the milk. Makes 6 to 8 side-dish servings (about 6 cups).

Nutrition Facts per serving for cheese, quick cheese, and beer-cheese variations: 311 cal., 21 g total fat (13 g sat. fat), 66 mg chol., 748 mg sodium, 13 g carbo., 1 g fiber, 18 g pro.
Daily Values: 83% vit. A, 39% vit. C, 54% calcium, 5% iron
Exchanges: ½ Milk, 1 Vegetable, 2 High-Fat Meat, 1 Fat

French Onion Soup

Minestrone `Best Loved`

This minestrone tastes better the day after it's made. After chilling, reheat the soup and add the cooked pasta and fresh spinach.

`Fast` `Low Fat`

Prep: 15 minutes **Cook:** 10 minutes
Makes: 8 servings (about 12 cups)

- 3 14-ounce cans beef broth
- 1 15-ounce can red kidney beans, rinsed and drained
- 1 15-ounce can garbanzo beans (chickpeas), rinsed and drained
- 1 14½-ounce can stewed tomatoes, undrained
- 1 11½-ounce can vegetable juice
- 1 6-ounce can tomato paste
- 2 teaspoons sugar
- 1 teaspoon dried Italian seasoning, crushed
- 1½ cups loose-pack frozen mixed vegetables (such as Italian blend)
- 2 cups cooked pasta, such as medium shell macaroni or mostaccioli
- 2 cups fresh spinach leaves, cut into strips
  Finely shredded Parmesan cheese (optional)

1. In a 4-quart Dutch oven combine beef broth, kidney beans, garbanzo beans, undrained tomatoes, vegetable juice, tomato paste, sugar, and Italian seasoning. Bring to boiling; add mixed vegetables. Reduce heat. Simmer, covered, about 10 minutes or until vegetables are tender.

2. Stir in cooked pasta and spinach; heat through. If desired, sprinkle with Parmesan cheese.

Make-ahead directions: Prepare as above through step 1. Cover and chill overnight. To serve, reheat soup over medium heat. Stir in cooked pasta and spinach; heat through.

Nutrition Facts per serving: 223 cal., 2 g total fat (0 g sat. fat), 0 mg chol., 1,152 mg sodium, 43 g carbo., 8 g fiber, 11 g pro.
Daily Values: 48% vit. A, 48% vit. C, 8% calcium, 18% iron
Exchanges: 2 Vegetable, 2 Starch

Vegetarian Chili

`Low Fat`

Prep: 20 minutes **Cook:** 20 minutes
Makes: 6 servings (about 10½ cups)

- 3 cloves garlic, minced
- 1 tablespoon cooking oil
- 2 14½-ounce cans chunky chili-style tomatoes or stewed tomatoes, undrained
- 1 12-ounce can beer or one 14-ounce can beef broth
- 1 cup water
- 1 8-ounce can tomato sauce
- 3 to 4 teaspoons chili powder
- 1 tablespoon snipped fresh oregano or 1 teaspoon dried oregano, crushed
- 1 tablespoon Dijon-style mustard
- 1 teaspoon ground cumin
- ½ teaspoon black pepper
  Several dashes bottled hot pepper sauce (optional)
- 3 15-ounce cans pinto beans, white kidney beans, and/or red kidney beans, rinsed and drained
- 2 cups fresh or frozen whole kernel corn
- ¾ cup shredded cheddar or Monterey Jack cheese (3 ounces) (optional)

1. In a 4-quart Dutch oven cook garlic in hot oil for 30 seconds. Stir in undrained tomatoes, beer, water, tomato sauce, chili powder, dried oregano (if using), mustard, cumin, pepper, and, if desired, hot pepper sauce. Stir in beans. Bring to boiling; reduce heat. Simmer, covered, for 10 minutes.

2. Stir in corn. Return to boiling; reduce heat. Simmer, covered, for 10 minutes more. Stir in fresh oregano, if using. If desired, top each serving with 2 tablespoons of the cheese.

Nutrition Facts per serving: 330 cal., 4 g total fat (0 g sat. fat), 0 mg chol., 1,586 mg sodium, 61 g carbo., 16 g fiber, 17 g pro.
Daily Values: 18% vit. A, 33% vit. C, 10% calcium, 18% iron
Exchanges: 1½ Vegetable, 3½ Starch, ½ Very Lean Meat

Soup Toppers and Stir Ins
Make a bowl of soup even more special by adding a simple garnish.

■ Purchased or homemade pesto or snipped fresh herbs are fragrant and lively toppers for creamy soups, such as potato and other vegetable soups, or thick stews and chowders.

■ Crumbled crispy bacon or roasted garlic is just the right addition for heartier soups.

■ Stir in a handful of dried tomatoes or a little crumbled Parmigiano-Reggiano cheese into simmering broth-based soups. The hot broth will soften the tomatoes and melt the cheese, bringing out the spunky flavor of these two ingredients.

■ Cool down spicy soups, such as chili, by topping with dairy sour cream.

Corn Chowder

If you want a cheesy chowder, add ½ cup shredded cheddar cheese with the bacon and stir until it melts.

Prep: 30 minutes **Cook:** 20 minutes
Makes: 6 side-dish servings (about 5½ cups)

6 **ears of fresh corn or 3 cups frozen whole kernel corn**
½ **cup chopped onion (1 medium)**
½ **cup chopped green sweet pepper**
1 **tablespoon cooking oil**
1 **14-ounce can chicken broth**
1 **cup cubed, peeled potato (1 medium)**
4 **teaspoons all-purpose flour**
¼ **teaspoon salt**
¼ **teaspoon black pepper**
1½ **cups milk**
3 **slices bacon, crisp-cooked, drained, and crumbled, or 2 tablespoons cooked bacon pieces**
2 **tablespoons snipped fresh parsley (optional)**

1. If using fresh corn, use a sharp knife to cut the kernels off the cobs (see photo, below); you should have about 3 cups corn. Set corn aside.

2. In a large saucepan cook onion and sweet pepper in hot oil until the onion is tender but not brown. Stir in the chicken broth and potato. Bring to boiling; reduce heat. Simmer, covered, for 10 minutes. Stir in corn. Cook, covered, about 10 minutes more or until potato and corn are tender, stirring occasionally.

3. In a small bowl combine flour, salt, and pepper. Stir milk into flour mixture; add to corn mixture in saucepan. Cook and stir until slightly thickened and bubbly. Cook and stir for 1 minute more. Add crumbled bacon; heat through. If desired, garnish each serving with parsley.

Nutrition Facts per serving: 184 cal., 6 g total fat (2 g sat. fat),
7 mg chol., 468 mg sodium, 28 g carbo., 2 g fiber, 7 g pro.
Daily Values: 4% vit. A, 33% vit. C, 9% calcium, 5% iron
Exchanges: 2 Starch, 1 Fat

Hold the ear of corn so an end rests on a cutting board. Using a sharp knife, cut along the cob across the base of the kernels from the top end to the bottom end.

Roasted Yellow Pepper Soup `Best Loved`

If desired, omit roasting the sweet peppers and substitute one 12-ounce jar roasted red sweet peppers that has been drained.

`Low Fat`

Prep: 55 minutes (includes roasting peppers)
Cook: 15 minutes **Cool:** 15 minutes
Makes: 6 to 8 side-dish servings (about 8 cups)

1 **cup chopped onion (1 large)**
4 **cloves garlic, minced**
1 **teaspoon olive oil**
5 **roasted yellow sweet peppers (see tip, page 519)**
3 **14-ounce cans vegetable broth or chicken broth**
1 **cup chopped potato**
1 **tablespoon snipped fresh oregano**
1 **teaspoon snipped fresh thyme**
Dairy sour cream (optional)
Fresh chives (optional)
Fresh thyme leaves (optional)

1. In a large saucepan cook onion and garlic in hot oil for 3 to 4 minutes or until tender. Stir in roasted sweet peppers, broth, and potato. Bring to boiling; reduce heat. Simmer, covered, for 15 minutes. Cool slightly; stir in oregano and thyme.

2. Place one-fourth of the pepper mixture in a food processor bowl or blender container. Cover and process or blend until almost smooth. Repeat with the remaining portions, one at a time, until all of the mixture is processed. Return all of the soup to saucepan; heat through. If desired, top with sour cream and garnish with chives and additional thyme.

Nutrition Facts per serving: 79 cal., 2 g total fat (0 g sat. fat),
0 mg chol., 816 mg sodium, 19 g carbo., 2 g fiber, 3 g pro.
Daily Values: 7% vit. A, 412% vit. C, 3% calcium, 7% iron
Exchanges: 2 Vegetable, ½ Starch

Fresh Tomato Soup

`No Fat`

Prep: 20 minutes **Cook:** 20 minutes **Cool:** 10 minutes
Makes: 4 side-dish servings (about 4 cups)

3 **medium tomatoes, peeled and quartered**
1½ **cups water**
½ **cup chopped onion (1 medium)**
½ **cup chopped celery (1 stalk)**

½ of a 6-ounce can (⅓ cup) tomato paste
2 tablespoons snipped fresh cilantro or basil
2 teaspoons instant chicken bouillon granules
1 teaspoon sugar
  Few dashes bottled hot pepper sauce
  Snipped fresh cilantro or basil (optional)

1. If desired, seed the tomatoes. In a large saucepan combine tomatoes, water, onion, celery, tomato paste, the 2 tablespoons cilantro, bouillon granules, sugar, and hot pepper sauce. Bring to boiling; reduce heat. Simmer, covered, about 20 minutes or until celery and onion are very tender. Remove from heat and cool for 10 minutes.

2. Place half of the tomato mixture in a blender container or food processor bowl. Cover and blend or process until smooth. Repeat with the remaining mixture. Return all of the soup to the saucepan; heat through. If desired, garnish with the additional cilantro.

Chilled Fresh Tomato Soup: Prepare as above, except after blending or processing, cover and chill soup for up to 24 hours. If desired, serve chilled soup topped with dairy sour cream.

Nutrition Facts per serving: 54 cal., 0 g total fat (0 g sat. fat), 0 mg chol., 744 mg sodium, 12 g carbo., 3 g fiber, 2 g pro.
Daily Values: 25% vit. A, 45% vit. C, 3% calcium, 5% iron
Exchanges: 2 Vegetable

Butternut Squash Soup with Ravioli

Add a mixed greens salad and warm crusty bread to serve this soup as a main-dish meal. Omit the molasses, if you like.

Fast

Start to Finish: 30 minutes
Makes: 5 side-dish servings (about 6½ cups)

2 pounds butternut squash
2 14-ounce cans vegetable broth
⅛ teaspoon ground red pepper
1 tablespoon butter or margarine
1 9-ounce package refrigerated cheese-filled ravioli
1 tablespoon molasses

1. Peel squash. Halve lengthwise. Remove seeds and discard. Cut squash into ¾-inch pieces.

2. In a large saucepan combine ½ cup *water*, squash, vegetable broth, and red pepper. Cook, covered, over medium heat for 20 minutes or until squash is tender.

3. Transfer one-fourth of the squash mixture to a blender container or food processor bowl. Cover and blend or process until smooth. Repeat with remaining portions, one at a time, until all of the mixture is blended.

4. Return blended mixture to the saucepan. Bring just to boiling; reduce heat. Simmer, uncovered, for 5 minutes. Add butter; stir until just melted.

5. Meanwhile, prepare the ravioli according to package directions; drain. Ladle hot soup into bowls. Divide cooked ravioli among the bowls. Drizzle with molasses.

Nutrition Facts per serving: 259 cal., 10 g total fat (5 g sat. fat), 52 mg chol., 933 mg sodium, 36 g carbo., 2 g fiber, 10 g pro.
Daily Values: 95% vit. A, 40% vit. C, 18% calcium, 10% iron
Exchanges: 2½ Starch, 2 Fat

Gazpacho

Low Fat

Prep: 40 minutes **Chill:** 2 to 24 hours
Makes: 6 to 8 side-dish servings (about 6 cups)

4 cups chopped, peeled tomatoes (4 large)
1 cup tomato juice or vegetable juice
1 cup beef broth
½ cup chopped, seeded cucumber
¼ cup finely chopped green sweet pepper
¼ cup finely chopped onion
2 tablespoons snipped fresh basil or 1 teaspoon dried basil, crushed
1 tablespoon lemon juice or lime juice
½ teaspoon ground cumin
¼ teaspoon bottled hot pepper sauce
1 clove garlic, minced
  Chopped avocado (optional)
  Olive oil (optional)

1. In a large bowl combine tomatoes, tomato juice, beef broth, cucumber, sweet pepper, onion, basil, lemon juice, cumin, hot pepper sauce, and garlic. Cover and chill for 2 to 24 hours. To serve, ladle soup into chilled bowls or mugs. If desired, top each serving with avocado and/or drizzle with a little olive oil.

Nutrition Facts per serving: 43 cal., 1 g total fat (0 g sat. fat), 0 mg chol., 297 mg sodium, 9 g carbo., 2 g fiber, 2 g pro.
Daily Values: 21% vit. A, 64% vit. C, 2% calcium, 5% iron
Exchanges: 2 Vegetable

Vichyssoise

Prep: 20 minutes **Cook:** 15 minutes **Chill:** 4 to 24 hours
Makes: 4 side-dish servings (about 3¼ cups)

- ⅔ **cup sliced leeks (2) or chopped onion (2 small)**
- 1 **tablespoon butter or margarine**
- 1½ **cups sliced, peeled potatoes**
- 1 **cup chicken broth**
- ⅛ **teaspoon salt**
   Dash white pepper
- 1¼ **cups half-and-half or light cream or milk**
   Dairy sour cream (optional)
   Fresh snipped chives or dill (optional)

1. In a medium saucepan cook leeks in hot butter until tender. Stir in potatoes, chicken broth, salt, and pepper. Bring to boiling; reduce heat. Simmer, covered, for 10 to 15 minutes or until potatoes are tender. Cool slightly.

2. Place potato mixture in a blender container or food processor bowl. Cover and blend or process until smooth; transfer mixture to a medium bowl. Stir half-and-half into potato mixture. If necessary, add more half-and-half to reach desired consistency. Cover and chill for 4 to 24 hours. If desired, serve topped with sour cream and garnish with chives.

Nutrition Facts per serving: 188 cal., 12 g total fat (7 g sat. fat), 36 mg chol., 334 mg sodium, 16 g carbo., 1 g fiber, 5 g pro.
Daily Values: 9% vit. A, 17% vit. C, 9% calcium, 5% iron
Exchanges: 1 Starch, 2½ Fat

Tropical Fruit Soup

This mint-scented soup is the perfect start to a springtime brunch.

Low Fat

Prep: 20 minutes **Chill:** 4 to 24 hours
Makes: 4 to 6 side-dish servings (about 4½ cups)

- 2 **cups cubed, peeled mango, papaya, and/or cantaloupe**
- ¾ **cup passion fruit nectar**
- 2 **teaspoons snipped fresh mint**
- 1½ **cups cubed pineapple**
- ¾ **cup papaya, mango, or guava nectar**
   Sliced strawberries (optional)
   Mint leaves (optional)

1. In a blender container or food processor bowl combine mango, passion fruit nectar, and mint. Cover and blend or process until nearly smooth; transfer to a large bowl. In the same blender container or food processor bowl combine the pineapple and papaya nectar. Cover and blend or process until nearly smooth; add to mango mixture in bowl, stirring to combine. Cover and chill for 4 to 24 hours. If desired, garnish each serving with strawberries and mint.

Nutrition Facts per serving: 121 cal., 1 g total fat (0 g sat. fat), 0 mg chol., 4 mg sodium, 31 g carbo., 3 g fiber, 1 g pro.
Daily Values: 67% vit. A, 94% vit. C, 2% calcium, 3% iron
Exchanges: 2 Fruit

Roasted Fruit Soup

Using a high oven temperature concentrates the mulled-fruit flavor of the pear, plums, cranberries, and apple in this gently spiced dessert.

No Fat

Prep: 10 minutes **Roast:** 35 minutes
Oven: 450°F **Makes:** 6 side-dish servings (5 cups)

- 1 **cup cranberries (4 ounces)**
- ½ **cup packed brown sugar**
- 1 **medium pear, cored and cut into thin wedges**
- 1 **medium cooking apple, such as Rome, Jonathan, or Fuji, cored and cut into wedges**
- 3 **plums, halved and pitted**
- 3 **cups cranberry-apple juice**
- 1 **tablespoon lemon juice**
- 2 **3-inch pieces stick cinnamon**

1. In a 3-quart rectangular baking dish stir together cranberries and brown sugar. Add pear and apple wedges. Roast, uncovered, in a 450° oven about 20 minutes or just until fruit is tender. Add plum halves. Roast, uncovered, for 15 minutes more or until fruit is tender and edges of fruit begin to brown or curl. Stir gently to combine.

2. Meanwhile, in a large saucepan combine cranberry-apple juice, lemon juice, and cinnamon sticks. Bring to boiling; reduce heat. Simmer, uncovered, for 10 minutes. Remove cinnamon sticks and discard. Gently stir roasted fruits and their juices into cooked mixture in saucepan. To serve, spoon warm fruit and juice mixture into small dessert bowls.

Nutrition Facts per serving: 185 cal., 0 g total fat (0 g sat. fat), 0 mg chol., 7 mg sodium, 47 g carbo., 3 g fiber, 1 g pro.
Daily Values: 1% vit. A, 81% vit. C, 3% calcium, 3% iron
Exchanges: 2 Fruit, 1 Other Carbo.

Chapter 22
Vegetables & Fruits

On the divider: Oven-Roasted Autumn Vegetables (see recipe, page 528)

Vegetables & Fruits

Artichokes with Butter Sauce

Start to Finish: 35 minutes **Makes:** 2 servings

> 2 artichokes (about 10 ounces each)
>   Lemon juice
> ¼ cup butter or margarine
> 1 teaspoon snipped fresh dill, tarragon, or oregano, or ¼ teaspoon dried dill, tarragon, or oregano, crushed
> 1 tablespoon lemon juice

1. Wash artichokes; trim stems and remove loose outer leaves. Cut off 1 inch from each top; snip off the sharp leaf tips (see photo, right). Brush the cut edges with a little lemon juice. In a large saucepan or Dutch oven bring a large amount of lightly salted water to boiling; add artichokes. Return to boiling; reduce heat. Simmer, covered, for 20 to 30 minutes or until a leaf pulls out easily. Drain artichokes upside down on paper towels.

2. Meanwhile, for butter sauce, melt butter. Stir in herb and the 1 tablespoon lemon juice. Turn artichokes right side up. Serve with butter sauce.*

*Note: To eat artichokes, pull off one leaf at a time and dip base of leaf into sauce. Draw the base of the leaf through your teeth, scraping off only the tender flesh. Discard remainder of leaf. Continue removing leaves until the fuzzy choke appears. Remove the choke by scooping it out with a spoon; discard choke. If you have trouble getting the choke out with a spoon, try loosening it with a grapefruit knife, then pulling it out with the spoon. Eat the remaining heart with a fork, dipping each piece into sauce.

Artichokes with Citrus Mayonnaise: Prepare artichokes as in step 1, above; chill thoroughly. Omit butter sauce. For citrus mayonnaise, combine ¼ cup mayonnaise or salad dressing; 2 teaspoons orange juice concentrate, thawed; and ⅛ teaspoon lemon-pepper seasoning. Cover and chill for 2 hours before serving with chilled artichokes.

Nutrition Facts per serving with butter sauce or citrus
mayonnaise: 278 cal., 25 g total fat (15 g sat. fat), 66 mg chol., 362 mg sodium, 15 g carbo., 7 g fiber, 4 g pro.
Daily Values: 23% vit. A, 30% vit. C, 6% calcium, 9% iron
Exchanges: 3 Vegetable, 4½ Fat

Artichokes with Sour Cream Sauce: Prepare artichokes as in step 1, above; chill thoroughly. Omit butter sauce. For sour cream sauce, combine ½ cup dairy sour cream; 1½ teaspoons milk; 1 teaspoon fresh dill, tarragon, or oregano, or ⅛ teaspoon dried dill, tarragon, or oregano, crushed; ½ teaspoon Dijon-style mustard; and dash onion powder. Cover and chill for 2 hours before serving with chilled artichokes.

Nutrition Facts per serving: 168 cal., 10 g total fat (6 g sat. fat), 22 mg chol., 149 mg sodium, 16 g carbo., 7 g fiber, 6 g pro.
Daily Values: 12% vit. A, 25% vit. C, 12% calcium, 9% iron
Exchanges: 3 Vegetable, 2 Fat

Using kitchen shears, cut 1 inch from the top of each artichoke. Next, carefully snip off sharp tips of leaves.

Asparagus with Almond Sauce

`Fast`

Start to Finish: 13 minutes **Makes:** 4 servings

> 1 pound asparagus spears or one 10-ounce package frozen asparagus spears
> 1 tablespoon butter or margarine
> 2 tablespoons sliced almonds
> 1¼ teaspoons cornstarch
> ½ cup water
> 2 teaspoons lemon juice
> ½ teaspoon instant chicken bouillon granules

1. Snap off and discard woody bases from fresh asparagus (see photo, below). If desired, scrape off scales. Cook fresh asparagus, covered, in a small amount of boiling lightly salted water for 3 to 5 minutes or until crisp-tender. (Or, cook frozen asparagus according to package directions.) Drain well; transfer to a serving platter.

2. Meanwhile, for sauce, melt butter in a small saucepan; add almonds. Cook and stir over medium-low heat for 3 to 5 minutes or until golden. Stir in cornstarch. Add water, lemon juice, bouillon granules, and dash *black pepper.* Cook and stir until thickened and bubbly. Cook and stir 2 minutes more. Spoon sauce over asparagus.

Nutrition Facts per serving: 73 cal., 6 g total fat (2 g sat. fat), 8 mg chol., 179 mg sodium, 3 g carbo., 1 g fiber, 3 g pro.
Daily Values: 4% vit. A, 26% vit. C, 2% calcium, 4% iron
Exchanges: 1 Vegetable, 1 Fat

Starting at the base and working toward the tip, bend the asparagus spear several times until you find a place where it breaks easily; snap off at that point.

Oriental Cashew Asparagus

`Fast`

Prep: 20 minutes **Cook:** 6 minutes **Makes:** 4 servings

>   1 pound asparagus spears
> 1½ cups quartered fresh button mushrooms
>   1 medium red onion, cut into thin wedges
>   ¼ cup chopped red sweet pepper
>   1 tablespoon butter or margarine
>   1 teaspoon cornstarch
>   2 tablespoons teriyaki sauce
>   1 tablespoon water
>   2 tablespoons cashew halves

1. Snap off and discard woody bases from fresh asparagus (see photo, page 511). If desired, scrape off scales. Bias-slice asparagus into 1-inch pieces (you should have 3 cups).

2. Place a steamer basket in a saucepan. Add water to just below the bottom of the basket. Bring water to boiling. Add asparagus to basket. Cover and reduce heat; steam for 2 minutes. Add mushrooms, onion, and sweet pepper. Cover and steam for 2 to 5 minutes more or until vegetables are crisp-tender. Remove basket; discard liquid.

3. In the same saucepan melt butter; stir in cornstarch and ¼ teaspoon *black pepper.* Add the teriyaki sauce and water. Cook and stir until thickened and bubbly. Return vegetables to saucepan; toss gently to coat. Top with cashews.

Nutrition Facts per serving: 105 cal., 6 g total fat (2 g sat. fat), 8 mg chol., 381 mg sodium, 11 g carbo., 3 g fiber, 5 g pro.
Daily Values: 23% vit. A, 46% vit. C, 3% calcium, 9% iron
Exchanges: 2 Vegetable, 1 Fat

Oriental Cashew Asparagus

Green Beans Amandine

`Fast`

Start to Finish: 30 minutes **Makes:** 3 servings

>   8 ounces green beans or one 9-ounce package frozen cut or French-cut green beans
>   2 tablespoons slivered almonds
>   1 tablespoon butter or margarine
>   1 teaspoon lemon juice

1. Cut fresh beans into 1-inch pieces (or, slice lengthwise for French-cut beans). Cook fresh green beans, covered, in a small amount of boiling salted water for 10 to 15 minutes (5 to 10 minutes for French-cut beans) or until crisp-tender. (Or, cook frozen beans according to package directions.) Drain; keep warm.

2. Meanwhile, in a small saucepan cook and stir almonds in melted butter over medium heat until golden. Remove from heat; stir in lemon juice. Stir almond mixture into beans.

Nutrition Facts per serving: 89 cal., 7 g total fat (3 g sat. fat), 11 mg chol., 45 mg sodium, 6 g carbo., 3 g fiber, 2 g pro.
Daily Values: 11% vit. A, 15% vit. C, 4% calcium, 5% iron
Exchanges: 1 Vegetable, 1½ Fat

Home-Style Green Bean Bake

If you don't want to use wax beans, just add another package or can of green beans.

Prep: 15 minutes **Bake:** 40 minutes
Oven: 350°F **Makes:** 6 servings

>   1 10¾-ounce can condensed cream of celery soup or cream of mushroom soup
>   ½ cup shredded cheddar cheese or American cheese (2 ounces)
>   1 2-ounce jar diced pimiento, drained (optional)
>   2 9-ounce packages frozen French-cut green beans, thawed and drained, or two 16-ounce cans French-cut green beans, drained
>   1 16-ounce can cut wax beans, drained
>   ½ of a 2.8-ounce can (¾ cup) French-fried onions

1. In a large bowl combine soup, cheese, and, if desired, pimiento. Stir in green beans and wax beans. Transfer to a 1½-quart casserole. Bake in a 350° oven for 35 minutes. Remove from oven and stir; sprinkle with French-fried onions. Bake about 5 minutes more or until heated through.

Nutrition Facts per serving: 155 cal., 8 g total fat (3 g sat. fat), 15 mg chol., 686 mg sodium, 14 g carbo., 3 g fiber, 5 g pro.
Daily Values: 14% vit. A, 8% vit. C, 12% calcium, 8% iron
Exchanges: 1½ Vegetable, ½ Starch, 1½ Fat

Green Beans Supreme `Best Loved`

A lemony sour cream sauce and a cheesy crumb topping dress up green beans.

Prep: 15 minutes **Bake:** 30 minutes
Oven: 350°F **Makes:** 8 servings

- **6** cups frozen, loose-pack cut green beans or three 14½-ounce cans cut green beans, drained
- **½** cup chopped onion (1 medium)
- **1** tablespoon butter or margarine
- **1** 8-ounce carton dairy sour cream
- **2** tablespoons all-purpose flour
- **½** teaspoon finely shredded lemon peel
- **¼** teaspoon black pepper
- **½** cup shredded American cheese (2 ounces)
- **⅓** cup fine dry bread crumbs
- **1** tablespoon butter or margarine, melted

1. If using frozen beans, place in a large saucepan with ½ inch water. Bring to boiling; reduce heat. Cook, covered, about 4 minutes or until just tender, stirring occasionally. Drain and set aside.

2. Meanwhile, in a small saucepan cook onion in 1 tablespoon butter until tender. In a large bowl stir together sour cream, flour, lemon peel, and pepper; stir in cooked or canned beans and onion. Transfer bean mixture to a 2-quart baking dish. Top with cheese. Combine bread crumbs and 1 tablespoon melted butter; sprinkle over cheese.

3. Bake in a 350° oven about 30 minutes or until heated through.

Nutrition Facts per serving: 169 cal., 12 g total fat (7 g sat. fat), 27 mg chol., 639 mg sodium, 13 g carbo., 3 g fiber, 5 g pro.
Daily Values: 19% vit. A, 14% vit. C, 13% calcium, 10% iron
Exchanges: 1½ Vegetable, ½ Starch, 2 Fat

Orange-Glazed Beets

You'll find that beet skins slip off easily once the beets have been cooked.

`Low Fat`

Prep: 30 minutes **Cook:** 35 minutes **Makes:** 4 servings

- **4** medium beets (1 pound) or one 16-ounce can sliced beets, drained
- **1** tablespoon butter or margarine
- **1** tablespoon brown sugar
- **1** teaspoon cornstarch
- **¼** teaspoon finely shredded orange peel
- **¼** cup orange juice

1. Cut off all but 1 inch of fresh beet stems and roots; wash. Do not peel. Cook, covered, in boiling salted water 35 to 45 minutes or until tender. Drain and cool slightly. Slip skins off beets and slice.

2. Meanwhile, melt butter in a medium saucepan. Stir in brown sugar and cornstarch. Stir in orange peel and orange juice. Cook and stir until thickened and bubbly. Cook and stir for 2 minutes more. Stir in cooked or canned beets; heat through.

Nutrition Facts per serving: 94 cal., 3 g total fat (2 g sat. fat), 8 mg chol., 116 mg sodium, 15 g carbo., 3 g fiber, 2 g pro.
Daily Values: 4% vit. A, 19% vit. C, 2% calcium, 5% iron
Exchanges: 1½ Vegetable, ½ Other Carbo., ½ Fat

Stuffed Zucchini

Prep: 30 minutes **Bake:** 25 minutes
Oven: 350°F **Makes:** 6 servings

- **6** medium zucchini
- **1** slightly beaten egg
- **1½** cups soft bread crumbs
- **½** cup finely shredded cheddar cheese or Parmesan cheese (2 ounces)
- **¼** cup finely chopped onion
- **1** tablespoon snipped fresh parsley
- **¼** teaspoon salt
- **⅛** teaspoon black pepper

1. In a Dutch oven cook whole zucchini, covered, in boiling lightly salted water for 5 minutes; drain and cool slightly. Cut a lengthwise slice off the top of each zucchini. Remove pulp with a spoon, leaving about a ¼-inch shell.

2. Chop enough of the pulp to measure 2 cups; place chopped pulp in a medium bowl. (Save remaining pulp for another use.) Stir the egg, bread crumbs, ¼ cup of the cheese, onion, parsley, salt, and pepper into the chopped pulp. Fill zucchini shells with pulp mixture. Place in a shallow baking pan.

3. Bake in a 350° oven for 20 minutes; sprinkle with the remaining ¼ cup cheese. Bake for 5 to 10 minutes more or until heated through.

Nutrition Facts per serving: 111 cal., 5 g total fat (2 g sat. fat), 45 mg chol., 233 mg sodium, 12 g carbo., 3 g fiber, 7 g pro.
Daily Values: 16% vit. A, 27% vit. C, 12% calcium, 8% iron
Exchanges: ½ Starch, ½ High-Fat Meat

Broccoli-Carrot Stir-Fry

If you don't have a wok, use a 10-inch skillet when stir-frying. If you'll be stir-frying more than 4 cups of ingredients, as in this recipe, you'll need a 12-inch skillet.

Fast

Start to Finish: 25 minutes **Makes:** 4 servings

   ⅓ **cup chicken broth or vegetable broth**
   1 **tablespoon balsamic vinegar**
   1 **teaspoon cornstarch**
   1 **tablespoon cooking oil**
   1 **teaspoon grated fresh ginger**
   1½ **cups thinly bias-sliced carrots (3 medium)**
   2 **cups broccoli florets**
   2 **tablespoons chopped walnuts, toasted (see tip, page 224)**

1. For sauce, in a small bowl stir together broth, balsamic vinegar, and cornstarch; set aside.

2. Pour oil into a wok or large skillet. (Add more oil as necessary during cooking.) Preheat over medium-high heat. Stir-fry ginger in hot oil for 15 seconds. Add carrots; stir-fry 1 minute. Add broccoli and stir-fry for 3 to 4 minutes or until vegetables are crisp-tender. Push vegetables from center of wok.

3. Stir sauce; add to center of wok. Cook and stir until thickened and bubbly. Stir all ingredients together to coat with sauce. Cook and stir about 1 minute more or until heated through. Sprinkle with nuts.

Nutrition Facts per serving: 94 cal., 6 g total fat (1 g sat. fat), 0 mg chol., 111 mg sodium, 9 g carbo., 3 g fiber, 3 g pro.
Daily Values: 243% vit. A, 64% vit. C, 4% calcium, 4% iron
Exchanges: 2 Vegetable, 1 Fat

Breaded Veggies

Prep: 25 minutes **Bake:** 20 minutes
Oven: 400°F **Makes:** 6 servings

   ½ **cup seasoned fine dry bread crumbs**
   2 **tablespoons grated Parmesan cheese**
   ¼ **teaspoon black pepper**
   1 **slightly beaten egg**
   1 **tablespoon milk**
   4 **cups cauliflower florets, broccoli florets, whole fresh button mushrooms, and/or packaged, peeled baby carrots**
   1 **tablespoon butter or margarine, melted**

1. Lightly grease a 15×10×1-inch baking pan; set aside. In a plastic bag combine bread crumbs, Parmesan cheese, and pepper. In a small bowl combine egg and milk.

2. Toss 1 cup of the vegetables in the egg mixture; add them to the plastic bag. Close bag and shake to coat well. Place coated vegetables on the prepared baking pan. Repeat with remaining vegetables. Drizzle melted butter over the coated vegetables.

3. Bake in a 400° oven about 20 minutes or until golden brown, stirring twice.

Nutrition Facts per serving: 93 cal., 4 g total fat (2 g sat. fat), 42 mg chol., 348 mg sodium, 11 g carbo., 2 g fiber, 5 g pro.
Daily Values: 3% vit. A, 52% vit. C, 6% calcium, 4% iron
Exchanges: 1 Vegetable, ½ Starch, ½ Fat

Broccoli-Cauliflower Bake

Prep: 20 minutes **Bake:** 15 minutes
Oven: 375°F **Makes:** 10 servings

   4 **cups broccoli florets***
   3 **cups cauliflower florets***
   1 **10¾-ounce can condensed cream of mushroom soup or cream of chicken soup**
   3 **ounces American cheese or process Swiss cheese, torn (¾ cup)**
   1 **tablespoon dried minced onion**
   ½ **teaspoon dried basil, thyme, or marjoram, crushed**
   ¾ **cup soft bread crumbs (1 slice)**
   1 **tablespoon butter or margarine, melted**

1. In a large saucepan cook broccoli and cauli-flower, covered, in a small amount of boiling lightly salted water for 6 to 8 minutes or until vegetables are almost crisp-tender. Drain well; remove from pan.

2. In the same saucepan combine soup, cheese, onion, and basil. Cook and stir until bubbly. Stir in the cooked vegetables. Transfer vegetable mixture to a 1½-quart casserole.

3. Combine bread crumbs and melted butter; sprinkle over vegetable mixture. Bake in a 375° oven 15 minutes or until heated through.

*Note: If you like, substitute frozen, loose-pack broccoli and cauliflower, thawed, for the fresh broccoli and cauliflower florets. Bake in a 375° oven 35 minutes or until heated through.

Nutrition Facts per serving: 100 cal., 6 g total fat (3 g sat. fat), 12 mg chol., 376 mg sodium, 7 g carbo., 2 g fiber, 4 g pro.
Daily Values: 13% vit. A, 61% vit. C, 9% calcium, 4% iron
Exchanges: 1½ Vegetable, 1½ Fat

Glazed Parsnips and Carrots

Fresh pears, dried cranberries, and orange juice add a pleasant fruity flavor to this winning combination of parsnips and carrots.

Fast

Start to Finish: 20 minutes **Makes:** 6 servings

- 8 **ounces parsnips, cut into thin bite-size strips (2¼ cups)**
- 8 **ounces carrots, cut into thin bite-size strips (2¼ cups)**
- ¾ **cup orange juice**
- ⅓ **cup dried cranberries**
- ½ **teaspoon ground ginger**
- 2 **firm ripe pears, peeled and sliced**
- ⅓ **cup pecan halves**
- 3 **tablespoons brown sugar**
- 2 **tablespoons butter or margarine**

1. In a large nonstick skillet combine parsnips, carrots, orange juice, dried cranberries, and ginger. Bring to boiling; reduce heat to medium. Cook, uncovered, for 7 to 8 minutes or until vegetables are crisp-tender and most of the liquid has evaporated, stirring occasionally.

2. Stir in pears, pecans, brown sugar, and butter. Cook, uncovered, for 2 to 3 minutes more or until vegetables are glazed.

Nutrition Facts per serving: 200 cal., 9 g total fat (3 g sat. fat), 11 mg chol., 59 mg sodium, 31 g carbo., 5 g fiber, 2 g pro.
Daily Values: 175% vit. A, 41% vit. C, 4% calcium, 5% iron
Exchanges: 1½ Vegetable, 1 Fruit, ½ Starch, 1½ Fat

Garden Vegetable Stir-Fry

Fast

Start to Finish: 30 minutes **Makes:** 4 servings

- ¼ **cup cold water**
- 2 **tablespoons soy sauce**
- 2 **teaspoons cornstarch**
- 1 **teaspoon sugar**
- 1 **teaspoon grated fresh ginger or ⅛ teaspoon ground ginger**
- ⅛ **teaspoon black pepper**
- 1 **cup green beans, bias-sliced into 1-inch pieces**
- 1½ **cups cauliflower, cut into ½-inch florets**
- 1 **tablespoon cooking oil**
- 1 **medium onion, cut into thin wedges**
- ½ **cup thinly bias-sliced carrot (1 medium)**
- 1 **small zucchini, halved lengthwise and cut into ¼-inch slices (1 cup)**

1. For sauce, in a small bowl stir together water, soy sauce, cornstarch, sugar, ginger, and pepper; set sauce aside.

2. In a medium saucepan cook green beans, covered, in boiling salted water for 2 minutes. Add cauliflower. Return to boiling; reduce heat. Simmer, covered, for 1 minute; drain and set aside.

3. Pour oil into a wok or large skillet. (Add more oil as necessary during cooking.) Preheat over medium-high heat. Add onion and carrot; stir-fry 2 minutes. Add beans, cauliflower, and zucchini; stir-fry 3 to 4 minutes or until vegetables are crisp-tender. Push vegetables from center of wok.

4. Stir sauce; add to center of wok. Cook and stir until thickened and bubbly. Stir all ingredients together to coat with sauce.

Nutrition Facts per serving: 81 cal., 4 g total fat (1 g sat. fat), 0 mg chol., 480 mg sodium, 10 g carbo., 3 g fiber, 3 g pro.
Daily Values: 82% vit. A, 38% vit. C, 3% calcium, 4% iron
Exchanges: 2 Vegetable, ½ Fat

Crunchy Cabbage

The peppy flavor of mustard and the crunch of pecans make this simple, yet special, vegetable dish good enough for company.

Fast

Start to Finish: 15 minutes **Makes:** 6 servings

- ¼ **cup water**
- 1 **teaspoon instant beef bouillon granules**
- 6 **cups packaged shredded cabbage with carrot (coleslaw mix)**
- ½ **cup sliced green onions (4)**
- ¼ **teaspoon salt**
- ¼ **teaspoon black pepper**
- ⅓ **cup chopped pecans**
- 2 **tablespoons butter or margarine, melted**
- 1 **teaspoon prepared mustard**
   Dash paprika

1. In a large saucepan combine water and bouillon granules; heat until dissolved. Stir in coleslaw mix, green onions, salt, and pepper. Cook, covered, over medium-low heat about 5 minutes or until crisp-tender, stirring once or twice. Drain, if necessary. Combine pecans, butter, and mustard; pour over cabbage mixture, tossing to combine. Sprinkle with paprika.

Nutrition Facts per serving: 104 cal., 9 g total fat (3 g sat. fat), 11 mg chol., 336 mg sodium, 7 g carbo., 3 g fiber, 2 g pro.
Daily Values: 98% vit. A, 31% vit. C, 5% calcium, 4% iron
Exchanges: 1½ Vegetable, 1½ Fat

Horseradish-Sauced Vegetables

The tang this dish gets from horseradish makes it perfect to serve with a thick, juicy grilled steak.

Prep: 20 minutes **Bake:** 15 minutes
Oven: 350°F **Makes:** 4 to 5 servings

- 1½ **cups cauliflower florets**
- 1½ **cups sliced carrots (3 medium)**
- 8 **ounces broccoli, cut into 1-inch pieces (1¾ cups)**
- ½ **cup mayonnaise or salad dressing**
- 2 **tablespoons finely chopped onion**
- 4 **teaspoons prepared horseradish**
- ¼ **cup fine dry bread crumbs**
- 1 **tablespoon butter or margarine, melted**
  Dash paprika

1. In a medium saucepan cook cauliflower and carrots, covered, in a small amount of boiling salted water for 5 minutes. Add broccoli. Cook about 5 minutes more or until vegetables are crisp-tender; drain.

2. Meanwhile, stir together mayonnaise, onion, horseradish, ⅛ teaspoon *salt,* and dash *black pepper;* stir into cooked vegetables. Transfer to a 1½-quart casserole.

3. In a small bowl combine bread crumbs, melted butter, and paprika; sprinkle over vegetable mixture. Bake in a 350° oven about 15 minutes or until heated through.

Nutrition Facts per serving: 287 cal., 26 g total fat (5 g sat. fat), 24 mg chol., 434 mg sodium, 14 g carbo., 4 g fiber, 3 g pro.
Daily Values: 246% vit. A, 72% vit. C, 6% calcium, 7% iron
Exchanges: 1½ Vegetable, ½ Starch, 5 Fat

Brown Sugar-Glazed Carrots

Fast **Low Fat**

Start to Finish: 25 minutes **Makes:** 4 servings

- 1 **pound medium carrots, parsnips, or turnips, peeled**
- 1 **tablespoon butter or margarine**
- 1 **tablespoon brown sugar**

1. Cut the carrots or parsnips in half, both crosswise and lengthwise. (Or, cut the turnips into bite-size pieces.)

2. In a medium saucepan cook carrots or parsnips, covered, in a small amount of boiling salted water for 8 to 10 minutes (10 to 12 minutes for turnips) or until crisp-tender. Drain; remove from pan.

3. In the same saucepan combine butter, brown sugar, and dash *salt.* Cook and stir over medium heat until combined. Add carrots, parsnips, or turnips. Cook, uncovered, about 2 minutes or until glazed, stirring frequently. Season to taste with *black pepper.*

Nutrition Facts per serving: 79 cal., 3 g total fat (2 g sat. fat), 8 mg chol., 102 mg sodium, 12 g carbo., 3 g fiber, 1 g pro.
Daily Values: 513% vit. A, 11% vit. C, 3% calcium, 3% iron
Exchanges: 2½ Vegetable, ½ Fat

Nutty Brussels Sprouts

Prep: 30 minutes **Cook:** 11 minutes **Makes:** 8 to 10 servings

- 1½ **pounds Brussels sprouts or three 10-ounce packages frozen Brussels sprouts**
- ⅓ **cup dried tomatoes (not oil-packed), snipped**
- 2 **tablespoons butter or margarine**
- 1 **cup chopped onion (1 large)**
- ¼ **cup pine nuts, toasted (see tip, page 224)**

1. Trim stems and remove any wilted outer leaves from fresh Brussels sprouts; wash. Cut any large sprouts in half lengthwise; set aside.

2. Pour enough boiling water over dried tomatoes to cover; let stand about 2 minutes or until softened. Drain well; set aside.

3. In a large skillet melt butter over medium heat. Add fresh or frozen Brussels sprouts and onion. Cook, covered, about 10 minutes (15 minutes for frozen sprouts) or until Brussels sprouts are nearly tender, stirring occasionally. (If necessary, reduce heat to medium-low to prevent overbrowning.) Uncover and cook for 1 to 2 minutes more or until Brussels sprouts are just tender. Season to taste with *salt* and *black pepper.* Sprinkle with tomatoes and pine nuts.

Nutrition Facts per serving: 99 cal., 6 g total fat (2 g sat. fat), 8 mg chol., 170 mg sodium, 11 g carbo., 4 g fiber, 4 g pro.
Daily Values: 16% vit. A, 95% vit. C, 4% calcium, 10% iron
Exchanges: 2 Vegetable, 1 Fat

Dried Tomato Talk

The flavor burst dried tomatoes add to a dish can't be matched by fresh tomatoes. You'll find dark red, flavor-rich dried tomatoes as halves or pieces; they may be dried or marinating in oil. Marinated dried tomatoes are ready to use once they've been drained, but dry ones need plumping. To plump dried tomatoes, cover them with boiling water, let stand 10 minutes, then drain and pat dry. Snip pieces with scissors if needed.

Collard Greens with Bacon

Prep: 30 minutes **Cook:** 1¼ hours **Makes:** 6 servings

- 1½ **pounds collard greens**
- 3 **slices bacon, chopped**
- 2 **cups water**
- 1 **7- to 8-ounce smoked pork hock**
- ½ **cup chopped onion (1 medium)**
- ½ **cup chopped green sweet pepper**
- 1 **teaspoon sugar**
- ¼ **teaspoon salt**
- ⅛ **teaspoon ground red pepper**
- 4 **cloves garlic, minced**
- **Red wine vinegar (optional)**

1. Wash collard greens thoroughly in cold water; drain well. Remove and discard stems; trim bruised leaves. Coarsely chop leaves to measure 6 cups; set aside.

2. In a large saucepan cook bacon until crisp. Remove bacon, reserving drippings in saucepan. Drain bacon and set aside. Add water, pork hock, onion, sweet pepper, sugar, salt, red pepper, and garlic to saucepan. Bring to boiling. Add chopped collard greens; reduce heat. Simmer, covered, about 1¼ hours or until greens are tender. Remove from heat. Remove pork hock. Cover greens; keep warm.

3. When cool enough to handle, cut meat off pork hock. Chop or shred meat; discard bone. Return meat to greens mixture along with cooked bacon; heat through. Serve with a slotted spoon. If desired, sprinkle each serving with a little vinegar.

Nutrition Facts per serving: 158 cal., 13 g total fat (5 g sat. fat), 22 mg chol., 267 mg sodium, 5 g carbo., 2 g fiber, 5 g pro.
Daily Values: 28% vit. A, 31% vit. C, 6% calcium, 2% iron
Exchanges: 1 Vegetable, ½ Medium-Fat Meat, 2 Fat

Corn Cakes with Chives `Best Loved`

`Fast`

Prep: 20 minutes **Cook:** 3 minutes per batch
Makes: 6 servings

- 2 **tablespoons all-purpose flour**
- 1½ **teaspoons baking powder**
- 1 **teaspoon sugar**
- ½ **teaspoon salt**
- 1 **cup boiling water**
- 1 **cup yellow cornmeal**
- ¼ **cup milk**
- ½ **cup frozen whole kernel corn**
- 1 **slightly beaten egg**
- 1 **tablespoon snipped fresh chives**
- 3 **tablespoons cooking oil**
- 1 **teaspoon snipped fresh chives or cilantro (optional)**
- ⅓ **cup dairy sour cream**

1. In a small bowl combine flour, baking powder, sugar, and salt; set aside.

2. In a medium bowl stir boiling water into cornmeal to make a stiff mush. Stir in milk until smooth. Stir in frozen corn, egg, and the 1 tablespoon chives. Add flour mixture to cornmeal mixture and stir just until combined.

3. In a large skillet heat 2 tablespoons of the oil over medium heat. Drop half of the batter by rounded tablespoons into hot oil, making 6 cakes. Cook for 3 to 4 minutes or until golden brown, turning once. Transfer corn cakes to a serving platter. Cover and keep warm. Add the remaining 1 tablespoon oil and repeat with the remaining batter to make a total of 12 corn cakes.

4. Meanwhile, if desired, stir the 1 teaspoon chives into sour cream; serve with the corn cakes. If desired, sprinkle with additional snipped chives.

Nutrition Facts per serving: 209 cal., 11 g total fat (3 g sat. fat), 41 mg chol., 317 mg sodium, 24 g carbo., 2 g fiber, 4 g pro.
Daily Values: 5% vit. A, 3% vit. C, 10% calcium, 8% iron
Exchanges: 1½ Starch, 2 Fat

Corn Cakes with Chives

Scalloped Corn **Best Loved**

Prep: 20 minutes **Bake:** 35 minutes **Oven:** 325°F
Stand: 10 minutes **Makes:** 6 to 8 servings

- 1 10-ounce package frozen whole kernel corn
- ½ cup chopped onion (1 medium)
- ½ cup chopped green or red sweet pepper (optional)
- 2 slightly beaten eggs
- 1 14¾- or 16-ounce can cream-style corn
- 1½ cups coarsely crushed saltine crackers (about 30 crackers)
- 1 cup milk
- 2 tablespoons butter or margarine, melted
- ¼ cup shredded cheddar cheese (optional)

1. Grease a 2-quart baking dish; set aside. In a medium saucepan combine frozen corn, onion, sweet pepper (if desired), ¼ cup *water*, and ¼ teaspoon *salt*. Bring to boiling; reduce heat. Simmer, covered, about 5 minutes or until vegetables are crisp-tender. Drain thoroughly.

2. Meanwhile, combine eggs, cream-style corn, 1 cup of the crushed crackers, and milk. Stir in cooked vegetables. Transfer corn mixture to prepared baking dish. Combine the remaining ½ cup crushed crackers and melted butter; sprinkle over the corn mixture.

3. Bake in a 325° oven for 35 to 40 minutes or until a knife inserted near center comes out clean. If desired, sprinkle with cheese. Let stand 10 minutes before serving.

Nutrition Facts per serving: 243 cal., 9 g total fat (4 g sat. fat), 85 mg chol., 531 mg sodium, 37 g carbo., 2 g fiber, 8 g pro.
Daily Values: 8% vit. A, 9% vit. C, 8% calcium, 8% iron
Exchanges: 2½ Starch, 1 Fat

Eggplant Parmigiana

Prep: 25 minutes **Bake:** 10 minutes
Oven: 400°F **Makes:** 4 servings

- 1 small eggplant (12 ounces)
- 1 beaten egg
- ¼ cup all-purpose flour
- 2 tablespoons cooking oil
- ⅓ cup grated Parmesan cheese
- 1 cup meatless spaghetti sauce
- ¾ cup shredded mozzarella cheese (3 ounces)

1. Wash and peel eggplant; cut crosswise into ½-inch slices. Combine egg and 1 tablespoon *water;* dip eggplant slices into egg mixture, then into flour, turning to coat both sides. In a large skillet cook eggplant, half at a time, in hot oil 4 to 6 minutes or until golden, turning once. (If necessary, add additional oil.) Drain on paper towels.

2. Place the eggplant slices in a single layer in a 2-quart rectangular baking dish.* (If necessary, cut slices to fit.) Sprinkle with Parmesan cheese. Top with the spaghetti sauce and the mozzarella cheese. Bake in a 400° oven for 10 to 12 minutes or until heated through.

*Note: If desired, omit the baking step. Wipe the skillet with paper towels. Arrange the cooked eggplant slices in the skillet; sprinkle with the Parmesan cheese. Top with spaghetti sauce and mozzarella cheese. Cook, covered, over medium-low heat for 5 to 7 minutes or until heated through.

Nutrition Facts per serving: 269 cal., 18 g total fat (6 g sat. fat), 76 mg chol., 660 mg sodium, 17 g carbo., 3 g fiber, 12 g pro.
Daily Values: 11% vit. A, 6% vit. C, 26% calcium, 7% iron
Exchanges: 2 Vegetable, ½ Starch, 1 High-Fat Meat, 2 Fat

Ratatouille

This Mediterranean dish featuring eggplant and tomatoes is equally delicious served cold.

Prep: 25 minutes **Cook:** 10 minutes **Makes:** 4 servings

- ½ cup chopped onion (1 medium)
- 1 clove garlic, minced
- 1 tablespoon olive oil or cooking oil
- 3 cups cubed, peeled eggplant
- 1 medium zucchini or yellow summer squash, halved lengthwise and cut into ¼-inch slices (1½ cups)
- 1 cup chopped, peeled tomatoes or one 7½-ounce can tomatoes, undrained and cut up
- ¾ cup chopped green sweet pepper (1 medium)
- 3 tablespoons dry white wine or water
- 1 tablespoon snipped fresh basil

1. In a large skillet cook onion and garlic in hot oil over medium heat until tender. Stir in eggplant, zucchini, tomatoes, sweet pepper, wine, ⅛ teaspoon *salt,* and ⅛ teaspoon *black pepper.* Bring to boiling; reduce heat. Simmer, covered, over medium-low heat about 10 minutes or until vegetables are tender. Uncover and cook about 5 minutes more or until most of the liquid has evaporated, stirring occasionally. Stir in basil.

Nutrition Facts per serving: 86 cal., 4 g total fat (1 g sat. fat), 0 mg chol., 82 mg sodium, 11 g carbo., 4 g fiber, 2 g pro.
Daily Values: 14% vit. A, 61% vit. C, 2% calcium, 5% iron
Exchanges: 2 Vegetable, 1 Fat

Mushroom Medley au Gratin

Prep: 35 minutes **Bake:** 15 minutes
Oven: 350°F **Makes:** 6 servings

> 2 tablespoons grated Parmesan cheese
> 2 tablespoons fine dry bread crumbs
> 2 teaspoons butter or margarine, melted
> 8 ounces fresh shiitake mushrooms
> 4 ounces fresh oyster mushrooms
> 1 pound fresh button mushrooms, sliced
> 1 clove garlic, minced
> 2 tablespoons butter or margarine
> 2 tablespoons all-purpose flour
> 2 teaspoons Dijon-style mustard
> 1½ teaspoons snipped fresh thyme or
>   ½ teaspoon dried thyme, crushed
> ¼ teaspoon salt
> ⅔ cup milk

1. Stir together Parmesan cheese, bread crumbs, and the 2 teaspoons butter; set aside.

2. Separate caps and stems from shiitake and oyster mushrooms. (Reserve stems to use in stock or discard.) Slice mushroom caps.

3. In a large skillet cook button mushrooms and garlic in the 2 tablespoons butter over medium-high heat about 5 minutes or until tender and most of the liquid has evaporated, stirring occasionally. Remove mushrooms and set aside, reserving drippings in skillet. Add the shiitake and oyster mushrooms to the skillet. Cook for 7 to 8 minutes or until tender and most of the liquid has evaporated, stirring occasionally. Stir in the flour, mustard, thyme, and salt. Add milk all at once. Cook and stir until thickened and bubbly. Cook and stir for 1 minute more. Stir in the button mushroom mixture.

4. Transfer mushroom mixture to a 1-quart au gratin dish or 1-quart casserole. Sprinkle with the bread crumb mixture. Bake in a 350° oven about 15 minutes or until heated through.

Nutrition Facts per serving: 124 cal., 9 g total fat (4 g sat. fat), 18 mg chol., 256 mg sodium, 8 g carbo., 1 g fiber, 7 g pro.
Daily Values: 6% vit. A, 1% vit. C, 7% calcium, 6% iron
Exchanges: 1½ Vegetable, 2 Fat

Kohlrabi with Honey Butter

`Fast` `Low Fat`

Prep: 15 minutes **Cook:** 4 minutes **Makes:** 4 servings

> 4 small kohlrabies (about 1 pound)
> ½ cup shredded carrot (1 medium)
> ¼ teaspoon finely shredded lemon peel
> 1 tablespoon lemon juice
> 1 tablespoon snipped fresh chives or parsley
> 2 teaspoons honey
> 1 tablespoon butter or margarine

1. Peel kohlrabies (see photo, below); cut into ¼-inch strips. Cook kohlrabi strips and carrot, covered, in a small amount of boiling salted water 4 to 6 minutes or until crisp-tender. Drain; keep warm. Combine lemon peel, lemon juice, chives, honey, and ⅛ teaspoon *black pepper;* pour over hot vegetables. Add butter; toss to coat.

Nutrition Facts per serving: 59 cal., 3 g total fat (2 g sat. fat), 8 mg chol., 46 mg sodium, 8 g carbo., 2 g fiber, 1 g pro.
Daily Values: 73% vit. A, 40% vit. C, 2% calcium, 2% iron
Exchanges: 1½ Vegetable, ½ Fat

To remove the woody fibers that compose the outer layer of a kohlrabi, use a sharp knife and peel off strips from top to bottom.

Roasting Sweet Peppers

You can use roasted sweet peppers in a variety of ways: Add them to soups or chili, puree them to use in pasta sauces, blend them with mayonnaise for a quick dip, or drizzle them with olive oil and balsamic vinegar to top toasted baguette slices. Follow these easy roasting directions.

Select firm sweet peppers; wash. Halve peppers lengthwise; remove stems, seeds, and membranes. Place pepper halves, cut side down, on a foil-lined baking sheet. Bake in a 425°F oven for 20 to 25 minutes or until skins are blistered and dark. (Or, broil 4 to 5 inches from heat for 8 to 10 minutes.) Carefully bring the foil up and around the pepper halves to enclose. Let stand about 15 minutes or until cool enough to handle. Use a sharp knife to loosen the edges of the skins from the pepper halves; gently and slowly pull off the skin in strips. Discard skin.

Dilled Peas and Walnuts

Start to Finish: 35 minutes **Makes:** 4 servings

> 2 **cups shelled peas or one 10-ounce package frozen peas**
> ¼ **cup chopped onion**
> 1 **tablespoon butter or margarine**
> 1½ **teaspoons snipped fresh dill or ½ teaspoon dried dill**
> ¼ **teaspoon salt**
> ¼ **teaspoon black pepper**
> 3 **tablespoons broken walnuts or slivered almonds, toasted (see tip, page 224)**

1. Cook fresh peas and onion, covered, in a small amount of boiling salted water for 10 to 12 minutes or until crisp-tender. (Or, cook frozen peas and onion according to the pea package directions.) Drain; return to saucepan. Stir in butter, dill, salt, and pepper; heat through. Sprinkle with walnuts.

Nutrition Facts per serving: 127 cal., 7 g total fat (2 g sat. fat), 8 mg chol., 180 mg sodium, 12 g carbo., 4 g fiber, 5 g pro.
Daily Values: 11% vit. A, 40% vit. C, 3% calcium, 7% iron
Exchanges: 1 Starch, 1 Fat

Peas and Mushrooms: Prepare as above, except cook 1½ cups sliced fresh mushrooms with the peas and onion. Omit dill and walnuts. If desired, stir 2 tablespoons chopped, roasted red sweet peppers into cooked peas and mushrooms.

Nutrition Facts per serving: 100 cal., 4 g total fat (2 g sat. fat), 8 mg chol., 182 mg sodium, 12 g carbo., 4 g fiber, 5 g pro.
Daily Values: 11% vit A, 40% vit. C, 2% calcium, 7% iron
Exchanges: 1 Starch, ½ Fat

Sugar Snap Peas with Orange-Ginger Butter   `Best Loved`

`Fast` `Low Fat`

Start to Finish: 25 minutes **Makes:** 4 servings

> 3 **cups fresh sugar snap peas or frozen loose-pack sugar snap peas**
> 1 **teaspoon grated fresh ginger**
> 1 **tablespoon butter or margarine**
> 1 **tablespoon orange marmalade**
> 1 **teaspoon cider vinegar**
> ⅛ **teaspoon black pepper**

1. Remove strings and tips from fresh peas. Cook fresh peas, covered, in a small amount of boiling salted water for 2 to 4 minutes or until crisp-tender. (Or, cook frozen peas according to package directions.) Drain well.

2. Meanwhile, in a small saucepan cook ginger in hot butter for 1 minute. Stir in marmalade, vinegar, and pepper; cook and stir until marmalade melts. Pour marmalade mixture over hot cooked peas; toss to coat.

Nutrition Facts per serving: 115 cal., 3 g total fat (2 g sat. fat), 8 mg chol., 53 mg sodium, 17 g carbo., 4 g fiber, 4 g pro.
Daily Values: 2% vit. A, 47% vit. C, 6% calcium, 10% iron
Exchanges: 3 Vegetable, 1 Fat

Snow Peas and Tomatoes

`Fast` `Low Fat`

Start to Finish: 10 minutes **Makes:** 6 servings

> 6 **cups fresh snow pea pods (about 1 pound)**
> 1 **large shallot, sliced**
> 2 **teaspoons peanut oil**
> ¼ **teaspoon toasted sesame oil**
> 1 **tablespoon teriyaki sauce**
> ½ **cup grape, cherry, and/or pear-shape red and/or yellow tomatoes, halved**
> 2 **teaspoons sesame seeds, toasted (see tip, page 224)**

1. Remove strings and tips from pea pods; set aside. In a 12-inch skillet cook shallot in hot peanut oil and sesame oil over medium heat until tender. Add pea pods and teriyaki sauce. Cook and stir for 2 to 3 minutes or until pea pods are crisp-tender. Add tomatoes; cook 1 minute more. Sprinkle with sesame seeds.

Nutrition Facts per serving: 58 cal., 2 g total fat (0 g sat. fat), 0 mg chol., 120 mg sodium, 7 g carbo., 2 g fiber, 3 g pro.
Daily Values: 5% vit. A, 66% vit. C, 3% calcium, 9% iron
Exchanges: 1½ Vegetable, ½ Fat

Snow Peas and Tomatoes

Creamed Peas and New Potatoes

`Fast`

Start to Finish: 30 minutes **Makes:** 4 servings

- 10 to 12 tiny new potatoes (1 pound)
- 1½ cups shelled peas or frozen loose-pack peas
- ¼ cup chopped onion
- 1 tablespoon butter or margarine
- 1 tablespoon all-purpose flour
- ½ teaspoon salt
  Dash black pepper
- 1 cup milk
  Snipped fresh chives or dill (optional)

1. Scrub potatoes; cut any large potatoes in half. Peel a narrow strip from around the center of each whole potato. In a medium saucepan cook potatoes, covered, in a small amount of boiling salted water for 8 minutes. Add fresh peas and cook for 10 to 12 minutes more or until tender. (If using frozen peas, cook potatoes 14 minutes; add peas and cook 4 to 5 minutes more.) Drain; return vegetables to saucepan.

2. Meanwhile, in a small saucepan cook onion in hot butter until tender. Stir in flour, salt, and pepper. Add milk all at once. Cook and stir until thickened and bubbly. Cook and stir 1 minute more. Stir into potatoes and peas; heat through. Season to taste. If desired, sprinkle with chives.

Nutrition Facts per serving: 194 cal., 5 g total fat (3 g sat. fat), 13 mg chol., 358 mg sodium, 31 g carbo., 5 g fiber, 8 g pro.
Daily Values: 11% vit. A, 57% vit. C, 10% calcium, 10% iron
Exchanges: 2 Starch, 1 Fat

Sweet-and-Sour Red Cabbage

`Fast`

Start to Finish: 15 minutes **Makes:** 3 to 4 servings

- 2 tablespoons brown sugar
- 2 tablespoons vinegar
- 2 tablespoons water
- 1 tablespoon cooking oil
- ¼ teaspoon caraway seeds
- ¼ teaspoon salt
  Dash black pepper
- 2 cups shredded red or green cabbage
- ¾ cup chopped apple (1 small)

1. In a large skillet combine the brown sugar, vinegar, water, oil, caraway seeds, salt, and pepper. Cook for 2 to 3 minutes or until hot, stirring occasionally. Stir in the cabbage and apple. Cook, covered, over medium-low heat about 5 minutes or until cabbage is crisp-tender, stirring occasionally. Serve with a slotted spoon.

Nutrition Facts per serving: 94 cal., 5 g total fat (1 g sat. fat), 0 mg chol., 202 mg sodium, 14 g carbo., 2 g fiber, 1 g pro.
Daily Values: 1% vit. A, 47% vit. C, 3% calcium, 3% iron
Exchanges: 1 Vegetable, ½ Other Carbo., 1 Fat

Creamy Potluck Potatoes `Best Loved`

Prep: 25 minutes **Bake:** 25 minutes **Oven:** 350°F
Stand: 5 minutes **Makes:** 10 servings

- 3 pounds potatoes, peeled and cut up (about 6 cups)
- 1 10¾-ounce can reduced-sodium condensed cream of chicken soup
- ½ cup dairy sour cream
- 1 3-ounce package cream cheese, softened
- 2 tablespoons butter or margarine, melted
- ¾ cup shredded cheddar cheese (3 ounces)
- ¼ cup sliced green onions (2)
- ¼ cup milk
- ¼ teaspoon garlic salt
- ¼ teaspoon black pepper

1. In a large saucepan cook potatoes, covered, in enough boiling salted water to cover for 10 to 12 minutes or until just tender. Drain; rinse with cold water. Drain again.

2. Meanwhile, in a large bowl stir together the soup, sour cream, cream cheese, and butter. Stir in ¼ cup of the cheddar cheese, 3 tablespoons of the green onions, the milk, garlic salt, and pepper. Stir in the cooked potatoes. Transfer mixture to a 2-quart rectangular baking dish.

3. Bake in a 350° oven for 25 to 30 minutes or until heated through. Sprinkle with the remaining ½ cup cheddar cheese. Let stand about 5 minutes or until cheese melts. Sprinkle with the remaining 1 tablespoon green onion.

Nutrition Facts per serving: 237 cal., 11 g total fat (7 g sat. fat), 32 mg chol., 275 mg sodium, 29 g carbo., 2 g fiber, 7 g pro.
Daily Values: 8% vit. A, 33% vit. C, 10% calcium, 7% iron
Exchanges: 2 Starch, 2 Fat

Scalloped Potatoes `Best Loved`

For a main dish, sprinkle 2 cups chopped cooked ham between the layers of potatoes.

Prep: 25 minutes **Bake:** 55 minutes
Oven: 350°F **Makes:** 4 servings

- ½ **cup chopped onion (1 medium)**
- 1 **clove garlic, minced**
- 2 **tablespoons butter or margarine**
- 2 **tablespoons all-purpose flour**
- ½ **teaspoon salt**
- ¼ **teaspoon black pepper**
- 1¼ **cups milk**
- 3 **medium round red or white, long white, or yellow potatoes (1 pound), peeled, if desired**

1. Grease a 1½-quart casserole; set aside. For sauce, in a small saucepan cook onion and garlic in butter until tender. Stir in flour, salt, and pepper. Add milk all at once. Cook and stir over medium heat until thickened and bubbly.

2. Thinly slice potatoes. Place half the sliced potatoes in the prepared casserole. Cover with half the sauce. Repeat potato and sauce layers.

3. Bake, covered, in a 350° oven for 40 minutes. Uncover and bake for 15 to 20 minutes more or until potatoes are tender.

Nutrition Facts per serving: 187 cal., 8 g total fat (5 g sat. fat), 22 mg chol., 397 mg sodium, 25 g carbo., 2 g fiber, 5 g pro.
Daily Values: 8% vit. A, 26% vit. C, 11% calcium, 6% iron
Exchanges: 1½ Starch, 1½ Fat

Cheesy Scalloped Potatoes: Prepare as above, except stir ¾ cup shredded white cheddar, American, or process Gruyère cheese (3 ounces) into thickened sauce until melted.

Nutrition facts per serving: 273 cal., 15 g total fat (9 g sat. fat), 44 mg chol., 529 mg sodium, 25 g carbo., 2 g fiber, 10 g pro.
Daily Values: 12% vit. A, 26% vit C, 26% calcium, 6% iron
Exchanges: 1½ Starch, 1½ Fat, 1 High-Fat Meat

Baked Potato Fans

Make cleanup easy by lining the baking dish with foil.

Prep: 10 minutes **Bake:** 65 minutes **Oven:** 350°F
Stand 5 minutes **Makes:** 4 servings

- 4 **medium baking potatoes (6 to 8 ounces each)**
- 3 **tablespoons butter or margarine, melted**
- ¼ **teaspoon garlic salt**
- ¼ **cup shredded cheddar cheese (1 ounce)**
- 3 **tablespoons snipped fresh chives or sliced green onions**
- 2 **tablespoons grated Parmesan cheese**

1. Scrub potatoes thoroughly with a brush; pat dry. Cut potatoes crosswise into thin slices, but do not cut all the way through (see photo, below). Place potatoes in a shallow baking dish or pan. Gently press potatoes down to fan slightly.

2. Combine melted butter and garlic salt; drizzle over potatoes. Bake, covered, in a 350° oven for 50 minutes. Uncover and bake about 15 minutes more or until tender. Transfer potatoes to a serving platter. Sprinkle with cheddar cheese, chives, and Parmesan cheese. Let stand about 5 minutes or until cheeses melt.

Nutrition Facts per serving: 245 cal., 13 g total fat (8 g sat. fat), 34 mg chol., 280 mg sodium, 27 g carbo., 3 g fiber, 7 g pro.
Daily Values: 11% vit. A, 43% vit. C, 11% calcium, 8% iron
Exchanges: 2 Starch, 2 Fat

Use the handles of wooden spoons, placed parallel to the length of the potato, to prevent your knife from cutting all the way through.

Baked Potatoes

`No Fat`

Prep: 5 minutes **Bake:** 40 minutes
Oven: 425°F **Makes:** 4 servings

- 4 **medium baking potatoes (6 to 8 ounces each)**
  Shortening, butter, or margarine (optional)

1. Scrub potatoes thoroughly with a brush; pat dry. Prick potatoes with a fork. (If desired, for soft skins, rub potatoes with shortening or wrap each potato in foil.)

2. Bake potatoes in a 425° oven 40 to 60 minutes (or in a 350° oven for 70 to 80 minutes) or until tender. Roll each potato gently under your hand. Using a knife, cut an X in each top. Press in and up on ends of each potato.

Baked Sweet Potatoes: Prepare as above, except substitute sweet potatoes or yams for the baking potatoes. If desired, serve with butter and cinnamon-sugar.

Nutrition Facts per serving for regular or sweet potatoes: 125 cal., 0 g total fat (0 g sat. fat), 0 mg chol., 12 mg sodium, 28 g carbo., 4 g pro.
Daily Values: 38% vit. C, 2% calcium, 13% iron
Exchanges: 2 Starch

Cottage-Fried Potatoes

`Fast`

Start to Finish: 25 minutes **Makes:** 4 servings

- 3 **tablespoons butter or margarine**
- 3 **medium potatoes (1 pound), thinly sliced**
- ¼ **teaspoon salt**
- ⅛ **teaspoon garlic powder**
- ⅛ **teaspoon black pepper**
- 1 **small onion, thinly sliced and separated into rings**

1. In a large skillet melt butter. (If necessary, add additional butter during cooking.) Layer sliced potatoes in skillet. Sprinkle with salt, garlic powder, and pepper. Cook, covered, over medium heat for 8 minutes. Add onion rings. Cook, uncovered, for 8 to 10 minutes more or until potatoes are tender and browned, turning frequently.

Nutrition Facts per serving: 168 cal., 9 g total fat (6 g sat. fat), 25 mg chol., 242 mg sodium, 19 g carbo., 2 g fiber, 3 g pro.
Daily Values: 7% vit. A, 27% vit. C, 2% calcium, 5% iron
Exchanges: 1½ Starch, 1 Fat

Parmesan Cottage-Baked Potatoes: Arrange potato slices and onion rings in a thin layer in a greased 15×10×1-inch baking pan. Melt butter; drizzle over potatoes. Omit salt. Combine garlic powder, pepper, and ¼ cup grated Parmesan cheese; sprinkle over the potatoes. Bake in a 450°F oven about 30 minutes or until browned, carefully turning potatoes once.

Nutrition Facts per serving: 197 cal., 11g total fat (7 g sat. fat), 30 mg chol., 213 mg sodium, 19 g carbo., 2 g fiber, 6 g pro.
Daily Values: 8% vit. A, 27% vit C, 10% calcium, 6% iron
Exchanges: 1½ Starch, ½ Lean Meat, 1 Fat

French Fries

For zesty fries like you get at your favorite fast-food place, combine ½ teaspoon seasoned salt and ½ teaspoon seasoned pepper; sprinkle lightly over the cooked fries.

Prep: 15 minutes **Fry:** 5 minutes per batch
Oven: 300°F **Makes:** 4 to 6 servings

- 4 **medium baking potatoes (6 to 8 ounces each)**
  Cooking oil or shortening for deep-fat frying
  Salt or seasoned salt (optional)

1. If desired, peel potatoes. To prevent darkening, immerse peeled potatoes in a bowl of ice water until ready to cut. Cut potatoes lengthwise into ⅜-inch-wide strips. Return strips to ice water.

2. In a heavy, deep, 3-quart saucepan or deep-fat fryer, heat oil to 365°F. To prevent splattering, pat potatoes dry. Using a spoon, carefully add potato strips, a few at a time, to hot oil. Fry for 5 to 6 minutes or until crisp and golden brown, turning once.

3. Using a slotted spoon, carefully remove french fries from hot oil; drain on paper towels. If desired, sprinkle with salt. Keep french fries warm in a 300° oven while frying remaining potatoes.

Nutrition Facts per serving: 224 cal., 19 g total fat (3 g sat. fat), 0 mg chol., 5 mg sodium, 15 g carbo., 1 g fiber, 2 g pro.
Daily Values: 20% vit. C, 2% calcium, 5% iron
Exchanges: 1 Starch, 3 Fat

Twice-Baked Potatoes

Prep: 20 minutes **Bake:** 62 minutes **Oven:** 425°F
Stand: 10 minutes **Makes:** 4 servings

- 1 **recipe Baked Potatoes (page 522)**
- ½ **cup dairy sour cream or plain yogurt**
- ¼ **teaspoon garlic salt**
- ⅛ **teaspoon black pepper**
  Milk (optional)
- 1 **tablespoon snipped fresh chives (optional)**
- 2 **¾-ounce slices cheddar cheese, halved diagonally**

1. Bake potatoes as directed; let stand about 10 minutes. Cut a lengthwise slice from the top of each baked potato; discard skin from slice and place pulp in a bowl. Scoop pulp out of each potato (see photo, below). Add the pulp to the bowl.

2. Mash the potato pulp with a potato masher or an electric mixer on low speed. Add sour cream, garlic salt, and pepper; beat until smooth. (If necessary, stir in 1 to 2 tablespoons milk to reach desired consistency.) Season to taste with *salt* and *black pepper.* If desired, stir in chives. Spoon mashed potato mixture into potato shells. Place in a 2-quart baking dish.

3. Bake in a 425° oven for 20 to 25 minutes or until lightly browned. Place a piece of cheese over each potato. Bake for 2 to 3 minutes more or until cheese melts.

Nutrition Facts per serving: 220 cal., 9 g total fat (5 g sat. fat), 22 mg chol., 151 mg sodium, 29 g carbo., 3 g fiber, 7 g pro.
Daily Values: 6% vit. A, 39% vit. C, 13% calcium, 14% iron
Exchanges: 2 Starch, 1½ Fat

Using a spoon, gently scoop out the cooked potato pulp, leaving a ¼-inch shell.

Easy Roasted Potatoes `Best Loved`

*To speed cooking time, roast potatoes in a
450°F oven about 25 minutes, stirring occasionally.*

Prep: 10 minutes **Bake:** 55 minutes
Oven: 325°F **Makes:** 4 servings

> 3 **medium round red or white potatoes
>   (1 pound), cut into eighths, or 10 to
>   12 tiny new potatoes (1 pound), halved**
> 2 **tablespoons olive oil or butter or margarine,
>   melted**
> ½ **teaspoon onion powder**
> ¼ **teaspoon garlic salt**
> ¼ **teaspoon black pepper**
> ⅛ **teaspoon paprika**

1. Place potatoes in a greased 9×9×2-inch baking
pan. Combine oil, onion powder, garlic salt, pepper, and paprika; drizzle over potatoes, tossing to
coat. Bake in a 325° oven for 45 minutes. Stir potatoes; bake 10 to 20 minutes more or until potatoes
are tender and brown on the edges.

Nutrition Facts per serving: 145 cal., 7 g total fat (1 g sat. fat),
0 mg chol., 68 mg sodium, 19 g carbo., 2 g fiber, 3 g pro.
Daily Values: 1% vit. A, 26% vit. C, 2% calcium, 9% iron
Exchanges: 1 Starch, 1½ Fat

Hash Brown Potatoes

`Fast`

Start to Finish: 30 minutes **Makes:** 4 servings

> 3 **medium potatoes (1 pound)**
> ¼ **cup finely chopped onion**
> ¼ **teaspoon salt**
> ⅛ **teaspoon black pepper**
> 3 **tablespoons butter or margarine**

1. Peel potatoes; coarsely shred to make 3 cups.
Rinse the shredded potatoes and pat dry with
paper towels. Combine shredded potatoes, onion,
salt, and pepper.

2. In a large skillet melt butter. Using a pancake
turner, pat potato mixture into skillet. Cook over
medium-low heat about 10 minutes or until bottom is crisp. Cut into 4 wedges; turn. Cook for
8 to 10 minutes more or until golden.

Nutrition Facts per serving: 152 cal., 9 g total fat (6 g sat. fat),
25 mg chol., 243 mg sodium, 16 g carbo., 1 g fiber, 2 g pro.
Daily Values: 7% vit. A, 21% vit. C, 1% calcium, 4% iron
Exchanges: 1 Starch, 1½ Fat

Potato-Fennel au Gratin

Prep: 25 minutes **Bake:** 55 minutes
Oven: 350°F **Makes:** 4 to 6 servings

> 1 **large fennel bulb (about 1 pound)**
> ½ **cup chopped onion (1 medium)**
> 4 **tablespoons butter or margarine**
> 2 **tablespoons all-purpose flour**
> ½ **teaspoon salt**
> ¼ **teaspoon black pepper**
> 1¼ **cups milk**
> 2 **large baking potatoes (about 10 ounces
>   each), thinly sliced**
> 2 **parsnips, peeled and thinly sliced**
> 2 **tablespoons finely shredded Parmesan cheese**
> 2 **slices rye and pumpernickel swirl bread, cut or
>   torn into 1- to 2-inch pieces (about 1¾ cups)**

1. Grease a 1½- or 2-quart baking dish; set aside.
To prepare fennel, cut off and discard upper stalks
(see photo, below). If desired, reserve some of the
feathery tops for garnish. Remove any wilted outer
layers and cut a thin slice from the fennel base.
Wash fennel and cut into quarters lengthwise;
remove core. Cut lengthwise into ¼-inch slices
(you should have 2 cups).

2. For sauce, in a small saucepan cook onion in
2 tablespoons of the butter until tender. Stir in
flour, salt, and pepper. Add milk all at once. Cook
and stir until thickened and bubbly.

3. Place half the sliced potatoes in the prepared
baking dish. Layer half of the parsnips and half
of the fennel over the potato slices. Cover with
half of the sauce. Repeat layers. Bake, covered,
in a 350° oven for 40 minutes.

4. Meanwhile, melt the remaining 2 tablespoons
butter. Stir in Parmesan cheese and bread pieces;
sprinkle over vegetable mixture. Bake, uncovered,
for 15 to 20 minutes more or until vegetables are
tender. If desired, garnish with fennel tops.

Nutrition Facts per serving: 373 cal., 16 g total fat (9 g sat. fat),
42 mg chol., 633 mg sodium, 52 g carbo., 17 g fiber, 9 g pro.
Daily Values: 13% vit. A, 52% vit. C, 20% calcium, 11% iron
Exchanges: 1 Vegetable, 3 Starch, 2½ Fat

Using a sharp knife, carefully
cut about 1 inch above the
bulb; discard the stalks. If
you like, save some of the
wispy leaves for garnishing.

Mashed Potatoes

Start to Finish: 35 minutes **Makes:** 4 servings

- 1⅓ **pounds baking potatoes, peeled and quartered**
- 2 **tablespoons butter or margarine**
- 2 **to 4 tablespoons milk**

1. In a medium saucepan cook potatoes and ½ teaspoon *salt,* covered, in enough boiling water to cover for 20 to 25 minutes or until tender; drain. Mash with a potato masher or beat with an electric mixer on low speed. Add butter. Season to taste with *salt* and *black pepper.* Gradually beat in enough milk to make mixture light and fluffy.

Nutrition Facts per serving: 147 cal., 6 g total fat (4 g sat. fat), 17 mg chol., 290 mg sodium, 21 g carbo., 2 g fiber, 3 g pro.
Daily Values: 5% vit. A, 27% vit. C, 2% calcium, 5% iron
Exchanges: 1½ Starch, 1 Fat

Duchess Potatoes: Prepare Mashed Potatoes as above, except decrease milk to 1 to 2 tablespoons. After adding milk, let mashed potatoes cool slightly. With an electric mixer on low speed, beat in 1 egg. Using a pastry bag with a large star tip, pipe potatoes into 4 mounds on a greased 15×10×1-inch baking pan. (Or, spoon 4 mounds onto the baking pan.) If desired, cover and chill potato mounds for up to 4 hours. Drizzle mounds with 2 tablespoons melted butter or margarine. Bake in a 450°F oven for 10 to 12 minutes or until lightly browned.

Nutrition Facts per serving: 218 cal., 14 g total fat (8 g sat. fat), 86 mg chol., 366 mg sodium, 21 g carbo., 2 g fiber, 4 g pro.
Daily Values: 11% vit. A, 27% vit. C, 2% calcium, 6% iron
Exchanges: 1½ Starch, 2½ Fat

Potato Primer

The type of potatoes you choose depends on the way you plan to cook them.

High-starch potatoes: Included are russet and purple potatoes, which have a light, mealy texture. They are best for baking, mashing, or frying. The fluffy quality that makes them good for these preparation methods makes them a poor choice for salads because they crumble when boiled.

Medium-starch potatoes: Round whites, long whites, and the yellow varieties are examples of these all-purpose potatoes. They are versatile and suitable for just about any dish.

Low-starch potatoes: Often called waxy potatoes, they are dense and hold their shapes, making them the ideal choice for soups, salads, and roasting. Round red and all new potatoes are low-starch varieties.

Sweet Potato Swirls

Yams, a tropically grown tuber with brownish skin and yellow to white starchy flesh, are not widely available in the United States. Usually the vegetables labeled as yams in supermarkets are a type of sweet potato. In any case, yams and sweet potatoes are interchangeable in recipes.

Prep: 40 minutes **Bake:** 15 minutes
Oven: 350°F **Makes:** 8 servings

- 4 **medium sweet potatoes or yams (2 pounds), peeled and quartered**
- ¼ **cup butter or margarine**
- 1 **to 2 tablespoons milk (optional)**
- 2 **eggs**
- 2 **tablespoons butter or margarine, melted**

1. In a large saucepan cook potatoes, covered, in enough boiling water to cover for 25 to 30 minutes or until tender; drain.

2. Mash potatoes with a potato masher or beat with an electric mixer on low speed. Add the ¼ cup butter. Season to taste with *salt* and *black pepper.* If desired, gradually beat in enough milk to make light and fluffy. Cool potatoes about 10 minutes. Stir eggs into cooled potato mixture until combined. Using a pastry bag with a large star tip, pipe potatoes into 8 mounds on a greased 15×10×1-inch baking pan. (Or, spoon 8 mounds onto the baking pan.)

3. Drizzle mounds with the 2 tablespoons melted butter. Bake in a 350° oven for 15 to 20 minutes or until tops are golden.

Make-ahead directions: Prepare as above through step 2. Cover and chill potato mounds for up to 4 hours. Continue as directed.

Nutrition Facts per serving: 218 cal., 11 g total fat (6 g sat. fat), 78 mg chol., 123 mg sodium, 28 g carbo., 3 g fiber, 4 g pro.
Daily Values: 418% vit. A, 28% vit. C, 3% calcium, 5% iron
Exchanges: 2 Starch, 1½ Fat

Duchess Potatoes

Candied Sweet Potatoes

Prep: 25 minutes **Bake:** 35 minutes
Oven: 375°F **Makes:** 6 servings

> 4 medium sweet potatoes or yams (2 pounds)
> or two 18-ounce cans sweet potatoes,
> drained
> ¼ cup packed brown sugar
> 3 tablespoons butter or margarine, melted
> ½ cup chopped nuts or tiny marshmallows

1. Peel fresh sweet potatoes; cut into 1½-inch chunks. Cook fresh sweet potatoes, covered, in enough boiling water to cover for 10 to 12 minutes or until just tender; drain. (Or, cut up canned sweet potatoes.)

2. Transfer potatoes to a 2-quart baking dish. Add brown sugar and melted butter; stir gently to combine.* Bake in a 375° oven for 30 to 35 minutes or until potatoes are glazed, stirring gently twice. Sprinkle with nuts; bake 5 minutes more.

Make-ahead directions: Prepare as above through step 2*. Cover and chill up to 24 hours. Uncover and bake as directed.

Nutrition Facts per serving: 268 cal., 13 g total fat (4 g sat. fat), 16 mg chol., 79 mg sodium, 37 g carbo., 4 g fiber, 3 g pro.
Daily Values: 398% vit. A, 27% vit. C, 4% calcium, 6% iron
Exchanges: 1½ Starch, 1 Other Carbo., 2 Fat

Candied Acorn Squash

Prep: 10 minutes **Bake:** 65 minutes
Oven: 350°F **Makes:** 2 servings

> 1 medium acorn squash (about 1¼ pounds)
> ¼ cup maple syrup or 3 tablespoons brown sugar
> 2 tablespoons butter or margarine, melted
> ½ teaspoon finely shredded orange peel (optional)
> ⅛ teaspoon ground cinnamon or ground nutmeg

1. Cut squash in half lengthwise; remove and discard seeds. Arrange the squash halves, cut side down, in a 2-quart baking dish. Bake in a 350° oven for 45 minutes. Turn the squash halves cut side up.

2. Meanwhile, in a small bowl stir together maple syrup, butter, orange peel (if desired), and cinnamon. Spoon syrup mixture into centers of squash halves. Bake for 20 to 25 minutes more or until squash is tender.

Nutrition Facts per serving: 299 cal., 12 g total fat (8 g sat. fat), 33 mg chol., 134 mg sodium, 49 g carbo., 3 g fiber, 2 g pro.
Daily Values: 23% vit. A, 34% vit. C, 10% calcium, 11% iron
Exchanges: 1½ Starch, 2 Other Carbo., 1½ Fat

Buttered Spaghetti Squash

Prep: 20 minutes **Bake:** 30 minutes
Oven: 350°F **Makes:** 6 servings

> 1 medium spaghetti squash (2½ to 3 pounds)
> ½ cup finely shredded Parmesan cheese
> 3 tablespoons butter or margarine, cut up
> ¼ teaspoon salt

1. Halve squash lengthwise; remove and discard seeds. Place squash halves, cut side down, in a large baking dish. Using a fork, prick the skin all over. Bake in a 350° oven for 30 to 40 minutes or until tender.

2. Remove squash pulp from shell (see photo, below). Toss pulp with ¼ cup of the Parmesan cheese, butter, and salt. Sprinkle with the remaining ¼ cup Parmesan cheese.

Nutrition Facts per serving: 132 cal., 9 g total fat (6 g sat. fat), 25 mg chol., 282 mg sodium, 10 g carbo., 0 g fiber, 4 g pro.
Daily Values: 8% vit. A, 4% vit. C, 12% calcium, 2% iron
Exchanges: ½ Starch, ½ Lean Meat, 1½ Fat

With a fork, carefully rake the stringy squash pulp from its shell, separating it into strands that look like spaghetti.

Squash, Pear, and Onion au Gratin Best Loved

Prep: 25 minutes **Bake:** 60 minutes
Oven: 350°F **Makes:** 6 servings

> 1½ pounds butternut, buttercup, or banana squash
> 1 large onion, sliced and separated into rings (1 cup)
> 1 tablespoon butter or margarine
> 1 medium pear, peeled and thinly sliced (1 cup)
> 3 tablespoons fine dry bread crumbs
> 3 slices bacon, crisp-cooked, drained, and crumbled
> 2 tablespoons chopped walnuts
> 1 tablespoon grated Romano cheese
> 1 tablespoon melted butter or margarine
> 2 tablespoons snipped fresh parsley (optional)

1. Peel squash; slice crosswise into ½-inch slices. (If using butternut squash, first cut the squash in half lengthwise.) Remove and discard seeds. Set squash aside.

2. Cook onion rings in the 1 tablespoon hot butter for 5 to 10 minutes or until tender.

3. Arrange half of the squash slices in the bottom of an 8×8×2-inch baking dish. Top with half of the pear slices. Repeat layers. Sprinkle lightly with *salt*. Cover with the cooked onions. Bake, covered, in a 350° oven about 45 minutes or until nearly tender.

4. Meanwhile, in a small bowl combine bread crumbs, bacon, walnuts, Romano cheese, and the 1 tablespoon melted butter; sprinkle over vegetables. Bake, uncovered, about 15 minutes more or until tender. If desired, sprinkle with parsley.

Nutrition Facts per serving: 153 cal., 8 g total fat (3 g sat. fat), 14 mg chol., 270 mg sodium, 20 g carbo., 1 g fiber, 3 g pro.
Daily Values: 146% vit. A, 35% vit. C, 7% calcium, 6% iron
Exchanges: 1½ Starch, 1 Fat

Squash, Pear, and Onion au Gratin

Spiced Vegetable-Stuffed Squash

Carrots, turnips, apples, and spices team with acorn squash for this tasty autumn side dish.

Low Fat

Prep: 20 minutes **Bake:** 80 minutes
Oven: 350°F **Makes:** 8 servings

> 2   medium acorn squash (1¼ pounds each)
> 1½ cups chopped turnips (2 small)
> 1   cup chopped carrots (2 medium)
> 1   tablespoon butter or margarine
> 1   tablespoon brown sugar
> ½   teaspoon ground cinnamon
> ¼   teaspoon salt
> ¼   teaspoon ground nutmeg
> 1   cup coarsely shredded, peeled apple

1. Cut squash in half lengthwise; remove and discard seeds. Arrange squash halves, cut side down, in a 3-quart rectangular baking dish. Bake in a 350° oven for 45 minutes. Turn squash halves cut side up. Bake for 20 to 25 minutes more or until squash is tender. Cut each squash half in half so you have 8 quarters. Carefully scoop the pulp out of each squash quarter, keeping shells intact and leaving a thin layer of squash in shells. Set shells aside. Place cooked pulp in a large bowl.

2. Meanwhile, in a covered saucepan cook turnips and carrots in boiling lightly salted water about 15 minutes or until very tender. Drain well. Add turnips and carrots to squash pulp in bowl. Coarsely mash vegetables with a potato masher.

3. Stir butter, brown sugar, cinnamon, salt, and nutmeg into mashed vegetables; fold in apple. Divide vegetable mixture evenly among squash shells. Return to baking dish. Bake for 15 to 20 minutes more or until heated through.

Nutrition Facts per serving: 86 cal., 2 g total fat (1 g sat. fat), 4 mg chol., 113 mg sodium, 18 g carbo., 3 g fiber, 1 g pro.
Daily Values: 85% vit. A, 26% vit. C, 5% calcium, 6% iron
Exchanges: 1 Starch

Gingered Jerusalem Artichokes

Wait until your dinner is ready to go on the table before you cook these slightly crunchy nibbles. Once cooked, they soften if they're not eaten right away.

Fast   Low Fat

Start to Finish: 15 minutes **Makes:** 4 servings

> 1   pound Jerusalem artichokes, peeled, if desired, and cut up
> 1   tablespoon butter or margarine
> 2   teaspoons grated fresh ginger
> ¼   cup Marsala, sherry, or apple juice

1. In a large skillet cook and stir artichokes in hot butter over medium-high heat for 5 to 6 minutes or until crisp-tender. Add ginger; cook for 30 seconds. Remove from heat; stir in Marsala. Season to taste with *salt*.

Nutrition Facts per serving: 110 cal., 3 g total fat (2 g sat. fat), 8 mg chol., 36 mg sodium, 16 g carbo., 1 g fiber, 2 g pro.
Daily Values: 3% vit. A, 5% vit. C, 1% calcium, 15% iron
Exchanges: 1 Starch, ½ Fat

Oven-Roasted Autumn Vegetables

Roasting vegetables in walnut oil and balsamic vinegar caramelizes their natural sugars and brings out their subtle sweetness (see photo, page 509).

Prep: 15 minutes **Bake:** 30 minutes
Oven: 425°F **Makes:** 4 to 6 servings

- 1 **large sweet potato or yam (10 ounces), peeled and cut into 1-inch cubes**
- 1 **large fennel bulb (1 pound), trimmed (see photo, page 524) and cut into wedges**
- 8 **ounces round red potatoes, quartered**
- 6 **ounces fresh shiitake mushrooms, halved**
- 4 **large shallots, quartered**
- 2 **tablespoons walnut oil**
- 2 **tablespoons balsamic vinegar**
- 1 **teaspoon coarse salt**

1. In a large roasting pan toss sweet potato, fennel, red potatoes, mushrooms, and shallots with the walnut oil, 1 tablespoon of the vinegar, and the salt. Roast in a 425° oven for 30 to 35 minutes or until vegetables are lightly browned and tender, stirring once or twice. Sprinkle with the remaining 1 tablespoon vinegar. Serve warm or at room temperature.

Nutrition Facts per serving: 209 cal., 7 g total fat (1 g sat. fat),
0 mg chol., 525 mg sodium, 35 g carbo., 5 g fiber, 4 g pro.
Daily Values: 245% vit. A, 49% vit. C, 6% calcium, 10% iron
Exchanges: 1 Vegetable, 2 Starch, 1 Fat

Caramelized Onions

Caramelized onions make a deliciously mellow topper for burgers or a flavorful side dish for meats, poultry, or fish.

Fast

Prep: 5 minutes **Cook:** 16 minutes **Makes:** 4 to 6 servings

- 2 **large sweet onions (such as Vidalia or Walla Walla), halved lengthwise and thinly sliced or cut into ¾-inch chunks**
- 2 **tablespoons butter or margarine**

1. In a large skillet cook onions, covered, in hot butter over medium-low heat for 13 to 15 minutes or until onions are tender, stirring occasionally. Uncover; cook and stir over medium-high heat for 3 to 5 minutes more or until onions are golden.

Nutrition Facts per serving: 84 cal., 6 g total fat (4 g sat. fat),
16 mg chol., 64 mg sodium, 7 g carbo., 1 g fiber, 1 g pro.
Daily Values: 5% vit. A, 7% vit. C, 2% calcium, 1% iron
Exchanges: 1½ Vegetable, 1 Fat

Fried Green Tomatoes

Prep: 10 minutes **Stand:** 15 minutes
Cook: 8 minutes per batch **Makes:** 6 servings

- 3 **medium, firm green tomatoes**
- ½ **cup all-purpose flour**
- ¼ **cup milk**
- 2 **beaten eggs**
- ⅔ **cup fine dry bread crumbs or cornmeal**
- ¼ **cup cooking oil**

1. Cut unpeeled tomatoes into ½-inch slices; sprinkle slices with ½ teaspoon *salt* and ¼ teaspoon *black pepper*. Let tomato slices stand for 15 minutes. Meanwhile, place flour, milk, eggs, and bread crumbs in separate shallow dishes.

2. Dip tomato slices in milk, then flour, then eggs, then bread crumbs. In a skillet fry half the coated tomato slices at a time in hot oil over medium heat for 4 to 6 minutes on each side or until brown. (If tomatoes begin to brown too quickly, reduce heat to medium-low. If necessary, add additional oil.) If desired, season to taste with additional *salt* and *black pepper.*

Nutrition Facts per serving: 194 cal., 12 g total fat (2 g sat. fat),
72 mg chol., 465 mg sodium, 18 g carbo., 1 g fiber, 5 g pro.
Daily Values: 10% vit. A, 24% vit. C, 5% calcium, 8% iron
Exchanges: 1 Vegetable, 1 Starch, 2 Fat

Smothered Okra

Prep: 20 minutes **Cook:** 20 minutes **Makes:** 4 servings

- ½ **cup chopped onion (1 medium)**
- ½ **cup chopped green sweet pepper**
- 2 **cloves garlic, minced**
- 2 **tablespoons butter or margarine**
- 8 **ounces whole okra, cut into ½-inch pieces (2 cups), or 2 cups frozen cut okra, thawed**
- 2 **cups chopped, peeled tomatoes (2 large)**
- ⅛ **teaspoon ground red pepper (optional)**
- 2 **slices bacon, crisp-cooked, drained, and crumbled (optional)**

1. In a large skillet cook and stir the onion, sweet pepper, and garlic in butter over medium heat about 5 minutes or until tender. Stir in okra, tomatoes, red pepper (if desired), ½ teaspoon *salt,* and ⅛ teaspoon *black pepper.* Bring to boiling; reduce heat. Simmer, covered, about 20 minutes for fresh okra (10 minutes for thawed okra) or until okra is very tender. If desired, sprinkle with bacon.

Nutrition Facts per serving: 106 cal., 7 g total fat (4 g sat. fat),
16 mg chol., 367 mg sodium, 12 g carbo., 4 g fiber, 2 g pro.
Daily Values: 25% vit. A, 72% vit. C, 6% calcium, 6% iron
Exchanges: 2½ Vegetable, 1 Fat

Selecting Fresh Vegetables

Take a few minutes in the supermarket's produce section and inspect each vegetable before you buy. Look for plump, crisp, bright-colored vegetables that are heavy for their size (this indicates moistness). Avoid vegetables that are bruised, shriveled, moldy, or blemished. Follow these guidelines for selecting and storing fresh vegetables. In most cases, wash vegetables just before using. For preparation and cooking information, see pages 540–544. See also pages 534–535 for descriptions of some less familiar vegetables and pages 470–471 for greens information.

Vegetable	Peak Season	How to Choose	How to Store
Asparagus	Available March through June with peak season in April and May; available year-round in some areas.	Choose firm, straight stalks with compact, closed tips. Avoid stalks that are very thin (less than $\frac{1}{8}$ inch) or very thick (more than $\frac{1}{2}$ inch) because they may be stringy.	Wrap the bases of fresh asparagus spears in wet paper towels and keep tightly sealed in a storage container in the refrigerator for up to 4 days.
Beans, green (snap or string)	Available from April through September; available year-round in some areas.	Select fresh beans that are bright-colored and crisp. Avoid bruised or scarred beans or ones that are rusty with brown spots or streaks. Bulging, leathery beans are old.	Refrigerate in a covered container for up to 5 days.
Beets	Available year-round with peak season from June through October.	Select small or medium beets; large beets tend to be pithy, tough, and less sweet.	Trim the beet greens, leaving an inch or two of stem. Do not cut the long root. Store unwashed beets in an open container in the refrigerator for up to 1 week.
Broccoli	Available year-round.	Look for firm stalks with deep green or purplish-green heads that are tightly packed. Avoid heads that are light green or yellowing.	Keep unwashed broccoli in a covered container in the refrigerator for up to 4 days.
Brussels sprouts	Available year-round with peak season from August through April.	Pick out the smaller sprouts that are vivid green; they will taste the sweetest. Large ones may be bitter.	Refrigerate in a covered container for up to 2 days.
Cabbage (green, Napa, red, or Savoy)	Available year-round.	The head should feel heavy for its size, and its leaves should be unwithered, brightly colored, and free of brown spots.	Refrigerate in a covered container for up to 5 days.
Carrots	Available year-round.	Check for straight, rigid, bright orange carrots.	Refrigerate in plastic bags for up to 2 weeks.
Cauliflower	Available year-round.	Look for solid heavy heads with bright green leaves. Avoid those with brown bruises or yellowed leaves.	Refrigerate in a covered container for up to 4 days.
Celery	Available year-round.	Look for crisp ribs that are firm, unwilted, and unblemished.	Refrigerate, tightly wrapped, for up to 2 weeks.
Cucumbers	Available year-round with peak season from late May through early September.	Select firm cucumbers without shriveled or soft spots. Edible wax is sometimes added to prevent moisture loss.	Keep salad cucumbers in refrigerator for up to 10 days. Pickling cucumbers should be picked and used the same day.

Selecting Fresh Vegetables *(continued)*

Vegetable	Peak Season	How to Choose	How to Store
Eggplant	Available year-round with peak season from July through September.	Look for plump, glossy eggplants. Skip any that are scarred or bruised. The cap should be fresh-looking and free of mold.	Refrigerate whole eggplants for up to 2 days.
Leeks	Available year-round.	Look for leeks with clean white ends and fresh, green-colored tops.	Refrigerate, tightly wrapped, for up to 5 days.
Mushrooms (all varieties)	Available year-round; morel mushrooms available from April through June.	Mushrooms should be firm, fresh, and plump and have no bruises. Size is a matter of preference. Avoid spotted or slimy mushrooms.	Store unwashed mushrooms in the refrigerator for up to 2 days. A paper bag or damp cloth bag lets them breathe so they stay firmer longer.
Okra	Available year-round with peak season from June through September.	Look for small, crisp, bright-colored pods without brown spots or blemishes. Avoid shriveled pods.	Refrigerate, tightly wrapped, for up to 3 days.
Onions (all varieties)	Availability determined by variety. Some varieties, such as white, red, pearl, and boiling onions, are available year-round. Various sweet onion varieties, such as Vidalia and Walla Walla, are available on and off throughout the year.	Select dry bulb onions that are firm, free from blemishes, and not sprouting.	Store in a cool, dry, well-ventilated place for several weeks.
Peas and Pea pods	**Peas:** Available January through June with peak season from March through May. **Pea pods:** Available from February through August.	Select fresh peas, snow peas, or sugar snap peas that are crisp and brightly colored. Avoid shriveled pods or those with brown spots.	Store, tightly wrapped, in the refrigerator for up to 3 days.
Peppers (hot or sweet)	Available year-round.	Fresh peppers, whether sweet or hot, should be brightly colored and have a good shape for the variety. Avoid shriveled, bruised, or broken peppers.	Refrigerate in a covered container for up to 5 days.
Potatoes	Available year-round.	Look for clean potatoes that have smooth, unblemished skins. They should be firm and have a shape that is typical for their variety. Avoid those that have green spots or are soft, moldy, or shriveled.	Store in a well-ventilated, dark place that is cool and slightly humid, but not wet, for several weeks. Bright lights cause potatoes to develop green patches that have a bitter flavor. Avoid refrigerating potatoes; cold temperatures cause them to turn overly sweet and to darken when cooked.
Root vegetables (parsnips, rutabagas, or turnips)	Available year-round. **Parsnips:** Peak season from November through March. **Rutabagas:** Peak season from September through March. **Turnips:** Peak season from October through March.	Choose vegetables that are smooth-skinned and heavy for their size. Sometimes parsnips, rutabagas, and turnips are covered with a wax coating to extend storage; cut off this coating before cooking.	Refrigerate for up to 2 weeks.

Selecting Fresh Vegetables *(continued)*

Vegetable	Peak Season	How to Choose	How to Store
Shallots	Available year-round.	Select dry shallots that are firm, free of blemishes, and not sprouting.	Store in a cool, dry, well-ventilated place for up to 1 month.
Squash, winter	Some varieties available year-round with peak season from September through March.	Avoid cracked or bruised squash.	Store whole squash in a cool, dry place for up to 2 months. Refrigerate cut squash, wrapped in plastic, for up to 4 days.
Sweet potatoes and Yams	Available year-round with peak season from October through January.	Choose small to medium, smooth-skinned potatoes that are firm and free of soft spots.	Store in a cool, dry, dark place for up to 1 week.
Tomatoes	Available year-round with peak season from June through early September.	Pick well-shaped, plump, fairly firm tomatoes.	Store at room temperature for up to 3 days. Do not store tomatoes in the refrigerator because they lose their flavor.
Zucchini and Summer squash	Some varieties available year-round with peak season from June through September.	Because of its tender skin, it is almost impossible for a zucchini to be blemish-free, but look for small ones that are firm and free of cuts and soft spots.	Refrigerate squash, tightly wrapped, for up to 5 days; fresh-from-the-garden squash may be stored for up to 2 weeks.

Selecting Fresh Fruit

When picking fruits, look for plumpness, tenderness, and bright color. Fruits should be heavy for their size and free from mold, mildew, bruises, cuts, or other blemishes. Some fruits are picked and shipped while still firm, so they may need additional ripening.

To ripen, place fruit in a small, clean paper bag. (A plastic bag is not recommended because it doesn't allow fruit to breathe and can produce mold on the fruit from trapped moisture.) Loosely close the bag and store it at room temperature. Feel free to mix varieties of fruit in the same bag. To speed up the ripening process, place a ripe apple or ripe banana in the bag with underripe fruit. Check fruit daily and remove any that yields to gentle pressure. Enjoy ripe fruit immediately or remove fruit from the bag and transfer it to the refrigerator for a few days to retard further ripening.

Fruit	Peak Season	How to Choose	How to Store
Apples	Available year-round with peak season from September through November.	Select firm apples, free from bruises or soft spots. Fruit is sold ready for eating. Select variety according to intended use.	Refrigerate for up to 6 weeks; store bulk apples in a cool moist place.
Apricots	Available from May through July.	Look for plump, fairly firm fruit with deep yellow or yellowish-orange skin.	Ripen firm fruit as directed above* until it yields to gentle pressure and is golden in color. Refrigerate ripe fruit for up to 2 days.
Avocados	Available year-round.	Avoid bruised fruit with gouges or broken skin. Soft avocados can be used immediately (and are especially good for guacamole).	Ripen firm fruit as directed above* until it yields to gentle pressure. Store ripened fruit in the refrigerator for up to 4 days.
Bananas	Available year-round.	Choose bananas at any stage of ripeness, from green to yellow.	Ripen at room temperature until they have a bright yellow color. Overripe bananas are brown.

Selecting Fresh Fruit *(continued)*

Fruit	Peak Season	How to Choose	How to Store
Berries	**Blackberries:** Available from June through August. **Blueberries:** Available from late May through October. **Boysenberries:** Available from late June through early August. **Raspberries:** Available year-round with peak season from May through September. **Strawberries:** Available year-round with peak season from June through September.	If picking your own, select berries that separate easily from their stems.	Refrigerate berries in a single layer, loosely covered, for up to 2 days. Rinse just before using.
Cantaloupe	Available year-round with peak season from June through September.	Select cantaloupe with a sweet, aromatic scent; a strong smell could indicate over-ripeness. It should feel heavy for its size. Avoid wet, dented, bruised, or cracked fruit.	Ripen as directed on page 531.* Refrigerate whole melon up to 4 days. Refrigerate cut fruit in a covered container or tightly wrapped for up to 2 days.
Carambolas (Starfruit)	Available from late August through February.	Look for firm, shiny-skinned, golden fruit. Some browning on the edge of the fins is natural and does not affect the taste.	Ripen as directed on page 531.* Refrigerate ripened fruit in a covered container or tightly wrapped for up to 1 week.
Cherries	**Sweet:** Available from May through August with peak season in June and July. **Tart:** Available from June through August with peak season in June and July.	Select firm, brightly colored fruit.	Refrigerate in a covered container for 2 to 3 days.
Cranberries	Available from October through December with peak season in November.	Fruit is ripe when sold. Avoid soft, shriveled, or bruised fruit.	Refrigerate for up to 4 weeks or freeze for up to 1 year.
Grapefruit	Available year-round.	Choose fully colored grapefruit with a nicely rounded shape. Juicy grapefruits will be heavy for their size.	Refrigerate for up to 2 weeks.
Grapes	Available year-round.	Look for plump grapes without bruises, soft spots, or mold. Bloom (a frosty white cast) is typical and doesn't affect quality.	Refrigerate in a covered container for up to 1 week.
Honeydew melon	Available year-round with peak season from June through September.	Choose honeydew that is smooth skinned and heavy for its size with a sweet, aromatic scent. Avoid wet, dented, bruised, or cracked fruit.	Ripen as directed on page 531.* Refrigerate whole melon up to 4 days. Refrigerate cut fruit in a covered container or tightly wrapped for up to 3 days.
Lemons	Available year-round.	Look for firm, well-shaped lemons with smooth, evenly yellow skin. Avoid bruised or wrinkled lemons.	Refrigerate for up to 2 weeks.
Limes	Available year-round.	Select firm, well-shaped, brightly colored limes. Avoid blemished, bruised, or shriveled skin.	Refrigerate for up to 2 weeks.

Selecting Fresh Fruit *(continued)*

Fruit	Peak Season	How to Choose	How to Store
Oranges	Available year-round.	Choose oranges that are firm and heavy for their size. Brown specking or a slight greenish tinge on the surface of an orange will not affect the eating quality.	Refrigerate for up to 2 weeks.
Peaches and Nectarines	Peaches: Available from May through September. **Nectarines:** Available from May through September with peak season from July through August.	Look for fruit with a golden-yellow skin and no tinges of green. Ripe fruit should yield slightly to gentle pressure.	Ripen as directed on page 531* and refrigerate for up to 5 days.
Pears	Available year-round.	Skin color is not always an indicator of ripeness because skin color of some varieties does not change much as the pears ripen. Look for pears without bruises or cuts. Choose a variety according to intended use.	Ripen as directed on page 531* until pear yields to gentle pressure at the stem end. Refrigerate ripened fruit for several days.
Pineapple	Available year-round with peak season from March through July.	Look for a plump pineapple with a sweet, aromatic smell at the stem end. It should be slightly soft to the touch, heavy for its size, and have deep green leaves.	Refrigerate for up to 2 days. Cut pineapple lasts a few more days if placed in a tightly covered container and refrigerated.
Plantains	Available year-round.	Choose undamaged plantains. Slight bruises are acceptable because the skin is tough enough to protect the fruit. Choose plantains at any stage of ripeness, from green to dark brown or black, depending on intended use.	Ripen plantains at room temperature according to directions on page 531.* Color will change from green to yellow-brown to black. Black plantains are fully ripe. The starchy fruit must be cooked before eating.
Plums	Available from May through October with peak season from June through July.	Find firm, plump, well-shaped fresh plums. Each should give slightly when gently pressed. Bloom (light gray cast) on the skin is natural and doesn't affect quality.	Ripen as directed on page 531* and refrigerate for up to 3 days.
Rhubarb	Available from February through June with peak season from April through June.	Look for crisp stalks that are firm and tender. Avoid rhubarb that looks wilted or has very thick stalks.	Wrap stalks tightly in plastic wrap and refrigerate for up to 5 days.
Watermelon	Available from May through September with peak season from mid-June through late August.	Choose watermelon that has a hard, smooth rind and is heavy for its size. Avoid wet, dented, bruised, or cracked fruit.	Watermelon does not ripen after picking. Refrigerate whole melon up to 4 days. Refrigerate cut fruit in a covered container or tightly wrapped for up to 3 days.

Beyond the Basic Vegetables

Broccoli raab

Bitter melon

Fennel

Jerusalem artichoke

Japanese eggplant

Bitter melon

Description: Bitter melon is similar in shape and size to a cucumber. The skin, however, is wrinkled and covered with a series of ridges and bumps. The flesh, which has a bitter, slightly sour flavor, ranges in color from pale yellow to yellow to pale green. The skin is edible, but remove and discard the seeds. Bitter melon actually is a fruit that is used like a vegetable when it is picked young and green. (To be considered a fruit, it has to turn a bright orange.)

Availability: Available in Asian or specialty produce markets sporadically throughout the year.

How to Choose: To use as a vegetable, select a brightly colored, firm, green to yellowish-green melon. Avoid a melon with blemishes or soft spots.

How to Store: Store at room temperature or in the refrigerator for a few days.

Broccoli raab (rabe) or Rapini

Description: Broccoli raab is approximately 6 to 9 inches in length with dark green leafy stalks and clusters of small buds that resemble broccoli. The flavor of the stems and leaves is sharp and somewhat bitter.

Availability: Available year-round in larger supermarkets or in specialty produce markets.

How to Choose: It is often sold in loose bunches. Choose sturdy, small stems with fresh-looking, crisp green leaves.

How to Store: Refrigerate in a plastic bag for up to 4 days.

Cactus leaves or Nopales

Description: These fleshy, oval-shape leaves are from the prickly pear cactus. Cooked cactus leaves, which have a mild, slightly tart flavor, have a soft texture and a slippery quality similar to that of cooked okra. Raw cactus leaves have a crisp texture.

Availability: Available year-round in larger supermarkets or in Mexican specialty markets.

How to Choose: Select small to medium, thin, bright green leaves. They may have tiny, sharp thorns or a few blemishes that need to be removed before using. (The leaves are usually sold with the thorns already removed.) Avoid leaves with wrinkled skin.

How to Store: Refrigerate in a plastic bag for up to 1 week.

Celeriac or Celery root

Description: This knobby, irregularly shaped root has brown skin. Its cream-colored flesh has a mild, celerylike flavor and a crisp texture.

Availability: Available from September through May.

How to Choose: Select small, firm celeriac free of soft spots.

How to Store: Remove and discard the stringy roots and leaves if present. Refrigerate in a plastic bag for up to 1 week. Peel before using.

Chayote or Mirliton

Description: Chayotes have a delicate, smooth skin with slight ridges and a moist pale green to white flesh that is mild tasting with a slight citrus tang. The skin and single flat seed in the center are edible, but can be discarded, if desired.

Availability: Available in some areas year-round.

How to Choose: Select small, firm pear-shape chayote with pale green skin. Avoid soft or blemished chayote.

How to Store: Refrigerate in a plastic bag for up to 2 weeks.

Fennel

Description: Both fennel's bulb and feathery foliage can be eaten. Bulbs range in color from white to pale green. When raw, bulbs have a light, licoricelike flavor and crunchy texture. When cooked, the flavor, as well as the texture, softens and becomes more delicate. The leaves have an even milder licoricelike flavor and can be snipped for use as fragrant additions to soups and salads.

Cactus leaves

Celeriac

Chayote

Tomatillo

Jicama

Kohlrabi (red and green)

Availability: Available from September through May.

How to Choose: Select fennel with a white to pale green, broad, bulbous base with bright green, fragrant leaves. The bulb should be firm and smooth without blemishes or cracks. The stalks should be crisp and have fresh-looking leaves.

How to Store: Refrigerate tightly wrapped for up to 5 days.

Japanese eggplant

Description: The narrow, slim Japanese eggplant has a mild, slightly sweet flesh with a tender texture. It has a slightly thinner skin and fewer seeds than a regular eggplant. Remove and discard the cap just before preparing. The skin and seeds are edible.

Availability: Available year-round in larger supermarkets or in specialty produce markets.

How to Choose: Select a long, slender eggplant with smooth purple to deep purple skin and a fresh-looking, tight cap. It should be firm and free from soft spots and blemishes.

How to Store: Refrigerate a whole eggplant for up to 2 days.

Jerusalem artichoke or Sunchoke

Description: Jerusalem artichokes resemble fresh ginger. The cream-colored flesh has a sweet and nutty flavor with a crisp texture. It can be eaten raw or cooked.

Availability: Available from October through March.

How to Choose: Select firm, brown-skinned Jerusalem artichokes. The shape can either be elongated and lumpy or round with fairly smooth skin. Avoid those with green-tinged skin, soft spots, or wrinkly skin.

How to Store: Refrigerate in a plastic bag for up to 1 week.

Jicama

Description: This bulb-shape root vegetable has a thin brown skin and white, crisp flesh that is juicy and slightly sweet. Peel and discard the skin just before using. Jicama can be used raw or cooked. When cooked, its texture and flavor softens a bit, but retains its crisp and juicy qualities.

Availability: Available year-round in larger supermarkets or in Mexican specialty markets.

How to Choose: Select a firm jicama with pale brown, unblemished skin. Choose one that feels heavy for its size.

How to Store: Refrigerate unpeeled jicama up to 3 weeks. Refrigerate cut jicama, tightly wrapped, for up to 1 week.

Kohlrabi

Description: Both its turnip-shape stem and leaves are edible. Both varieties, red and green, have white flesh that has a mild, sweet taste similar to a turnip.

Availability: Available from May through October.

How to Choose: Green kohlrabi should be white to pale green; red kohlrabi bulbs should be light to deep purple in color. Choose small to medium-size bulbs that seem heavy. Kohlrabi that is 3 inches in diameter or larger will likely have a woody, unpleasant texture. Avoid blemished or soft bulbs.

How to Store: Refrigerate tightly wrapped for up to 4 days.

Tomatillo or Mexican green tomato

Description: Tomatillos are small, round, pale green to white, and covered with a thin, papery husk. The flesh has an acidic flavor with a hint of citrus tang. The seeds are edible.

Availability: Available year-round.

How to Choose: Select firm, pale to bright olive-green tomatillos with tight fitting, dry husks that are green to light tan in color. Avoid shriveled or bruised tomatillos.

How to Store: Refrigerate, covered, for up to 10 days.

Beyond the Basic Fruits

Black Mission fig

Calimyrna fig

Asian pear

Guava

Horned melon

Asian pear

Description: These round pears have bright white flesh with a crisp, juicy texture that is not softened by cooking and baking. Depending on the variety, flavor can range from sweet to winelike to tart.

Availability: Available from August through October.

How to Choose: Select fruit that is firm to the touch. Skin color ranges from golden brown to pale yellow-green. Asian pears are usually sold ripe and ready to eat.

How to Store: Because Asian pears generally are ripe when you buy them, store for up to 1 month in the refrigerator.

Blood orange

Description: This variety of orange contains juicy, sweet segments with an intense orange flavor. The flesh color can be bright red, reddish-orange, or red-streaked white. They contain some seeds, which should be removed.

Availability: Available on a limited basis from December through June.

How to Choose: Select small, well-formed fruit that is heavy for its size and has healthy, blushing orange-red skin.

How to Store: Keep in the refrigerator for up to 2 weeks.

Cactus pear or Prickly pear

Description: The egg-shape fruit is covered with a thick, spiny skin. The bright red flesh is juicy and mildly sweet with a melonlike aroma. The soft porous flesh often contains small seeds, some of which are tiny enough to be edible (remove seeds, if desired).

Availability: Available from September through April.

How to Choose: The skin color ranges from green to orange to purple to red. The orange variety is thought to be the sweetest. Look for fairly firm fruit without soft spots. Although most cactus pears have had their spines removed, be sure to handle them carefully.

How to Store: Ripen at room temperature until fruit is slightly soft, then refrigerate and use within a few days.

Feijoa or Pineapple guava

Description: The flesh of the oval-shape fruit ranges in color from pale yellow to green. It has a sweet and tangy flavor with a texture similar to that of a ripe pear. The seeds in the jelly-like center are edible, but peel and discard the bitter skin.

Availability: Available spring through early winter.

How to Choose: Select small, slightly soft fruit with bright green skin and a fragrant aroma. Unripe fruit will be very firm.

How to Store: Ripen at room temperature for several days or until the fruit is slightly soft. Refrigerate ripe fruit up to 2 days.

Fig (Black Mission or Calimyrna)

Description: A Black Mission fig has dark purple skin and a pink interior with a sweet, hearty flavor and extremely small, edible seeds; it is available fresh or dried. A Calimyrna fig is the larger of the two varieties and has greenish-yellow skin, a pale pink or white interior with a sweet, nutlike flavor, and edible seeds. It is most commonly found dried, but occasionally is available fresh.

Availability: Fresh figs are available from July through September. Dried figs are available year-round.

How to Choose: Fresh figs are extremely delicate. Look for somewhat firm fruit with a plump, teardrop shape and good color for the variety. Avoid bruised, very soft, very hard,

Blood orange

Cactus pear

Feijoa

Kiwifruit (green)

Kiwifruit (golden)

Kumquat

overly dry, or split fruit, and those with flattened sides or signs of mold. Fresh figs should have a fragrant aroma. A sour odor means the fruit has begun to ferment and spoil.

How to Store: Place fresh figs in a single layer in a paper-towel-lined container. Refrigerate up to 3 days. Store dried figs in an airtight container and refrigerate for up to 6 months or store in freezer up to 1 year.

Guava

Description: Guavas are oval in shape and have skin that ranges from yellow to green in color. They range in size from 1 to 4 inches in diameter. Flesh can be off-white to red in color. The flavor is tangy and sweet. The seeds are edible but usually are discarded.

Availability: Generally available year-round with the exception of early spring.

How to Choose: Choose fruit that is slightly soft and fragrant. Avoid a guava that is overly soft or bruised.

How to Store: Ripen at room temperature until slightly soft. Refrigerate ripe fruit for up to 5 days.

Horned melon

Description: The shell of this oval-shape fruit is covered with spikes. The green, jellylike flesh has a tart flavor with a hint of sweetness. The seeds are edible but the shell is not.

Availability: Available on a limited basis throughout the year in supermarkets that have a specialty produce section.

How to Choose: Select bright orange to bright yellow fruit that has intact spikes. Avoid fruit that is blemished or has soft spots.

How to Store: Store at room temperature for up to 6 months. Do not refrigerate.

Kiwifruit

Description: This egg-shape fruit has edible brown, fuzzy skin. The flesh is either green or golden and is flecked with tiny, edible black seeds. Both varieties have a refreshingly sweet, yet tangy flavor.

Availability: Available year-round.

How to Choose: Select fruit that yields to gentle pressure and is free of bruises or soft spots. (Note: Do not add kiwi to gelatin salads because it contains an enzyme that prevents the gelatin from setting up properly.)

How to Store: Ripen kiwi at room temperature until it yields to gentle pressure. Store ripe fruit in the refrigerator for 2 to 3 weeks.

Kumquat or Chinese orange

Description: This small (1 to 2 inches in length), oval citrus fruit has bright orange skin, pale orange meat, and a combination of sweet and tart flavors. The entire fruit, including the tangy skin and tiny seeds, is edible.

Availability: Available from November through June.

How to Choose: Choose firm, bright orange kumquats with perfectly smooth skin. Avoid fruit that is wrinkled and/or dull in appearance.

How to Store: Hold this fruit at room temperature for up to 1 week, or refrigerate in a plastic bag for up to 3 weeks.

Beyond the Basic Fruits *(continued)*

Mango

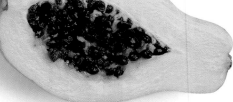

Papaya

Pummelo

Pomegranate

Mango

Description: Mangoes range greatly in size (from 6 ounces to 4 pounds) and vary in shape from round to kidney to oblong. This tropical fruit's flesh is a deep golden color with a juicy texture, spicy flavor, and perfumelike fragrance.

Availability: Available from April through September. Look for the fruit in larger supermarkets with a specialty produce section and specialty produce markets sporadically throughout the remainder of the year.

How to Choose: Depending on variety, skin color can range from green to yellow with tinges of red. When ripe, a mango should smell fruity and feel fairly firm when gently pressed. Avoid bruised or blemished fruit or a mango that is too soft. (To prepare a mango, see the note on page 481.)

How to Store: Ripen at room temperature until the fruit is slightly soft when gently pressed. Refrigerate ripe mangoes for up to 5 days.

Papaya

Description: The golden-orange meat of this pear-shape fruit is fragrant and sweet. The texture is creamy and smooth with a spoonable consistency. The seed cavity contains many tiny black seeds that are edible but often are discarded. Discard the peel.

Availability: Available year-round.

How to Choose: Skin color ranges from greenish-yellow to yellow-orange. Choose fruit that is at least half yellow and feels somewhat soft when pressed. The skin should be smooth and free from bruises and soft spots.

How to Store: Ripen firm fruit at room temperature until it's mostly yellow in color and yields slightly to gentle pressure. Refrigerate ripe fruit in a covered container up to 3 days.

Passion fruit

Description: The flesh of this egg-shape tropical fruit is golden or pink in color with a generous amount of tiny, edible seeds. It has a tangy, yet sweet taste and a tropical, perfumy fragrance.

Availability: Available from January through July.

How to Choose: Choose passion fruit that is small and firm. Ripe fruit has a purple, pink, or yellow skin that is shriveled and dented.

How to Store: Ripen smooth-skinned fruit at room temperature until it looks shriveled. Refrigerate ripe fruit for up to 1 week.

Peach (white)

Description: One variety of white peaches has the familiar round shape with golden-yellow to orange skin that sometimes has a red blush. Another variety has a flattened round shape, resembling a doughnut, and pale-yellow skin with a red blush. The flesh of both varieties is white or light in color with a mild, sweet peach flavor.

Availability: The flattened variety is only available from late June through mid-July; the round variety is available from June through September.

How to Choose: Select peaches that are well-shaped and slightly soft when pressed, with no soft spots or blemishes.

How to Store: Ripen at room temperature until slightly soft when pressed. Refrigerate ripe fruit for up to 5 days.

Passion fruit

White peaches

Plantain

Hachiya persimmon

Fuyu persimmon

Quince

Persimmon (Hachiya or Fuyu)

Description: The acorn-shaped Hachiya persimmon has soft, red-orange meat that is very sweet. The smaller and more round Fuyu has crisp, red-orange meat that has a sweet and slightly spicy flavor. Both have smooth, red-orange skin.

Availability: Both varieties are available fresh from mid-September through December.

How to Choose: A persimmon should have a green cap. A Hachiya should be soft to the touch, while a Fuyu persimmon should feel firm.

How to Store: Ripen the Hachiya variety at room temperature until soft. Refrigerate the ripe fruit and use within a few days. The Fuyu variety will remain firm and crisp. Refrigerate ripe Fuyu and use within a few days.

Plantain

Description: Plantains resemble bananas but have a thick, green skin. They are longer in shape than a banana and are square at the ends. Plantains should be cooked. The light-colored meat has a mild, starchy flavor. Plantains are often used in place of potatoes.

Availability: Available year-round.

How to Choose: Select plantains that are plump and undamaged. Do not be concerned with slight bruises or blemishes. Plan ahead when buying plantains. It takes about 1 week for them to turn from totally green to yellow-brown and another 1 to 2 weeks until the plantains are black and fully ripe.

How to Store: Ripen plantains at room temperature.

Pomegranate

Description: Pomegranates, generally the size and shape of an orange, contain hundreds of crunchy, red seeds that are embedded in white membranes and surrounded by a thick skin. When cut into, the seeds produce a deep-red juice with a sweet, delicate flavor. Use the seeds as you would nuts.

Availability: Available from September through December.

How to Choose: Select firm fruit with shiny, bright-red skin that shows no signs of shriveling. Choose a large fruit that feels heavy for its size.

How to Store: Pomegranates in the supermarket should be sold ready to eat. Use immediately or store for several weeks in the refrigerator. Store seeds in a freezer container or freezer bag for up to 1 year.

Pummelo or Chinese grapefruit

Description: Pummelos are similar in appearance to a jumbo grapefruit. The flesh color ranges from yellow to red. They contain juicy segments that have a sweet-tart taste.

Availability: Available from November through February.

How to Choose: Select fruit that is heavy for its size and has thick skin that is greenish to yellow. Avoid soft fruit.

How to Store: Store for up to 2 weeks in the refrigerator.

Quince

Description: This round or oval-shape fruit has smooth or woolly skin, which generally is peeled off and discarded. Quinces taste better cooked than raw. When raw, the hard, light-colored flesh has a dry texture and unpleasant tart flavor. When cooked, quinces taste like mild, sweet apples and have the soft texture of cooked apples.

Availability: Available from September through December.

How to Choose: Select firm fruit that has yellow skin and a knob at one end of the fruit.

How to Store: Ripen quince at room temperature until skin is an even yellow color, with no signs of green. Refrigerate ripe quince for up to 2 weeks.

Cooking Fresh Vegetables

There are several basic ways to cook fresh vegetables—on the range top (cooking or steaming), in the oven, and in the microwave oven. Keep in mind that cooking and steaming timings may vary, depending on the particular vegetable. The amounts given on the chart yield enough cooked vegetables for 4 servings, except where noted. Wash fresh vegetables with cool, clear tap water; scrub firm vegetables with a clean produce brush. To steam vegetables, place a steamer basket in a saucepan. Add water to just below the bottom of the steamer basket. Bring to boiling. Add vegetables to steamer basket. Cover and reduce heat. Steam for the time specified in the chart or until desired doneness. To microwave vegetables, use a microwave-safe baking dish or casserole and follow the directions in the chart, keeping in mind that timings may vary depending on the microwave oven.

Vegetable and Amount	Preparation (Yield)	Conventional Cooking Directions	Microwave Cooking Directions
Artichokes, baby 1 pound (6 to 8 whole)	Wash; trim stems. Cut off one-fourth from tops. Remove outer leaves until pale green petals are reached. Cut into halves or quarters. Cut out fuzzy centers, if necessary.	Cook, covered, in a large amount of boiling salted water for 15 minutes or until tender. (Or steam for 15 to 20 minutes.)	Place in a casserole with 2 tablespoons water. Microwave, covered, on 100% power (high) for 6 to 9 minutes or until tender.
Artichokes 2 (10 ounces each) (2 servings)	Wash; trim stems. Cut off 1 inch from tops; snip off sharp leaf tips (see top photo, page 511). Brush cut edges with lemon juice.	Cook, covered, in a large amount of boiling salted water for 20 to 30 minutes or until a leaf pulls out easily. (Or steam for 20 to 25 minutes.) Invert artichokes to drain.	Place in a casserole with 2 tablespoons water. Microwave, covered, on 100% power (high) for 7 to 9 minutes or until a leaf pulls out easily, rearranging artichokes once. Invert artichokes to drain.
Asparagus 1 pound (18 to 24 spears)	Wash; break off woody bases where spears snap easily (see bottom photo, page 511). If desired, scrape off scales. Leave spears whole or cut into 1-inch pieces. (2 cups pieces)	Cook, covered, in a small amount of boiling salted water for 3 to 5 minutes or until crisp-tender. (Or steam for 3 to 5 minutes.)	Place in a baking dish or casserole with 2 tablespoons water. Microwave, covered, on 100% power (high) for 3 to 6 minutes or until crisp-tender, rearranging or stirring once.
Beans (green, Italian green, purple, or yellow wax) 12 ounces	Wash; remove ends and strings. Leave whole or cut into 1-inch pieces. (2½ cups pieces) For French-cut beans, slice lengthwise.	Cook, covered, in a small amount of boiling salted water for 10 to 15 minutes for whole or cut beans (5 to 10 minutes for French-cut beans) or until crisp-tender. (Or steam whole, cut, or French-cut beans for 18 to 22 minutes.)	Place in a casserole with 2 tablespoons water. Microwave, covered, on 100% power (high) for 8 to 12 minutes for whole or cut beans (7 to 10 minutes for French-cut beans) or until crisp-tender, stirring once.
Beets 1 pound (4 medium)	For whole beets, cut off all but 1 inch of stems and roots; wash. Do not peel. (For microwaving, prick the skins of whole beets.) Or peel beets; cube or slice. (2¾ cups cubes)	Cook, covered, in boiling salted water for 35 to 45 minutes for whole beets (about 20 minutes for cubed or sliced beets) or until tender. Slip skins off whole beets.	Place in a casserole with 2 tablespoons water. Microwave whole, cubed, or sliced beets, covered, on 100% power (high) for 9 to 12 minutes or until tender, rearranging or stirring once. Slip skins off whole beets.
Broccoli 12 ounces	Wash; remove outer leaves and tough parts of stalks. Cut lengthwise into spears or cut into 1-inch florets. (3 cups florets)	Cook, covered, in a small amount of boiling salted water for 8 to 10 minutes or until crisp-tender. (Or steam for 8 to 10 minutes.)	Place in a baking dish with 2 tablespoons water. Microwave, covered, on 100% power (high) 5 to 8 minutes or until crisp-tender, rearranging or stirring once.

Cooking Fresh Vegetables *(continued)*

Vegetable and Amount	Preparation (Yield)	Conventional Cooking Directions	Microwave Cooking Directions
Brussels sprouts 12 ounces	Trim stems and remove any wilted outer leaves; wash. Cut large sprouts in half lengthwise. (3 cups)	Cook, covered, in enough boiling salted water to cover for 10 to 12 minutes or until crisp-tender. (Or steam for 10 to 15 minutes.)	Place in a casserole with $\frac{1}{4}$ cup water. Microwave, covered, on 100% power (high) for 5 to 7 minutes or until crisp-tender, stirring once.
Cabbage Half of a $1\frac{1}{2}$-pound head	Remove wilted outer leaves; wash. Cut into 4 wedges or coarsely chop. (3 cups coarsely chopped)	Cook, uncovered, in a small amount of boiling water for 2 minutes. Cover; cook for 6 to 8 minutes more for wedges (3 to 5 minutes for pieces) or until crisp-tender. (Or steam wedges for 10 to 12 minutes.)	Place in a baking dish or casserole with 2 tablespoons water. Microwave, covered, on 100% power (high) for 9 to 11 minutes for wedges (4 to 6 minutes for pieces) or until crisp-tender, rearranging or stirring once.
Carrots 1 pound	Wash, trim, and peel or scrub. Cut into $\frac{1}{4}$-inch slices or into strips. ($2\frac{1}{2}$ cups slices)	Cook, covered, in a small amount of boiling salted water for 7 to 9 minutes for slices (4 to 6 minutes for strips) or until crisp-tender. (Or steam slices for 8 to 10 minutes or strips for 5 to 7 minutes.)	Place in a casserole with 2 tablespoons water. Microwave, covered, on 100% power (high) for 6 to 9 minutes for slices (5 to 7 minutes for strips) or until crisp-tender, stirring once.
Carrots (packaged, peeled baby carrots or small carrots with tops) 1 pound	Wash; trim and scrub if necessary. ($3\frac{1}{2}$ cups)	Cook, covered, in boiling salted water for 8 to 10 minutes or until crisp-tender. (Or steam for 8 to 10 minutes.)	Place in a casserole with 2 tablespoons water. Microwave, covered, on 100% power (high) for 7 to 9 minutes or until crisp-tender, stirring once.
Cauliflower 12 ounces	Wash; remove leaves and woody stem. Leave whole or break into florets. (3 cups florets)	Cook, covered, in a small amount of boiling salted water for 10 to 15 minutes for head (8 to 10 minutes for florets) or until crisp-tender. (Or steam head or florets for 8 to 12 minutes.)	Place in a casserole with 2 tablespoons water. Microwave, covered, on 100% power (high) for 9 to 11 minutes for head (7 to 10 minutes for florets) or until crisp-tender, turning or stirring once.
Celeriac 1 pound	Wash; trim off the leaves and ends. Peel off hairy brown skin. Cut into strips. ($3\frac{1}{2}$ cups strips)	Cook, covered, in a small amount of boiling salted water for 5 to 6 minutes or until crisp-tender. (Or steam for 5 minutes.)	Place in a casserole with 2 tablespoons water. Microwave, covered, on 100% power (high) for 4 to 5 minutes or until crisp-tender, stirring once.
Celery 5 stalks	Remove leaves; wash stalks. Cut into $\frac{1}{2}$-inch slices. ($2\frac{1}{2}$ cups slices)	Cook, covered, in a small amount of boiling salted water for 6 to 9 minutes or until crisp-tender. (Or steam for 7 to 10 minutes.)	Place in a casserole with 2 tablespoons water. Microwave, covered, on 100% power (high) for 6 to 10 minutes or until crisp-tender, stirring once.
Chayote 1 pound	Wash, peel, halve lengthwise, and remove seed; cube. (2 cups cubes)	Cook, covered, in a small amount of boiling salted water about 5 minutes or until crisp-tender. (Or steam about 8 minutes.)	Place in a casserole with 2 tablespoons water. Microwave, covered, on 100% power (high) for 5 to 6 minutes or until crisp-tender, stirring once.

Cooking Fresh Vegetables *(continued)*

Vegetable and Amount	Preparation (Yield)	Conventional Cooking Directions	Microwave Cooking Directions
Corn 4 ears	Remove husks. Scrub with stiff brush to remove silks; rinse. Cut kernels from cob. (2 cups kernels)	Cook, covered, in a small amount of boiling salted water for 4 minutes. (Or steam for 4 to 5 minutes.)	Place in a casserole with 2 tablespoons water. Microwave, covered, on 100% power (high) 5 to 6 minutes, stirring once.
Corn on the cob (1 ear equals 1 serving)	Remove husks from fresh ears of corn. Scrub with a stiff brush to remove silks; rinse.	Cook, covered, in enough boiling lightly salted water to cover for 5 to 7 minutes or until tender.	Wrap each ear in waxed paper; place on microwave-safe paper towels in microwave. Microwave on 100% power (high) 3 to 5 minutes for 1 ear, 5 to 7 minutes for 2 ears, or 9 to 12 minutes for 4 ears, rearranging once.
Eggplant 1 pound	Wash and peel. Cut into $\frac{3}{4}$-inch cubes. (5 cups cubes)	Cook, covered, in a small amount of boiling water for 4 to 5 minutes or until tender. (Or steam for 4 to 5 minutes.)	Place in a casserole with 2 tablespoons water. Microwave, covered, on 100% power (high) for 6 to 8 minutes or until tender, stirring once.
Fennel 2 bulbs	Cut off and discard upper stalks, including feathery leaves (see photo, page 524). Remove wilted outer layer of stalks; cut off a thin slice from base. Wash; cut fennel lengthwise into quarters. (2$\frac{1}{2}$ cups quarters)	Cook, covered, in a small amount of boiling water for 6 to 10 minutes or until tender. (Or steam for 6 to 8 minutes.)	Place in a casserole with $\frac{1}{4}$ cup water. Microwave, covered, on 100% power (high) for 6 to 8 minutes or until tender, rearranging once.
Greens (beet or chard) 12 ounces	Wash thoroughly in cold water; drain well. Remove stems; trim bruised leaves. (12 cups torn)	Cook, covered, in a small amount of boiling salted water for 8 to 10 minutes or until tender.	Not recommended.
Greens (kale, mustard, or turnip) 12 ounces	Wash thoroughly in cold water; drain well. Remove stems; trim bruised leaves. (12 cups torn)	Cook, covered, in a small amount of boiling salted water for 20 to 25 minutes or until tender.	Not recommended.
Jerusalem artichokes (Sunchokes) 1 pound	Wash, trim, and peel or scrub. Cut into $\frac{1}{4}$-inch slices. (2 cups slices)	Cook, covered, in a small amount of boiling salted water for 7 to 9 minutes or until tender. (Or steam for 10 to 12 minutes.)	Place in a casserole with 2 tablespoons water. Microwave, covered, on 100% power (high) for 5 to 7 minutes or until tender, stirring once.
Jicama 10 ounces	Wash, trim, and peel. Cut into $\frac{1}{2}$-inch cubes. (2 cups cubes)	Cook, covered, in a small amount of boiling salted water about 5 minutes or until crisp-tender. (Or steam about 5 minutes.)	Place in a casserole with 2 tablespoons water. Microwave, covered, on 100% power (high) for 5 minutes or until crisp-tender, stirring once.
Kohlrabi 1 pound	Cut off leaves; wash. Peel (see photo, page 519); chop or cut into strips. (3 cups strips)	Cook, covered, in a small amount of boiling salted water for 4 to 6 minutes or until crisp-tender. (Or steam about 6 minutes.)	Place in a casserole with 2 tablespoons water. Microwave, covered, on 100% power (high) for 5 to 7 minutes or until crisp-tender, stirring once.
Leeks 1$\frac{1}{2}$ pounds	Wash well; remove any tough outer leaves. Trim roots from base. Slit lengthwise and wash well. Cut into $\frac{1}{2}$-inch slices. (3 cups slices)	Cook, covered, in a small amount of boiling salted water for 4 to 5 minutes or until tender. (Or steam slices for 4 to 5 minutes.)	Place in a casserole with 2 tablespoons water. Microwave, covered, on 100% power (high) for 4 to 6 minutes or until tender, stirring once.

Cooking Fresh Vegetables *(continued)*

Vegetable and Amount	Preparation (Yield)	Conventional Cooking Directions	Microwave Cooking Directions
Mushrooms 1 pound	Wash mushrooms with a damp towel or paper towel. Leave whole or slice. (6 cups slices)	Cook sliced mushrooms, covered, in 2 tablespoons butter or margarine about 5 minutes. (Or steam whole mushrooms for 10 to 12 minutes.)	Place mushrooms in a casserole with 2 tablespoons butter or margarine. Microwave, covered, on 100% power (high) for 4 to 6 minutes, stirring twice.
Okra 8 ounces	Wash; cut off stems. Cut into 1/2-inch slices. (2 cups slices)	Cook, covered, in a small amount of boiling salted water for 8 to 10 minutes or until tender.	Place in a casserole with 2 tablespoons water. Microwave, covered, on 100% power (high) for 4 to 6 minutes or until tender, stirring once.
Onions, boiling or pearl 8 ounces boiling onions (10 to 12) 8 ounces pearl onions (24 to 30)	Peel boiling onions. (Peel pearl onions after cooking.) (2 cups)	Cook, covered, in a small amount of boiling salted water for 10 to 12 minutes for boiling onions, 8 to 10 minutes for pearl onions. (Or steam 12 to 15 minutes for boiling onions, 10 to 12 minutes for pearl onions.)	Place in a casserole with 2 tablespoons water. Microwave, covered, on 100% power (high) for 3 to 5 minutes.
Parsnips 12 ounces	Wash, trim, and peel or scrub. Cut into 1/4-inch slices. (2 cups slices)	Cook, covered, in a small amount of boiling salted water for 7 to 9 minutes or until tender. (Or steam for 8 to 10 minutes.)	Place in a casserole with 2 tablespoons water. Microwave, covered, on 100% power (high) for 4 to 6 minutes or until tender, stirring once.
Peas, edible pod (snow peas or sugar snap peas) 8 ounces	Remove strings and tips; wash. (2 cups)	Cook, covered, in a small amount of boiling salted water for 2 to 4 minutes or until crisp-tender. (Or steam for 2 to 4 minutes.)	Place in a casserole with 2 tablespoons water. Microwave, covered, on 100% power (high) for 3 to 5 minutes or until crisp-tender, stirring once.
Peas, green 2 pounds	Shell and wash. (3 cups shelled)	Cook, covered, in a small amount of boiling salted water for 10 to 12 minutes or until crisp-tender. (Or steam for 12 to 15 minutes.)	Place in a casserole with 2 tablespoons water. Microwave, covered, on 100% power (high) for 6 to 8 minutes or until crisp-tender, stirring once.
Peppers, sweet 2 large	Wash. Remove stems, seeds, and membranes. Cut into rings or strips. (2 1/2 cups rings or strips)	Cook, covered, in a small amount of boiling salted water for 6 to 7 minutes or until crisp-tender. (Or steam for 6 to 7 minutes.)	Place in a casserole with 2 tablespoons water. Microwave, covered, on 100% power (high) for 4 to 6 minutes or until crisp-tender, stirring once.
Potatoes 1 pound	Wash and peel. Remove eyes, sprouts, or green areas. Cut into quarters or cubes. (2 3/4 cups cubes)	Cook, covered, in enough boiling salted water to cover for 20 to 25 minutes for quarters (about 15 minutes for cubes) or until tender. (Or steam about 20 minutes.)	Place in a casserole with 2 tablespoons water. Microwave, covered, on 100% power (high) for 8 to 10 minutes or until tender, stirring once.
Rutabagas 1 pound	Wash and peel. Cut into 1/2-inch cubes. (3 cups cubes)	Cook, covered, in a small amount of boiling salted water for 18 to 20 minutes or until tender. (Or steam for 18 to 20 minutes.)	Place in a casserole with 2 tablespoons water. Microwave, covered, on 100% power (high) for 11 to 13 minutes or until tender, stirring 3 times.

Cooking Fresh Vegetables *(continued)*

Vegetable and Amount	Preparation (Yield)	Conventional Cooking Directions	Microwave Cooking Directions
Spinach 1 pound	Wash and drain; remove stems. (12 cups torn)	Cook, covered, in a small amount of boiling salted water for 3 to 5 minutes or until tender, beginning timing when steam forms. (Or steam 3 to 5 minutes.)	Place in a casserole with 2 tablespoons water. Microwave, covered, on 100% power (high) for 4 to 6 minutes or until tender, stirring once.
Squash (acorn, delicata, golden nugget, or sweet dumpling) One 1¼-pound (2 servings)	Wash, halve, and remove seeds.	Place squash halves, cut side down, in a baking dish. Bake in a 350°F oven for 45 minutes. Turn cut side up. Bake for 20 to 25 minutes more or until tender.	Place squash halves, cut side down, in a baking dish with 2 tablespoons water. Microwave, covered, on 100% power (high) for 7 to 10 minutes or until tender, rearranging once. Let stand, covered, 5 minutes.
Squash (banana, buttercup, butternut, Hubbard, or turban) One 1½-pound or a 1½-pound piece	Wash, halve lengthwise, and remove seeds.	Place squash halves, cut side down, in a baking dish. Bake in a 350°F oven for 30 minutes. Turn cut side up. Bake, covered, for 20 to 25 minutes more or until tender.	Place squash halves, cut side down, in a baking dish with 2 tablespoons water. Microwave, covered, on 100% power (high) for 9 to 12 minutes or until tender, rearranging once.
Squash (pattypan, sunburst, yellow, or zucchini) 12 ounces	Wash; do not peel. Cut off ends. Cut into ¼-inch slices. (3 cups slices)	Cook, covered, in a small amount of boiling salted water for 3 to 5 minutes or until crisp-tender. (Or steam for 4 to 6 minutes.)	Place in a casserole with 2 tablespoons water. Microwave, covered, on 100% power (high) for 4 to 5 minutes or until crisp-tender, stirring twice.
Squash (spaghetti) One 2½- to 3-pound	Wash, halve lengthwise, and remove seeds.	Place squash halves, cut sides down, in a baking dish. Bake in a 350°F oven for 30 to 40 minutes or until tender.	Place squash halves, cut side down, in a baking dish with ¼ cup water. Microwave, covered, on 100% power (high) for 17 to 20 minutes or until tender, rearranging once.
Sweet potatoes 1 pound	Wash and peel. Cut off woody portions and ends. Cut into quarters or cubes. (2¾ cups cubes) (For microwaving, cut into quarters.)	Cook, covered, in enough boiling salted water to cover for 25 to 30 minutes or until tender. (Or steam for 20 to 25 minutes.)	Place in a casserole with ½ cup water. Microwave, covered, on 100% power (high) for 10 to 13 minutes or until tender, stirring once.
Turnips 1 pound	Wash and peel. Cut into ½-inch cubes or strips. (2¾ cups cubes)	Cook, covered, in a small amount of boiling salted water for 10 to 12 minutes or until tender. (Or steam for 10 to 15 minutes.)	Place in a casserole with 2 tablespoons water. Microwave, covered, on 100% power (high) for 10 to 12 minutes or until tender, stirring once.

Chapter 23
Index & Metric

A

Almonds.
Almond Macaroons, 214 `Low Fat`
Almond Sponge Cake, 165 `Low Fat`
Asparagus with Almond Sauce, 511 `Fast`
Chocolate-Almond Ice Cream, 258
Cranberry-Almond Cereal Mix, *96* `Fast`
Green Beans Amandine, 512 `Fast`
Nutty Spritz, 226
Trout Amandine, 289
Amaretti Gelato, 259

Angel food cakes.
Angel Food Cake, 169 `No Fat`
Chocolate Angel Food Cake, 169 `No Fat`
egg whites, beating, 169
Honey Angel Food Cake, 169 `No Fat`
tips for success, 169
Antipasto, Lemony Marinated, *67*

Appetizers.
Appetizer Cheesecake, 74, *75*
appetizers needed, calculating, 61
Brie en Croûte, *72*
Brie en Croûte with Caramelized Onions, 73
Buffalo Wings, 70
Citrus Seafood Cocktail, 76
Cowboy Caviar, 67
Crostini with Tapenade, 66 `Fast`
Egg Rolls, 76
Fruit with Prosciutto, *71*
Fruity Beef Kabobs, *71* `Low Fat`
Herbed Leek Tart, 75
Lemony Marinated Antipasto, *67*
Lower-Fat Appetizer Cheesecake, 75
Nachos, 64 `Fast`
Onion Rings, 73 `Fast`
Oysters Rockefeller, 73
Peppercorn-Cheese Melt, *71*
Pesto Roll-Ups, *71*
Phyllo Triangles, 74
Pork Filling, 76
Potato Skins, 60
Prosciutto-Stuffed Mushrooms, 61
Quesadillas, 66 `Fast`
Quick Pizza Breadsticks, 70 `Fast` `Low Fat`
Rumaki, 72
Sausage Bites, 69 `Fast`

Appetizers. *(continued)*
Smoky Cheese Ball, 66
Spinach Phyllo Triangles, 74
Stuffed Mushrooms, 61
Swiss Fondue, 68

Apples and apple juice. *See also* Applesauce
Apple Bread, 119
Apple Butter, 191 `No Fat`
Apple Cake, 160
Apple-Cinnamon Rolls, 145
Apple-Cranberry Filling, 205
Apple Crisp (see Fruit Crisp), 246
Apple Crumb Pie, 399
Apple-Glazed Lamb Chops, 308 `Fast` `Low Fat`
Apple Pie, 399
Apple-Rice Salad, 462
Baked Apples, 243 `Low Fat`
canning and freezing, 194–195
Caramel Apple Crepes, 245
Caramel Apple Pudding Cake, 245
Caramel Apple Sauce, 245
coring, 244
Double-Apple Coffee Cake, 125
Fruit-Filled Oatmeal Bars, 205
Harvest Stuffing, 442
Layered Cranberry-Apple Mold, 466 `Low Fat`
Oven-Roasted Honey-and-Apple Ribs, 350
Polenta-Pecan Apple Cobbler, 243
Ribs with Apples and Sauerkraut, 233
selecting fresh, 531
Saucy Apple Dumplings, *244*
Waldorf Salad, 465 `Fast`

Applesauce.
Applesauce, 191 `Low Fat`
Applesauce Bars, 206
Applesauce Spice Cake, 158
canning and freezing, 191
Appliances, 8, 14–15

Apricots.
Apricot Filling, 205
Apricot-Glazed Pork, 343 `Low Fat`
Apricot Icing, 209
Apricot-Mustard Pork Chops, 310
Apricot-Sauced Pork Medallions, 346 `Fast` `Low Fat`
Apricot Upside-Down Cake, 164
Apricot Vinaigrette, 468 `Fast`
Baked Coconut Shrimp with Curried Apricot Sauce, *294*

Apricots. *(continued)*
Brandied Cranberry-Apricot Bars, *206*
canning and freezing, 194–195
Festive Cranberry-Apricot Pie, *402*
Fruit-Filled Oatmeal Bars, 205
selecting fresh, 531
Spiced Apricot Bars, *209* `Low Fat`

Artichokes.
Artichokes with Butter Sauce, 511
Artichokes with Citrus Mayonnaise, 511
Artichokes with Sour Cream Sauce, 511
Artichoke-Turkey Casserole, 434 `Low Fat`
Baked Artichoke-Spinach Dip, 63
Chicken and Artichokes with Wine Sauce, 427 `Fast`
Cornish Game Hens with Artichokes and Potatoes, 445
Garlic Chicken with Artichokes, 239 `Low Fat`
removing leaves from, 511
Arugula Pasta, Fresh Tomato and, 394 `Fast` `Low Fat`
Asian pear, about, 536

Asparagus.
Asparagus with Almond Sauce, 511 `Fast`
canning and freezing, 196–197
Fettuccine with Vegetables and Prosciutto, 385 `Fast` `Low Fat`
Ham-Asparagus Strata, *273*
Lemon Cream-Sauced Pasta with Asparagus and Squash, *395* `Fast`
Lemony Fettuccine Alfredo with Asparagus, 396
Orange Roughy with Lemon Sauce, *285* `Fast` `Low Fat`
Oriental Cashew Asparagus, *512* `Fast`
removing bases from, 511
Rotini and Sweet Pepper Primavera, *393* `Fast` `Low Fat`
selecting fresh, 529
Avocado Salsa, 291
Avocados, selecting fresh, 531

B

Bacon.
Collard Greens with Bacon, 517
Cooking Bacon, 352 `Fast`
Deluxe Eggs Benedict, 264
Eggs Benedict, *264*

Note: Numbers in italics indicate photo pages for finished dishes.

Index

548

Note: Numbers in italics indicate photo pages for finished dishes.

Note: Numbers in italics indicate photo pages for finished dishes.

Index

552

Note: Numbers in italics indicate photo pages for finished dishes.

Index

554

Note: Numbers in italics indicate photo pages for finished dishes.

Index

556

Note: Numbers in italics indicate photo pages for finished dishes.

Note: Numbers in italics indicate photo pages for finished dishes.

Note: Numbers in italics indicate photo pages for finished dishes.

Index

562

Note: Numbers in italics indicate photo pages for finished dishes.

Index

564

Note: Numbers in italics indicate photo pages for finished dishes.

Index

566

Note: Numbers in italics indicate photo pages for finished dishes.

Index

567

Index

568

Note: Numbers in italics indicate photo pages for finished dishes.

Index

570

Note: Numbers in italics indicate photo pages for finished dishes.

Index

572

Note: Numbers in italics indicate photo pages for finished dishes.

Metric Information

The charts on this page provide a guide for converting measurements from the U.S. customary system, which is used throughout this book, to the metric system.

Product Differences

Most of the ingredients called for in the recipes in this book are available in most countries. However, some are known by different names. Here are some common American ingredients and their possible counterparts:

- Sugar (white) is granulated, fine granulated, or castor sugar.
- Powdered sugar is icing sugar.
- All-purpose flour is enriched, bleached or unbleached white household flour. When self-rising flour is used in place of all-purpose flour in a recipe that calls for leavening, omit the leavening agent (baking soda or baking powder) and salt.
- Light-colored corn syrup is golden syrup.
- Cornstarch is cornflour.
- Baking soda is bicarbonate of soda.
- Vanilla or vanilla extract is vanilla essence.
- Green, red, or yellow sweet peppers are capsicums or bell peppers.
- Golden raisins are sultanas.

Volume and Weight

The United States traditionally uses cup measures for liquid and solid ingredients. The chart below shows the approximate imperial and metric equivalents. If you are accustomed to weighing solid ingredients, the following approximate equivalents will be helpful.

- 1 cup butter, castor sugar, or rice = 8 ounces = $\frac{1}{2}$ pound = 250 grams
- 1 cup flour = 4 ounces = $\frac{1}{4}$ pound = 125 grams
- 1 cup icing sugar = 5 ounces = 150 grams

Canadian and U.S. volume for a cup measure is 8 fluid ounces (237 ml), but the standard metric equivalent is 250 ml.

1 British imperial cup is 10 fluid ounces.

In Australia, 1 tablespoon equals 20 ml, and there are 4 teaspoons in the Australian tablespoon.

Spoon measures are used for smaller amounts of ingredients. Although the size of the tablespoon varies slightly in different countries, for practical purposes and for recipes in this book, a straight substitution is all that's necessary. Measurements made using cups or spoons always should be level unless stated otherwise.

Common Weight Range Replacements

Imperial / U.S.	Metric
$\frac{1}{2}$ ounce	15 g
1 ounce	25 g or 30 g
4 ounces ($\frac{1}{4}$ pound)	115 g or 125 g
8 ounces ($\frac{1}{2}$ pound)	225 g or 250 g
16 ounces (1 pound)	450 g or 500 g
$1\frac{1}{4}$ pounds	625 g
$1\frac{1}{2}$ pounds	750 g
2 pounds or $2\frac{1}{4}$ pounds	1,000 g or 1 Kg

Oven Temperature Equivalents

Fahrenheit Setting	Celsius Setting*	Gas Setting
300°F	150°C	Gas Mark 2 (very low)
325°F	160°C	Gas Mark 3 (low)
350°F	180°C	Gas Mark 4 (moderate)
375°F	190°C	Gas Mark 5 (moderate)
400°F	200°C	Gas Mark 6 (hot)
425°F	220°C	Gas Mark 7 (hot)
450°F	230°C	Gas Mark 8 (very hot)
475°F	240°C	Gas Mark 9 (very hot)
500°F	260°C	Gas Mark 10 (extremely hot)
Broil	Broil	Grill

*Electric and gas ovens may be calibrated using celsius. However, for an electric oven, increase celsius setting 10 to 20 degrees when cooking above 160°C. For convection or forced air ovens (gas or electric) lower the temperature setting 25°F/10°C when cooking at all heat levels.

Baking Pan Sizes

Imperial / U.S.	Metric
9×1$\frac{1}{2}$-inch round cake pan	22- or 23×4-cm (1.5 L)
9×1$\frac{1}{2}$-inch pie plate	22- or 23×4-cm (1 L)
8×8×2-inch square cake pan	20×5-cm (2 L)
9×9×2-inch square cake pan	22- or 23×4.5-cm (2.5 L)
11×7×1$\frac{1}{2}$-inch baking pan	28×17×4-cm (2 L)
2-quart rectangular baking pan	30×19×4.5-cm (3 L)
13×9×2-inch baking pan	34×22×4.5-cm (3.5 L)
15×10×1-inch jelly roll pan	40×25×2-cm
9×5×3-inch loaf pan	23×13×8-cm (2 L)
2-quart casserole	2 L

U.S. / Standard Metric Equivalents

$\frac{1}{8}$ teaspoon = 0.5 ml	
$\frac{1}{4}$ teaspoon = 1 ml	
$\frac{1}{2}$ teaspoon = 2 ml	
1 teaspoon = 5 ml	
1 tablespoon = 15 ml	
2 tablespoons = 25 ml	
$\frac{1}{4}$ cup = 2 fluid ounces = 50 ml	
$\frac{1}{3}$ cup = 3 fluid ounces = 75 ml	
$\frac{1}{2}$ cup = 4 fluid ounces = 125 ml	
$\frac{2}{3}$ cup = 5 fluid ounces = 150 ml	
$\frac{3}{4}$ cup = 6 fluid ounces = 175 ml	
1 cup = 8 fluid ounces = 250 ml	
2 cups = 1 pint = 500 ml	
1 quart = 1 litre